MW01226017

# THE WALL STREET JOURNAL GUIDES TO BUSINESS TRAVEL

# USA & CANADA

Fodor's Travel Publications, Inc.
New York and London

First Edition

ISBN 0–679–01983–9

## The Wall Street Journal Guides to Business Travel: USA & Canada

**Series Editor:** Edie Jarolim
**Assistant Series Editor:** Caroline Haberfeld
**Contributing Editors:** Julia Lisella, Gloria McDarrah
**Art Director:** Fabrizio La Rocca
**Map Editor:** Suzanne Brown
**Assistant Map Editor:** Mark von Schlegell
**Cartographer:** David Lindroth

**Design:** Vignelli Associates

## Special Sales

# CONTENTS

## Cities

# INTRODUCTION

An executive once told me he doesn't travel anymore, he just goes from place to place. I wish I had his name so I could send him a copy of *The Wall Street Journal Guides to Business Travel*. Knowing your way around—knowing where to be at the right time, and where to get what you need *when you need it*—can save time and money. It could also save a deal. And it could put the joy back into travel.

For two years the world's #1 travel expert (Fodor's) and the world's #1 business authority (*The Wall Street Journal*) have been working to produce a series of guides that will give business travelers the savvy to succeed away from home. The result? The most comprehensive business travel guides ever published—the first that really qualify as an essential business tool.

It's useful pointing out the top hotels, although most of you already know where they are, at least in cities you visit regularly. What the *Journal* guides do, in addition, is rate each property for 29 different services of critical interest to business travelers—from fitness facilities to modem phone jacks, secretarial services, dry-cleaning and pressing, hairdryers, and in-room checkout.

We're also thorough—some would say fanatical—enough to tell you about the bed lighting. And the desk lighting. And the desks themselves. Not just whether they exist, but how good they are.

It's helpful to know the top restaurants, but only in the *Journal's* business travel guides will you find out whether tables are spaced far enough apart for confidential talks, or whether the ambience is best for hammering out a contract or for celebrating a deal. And only in the *Journal* guides will you learn about the current power-breakfast scene.

Not everyone is a CEO and not everyone (alas) is on a company expense account. And so, among reviews of hotels and restaurants are names of smaller, less obvious properties that keep standards up and prices down. We give stars to the best of the upscale restaurants and hotels, and we give stars to the best of the moderately priced ones, too.

We've tried to anticipate other needs as well. Such as where to find a late-night pharmacy, a gift basket, a tux. Or where to get slides made up an hour before a critical presentation. Or where to unwind—alone or with a client—after work.

And for a free afternoon, we suggest some fun ways to spend your time: Museum-hopping, yes, but also jogging, shopping, people-watching—ideas for speeding up the pace or slowing down.

*The Wall Street Journal Guides to Business Travel* are both for first-time travelers and frequent flyers; for traditionalists and trend-spotters; for long-term visitors and travelers on the run. Writers express their opinions with no holds barred, their goal being not so much to impose their tastes on you as to give you the information you need to make your own informed choices. Every property has been reviewed in person, virtually always by a long-time resident with an insider's way of looking at things. The result is an invaluable series of guides that satisfy the personal and professional needs of business travelers—those who never just go from here to there.

While every care has been taken to ensure the accuracy of the information in this guide, time brings change, and consequently the publisher cannot accept responsibility for errors that may occur. Prudent travelers will therefore want to call ahead to verify prices and other "perishable" information.

We encourage you to write and share your thoughts with us—positive or otherwise. We promise to take your comments seriously, to investigate all complaints, and to make changes when the facts warrant it. Write to Edie Jarolim, Editor, *The Wall Street Journal Guides to Business Travel*, Fodor's Travel Publications, 201 E. 50th Street, New York, NY 10022.

Michael Spring
Editorial Director
Fodor's Travel Publications

# INTERNATIONAL DIALING CODES

| | | |
|---|---|---|
| **Argentina** 54 | Athens 1 | **Nigeria** 231 |
| Buenos Aires 1 | **Hong Kong** 852 | Lagos 1 |
| **Australia** 61 | Hong Kong 5 | **Norway** 47 |
| Melbourne 3 | Kowloon 3 | Oslo 2 |
| Sydney 2 | **Hungary** 36 | **Pakistan** 92 |
| **Austria** 43 | Budapest 1 | Islamabad 51 |
| Vienna 1 | **India** 91 | **Panama*** 507 |
| **Belgium** 32 | Bombay 22 | **Peru** 51 |
| Brussels 2 | New Delhi 11 | Lima 14 |
| **Bolivia** 591 | **Indonesia** 62 | **Phillipines** 63 |
| Santa Cruz 33 | Jakarta 21 | Manila 2 |
| **Brazil** 55 | **Iran** 98 | **Poland** 48 |
| Brasilia 61 | Teheran 21 | Warsaw 22 |
| Rio de Janeiro 21 | **Iraq** 964 | **Portugal** 351 |
| **Brunei*** 673 | Baghdad 1 | Lisbon 1 |
| **Chile** 56 | **Ireland** 353 | **Romania** 40 |
| Santiago 2 | Dublin 1 | Bucharest 0 |
| **China, Rep. of** 86 | **Israel** 972 | **Saudia Arabia** 966 |
| Beijing 1 | Jerusalem 2 | |
| Canton 20 | Tel Aviv 3 | Riyadh 1 |
| Shanghai 21 | **Italy** 39 | **Singapore*** 65 |
| **Colombia** 57 | Florence 55 | **South Africa** 27 |
| Bogota 1 | Milan 2 | Cape Town 21 |
| **Czechoslavakia** 42 | Rome 6 | Pretoria 12 |
| | **Japan** 81 | **Spain** 34 |
| Prague 2 | Nagoya 52 | Barcelona 3 |
| **Denmark** 45 | Osaka 6 | Madrid 1 |
| Copenhagen 1 or 2 | Tokyo 3 | **Sweden** 46 |
| | **Jordan** 962 | Stockholm 8 |
| **Ecuador** 593 | Amman 6 | **Switzerland** 41 |
| Quito 2 | **Kenya** 254 | Geneva 22 |
| **Egypt** 20 | Nairobi 2 | Zurich 1 |
| Cairo 2 | **Korea, Rep. of** 82 | **Taiwan** 886 |
| **El Salvador*** 503 | Seoul 2 | Taipei 2 |
| **Ethiopia** 251 | **Kuwait*** 965 | **Thailand** 66 |
| Addis Ababa 1 | **Libya** 218 | Bangkok 2 |
| **Finland** 358 | Tripoli 21 | **Turkey** 90 |
| Helsinki 0 | **Liechtenstein** 41 | Istanbul 1 |
| **France** 33 | All points 75 | **United Arab** |
| Lyon 7 | **Luxembourg*** 352 | **Emirates** 971 |
| Marseille 91 | **Malaysia** 60 | Abu Dhabi 2 |
| Paris 13, 14, or 16 | Kuala Lumpur 3 | Dubai 4 |
| **Germany, Eastern**† 37 | **Mexico** 52 | **United Kingdom** 44 |
| | Mexico City 5 | Edinburgh 31 |
| Berlin 2 | **Netherlands** 31 | London 71 or 81 |
| **Germany, Western**† 49 | Amsterdam 20 | **USSR** 7 |
| | The Hague 70 | Leningrad 812 |
| Berlin 30 | Rotterdam 10 | Moscow 95 |
| Bonn 228 | **New Zealand** 64 | **Venezuela** 58 |
| Cologne 221 | Auckland 9 | Caracas 2 |
| Frankfurt 69 | Wellington 4 | **Yugoslavia** 38 |
| Munich 89 | **Nicaragua** 505 | Belgrade 11 |
| **Greece** 30 | Managua 2 | |

*\* no city code required*
*† the former divisions of Germany are still reflected in separate telephone country codes and Berlin city codes*

# USA & CANADA TIME ZONES AND AREA CODES

**PACIFIC STANDARD TIME**

4:00 AM (-8 hours)

**MOUNTAIN STANDARD TIME**

5:00 AM (-7 hours)

**Clocks show AM times when**

## WORLD TIME ZONES

Algiers, **54**
Anchorage, **16**
Athens, **61**
Atlanta, **32**
Auckland, **14**
Baghdad, **63**
Bangkok, **2**
Beijing, **6**
Berlin, **55**
Bogotá, **34**
Boston, **29**
Brussels, **48**
Budapest, **58**

Buenos Aires, **38**
Caracas, **35**
Chicago, **25**
Copenhagen, **46**
Dallas, **23**
Delhi, **67**
Denver, **21**
Dublin, **41**
Edmonton, **20**
Frankfurt, **49**
Geneva, **51**
Hong Kong, **8**
Honolulu, **15**
Istanbul, **60**

Jakarta, **5**
Jerusalem, **62**
Johannesburg, **66**
Lima, **36**
Lisbon, **43**
London (Greenwich), **42**
Los Angeles, **19**
Madrid, **44**
Manila, **9**
Mecca, **64**
Mexico City, **22**
Miami, **33**
Milan, **52**
Montréal, **28**

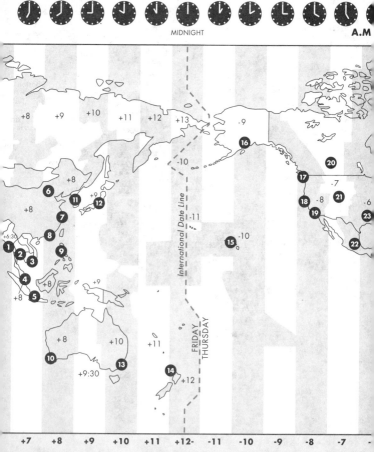

MIDNIGHT                                        A.M

International Date Line

FRIDAY
THURSDAY

+7   +8   +9   +10   +11   +12-   -11   -10   -9   -8   -7

Numbers below vertical bands relate each zone to Greenwich Mean Time (0 hrs.).
Local times frequently differ from these general indications,
as indicated by light-face numbers on map.

# FREQUENT FLYER AFFILIATIONS: HOTELS

| AIRLINES | Adams Mark | Colony | Compri | Courtyard Inns | Canadian Pacific | Doubletree | Hilton | Holiday Inn | Hyatt | InterContinental | Lodge Inn | Marriott |
|---|---|---|---|---|---|---|---|---|---|---|---|---|
| **Air Canada/** Aeroplan | ✓ | | | ✓ | ✓ | | | | | | | |
| **Alaska Airlines/** Gold Coast | | | | | | | | | | | | |
| **Aloha Airlines/** Aloha Pass | | ✓ | | | | | | | | | | |
| **American Airlines/** AAdvantage | | | | | | | ✓ | | ✓ | | | ✓ |
| **America West/** Flight Fund | | | ✓ | | | ✓ | | | | | | ✓ |
| **Canadian Airlines Int'l./** Canadian Plus | | | | ✓ | | | | | | | ✓ | ✓ |
| **Continental** | | | ✓ | | | ✓ | | | | | | ✓ |
| **Delta/** Frequent Flyers | | | | | | ✓ | | | | | | ✓ |
| **Hawaiian Airlines/** Gold Pass | | | | | | | | | | | | |
| **Midway/** Flyers First | | | | | | | | | ✓ | | | |
| **Midwest Express/** Frequent Flyers | | | | | | | | | | | | |
| **Northwest/** World Perks | | | | | | | | | ✓ | | | ✓ |
| **Pan Am/** World Pass | | | | | | | | | | ✓ | | |
| **TWA/** Frequent Flyers | ✓ | | | | | | ✓ | | | | | ✓ |
| **United/** Mileage Plus | | | | | | | ✓ | ✓ | | | | |
| **USAir/** Frequent Traveler | | | | | | | ✓ | ✓ | | | | ✓ |

| Ming Court | Omni | Radisson | Ramada | Red Lion | Sheraton | Stouffer | Westin | West Mark | Wyndham | Car Rentals | Alamo | Avis | Budget | Dollar | Hertz | National | Tilden | Thrifty |
|---|---|---|---|---|---|---|---|---|---|---|---|---|---|---|---|---|---|---|
| ✓ |  | ✓ |  |  | ✓ |  | ✓ |  |  |  |  | ✓ |  |  | ✓ |  |  |  |
|  |  |  |  | ✓ |  |  |  |  | ✓ |  | ✓ |  | ✓ |  |  | ✓ |  |  |
|  |  |  |  |  | ✓ |  |  |  |  |  |  |  | ✓ |  |  |  |  |  |
|  |  |  |  |  | ✓ |  |  |  | ✓ |  |  | ✓ |  |  | ✓ |  |  |  |
|  |  |  |  | ✓ |  |  |  |  |  |  |  |  | ✓ |  |  |  |  | ✓ |
|  |  |  | ✓ |  |  |  |  |  |  |  |  |  | ✓ |  |  |  | ✓ | ✓ |
|  |  | ✓ |  |  |  |  |  |  | ✓ |  |  |  |  |  |  | ✓ | ✓ | ✓ |
|  |  |  |  |  |  |  |  |  |  |  | ✓ | ✓ |  |  |  | ✓ |  |  |
|  |  |  |  |  | ✓ |  |  |  |  |  |  | ✓ |  | ✓ |  |  |  |  |
|  | ✓ |  |  |  |  |  |  |  |  |  |  |  | ✓ |  |  |  |  | ✓ |
|  |  |  |  |  |  |  |  |  |  |  |  |  |  |  |  | ✓ |  |  |
|  |  | ✓ |  |  |  |  |  | ✓ |  |  |  |  | ✓ |  |  | ✓ |  |  |
|  |  |  |  |  | ✓ |  |  |  |  |  | ✓ | ✓ | ✓ |  |  |  |  |  |
|  |  |  |  |  |  |  |  |  |  |  |  |  |  |  |  | ✓ |  | ✓ |
|  |  |  |  |  |  |  |  | ✓ |  |  |  |  |  |  | ✓ | ✓ |  |  |
|  | ✓ | ✓ |  |  |  | ✓ | ✓ |  |  |  |  |  |  |  |  | ✓ | ✓ | ✓ |

# THE WINE ADVOCATE'S VINTAGE GUIDE,

| | Regions | '70 | '71 | '72 | '73 | '74 | '75 | '76 | '77 |
|---|---|---|---|---|---|---|---|---|---|
| **BORDEAUX** | Medoc/Graves | 90R | 83R | 55C | 58C | 70C | **89E** | 82R | 60C |
| | Pomerol St. Emilion | 87R | 87R | 60C | 55C | 65C | **88R** | 80R | 55C |
| | Sauternes/Barsac | 84R | 86R | 55C | 65C | 50C | **88T** | 87R | 50C |
| **BURGUNDY** | Côte de Nuits (Red) | 82C | 87R | 86R | 58C | 64C | 50C | 86T | 60C |
| | Côte de Beaune (Red) | 82C | 87R | 83R | 60C | 62C | 50C | 86T | 55C |
| | White | 83C | 83C | 84C | 84R | 75C | 65C | 86C | 80C |
| **RHONE** | North-Côte Rôtie Hermitage | **90R** | 84R | 86R | 72R | 70C | 73C | 82R | 72R |
| | South-Châteauneuf du Pape | **88R** | 82C | 86C | 74C | 70C | 60C | 75C | 70C |
| | Beaujolais | - | - | - | - | - | - | 86C | 50C |
| | Alsace | 80C | **90R** | 55C | 75C | 74C | 82C | **90R** | 70C |
| | Loire Valley | - | - | - | - | - | - | 86C | 70C |
| | Champagne | 85C | **90C** | N.V. | 82C | N.V. | **90R** | **90R** | N.V. |
| **ITALY** | Piedmont | 84R | **90R** | 50C | 70R | 85T | 65C | 67C | 67C |
| | Chianti | 84C | **88C** | 50C | 68C | 80R | 84C | 60C | 72C |
| | Germany | 80C | **90R** | 50C | 67C | 60C | 85R | **90R** | 70C |
| | Vintage Port | **90R** | N.V. | 78C | N.V. | N.V. | 82C | N.V. | **98T** |
| **SPAIN** | Rioja | **90R** | 74C | 67C | 86R | 65C | 84R | 86R | 70C |
| | Penedes | - | - | - | - | - | - | - | - |
| **AUST** | New So. Wales & Victoria | - | - | - | - | - | - | - | - |
| **CALIFORNIA N. COAST** | Cabernet Sauvignon | **92R** | 70C | 65C | **88R** | **90R** | 85R | 85T | 84R |
| | Chardonnay | 83C | 82C | 84C | 85C | 75C | 86C | 80C | 83C |
| | Zinfandel | 86C | 60C | 50C | 86C | **88C** | 80C | 87C | 85R |
| | Pinot Noir | - | - | - | - | - | - | - | - |
| **WASH ORE** | Pinot Noir | - | - | - | - | - | - | - | - |
| | Cabernet Sauvignon | - | - | - | - | - | - | - | - |

**Key: 90-100** = Excellent, **80-89** = Very Good, **70-79** = Average,
**60-69** = Below Average, **Below 60** = Poor
**Symbols: C** = Caution, may now be too old, **E** = Early maturing, **T** = Tannic wines,
**R** = Ready to drink, **N.V.** = Non-vintage, **Bold Print** = The best vintages.

| '78 | '79 | '80 | '81 | '82 | '83 | '84 | '85 | '86 | '87 | '88 | '89 |
|-----|-----|-----|-----|-----|-----|-----|-----|-----|-----|-----|-----|
| 87R | 86R | 72R | 85E | 98E | 85E | 74R | 87E | 98T | 78R | 86T | 92E |
| 82R | 87R | 72C | 84R | 98R | 85R | 59C | 89R | 88F | 82R | 88T | 97E |
| 75R | 75R | 85R | 85R | 75R | 88T | 70C | 85R | 95T | 70R | 98T | 94E |
| 88R | 77C | 84R | 72T | 82R | 85T | 78R | 96E | 80T | 86R | 88T | 88E |
| 86R | 77R | 78R | 74E | 80R | 85T | 75R | 90R | 78R | 84R | 89E | 87E |
| 90R | 86R | 75R | 86R | 90R | 85C | 80R | 89R | 90R | 79R | 82R | 92R |
| 95T | 87R | 83R | 75C | 85R | 89T | 75E | 90E | 84T | 86E | 92E | 96E |
| 95R | 88R | 83R | 88R | 70C | 87R | 72C | 88E | 86T | 60C | 90R | 95E |
| 84C | 80C | 60C | 83C | 75C | 86C | 75C | 87C | 84C | 85R | 86R | 92E |
| 80C | 84R | 80C | 86R | 82C | 92R | 75R | 88R | 82R | 83R | 86R | 93R |
| 85C | 83C | 72C | 82C | 84C | 84C | 68C | 88R | 87R | 82R | 88R | 92R |
| N.V. | 88R | N.V. | 84R | 90R | 84R | N.V. | 87E | 85E | N.V. | N.V. | 89E |
| 95T | 86R | 70R | 80R | 92E | 75C | 65C | 92E | 78R | 85E | 92T | 92E |
| 85C | 75C | 70C | 82C | 86R | 80R | 60C | 93R | 84R | 73R | 90E | 72C |
| 72C | 84R | 65R | 82R | 80R | 90R | 70R | 85R | 80R | 82R | 89R | 90E |
| 83E | N.V. | 84T | N.V. | 86T | 90E | N.V. | 90E | N.V. | N.V. | N.V. | N.V. |
| 84R | 79R | 75R | 87R | 92R | 74R | 78R | 82R | 83E | 82E | 87E | 90E |
| - | - | 85R | 84R | 87R | 85R | 86R | 85R | 77R | 88E | 87E | 88E |
| - | - | 88R | 85E | 83R | 76E | 84R | 86R | 90E | 87E | 85E | 88E |
| 86R | 80R | 86R | 85R | 86R | 82T | 90R | 94T | 89T | 92E | 75E | 82E |
| 86C | 83C | 88C | 86C | 85C | 85C | 88C | 84C | 90R | 75R | 89R | 76R |
| 86R | 83R | 82R | 82R | 80R | 78R | 88R | 88E | 87E | 90R | 82R | 83R |
| 84R | 80C | 86R | 83C | 84C | 85C | 85R | 86E | 84R | 86E | 87R | 85R |
| - | - | 86C | 86C | 84C | 90C | 65C | 90R | 85R | 72R | 84R | 84E |
| - | - | - | - | 78C | 92E | 72C | 86T | 78R | 85E | 88E | 92E |

Robert M. Parker is one of the most influential wine critics in the world. His chart is reprinted from his bi-monthly newsletter, *The Wine Advocate*, P.O. Box 311, Monkton, MD 21111.
Copyright © 1990 by Robert M. Parker, Jr.

# TOLL-FREE NUMBERS

## Car Rentals

Ajax, 800/252-9756
Alamo, 800/327-9635
American, 800/527-0202
Avis, 800/331-1212
Budget, 800/527-0700
Dollar, 800/421-6878
Enterprise, 800/325-8007
General, 800/327-7607
Hertz, 800/654-3131
National, 800/328-4657
Sears, 800/527-0770
Thrifty, 800/367-2277

## Airlines

Air Canada, 800/776-3000
American, 800/433-7300
British Airways, 800/247-9297
Continental, 800/525-0280
Delta, 800/221-1212
Midway, 800/621-5700
Northwest, 800/225-2525
Pan Am, 800/221-1111
Southwest, 800/531-5601
Trump Shuttle, 800/247-8786
TWA, 800/221-2000
United, 800/241-6522
USAir, 800/428-4322

## Hotels

Adams Mark, 800/231-5858
Best Western, 800/528-1234
Clarion, 800/252-7466
Colony, 800/367-6046
Comfort, 800/228-5150
Compri, 800/426-6774
Days Inn, 800/547-7878
Doubletree, 800/528-0444
Four Seasons, 800/332-3442
Hilton, 800/445-8867
Holiday Inn, 800/465-4329
Hyatt & Resorts, 800/233-1234
InterContinental, 800/327-0200
Marriott, 800/228-9290
Meridien, 800/543-4300
Quality, 800/228-5151
Radisson, 800/333-3333
Ramada, 800/228-2828
Red Lion, 800/547-8010
Ritz-Carlton, 800/241-3333
Sheraton, 800/325-3535
Stouffer, 800/468-3571
Westin Hotels & Resorts, 800/228-3000
Wyndham, 800/822-4200

# THE WALL STREET JOURNAL AWARDS

Our dining and lodging critics were asked to list their favorite restaurants and hotels from three price categories: Very Expensive (*$$$$*), Expensive (*$$$*), and Moderate (*$$*).

## Atlanta

*Best Hotels*
Ritz-Carlton, Buckhead, *$$$$*
Colony Square Hotel, *$$$*
Atlanta Airport Hilton, *$$*

*Best Restaurants*
Nikolai's Roof, *$$$$*
Savannah Fish Company, *$$$*

## Baltimore

*Best Hotels*
Harbor Court, *$$$$*
Tremont Hotel, *$$$*
Tremont Plaza, *$$*

*Best Restaurants*
The Conservatory, *$$$$*
The Brass Elephant, *$$$*
Kawasaki, *$$*

## Boston

*Best Hotels*
Four Seasons, *$$$$*
Le Meridien, *$$$*
The 57 Park Plaza, *$$*

*Best Restaurants*
Le Marquis de LaFayette, *$$$$*
Biba, *$$$*
Legal Seafoods, *$$*

## Chicago

*Best Hotels*
The Drake, *$$$$*
Richmont, *$$$*

*Best Restaurants*
The Everest Room, *$$$$*
Printer's Row, *$$$*
Berghoff, *$$*

## Cincinnati

*Best Hotels*
Cincinnatian, *$$$$*
The Garfield, *$$*

*Best Restaurants*
Maisonette, *$$$$*
The Precinct, *$$$*
The Phoenix, *$$*

## Cleveland

*Best Hotels*
Stouffer Tower City Plaza, *$$$$*
Glidden House, *$$$*

*Best Restaurants*
Burgess Grand Cafe, *$$$$*
Ninth Street Grill, *$$$*
Miller's Dining Room, *$$*

## Dallas/Fort Worth

*Best Hotels*
The Adolphus, *$$$$*
Hyatt Regency Dallas at Reunion, *$$$*
Embassy Suites Airport, *$$*

*Best Restaurants*
Routh Street Cafe, *$$$$*
Saint-Emilion, *$$$*
Joe T. Garcia's, *$$*

## Denver

*Best Hotels*
The Brown Palace, *$$$$*
Hyatt Regency Tech Center, *$$$*

*Best Restaurants*
Tante Louise, *$$$$*
Chez Thoa, *$$$*

## Detroit

| *Best Hotels* | *Best Restaurants* |
|---|---|
| Ritz-Carlton, Deerborn, $$$$ | The Whitney, $$$$ |
| | The Rattlesnake Club, $$$ |
| Drury Inn, $$ | Sweet Lorraine's Cafe, $$ |

## Houston

| *Best Hotels* | *Best Restaurants* |
|---|---|
| Four Seasons, $$$$ | Café Annie, $$$$ |
| Houstonian, $$$ | Damian's, $$$ |
| Holiday Inn Crowne Plaza, $$ | Churrascos, $$ |

## Indianapolis

| *Best Hotels* | *Best Restaurants* |
|---|---|
| Cantebury, $$$$ | Something Different, $$$ |
| Radisson Plaza, $$$ | |
| Holiday Inn Union Station, $$ | |

## Kansas City

| *Best Hotels* | *Best Restaurants* |
|---|---|
| Ritz-Carlton, $$$$ | American, $$$$ |
| Radisson Suite Hotel, $$$ | Cafe Allegro, $$$ |
| | Arthur Bryants, $$ |

## Las Vegas

| *Best Hotels* | *Best Restaurants* |
|---|---|
| Desert Inn, $$$$ | La Vie En Rose, $$$$ |
| Alexis Park, $$$ | Aristocrat, $$$ |
| Golden Nugget, $$ | Savoia, $$ |

## Los Angeles

| *Best Hotels* | *Best Restaurants* |
|---|---|
| Hotel Bel-Air, $$$$ | Patina, $$$$ |
| New Otani Hotel | Citrus, $$$ |
| and Gardens, $$$ | Locanda Veneta, $$ |

## Memphis

| *Best Hotels* | *Best Restaurants* |
|---|---|
| Peabody, $$$$ | Chez Phillipe, $$$$ |
| Omni Memphis, $$$ | Hemming's, $$$ |
| | La Pâtisserie, $$ |

## Miami

| *Best Hotels* | *Best Restaurants* |
|---|---|
| Grand Bay, $$$$ | Vinton's, $$$$ |
| Sofitel, $$$ | Stefano's, $$$ |
| St. Michel, $$ | JJ's, $$ |

## Minneapolis/St. Paul

| *Best Hotels* | *Best Restaurants* |
|---|---|
| Marquette Hotel, $$$$ | Goodfellows, $$$$ |
| The St. Paul Hotel, $$$ | D'Amico Cucina, $$$ |
| | Dakota, $$ |

## Montréal

**Best Hotels**
Four Seasons/Le Quatre
  Saison, $$$$
Delta, $$$
Le Nouvel Hôtel, $$

**Best Restaurants**
Café de Paris, $$$$
Le Mas des Oliviers, $$$

## New Orleans

**Best Hotels**
Windsor Court, $$$$
Pontchartrain, $$$
Le Richelieu, $$

**Best Restaurants**
Henri, $$$$
Gautreau's, $$$
Galatoire's, $$

## New York

**Best Hotels**
Carlyle, $$$$
Sherry Netherland, $$$
Algonquin, $$

**Best Restaurants**
Lutèce, $$$$
Montrachet, $$$
Union Square Café, $$

## Philadelphia

**Best Hotels**
Hotel Atop the Bellevue,
  $$$$
The Holiday Inn Center
  City, $$$

**Best Restaurants**
The Fountain at the Four
  Seasons Hotel, $$$$
Deux Cheminées, $$$
White Dog Café, $$

## Phoenix

**Best Hotels**
Ritz-Carlton, $$$$
Westcourt in the Buttes,
  $$$
Executive Park, $$

**Best Restaurants**
La Hacienda, $$$$
Eddie's Grill, $$$
The Stockyards, $$

## Pittsburgh

**Best Hotels**
Vista International, $$$$
Westin William Penn, $$$
Holiday Inn at University
  Center, $$

**Best Restaurants**
Jake's Above the Square,
  $$$$
Juno Trattoria, $$

## St. Louis

**Best Hotels**
Hotel Majestic, $$$$
Stouffer Concourse, $$$
Drury Inn-St. Louis Union
  Station, $$

**Best Restaurants**
Tony's, $$$$
Riddle's Penultimate Cafe
  & Wine Bar, $$

## San Diego

**Best Hotels**
Hotel del Coronado, $$$$
San Diego Marriott Hotel
  & Marina, $$$

**Best Restaurants**
Top o' the Cove, $$$$
Salvatore's, $$$
Café Pacifica, $$

## San Francisco

**Best Hotels**
Mandarin Oriental, $$$$
Prescott, $$

**Best Restaurants**
Masa's, $$$$
Stars, $$$
Fog City Diner, $$

## Seattle

*Best Hotels*
Four Seasons Olympic, *$$$*
Alexis, *$$$*
Edgewater Inn, *$$*

*Best Restaurants*
Sheraton's Fullers, *$$$$*
Elliott's, *$$$*

## Toronto

*Best Hotels*
The Four Seasons Toronto,
  *$$$$*
Sheraton Centre, *$$$*
Novotel Toronto Centre, *$$*

*Best Restaurants*
Pronto, *$$$$*
Bistro 990, *$$$*
The Avocado Club, *$$*

## Vancouver

*Best Hotels*
Le Meridien, *$$$$*
Wedgewood, *$$$*

*Best Restaurants*
Chartwell, *$$$$*
Bishop's, *$$$*
Chez Thierry, *$$*

## Washington, DC

*Best Hotels*
The Willard, *$$$$*
The Jefferson, *$$$*
Hotel Washington, *$$*

*Best Restaurants*
Jockey Club, *$$$$*
Doninique's, *$$$*
Le Gaulois, *$$*

# CEO AWARDS

This is our first annual poll of the nation's top CEOs. Recommendations are limited to cities included in the guide. Not all places are reviewed by our critics.

## William W. Adams
*Chairman*
*Armstrong World Industries*
*Lancaster, Pennsylvania*

**Restaurants**
Tio Pepe, Baltimore
Louie's Bookstore and Cafe, Baltimore
The Fountain, Philadelphia
Aux Beaux Champs, Washington, DC
**Hotels**
Four Seasons, Philadelphia
Four Seasons, Washington, DC

## Rand V. Araskog
*Chairman*
*ITT Corporation*
*New York, New York*

**Restaurants**
Elio's, New York
Salvatore's, San Diego
**Hotels**
Ritz-Carlton, Washington, DC

## James K. Baker
*Chairman*
*ARVIN Industries Inc.*
*Columbus, Indiana*

**Restaurants**
Ninfa's, Houston
The Greenhouse, Indianapolis
Peter's, Indianapolis
Mrs. Simpson's, Washington, DC

## Bill Bindley
*President*
*Bindley Western Industries*
*Indianapolis, Indiana*

**Restaurants**
Locke-Ober Cafe, Boston
George's Place, Indianapolis
La Scala, Los Angeles
Joe's Stone Crab, Miami
Le Cirque, New York
**Hotels**
Le Meriden, Boston
Beverly Hills, Los Angeles
Sherry Netherland, New York

## Arthur M. Bjontegard, Jr.
*President*
*S.C. National Corporation*
*Columbia, South Carolina*

**Restaurants**
Locke-Ober Cafe, Boston
Bookbinders, Philadelphia
**Hotels**
Ritz-Carlton, Boston

## Harry G. Bubb
*Chairman*
*Pacific Mutual Life Insurance Company*
*Newport Beach, California*

**Restaurants**
Jimmy's, Los Angeles
Amelio's, San Francisco
Donatello, San Francisco
**Hotels**
Bel Air, Los Angeles

## M. Anthony Burns
*Chairman, President, and CEO*
*Ryder Systems, Inc.*
*Miami, Florida*

**Restaurants**
Buckhead Diner, Atlanta
Pano's and Paul's, Atlanta
Routh St. Cafe, Dallas
L' Orangerie, Dallas
Spago, Los Angeles
Grand Cafe, Miami
Max's Place, Miami
Aureole, New York
Gotham Bar and Grill, New York
Le Cirque, New York
**Hotels**
Crescent Court, Dallas
Mansion on Turtle Creek, Dallas
Regent Beverly Wilshire, Los Angeles
Grand Bay, Miami
InterContinental, Miami
Omni Royal Orleans, New Orleans
Helmsley Palace, New York
Plaza Athenée, New York
Four Seasons, Washington, DC
Hay Adams, Washington, DC
Windsor Court, Washington, DC

## Dr. William J. Catacosinos
*Chairman and CEO*
*Long Island Lighting Company*
*Hicksville, New York*

**Restaurants**
Paola's, New York
Sistina, New York
**Hotels**
Mansion on Turtle Creek, Dallas
Four Seasons, Washington, DC

## James C. Chapman
*President*
*Outboard Marine Corporation*
*Waukegan, Illinois*

**Restaurants**
Carlos', Chicago
Pronto, Chicago
The Forge, Miami
**Hotels**
Bally's Las Vegas, Las Vegas
Peabody, Memphis
Jefferson, Washington, DC

## Richard A. Clarke
*Chairman*
*Pacific Gas and Electric*
*San Francisco, California*

**Restaurants**
Le Bernardin, New York
**Hotels**
Mansion on Turtle Creek, Dallas
Westin, Washington, DC

## W. H. Clark
*Chairman*
*Nolco Chemical Company*
*Naperville, Illinois*

**Restaurants**
Alfredo's, Chicago
Como Inn, Chicago
**Hotels**
Stanford Court, San Francisco

## R. K. Crutsinger
*President*
*Wetterau Inc.*
*Hazelwood, Missouri*

**Restaurants**
Anthony's, St. Louis
Dominic's, St. Louis
Tony's, St. Louis

## Robert Deffeyes
*Senior Vice Pres. of Technologies*
*Carlisle Companies*
*Syracuse, New York*

**Restaurants**
Joe T. Garcia's, Ft. Worth
Benihana Village, Las Vegas
Brennan's, New Orleans
Hurlingham's, New York
Anthony's Star of the Sea, San Diego
Top o' the Cove, San Diego
Blue Fox, San Francisco
Castagnola, San Francisco
**Hotels**
Adolphus, Dallas
Mansion on Turtle Creek, Dallas
New York Hilton at Rockefeller Center, New York

Sea Lodge, San Diego
Hotel Fairmont, San Francisco

## Ted Enloe
*President*
*Lomas Financial Corp.*
*Dallas, Texas*

**Restaurants**
Veni Vidi Vici, Atlanta
Calluaud's, Dallas
Routh Street Cafe, Dallas
The Box Tree, New York
Il Cantinori, New York
Le Grenouille, New York
Primavera, New York
Toscana, New York
**Hotels**
Crescent Court, Dallas
Mansion on Turtle Creek, Dallas
Regency, New York

## Robert F. Erburu
*Chairman*
*Times Mirror Co.*
*Los Angeles, California*

**Restaurants**
Citrus, Los Angeles
L' Orangerie, Los Angeles
Aurora, New York
Le Lion d'Or, Washington, DC
**Hotels**
Ritz-Carlton, Boston
Helmsley Palace, New York
Fairmont, San Francisco
Madison, Washington, DC

## Lynn M. Ewing, Jr.
*General Counsel*
*Ewing, Carter, McBeth, Smith, Gosnell,*
*Vickers & Hoberock*
*Nevada, Missouri*

**Restaurants**
Jockey Club, Washington, DC
Tony's, St. Louis
Campton Place, San Francisco
**Hotels**
Hay Adams, Washington, DC

## J. Carter Fox
*President*
*Chesapeake Corp.*
*West Point, Virginia*

**Restaurants**
Oggie, New York
**Hotels**
Brown Palace, Denver
Huntington, San Francisco
Four Seasons, Washington, DC

## William W. Gaston
*President*
*Gold Kist, Inc.*
*Atlanta, Georgia*

**Restaurants**
Pano's and Paul's, Atlanta
103 West, Atlanta
**Hotels**
Ritz-Carlton Buckhead, Atlanta
Ritz-Carlton Atlanta, Atlanta
Brown Palace, Denver
Arizona Biltmore, Phoenix
Hay Adams, Washington, DC

## A. Frederick Gerstell
*President*
*CalMat Co.*
*Los Angeles, California*

**Restaurants**
Cricket's, Chicago
Le Chardonnay, Los Angeles
Bouley, New York
Primavera, New York
**Hotels**
Mayfair Regent, Chicago
Regent Beverly Wilshire, Los Angeles
Lowell, New York
Hay Adams, Washington, DC

## A. F. Giacco
*Chairman*
*Himont, Inc.*
*Wilmington, Delaware*

**Restaurants**
Giambelli 50, New York
**Hotels**
Park Lane, New York
Fairmont, San Francisco

## Nelson Harris
*President*
*Pittway Corp.*
*Northbrook, Illinois*

**Restaurants**
Arnie's, Chicago
Chestnut Street Grill, Chicago
Spiaggia, Chicago
Harvey's, Washington, DC
**Hotels**
Ritz-Carlton, Boston
Drake, Chicago
Ritz-Carlton, Washington, DC

## Robert J. Haugh
*Vice Chairman*
*The St. Paul Companies, Inc.*
*St. Paul, Minnesota*

**Restaurants**
Legal Seafoods, Boston
Cliff Young's, Denver

Asti, New York
The Courtyard, San Francisco
Mrs. Simpson's, Washington, DC

## Ross B. Kenzie
*Chairman (Retired)*
*Goldome*
*Buffalo, New York*

**Restaurants**
The Four Seasons, New York
Harvey's, Washington, DC
**Hotels**
The Pierre, New York

## Lawrence P. Klamon
*President*
*Fuqua Industries, Inc.*
*Atlanta, Georgia*

**Restaurants**
La Grotta, Atlanta
Pano's and Paul's, Atlanta
Lafayette, New York
Primavera, New York
**Hotels**
Ritz-Carlton Buckhead, Atlanta

## George V. MacGowan
*Chairman of the Board*
*Baltimore Gas & Electric*
*Baltimore, Maryland*

**Restaurants**
103 West, Atlanta
Milton Inn, Baltimore
**Hotels**
Harbor Court, Baltimore

## Donald H. Mitzel
*President (retired)*
*First Federal of Michigan*
*Birmingham, Michigan*

**Restaurants**
Joe Muer's, Detroit
The Lark, Detroit
Joe's Stone Crab, Miami

## J. Terrance Murray
*Chairman*
*Fleet/Norstar Financial Corporation*
*Providence, Rhode Island*

**Hotels**
Boston Harbor Hotel at Rowes Wharf, Boston

## Eugene R. Olson
*Chairman*
*Deluxe Corporation*
*St. Paul, Minnesota*

**Restaurants**
Anchorage, Minneapolis

**Hotels**
The Plaza, New York

**John Pomerantz**
*Chairman*
*Leslie Fay Companies*
*New York, New York*

**Hotels**
Ritz-Carlton, Chicago

**Seymour S. Preston III**
*President*
*Atochem North America, Inc.*
*Philadelphia, Pennsylvania*

**Restaurants**
Maison Robert, Boston
Joe's Stone Crab, Miami
Gloucester House, New York
Di 'Lullo's Centro, Philadelphia
**Hotels**
Ritz-Carlton, Boston
Four Seasons, Philadelphia

**Thomas R. Ricketts**
*Chairman*
*Standard Federal Bank*
*Troy, Michigan*

**Restaurants**
The Lark, Detroit
Joe Meur's, Detroit
Le Bernardin, New York
La Caravelle, New York
L'Etoile, San Francisco
Kan's, San Francisco
Le Lion D'Or, Washington, DC
Maison Blanche, Washington, DC
**Hotels**
Hyatt Regency Dearborn, Detroit
Waldorf-Astoria, New York
Mandarin Oriental, San Francisco
Stanford Court Stouffer, San Francisco
Hay Adams, Washington, DC
Madison, Washington, DC

**Robert D. Rogers**
*President and CEO*
*Texas Industries, Inc.*
*Dallas, Texas*

**Restaurants**
Mr. K's, Washington, DC
**Hotels**
Mansion on Turtle Creek, Dallas
Bel Air, Los Angeles

**Richard D. Wood**
*Chairman*
*Eli Lilly & Co.*
*Indianapolis, Indiana*

**Restaurants**
Benvenuti, Indianapolis
Le Regence, New York
**Hotels**
Canterbury, Indianapolis
Plaza Athenée, New York

## John F. Woodhouse
*Chairman*
*Sysco Corporation*
*Houston, Texas*

**Restaurants**
Locke-Ober Cafe, Boston
Rotisserie Beef and Bird, Houston
Leopard, New York
**Hotels**
Ritz-Carlton, Boston
Warwick, Houston
Waldorf-Astoria, New York

## Douglas C. Yearley
*Chairman*
*Phelps Dodge Corporation*
*New York, New York*

**Restaurants**
Ritz-Carlton, Phoenix
**Hotels**
Drake, Chicago
Bel Air, Los Angeles
Jefferson, Washington, DC

# TWO-YEAR CALENDAR

## 1991

### January
| S | M | T | W | T | F | S |
|---|---|---|---|---|---|---|
|   |   | 1 | 2 | 3 | 4 | 5 |
| 6 | 7 | 8 | 9 | 10 | 11 | 12 |
| 13 | 14 | 15 | 16 | 17 | 18 | 19 |
| 20 | 21 | 22 | 23 | 24 | 25 | 26 |
| 27 | 28 | 29 | 30 | 31 |   |   |

### February
| S | M | T | W | T | F | S |
|---|---|---|---|---|---|---|
|   |   |   |   |   | 1 | 2 |
| 3 | 4 | 5 | 6 | 7 | 8 | 9 |
| 10 | 11 | 12 | 13 | 14 | 15 | 16 |
| 17 | 18 | 19 | 20 | 21 | 22 | 23 |
| 24 | 25 | 26 | 27 | 28 |   |   |

### March
| S | M | T | W | T | F | S |
|---|---|---|---|---|---|---|
|   |   |   |   |   | 1 | 2 |
| 3 | 4 | 5 | 6 | 7 | 8 | 9 |
| 10 | 11 | 12 | 13 | 14 | 15 | 16 |
| 17 | 18 | 19 | 20 | 21 | 22 | 23 |
| $^{24}/_{31}$25 | 26 | 27 | 28 | 29 | 30 |   |

### April
| S | M | T | W | T | F | S |
|---|---|---|---|---|---|---|
|   | 1 | 2 | 3 | 4 | 5 | 6 |
| 7 | 8 | 9 | 10 | 11 | 12 | 13 |
| 14 | 15 | 16 | 17 | 18 | 19 | 20 |
| 21 | 22 | 23 | 24 | 25 | 26 | 27 |
| 28 | 29 | 30 |   |   |   |   |

### May
| S | M | T | W | T | F | S |
|---|---|---|---|---|---|---|
|   |   |   | 1 | 2 | 3 | 4 |
| 5 | 6 | 7 | 8 | 9 | 10 | 11 |
| 12 | 13 | 14 | 15 | 16 | 17 | 18 |
| 19 | 20 | 21 | 22 | 23 | 24 | 25 |
| 26 | 27 | 28 | 29 | 30 | 31 |   |

### June
| S | M | T | W | T | F | S |
|---|---|---|---|---|---|---|
|   |   |   |   |   |   | 1 |
| 2 | 3 | 4 | 5 | 6 | 7 | 8 |
| 9 | 10 | 11 | 12 | 13 | 14 | 15 |
| 16 | 17 | 18 | 19 | 20 | 21 | 22 |
| $^{23}/_{30}$24 | 25 | 26 | 27 | 28 | 29 |   |

### July
| S | M | T | W | T | F | S |
|---|---|---|---|---|---|---|
|   | 1 | 2 | 3 | 4 | 5 | 6 |
| 7 | 8 | 9 | 10 | 11 | 12 | 13 |
| 14 | 15 | 16 | 17 | 18 | 19 | 20 |
| 21 | 22 | 23 | 24 | 25 | 26 | 27 |
| 28 | 29 | 30 | 31 |   |   |   |

### August
| S | M | T | W | T | F | S |
|---|---|---|---|---|---|---|
|   |   |   |   | 1 | 2 | 3 |
| 4 | 5 | 6 | 7 | 8 | 9 | 10 |
| 11 | 12 | 13 | 14 | 15 | 16 | 17 |
| 18 | 19 | 20 | 21 | 22 | 23 | 24 |
| 25 | 26 | 27 | 28 | 29 | 30 | 31 |

### September
| S | M | T | W | T | F | S |
|---|---|---|---|---|---|---|
| 1 | 2 | 3 | 4 | 5 | 6 | 7 |
| 8 | 9 | 10 | 11 | 12 | 13 | 14 |
| 15 | 16 | 17 | 18 | 19 | 20 | 21 |
| 22 | 23 | 24 | 25 | 26 | 27 | 28 |
| 29 | 30 |   |   |   |   |   |

### October
| S | M | T | W | T | F | S |
|---|---|---|---|---|---|---|
|   |   | 1 | 2 | 3 | 4 | 5 |
| 6 | 7 | 8 | 9 | 10 | 11 | 12 |
| 13 | 14 | 15 | 16 | 17 | 18 | 19 |
| 20 | 21 | 22 | 23 | 24 | 25 | 26 |
| 27 | 28 | 29 | 30 | 31 |   |   |

### November
| S | M | T | W | T | F | S |
|---|---|---|---|---|---|---|
|   |   |   |   |   | 1 | 2 |
| 3 | 4 | 5 | 6 | 7 | 8 | 9 |
| 10 | 11 | 12 | 13 | 14 | 15 | 16 |
| 17 | 18 | 19 | 20 | 21 | 22 | 23 |
| 24 | 25 | 26 | 27 | 28 | 29 | 30 |

### December
| S | M | T | W | T | F | S |
|---|---|---|---|---|---|---|
| 1 | 2 | 3 | 4 | 5 | 6 | 7 |
| 8 | 9 | 10 | 11 | 12 | 13 | 14 |
| 15 | 16 | 17 | 18 | 19 | 20 | 21 |
| 22 | 23 | 24 | 25 | 26 | 27 | 28 |
| 29 | 30 | 31 |   |   |   |   |

## 1992

### January
| S | M | T | W | T | F | S |
|---|---|---|---|---|---|---|
|   |   |   | 1 | 2 | 3 | 4 |
| 5 | 6 | 7 | 8 | 9 | 10 | 11 |
| 12 | 13 | 14 | 15 | 16 | 17 | 18 |
| 19 | 20 | 21 | 22 | 23 | 24 | 25 |
| 26 | 27 | 28 | 29 | 30 | 31 |   |

### February
| S | M | T | W | T | F | S |
|---|---|---|---|---|---|---|
|   |   |   |   |   |   | 1 |
| 2 | 3 | 4 | 5 | 6 | 7 | 8 |
| 9 | 10 | 11 | 12 | 13 | 14 | 15 |
| 16 | 17 | 18 | 19 | 20 | 21 | 22 |
| 23 | 24 | 25 | 26 | 27 | 28 | 29 |

### March
| S | M | T | W | T | F | S |
|---|---|---|---|---|---|---|
| 1 | 2 | 3 | 4 | 5 | 6 | 7 |
| 8 | 9 | 10 | 11 | 12 | 13 | 14 |
| 15 | 16 | 17 | 18 | 19 | 20 | 21 |
| 22 | 23 | 24 | 25 | 26 | 27 | 28 |
| 29 | 30 | 31 |   |   |   |   |

### April
| S | M | T | W | T | F | S |
|---|---|---|---|---|---|---|
|   |   |   | 1 | 2 | 3 | 4 |
| 5 | 6 | 7 | 8 | 9 | 10 | 11 |
| 12 | 13 | 14 | 15 | 16 | 17 | 18 |
| 19 | 20 | 21 | 22 | 23 | 24 | 25 |
| 26 | 27 | 28 | 29 | 30 |   |   |

### May
| S | M | T | W | T | F | S |
|---|---|---|---|---|---|---|
|   |   |   |   |   | 1 | 2 |
| 3 | 4 | 5 | 6 | 7 | 8 | 9 |
| 10 | 11 | 12 | 13 | 14 | 15 | 16 |
| 17 | 18 | 19 | 20 | 21 | 22 | 23 |
| $^{24}/_{31}$25 | 26 | 27 | 28 | 29 | 30 |   |

### June
| S | M | T | W | T | F | S |
|---|---|---|---|---|---|---|
|   | 1 | 2 | 3 | 4 | 5 | 6 |
| 7 | 8 | 9 | 10 | 11 | 12 | 13 |
| 14 | 15 | 16 | 17 | 18 | 19 | 20 |
| 21 | 22 | 23 | 24 | 25 | 26 | 27 |
| 28 | 29 | 30 |   |   |   |   |

### July
| S | M | T | W | T | F | S |
|---|---|---|---|---|---|---|
|   |   |   | 1 | 2 | 3 | 4 |
| 5 | 6 | 7 | 8 | 9 | 10 | 11 |
| 12 | 13 | 14 | 15 | 16 | 17 | 18 |
| 19 | 20 | 21 | 22 | 23 | 24 | 25 |
| 26 | 27 | 28 | 29 | 30 | 31 |   |

### August
| S | M | T | W | T | F | S |
|---|---|---|---|---|---|---|
|   |   |   |   |   |   | 1 |
| 2 | 3 | 4 | 5 | 6 | 7 | 8 |
| 9 | 10 | 11 | 12 | 13 | 14 | 15 |
| 16 | 17 | 18 | 19 | 20 | 21 | 22 |
| $^{23}/_{30}$ $^{24}/_{31}$25 | 26 | 27 | 28 | 29 |   |   |

### September
| S | M | T | W | T | F | S |
|---|---|---|---|---|---|---|
|   |   | 1 | 2 | 3 | 4 | 5 |
| 6 | 7 | 8 | 9 | 10 | 11 | 12 |
| 13 | 14 | 15 | 16 | 17 | 18 | 19 |
| 20 | 21 | 22 | 23 | 24 | 25 | 26 |
| 27 | 28 | 29 | 30 |   |   |   |

### October
| S | M | T | W | T | F | S |
|---|---|---|---|---|---|---|
|   |   |   |   | 1 | 2 | 3 |
| 4 | 5 | 6 | 7 | 8 | 9 | 10 |
| 11 | 12 | 13 | 14 | 15 | 16 | 17 |
| 18 | 19 | 20 | 21 | 22 | 23 | 24 |
| 25 | 26 | 27 | 28 | 29 | 30 | 31 |

### November
| S | M | T | W | T | F | S |
|---|---|---|---|---|---|---|
| 1 | 2 | 3 | 4 | 5 | 6 | 7 |
| 8 | 9 | 10 | 11 | 12 | 13 | 14 |
| 15 | 16 | 17 | 18 | 19 | 20 | 21 |
| 22 | 23 | 24 | 25 | 26 | 27 | 28 |
| 29 | 30 |   |   |   |   |   |

### December
| S | M | T | W | T | F | S |
|---|---|---|---|---|---|---|
|   |   | 1 | 2 | 3 | 4 | 5 |
| 6 | 7 | 8 | 9 | 10 | 11 | 12 |
| 13 | 14 | 15 | 16 | 17 | 18 | 19 |
| 20 | 21 | 22 | 23 | 24 | 25 | 26 |
| 27 | 28 | 29 | 30 | 31 |   |   |

# Atlanta

*by Robin Hohman*

From the gold-covered dome of the state capitol to the trendiest nightspots in Buckhead, Atlanta is a combination of old Southern traditions and new moneyed power. It's southern, because it's in the South, but there are so many transplanted northerners that regional differences seem to matter less and less. Ask anybody working in Atlanta where they're from, and there's a good chance it's somewhere else.

Since the 1960s, business leaders have worked hard to combat northern perceptions of the South as a backward and racist region. Atlantans like to say it's a city too busy to hate, and, for the most part, that seems to be true. Atlanta businesspeople are primarily interested in getting ahead, in broadening the city's economic base, and in encouraging business travel and tourism.

Now a major airline hub, Atlanta had formerly been a railroad town. Soon after Hardy Ivy, the first settler, put down stakes here in 1833, it became known as Terminus, because the railroad line ended here. It became Marthasville a decade later and Atlanta soon after that, in 1845.

As a railroad and trade center, its importance to the Confederacy during the Civil War wasn't lost on the Union. Most of the city was burned by Gen. Sherman's forces before they began the famous march to the sea in 1864.

It was rebuilt rapidly after the war, and has been an important commercial center ever since. Coca-Cola and Georgia Pacific, among other commercial giants, call Atlanta home.

Atlanta scored a major coup when it earned the right to host the 1996 summer Olympics. In anticipation, the city began building the Georgia Dome, which will become home to the Atlanta Falcons football team in 1992 and a major site for some of the games. Organizers expect about 84,000 jobs to be created in preparation for the event.

## Top Employers

| Employer | Type of Enterprise | Parent*/ Headquarters |
|----------|--------------------|------------------------|
| **AT&T** | Communications | Baskin Ridge, NJ |

| | | |
|---|---|---|
| **Atlanta Newspapers** | Daily newspaper | Atlanta |
| **The Coca-Cola Co.** | Soft drink manufacturer | Atlanta |
| **Delta Air Lines** | Airline | Atlanta |
| **General Motors** | Automobile manufacturer | Dearborn, MI |
| **Georgia Power** | Utility | Atlanta |
| **IBM** | Computers | Armonk, NY |
| **Lockheed Aeronautical Systems Co.** | Airplane manufacturer | Burbank, CA |
| **Rich's, Inc.** | Department store | Campeau/Toronto |
| **Southern Bell Telephone & Telegraph** | Telecommuni- cations | BellSouth/Atlanta |

*\*if applicable*

## ESSENTIAL INFORMATION

### Climate

Allergy sufferers alert: Atlanta's mostly mild tempera-tures, with two rainy seasons, one in winter and one in summer, are fodder for more than just good cotton. If pol-len was a cash crop, Atlanta alone could pay off the nation-al debt. If you suffer from allergies or asthma, bring your medication, and be prepared to use it.

What follows are average daily maximum and minimum temperatures for Atlanta.

| | | | | | | | | |
|---|---|---|---|---|---|---|---|---|
| **Jan.** | 52F 36 | 11C 2 | **Feb.** | 54F 38 | 12C 3 | **Mar.** | 63F 43 | 17C 6 |
| **Apr.** | 72F 52 | 22C 11 | **May** | 79F 61 | 26C 16 | **June** | 86F 67 | 30C 19 |
| **July** | 88F 70 | 31C 21 | **Aug.** | 86F 70 | 30C 21 | **Sept.** | 83F 65 | 28C 18 |
| **Oct.** | 72F 54 | 22C 12 | **Nov.** | 61F 43 | 16C 6 | **Dec.** | 52F 38 | 11C 3 |

### Airport

**Hartsfield International Airport** is located 10 miles south of downtown.

### Airport Business Facilities

**Mutual of Omaha Business Service Center** (South Terminal next to the security checkpoint, tel. 404/761–0106) has fax machines, photocopying, notary public, ticket pickup, Western Union, and travel insurance.

## Airlines

**Delta Air Lines** is based in Atlanta.

**American,** tel. 404/521–2655 or 800/433–7300.
**Continental,** tel. 404/436–3300 or 800/525–0280.
**Delta,** tel. 404/765–5000 or 800/221–1212.
**Northwest,** tel. 800/225–2525.
**Pan Am,** tel. 800/221–1111.
**TWA,** tel. 404/522–5738 or 800/221–2000.
**United,** tel. 404/394–2234 or 800/241–6522.
**USAir,** tel. 800/428–4322.

## Between the Airport and Downtown

*By Taxi*
Taxis take 20 minutes if there's no traffic, 35–45 minutes in rush hour (6–9 AM, 3:30–6:30 PM). The cost between the airport and downtown hotels is set by the city; at press time it was $15 for one person, $16 for two people, and $18 for three.

*By Train*
This is the fastest, cheapest, most reliable way to go, especially during rush hours. MARTA trains take about 13 minutes to get downtown from a terminal near the Delta baggage claim carousels 8 and 9. Airport trains run on the north/south line; if you want to get to, or are coming from, an east/west stop, switch at the downtown Five Points Station. Trains leave for the airport every 12 minutes from Five Points. MARTA operates 5 AM–12:30 AM, Mon.–Sat., and 6 AM–midnight, Sun. Cost: 85¢. You need exact change or a token purchased from the machines. For MARTA schedule information call 404/848–4711.

*By Shuttle Bus*
**The Atlanta Airport Shuttle** (tel. 404/525–2177) takes about 20 minutes and stops at major downtown hotels. Cost: $7 one way, $12 round trip, higher to midtown and suburbs.

*By Limousine*
This is a more comfortable way to get to the airport than taxi, but you must reserve in advance and pay a 6% service tax. Prices run between $40 and $50, plus tax and tip. (*See* Important Addresses and Numbers below, for some company names.)

## Car Rentals

The following companies have booths in the airport:

**Ace Rent-A-Car,** tel. 404/530–2210 or 800/533–6489.
**Atlanta Rent-A-Car,** tel. 404/297–0990.
**Avis,** tel. 404/530–2700 or 800/331–1212.
**Budget,** tel. 404/530–3000 or 800/527–0700.
**Hertz,** tel. 404/530–2900 or 800/654–3131.
**National,** tel. 404/530–2800 or 800/328–4657.
**Snappy,** tel. 404/968–0255.
**Southern Rent-A-Car,** tel. 404/436–2722.

## Emergencies

*Doctors*
**Piedmont Minor Emergency Clinic** (3115 Piedmont Rd. NE, tel. 404/237–1755) is open 8 AM–8 PM Mon.–Sat.,

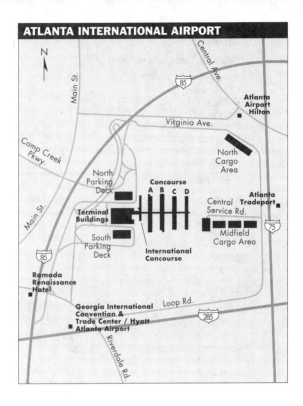

noon–8 Sun. **Medical Associations of Atlanta** (874 W. Peachtree St. NE, tel. 404/881–1714) is a physician referral service.

*Dentists*
**Northern District Dental Society** (tel. 404/270–1635) is a free dental referral service, with someone always on call.

*Hospitals*
**Piedmont Hospital** (1968 Peachtree Rd. N.W., tel. 404/350–2222).

## Important Addresses and Numbers

**Audiovisual rentals.** Audio Visual Services (811 Marietta St. NW, tel. 404/875–7555), Image America (771 Miami Circle NE, tel. 404/266–3340).

**Chamber of Commerce** (234 International Blvd. NW, tel. 404/880–9000).

**Computer rentals.** Computer Business Solutions (2260–R Northwest Pkwy., Marietta, tel. 404/952–9930), PCR Personal Computer Rentals (1874 Piedmont Ave. NE, tel. 404/874–5394).

**Convention and exhibition centers** (233 Peachtree St. NE, tel. 404/521–6600).

**Fax service.** Action Fax (3620 DeKalb Technology Pkwy., Doraville, tel. 404/452–0502) will direct you to the closest facsimile station in the city.

**Formal-wear rentals.** Men's: Mitchell's Formal Wear (3976 Peachtree Rd., tel. 404/261–0761), Women's: Women's Overnight Sensations (4920 Roswell Rd. NW, tel. 404/250–0711).

**Gift shops.** Gift Baskets: Christie's Baskets (442 Sherwood Oaks Rd., tel. 404/469–6408), Flowers: Execu-Flower Service (5299 Roswell Rd. NE, tel. 404/252–5151).

**Graphic design studios.** Atlanta Graphics Center (6456 Warren Dr., Norcross, tel. 404/448–3920), Executive Arts (1916 Piedmont Rd. NE, tel. 404/325–0087).

**Hairstylists.** Unisex: Fugi's Hair Designers (in the Marriott Marquis at Peachtree Center, tel. 404/524–6622), Lenox Hair Studio (3355 Lenox Rd NE, tel. 404/261–8832).

**Health and fitness clubs.** *See* Fitness, below.

**Information hot lines.** Concert information (tel. 404/633–9623), movie listings (tel. 404/222–2070), sports scores (tel. 404/222–2030).

**Limousine services.** A-1 Limousine Services (tel. 404/299–2388 or 800/672–5466), Executive Limousine Service (tel. 404/763–1000 or 800/241–3943).

**Liquor stores.** Elite Liquor Store (1163 Peachtree St. NE, tel. 404/892–7892), Peachtree Road Package Store (1893 Peachtree Rd. NE, tel. 404/351–2994).

**Mail delivery, overnight.** DHL Worldwide Express (tel. 404/997–1635), Federal Express (tel. 404/321–7566), TNT Skypak (tel. 404/991–9191), United Parcel Service (tel. 404/432–9494), U.S. Postal Service Express Mail (404/765–7486).

**Messenger services.** Central Delivery Service of Atlanta (tel. 404/892–1350), Georgia Messenger Service Inc. (tel. 404/681–3278).

**Office space rentals.** Executive Office Center (3525 Piedmont Rd. N.E., tel. 404/233–0055), Secretariat Executive Center (3355 Lenox Rd. NE, Suite 750, tel. 404/262–2121).

**Pharmacies, 24-hour.** Treasury Drug (1061 Ponce de Leon Ave. NE, tel. 404/876–0381), Bells Ferry (1250 N. Cobb Dr., Marietta, tel. 404/427–7344).

**Radio stations, all-news.** WCNN 680 AM; WGST 640 AM.

**Secretarial services.** Convention Connection (1 CNN Center, Suite 553, tel. 404/872–1268), Manpower (260 Peachtree St. NW, Suite 900, tel. 404/659–3565).

**Stationery supplies.** Brown Office Supply Services (477 Peachtree St. NE, tel. 404/892–4770), Franklin's Printing Office Supplies and Copy Service will pick up and deliver (123 Peachtree St. NE, tel. 404/523–6931).

**Taxis.** Yellow Cabs (tel. 404/521–0200), Checker Cab (tel. 404/351–1111).

**Train information.** Amtrak (1688 Peachtree St. NW, tel. 404/881–3060), MARTA hot line (tel. 404/848–5072).

**Travel agents.** AAA Travel Agency (1100 Spring St. NW, tel. 404/843–4500), Maritz Travel (5605 Glen Ridge Dr., Suite 200, tel. 404/522–6515 or 800/334–6718).

**Weather.** Weather Line, WYNX (tel. 404/436–1550).

## LODGING

Atlanta is a big convention town, which room availability and rates reflect. Prices change according to season and are usually higher in the late winter and spring when most conventions are held.

Buckhead is a trendy, expensive area, about four miles north of downtown, with numerous restaurants and the best stores. If you have business in midtown—between Buckhead and downtown—this is where you'll want to stay, though there's little nightlife or shopping here. Downtown can be very expensive, and gets very crowded during conventions and trade shows, but you can get around easily and won't need a car. The downtown and midtown hotel complexes are fairly safe, but it's best to be cautious walking around in these areas at night. An active street life keeps uptown Buckhead a safer bet.

Airport hotels cost 30–50% less than those downtown, but they're smaller and don't offer as many business services. Most provide a free shuttle bus to and from Hartsfield International, and downtown Atlanta is a 15-minute ride on a MARTA train, so a car is unnecessary if you stay in the airport area.

All of the hotels listed below offer corporate rates and weekend discounts; inquire when making reservations.

Highly recommended lodgings in each price category are indicated by a star ★.

| Category | Cost* |
| --- | --- |
| *$$$$* (Very Expensive) | over $150 |
| *$$$* (Expensive) | $105–$150 |
| *$$* (Moderate) | under $105 |

*All prices are for a standard double room, single occupancy, excluding 11% tax.*

*Numbers in the margin correspond to numbered hotel locations on the Atlanta Lodging and Dining maps.*

### Buckhead

❶ **Embassy Suites Hotel-Buckhead.** This quiet and comfort-
*$$$* able all-suites hotel, in a pleasant if predictable atrium setting, offers many in-room extras geared specifically to the busy business traveler. Each double and king suite is equipped with a kitchen area, three sinks, a microwave oven, a small refrigerator, and a coffeemaker with coffee— good if you plan to do a lot of in-room business and don't want to have to call room service all the time. Living/dining areas have a sofa bed, an overstuffed chair, a dining table, and an extra phone. An all-you-can-eat breakfast and a cocktail hour are included in the suite price. For more space, ask for a room with a double bed, larger than those with kings. *3285 Peachtree Rd. NE, 30305, tel. 404/261–*

# GREATER ATLANTA

**Lodging**

Atlanta Airport Hilton, **7**

Atlanta Marriott Gwinnett Place, **4**

Colony Square Hotel, **6**

Embassy Suites Hotel-Buckhead, **1**

Hyatt Atlanta Airport, **9**

Ramada Renaissance Hotel/Atlanta-Airport, **8**

Ritz-Carlton Buckhead, **2**

**Dining**

The Dining Room, **2**

Harry Baron's, **3**

Houston's, **5**

# DOWNTOWN ATLANTA

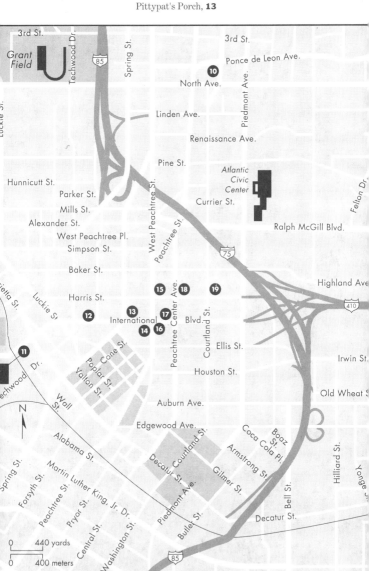

*7733 or 800/362–2779, fax 404/261–7733, ext. 2198. Gen. manager, Ken Powers. 328 suites. AE, CB, D, DC, MC, V.*

★ ❷ **Ritz-Carlton, Buckhead.** This is simply the most luxurious
$$$$ hotel in Atlanta, the place where the high-powered mon-eyed people meet. Some may find the white-gloved staff overattentive, but most appreciate the full service for both business and personal needs. Dark wood paneling, high-pile oriental rugs, and quality antique reproductions and paintings give the lobby the feel of an Old World hotel. Rooms are similarly elegant, with richly patterned drap-eries and spreads, and high four-poster beds with claw-and-ball feet. Twin rooms are small, but as gracefully dec-orated as the larger kings and suites. Views are not spec-tacular—rooms overlook the Phipps Plaza and Lenox Square shopping centers. But you can walk to these two malls, which are the best in Atlanta. The hotel's dining room is well worth trying (*see* Dining, below), the Lobby Lounge is a fine place to entertain a client, and the Café Bar offers jazz in the evenings (*see* After Hours, below, for both). *3434 Peachtree Rd. NE, 30326, tel. 404/237–2700 or 800/241–3333, fax 404/239–0078. Gen. manager, Ed Staros. 555 rooms, 14 suites. AE, CB, D, DC, MC, V.*

## Downtown

❶❾ **Atlanta Hilton and Towers.** This fashionable hotel is aimed
$$$ at people who are willing to forgo some business services for a downtown location in an elegant setting. On the Tow-ers level, floors 26–28, you'll get extra-plush rooms, a bet-ter selection of bath toiletries, access to the Towers lounge, plus Continental breakfast, afternoon hors d'oeuvres, and self-serve cocktails from the wet bar in the lounge. The less expensive business-class section on the fifth floor has fewer VIP services than the Towers level, but offers complimentary Continental breakfast and pri-vate check-in and check-out. Nikolai's Roof (*see* Dining, below) is one of Atlanta's best restaurants and Trader Vic's (*see* After Hours, below) features its trademark ex-otic drinks. *255 Courtland St., 30303, tel. 404/659–2000 or 800/445–8667, fax 404/ 222–2868. Gen. manager, An-dre Schaeffer. 1,220 rooms, 60 suites. AE, CB, D, DC, MC, V.*

❶❽ **Atlanta Marriott Marquis.** Designed by Atlanta architect
$$$$ John Portman, the Marquis atrium is a towering maze of pink walls and black railings, punctuated by the trade-mark glass elevators constantly on the move. Rooms above the 10th floor have the best views; ask to face north to see the city, south to view the airport. The location, setting, and service here are first rate; the staff is large and friend-ly. However, the furnishings in some of the less expensive rooms seem tacky and out of date. In an ongoing renova-tion begun in 1990, richer, darker furniture was added to over half the rooms. The more expensive suites are well equipped. Concierge-level guests receive an ample Conti-nental breakfast and hors d'oeuvres in the concierge lounge. Champions (*see* Dining, below) is a fun place for a casual meal or drink. *265 Peachtree Center Ave., 30303, tel. 404/521–0000 or 800/228–9290, fax 404/586–6299. Gen. manager, Ted Renner. 1,674 rooms, 80 suites. AE, CB, D, DC, MC, V.*

❶❷ **Comfort Inn Hotel.** Despite the Comfort Inn's $2.5-million
$$ renovation when it changed hands in late 1989 (it used to

# ATLANTA HOTEL CHART

| HOTELS | Price Category | Business Services | | | | | | | | Desk | Desk lighting | Bed lighting |
| | | Banquet capacity | No. of meeting rooms | Secretarial services | Audiovisual equipment | Teletype news service | Computer rentals | In-room modem phonejack | All-news cable channel | | | |
|---|---|---|---|---|---|---|---|---|---|---|---|---|
| Airport Hilton | $$ | 570 | 22 | ✓ | ✓ | ✓ | ✓ | ✓ | ✓ | ● | ◐ | ◐ |
| Colony Square | $$$ | 1500 | 14 | ✓ | ✓ | - | ✓ | - | ✓ | ◐ | ● | ◐ |
| Comfort Inn | $$ | 0 | 4 | - | ✓ | - | - | - | ✓ | ● | ◐ | ● |
| Embassy Suites Hotel-Buckhead | $$$ | 200 | 5 | ✓ | ✓ | - | ✓ | ✓ | ✓ | ● | ● | ● |
| Hilton and Towers | $$$ | 1700 | 49 | ✓ | ✓ | - | ✓ | - | ✓ | ◐ | ◐ | ● |
| Hyatt Atlanta Airport | $$ | 500 | 11 | ✓ | ✓ | - | ✓ | - | ✓ | ● | ● | ● |
| Hyatt Regency | $$$$ | 1400 | 37 | ✓ | ✓ | ✓ | ✓ | ✓ | ✓ | ◐ | ● | ● |
| Marriott Gwinnett Place | $$ | 1000 | 13 | ✓ | ✓ | - | ✓ | ✓ | ✓ | ● | ● | ◐ |
| Marriott Marquis | $$$$ | 2150 | 46 | ✓ | ✓ | - | ✓ | ✓ | ✓ | ● | ● | ● |
| Omni Hotel at CNN Center | $$ | 2000 | 99+ | ✓ | ✓ | ✓ | ✓ | ✓ | ✓ | ◐ | ● | ◐ |
| Ramada Renaissance | $$ | 620 | 23 | - | ✓ | - | ✓ | - | ✓ | ● | ◐ | ◐ |
| Ritz-Carlton Atlanta | $$$$ | 240 | 15 | ✓ | ✓ | ✓ | ✓ | ✓ | ✓ | ● | ● | ● |
| Ritz-Carlton Buckhead | $$$$ | 500 | 25 | ✓ | ✓ | ✓ | ✓ | ✓ | ✓ | ● | ● | ● |
| Westin Peachtree Plaza | $$$$ | 2800 | 41 | ✓ | ✓ | ✓ | ✓ | ✓ | ✓ | ● | ● | ● |

$$$$ = over $150, $$$ = $105 -$150, $$ = under $105.
● good, ◐ fair, ○ poor.
All hotels listed here have photocopying and fax facilities.

| In-Room Amenities | | | | | | | | | | | Hotel Amenities | | | | | | |
|---|---|---|---|---|---|---|---|---|---|---|---|---|---|---|---|---|---|
| Nonsmoking rooms | In-room checkout | Minibar | Pay movies | VCR/Movie rentals | Hairdryer | Toiletries | Room service | Laundry/Dry cleaning | Pressing | | Concierge | Barber/Hairdresser | Garage | Courtesy airport transport | Sauna | Pool | Exercise room |
| ✓ | ✓ | ✓ | ✓ | - | ✓ | ◐ | ● | ● | ● | | ✓ | ✓ | ✓ | ✓ | ✓ | ● | ● |
| ✓ | ✓ | - | ✓ | - | - | ● | ● | ● | ● | | ✓ | ✓ | ✓ | - | - | ● | ◐ |
| ✓ | - | - | ✓ | - | - | ○ | ◐ | ○ | - | | - | - | ✓ | - | ✓ | ◐ | - |
| ✓ | ✓ | ✓ | ✓ | - | - | ◐ | ● | ◐ | ◐ | | ✓ | - | ✓ | - | ✓ | ● | ◐ |
| ✓ | ✓ | ✓ | ✓ | - | - | ◐ | ● | ● | ● | | ✓ | ✓ | ✓ | - | ✓ | ● | ◐ |
| ✓ | - | - | ✓ | - | - | ○ | ◐ | ● | ● | | ✓ | - | ✓ | ✓ | ✓ | ○ | ○ |
| ✓ | ✓ | ✓ | ✓ | - | ✓ | ◐ | ● | ● | ◐ | | ✓ | ✓ | ✓ | - | ✓ | ○ | ○ |
| ✓ | ✓ | - | ✓ | - | - | ○ | ◐ | ● | ● | | ✓ | - | ✓ | - | ✓ | ● | ◐ |
| ✓ | ✓ | - | ✓ | - | ✓ | ◐ | ● | ● | ● | | ✓ | - | ✓ | - | ✓ | ● | ● |
| ✓ | ✓ | ✓ | ✓ | - | - | ○ | ◐ | ● | ● | | ✓ | - | ✓ | - | ✓ | ● | ● |
| ✓ | ✓ | - | ✓ | - | ✓ | ○ | ◐ | ● | ● | | ✓ | - | ✓ | ✓ | ✓ | ● | ● |
| ✓ | ✓ | ✓ | - | ✓ | ✓ | ○ | ● | ● | ● | | ✓ | - | ✓ | - | ✓ | - | - |
| ✓ | ✓ | ✓ | ✓ | - | ✓ | ○ | ● | ● | ● | | ✓ | ✓ | ✓ | - | ✓ | ● | ● |
| ✓ | ✓ | ✓ | ✓ | - | - | ○ | ● | ◐ | ◐ | | ✓ | - | ✓ | - | ✓ | ● | ● |

**Room service:** ● 24-hour, ◐ 6AM-10PM, ○ other.
**Laundry/Dry cleaning:** ● same day, ◐ overnight, ○ other.
**Pressing:** ● immediate, ◐ same day, ○ other.

be the Hotel Ibis), its main attraction is still its price. During convention time, this hotel is booked. Yet it offers few business services and very basic rooms with limited storage space: only one desk drawer, no closets. A very narrow open-sided armoire is provided for clothing. Bathrooms, however, are extra large, and double rooms are fairly spacious. Although it's close to bustling Peachtree Street, the hotel is in a seedier part of town, across from the Greyhound bus station. Security people are visible, walking around with two-way radios. Women traveling alone may be uneasy in this neighborhood. *101 International Blvd., 30303, tel. 404/524–5555 or 800/535–0707. Gen. manager, Ian Saucer. 260 rooms. AE, CB, D, DC, MC, V.*

**⑮** **Hyatt Regency Atlanta.** You pay for the name, location, and convention services here; luxurious rooms and ele-
$$$$ gant surroundings are not part of the package. The hotel's public areas are not in great condition, nor are the rooms; their Danish modern furnishings have seen better days, and the color scheme is dark and somewhat depressing, like the spiny greenery in the center atrium. There are no desk phones, some rooms have tables instead of desks, and there are few in-room extras. If working in your room is less important than a good location (right near the Apparel and Merchandise marts), and you'd rather mingle with the convention crowd at night than hole up in your room, the Hyatt will meet your needs. *265 Peachtree St., 30303, tel. 404/577–1234 or 800/228–9000, fax 404/588–4137. Gen. manager, Steve Mills. 1,279 rooms, 59 suites. AE, D, DC, MC, V.*

**⑪** **Omni Hotel at CNN Center.** A downtown hotel in the com-
$$ plex that houses CNN, The Omni Coliseum, some foreign consulates, and the Associated Press, the Omni seems crowded only during Hawks games and the NCAA tournament. That's no reflection on the hotel's quality, because you get more for less here than you do at other downtown hotels, especially those on Peachtree Street. The Omni is an attractive establishment: the public spaces are huge and airy, and the staff is willing and attentive. Some of the suites are extremely large, at reasonable prices. Hallways are long and wide, adorned with crisp black-and-white movie stills from the MGM Library (now owned by the Turner Broadcasting System, which also owns the complex). Rooms are comfortable and spacious, if the furniture is a bit on the tacky side. There are balconies in some rooms, and all rooms have desks or tables with adequate lighting. The Bugatti Restaurant (*see* Dining, below) is highly recommended for its fine northern Italian fare. *100 CNN Center, 30305, tel. 404/659–0000 or 800/843–6664, fax through hotel switchboard. Gen. manager, William M. Thompson. 470 rooms, 29 suites. AE, CB, D, DC, MC, V.*

**★ ⑯** **Ritz-Carlton, Atlanta.** For all its beauty and Old World
$$$$ charm, the downtown Ritz-Carlton is still not quite as lavish as its uptown cousin in Buckhead, but plenty of quality reproduction antiques, crystal chandeliers, Chinese lamps, plush rugs, and extensive in-room extras make this the second most luxurious hotel in town. Service, for business or pleasure, is impeccable. The deluxe accommodations are larger than the standard ones, with better views. Rooms on the Japanese floor come with tea service, slip-

pers, and Japanese porcelain dishes. There's no health club on premises (although one is planned), but guests can use facilities in the nearby Georgia Pacific building and the pool at the Westin Peachtree Plaza. The Café (*see* Business Breakfasts, below) offers an elegant setting for business meals. *181 Peachtree St. NE, 30303, tel. 404/659-0400 or 800/241-3333, fax 404/688-0400. Gen. manager, Darrell Sheaffer. 454 rooms, 22 suites. AE, CB, D, DC, MC, V.*

★ ⑭  **The Westin Peachtree Plaza.** This 73-floor glass cylinder in
$$$$ the heart of the business district is the tallest hotel in North America. Public areas are plush and luxurious, with gleaming marble, polished wood with brass accents, and handsome floral arrangements; the plaza's shops, restaurants, and lounges all display similar high-tech elegance. Guest rooms are angled around the center elevators; it can be a bit dizzying to walk in circles to find your room. Accommodations are smaller than in other luxury hotels, but floors above 46 offer spectacular city views (those facing north or south are the best). Floors 15 and 16 have the worst views, and tables instead of desks, but cost appreciably less. There are desks in most of the other rooms, and all are decorated with overstuffed chairs, modernistic furniture, and imported marble in the bathrooms. The staff is helpful and attentive. At the top of the building, the revolving Sun Dial restaurant is a good steakhouse with a great view, and The Savannah Fish Company serves up excellent seafood (*see* Dining, below, for both). *210 Peachtree at International Blvd. NE, 30303, tel. 404/659-1400 or 800/228-3000, fax 404/589-7424. Gen. manager, Herman Gammeter. 1,074 rooms, 48 suites. AE, CB, D, DC, MC, V.*

## Midtown

★ ⑥  **Colony Square Hotel.** In the heart of the midtown business
$$$ district, across from the Woodruff Arts Center and near the High Museum of Art, the Colony Square is superfunctional. A full-service meeting site connected to a mini shopping mall, it offers just about everything you'll need except, possibly, excitement. The ambience here, like the hushed mauves and dusty blues throughout, is restrained. The towering main lobby and long, narrow corridors give the feel of an apartment building more than of a bustling hotel. Rooms are spacious and comfortable, if somewhat plain, and business amenities are good, especially on Colony Club floors, where suites have two telephones with three separate lines. Trellises (*see* Business Breakfasts, below) is a good spot for an early morning meeting. Overall, the value-to-price ratio here is much higher than on downtown Peachtree Street. *Peachtree at 14th St. NE, 30361, tel. 404/892-6000 or 800/422-7895, fax 800/876-3276. Gen. manager, Mark Hancock. 466 rooms, 34 suites. AE, CB, DC, MC, V.*

## Gwinnett County

④  **Atlanta Marriott Gwinnett Place.** This is an attractive 17-
$$ story hotel about 25 miles northeast of downtown Atlanta, where you get more for less. A comfortable main lobby with cozy, overstuffed furniture lends a relaxed, easygoing atmosphere to this business-efficient hotel. Rooms are pleasant and, with two phones and a desk in each, well suited for the business traveler. Ten guest rooms are

equipped with computers, software, color monitors, and printers. Hallway lighting is inadequate, though, and women traveling alone may be uncomfortable here at night. New lighting and room renovations are in process. *1775 Pleasant Hill Rd., Duluth, 30136, tel. 404/923–1775 or 800/228–9290, fax 404/923–1775, ext. 7102 for hotel business, ext. 7103 for guests. Gen. manager, Kevin Regan. 295 rooms, 5 suites. AE, CB, D, DC, MC, V.*

## Airport

★ ❼ **Atlanta Airport Hilton.** A full-service hotel practically
$$ touching the airport, the Hilton is high-tech yet comfortable. The exterior is contemporary stone-and-glass, but rooms are plush, well equipped, and exceedingly clean. Corner rooms, called Executive rooms, are very large; rooms –04 and –20 on each floor have extra-big tubs and stall showers. Better, more expensive accommodations are on the Towers level, with higher ceilings, bathroom TVs, access to the Towers lounge, and free Continental breakfast and afternoon hors d'oeuvres. *1031 Virginia Ave., Hapeville, 30354, tel. 404/767–9000 or 800/445–8667, fax 404/768–0185. Gen. manager, Jim Haughney. 501 rooms, 4 suites. AE, CB, D, DC, MC, V.*

❾ **Hyatt Atlanta Airport.** A cozy lobby with exotic flowers,
$$ reproduction antiques, a marble floor, and a decorative fountain give the Hyatt an ambience that's closer to downtown luxury than that at other airport hotels; it's not as well equipped for business travelers, however. Don't let the hospital-like basic brick exterior throw you; the hotel was formerly the Holiday Inn Crowne Plaza before it changed hands in mid-1989. A $5-million renovation blends the stark modern architecture with comfortable furnishings. Rooms, decorated in easy-to-take muted greens, are better than those at most mid-priced hotel chains. And more executive frills were laid on for the hotel's Regency Club level, opened in late 1990. The hotel's biggest draw for business travelers is that it's connected to the Georgia International Convention and Trade Center, with 17 meeting rooms and a 40,000-square-foot exhibit hall. *1900 Sullivan Rd., College Park, 30337, tel. 404/991–1234 or 800/228–9000, fax 404/991–5906. Gen. manager, Valerie Ferguson. 400 rooms, 9 suites. AE, CB, D, DC, MC, V.*

❽ **Ramada Renaissance Hotel/Atlanta-Airport.** If you're look-
$$ ing for a basic, moderately priced room close to I-85—and little else—this is the place to come. The layout is motel-modern, with small rectangular rooms radiating from the hall. Furnishings are too large for the rooms, so an extra chest of drawers is placed in the closet. There's some attempt at atmosphere in the main lobby, with a touch of Ramada burgundy to set off natural stone columns, but results are mixed. The staff can be less than friendly—unusual for Atlanta. *4736 Best Rd., College Park, 30337, tel. 404/762–7676 or 800/228–9898, fax 404/ 763–1913. Gen. manager, Chris Steinfals. 496 rooms, 57 suites. AE, CB, D, DC, MC, V.*

## DINING

Atlanta has restaurants for almost every taste, and often at prices lower than those in other major metropolitan areas. Most hotel restaurants offer decent American fare, and there are good French and Italian restaurants throughout the city. Greek, Vietnamese, Korean, Indian, Thai, Spanish, and Mexican food are available, but not always authentic. Fresh seafood is hard to come by, except at a few downtown restaurants. Good Southern cooking is equally hard to find in this convention city, as is real down-home barbecue. The local celebrity crowd favors the trendy theme bistros and cafés in uptown Buckhead. Downtown and midtown fare is geared to traditional American palates.

Highly recommended restaurants in each price category are indicated by a star ★.

| Category | Cost* |
|----------|-------|
| *$$$$* (Very Expensive) | over $40 |
| *$$$* (Expensive) | $25–$40 |
| *$$* (Moderate) | under $25 |

*per person, including appetizer, entrée, and dessert, and excluding drinks, service, and 6% sales tax.*

*Numbers in the margin correspond to numbered restaurant locations on the Atlanta Lodging and Dining maps.*

### Business Breakfasts

Atlanta offers a number of good hotel dining rooms for breakfast meetings. **The Café** in the Ritz-Carlton (tel. 404/659–0400) is cheerful and relaxed; menus run from griddle cakes and grits to Scottish smoked salmon; special fitness menus are also available. **Trellises,** in the Colony Square Hotel (tel. 404/892–6000), small and low-key, is one of the few full service restaurants in the midtown business district. Its tables and chairs are strategically placed for private conversation. The breakfast menu offers everything from bagels and lox to eggs Benedict. **The Atrium Café** (tel. 404/521–0000), on the garden level of the Atlanta Marriott Marquis, adjacent to Peachtree Center, offers a breakfast buffet with a variety of freshly baked breads, grits, and eggs prepared to order.

**Cracker Barrel** (2160 Delk Rd., SE, Marietta, tel. 404/951–2602), in an old country store setting, is not the place to impress people—unless they love homemade hotcakes dripping with real maple syrup, big slabs of bacon, eggs, and grits, and a huge hunk of watermelon for dessert. Nine separate restaurants ring the city, all about 20 minutes from downtown. They open at 6 AM; on Sunday, arrive before noon to avoid the after-church crowd. **The Waffle House** (2581 Piedmont Rd. NE, tel. 404/261–4475, various other locations) doesn't look like much, but it's open 24 hours a day, makes pecan waffles just right, and always has good, fresh coffee.

## Buckhead

★ ❷ **The Dining Room.** Soft linens and lavish flower arrange-
$$$$ ments set the tone for this elegant eatery that features
Chef Gunter Seeger's thoughtfully prepared nouvelle cuisine. The atmosphere is a bit stiff and the service somewhat cold, but if you want to make an impression, this is
the place to come. Menus are prix fixe, and change daily.
Popular appetizers include Olympia oysters in chive vinaigrette, and white Alaska salmon cake with citrus vinaigrette. Choice entrées include bass in red wine sauce, and
Jamison farm lamb with cabbage. Lime mousse with piña
colada sorbet and dark chocolate mousse with huckleber-
ry compote are among the excellent desserts. The wine
list is consistently strong. *Ritz-Carlton, Buckhead, 3434
Peachtree Rd., tel. 404/237-2700. Formal dress; jacket
and tie required. Reservations required. AE, CB, D, DC,
MC, V. Closed Sun. and holidays. Dinner only.*

❸ **Harry Baron's.** Probably the only kosher-style deli in the
$$ country that serves grits, Harry Baron is nevertheless
authentic in decor—that is, there isn't any, just the usual
salamis hanging over the glassed-in deli counter. You
don't come here to entertain but to satisfy a craving for
a Hebrew National hot dog with steaming sauerkraut, a
pastrami on rye, or a Dr. Brown's soda. There are plenty
of overstuffed sandwiches on the menu, some of them fea-
turing unusual combinations. Challah bread, borscht, ba-
gels, and lox are all available for takeout. *Phipps Plaza,
Buckhead, tel. 404/261-5288. Casual dress. No reserva-
tions. No credit cards; out-of-town checks accepted.
Closed Thanksgiving, Christmas, New Year's.*

❺ **Houston's.** Part of a national, Texas-based chain, Hous-
$$ ton's serves up hearty portions of American standards
as well as some Southwest specialties. Deep burgundies,
dark woods, and brass accents give this place a clubby feel.
Parties of three or more should ask for the roomier round
tables in the middle of the restaurant. Try roasted chicken
with black bean sauce, or the Texas burger smothered in
chili, grated cheddar, onions, and jalapeño peppers. This
is not a place to discuss business—the noise level is fairly
high, with a constant din of soft rock in the background.
The wine menu is extremely limited, the beer selection is
better, and there's plenty of top-notch hard stuff. *2166
Peachtree St., tel. 404/351-2442. Casual dress, no cut-
offs. No reservations. AE, CB, DC, MC, V. Closed
Thanksgiving, Christmas.*

## Downtown

⓫ **Bugatti Restaurant.** Oversized posters of the vintage cars
$$$ for which this restaurant was named line the walls of
Bugatti, which specializes in cuisine from northern Italy.
The large, high-back leather chairs and the well-spaced
tables make it a good choice for relaxing and private busi-
ness discussions. Zuppa di pesce, the house specialty, fea-
tures fish, shrimp, and mussels in a tomato base. Veal
lovers can find several different kinds of scaloppine, as well
as a good standard veal Parmesan. Another favorite is the
Italian Connection, which comes with medallions of veal,
beef, and jumbo shrimp. The wine selection is strong and
varied. *Omni Hotel, 100 CNN Center, tel. 404/659-0000.*

*Casual dress. Reservations accepted. AE, CB, D, DC, MC, V. Closed Sun.*

**⑱ Champion's.** More than 22 television sets, usually tuned to
$$ ESPN or the game of the day, make this a good place for
sports fans to relax with colleagues or dine alone. The
large, airy bar/restaurant is decorated with sports post-
ers and memorabilia. Food is basic bar fare, featuring
well-prepared nachos, salads, sandwiches, and burgers.
There's a very decent chili with red beans and a good se-
lection of beers and ales to chase it down. *Garden Level,
Marriott Marquis, 265 Peachtree Center Ave., tel. 404/
586-6359. Casual dress. Reservations suggested for lunch
weekdays. AE, D, DC, MC, V.*

**⑰ Dailey's.** This converted two-story warehouse has a good
$$$ bar and grill downstairs, and finer dining upstairs. The
basic bar menu is supplemented with some more imagina-
tive dishes, like baked salmon in parchment with garlic
butter and fresh dill, or avocado pasta. The larger upstairs
menu features veal, duck, and seafood entrées, and a dessert bar. The dining room is private but dark, especially at
night when candles are the main light source. Service is
not speedy: Be prepared to wait up to 90 minutes to be
seated for dinner, 20 for lunch. *17 International Blvd., tel.
404/681-3303. Casual but neat dress. No reservations.
AE, CB, DC, MC, V. Closed Christmas Eve, Christmas,
Thanksgiving.*

**★ ⑲ Nikolai's Roof.** This restaurant takes its cue from the opu-
$$$$ lent lifestyle of the last Czar of Russia, and the czar's pas-
sion for French food and wine. In an intimate setting, with
a fine view of the city, Chef Philippe Haddad serves up a
five-course, prix-fixe meal in classic French style, with a
liberal sprinkling of Russian specialties. The menu
changes monthly, and might offer an appetizer of pirozh-
kis followed by borscht, a house salad, roasted rack of
lamb served with white basil butter and garlic demi-glaze,
and a dessert soufflé. Russian vodkas are available, of
course, and there are nearly 200 wines, in all price ranges.
This is a restaurant for celebrating, entertaining, or im-
pressing, but reserve early; there's usually a three-week
wait for Saturday night, and during convention time you
could wait a month for a table. *255 Courtland St., atop the
Atlanta Hilton and Towers, tel. 404/659-3282. Jacket and
tie required. Reservations required. AE, CB, D, DC, MC,
V. Closed Christmas and New Year's Day. Dinner only,
two seatings nightly: at 6:30 and 9:30.*

**⑬ Pittypat's Porch.** This is *the* place for traditional, down-
$$$ home Southern cooking. The entrance to this Atlanta in-
stitution re-creates a pre-Civil War plantation porch, and
allows a rocking-chair view of the plain 18th-century-style
dining area below. The menu reflects the German, En-
glish, and French heritage of many Southern settlers.
Smoked pork loin and marinated venison and buffalo are
good choices among a variety of game and seafood dishes;
all entrées include a 39-item all-you-can-eat hors d'oeuvre
sideboard. The wine list is short, but why not try a mint
julep or an Ankle Breaker—rum, wild cherry brandy, or-
ange juice, and grenadine? This is a place to indulge; ta-
bles are tightly placed and the noise level makes it more
suitable for relaxing or entertaining than for discussing
serious business. *25 International Blvd., tel. 404/525-
8228. Casual dress. No reservations. AE, CB, DC, MC,*

*V. Closed Thanksgiving, Christmas, New Year's Day.
Dinner nightly, lunch only by appointment for 40 or
more.*

★ ⑭ **Savannah Fish Company.** The seafood served here is flown
$$$ in daily from the coast. Whether it's a bucket of Little
Neck clams in white wine sauce or red snapper fried in
just the right amount of butter, Chef Gerhardt Wind be-
lieves in excellence through simplicity. The daily menu re-
flects the day's catch, but there's always a full range of
regional favorites, such as baby Boston scrod and lemon
sole from the Northeast, or grouper and sea trout from
the Southern coast. Be sure to try the famous Savannah
Fish Stew, a bouillabaisse of yesterday's fish stock, brim-
ming with julienne vegetables, and a touch of saffron and
pernod. The decor is as fresh and appealing as the menu,
with a 100-foot glassed-in waterfall, huge pots of yellow
daisies, and a sumptuous white-tiled oyster bar. Always
crowded during convention time, it's still a good place to
discuss business or simply relax after work. *Westin Peach-
tree Plaza, Peachtree & International Blvd. NE, tel. 404/
589-7456. Casual but neat. No reservations. AE, CB, D,
DC, MC, V. Closed Christmas.*

⑭ **Sun Dial Restaurant.** As the name suggests, this restau-
$$$$ rant revolves, offering spectacular views of Atlanta from
73 floors above the city. Tables are crowded together in
this popular eatery, but business talks are possible on a
slow night, when you can ask to be seated apart from other
diners. Among the excellent American specialties are
smoked prime ribs, T-bone steaks, and lamb chops. The
wine list is strong and varied, with selections from Cali-
fornia, Italy, and France. Desserts range from simple
cheesecake to the baroque Cloud Duster—marble pound
cake filled with hazelnut-chocolate ice cream and topped
with hot Southern Comfort sauce. Request a window seat
and the staff will try to accommodate you—but there are
no guarantees. *Westin Peachtree Plaza Hotel, Peachtree
St. & International Blvd. NE, tel. 404/589-7506, ext.
7200. No jeans, no sneakers, men's shirts must have col-
lars. Reservations advised. AE, CB, D, DC, MC, V.*

## Midtown

★ ⑩ **The Abbey.** Waiters are dressed in monk's habits in this
$$$$ converted church built in 1915 with stained glass windows
and vaulted ceilings. Tables are private enough for seri-
ous business discussions, but it's the sophisticated menu
that brings most locals here. Among the recommended en-
trées are pheasant breast with sweetbreads in Madeira,
and venison medallions in port sauce with sweet potato
puree. For lighter fare, try the sautéed grouper with juni-
per berries in grapefruit sauce. The wine list is also com-
mendable. *163 Ponce de Leon Ave. NE, tel. 404/876-8532.
No jeans or tennis shoes; jacket optional. Reservations
advised. AE, CB, D, DC, MC, V. Closed all legal holi-
days. Dinner only.*

## FREE TIME

### Fitness

*Hotel Facilities*

The **Atlanta Marriott Marquis** has a fully equipped health club, with an indoor/outdoor pool, sauna, and massages. The daily fee for nonguests is $5. The **Westin Peachtree – Plaza** is also fully equipped, with exercise bikes, Stairmaster, weight room, swimming pool, and sauna; massages are often available at an hour's notice. The cost (without massage) for nonguests is $7 per day or $20 per week.

*Health Clubs*

The **Atlanta Health and Racquet Club** (1775 Water Pl., tel. 404/952–3200) has the best facilities, including the regulation-size basketball court where the Atlanta Hawks practice when they're in town. Guest passes are $15 a day. Very close seconds are the **Sporting Club** (1515 Sheraton Rd., tel. 404/325–2700) and the newer **Sporting Club at Windy Hill** (300 Interstate North Parkway, tel. 404/953–1100). Rates for nonmembers are $20 a day ($11 if you are accompanied by a member), but the range of equipment and activities available is excellent.

*Jogging*

The best downtown jogging route is in **Piedmont Park,** about a 3½-mile run around ball fields, tennis courts, and Piedmont Lake. Call the **Atlanta Track Club** (3097 Shadowlawn Ave., tel. 404/231–9064) for alternatives.

### Shopping

There are more than 22 malls in the greater Atlanta area, as well as an abundance of small shops. In Buckhead, **Lenox Square** (3393 Peachtree Rd. NE) boasts more than 200 shops, including high-fashion designer stores such as Louis Vuitton, Guy Laroche, and Brooks Brothers, as well as Macy's, Neiman Marcus, and Rich's. Adjacent, **Phipps Plaza** (3500 Peachtree at Lenox Rd.) counters with Sak's Fifth Avenue, Lord & Taylor, Tiffany & Co., Godiva Chocolates, Mark Cross, Abercrombie & Fitch, and more than 50 other high-priced specialty stores. Downtown, the **Peachtree Center Shopping Mall** (231 Peachtree St. NE) has more than 70 shops and restaurants, ranging from upscale designer stores to touristy gift boutiques.

More than $100 million was spent to redevelop **Underground Atlanta** (Peachtree St. and Central Ave. at Alabama St.), a megashopping complex with space for 130 shops, restaurants, and nightclubs—but it hasn't really caught on yet. Several shops closed down soon after opening, and the city is fighting to promote the concept. Expect to find plenty of "Southern" souvenirs that say "Hi, ya'll, from Atlanta." There's adequate parking, but streets are congested; consider taking a MARTA Peachtree Trolley bus from downtown.

### Diversions

**Atlanta Botanical Garden** (Piedmont Rd. between 14th St. and Monroe Dr., tel. 404/876–5858) features both exotic and endangered plants, including a restored hardwood forest, vegetable rows, and Japanese gardens. In spring the blooming dogwoods are especially beautiful.

**Chastain Park** (216 W. Wieuca Rd., tel. 404/255–0723) and **Sugar Creek** (2706 Bouldercrest Rd., tel. 404/241–7671) are two of the best public golf courses, with carts and rental clubs available.

**DeKalb Farmers Market** (3000 E. Ponce de Leon Ave., Decatur, tel. 404/377–6400) has 106,000 square feet of fresh fruits, cheeses, and delicacies from around the world. Closed Mon.

**High Museum of Art** (1280 Peachtree St., tel. 404/892–3600), Atlanta's major museum, features permanent exhibits on the decorative arts and African folk arts, as well as changing special exhibits.

**Martin Luther King, Jr., National Historic District** (along Auburn Ave.) is a memorial to the life and death of the civil rights leader. It encompasses the **Center for Nonviolent Social Change** (449 Auburn Ave., tel. 404/524–1956), a community-oriented education center with a museum, library, and souvenir gift shop; tours of the district are offered here. Next to the Center is the **Ebenezer Baptist Church** (407 Auburn Ave.), where three generations of the King family preached. Adjacent to it is Dr. King's white marble tomb, with an eternal flame. A few doors up the street is Dr. King's birthplace (501 Auburn Ave., tel. 404/331–3919), which is managed by the National Park Service and open daily.

**Museum of the Jimmy Carter Library** (Carter Presidential Center, 1 Copenhill Ave. NE, tel. 404/331–3942) features photos, videotapes, and other memorabilia from the native Georgian's days at the White House.

**Piedmont Park** (Piedmont Ave. between 10th and 14th Sts.) is closed to automobile traffic, and is a popular spot to picnic, jog, or bicycle.

## Professional Sports

The **Braves,** Atlanta's baseball team (tel. 404/577–9100), and the **Falcons,** the city's football team (tel. 404/261–5400), play at the Atlanta/Fulton County Stadium. Atlanta's basketball players, the **Hawks** (tel. 404/681–3605), appear at the Omni Coliseum.

## The Arts

Atlanta offers high-quality symphony, ballet, and regional theater. The city's young, moneyed population also helps attract top rock groups in the largest arena in town, the **Omni Coliseum** (100 Techwood Dr. NW, tel. 404/681–2100). Traditionalists can hear the Atlanta Symphony Orchestra and the Atlanta Opera Association at **Symphony Hall** in the **Woodruff Arts Center** (1280 Peachtree St. NE, tel. 404/892–2414); there are also free classical concerts in the summer at **Chastain and Piedmont parks.** The **Alliance Theater,** also at the Woodruff Arts Center, presents a mix of classic Broadway musicals, comedies, and drama.

The **Fox Theatre** (660 Peachtree St., tel. 404/881–2000), built in the 1920s and now a national landmark, is still a grand showcase for current films, Broadway hits, and popular music. The Atlanta Ballet, which has a repertoire ranging from classical to modern, used to perform at the Fox, but now may be seen at the **Atlantic Civic Center** (395 Piedmont Ave. NE, tel. 404/523–1879).

For listings, check *Atlanta* magazine, Friday's *Atlanta Journal-Constitution*, or *Creative Loafing*, a free tabloid distributed throughout the city.

Ticket agencies include **Ticket Master** (1 Georgia Center, 600 W. Peachtree St., Suite 2550, tel. 404/249–6400) and **Turtle's Records & Tapes** (2385 Peachtree Rd. NE, tel. 404/261–8130; ask about other outlets throughout the city).

## After Hours

*Bars and Lounges*
The lounges at the **Ritz Carlton Atlanta** (tel. 404/659–0400) and **Buckhead** (tel. 404/237–2700) are both elegant and perfect for a quiet drink with a client. If you want to have a late-night sandwich or relax over a fresh draft, head for **Manuel's Tavern** (602 N. Highland Ave., tel. 404/525–3447). **Trader Vic's Mai Tai Bar** at the Atlanta Hilton and Towers (Courtland & Harris Sts. NE, tel. 404/659–2000) is mostly visited by the convention crowd, who come here to taste the best tropical drinks in town, including the bar's famous namesake.

*Blues Clubs*
The most popular club for New Orleans–style blues is **Blind Willie's** (818 N. Highland Ave., tel. 404/456–4433). **Blues Harbor** (3179 Peachtree Rd., tel. 404/261–6717) wails nightly with Chicago-style blues.

*Country Music Clubs*
**Miss Kitty's Saloon & Dance Hall** (Underground Atlanta, tel. 404/524–4614) combines traditional country and western with today's Southern rock.

*Jazz Clubs*
Upscale, laid-back jazz aficionados will appreciate the combo at **The Café Bar** at the Ritz-Carlton Buckhead (tel. 404/237–2700). Somewhat gimmicky, **Dante's Down the Hatch** (3380 Peachtree Rd., tel. 404/266–1600) features The Paul Mitchell Trio, fondue, and wine in the "hold" of a replica of a sailing ship. **Walter Mitty's Jazz Café** (816 N. Highland Ave., tel. 404/876–7115) offers high style for a well-to-do crowd.

*Rock Clubs*
**The Cotton Club** (1021 Peachtree St., tel. 404/874–2523) is a loud, contemporary rock club. **The Metroplex** (388 Marietta St., tel. 404/523–1468) screams nightly with heavy metal, punk, reggae, and new wave music.

*For Singles*
**Atkins Park Bar & Grill** (794 N. Highland Ave., tel. 404/876–7249) is an old-time neighborhood bar, where a casually dressed, mostly young (20s and 30s) clientele come to drink, eat, and listen to rock. **Confetti** (3909 Roswell Rd., tel. 404/237–4238) is a good place to drink, dance, and meet upscale singles.

# Baltimore

*by Francis X. Rocca*

As Bostonians have been characterized as "proper," Baltimoreans have borne the epithet "amiable"—a still accurate assessment of the southern-style hospitality of the city. Baltimore has a charm and sophistication derived from a density of cultural and educational resources, including the state theater of Maryland, nationally respected art galleries and museums, Johns Hopkins University, and the Peabody Conservatory of Music. The city has been a major port since its harbor was dredged in the 18th century; fittingly, its most symbolic buildings are waterside: Fort McHenry, where the original "Star Spangled Banner" flew during the War of 1812, and the World Trade Center and adjoining pavilions of Harborplace, which heralded the renaissance of the area in the 1970s and '80s.

Baltimore's manufacturing industries, including such giants as Bethlehem Steel and General Motors, maintain a large though diminishing presence in the city's economy. Biotechnology, centering on the research at Johns Hopkins University, high-technology (Martin Marietta and Westinghouse), and service industries (including banking and tourism) increasingly characterize the economic profile of the city. And Baltimore still figures as a major port, the seventh largest in the country, handling 3,000 ships from 50 countries every year.

One of the reasons employers stay and expand here is the high quality of life, attributable to an old but well-preserved infrastructure and a cost of living among the lowest in the Boston–New York–Washington megalopolis. The downtown renewal projects have halted the middle-class flight that exacerbated urban decay in the '50s and '60s, and tourism is gaining. Planning that started 30 years ago for redevelopment has borne fruit in the last decade, most notably in the shiny hotels, arcades, office buildings, and museums of the Inner Harbor.

## Top Employers

| Employer | Type of Enterprise | Parent*/ Headquarters |
| --- | --- | --- |
| **Baltimore Gas & Electric** | Utility | Baltimore |

| Bethlehem Steel | Steel | Bethlehem, PA |
|---|---|---|
| C&P Telephone | Telecommunications | Baltimore |
| General Motors Truck & Bus Group | Automotive production | General Motors, Corp./ Pontiac, MI |
| Giant Food | Retail | Baltimore |
| Marriott | Hospitality industry | Washington, DC |
| Martin Marietta Aero & Naval Systems | Defense industry | Martin Marietta, Corp./ Bethesda, MA |
| Maryland National Bank | Financial services | Baltimore |
| Westinghouse Electric | Financial services, broadcasting, electronics | Pittsburgh |

*\*if applicable*

## ESSENTIAL INFORMATION

### Climate

What follows are the average daily maximum and minimum temperatures for Baltimore.

| Jan. | 43F 29 | 6C −2 | Feb. | 43F 29 | 6C −2 | Mar. | 52F 36 | 11C 2 |
|---|---|---|---|---|---|---|---|---|
| Apr. | 63F 45 | 17C 7 | May | 74F 56 | 23C 13 | June | 83F 65 | 28C 18 |
| July | 86F 70 | 30C 21 | Aug. | 85F 67 | 29C 19 | Sept. | 79F 61 | 26C 16 |
| Oct. | 67F 50 | 19C 10 | Nov. | 54F 40 | 12C 4 | Dec. | 45F 31 | 7C −1 |

### Airport

**Baltimore/Washington International** (BWI) is 10 miles south of Baltimore off Rte. 295 (Baltimore-Washington Pkwy.) in Anne Arundel County, MD.

### Airport Business Facilities

**Mutual of Omaha Business Service Center** (upper level at the entrance to Pier C, tel. 301/859–5997) has fax machines, photocopying, notary public, secretarial service, ticket pickup, baggage storage, Western Union, travel insurance, cash advance, phone suites, and a conference room holding up to 26 people. The **Airport Authority** (tel. 301/859–7024) will lease its large conference room in advance.

### Airlines

Baltimore is a hub city for USAir.

**American,** tel. 301/850–5800 or 800/433–7300.
**Continental,** tel. 301/337–2061 or 800/525–0280.

**Delta,** tel. 301/768–9000 or 800/221–1212.
**Northwest,** tel. 800/225–2525 or 800/447–4747.
**TWA,** tel. 301/338–1156 or 800/221–2000.
**United,** tel. 301/850–4557 or 800/241–6522.
**USAir,** tel. 301/727–0825 or 800/428–4322.

## Between the Airport and Downtown

Since 1980, train service (both Amtrak and MARC) has been the fastest and most cost-effective way from the airport into town. Direct transportation questions to BWI's Ground Transportation Desk, tel. 301/859–7545.

*By Taxi*
The ride into town via I-295 takes 15–20 minutes. Airport taxis stand by for arriving flights. Cost: $12–$15.

*By Train*
Two railways serve this route: Amtrak trains (tel. 800/ USA–RAIL) run between Baltimore's Penn Station at N. Charles St. and Mt. Royal Ave., and the BWI airport rail station. The trip takes approximately 12 minutes and costs $6.25. Maryland Area Rail Commuter (MARC) trains (tel. 800/325–RAIL) make the same trip, Mon.– Fri., from 7 AM–10 PM in about 20 minutes, for $2.75. There is free and continual shuttle bus service between the BWI Airport Rail Station and the airport terminal, less than 10 minutes away.

*By Van*
Shuttle Express (tel. 301/859–0800) provides motorcoach service every ½-hour from 6 AM–11 PM between the airport and downtown hotels. The ride takes 20–30 minutes. Cost: $5.75 or $6.75, depending on the hotel.

*By Limousine*
Carey Limousines (tel. 800/336–4646 or 301/837–1234) should be reserved 24 hours in advance. Cost: not including tip, tolls, and 8% tax, for a sedan, $38; for a regular limousine, $43; for a stretch limousine, $49. Cellular phones are available. (Also *see* Important Addresses and Numbers, below.)

## Car Rentals

The following companies have outlets in the BWI terminal:
**Avis,** tel. 301/859–1680 or 800/331–1212.
**Budget,** tel. 301/859–0850 or 800/527–0700.
**Dollar,** tel. 301/684–2020 or 800/421–6868.
**Hertz,** tel. 301/850–7400 or 800/654–3131.
**National,** tel. 301/859–8860 or 800/328–4567.

## Emergencies

*Doctors*
The **CMC Inc. Clinic** (16 S. Eutaw St., tel. 301/752–3010) is open 24 hours daily except Sun. 1 AM–Mon. 7 AM. **Ask-A-Nurse** (tel. 301/760–8787) is a free, 24-hour physician referral and health information service.

*Dentists*
**Ask-A-Nurse,** *see* above.

*Hospitals*

**The Johns Hopkins Hospital** (600 N. Wolfe St., tel. 301/955–2280), **Maryland General Hospital** (827 Linden Ave., tel. 301/225–8100), **The Mercy Medical Center** (301 St. Paul Pl., tel. 301/332–9477), **University of Maryland Hospital** (22 S. Greene St., tel. 301/328–2121).

## Important Addresses and Numbers

**Audiovisual rentals.** Audiovisual Service (3401 Chestnut Ave., tel. 301/467–3620), Nelson C. White (8818 Orchard Tree Ln., Towson, tel. 301/339–7555).

**Chamber of Commerce** (100 W. Pennsylvania Ave., tel. 301/825–6200).

**Computer rentals.** Computer Rentals of Maryland (2205 Maryland Ave., tel. 301/366–5088), Computerental Corp. (2 E. Wheeling St., tel. 301/366–5088).

**Convention and exhibition center.** Baltimore Convention Center and Festival Hall (1 E. Pratt St., tel. 301/659–7000).

**Fax service.** Mail Boxes Etc. (911 S. Charles St., tel. 301/752–8110; and 808 Guilford Ave., tel. 301/783–1555).

**Formal-wear rentals.** Hiken Formal Wear (1646 E. Baltimore St., tel. 301/563–1414).

**Gift shops.** Chocolates: Godiva Chocolatier (Gallery at Harborplace, tel. 301/332–0931); Flowers: Harborplace Flower Market (Light St. Pavillion, Harborplace, tel. 301/685–5565).

**Graphic design studios.** Madison West Design (10 W. Madison St., tel. 301/962–1588).

**Hairstylist.** Unisex: Rainbow Hair Design (Gallery at Harborplace, tel. 301/332–0433).

**Health and fitness clubs.** *See* Fitness, below.

**Information hot lines.** Call 301/893–3000 from a touch-tone phone; when asked, enter the appropriate four-digit access code: national sports update, 1300; national news, 1210; business news, 1220; stock market update, 1222; currency, commodities, and precious metals update, 1224; theater and music, 1413.

**Limousine service.** Carey Limousines (tel. 301/837–1234 or 800/336–4646).

**Liquor stores.** Bun Penny (Light St. Pavillion, Harborplace, tel. 301/547–1660), Gallery Wine & Liquors (13 W. Centre St., tel. 301/752–1383).

**Mail delivery, overnight.** DHL Worldwide Express (tel. 301/247–6622), Federal Express (tel. 301/792–8200 for all locations), TNT Skypak (tel. 301/787–1122), United Parcel Service (tel. 301/792–9900), U.S. Postal Service Express Mail (tel. 301/347–4352).

**Messenger services.** ACME Delivery and Messenger Service (tel. 301/945–3900), Harbor City Courier (tel. 301/528–9111), Maryland Messenger Service (tel. 301/837–5550).

**Office space rental.** Headquarters (200 E. Pratt St., tel. 301/659–0055).

**Pharmacy, late-night.** Rite Aid (1100 Light St., tel. 301/539–7636).

**Radio stations, all-news.** WBAL, 1090 AM.

**Secretarial services.** Able Temporaries (2 N. Charles St., tel. 301/685–8189), Kelly Services (1 N. Charles St., tel. 301/685–3195).

**Stationery supplies.** Ginns Office Products (N. Charles and Baltimore Sts., tel. 301/385–1000).

**Taxis.** Yellow Cab (tel. 301/685–1212).

**Theater tickets.** *See* The Arts, below.

**Train information.** Amtrak (tel. 301/539–2112 or 800/872–7245), Maryland Area Rail Commuter (MARC, tel. 800/325–RAIL), Pennsylvania Station (North Charles St. and Mt. Royal Ave., tel. 301/291–4265).

**Travel agents.** American Express Travel Service (23 W. Baltimore St., tel. 301/539–7300), Charles Center Travel (810 Light St., tel. 301/962–1011).

**Weather** (tel. 301/936–1212, local; tel. 301/893–3000, ext. 1605, national).

## LODGING

Since the redevelopment of the Inner Harbor neighborhood and the ensuing revival of all downtown, competition between hotels has become keen and the level of service high, while prices have been restrained. Between the Inner Harbor and the Washington Monument in Mt. Vernon Square, a mile to the north, lie most of the major office buildings and most of the downtown hotels listed below.

All hotels listed below offer corporate rates and weekend discounts; inquire when making reservations.

Highly recommended lodgings in each price category are indicated by a star ★.

| Category | Cost* |
|---|---|
| *$$$$* (Very Expensive) | over $175 |
| *$$$* (Expensive) | $140–$175 |
| *$$* (Moderate) | under $140 |

*All prices are for a standard double room, single occupancy, excluding 12% Maryland hotel tax.*

*Numbers in the margin correspond to numbered hotel locations on the Baltimore Lodging and Dining map.*

### Downtown

★ ⓰ **Harbor Court.** Despite a slightly inconvenient location, on
*$$$$* the west side of the Inner Harbor, this eight-story, red-brick hotel has eclipsed the Peabody Court as the most prestigious hotel in town. CEOs are likely to stay here and lodge their subordinates elsewhere. Built in 1986, the ho-

tel strives for an English country house look. A ground-floor library, stocked with collectors' editions, is the domain of a concierge who heads an obliging staff. The guest rooms reflect the expensive, meticulous look of the public areas: 18th-century English landscapes on the walls, marble floors in the bathrooms. The business class rooms have canopied, four-poster beds. The most desirable rooms have a harbor view. Courtyard rooms are quieter, except for the occasional screech of peacocks. Least desirable are the rooms on the north side with a city view. The hotel's restaurant, Hampton's (*see* Dining, below), is well worth a visit. *550 Light St., 21202, tel. 301/234–0550 or 800/824–0076, fax 301/659–5925. Gen. manager, Donald Raines. 195 rooms, 8 suites. AE, CB, D, DC, MC, V.*

**⑮ Hyatt Regency.** The street it's on is practically a highway
$$$ and therefore difficult to cross, but the Hyatt has unenclosed skyways that link it to the convention center and the Harborplace Mall. While the Harbor Court next door (*see* above) strives for the ambience of a country inn in the big city, the Hyatt has the impersonal ambience of an airport hotel in a downtown location. The reserved though polite staff does little to dispel the somewhat desolate atmosphere. The lobby is the chain's trademark atrium, complete with glass elevators. Guest rooms are standard, with small tables instead of proper desks; the views are of the harbor or the city. The hotel dining room, Berry & Elliot's (*see* Dining, below), has good views and good food—a rare combination. Frequent-stay (Gold Passport) participants get hair-dryers and newspapers in their rooms, and may use the health club free of charge. *300 Light St., 21202, tel. 301/528–1234 or 800/233–1234, fax 301/685–3362. Gen. manager, Richard Morgan. 487 rooms, 9 suites. AE, CB, D, DC, MC, V.*

**⑫ Lord Baltimore Radisson Plaza.** The best feature of this
$$$ 23-floor hotel, built in 1928, is the cavernous Art Deco lobby with dark green walls and carved brown-and-gold moldings, all dimly lighted by frosted-glass sconces. Jazz Age elegance does not extend to the guest rooms, renovated in 1986, which are slightly cramped, as are the unmodernized bathrooms. Rooms on the south side have the best views: from the top three floors you can see the water. East side rooms face a wall and an alley below. This is a quiet, clean, and comfortable place, favored by tourists, airline pilots, and business travelers who want a central location. The staff is polite but harried. *20 W. Baltimore St., 21202, tel. 301/539–8400 or 800/333–3333, fax 301/625–1060. Gen. manager, William Gillette. 440 rooms, 4 suites. AE, CB, D, DC, MC, V.*

**⑬ Marriott Inner Harbor.** This modern, 10-story hotel, built
$$$$ in 1985, is one of the city's largest. The public areas, brightly lighted and decorated in a nondescript contemporary style, are surprisingly quiet given the hotel's clientele of conventioneers and tourist families. The Festival Hall convention facility is only a block away, and as of 1992 the New Orioles stadium will be right next door. The view of that construction site (from even-numbered guest rooms) is preferable to the view of the garage (from odd-numbered rooms). The rooms, which were redecorated in 1988, are adorned with nature photographs and a rather dramatic color scheme dominated by expanses of jade green. Tenth-floor guests enjoy concierge privileges, such

# BALTIMORE

## Lodging

Guest Quarters Suite Hotel-BWI, 22
Harbor Court, 16
Holiday Inn BWI, 23
Hyatt Regency, 15
Lord Baltimore Radisson Plaza, 12
Marriott BWI, 24
Marriott Inner Harbor, 13
Omni Inner Harbor, 11
Peabody Court, 6
Sheraton Inner Harbor, 14
Stouffer Harborplace, 17
Tremont Hotel, 9
Tremont Plaza, 10

## Dining

Acropolis, 21
Akbar, 4
L'Auberge, 20
Bandaloops, 18
Berry & Elliot's, 15
Bertha's, 25
The Brass Elephant, 3
Café des Artistes, 1
The Conservatory, 6
Da Mimmo, 19
Hamptons, 16
Kawasaki, 8
The Prime Rib, 5
Tio Pepe, 7
Windows, 17

# BALTIMORE HOTEL CHART

| HOTELS | Price Category | Business Services / Banquet capacity | No. of meeting rooms | Secretarial services | Audiovisual equipment | Teletype news service | Computer rentals | In-room modem phone jack | All-news cable channel | Desk | Desk lighting | Bed lighting |
|---|---|---|---|---|---|---|---|---|---|---|---|---|
| Guest Quarters Suite Hotel-BWI | $$ | 200 | 11 | ✓ | ✓ | - | ✓ | ✓ | ✓ | fair | fair | fair |
| Harbor Court | $$$$ | 200 | 8 | ✓ | ✓ | ✓ | ✓ | ✓ | ✓ | fair | fair | fair |
| Holiday Inn-BWI | $$ | 325 | 10 | - | ✓ | - | - | - | ✓ | fair | fair | fair |
| Hyatt Regency | $$$ | 1400 | 19 | ✓ | ✓ | - | - | ✓ | ✓ | poor | poor | fair |
| Lord Baltimore Radisson Plaza | $$$ | 400 | 6 | - | ✓ | - | - | - | ✓ | fair | good | fair |
| Marriott BWI | $$$ | 960 | 14 | ✓ | ✓ | - | ✓ | ✓ | ✓ | fair | fair | fair |
| Marriott Inner Harbor | $$$$ | 550 | 17 | ✓ | ✓ | - | ✓ | ✓ | ✓ | fair | fair | fair |
| Omni Inner Harbor | $$$ | 1000 | 20 | ✓ | ✓ | - | - | ✓ | ✓ | good | good | good |
| Peabody Court | $$$$ | 200 | 7 | ✓ | ✓ | ✓ | ✓ | ✓ | ✓ | good | fair | good |
| Sheraton Inner Harbor | $$$ | 600 | 8 | ✓ | ✓ | - | ✓ | ✓ | ✓ | fair | good | fair |
| Stouffer Harborplace | $$$$ | 200 | 10 | ✓ | ✓ | - | ✓ | - | ✓ | fair | good | good |
| Tremont Hotel | $$$ | 0 | 3 | ✓ | ✓ | - | ✓ | ✓ | - | good | good | good |
| Tremont Plaza | $$ | 225 | 5 | - | ✓ | - | - | ✓ | - | fair | fair | fair |

**$$$$** = over $175, **$$$** = $140-$175, **$$** = under $140.
● good, ◐ fair, ○ poor.
All hotels listed here have photocopying and fax facilities.

| In-Room Amenities | | | | | | | | | | Hotel Amenities | | | | | | |
| Nonsmoking rooms | In-room checkout | Minibar | Pay movies | VCR/Movie rentals | Hairdryer | Toiletries | Room service | Laundry/Dry cleaning | Pressing | Concierge | Barber/Hairdresser | Garage | Courtesy airport transport | Sauna | Pool | Exercise room |
|---|---|---|---|---|---|---|---|---|---|---|---|---|---|---|---|---|
| ✓ | ✓ | – | – | ✓ | – | ◐ | ◐ | ● | ◐ | – | – | – | ✓ | ✓ | ● | ● |
| ✓ | ✓ | ✓ | ✓ | ✓ | ✓ | ● | ● | ● | ● | ✓ | ✓ | ✓ | – | ✓ | ● | ● |
| ✓ | – | – | ✓ | – | ✓ | ○ | ◐ | ○ | ◐ | ✓ | – | – | ✓ | – | ○ | ◐ |
| ✓ | – | ✓ | ✓ | – | – | ◐ | ◐ | ● | ● | ✓ | ✓ | ✓ | – | ✓ | ◐ | ◐ |
| ✓ | – | – | – | – | – | ◐ | ◐ | ◐ | ○ | ✓ | – | – | – | ✓ | – | ◐ |
| ✓ | ✓ | – | – | – | – | ◐ | ● | ● | ● | ✓ | – | – | ✓ | – | ● | ● |
| ✓ | – | ✓ | – | – | – | ○ | ● | ● | ● | ✓ | – | ✓ | – | ✓ | ● | ◐ |
| ✓ | ✓ | ✓ | – | – | ✓ | ○ | ◐ | ● | ● | ✓ | – | – | ✓ | – | ○ | ○ |
| ✓ | ✓ | ✓ | – | ✓ | ✓ | ● | ◐ | ○ | ● | – | – | – | – | – | – | – |
| ✓ | ✓ | ✓ | ✓ | ✓ | – | ◐ | ◐ | ● | ● | ✓ | – | ✓ | – | – | ◐ | ◐ |
| ✓ | – | ✓ | ✓ | – | – | ● | ● | ● | ◐ | ✓ | ✓ | ✓ | – | ✓ | ● | ● |
| – | – | ✓ | ✓ | ✓ | – | ◐ | ◐ | ● | ● | ✓ | – | – | – | – | – | – |
| ✓ | – | – | ✓ | – | ✓ | ◐ | ◐ | ● | ◐ | ✓ | – | ✓ | – | ✓ | ○ | ● |

**Room service:** ● 24-hour, ◐ 6AM-10PM, ○ other.
**Laundry/Dry cleaning:** ● same day, ◐ overnight, ○ other.
**Pressing:** ● immediate, ◐ same day, ○ other.

as terry robes. *Pratt and Eutaw Sts., 21201, tel. 301/962–0202 or 800/228–9290, fax 301/962–8585. Gen. manager, Bill Denzer. 525 rooms, 14 suites. AE, CB, D, DC, MC, V.*

**⑪ Omni Inner Harbor.** Many convention-goers and bus touring groups stay at this colossal hotel, which has two towers, one 24-stories, the other 27-stories high. Inner Harbor is more than six blocks away, but you can get there by skywalk, stopping if you like at the convention center or the Baltimore Arena. The lobby is small and rather gloomy. Standard-issue furnishings crowd the guest rooms. The best views are of Liberty Street, to the west; rooms to avoid are on the fifth floor of the south tower, which gets the worst of Arena noise. Guests on the top three floors of the north tower can use the 22nd floor lounge, which offers Continental breakfast and concierge service. The staff always seems busy but is usually quite pleasant. *101 W. Fayette St., 21201, tel. 301/752–1100 or 800/843–6664, fax 301/752–0832. Gen. manager, Joseph Kane. 714 rooms, 8 suites. AE, CB, D, DC, MC, V.*

**⑥ Peabody Court.** This ornate, 13-story landmark, built as an apartment house in 1924, was converted to a luxury hotel in 1985. It's a favorite of upscale business travelers, rivaled only by the Harbor Court (*see* above). Its location, on elegant Mt. Vernon Square, is exceptional. Restaurants and the Peabody Conservatory of Music are nearby, and major office buildings are less than a mile away. The staff is attentive. The hotel's lobby is distinguished by a library with dark wood paneling reminiscent of a men's club. Guest rooms are decorated largely in pastels, with horticultural prints on the walls. Naturally, park views are best, alley views worst. *612 Cathedral St., 21201, tel. 301/727–7101 or 800/732–5301, fax 301/539–7908. Gen. manager, Tom Kamerer. 104 rooms, 10 suites. AE, CB, DC, MC, V.*

**⑭ Sheraton Inner Harbor.** Adjacent to the Convention Center, with all the bustle and traffic that implies, this well-run hotel maintains a relaxed atmosphere nonetheless. The chrome and glass look of the lobby is like a thousand others, but on bright days the lobby can be filled with light. Standard rooms, among the smallest in a major downtown hotel, were all renovated in 1990. One notable service: the only certified kosher hotel kitchen in Baltimore, available for functions and room service by arrangement. Another attraction is Impulse, a nightclub (*see* After Hours, below). *300 S. Charles St., 21201, tel. 301/962–8300 or 800/325–3535, fax 301/962–8211. Gen. manager, Michael Whipple. 339 rooms, 20 suites. AE, CB, D, DC, MC, V.*

**⑰ Stouffer Harborplace.** The upscale, business-oriented Harborplace serves a clientele of business travelers, conventioneers, and tourists. It's across the street from the shopping pavilions where the Inner Harbor area's renaissance began. Guest rooms are light and cheerful, but the furnishings—oversized pieces of stained mahogany veneer accented with brass—take up an inordinate amount of space. Bathrooms have phones and black-and-white TVs. Rooms with harbor views are the most popular. Service at the hotel is uniformly quick and businesslike; do not expect anyone to remember your name, except perhaps on the 12th-floor concierge level, accessible only by card-key, where you can have free breakfast and snacks (and cocktails at a charge) in a staffed club room. *202 E. Pratt St., 21202, tel. 301/547–1200 or 800/468–3571, fax 301/539–5780. Gen. manager, Allan Villaverde. 622 rooms, 60 suites. AE, CB, D, DC, MC, V.*

★ **⑨** **Tremont Hotel.** The 13-story Tremont, built in the '60s as
$$$ an apartment house on an unusually quiet downtown block, was converted in 1983 into a cozy European-style all-suites hotel. The accommodations have all been renovated and have reproduction Queen Anne-style furnishings; kitchens are well equipped. Room phones have conference and speaker functions. Rooms with views of the north, including the Washington Monument, are preferable to those overlooking shady Pleasant Street. The level of service is high: the concierge will arrange transportation, in most cases free of charge, to and from meetings. Staff will also do guests' personal shopping for groceries or clothing. The excellent 8 East restaurant (*see* Dining, below) is highly recommended. *8 East Pleasant St., 21202, tel. 301/576–1200 or 800/638–6266, fax 301/685–1212. Gen. manager, Helma O'Keefe. 60 suites. AE, CB, DC, MC, V.*

★ **⑩** **Tremont Plaza.** In 1984, the owners of the Tremont Hotel
$$ (*see* above) converted this 37-story apartment building into another all-suites hotel. This one is in the heart of the business district, five blocks north of the Inner Harbor. The building's plain gray facade and the tiny brass-and-marble lobby belie the ample and tasteful guest rooms, decorated in earth tones. The staff is friendly but not oppressive. Suites come in various configurations, all boasting fully outfitted kitchens. Rooms whose numbers end in -06 have the best views, of the city and the small park in the center of St. Paul Place. The concierge floors, 30 and above, have bigger rooms and provide free breakfast and cocktails. Tugs is a respectable seafood restaurant, but the hotel's culinary distinction lies in its gourmet delicatessen. *222 St. Paul Pl., 21202, tel. 301/727– 2222 or 800/ 638–6266, fax 301/685–4216. Gen. manager, Beth Barnes. 193 suites, 33 business class. AE, CB, DC, MC, V.*

## Airport

**㉒** **Guest Quarters Suite Hotel-BWI.** The main attraction of
$$ this eight-story all-suite hotel, opened in 1987, is the size and layout of the units. Every one of them has a living room, at a price competitive with those of standard rooms elsewhere—which makes holding a meeting in one's room a convenient option. All suites have refrigerators, and microwaves are available. The Atrium Café is an attractive place to eat, and full breakfast is included in the hotel rate. *1300 Concourse Dr., Linthicum 21090, tel. 301/850–0747 or 800/424–2900, fax 301/859–0816. Gen. manager, Tim Benolken. 251 suites. AE, CB, D, DC, MC, V.*

**㉓** **Holiday Inn BWI.** This is livelier than the other airport
$$ hostelries, thanks to both a dance club (oldies rock) and a piano bar. The seven-story brick building is fifteen years old, but was remodeled in 1988 to keep up its tidy, generic appearance. *890 Elkridge Landing Rd., Linthicum 21090, tel. 301/859–8400 or 800/465–4329, fax 301/859–8400 x1196. Gen. manager, Kevin Richards. 254 rooms, 2 suites. AE, CB, D, DC, MC, V.*

**㉔** **Marriott BWI.** Built in 1988, this ten-story brick building
$$$ is the biggest, newest, and most accommodating hotel

near the airport, with a standard of service (personal and business-related) equal to that of several downtown hotels. The Champions Sports Bar is one of a popular national chain. *1742 W. Nursery Rd., 21240, tel. 301/859–8300 or 800/228–9290, fax 301/859–8300 (same switchboard). Gen. manager, James Kappel. 310 rooms, 4 suites. AE, CB, D, DC, MC, V.*

## DINING

The business community in Baltimore favors conservative, long-established restaurants, typified by the John Eager Howard Room, where traditional American fare like prime rib and roast lamb are served. Baltimore is a noted seafood mecca, and you'll usually do very well by ordering any preparation with crab (especially crab cakes). If you have time to look around the Inner Harbor shopping and market pavilions, check out the offerings at the fresh seafood stands, where spicy steamed shrimp is an outstanding specialty. The restaurants listed here are all within walking distance of the major downtown hotels or just a short cab-ride away.

Highly recommended restaurants in each price category are indicated by a star ★.

| Category | Cost* |
| --- | --- |
| *$$$$* (Very Expensive) | over $30 |
| *$$$* (Expensive) | $20–$30 |
| *$$* (Moderate) | under $20 |

*per person, including appetizer, entrée, and dessert, but excluding drinks, service, and 9% sales tax.*

*Numbers in the margin correspond to numbered restaurant locations on the Baltimore Lodging and Dining map.*

### Business Breakfasts

**Café Brighton,** in the Harbor Court Hotel (550 Light St., tel. 301/234–0550) is a good choice for any meal, but breakfast is especially pleasant. Service is quick and cheerful and there is just enough noise to make conversation confidential. Cheese blintzes with blackcurrant sauce liven up an ordinary, well-executed menu. **8 East** (8 E. Pleasant St., tel. 301/576–1199) is a modestly elegant retreat right around the corner from many of Baltimore's major office buildings. It's a good place for an early meeting—breakfast is served from 6:30 on weekdays. Try the crabmeat omelet with cheddar cheese. **Peabody's** (612 Cathedral St., tel. 301/727–7101) has dark wood-paneled walls, brass, frosted-glass "gas" lamps, and black-marble tables that evoke the late-19th century. Equally fine for a meeting or breakfast alone, the dining rooms of the Peabody Court Hotel are not hushed, but quiet enough to talk or read in.

Three restaurants recommended for lunch and dinner (*see* below) are also suitable for breakfast meetings: the **Conservatory** (Peabody Court Hotel, tel. 301/727–7101), the **John Eager Howard Room** (Hotel Belvedere, N. Charles and Chase Sts., tel. 301/332–1000), and **Windows** (Stouffer

Harborplace Hotel, tel. 301/547–1200). **Cascades** (Hyatt Regency Hotel, tel. 301/528–1234) offers convenience, prompt service, unobjectionable cuisine and an absence of distractions.

## Downtown/Inner Harbor

**⑮** **Berry & Elliot's.** From 14 floors above the Inner Harbor,
**$$$** the views are impressive, especially at a windowside table at this dining room of the Hyatt Regency. Many conventioneers who stay at the hotel eat here, and the atmosphere tends to be bustling. It's not super noisy, but neither is it conducive to serious business conversation. The waiters are responsive and trustworthy. The kitchen is inconsistent, but beef is generally reliable, and so are some seafood dishes. The "Side-by-Side" *petite filet* and crab cake is a standard the chefs cannot afford to get wrong. They also do a good job with Salmon Streudel—salmon flavored with boursin cheese, wrapped in a flaky phyllo dough, and covered with dill sauce. California labels dominate the wine list, along with a few German and Italian names. After dinner, a DJ plays light Top 40 dance music. *300 Light St., tel. 301/528–1234. Jacket and tie advised. Reservations required. AE, CB, D, DC, MC, V.*

**㉕** **Bertha's.** All over the region, visitors will see the bumper
**$$** sticker "Eat Bertha's Mussels"—come here to find out why that slogan is so enthusiastically displayed. This family-run establishment on Fell's Point, first opened as a bar in 1972, has gradually expanded into two cozy but uncramped dining rooms. The ballyhooed mussels are the outstanding item on the menu. They come steamed, with a choice of eight butter-based sauces (such as a garlic sauce with capers) or as a Turkish appetizer, stuffed with sweet-and-spicy rice. Stuffed shrimp, crab cakes, and paella Valenciana are other good options. The Scottish afternoon tea (featured every day except Sunday) offers a hearty repast. Come to Bertha's for local color, not for a serious talk. *734 S. Broadway, tel. 301/327–5795. Dress: casual. Reservations required for tea, accepted at other times only for parties of 6 or more. MC, V.*

**★ ⑥** **The Conservatory.** On the northern edge of the business
**$$$$** district, this elegant, glass-enclosed rooftop dining room in the Peabody Court Hotel affords lovely views of Mt. Vernon Square and the Washington Monument. At breakfast on a clear day, the sun shines through its glass walls. This is an impressive site for meetings; service is discreet and alert, but stately, and dinner can take up to three hours. This is the place to celebrate a special occasion in a dignified setting, with dark green draperies and upholstery and plenty of space between the candlelit tables. Dishes are memorable for their high quality rather than their innovative preparation, yet some combinations are creative. A small piece of lobster baked in a timbale makes a lively accompaniment to sea scallops in saffron-vermouth cream sauce. Wild fowl ravioli sits well alongside breast of duck—in its own *jus* as well as a mushroom sauce. *612 Cathedral St., tel. 301/727–7101. Jacket and tie required. Reservations required. AE, CB, DC, MC, V. No lunch; closed Sun. dinner.*

**⑯** **Hamptons.** A view of the Inner Harbor and the distinctive
**$$$$** National Aquarium building provide an impressive backdrop for this elegant dining room of the Harbor Court ho-

tel, which serves up a sophisticated mix of nouvelle American and Continental specialties. Sheraton-style tables, set with bowls of dahlias, are set far apart in a dining room styled after an English country house. The atmosphere is sedate and dignified, perfect for quiet conversation. The waiters are helpful but not long-winded. Try the red snapper poached in white wine, topped with crab meat, and served with a leek and butter sauce. A fine bouillabaisse is loaded with crab, mussels, clams, white fish, vegetables, and herbs. Avoid the scallops, which are sometimes overcooked. The wine list focuses on French and American labels. On Sundays, the champagne brunch is always well done. *550 Light St., tel. 301/234–0550. Jacket and tie required. Reservations required. AE, CB, D, DC, MC, V. Closed Mon.*

★ ❼ **Tio Pepe.** The whitewashed stone walls of these cellar din-
$$$ ing rooms reflect the candlelight that illuminates this Baltimore institution. It's usually busy; if you're seeking a quiet spot for a talk, request a table in the Shawl Room, which is relatively subdued. The restaurant is less than a mile from the Inner Harbor and a few blocks from many office buildings and hotels. It has been in the same family—some of whose members live upstairs—for 22 years, and the service is accordingly a bit familiar, even casual. But it is well-informed and prompt. The consistently reliable menu represents every region of Spain. There is the staple paella Valenciana (chicken, sausage, shrimp, clams, and mussels with saffron rice), or a special Basque preparation of red snapper with clams, mussels, asparagus, and boiled egg. The wine list favors Spanish labels; the selection is limited, but fairly priced. A pricier Reserve list is also available. *10 E. Franklin St., tel. 301/539–4675. Jacket and tie required at dinner. Reservations required. AE, MC, V.*

❶❼ **Windows.** Through large picture windows you can watch,
$$$ from five floors up, the goings-on at Inner Harbor at this rather understated but upscale restaurant. Nouvelle American cuisine is served up by an obliging staff to the relaxed patrons whose casual dress seems appropriate in a dining room of a resort hotel (Stouffer Harborplace). The tables are well spaced, and serious conversations won't be overheard. The service is pleasantly attentive. The house specialty is the three-item seafood grill, which typically includes two fish (often tuna and either swordfish or salmon) and a shellfish (jumbo shrimp or softshell crab) in a tarragon vinaigrette. The kitchen is also justly proud of the shrimp stuffed with crabmeat, prepared in a flaky phyllo dough in a caviar sauce. The wine list is heavily American, mostly California labels, with one Maryland vintage. *202 E. Pratt St., tel. 301/547–1200. Jacket and tie advised. Reservations advised. AE, CB, D, DC, MC, V.*

## Mt. Vernon

❹ **Akbar.** This small Indian restaurant, a few steps below
$$ street level on busy Charles Street, is a good place to relax after work. House specialties are the spicy tandoori chicken marinated in yogurt, herbs, and pungent spices, then barbecued in a clay oven; and some exceptional vegetarian dishes, such as alu Gobi masala, a cauliflower and potato blend with onions and tomatoes. The place is always crowded and the noise tends to rise above the continuous

Indian background music. Service can be rushed but is consistently polite. The wine list is brief and undistinguished. *823 N. Charles St., tel. 301/539–0944. Dress: Casual but neat. Reservations advised. AE, CB, DC, MC, V.*

★ ❸ **The Brass Elephant.** Right on busy Charles Street, this
$$$ grand pre-Civil War rowhouse serves well-prepared northern Italian cuisine in several dining rooms sporting brass elephant wall sconces. Two wood-paneled rooms—The Teak Room and the Oak Room—are the quietest and noisiest, respectively. The most eccentric room is an atrium meant to suggest a Venetian café with moss painted on its pink walls. The young waiters and waitresses are polite and enthusiastic. The chef/owner's specialty is veal Valdostano—a cutlet sautéed with butter, shallots, mushrooms, cream, white wine, and Fontina cheese. The extensive wine list won an award from the *Wine Spectator. 924 N. Charles St., tel. 301/547–8480. Jacket and tie advised. Reservations required. AE, CB, DC, MC, V.*

★ ❽ **Kawasaki.** Located on a street with fine art galleries and
$$ shops, yet within the business district, this brightly lighted and lively dining room is a good setting for a weekday lunch on one's own, or a convivial dinner. The service is courteous and soft-spoken. The sushi and sashimi are the best in town, and you can watch their preparation at the sushi bar in the front dining room. For those who can never remember the names of their favorite sushi, the menu is illustrated. Consider a glass of Japanese beer .with dinner, and some sake afterwards. *413 N. Charles St., tel. 301/659–7600. Dress: Casual but neat. Reservations advised. AE, MC, V. Closed Sun.*

❺ **The Prime Rib.** Popular with an earlier generation of busi-
$$$$ ness patrons when it opened in 1965, this upscale restaurant remains a favorite of locals and out-of-towners. The dimly lighted dining room is bustling and crowded, with tables close together under low ceilings. Bankers and lawyers are much in evidence, but you'll also see chic couples enjoying an evening out. Just north of Mt. Vernon Square, the restaurant is a short taxi ride from the major hotels and most offices. The service is swift, polite, and informative. Not that there is much to explain about the traditional menu, including the prime rib—flawless, except for an occasional overripe tomato garnish—and an even better filet Mignon. Oysters Rockefeller and smoked trout are recommended appetizers. The wine list is surprisingly short, and predominantly Californian. *1101 N. Calvert St., tel. 301/539–1814. Jacket and tie required. Reservations required. AE, CB, D, DC, MC, V.*

## Environs

㉑ **Acropolis.** Located in Greektown, 15 minutes by cab from
$$ the major hotels, the Acropolis has an informal air, suitable for relaxed discussion but better for simply relaxing. The dining room, with murals of Greece on the walls and Greek music playing in the background, is filled largely with families. The generously sized dishes are distinguished by fresh seafood, notably rockfish and red snapper. There are several lamb dishes, including two pounds of moist chops. There is a good selection of Greek wines, including retsinas. The staff is well-informed and efficient. *4718 Eastern Ave., tel. 301/675–3384 or 675–7882. Dress:*

*Casual. Reservations required. AE, DC, MC, V. Closed Mon.*

**㉠ L'Auberge.** Half a mile east of the Inner Harbor, in the
$$$ slightly shabby northern part of Fells Point (*see* Diversions, below), is this small French restaurant, with exposed beams and wainscoted walls. Highly regarded, but not usually crowded, it's a good place for a small private meeting. The service suffers only from a sometimes-intrusive attentiveness. The kitchen handles duck commendably, in one version, roasted in fig sauce. Tournedos of beef is a popular entrée, prepared with foie gras, artichoke, and mushrooms. *505 S. Broadway, tel. 301/732–1151. Jacket and tie required. Reservations required. AE, MC, V. Closed Sun.*

**㉑ Bandaloops.** If you want to see where young Baltimoreans
$$ go for a casual California-style meal, take a five-minute ride south from the Inner Harbor to this informal and lively restaurant, housed in a building so narrow that it might be mistaken for a box car. The bar in the front room is usually crowded, but the waiters maintain an amiable reserve and execute their duties commendably. The menu features salads and sandwiches. Oysters are a house specialty; they are recommended in combination with steak, or with Cajun shrimp and spinach pasta covered with tomato-pepper butter. The wine list is heavily Californian, with some Chilean and Spanish labels. *1024 S. Charles St., tel. 301/727–1355. Dress: Casual but neat. Reservations required. AE, MC, V. Closed Sun.*

**❶ Café des Artistes.** This formal French restaurant is worth
$$$ the 15-minute taxi ride north from downtown to the residential Mt. Washington neighborhood. Candles glow in the lovely room with deep-green carpets and wallpaper; hand-painted china picks up coral tones in the decor. It's too quiet for a large group, but it's fine for private discussions. Jazz from a grand piano provides a soothing background. Try the onion soup, escargot, or tender scallops with tomatoes and saffron. *1501 Sulgrave Ave., tel. 301/664–2200. Jacket and tie required. Reservations advised. AE, CB, DC, MC, V. Closed Sun. lunch.*

**㉒ Da Mimmo.** This is Little Italy's best and most expensive
$$$$ Italian restaurant. It's a five minute cab ride from downtown, but a trip worth taking. The room is a bit noisy, and the tables are too close together, but you'll find all the old standards of southern Italian cuisine handled with practiced ease. The seafood is consistently good: shrimp and red snapper, in their various guises, are both recommended. Clams casino (diced and prepared with bacon) is a favorite appetizer. Pastas are reliably fresh and not overcooked. The staff is professional but friendly. The list of Italian wines is, like the menu, the best in the neighborhood. *217 S. High St., tel. 301/727–6876. Jacket and tie advised. Reservations required. AE, CB, DC, MC, V.*

## FREE TIME

### Fitness

*Hotel Facilities*
The **Harbor Court** (tel. 301/234–0550) has by far the best facilities, including racquetball and outdoor tennis courts; nonguests pay $10 a day.

*Health Clubs*

Many hotels give their guests privileges at the **Downtown Athletic Club** (210 E. Centre St., 301/547–6984), which accepts other guest members for a day rate of $15. The **Baltimore Racquet and Fitness Club** (218 N. Charles St., tel. 301/625–6400) also takes guest members on a daily basis of $10.

*Jogging*

The track at Rash Field, on the south side of the Inner Harbor, adjacent to the Science Center and Federal Hill Park, is convenient and scenic.

## Shopping

**Antique Row** comprises the 700 and 800 blocks of N. Howard Street and the 200 block of West Read Street. There are more than three dozen first-rate shops for furniture, art, books, and sundry collectibles at prices that are not low, but are negotiable.

The Pratt Street and Light Street pavillions of **Harborplace,** and the **Gallery mall,** right across from Pratt Street, contain more than 110 specialty shops, selling everything from business attire (Ann Taylor, Brooks Brothers, etc.) to children's toys and gourmet foods. There are also some 60 eateries, from fast food stalls to expensive restaurants. (For information about both, tel. 301/332–4191.)

## Diversions

**Fells Point,** east of the Inner Harbor, is an 18th-century neighborhood with cobblestone streets, a tugboat pier, good seafood restaurants, lively bars, and a number of boutiques in converted warehouses on Brown's Wharf.

**Museum Row** (800 E. Lombard St., tel. 301/396–3279) in Little Italy includes two restored buildings: the elegant Carroll Mansion, home of a signer of the Declaration of Independence, and the more modest 1840 House next door, where costumed interpreters perform historical skits.

**The National Aquarium** (Pier Three, Inner Harbor, tel. 301/576–3810) holds 500 species of fish and marine mammals in one million gallons of water. On the top floor, spectacular birds and reptiles are kept in an artificial rain forest.

**North Charles Street,** from Baltimore Avenue to the Washington Monument on Mt. Vernon Square, is an uphill walk of about a ½ mile, with a number of interesting art galleries and shops.

The **Walters Art Gallery** (Charles and Centre Sts., tel. 301/547–ARTS) is a nationally recognized museum, with an outdoor sculpture court and a fine collection that's especially strong in Renaissance and 19th-century paintings.

**Top of the World** (Pier Two, Inner Harbor, tel. 301/837–4515), on the 27th floor of the World Trade Center, is the world's tallest pentagonal building, and the place to view the city and environs.

## Professional Sports

**Soccer. Blast,** Arena, tel. 301/347–2010; **Baseball. Orioles,** Memorial Stadium, tel. 301/338–1300; **Hockey. Skipjacks,** Arena, tel. 301/347–2010; **Indoor Lacrosse. Thunder,** Arena, tel. 301/347–2010.

## The Arts

Pre-New York runs and roadshows of Broadway hits are the usual fare at the **Mechanic Theatre** (Baltimore and Charles Sts., tel. 301/625–1400) and occasionally at the **Lyric** (Mt. Royal Ave. and Cathedral St., tel. 301/485–6000), which usually is reserved for opera. **Center Stage** (N. Calvert and Monument Sts., tel. 301/332–0033) is the State Theater of Maryland, and its repertory ranges from Shakespeare to Sam Shepard. The Baltimore Symphony performs at **Meyerhoff Hall** (Cathedral and Preston Sts., tel. 301/783–8000). Distinguished guests join the students and faculty at the **Peabody Conservatory** (E. Mt. Vernon Pl. and Charles Sts., tel. 301/659–8124) for concerts, recitals, and opera performances in the school's Friedberg Hall.

At most hotels, guests can ask the concierge to obtain theater tickets; otherwise, Ticket Center (tel. 301/481–6000) has tickets to concerts and peformances around the area.

## After Hours

When Baltimore business people invite clients for a drink after work, they usually head for one of the hotel bars, perhaps in the Belvedere, Peabody, or Harbor Court. For a more boisterous kind of evening, the bars around the Broadway and Thames intersection (on the Fells Point waterfront) attract a younger crowd Thursday through Saturday nights.

*Bars and Lounges*
**On the Thirteenth Floor** (Belvedere Hotel, N. Charles and Chase Sts., tel. 301/332–1000) attracts all ages with music to dance to and a grand view of the harbor. The top-floor **Conservatory Lounge** (Peabody Court Hotel, tel. 301/727–7101) draws a dressy crowd of thirtyish and older patrons to its view of the illuminated Washington Monument, and the elegant Mt. Vernon neighborhood that surrounds it; jazz piano Fri. and Sat. nights. **The Explorer's Club** (Harbor Court Hotel, tel. 301/234–0550) has piano music every night, and a full jazz band on Fri. and Sat.; the setting is 19th-century colonial Africa, complete with elephant tusks and leopard-skin chairs.

*Comedy Clubs*
**The Charm City Comedy Club** (102 Water St., tel. 301/576–8558) and the **Comedy Factory of Maryland** (36 Light St., tel. 301/523–3837) are both convenient to downtown.

*Jazz Clubs*
**Blues Alley** (1225 Cathedral St., tel. 301/837–2288) is a spinoff of a Washington, D.C., supper club; it's seen the likes of Dizzy Gillespie, Mel Torme, and Wynton Marsalis.

*For Singles*
**Impulse** (Sheraton Inner Harbor Hotel, tel. 301/962–8300) is a high-energy dance club with flashy lighting effects. **Bertha's** (734 S. Broadway, tel. 301/327–5795) is the best known of a group of meeting places on the Fells Point waterfront.

# Boston

*by Mary Frakes*

Boston is a paradox. Often called one of the most European of U.S. cities, it is nevertheless best known as the birthplace of the American Revolution. Tradition is knit into its bones, in the red-brick Victorian bow-front townhouses of Beacon Hill and the Back Bay, yet its economy has been closely linked to the most modern of industries, high-tech. Known for its conservative tastes in art and fashion—remnants of the days when being "banned in Boston" could boost book or ticket sales elsewhere—the city has universities that still produce some of the most challenging new minds of each generation. The slick and the staid exist side by side in a city on a human scale, which has assimilated—sometimes uneasily—different cultures without losing its unique character.

The "Massachusetts miracle"—the economic recovery of the 1980s—has ended, and Boston's major industries are struggling to cope with hard times, mergers, and downsizing.

A classic example is high technology, which fueled much of Boston's growth in the previous decade as the area's universities turned out computer whizzes. Employment in the computer industry was lower in 1989 than it was at the decade's beginning, reflecting increased domestic and foreign competition. Several of the largest companies along Route 128, the high-tech beltway outside the city limits, have been the victims of mergers or takeovers.

Defense companies, which profited from the Reagan administration's largesse in defense spending, are nervous about an extended downturn, though their emphasis on research and development makes them less vulnerable than hardware manufacturers. Financial services and construction have been hard-hit by a sluggish real estate market, though construction jobs are expected to pick up in several years once major public works, such as the third harbor tunnel and reconstruction of the Central Artery, begin.

The service sector has expanded steadily, though the state's poor economic health has slowed even that growth. However, the more optimistic economists say a depressed economy should help hold down costs and thus make it easier for businesses to find labor and space.

Boston's primary growth product remains brains: The city's more than 50 colleges and universities have traditionally supplied the rest of the nation with thinkers and leaders in every field. That emphasis on intellectual achievement, coupled with a strong sense of history and an increasingly diverse ethnic population, has created a city where world-class musical groups and art museums coexist with such big-city problems as racism and poverty.

## Top Employers

| Employer | Type of Enterprise | Parent*/ Headquarters |
|---|---|---|
| **Amoskeag Co.** | Real estate development | Boston |
| **Digital Equipment Corp.** | Computers | Maynard, MA |
| **EG & G Inc.** | Electronics | Wellesley, MA |
| **General Cinema Corp.** | Movie theaters | Newton, MA |
| **Gillette Co.** | Personal products | Boston |
| **New England Telephone and Telegraph** | Telecommunications | Boston |
| **Raytheon Corp.** | Defense contractor | Lexington, MA |
| **Sheraton Corp.** | Hotels | Boston |
| **Stop and Shop** | Grocery chain | Braintree, MA |
| **Wang Laboratories, Inc.** | Computers | Lowell, MA |

*if applicable*

## ESSENTIAL INFORMATION

### Climate

What follows are the average daily maximum and minimum temperatures for Boston.

| | | | | | | | | |
|---|---|---|---|---|---|---|---|---|
| **Jan.** | 36F | 2C | **Feb.** | 38F | 3C | **Mar.** | 43F | 6C |
| | 20 | −7 | | 22 | −6 | | 29 | −2 |
| **Apr.** | 54F | 12C | **May** | 67F | 19C | **June** | 76F | 24C |
| | 38 | 3 | | 49 | 9 | | 58 | 14 |
| **July** | 81F | 27C | **Aug.** | 79F | 26C | **Sept.** | 72F | 22C |
| | 63 | 17 | | 63 | 17 | | 56 | 13 |
| **Oct.** | 63F | 17C | **Nov.** | 49F | 9C | **Dec.** | 40F | 4C |
| | 47 | 8 | | 36 | 2 | | 25 | −4 |

### Airport

**Logan International Airport** is 3 miles southwest of downtown Boston.

## Airport Business Facilities

**Mutual of Omaha Business Service Center** (Terminal C, tel. 617/569–4635) has fax machines, photocopying, notary public, secretarial service, ticket pickup, Western Union, travel insurance, cash advance, phone suites, and two conference rooms.

## Airlines

Other than the Trump and Pan Am shuttles to New York, which operate hourly, the most frequent service by national carriers flying into Logan is offered by Delta and USAir. The following airlines serve Logan Airport:

**American,** tel. 617/338–6755 or 800/334–7400.
**Continental,** tel. 617/569–8400 or 800/231–0856.
**Delta,** tel. 617/567–4100 or 800/221–1212.
**Midway,** tel. 800/621–5700.
**Northwest,** tel.617/267–4885 or 800/225–2525.
**Pan Am,** tel. 800/221–1111.
**Trump Shuttle,** tel. 800/247–8786.
**TWA,** tel. 617/367–2800 (domestic), 617/367–2808 (international), or 800/221–2000.
**United,** tel. 800/241–6522.
**USAir,** tel. 617/482–3160 or 800/428–4322.

## Between the Airport and Downtown

Although Logan airport is only 3 miles from downtown, it includes a stretch under Boston Harbor in a two-lane tunnel. There can be massive traffic jams, not only during rush hour (8–10AM and 4–6 PM) but at peak weekend travel times (Sunday evenings). Depending on city traffic and tunnel conditions, it can take anywhere from five minutes to an hour to get downtown.

If you don't have a lot of luggage and it's rush hour, the fastest way to get downtown is either via the water shuttle or the MBTA subway system, called "the T." For direct service to your hotel, an airport shuttle bus serves many area hotels. For information about ground transportation to and from Logan International, call 617/561–1769 or 800/ 235–6426.

*By Taxi*
There are cab stands outside each terminal. Barring major traffic delays, the trip should take 5–15 minutes to downtown. Cost: about $15, though a flat rate is available if a cab is shared.

*By Helicopter*
**Hub Express** (tel. 800/962–4744) links Logan's Terminal B with Boston City Heliport, near the World Trade Center, and four suburban sites: the New England Executive Park in Burlington (Rte. 128, north of the city); Waltham's Vista International Hotel; Norwood Municipal Airport; and the Sheraton Boxborough (Rte. 495). Each site has hourly service Mon.–Fri., 6 AM–8:30 PM. Cost: $59 basic fare; Trump Shuttle passengers fly free to downtown Boston, pay $10 to Rte. 128, and $20 to Boxborough; passengers on some routes of American, United, TWA, USAir, Delta, Midway, and Midwest Express pay $20 with advance reservations.

*By Subway*
The **MBTA's Blue Line,** which operates 5:30 AM–1 AM, links the airport with commuter rail service, downtown bus terminals, and interstate train service. The T runs about every 10 minutes and takes about 5 minutes to downtown. Free shuttle buses connect the subway terminal with all airline terminals. Cost: 75¢.

*By Bus*
**Airways Transportation** (tel. 617/267–2981) has regularly scheduled daily service to most major Boston hotels. Cost: $6.50.

*By Water Shuttle*
A small (50-passenger) ferry between Logan Airport and Rowes Wharf in downtown Boston operates every 15 minutes Mon.–Fri., 6 AM–8 PM and every half-hour weekends, noon–8, except July 4, Thanksgiving, and Christmas. Travel time is about 7 minutes. Cost: $7.

## Car Rentals

The following companies have booths at the airport:

**American,** tel. 617/569–3550 or 800/527–0202.
**Avis,** tel. 617/424–0800 or 800/331–1212.
**Budget,** tel. 617/561–2300 or 800/527–0700.
**Dollar,** tel. 617/569–5300 or 800/421–6878.
**Hertz,** tel. 617/569–7272 or 800/654–3131.
**Thrifty,** tel. 617/569–6500 or 800/367–2277.

## Emergencies

*Doctors*
**Beth Israel Hospital** has a physician referral service (330 Brookline Ave., tel. 617/735–5356), as does **New England Baptist Hospital** (125 Parker Hill Ave., tel. 800/447–5558).

*Dentists*
**The Dental Cooperative of Massachusetts** (tel. 617/262–9734) offers a dental referral service. The **New England Medical Center** (750 Washington St., tel. 617/956–5472), affiliated with Tufts University, has a dental clinic, as does **Massachusetts General Hospital** (55 Fruit St., tel. 617/726–5508).

*Hospitals*
**Massachusetts General** (55 Fruit St., tel. 617/726–2000), **Beth Israel Hospital** (330 Brookline Ave., tel. 617/735–3337), **Brigham and Women's Hospital** (75 Francis St., tel. 617/732–5500), **New England Medical Center** (750 Washington St., tel. 617/956–5000).

## Important Addresses and Numbers

**Audiovisual rentals.** A.D. Handy (44 Bromfield St., tel. 617/542–3954), Mass Audio Visual Equipment (1167 Massachusetts Ave., Arlington, tel. 617/646–5410), Projection Video Services (39 Dalton St., tel. 617/262–3664).

**Chamber of Commerce** (600 Atlantic Ave., tel. 617/227–4500).

**Computer rentals.** Rentex Office Equipment (337 Summer St., tel. 617/423–5567), City Office Equipment (66 L St., South Boston, tel. 617/542–8378), PCR Personal Computer Rentals (10 Cedar St., Suite 19, Woburn, tel. 617/933–5993).

**Convention and exhibition centers.** Bayside Exposition Center (200 Mt. Vernon St., Dorchester, tel. 617/825–5151), John B. Hynes Veterans Memorial Convention Center (Prudential Tower, Suite 225, tel. 617/954–2300), World Trade Center Boston (Commonwealth Pier, tel. 617/439–5000).

**Fax service.** Copy Cop (2 locations: 260 Washington St., tel. 617/367–3370, 815 Boylston St., tel. 617/267–9267).

**Formal-wear rentals.** Formalwear Ltd. (15 Elm St., Waltham, tel. 617/899–5727), Read and White (54 Chauncy St., tel. 617/542–7444).

**Gift shops.** Gift Baskets: Beaubasket (1250 Washington St., Norwood, tel. 617/769–7755), Candy: The Chocolate Truffle (100 Tower Office Park, Suite I, Woburn, tel. 617/933–4616), Flowers: Winston Flowers, 131 Newbury St., tel. 617/536–6861).

**Graphic design studios.** Bezdek Design (24 Mt. Auburn St., Cambridge, tel. 617/547–6609), Independent Design Studios (451 D St., tel. 617/439–4944), Woodard/Black (419 Western Ave., tel. 617/782–3050).

**Hairstylists.** Unisex: Cramer's Hair Studio (Copley Place Shopping Center, tel. 617/267–4146), MJN at Harringtons (883 Boylston St., tel. 617/262–5587).

**Health and fitness clubs.** *See* Fitness, below.

**Information hot lines.** Boston Tourism and Convention Center (tel. 617/536–4100), Boston Globe Sports Scoreboard (tel. 617/265–6600), Ticketmaster Concert Line (tel. 617/332–9000), Boston Jazz Line (tel. 617/262–1300).

**Limousine services.** Ambassador Services (tel. 617/227–7844), Fifth Avenue Limousine Service of Boston (tel. 617/286–1590 or 800/343–2071).

**Liquor stores.** Merchants Wine and Spirits (6 Water St., tel. 617/523–7425), Marty's (193 Harvard Ave., Brighton, tel. 617/782–3250), Simmons Package Store (210 Cambridge St., tel. 617/227–2223).

**Mail delivery, overnight.** DHL Worlwide Express (tel. 617/846–8901), Federal Express (tel. 617/542–6142), TNT Skypak (617/884–9780), UPS (tel. 617/561–8483), U.S. Postal Service Express Mail (tel. 617/654– 5676).

**Messenger services.** Boston Bicycle Couriers (tel. 617/426–7575) delivers within Boston, Statewide Delivery (tel. 617/242–9005) delivers outside Boston.

**Office space rental.** Headquarters (2 locations: 50 Milk St., tel. 617/451–6868, World Trade Center, tel. 617/439–5300).

**Pharmacies, late-night.** Back Bay Pharmacy (1130 Boylston St., tel. 617/267–5331), Phillips Drug (155 Charles St., tel. 617/523–1028 or 523–4372).

**Radio stations, all-news.** WEEI, 590 AM; WHDH, 850 AM.

**Secretarial services.** Drake International (80 Boylston St., Suite 333, tel. 617/542–7812), Office Support Management (715 Boylston St., 5th floor, tel. 617/262–5464), Staff Builders Convention Services (18 Tremont St., tel. 617/523–1880).

**Stationery supplies.** Back Bay Stationers (2 locations: 711 Boylston St., tel. 617/267–0445, 85 Arch St., tel. 617/542–0001).

**Taxis.** Boston Cab Association (tel. 617/536–5010), Boston City Taxicab Co. (tel. 617/859–0855), Checker Cab (tel. 617/536–7000), Independent Taxi Operators Association (tel. 617/426–8700), Red & White Cab (tel. 617/742–9090), Town Taxi (tel. 617/536–5000).

**Theater Tickets.** *See* The Arts, below.

**Train information.** Amtrak (tel. 617/482–3660 or 800/392–6099), Commuter Rail (tel. 617/227–5070 or 800/392–6099). Trains for destinations north leave from North Station (150 Causeway St.); those heading south go from South Station (Atlantic Ave. and Summer St.).

**Travel agents.** Crimson Travel (3 locations: 53 State St., tel. 617/742–7060; 245 Summer St., tel. 617/720–2300; 2 Government Center Plaza, tel. 617/742–8500), Garber Travel (4 locations: 1047 Commonwealth Ave., tel. 617/787–0600; 44 School St., tel. 617/723–4400; 265 Franklin St., tel. 617/439–6773; Prudential Center Plaza, tel. 617/437–7200),

**Weather** (tel. 617/923–1234).

## LODGING

Business travelers generally stay either downtown or near the Hynes Convention Center at Copley Square. Downtown is closer to Logan Airport and rail transportation, and most convenient for the financial district. The area around the convention center in the more residential Back Bay neighborhood is handy for conventioneers and those doing business with the major insurance companies. A few of the hotels listed are in the theater district, just about halfway between downtown and Back Bay. Hotel rates in Boston rival those of bigger cities, and most rates do not include parking, which can cost $10–$20 a night. The busiest times of the year are June, when students from the city's many colleges graduate, and fall, when students return and tourists come to see the foliage. Most of Boston's older hotels, like the Parker House, are situated in the financial district. Boston's newer mega hotels are for the most part centered around the Prudential Center in the Back Bay.

All the hotels listed below offer corporate rates and weekend discounts; inquire when making reservations.

Highly recommended lodgings in each price category are indicated by a star ★.

| Category | Cost* |
|---|---|
| $$$$ (Very Expensive) | over $180 |
| $$$ (Expensive) | $110–$180 |
| $$ (Moderate) | under $110 |

*All prices are for a standard double room, single occupancy, excluding 9.7% tax.*

*Numbers in the margin correspond to numbered hotel locations on the Boston Lodging and Dining map.*

## Downtown/Center City

★ **㉙**
$$$$
**Boston Harbor Hotel.** If a room with a view is your top priority, it's hard to beat having a choice of either Boston Harbor or the heart of downtown. But the real advantage here is the ease of access to Logan Airport; this is the downtown terminus for the seven-minute water shuttle across the harbor. This newest of Boston's luxury hotels (1987) is also within walking distance of the financial district. The lobby features an antique map collection, oil portraits, and salmon and gray marble. The decor of the public areas and rooms is upscale Anglophile. Guest rooms, decorated with mahogany reproductions, are on floors 8–16; the Rotunda suites have a view of both harbor and city, though the room configuration can be awkward. Oversize club chairs and floor lamps are good for lounging and reading. In summer, there's a small outdoor terrace café, and the Rowes Wharf Bar has an outstanding selection of single-malt Scotches. *Small Luxury Hotels. 70 Rowes Wharf, 02110, tel. 617/439–7000 or 800/752–7077, fax 617/330–9450. Gen. manager, Francois Nivaud. 206 rooms, 24 suites. AE, CB, D, DC, MC, V.*

**㉕**
$$$$
**Bostonian.** Only minutes from Logan Airport, this small, European-style luxury hotel occupies three historic buildings across from Faneuil Hall. Converted to hotel use over the last decade, the somewhat undersized rooms were renovated in 1989. All have balconies and original watercolors. Weekend traffic in tourist season can be noisy, so try to avoid rooms closest to the Central Artery. Rooms in the oldest of the buildings (the Harkness) have working fireplaces and beamed ceilings; those in the other buildings mix contemporary metal with Chippendale reproductions. Some suites have whirlpool baths. Seasons, the hotel restaurant (*see* Dining, below), is excellent. *Fisher Hotel Group. Faneuil Hall Marketplace, 02109, tel. 617/523–3600 or 800/343–0922, fax 617/523–2454. Gen. manager, Timothy Kirwan. 153 doubles, 10 suites. AE, DC, MC, V.*

**㉒**
$$$
**Lafayette Hotel.** This luxury hotel, built in 1985, does its best to ignore the fact that it's located on the edge of the so-called Combat Zone—a downtown area within walking distance of Quincy Market, South Station, and the financial district. Though the Zone is being gentrified, walking at night is still not recommended. The lobby is on the second floor, away from the street level, and the atmosphere is sedate, with impressive flower arrangements, mahogany furniture, and soft music. Chippendale reproduction furniture, marble-topped nightstands, and botanical prints give the rooms a traditional feel, and upholstered armchairs are comfortable for lounging. The corner suites on

each floor are the most spacious, and odd-numbered rooms up to 37 have a view of the statehouse. The three butler-staffed concierge floors have juicers, hair-dryers, and robes in each room plus access to the central lounge, which features a complimentary Continental breakfast and afternoon tea, a billiard table, and a small sundeck. The formal dining room, Le Marquis de Lafayette, is one of the best restaurants in the city (*see* Dining, below). *Swissotel. 1 Ave. de Lafayette, tel. 617/451–2600 or 800/992–0124, fax 617/451–0054. Gen. manager, Liam Madden. 320 doubles, 44 suites, 117 business class. AE, CB, D, DC, MC, V.*

★ ❷ **Le Meridien.** When Air France converted the former Fed-
$$$  eral Reserve Bank into a hotel in 1981, it managed to blend ornate Renaissance revival granite-and-limestone architecture with traditional French elegance. The low-ceilinged, contemporary marble lobby is a striking counterpoint to the ornate marble carving over the door frames and gilded ceilings elsewhere in the building. In the heart of the financial district, Le Meridien is convenient to the airport, South Station, the north-south expressway (the Central Artery), and the Massachusetts Turnpike. Rooms on the top three of the nine floors have sloping glass windows with panoramic city views. Suites have recently been renovated, but you must specify if you want a desk in the room. Rooms on the third floor are smaller than the others, and those near the health club can be noisy; there are some bi-level loft suites on the second floor. The Julien lounge, a piano bar with N.C. Wyeth murals of American political figures, and the Julien restaurant (*see* Dining, below) are both favorites of the city's business leaders. Café Fleuri (*see* Business Breakfasts, below) draws them in in the morning. *250 Franklin St., 02110, tel. 617/451–1900 or 543-4300, fax 617/423–3844. Gen. manager, Hugues Jaquier. 304 doubles, 22 suites, AE, CB, D, DC, MC, V.*

❷ **Parker House.** The lobby, with its ornately embossed
$$$  brass elevator doors and elaborately carved ceiling friezes, looks as grand as the original hotel, built in 1854, where Charles Dickens stayed and Parker House rolls were created in the kitchen. The present hotel, built in 1927, has long been associated with politics; John F. Kennedy announced his presidential candidacy here, and proximity to the statehouse means a clientele rife with government officials. It's also close to Boston Common and around the corner from the Downtown Crossing shopping area; you might have to contend with congested traffic if you have a rush hour appointment, but not much noise filters up to the rooms at night (the quietest rooms face School Street). As with many older hotels, room size can vary greatly. Desks are marble-topped and decor is traditional. Parker's dining room, with its crystal chandeliers, mahogany paneling, and wing chairs, is a mecca for political wheeling and dealing at lunch. *Omni Hotels. 60 School St., 02108, tel. 617/227–8600 or 800/843–6664, fax 617/ 742–4729. Gen. manager, Laurence Jeffrey. 476 doubles, 70 suites. AE, CB, D, DC, MC, V.*

## Back Bay

❸ **Back Bay Hilton.** This triangular, concrete 26-story hotel,
$$$  built in 1982, is just around the corner from the Hynes Convention Center; as a result, its primary market is conventioneers and business travelers. One of the virtues of

# BOSTON

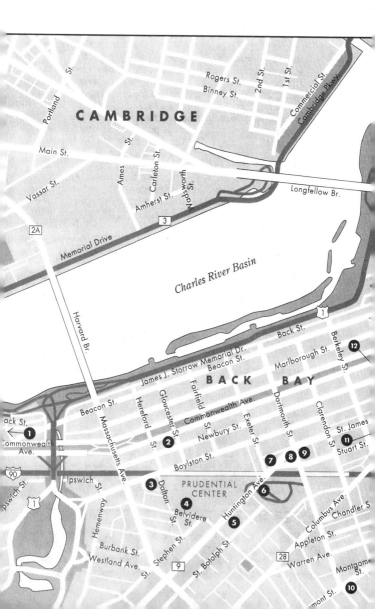

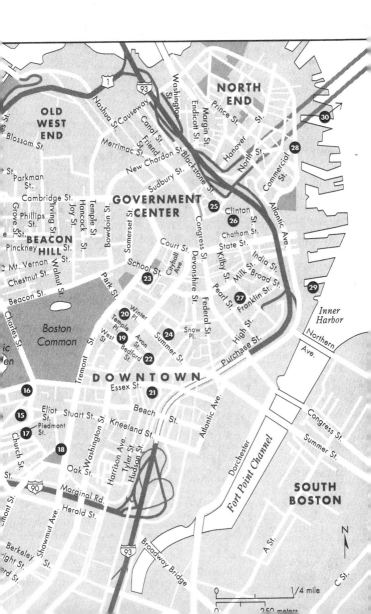

# BOSTON HOTEL CHART

| HOTELS | Price Category | Business Services Banquet capacity | No. of meeting rooms | Secretarial services | Audiovisual equipment | Teletype news service | Computer rentals | In-room modem phone jack | All-news cable channel | Desk | Desk lighting | Bed lighting |
|---|---|---|---|---|---|---|---|---|---|---|---|---|
| Back Bay Hilton | $$$ | 250 | 14 | - | ✓ | - | ✓ | - | - | - | - | ◐ |
| Boston Harbor | $$$$ | 120 | 7 | ✓ | ✓ | - | - | ✓ | ✓ | ● | ◐ | ◐ |
| Bostonian | $$$$ | 75 | 2 | ✓ | ✓ | - | - | ✓ | ✓ | ○ | ○ | ◐ |
| Boston Park Plaza | $$ | 1500 | 35 | - | ✓ | - | - | - | ✓ | ○ | - | ● |
| Colonnade | $$$ | 350 | 7 | ✓ | ✓ | - | - | ✓ | ✓ | ● | ● | ◐ |
| Copley Plaza | $$$ | 1000 | 9 | ✓ | ✓ | - | ✓ | ✓ | - | ◐ | ◐ | ◐ |
| Copley Square | $$ | 40 | 1 | - | - | - | - | - | - | - | - | ● |
| The 57 Park Plaza/ Howard Johnson | $$ | 600 | 11 | ✓ | ✓ | - | - | - | ✓ | ◐ | ● | ◐ |
| Four Seasons | $$$$ | 300 | 6 | ✓ | ✓ | - | - | ✓ | ✓ | ● | ● | ● |
| Guest Quarters Suite Hotel | $$$ | 160 | 8 | - | ✓ | - | - | ✓ | ✓ | ◐ | ● | ◐ |
| Lafayette | $$$ | 300 | 16 | ✓ | ✓ | - | - | ✓ | ✓ | ● | ● | ◐ |
| Logan Airport Hilton | $$$ | 250 | 21 | - | ✓ | - | - | ✓ | ✓ | ◐ | ◐ | ◐ |
| Marriott Copley Place | $$$$ | 2200 | 37 | ✓ | ✓ | - | - | - | ✓ | ◐ | ● | ◐ |
| Le Meridien | $$$ | 250 | 8 | ✓ | ✓ | ✓ | ✓ | ✓ | ✓ | ◐ | ● | ● |
| Parker House | $$$ | 300 | 14 | - | ✓ | - | - | - | ✓ | ● | ● | ◐ |
| Ritz-Carlton | $$$$ | 275 | 12 | ✓ | ✓ | - | ✓ | - | ✓ | ○ | ◐ | ◐ |
| Sheraton Boston Hotel and Towers | $$$ | 1160 | 41 | ✓ | ✓ | - | ✓ | ✓ | ✓ | - | - | ● |
| Tremont House | $$ | 350 | 7 | ✓ | ✓ | - | ✓ | - | ✓ | ◐ | ◐ | ◐ |
| Westin | $$$$ | 1400 | 24 | - | ✓ | - | - | ✓ | ✓ | ◐ | ◐ | ◐ |

**$$$$** = over $180, **$$$** = $110-$180, **$$** = under $110.
● good, ◐ fair, ○ poor.
All hotels listed here have photocopying and fax facilities.

| **In-Room Amenities** | | | | | | | | | | **Hotel Amenities** | | | | | | |
|---|---|---|---|---|---|---|---|---|---|---|---|---|---|---|---|---|
| Nonsmoking rooms | In-room checkout | Minibar | Pay movies | VCR/Movie rentals | Hairdryer | Toiletries | Room service | Laundry/Dry cleaning | Pressing | Concierge | Barber/Hairdresser | Garage | Courtesy airport transport | Sauna | Pool | Exercise room |
| ✓ | - | - | ✓ | - | ✓ | ● | ◐ | ● | ● | ✓ | - | ✓ | - | - | ● | ● |
| ✓ | - | ✓ | ✓ | ✓ | ✓ | ● | ● | ● | ◐ | ✓ | ✓ | ✓ | - | ✓ | ● | ● |
| ✓ | - | ✓ | ✓ | ✓ | ✓ | ● | ● | ● | ◐ | ✓ | - | - | ✓ | - | - | - |
| ✓ | ✓ | - | ✓ | - | - | ○ | ● | ● | ◐ | ✓ | ✓ | ✓ | - | - | - | - |
| ✓ | - | ✓ | ✓ | ✓ | ✓ | ● | ● | ● | ◐ | ✓ | - | ✓ | - | - | ○ | ◐ |
| ✓ | ✓ | ✓ | ✓ | ✓ | ✓ | ◐ | ◐ | ● | ◐ | ✓ | - | ✓ | - | - | - | - |
| ✓ | - | ✓ | ✓ | - | ✓ | ◐ | - | ● | ◐ | ✓ | - | - | - | - | - | - |
| ✓ | ✓ | ✓ | - | - | - | ○ | ◐ | ● | ● | - | ✓ | ✓ | - | ✓ | ◐ | - |
| ✓ | - | ✓ | - | - | ✓ | ● | ● | ● | ● | ✓ | - | ✓ | - | ✓ | ● | ● |
| ✓ | ✓ | ✓ | ✓ | ✓ | - | ◐ | ◐ | ● | ◐ | ✓ | - | ✓ | - | ✓ | ○ | - |
| ✓ | ✓ | ✓ | ✓ | ✓ | - | ◐ | ● | ● | ◐ | ✓ | - | ✓ | - | ✓ | ◐ | ○ |
| ✓ | ✓ | ✓ | - | - | - | ○ | ○ | ● | ● | ✓ | - | - | - | - | ○ | - |
| ✓ | ✓ | - | ✓ | - | - | ● | ● | ● | ● | ✓ | - | ✓ | - | ✓ | ● | ● |
| ✓ | ✓ | ✓ | ✓ | - | - | ● | ● | ◐ | ◐ | ✓ | - | - | - | ✓ | ● | ● |
| ✓ | ✓ | - | ✓ | ✓ | - | ◐ | ◐ | ◐ | ○ | ✓ | ✓ | - | - | - | - | - |
| ✓ | - | ✓ | - | ✓ | ✓ | ● | ● | ● | ● | ✓ | ✓ | ✓ | - | ✓ | - | ● |
| ✓ | ✓ | - | ✓ | ✓ | - | ◐ | ● | ● | ◐ | ✓ | ✓ | - | - | - | ● | ● |
| ✓ | - | ✓ | - | - | - | ○ | ◐ | ● | ◐ | - | - | - | - | - | - | - |
| ✓ | ✓ | ✓ | ✓ | - | - | ◐ | ● | ● | ◐ | ✓ | - | - | - | - | ◐ | ● |

**Room service:** ● 24-hour, ◐ 6AM-10PM, ○ other.
**Laundry/Dry cleaning:** ● same day, ◐ overnight, ○ other.
**Pressing:** ● immediate, ◐ same day, ○ other.

large chains is consistency, and you'll find few surprises at this Hilton. New management has promised to redo the rooms' uninspiring decor, including the ubiquitous round-table with overhead light and two side chairs. Rooms are soundproofed, the elevator is enclosed by glass partitions, and there are only 16 rooms per floor, so it's one of the quietest hotels around. The rooms on the north side of the uppermost floors have a view of the Charles River; corner rooms are largest and have balconies. The health club is one of the best of the hotel fitness facilities; hotel guests pay a minimal charge. *40 Dalton St., 02115, tel. 617/236–1100 or 800/874–0663, fax 617/236–1506. Gen. manager, Alan Lewis. 337 doubles, 3 suites. AE, CB, D, DC, MC, V.*

**5** **Colonnade.** Built in 1972 and renovated in 1989–90, this is
**$$$** where Gerald Ford stayed to open the city's Bicentennial celebration. The exterior has all the charm of a concrete bunker, but the interior is that of a small luxury hotel. Rooms feature either contemporary oak furniture with black accents and coppery autumn colors, or mahogany furniture with a rose and black color scheme; executive suites have a dining table and sitting area. Bathrooms are on the small side; the newer ones with an Art Deco look seem larger. Rooms on the north side overlook the Christian Science Monitor building's reflecting pool and the Prudential Center; rooms facing south get less street noise. The Hynes Convention Center, Symphony Hall, and Copley Place shopping are nearby. Zachary's, the hotel's sleek gray and black dining room, is well regarded. Don't expect to use the rooftop pool except in summer; it's not enclosed. *Preferred Hotels. 120 Huntington Ave., 02116, tel. 617/424–7000 or 800/962–3030, fax 617/424–1717. Gen. manager, Sayed Saleh. 277 doubles, 11 suites. AE, CB, DC, MC, V.*

**9** **Copley Plaza.** A major renovation program in 1989 gave
**$$$** new sparkle to this aging turn-of-the-century dowager. The gray-stone building, adorned with a bow-front, was designed by Henry Hardenbergh, architect of New York City's Plaza Hotel. The public areas now shine with bright lighting, gleaming gold leaf, pink marble, and ornately carved ceilings; the Grand Ballroom is straight out of 18th-century Vienna. The refurbished rooms, spread over seven floors, have a bland, uniformly beige decor and don't live up to the grandeur downstairs—though they are spacious, particularly the suites. Quietest rooms are in the central corridor, but they have the worst views; best views are in front, overlooking Copley Square and Trinity Church. The Plaza Dining Room (*see* Dining, below) and the Plaza Bar (*see* After Hours, below) with their leaded-glass doors and clublike atmosphere, are institutions. *138 St. James Ave., 02116, tel. 617/267–5300 or 800/826–7539, fax 617/267–7668. Gen. manager, Jan Chovanec. 287 doubles, 109 singles, 44 suites. AE, CB, DC, MC, V.*

**7** **Copley Square.** You won't impress anyone by staying here,
**$$** except maybe your accountant. However, in a city where hotel rates tend to be high, this has always been a mecca for those seeking a reputable hotel bargain. Built in 1891 and renovated most recently in 1985, it appeals to many European travelers who like its intimate scale and often opt for the less expensive, shared bathrooms. The hotel bears the scars of age—chipped molding; relatively small, 1940s-era bathrooms; dark, mismatched furniture; indi-

vidual window-unit air conditioners; and an old steam-heat radiator system. However, it's clean and it's convenient to the Hynes Convention Center and Back Bay. Single rooms can be odd-shaped and small; best bets are the corner rooms, which are the largest, and rooms ending in 10 and 11, which have newer bathrooms. Courtyard rooms on upper floors are quietest. In the basement is Café Budapest, an appealing Hungarian restaurant with a romantic atmosphere. *Saunders Hotels. 47 Huntington Ave., 02116, tel. 617/536–9000 or 800/225–7062, fax 617/267–3547. Gen. manager, Jose Estrompa. 46 singles, 54 doubles, 11 suites. Coffeemakers in rooms. AE, CB, D, DC, MC, V.*

**❻ Marriott Copley Place.** This and the Westin (*see* below) are
$$$$ the two behemoths of Copley Place. One of the city's largest hotels, this 38-story modern structure was built in 1984, along with the rest of the posh Copley Place shopping complex. Most of the hotel's clientele is drawn from the big conventions at the nearby Hynes Center. The cavernous lobby is sleek pink-and-gray marble. Rooms feature Queen Anne-style furniture and pastel colors. The concierge floor has a complimentary Continental breakfast, hors d'oeuvres, and dessert, as well as concierge service. A Charles River view is available on the 30th floor and above. It's big, it's efficient, and it's not far from the Prudential Center. *110 Huntington Ave., 02116, tel. 617/236–5800 or 800/228–9290, fax 617/424–9378. Gen. manager, Jurgen Giesbert. 1001 doubles, 77 suites, 69 business class. AE, CB, D, DC, MC,V.*

**❶❷ Ritz-Carlton.** Visiting royalty and heads of state stay here
$$$$ (the Aga Khan, Prince Charles, and the Kennedys, for example). Until the nearby Four Seasons opened, this was *the* place to stay in Boston. It was built in 1927, expanded in 1981 to add condominiums and additional rooms, and renovated in 1985. Service is the top priority here; the staff-to-guest ratio is high, and it's the only place in town that still has white-gloved elevator operators (who double as security guards). Some of the white-and-gold French Provincial furnishings are a touch old-fashioned, such as the vanity tables that serve as desks in some rooms. Newer rooms have bigger baths and floor-to-ceiling windows; however, many people still choose the older section, which has a pantry on all floors, buttons for calling the butler, and some working fireplaces. Interior courtyard rooms have no view, and you can't be guaranteed one of the coveted rooms facing the Public Garden even if you request it. The Ritz Café (*see* Business Breakfasts, below) hosts many movers and shakers in the morning, the hotel Dining Room attracts the same affluent crowd for lunch and dinner (*see* Dining, below), and the hotel bar (*see* After Hours, below) brings them in later in the evening. *15 Arlington St., 02117, tel. 617/536–5700 or 800/241–3333, fax 617/536–1335. Gen. manager, Sigi Brauer. 168 doubles, 68 singles, 42 suites. AE, CB, D, DC, MC, V.*

**★ ❹ Sheraton Boston Hotel and Towers.** If you're staying at the
$$$ Sheraton and attending a convention at the Hynes, you could stay indoors for your entire trip. The 29-story hotel has a direct link with not only the convention center but also the Prudential Center complex. It gets a lot of business from conventioneers, the city's consular corps, soloists at nearby Symphony Hall, and visiting sports teams. Rooms are large, modern, and comfortable, especially on

the four Towers floors, which have their own separate staff, a private lounge, complimentary Continental breakfast and hors d'oeuvres, and small conference rooms. Lanai suites open onto the skylit pool, which has a roof that opens in summer. Rooms above the 15th floor in the north tower overlook the Charles River; corner suites may have a four-poster bed, a wet bar, and a pantry. The business center, complete with desktop publishing facilities, is convenient to the convention center entrance. *39 Dalton St., Prudential Center, 02199, tel. 617/236–2000 or 800/325–3535, fax 617/236–1702. Gen. manager, Stephen Foster. 1,085 doubles, 45 suites, 120 business class. Voicemail messages in rooms, in-house graphics service. AE, CB, D, DC, MC, V.*

**❽** **Westin.** This 36-story hotel in the Copley Place office/
**$$$$** shopping complex has all the conveniences—and impersonality—of a big-city chain facility. Built in 1983, it rivals the Marriott in height; rooms above the 16th floor have a good view of the Charles River (corner rooms have the best panorama as well as sitting areas). Even-numbered floors have bleached oak furniture, the odd floors mahogany; both include Colonial armoires for the TV and either a burgundy or gray color scheme. The bottled water in the bathrooms is a nice touch, as are operative windows and voice-mail messages. Floors 24–29 are the corporate floors, which have added perks such as complimentary breakfast. The hotel restaurant, Turner Fisheries (*see* Dining, below), is a fine setting for a business talk. *10 Huntington Ave., 02116, tel. 617/262–9600 or 800/228–3000, fax 617/424–7483. Gen. manager, David C. King. AE, CB, D, DC, MC, V.*

## Brighton

**❶** **Guest Quarters Suite Hotel.** This 1985 post modern hotel is
**$$$** five miles west of downtown, a trip that can take up to a half hour when traffic is heavy. However, it's the only Boston hotel that concentrates so heavily on suites; all but 22 rooms have a separate sitting room and kitchenette, and the executive suites have a small conference table. As a result, the hotel is popular with recruiters, government officials, and business travelers who must hold small seminars or stay for extended periods. All rooms have a view of the Charles River and either Harvard or Boston; the river's proximity is underlined by the rowing scull that hangs in the skylit atrium lobby. The bi-level loft rooms on the upper floors are the most expensive. A courtesy van from the water shuttle and complimentary Continental breakfast are pluses, and there's a cabaret nightly at Scullers (*see* After Hours, below), the hotel's restaurant. *400 Soldiers Field Rd., Brighton, 02134, tel. 617/783–0090 or 800/424–2900, fax 617/673–0987. Gen. manager, Mark Fallon. 22 doubles, 320 suites. AE, CB, D, DC, MC, V.*

## Theater District

**❸** **Boston Park Plaza.** The lobby here speaks of the days
**$$** when the Boston Park Plaza was the flagship for the Statler hotels: all cream and gilt molding, with ornate wrought iron and mahogany railings on the mezzanine balconies. Built in 1927, the hotel is showing a bit of age these days, but the location is still a good one: adjacent to the theater district and a block from the Public Garden. Some

smaller rooms have been merged into one and are spacious; others are still small. Be sure to ask for an outside room, which looks out over the city. The upgraded Plaza Towers rooms have extra amenities, complimentary Continental breakfast, and access to a lounge and meeting room. Furnishings are ersatz Oriental bamboo or light Colonial-style pine with abstract pastels; bathrooms are somewhat cramped. The Terrace Room hosts the Forbidden Broadway comedy revue (*see* After Hours, below). *Saunders Hotels. 64 Arlington St., 02117, tel. 617/426–2000 or 800/225–2008, fax 617/426–5545. Gen. manager, Joseph N. Malone. 873 doubles, 25 suites, 82 business class. Voicemail service in rooms. AE, CB, D, DC, MC, V.*

★ **⓱** **The 57 Park Plaza Hotel/Howard Johnson.** Even though
$$ the rooftop sign says Howard Johnson's, don't look for an orange roof or fried clams; this is an independently owned hotel. The lobby proclaims the difference with streamlined black lacquer Deco furniture, mirrors, frosted glass torchères, and soft rose and blue upholstery. Close to New England Medical Center, Chinatown, and the theater district, it caters to business travelers and families looking for a downtown bargain. All rooms in this big, 1970s-style concrete box are the same size and have balconies; the decor is contemporary, with soft pink and gray pastels and black lacquer trim on mahogany or light oak furnishings. Suites have small bathtubs. Executive rooms include a snack box, complimentary newspapers, and hair-dryers in the bathroom. If you don't want to pay for luxuries but need a comfortable, modern facility, this is a good choice. *200 Stuart St., 02116, tel. 617/482–1800 or 800/654–2000, fax 617/451–2750. Gen. manager, Donald Walsh. 276 doubles, 26 suites, 24 business class. Free parking. AE, CB, D, DC, MC, V.*

★ **⓰** **Four Seasons Hotel.** Rivaling the traditional Ritz as
$$$$ Boston's finest hotel, the Four Seasons has a superb location, across from the Public Garden, only a few blocks from the theater district, and equidistant from the Hynes Center and the financial district. The hotel occupies eight of this 1985 building's 15 stories; the other floors feature luxury condominiums. Oil portraits of proper Bostonians decorate the rather impersonal but antique-filled lobby. In the guest rooms, contemporary blond wood furnishings, brass touches, and spacious baths are the norm. Rooms in the front, including all of the suites, have a garden view. Fresh flowers and shaving/makeup mirrors in the bathrooms, free disposable bathing suits in the health clubs, and shaving kits on request are typical of the hotel's thoughtfulness. Shoeshines, newspapers, and limos to downtown are complimentary. The staff is not only efficient but friendly. The hotel dining room, Aujourd'hui (*see* Dining, below) is excellent. This is as glamorous as Boston gets, which is not very. *200 Boylston St., 02116, tel. 617/338–4400 or 800/332–3442, fax 617/423–0154. Gen. manager, Robin Brown. 272 doubles, 13 suites, 3 business class. AE, CB, DC, MC, V.*

**⓲** **Tremont House.** In its 66 years, this theater district hotel
$$ with grandiose meeting spaces has been the national headquarters for the Elks. A down-at-the-heels has-been until a 1984 renovation, the Tremont now is a good choice for travelers on a budget. Rooms have dark Colonial furnishings and vary greatly in size (some are tiny), but the

ones on the upper floors of the west side overlook Back Bay. If you're concerned about noise, avoid the sixth floor, which is over the banquet area. The hotel also includes the Stage Deli, a sandwich place that stays open late; a 1950s-style rock 'n' roll bar; and the Roxy nightclub (*see* After Hours, below). The area is being revitalized, but it's best to be judicious late at night. *Quality Inns. 275 Tremont St., tel. 617/426-1400 or 800/228-5151, fax 617/482-6730. Gen. manager, Gregory Hargrave. 234 doubles, 34 suites. Bus tour office. AE, CB, D, DC, MC, V.*

## Airport

**③⓪** **Logan Airport Hilton.** The only airport hotel in Boston,
*$$$* this four-building complex immediately adjacent to the airport was renovated in 1989. The newest building is a 14-story tower; the oldest section, a two-story structure, houses the pool. *Logan International Airport, East Boston, 02128, tel. 617/569-9300 or 800/445-8667, fax 617/569-3981. Gen. manager, Richard Eaton, 542 doubles, 5 suites, 24-hour shuttle to airport. AE, CB, DC, MC, V.*

# DINING

The quality of Boston dining has come a long way from the days of bland, overcooked seafood and heavy cream sauces. Interest in fine dining began about a decade ago in hotel dining rooms, many of which continue to be notable for their ambience and high quality. However, some of the best new entries are bistros that appeal to the Bostonian common-sense ethos of good quality at a good price. Though many of these bistros—Biba's, Hammersley's, Cornucopia—are expensive, the menus are flexible enough to allow for moderately priced dining as well. Chef/owners, many of whom started in the large hotel rooms and have since opened places of their own, are bringing creativity and flair to menus that emphasize good-sized portions, seasonal local foods, and inventive techniques and ingredients.

Highly recommended restaurants in each price category are indicated by a star ★.

| Category | Cost* |
| --- | --- |
| *$$$$* (Very Expensive) | over $45 |
| *$$$* (Expensive) | $30–$45 |
| *$$* (Moderate) | under $30 |

*per person, including appetizer, entrée, and dessert, but excluding drinks, service, and 5% sales tax.*

*Numbers in the margin correspond to numbered restaurant locations on the Boston Lodging and Dining map.*

## Business Breakfasts

**Café Fleuri** (tel. 617/451–1900) has the best Sunday brunch in town, and the regular breakfast isn't shabby, either. The location, in the Meridien Hotel in the financial district, makes it perfect for a working breakfast in a cheerful, skylit atrium setting. The menu includes more than just the eggs-and-bacon standards. **Ritz Café** (tel.

617/536–5700) in the Ritz-Carlton is where power break-fasts are the norm for politicians, financiers, and executives of all stripes—not to mention people getting fueled up for a day of shopping on Newbury Street. The Scotch salmon is always popular, as are the eggs Benedict and steak with eggs. Window seats are popular and difficult to get.

For more casual morning dining the bustling **Café Tremont** (60 School St., tel. 617/ 227–8600) is convenient to the statehouse and downtown; it also has a self-serve takeout pastry counter. **Rebecca's** (21 Charles St., tel. 617/742–9747) specializes in baked goods and people-watching on Beacon Hill. **Charlie's Sandwich Shoppe** (429 Columbus Ave., tel. 617/536–7669) opens at 6 AM weekdays and is usually packed with people ordering the enormous portions of down-home food, especially the pancakes. **Au Bon Pain,** which specializes in croissants, muffins, and pastries, has a number of outlets, both takeout and eat-in, all over the city.

## Downtown

⑲ **Cornucopia.** It took a pioneering spirit to open an upscale
$$$ restaurant on a side street off Downtown Crossing near the slowly gentrifying Combat Zone, but the gamble has paid off. This two-level Art Deco room is warm and appealing, with geometric-patterned stained-glass chandeliers over oak tables. The imaginative New American menu changes monthly, but often reflects a balance of East and West, such as sesame-crusted catfish with fried Chinese noodles in a spicy Thai sauce; or dishes that star New England ingredients, such as grilled pork chop with apples, sausage, and sage stuffing. The restaurant places great importance on wine and even suggests ones to accompany specific dishes. There is a good selection of wines by the glass. Women alone should be careful at night in this neighborhood. The downstairs can be a bit noisy; if you want serious conversation, go upstairs. *15 West St., tel. 617/338–4600. Dress: casual but neat. No reservations. AE, DC, MC, V. Closed Sun. and for dinner Mon.*

㉔ **Dakota's.** Located in the Downtown Crossing shopping
$$$ area, this Texas-influenced grill aims squarely at a straightforward business clientele. The room is quietly comfortable, with black wainscoting, salmon and cream marble floor, and brass sconces—the food may be southwestern, but the look is sedate Boston. The menu includes standards such as roast chicken, grilled rainbow trout, swordfish, and haddock; Southwest accents include venison sausage quesadillas, tortilla soup, and crab cakes made with minced serrano peppers. On the lobby level of the 101 Arch Street building, Dakota's is a bit difficult to find, and service can be haphazard. *34 Summer St., tel. 617/737–1777. Jacket and tie suggested. AE, MC, V. Closed Mon.*

㉖ **Durgin-Park.** Diners who come to this Quincy Market res-
$$ taurant have to be hungry enough to cope with enormous portions and have the time to stand in line for them. Durgin-Park has been serving hearty New England fare since the 1830s, when the building was a working produce and meat market instead of a tourist attraction; it requires only a little imagination to picture burly working men sit-

ting around communal tables and chowing down. The communal tables are still here, as are homey old New England dishes such as Indian pudding and huge haunches of prime rib. Lunch is a little calmer than dinner, though both are crowded during peak tourist seasons; poor ventilation in summer can leave you sweaty after all that vigorous eating. It would be difficult to do business here, especially when you're elbow-to-elbow with strangers, but the atmosphere is uniquely old Boston. *340 Faneuil Hall Marketplace, North Market Building, tel. 617/227–2038. Casual dress. No reservations. No credit cards.*

**㉗** **Julien.** When the former Federal Reserve Bank became
$$$$ the Hotel Meridien, the owners turned part of it into a formal dining room, and some say it's still where the money is; the clientele draws heavily on the financial district. High ceilings, a limestone balcony, crystal chandelier, and heavy silver befit the elegant room, and wing chairs afford plenty of privacy for important discussions. Owned by Air France, the restaurant is a culinary collaboration between a young American chef and a four-star consulting chef from France; the result is a French-oriented menu that makes extensive use of local ingredients and cooking techniques that give lighter results than the traditional cream-laden Escoffier-style fare. Dishes change seasonally, but might include duck glazed with a Caribbean-spiced caramel sauce, pomegranate seeds, and watercress; or roasted lobster with artichoke hearts and lemon verbena juice. The wine list is largely French and well selected. *250 Franklin St., tel. 617/451–1900. Jacket and tie required. Reservations required. Dinner only on weekends and July–Aug. AE, CB, D, DC, V.*

★ **㉒** **Le Marquis de Lafayette.** Although it's located on the edge
$$$$ of the Combat Zone, the Lafayette Hotel's dining room has an upscale image and a clientele of top-echelon businesspeople. French consulting chef Louis Outhier created the menu, and the atmosphere is that of an English club, with hunting prints and oil portraits on the walls, and crested china and a long-stemmed rose in a crystal vase on each table. Formally attired waiters provide deft, unobtrusive service. The seasonal menu might include a breast of pheasant with potato and pheasant hash, poached foie gras in lentils, or grouper steak with fried lotus root. The banquettes in the rear of the small room, shielded from the entrance, afford the most privacy. *1 Ave. de Lafayette, tel. 617/451–2600. Jacket and tie required. Reservations advised. AE, CB, DC, MC, V.*

**㉑** **Mei Lei Wa.** If you've been negotiating into the late night,
$$ the Cantonese food here just might be able to break up the stalemate. There are not a lot of late-night choices in Boston, and Mei Lei Wa, by contrast, is open till 4 AM and takes credit cards—a rare combination in Chinatown. The decor is standard Chinese restaurant—unadorned. Especially good are the roast duck, which has crispy skin flavored with cinnamon, cloves, and anise; and clams in black-bean sauce. *21 Edinboro St., tel. 617/482–6840. Casual dress. AE, DC, MC, V.*

★ **㉘** **Restaurant Jasper.** Owner Jasper White, who trained a
$$$$ number of the city's best chefs when he was at Seasons (*see below*), has won a national reputation with his updated New England specialties since he opened this restaurant on the waterfront. A loyal business clientele

dominates this subdued Art Deco room, decorated in chic black and white, with exposed brick walls that hark back to the time when this space was occupied by a molasses factory. Dishes change almost nightly, but lean heavily on local game and seasonal produce. Typical fare might be as nouvelle as a salad of grilled duck with cranberries and spiced nuts, or as traditional as a New England boiled dinner cooked to perfection. Desserts such as a superb crème brulée or chocolate bread pudding may be New England inspired, but are anything but Puritan. *240 Commercial St., tel. 617/523–1126. Reservations required. Jacket and tie required. AE, CB, DC, MC, V. Dinner only.*

**29** **Rowe's Wharf.** If you want a waterfront view of Boston
**$$$** Harbor without the noise and mediocre food of tourist-ridden megarestaurants, this is the place. Though it was built in 1987, this large dining room of the Boston Harbor Hotel is replete with traditional touches such as upholstered armchairs, gathered swag curtains, mahogany paneling, and shaded wall sconces. It's a comfortable, low-key setting for thoughtful discussions, as well as a good choice for a working breakfast or lunch. Though the room itself is large, pillars and banquettes break the space into a gallery of smaller areas, and one section is set aside for more casually dressed diners. The food is subdued New American, with entrées such as fricassee of lobster and sea scallops on fresh herb pasta, and duck breast with a leek confit and honey-ginger glaze. Some of the items are designated as being heart healthy. *70 Rowe's Wharf, tel. 617/439–7000. Jacket suggested. Reservations suggested. AE, CB, DC, MC, V.*

**25** **Seasons.** This highly respected restaurant has been the
**$$$$** training ground for some of Boston's best-known chefs. Located in the Bostonian Hotel, it is close to both the financial district and City Hall; it's also only minutes from Logan airport, making it perfect for a business breakfast on the way out of town. Chef William Poirier has upheld the restaurant's tradition of excellence with a menu of New American cuisine with well-executed exotic touches. The menu changes seasonally; the duckling with ginger and scallions has been a perennial favorite, but a winter menu might also include caraway venison with wood mushrooms and cheese pierogi, or swordfish with chickpeas, eggplant, and taramosalata. The wine list is exclusively—and comprehensively—American, and the waiters, many of whom have been on the staff for years, are knowledgeable enough to make excellent recommendations. Large windows overlook the Faneuil Hall bustle, and the overhead ceiling draperies are drawn back at night for a view of the sky. *North and Blackstone Sts., tel. 617/523–3600. Jacket required. Reservations suggested. AE, DC, MC, V.*

## Back Bay

**11** **Grill 23.** The gray suits of insurance, the law, and banking
**$$$$** are prominent at this dining room in the renovated Salada Tea building. This is a classic steak house, from the mahogany paneling, gigantic marble columns, and white-jacketed waiters, right down to the brass plaques on the bar that identify the favorite seats of its regular customers. Best tables are around the lower-level dining room. The house salad, a melange of vegetables, is rightly

praised, and the menu concentrates on doing one thing well: grilling meat and seafood. Typical dishes include a mixed grill and beef Wellington. If you want a burger for lunch, you'll have to come early; inexplicably for a steak house, they can run out. *161 Berkeley St., tel. 617/542–2255. Jacket and tie advised. Reservations suggested. AE, CB, D, DC, MC, V. Closed Sun. dinner only Fri. and Sat.*

❷ **L'Espalier.** When Moncef Meddeb announced he was sell-
$$$$ ing this temple of Boston haute cuisine, Boston feared the new owner wouldn't keep up Meddeb's high standards. However, Frank McClelland, Meddeb's second in command, has upheld the tradition of fine cuisine in this elegant spot that occupies two floors of a renovated Back Bay townhouse. Marble fireplaces grace each of the three rooms; the mahogany-paneled dining room upstairs is clubby, while the other two dining rooms have a lighter feel. A three-course prix fixe menu might include such New American dishes as roast rack of lamb with a maple mustard crust served with an apple-and-goat-cheese tart and a shallot rosemary sauce, or grilled tuna and swordfish with shrimp risotto and olive basil butter. The atmosphere is quiet, and the intimate feel appropriate for important business dinners. A tasting menu is available on request. There's a well-selected wine list, and service is punctilious. *30 Gloucester St., tel. 617/262–3023. Jacket and tie required. Reservations required. AE, MC, V. Closed Sun.*

❾ **Plaza Dining Room.** The Edwardian dining room at the
$$$$ Copley Plaza Hotel has always been elegant, but it has taken on additional luster after a recent refurbishing by new owners and the importation of two top chefs from Le Marquis de Lafayette. High-backed, tapestry-covered chairs, crystal chandeliers, a lavishly molded ceiling, and mahogany Palladian-arched mirrors create a formal atmosphere suitable for the most serious business dinners, while a baby grand plays discreetly in the background. The extensive menu lists seasonal dishes that are classically French with some innovative touches. For example, fillet of salmon is served with cepes mushrooms and leeks flavored with walnut oil; warm oysters are topped with caviar; and roasted rack of lamb is accented with salt-cured lemon peels and sweet garlic. The wine list is designed to impress, and the library at the entrance is perfect for an after-dinner brandy. Service is meticulous. *138 St. James Ave., tel. 617/267–5300. Jacket and tie required. Reservations advised. AE, CB, DC, MC, V.*

⓬ **Ritz Dining Room.** This is where generations of Bostoni-
$$$$ ans have come to celebrate special occasions. After more than a half century, the dining room of the Ritz-Carlton has perfected its regal ways; the service is efficient, the white and gold decor properly refined. The view of the Public Garden is exquisite, the Sunday brunch is lavish, conversations and the dinner music from the white grand piano are discreetly subdued, and the array of silverware offers the perfect opportunity to demonstrate one's social aplomb. The kitchen focuses on such classic Continental fare as steak Diane and Dover sole in a lemon-butter sauce, and long-time local favorites like lobster in bourbon sauce. This is not the place to impress someone with cutting-edge tastes. *15 Arlington St., tel. 617/536–3700.*

*Jacket and tie required. Reservations required. AE, CB, D, DC, MC, V.*

**❽** **Turner Fisheries.** Businesspeople come to Turner Fisher-
**$$** ies, in the Westin at Copley Place, for fresh, well-prepared
seafood served in a comfortable, spacious room. Booths
are paneled with gray wainscoting, and the room is
adorned with mahogany sideboards and green-shaded
lamps. Subdued contemporary jazz fills in the back-
ground. Locals usually begin with the chowder, which
packs a rich punch. Seafood items can be ordered broiled,
grilled, fried, baked, or blackened; other specialties in-
clude several kinds of smoked fish and steamed mussels
served with a choice of sauces. There's plenty of privacy,
especially in the booths, and the atmosphere is conducive
to quiet talk. *10 Huntington Ave., tel. 617/424–7425.
Dress: casual but neat. AE, CB, D, DC, MC, V.*

## South End

**★ ❿** **Hamersley's Bistro.** This small storefront in the up-and-
**$$$** coming South End is known for its innovative yet unpre-
tentious fare. Chef/owner Gordon Hamersley creates his
hearty stews and braised dishes in an open kitchen at the
back of the intimate restaurant. The black-and-white decor is simple but enlivened with posters. Specialties on the
seasonal menu include a delectable lemon-garlic roasted
chicken and a grilled mushroom and garlic sandwich; Sunday nights are prix fixe with slightly lower prices. The
wine list has reasonably priced entries from Portugal,
Spain, and Australia, as well as from France and the U.S.
The noisy, informal atmosphere and small size make
Hamersley's unsuitable for heavy-duty business negotiations. For women alone, the surrounding neighborhood
can still be dicey after dark; it's best to take a cab directly
to and from the restaurant. *578 Tremont St., tel. 617/267–
6068. Dress: casual but neat. Reservations advised, especially on weekends. AE, MC, V.*

## Theater District

**⓰** **Aujourd'hui.** This temple of understated elegance, the for-
**$$$$** mal dining room of the Four Seasons Hotel, has been
around for less than a decade, but it has become one of the
power rooms in town. Tables overlooking the Public Garden are especially sought after. All tables are discreetly
separated for important discussions, the carpet is thick,
the staff is reverent. The food is anything but cold roast
Boston; chef Mark Baker has earned a reputation for an
inventive hand with regional ingredients and New American recipes. Though entrées such as braised lobster
ragout with grilled corn and sauvignon blanc, or rack of
lamb with kalamata olives and goat cheese ravioli can
sometimes be extremely rich, the menu, which changes
seasonally, also contains low-calorie, low-cholesterol spa
cuisine. Aujourd'hui is also recommended for breakfast
meetings. *200 Boylston St., tel. 617/338–4400. Jacket and
tie advised. Reservations advised. AE, DC, MC, V.*

**★ ⓮** **Biba.** Chef Lydia Shire's culinary innovations were so re-
**$$$** nowned that her casual restaurant, opened in 1989, quick-
ly became a Boston favorite. She serves up earthy dishes
that borrow inspiration from all five continents and can be
as simple as spaghetti with breadcrumbs or as arty as
wood-roasted swordfish with zucchini flowers and shrimp

risotto. The eclectic decor combines Turkish-pattern upholstery on the banquettes, a spectacular redrailed staircase, and a cryptic mural of well-fed diners. The informal atmosphere encourages spontaneous conversations with people at the next table; this is not a place for private discussions. Menu items are grouped not as appetizers, salads, vegetables, entrées, and desserts, but as "meats" or "legumina" or the challenging "offal"; the format encourages grazing—combining small, inexpensive portions. The extensive wine list emphasizes adventurous selections from lesser-known areas rather than renowned older vintages. The downstairs bar, where street-level windows offer interesting people-watching, is good for late-night snacks or single diners. *272 Boylston St., tel. 617/426–7878. Dress: casual but neat. Reservations advised. AE, MC, V.*

★ ⓯ **Legal Seafood.** "If it isn't fresh, it isn't Legal" is this Boston institution's slogan. And that freshness is what keeps drawing crowds to this restaurant located in the theater district, despite waits for a table so long you could go out and dig your own clams. Legal restaurants (there are branches in Cambridge and several other suburbs) get the top of the catch. This wood-paneled restaurant is open and airy, with large windows that let in lots of light. Most entrées are of the standard fried-boiled-broiled-grilled variety with few elaborate sauces. The renowned clam chowder comes in a calorie-reduced version, and the fried calamari taste like seafood instead of rubber bands. Don't bring a client if you're in a hurry or are uncomfortable being served before he or she is; dishes come out whenever they're ready. *27 Columbus Ave., tel. 617/426–4444. Casual dress. No reservations. AE, CB, D, DC, M, V.*

⓴ **Locke-Ober Café.** After more than 100 years, this is still the place where old-line Brahmins can find food that conforms with Boston tradition. The decor is solid and comfortable as well, featuring mahogany paneling, lace curtains, and brass trim. Tables are well spaced so conversations can be confidential. The location is conveniently near downtown, just off the Common. The specialty is lobster Savannah, a generous portion of shellfish in a rich cream sauce, but grilled chops, Dover sole, and finnan haddie are also menu staples. The Men's Bar downstairs is now open to women, though the female nude portrait that gets draped in black when Harvard loses to Yale is still there. *4 Winter Place, tel. 617/542–1340. Jacket and tie required. Reservations required. AE, CB, DC, MC, V.*

## FREE TIME

### Fitness

*Hotel Facilities*

**The Westin** (tel. 617/262–9600) offers a $7 day-pass for nonguests, which includes the use of the pool and equipment room. The excellent facilities at the **Back Bay Hilton** (tel. 617/262–2050) are run by FitCorp (*see* below), and are available to nonguests for $12 per day.

*Health Clubs*

In addition to the fitness center at the Back Bay Hilton, noted above, **FitCorp** has a downtown facility (133 Federal St., tel. 617/542–1010), also charging a $12 per-visit rate.

The **Spa at the Heritage** (75 Park Plaza, tel. 617/426–6999) has a $25 per-visit rate, plus discounts on aerobics classes and complimentary day passes for guests of the Ritz-Carlton, Copley Plaza, and Park Plaza hotels. **Boston Athletic Club** (653 Summer St., tel. 617/269–4300) allows travelers staying at a Boston hotel access to Nautilus equipment and tennis, racquetball, and basketball courts on a $20 per-visit rate. The **Greater Boston YMCA's** facilities (316 Huntington Ave., tel. 617/536–7800), are available to members of other Ys free with a photo ID.

*Jogging*
The **Esplanade,** which runs from Charles Street the length of the city along the Charles River, is the city's best route; at rush hour, though, you'll have to contend with exhaust fumes from Storrow Drive. **Boston Common** and the **Public Garden** also are popular, but to be avoided after dark.

## Shopping

Some of the best souvenirs to take home from Boston are edible—maple syrup and live lobsters packed to travel have long been favorites. Most of the city's tourist attractions carry replicas of documents or artifacts of the Revolutionary War era.

The most popular shopping areas for visitors are the **Quincy Market/Faneuil Hall** "festival marketplace" developments, just off Atlantic Avenue, along the waterfront near City Hall. The most expensive shopping is along **Newbury Street,** which has fashion boutiques, furriers, art galleries, home design stores, and small cafés; **Boylston Street,** where designer names such as Hermes, Saint Laurent, and Escada have appeared in recent years; and **Copley Place,** an indoor mall that houses Gucci, Louis Vuitton, Tiffany, and Neiman Marcus. The Downtown Crossing area has the city's two major department stores: **Jordan Marsh** (450 Washington St., tel. 617/357–3000) and **Filene's** (426 Washington St., tel. 617/357–2100), which is above but no longer affiliated with **Filene's Basement,** whose automatic markdowns have created some legendary shopping frenzies.

Other highly regarded stores include **Louis Boston** (234 Berkeley St., tel. 617/965–6100) and **Brooks Brothers** (46 Newbury St., tel. 617/267–2600) for menswear; **Suzanne** (35 Newbury St., tel. 617/266–4146) and **Charles Sumner** (16 Newbury St., tel. 617/536–6225) for designer women's clothing; **Shreve, Crump and Low** (350 Boylston St., tel. 617/267–9100) for jewelry, silver, china, and antiques; and **FAO Schwarz** (338 Boylston St., tel. 617/266–5101) for toys.

## Diversions

The red-brick bowfront townhouses and cobblestone streets of **Beacon Hill,** which date back to the early 1800s, are good territory for exploring on foot and absorbing the proper Bostonian atmosphere. Louisburg Square, at one end of Mount Vernon Street, has been home to William Dean Howells and the Bronson Alcotts; the enclosed patch of green is open only to the adjacent residents.

The 50-acre **Boston Common,** where colonials grazed cattle, and the adjacent **Public Garden** provide green space in the city's heart. The Public Garden, with its carefully tended formal plantings and summer swan-boat rides on a small pond, is the oldest botanical garden in the United States. Neither the Common nor the Garden, however, is recommended after dark.

Old Granary Burying Ground and nearby Park Street Church, at Boylston and Tremont streets, mark the beginning of the city's **Freedom Trail,** a walking tour that follows a line of red bricks to the city's most historic sites; a map is available at the Visitors' Information Booth just across the street on the corner of Boston Common. The church was the place where William Lloyd Garrison campaigned against slavery; the burying ground holds the remains of Samuel Adams, John Hancock, Paul Revere, and the victims of the Boston Massacre.

Across the river from Boston is busy **Harvard Square** and **Harvard Yard,** though there's little room to "pahk your cah." Take a break at one of the many bookstores or cafés there.

The **Museum of Fine Arts** (465 Huntington Ave., tel. 617/267–9300) is one of the country's outstanding museums, with extensive collections of Asian and Egyptian artifacts, American fine and decorative arts, and Impressionist paintings. On the Fenway Park side is the Tenshin Garden, a Japanese meditation area.

The **New England Aquarium** (Central Wharf, tel. 617/973–5200) has some of the most engaging performers in the city. A four-story, 187,000-gallon observation tank houses sharks and other inhabitants of the deep. Dolphin and sea lion shows take place aboard the floating pavilion *Discovery*.

At the **Old North Church** (193 Salem St., tel. 617/523–6676), lanterns that signaled "one if by land and two if by sea" prompted Paul Revere's famous ride. The church is in the North End, an Italian enclave that is rapidly being gentrified.

The **Old Statehouse** (206 Washington St., tel. 617/720–3290) served as the seat of Colonial government until the Revolution and as the capitol of the commonwealth until a new state house was built on Boston Common. It now holds a collection of marine memorabilia and Revolutionary War artifacts. In front is a circle of cobblestones that mark the site of the Boston Massacre, when a group of British soldiers fired into a crowd of jeering colonials.

The original **Paul Revere House** (19 North Sq., tel. 617/523–1676) is hidden beneath restoration clapboard and practically none of the furnishings belonged to the famous patriot and silversmith, but it is the site of the oldest house in Boston. Tours are self guided.

The **Quincy Market** area, prior to the 1970s renovation, was filled with produce and meat vendors rather than boutiques and trendy cafés. Some of the original vendors are still here, though. **Faneuil Hall** (pronounced "Fan'l"), at one end of Quincy Market, distinguished by a grasshopper weathervane, has since Colonial days been the scene of political debates; it houses a number of historic paintings, including a Gilbert Stuart portrait of George Washington. The street level is packed with shops geared to tourists.

The *USS Constitution*'s (Charlestown Navy Yard, tel. 617/426 1812) voyages now are limited to July 4, when the ship is taken into Boston Harbor. Undefeated during its service against pirates and in the War of 1812, it now is a floating history lesson. Guided tours.

## Professional Sports

**Basketball.** Boston Celtics (Boston Garden, tel. 617/523–3030); **Baseball.** Boston Red Sox (Fenway Park, tel. 617/267–8661); **Hockey.** Boston Bruins (Boston Garden, tel. 617/227–3223); **Football.** New England Patriots (Sullivan Stadium, Foxboro, tel. 617/543–1776).

## The Arts

No matter what art forms a visitor prefers, Boston is a cultural mecca. Its musical resources are particularly rich. It is home to the world-renowned **Boston Symphony Orchestra,** which appears at Symphony Hall. The **New England Conservatory of Music** is affiliated with Jordan Hall. For opera, head for the **Opera Company** of Boston's home at the Opera House. Contemporary **jazz** can be heard at the Berklee Performance Center. Boston's reputation as a tryout ground for Broadway productions has faded in recent years, but **touring companies** still get booked into the large downtown theaters, such as the Colonial, Shubert, Wilbur theaters, and the Wang Center for the Performing Arts. The number of art film houses has dwindled substantially, but various universities and organizations sponsor a number of film series.

**Bostix** (Faneuil Hall Marketplace, tel. 617/723–5181) sells half-price tickets for same-day theater productions. No sales are made by phone. Most ticket brokers charge a service fee and take major credit cards. Among them are: **Ticketmaster** (tel. 617/931–2000); **Ticketmaster of New England** (tel. 617/787–8000); **Concert Charge, Sport-Charge, TheatreCharge** (tel. 617/497–1118); **Concertix,** (tel. 617/876–7777); **Charg-Tix** (617/542–8511); **Teletron** (617/720–3434 or 800/382–8080).

**Berklee Performance Center,** 136 Massachusetts Ave., tel. 617/266–1400.
**Colonial Theatre,** 106 Boylston St., tel. 617/426–9366.
**Jordan Hall,** 33 Gainsborough St., tel. 617/536–2412.
**Opera House,** 539 Washington St., tel. 617/426–5300.
**Shubert Theatre,** 265 Tremont St., tel. 617/426–4520.
**Symphony Hall,** 301 Massachusetts Ave., tel. 617/266–1492.
**Wang Center for the Performing Arts,** 268 Tremont St., tel. 617/482–2595.
**Wilbur Theatre,** 246 Tremont St., tel. 617/426–1988.

## After Hours

Boston's Puritan founders bequeathed a tradition of ending evenings early, but that has begun to change a bit. Because of the large student population, the rock scene is lively, and in recent years, clubs catering to an older audience have opened, particularly some excellent jazz clubs.

And Boston is one of the great breeding grounds for standup comedy; Jay Leno got his start here, for one. The *Boston Globe*'s Thursday Calendar section provides extensive listings of current and coming events, as does the weekly *Boston Phoenix*.

### Bars and Lounges

The **Bay Tower Room** (60 State St., tel. 617/723–1666) has a subdued yet glamorous atmosphere and a stunning view of downtown Boston. The **Bull and Finch Pub** (84 Beacon St., tel. 617/227–9605), the model for the TV series *Cheers*, is good for a beer and a sandwich. The bar upstairs in the **Hampshire House** (84 Beacon St., tel. 617/227–9600) has a fireplace where you can relax with a glass of port. The clubby **Ritz Bar** at the Ritz-Carlton (tel. 617/536–5700) has long been a favorite of the city's powerful; try for a window table. **St. Cloud** (Tremont and Clarendon Sts., tel. 617/353–0202) draws an upscale crowd, as does **Rocco's** (5 S. Charles St., tel. 617/723–6800), which is close to the theater district.

### Cabarets

**Forbidden Broadway** in the Terrace Room of the Boston Park Plaza Hotel (tel. 617/426–2000) has been skewering theatrical icons for years and is updated annually to spoof the latest hits. One of the best bargains in town is the **Theatre Lobby and Cabaret** (216 Hanover St., tel. 617/227–9872), which has a café, a lively revue, and a lounge with live entertainment on the weekends. The **Plaza Bar** at the Copley Plaza (tel. 617/267–5300) has a cabaret format with lush Indo-Anglo decor; seating is a bit crowded. **Sculler's** at the Guest Quarters Suite Hotel (tel. 617/783–0090) features both local and national performers. **Club Cabaret at the Club Café** (209 Columbus Ave., tel. 617/536–0972) is the most theatrical of the city's cabarets and books everything from folk singers to female impersonators.

### Comedy Clubs

**Comedy Connection** (76 Warrenton St., tel. 617/426–6339) has long been one of Boston's premier comedy clubs, booking top national comedians. Its neighbor, **Nick's Comedy Stop** (100 Warrenton St., tel. 617/482–0930), concentrates more on local comics. **Dick Doherty's Comedy Vault** (124 Boylston St., tel. 617/267–6626) includes improvisational comedy as well as magic acts.

### Jazz Clubs

Some of the best clubs are across the river in Cambridge. The Charles Hotel's sleek **Regattabar** (1 Bennett St., tel. 617/876–7777) books top-flight national acts. **Nightstage** (823 Main St., tel. 617/497–8200) boasts excellent acoustics and sight lines for an interesting mix of jazz, blues, world music, and rock. There are the two-hour **Jazzboat** cruises on Boston Harbor on Fridays from June–Sept., departing from Central Wharf (tel. 617/876–8742). **Diamond Jim's Piano Bar** hosts a singalong Wed.–Sat. (710 Boylston St., tel. 617/566–8651).

### For Singles

**Zanzibar** (1 Boylston Place, tel. 617/451–1955), open Wed.–Sat., an upscale mix of faux marble, rattan furniture, and palm trees, leans toward financial-district late-baby-boomer types who still like to shake a tailfeather. **Citi** (15

Lansdowne St., tel. 617/262–2424), open Thurs.–Sun., is all neon disco, light show, and elbow-to-elbow dancing. The **Roxy** (279 Tremont St., tel. 617/227–7699), open Thurs.–Sat., is a palatial setting with two tiers of supper-club-style banquettes and tables with a surprising mix of contemporary pop interspersed with an occasional big-band set.

# Chicago

*by Elizabeth Gardner*

For many, the name "Chicago" still conjures up images of gangsters and tommy guns, stockyards and packing-houses; in the popular imagination it's a grimy industrial town whose climate is severe and whose denizens are rough-and-ready workmen. Few non-Chicagoans know that the city's motto is *Urbs in Horto*, "City in a Garden," and first-time visitors are often astonished to see Grant Park's acres of blooms, sailboats gliding on Lake Michigan, and lush green parkland along the lakefront; to find elegant and sophisticated shops along Michigan Avenue's Magnificent Mile; and to view handsome and impressive buildings, old and new, designed by world-class architects.

Like many American cities, Chicago prospered in the 1980s as middle-class urban pioneers migrated from the safety of the suburbs back to the city. In the 1960s, Lincoln Park, along the lakefront north of downtown, was plagued by crime and blight; now it's inhabited by bankers, physicians, lawyers, and other professionals who restored the 1890s-vintage two-family houses and are snapping up new $300,000 town houses. Upscale buyers are spilling into adjacent neighborhoods to the north and west as well, even invading a former industrial corridor along the Kennedy Expressway. The city's many ethnic neighborhoods on the northwest, west, and south sides— black, Mexican, Polish, Irish, Italian, Ukrainian, and Indian, to name a few—remain relatively stable, and gentrification has not yet disenfranchised the poor.

Chicago's almost even split between black and white residents (about 40% of each, with the remaining 20% divided among Hispanic and "other") doesn't diminish political acrimony and violence, though visitors are unlikely to encounter overt racism in the downtown and Near North Side neighborhoods that contain the city's major hotels and businesses.

Chicago enjoys a diverse economy. Although packing-houses, factories, and steel mills are gone, many corporate greats, including Quaker Oats, Helene Curtis, and Johnson Publishing, remain. The city is a hub for retailing, banking and insurance, commodities trading, drug and hospital supply companies, advertising, printing, and educational publishing. The suburbs to the north and west are home to many corporate headquarters. Chicago also has a large concentration of high-tech medical centers, including Rush-Presbyterian-St. Lukes, Northwestern Memorial Medical Center, Loyola University Medical Center, and the University of Chicago Hospitals.

The community was shaken when Sears Roebuck, the city's largest employer, threatened to leave Illinois for more hospitable economic climes. A package of tax breaks and incentives persuaded the company to stay in the Chicago area.

The center of Chicago business is the Loop, so-called because of the elevated train tracks that loop around its borders (Lake St., Wabash Ave., Van Buren St., and Wells St.). The Loop is home to the financial district, several major retailers, City Hall, and state and federal offices. (Helmut Jahn's futuristic State of Illinois Building at Randolph and Clark streets, also called Spaceship Chicago, is part of the redevelopment of the north Loop.) Most of the city's historic skyscrapers are in this area. The Loop deteriorated in the 1960s and 1970s as major retailers fled and downtown movie theaters were taken over by porno and kung-fu flicks, but it's slowly being reclaimed by new development and renovation.

Rampant office and hotel development is reshaping Chicago's other main business district, North Michigan Avenue. Travelers are likely to see scaffolding and torn-up streets for several years to come.

## Top Employers

| Employer | Type of Enterprise | Parent*/ Headquarters |
|---|---|---|
| **Abbott Laboratories** | Health care supply | Abbott Park, IL |
| **Baxter International** | Health care supply | Deerfield, IL |
| **Commonwealth Edison** | Utility | Chicago |
| **Dominick's Finer Foods** | Grocery | Chicago |
| **Illinois Bell** | Telephone | Ameritech/ Chicago |
| **Jewel Food Stores** | Grocery | American Stores Co./Salt Lake City, UT |
| **Marshall Field** | Retail | Dayton-Hudson Corp./Minneapolis |
| **Sears Roebuck and Co.** | Retail | Chicago |
| **United Airlines** | Transportation | UAL Corp./Elk Grove Village, IL |

*if applicable

## ESSENTIAL INFORMATION

### Climate

Strong winds off Lake Michigan can be pleasantly cool in the summer or bone-chilling in the winter. (Chicago's nickname, The Windy City, was inspired not by the weather but by the hot air emitted by its politicians.) The height of summer usually brings temperatures in the 80s and 90s and humidity up to 100%. Winter temperatures range from the mid-30s to well below zero and can change from one to the other overnight. Snow has been scarce for the past few years, but the occasional blizzard and other sudden storms often cause travel delays.

What follows are the average daily maximum and minimum temperatures for Chicago.

| Jan. | 32F | 0C | Feb. | 34F | 1C | Mar. | 43F | 6C |
|------|-----|-----|------|-----|-----|------|-----|-----|
|      | 18  | −8  |      | 20  | −7  |      | 29  | −2  |
| Apr. | 55F | 13C | May | 65F | 18C | June | 75F | 24C |
|      | 40  | 4   |     | 50  | 10  |      | 60  | 16  |
| July | 81F | 27C | Aug. | 79F | 26C | Sept. | 73F | 23C |
|      | 66  | 19  |      | 65  | 18  |       | 58  | 14  |
| Oct. | 61F | 16C | Nov. | 47F | 8C | Dec. | 36F | 2C |
|      | 47  | 8   |      | 34  | 1   |      | 23  | −5  |

### Airports

Chicago is served by two major airports. **O'Hare International Airport,** about 20 miles northwest of downtown, is one of the world's busiest. All major airlines, both national and international, serve O'Hare. It's big and sprawling; expect a walk of up to 20 minutes if you have to change carriers. Free shuttle buses on the lower (arrival) level take passengers from terminal to terminal and to remote parking lots. **Midway Airport,** about seven miles southwest of downtown, is more pleasant—much smaller and less congested. It's a hub for Midway Airlines, but other carriers use it as well. Some commuter planes and private aircraft fly out of tiny **Meigs Field,** on the lakefront just south of downtown.

### Airport Business Facilities

**O'Hare International Airport.** The **O'Hare Hilton Hotel** (across the street from Terminal 2, tel. 312/686–8000) has a business center on the lower level with fax machines, photocopying, notary public, secretarial service, cash advance, and conference rooms with catering service. It also has day rates for rooms and a health club. **Skyberg** (in the Rotunda between Terminals 2 and 3, tel. 312/686–6101) has five conference rooms with catering service, and fax machines, photocopier, and secretarial services.

**Midway Airport.** There are no business facilities at this airport.

### Airlines

All major domestic airlines serve Chicago, and it is a hub city for United, Midway, and American.

**Air Canada,** tel. 800/422–6232.
**American,** tel. 800/433–7300.
**British Airways,** tel. 800/247–9297.
**Continental,** tel. 312/686–6500 or 800/525–0280.
**Delta,** tel. 312/346–5300 or 800/221–1212.
**Midway,** tel. 312/767–3400 or 800/621–5700.
**Northwest,** tel. 312/349–4900 or 800/225–2525.
**Pan Am,** tel. 800/221–1111.
**TWA,** tel. 312/938–3000 or 800/221–2000.
**United,** tel. 312/569–3000 or 800/241–6522.

## Between the Airport and Downtown

*By Taxi*
Metered taxis connect both airports to Near North Side and downtown Chicago. Each O'Hare terminal has a taxi stand; there is one taxi stand at Midway. Cost from O'Hare: $20–$30, plus tip; from Midway: about $12, plus tip. The Kennedy Expressway is the only route from O'Hare to the city; the trip takes 20–30 minutes at best, but can stretch to more than an hour during rush hours (7–9 AM and 3:30–7:30 PM) or bad weather. From Midway, the best route is north on Cicero Avenue to the Stevenson Expressway, then east to Lake Shore Drive and north to downtown and the Near North Side. The trip takes 20–30 minutes.

*By Bus*
**Continental Air Transport** minivans (tel. 312/454–7799) connect most major hotels with both Midway and O'Hare. The fare from O'Hare is $10.75; from Midway, $8. The O'Hare trip can take more than an hour because buses make several stops en route; the Midway run takes about 30 minutes. Vans operate from O'Hare from 6 AM to 11:30 PM, from Midway from 8 AM to 8:30 PM. Check with the company for exact travel times.

*By Public Transportation*
The Chicago Transit Authority's rapid transit station at O'Hare is in the underground concourse near terminal 3; you can reach it from any terminal without going outside.

If you're heading to the Near North Side or downtown and don't have much luggage, this is an inexpensive way to go, and, at rush hour, probably the fastest. Cost: $1.25. The first stop downtown is at Washington and Dearborn streets; the trip takes 40–50 minutes. From here you can take a taxi to your hotel or change to other rapid transit lines. Note, however, that the CTA train is best avoided late at night. There is no convenient public transportation from Midway Airport.

## Car Rentals

All major national companies have booths at O'Hare and Midway.

**Avis,** tel. 312/694–5600 or 800/331–1212.
**Budget,** tel. 312/686–6800 or 800/527–0700.
**Hertz,** tel. 312/686–7272 or 800/654–3131.
**National,** tel. 312/694–4640 or 800/227–7368.
**Sears,** tel. 312/686–6780 or 800/527–0770.
**Thrifty,** tel. 708/298–3383 or 800/367–2277.

## Emergencies

*Doctors*
Northwestern Memorial Hospital's **HealthPlus** (Two Illinois Center Concourse, 233 N. Michigan Ave., tel. 312/649–2390) is open 8–6.

*Dentists*
The **Chicago Dental Society Emergency Service** (tel. 312/726–4321) makes 24-hour referrals.

*Hospitals*
In the Near North Side, **Northwestern Memorial Hospital** (Superior St. at Fairbanks Ct., tel. 312/908–2000); near the Loop, **Rush-Presbyterian-St. Lukes Medical Center** (1753 W. Congress Pkwy., tel. 312/942–5000).

## Important Addresses and Numbers

**Audiovisual rentals.** Mills Recording Systems (316 N. Michigan Ave., tel. 312/332–4116), Video Replay, (118 W. Grand Ave., tel. 312/822–0221).

**Chamber of Commerce** (200 N. LaSalle St., tel. 312/580–6900).

**Computer rentals.** Computerland (153 E. Ohio St., tel. 312/661–0160), Computer Rental Centers (130 E. Randolph St., tel. 312/938–0087).

**Convention and exhibition center** (McCormick Pl., 2300 S. Lake Shore Dr., tel. 312/791–7000).

**Fax services.** Instant Printing Centers (200 S. Clark St., the Loop, tel. 312/726–6275; 180 N. LaSalle St., the Loop, tel. 312/263–6212; at the Merchandise Mart, tel. 312/670–2330).

**Formal-wear rentals.** Gingiss Formal Wear (185 N. Wabash Ave., tel. 312/263–7071), Seno Formal Wear (6 E. Randolph St., tel. 312/782–1115).

**Gift shops.** Chocolates: Godiva (10 S. LaSalle St., tel. 312/855–1588; Water Tower Place, 845 N. Michigan Ave., tel. 312/280–1133), Neuchatel (Avenue Atrium, 900 N. Michigan Ave., tel. 312/787–1301); Florists: Alice's Garden

(Avenue Atrium, 900 N. Michigan Ave., tel. 312/649–2100), Amlings (151 E. Wacker Dr., tel. 312/265–4647; 2 N. Riverside Plaza, tel. 312/265–4647).

**Graphic design studio.** Artisan (575 W. Madison St., tel. 312/902–2969).

**Hairstylists.** Unisex: The Beauty Salon at Marshall Field (835 N. Michigan Ave., Water Tower Place, tel. 312/951–9054; 111 N. State St., the Loop, tel. 312/781–3651), Palmer House Hair Salon (17 E. Monroe St., tel. 312/201–0202), Jonathan's (875 N. Michigan Ave., tel. 312/664–9119).

**Health and fitness clubs.** *See* Fitness, below.

**Information hot lines.** Time (tel. 312/976–1616), financial markets (tel. 312/976–8100), stock market (tel. 312/976–3434), traffic (tel. 312/976–8646), sports (tel. 312/976–8383), toll-free entertainment information (tel. 312/FINEART).

**Limousine services.** Chicago Limousine Service (tel. 312/726–1035), Gold Coast Regency (tel. 312/227–1000).

**Liquor stores.** Chalet Wine and Cheese Shop (40 E. Delaware Pl., tel. 312/787–8555), Sam's Wines and Liquors (1000 W. North Ave., tel. 312/664–4394), Zimmerman's (213 W. Grand Ave., tel. 312/332–0012). Both Sam's and Zimmerman's deliver large orders.

**Mail delivery, overnight.** DHL Worldwide Express (tel. 708/456–3200), Federal Express (tel. 312/559–9000), TNT Skypak (312/992–2090), UPS (tel. 708/990–2900), U.S. Post Office Express Mail (tel. 312/765–3525).

**Messenger services.** Arrow (tel. 312/489–6688), Cannonball (tel. 312/829–1234).

**Office space rental.** U.S. Office (333 W. Wacker Dr., tel. 312/444–2000).

**Pharmacies, late-night.** Walgreen's (757 N. Michigan Ave., tel. 312/664–8686, open 24 hours; 25 S. Wabash Ave., tel. 312/641–1856).

**Radio stations, all-news.** WBBM 780 AM; WMAQ 670 AM.

**Secretarial services.** A-EC Secretarial Services (39 S. LaSalle St., tel. 312/236–6847), Executive Word Processing (612 N. Michigan Ave., tel. 312/337–7535), The Paper Works (105 W. Madison St., tel. 312/726–3442).

**Stationery supplies.** Order from Horder (111 W. Washington Blvd., tel. 312/648–7216; 211 E. Ontario St., tel. 312/648–7223; and Merchandise Mart Plaza, tel. 312/648–7205).

**Taxis.** Flash Cabs (tel. 312/561–1444), Yellow and Checker cabs (tel. 312/829–4222).

**Theater tickets.** *See* The Arts, below.

**Train information.** Amtrak (Jackson and Canal Sts., tel. 800/872–7245), Metropolitan Rail, suburban commuter trains (tel. 312/836–7000).

**Travel agents.** AAA Travel Agency (111 E. Wacker Dr., tel. 312/861–0771), Ask Mr. Foster (645 N. Michigan

Ave., tel. 312/828–9230; 203 N. LaSalle St., tel. 312/726–4799).

**Weather** (tel. 312/976–1212).

## LODGING

Chicago hotels are clustered in three main areas: the Loop, or downtown; Michigan Avenue and the Near North Side (that is, near the Loop); and around O'Hare Airport.

In general, the glossiest and most expensive hotels are in the Near North Side, where there has been a surge of hotel construction in the last decade. Many trade associations, advertising agencies, publishers, and television studios have their offices here. Michigan Avenue, the main drag of the Near North Side, is also Chicago's shopping mecca. Just to the west of the Near North Side is the River North neighborhood, Chicago's SoHo, bounded by Clark Street on the east and the Chicago River on the west. Art galleries abound here, along with boutiques and photography and design studios.

The Loop, or downtown, is home to city, state, and federal government offices, the financial district, and many law firms. Most Loop hotels are older and often less expensive than those in the Near North Side. Major cultural attractions—Orchestra Hall, the Art Institute, the Field Museum of Natural History, the Auditorium Theater, and the Lyric Opera—are all in the Loop, as are many of Chicago's renowned architectural masterpieces.

The Merchandise Mart, a magnet for wholesale buyers, is at the Chicago River between Wells and Orleans streets, about equidistant between downtown and the Near North Side. The nearest hotels are the Nikko and the Holiday Inn Mart Plaza.

McCormick Place, south of the Loop on the lakefront, is the largest convention center in the nation. Only one hotel, the McCormick Center, is within walking distance of McCormick Place, but all major trade shows provide free shuttle service to Loop and Near North hotels. McCormick Place is 10–15 minutes by taxi from most hotels. The McCormick Place Annex is right across Lake Shore Drive from the main building.

Women traveling alone may prefer to stay in the Near North Side; despite City Hall's efforts at rejuvenation, the Loop tends to be deserted and a little spooky at night.

A number of the hotels listed below offer corporate rates and weekend discounts; inquire when making reservations.

Highly recommended lodgings in each price category are indicated by a star ★.

| Category | Cost* |
|---|---|
| $$$$ (Very Expensive) | over $150 |
| $$$ (Expensive) | $100–$150 |
| $$ (Moderate) | under $100 |

*All prices are for a standard double room, single occupancy, excluding 12.4% tax.*

*Numbers in the margin correspond to numbered hotel locations on the Chicago Dining and Lodging maps.*

## Near North Side/Michigan Avenue

★ ❷ **Claridge.** If you're paying your own expenses and looking
$$$ for something simple but comfortable, this small, recently renovated 1930s hotel is a good value. Public areas are tastefully decorated in dark wood and green marble; the attractive contemporary-style guest rooms tend toward mauves, grays, and other neutral colors. Corner rooms are the most spacious. In-room amenities aren't lavish, but almost any toilet article is available from the concierge. Most business needs can be accommodated, too. The Gold Coast location is quiet, but offers easy access to the Rush Street singles scene and North Michigan Avenue. The house restaurant, J.P.'s, serves outstanding, moderately priced seafood. *A Golden Tulip hotel. 1244 N. Dearborn Pkwy., 60610, tel. 312/787–4980 or 800/245–1258, fax 312/266–0978. Gen. manager, Michael Depoy. 173 rooms, 3 suites. AE, CB, D, DC, MC, V.*

★ ❻ **Drake.** The grandest of Chicago's landmark hotels, the
$$$$ Drake is popular with upscale business travelers and visiting heads of state. Built on the lakefront in the style of an Italian Renaissance palace, the hotel opened in 1920 and has been listed in the National Register of Historic Places since 1981. The location across from Oak Street Beach offers easy access to the lakefront jogging path. Public areas are lavishly decorated, with oak accents and crystal chandeliers; the lobby boasts a spectacular marble fountain. Rooms are generally spacious and decorated in traditional style, with floral prints and comfortable, upholstered furniture; lakefront views cost more, but non-lakefront rooms tend to be bigger. Bathrooms include robes, hairdryers, and scales. The staff is friendly and helpful; elevators are a little slow despite the presence of elevator operators. The Cape Cod Room and the Oak Terrace (*see* Business Breakfasts, below) serve reliable fare; there's tea in the Palm Court in the late afternoon. *A Hilton International hotel. 140 E. Walton Pl., 60611, tel. 312/787–2200 or 800/445–8667, fax 312/787–1431. 535 rooms, 65 suites. Gen. manager, Victor Burt. AE, CB, D, DC, MC, V.*

❼ **Four Seasons.** A hotel-within-a-skyscraper, this lavish
$$$$ $300-million hostelry has a seventh-floor lobby with the ambience and attention to detail of an 18th-century English manor house, complete with a wood-burning fireplace. Handcrafted woodwork, luxurious, Oriental-style floral carpets, and botanical prints are featured throughout public areas and rooms. There's even a touch of humor—life-size Seward Johnson sculptures of travelers and workmen. Standard rooms are small, though bathrooms are large and well appointed. Most rooms have ter-

# NEAR NORTH SIDE CHICAGO

N. Sedgwick St.

W. Goethe St.

N. Wells St.

W. Division St.

N. Ed Julie Sr.

Seward
Park

N. Orleans St.

N. Hudson Ave.

N. Franklin St.

W. Chicago Ave.

W. Superior St.

W. Huron St.

W. Erie St. **16**

**15**

W. Ohio St.

W. Grand St.

**20**

**2**

W. Illinois St.

North Branch

W. Hubbard St.

W. Kinzie

# DOWNTOWN CHICAGO

**Lodging**

Chicago Hilton and Towers, **38**

Fairmont, **30**

Holiday Inn Mart Plaza, **23**

Hotel Nikko, **25**

Hyatt Regency Chicago, **28**

McCormick Center Hotel, **39**

Midland, **34**

Palmer House, **33**

Swiss Grand Hotel, **29**

**Dining**

Berghoff, **36**

Billy Goat Tavern, **27**

The Everest Room, **35**

Harry Caray's, **24**

Nick's Fishmarket, **32**

Printer's Row, **37**

Shaw's Crab House and Blue Crab Lounge, **26**

Walnut Room, **31**

# CHICAGO HOTEL CHART

| HOTELS | Price Category | Business Services / Banquet capacity | No. of meeting rooms | Secretarial services | Audiovisual equipment | Teletype news service | Computer rentals | In-room modem phone jack | All-news cable channel | Desk | Desk lighting | Bed lighting |
|---|---|---|---|---|---|---|---|---|---|---|---|---|
| Chicago Hilton and Towers | $$$$ | 2100 | 55 | ✓ | ✓ | - | ✓ | ✓ | ✓ | ◐ | ● | ● |
| Claridge | $$$ | 60 | 4 | ✓ | ✓ | - | ✓ | ✓ | - | ◐ | ● | ● |
| Drake | $$$$ | 535 | 29 | ✓ | ✓ | ✓ | ✓ | ✓ | ✓ | ◐ | ● | ● |
| Fairmont | $$$$ | 1600 | 14 | ✓ | ✓ | - | ✓ | ✓ | ✓ | ◐ | ● | ● |
| Four Seasons | $$$$ | 500 | 18 | ✓ | ✓ | - | ✓ | ✓ | ✓ | ● | ● | ● |
| Holiday Inn Mart Plaza | $$$ | 700 | 14 | - | ✓ | - | - | ✓ | ● | ◐ | ◐ | ● |
| Hotel Nikko | $$$$ | 700 | 11 | ✓ | ✓ | - | ✓ | ✓ | ● | ● | ● | ● |
| Hyatt Regency Chicago | $$$$ | 2600 | 72 | ✓ | ✓ | - | ✓ | ✓ | ✓ | ○ | ◐ | ● |
| Hyatt Regency O'Hare | $$$$ | 1500 | 45 | ✓ | ✓ | - | ✓ | ✓ | ✓ | ● | ● | ● |
| Le Meridien | $$$$ | 130 | 6 | ✓ | ✓ | - | ✓ | ✓ | ✓ | ● | ◐ | ● |
| Mayfair Regent | $$$$ | 50 | 3 | ✓ | ✓ | - | ✓ | - | ✓ | ◐ | ● | ● |
| McCormick Center | $$$ | 1000 | 20 | - | ✓ | - | - | - | ✓ | ◐ | ◐ | ● |
| Midland | $$$ | 450 | 12 | ✓ | ✓ | - | ✓ | ✓ | ✓ | ○ | ○ | ● |
| O'Hare Hilton | $$$ | 275 | 56 | ✓ | ✓ | - | ✓ | ✓ | ✓ | ◐ | ◐ | ◐ |
| Omni Ambassador East | $$$$ | 120 | 11 | ✓ | ✓ | - | ✓ | - | ✓ | ● | ● | ● |
| Palmer House | $$$ | 1600 | 68 | ✓ | ✓ | - | ✓ | ✓ | ✓ | ○ | ◐ | ● |
| Park Hyatt | $$$$ | 150 | 6 | ✓ | ✓ | ✓ | ✓ | ✓ | ✓ | ● | ● | ● |
| Radisson Suite Hotel O'Hare Airport | $$$ | 725 | 8 | - | ✓ | - | - | ✓ | ✓ | ● | ● | ● |

$$$$ = over $150, $$$ = $100-$150, $$ = under $100.
● good, ◐ fair, ○ poor.
All hotels listed here have photocopying and fax facilities.

| In-Room Amenities | | | | | | | | | | Hotel Amenities | | | | | | |
| Nonsmoking rooms | In-room checkout | Minibar | Pay movies | VCR/Movie rentals | Hairdryer | Toiletries | Room service | Laundry/Dry cleaning | Pressing | Concierge | Barber/Hairdresser | Garage | Courtesy airport transport | Sauna | Pool | Exercise room |
|---|---|---|---|---|---|---|---|---|---|---|---|---|---|---|---|---|
| ✓ | ✓ | ✓ | ✓ | ✓ | - | ● | ● | ● | ● | ✓ | ✓ | ✓ | - | ✓ | ● | ● |
| ✓ | - | ✓ | ✓ | ✓ | ✓ | ◐ | ◐ | ● | ● | ✓ | - | - | - | - | - | - |
| ✓ | ✓ | ✓ | ✓ | - | - | ● | ● | ● | ◐ | ✓ | ✓ | ✓ | - | - | - | - |
| ✓ | - | ✓ | - | - | ✓ | ◐ | ● | ● | ● | ✓ | ✓ | ✓ | - | - | - | - |
| ✓ | ✓ | - | ✓ | - | - | ● | ● | ● | ● | ✓ | ✓ | ✓ | - | ✓ | ● | ● |
| ✓ | - | - | ✓ | - | - | ○ | ◐ | ● | ● | - | ✓ | ✓ | - | - | ◐ | ◐ |
| ✓ | ✓ | ✓ | ✓ | - | - | ● | ● | ● | ● | ✓ | - | ✓ | - | ✓ | - | ● |
| ✓ | ✓ | ✓ | ✓ | - | - | ● | ● | ● | ● | ✓ | ✓ | ✓ | - | - | - | - |
| ✓ | ✓ | - | ✓ | ✓ | - | ◐ | ● | ● | ● | ✓ | ✓ | ✓ | ✓ | ✓ | ◐ | ● |
| ✓ | ✓ | ✓ | - | ✓ | ✓ | ● | ● | ◐ | ● | ✓ | - | ✓ | - | - | - | - |
| ✓ | - | ✓ | - | - | ✓ | ◐ | ● | ● | ● | ✓ | ✓ | - | - | - | - | - |
| ✓ | - | ✓ | ✓ | - | - | ◐ | ◐ | ● | ◐ | ✓ | - | ✓ | - | ✓ | ◐ | ● |
| ✓ | - | ✓ | ✓ | - | ✓ | ○ | ◐ | ● | - | ✓ | ✓ | - | - | - | - | ◐ |
| ✓ | ✓ | - | ✓ | - | - | ◐ | ● | ● | ◐ | - | - | ✓ | - | - | - | ◐ |
| ✓ | ✓ | - | ✓ | - | ✓ | ◐ | ● | ● | - | ✓ | ✓ | ✓ | - | - | - | - |
| ✓ | ✓ | ✓ | ✓ | - | - | ○ | ◐ | ● | ◐ | ✓ | ✓ | ✓ | - | ✓ | ◐ | ● |
| ✓ | - | ✓ | ✓ | - | ✓ | ● | ● | ● | ● | ✓ | ✓ | ✓ | - | - | - | - |
| ✓ | - | ✓ | ✓ | - | - | ◐ | ○ | ● | ◐ | - | - | ✓ | ✓ | ✓ | ● | ● |

**Room service:** ● 24-hour, ◐ 6AM-10PM, ○ other.
**Laundry/Dry cleaning:** ● same day, ◐ overnight, ○ other.
**Pressing:** ● immediate, ◐ same day, ○ other.

# CHICAGO HOTEL CHART

| HOTELS | Price Category | Business Services Banquet capacity | No. of meeting rooms | Secretarial services | Audiovisual equipment | Teletype news service | Computer rentals | In-room modem phone jack | All-news cable channel | Desk | Desk lighting | Bed lighting |
|---|---|---|---|---|---|---|---|---|---|---|---|---|
| **Richmont** | $$$ | 30 | 1 | - | - | - | - | - | ✓ | ◐ | ● | ● |
| **Ritz-Carlton** | $$$$ | 640 | 6 | ✓ | ✓ | - | ✓ | ✓ | ✓ | ◐ | ● | ● |
| **Hotel Sofitel Chicago at O'Hare** | $$$$ | 700 | 11 | ✓ | ✓ | ✓ | ✓ | ✓ | ✓ | ● | ● | ● |
| **Swiss Grand** | $$$$ | 450 | 31 | ✓ | ✓ | ✓ | ✓ | - | ✓ | ● | ● | ● |

$$$$ = over $150, $$$ = $100–$150, $$ = under $100.
● good, ◐ fair, ○ poor.
All hotels listed here have photocopying and fax facilities.

| In-Room Amenities | | | | | | | | | | Hotel Amenities | | | | | | |
| Nonsmoking rooms | In-room checkout | Minibar | Pay movies | VCR/Movie rentals | Hairdryer | Toiletries | Room service | Laundry/Dry cleaning | Pressing | Concierge | Barber/Hairdresser | Garage | Courtesy airport transport | Sauna | Pool | Exercise room |
|---|---|---|---|---|---|---|---|---|---|---|---|---|---|---|---|---|
| ✓ | ✓ | ✓ | ✓ | – | – | ◐ | ◐ | ● | ● | – | – | – | – | – | – | – |
| ✓ | ✓ | ✓ | ✓ | ✓ | ✓ | ● | ● | ● | ● | ✓ | – | ✓ | – | – | ● | ● |
| ✓ | ✓ | ✓ | ✓ | – | – | ● | ◐ | ● | ● | ✓ | – | ✓ | ✓ | ✓ | ● | ● |
| ✓ | ✓ | ✓ | – | – | ✓ | ● | ● | ● | ● | ✓ | – | ✓ | – | ✓ | ● | ● |

**Room service:** ● 24-hour, ◐ 6AM-10PM, ○ other.
**Laundry/Dry cleaning:** ● same day, ◐ overnight, ○ other.
**Pressing:** ● immediate, ◐ same day, ○ other.

rific views of the city or the lake; there's no extra charge for a lake view. The Four Seasons has one of the more luxurious health clubs in town, and an excellent restaurant, The Seasons (*see* Business Breakfasts, below), that features creative American cuisine. The Avenue Atrium, the more upscale of Michigan Avenue's two vertical malls, is in the same building. *A Four Seasons hotel. 120 E. Delaware Pl., tel. 312/280–8800 or 800/332–3442, fax 312/280–9184. Gen. manager, Hans Williman. 344 rooms, 121 suites, 16 apartments. AE, CB, D, DC, MC, V.*

**❺** **Mayfair Regent.** A small hotel in the European tradition,
**$$$$** the Mayfair Regent is popular with visiting concert artists. It's on the lakefront, and many of its well-appointed rooms have spectacular views to the north and east, though a number of south-facing rooms look onto the backs of other buildings. A recent management change has brought a less formal ambience and less stringent standards of service, but the multilingual staff remains highly attentive to travelers' needs. Rooms have phones at bedside, on desks, and in the bathrooms, which are also equipped with makeup and shaving mirrors and scales. Of the Regent's two restaurants, the Ciel Bleu (*see* Business Breakfasts, below), on the top floor, offers expensive, adequate French food in a beautiful setting. *181 E. Lake Shore Dr., 60611, tel. 312/787–8500 or 800/545–4000, fax 312/664–6194. Gen. manager, Michael Burchett. 200 rooms, 30 suites. AE, CB, D, DC, MC, V.*

**❸** **Le Meridien.** High-tech is the hallmark of this sleek gray
**$$$$** midrise building, completed in 1988. Services are what you'd expect from a hotel in this price category: Each guest room has a CD player, videocassette recorder, and several two-line phones, with a hot line to the video-rental store next door. Walls are extra thick, and the music systems have preset volume controls so that your neighbors won't blast you out. Every room lamp is on a rheostat for perfect lighting conditions. Phones are equipped for conference calling. Separate bathtubs and showers are standard in all bathrooms. The hotel's equally glossy meeting rooms have state-of-the-art audiovisual equipment operated through space-age control panels. Public areas feature gray marble, original photographs by Robert Mapplethorpe, and piped-in classic jazz. *21 E. Bellevue Pl., 60611, tel. 312/266–2100 or 800/266–2101, fax 312/266–2141. Gen. manager, Ken Withrow. 247 rooms, 41 suites. AE, CB, DC, MC, V.*

**❶** **Omni Ambassador East.** The renowned Pump Room, the
**$$$$** restaurant where celebrities have their pictures taken in Booth One, put the Ambassador East on the map; elegance, charm, and gracious service keep it there. Located in the residential Gold Coast neighborhood, it's slightly off the beaten business track (about a 10–15 cab ride from the Loop); it's popular with movie stars and other celebrities, as well as with business travelers who want to get away from the bustle of the Loop and Michigan Avenue. The lobby has an Old World elegance, with crystal chandeliers, marble floors, and curving banisters. Rooms have reproductions of 19th-century American furnishings. They vary in size and shape, consistent with the building's 1920s vintage, but all are comfortable. Many members of the staff have been here a long time. *1301 N. State Pkwy.,*

60610, tel. 312/787-7200 or 800/842-6664, fax 312/787-4760. Gen. manager, David Colella. 275 rooms, 52 suites. AE, CB, DC, MC, V.

**⑫ Park Hyatt.** Behind the unprepossessing façade of this
$$$$ high rise are extremely luxurious (and costly) rooms, a plush, comfortable lobby filled with overstuffed armchairs, and one of the best French restaurants in the city. La Tour (*see* Business Breakfasts, below) looks out on the historic Water Tower, and is a popular spot for all types of power meals, particularly breakfast and lunch. All guest rooms were refurbished in 1989, and are done in subtle tones of peach, beige, and green. Fruit baskets, cookies, and thrice-daily maid service are standard. Bathrooms have high quality fixtures and toiletries, as well as telephones and televisions. There's no health club, but guests can request exercise bikes and rowing machines in their rooms. The Park Hyatt is a favorite with upscale corporate travelers, politicians, and movie stars. You get the kind of luxury you'd expect for the steep price tag. *800 N. Michigan Ave., 60611, tel. 312/280-2222 or 800/228-9000, fax 312/280-1963. Gen. manager, Marc Ellin. 255 rooms, 43 suites. AE, CB, DC, MC, V.*

**★ ⑲ Richmont.** This is an intimate establishment in recently
$$$ renovated quarters convenient to North Michigan Avenue. Charming rather than luxurious, comfortably rather than elegantly appointed, the Richmont offers an excellent value. It's not well equipped for meetings or other business needs, but is a good choice for someone who doesn't need these services. Continental breakfast and hors d'oeuvres at cocktail time are included in the basic room rate. The hotel restaurant is the delightful Rue St. Clair, an "American bistro." *162 E. Ontario St., 60611, tel. 312/787-3580 or 800/621-8055, fax 312/787-1299. Gen. manager, Frances Moore. 193 rooms, 26 suites. AE, CB, D, DC, MC, V.*

**⑪ Ritz-Carlton.** Like its sister hotel, the Four Seasons, the
$$$$ Ritz occupies space in a skyscraper that also houses a vertical shopping mall, Water Tower Place. Built in the 1970s, the hotel has a 12th-floor lobby with a skylighted fountain surrounded by bronze sculptures, modern chandeliers, and lots of plants. Rooms are spacious; most have been recently redecorated. Twin sinks are standard in each bathroom. The excellent health club includes a 52-foot lap pool; it's also used by residents of the condominiums that occupy the upper floors of the building. The Bar (*see* After Hours, below) is highly regarded among the club-going crowd for its live music and dancing; the Dining Room is one of Chicago's finer restaurants; and The Café (*see* Business Breakfasts, below) is a good place for an early meeting. *A Four Seasons hotel. 160 E. Pearson St., 60611, tel. 312/266-1000 or 800/332-3442, fax 312/266-9498. Gen. manager, Nicholas Mutton. 431 rooms, 81 suites. AE, CB, DC, MC, V.*

## Downtown/The Loop

**㊳ Chicago Hilton and Towers.** This massive, opulent conven-
$$$$ tion hotel was built in 1927 and had a $200-million renovation in 1985. Its facilities, amenities, and South Michigan Avenue location make it a good choice for business travelers, though you may want to steer clear if the hotel is holding more than one large meeting; restaurants and other

facilities can become congested. The 1,543 rooms include 626 double-doubles, which have two double beds and two bathrooms. Most popular rooms are those with one king-size bed and a view of Lake Michigan. Business travelers prefer the more expensive Towers rooms, which have a service desk on each floor, complimentary Continental breakfast, a lounge with honor bar, and extensive business services. Bathtubs in all the rooms tend to be small. A state-of-the-art health club, featuring Universal weight machines, saunas, and a 60-foot lap pool, makes this hotel worth the stay. The Grand Ballroom, a tribute to the French Empire, is worth a look even if you're not staying here. Kitty O'Shea's (*see* After Hours, below) is a fun place to relax at the end of the day. *720 S. Michigan Ave., 60605. tel. 312/922–4400 or 800/445–8667, fax 312/922–5240. Gen. manager, Gerhardt Seibert. AE, CB, D, DC, MC, V.*

**30 Fairmont.** This 45-story, neoclassic, pink granite struc-
**$$$$** ture is one of Chicago's most attractive new hotels (late 1980s), and offers wonderful lake or city views in all accommodations. The unusually spacious rooms are comfortably furnished in a variety of period styles; antiques and original artwork grace the public areas. All bathrooms include TV set, telephone, scale, an oversize tub, and separate shower. Windows can be opened slightly to get the fresh lake breezes—an unusual feature in a high-rise hotel; another plus is extra-long beds. Clever design places every room no more than four doors from an elevator. An Art Deco lounge offers evening cabaret entertainment. *200 N. Columbus Dr., 60601, tel. 312/565–8000 or 800/527–4727, fax 312/856–1032. Gen. manager, Wolf Lehmkuhl. 694 rooms, 66 suites. AE, CB, DC, MC, V.*

**23 Holiday Inn Mart Plaza.** Situated atop the Apparel Center
**$$$** and next door to the Merchandise Mart, this 1970s hotel principally serves business travelers. Rooms are standard-issue Holiday Inn, comfortable but not lavish; bathrooms are spacious. There's no health club, but there is a heated indoor swimming pool. If you have business at the Mart, the location may make up for the relative lack of amenities and business services. *350 N. Orleans St., 60654, tel. 312/836–5000 or 800/465–4329, fax 312/836–0223. Gen. manager, William J. Horine. 525 rooms, 14 suites. AE, CB, D, DC, MC, V.*

**★ 25 Hotel Nikko.** One of Chicago's newest and most beautiful
**$$$$** hotels, the Nikko is on the Chicago River, about four blocks west of the main hotel district, and convenient to the Merchandise Mart. Exquisite pieces of Oriental art decorate the public areas; the south side of the lobby is glassed in, giving views of a traditional Japanese garden and a riverfront park. Dark grays and black predominate in the design scheme. The standard, contemporary-style rooms have marble baths, separate dressing areas, and full-length mirrors; visitors can also request rooms with traditional Japanese decor and tatami sleeping mats. The three top floors have their own check-in and check-out, a special concierge, and complimentary breakfast and hors d'oeuvres. Business services include a library and executive lounge. One of the Nikko's two restaurants, Benkay, is esteemed locally for its fine Japanese food. *Owned by Japan Air Lines. 320 N. Dearborn St., 60610, tel. 312/744–1900 or 800/645–5687, fax 312/527–2650. Gen. manager,*

*Pete Dangerfield. 425 rooms, 26 suites. AE, CB, D, DC, MC, V.*

**㉘ Hyatt Regency Chicago.** It's alarmingly easy to get lost in
$$$$ this huge convention hotel, which is divided into East and
West Towers. The Hyatt is one of three hotels in the Illinois Center complex (the others are the Fairmont and the
Swiss Grand). You'll be comfortably housed if you stay
here to attend a meeting, but if your business is elsewhere, you may prefer one of the smaller, less crowded hotels. Accommodations are adequate but not luxurious,
though amenities include hair dryers and access to a
brand-new health club in Illinois Center. A club floor offers free Continental breakfast, concierge, and a lounge.
Catch a Rising Star Comedy Club (*see* After Hours, below)
is on the premises. *151 E. Wacker Dr., 60601, tel. 312/565–
1234 or 800/233–1234, fax 312/565–2966. Gen. manager,
Rod Young. 2,033 rooms, 175 suites. AE, CB, D, DC, MC,
V.*

**㉞ Midland.** This small hotel in the heart of the financial dis-
$$$ trict was built as a men's club in the 1920s. The Beaux
Arts lobby has vaulted arches and a gold-leaf ceiling.
Rooms are small but comfortable and were recently redec-
orated with black lacquer furniture and tones of mauve
and gray; amenities aren't lavish. The clientele is predom-
inantly business travelers. There's a free English-style
taxi to downtown locations and a complimentary breakfast
buffet. The taxi also transports joggers to the lakefront
jogging path weekday mornings at 6:30, and provides
them with Walkmans and orange juice. The exercise room
is limited to a few weight machines, but guests have free
access to the Randolph Combined Fitness Center a few
blocks away. The 12 meeting rooms have been decorated
in the styles of various Chicago architects, including
Frank Lloyd Wright and Louis Sullivan. Staff is friendly
and helpful. *A Grand Tradition hotel. 172 W. Adams St.,
60603, tel. 312/332–1200 or 800/621–2360 (outside Illi-
nois), fax 312/332–5909. Gen. manager, Myron Levy. 257
rooms, 4 full suites, 50 executive junior suites. AE, CB,
D, DC, MC, V.*

**㉝ Palmer House.** Built more than 100 years ago by Chicago
$$$ merchant Potter Palmer, this landmark hotel in the heart
of the Loop has some of the most ornate and elegant public
areas in the city. The gilded Victorian lobby, up a flight of
stairs from the street-level concourse, is worth a visit even
if you're staying elsewhere. The clientele is a mix of tourists and business travelers; the atmosphere can be hectic
and the service a little brusque during peak times. Recently renovated rooms are comfortable though not luxurious; if you're not staying in the Towers executive floors,
you're likely to have to do your work on the bed. Smallish
bathrooms include full-length mirrors. The hotel has sev-
en restaurants, among them the French Quarter, a good
place for a business breakfast. *A Hilton property. 17 E.
Monroe St., 60603, tel. 312/726–7500 or 800/445–8667, fax
312/947–1707. Gen. manager, James Claus. 1,600 rooms,
88 suites, 500 corporate class. AE, CB, D, DC, MC, V.*

**㉙ Swiss Grand Hotel.** Despite its size, this sleek, triangular,
$$$$ 45-story hotel, designed by Chicago architect Harry
Weese and opened in 1988, offers a quiet European ambience, as well as spacious rooms, and services designed
specifically for the business traveler. The business center

includes a library of current business and trade magazines, as well as up-to-the-minute stock exchange reports. Each guest room has two-line phones, an oversize writing desk, and a separate seating area. Among the state-of-the-art meeting rooms is a theater with banked seats. You can buy fresh bread and pastries at the in-house bakery, which also supplies them to the hotel's restaurants. *A Swissotel property. 323 E. Wacker Dr., 60601, tel. 312/565-0565 or 800/654-7263, fax 312/565-0540. Gen. manager, Costas Vafoupoulos. 625 rooms, 34 suites. AE, CB, D, DC, MC, V.*

## McCormick Place

**39** **McCormick Center Hotel.** This isolated high rise is the
**$$$** only place to stay if you have to shuttle back and forth more than a few times a day between your hotel and a trade show at the McCormick Place convention center, right across the street. Rooms are attractively furnished, following a recent renovation. Several restaurants and a health club can take care of basic needs, but for culture, nightlife, really good food, and easy access to the major business areas, you're better off staying in the Loop or Near North Side, where you can get equally nice accommodations at similar prices. That said, it should be noted that the hotel does provide complimentary limousine service to the business districts. *451 E. 23rd St., 60616, tel. 312/791-1900 or 800/621-6909, fax 312/791-0634. Gen. manager, Joseph Duellman. 650 rooms, 40 suites. AE, CB, D, DC, MC, V.*

## O'Hare Airport

**$$$$** **Hotel Sofitel Chicago at O'Hare Airport.** This luxury hotel, opened in 1987, has public areas richly appointed with marble, wood, glass, and Oriental rugs. Rooms are furnished in country French–style, with light-wood furniture and floral prints. There's a 24-hour concierge, and turndown service includes a red rose and a chocolate truffle. An in-house French bakery is a good place to pick up last-minute gifts. Business services are exceptionally good for the airport area. *5550 N. River Rd., Rosemont, 60018, tel. 708/678-4488 or 800/233-5959, fax 708/678-4244. Gen. manager, Pierce Johnson. 305 rooms, 16 suites. AE, CB, D, DC, MC, V.*

**$$$$** **Hyatt Regency O'Hare.** You can't miss the quartet of shiny copper-color towers that mark this institution among O'Hare-area hotels. In typical Hyatt style, a central atrium soars eight stories to the glass roof, and elevators are glass-enclosed. Both the lobby and guest rooms have been recently outfitted with new carpeting and furniture; two club floors offer concierge service and a private lounge with honor bar. A new ballroom was just added. A good health club has a dome-enclosed swimming pool, exercise machines, Jacuzzi, and sauna. There are three restaurants, including a revolving dining room on the top of the hotel. *9300 W. Bryn Mawr Ave., Rosemont, 60018, tel. 708/696-1234 or 800/233-1234, fax 708/696-1418. Gen. manager, Paul Tang. 1,100 rooms, 60 suites, 400 business class. AE, CB, D, DC, MC, V.*

**$$$** **O'Hare Hilton.** The only hotel within walking distance of the airport (connected to the terminals by an underground walkway), this cement pile tends to fill up without even trying, especially when bad weather delays flights overnight. As a result, it doesn't try terribly hard. You can get a perfectly comfortable basic room, but amenities are scarce for the price. If you need more than a place to sleep and have time to shop around, look farther afield. *Box 66414, O'Hare International Airport, 60666, tel. 312/686–8000 or 800/445–8667, fax 312/686–0073. Gen. manager, Bruce Ulrich. 885 rooms. AE, CB, DC, MC, V.*

$$$ **Radisson Suite Hotel O'Hare Airport.** This low rise has two-room suites furnished in a comfortable, homelike style, with casual light-wood furnishings. Each living room has a kitchen area with a wet bar, refrigerator, microwave, sofabed, and dining table with four chairs. Each suite has two television sets and two phones. Room service hours are limited. Room rates include an American-style breakfast and complimentary evening cocktails. *5500 N. River Rd., Rosemont, 60018, tel. 708/678–4000 or 800/333–3333, fax 708/671–3059. Gen. manager, Mark Marotta. 296 suites. AE, CB, D, DC, MC, V.*

## DINING

The list below concentrates on restaurants in the Loop, Near North Side, and River North neighborhoods, where business travelers are likely to be staying. Proximity dictates the stamping grounds for locals—financiers dine in the Loop near the banking district; politicians eat near City Hall; advertising and public relations people gather at eateries on North Michigan Avenue. Brownbagging is also popular among the city's professionals; Chicago is a get-down-to-business city where lunch hour is likely to last no more than 60 minutes.

Virtually every type of dining experience is available in this former steak-and-potatoes city. Some of Chicago's notable restaurants are in its hotels, such as La Tour in the Park Hyatt. But for a real taste of Chicago dining, it's best to leave your hotel room and explore.

Highly recommended restaurants are indicated by a star ★.

| Category | Cost* |
|---|---|
| $$$$ (Very Expensive) | over $40 |
| $$$ (Expensive) | $26–$40 |
| $$ (Moderate) | $13–$25 |
| $ (Inexpensive) | under $13 |

*per person, including appetizer, entrée, and dessert, but excluding drinks, service, and 8.5% sales tax.*

*Numbers in the margin correspond to numbered restaurant locations on the Chicago Lodging and Dining maps.*

### Business Breakfasts

For breakfast meetings, local businesspeople generally prefer hotel restaurants. Of these, the Mayfair Regent's **Ciel Bleu** (tel. 312/787–8500) has good food and a superb view. Other spots with plush, pleasant surroundings, good food, and an atmosphere conducive to talk include

**The Seasons** at the Four Seasons (tel. 312/280–8800), **The Café** at the Ritz-Carlton (tel. 312/266–1000), and **Oak Terrace,** at the Drake (tel. 312/787–2200).

**La Tour,** at the Park Hyatt (tel. 312/280–2230), is the most popular spot in town for power breakfasts, partly because of the "see and be seen" floor-to-ceiling windows that look out on North Michigan Avenue's Water Tower Park. The menu features standard breakfast fare (eggs, fresh fruit, and pastries), but everything is well prepared and beautifully presented.

**Lou Mitchell's** (565 W. Jackson Blvd., tel. 312/939–3111), one of the city's great breakfast spots, features fresh double-yolked eggs in 14 kinds of omelets, as well as pancakes, French toast, and Belgian waffles. Be prepared to stand in line, and to be seated at a long communal table. It's not ideal for meetings, but fun if you have extra time and don't mind a side trip to the west Loop.

## The Loop

★ ㊱  **Berghoff.** This bustling Loop institution serves German
$$ food in a huge wood-panel dining room where historic photographs of the area hang. A menu of classics (Wiener schnitzel, sauerbraten) are augmented by American favorites. Berghoff Beer (light and dark) is on tap, as is rootbeer. Because it's a popular lunch spot with the business crowd, expect a wait of about 15 minutes at midday; the noise level does not permit serious discussions. The food varies from competent to excellent. The brisk efficiency of the service, delivered by formally dressed and very correct waiters, does not encourage lingering over coffee. *17 W. Adams St., tel. 312/427–3170. Casual dress. Reservations accepted for parties of 6 or more. AE, MC, V.*

★ ㉟  **The Everest Room.** On the 40th floor of a high rise in the
$$$$ heart of the financial district, the Everest Room is arguably the best French restaurant in town. Meals are graciously served in an elegant setting with a spectacular view. Chef Jean Joho combines classic French techniques with those of his native Alsace. Entrées change frequently; among recent offerings were fish fillet wrapped and roasted in potato with thyme; yellowfin tuna tournedos sautéed medium rare with shallots; and breast of squab with truffle coulis and Napa cabbage. A fine wine list, including many Alsatian vintages, complements the menu. Service is polished and efficient; prices are high. This is a place to come to celebrate a deal; one would not want to be distracted from the food by a business discussion. *440 S. LaSalle St., tel. 312/663–8920. Jacket and tie required. Reservations required. AE, DC, MC, V. Closed Sun., holidays.*

㉜  **Nick's Fishmarket.** This dark room has the feel of a tradi-
$$$ tional club, furnished in leather and wood and adorned with sports paintings. Phones can be requested and plugged into jacks at each booth. The large seafood menu often includes catfish, frog legs, Hawaiian opakapaka, and abalone. Although ingredients are fresh, they can be overcooked; share your concern with the efficient wait staff. A few pasta and beef dishes are also available. *1 First National Plaza, tel. 312/621–0200. Jacket and tie recommended. Reservations advised. AE, DC, MC, V. Closed Sun., holidays.*

★ **③** **Printer's Row.** Located in and named after the recently
$$$  chic loft neighborhood in the South Loop, this warm and
attractive restaurant offers some of the most interesting
and satisfying American cuisine in Chicago. Polished,
dark wood and neutral colors provide a quiet backdrop for
owner and chef Michael Foley's constantly changing fare.
New ideas and approaches bring forth such creative
dishes as grilled mallard duck with radicchio and endive in
port wine sauce, and ragout of sweetbreads with aromatic
vegetables and pasta. Daily specials augment the menu
and include at least one dish low in fat and sodium. An ex-
cellent wine list features a large selection of fine ports, co-
gnacs, and armagnacs. Tables are well spaced and the
noise level is low; this is a good place for business discus-
sions. *550 S. Dearborn St., tel. 312/461–0780. Jacket re-
quired. Reservations recommended, required on week-
ends. AE, CB, D, DC, MC, V. No lunch Sat., closed Sun.*

**③** **Walnut Room.** Marshall Field's dining room, with its wood
$$  archways and beams and Oriental screens and carpets, is
reminiscent of a Victorian-era English tearoom. Long a
haven for businesspeople seeking a relaxed, unhurried
lunch spot, the Walnut Room serves standard, comforting
fare: beef tenderloin tips Stroganoff, Field's own chicken
pot pie, roast free-range chicken, and a fresh fish of the
day, as well as a large selection of salads and sandwiches.
A traditional English tea, complete with scones and
Devonshire cream, is served at 3 PM. Bar service is available, too. Avoid the Walnut Room during Christmas season unless you want to battle the crowds who come to have
lunch under Field's two-story Christmas tree. *111 N.
State St., tel. 312/781–1000. Casual dress. No reservations. AE, MC, V. No dinner. Closed Sun., holidays.*

## Near North Side

★ **⑭** **Avanzare.** This chic Italian restaurant has two handsome
$$$  rooms dominated by traditional brass accents, leather
banquettes, and marble floors; a full-length mirrored bar
separates the dining rooms. The main room tends to be
noisy; for serious discussions, try to get a table on the
mezzanine. A dozen carefully prepared pastas appear on
the regular menu, but the best offerings are usually on a
list of daily specials. Entrées might include ravioli stuffed
with mushrooms in shallot butter sauce, or succulent
braised baby pheasant with fennel. The tuna carpaccio ap-
petizer, paper-thin slices of raw tuna in soy sauce with av-
ocado and sweet onion, is a good starter. The freshness
and quality of the ingredients is outstanding. Reason-
ably priced Italian wines are available by the glass or
the bottle. *161 E. Huron St., tel. 312/337–8036. Casual
dress. Reservations recommended. AE, CB, DC, MC, V.*

**㉗** **Billy Goat Tavern.** A favorite hangout for reporters from
$  the *Chicago Tribune*, just across the street, this self-serv-
ice bar-and-grill features the "chizboorgers" made famous
by John Belushi on "Saturday Night Live" in the 1970s.
Come for the atmosphere, a quick bite, and a cold brew
that won't set you back a day's pay. *430 N. Michigan Ave.
(lower level), tel. 312/222–1525. Casual dress. No reser-
vations. No credit cards.*

**⑩** **Chestnut Street Grill.** Modeled after the famous Tadich
$$$  Grill in San Francisco, this Water Tower Place establish-
ment serves some of the best fresh seafood you'll find in

the Chicago area. Offerings vary from day to day; the catch is flown in from the coasts and prepared in a variety of ways, including charcoal-grilled. An excellent sourdough bread starts each meal; a few nonfish dishes, salads, and a selection of low-calorie, low-sodium dishes round out the menu. The restaurant is attractive, with tile floors, dark wood, and reproductions of details from buildings by notable Chicago architects—for example, the ornamental ironwork of Louis Sullivan. The brisk and efficient service also makes it a popular setting for business lunches; tables in the back tend to be quietest. *845 N. Michigan Ave., tel. 312/280–2720. Casual dress. Reservations accepted for lunch, and at dinner for 6 or more. AE, CB, D, DC, MC, V.*

**❽** **Crickets.** The ladies who lunch tend to lunch at this Chica-
**$$$$** go institution, something you wouldn't guess from the atmosphere—a dark, crowded room with toy airplanes, tanks, cars, and industrial signs hanging from the ceiling. Tables in this trendy spot (trendy, that is, for a middle-aged corporate crowd) are close together; sharing conversations with those nearby is inevitable and considered part of the fun. The eclectic menu features traditional French dishes: appetizers usually include pâté maison, baked oysters, and ragout of snails. Popular entrées include veal medallions with wild mushroom sauce, tournedos of beef with Zinfandel shallot sauce, and sweetbread medallions with tarragon-truffle sauce. For dessert, try Crickets's original cheesecake. Some wines are available by the glass; the wine list is extensive. *100 E. Chestnut St., tel. 312/280–2100. Jacket required. Reservations required. AE, CB, DC, MC, V. Closed for dinner, Sun., some holidays.*

**⓰** **The Eccentric.** Restaurateur Richard Melman has teamed
**$$** up with talk-show host Oprah Winfrey to open this aptly named adventure in dining. The pair built a combination of French café, Italian coffeehouse, and English pub into a space formerly occupied by a car dealership; the restaurant can seat about 400. Works by local artists adorn the walls. The food is surprisingly good, given the novelty value of the enterprise. Steaks and chops stand out, as do Oprah's mashed potatoes with horseradish (the only dish on the menu attributed directly to her). For dessert, try the butterscotch or bittersweet chocolate pot de crème. There is a selection of wines by the glass, as well as a variety of designer beers. And keep an eye out for Oprah. *159 West Erie St., tel. 312/787–8390. Casual dress. No reservations. Closed Sun. AE, CB, DC, M, V.*

**⓯** **Ed Debevic's.** This imitation 1950s diner serves a swell
**$** meatloaf, along with other diner fare, in a high-camp atmosphere that features gum-chewing, wisecracking waitresses, Jell-o salads, and "Ed Debevic's Beer, Aged in Its Own Bottle." Try the exemplary tuna sandwich and the homemade cream pies. A cult spot, Ed's tends to be packed evenings and weekends, but may be a good bet for a quick lunch during the week. Rock 'n' roll in the main room can make it difficult to talk; conversation is easier in the back room, where the noisiest things are the televisions tuned to the soaps and vintage sitcoms. Ed's is in the heart of the River North gallery neighborhood, just west of the Near North Side. Your meal here is likely to make an amusing anecdote for your co-workers back home. *640*

*N. Wells St., tel. 312/664–1707. Casual dress. No reservations; the wait may be substantial. No credit cards. Closed some holidays.*

★ ⑬ **Eli's The Place for Steak.** The lounge and dining room of
$$$ this Chicago institution have the ambience of a private club, with soft lights, thick carpets, and lots of leather and warm woods—a good setting for quiet conversation. Eli's developed its outstanding reputation through an unflagging commitment to top-quality ingredients, prepared precisely to the customer's taste in generous portions. Prime aged steaks are the specialty of the house; you'll also find superb, thickly cut veal chops and splendid calves' liver. For dessert, order Eli's cheesecake, now sold nationally in countless varieties. *215 E. Chicago Ave., tel. 312/642–1393. Jacket required. Reservations required. AE, DC, MC, V. Closed holidays.*

★ ㉑ **Gordon.** A favorite spot for Chicago's power-lunch crowd—
$$$$ it is quiet and well located in the River North loft district—Gordon consistently offers some of the city's most innovative contemporary American fare. Rococo furnishings include Oriental rugs and swag curtains along the walls; tables have fresh flowers. The menu changes often; popular entrées include seared tuna with red-tomato-and-chive vinaigrette, grilled beef tenderloin with cabernet-braised mushrooms and marjoram, and roasted sweetbreads with chanterelle mushrooms, prosciutto, and chardonnay. There's a respectable wine list, with a good selection available by the glass. Service is friendly and efficient. On weekends, there's piano music and dancing. *500 N. Clark St., tel. 312/467–9780. Jacket required. Reservations required. AE, CB, DC, MC, V. Closed holidays.*

㉔ **Harry Caray's.** Holy cow! It's a celebrity restaurant
$$$ where the food is decent and the owner, the veteran Chicago Cubs announcer, really stops by now and then. The menu is Italian-American; steaks and chops share the bill with pastas, veal dishes, salads, and cold platters. Baseball memorabilia decorate the walls. This is a good after-work spot for sports fans who don't take the dining experience too seriously. *33 W. Kinzie St., tel. 312/465–9269. Casual dress. AE, CB, D, DC, MC, V. Closed some holidays.*

★ ⑱ **Hatsuhana.** Many sushi and sashimi lovers regard this
$$$ restaurant as the best of its kind in Chicago; its broad selection of fish is infallibly fresh and carefully prepared. The decor is characteristically Japanese—tasteful and streamlined; diners sit at a long, angled sushi bar or at wooden tables. Appetizers include broiled spinach in sesame-soy sauce, and steamed egg custard with shrimp, fish, and vegetables. Daily specials might include steamed baby clams in sake, and king mackerel with soybean paste. Service can be unpredictable. *160 E. Ontario St., tel. 312/280–8287. Casual dress. Reservations recommended. AE, DC, MC, V. Closed Sun., holidays, and Sat. lunch.*

⑳ **Honda.** Owned and operated by a Tokyo restaurateur,
$$$ Honda offers one of the most varied Japanese menus in the city. Its sushi and sashimi are among Chicago's best; it also lays claim to one of the country's first kushi bars, where vegetables and morsels of meat and seafood are grilled or deep-fried. Customers sit at the kushi bar or

sushi bar, or in one of several dining rooms. Call a day in advance to reserve a tatami room, where diners remove their shoes and sit on the floor (a well under the table lets you stretch your legs). Visiting Japanese will find a large array of familiar dishes, including *chawan mushi* (steamed vegetables and fish in an egg custard) and *chasoba* (noodles in cold green tea). Sukiyaki is prepared for you at your table. Service can be uncoordinated, especially when large parties order a variety of entrées. *540 N. Wells St., tel. 312/923–1010. Casual dress. Reservations accepted. Closed Sun., Sat. lunch. AE, CB, DC, MC, V.*

**❾** **The 95th.** Splendidly situated at the top of Chicago's third-**$$$$** tallest building, The 95th will impress clients with its spectacular view and elegant atmosphere, created by subdued lighting, lavish place settings, and contemporary-style chandeliers. The food's good, too. The entrées emphasize seafood and poultry, with dishes like Gulf shrimp with spinach linguine in tomato-basil butter, and roasted quail with ratatouille and rosemary butter. The wine list is large and reasonably priced, and there's a good choice by the glass. Spacious and quiet, The 95th is a good spot to talk business, as long as you can keep from looking out the window. An adjoining bar and lounge (*see* After Hours, below) is often crowded, but never frantic, and offers equally spectacular views. *John Hancock Building, 875 N. Michigan Ave., tel. 312/987–9596. Jacket required at dinner. Reservations recommended; weekend reservations required. AE, CB, DC, MC, V.*

**⓱ ㉒** **Pizzeria Uno/Due.** Chicago deep-dish pizza originated in **$** these two informal restaurants. Still run by the original owner, Ike Sewell, Uno has been remodeled to resemble its franchised cousins in other cities, but its pizzas retain their light crust and distinctive tang. Those not accustomed to pizza on a Chicago scale may want to skip the salad. Beer and soft drinks can be ordered by the pitcher. The wait is usually shorter at Pizzeria Due, which is a block away and has the same menu, more traditional decor, and longer hours. Some say Uno's pizza is better, but both establishments offer about the best in town. *Uno, 29 E. Ohio St., tel. 312/321–1000; Due, 619 N. Wabash Ave., tel. 312/943–2400. Casual dress. No reservations; phone-ahead orders accepted weekdays only. AE, DC, MC, V.*

**㉖** **Shaw's Crab House and Blue Crab Lounge.** This New En-**$$$** gland–style crab house has a large room with exposed brick and wood, and an adjoining lounge with an oyster bar. Both are very popular, and tend to be packed at peak hours; come for after-work relaxation rather than quiet conversation. Appetizers include fried calimari, steamed blue mussels, and Maryland crab cakes. In addition to the standard shellfish dishes—simply and honestly prepared—are such daily fresh fish specials as grilled Hawaiian tuna with purslane and tomato relish, and grilled Pacific king salmon with herb marinade. A few chicken and beef items are also available. *21 E. Hubbard St., tel. 312/ 527–2722. Casual dress. Reservations accepted for lunch only; the wait at dinner can be substantial. AE, DC, MC, V. Lounge closed Sun.*

**★ ❹** **Spiaggia.** This softly lighted, rose-color dining room at the **$$$$** north end of the chic Magnificent Mile vies with trendy New York or Los Angeles eateries for sophistication, quality of food—and price. The ambience is quietly elegant, service is gracious and knowledgeable, and business-people come here to make an impression. Variations on Northern Italian cuisine include crisp pizza with a paper-thin crust and topped with duck and goat cheese; ravioli filled with lobster meat in a delicate sauce; and paper-white grilled veal chop with rosemary. The large, all-Italian wine list is excellent, but yields few bargains. Café Spiaggia, next door, offers many of the same dishes at lower prices. *1 Magnificent Mile (Oak St. at Michigan Ave.), tel. 312/280-2750. Jacket required; no denim. Reservations recommended. AE, CB, D, DC, MC, V. No lunch Sun.*

## FREE TIME

### Fitness

*Hotel Facilities*
Good hotel fitness clubs are at the **Hilton** (tel. 312/922–4400), which has the best pool, and the **Nikko** (tel. 312/744–1900), which has an excellent selection of aerobic and weight machines, but no pool. However, neither is available to nonguests. Hotels without facilities often have agreements with local clubs.

*Health Clubs*
Many of the health clubs listed have arrangements with hotels for use of their facilities; inquire at your hotel. **Downtown Sports Club** (441 N. Wabash Ave., tel. 312/644–4880), with a day rate of $12, has agreements with several hotels. The top Chicago sports clubs do not accept non-members, but the following, all convenient and well equipped, take visitors on a per-diem basis: **Onterie Fitness Center** (466 E. Ontario St., tel. 312/642–0031), cost $10; **Charlie Club** (112 S. Michigan Ave., tel. 312/726–0510), cost $15; **Chicago Health and Racquet Clubs** (25 E. Washington Blvd., tel. 312/327–7755), cost $10; **Grand Ohio Athletic Club** (211 E. Ohio St., tel. 312/661–0036), cost $10; **Combined Fitness Center** (1235 N. LaSalle St., tel. 312/787–8400), cost $10.

*Jogging*
There's a 19-mile running and bicycle path, with mileage markers, along the lakefront through Lincoln and Grant parks. Enter at Oak Street Beach (across from the Drake Hotel) or at Grand Avenue (underneath Lake Shore Drive), or by going through Grant Park on Monroe Street or on Jackson Boulevard. It's well used in the early morning and late afternoon, especially north from the Loop, but be wary after dark and in the sparsely populated section south of McCormick Place.

### Shopping

The two main shopping areas are **North Michigan Avenue** (also called the Magnificent Mile), between the Chicago River and Oak Street, and **the Loop.**

The city's two largest department stores, **Marshall Field** and **Carson Pirie Scott,** anchor the Loop's State Street–Wabash Avenue area (which has declined since the years when it was known as "State Street, that great street"). Marshall Field (111 N. State St., at the corner of Randolph

St., tel. 312/781–1000) is in the midst of a $110-million renovation; the bargain basement has been replaced with "Down Under," a series of small boutiques that sell clothing, luggage, picture frames, Chicago memorabilia, and Field's famous Frango mints, which many consider to be Chicago's greatest edible souvenirs. Second only to Marshall Field for many years, Carson Pirie Scott (1 S. State St., tel. 312/641–7000), the work of architect Louis Sullivan, is protected by landmark status, and well worth visiting for its ornate iron scrollwork.

The Magnificent Mile, Chicago's most glamorous shopping district, stretches along Michigan Avenue from the Chicago River to Oak Street. It's lined on both sides with some of the most sophisticated names in retailing: **Tiffany** (715 N. Michigan Ave., tel. 312/944–7500), **Gucci** (900 N. Michigan Ave., tel. 312/664–5504), **Chanel** (990 N. Michigan Ave., tel. 312/787–5500), **I. Magnin** (830 N. Michigan Ave., tel. 312/751–0500), and **Bonwit Teller** (875 N. Michigan Ave., tel. 312/751–1800), to name just a few.

Aside from dozens of designer shops, Michigan Avenue also features two "vertical malls." **Water Tower Place** (835 N. Michigan Ave., tel. 312/440–3165) contains branches of Lord & Taylor and Marshall Field, as well as seven floors of specialty stores. The **Avenue Atrium** (900 N. Michigan Ave., tel. 312/915–3916) houses the new Chicago branch of Bloomingdale's, along with dozens of smaller boutiques. Generally, the merchandise found here is more sophisticated, and more expensive, than that in Water Tower Place.

## Diversions

The **ArchiCenter** (330 S. Dearborn St., tel. 312/782–1776) is the starting point for guided tours of the city's buildings and historic homes, led by the Chicago Architecture Foundation; also available here are maps of Chicago landmarks so that you can take your own architectural tour of the Loop.

The **Art Institute** (Michigan Ave. at Adams St., tel. 312/443–3600) has a world-renowned collection of French Impressionist art, as well as outstanding medieval and Renaissance works, Asian art, and photography.

Even if your business doesn't take you there, the Art Moderne–style **Chicago Board of Trade** (141 W. Jackson St.) is worth a visit for its stunning 1930s lobby.

The **Field Museum of Natural History** (Lake Shore Dr. at Roosevelt Rd., tel. 312/922–9410), the **Shedd Aquarium** (1200 S. Lake Shore Dr., tel. 312/939–2426), and the **Adler Planetarium** (1300 S. Lake Shore Dr., tel. 312/322–0304) occupy the same peninsula just south of the Loop, jutting out into Lake Michigan. If a visit to this neighborhood gives you museum overload, the adjoining park is a good place to walk and take in a great view of the skyline.

The **Museum of Contemporary Art** (237 E. Ontario St., tel. 312/280–2660) concentrates on works created after 1940.

**Navy Pier,** at the far eastern end of Grand Avenue, juts out almost a mile into Lake Michigan, and is used exclusively by walkers, joggers, and cyclists. It's a good place to get away from it all on a sunny day and enjoy the lake breezes, the cry of the gulls, and spectacular views of downtown and Near North skylines. If you're at McCormick Place, the serene promenade between the convention center and the lakefront is another good "time out" spot.

The small **Terra Museum** (664 N. Michigan Ave., tel. 312/664–3939) contains an excellent collection of American art, including pieces by Whistler, Sargeant, Hopper, Avery, Stella, and Wyeth.

## Professional Sports

Chicago's hockey team, the **Black Hawks,** (tel. 312/733–5300) and basketball team, the **Bulls** (tel. 312/943–5800) play at the Chicago Stadium. The city's football club, the **Bears** (tel. 312/663–5100) plays at Soldier Field. For baseball, see the **Cubs** (tel. 312/878–2827) at Wrigley Field, and the **White Sox** (tel. 312/924–1000) at Comiskey Park.

## The Arts

The Chicago Symphony is internationally renowned, and the city's Lyric Opera is one of the best opera companies in the United States today. In addition, the Auditorium Theater holds a variety of first-rate subscription concerts and recital series throughout the year. Although road-show productions of Broadway hits come to Chicago, the true vigor of the city's theater springs from the multitude of small ensembles that have made a home here, ranging from the critically acclaimed Steppenwolf Company to the often satirical Body Politic.

Tickets for concerts and plays are available through **Theater Tix** (tel. 312/902–1919), **Ticketmaster** (tel. 312/559–1212), and **Ticketron** (tel. 312/902–1919). For a full listing of current attractions, call **Curtain Call** (tel. 312/977–1755). For half-price tickets on the day of the performance, check the **Hot Tix booth** (24 S. State St., no telephone).

**Auditorium Theater,** 70 E. Congress Pkwy., tel. 312/922–2110.
**Body Politic Theater,** 2261 N. Lincoln Ave., tel. 312/871–3000.
**Chicago Symphony,** Orchestra Hall, 220 S. Michigan, tel. 312/435–8122.
**Lyric Opera,** 20 N. Wacker Dr., tel. 312/332–2244.
**Steppenwolf Theater Company,** 2851 N. Halsted St., tel. 312/472–4141.

## After Hours

Hotel bars are popular among businesspeople looking for a quiet drink and a place to talk; the atmosphere at the Park Hyatt (tel. 312/280–2222), the Four Seasons (tel. 312/280–8800), and the Drake (tel. 312/787–2200) is particularly pleasant. Nightlife options listed below are within an easy walk or short cab ride of the downtown and Near North Side hotels. The Near North is very lively on weekends, as are two lakefront neighborhoods—Lincoln Park and Lakeview. Women on their own will feel more at ease on North Michigan Avenue than in the Loop, which tends to be deserted after dark.

### Bars and Lounges

**The Bar** at the Ritz-Carlton (tel. 312/266–1000) is popular with sophisticated clubbers; **Kitty O'Shea's** at the Hilton (tel. 312/922–4400) re-creates the atmosphere of an Irish pub. For a great view, try the bar at **The 95th,** in the John Hancock Building (tel. 312/987–9596).

### Blues Clubs

**Blue Chicago** (937 N. State St., tel. 312/642–6261) is the best blues club in the Near North Side; in the Loop, check out **Buddy Guy's Legends** (754 S. Wabash Ave., tel. 312/427–1190), run by one of Chicago's own blues legends.

### Cabarets

**Milt Trenier's Lounge** (610 Fairbanks Ct., tel. 312/266–6226) is lounge cabaret with a jazz quintet on the weekends.

### Comedy Clubs

**Second City** (1608 N. Wells St., tel. 312/642–8189), the granddaddy of them all (and some say past its prime), is a short cab ride from the Near North Side; there are usually two different revues playing at the same time. Also try **Chicago Improv** (504 N. Wells St., tel. 312/782–6387), or **Catch a Rising Star** (Hyatt Regency, tel. 312/565–4242).

### Jazz Clubs

The **Jazz Showcase,** in the Blackstone Hotel (tel. 312/427–4300), books name acts for serious listeners; don't come here if you want background music. For boisterous after-work and noon jazz, try **Andy's** (11 E. Hubbard St., tel. 312/642–6805). For something more intimate, go to the **Gold Star Sardine Bar** (680 N. Lake Shore Dr., tel. 312/664–4215).

### For Singles

Chicago's famous Rush Street singles scene, popular with professionals in their 20s, is actually on Division Street between Clark Street and State Street. Its legendary singles bars include **Mother's** (26 W. Division St., tel. 312/642–7251) and **Butch McGuire's** (20 W. Division St., tel. 312/337–9080). **Eddie Rocket's** (9 W. Division St., tel. 312/787–4881) has dancing. For a more "amusement park" atmosphere that gives you something to do besides cruise, try the **North Pier** development, on the river at 455 East Illinois Street, which combines bars, museums, shops, restaurants, and miniature golf.

# Cincinnati

*by Sara Pearce*

Cincinnati is proof that geography is destiny. In 1788, when riverboats were the prime means of cargo transport, the city was founded on the Ohio River. By the mid-19th century the city built on seven hills became the nation's largest producer of beer and the world's largest hog market (earning it the nickname "Porkopolis"). Although the river is no longer a real economic force, it's still a major part of the city's profile. Most downtown activity from professional baseball to dining is on or within a few blocks of the riverfront. New luxury apartment complexes and high-rise office buildings now are being built along both sides of the river.

Just as important to Cincinnati as the river is its location on the edge of Dixie. This is a Midwestern city with a Southern sense of hospitality and propriety. The flap over the display of nude photographs by Robert Mapplethorpe in an exhibit at the Contemporary Art Center in early 1990 is just a recent and widely publicized example of the city's conservative nature.

Cincinnati went through a bad period at the turn of the century, when railroads overtook riverboats as freight carriers, but after World War II, having slowly turned to manufacturing, the city once again became one of the Midwest's major industrial and commercial centers. These days there are signs of weakness, but overall the economy of Cincinnati is holding up. Unemployment is below 5%, the economy has diversified over the past seven years, and the two biggest employers, GE Aircraft Engines and Procter & Gamble, are prospering.

Delta Air Lines' expansion of its Cincinnati hub in 1986 has allowed local companies to expand operations outside Cincinnati and has drawn new firms, such as Heinz Pet Products.

Ties to Japan are growing. Japanese contractors and U.S.-Japanese joint ventures are setting up in Cincinnati as a midpoint between Honda's U.S. plant, 80 miles northeast in Marysville, Ohio, and Toyota's U.S. plant, 70 miles south in Georgetown, Kentucky.

Financier Carl Lindner, an industry by himself, manages $10 billion in investments from Cincinnati, and has moved the headquarters of three of his companies here—Penn Central, Chiquita Brands, and John Morrell.

Less sanguine prospects face downtown retailers, whose businesses continue to weaken, leaving streets almost abandoned after dark. General Motors closed two local plants in 1987 and 1988, putting 6,000 people out of work. Federated Department Stores and Allied Stores filed for Chapter 11 protection from creditors. Kroger Company took on $2 billion in debt and laid off 300 employees to avoid a takeover.

## Top Employers

| Employer | Type of Enterprise | Parent*/ Headquarters |
|---|---|---|
| Armco Inc. | Coated and specialty steels | Parsippany, NJ |
| Bethesda Hospital, Inc. | Hospital care and retirement | Cincinnati |
| Cincinnati Bell Telephone Co. | Telecommunications | Cincinnati |
| Cincinnati Gas & Electric | Utilities | Cincinnati |
| Cincinnati Milacron | Process manufacturing | Cincinnati |
| Ford Motor Co. | Automobiles and trucks | Dearborn, MI |
| GE Aircraft Engines | Jet-engine manufacturers | General Electric Co./Stamford, CT |
| Kroger Co. | Food stores | Cincinnati |
| Procter & Gamble Co. | Consumer products | Cincinnati |
| Thriftway Inc. | Food and drug stores | Cincinnati |
| University of Cincinnati | Education | Cincinnati |

*if applicable

## ESSENTIAL INFORMATION

### Climate

What follows are the average daily maximum and minimum temperatures for Cincinnati.

| | | | | | | | | |
|---|---|---|---|---|---|---|---|---|
| Jan. | 38F | 3C | Feb. | 40F | 4C | Mar. | 49F | 9C |
| | 21 | −6 | | 23 | −5 | | 32 | 0 |
| Apr. | 61F | 16C | May | 72F | 22C | June | 81F | 27C |
| | 43 | 6 | | 52 | 11 | | 61 | 16 |
| July | 85F | 29C | Aug. | 83F | 28C | Sept. | 77F | 25C |
| | 65 | 18 | | 63 | 17 | | 58 | 14 |
| Oct. | 65F | 18C | Nov. | 50F | 10C | Dec. | 40F | 4C |
| | 47 | 8 | | 36 | 2 | | 27 | −3 |

## Airport

**Greater Cincinnati International Airport** is in northern Kentucky, 12 miles southeast of downtown off I–275.

## Airport Business Facilities

An unmanned business center in Terminal C has fax and photocopy machines, phone cubicles, round tables, and an informal conference room.

## Airlines

Cincinnati is a hub city for Delta Airlines, Comair.

**American,** tel. 513/621–6200 or 800/433–7300.
**Comair,** tel. 800/354–9822.
**Delta,** tel. 513/721–7000 or 800/221–1212.
**Northwest,** tel. 800/225–2525.
**Pan Am,** tel. 800/221–1111.
**TWA,** tel. 513/381–1600 or 800/221–2000.
**United,** tel. 800/241–6522.
**USAir,** tel. 513/621–9220 or 800/428–4322.

## Between the Airport and Downtown

*By Taxi*
Taxis are available 24 hours at the three baggage claim areas. The ride takes 15–20 minutes at nonpeak hours, up to 30 minutes at rush hour (6–8 AM from the airport and 4–7 PM from the city). If you're heading downtown, the most direct route is I–275 E to I–75 N to the downtown exits. Cost: $18 per cab (1–4 passengers) plus tip.

*By Bus*
**Jetport Shuttle Express** (tel. 606/283–3702) stops at every terminal and most of the major downtown hotels, and therefore takes about 10 minutes longer than a taxi. The buses leave the airport and The Westin Hotel downtown every 30 minutes on the hour and half hour from 6 AM–11 PM daily. Cost: $8 one way, $12 round-trip.

*By Van*
**Door to Door Transportation Services** (tel. 513/641–0088) picks up at the airport 5 AM–midnight daily. Reservations should be made 48 hours in advance. Cost: about $14 per person to downtown.

## Car Rentals

The following companies have offices at or near the airport.

**Alamo,** tel. 606/586–8050 or 800/327–9633.
**Avis,** tel. 606/283–3773 or 800/331–1212.
**Budget,** tel. 606/283–1166 or 800/527–0700.
**Hertz,** tel. 606/283–3535 or 800/654–3131.
**National,** tel. 606/283–3655 or 800/227–7368.
**Sears,** tel. 606/283–1188 or 800/527–0770.
**Snappy,** tel. 606/525–9200 or 800/669–4800.
**Thrifty,** tel. 606/689–5200 or 800/367–2277.

## Emergencies

*Doctors*
**Academy of Medicine of Cincinnati** (320 Broadway, tel. 513/721–2345) offers referrals on weekdays.

*Dentists*
**Cincinnati Dental Society** (9200 Montgomery Rd., tel. 513/984–3443) has a 24-hour emergency referral service.

*Hospitals*
**Christ Hospital** (2139 Auburn Ave., tel. 513/369–2000), **St. Elizabeth Medical Center-North** (401 E. 20th St. Covington, KY, tel. 606/292–4000), **University Hospital,** (234 Goodman St., tel. 513/872–3100).

## Important Addresses and Numbers

**Audiovisual rentals.** Cavalier Audio Visual (Clarion Hotel, 141 W. 6th St., tel. 513/961–3900), David Douglas, 24-hour service (906 Dalton St., tel. 513/421–1300).

**Chamber of Commerce** (441 Vine St., Carew Tower, Suite 300, downtown, tel. 513/579–3100).

**Computer rentals.** ROM Rentals (8790 Governor's Hill Dr., tel. 513/677–2323).

**Convention and exhibition centers.** Albert B. Sabin Cincinnati Convention Center (5th and Elm Sts., tel. 513/352–3750), Cincinnati Gardens (2250 Seymour Ave, tel. 513/631–7793), Drawbridge Inn and Convention Center (I–75 and Buttermilk Pike, Ft. Mitchell, KY, tel. 606/341–2800).

**Fax services.** Cincinnati Bell Phone Center (201 E. 4th St., tel. 513/397–5600), Queensgate Express-Arnco Printing (Mercantile Center, 120 E. 4th St., tel. 513/421–3445; 10 Fountain Square Plaza, tel. 513/241–0044).

**Formal-wear rentals.** All About Tuxedos (225 E. 6th St., tel. 513/721–6770).

**Gift shops.** Chocolates: Galerie au Chocolat (Westin Hotel, tel. 513/421–4466); Flowers: Julius Baer (24 E. 4th St., tel. 513/621–3662).

**Graphic design studios.** Butz Gaskins (1994 Madison Rd., tel. 513/321–7002), Design Team I (49 E. 4th St., tel. 513/381–4774), Deskey (2534 Victory Pkwy., tel. 513/861–6600).

**Hairstylists.** Unisex: Fourth Street Salon (113 W. 4th St., tel. 513/721–7333), Saks Fifth Avenue Beauty Salon (5th and Race Sts., tel. 513/421–6900).

**Health and fitness clubs.** *See* Fitness, below.

**Information hot lines.** Call Cincinnati Bell Telephone Talking Yellow Pages (tel. 513/333–4444) and punch in the four-digit category code listed in the phone book for the service you want, or wait for an operator to assist you.

**Limousine services.** Cincinnati Limousine has 24-hour service (8639 Beechmont Ave., tel. 513/474–5870), Executive Transportation also has 24-hour service (629 York St., Newport, KY, tel. 606/261–8841).

**Liquor stores.** Liquor is sold only through state liquor stores. Ohio State Liquor Store (612 Race St., tel. 513/651–3927).

**Mail delivery, overnight.** DHL Worldwide Express (tel. 513/241–8040), Federal Express (tel. 513/530 5660), TNT Skypak (tel. 606/525–2900), UPS (tel. 513/241–5161), U.S. Postal Service Express Mail (tel. 513/292–3131).

**Messenger services.** City Dash (4586 Paddock Rd., tel. 513/641–2000), Priority Dispatch (123 E. Liberty St., tel. 513/421–3800).

**Office space rental.** Personal Assistant (120 E. 4th St., Suite 940, tel. 513/784–1115).

**Pharmacy, late-night.** Walgreen's (1 W. Corry St., University Plaza Shopping Center, tel. 513/751–3444).

**Radio stations, all-news.** WLW 700 AM and WCKY 1530 AM.

**Secretarial services.** Manpower Temporary Services (600 Vine St., tel. 513/621–0788), Personal Assistant (120 E. 4th St., Suite 940, tel. 513/784–1115).

**Stationery supplies.** Gibson & Perin (121 W. 4th St., tel. 513/621–2592 or 138 E. 6th St., tel. 513/241–0495).

**Taxis.** Yellow Cab (tel. 513/241–2100 or 513/681–5100).

**Theater tickets.** *See* The Arts, below.

**Train information.** Amtrak (1901 River Rd., tel. 513/921–4172, 9:30 AM–5 PM weekdays, or 800/872–7245, 24 hours).

**Travel agents.** Pier 'n Port (580 Walnut St., tel. 513/421–7447), Provident (Atrium II, Suite 2800, 221 E. 4th St., tel. 513/621–4900).

**Weather** (tel. 513/333–4444, ext. 2400).

## LODGING

Most business travelers stay downtown, a compact 10-block area; Procter & Gamble's world headquarters, the Convention Center, Riverfront Stadium (home of the Reds and Bengals), the Music Hall (home of the symphony, ballet, and opera), and the Maisonette (Cincinnati's premier French restaurant), are all within 10 minutes by foot of any downtown hotel. Most hotels are connected, both to each other and to businesses and shops, by the city's system of enclosed and partially sheltered skywalks.

Accommodations lean toward large, well-tended chain hotels, but there are a few small, independent hotels with character that are worth seeking out.

Most hotels listed here offer special corporate rates and weekend discounts; inquire when making reservations.

Highly recommended lodgings in each price category are indicated by a star ★.

| Category | Cost* |
|---|---|
| *$$$$* (Very Expensive) | over $130 |
| *$$$* (Expensive) | $90–$130 |
| *$$* (Moderate) | under $90 |

*\*All prices are for a standard double room, single occupancy, excluding 10% sales tax in Cincinnati; 8.15%–8.75% sales tax in Kentucky.*

*Numbers in the margin correspond to numbered hotel locations on the Cincinnati Lodging and Dining map.*

## Downtown

★ ❾  
*$$$$*  
**Cincinnatian Hotel.** In 1987, this eight-story Victorian limestone building was gutted and transformed into a bright and elegant hostelry. The original 1882 marble-and-walnut staircase adds intimacy to an interior anchored by a skylighted, eight-story atrium and decorated in a striking color combination of purple, terra-cotta, mahogany, and tan. Large-scale contemporary paintings and prints abound. Many of the rooms around the atrium have small, bay-shape balconies painted lavender. Private areas are more subdued: Rooms are furnished with sleek gray-and-black desks, armoires, and plump, upholstered chairs and sofas. All bathrooms have telephones and separate dressing areas with hair dryers. You're as likely to see a CEO as you are to see a film star in this deluxe establishment. The concierge and the rest of the youthful staff are friendly and dedicated. The hotel's Palace restaurant (*see* Dining, below) is noted for sophisticated new American cuisine. *Fisher Hotels Group. 601 Vine St., 45202, tel. 513/381–3000 or 800/942–9000; in OH, 800/332–2020; fax 513/651–0256. Gen. manager, Denise Vandersall. 128 singles, 11 doubles, 8 suites. AE, D, DC, MC, V.*

❺  
*$$$*  
**Clarion.** This two-tower high rise, built in 1968, is across the street from the convention center. The cavernous lobby is a maze of nooks and crannies, with the city's skywalk connecting to it on the second floor. Standard rooms in the 21-story South Tower are small and have low ceilings, decorated in a contemporary style. They are tidy but nondescript, with gray-blue carpets, pastel art prints, and floral fabrics. Bathrooms are tiny, and a recessed area outside the bathroom is the only closet space. Rooms in the 31-story North Tower are the same size but are more traditional, furnished with wingback chairs, wood headboards, and carved wooden bureaus. All guests have free access to Moore's Nautilus (*see* Fitness, below), a fitness center just off the second floor via the skywalk. There is also an outdoor pool, the only one downtown. Even-numbered rooms in the South Tower offer the best views of the city. The executive floors (28–31) have a concierge, small private lounge, a library with a river view, and express check-out. *141 W. 6th St., 45202, tel. 513/352–2100 or 800/252–7466, fax 513/352–2148. Gen. manager, Bob Hoeb. 346 singles, 510 doubles, 32 suites. AE, D, DC, MC, V.*

★ ❹  
*$$*  
**The Garfield House.** This boxy 16-story all-suites property, built in 1982 and renovated 1989–90, is adjacent to Piatt Park, a pretty two-block stretch of green. Even the smallest suites in this establishment—which was originally an apartment building—have a fully equipped kitchen,

a living room with a dining area, and a bedroom. Floor plans for the suites vary and each is decorated differently. Some accommodations have balconies, others have dens, libraries, or offices. There are TVs in all bedrooms and living rooms, and even a miniature one on the wall above the bathroom sink. Kitchens are fully stocked, and a deli/grocery off the lobby carries all the necessaries. Governor's Suites, on the 15th floor, are more spacious and feature such amenities as VCRs (you can rent tapes downstairs). The bilevel, glass-roofed fitness center boasts a panoramic view of downtown. The staff is friendly and accommodating. *2 Garfield Pl., 45202, tel. 513/421–3355, fax 513/421–3729. Gen. manager, Philip Kinnison. 110 suites. AE, D, DC, MC, V.*

**❻ Hyatt Regency Cincinnati.** This 22-story hotel, opened
$$$$ across the street from the convention center in 1985, is clean and crisp. Water splashes from a two-story marble fountain in the glass-roof atrium, which is filled with potted trees, plump sofas, and hanging plants, and lined with shops. Rooms, redecorated in 1989, are spacious, but furnishings are standard. You can request a view of the river or city (the best views are from the top three floors). Guests on the Regency Club level (21st floor) have their own concierge and a lounge where breakfast and cocktail snacks are served. Women often are booked on this floor because it is only accessible with an elevator passkey; rooms include such extras as hair dryers and makeup mirrors. Service is efficient, if not especially friendly. The convention center is connected to the hotel via a skywalk. Findlay's (*see* Business Breakfasts, below) is fine for a relaxing breakfast. *151 W. 5th St., 45202, tel. 513/579–1234, or 800/233–1234, fax 513/579–0107. Gen. manager, Sheldon Fox. 232 singles, 231 doubles, 22 suites. AE, D, DC, MC, V.*

**❼ Omni Netherland Plaza.** Opened in 1930 and restored in
$$$$ 1983, this 29-story hotel is a monument to Art Deco style. The lobby and two-story Palm Court bar (*see* After Hours, below) are sleek and curvy, with Rookwood tile friezes, marble stairs, brass torchères, and Brazilian rosewood paneling. The walls and ceilings are trimmed in shades of green and lilac, colors reflected in the boldly patterned rugs. Unfortunately, the rooms don't carry on the Art Deco theme. Single and deluxe rooms are tiny, poorly furnished, and have small, outdated bathrooms. Executive and club rooms are larger and have some of the Art Deco style, with sleek tables and desks, and peach-color walls. Rooms ending in 40 have a view of Fountain Square; the largest rooms are on the sixth and seventh floors. The hotel is adjacent to the 49-story Carew Tower, which houses a parking garage, offices, and shops. There are no fitness facilities, but guests are provided with passes to the Y a few blocks away. Orchids (*see* Dining, below) is a popular spot for dinner. *5th and Race Sts., 45202, tel. 513/421–9100 or 800/843–6664, fax 513/421–4291. Gen. manager, Mark F. Kenney. 401 singles, 220 doubles, 14 suites. AE, D, DC, MC, V.*

**❽ Terrace Hilton.** Although the red brick, 1948 structure
$$$ housing the Hilton is 18 stories high, the hotel actually is a narrow 10-story box perched atop seven windowless floors filled with offices. The long, marble and wood-panel lobby on the eighth floor opens up to a spacious, bright restau-

# CINCINNATI

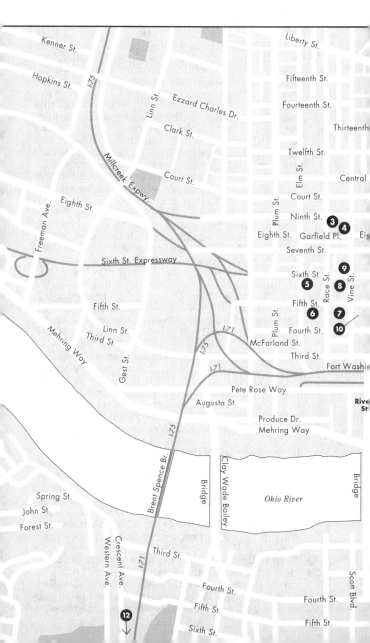

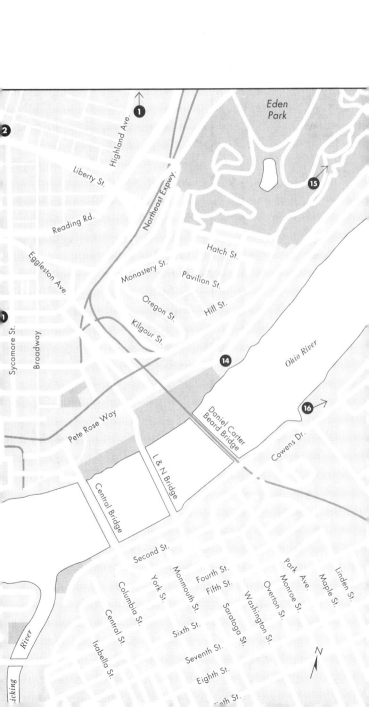

# CINCINNATI HOTEL CHART

| HOTELS | Price Category | Business Services — Banquet capacity | No. of meeting rooms | Secretarial services | Audiovisual equipment | Teletype news service | Computer rentals | In-room modem phone jack | All-news cable channel | Desk | Desk lighting | Bed lighting |
|---|---|---|---|---|---|---|---|---|---|---|---|---|
| Cincinnatian | $$$$ | 90 | 4 | ✓ | ✓ | ✓ | ✓ | - | ✓ | ● | ● | ◖ |
| Clarion | $$$ | 1000 | 16 | ✓ | ✓ | - | ✓ | - | ✓ | ● | ● | ● |
| Garfield House | $$ | 0 | 1 | ✓ | ✓ | - | ✓ | ✓ | ✓ | ● | ● | ● |
| Hyatt Regency | $$$$ | 1300 | 19 | ✓ | ✓ | - | - | - | ✓ | - | - | ○ |
| Mariemont Inn | $$ | 200 | 1 | ✓ | - | - | - | - | - | - | - | ◖ |
| Omni Netherland Plaza | $$$$ | 1000 | 28 | ✓ | ✓ | ✓ | ✓ | ✓ | ✓ | ◖ | ◖ | ◖ |
| Radisson Inn Airport | $$ | 450 | 8 | - | ✓ | - | - | ✓ | ✓ | ● | ◖ | ◖ |
| Terrace Hilton | $$$ | 300 | 7 | ✓ | ✓ | - | ✓ | ✓ | ✓ | ● | ● | ◖ |
| Vernon Manor | $$ | 170 | 7 | - | ✓ | - | - | ✓ | ✓ | ● | ● | ◖ |
| Westin | $$$$ | 1000 | 16 | ✓ | ✓ | - | ✓ | ✓ | ✓ | ● | ◖ | ◖ |

$$$$ = over $130, $$$ = $90-$130, $$ = under $90.
● good, ◖ fair, ○ poor.
All hotels listed here have photocopying and fax facilities.

| In-Room Amenities | | | | | | | | | | Hotel Amenities | | | | | | |
| Nonsmoking rooms | In-room checkout | Minibar | Pay movies | VCR/Movie rentals | Hairdryer | Toiletries | Room service | Laundry/Dry cleaning | Pressing | Concierge | Barber/Hairdresser | Garage | Courtesy airport transport | Sauna | Pool | Exercise room |
| --- | --- | --- | --- | --- | --- | --- | --- | --- | --- | --- | --- | --- | --- | --- | --- | --- |
| ✓ | - | ✓ | ✓ | - | ✓ | ● | ● | ● | ● | ✓ | - | - | - | - | - | - |
| ✓ | - | - | ✓ | - | - | ◐ | ● | ● | ◐ | ✓ | ✓ | - | ✓ | ✓ | ◐ | ● |
| - | - | - | ✓ | - | - | ● | - | ● | ● | - | - | ✓ | - | - | - | ● |
| ✓ | - | - | ✓ | - | - | ● | ◐ | ● | ● | ✓ | ✓ | ✓ | - | ✓ | ● | ● |
| - | - | - | - | ✓ | ✓ | ◐ | ● | ● | ● | - | ✓ | - | - | - | - | - |
| ✓ | ✓ | ✓ | ✓ | ✓ | - | ◐ | ● | ● | ● | ✓ | ✓ | ✓ | - | - | - | - |
| ✓ | - | - | ✓ | - | - | ◐ | ● | ◐ | ◐ | - | - | - | ✓ | - | ● | ◐ |
| ✓ | ✓ | - | ✓ | - | - | ◐ | ● | ● | ◐ | ✓ | ✓ | - | - | ✓ | - | ● |
| ✓ | - | - | ✓ | - | - | ● | ◐ | ● | ● | - | ✓ | - | - | - | - | - |
| ✓ | ✓ | ✓ | ✓ | - | - | ● | ● | ● | ● | ✓ | ✓ | ✓ | - | ✓ | ● | ● |

**Room service:** ● 24-hour, ◐ 6AM–10PM, ○ other.
**Laundry/Dry cleaning:** ● same day, ◐ overnight, ○ other.
**Pressing:** ● immediate, ◐ same day, ○ other.

rant enclosed on two sides by a plant-filled terrace. Standard single and double rooms are small, but large windows and full-length mirrors on the closet doors make the accommodations slightly less claustrophobic. The double rooms with two double beds are much more comfortable, and corner rooms have terrific views (even from the bathrooms, where large windows stretch across the vanity) of downtown and the surrounding hillside neighborhoods. Request a redecorated room; those that haven't been redone have worn furnishings and garish colors. New rooms feature comfortable chairs, armoires, brass lamps, a beige and teal palette, and marble-tiled bathrooms. Rooms on the 19th floor, once apartments, are the largest. The circular rooftop Gourmet Room has lost some of its cachet, but the adjacent Panorama Lounge (*see* After Hours, below) is a small, romantic bar with a view of downtown and live piano music. *15 W. 6th St., 45202, tel. 513/381–4000 or 800/445–8667, fax 513/381–5158. Gen. manager, Jan Larsen. 298 singles, 31 doubles, 10 suites. AE, D, DC, MC, V.*

★ ⑩ **Westin.** Located on Fountain Square and boasting a
$$$$ plazalike atrium, the modern, granite-and-glass, 13-story Westin is one of downtown's most visible hotels. TV broadcasts, musical performances, and exhibits often take place on the square and in the Westin's atrium. The spacious rooms were all redecorated in 1989 in a soothing mauve-and-gray color scheme, and furnished in a modern style. Fountain View rooms overlook the square, downtown, and the hillside neighborhoods (the rooms ending in 26 are the hotel's largest double rooms). Queen City rooms, in the back of the hotel, face neighboring buildings (ask for a room ending in 06 for extra space). The rooftop health club is the best in a downtown hotel (*see* Fitness, below). Guests staying on executive floors have concierge service and complimentary breakfast in a lounge overlooking the square. Women usually are booked in rooms closest to the elevators so that they don't have to walk the long corridors alone. *Fountain Square South, 5th and Vine Sts., 45202, tel. 513/621–7700 or 800/228–3000, fax 513/421–6869. Gen. manager, Larry Alexander. 325 singles, 123 doubles, 18 suites. AE, D, DC, MC, V.*

## Mariemont

⑯ **Mariemont Inn.** This Tudor-style inn is on the main square
$$ of Mariemont, a tranquil, planned community, 9 miles east of Cincinnati, that was built in 1924 to resemble an old English village. The lobby of the three-story inn is paneled with hand-carved oak and crisscrossed with thick ceiling beams, anchored with hefty posts. Some rooms have antiques and four-poster beds. The furniture is massive enough to make all rooms (especially the singles) feel cramped, but the homeyness of the inn, the beauty of the tree-lined neighborhood, and the friendliness of the staff make this a popular place with businesswomen and older executives. It's a quick ride from downtown via Rte. 50 E. The city's Nos. 11 and 28 Metro buses run regularly to and from downtown with a stop in front of the hotel. The National Exemplar restaurant on the first floor is a favorite breakfast spot for local families. *A Best Western hotel. 6880 Wooster Pike, 45227, tel. 513/271–2100 or 800/528–1234, fax 513/271–1057. Gen. manager, Bonnie Malone. 42 singles, 14 doubles, 4 suites. AE, D, DC, MC, V.*

## Uptown

**❶ Vernon Manor.** Built in 1924, this small seven-story hotel
**$$** with an Elizabethan brick-and-stone exterior, was con-
verted to an apartment house during the 1970s, then
turned back into a hotel in the '80s. It is dowdy and out of
the way, 5 miles north of downtown, but it is in the heart
of Cincinnati's hospital row and within five minutes of
Xavier University and the University of Cincinnati. It also
is within minutes of the businesses along Spring Grove
Avenue (Jergens, Kahn's, and P&G's Ivorydale Technical
Center) and the Cincinnati Zoo (where performers such as
Mel Torme and Ray Charles have performed during the
summer Jazzoo concert series). In 1989, the spacious high-
ceiling rooms were redecorated in shades of rose and
Wedgwood blue, furnished in Queen Anne style, and
adorned with botanical and wildlife prints. Front and
back rooms get the most light, and front rooms on the sev-
enth floor have the best view of downtown. Noisiest rooms
face Burnet Avenue, much traveled by ambulances and
police cars. The bargain-price minisingles are almost as
small as Pullman berths, but they are popular with medi-
cal students interviewing for jobs. The neighborhood is
tatty, but halfway down the street you'll find the peaceful
gardens of the Civic Garden Center and Hauck Botanical
Gardens. *400 Oak St., 45219, tel. 513/281–3300 or 800/543–
3999, fax 513/281–8933. Gen. manager, Shawn Zaczek. 25
minisingles, 51 singles, 32 doubles, 55 suites. AE, D, DC,
MC, V.*

## Airport

**❶❷ Radisson Inn Airport Cincinnati.** The boxy, red-brick and
**$$** concrete hotel was built in 1986 across the street from the
airport terminals. It is the only hotel at the airport so it
serves airline crews, late arrivals, and executives who
want to whisk in and out of town quickly. The hangarlike
lobby houses a restaurant, indoor pool, whirlpool, fitness
area, and sunken piano bar in a garden setting that is closer in style to a shopping mall than to a hotel. The sounds of
planes taking off and landing can be distracting; rooms off
the lobby are the noisiest, rooms in the eight-story tower
are quieter but slightly smaller. Furnishings are standard, bathrooms are small. The staff is geared to the needs
of its business clientele and is eager to please. *Greater
Cincinnati International Airport, Box 75108, Hebron,
KY, 45275–0108, tel. 606/371–6166 or 800/333–3333, fax
606/371–9863. Gen. manager, Peter Platz. 179 singles, 30
doubles, 5 suites. AE, D, DC, MC, V.*

## DINING

You can eat well in Cincinnati in every price range, and
enjoy cuisines ranging from new American to Cajun, Middle Eastern, and Thai. Classic French food is popular, too,
but in an updated version with lighter sauces and less
fussy presentations. Hotel restaurants, such as the Palace
in The Cincinnatian and Orchids in The Omni Netherland
Plaza, are noted for new American cuisine, as are some
half-dozen independent restaurants. Dining rooms with
views have always been popular in this city built on seven
steep hills; during the late '80s, river restaurants, many

of them floating on the Kentucky side of the river, became popular, too. Although the views can be wonderful, the food is usually undistinguished, so your best bet is to stop by for a drink.

Only a handful of German restaurants testify to Cincinnati's German heritage, but street cart vendors downtown hawk bratwurst and mettwurst, and every neighborhood has at least one butcher who still makes sausage.

The famous Cincinnati chili, more like a meat sauce served over spaghetti, is spiced with cinnamon and chocolate, and served at numerous downtown outlets of the two biggest chili chains: Skyline and Gold Star.

Highly recommended restaurants in each price category are indicated by a star ★.

| Category | Cost* |
|---|---|
| *$$$$* (Very Expensive) | over $50 |
| *$$$* (Expensive) | $30–$50 |
| *$$* (Moderate) | under $30 |

*\*per person, including appetizer, entrée and dessert, but excluding drinks, service, and 5% sales tax.*

*Numbers in the margin correspond to numbered restaurant locations on the Cincinnati Lodging and Dining map.*

## Business Breakfasts

**Palace Restaurant.** This beautifully appointed room (*see* Downtown, below) is where the city's movers and shakers are coddled during leisurely power breakfasts featuring fresh-ground Kona coffee, poached eggs in brioche with chive hollandaise, oat bran pancakes, and French toast with warm mandarin oranges. For the health conscious, the menu includes under-350-calorie dishes such as poached eggs on seven-grain bread and homemade granola. A Japanese breakfast of miso soup, rice, a boiled vegetable, rolled egg, and green tea is also available. *Cincinnatian Hotel, tel. 513/381–6006.*

**Harvey D's.** Plants and white trellises lend a gardenlike atmosphere to this cheerful breakfast spot where roomy booths are upholstered in bright red. Just off the skywalk system in the Fifth Street Arcade, between the Terrace Hilton and Clarion hotels, it's popular with conventioneers and businesspeople. Puffy, oven-baked German pancakes are the specialty, but crunchy waffles, light buttermilk pancakes, delicate crêpes, and four-egg omelets also are popular. Service is snappy, servings are generous, and Egg Beaters are available for cholesterol counters. *124 W. Convention Way (on the skywalk), tel. 513/721–5858.*

**Gourmet de Paris.** Freshly baked baguettes and a variety of filled croissants lure early risers to take out or dine in at two casual locations, both within walking distance of the convention center, major downtown hotels, and businesses. Decor is minimal: white walls, white tile, wooden counters and tables, and bright photographs of food. The staff is efficient but occasionally grumpy. *309 Vine St., tel. 513/381–3338; 205 W. 4th St., tel. 513/381–5666.*

**Busken Bakery** (210 E. 6th St., tel. 513/621–4505), a stone's throw from Procter & Gamble, attracts employees there with its early hours (it opens at 6:30 AM), freshly baked muffins, thick cake doughnuts, and full breakfast menu. The roomy, plant-filled **Findlay's** in the Hyatt Regency (tel. 513/579–1234) also opens at 6:30 AM and offers everything from buckwheat waffles and fresh-squeezed orange juice to steaks and yogurt-fruit shakes in a relaxing, plant-filled room just off the hotel's atrium. Lawyers, police officers, and stock analysts flock to **Izzy's** deli (612 Main St., tel. 513/241–6246) for a quick breakfast (or takeout order) of juice and bagels with cream cheese. Advertising and marketing executives frequent **Henry's on the Skywalk** in the Chiquita Center (250 E. 5th St., tel. 513/421–3354) for omelets and homemade muffins. Service is quick and the location is convenient to the skywalks.

## Downtown

★ ❷ **Grammer's Restaurant.** The dining rooms of this old-time
$$ German café are decorated with memorabilia from the dozens of breweries that once stood in the neighborhood. The most attractive room is the bar room, with its handset ceramic tile floor, kitschy Rhineland mural, copper-top bar, and shimmering beveled glass windows. Bentwood chairs are pushed up to small café tables (spaced well apart) covered with white cloths and bouquets of fresh flowers. The menu features such German specialties as sauerbraten with spatzle, and Wiener schnitzel, along with contemporary American fare such as walleye pike with tomato and basil, and grilled turkey Southwestern style. This neighborhood, the center of Cincinnati's German community when Frank Grammer opened the restaurant in 1911, is now one of the city's shabbiest. Although it is within walking distance of downtown, it's best to take a taxi or drive (the parking lot is always attended). *1440 Walnut St., tel. 513/721–6570. Casual but neat. Reservations advised. AE, DC, MC, V. Closed Sun., New Year's Day, and Christmas.*

★ ⓫ **Maisonette.** Don't let the facade of this somber turn-of-
$$$$ the-century townhouse, flanked by fast-food outlets, fool you. Inside, marbleized woodwork, fabric wall panels, and upholstery are elegantly decorated in flattering shades of salmon. Crystal chandeliers illuminate the large tables, which are covered with white damask and set with Villeroy & Boch china and monogrammed silver. Captains, dressed in tuxedo jackets, and other staff members are always attentive. Of the dining room's three sections, the center is the place to see and be seen. All courses are served tableside from rolling carts. The menu takes a conservative French tack, but many dishes now have light sauces, and there's a section of low-fat "Svelte Cuisine" specialties such as broiled Dover sole with lobster-chive sauce. Traditional favorites such as crabmeat cocktail, sautéed duck liver, chateaubriand, and roast rack of lamb are always on offer. More adventuresome palates may try braised chicken in raspberry vinegar sauce, or poached scallops on tomato mousse with curry sabayon sauce. The wine list, an award winner, emphasizes French vintages.

*114 E. 6th St., tel. 513/721–2260. Jacket and tie required. Reservations required. AE, DC, MC, V. Closed Sun., New Year's Day, first 2 weeks of July, Thanksgiving, and Christmas.*

**⑩ Montgomery Inn at The Boathouse.** This restaurant on the
**$$** Ohio River has a warm, lively atmosphere; local TV people, professional athletes, and business types come here to unwind. The decor features sports memorabilia, including a full-size rowing scull hanging over the second-floor bar, which is the center of the hubbub. Floor-to-ceiling windows offer views of the river, the city, and the Kentucky hills. Although it's said that Bob Hope has the house specialty, meaty ribs with sweet barbecue sauce, shipped monthly to California, the grilled duck and barbecue chicken are better bets. The thick, homemade potato chips are recommended, and the Greek salad is preferable to the bland house salad. Even with reservations there is often a short wait. You can walk here from downtown, but it's easier and safer to take a taxi or drive (there's plenty of parking). *925 Eastern Ave. (on the Ohio River in the Olympic rowing facility at Sawyer Point Park), tel. 513/721–7427. Casual dress. Reservations advised. AE, MC, V. Closed New Year's Day, Thanksgiving, Christmas Eve, and Christmas Day.*

**⑪ La Normandie Grill.** Businesspeople flock to this quintes-
**$$** sential chop house—beamed ceilings, plank floors, rough wood paneling, wooden booths—in the basement of a center city townhouse. La Normandie shares a kitchen and superb wine list with another restaurant (*see* Maisonette, above). Most people come for the well-marbled steaks, juicy chops, thick slabs of calves liver, and hefty hamburgers, but the menu also features chicken and fresh seafood. All the trimmings—warm crusty bread, pungent Greek salads, Parmesan-laced whipped potatoes, sweet fried onion strings—are equally fine. The bar, lined with caricatures of local and national celebrities, is packed afternoon and night. While waiting for tables, customers eat peanuts and toss the empty shells on the floor. You can talk business here, but it's not the place for quiet negotiations. *118 E. 6th St., tel. 513/721–2761. Casual but neat. Reservations accepted (and advised) for dinner only. AE, DC, MC, V. Closed Sun., New Year's Day, first week of July, Thanksgiving, and Christmas.*

**⑦ Orchids.** A stylish Art Deco setting, well-spaced tables,
**$$$** and nicely prepared contemporary American cuisine make this a popular place, especially with lawyers, accountants, and corporate executives who work nearby. If conversation is important, avoid the tables closest to the pianist. Brazilian rosewood paneling, pastoral murals, and etched glass lighting fixtures set the stage for luxurious dining. House favorites include Minnesota wild rice soup, a salad of Kentucky bibb lettuce with brioche croutons, and grilled chicken with pecan rice. The nutritional lowdown is given for such Spa Cuisine dishes as warm smoked chicken breast with walnut-tarragon vinaigrette, and yellow-fin tuna with marinated shrimp. The extensive wine list is evenly divided between domestic and foreign vintages. Service is discreet. *Omni Netherland Plaza Hotel, 35 W. 5th St., tel. 513/421–1772. Jacket and tie required. Reservations advised. AE, D, DC, MC, V. Closed Sun.*

**❾ The Palace.** This chic and elegant hotel dining room has a
$$$$ contemporary American outlook in its cuisine and atmosphere. The long, softly lighted room is furnished with oak
armchairs, tufted banquettes, and bold contemporary
prints. Cream-color damask, heavy silver, pink linen nap
kins, gray and-white china, and fresh flowers adorn the
well-spaced tables. The staff is young, energetic, and
smartly turned out in tuxedo trousers and starched white
jackets. The seasonal menu features such dishes as mesquite duck salad with peppercorn vinaigrette, oysters on
the half shell with three pestos, and veal medallions with
saffron-tomato butter. Menu items marked by a chef's hat
with a red heart—for example, spinach salad with gar-
licky clams or pan-seared chicken—are low cholesterol.
*Cincinnatian Hotel, 601 Vine St., tel. 513/381–6006.*
*Jacket and tie advised. Reservations advised. AE, D, DC,*
*MC, V. Closed for dinner New Year's Day.*

**★ ❸ The Phoenix.** Built in 1893 as a private men's club, The
$$ Phoenix fell into disrepair, but in 1987, it was gutted and
restored to its former elegant state. Now this public meet-
ing and dining facility attracts media people, lawyers,
stockbrokers, and corporate executives to its two dining
rooms with 22-foot-high ceilings and tall windows. The
President's Room is trimmed in oak (with a handcarved
bookcase along the entire back wall), papered in rose and
blue, furnished with oak armchairs, and hung with sky-
blue velvet curtains. The adjacent Chef's Dining Room
has an open kitchen and similar furnishings, but bolder
colors give it a more modern feel. The seasonal menu fea-
tures such new American dishes as grilled marinated egg-
plant, Sonoma goat cheese ravioli, grilled chicken breast
sandwich with mustard aioli, and roasted game hen with
honey-ginger glaze. The service is deft. *812 Race St., tel.*
*513/721–2255. Jacket and tie advised. Reservations re-*
*quired. AE, DC, MC, V. Closed Sun., for dinner Mon.,*
*and New Year's Day, July 4, Christmas Eve, Christmas,*
*and Thanksgiving.*

## Mount Lookout

**★ ⓯ The Precinct.** This Victorian, red-brick police station,
$$$ built in 1901, is now the haunt of politicians, entertainers,
lawyers, bankers, and professional athletes who crave a
basic meat-and-potatoes meal. Even on week nights, cars
back up along Delta Avenue, a 10-minute ride from downtown along Columbia Parkway East, awaiting parking at-
tendants. Photos of celebrity clients line the cramped
entrance to the two small front dining rooms, usually
packed with regulars. Overcrowded seating arrangements and tableside preparation of many house specialties
puts the wait staff—and anyone wishing to converse quietly—at a disadvantage, but they usually rise above it.
The steaks—porterhouse, strip, filet Mignon—rival
those at America's top steakhouses. There is a roster of
steaks named in honor of local athletes, such as Bengal
quarterback Boomer Esiason (blackened strip with ancho
chili sauce). The rest of the menu follows the fashions,
winding its way through every food trend of the last decade from Cajun to Southwestern. *Delta Ave. at Columbia*
*Pkwy., tel. 513/321–5454. Casual but neat. Reservations*

*advised. AE, D, DC, MC, V. Dinner only. Closed New Year's Day, Thanksgiving, Christmas.*

## FREE TIME

### Fitness

*Hotel Facilities*

The **Westin Hotel** is the only downtown hotel with a complete fitness center, including an indoor pool, whirlpool, workout room, sauna, and daily aerobics classes. It is open to nonguests for a day fee of $10.

*Health Clubs*

The renovated **Central Parkway YMCA** (Central Pkwy. and Elm St., tel. 513/241–5348) offers a $6 one-day membership. There is a pool, exercise room, Nautilus room, racquetball court, indoor track, gymnasium, and sauna. The offerings are less extensive at **Moore's Nautilus** (609 Rusconi Pl., tel. 513/381–2323), day fee $8, and **Venice Beach East** (Longworth Hall, 700 W. Pete Rose Way, tel. 513/651–9300), one-day membership $6.

*Jogging*

The 4-mile paved **Riverwalk** begins at the entrance of Sawyer Point Park, downtown, and follows the river across the Suspension Bridge to Covington, Kentucky, along that city's historic Riverside Drive.

### Shopping

The best and most compact shopping area downtown is along **Fourth, Fifth, and Sixth streets** (between Main St. and Central Ave.). Here you'll find two good department stores, Lazarus and Saks Fifth Avenue, and A.B. Clossen, which has a fine selection of gifts. The Contemporary Arts Center Bookstore is also worth browsing. Outside downtown, shopping is convenient at **Hyde Park Square** (Erie Ave. and Edwards Rd., a 10-minute taxi ride from downtown) and **Kenwood Towne Centre** (Montgomery Rd., a 20-minute taxi ride from downtown).

For the latest looks, try **Dino's For Men** (6th and Race Sts., tel. 513/421–5692 or Kenwood Towne Centre, tel. 513/984–0660), **Gidding-Jenny** (18 W. 4th St., women only, tel. 513/421–6400), **Henry Harris** (420 Race St., women only, tel. 513/721–7100), and **Rags 2 Riches,** for men and women, (2728 Vine St., tel. 513/861–8067).

Also worth checking: **Ohio Book Store** (726 Main St., tel. 513/621–5142); **Galerie au Chocolat** and the other shops in the Westin hotel (tel. 513/421–4466); the art galleries along Fourth Street between Central Avenue and Race Street; historic **Findlay Market House** and the open-air food mart, Wed.–Sat. (1700 Elm St.); and **MainStrasse Village,** in Covington, KY (along 5th, 6th, and 7th Sts. between Main and Philadelphia Sts.), a restored 19th-century German neighborhood across the river from downtown, hosting somewhat touristy but charming gift shops.

### Diversions

**BB Riverboats** (foot of Madison St., Covington, KY, tel. 606/261–8500) will take you sightseeing year-round on the

Ohio River on lunch, dinner, and dancing cruises of varying lengths.

**Cincinnati Art Museum** (Art Museum Dr., Eden Park, tel. 513/721–5204) has a particularly fine Near East collection, and one of the largest collections of Gainsboroughs in any American museum. It also houses fine examples of the locally produced Rookwood pottery and works by the Cincinnati School painters.

**Cincinnati Zoo and Botanical Gardens** (Vine St. and Erkenbrecher Ave., tel. 513/281–4700) features 62 acres of beautifully landscaped grounds, white Bengal tigers, an outdoor gorilla exhibit, the nation's first Insect World exhibit building, and a butterfly garden.

**College Football Hall of Fame** (Mason, OH, 20 miles north of downtown, tel. 513/398–5410) is a monument to Knute Rockne's game: you can hear one of his pep talks, watch film clips of famous games, and maybe even kick your own field goal.

**Contemporary Arts Center** (115 E. 5th St., tel. 513/721–0390) features cutting-edge art with changing exhibitions (there is no permanent collection) and contemporary musical performances.

**Hauck Botanic Garden** (Reading and Taft Rds.) has 8 acres of gardens adjacent to the herb and flower gardens of The Civic Garden Center. Bring lunch and dine on the tiered terrace.

**Krohn Conservatory** (Eden Park, tel. 513/352–4086), with its ornate, Victorian glass dome, houses more than 1,500 plants representing 250 species and varieties. The seasonal displays are extremely popular, which often means waiting in line.

**Spring Grove Cemetery and Arboretum** (4521 Spring Grove Ave., tel. 513/681–6680) is the permanent home of such prominent Cincinnatians as soap makers Gamble and Procter, and grocery-chain founder Barney Kroger. The cemetery is listed on the National Register of Historic Places and is filled with picturesque mausoleums and flower gardens.

## Professional Sports

Cincinnati's baseball club, the **Reds** (tel. 513/421–4510) and its football team, the **Bengals** (tel. 513/621–3550) play at Riverfront Stadium.

## The Arts

Music dominates Cincinnati's arts scene, with the Cincinnati Symphony Orchestra and Cincinnati Pops Orchestra performing year-round at Music Hall and Riverbend Music Center (their summer outdoor home). Music Hall also hosts May Festival (the oldest choral festival in the Western Hemisphere), opera, and ballet. The Playhouse in the Park offers year-round productions of musicals and dramas in its two theaters. A variety of small dance, music, and theater groups round out the scene with performances at The Dance Hall, Ensemble Theater, Taft Theater, and the historic Showboat Majestic.

During the warm months, there is free outdoor entertainment—music, theater, comedy—at Fountain Square and Sawyer Point Park, and in the city's other parks.

Ticket agencies include **CSO Ticket Store** (4th and Walnut Sts., tel. 513/381–3300) and **Ticketmaster** (all Lazarus and All About Sports stores, tel. 513/721–6100).

**The Dance Hall,** 2728 Vine St., tel. 513/751–2800.
**Ensemble Theater,** 1127 Vine St., tel. 513/421–3556.
**Music Hall,** 1241 Elm St., tel. 513/721–8222.
**Playhouse in the Park,** 962 Mount Adams Dr., tel. 513/421–3888.
**Riverbend Music Center,** 6295 Kellogg Ave. at Coney Island, tel. 513/232–6220.
**Showboat Majestic,** on the Ohio River at the Public Landing, downtown, tel. 513/241–6550.
**Taft Theater,** 317 E. 5th St., tel. 513/381–3784.

## After Hours

Nightlife downtown centers on the hotels and the riverfront. Uptown, it's in the small bars and lounges that line the neighborhoods of Mount Adams (a hilly San Francisco look-alike) and Clifton (site of the University of Cincinnati). Generally, older, well-heeled types go downtown; the younger crowd gathers uptown; and businesspeople visit the places along the river.

*Bars and Lounges*
Perched on a Mount Adams hillside, **The Incline** (Highland Towers, 1071 Celestial St., tel. 513/241–4455) is an elegant, tiered room with a circular bar and a view of downtown, the river, and the sunset. The bar at the swanky, Art Deco **Palm Court** (Omni Netherland Plaza Hotel, tel. 513/421–9100), is a busy yet relaxing place to wind down after work. But the coziest and most overlooked bar is the plush **Panorama Lounge,** adjacent to the rooftop Gourmet Room restaurant in the Terrace Hilton Hotel (tel. 513/381–4000), where there's light jazz and popular standards on the piano. For an offbeat setting, stop by **Rookwood Pottery** (1077 Celestial St., tel. 513/721–5456), where you sit among kilns once used to fire tiles and pottery.

*Comedy Clubs*
**Caddy Shack** (230 W. Pete Rose Way, tel. 513/721–3636) is run by the owner of Caddy's, a '50s theme restaurant/bar next door. Headliners often turn up on the late-night talk shows after you've seen them here.

*Jazz Clubs*
**Blue Wisp Lounge** (19 Garfield Pl. between Race and Vine Sts., tel. 513/721–9801), in the basement of the Presidential Plaza Building, showcases the house's 16-piece big band, local musicians, and out-of-town guests. Uptown, the seedy **Greenwich Tavern** (2440 Gilbert Ave., tel. 513/221–6764) features locals on week nights and nationally known acts on weekends. Across the river, listen to the Dee Felice Trio and Dixieland jazz while dining on jambalaya and crawfish étouffée at **Dee Felice's Café** (529 Main St., Covington, KY, tel. 606/261–2365).

*For Singles*
The **Blind Lemon** (936 Hatch St., tel. 513/241–3885) has people waiting to get in year-round, but during warm

weather it is even more crowded with young professionals and aging baby boomers crowding the small patio to listen to contemporary, folk, and jazz music. Nightly fireworks, frequent sightings of movie stars, and a sizzling disco make **La Boom,** on the top floor of the floating Waterfront (14 Pete Rose Pier, Covington, KY, tel. 606/581–1414), a trendy place to be seen along the river; you'll find an all-ages crowd.

# Cleveland

*by Mary E. Mihaly*

Called the "Comeback City" by the national press, this city of 536,000, built on the banks of the Cuyahoga River, has seen a lot of changes for the better lately. The downtown area has been going through a renaissance—at a cost, over five years, of a staggering $10 billion. The most dramatic change so far has happened in the Flats, Cleveland's historic industrial district on the Cuyahoga riverfront, where Sherwin and Williams Paints made their fortunes, as did John D. Rockefeller. (Margaret Bourke-White found beauty in the smokestacks and furthered her legendary career photographing them.) Today, the area teems with restaurants, boutiques, and clubs and supports a $300-million river-dependent industrial economy.

After a long abatement controversy, developer Richard Jacobs completed plans to transform Public Square with two new hotel/office complexes, including a swank Hyatt Regency, at a cost of nearly $1 billion. Tower City, part of Cleveland's landmark Terminal Tower complex, is going ahead with its total development plan that includes a Ritz-Carlton Hotel and, supplementing a new, upscale retail project, Ohio's first Neiman-Marcus store. The Convention Center's $28-million renovation is complete, and the International Exposition Center has made it into *The Guinness Book of World Records* as the largest expo facility. Life in Cleveland is also enhanced by the acclaimed Cleveland Orchestra, the Cleveland Museum of Art, and, due to open in 1992, the Rock and Roll Hall of Fame and Museum, designed by architect I. M. Pei.

Cleveland has always been marked by ethnic diversity—some 60 nationalities are represented here—and the result is a collection of city neighborhoods with their own strong identities and personalities. Real estate values have been appreciating as young professionals move into suburbs—the pastoral towns of the Chagrin Valley to the east, the lakefront communities to the west, and the fast-growing suburbs to the south.

## Top Employers

| Employer | Type of Enterprise | Parent*/ Headquarters |
|---|---|---|
| American Greetings Corp. | Greeting cards | Cleveland |
| Ameritrust Corp. | Banking | Cleveland |
| BP America | Oil | Cleveland |
| Cleveland Clinic Foundation | Hospital | Cleveland |
| Ford Motor Co. | Automotive | Detroit |
| Lubrizol Inc. | Chemicals manufacturer | Cleveland |
| NASA Lewis Research Center | Space research | NASA/ Washington, DC |
| National City Corp. | Banking | Cleveland |
| Sherwin Williams Co. | Paints and chemicals manufacturer | Cleveland |

*if applicable*

## ESSENTIAL INFORMATION

### Climate

What follows are the average daily maximum and minimum temperatures for Cleveland.

| | | | | | | | | |
|---|---|---|---|---|---|---|---|---|
| Jan. | 36F | 2C | Feb. | 38F | 3C | Mar. | 45F | 7C |
| | 22 | −6 | | 22 | −6 | | 29 | −2 |
| Apr. | 59F | 15C | May | 72F | 22C | June | 81F | 27C |
| | 38 | 3 | | 49 | 9 | | 59 | 15 |
| July | 85F | 29C | Aug. | 83F | 28C | Sept. | 76F | 24C |
| | 63 | 17 | | 61 | 16 | | 56 | 13 |
| Oct. | 65F | 18C | Nov. | 50F | 10C | Dec. | 38F | 3C |
| | 45 | 7 | | 34 | 1 | | 25 | −4 |

### Airports

**Hopkins International Airport,** Cleveland's main airport, is about 6 miles southwest of downtown. **Burke Lakefront Airport** is a commuter airport on downtown's northeast fringe, a ½ mile from city center. It primarily services private aircraft and small, intrastate shuttles.

### Airlines

Cleveland is a minihub for USAir and a hub for Continental.

**American,** tel. 216/881–4341 or 800/433–7300.
**Central States,** tel. 216/289–9400 or 800/827–5050.
**ComAir (Delta connection),** tel. 800/354–9822.
**Continental,** tel. 216/771–8419 or 800/525–0280.
**Delta,** tel. 216/221–1212 or 800/221–1212.

**Midway,** tel. 800/621–5700.
**Northwest,** tel. 800/225–2525.
**Pan Am,** tel. 800/221–1111.
**TWA,** tel. 216/781–7950 or 800/221–2000.
**United,** tel. 216/356–1311 or 800/241–6522.
**USAir,** tel. 216/696–8050 or 800/428–4322.

## Between the Airport and Downtown

Hopkins International is a 25-minute drive from downtown on I–71. Add another 15 minutes during rush hours. Travelers arriving from 7 to 9 AM will find the RTA Rapid Transit a more predictable and less exasperating option than a taxi. The trip from Burke, only 5–10 minutes from city center, is not subject to the vagaries of traffic.

*By Rapid Transit Train*
**RTA** trains (tel. 216/621–9500) leave Hopkins every 20 minutes, 24 hours a day, and arrive at the Tower City terminal, in the heart of downtown, in 25 minutes. Cost: $1.

*By Taxi*
Unlike most larger cities, Cleveland is not a taxi town. One of the city's few taxi stands is located at Hopkins. The trip downtown from Hopkins costs about $17, more during rush hours. The drive to the eastern suburbs takes 40–65 minutes and costs about $25, depending on the suburb. The 5–10 minute trip from Burke Airport costs $2–$4; add 15–20 minutes and up to $10 for suburban destinations.

## Car Rentals

The following companies have booths in Hopkins or Burke airports:

**Avis,** tel. 216/265–3700 (Hopkins) or 800/331–1212.
**Budget,** tel. 216/433–4433 (Hopkins), 216/574–9870 (Burke), or 800/527–0700.
**Dollar,** tel. 216/267–3133 (Hopkins) or 800/421–6878.
**Hertz,** tel. 216/267–8900 (Hopkins) or 800/654–3131.
**Thrifty,** tel. 216/267–6811 (Hopkins) or 800/367–2277.

## Emergencies

*Doctors*
The **Academy of Medicine** (tel. 216/231–5000) will provide names of three member physicians by phone, basing their referrals on the nature of the caller's illness and other personal preferences (gender of doctor, location, etc.). Physician referrals can also be obtained from westside **Fairview General Hospital** (tel. 216/476–7000) and eastside **Meridia Medline** (tel. 216/449–4533).

*Dentists*
Referrals for emergency dental services are made by the **Greater Cleveland Dental Society** (526 Superior Ave. NE, tel. 216/241–4158).

*Hospitals*
Emergency facilities, including a trauma center, are located just southeast of outside downtown at **St. Vincent Charity Hospital and Medical Center** (2351 E. 22nd St., tel. 216/363–2536; Trauma Center, tel. 216/781–8985). Emergencies are also treated on the Near West Side, two minutes from downtown, at **Lutheran Medical Center** (2609

Franklin Blvd., tel. 216/363–2128). Other emergency centers include **MetroHealth System** (3395 Scranton Rd., tel. 216/459–4145), five minutes west of downtown.

## Important Addresses and Numbers

**Audiovisual rentals.** Colortone (24 Public Sq., tel. 216/241–0858), Eighth Day Sound Systems (1305 W. 80th St., tel. 216/961–2900).

**Chamber of Commerce.** Greater Cleveland Growth Association (Huntington Bldg., 925 Euclid Ave., tel. 216/621–3300).

**Computer rentals.** Cleveland Typewriter and Computer Co. (1955 Lee Rd., tel. 216/371–2500), International Computer Exchange (24950 Great Northern Corporate Center, tel. 216/779–2200).

**Convention and exhibition centers.** Cleveland Convention Center (1220 E. 6th St., tel. 216/348–2200), International Exposition Center (6200 Riverside Dr., tel. 216/676–6000).

**Fax services.** ABC Document Facsimile Express (510 Superior Ave., tel. 216/696–5964), Headquarters Companies (25000 Great Northern Corporate Center, tel. 216/777–0000 or 23200 Chagrin Blvd., tel. 216/831–8220), Kinko's Copies (1832 Euclid Ave., tel. 216/589–5679).

**Formal-wear rentals.** American Commodore Tuxedo (1122 Euclid Ave., tel. 216/241–0440), Joseph Scafidi (Huntington Bldg., 925 Euclid Ave., tel. 216/579–9500).

**Gift shops.** Chocolates: Malley's Chocolates (BP Bldg., Public Sq., tel. 216/348–1010); Florists: Alexander's Flowers (BP Bldg., Public Sq., tel. 216/292–4500), Statler Florist (Statler Office Tower, E. 12th St. and Euclid Ave., tel. 216/771–7673); Gifts: Omni Shop (The Arcade, 401 Euclid Ave., tel. 216/781–3444), Cleveland Reflections (The Arcade, 401 Euclid Ave., tel. 216/566–1566).

**Graphic design studios.** Ade Skunta & Co. (700 St. Clair Ave. NW, tel. 216/241–0730), Common & Kotowski (5311 Franklin Blvd., tel. 216/281–5150), Epstein, Gutzwiller & Partners (11427 Bellflower Rd., tel. 216/421–1600).

**Hairstylists.** Unisex: Arcade Style Shop (401 Euclid Ave., tel. 216/861–3238), La Coiffe (The Pavilion Mall, 24049 Chagrin Blvd., tel. 216/831–1105), Dino Palmieri Salon (The Galleria, 100 Erieview Plaza, tel. 216/623–0707), John's Markfrank (Halle Bldg., 1228 Euclid Ave., tel. 216/781–1199).

**Health and fitness clubs.** *See* Fitness, below.

**Information hot lines.** Convention and Visitors Bureau (tel. 216/621–7981), Jazz line (tel. 216/421–2266), Ticketron event line (tel. 216/771–1007).

**Limousine services.** American Limousine Service (tel. 216/221–9330), Beal Street Limousine (tel. 216/835–5466), Hopkins Airport Limousine Service (tel. 216/267–8282).

**Liquor stores.** Hard liquor can be purchased only at State liquor stores (514 Prospect Ave., tel. 216/621–1184; 2539

Lorain Ave., tel. 216/241–0954; 17116 Chagrin Blvd., tel. 216/561–0495); for wine and beer, Hinman's at the Hoyt (700 W. St. Clair Ave., tel. 216/621–2202), Shaker Square Beverage (Halle Bldg. 1228 Euclid Ave., tel. 216/241–0444).

**Mail deliveries, overnight.** DHL Worldwide Express (tel. 216/671–4700), Federal Express (tel. 800/238–5355), TNT Skypak (tel. 216/826–3366), UPS (tel. 216/826–3320), U.S. Postal Service Express Mail (tel. 216/443–4409).

**Messenger services.** Bonnie Speed Delivery (tel. 216/696–6033), Professional Delivery & Courier (tel. 216/566–0058), Quicksilver Messenger Service (tel. 216/687–1616).

**Office space rentals.** Headquarters Companies (25000 Great Northern Corporate Center, tel. 216/777–0000 or 23200 Chagrin Blvd., tel. 216/831–8220), Office Place (24200 Chagrin Blvd., tel. 216/464–7520), Statler Exec Suite (1127 Euclid Ave., tel. 216/566–8050).

**Pharmacies, late-night.** Chesterfield Pharmacy (1799 E. 12th St., tel. 216/621–1448), Downtown Leader Drug (1400 E. 9th St., tel. 216/621–0132), Revco Discount Drug (15029 Snow Rd., tel. 216/676–4380), Tower City Drug (1030 Terminal Tower, tel. 216/566–9157).

**Radio stations, all-news.** WCPN FM 90.3, WERE AM 1300, WNIR FM 100.1, WWWE AM 1100.

**Secretarial services.** Bureau of Office Services (Marion Bldg., 1276 W. 3rd St., tel. 216/781–1855), Erieview Word Processing Center (Superior Bldg., tel. 216/621–0290), Statler Office Services (1127 Euclid Ave., tel. 216/566–8050).

**Stationery supplies.** Burrows Bros. Stationers (601 Euclid Ave., tel. 216/861–1400), Checker Office Products (1430 Euclid Ave., tel. 216/579–1280), Superior Office Products (75 Public Sq., tel. 216/566–1800).

**Taxis.** AmeriCab (tel. 216/881–1111), Yellow-Zone Cab (tel. 216/623–1500).

**Theater tickets.** *See* The Arts, below.

**Train information.** Greater Cleveland RTA (Customer Service Center, BP America Parking Garage, Euclid Ave. at Public Sq., tel. 216/621–9500), Amtrak (200 Cleveland Memorial Shoreway NE, tel. 216/696–5115 or 800/872–7245).

**Travel agents.** American Express (1925 E. 9th St., tel. 216/241–4575), Ask Mr. Foster Travel Service (200 Public Sq., tel. 216/586–6087), Thomas Cook Travel (925 Euclid Ave., tel. 216/621–3220).

**Weather** (tel. 216/931–1212).

## LODGING

Cleveland is experiencing a boom in hotel construction, with some of the country's most prestigious hotel names becoming part of the cityscape. A Ritz-Carlton has been completed at Tower City, and ground has been broken for a Hyatt Regency on Public Square, a Fisher Hotel at Playhouse Square, and a deluxe Marriott at Public Square. Hotels are also expected as spinoff developments from planned and current projects in the Flats, Gateway, and North Coast Harbor.

Most of the building boom is happening downtown, a 20-block area bounded by Lake Erie to the north, freeways to the south, the Flats and the Cuyahoga River to the west, and the fast-expanding Cleveland State University to the east. The nerve center is Public Square, a four-quadrant park anchored by Terminal Tower, Cleveland's most famous landmark, and the attached Tower City complex of stores, offices, and restaurants.

University Circle, a 15-minute drive to the east, is an area of cultural, medical, and educational institutions, set in 5 square miles of lush greenery. Grand old homes are sprinkled throughout the neighborhood, which is a perfect jumping-off point for meetings held at the think-tank companies that mark the eastern suburbs. High-tech industries of Solon, Beachwood, and the Wickliffe/Willoughby corridor are a short freeway drive away.

The airport area hotels, southwest of downtown, are popular with groups on retreats and those coming together for brief (one- or two-day) regional meetings. What keeps the rooms at these hotels in demand, in addition to proximity to the airport, is quick access to the NASA Lewis Research Center, and, just 10 minutes away, the hundreds of offices and corporate headquarters in suburban Independence.

Although changes are under way, Cleveland's accommodations are not yet on a par with those of other comparably sized cities. For example, there was no suite hotel in town until 1990, and business amenities that would be considered standard in many places are either missing or are big news here.

Most hotels listed here offer special corporate rates and weekend discounts; inquire when making reservations.

Highly recommended lodgings in each price category are indicated by a star ★ .

| Category | Cost* |
|----------|-------|
| *$$$$* (Very Expensive) | over $140 |
| *$$$* (Expensive) | $75–$140 |
| *$$* (Moderate) | under $75 |

*\*All prices are for a standard double room, single occupancy, excluding a 7% sales tax and a 6% bed tax.*

*Numbers in the margin correspond to numbered hotel locations on the Cleveland Lodging and Dining map.*

## Downtown

★ ⑯ **Radisson Suite Hotel.** A former apartment complex across
*$$$$* the street from Chester Park made its debut in March 1990 as Cleveland's first all-suite hotel. The $20-million renovation created 252 two-room suites, a ballroom, conference and meeting space, and a new marble facade at the East 12th Street entrance. The decor is modern but warmly ele-

# CLEVELAND

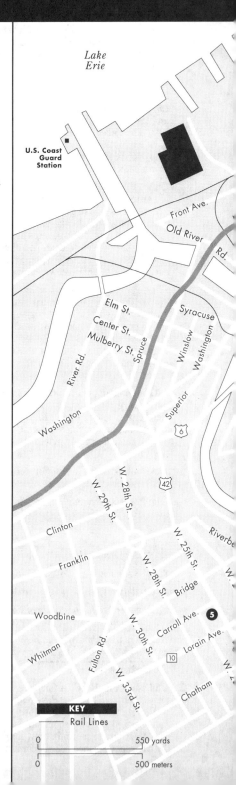

## Lodging

## Dining

Lake
Erie

U.S. Coast
Guard
Station

Front Ave.

Old River

Rd.

Elm St.

Center St.

Mulberry St.

Spruce

Syracuse

Winslow

Washington

River Rd.

Washington

Superior

6

W. 28th St.

W. 29th St.

42

Clinton

Franklin

W. 25th St.

W. 28th St.

Bridge

Riverbe

Woodbine

W. 30th St.

Carroll Ave.

10

Lorain Ave.

Whitman

Fulton Rd.

W. 33d St.

Chatham

**KEY**

— Rail Lines

0            550 yards

0            500 meters

# CLEVELAND HOTEL CHART

| HOTELS | Price Category | Business Services | | | | | | | | | | |
| --- | --- | --- | --- | --- | --- | --- | --- | --- | --- | --- | --- | --- |
| | | Banquet capacity | No. of meeting rooms | Secretarial services | Audiovisual equipment | Teletype news service | Computer rentals | In-room modem phone jack | All-news cable channel | Desk | Desk lighting | Bed lighting |
| **Airport Marriott** | $$$ | 400 | 15 | ✓ | ✓ | - | - | ✓ | ✓ | ◐ | ● | ● |
| **Glidden House** | $$$ | 150 | 2 | ✓ | ✓ | - | - | ✓ | ✓ | ◐ | ● | ● |
| **Pierre Radisson Inn Airport** | $$ | 200 | 4 | - | ✓ | - | ✓ | ✓ | ✓ | ● | ◐ | ◐ |
| **Radisson Suite** | $$$$ | 180 | 3 | - | ✓ | - | - | ✓ | ✓ | ● | ● | ● |
| **Residence Inn by Marriott** | $$$ | 20 | 1 | - | ✓ | - | - | ✓ | ✓ | ● | ● | ● |
| **Ritz-Carlton** | $$$$ | 330 | 8 | ✓ | ✓ | - | ✓ | ✓ | ✓ | ● | ● | ● |
| **Sheraton Cleveland City Centre** | $$$ | 750 | 16 | - | ✓ | - | - | ✓ | ✓ | ● | ◐ | ◐ |
| **Stouffer Tower City Plaza** | $$$$ | 1700 | 29 | ✓ | ✓ | - | ✓ | ✓ | ✓ | ● | ◐ | ◐ |

$$$$ = over $140, $$$ = $75-$140, $$ = under $75.
● good, ◐ fair, ○ poor.
All hotels listed here have photocopying and fax facilities.

| In-Room Amenities | | | | | | | | | | Hotel Amenities | | | | | | |
| Nonsmoking rooms | In-room checkout | Minibar | Pay movies | VCR/Movie rentals | Hairdryer | Toiletries | Room service | Laundry/Dry cleaning | Pressing | Concierge | Barber/Hairdresser | Garage | Courtesy airport transport | Sauna | Pool | Exercise room |
|---|---|---|---|---|---|---|---|---|---|---|---|---|---|---|---|---|
| ✓ | ✓ | - | ✓ | ✓ | ✓ | ◐ | ◐ | ● | ● | ✓ | - | - | ✓ | ✓ | ● | ◐ |
| ✓ | ✓ | - | ✓ | - | - | ○ | - | ● | ◐ | - | - | - | - | - | - | - |
| ✓ | ✓ | - | ✓ | - | ✓ | ○ | ◐ | ● | ● | ✓ | - | - | ✓ | - | ◐ | ◐ |
| ✓ | - | ✓ | ✓ | - | ✓ | ◐ | ◐ | ● | ● | ✓ | - | ✓ | - | ✓ | ● | ● |
| ✓ | - | - | - | ✓ | ✓ | ○ | - | ● | ● | - | - | - | ✓ | - | ● | ● |
| ✓ | - | ✓ | ✓ | - | ✓ | ● | ● | ● | ● | ✓ | ✓ | ✓ | ✓ | ✓ | ● | ● |
| ✓ | ✓ | - | ✓ | - | - | ◐ | ◐ | ◐ | ◐ | ✓ | ✓ | ✓ | - | - | - | - |
| ✓ | - | ✓ | ✓ | - | ✓ | ● | ● | ◐ | ◐ | ✓ | ✓ | ✓ | - | ✓ | ◐ | ● |

**Room service:** ● 24-hour, ◐ 6AM-10PM, ○ other.
**Laundry/Dry cleaning:** ● same day, ◐ overnight, ○ other.
**Pressing:** ● immediate, ◐ same day, ○ other.

gant with decidedly private club-style furnishings. The hotel lobby, located on the fifth floor (the first four floors are offices), is expansive and, because it is not located at street level, is devoid of loiterers and street noise, creating a tone of exclusivity. In-room amenities include two remote-control TV sets, work station, wet bar, and two phones with modem hookups. Suites are sufficiently spacious for extended stays, and each includes a large bathroom and kitchenette. Also available to guests is a world-class health club, as well as good dining options and complimentary breakfast in the Grill Restaurant. *1706 E. 12th St., 44114, tel. 216/523–8000, fax 216/861–1266. Gen. manager, Vern Fuller. 252 suites. AE, D, DC, MC, V.*

**❽ Ritz-Carlton Hotel.** Opened in November 1990 in Tower
$$$$ City, a huge office, shopping, and entertainment complex, this Ritz-Carlton has all the characteristics of the upscale chain. It's opulently furnished, with original 18th- and 19th-century art and antiques in the lobby. Rooms feature antique reproductions, custom-made to complement the decor of the public spaces; baths are marble, and those in suites have Jacuzzis. Guests on The Club floor have access to the Club Lounge, where complimentary meals and snacks are served, including a light lunch. The Café restaurant affords views of the Cuyahoga River and the historic Flats district; the lobby lounge has a working fireplace and is a good spot to meet associates for a drink. The staff is eager to prove that this new member lives up to the chain's reputation for superlative service. (The hotel opened too recently for us to give it a star.) *Tower City, 44113, tel. 216/736–7171 or 800/241–3333. Gen. manager, Cheryl O'Connor. 187 rooms, 21 suites. AE, D, DC, MC, V.*

**❿ Sheraton Cleveland City Centre Hotel.** The former Bond
$$$ Court Hotel, 20 paces from the newly remodeled Cleveland Convention Center, has been transformed into a Sheraton geared specifically to business travelers, with upgraded communications systems and additional phones and work spaces in all rooms. The refurbishment brought crystal-chandelier lighting and two waterfalls to the lobby. Rooms are spacious and pleasant if not luxurious; a work station and a business lounge are available on the executive level. Conference facilities now accommodate up to 1,000 people, and 18 meeting rooms have new decor and updated audiovisual capabilities. The lobby is relatively quiet for a hotel catering to a convention trade. *777 St. Clair Ave., 44114, tel. 216/771–7600; in Ohio, 800/321–1090; 800/325–3535; fax 216/771–5129. Gen. manager, Michael Burin. 307 doubles, 45 suites, 8 larger doubles on the executive level. AE, D, DC, MC, V.*

**★ ❾ Stouffer Tower City Plaza Hotel.** In a city that's generally
$$$$ lacking upgraded business facilities, this posh establishment offers many conveniences for business travelers, including telephones at bedside, desk, and bathroom; a fourth-floor business center; limousine service to the Playhouse Square theaters; and guest privileges at the nearby 13th Street Racquet Club (*see* Fitness, below). The 60-year-old hotel, easily the most opulent in town, recently underwent a $35-million renovation and now has its own fitness area and executive floors with library, speaker phones with call waiting, and Club Lounge. Rooms are large and quietly elegant; many have marble baths. Gold-

leaf banisters, marble pillars, and ornate chandeliers create an aura of opulence in the lobby, which connects directly to Tower City's rapid transit station, banks, 11 movie theaters, restaurants, and The Avenue shopping mall. French Connection (*see* Dining, below) is a top-notch restaurant. A convenient location, personalized services, and lush accommodations make Stouffer's the top choice. *24 Public Sq., 44113, tel. 216/696–5600, fax 216/696–0432. Gen. manager, Edward Chanatry. 271 singles, 170 doubles, 50 suites. AE, D, DC, MC, V.*

## University Circle

★ **⑰** **Glidden House Hotel.** Guests in this French Gothic-style
$$$ mansion, 15 minutes east of downtown in the heart of University Circle, are within a few minutes' walk of the Cleveland Museum of Art, the Museum of Natural History, and Severance Hall, home of the Cleveland Orchestra. Built in 1910 by the Glidden family (of Glidden Paint Co.), the house was converted to a hotel on a bed-and-breakfast theme in 1989. Public spaces have hand-carved woodwork, beamed ceilings, and Oriental rugs; there's also a large sun porch, and an ornate stone fireplace in the dining area. Somewhat unexpected in this rustic setting are the banquet facilities and conference rooms. To attract a business clientele, the owners decided to make the rooms less frilly than those often found in bed-and-breakfasts; they instead refinished the original dark wood in the house, setting a quiet, serious tone. The single rooms, which vary in size, may be the best choice for business travelers; double rooms are rather cramped, with little work space. *Treadway Inns of America. 1901 Ford Dr., 44106, tel. 216/231–8900, fax 216/231–2130. Gen. manager, Paul Eddington. 20 doubles, 33 singles, 8 suites. AE, D, DC, MC, V.*

## Airport

**④** **Cleveland Airport Marriott.** Located just off I–480, mid-
$$$ way between downtown and Hopkins Airport, this 30-year-old hotel is a five-minute drive from the bustling Independence business area at the I–77/Rockside Road interchange. Marriott recently added a new, 51-room concierge level with larger rooms, valet services, and complimentary Continental breakfast. Business travelers can request telephones with conference call and speaker capabilities. Although this is the oldest airport hotel, it is the most plush and offers the most amenities for business travelers. Suites are spacious and luxurious, with mahogany furniture, set against a bold maroon and forest green color scheme with navy accents. First-floor courtyard rooms are breezy and in demand during warm months. *4277 W. 150th St., 44135, tel. 216/252–5333 or 800/228–9290, fax 216/251–1508. Gen. manager, Jack Jones. 379 rooms, 3 suites. AE, CB, D, DC, MC, V.*

**❷** **Pierre Radisson Inn Airport.** This six-story hotel, opened
$$ in 1989, features an open, airy lobby and spacious, comfortable rooms. With four meeting rooms but no large ballroom, the Pierre Radisson is a good choice for someone who wants the amenities of a large hotel without the expected foot traffic. A small, quiet lounge just off the lobby is conducive to business talks. A floor of executive rooms and suites offers additional amenities. One deluxe suite features a Jacuzzi in the bedroom. All rooms are equipped

for computer and modem hookup, as well as in-room checkout. *25070 Country Club Blvd., 44070, tel. 216/734–5060 or 800/333–3333, fax 216/734–5471. Gen. manager, Mike McCurdy. 87 singles, 46 doubles, 7 suites. AE, CB, D, DC, MC, V.*

**❸** **Residence Inn by Marriott.** Twelve separate townhouses,
**$$$** each with eight units, make up this facility created for businesspeople who need extended-stay lodgings. Hopkins Airport, the International Expo Center, the NASA compound, and the MetroParks—the huge park system that almost surrounds the city—are all within a five-minute drive. Penthouse suites offer two bathrooms, a hideaway bed in the dining room, and an upstairs bedroom. Kitchens in all units have a full range of appliances. Extras include complimentary Continental breakfast in the gatehouse, grocery shopping services, newspapers, laundry facilities, VCRs, and movie rentals. The exercise area has a pool, heated spa, and paddle tennis, basketball, and volleyball courts. *17525 Rosbough Dr., 44130, tel. 216/234–6688 or 800/331–3131, fax 216/234–3459. Gen. manager, Mark Hemmer. 52 singles, 26 doubles, 26 suites. AE, D, DC, MC, V.*

## DINING

*by Gail Ghetia*

Perhaps because Cleveland was a transplant city for many European cultures and a base for blue-collar workers, the local version of hospitality often includes generous portions and genuine ethnic cuisines.

Near downtown in the Flats is a bustling nighttime entertainment hub, with restaurants on both sides of the Cuyahoga River. Other notable restaurants are on the near West Side in the historic Ohio City and Tremont neighborhoods; and on the eastern edge of the city, in Slavic Village and the culturally diverse University Circle area.

Highly recommended restaurants in each category are indicated by a star ★ .

| Category | Cost* |
|---|---|
| *$$$$* (Very Expensive) | over $30 |
| *$$$* (Expensive) | $20–$30 |
| *$$* (Moderate) | under $20 |

*\*per person, including appetizer, entrée, and dessert, but excluding drinks, service, and 7% sales tax.*

*Numbers in the margin correspond to numbered restaurant locations on the Cleveland Lodging and Dining map.*

### Business Breakfasts

Most local businesspeople meet at small coffee shops in or near their office buildings. Adjacent to Stouffer Tower City Plaza Hotel is **The Brasserie** (24 Public Sq., tel. 216/696–5600), which opens at 6:30 AM. Breakfast meetings go upscale at **Burgess Grand Café** (tel. 216/574–2232, *see* below), which offers such specialties as orange brandied French toast, oatmeal pecan pancakes, and salmon hash.

The **Colonnade Cafeteria** (tel. 216/861–7522, *see* below) begins serving breakfast at 7AM. The **Garden Restaurant** (668 Euclid Ave., tel. 216/861–1853), in the Atrium Office Plaza, offers standard fare and daily specials from 6AM on weekdays, 7AM on Saturday. The **French Bakery & Bistro** (100 Erieview Plaza, tel. 216/241–4215), in The Galleria, has oversize muffins, fresh croissants, and delicious coffees and teas. For breakfast-to-go, try the muffins or croissants at **Hinman's at the Hoyt** (700 W. St. Clair, tel. 216/621–2202).

## Downtown

**⑭** **Colonnade Cafeteria.** The bankers and investment counse-
**$$** lors who work in the Ohio Savings Plaza find the Colonnade a perfect weekday spot for an inexpensive solo breakfast or lunch. Public Square is a leisurely 10-minute walk away. The cafeteria's three dining rooms are decorated in '50s style, with laminate tabletops, vinyl upholstery, turquoise woodwork, and flying-saucer-shaped light fixtures. There are four soups daily (one with no salt), at least eight side dishes, and no-nonsense entrées like meatloaf with mashed potatoes, and pork pepper steak with rice. Four cashier's lines keep the wait to a minimum. *Ohio Savings Plaza, 1801 E. 9th St., tel. 216/861–7522. Casual dress. No reservations. No credit cards. Closed weekends and for dinner weekdays.*

**❾** **French Connection.** Cleveland is headquarters for the
**$$$$** Stouffer Restaurant and Hotel Company, and this flagship dining room in the Stouffer Tower City Plaza Hotel (attached to Cleveland's landmark Terminal Tower) is the best they have to offer. Upholstered armchairs, intimate dining spaces, and a subdued atmosphere make this an ideal spot for a quiet business discussion. Creatively classic versions of French specialties include roast rack of lamb with artichoke hearts and potatoes boulangerie (braised with onions), fricassee of lobster with dill and cucumber, and sautéed Dover sole with capers and minced parsley. The wine list features more than 100 domestic and imported vintages. *Stouffer Tower City Plaza Hotel, 24 Public Sq., tel. 216/696–5600. Jacket and tie required. Reservations advised. AE, CB, D, MC, V.*

**⑫** **Gershwin's.** The only restaurant in the high-rise head-
**$$$** quarters of British Petroleum America draws a diverse business crowd from Public Square, the courthouse, and BPA itself. Gershwin's is usually busy, but its warmth and liveliness provide a good setting for solidifying business relationships, if not for serious discussion. New American fare is served in a trendy, three-tiered dining room with black-and-white checkerboard floor and etched glass walls. Consider starting with raw bar fare: littleneck clams, Chesapeake Bay oysters, shrimp, or snow crab claws. The eclectic menu includes pizzas, pastas, burgers, salads, and chicken and seafood dishes. The bar is a good spot for solo dining. There's a piano player in the evenings. *BP America Bldg., 200 Public Sq., tel. 216/771–4377. Jacket and tie. Reservations required. AE, D, MC, V. Closed Sun.*

**★ ⑮** **Ninth St. Grill.** A well-dressed, affluent crowd, including
**$$$** advertising and publishing people, gathers at this restaurant in The Galleria at Erieview, an upscale central city mall close to the Federal Office Building and a 15-minute

walk from Public Square. A casual, somewhat eclectic menu—including grilled seafood, chicken, and steaks, as well as pastas—is served all day. The attractive dining room has a high coffered ceiling, rose neon lighting behind sandblasted glass casts, and well-placed wall sconces and spotlights. Tables are far apart, and the high ceilings and hard surfaces make for a good noise level for privacy. Try the curry raisin bread; the Indonesian chicken satay, grilled with sweet red peppers, and dipped in a spicy peanut sauce; or the grilled chicken sandwich, marinated in olive oil, lemon, and shallots. A small but respectable selection of wines is offered by the glass. *100 Erieview Plaza, tel. 216/579–9919. Jacket and tie advised. Reservations required for 6 or more at lunch; suggested for dinner. AE, MC, V. Closed Sun.*

## Warehouse District

**❼ Burgess Grand Café.** This bright, upbeat bistro is in the
$$$$ 19th-century Burgess Grocers Building in the downtown warehouse district. Leaded glass panels and black-and-white tile floors evoke the Victorian era, but the menu—a blend of classic Italian and French, with current regional American specialties—bridges past and present. Lunch selections include such inspired combinations as linguine with poached bay scallops in lime beurre blanc with julienne of leek, tomato, and fresh chives. Dinner choices are equally flavorful, for example, the breast of chicken sautéed with sun-dried tomatoes and artichoke hearts in a porcini mushroom sauce. Burgess is near Public Square, and offers comfortable seating in booths or at well-spaced tables. This is a good place for business entertaining. After dinner, on Wednesdays, Fridays, and Saturdays, you can listen to live jazz at the bar (*see* After Hours, below). *1406 W. 6th St., tel. 216/574–2232. Jacket and tie advised. Reservations required. AE, MC, V. Closed Christmas, New Year's Day.*

## The Flats

**⓫ Jim's Steak House.** Cleveland's steak lovers know the way
$$$ to Jim's, operated by the same family for 60 years and recently restored to its 1930s splendor, complete with diffused lighting and a red-and-black zebra print carpet. Service is helpful but not obtrusive. Windows on three sides afford wonderful views of the river traffic on Collision Bend. The filet Mignon is the local favorite, but trout flown in daily, lobster, and broiled salmon are popular as well. The relaxing waterfront setting, away from the formality of downtown restaurants, makes it a good place for getting to know associates. If you call ahead, you can arrange for free van service from downtown. *1800 Scranton Rd., tel. 216/241–6343. Jacket and tie suggested. Reservations suggested. AE, D, MC, V. Closed Sun.*

**❻ Sammy's.** Energy meets elegance in this 80-seat see-and-
$$$$ be-seen restaurant in the Flats, serving Continental and American cuisine with an emphasis on regional ingredients. Sammy's neon logo makes the restaurant easy to spot; the dining room is one flight up from the entrance. The city's in-crowd gathers at this former industrial space, with exposed brick, hardwood floors, beams, and painted ductwork. Dining areas are delineated by wooden railings surrounding each level of the three-tiered space;

tables are large and well spaced, and the upholstered armchairs are comfortable. At lunch, try the grilled chicken breast with caramelized onions and melted Jarlsberg on a croissant. For dinner, there's a popular grilled loin of venison in English mustard marinade, served with braised spinach, red onion, and oven-roasted potatoes. The signature dessert is *boule de neige*, a "snowball" of whipped cream on a pastry base. The award-winning wine list has a notable selection of chardonnays. A jazz pianist performs at noon; a jazz combo plays in the evening. *1400 W. 10th St., tel. 216/523–5560. Jacket and tie suggested. Reservations advised. AE, D, DC, MC, V. Closed Sun.*

## North West Side

**⑤** **Great Lakes Brewing Co.** Microbreweries—small compa-
**$$** nies that produce and serve their own beer—are an emerging trend throughout the country, and it's easy to see why at this amiable, 150-seat brew-pub in the historic Ohio City district, about a mile west of downtown. Beer fermentation and kegging take place in the cellar dining section; large brew vats are in glass-enclosed work areas visible from the main room. The crowd in the dining area, which features lots of dark wood, ceiling fans, and planked wood flooring, is friendly to the point of rowdiness. On the pub-style menu, sausage, liverwurst, chili, and cheeses are all good choices; other popular dishes include beer-poached shrimp, Stilton cheese soup, and beef stew with a touch of beer. Adjacent to the open-air Westside Market, this is a great spot to relax after work (*see* After Hours, below). *2516 Market St., tel. 216/771–4404. Casual dress. Reservations advised. AE, D, MC, V. Closed Sun., Thanksgiving, Christmas, New Year's Day.*

**⑬** **Miracles'.** The adventurous chef in this spruced-up store-
**$$** front across from Lincoln Park in the Tremont neighborhood, only a few minutes' cab ride from downtown, produces unusual variations on ethnic themes—some more successful than others. The simple, streamlined dining room, with a few framed prints on the walls, seats about 40. This is not a place for formal business dining, but for joining locals on an adventure in ethnic dining. Try the Reuben sandwich served between two potato pancakes. Daily specials include Mexican, Middle Eastern, Polish, and vegetarian entrées, pastas, and cooked-to-order steaks. Homemade frozen custard is the favorite dessert. *2391 W. 11th St., tel. 216/621–6419. Reservations recommended. Casual dress. AE, MC, V. Closed Mon.; dinner Sun.*

## East of Downtown

**⑱** **Parker's.** Chef-owner Parker Bosley incorporates indige-
**$$$$** nous Ohio ingredients into his classic French menu, using organically grown produce and chemical-free meats. Located in Cleveland's Slavic Village, a 10–15 minute ride from downtown, this 12-table dining room is simply and soothingly decorated in grays and mauves. The quiet, formal setting and efficient but unobtrusive service make this a good place for business discussions. Corner tables near the front door are most secluded. Inspired appetizers have a seasonal slant, such as fall harvest turnip soup, or rabbit terrine seasoned with fresh rosemary. Ohio farm-raised rack of lamb is served in puff pastry, with parsnip

purée; roast duck comes with blackcurrant sauce and savoy cabbage. The seasonal dessert list is always rounded out with several lemon-flavored selections: lemon tart, lemon ice, and hot lemon soufflé are favorites. The wine list is extensive. *6802 St. Clair Ave., tel. 216/881–0700. Jacket and tie required. Reservations required. AE, MC, V. Closed Sun. Dinner only.*

## Suburbs

★ ❶  **Miller's Dining Room.** If you're into comfort food and fami-
$$  ly-style dining, make a foray into suburban Lakewood, an easy 10-mile drive west of downtown. In a freestanding white brick building with an ample parking lot set off by a decorative fence, Miller's has been serving lunch and dinner daily since 1950. Signature items include carrot salad, sticky buns, and chicken á la king served in a basket made of fried shredded potatoes. Most diners choose one of 10 daily specials, which might include meatloaf, fried lake perch, or roast turkey. The place is a bit noisy, but you wouldn't be overheard if you wanted to talk shop. Motherly waitresses bustle about a room decorated with lace curtains. The reception/waiting area has sofas, coffee tables, and a small electric organ. *16707 Detroit Ave., Lakewood, tel. 216/221–5811. Casual dress. Reservations suggested, especially on weekends. No credit cards.*

★ ❶⑨  **Z Contemporary Cuisine.** On the ground floor of an office
$$$  building in Shaker Heights, an upscale suburb about 12 miles east of downtown, Z has a minimalist interior, with predominantly off-white tones, which lets the contemporary California cuisine take the stage. Uncharacteristically for this type of restaurant, portions are large, and the serving staff is unpretentious. There are two private, glassed-in dining rooms where business conversations can be seen but not heard. The warm lettuce and three-mushroom salad with pistachios is good for a starter. Both grilled free-range chicken and grilled salmon with olive/basil sauce are excellent. A very good selection of French and California wines is available by the glass. If you have room after the complimentary chocolate truffles, try some fresh sorbet and one of the interesting dessert wines. *Tower East Office Bldg., 20600 Chagrin Blvd., Shaker Heights, tel. 216/991–1580. Jacket and tie required. Reservations required. AE, DC, MC, V. Closed Sun.; for lunch, Mon.*

## FREE TIME

## Fitness

*Hotel Facilities*
None of the hotels listed above has fitness facilities available to nonguests.

*Health Clubs*
**One to One Fitness** (2130 Adelbert Rd., tel. 216/368–1121), 15 minutes from downtown, has computerized exercise equipment and a lap pool. Downtown, **One Fitness Center, YMCA** (1375 E. 9th St., tel. 216/781–5510) has an outdoor track as well as a wide array of fitness equipment. **13th Street Racquet Club** (1901 E. 13th St., tel. 216/696–1365) has racquetball courts, squash courts, and an indoor

track. All three clubs offer day rates that vary according to the facility requested.

*Jogging*

The most scenic run downtown is a 3-mile route along **North Marginal Road,** following the Lake Erie shoreline east from East 9th Street. For longer runs through the most lush greenery in northern Ohio, follow paths in the **Cleveland Metroparks** that nearly circle the city; contact the Metroparks office (tel. 216/351–6300) for information on jogging and bike routes.

## Shopping

A new shopping mall at **Tower City** (tel. 216/771–5577) features downtown's most upscale boutiques; Neiman-Marcus is slated to open across the street, behind (just west of) the mall. Antiques shops, boutiques, and art galleries line **The Old Arcade,** which celebrated its 100th birthday in May 1990, and is the largest and most decorative of three arcades along Euclid Avenue. **The Galleria at Erieview** (tel. 216/861–4343) is another upscale shopping mall, with men's and women's fashions, and shops such as Williams-Sonoma and Banana Republic.

## Diversions

Downtown is home to a variety of **art galleries.** Collectors travel from across the country to attend auctions at the exclusive **Wolf's Gallery** (1239 W. 6th St., tel. 216/575–9653) in the Warehouse District. The **Cleveland Center for Contemporary Art** (8499 Carnegie Ave., tel. 216/421–8671) recently moved into its new, 20,000-square-foot space. **The Bonfoey Col's** (1710 Euclid Ave., 216/621–0178) displays etchings, lithographs, reproduction prints, posters, and contemporary paintings. **The Animated Art Gallery** (200 Public Sq., tel. 216/621–0330), in the BP Building, offers artistic comic relief. Wolf's, Bonfoey, and The Animated Art Gallery are within a 15-minute walk of one another.

**The Cleveland Museum of Art** (11150 East Blvd., tel. 216/421–7340) is one of the top art museums in the country, known for its Oriental art collection and its modern art holdings.

**Crawford Auto-Aviation Museum** (10825 East Blvd., tel. 216/721–5722) is home to the only remaining Chitty Bang-Bang antique auto, the first DeLorean, and several dozen other meticulously restored cars. Also in its collection is the first U.S. airmail plane.

It's a 30-minute drive to **Holden Arboretum** (9500 Sperry Rd., Kirtland, tel. 216/946–4400), a lovely 2,900-acre nature preserve with 6,000 varieties of trees, shrubs, and vines, as well as hiking and cross-country ski trails.

**NASA Lewis Research Center Visitor Center** (21000 Brookpark Rd., tel. 216/433–4000) is one of four NASA visitor centers in the country. Located on the NASA compound 20 minutes southwest of Cleveland, the center features space exploration exhibits and displays on aeronautical propulsion and solar energy. On Wednesdays there are special tours of selected research facilities in the 150-building compound.

Phase I of **North Coast Harbor** lakefront park was completed in 1988. Located at the foot of East 9th Street, the inner harbor and park hosts special events and has moorings for boats, a promenade area, and a restaurant. By 1994 (two years before Cleveland's Bicentennial), the Great Lakes Museum of Science and Technology will open here, featuring hands-on exhibits focusing on Great Lakes technology and the lake environment.

A variety of **tours** of the city and surrounding areas are available. **The Convention and Visitors Bureau of Greater Cleveland** (Terminal Tower, tel. 216/621–4110) leads 90-minute walking tours for those interested in a closer look at downtown architecture. **The Hidden City Revealed: A Walking Tour** (Committee for Public Art, 1220 W. 6th St., tel. 216/621–5330) is a free self-guided tour of Cleveland's historic Warehouse District and the city's first neighborhoods. Pick up a copy at the Development Corporation Office on the first floor of the Rockefeller Building at the corner of West 6th Street and Superior. The **Goodtime II** (E. 9th St. pier, tel. 216/861–5110) gives narrated **cruises** up the Cuyahoga River and into Lake Erie.

**Western Reserve Historical Society** (10825 East Blvd., tel. 216/721–5722) displays antique furniture and decorative arts in 20 period rooms (1770–1920). Also open to the public is the Chisholm Halle Costume Wing, a collection of 20,000 women's garments from 1750 to the present.

**West Side Market** (1729 W. 25th St., tel. 216/664–3386), built in 1912, is a fresh-food bazaar with booths selling everything from vegetables to pierogies and strudel. The structure still has its original red quarry tile floor and herringbone-patterned ceiling. The 137-square-foot clock tower, modeled after medieval Italian churches, is a beacon to shoppers.

## Professional Sports

The **Cleveland Browns** (tel. 216/696–3800) football team appears at the Cleveland Municipal Stadium. The **Cleveland Cavaliers** (tel. 216/659–9100), the city's basketball team, play at Richfield Coliseum, as do the **Cleveland Crunch** (tel. 216/349–2090), the town's soccer team. The baseball club, the **Cleveland Indians** (tel. 216/861–1200), plays at the Municipal Stadium.

## The Arts

**Severance Hall** is the home of Cleveland's world-renowned Cleveland Orchestra. **DanceCleveland** in Playhouse Square is the base for the nationally recognized Cleveland Ballet. Classical and modern drama are performed at the three-theater **Cleveland Play House** on the near East Side. Traveling Broadway shows, concerts, and other performances are featured year-round at both the **Hanna Theater** and **Playhouse Square theaters**. Great Lakes Theater Festival specializes in Shakespeare. **Karamu House Theatre** features contemporary drama. For pop and rock concerts, the outdoor **Nautica stage** in the Flats hosts top-name performers; downtown, the **Music Hall** and the **Cleveland Public Auditorium,** part of the Cleveland Convention Center complex, cater to the same audiences.

Tickets are available through **Ticketron** (6701 Rockside Rd., tel. 216/524–0000 or 800/225–7337) or by calling locations listed below. Ticketron outlets are also located at May Company department stores, Public Hall, and The Galleria.

**Cleveland Play House** (includes the Bolton, Brooks and Drury theaters), 8500 Euclid Ave., tel. 216/765–7000.

**Cleveland Public Auditorium,** 1200 E. 6th St., tel. 216/348–2229.

**DanceCleveland,** 1422 Euclid Ave., Suite 611, tel. 216/861–2213.

**Great Lakes Theater Festival,** 1501 Euclid Ave., tel. 216/771–3999.

**Hanna Theater,** 2067 E. 14th St., tel. 216/621–5000.

**Karamu House Theatre,** 2355 E. 89th St., tel. 216/795–7070.

**Music Hall,** 1220 E. 6th St., tel. 216/348–2229.

**Nautica,** west bank in the Flats, tel. 216/247–2722.

**Playhouse Square** (includes Ohio, Palace, and State theaters), 1519 Euclid Ave., tel. 216/241–6000.

**Severance Hall,** 11001 Euclid Ave., tel. 216/231–1111.

## After Hours

The Flats is the hottest area in Cleveland, with dance clubs, fine dining, and patio bars along the Cuyahoga River. On the west bank, evening entertainment options include the **Nautica** stage with classical, jazz, rock, and pop performances during the summer, and the newly renovated **Powerhouse** complex with restaurants, shops, and **The Improv** comedy hall. During summer months, the outdoor **Party in the Park** music series, sponsored by the Greater Cleveland Growth Association, is held at a rotating schedule of downtown parks.

*Bars and Lounges*
In central downtown, sophisticated **Gershwin's** (200 Public Sq., tel. 216/771–4377) is a good place for business talks. **Getty's** (1422 Euclid Ave., tel. 216/771–1818), in downtown's Playhouse Square neighborhood, is also quiet and upscale; its clientele is mostly businesspeople. The lounge at the **Haymarket Restaurant** behind Tower City (123 Prospect Ave. NW, tel. 216/241–4220), located in an old bank vault, is another sophisticated spot for unwinding. In warm weather, the al fresco lounge at the **Watermark** (1250 Old River Rd., in the Flats, tel. 216/241–1600) offers sophisticated drinking and dining on the banks of the Cuyahoga River. The noisy **Roxy Bar and Grill** (1900 E. 9th St., tel. 216/523–5580), upscale **Ninth Street Grill** (Galleria, 1301 E. 9th St., tel. 216/579–9919), and **Sweetwater's Cafe Sausalito** (Galleria, 1301 E. 9th St., tel. 216/696–2233) supply neon and plenty of company during happy hour, especially Fridays after 6 PM. Just west of the city, the **Great Lakes Brewing Co.** (tel. 216/771–4404), Cleveland's only brew-pub, is less crowded and the beer is always fresh. For more of a shot-and-beer atmosphere, raunchier and less upscale, try **Flat Iron Café** (1114 Center St., tel. 216/696–6968) and **Harbor Inn Café** (1219 Main Ave., tel. 216/241–3232), both on the west bank of the Flats.

## Comedy Clubs

**Hilarities Comedy Club,** in the historic Warehouse District (1230 W. 6th St., tel. 216/781–7733), features both well-known comics and newcomers. Scheduling for comics appearing at **The Improv** in the Powerhouse (2000 Sycamore, tel. 216/696–4677) is handled by the main Improv in Los Angeles; comics appearing here are big names.

## Jazz Clubs

**Fulton Avenue Café** (1835 Fulton Ave., tel. 216/522–1835), located on the near West Side, is open nightly for jazz, blues, and reggae. **Club Isabella** (2025 Abington Rd., tel. 216/229–1177) in University Circle, about 15 minutes east of downtown, features jazz performers, Monday–Saturday. The classiest jazz setting is at **Burgess Grand Café** (tel. 216/574–2232).

## For Singles

The Flats is the most popular destination for singles. Dance clubs, including **Club Coconuts** (1148 Main Ave., tel. 216/579–9960), **The Beach Club** (1064 Old River Rd., tel. 216/241–1587), and **Cleveland Playdium** (1001 Front Ave., tel. 216/579–9717) cater to a young crowd, especially on weekends. **Aquilon** (1575 Merwin Ave., tel. 216/781–1575) is known for more sophisticated (though never quiet) dancing and cocktails—not a club for the denim crowd. **Shooters** (1148 Main Ave., tel. 216/861–6900) is a restaurant and bar popular with singles, couples, and families alike. At any Flats club or restaurant, expect a mob scene on weekends.

# Dallas/Fort Worth

*by Jeff Siegel*

Dallas is neither the cowtown depicted in numerous Western movies, nor the cutthroat oil town of the "Dallas" TV series.

Founded as an Indian trading post in 1841, it was settled in 1855 by a group of French, Belgians, and Swiss, who came with dreams of a Utopian colony that never quite worked out. But the culture they brought helped transform the frontier town into the modern metropolis it is today.

Fort Worth, by contrast, was a major cattle-drive point in the last century, and it retains a good deal of the down-home friendliness of a Western frontier town. During the westward expansion, a garrison was based here to protect settlers; although it was never a fortress, it was later named Fort Worth for Gen. William Worth, a hero of the Mexican War.

As the Southwestern economy collapsed in the second half of the 1980s, the Metroplex (the local term for Dallas, Fort Worth, and the area between them) seemed to be riding out the storm. But instead of learning from the mistakes made in Houston and New Orleans, the area's bankers continued to lend money to the area's real estate developers, who continued to build. The result? Major, locally owned banks and savings and loans were wiped out, and the construction industry floundered.

The key to recovery, local leaders say, lies in how carefully the government manages all of its foreclosed properties. How the volatile situation in the Gulf will impact on Texas's economy is also for the future to determine. In the meantime, several major national companies have moved to the area in the past few years—Exxon to Las Colinas, J.C. Penney to Richardson, and GTE to Irving—and that has helped the economy.

## Top Employers

| Employer | Type of Enterprise | Parent*/ Headquarters |
|---|---|---|
| **AMR Corp.** | Airlines | Fort Worth |
| **Burlington Northern** | Transportation | Dallas |

| Dresser Industries | Oil field services | Dallas |
|---|---|---|
| Electronic Data Systems | Computers | Dallas |
| Halliburton Industries | Oil | Dallas |
| J.C. Penney | Retailer | Dallas |
| LTV | Holding company | Dallas |
| Kimberly-Clark | Consumer goods | Irving, TX |
| Texas Instruments | Computers | Dallas |
| Texas Utilities | Utilities | Dallas |

*if applicable*

## ESSENTIAL INFORMATION

### Climate

What follows are the average daily maximum and minimum temperatures for Dallas and Fort Worth.

| Jan. | 56F | 13C | Feb. | 61F | 16C | Mar. | 67F | 19C |
|---|---|---|---|---|---|---|---|---|
| | 36 | 2 | | 40 | 4 | | 47 | 8 |
| Apr. | 76F | 24C | May | 83F | 28C | June | 90F | 32C |
| | 56 | 13 | | 63 | 17 | | 72 | 22 |
| July | 94F | 34C | Aug. | 94F | 34C | Sept. | 88F | 31C |
| | 76 | 24 | | 74 | 23 | | 68 | 20 |
| Oct. | 79F | 26C | Nov. | 67F | 19C | Dec. | 58F | 14C |
| | 58 | 14 | | 47 | 8 | | 38 | 3 |

### Airports

**Dallas-Fort Worth International** (DFW), with its Airtrans intraterminal subway system, is the main airport for both cities. DFW is 13 miles northwest of downtown Dallas and 17 miles northeast of downtown Fort Worth. Try to avoid changing planes at DFW if it means transferring between any of the five terminals. The Airtrans trains are inconvenient at best, and the walk is always too long, particularly with luggage.

Dallas' **Love Field,** six miles from downtown, is smaller and more convenient for Dallas passengers, but it is serviced only by Southwest. (Continental has received federal permission, but hasn't started service as of press time.) **Suburban Addison Airport,** 14 miles north of downtown Dallas, is a major commuter and general aviation facility.

### Airport Business Facilities

The **Hyatt** (near the American Airlines terminal, tel. 214/453–1234) has fax machines, photocopying, a fitness center, and day rates for rooms with bed, desk, and telephone.

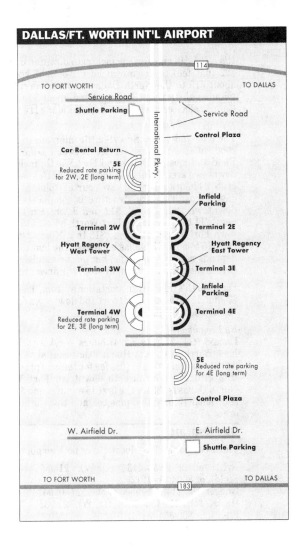

## DALLAS/FT. WORTH INT'L AIRPORT

114

TO FORT WORTH · TO DALLAS

Service Road

Shuttle Parking

International Pkwy.

Service Road

Control Plaza

Car Rental Return

**5E**
Reduced rate parking
for 2W, 2E (long term)

Infield
Parking

Terminal 2W · Terminal 2E

Hyatt Regency
West Tower

Hyatt Regency
East Tower

Terminal 3W · Terminal 3E

Infield
Parking

Terminal 4W · Terminal 4E
Reduced rate parking
for 2E, 3E (long term)

**5E**
Reduced rate parking
for 4E (long term)

Control Plaza

W. Airfield Dr. · E. Airfield Dr.

Shuttle Parking

TO FORT WORTH · TO DALLAS
183

## Airlines

Dallas-Fort Worth International is a major hub for American Airlines (the airline's headquarters are a mile and a half away); Love Field is home to Southwest.

**American,** tel. 214/267–1151 or 800/433–7300.
**Continental,** tel. 214/263–0523 or 800/525–0280.
**Delta,** tel. 214/630–3200 or 800/221–1212.
**Southwest,** tel. 214/640–1221 or 800/531–5601.

## Between the Airports and Downtown

The trip from Dallas-Fort Worth International and downtown Dallas and Fort Worth takes 20–40 minutes, depending on rush-hour (6:30 AM–8:30 AM and 4 PM–6:30 PM) conditions.

*By Taxi*

It's a $25 cab ride (on the meter) to downtown Dallas and $22 (flat fee) to downtown Fort Worth. Expect to pay about $15 to the North Dallas business corridor (10–20 minutes along the LBJ Fwy.) and about $10 to the Las Colinas office sprawl (10–20 minutes along Hwy. 114).

*By Bus*

The blue-and-yellow **SuperShuttle** minivans (tel. 817/329–2000) offer scheduled service between DFW and Love Field and most of Dallas and Fort Worth, including both downtown areas, North Dallas, and Las Colinas. They operate 24 hours a day and have courtesy phones at the baggage areas. The fare structure is complicated: $10 to a downtown Dallas hotel, $12 to a downtown Dallas business, $11 to a downtown Fort Worth hotel, $18 to a downtown Fort Worth business, $12 to a North Dallas hotel, and $15 to a North Dallas business. The length of the trip depends not only on traffic, but on the number of passengers in the van and how many stops the driver has to make.

Fort Worth's public transportation system, The T, offers a $7 shuttle between the airport and downtown from 5 AM to 10 PM. The trip takes about an hour.

*By Limousine*

**Limaxi** (tel. 214/748–6294) offers service to Dallas and Fort Worth in stretch Hondas that seat six. The fare to downtown Dallas is $35 (flat fee for the car) plus $2 toll and 20% gratuity. The fare to downtown Fort Worth and North Dallas is $35 for the first 15 minutes and $10 for each additional 15 minutes, plus toll and tip. Corporate rates are available.

## Car Rentals

These companies have locations at both airports.

**Avis,** tel. 214/574–4130 (DFW), 214/357–0301 (Love Field), or 800/331–1212.
**Budget,** tel. 214/871–9500 or 800/527–0700.
**Hertz,** tel. 214/453–0370 (DFW), 214/350–7071 (Love Field), or 800/654–3131.
**National,** tel. 214/574–3400 (DFW), 214/357–0478 (Love Field), or 800/227–7368.

These companies have locations near both airports, and operate shuttle services between the terminals and their sites.

**Enterprise,** tel. 214/986–1890 (DFW), 214/358–8831 (Love Field), or 800/325–8007.
**Snappy,** tel. 817/577–2655 (DFW), 214/357–8167 (Love Field), or 800/321–7159.
**Thrifty,** tel. 214/929–1320 (DFW) or 214/357–2821 (Love Field).

## Emergencies

**Prologue** (tel. 214/256–2283 or 800/362–8677) is a free referral service for doctors and dentists.

*Doctors*

**PrimaCare** (tel. 214/263–0190) has 16 clinics, open 8 AM–10 PM daily.

*Dentists*

**Horizon Dental Centers** has several locations in Dallas County (downtown Dallas, tel. 214/720–7770) and six in Tarrant County (east Fort Worth, tel. 817/451–8825). **The Dallas County Dental Society** (tel. 214/654–7367) provides emergency service after 5 PM and on weekends. **The Fort Worth District Dental Society** (tel. 817/924–7111) offers 24-hour emergency service.

*Hospitals*

**Baylor University Medical Center** (3500 Gaston Ave., Dallas, tel. 214/820–0111) is five minutes from downtown. **Humana Hospital Medical City Dallas** (7777 Forest La., Dallas, tel. 214/661–7000) is in the heart of the North Dallas corridor. **All Saints Episcopal Hospital** (1400 8th Ave., Fort Worth, tel. 817/926–2544) is five minutes from downtown.

## Important Addresses and Numbers

**Audiovisual rentals.** AVW Audio Visual (2233 Irving Blvd., Dallas, tel. 214/638–0024), J&S Audio Visual Communications (4407 Beltwood Pkwy. N., No. 112, Dallas, tel. 214/239–9133), Texas Audio Visuals (1822 N. Sylvania Ave., Fort Worth, tel. 817/831–3116).

**Chambers of Commerce.** Dallas Chamber of Commerce (1201 Elm St., Suite 2000, Dallas, tel. 214/746–6600), North Dallas Chamber of Commerce (10707 Preston Rd., Dallas, tel. 214/368–6486), Fort Worth Chamber of Commerce (777 Taylor St., Fort Worth, tel. 817/336–2491).

**Computer rentals.** First National Computer (4843 Keller Springs Rd., Dallas, tel. 214/380–8700), InfoRent (5001 Infomart, Dallas, tel. 214/746–5030), Computer Store (2700-B W. Berry St., Fort Worth, tel. 817/924–7772).

**Convention and exhibition centers.** Dallas Convention Center (650 S. Griffin St., Dallas, tel. 214/658–7000), Dallas Market Center (2100 Stemmons Fwy., Dallas, tel. 214/655–6100), Infomart (1950 Stemmons Fwy., Dallas, tel. 214/746–3500), Reunion Arena (777 Sport St., Dallas, tel. 214/658–7070), Tarrant County Convention Center (1111 Houston St., Fort Worth, tel. 817/332–9222), Will Rogers Memorial Center (330 W. Lancaster St., Fort Worth, tel. 817/870–8150).

**Fax services.** ActionFax (6390 LBJ Fwy., Dallas, tel. 214/661–2913), Alphagraphics (Renaissance Tower, Dallas, tel. 214/698–0556; 777 Main St., Fort Worth, tel. 817/870–2660).

**Formal-wear rentals.** Culwell & Son (13020 Preston Rd., Dallas, tel. 214/661–8282), Al's Formal Wear (315 Throckmorton St., Fort Worth, tel. 817/335–9493).

**Gift shops.** Chocolates: Godiva Chocolatier (73 Highland Park Ave., Dallas, tel. 214/559–0397; 13350 Dallas Pkwy., Dallas, tel. 214/458–1821), Russel Stover (800 Houston St., Fort Worth, tel. 817/332–3434); Florists: Liland's (2101 Abrahms Rd., Dallas, tel. 214/823–9505), John A. Winters (1021 N. Sylvania Ave., Fort Worth, tel. 817/831–1281.

**Graphic design studios.** The Artwerks Group (6116 N. Central Exp., Dallas, tel. 214/361–7750), Laser Publications (5005 Birch Hollow La., Fort Worth, tel. 817/294–7107).

**Hairstylists.** Unisex: Toni & Guy (443 North Park Center, Dallas, tel. 214/750–0067), Skiles (Tandy Center, Fort Worth, tel. 817/870–2588).

**Health and fitness clubs.** *See* Fitness, below.

**Limousine services.** Dallas-Fort Worth Limousines (tel. 817/467–5355), Limaxi (tel. 214/748–6294).

**Liquor stores.** Marty's (3316 Oak Lawn Ave., Dallas, tel. 214/526–7796), Sigel's (5757 Greenville Ave., Dallas, tel. 214/739–4012), Majestic (4520 Camp Bowie Blvd., Fort Worth, tel. 817/731–0634).

**Mail delivery, overnight.** DHL (tel. 214/471–1999, Dallas) Federal Express (tel. 214/358–5271, Dallas; tel. 817/332–6293, Fort Worth; or 800/238–5355), Purolator (tel. 800/645–3333), TNT Skypack (tel. 214/929–8720, Dallas), U.S. Postal Service Express Mail (tel. 214/760–4640, Dallas; tel. 817/625–3616, Fort Worth).

**Messenger service.** Dial-A-Messenger (tel. 214/630–2921, Dallas; tel. 214/263–1316, Fort Worth).

**Office space rentals.** Executive Suites of Dallas (1440 W. Mockingbird La., Suite 205, Dallas, tel. 214/634–4428), Fort Worth Executive Center (Fort Worth Club Tower, Fort Worth, tel. 817/336–0800).

**Pharmacies, late-night.** Eckerd Drugs (7028 Greenville Ave., Dallas, tel. 214/369–3706; 2414 Jacksboro Hwy., Fort Worth, tel. 817/626–8255).

**Radio stations, all news.** KRLD 1080AM; KDBN 1480AM, business news.

**Secretarial services.** Parkway Professional Suites (5050 Quorum Dr., Suite 700, Dallas, tel. 214/980–4126), Professional Suites (1700 Pacific Ave., Dallas, tel. 214/922–9888), Summit Secretarial Services (307 W. 7th St., Suite 1800, Fort Worth, tel. 817/332–7096).

**Stationery supplies.** Bizmart (2998 Stemmons Fwy., Dallas, tel. 214/637–6110; 6732 Camp Bowie, Fort Worth, tel. 817/732–1503).

**Taxis.** Executive Taxi (tel. 214/554–1212, Dallas and Mid-Cities), Terminal Taxi (tel. 214/350–4445, Dallas), American Taxi Cab (tel. 817/429–8829, Fort Worth).

**Theater tickets.** *See* The Arts, below.

**Train information.** Amtrak, Dallas (Union Station, 400 S. Houston Ave., tel. 214/653–1101 or 800/872–7245), Amtrak, Fort Worth (Union Station, 1601 Jones St., tel. 817/334–0268 or 800/872–7245).

**Travel agents.** Maritz Travel (11353 Emerald St., Dallas, tel. 214/484–1010), Travel Service Everywhere (306 Main St., Fort Worth, tel. 817/332–7434 or 800/433–5703).

**Weather** (tel. 214/787–1111).

# LODGING

The Dallas-Fort Worth area has not one central business district but four: downtown Fort Worth, downtown Dallas, North Dallas, and Las Colinas. Real estate business might bring you to any of these locales. Downtown Dallas also has banking and oil service–related firms, while North Dallas, which runs east–west along LBJ Freeway, about 10 miles north of downtown, has a concentration of the city's high-tech industry. Fort Worth is home to a number of investment concerns. A good many banks are sited in the planned Las Colinas development, located midway between Dallas and the Dallas Fort Worth International Airport; this area has more office space than any Texas city except Dallas and Houston.

With the exception of the Mansion on Turtle Creek, all the hotels listed below offer corporate rates and weekend discounts; inquire when making reservations.

Highly recommended lodgings in each price category are indicated by a star ★ .

| Category | Cost* |
| --- | --- |
| $$$$ (Very Expensive) | over $175 |
| $$$ (Expensive) | $111–$175 |
| $$ (Moderate) | under $111 |

*All prices are for a standard double room, single occupancy, excluding 13% tax.*

*Numbers in the margin correspond to numbered hotel locations on the Dallas and Fort Worth Lodging and Dining maps.*

## Downtown and Near Downtown Dallas

★ ❷⓿ **Adolphus Hotel.** This old-fashioned hotel has been a fix-
$$$$ ture in the heart of downtown for more than 75 years, and remains the place of choice for visitors who care about charm and class. A complete renovation a few years ago restored much of its turn-of-the-century comfort, luxury, and service. Guests range from celebrities like rocker Tom Petty to visiting oil executives. The most elegant rooms include four-poster beds and original art. Most rooms have a refrigerator and a second phone in the bathroom. The hotel offers a variety of advantages: a central location minutes from anything of importance downtown; complimentary limousine service anywhere downtown; and complete in-house audiovisual services. There's also one of Dallas's most highly rated (and expensive) restaurants, The French Room. Suites cost more than $1,000 a night. *1321 Commerce St., 75202, tel. 214/742–8200; 800/221–9083; in Texas, 800/441–0574; fax 214/747–3532. Gen. manager, Jeff Trigger. 413 rooms, 21 suites. AE, CB, MC, V.*

❷❺ **Fairmont Hotel.** The Dallas outpost of the ritzy national
$$$$ chain attracts everyone from society matrons, who like being next door to the Dallas Museum of Art, to visiting stockbrokers, who like the Fairmont's four-star touches. The two-tower building (one tower is 24 stories high, the other 19), which occupies a city block on the northwest edge of downtown, underwent a multimillion dollar reno-

vation in the past few years, and every room was refurbished and modernized in earth tones. The ornate lobby features plush carpeting and bright wall hangings. The Fairmont is now considered to be on par with the Adolphus. The Pyramid Room is noted for its Continental cuisine. The Venetian Room, a supper club, features live music. *1717 N. Akard St., 75201. tel. 214/720-2020 or 800/527-4727, fax 214/720-5269. Gen. manager, Rolf Schraegle. 500 rooms, 50 suites. AE, CB, DC, MC, V.*

★ **㉙** **Hyatt Regency Dallas at Reunion.** This 50-story glass-and-
$$$ steel tower with the tennis ball on top is one of the tallest buildings in the city, and has become a recognizable part of Dallas's skyline. On a clear day, the view from the revolving lounge at the top of the ball extends past Fort Worth. Rooms, furnished in earth tones, are a step up from those in most Hyatts, and each one has a view of the waterfalls in the atrium. The on-site shops, arranged in bazaarlike fashion throughout the entire building, are as good as any in Dallas. The hotel is adjacent to Reunion Arena, home of the NBA's Dallas Mavericks and host to conventions and special events (which means guests can range from rowdy conventioneers to conservative church groups). On the negative side, the Hyatt is tucked on the southwestern edge of downtown, six blocks from the city center, and the neighborhood is not a good place to wander after dark. *300 Reunion Blvd., 75207, tel. 214/651-1234 or 800/228-9000, fax 214/742-8126. Gen. manager, Todd Martin. 943 rooms. AE, MC, V.*

**㉗** **Loews Anatole.** This plush, modern hotel is one of the best
$$$$ examples of what Dallas was like in the 1980s, when insolvent was never used in the same sentence with savings and loan. Both Ronald Reagan (during the 1984 Republican convention) and Bruce Springsteen (during his "Born in the USA" tour) stayed here. The Anatole's lobby/atrium is all glass, chrome, and tile. The hotel gets tonier— some would say more ostentatious—from there. Rooms on the concierge floor feature Continental breakfast, free use of the hotel's health clubs, and complimentary cocktails. Rooms have separate sitting areas with desks; many have two phones. The location on the city's trade-show corridor, minutes from convention locations and a 10-minute cab ride from downtown, is a plus. The neighborhood on the west side of the hotel is not the best. *2201 Stemmons Fwy., 75207, tel. 214/748-1200 or 800/223-0888, fax 214/761-7242. Gen. manager, John Thacker. 1,475 rooms, 145 suites. AE, CB, DC, MC, V.*

**㉘** **The Mansion on Turtle Creek.** The Mansion, built as a pala-
$$$$ tial private home, serves as a lobby and restaurant to an adjoining, nine-story tower in a quiet residential neighborhood about 10 minutes from downtown. The staff's reputation for service is legendary, and tales abound of the extraordinary lengths to which employees go for the cadre of regular guests. If you're not a regular, though, the service can be abrupt. All rooms, decorated in Southwestern colors, open onto balconies or private patios; bathrooms are fitted with Italian marble. The lobby boasts antique furnishings, paintings, and sculpture. This is where the rich and powerful stay, from cotton and oil barons to world celebrities. The hotel's restaurant serves innovative Southwestern cuisine, and is also a good place for business breakfasts (*see* Dining, below). *A Rosewood ho-*

# GREATER DALLAS

**Lodging**

Dallas Parkway Hilton, **11**

D-FW Hilton Executive Conference Center, **1**

Doubletree at Lincoln Center, **13**

Embassy Suites DFW Airport, **3**

Four Seasons Hotel and Resort, **5**

Grand Kempinski Dallas, **8**

Hyatt Regency DFW, **2**

Marriott Mandalay at Los Colinas, **6**

Marriott Quorum, **9**

Westin Galleria, **12**

**Dining**

Blue Mesa Grill, **10**

Cacheral, **4**

Celebration, **15**

Gershwin's, **14**

May Dragon, **7**

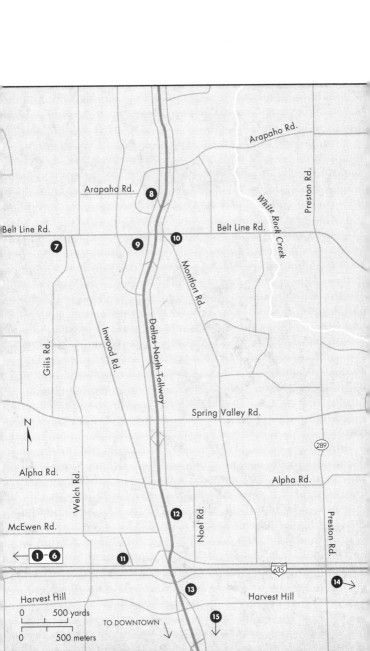

# DOWNTOWN DALLAS

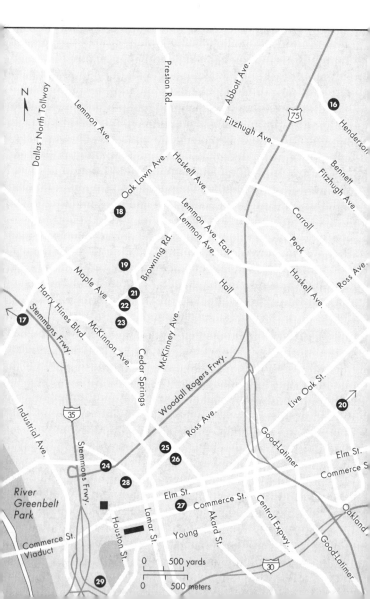

*tel. 2821 Turtle Creek Blvd., 75219, tel. 214/559–2100 or 800/223–6800, fax 214/528–4187. Gen. manager, Philip Wood. 128 rooms, 14 suites. AE, CB, DC, MC, V.*

**㉓** **Stoneleigh Hotel.** In the mid-1980s, this former luxury
**$$$** apartment hotel underwent its first renovation in almost 30 years. The lobby's original brass chandeliers, parquet floor, and marble columns were restored, and rooms were comfortably refurnished in tasteful tones of green and brown. Today, the Stoneleigh looks much like many of the small, well-appointed hotels that dot New York's best neighborhoods. It's in the Turtle Creek section, a 10-minute cab ride from downtown or the Market Center corridor, and just blocks away from the McKinney Avenue shopping and restaurant district. What the Stoneleigh lacks in business services it makes up for in comfort. The rooms are bigger than those in most chain hotels, and many have living rooms and kitchens. *2927 Maple Ave., 75201, tel. 214/871–7111; 800/255–9299; in Texas; 800/336–4242; fax 214/871–7111, ext. 1213. Gen. manager, Gary Bruton. 140 rooms, 10 suites. AE, MC, V.*

## North Dallas

**⓫** **Dallas Parkway Hilton.** This 15-story stucco building is
**$$** tucked away behind some service roads, next to an auto dealership. The building is a startling shade of pink, but it's one of the few places in North Dallas where you can get a reasonably priced room. Lobby and rooms are standard Hilton. Colors are assembly-line hues of pink, tan, and beige, and furniture seems flimsy. The hotel business center (open weekdays 8 AM–5 PM) handles most secretarial services. Amenities on the Hilton Club Floor include free local phone calls. Guests can purchase temporary membership to the International Athletic Club, a few blocks north, for $7. *4801 LBJ Fwy., 75244, tel. 214/661–3600 or 800/445–8667, fax 214/385–3156. Gen. manager, Mike Meehan. 296 rooms, 13 suites. AE, CB, DC, MC, V.*

**⓭** **Doubletree at Lincoln Centre.** The former Lincoln Hotel,
**$$$** on the south side of the LBJ Freeway and east of the Dallas North Tollway, is a convenient base for shopping and doing business. The tinted glass-and-steel building is attached to the three-tower Lincoln Centre office complex by skyways. It's fancier now than when it was the Lincoln, and room rates have risen accordingly. The spacious, high-ceiling lobby overlooks a lake. Rooms are on the small side, though, and the furniture is standard hotel issue—thinly padded arms on the chairs and inexpensively constructed desks and tables. Guests can purchase a temporary membership for the health club facilities in the Lincoln City Club in the adjacent complex. The hotel restaurant, Crockett's, handles Southwestern cuisine respectably. *5410 LBJ Fwy., 75240, tel. 214/934–8400 or 800/528–0444, fax 214/701–5244. Gen. manager, Joe Palmieri. 509 rooms, 21 suites. AE, MC, V.*

**★ ⑧** **Grand Kempinski Dallas.** This 15-story establishment (the
**$$$$** former Registry Hotel) might be the best business hotel in North Dallas; it's certainly the most impressive. Owned by Lufthansa's hotel division, this luxury hostelry is maintained with Teutonic efficiency. It's a blend of the European grand hotel tradition and Southwestern high tech, with a large marble-tile lobby, a business center, and a health club with better equipment than that of many pri-

# FORT WORTH

**Lodging**
Hilton Fort Worth, **36**
Green Oaks Inn, **30**
Worthington Hotel, **34**

**Dining**
Joe T. Garcia's, **33**
Saint-Emilion, **31**
Tours, **32**
Winfield '08's, **35**

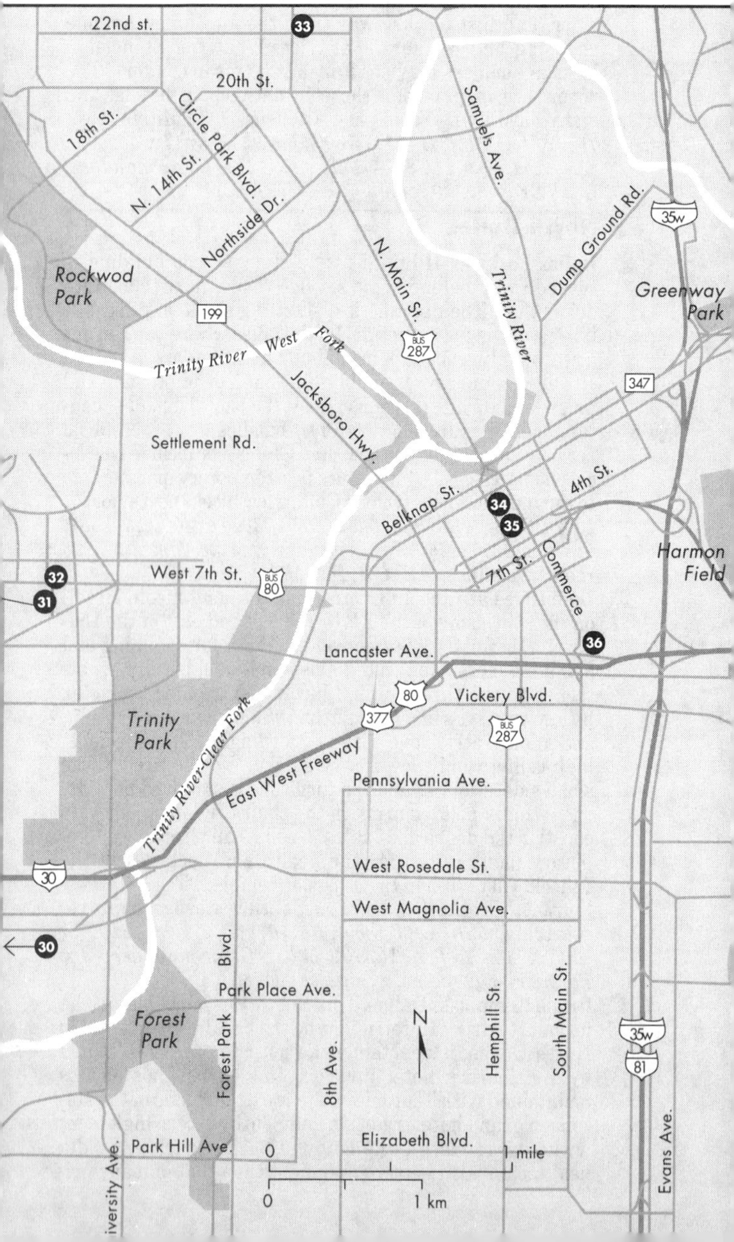

vate facilities. In addition to the usual secretarial services, the business center includes extensive audiovisual services. On the concierge floors (14 and 15) each room has three phones and fresh flowers. *15201 Dallas Pkwy., 75248, tel. 214/386–6000; 800/527–1690; in Texas, 800/442–2039, fax 214/991–6937. Gen. manager, Michael Spencer. 492 rooms, 37 suites. AE, DC, MC, V.*

**❾** **Marriott Quorum.** This seven-year-old Marriott property
**$$$** fits in nicely with the other glass-and-steel buildings along the Dallas North Parkway. The 12-story hotel finished a room renovation program in 1989. The lobby, a mix of off-white marble and natural wood, isn't as big as many others in North Dallas. Rooms are standard issue, outfitted in shades of green and mauve; king corner accommodations are most spacious. The hotel is just south of Belt Line Road, convenient to both Prestonwood Town Center and The Galleria, and right around the corner from the bars and restaurants that line Belt Line Road in Dallas and Addison. The hotel's nightclub is popular with the younger, professional crowd that stays at the Quorum, and many of the guests are lawyers and real estate developers who do business in the silver towers along the Parkway. *14901 Dallas Pkwy., Addison, 75240, tel. 214/661–2800 or 800/228–9290, fax 214/934–1731. Gen. manager, Stephen Benkowitz. 537 rooms, 10 suites. AE, MC, V.*

**⓬** **Westin Galleria.** The 21-story Westin helped pioneer a tru-
**$$$** ly Dallas concept—the hotel/shopping mall. It's one of the anchors at The Galleria, where Macy's is the most downscale department store. There's a mall entrance on the second floor of the hotel, near the meeting rooms. It's not the swankiest spot in North Dallas, and it's starting to fray at the far edges. The lobby, for instance, is surprisingly small, and checking out can take time on busy days. Rooms are small, too, but the location, right in the middle of the North Dallas business center, couldn't be better. *13340 Dallas Pkwy., Addison, 75240, tel. 214/934–9494 or 800/228–3000, fax 214/851–2869. Gen. manager, Steve Shalit. 417 rooms, 14 suites. AE, DC, MC, V.*

## DFW International Airport/Las Colinas

**❶** **D-FW Hilton Executive Conference Center.** This is the
**$$$** loneliest hotel in the Dallas-Fort Worth area, isolated in a prairie 2½ miles north of DFW International Airport. Rooms are standard Hilton, but the business and recreational facilities are outstanding—an amphitheater, a 14,000-square-foot exhibit hall, teleconferencing and satellite capabilities, 24-hour access to audiovisual services, a two-level fitness center with tennis and racquetball courts, and even an affiliation with the neighboring Austin Ranch for Texas-style entertainment and parties. Hilton has made an effort to deal with the hotel's remote location; there is a free shuttle service to the airport, and rental cars can be picked up and dropped off at a site at the hotel. Still, don't get any cravings for pizza late at night. *Box 759, Grapevine, 76051, tel. 817/481–8444 or 800/645–1019, fax 817/481–3160. Gen. manager, Juan Aquinde. 411 rooms. AE, CB, DC, MC, V.*

**★ ❸** **Embassy Suites DFW Airport.** This goofy-looking hotel—
**$$** it has a cupola, and extended eaves—is one of the best business values in the Dallas-Fort Worth area. Functional rather than fancy, it features a prime location at the south

# DALLAS/FORT WORTH

| HOTELS | Price Category | Business Services / Banquet capacity | No. of meeting rooms | Secretarial services | Audiovisual equipment | Teletype news service | Computer rentals | In-room modem phone jack | All-news cable channel | Desk | Desk lighting | Bed lighting |
|---|---|---|---|---|---|---|---|---|---|---|---|---|
| **Adolphus** | $$$$ | 750 | 17 | ✓ | ✓ | - | ✓ | ✓ | ✓ | ◐ | ● | ● |
| **Dallas Parkway Hilton** | $$ | 450 | 23 | ✓ | ✓ | - | ✓ | ✓ | ✓ | ● | ◐ | ◐ |
| **DFW Hilton Executive Conference Center** | $$$ | 900 | 30 | ✓ | ✓ | - | - | ✓ | ✓ | ● | ◐ | ◐ |
| **Doubletree at Lincoln Centre** | $$$ | 1200 | 21 | ✓ | ✓ | - | - | ✓ | ✓ | ● | ● | ◐ |
| **Embassy Suites DFW Airport** | $$ | 400 | 10 | ✓ | ✓ | - | - | - | ✓ | ● | ● | ◐ |
| **Fairmont** | $$$$ | 180 | 24 | ✓ | ✓ | - | ✓ | ✓ | ✓ | ◐ | ◐ | ◐ |
| **Four Seasons Hotel and Resort** | $$$ | 300 | 26 | ✓ | ✓ | - | ✓ | ✓ | ✓ | ● | ◐ | ◐ |
| **Grand Kempinski** | $$$$ | 3000 | 22 | ✓ | ✓ | - | - | ✓ | ✓ | ● | ● | ◐ |
| **Green Oaks Inn** | $$ | 450 | 16 | - | ✓ | - | - | - | ✓ | ● | ◐ | ◐ |
| **Hilton Fort Worth** | $$ | 600 | 15 | ✓ | ✓ | - | - | - | ✓ | ◐ | ◐ | ◐ |
| **Hyatt Regency Dallas at Reunion** | $$$ | 3000 | 12 | ✓ | ✓ | ✓ | - | ✓ | ✓ | ● | ● | ◐ |
| **Hyatt Regency DFW** | $$$ | 1800 | 80 | ✓ | ✓ | - | - | ✓ | ✓ | ● | ● | ● |
| **Loews Anatole** | $$$$ | 3600 | 80 | ✓ | ✓ | ✓ | ✓ | ✓ | ✓ | ● | ● | ● |
| **The Mansion on Turtle Creek** | $$$$ | 145 | 5 | ✓ | ✓ | - | ✓ | ✓ | ✓ | ● | ● | ● |
| **Marriott Mandalay at Las Colinas** | $$$$ | 450 | 14 | - | ✓ | - | - | ✓ | ✓ | ● | ◐ | ◐ |
| **Marriott Quorum** | $$$ | 700 | 10 | ✓ | ✓ | - | ✓ | ✓ | ✓ | ● | ◐ | ◐ |
| **Stoneleigh** | $$$ | 230 | 3 | ✓ | ✓ | - | - | ✓ | ✓ | ◐ | ● | ◐ |
| **Westin Galleria** | $$$ | 1690 | 20 | - | ✓ | - | - | ✓ | ✓ | ● | ● | ◐ |
| **The Worthington** | $$$ | 950 | 17 | - | ✓ | - | - | - | ✓ | ◐ | ◐ | ◐ |

**$$$$** = over $175, **$$$** = $111 -$175, **$$** = under $111.
● good, ◐ fair, ○ poor.
All hotels listed here have photocopying and fax facilities.

| In-Room Amenities | | | | | | | | | | Hotel Amenities | | | | | | |
|---|---|---|---|---|---|---|---|---|---|---|---|---|---|---|---|---|
| Nonsmoking rooms | In-room checkout | Minibar | Pay movies | VCR/Movie rentals | Hairdryer | Toiletries | Room service | Laundry/Dry cleaning | Pressing | Concierge | Barber/Hairdresser | Garage | Courtesy airport transport | Sauna | Pool | Exercise room |
| ✓ | ✓ | - | - | - | ✓ | ● | ● | ● | ● | ✓ | ✓ | ✓ | - | - | - | - |
| ✓ | - | - | - | - | ✓ | ◐ | ◐ | ◐ | ◐ | - | - | - | - | ✓ | ◐ | - |
| ✓ | ✓ | - | ✓ | - | - | ● | ◐ | ◐ | ◐ | ✓ | - | - | ✓ | ✓ | ● | ● |
| ✓ | ✓ | - | ✓ | ✓ | - | ● | ◐ | ◐ | ◐ | ✓ | - | ✓ | - | ✓ | ◐ | - |
| ✓ | - | ✓ | - | - | - | ◐ | ◐ | ◐ | ◐ | - | - | - | ✓ | ✓ | ◐ | - |
| ✓ | ✓ | - | - | - | - | ● | ● | ● | ● | ✓ | - | - | - | - | - | - |
| ✓ | ✓ | - | - | - | ✓ | ● | ◐ | ◐ | ● | ✓ | ✓ | - | - | ✓ | ● | ● |
| ✓ | ✓ | - | ✓ | ✓ | - | ● | ◐ | ◐ | ◐ | ✓ | ✓ | - | - | ✓ | ● | ● |
| ✓ | - | - | ✓ | - | - | ◐ | ◐ | ◐ | ◐ | ✓ | - | - | - | ✓ | ● | ● |
| ✓ | - | ✓ | ✓ | - | - | ● | ● | ◐ | ◐ | - | - | ✓ | - | ✓ | ◐ | - |
| ✓ | - | ✓ | ✓ | - | - | ● | ● | ◐ | ◐ | ✓ | - | ✓ | ✓ | - | ● | ● |
| ✓ | ✓ | ✓ | ✓ | ✓ | ✓ | ◐ | ◐ | ● | ● | ✓ | ✓ | ✓ | ✓ | ✓ | ◐ | ◐ |
| ✓ | - | ✓ | ✓ | - | ✓ | ● | ● | ◐ | ● | ✓ | ✓ | - | ✓ | ✓ | ● | ● |
| ✓ | - | - | - | ✓ | ✓ | ● | ● | ● | ● | ✓ | - | - | - | ✓ | ● | - |
| ✓ | ✓ | - | ✓ | - | - | ● | ◐ | - | - | ✓ | - | ✓ | - | ✓ | ◐ | ● |
| ✓ | ✓ | - | ✓ | ✓ | ✓ | ◐ | ◐ | ● | ● | ✓ | - | ✓ | - | ✓ | ◐ | ● |
| - | ✓ | ✓ | ✓ | - | - | ◐ | ◐ | ◐ | ◐ | ✓ | ✓ | ✓ | ✓ | - | ○ | - |
| ✓ | ✓ | ✓ | ✓ | ✓ | - | ◐ | ● | ◐ | ◐ | ✓ | ✓ | ✓ | ✓ | ✓ | ◐ | ● |
| ✓ | - | - | ✓ | - | - | ● | ● | ● | ● | ✓ | - | ✓ | - | ✓ | ● | ● |

**Room service:** ● 24-hour, ◐ 6AM-10PM, ○ other.
**Laundry/Dry cleaning:** ● same day, ◐ overnight, ○ other.
**Pressing:** ● immediate, ◐ same day, ○ other.

entrance to DFW International, minutes from the terminals and halfway between Dallas and Fort Worth. Standard Embassy Suites have separate bedrooms and sitting rooms. There's free breakfast, an audiovisual service center, and a courtesy bus to the nearby Centerpoint Athletic Club, which hotel guests can use on a per-diem basis. *4650 W. Airport Fwy., Irving, 75062, tel. 214/790-0093 or 800/ 362-2779, fax 214/790-4768. Gen. manager, Josef Puhringer. 308 rooms. AE, MC, V.*

**❺** **Four Seasons Hotel and Resort.** This hotel looks like a
**$$$** Frank Lloyd Wright–designed country club, with low ceilings, earth-hugging shapes, and earth colors. It takes up a large portion of the Las Colinas office center—some 300 rooms and suites, a couple of golf courses, a separate building for the health club, an amphitheater, and a media center providing design, print, and graphic services. Each room has a balcony that overlooks the TPC course (site of the Professional Golfers' Association's GTE Byron Nelson Classic) and oversized bathrooms, some with separate showers and bathtubs. There are two sets of rates: the standard European plan and the conference plan, which includes meals, use of the health and conference facilities, gratuities, and airport transportation. *4150 N. MacArthur Blvd., Irving, 75038, tel. 214/717-0700 or 800/ 332-3442, fax 214/717-2550. Gen. manager, Jim Fitzgibbon. 312 rooms, 3 suites. AE, CB, DC, MC, V.*

**❻** **Hyatt Regency DFW.** An air of hustle and bustle pervades
**$$$** this Hyatt, the largest airport hotel in the world. The hotel has two towers, 14 stories on the east side, 13 stories on the west. Guests can register at either (unless they are part of a group). Rooms are relatively spacious and somewhat above standard issue. The Hyatt also has its own Airtrans courtesy van station and provides shuttle service to the terminals. The Business Communications Center features a 24-hour dictation service. Guests can also use the Hyatt Bear Creek Golf and Racquet Club, five minutes away at the southern edge of the airport; resort/hotel packages are available. *Box 619014, DFW Airport, 75261, tel. 214/453-8400 or 800/228-9000, fax 214/453-0638. Gen. manager, Abdul Suleman. 1,320 rooms, 49 suites. AE, MC, V.*

**❻** **Marriott Mandalay at Las Colinas.** Marriott bought the
**$$$$** Mandalay several years ago, and since then has toned down the Oriental motif (although bronze Siamese elephants still greet guests at the door) and upgraded the business services. The Mandalay is well located, in the middle of Las Colinas near shopping, the monorail, and the canal (with its water taxis). The regal-looking lobby is decorated in beige and gold and boasts a fountain. Many rooms have an Oriental motif and are comfortably furnished with sitting areas. King single rooms are exceptionally spacious. The Mandalay is well known for its weekend specials, one of which includes golf at nearby Fossil Creek. Weekend discounts can be as much as half the weeknight rate. The hotel's French restaurant, Enjolie, is among the trendiest in the Dallas area. *221 E. Las Colinas Blvd., Irving, 75039, tel. 214/556-0800 or 800/228-9290, fax, 214/869-9053. Gen. manager, Jim Kauffman. 322 rooms, 98 suites. AE, MC, V.*

## Fort Worth

**30** **Green Oaks Inn.** From the outside, it looks like a motel
**$$** from a 1950s travelogue, but the interior is clean, the staff
is efficient, and most business travelers consider this the
leading business hotel in west Fort Worth. The lobby is
low-ceilinged, with brick walls and a fireplace. Rooms are
nondescript but quiet and decently furnished. The ball-
room holds 1,000. It's a five-minute drive to Carswell Air
Force Base and General Dynamics's Fort Worth division,
and 10 minutes to downtown Fort Worth along the West
Freeway. Ridgemar Mall is across the street. An on-site
American Airlines AAirlink office lets passengers check in
for their flights at the hotel. *A Kahler hotel. 6901 West
Fwy., 76116, tel. 817/738–7311; 800/433–2174; in Texas,
800/772–2341; fax 817/377–1308. Gen. manager, Her-
mann Jung. 273 rooms, 9 suites. AE, MC, V.*

**36** **Hilton Fort Worth.** An extensive renovation began in 1990
**$$** for this 12-story property on the south edge of downtown,
near I–30, and across from the Fort Worth Water Gar-
dens. Ask for an updated room. The hotel isn't as centrally
located as several others downtown, and it's a healthy
walk to Sundance Square. However, the Tarrant County
Convention Center is only three blocks from here. The
lobby, decorated in Southwestern pinks, is narrow and
can get crowded at check-out time. The Hilton's business-
floor service includes free local calls and the chain's
corporate amenities. *1701 Commerce St., 76102, tel. 817/
335–7000 or 800/445–8667, fax 817/335–7850. Gen. manager, Nelson Barnes. 424 rooms, 10 suites. AE, MC, V.*

**★ 34** **The Worthington Hotel.** Built in 1981, this white lump of a
**$$$** building is one of the newest in a downtown that prides it-
self on its 19th-century roots. It is, nonetheless, Fort
Worth's preeminent luxury hotel, with two waterfalls in
the lobby, high tea every afternoon from 3 to 5, and rooms
with separate sitting areas. The lobby's contemporary
look is carried through to the room, which are decorated in
pastels, with comfortable furnishings. Closets are extra
large. The Worthington is part of Sundance Square, the
center of the city's efforts to invigorate its downtown with
upscale shops and restaurants. It's also across the street
from the Tandy Center Shopping mall and six blocks from
the Tarrant County Convention Center. The health club
includes an indoor pool and workout classes for guests.
The Reflections restaurant, serving nouvelle cuisine in an
Art Deco room, is the leading Fort Worth power lunch
spot. *200 Main St., 76102, tel. 817/870–1000; 800/433–
5677; in Texas, 800/772–5977; fax, 817/332–5679. Gen.
manager. Robert Jameson. 438 rooms, 69 suites. AE,
MC, V.*

## DINING

Eating out is a social event in the Dallas-Fort Worth area.
People go to restaurants to be seen and to impress others,
and they very often dress up to do it. The food is often inci-
dental (which explains why this area is one of the last bas-
tions of nouvelle cuisine).

The Dallas-Fort Worth area is best known for two kinds of
cuisine: Southwestern—a "nouvelle Mexican" style, often

involving mesquite grilling as well as unusual combinations and the use of native American ingredients such as blue corn—pioneered by such Dallas chefs as Stephen Pyles at Routh Street Café and Dean Fearing at The Mansion on Turtle Creek; and Tex-Mex, a heavier North Texas derivative of traditional Mexican cooking that features enchiladas and fajitas. The chicken and sour cream enchilada, for instance, was invented in this area, and the ultimate Tex-Mex restaurant is Fort Worth's Joe T. Garcia's.

Thanks to Texas's Baptist heritage, all of Dallas (except for downtown and near north areas) and almost every suburban city between Dallas and Fort Worth is dry (Fort Worth itself is wet). There is no BYOB, either. Some restaurants get around the law by asking patrons to pay an additional fee to join the restaurant's private club.

Remember two names—the Dixie House and Black-Eyed Pea—if you want to eat but don't want to make a production out of it. These popular chain restaurants, located throughout the Dallas-Fort Worth area, feature home-style cooking (the chicken-fried steak is as good as anything in a diner in West Texas) at reasonable prices.

Highly recommended restaurants in each price category are indicated by a ★.

| Category | Cost* |
| --- | --- |
| *$$$$* (Very Expensive) | over $50 |
| *$$$* (Expensive) | $25–$50 |
| *$$* (Moderate) | under $25 |

*\*per person, including appetizer, entrée, and dessert, but excluding drinks, service, and 8% sales tax.*

*Numbers in the margin correspond to numbered restaurant locations on the Dallas-Fort Worth Lodging and Dining maps.*

## Business Breakfasts

Power breakfasts are not very popular in this rather traditional area, where people prefer to do their wheeling and dealing a bit later in the day. The main exception to this rule is **The Mansion on Turtle Creek** (214/526–2121); important matters are discussed over everything from fruit platters and bagels and lox to huevos rancheros and raspberry buttermilk pancakes in the mansion's sunny, tile-floor Promenade Room. Reservations (preferably a day in advance) are required; breakfast is served weekdays from 7–10:30, weekends until 11:30.

## Downtown Dallas

 **Dakota's.** An elevator on Akard Street takes guests down *$$$* to this wood-paneled dining room, a popular lunch spot for local businesspeople; the modern but clublike room never gets too crowded or noisy for serious talk. The menu features New American food, combining the best elements of Southwestern and nouvelle cuisines. (In other words, Dakota's serves vegetables like jicama, but doesn't make a meal out of them.) The best entrées are mesquite grilled: try the smoked pork tenderloin or the swordfish. The wine list, though expensive, offers some interesting California choices. The restaurant has valet parking, and is extremely popular with couples on the weekend. *600 N. Akard St., tel. 214/740–4001. Jacket and tie suggested. Reservations required. AE, MC, V.*

**㉒ Lawry's, The Prime Rib.** The menu is extremely limited
**$$$** and the waitresses dress in kitschy 19th-century costumes, but Dallas adores this entry from the national chain. It's almost always busy at lunch and dinner, particularly with older businessmen dining together or with their families; you're likely to be taken here if your Dallas business contact is fairly traditional. Sandwiches are served at lunch, but roast beef is the only entrée offered at dinner. The prime rib lives up to Lawry's reputation, and the Victorian library atmosphere works well. But the side dishes, served à la carte, are undistinguished. *3008 Maple Ave., tel. 214/521–7777. Jacket and tie required. Reservations required. AE, MC, V.*

**⑲ The Mansion on Turtle Creek.** This opulent restaurant
**$$$$** helped pioneer Southwestern cuisine, and it is a mecca for the beautiful, celebrated, and powerful in the Dallas-Fort Worth area. Located some 15 minutes from downtown, in a hotel of the same name, the Mansion is one of the city's premier power lunch spots, and the only place for a power breakfast. But don't expect to be treated well (or even civilly) unless you are known to the staff—which is a shame, as the cooking is as good as any in the city. A different menu is featured daily. Chef Dean Fearing's vision of Southwestern cuisine features such specialties as tortilla soup, warm lobster tacos, and halibut with cashews in a basil sauce, all stunningly presented. *2821 Turtle Creek Blvd., tel. 214/526–2121. Jacket and tie required. Reservations required. AE, DC, MC, V.*

**⑱ Mucky Duck.** This is a surprisingly near-authentic En-
**$$** glish pub (even though it's in the back of a shopping center), complete with dart boards, an Irish bartender who can talk about "The Troubles," legitimate pub grub, and Fuller Extra Special Bitter on tap. Mucky Duck is a neighborhood hangout for young professionals in the affluent Turtle Creek area, 15 minutes north of downtown Dallas, and never gets too raucous (although there is live folk-rock music Thursday through Sunday nights). It's popular, too, with students from Southern Methodist University. Come for lunch (try the shepherd's pie) or to unwind after work; it's even possible to talk business over a pint. Women seem to feel especially comfortable here. *3102 Welborn St., Suite 100, tel. 214/522–7200. Casual dress. No reservations. AE, MC, V.*

**㉔ Newport's.** The Dallas-Fort Worth area, some 300 miles
**$$** from the nearest ocean, is not famous for seafood, but Newport's, a fashionable and upscale spot on lower McKinney Avenue, just minutes from downtown Dallas, is among the best of the lot. The fish is flown in fresh daily, and the menu and prices change depending on the day's catch. The restaurant was part of an old brewery and has lots of exposed brick and wood and an open kitchen. It is popular among calorie-conscious executives at lunch; somewhat off the beaten path, Newport's never gets too noisy to preclude business discussion. Menu specialties include grilled fresh grouper and swordfish. *703 McKinney*

*Ave., tel. 214/954–0220. Jacket suggested. Reservations suggested. AE, MC, V.*

**㉘** **The Palm.** The Dallas outpost of this steak-and-lobster
$$$$ chain is the place in Big D for a power lunch. It's almost
impossible to walk into the downtown location at lunchtime and not recognize a face from the papers or television; Southwest Airlines chairman Herb Kelleher likes
The Palm so much that the restaurant has reserved a
Southwest Airlines room. The service and decor are much
the same as at the Palms in New York, Washington, and
Los Angeles—caricatures of customers on the dark wall
and waiters who graduated from the Don Rickles School of
Charm and go out of their way to ignore women dining
without men. The lunch menu is unexceptional; the dinner
menu features all of the things The Palm is famous for, including 12-pound lobsters and steaks the size of
placemats. *701 Ross Ave., tel. 214/698–0470. Jacket suggested. Reservations suggested. AE, DC, MC, V.*

**★ ㉑** **Routh Street Café.** Chef Stephen Pyles's restaurant is as
$$$$ good as everyone says it is. Opened in 1985, Routh Street
Café now ranks with top-class restaurants all over the
world. The staff is pleasant, too. It's an ideal place to entertain clients, talk business, or just enjoy an outstanding
meal. The five-course, fixed-priced menu offers several
choices for each course; options change daily. The cuisine
is Southwestern: Try the tamale tart for a starter and the
barbecued rib-eye steak as an entrée. Weekend reservations must be made at least one week in advance. Pyles has
opened a more casual restaurant, Baby Routh, a few
blocks down the street, to handle the overflow. *3005 Routh
St., tel. 214/871–7161. Jacket and tie required. Reservations required. Dinner only. Closed Sun. and Mon. AE,
MC, V.*

## North Dallas

**⑩** **Blue Mesa Grill.** This is the quintessential Dallas restau-
$$ rant, where fashion-conscious people come more for the
atmosphere than for the food. Customers come to sit in
one of the cowhide-covered booths; to relax at a table in
front of the Texas-sized fireplace; or to drink a blue mar-
garita (this is one of the few wet areas in dry North Dal-
las). The cuisine is modeled on Mark Miller's Coyote Café
in Santa Fe, but fortunately it is not as trendy. There are
fajitas to go along with the corn pasta, cheese chili
rellenos, fried yam chips, and duck-filled *taquitos* (similar
to tacos). Blue Mesa is a popular lunch spot for many exec-
utives who work in North Dallas along the crowded
tollway/parkway corridor; the atmosphere is more laid
back at dinner. *5100 Belt Line Rd., Village on the Park-
way, Addison, tel. 214/934–0165. Casual but neat. No res-
ervations. AE, MC, V.*

**⑦** **May Dragon.** One of the most popular business lunch spots
$$ in North Dallas, this moderately priced Chinese restaurant is always crowded with men in three-piece suits talk-
ing to other men in three-piece suits. It isn't noisy, it isn't
trendy, and it's not a place to impress clients with elegant
decor or fine cuisine. But the service is impeccable, the atmosphere is comfortable, and it's possible to make deals
here. The menu mixes Hunan and Szechuan, which means
it offers such dishes as lobster in ginger root-and-scallion
sauce, and beef stir-fried with vermicelli. *4848 Belt Line*

*Rd., Addison, tel. 214/392–9998. Casual but neat. Reservations suggested. AE, MC, V.*

## Near North Dallas

**⑭** **Gershwin's.** This major yuppie watering hole is the fron-
**$$$** tier between wet and dry Dallas. On Friday and Saturday
nights, the crowd at the bar stretches from the front door
to the kitchen; don't even think about trying to have a seri-
ous discussion here. The restaurant has a New Orleans fla-
vor, both in its menu—with plenty of fresh grilled fish
including the obligatory blackened redfish—and in its de-
cor—neo-French Quarter, with brick walls, plenty of
glass, and a piano player. There's also a creditable bread
pudding. The tables in back, adjacent to the kitchen, are
the most private. The wine list is adequate, but over-
priced. *8442 Walnut Hill La., tel. 214/373–7171. Casual
but neat. AE, MC, V.*

## East Dallas

**⑯** **Bohemia.** The Dallas-Fort Worth area (with its Scottish-
**$$** Irish heritage) doesn't have many great ethnic restaurants. This intimate, candlelit dining room, serving East
European–style cuisine, is one of the exceptions. The Bo-
hemia, which has about a dozen tables, takes up the front
room of a two-story house between the boutique-filled
shops of the pricey Upper McKinney Avenue neighborhood and a decidedly more blue-collar section of East Dallas. It is not part of the city's trendy dining scene; the
crowd is older and quieter than at other, similarly priced
restaurants. Highlights of the Czech-influenced menu include marvelously light dumplings that come with every
meal, beef Prague (a type of stew), and very traditional
Wiener schnitzel and chicken paprika. The short, inexpensive wine list features East European labels. *2810 N.
Henderson Ave., tel. 214/826–6290. Casual but neat. Dinner only. Reservations required. Closed Mon., Tues.,
and the week between Christmas and New Year's. AE,
MC, V.*

**⑳** **Lakewood Plaza Grill.** There's nothing spectacular about
**$$$** this two-level neighborhood spot in the Lakewood section,
a 15-minute cab ride from downtown Dallas—just a good
meal in comfortable surroundings. The decor is glass with
black-and-white tile, the service is usually efficient, and
it's possible to have dinner and to talk without being both-
ered by overzealous waiters. Try to get a table upstairs,
where it's quieter and more secluded. The menu is eclec-
tic, with choices as simple as hamburgers and salads shar-
ing space with items like venison sausage. Any of the
grilled chicken specialties is worth sampling. The wine
list, with Texas and California selections, is good. *6334
LaVista Dr., tel. 214/826–5226. Casual but neat. No res-
ervations. AE, DC, MC, V.*

## West Dallas

**★ ⑮** **Celebration.** This is one of the few places in the Dallas area
**$$** to get an honest meal at a moderate price, which explains
why customers wait for up to an hour almost every night;
come before 6:30 or after 9 if you want to avoid the crowds.
The restaurant, in a renovated house in a residential
neighborhood near Love Field, is a good choice for a leisurely, casual meal after a day of serious meetings. Ask

for a booth; they're farther from the large tables with yelling children. The menu features traditional Texas/Southern cooking—chicken-fried steak, meat loaf, fried catfish, and pot roast—combined with daily specials, bowls of vegetables, and a wine list with several Texas selections. The food is served family style, and most entrées are all-you-can-eat. There is also a newer location in Fort Worth, in the old Crystal Ice House near the Cultural District. *4503 W. Lovers La., tel. 214/351–5681. Casual dress. Reservations required for parties of 6 or more. AE, MC, V.*

## Fort Worth

★ ③③ **Joe T. Garcia's.** This is the ultimate Tex-Mex restaurant,
$$ where cowboy-boot-clad customers drink Mexican beer and the bartenders mix potent margaritas. Don't plan on doing any business here; rather, celebrate after it's done. Joe T's, as it is fondly known, doesn't take credit cards, doesn't accept reservations, and doesn't serve anything other than beef and chicken fajitas and cheese enchiladas. There's usually a wait for tables, and on Saturday nights the wait can stretch to an hour. Don't be deterred by the location: a ramshackle old house in north Fort Worth a few blocks south of the Stockyards. In spring or fall it's pleasant to eat outside on the patio. *2201 N. Commerce St., tel. 817/624–0266. Casual dress. No reservations. No credit cards.*

★ ③① **Saint-Emilion.** It doesn't look like much from the outside,
$$$ but this tiny, buff-color brick building nestled between doctors' offices in west Fort Worth is one of the two or three best restaurants in Tarrant County. Saint-Emilion serves a variety of purposes: as a power dining spot (the service defines discreet), as a place to be seen, and as the site for country French cooking few would expect in a city whose nickname is Cowtown. There are two fixed-price menus at dinner and one at lunch, featuring roasted duck, rack of lamb, and veal dishes. Chef Patrice de Faveri prepares entrées in the open in the comfortable main dining room, and the wine list includes some good values in Bordeaux. *3617 W. 7th St., tel. 817/737–2781. Casual but neat. Reservations required. Closed Sun. and Mon. lunch. AE, MC, V.*

③② **Tours.** The cuisine here is an unlikely combination of
$$$ Southwestern influences and traditional French cooking, but it is more than successful. The menu changes weekly, but it can include dishes such as veal sweetbreads, trout meunière, and fettucine with mushrooms and bacon. The dining room is frilly in a pleasant, un-Texaslike way, with attention to detail; service can be slow, however. If you have time, this is a dignified setting for a discussion without distractions. A more basic menu is on offer at the bar, which stays open until midnight. The weekend brunch, served from 11 AM–2 PM weekends, is recommended. *3500 W. 7th St., tel. 817/870–1672. Casual but neat. Reservations suggested on weekends. Closed for dinner Sun. AE, MC, V.*

③⑤ **Winfield '08's.** One of the best of the new restaurants in
$$ Sundance Square in downtown Fort Worth, Winfield '08's is extremely popular at lunch time. The menu is nothing to get excited about—hamburgers and salads—but the desserts are interesting, and the daily specials are reasonably priced and more than competently prepared. Service

is professional. The newly restored building started life as the 50-room Savoy Hotel in 1908; the Winfield in the restaurant's name refers to Winfield Scott, the Fort Worth tycoon who built the hotel. The dining room's brass and green decor is in keeping with the Victorian style of the original structure. *301 Main St., tel. 817/870–1908. Casual dress. No reservations. AE, MC, V.*

## Arlington

**4** **Cacharel.** Located on the ninth floor of an office building
**$$$** overlooking the Six Flags Over Texas amusement park, Cacharel is easily the best restaurant in the Mid-Cities, serving simple, country French food in an unintimidating atmosphere. The three-course, fixed-price menu at lunch and dinner includes a choice of fresh seafood, beef, or veal. The duck braised with blackcurrant sauce is worth the 20-minute drive from Dallas or Fort Worth. Cacharel, long a favorite with the local television community, is probably the best spot for a proper business dinner in an area filled with chains and fast-food restaurants. *2221 E. Lamar Blvd., Arlington, tel. 817/640–9981. Jacket and tie suggested. Reservations required. AE, MC, V.*

## FREE TIME

### Fitness

*Hotel Facilities*
Most of the area's hotel facilities are open only to guests at the hotel. An exception in Fort Worth is the first-rate health club at the **Worthington** (tel. 817/870–1000); nonguests pay $7 per day.

*Health Clubs*
The **Downtown Dallas YMCA** (601 N. Akard St., tel. 214/954–0500) is well equipped to provide a variety of workouts, offering a pool, running track, squash and racquetball courts, free-weight and machine rooms, and aerobics classes. The fee for nonmembers is $10 per day.

*Jogging*
In Dallas, the best place to go jogging is along the 12-mile path around east Dallas's White Rock Lake, site of the annual White Rock Marathon. In Fort Worth, try the 7-mile course west along the Trinity River from downtown to the Cultural District.

### Shopping

*Dallas*
The glitzy **Galleria** (tel. 214/702–7100) and its 185 stores (including Macy's, tel. 214/851–3300; and Marshall Field, tel. 214/851–1461) is the top attraction in North Dallas, while the **Valley View Center** (tel. 214/661–2424) is less than a mile away. The flagship **Neiman Marcus** (1618 Main St., tel. 214/741–6911) has been a downtown landmark for more than 80 years and still attracts many of Dallas's wealthiest shoppers. The **McKinney Avenue** district near downtown includes an Espirit (2425 McKinney Ave., tel. 214/871–8989) superstore for casual women's clothing; the posh Crescent (tel. 214/871–5150) (with Stanley Korshak, a retailer who provides space to designer shops like Ralph Lauren and Donna Karan, as the anchor) across the street; and the Paris-based men's boutique Hippolyte (2800

Routh St., tel. 214/855-5081) a few blocks away in the Quadrangle. **NorthPark Center** (tel. 214/363-7441) on Northwest Highway includes a ritzy Neiman's (No. 400, tel. 214/363-8311) and one of the largest Limited's (women's sportswear) (No. 452, tel. 214/363-7528) in the country among its 150 shops.

It's also possible to save as much as 50% on cowboy boots at outlet stores such as Just Justin (1505 Wycliff Ave., tel. 214/630-2858).

*Fort Worth*

In downtown Fort Worth, the twin-towered **Tandy Center** (tel. 817/390-3717) features three levels of shops, a privately operated subway, and an ice-skating rink. At the nearby **Sundance Square,** shops and boutiques fill up a two-block area.

The **Stockyards District** in Fort Worth includes about a dozen places to stock up on Western-style souvenirs.

## Diversions

*Dallas*

The **Dallas Museum of Art** (1717 N. Harwood St., tel. 214/922-1200) is best known for its contemporary-style building by architect Edward Larabec Barnes (it's the linchpin of the downtown Arts District), and for its Wendy and Emery Reeves Collection of objets d'art and furniture. The collection is displayed in a room resembling the Reeves's Mediterranean villa.

**Fair Park,** in south Dallas, is the site of the Cotton Bowl stadium, the Starplex outdoor amphitheater, and a handful of museums, including the Science Place and Museum of Natural History.

The **Sixth Floor** (411 Elm St., tel. 214/653-6666) is on the sixth floor of the old Texas School Book Depository, where Lee Harvey Oswald waited in ambush for President John F. Kennedy. The 9,000-square-foot exhibit on Kennedy and his death is a moving experience.

The **Swiss Avenue Historic District** of houses and mansions stretches for three miles from downtown to Lakewood in east Dallas. The first eight blocks (before Baylor Medical Center) are lined with Victorian gingerbread homes; the last mile (between Munger Ave. and La Vista St.) has dozens of mansions and town houses. Pick up a map of the district at the Dallas Convention & Visitor's Bureau (1201 Elm St., Suite 2000, tel. 214/746-6672.)

*Fort Worth*

The **Amon Carter Museum** (3501 Camp Bowie Blvd., tel. 817/738-1933) has the world's leading collection of Frederic Remington and Charles Russell paintings and sculptures, and several noteworthy Georgia O'Keeffes.

The **Fort Worth Stockyards** in north Fort Worth, designated a national historic district in 1976, includes the Cowtown Coliseum rodeo arena (tel. 817/625-1025), Billy Bob's Texas honky-tonk (*see* After Hours, below), and a live cattle auction at 10 AM each Monday.

**Kimbell Art Museum** (3333 Camp Bowie Blvd., tel. 817/332-8451) is one of the best small art museums in the

United States. It is also one of the richest, with the second-largest acquisition budget in the country. Expect to see one or two outstanding examples from each major period from the Renaissance to the early 20th century.

## Professional Sports

For football, see the **Dallas Cowboys** at Texas Stadium in Irving (tel. 214/556–2500). Dallas's basketball team, the **Dallas Mavericks,** plays at Reunion Arena (tel. 214/658–7068). Also at Reunion Arena are the **Dallas Sidekicks,** the city's soccer team (tel. 214/361–5425). **Mesquite Championship Rodeo** competitions take place at MCR Arena in Mesquite (tel. 214/285–8777). The region's baseball club, the **Texas Rangers,** plays at Arlington Stadium (tel. 817/273–5100).

## The Arts

The Dallas-Fort Worth area offers all of the entertainment options you'd expect in a major regional metropolitian area. The **Fort Worth Ballet** (tel. 817/763–0207) performs at the Tarrant County Convention Center Theater; the home of the **Dallas Opera** (tel. 214/979–0123) is the Music Hall at Fair Park; the **Dallas Symphony Orchestra** (tel. 214/692–0203) plays in the new Morton H. Myerson Center in the Arts District. There's a lively theater scene, led by the **Dallas Theater Center** and the **Majestic Theater,** and Fort Worth's **Casa Manana,** as well as its offbeat **Hip Pocket Theater.** All the major pop groups that visit the area play at the large **Starplex Amphitheater.**

Ticket agencies include Texas Tickets (8840 N. Central Expressway, Dallas, tel. 214/696–8001 or 800/882–9600) and First Row Tickets (11613 N. Central Expressway, Dallas, tel. 214/750–7555). Scalping, incidentally, is legal in Texas.

**Casa Manana Playhouse,** 3101 W. Lancaster Ave., Fort Worth, tel. 817/332–9319.
**Dallas Theater Center,** 3636 Turtle Creek Blvd., Dallas, tel. 214/526–8857.
**Hip Pocket Theater,** 1627 Fairmount Ave., tel. 817/927–2833.
**Majestic Theater,** 1925 Elm St., Dallas, tel. 214/692–9090.
**Morton H. Myerson Center,** Pearl and Munger Sts., Dallas, tel. 214/565–9100.
**Music Hall at Fair Park,** tel. 214/565–1116.
**Starplex Amphitheater,** 1818 First Ave., Dallas, tel. 214/421–1111.
**Tarrant County Convention Center Theater,** 1111 Houston St., Fort Worth, tel. 817/332–9222.

## After Hours

This area isn't as strong for live music as Austin is, but the club scene is more than healthy. In Dallas, it ranges from the neopunk bars of Deep Ellum, an entertainment district just east of downtown, to the country-and-western spots along Greenville Avenue, to the Yuppie nightclubs in the downtown West End development. In Fort Worth, downtown's Caravan of Dreams offers an eclectic mix of jazz, funk, and new music. In the Stockyards, there are a host of honky-tonks, led by Billy Bob's Texas.

*Bars and Lounges*

**Dallas.** The **Library** at the Omni Melrose (3015 Oak Lawn Ave., tel. 214/521–5151) is perfect for a power drink: It's proper, quiet, and sedate. The **Stoneleigh P.** (2926 Maple Ave., tel. 214/871–2346) is more relaxed and informal. The **Scoreboard Sports Bar & Grill** (4872 Belt Line Rd., Addison, tel. 214/788–5444) is one of the few places to get a drink in the dry North Dallas area.

**Fort Worth.** The **Main Street Bar and Grille** (318 Main St., tel. 817/870–9165) stays open until 2 AM on weekends.

*Cabaret*

**Dallas. Barney Oldfield's** (Sheraton Mockingbird, 1893 W. Mockingbird La., tel. 214/634–8850) is a Las Vegas-style showroom with dinner and dancing.

*Comedy Clubs*

**Dallas. The Improv** (Corner Shopping Center, 8910 N. Central Expressway, tel. 214/750–5858; 4980 Belt Line Rd., Addison, tel. 214/404–8501) features national acts. Dinner reservations are required. In Tarrant County, try the **Comedy Corporation** (Lincoln Square II, Arlington, tel. 817/792–3700) and the **Funny Bone** (Arkansas and Hwy. 360, Arlington, tel. 817/265–2277).

*Jazz Clubs*

**Dallas.** The venerable **Poor David's Pub** (1924 Greenville Ave., tel. 214/821–9891) books more Texas blues and rock acts than jazz, but probably is the best live music spot in Dallas—folding chairs and all.

**Fort Worth.** The **Caravan of Dreams Performing Arts Center** (312 Houston St., tel. 817/877–3000) has a national reputation.

*For Singles*

**Dallas. 8.0** (2800 Routh St., tel. 214/979–0800) tops the McKinney Avenue scene, where the young and the beautiful gather. In the West End, **Dick's Last Resort** (1701 N. Market St., tel. 214/747–0001) is rowdy without being too redneck. **Dallas Alley** (West End Marketplace, tel. 214/988–9378) offers a variety of music, from blues to pop.

**Fort Worth. Billy Bob's Texas** (2520 Rodeo Plaza, tel. 817/624–7117) must be seen to be believed—a Disneyland of longneck beers and country music. The popular **White Elephant Saloon** in the Stockyards (106 E. Exchange Ave., tel. 817/624–1887), is a country-and-western bar, and trendy **West Side Stories** (3900 Hwy. 377 S., tel. 817/560–7632) is a group of nightclubs offering rock, blues, and pop.

# Denver

*by Penelope Purdy*

Denver is a young city, full of energetic people who live here partly because they enjoy being close to the mountains and to the city's numerous parks—to ski, hike, bicycle, or just enjoy the outdoors.

Denver's climate is surprisingly mild, and the city's architecture, especially in the two primary business areas—downtown and the Denver Technology Center—reflects Denverites' love of the out-of-doors. Downtown, a mix of brick and stone 19th-century low rises and steel-and-glass towers constructed during the late 1970s and early 1980s, is home to the one-mile-long outdoor 16th Street Mall, one of the most successful pedestrian malls in the United States. The Denver Tech Center, a cluster of modern office developments in the city's southeast quadrant, is arranged like a college campus, with large green lawns and tree-lined streets flanking modernist steel-and-glass midrises.

Yet in its recent past, Denver has been a troubled city. As the Rocky Mountains' business and financial center, the city boomed during the late 1970s. An energy-hungry nation encouraged petroleum companies to explore the region's vast oil and natural gas reserves, and Denver experienced a rush for black gold much like the original gold and silver rushes that first attracted settlers here in the 1850s. But the community was hard-hit when oil prices collapsed in the mid-1980s, forcing Colorado companies to diversify in order to survive.

Today's business climate is much improved. The Mile High City (elevation 5,280 feet) is much less dependent on the volatile natural resources industries, and its primary industries now include light manufacturing, wholesale trade and distribution, telecommunications, transportation, tourism, finance, aerospace, and computer and biomedical technologies.

Nationally known firms based in the Denver area include telecommunications giant U S West, beer brewer Adolph Coors, rubber products manufacturer Gates Corporation, cable television leader Tele-Communications, movie theater and cable TV conglomerate United Artists Entertainment, and herbal tea maker Celestial Seasonings. However, the backbone of the city's business community is formed by small businesses that collectively employ more people than any single, large enterprise in the state.

## Top Employers

| Employer | Type of Enterprise | Parent*/ Headquarters |
|---|---|---|
| AT&T | Telecommunications | New York City |
| Continental Airlines | Transportation | Texas Air Corp./ Houston |
| Adolph Coors Co. | Beer brewing | Golden, CO |
| EG&G/Rocky Flats | Nuclear weapons | U.S. Department of Energy/ Washington, DC |
| IBM | Computers | New York City |
| King Soopers | Grocery chain | Kroger Co./Cincinnati |
| Martin Marietta | Aerospace engineering | Bethesda, MD |
| Storage Technology Corp. | Computers | Louisville, CO |
| United Airlines | Transportation | UAL Inc./ Chicago |
| U S West Inc. | Telecommunications | Englewood, CO |

*if applicable

## ESSENTIAL INFORMATION

### Climate

Denver boasts 300 days of sunshine; winters are mild with temperatures dropping below zero only a couple of days in January. The city's air quality is acceptable to good most of the year, but can become very poor on warm days in the winter months, from late November to late February.

What follows are the average daily maximum and minimum temperatures for Denver.

| Jan. | 42F | 6C | Feb. | 44F | 7C | Mar. | 51F | 11C |
|---|---|---|---|---|---|---|---|---|
| | 17 | −8 | | 19 | −7 | | 24 | −4 |
| Apr. | 60F | 16C | May | 69F | 21C | June | 80F | 27C |
| | 33 | 1 | | 44 | 7 | | 53 | 12 |
| July | 87F | 31C | Aug. | 87F | 31C | Sept. | 78F | 26C |
| | 59 | 15 | | 57 | 14 | | 48 | 9 |
| Oct. | 66F | 19C | Nov. | 53F | 12C | Dec. | 46F | 8C |
| | 37 | 3 | | 26 | −3 | | 21 | −6 |

### Airport

**Stapleton International Airport** is 15 minutes northeast of downtown and 25 minutes due north from the Denver Tech

Center. Stapleton operates with tolerable efficiency. In bad weather, however, technical requirements force the world's sixth busiest airport to use only one runway, so wintertime delays can be exasperating.

## Airport Business Facilities

**Ace Cash Express Money Services** (Second level between Concourses C and D, tel. 303/394–2112) has fax machines, photocopying, Western Union, cash advance, and check cashing. It also sells traveler's checks, money orders, and Amex moneygrams.

## Airlines

The air travel business in Denver is dominated by close rivals Continental and United.

**America West Airlines,** tel. 303/571–0738 or 800/247–5692.
**Continental,** tel. 303/398–3000 or 800/525–0280.
**Delta,** tel. 303/696–1322 or 800/221–1212.
**United,** tel. 303/398–4141 or 800/241–6522

## Between the Airport and Downtown

*By Taxi*
Taxi stands are on the lower level, outside door No. 5. The ride is about 15 minutes to downtown and 25 minutes to Denver Tech Center. Cost: to downtown, $10–$12; to the Denver Tech Center, $15–$18.

*By Shuttle*
Many hotels operate shuttles to the airport. Denver Airport Limousine (tel. 303/398–2284) operates a shuttle van that takes 15 minutes to downtown, cost $5, and about 20–25 minutes to the Denver Tech Center, cost $7.

*By Bus*
Regional Transportation District (RTD or the Ride) buses leave from Stapleton's lower level and take 20–30 minutes to downtown. Schedule information is available by calling tel. 303/778–6000. Cost: Basic fare is 50¢, but rises to $1 during rush hour (6–9AM and 4–6PM.).

## Car Rentals

The following rental car companies have offices or booths at the terminal:

**Avis,** tel. 303/398–3725 or 800/331–1212.
**Budget,** tel. 303/341–2277 or 800/527–0700.
**Hertz,** tel. 303/355–2244 or 800/654–3131.
**National,** tel. 303/321–7990 or 800/227–7368.

## Emergencies

*Doctor or Dentist*
**Dial-4-Health** offers a doctor and dentist referral service (tel. 303/443–2584).

*Hospitals*
**Denver General Hospital** (777 Bannock St., tel. 308/893–6000), **St. Joseph Hospital** (1835 Franklin St., tel. 303/837–1240).

## Important Addresses and Numbers

**Audiovisual rentals.** Audio Visual Rentals (1515 Cleveland Pl., tel. 303/893–9078), Colorado Visual Aids (424 Lincoln St., tel. 303/778–1111), J&S Communications (8745 E. Orchard Rd., tel. 303/779–8989 or 800/356–2466).

**Chambers of Commerce.** Denver Metro Convention and Visitors Bureau (225 W. Colfax Ave., tel. 303/892–1112 or 800/888–1990), Downtown Denver (511 16th St., tel. 303/534–6161), Greater Denver Chamber of Commerce (1600 Sherman St., tel. 303/894–8500).

**Computer rentals.** Active Computer Group (6440 E. Hampden Ave., tel. 303/691–2330), Business Computer (7000 Broadway, tel. 303/426–4100), Champion Computer (5555 DTC Blvd., Greenwood Village, tel. 303/773–1909).

**Convention and exhibition centers.** Colorado Convention Center (14th St., between Stout and Welton Sts., tel. 303/640–8000), Currigan Exhibition Hall (14th St., between Stout and Champa Sts., tel. 303/640–5106); for information about either center, call the Denver Metro Visitors and Convention Bureau (tel. 303/892–1112), Denver Merchandise Mart (451 E. 58th St., tel. 303/292–6278).

**Fax services.** Autotype Word Processing Service (717 17th St., No. 1510, tel. 303/298–1676), Center Copy Printing and Typesetting (303 16th St., tel. 303/623–3161), Facsimile Telecopy Transmission Services (7730 E. Belleview Ave., tel. 303/771–8686), HQ Headquarters Companies (999 18th St., tel. 303/298–9000).

**Formal-wear rentals.** President Tuxedo (Tabor Center, 1201 16th St., tel. 303/629–5475), Randalls' (7400 E. Hampden Ave., tel. 303/779–6119).

**Gift shops.** Confectioners: Enstrom Candies (201 University Ave., tel. 303/322–1005); Flowers: Bouquets Ltd. (2908 E. 6th Ave., tel. 303/333–5500); Gourmet Foods: Business Basket Business, specializes in gift packs for business clients and hosts, including gourmet foods (1732 Blake St., tel. 303/295–7714).

**Graphic design studios.** Ahrens & Whitlock (1860 Blake St., Suite 640, tel. 303/292–2100), Croce Advertising (1624 Market St., tel. 303/534–3501), Weber Design (1439 Larimer St., tel. 303/892–9816).

**Hairstylists.** Unisex: The Barbers, appointments recommended (17th St. at Arapahoe St., tel. 303/572–0908), Salon Mercades, walk-ins welcome (Beau Monde Shopping Mall, 8081 E. Orchard Rd., tel. 303/741–0606).

**Health and fitness clubs.** *See* Fitness, below.

**Information hot lines.** Convention information (tel. 303/892–1112), tourist information (tel. 303/892–1505), road conditions: mountains and west (tel. 303/639–1111), road conditions: east, north, and south (tel. 303/639–1234).

**Limousine services.** Colorado Limousine Service (tel. 303/832–7155, many drivers speak foreign languages), Presidential Limousine (tel. 303/698–1114), Renaissance

Classic Car Rental Services (tel. 303/830–6657, antique and luxury cars).

**Liquor stores.** Argonaut Liquors (700 E. Colfax Ave., tel. 303/831–7788), Brooks Tower Liquors (1020 15th St., tel. 303/629–6707), Downtown Wine and Spirits (1815 Arapahoe St., tel. 303/295–0295), High Spirits (800 E. Quincy Ave., tel. 303/771–1077), International Wine and Spirit (8200 S. Quebec St., Englewood, tel. 303/740–9463), Watson's at the Tabor Center (1201 16th St., tel. 303/893–6767). All Colorado liquor stores are closed on Sundays. Grocery stores sell only 3.2 beer.

**Mail delivery, overnight.** DHL Worldwide Express (tel. 303/377–2433), Federal Express (tel. 303/892–7981), TNT Skypak (tel. 303/373–2556), UPS (tel. 303/429–3340), U.S. Postal Service Express Mail (tel. 303/297–6636).

**Messenger services.** Champion Messenger Service (tel. 303/333–7874), Speedy Messenger Service (tel. 303/292–6000), Tech Center Couriers (tel. 303/770–9616).

**Office space rentals.** Capitol Suites (303 E. 17th Ave., tel. 303/832–1882), Executives Suites at DTC (8400 E. Prentice Ave., tel. 303/771–9926), Tabor Center Executive Suites (1200 17th St., tel. 303/572–6050).

**Pharmacies, late-night.** Pencol Medisave Pharmacy (3535 Cherry Creek Dr., tel. 303/388–3613) has a 24-hour answering service, Walgreen's (2000 E. Colfax Ave., tel. 303/331–0917).

**Radio stations, all-news.** KDEN 1340 AM; KOA 85 AM.

**Secretarial services.** Affiliated Executives Systems (5299 DTC Blvd., tel. 303/773–0711; 6860 S. Yosemite Circle, tel. 303/773–3131), Autotype Word Processing (717 17th St., tel. 303/298–1676), Corporate Office Concepts (6200 S. Syracuse Way, tel. 303/779–6700), Executive Business Services (1675 Broadway, tel. 303/892–6799).

**Stationery supplies.** Affiliated Executive Systems (5299 DTC Blvd., Greenwood Village, tel. 303/793–5900), Arapahoe Office Express (1147 Broadway, tel. 303/620–9900), Colorado Stationers (6630 S. Yosemite St., Englewood, tel. 303/796–7242), Hilb Office Products (1529 Market St., tel. 303/595–3380).

**Taxis.** Metro Cab (tel. 303/333–3333), Yellow Cab (tel. 303/777–7777), Zone Cab (tel. 303/444–8888). The best place to find a taxi is in front of a major hotel; calling for one can involve a wait of 20 minutes or longer.

**Theater tickets.** *See* The Arts, below.

**Train information.** Amtrak (Union Station, 17th and Wynkoop Sts., tel. 303/892–1442 or 800/872–7245).

**Travel agents.** American Express Travel Services (555 17th St., tel. 303/298–7100), Corporate Travel Services (1675 Broadway, tel. 303/592–4590; 7887 E. Belleview Ave., tel. 303/694–3322), Professional Travel (1625 Broadway, tel. 303/623–4117; 7720 E. Belleview Ave., tel. 303/770–9744).

**Weather** (tel. 303/639–1515).

## LODGING

Denver's hotels are clustered, like the business community, primarily in two areas: downtown and the Denver Tech Center. Picking a hotel close to your business destination will spare you a lot of driving, particularly along the overused I–25 corridor. Most of the city's high-tech companies are located near the Denver Tech Center; most oil companies, banks, and stock brokerages are located downtown. The majority of Denver hotels are chain-owned, but there are some locally owned, older properties, like the Brown Palace and the Oxford Alexis, that combine the warmth and charm of old Denver with modern amenities. Since the completion of the Colorado Convention Center in 1990, numerous Denver-area hotels have undergone extensive renovations.

Most hotels listed here offer special corporate rates and weekend discounts; inquire when making reservations.

Highly recommended lodgings in each price category are indicated by a star ★.

| Category | Cost* |
| --- | --- |
| *$$$$* (Very Expensive) | over $150 |
| *$$$* (Expensive) | $100–$150 |
| *$$* (Moderate) | under $100 |

*All prices are for a standard double room, single occupancy, excluding tax and service charge.*

*Numbers in the margin correspond to numbered hotel locations on the Denver Lodging and Dining maps.*

### In or Near Downtown

★ ⓰
$$$$

**Brown Palace.** Built in 1892 by pioneer Denver businessman Henry C. Brown from native Colorado brownstone, this Romanesque, 10-story, flatiron-shaped hotel with terra-cotta trim is among the most historic sites in the city. The spacious lobby, rising eight stories and covered by a giant stained-glass skylight, invites guests to relax in big, red couches or numerous leather chairs; you might also see a local journalist interviewing a visiting ambassador, or important politicians conferring here. Rooms and suites are furnished in Victorian style, with antique reproductions. All the accommodations are different, but guests can expect thick carpets, fine linen drapes, brass lamps, and hardwood coffee tables. Suites are large enough to host a meeting of 15 or more. Recent renovations have updated the bathrooms, which, though small, offer all modern conveniences. The Brown has the best reputation for service of any Denver hotel, and it's located at the main crossroads of downtown's financial district. Ellyngton's (*see* Business Breakfasts, *below*) suits those looking for an elegant breakfast setting, and The Ship Tavern (*see* After Hours, *below*) is good for after-dinner drinks. *A Preferred Hotel. 321 17th St., 80202, tel. 303/297–3111 or 800/321–2599, fax 303/293–9204. Gen. manager, Peter Abey. 230 rooms, 21 suites. AE, CB, DC, MC, V.*

**㉓ Burnsley.** This 16-story, Bauhaus-style tower, on the edge
**$$** of downtown, has become popular with upper-echelon ex-
ecutives since its major facelift of the 1980s. The long, nar-
row lobby is serene enough for a guest to read the
newspaper, but too small for anyone to comfortably host a
business discussion. All rooms and suites feature outdoor
balconies, which are usable most of the year. Even-num-
bered rooms on floor 10 and above offer stunning, northern
views of downtown and the Rockies, but some are painted
an unappealing shade of green. Rooms facing south don't
have the view, but are painted a more palatable light-rose
color. All rooms are well appointed with soft carpets, firm
beds, large writing desks, and full kitchens. The suites
also boast two television sets—one in the living area and
one in the bedroom. Downtown skyscrapers are within
walking distance. The residential neighborhood around
the hotel is safe during the day, but strolls after dark are
not recommended. The hotel's intimate bar, featuring live
jazz, makes single guests feel welcome. *1000 Grant St.,
80203, tel. 303/830–1000 or 800/231–3915, fax 303/830–
7676. Gen. manager, Joy Burns. 82 suites. AE, CB, DC,
MC, V.*

**㉗ Cambridge Club Hotel.** Secluded on a tree-lined side street
**$$** a ½ block from the gold dome of Colorado's state capitol,
this four-story, 1960s-era luxury suite hotel has become a
favorite with political lobbyists, chief executives, and
touring celebrities who would rather keep their wherea-
bouts unknown. The financial district, the 16th Street
Mall, and City Hall all are within easy walking distance.
Guests are greeted personally by the concierge. The lobby, decorated with light-wood paneling, is a quiet retreat
in which to watch the fire in the hearth, or to chat with
business associates. Each of the hotel's 26 one- and two-
bedroom suites is individually decorated, so no two rooms
are alike. Elements they share, however, include plush
carpeting, a firm bed, cozy reading chairs, and enough
room to hold a meeting with a few colleagues. The Cambridge is not equipped for large conferences. The staff is
soft-spoken and courteous. *1560 Sherman St., 80203, tel.
303/831–1252 or 800/752–1252. Dial main number for fax
access. Gen. manager, Frank Casados. 27 suites. AE,
DC, MC, V.*

**㉕ Comfort Inn/Downtown.** Travelers on a limited budget
**$$** will appreciate the Comfort Inn's reasonable prices and
convenient location. Built in 1959, the metallic-skinned
high rise directly faces 17th Street's financial houses, and
is within walking distance of the Colorado Convention
Center. The lobby decor is eclectic, to put it kindly, with a
mismatched ensemble of orange-striped sofas, brown-
spotted chairs, and a green patterned rug. Large win-
dows face two busy streets. Guest rooms are spartan, dec-
orated in dark colors, and lack the warmth of finer hotels.
With all of its drawbacks in decor, the Comfort Inn is
spanking clean and has an energetic staff, and can be ac-
counted one of the best buys in its price range. Rooms on
the upper floors are subject to the least street noise. Rates
include Continental breakfast and cocktails. *401 17th St.,
80202, tel. 303/296–0400 or 800/228–5150, fax 303/293–
9204. Gen. manager, Robert Holston. 224 rooms. AE, CB,
DC, MC, V.*

# DOWNTOWN DENVER

**Lodging**
Brown Palace , **16**
Burnsley, **20**
Cambridge Club
Hotel, **17**
Comfort Inn/
Downtown, **15**
Days Inn/Capitol
Hill, **21**
Embassy Suites/Denver
Place, **8**
Executive Tower
Inn, **6**

Hotel Denver
Downtown, **13**
Hyatt Regency
Denver/Downtown, **10**
Marriott-City
Center, **9**
Oxford Alexis, **3**
Radisson, **14**
Westin/Tabor Inn, **7**

**Dining**
Augusta, **7**
Buckhorn Exchange, **2**
Cliff Young's, **18**
Marlowe's, **12**
Paramount Café, **11**
Racine's, **19**
Tandoor Cuisine of
India, **4**
Zenith's, **1**

# GREATER DENVER

㉑ **Days Inn/Capitol Hill.** Simple, efficient, and affordable,
$$ the white, boxlike Days Inn is located in a commercial district southeast of the core downtown area, a brisk stroll from the state capitol, but a taxi ride from the core financial area and the Colorado Convention Center. Solo walks after dark are discouraged in this neighborhood. The lobby is serviceable but not inviting; the best place for business discussions is the hotel's coffee shop. Despite the tacky carpets and standard-issue wall prints, Days Inn provides a comfortable night's rest to travelers on a limited budget. *1150 E. Colfax Ave., 80218, tel. 303/831–7700 or 800/325–2525, fax 303/894–9193. Gen. manager, Larry Hammell. 143 rooms, 6 suites. AE, CB, D, DC, MC, V.*

❽ **Embassy Suites/Denver Place.** Built in 1983, the Embassy
$$$ Suites has become a favorite of television production crews and casts in town to shoot segments of "Perry Mason" and other TV shows. Housed in a gray-glass, ultramodern skyscraper, Embassy Suites is connected by skywalks to adjacent office towers, and is within walking distance of the financial district, the 16th Street Mall, and the shops at the Tabor Center. Since all rooms are suites, guests have considerably more elbow room than in standard hotel accommodations. Women business travelers are likely to appreciate the hotel's added security measures. Breakfast is complimentary and made-to-order. Suites on upper floors have spectacular views. Rooms on the lower levels, particularly right above the bar, are noisy. *1881 Curtis St., 80202, tel. 303/297–8888 or 800/572–5566, fax 303/298–1103. Gen. manager, Ian Van Riemsdyk. 335 suites. AE, D, MC, V.*

❻ **Executive Tower Inn.** Across the street from the Denver
$$ Center for the Performing Arts, the Executive Tower is close to downtown's theaters and concert halls, as well as to the Colorado Convention Center. The hotel has the active traveler in mind, and facilities include an exceptional in-house health club, with pool, weight room, and squash and tennis courts. Although a 1989 renovation enlivened the appearance of this 16-story modernist structure, it still suffers a bit from an overuse of earth tones in the rooms. The lobby, featuring rough brownstone planters and walls, is a good place to relax with a cocktail, but a bit too confined for confidential conversation. All upper-level rooms have unobstructed views either of the mountains or the city skyline. *1405 Curtis St., 80202, tel. 303/571–0300 or 800/525–6651, fax 303/825–4301. Gen. manager, Harold Levin. 337 rooms, 23 suites. AE, CB, DC, MC, V.*

⓭ **Hotel Denver Downtown.** Built in 1972, this white, mod-
$$ ernist hotel caters mostly to businesspeople attending large gatherings at the nearby Colorado Convention Center. The hotel has the cookie-cutter look of a large, mid-priced chain, including unimaginative rust-color room appointments and smallish guest bathrooms. The lobby has plenty of chairs, but can become noisy with the traffic of the close-by check-in counter and of the busy street outside; in fact, it seems more like an airport waiting room than a hotel lobby. The building's location provides good mountain and city views from the north-facing rooms. The hotel's restaurant is okay for a quick bite. *1450 Glenarm Pl., 80202, tel. 303/573–1450 or 800/465–4329, fax 303/*

# DENVER HOTEL CHART

| HOTELS | Price Category | Banquet capacity | No. of meeting rooms | Secretarial services | Audiovisual equipment | Teletype news service | Computer rentals | In-room modem phone jack | All-news cable channel | Desk | Desk lighting | Bed lighting |
|---|---|---|---|---|---|---|---|---|---|---|---|---|
| Brown Palace | $$$$ | 750 | 16 | ✓ | ✓ | - | ✓ | ✓ | ✓ | ● | ● | ◐ |
| Burnsley | $$$ | 0 | 2 | - | - | - | - | ✓ | - | ● | ● | ◐ |
| Cambridge Club | $$$ | 0 | 0 | ✓ | ✓ | - | - | ✓ | - | ◐ | ● | ◐ |
| Comfort Inn/ Downtown | $$ | 20 | 2 | ✓ | ✓ | - | ✓ | ✓ | ✓ | ◐ | ○ | ○ |
| Days Inn/ Capitol Hill | $$ | 225 | 4 | - | ✓ | - | - | ✓ | ✓ | ◐ | ◐ | ◐ |
| Embassy Suites/ Denver Place | $$$ | 250 | 4 | ✓ | ✓ | - | - | ✓ | ✓ | ◐ | ◐ | ◐ |
| Executive Tower Inn | $$ | 500 | 12 | ✓ | ✓ | - | - | ✓ | ✓ | ◐ | ◐ | ◐ |
| Hilton South | $$ | 500 | 13 | - | ✓ | - | - | ✓ | ✓ | ◐ | ◐ | ◐ |
| Hotel Denver Downtown | $$ | 400 | 16 | - | ✓ | - | - | ✓ | ✓ | ◐ | ○ | ◐ |
| Hyatt Regency Denver/Downtown | $$$ | 800 | 12 | - | ✓ | - | ✓ | ✓ | ✓ | ◐ | ◐ | ○ |
| Hyatt Regency Tech Center | $$$ | 1200 | 19 | ✓ | ✓ | - | - | ✓ | ✓ | ◐ | ◐ | ◐ |
| Loews Giorgio | $$$$ | 200 | 5 | ✓ | ✓ | - | - | ✓ | ✓ | ● | ◐ | ◐ |
| Many Mansions | $$ | 50 | 1 | - | - | - | - | ✓ | ✓ | ◐ | ● | ◐ |
| Marriott- City Center | $$$ | 1300 | 25 | ✓ | ✓ | - | - | ✓ | ✓ | ◐ | ◐ | ◐ |
| Oxford Alexis | $$$ | 110 | 6 | ✓ | ✓ | - | - | ✓ | ✓ | ◐ | ◐ | ◐ |
| Radisson | $$ | 1300 | 16 | ✓ | ✓ | - | - | ✓ | ✓ | ◐ | ◐ | ◐ |
| Registry | $$ | 575 | 5 | ✓ | ✓ | ✓ | - | ✓ | ✓ | ◐ | ◐ | ◐ |
| Sheraton Denver Tech Center | $$$ | 1000 | 23 | ✓ | ✓ | - | ✓ | ✓ | ✓ | ◐ | ○ | ○ |
| Westin/Tabor Center | $$$ | 600 | 20 | ✓ | ✓ | - | ✓ | ✓ | ✓ | ● | ● | ● |

**$$$$** = over $150, **$$$** = $100-$150, **$$** = under $100.
● good, ◐ fair, ○ poor.
All hotels listed here have photocopying and fax facilities.

| In-Room Amenities | | | | | | | | | | Hotel Amenities | | | | | | |
| Nonsmoking rooms | In-room check-out | Minibar | Pay movies | VCR/Movie rentals | Hairdryer | Toiletries | Room service | Laundry/Dry cleaning | Pressing | Concierge | Barber/Hairdresser | Garage | Courtesy airport transport | Sauna | Pool | Exercise room |
|---|---|---|---|---|---|---|---|---|---|---|---|---|---|---|---|---|
| ✓ | ✓ | ✓ | ✓ | - | ✓ | ● | ● | ● | ● | ✓ | ✓ | ✓ | ✓ | - | - | - |
| - | - | ✓ | - | - | - | ● | ◐ | ● | ● | ✓ | - | ✓ | - | - | ◐ | - |
| - | ✓ | ✓ | - | ✓ | - | ● | ◐ | ● | ● | ✓ | - | ✓ | - | - | - | - |
| ✓ | - | - | ✓ | - | - | ○ | ◐ | ● | ● | - | - | ✓ | - | - | - | - |
| ✓ | ✓ | - | - | - | - | ○ | ◐ | ◐ | ◐ | - | - | - | ✓ | - | ○ | - |
| ✓ | ✓ | ✓ | - | - | - | ● | ● | ● | ● | - | ✓ | ✓ | - | ✓ | ◐ | ● |
| ✓ | - | - | - | - | - | ◐ | ◐ | ● | ● | - | ✓ | ✓ | ✓ | ✓ | ● | ● |
| ✓ | ✓ | ✓ | - | - | - | ◐ | ● | ● | ● | ✓ | - | - | ✓ | ✓ | ● | ◐ |
| ✓ | ✓ | ✓ | ✓ | - | - | ◐ | ◐ | ● | ● | - | - | ✓ | ✓ | - | ◐ | - |
| ✓ | ✓ | ✓ | ✓ | - | ✓ | ◐ | ◐ | ● | ● | ✓ | - | ✓ | - | - | ◐ | - |
| ✓ | ✓ | ✓ | - | - | - | ● | ◐ | ● | ◐ | ✓ | - | ✓ | ✓ | - | ● | ◐ |
| ✓ | ✓ | - | ✓ | - | - | ◐ | ◐ | ● | ● | ✓ | - | - | ✓ | - | - | - |
| ✓ | - | ✓ | - | ✓ | ✓ | ◐ | ○ | ● | ● | - | - | ✓ | ✓ | ✓ | - | - |
| ✓ | ✓ | - | - | - | - | ● | ◐ | ● | ● | ✓ | - | ✓ | ✓ | ✓ | ● | ● |
| - | - | ✓ | - | - | ✓ | ● | ● | ● | ● | ✓ | ✓ | ✓ | ✓ | ✓ | - | ● |
| ✓ | ✓ | ✓ | ✓ | - | - | ◐ | ◐ | ● | ● | ✓ | ✓ | ✓ | - | - | ◐ | ◐ |
| ✓ | - | ✓ | ✓ | - | - | ◐ | ● | ● | ● | ✓ | - | ✓ | ✓ | ✓ | ● | ● |
| ✓ | - | ✓ | ✓ | ✓ | - | ● | ● | ● | ● | ✓ | ✓ | - | ✓ | ✓ | ● | ● |
| ✓ | ✓ | ✓ | ✓ | - | ✓ | ◐ | ● | ● | ● | ✓ | - | - | ✓ | ✓ | ● | ● |

**Room service:** ● 24-hour, ◐ 6AM–10PM, ○ other.
**Laundry/Dry cleaning:** ● same day, ◐ overnight, ○ other.
**Pressing:** ● immediate, ◐ same day, ○ other.

*572–1113. Gen. manager, Russ Finch. 400 rooms, 12 suites. AE, CB, D, DC, MC, V.*

**10**
**$$$**
**Hyatt Regency Denver/Downtown.** Linked to office buildings that face the core financial district, the 1980-era downtown Hyatt is conveniently located for bankers, stockbrokers, and government regulators with business on 17th Street, Denver's "Wall Street of the West." The Hyatt staff had some trouble adjusting when the hotel (formerly the Fairmont) changed management in the late 1980s, but travelers report that most service problems have been solved and the hotel is again worth a stay. The main entrance leads into a spacious lobby with low, comfortable sofas and chairs. With cocktails served from the well-staffed lobby bar, the Hyatt's main floor gives its guests a nice place to relax or talk business. The rose and pale-green color scheme is repeated throughout the hotel, and is just subtle enough not to become boring. The rooms are clean and up-to-date, if unoriginal; bathrooms could do with better lighting. *1750 Welton St., 80202, tel. 303/295–1200 or 800/233–1234, fax 303/292–2472. Gen. manager, John Schafer. 513 rooms, 27 suites. AE, CB, DC, MC, V.*

**28**
**$$$$**
**Loews Giorgio.** The most prominent feature of the 11-story Giorgio is its consistent, almost unrelenting, Italian Baroque motif—at odds with the hotel's simple, steel-and-black-glass facade. The cozy lobby includes a marble fireplace and Baroque paintings, while rooms feature large, comfortable chairs with brocade coverings. Built in 1987, the Giorgio has large guest bathrooms that feature soft lighting and big bathtubs. It also has earned a good reputation for service in the few years it's been open. Located halfway between downtown and the Denver Tech Center, the hotel is a convenient base for people who have business in both commercial districts. But the immediate surroundings—mostly strip shopping centers and apartment complexes—give the hotel a less businesslike feel than its competitors in either primary business area. Room rates include a complimentary breakfast—with, of course, Italian pastries. *4150 E. Mississippi Ave., 80222, tel. 303/782–9300 or 800/223–0607, fax 303/782–9300, ext. 7576. Gen. manager, C. E. Buckley. 200 rooms, 19 suites. AE, CB, DC, MC, V.*

**24**
**$$**
**Many Mansions.** A 1960s-era mid-rise nestled in a quiet residential neighborhood 15 minutes from downtown, Many Mansions has the feel of a comfortable, mid-priced apartment house converted to hotel use. That makes it ideal for people staying in Denver for an extended period and looking for an alternative to chain hotels. Its one- and two-bedroom suites include a dining area, full kitchen, and outdoor balcony, and are modestly decorated with pastel carpets and floral bedspreads. Suites are roomy enough to accommodate a small meeting; the hotel lobby is too small to offer a good place to sit and chat. Guests can use the Penthouse Clubroom to entertain. Free transportation is provided to destinations within a 15-minute drive of the hotel. Upper-level rooms that face Steele Street are quieter than those overlooking 13th Avenue. *1313 Steele St., 80206, tel. 303/355–1313 or 800/225–7829. Dial main number for fax access. Gen. manager, David Sackman. 36 suites. AE, D, MC, V.*

**⑨ Marriott-City Center.** The hotel occupies only 20 of the 40
$$$ stories in this 1982-vintage steel-and-glass skyscraper,
with the remaining floors dedicated to offices of local com-
panies. The structure's all-black exterior has earned it the
nickname "the Darth Vader building." Fortunately, the
interior is more appealing, and includes plum-color car-
pets and chairs in the lobby bar, a predictable marble-fa-
cade check-in counter, and a small army of eager bellhops.
The plum-and-rose color scheme is repeated in several of
the rooms: furnishings are comfortable, nothing out of the
ordinary. The Marriott is a favorite with convention-
goers; it is near the Colorado Convention Center, and its
large, lower-level ballrooms host numerous trade group
conclaves. Breakfast buffet at Marjolaines' restaurant on
the lower level begins at 6:30 AM weekdays, and 7 AM week-
ends, and is ideal for talks before the day's events swing into
high gear. The taxi stand in front of the hotel is one of the
few sure, convenient places to find a cab downtown. *1701
California St., 80202, tel. 303/297-1300 or 800/228-9290,
fax 303/298-7474. Gen. manager, David Pease. 612
rooms. AE, CB, DC, MC, V.*

**★ ❸ Oxford Alexis.** Visiting this hotel is like entering a time
$$$ machine that takes you back to 1891, when architect
Frank Edbrooke (who also designed the Brown Palace)
built this grande dame from native stone with wrought-
iron and terra-cotta accents. The exterior has been faithfully preserved, while inside the hardwood and tile floors
and marble registration counter have been restored. The
massive, original Victorian oil paintings are also in keeping with the hotel's spirit. Each room is individually appointed in French and English antiques; one room's
attraction may be a turn-of-the-century writing desk,
another's may be a Queen Anne chair. Bathrooms have
been modernized but are a bit small. Historic Union Station is less than a block away, and the financial district and
16th Street Mall are within walking distance. *1600 17th
St., 80202, tel. 303/628-5400 or 800/228-5838, fax 303/
628-5413. Gen. manager, Peter White. 81 rooms. AE, CB,
DC, MC, V.*

**⑭ Radisson.** One of the earliest commissioned works of
$$ famed architect I.M. Pei (who also designed Denver's 16th
Street Mall), the Radisson is a monument to the 1960s
Brutalist building style. The 22-story structure is long
and narrow, and rises directly above the 16th Street pe-
destrian mall. An extensive renovation in 1990 converted
some of the cramped, conventioneer-style rooms into spa-
cious suites, and added new carpets and furnishings. The
new earth-tone decor is pleasantly subtle, and the bath-
room lighting is much improved. The Radisson is well lo-
cated, within walking distance of the Colorado
Convention Center, the financial district, the state capi-
tol, and City Hall. The layout of the hotel may confuse
guests initially, since the registration desk and meeting
rooms are on the second level, and it's hard to find a bell-
hop to ask directions. *1550 Court Pl., 80202, tel. 303/893-
3333 or 800/333-3333, fax 303/623-0303. Gen. manager,
Tom Driscoll. 750 rooms. AE, CB, DC, MC, V.*

**❼ Westin/Tabor Center.** Built in 1982, this 20-story green
$$$ glass and stone hotel is one of Denver's newest landmarks.
The lobby, which is on the second level, suffers from a su-

perabundance of pink marble, but it offers single guests a comfortable place to relax and listen to live music—unless noise from the registration desk is excessive when large groups are checking in. Decorated in maroon and subtle green, the Westin's rooms are spacious, well lighted, and well kept; they also offer good views. Upgraded rooms on the concierge level have such perks as a sizable writing desk with good lighting, and a telephone and television in the large bathroom. Considered one of downtown's most modern, upscale hotels, the Westin attracts sports celebrities, corporate executives, and nationally known politicians. Augusta (*see* Dining, below), an award-winning restaurant, is housed on the lobby level. The Westin's indoor tunnels connect it to the chic shops at the Tabor Center, as well as to a post office-pharmacy-liquor store-convenience store called Watson's. *1672 Lawrence St., 80202, tel. 303/572–9100 or 800/228–3000, fax 303/572–7288. Gen. manager, William Quinn. 420 rooms. AE, CB, D, DC, MC, V.*

## In or Near Denver Tech Center

**③①** **Denver Hilton South.** Set on a large lawn amid numerous
**$$** small trees, this six-story, brick hotel blends in well with the campuslike surroundings of the Denver Tech Center. Its location just off the Interstate puts the ranch-style hotel only minutes away from some of the largest companies in the metro area, including the corporate headquarters for U S West and the regional offices of AT&T. The ranch motif continues inside; the lobby is colored like a Southwestern sunset, in subtle purples, tans, and oranges, and boasts a large fireplace; there's plenty of room to sit and chat here. Both guest rooms and baths are of average size, but appointed in pleasing aqua and rose colors. The writing desk, placed near the floor-to-ceiling windows, captures the natural light during the day; after dark, however, the desk's lighting is a bit dim. West-facing rooms offer mountain views; rooms facing south offer views of Pikes Peak, 65 miles to the southwest. Avoid rooms that face the pool area; they get far too much noise. The hotel's biggest drawback is the rambling layout; it's a long walk from rooms to the registration desk, an annoyance even though guests can park close to their quarters. *7801 E. Orchard Rd., Englewood, 80111, tel. 303/779–6161 or 800/327–2242, fax 303/850–0103. Gen. manager, Gerald Valone. 306 rooms, 5 suites. AE, CB, DC, MC, V.*

**★ ㉙** **Hyatt Regency Tech Center.** Built in 1985, this 12-story
**$$$** glass and pink stone hotel has earned a good reputation for service among business travelers, who make up 80% of its clientele. Located in the heart of the Denver Tech Center, the Hyatt Regency is within walking distance of several major cable television and entertainment companies. The lobby has a winding staircase that leads to the meeting-room level and also divides the space into some cozy seating areas. Most rooms are appointed with rose- or light-plum furnishings, colors apparently popular with interior designers of the mid-1980s. Suites are exceptionally fine, featuring a large living-room area and sizable bedroom and bath. The dining table seats up to six people and doubles as a large desk or work area. The 11th floor offers added security for guests. Rooms on the northwest side have the best views of downtown, with the Rockies as a

backdrop. *7800 E. Tufts Ave., 80237, tel. 303/779–1234 or 800/233–1234, fax 303/850–7164. Gen. manager, David Beecham. 450 rooms. AE, CB, DC, MC, V.*

**③⓪** **Sheraton Denver Tech Center.** Surrounded by office devel-
**$$$** opments, the Sheraton offers easy access to corporate Denver, as well as to the numerous trade conferences held in its ballrooms. A recent renovation added an 11-story wing to the original 1970s-vintage, five-story structure, plus a secure floor to make female guests more comfortable. It's a fair hike from the registration desk to the elevators that lead to the new wing, but these rooms are definitely preferred—they are brighter, have better desk and bathroom lighting, and a pleasing pastel decor. Older rooms are steeped in outdated dark green, and rooms with balconies facing the restaurants are noisy. If you get placed in the older wing, ask for a room with a window facing out, preferably west or northwest. Additional amenities, such as free fax service, are available with room upgrades. *4900 DTC Pkwy., 80237, tel. 303/779–1100 or 800/552–7030, fax 303/779–1100, ext. 202. Gen. manager, William Zollars. 623 rooms. AE, MC, V.*

### Airport

**㉖** **Registry.** This hotel, across the street from Stapleton In-
**$$** ternational Airport, is a favorite with airline crews and just-in-for-the-night travelers. Free shuttle buses circulate between the hotel and the airport check-in counters every 15 minutes, 24 hours a day. The drawback to this convenient location is the occasional roar of jets, which can be particularly annoying when planes are routed over the hotel. A 1989 renovation gave the Registry new carpets, new fixtures, a pleasant rose-and-cream color scheme, a new name, and a much-improved attitude about service. The now spacious bathrooms particularly benefited from the makeover. The dimly lighted lobby, however, still feels cramped. *3203 Quebec St., 80237, tel. 303/321–3333 or 800/ 247–9810, fax 303/321–3333. Gen. manager, Steven Hronek. 574 rooms. AE, CB, D, DC, MC, V.*

## DINING

Denver once was a beef-hungry town, but as health-conscious tastes evolved, a cornucopia of new restaurants opened, offering consumers a variety of fresh fish, salads, and ethnic and contemporary American cuisine. The most pleasant surprise is the reasonable prices, even at the fanciest places. Because Denver is a Western town, casual attire is acceptable in most restaurants; jacket and tie are recommended only in the better establishments.

Highly recommended restaurants in each price category are indicated by a star ★.

| Category | Cost* |
| --- | --- |
| $$$$ (Very Expensive) | over $35 |
| $$$ (Expensive) | $25–$35 |
| $$ (Moderate) | under $25 |

*per person, including appetizer, entrée, and dessert, but excluding drinks, service, and 7.5% sales tax.*

*Numbers in the margin correspond to numbered restaurant locations on the Denver Lodging and Dining maps.*

## Business Breakfasts

**Ellyngton's.** Local businesspeople often invite clients to breakfast in this dining room of the historic Brown Palace Hotel. White-linen tablecloths, brass chandeliers, and a tuxedoed wait staff set a tone of elegance. On bright summer days, Colorado sunshine floods the room. The staff is attentive, but not overly so. Breakfast starts with fresh fruits and juices; also on the menu are home-baked pastries, granola parfait, hot Irish oatmeal, omelets, and specialties such as smoked Oregon sockeye salmon. *321 17th St., tel. 303/297–3111.*

**Egg Shell.** In addition to the usual omelets and french toast, the Egg Shell has low-fat dishes. Denver's joggers favor the legendary pancakes, which taste rich but actually are quite healthful. Tucked inside a renovated historic building in downtown Denver, this place offers pleasant surroundings for a business meeting, but is packed with patrons 7:15–8:30 AM; be there earlier or later to avoid waiting up to 45 minutes for a table. *1520 Blake St., tel. 303/623–7555.*

**Harvest.** In the Denver Tech Center, the Harvest caters mostly to the health-conscious, offering an interesting variety of homemade breads, muffins, granolas, yogurts, omelets, pancakes, tofus mixed with spicy vegetables and brown beans, and rice dishes with a zesty Mexican-style salsa. A variety of fruit-and-protein shakes make filling meals in themselves (the strawberry one is particularly recommended). The blueberry muffins are not to be missed. Smoking is not permitted. Private booths are available, but the "commons table" creates a casual atmosphere for single diners and those on the run. *7730 E. Belleview Ave., Denver Tech Center, tel. 303/779–4111.*

**Racine's.** In a new, adobe-style building near downtown, this casual eatery has become a favorite Denver power-breakfast spot; it's a good place for a quiet talk against a backdrop of cacti, Indian weavings, and buffalo skulls. You can start your day here with a granola, fresh fruit, bread platter—or face the world after a chili-and-tortilla dish called the Southwestern Sun breakfast. *850 Bannock St. (at Speer Blvd.), tel. 303/595–0148.*

Other breakfast options include the two downtown locations of **Delectable Egg** (1642 Market St., tel. 303/572–8156; 1625 Court Pl., tel. 303/892–5720); both casual places offer dishes ranging from shepherd's pie to omelets to Mexican-style huevos rancheros. For an informal or solo Continental breakfast, **Market** (1455 Larimer St., tel. 303/534–5140) has a good selection of freshly made pastries, and an eye-opening array of espresso, teas, and coffees.

## Downtown

$$$$ **Augusta.** This award-winning restaurant on the lobby level of the Westin Hotel/Tabor Center offers an excellent atmosphere for business entertaining. China table settings, velvet chairs, and black lacquer fixtures create an atmosphere that's sophisticated but not ostentatious. Win-

dowside tables offer fine city views. Entrées on the Northwest American menu include succulent silver salmon, broiled tiger prawns in red or yellow curry, roast duckling, Colorado rack of lamb, and 18-ounce T-bone steak. The wine list is extensive and varied. The staff is discreet, and the tables are well separated—all of which allows for serious business discussion. *1672 Lawrence St., tel. 303/ 572–9100. Jacket and tie recommended. Reservations advised. AE, CB, D, DC, MC, V. Closed Sun. and Mon., Sat. lunch.*

**➋ Buckhorn Exchange.** This place looks like a set for a Western movie, as well it should. Opened in 1893, it claims to be
$$$$ Denver's oldest surviving restaurant and tavern. It's in a brick and wooden building, with old wagon wheels lining the sidewalk by the entrance. Floors are of rough hardwood, tables are covered with red-and-white checked cloths, and the huge, carved cherry wood bar on the upper level is authentic Victorian handwork. Old photos, maps, hunting rifles, and dozens of stuffed animal heads complete the picture. The menu is almost exclusively meat; specialties include wild game, such as buffalo and elk steaks, as well as quail and rabbit dishes. The wine list is limited. The casually dressed staff is energetic and friendly, but the noise level can rise to annoying heights; this is a place to relax after work, not one in which to attempt a serious discussion. The restaurant's main drawback is its location in a neighborhood that's sliding into seediness. *1000 Osage St., tel. 303/534–9505. Casual dress. Reservations advised. AE, CB, D, DC, MC, V. Closed Sat. and Sun. lunch.*

**★ ⓭ Cliff Young's.** Specializing in fine American cuisine, Cliff
$$$$ Young's is noted for its intimate atmosphere and discreet, efficient service. Large windows in the renovated building let in plenty of natural light, but translucent white-linen curtains filter out street distractions. You walk through a lounge with comfortable chairs and a dark hardwood bar to reach the elegant Art Deco dining room. The excellent fare usually includes free-range veal, medallions of beef, and several fish and salad dishes. A particular favorite is venison, covered with a subtly sweet combination of pineapple, berry, and walnut sauces. There's live piano and violin music nightly. The neighborhood can be off-putting, especially at night, so it's wise to let the valet park your car. *700 E. 17th Ave., tel. 303/831–8900. Jacket and tie recommended. Reservations advised. AE, CB, D, DC, MC, V. Closed Sun., Sat. lunch*

**㉓ Juanita's.** When Denverites crave Mexican food, they head
$$ to Juanita's, a casual cantina that attracts a local crowd, usually attired in blue jeans. Located east of downtown along 17th Avenue's emerging restaurant row, Juanita's features moderate to spicy salsas, giant burritos, salads, soups, seafood, and some of the best chili in town. In warm weather, Juanita's outdoor patio is a great spot for relaxing. The room, which can only be described as neon Mexican, has Southwestern pastel walls, small booths with seats that look like church pews, and a giant, red neon cactus. It can get very noisy at dinner, but that only seems to add to the fun; this isn't the place for quiet business talks. *1700 Vine St., tel. 303/333–9595. Casual dress. Reservations not needed. AE, MC, V.*

**⑫ Marlowe's.** Local businesspeople find Marlowe's light-oak
$$ tables and open atmosphere a good setting for informal
business get-togethers. The fare is simple and hearty, fea-
turing salads, pastas, and grilled dishes, including many
low-fat items. All portions are large; even individual sal-
ads are big enough to feed the average American family.
The veal chop is popular, as is the linguine and the
Cobb salad. Located in a historic, gray stone building,
Marlowe's has large windows that let in lots of light.
During warm weather, preferred seating is on the restau-
rant's patio, facing the 16th Street Mall. Lunchtime
crowds are large, so it's wise to arrive early. *511 16th St.
(entrance faces Glenarm Pl.), tel. 303/595–3700. Casual
dress. Reservations usually not accepted at lunchtime.
AE, CB, DC, MC, V. Closed Sun.*

**⑪ Paramount Café.** A noisy bistro that attracts the younger
$$ set, the Paramount is one of the best people-watching
places in town. Rock'n'roll blares from the loudspeakers,
the tables are packed close together, the staff dresses in
sweatshirts, and patrons all seem to wear Vuarnet sunglasses. The energized atmosphere is pure urban funk.
It's a good place to relax with close associates, but not to
transact serious business. The Paramount serves burgers, burritos, salads, sandwiches, and blue-plate specials.
*511 16th St. (entrance faces 16th Street Mall), tel. 303/
893–2000. Casual dress. No reservations. AE, CB, DC,
MC, V. Closed Sun.*

**④ Tandoor Cuisine of India.** A variety of exotic dishes are
$$$ featured at this intimate restaurant nestled in a historic
building in lower downtown. Red carpets, brass fixtures,
and carved hardwood chairs and tables set the mood for
the Indian fare, which includes curries, pakoras, and ka-
bobs; the vegetarian selection is large. Entrées are accom-
panied by *dal* (lentil soup), salad, rice, and crispy papa-
dum bread. The tandoori chicken is a favorite with local
patrons, but the restaurant also serves some traditional
American foods like steaks for those with less adventur-
ous tastes. Secluded tables allow for quiet business meet-
ings. There is a lunch buffet on weekdays. *1514 Blake St.,
tel. 303/572–9071. Casual dress. Reservations advised.
AE, CB, DC, MC, V.*

**★ ㉕ Tante Louise.** Long a favorite of Denverites who want to
$$$$ combine good food and private conversation, this quaint
restaurant, about 15 minutes east of downtown, is notable
for its understated good taste. There are several small din-
ing rooms—all elegantly appointed with linen table cloths
and silver place settings—so it's easy to find a nook or
cranny to discuss business. About a third of the menu is
French, another third New American, and the rest con-
sists of tasty low-fat dishes. The delicate angel hair pasta
and grilled salmon in beurre blanc are recommended.
Service is crisp but friendly. *4900 E. Colfax Ave., tel. 303/
355–4488. Reservations advised. Business or formal at-
tire suggested. AE, CB, DC, MC, V. Closed lunch and
Sun.*

**① Zenith's.** Although this trendy downtown spot bills itself
$$$ as "an American grill," it dishes up specialties like jumbo
ravioli and charbroiled bobwhite quail with Texas barbe-
cue sauce. Its location atop the six-story Tivoli tower—
a renovated Victorian brewery—provides exceptional
views, particularly as the sun fades over the mountains

and the city lights are turned on. Tables are spaced far apart and the young staff is energetic and eager to please, making this a good place to have a talk with clients or associates. The open, airy room with its pastel color scheme is in keeping with the Southwestern style that is the current rage in town. *901 Larimer St., tel. 303/629–1989. Casual dress. Reservations advised. AE, MC, V. Closed Sun., Sat. lunch.*

## Denver Tech Center

★ ③② **Château Pyrenees.** Opened in 1974, this formal restaurant
$$$$ still offers the best locale for fine dining in the Denver Tech Center area. Its location, just off Interstate 25, makes it easy to find; and the building, with its turrets and wooden shingles, looks decidedly out of place amid the surrounding fast food outlets. Plush booths in the large, open dining area, graced by a crystal chandelier and an antique grand piano, allow for quiet discussions. Tuxedoed waiters provide efficient if somewhat stiff service. The French name of this establishment belies the diversity of its menu, which includes a variety of Continental dishes. Quail with wild rice and lamb chops with artichokes are particularly noteworthy. *6538 S. Yosemite Circle, tel. 303/770–6660. Business or formal attire suggested. Reservations advised. AE, CB, DC, MC, V.*

③⓪ **Campari's.** This cheerful, Mediterranean-style restau-
$$$ rant, with its patterned tile floors and pastel tones, is a good spot for business lunches, if it's a bit too casual for serious business entertaining. On the ground level of the Sheraton Tech Center, Campari's draws heavily on convention and local business clientele (the restaurant has its own entrance on the north side of the Center, so it's possible to avoid the confusion of the lobby and convention areas); secluded booths provide privacy for important discussions, and tables are well spaced for confidential conversation. The Northern Italian menu includes good pasta selections, such as linguine with clams; the pasta is made on the premises. Veal dishes and fresh seafood entrées such as scallops and salmon in a tasty fish broth are also recommended. The wine list has some nice bottles from Northern Italy. The best desserts are the restaurant's own gelati and sorbets. *4900 DTC Pkwy., tel. 303/779–1100. Casual dress. Reservations advised. AE, MC, V.*

②⑨ **Centennial.** Located in the penthouse of the Hyatt Regency
$$$ Tech Center, this restaurant may have the best mountain views in Denver. From its west-side tables, on a clear day guests can see a 120-mile sweep of the Rocky Mountains, from Long's Peak to the north to Pike's Peak far to the south. (The scene is less pleasing on some winter days, when smog covers the city.) If the quality of the food doesn't quite match that of the view, the menu is diverse, featuring salads and seafood items that appeal to the health-conscious diner—a category that includes many young cable TV executives who work nearby. Popular dishes include blackened scallops, and veal with mushrooms. The Southwestern-style decor perfectly complements the open, atrium-style setting. Tables and booths are secluded, so conversations remain private. The small bar near the entrance is a comfortable place for a single woman to enjoy a quiet drink. *7800 E. Tufts Ave., in*

*the Denver Tech Center, tel. 303/779–1234. Jacket and tie advised; casual attire acceptable. Reservations advised. AE, CB, D, DC, MC, V. Closed Sat. lunch, Sun. dinner.*

## Cherry Creek

★ **㉗** **Chez Thoa.** Since the mid-1970s, Denver has seen a mod-
**$$$** est rise in restaurants serving Southeast Asian foods, and this place, owned by Thoa Fink, is the best. Thoa's establishment cooks up French and Vietnamese food in an elegant setting. The large open dining room has private booths and tables spaced far enough apart for private business meetings. White linen tablecloths, leather chairs, and a nattily attired wait staff create a formal atmosphere. The menu features such flavorful items as Oriental dumplings and steamed fish in ginger sauce. Nightly pork or duck specials are always excellent choices. Many dishes are especially created for health-conscious customers. Located in the Cherry Creek shopping district, Chez Thoa's is a good halfway meeting point between downtown and the Denver Tech Center. *158 Fillmore St., tel. 303/ 355–2323. Jacket and tie recommended. Reservations advised. AE, DC, MC, V. Closed Sun., Sat. lunch.*

## Outlying Areas

**㉒** **The Fort.** This restaurant's panoramic view of Denver is
**$$$$** itself worth the 30-minute drive from downtown. Located in the foothills of the Rocky Mountains, the Fort is modeled after an historic adobe trading post. Admittedly, it's somewhat touristy: A tepee marks the entrance and a giant sculpture of a mythical snake stands on the red rocks above the restaurant. Wooden tables and earth tones pick up the Old Southwest motif indoors. The fare matches the ambience: Specialties include buffalo, elk, quail, trout, salmon, and catfish. The buffalo sausage is spicy; the pinion nuts that coat the catfish add zest to an old favorite. Rocky Mountain "oysters" are a local oddity for the courageous to try. The restaurant seats up to 350, but tables are arranged to maximize patrons' privacy. *19192 State Hwy. 8, south of Morrison, tel. 303/697–4771. Casual dress. Reservations advised. AE, CB, D, DC, MC, V.*

## FREE TIME

### Fitness

*Hotel Facilities*
Hotel health clubs in Denver are not open to nonguests; most hotels without their own facilities have arrangements with downtown health clubs.

*Health Clubs*
The **International Athletic Club** (1630 Welton St., tel. 303/ 623–2100) has a rooftop running track, providing a safe place to run at night under the city lights. Rates are $10 a day; on the third Friday and fourth Saturday of every month admission is free. **Oxford Club** (17th and Wynkoop Sts., downtown, tel. 303/628–5444) also charges nonmembers $10 for day use, as does the **Sporting Club** (2 locations: 500 S. Cherry St., east of Cherry Creek shopping mall, tel. 303/399–3050; 5151 DTC Blvd., Denver Tech Center, tel. 303/779–0700).

*Jogging*

**City Park,** about 10 minutes east of downtown, offers good opportunities for a run with a view. A path around the lake is nice for a short jog (about ½ mile); more ambitious runners should move west beyond the lake, toward the park's playgrounds and gardens. (Note: it's not safe to run here at night.) The **Denver Tech Center** is set up like a college campus, with lots of open green space and gently curving streets. Most hotels in the area provide jogging maps or directions on running through the Center. Keep Denver's altitude in mind when going for a run; those not used to the city's rarified air may find themselves feeling headachy, nauseated, and short of breath.

## Shopping

**The Shops at the Tabor Center** (tel. 303/534–2141), in the 16th Street Mall between Arapahoe and Larimer Streets, adjacent to the Westin Hotel, is a slick, modern, glass structure with tenants as diverse as **Brooks Brothers,** the **Sharper Image,** and a Western and Indian jewelry store called **Silver Heels. Larimer Square** (tel. 313/534–2367), west of the Tabor Center, along Larimer Street between 15th and 14th streets, is a group of historic buildings housing gift shops, art galleries, and affordable clothiers. **Cherry Creek** shopping center, located halfway between downtown and the Denver Tech Center, offers Denver's most upscale shopping options. It's divided into two sections: **North Cherry Creek** includes **Auer's** (2100 St. Paul St., tel. 303/327–0404), a high-fashion woman's clothing store, and **Lawrence Covell** (225 Steel St., tel. 303/320–1023), featuring imported European clothing for men and women, as well as numerous chic restaurants and boutiques. Across 1st Avenue from this district is the **Cherry Creek shopping center** (1st Ave. and University Blvd., tel. 303/388–2522), which has recently expanded to include **Saks Fifth Avenue, Lord & Taylor,** and **Neiman-Marcus.**

The mall closest to the Denver Tech Center, **Marina Square** (8101 E. Belleview Ave., tel. 303/773–8622), features several tony clothing and gift stores.

## Diversions

The **Colorado State Museum** (13th St. and Broadway, tel. 303/866–3681), an ultramodern structure, features colorful exhibits that tell the story of Colorado's pioneer era.

The **Denver Art Museum** (14th and Bannock Sts., tel. 303/575–2793), near City Hall, in a modern building, displays excellent examples of North and South American Indian art, as well as classical, modern, and Oriental works.

The **Denver Zoo** (tel. 303/331–4110), located near the Natural History Museum, has an exceptional collection of predatory cats, including the rare snow leopard from the Himalayas.

The **Museum of Western Art** (1727 Tremont Pl., downtown, tel. 303/296–1880), housed in a Victorian structure that used to be a bordello, exhibits original paintings and sculpture from the Civil War through World War II. Included are master works by such American artists as Bierstadt, Remington, and O'Keeffe.

For a **scenic drive,** a year-round tour follows I–70 for 60 miles west to the Georgetown turnoff, goes through that historic mining town, and winds up a narrow road with good views to Guanella Pass. At the top of the pass, which is above the timberline, you'll have a close-up view of the west side of Mt. Evans, with its rugged sawtooth ridge. From the pass, descend south for several miles to U.S. 285. At the intersection, go left (east). The road winds through scenic mountain canyons before reentering Denver, where it hooks up with I–25. At the I–25 intersection, go south to reach the Denver Tech Center and north to return to downtown. Drive time is around 3½ hours. Call ahead for road-condition information (tel. 303/639–1111); do not go if the roads are icy, snowy, or otherwise impaired.

Colorado's **ski** season traditionally starts in November and lasts into early June. The closest resorts are in Summit County: Breckenridge, Copper Mountain, Arapahoe Basin, and Keystone. Most open about 9 AM and close about 4 PM, but Keystone's well-lighted runs remain open until 10 PM. To reach the Summit County ski areas, follow I–70 west for about an hour and a half, passing through the 1.7-mile-long Eisenhower tunnel. You can rent equipment at the resorts or at Gart Bros. sporting goods (1000 Broadway, a few blocks south of downtown, tel. 303/861–1112) or at Breeze Ski rentals in west Denver (11355 W. 6th Ave., tel. 303/232–7547).

**U.S. Mint** (320 W. Colfax at Cherokee St., tel. 303/844–3582), the one place in Denver that's really making money, attracts more tourists than any other single institution in town. It has one of the nation's largest stocks of gold bullion. Tours are free, but lines are long.

Stroll through **Washington Park** (S. Downing and E. Virginia Sts.) as a break from the work day. It's virtually unknown to tourists but well frequented by Denver's joggers and lollers.

## Professional Sports

**Football. Denver Broncos,** Mile High Stadium (tel. 303/433–7466). **Basketball. Denver Nuggets,** McNichols Arena (tel. 303/893–3865).

## The Arts

The **Denver Center for the Performing Arts** (13th and Curtis Sts., tel. 303/893–3272; box office, 303/893–4100) is a modern complex that houses most of the city's large concert halls and live theaters, including **Boettcher Concert Hall** (tel. 303/893–4111), home of the **Colorado Symphony Orchestra** (tel. 303/893–3272); **Denver Center Theater Company** (tel. 303/893–4100), the city's largest theatrical company; and **Robert Garner Attractions** (performance information, tel. 303/893–3272; box office, 303/893–4100), which produces Broadway-style plays. The **Denver Chamber Orchestra** performs at century-old **Trinity Methodist Church** (18th St. and Broadway, downtown, tel. 303/825–4911). Rock and pop music fans will find their favorite stars performing at **McNichols Arena** (1635 Clay St., tel. 303/572–4703) during the winter, and at the famed **Red Rocks** (west of Denver, near Morrison) and **Fiddler's**

**Green** (6350 Greenwood Plaza Blvd., southeast of Denver Tech Center, tel. 303/741–5000) outdoor amphitheaters during the summer. Call Ticketmaster (*see* below) for information.

The **Ticket Bus**, a red double-decker parked on 16th Street at Curtis Street, sells tickets to most downtown events; no phone, open 10–6 weekdays. **Ticketmaster** (tel. 303/290–8497) has tickets for most sporting, musical, and theatrical events in Denver.

## After Hours

Those planning to go out for drinks with business contacts or associates should take note: The city's altitude works to exacerbate the effect of alcohol on the system. You'll get drunk much more quickly here. It's best to decrease your usual intake—especially if you plan to drive.

*Bars and Lounges*
**The Ship Tavern** (tel. 303/297–3111), in the elegant Brown Palace hotel, downtown, is top choice for quiet drinks after work. **The Peppermill** (8100 E. Orchard Rd., tel. 303/741–1626) is a favorite gathering spot for business types who work in the Denver Tech Center. Across the South Platte River from downtown, **My Brother's Bar** (2376 15th St., just north of the Forney Museum, tel. 303/455–9991) is a popular tavern with a beer and burger menu, and classical music on the sound system. The bar has no sign outside, but it is still not hard to locate.

*Rock Clubs*
**Basin's Up** (1427 Larimer St., tel. 303/623–2104) is loud, noisy, and crowded, especially on weekends. It features good live rock and attracts a late 20s–early 40s crowd.

*Country-Western Music Clubs*
**Grizzly Rose** (5450 N. Valley Hwy., tel. 303/295–1330) promises a foot-stomping good time on a huge dance floor. Music ranges from crossover, rocklike renditions to fiddle-playing, two-step Texas swing tunes. Jammed on weekends with patrons decked out in Stetsons and boots.

*Comedy Clubs*
**Comedy Works** (1226 15th St., tel. 303/595–3637) is especially popular on weekends, when it features nationally known stand-up comics.

# Detroit

*by Richard Bak*

Despite hosting a Super Bowl and a National Republican Convention in the 1980s, Detroit suffers from a shortage of downtown hotels and a negative image that works against the city's drawing the kind of high profile events it desires. Nevertheless, downtown's renaissance, although slowed in the recession of the 1980s, is still continuing. New building has been extensive, with the $750-million waterfront Renaissance Center complex as the focus of a revitalized downtown, and old buildings are gaining new life as commercial centers. The refurbished theater district is flourishing; a new elevated monorail system makes a circuit around the central business district in 14 minutes; and the Cobo Exhibition/Convention Center completed a $225 million expansion in 1989.

Foreign competition and the recession of the early '80s have forced Detroit to broaden its economic base with a range of high-tech and service companies, many of them foreign-owned. Although the "Big Three" of General Motors, Ford, and Chrysler are all headquartered hereabouts, the center of U.S. automaking is slowly sliding south along I-75, with Honda (Ohio), Subaru-Isuzu (Indiana), Toyota (Kentucky), and Nissan (Tennessee) all opening production plants in the last decade.

Today, nearly 400 foreign firms—most of them joint ventures—employ more than 33,000 people in and around Detroit, including Mazda, whose presence would have been unthinkable in the '70s. Now it's accepted as part of Detroit's growth in the global marketplace.

Despite being the largest port city on the Canadian border, Detroit is still struggling to realize the full potential of the U.S./Canada Free Trade Agreement, which by 1998 will lift all tariffs and duties on products exchanged between the world's two largest trade partners. Because Detroit already handles 25% of the nearly $170 billion worth of goods that annually flow between the two countries, the agreement makes the city a logical choice for facilitating new and expanded products and services.

## Top Employers

| Employer | Type of Enterprise | Parent*/ Headquarters |
|---|---|---|
| Chrysler Corp. | Automobile manufacturing | Warren, MI |
| Detroit Edison Co. | Utility | Detroit |
| Ford Motor Co. | Automobile manufacturing | Dearborn, MI |
| Fruehauf Corp. | Auto parts | Southfield, MI |
| General Motors Corp. | Automobile manufacturing | Detroit |
| K-Mart Corp. | General merchandising | Troy, MI |
| Masco Corp. | Auto parts | Taylor, MI |
| NBD Bancorp Inc. | Banking | Detroit |
| The Stroh Brewery Co. | Beer | Detroit |
| Unisys Corp. | Auto parts | Southfield, MI |

*if applicable

## ESSENTIAL INFORMATION

### Climate

What follows are the average daily maximum and minimum temperatures for Detroit.

| | | | | | | | | |
|---|---|---|---|---|---|---|---|---|
| **Jan.** | 31F | −1C | **Feb.** | 32F | 0C | **Mar.** | 43F | 6C |
| | 20 | −7 | | 18 | −8 | | 27 | −3 |
| **Apr.** | 56F | 13C | **May** | 67F | 19C | **June** | 77F | 25C |
| | 38 | 3 | | 49 | 9 | | 58 | 14 |
| **July** | 83F | 28C | **Aug.** | 81F | 27C | **Sept.** | 74F | 23C |
| | 63 | 17 | | 63 | 17 | | 56 | 13 |
| **Oct.** | 61F | 16C | **Nov.** | 47F | 8C | **Dec.** | 36F | 2C |
| | 45 | 7 | | 34 | 1 | | 25 | −4 |

### Airports

**Metropolitan Airport** is located in Romulus, 26 miles southwest of downtown. Southwest Airlines routes roughly half of its flights through **City Airport** on the east side, 10 miles from downtown.

### Airport Business Facilities

**Teleticket** (in the North, South, and International Terminals, tel. 313/942–4731) has ticket pickup and travel insurance. The North and South terminal locations also have fax and photocopying services; the South terminal location has baggage storage. **Marriott Airport Hotel** (upper level, between Concourses D and E, tel. 313/941–9400) has fax machines, photocopying, secretarial service, notary public, baggage storage, conference rooms with catering service, and day rates for rooms.

## Airlines

Detroit is a hub city for Midway, Northwest, and Southwest Airlines.

**American,** tel. 800/433–7300.
**Braniff,** tel. 800/272–6433.
**Continental,** tel. 313/963–4600 or 800/525–0280.
**Delta,** tel. 313/355–3200 or 800/221–1212.
**Great Lakes,** tel. 800/554–5111.
**Midway,** tel. 800/621–5700.
**Northwest,** tel. 313/962–2002 or 800/225–2525.
**Pan Am,** tel. 800/221–1111.
**Piedmont,** tel. 800/251–5720.
**Southwest,** tel. 313/562–1221.
**TWA,** tel. 313/962–8650 or 800/221–2000.
**United,** tel. 800/631–1500.
**USAir,** tel. 313/963–8340 or 800/428–4322.

## Between the Airport and Downtown

*By Taxi*
Taxis take 30–40 minutes at nonpeak hours and 45–60 minutes at rush hour (7:30–8:30 AM from the airport, 4–6:30 PM from downtown). Cost: $26 plus tip.

*By Bus*
Commuter Transportation Company (tel. 313/941–9391) operates nonstop buses from the airport to major downtown hotels from 6 AM to 11 PM. Depending on your hotel stop, the ride can take up to 15 minutes longer than by taxi. Cost: $12 one way; $22 round-trip. Buses leave every ½ hour weekdays, every hour weekends.

*By Limousine*
Carey Cars (1542 E. Grand Blvd., tel. 313/885–2600) offers 24-hour service to or from the airport. Cost: $90 one way, including tip. Also *see* Important Addresses and Numbers, below.

## Car Rentals

The following companies have offices at or near Metropolitan Airport; Avis, Hertz, and National also have offices at or near City Airport.

**Alamo,** tel. 313/941–8420 or 800/327–9633.
**American International,** tel. 800/527–0202.
**Avis,** tel. 313/942–3450 or 800/331–1212.
**Budget,** tel. 313/941–8804 or 800/527–0700.
**Dollar,** tel. 313/729–6800 or 800/421–6868.
**Hertz,** tel. 313/941–4747 or 800/654–3131.
**National,** tel. 313/941–7000 or 800/328–4567.
**Sears,** tel. 800/527–0770.
**Snappy,** tel. 800/762–7791.
**Thrifty,** tel. 313/946–7830 or 800/367–2277.

## Emergencies

*Doctors*
**Henry Ford Medical Centers** (2799 W. Grand Blvd., tel. 313/876–2600), **Samaritan Health Center** (5555 Conner Ave., tel. 313/579–4000).

*Dentists*

**Dr. Golden Dental Centers** (115 State St., tel. 313/963–3336), **Penobscot Dental Associates** (1645 Griswold, Suite 224, tel. 313/963–8800).

*Hospitals*

**Henry Ford Hospital** (2799 W. Grand Blvd., tel. 313/876–2600), **Harper Hospital** (4201 St. Antoine St., tel. 313/745–8040).

## Important Addresses and Numbers

**Audiovisual rental.** Gavco Audio Visual (1 Washington Blvd., tel. 313/567–2155).

**Chamber of Commerce** (600 W. Lafayette St., tel. 313/964–4000).

**Computer rental.** Paramount Computer Rentals (797 E. Big Beaver Rd., Troy, tel. 313/524–7368 or 800/727–3685).

**Convention and exhibition center.** Cobo Hall Conference/Exhibition Center (1 Washington Blvd., tel. 313/224–1010).

**Fax services.** Three D Express Fax Service (155 W. Congress St., tel. 313/963–3303), Kinko's Copies (781 E. Big Beaver Rd., Troy, tel. 313/680–0280 and 28641 Northwestern Hwy., Southfield, tel. 313/355–5670).

**Formal-wear rentals.** Brothers Formal Wear (22198 Michigan Ave., Dearborn, tel. 313/278–2244) also rents men's street suits; Dobby's Mens Formal Wear (28755 Plymouth Rd., Livonia, tel. 313/425–7070) offers 24-hour phone order service.

**Gift shops.** Chocolates: Sanders (621 Griswold Ave., tel. 313/964–2740); Flowers: Alexander's Flowers (546 Moore, tel. 313/963–9400), Silver's (151 W. Fort, tel. 313/963–0000).

**Graphic design studios.** Bromley Chapin Design (100 Renaissance Center, tel. 313/259–2661), Graphic House Inc. (672 Woodbridge, tel. 313/259–7790).

**Hairstylists.** Men: Golden Razor Salon (300 River Pl., tel. 313/567–6677), Unisex: Vento's (200 Renaissance Center, tel. 313/259–1490) has booths and a Jacuzzi.

**Health and fitness clubs.** *See* Fitness, below.

**Information hot lines.** The Detroit Visitor Information Center's "What's Line" for daily events, (tel. 313/298–6262), Detroit Public Library's TIP Line, a community information/referral service (tel. 313/833–4000).

**Limousine services.** Starfire Limousine Service (tel. 313/839–0774), United Limousine Service (tel. 313/365–0970).

**Liquor stores.** Leland Commissary Market (400 Bagley, tel. 313/962–9231), Park & Sibley Market (2601 Park, tel. 313/964–3257).

**Mail delivery, overnight.** Airborne Express (tel. 313/946–6800), DHL Worldwide Express (tel. 313/388–7200), Express Mail (tel. 313/226–8681), Federal Express (tel. 313/961–8771), TNT Skypak (tel. 313/941–8200), UPS (tel. 313/261–8500).

**Messenger services.** PDQ Courier System (tel. 313/965–9600), Professional Delivery (tel. 313/964–6645).

**Office space rentals.** HQ Services & Offices (400 Renaissance Center, tel. 313/259–5422), Professional Suite Management Services (2180 Penobscot Bldg., tel. 313/962–0184).

**Pharmacy, late-night.** Perry Drug Store (5650 Schaefer, Dearborn, tel. 313/581–3280).

**Radio station, all-news.** WWJ AM 950.

**Secretarial services.** Entech Services (100 Renaissance Center, tel. 313/567–0050), HQ Services & Offices (400 Renaissance Center, tel. 313/259–5422).

**Stationery supplies.** Gail's General Office Supply (144 Penobscot Bldg., tel. 313/962–7983), Silver's (151 W. Fort, tel. 313/963–0000).

**Taxis.** Checker Cab (tel. 313/963–7000), Detroit Cab (tel. 313/841–6000).

**Theater tickets.** *See* The Arts, below.

**Train information.** Amtrak Station (16121 Michigan Ave., Dearborn, tel. 313/336–5407; general info., tel. 313/963–1396).

**Travel agents.** Kirby Travel Service (1 Kennedy Sq. Bldg., tel. 313/963–3965), Thomas Cook Travel (300 Renaissance Center, tel. 313/259–3100).

**Weather** (tel. 313/941–7192).

## LODGING

Lodgings in the Detroit area range from the functional to the futuristic. The airport motels that crowd industrial Romulus are adequate if uninspiring, though many are upgrading their facilities and services to take advantage of the continuing boom in air traffic. Downtown remains the center for banking, law, and the convention trade, so business people continue to frequent luxury hotels like the Westin and Omni. Dearborn—home to the Ford Motor Company and just 15 minutes from downtown, the airport, and the office silos of Southfield—has evolved into a popular alternative because of its location and first-class accommodations like the Ritz-Carlton. Troy is a more convenient place if you're doing business in the northern suburbs, home to many corporate offices, tony restaurants and shops, and two of Detroit's professional sports teams (the Pistons in Auburn Hills and the Lions in Pontiac). The biggest drawback is the 50-minute expressway ride from Troy to Metropolitan Airport, a trip that can take twice as long during bad weather or rush hour.

A number of the hotels listed below have corporate rates and/or weekend discounts. Inquire when making reservations.

Highly recommended lodgings in each price category are indicated by a star ★.

| Category | Cost* |
| --- | --- |
| $$$$ (Very Expensive) | over $100 |
| $$$ (Expensive) | $76–$100 |
| $$ (Moderate) | under $76 |

*All prices are for a standard double room, single occupancy excluding 11% tax.*

*Numbers in the margin correspond to numbered hotel locations on the Detroit Lodging and Dining maps.*

## Downtown/Center City

**⑨** **Days Inn–Detroit Downtown.** This attractive and crisply ef-
$$ ficient motor inn, just three blocks from Cobo Convention
Center and the Joe Louis Arena, is a sleeper in every
sense of the word. Seasoned conventioneers and business-
people know it as a convenient, inexpensive alternative to
downtown's pricey luxury hotels. The public areas and
guest rooms throughout its 16 floors are tastefully deco-
rated in dark green and burgundy floral wallpaper and
mahogany furniture. Extras include a complimentary
Continental breakfast served daily, two-line telephones in
each room, a free hotel shuttle van to local restaurants, a
weekday cocktail hour, and a friendly, responsive staff.
*231 Michigan Ave., 48226, tel. 313/965–4646 or 800/325–
2525. Gen. manager, Bruce Jackson. 197 rooms, 89
suites. AE, CB, D, MC, V.*

**⑮** **Omni International.** Many of the Omni's problems since it
$$$$ opened in 1985 have been attitudinal in nature, including a
staff that often confuses personal service with personal fa-
vors. That aside, this 21-story high rise—part of the
Millender Center's "vertical neighborhood" of shops, of-
fices, and apartments—has much to recommend it. A
skywalk links it to the Renaissance Center office/retail
complex, while a People Mover (Detroit's monorail serv-
ice) station puts all of downtown within easy reach. The
Omni's standard rooms are all the same: spacious, luxuri-
ous, with three telephones and two TVs, including one of
each in the cavernous bathrooms. The only real choice is
which side of the hotel you prefer. Rooms facing north of-
fer a view of the Detroit River and Windsor; those facing
south offer downtown. Either is just fine. The hotel's res-
taurant draws a downtown business trade in the morning
(*see* Business Breakfasts, below). *333 E. Jefferson Ave.,
48226, tel. 313/222–7700 or 800/843–6664, fax 313/222–
6509. Gen. manager, Ernest Wooden. 240 rooms, 15
suites. AE, CB, D, MC, V.*

**★ ⑬** **Hotel Pontchartrain.** The Pontch has it all: location, looks,
$$$$ and a loyal following of engineers, contractors, and what-
ever professional group is attending this week's conven-
tion at Cobo Center, directly across the street. The 1984
renovation of this 25-story hotel has produced a pleasantly
indulgent ambience not unlike that of an elegant but infor-
mal country house. The public areas are done in sparkling
marble and glass, accentuated by plants, floral arrange-
ments, crystal chandeliers, and intimate furniture group-
ings. The rooms, decorated in neutral colors, are so airy
that the modern furnishings seem almost spartan. Rooms
on the upper floors offer a panoramic view of the city and
Detroit River. The staff, which provides maid service

twice daily, is exceptional even for a luxury hotel, and the lobby boasts the best piano bar in town (*see* After Hours, below). One of the Pontch's few drawbacks is the neighboring firehouse, whose bells and sirens can make sleepless nights a real possibility for guests in the back of the hotel. *A Preferred Hotel, 2 Washington Blvd., 48226, tel. 313/965–0200 or 800/537–6624, in MI 800/247–3816, fax 313/965–9464. Gen. manager, Martin Svigar. 415 rooms, 34 suites. AE, CB, D, MC, V.*

**❾** **Hotel St. Regis.** The St. Regis is a mixture of attractive Old
**$$$$** World-style rooms and new sections, reflecting the property's recent shift from a European- to American-style hotel. The 6-story hotel doubled its room count in 1988, a retrofit that included halving many existing rooms. The results are standard doubles that are nicely done in blues and browns, but cramped and noisy because of the new, thinner walls. The suites remain sumptuous, though. Each boasts a Jacuzzi, three TVs, a large parlor area, and a table with six chairs. Because the St. Regis is connected by enclosed walkway to General Motors' world headquarters and is a block from the Fisher Theatre, the guest list is an odd mix of entertainment and corporate types. In the lobby dining room (*see* Business Breakfasts, below) you're liable to see anyone from Bob Hope to GM chairman Roger Smith. *3071 W. Grand Blvd., 48202, tel. 313/873–3000 or 800/223–5560, fax 313/873–3000, ext. 7116. Gen. manager, David Ong. 202 rooms, 22 suites. AE, CB, D, MC, V.*

**⓳** **Shorecrest Motor Inn.** In many ways the rooms in this 2-
**$$** story motel resemble those jerry-built affairs one finds in the basement of a suburban development home: paneled walls, tacky carpeting, even management's admonition not to have any guests after 11 PM. All that's missing is the gas meter on the wall. But as the motel proclaims: "We sell sleep." So far the Shorecrest, which has been going strong since 1958, has had no shortage of buyers. Most of them are drawn by the inn's prices and convenient location—just two blocks from the Renaissance Center and within walking distance of most downtown ports of call. This is basic lodging. The beds are comfortable and everything works, though if you want a tub instead of a shower stall, you'll have to pay for the difference between an economy and standard room. *1316 E. Jefferson Ave., 48207, tel. 313/568–3000 or 800/992–9616, fax 313/568–3002, ext. 260. Gen. manager, Bruce Slezak. 54 rooms. AE, CB, D, MC, V.*

**⓰** **The Westin Hotel-Renaissance Center Detroit.** The 73-story
**$$$$** Westin is the midwest's tallest hotel, with a wraparound design that affords every room a waterfront view of the city and of Windsor, Ontario. Rates are lofty, too, considering the wedge-shaped standard rooms and ordinary modern furnishings. But if being centrally located is what you're after, The Westin—within walking distance of every important downtown destination—is the place. Despite a costly remodeling of the eight-story-high brass-and-marble lobby, confused hotel patrons are still bumbling into the adjacent Renaissance Center, an office/retail complex with a bewildering array of levels, walkways, and towers. The trials of finding your way around here at the top-floor revolving Summit Restaurant make it an

# GREATER DETROIT

**Lodging**
Airport
Hilton Inn, **8**
Drury Inn, **2**
Ramada Metro-
Airport, **7**
Ritz-Carlton,
Dearborn, **6**

**Dining**
Les Auteurs, **4**
Golden Mushroom, **5**
The Lark, **1**
Sweet Lorraine's
Café, **3**

# DOWNTOWN DETROIT

establishment many businesspeople visit more for the view than the food. The River Bistro (*see* Dining, below) is the place to go to eat. *Renaissance Center, Jefferson Ave. at Randolph St., 48243, tel. 313/568–8000 or 800/228–3000, fax 313/568–8666. Gen. manager, Taylor Terao. 1,350 rooms, 50 suites. AE, CB, MC, V.*

## Airport

**❽ Airport Hilton Inn.** The 4-story Hilton, completely re-
$$$  novated over the last four years, remains a favorite of business groups because of its airport location and above-par banquet and convention facilities. The poor reputation of its restaurant is offset by larger-than-average rooms, lighted tennis courts, and a Federal Express drop-off box. *31500 Wick Rd., Romulus, 48174, tel. 313/292–3400 or 800/445–8667, fax 313/721–8870. Gen. manager, Hassan Ghalam. 266 rooms, 4 suites. AE, CB, D, MC, V.*

**❼ Ramada Metro Airport.** You won't get a chocolate on your
$$  pillow at this clean and comfortable four-story inn, a half mile from the airport. But you can get a candy bar at the vending machines anchoring each hallway. (However, you may not want to sleep near the sound of those machines, so avoid rooms 3 and 4 on each floor.) All the rooms are uniformly cozy, with oversized beds and plenty of towels; rooms set aside for women travelers have special toiletries and makeup mirrors. *8270 Wickham Rd., Romulus, 48174, tel. 313/729–6300 or 800/272–6232, fax 313/722–8740. Gen. manager, Preston Swain. 236 rooms, 7 suites. AE, CB, D, MC, V.*

## Suburbs

**★ ❷ Drury Inn.** This 4-story inn, built in 1984, underwent a
$$  complete facelift in 1990, though regulars are still wondering why. The Drury, close to Troy's business center, has built a local following with its enthusiastic service, tasteful decor, and moderate prices. The large standard rooms are clean to the point of sterility. Light sleepers should ask for even-numbered rooms on the east side of the inn, away from busy I-75. Herschel's American Deli, the northern suburbs' best 24-hour restaurant, is adjacent. Or you can choose the inn's hospitable and free quick-start breakfast of hot cereals, muffins, fruit, and seasonal surprises, served daily. *575 W. Big Beaver Rd., Troy, 48084, te . 313/528–3330 or 800/325–8300, fax 313/528–3330, ext. 479. Gen. manager, Christine English. 154 rooms. AE, CB, D, MC, V.*

**★ ❻ Ritz-Carlton, Dearborn.** Detroit's newest luxury hotel,
$$$$  filled to its sumptuous rafters with marble, polished wood, Persian rugs, and blazing chandeliers, is an 11-story salute to old European elegance. It's geared toward the upper 5% of the business class, though, since it opened in 1989, guests have also included Tom Cruise, Joan Collins, and the Rolling Stones. From the formal doormen to the attentive staff, the service is impeccable. Rooms throughout are done in restful peach or blue hues and boast marble and brass bathrooms. Traditional English afternoon tea and hors d'oeuvres are served in the lobby lounge throughout the day. The Ritz is steps away from Ford Motor headquarters, adjacent to the 200-store Fairlane Town

# DETROIT HOTEL CHART

| HOTELS | Price Category | Business Services — Banquet capacity | No. of meeting rooms | Secretarial services | Audiovisual equipment | Teletype news service | Computer rentals | In-room modem phone jack | All-news cable channel | Desk | Desk lighting | Bed lighting |
|---|---|---|---|---|---|---|---|---|---|---|---|---|
| Airport Hilton Inn | $$$ | 700 | 12 | ✓ | ✓ | – | ✓ | – | ✓ | ● | ● | ● |
| Days Inn-Downtown | $$ | 150 | 4 | – | – | – | – | ✓ | – | ● | ● | ● |
| Drury Inn | $$ | 0 | 4 | ✓ | – | – | ✓ | ✓ | ✓ | ● | ● | ● |
| Hotel Pontchartrain | $$$$ | 200 | 8 | ✓ | ✓ | ✓ | ✓ | ✓ | – | ◑ | ● | ● |
| Hotel St. Regis | $$$$ | 450 | 11 | ✓ | – | ✓ | ✓ | ✓ | ✓ | ◑ | ● | ● |
| Omni International | $$$$ | 275 | 6 | ✓ | ✓ | – | ✓ | ✓ | – | ● | ● | ● |
| Ramada Metro Airport | $$ | 300 | 11 | ✓ | ✓ | ✓ | ✓ | ✓ | ✓ | ● | ● | ● |
| Ritz-Carlton Dearborn | $$$$ | 850 | 12 | ✓ | ✓ | ✓ | ✓ | ✓ | ✓ | ● | ● | ● |
| Shorecrest Motor Inn | $$ | 0 | 0 | – | – | – | – | – | – | ● | ◑ | ● |
| Westin Hotel Renaissance Center | $$$$ | 5000 | 28 | ✓ | ✓ | ✓ | ✓ | – | – | ● | ● | ● |

$$$$ = over $100, $$$ = $76-$100, $$ = under $76.
● good, ◑ fair, ○ poor.
All hotels listed here have photocopying and fax facilities.

| In-Room Amenities | | | | | | | | | | Hotel Amenities | | | | | | |
| Nonsmoking rooms | In-room checkout | Minibar | Pay movies | VCR/Movie rentals | Hairdryer | Toiletries | Room service | Laundry/Dry cleaning | Pressing | Concierge | Barber/Hairdresser | Garage | Courtesy airport transport | Sauna | Pool | Exercise room |
|---|---|---|---|---|---|---|---|---|---|---|---|---|---|---|---|---|
| ✓ | – | – | ✓ | – | ✓ | ◑ | ◑ | ◑ | ● | – | – | – | ✓ | ✓ | ◑ | ◑ |
| ✓ | – | – | ✓ | – | – | ◑ | – | – | – | – | – | ✓ | – | ✓ | ● | ◑ |
| ✓ | – | – | ✓ | ✓ | – | ◑ | – | ● | ◑ | – | – | ✓ | – | ◑ | ◑ | – |
| ✓ | – | – | ✓ | ✓ | ✓ | ● | ● | ● | ● | ✓ | ✓ | ✓ | ✓ | ✓ | ◑ | ● |
| ✓ | ✓ | – | ✓ | – | – | ● | ◑ | ● | – | ✓ | ✓ | ✓ | – | ✓ | ● | ● |
| ✓ | ✓ | ✓ | ✓ | – | – | ● | ◑ | ● | ◑ | – | – | – | – | ✓ | ● | ◑ |
| ✓ | ✓ | ✓ | – | ✓ | – | ● | ● | ● | ○ | ✓ | – | ✓ | – | ✓ | ● | ● |
| – | – | ✓ | – | – | ✓ | ◑ | ○ | ◑ | ◑ | – | – | – | ✓ | – | – | – |
| ✓ | ✓ | ✓ | – | ✓ | – | ● | ● | ● | ● | – | ✓ | ✓ | – | ✓ | ● | ● |

**Room service:** ● 24-hour, ◑ 6AM-10PM, ○ other.
**Laundry/Dry cleaning:** ● same day, ◑ overnight, ○ other.
**Pressing:** ● immediate, ◑ same day, ○ other.

Center, and astride a freeway system that connects you with downtown, the airport, and the western suburbs. The hotel's dining room is a fine setting for early morning negotiations (*see* Business Breakfasts, below). Other than the service, that at times can border on the suffocating (not a common problem in most hotels), the Ritz's only flaw might be the pedestrian view, which even from the top floors can't come close to matching the elegance inside. *300 Town Center Dr., Dearborn, 48126, tel. 313/441–2000 or 800/241–3333, fax 313/441–2051. Gen. manager, Paul O. Westbrook. 308 rooms, 13 suites. AE, CB, D, MC, V.*

# DINING

Blame it on generations of autoworkers getting up before dawn and grabbing a cup of coffee hurrying down to the plant, but a lot of Detroiters have never really gotten into the habit of eating breakfast, much less conducting business around it. Thankfully, such blue-collar sensibilities don't extend to lunch and dinner. Keith Famie of Les Auteurs, and The Rattlesnake Club's Jimmy Schmidt are just two of the nationally known chefs working in a city that boasts fine dining. In fact, the following list is just a sampling of the metropolitan area's many good restaurants.

Highly recommended restaurants in each price category are indicated by a star ★.

| Category | Cost* |
|---|---|
| $$$$ (Very Expensive) | over $25 |
| $$$ (Expensive) | $20–$25 |
| $$ (Moderate) | under $20 |

*per person, including appetizer, entrée, and dessert, but excluding drinks, service, and 4% sales tax.*

*Numbers in the margin correspond to numbered restaurant locations on the Detroit Lodging and Dining maps.*

### Business Breakfasts

**The Restaurant at the Ritz-Carlton** (tel. 313/441–2000) is the best place in Detroit for a formal breakfast. It offers service and comforts you expect from its name. The old-English decor is highlighted by oriental rugs, deep couches, and paintings of the Gainsborough variety. A plus is its long breakfast hours—from 6:30 to 11:30 AM daily. A minus is its back-to-back banquettes that can work against private conversations. Lunch and dinner at **The Dining Room** in the Hotel St. Regis (tel. 313/873–3000) are nothing to excite the palate, but the traditional London club ambience makes it fun for breakfast. And there's always the chance that an entertainer performing at nearby Fisher Theatre and staying at the hotel will be seated nearby. Otherwise, early morning crowds of mid-level auto executives, intent on their newspapers, congregate here before trooping across the street to GM headquarters to work.

**333 East** at the Omni Hotel (tel. 313/222–7404) started out well in 1985, but has since become a little slack in its service and uninspired in menu offerings. It still does an adequate breakfast at a very convenient downtown location—a walkway's stroll from the Renaissance Center and the main City Hall building. If you're breakfasting alone downtown, try the freshly baked muffins and scones at **Britt's Café** in the basement of Silver's (151 W. Fort, tel. 313/963–4866). If you're in Dearborn or headed for the airport from downtown, stop at **Judy's Café** (15714 W. Warren, tel. 313/581–8185), noted for its omelets.

## Downtown

**⑪** **Joe Muer's.** This is a Detroit institution, an old-fashioned
**$$$$** fish house where families have been bringing their children and grandchildren for generations. Not much has changed over the years at this cavernous emporium of red leather, wood, and brick, set off with nautical touches throughout. It has excellent, respectful, Old World service and delicious soups and chowders. The fish—Dover sole, Norwegian salmon, and Canadian walleye and whitefish—is always fresh and is usually fried or broiled. Dishes such as crab cakes and mussels will appear on the list from time to time. Nothing fancy here, just the best of simple, good food. *200 Gratiot Ave., tel. 313/567–1088. Dress: casual at lunch; jacket and tie recommended at dinner. Reservations suggested. AE, D, MC, V. Dinner only Sat.; closed Sun.*

**⑭** **London Chop House.** After a low period in the '80s when it
**$$$$** was on the verge of closing, Detroit's version of Sardi's has been completely refurbished and is slowly regaining lost ground. The Chop, whose walls are covered with Hy Vogel cartoons of celebrities, has always been as much a place to people-watch as to eat. This is where Lee Iacocca, lunching in the famous Booth One, was summoned to take the call telling him that Congress had voted to bail out the failing Chrysler Corporation. The menu changes frequently, but still includes the house favorites—chopped steak and a "mess of smelt." The restaurant's best features may be a wine list that matches anything in New York or San Francisco and a bar where Clark Gable, Elizabeth Taylor, Liza Minelli, and other stars have sipped. *155 W. Congress St., tel. 313/962–0277. Jacket and tie required. Reservations required. AE, CB, D, MC, V.*

**⑱** **Opus One.** This bright new star opened without fanfare in
**$$$** 1987 and has become a popular lunch and dinner spot for some of the biggest deal makers and politicians in town, edging out the London Chop House. The room is an elegant mix of mahogany trim, Art Deco mirrors, marble floors, etched glass, and tapestry-upholstered banquettes. The cuisine blends California nouvelle and traditional European styles. You might start with light seafood dumplings in a mousselline sauce, followed by boneless guinea hen. Also recommended are pasta dishes with delicate combinations of seafood, wine, and cream, and a salad with slivers of meat of three game birds. *565 E. Larned, tel. 313/961–7766. Jacket and tie recommended. Reservations recommended. AE, D, MC, V. Dinner only, Sat.; closed Sun.*

**★ ⑳** **The Rattlesnake Club.** Owner Jimmy Schmidt, who be-
**$$$** came a culinary darling in the early 1980s at the London

Chop House, returned to Detroit to open this bright, airy, and lively restaurant in 1988. Focal points of the room are the 10-foot-high windows that overlook the Detroit River and the Windsor skyline. One of the most innovative young chefs in the country, Schmidt is the inventor of white-chocolate ravioli desserts, guaranteed to satisfy your sweet tooth. Worthwhile offerings include salmon carpaccio, little neck clams in fennel butter, and beef tenderloin with blue corn tortillas. Although service in the main dining room can be erratic, the grill is inexpensive and quick. There's also outdoor dining and live jazz on the patio during the summer. *300 River Place, tel. 313/567–4400. Dress: casual. Reservations recommended. AE, D, MC, V.*

**⓱** **River Bistro.** Of the restaurants in the Westin Hotel, the
$$$ Summit is noted for its view, the River Bistro for its food. The room is brightly lighted and lined with colorful acrylic paintings. There is a massive cast-iron fountain in the middle of the room. Overseeing some of the crispest service in town and a short but solid wine list is the attentive maître d'hotel, Joseph Calemme, a fixture on the Detroit scene for the last 20 years. The cuisine runs the gamut from fish, to pasta, veal, and beef entrées with a menu that changes daily. A house specialty is the complimentary roasted bulb of garlic, which diners spread on bread with butter. Simple but well-prepared dishes such as roast chicken with rosemary, smoked duck sausage, and rack of lamb in mustard are mainstays. *Lower Promenade, Renaissance Center, tel. 313/568–8110. Dress: casual at lunch; jacket and tie recommended at dinner. Reservations recommended. AE, CB, D, MC, V. Closed Sun.*

**★ ⓾** **The Whitney.** The most opulent restaurant in Detroit, this
$$$$ was the 19th-century mansion of lumber baron David Whitney. The former libraries, living rooms, and ballrooms are trimmed in carved ebony, cherry, and mahogany woods, and have Tiffany lamps, Delft pottery, and marble fireplaces. The service is attentive, crisp, and formal; tables are well spaced for privacy, and everything speaks of high polish and quality. The food is very good, though it can't quite live up to the superlative surroundings. The menu leans toward nouvelle American with occasional Continental touches: chicken stuffed with smoked cheese and ham, and wild game sausage are good choices. The Whitney has a first-rate wine list and, on the top floor, a night-club bar with a jazz pianist and vocalist (*see* After Hours, below). *4421 Woodward Ave., tel. 313/832–5700. Jacket and tie recommended. Reservations required. AE, MC, V. Closed lunch Sat.*

## Suburbs

**❺** **Golden Mushroom.** Although it's a 20-minute drive from
$$$$ downtown, the Mushroom has drawn a local following that fills its comfortably spaced booths and tables. Milos Cihelka, one of Detroit's best younger chefs, supervises the kitchen, which is noted for regional American specialties and updated Continental favorites, ranging from a delicate pasta with morels, truffles, or lobster to impeccable fish dishes. Cihelka's forte is his preparation of wild game; his pâté de foie gras ranks high as well. An excellent wine list rounds out what has consistently been rated one of Detroit's top dining experiences. *18100 W. 10 Mile Rd.,*

Southfield, tel. 313/559–4230. *Dress: jacket and tie advised. Reservations required. AE, CB, D, MC, V. Closed Sun.*

★ ❶ **The Lark.** Thirty minutes from downtown, The Lark is
$$$$ generally regarded as the western suburbs' best restaurant. Owners Jim and Mary Lark, avid travelers, bring back mementos from every place they go, but the central theme and decor is that of an elegant Portuguese country inn. You'll see flowered tile work, rustic heavy wood, high-back leather chairs, peasant earthenware table settings, and a huge chandelier near the hearth. The food is traditional Continental cuisine with an American flair. Guests select their appetizers from a rolling cart, and can ask for seconds. House specialties include rack of lamb, each serving of which has its own numbered tag to take home, much like the pressed duck at Paris's Tour d'Argent. Also highly recommended is the prime rib with bone. The ambience and a spectacular wine list make this the place to celebrate the closing of a deal. *6430 Farmington Rd., West Bloomfield, tel. 313/661–4466. Jacket and tie recommended. Reservations required. AE, CB, D, MC, V. Dinner only Tues.–Sat.*

❹ **Les Auteurs.** Owner-chef Keith Famie has achieved nation-
$$$ al prominence with his contemporary American culinary style in this casual restaurant in Royal Oak, about 15 minutes from downtown Detroit. Sheets of white paper overlay the tablecloths, anchored by a jar of crayons for doodling. The kitchen opens onto the dining area so that guests can watch the staff cook. High ceilings, low lighting, and a soaring glass front all give Les Auteurs an open, airy feel. The food, ranging from Famie's trademark black bean cake with smoked chicken to his delicate one-serving pizzas of duck confit, is superior. An upscale suburban clientele from Grosse Pointe and Birmingham wait in line to be seated here. *222 Sherman Drive, Washington Sq. Plaza, Royal Oak, tel. 313/544–2887. Dress: casual. No reservations. MC, V. Closed Sun. dinner.*

★ ❸ **Sweet Lorraine's Café.** This restaurant, 20 minutes from
$$ downtown, is a breezily attractive place with more experimental dishes than anywhere else in the area. Look for items such as salmon mousse stuffed in phyllo triangles on a lemon-peppercorn sauce, salmon in a cilantro beurre-blanc, or chicken breast coated in ground pecans and sautéed and served in a cream mustard sauce. There's also a good selection of sandwiches and hamburger made with ground Porterhouse steak. Wines are available by the glass. The room is decorated with pretty Mediterranean colors. The noise level is higher-than-normal. *29101 Greenfield, Southfield, tel. 313/559–5985. Dress: very casual. No reservations needed. AE, MC, V. Closed Sun.*

## FREE TIME

### Fitness

*Hotel Facilities*
One-day passes are available for $7 at the **Fitness Center** inside the Omni Hotel, which offers an aerobics studio, outdoor running track, weight-lifting equipment, and indoor pool.

*Health Clubs*

The **Dearborn Racquet & Health Club** (2727 S. Gulley Rd., Dearborn, tel. 313/562–1296), 20 minutes from downtown, has Nautilus equipment, 11 indoor tennis and racquetball courts, aerobics, whirlpools, saunas, and a sunning patio for $5 a day. Serious weightlifters train at the **Powerhouse Gym** (16251 Woodward, Highland Park, tel. 313/868–3411), 10 minutes from downtown.

*Jogging*

The most popular running path is a 7-mile circuit around the perimeter of scenic **Belle Isle,** itself a 3-mile jog from downtown. The island also has a ¼-mile cinder track.

## Shopping

**Trappers Alley Festival Marketplace** (508 Monroe St., tel. 313/963–5445) in Greektown has more than 70 stores, restaurants, and gift shops. Dearborn's **Fairlane Town Center** (300 Town Center Dr., tel. 313/593–3330) has 10 movie theaters, 25 restaurants, and 200 shops, including Saks Fifth Avenue and Lord & Taylor. The toniest shopping can be found at **Somerset Mall** (2801 W. Big Beaver Rd., Troy, tel. 313/643–6360), which has stores like Laura Ashley, Brooks Brothers, and Gucci.

The Detroit area boasts a pair of oversized, browser-friendly bookstores. You can pull up a chair at **Borders Book Shop** (31150 Southfield Rd., Southfield, tel. 313/644–1515), whose wide selection, service, discounts, and free gift-wrapping are worth the 20-minute trip from downtown. **John K. King Books** (901 W. Lafayette, tel. 313/961–0622) offers 600,000 used and rare books, antiques, and art prints in a five-story former glove factory.

## Diversions

The **People Mover,** an elevated monorail that follows a 14-minute, 2.9-mile circular path through 13 downtown stations, is a leisurely, inexpensive way to explore the central business district.

**Belle Isle** (tel. 313/267–7115) is a 1000-acre island park 3 miles from downtown. Among the attractions are an **Aquarium** (tel. 313/267–7159) and a 25-acre **Zoo** (tel. 313/267–7160 or 398–0903).

**Hart Plaza,** a block west of the Renaissance Center on Jefferson Ave., is a popular place to skate during the winter, sunbathe during the summer, and stroll or people-watch anytime. Ethnic festivals are held here each summer.

Admission is free at the **Detroit Institute of Arts** (5200 Woodward Ave., tel. 313/833–7900), one of the country's five largest fine arts museums. There's a wonderful series of Diego Rivera murals in the enclosed courtyard (the artist depicted himself and his friends as workers in the paintings), as well as master works by Breughel and Van Gogh.

## Professional Sports

**Football.** Lions, Pontiac Silverdome (tel. 313/335–4151). **Basketball.** Pistons, The Palace in Auburn Hills (tel. 313/377–0100). **Hockey.** Red Wings, Joe Louis Arena (tel. 313/

567–6000). **Baseball.** Tigers, Tiger Stadium (tel. 313/963–9944).

## The Arts

The Detroit Symphony has moved back into the recently refurbished **Orchestra Hall** (3711 Woodward Ave., tel. 313/833–3700). The **Meadow Brook Music Festival** (Oakland University, Rochester, tel. 313/377–2010) is the symphony's summer home. The **Fox Theater** (2211 Woodward Ave., tel. 313/965–7100), a 1927 movie palace restored to its glittering Byzantine-style opulence, is home to touring Broadway shows and musical performers. **The Fisher Theatre** (Fisher Bldg., W. Grand Blvd. and Second St., tel. 313/872–1000) and the **Birmingham Theater** (211 S. Woodward Ave., Birmingham, tel. 313/644–3533) put on Off-Broadway-type shows, both dramas and musicals; The **Detroit Repertory Theater** (13103 Woodrow Wilson Ave., tel. 313/868–1347) tends towards gritty realism, with some avant garde productions.

For tickets phone **TicketMaster** (tel. 313/645–6666). There also are ticket booths in the Omni and Westin hotels.

## After Hours

Downtown and the riverfront contain some of the area's best night spots. Many are former speakeasies or converted warehouses, reflecting Detroit's rowdy lunch-bucket past. Greektown is a heavily traveled area but still lots of fun. The theater district along Woodward also has an active night life. North of this district though, proceed with caution, until you reach the trendy suburbs, like Royal Oak and Birmingham.

For the most comprehensive listing of events, pick up a copy of *Detroit Monthly*.

*Bars and Lounges*
For a quiet drink with a colleague or business contact after work, the two best places are the piano bar at the **Hotel Pontchartrain** (tel. 313/965–0200) and the top floor nightclub/bar at **The Whitney** restaurant (tel. 313/832–5700). In contrast, the **Mykonos Supper Club** (454 E. Lafayette, tel. 313/965–3737), where the dancing, ouzo-fueled patrons are as entertaining as the belly dancers and bouzouki band, is one of Greektown's wildest stops. A much mellower crowd gathers in the piano bar at the landmark **Caucus Club** (in the Penobscot Bldg., 150 W. Congress, tel. 313/965–4970). Irish ales and folk songs are on tap at the **Old Shillelagh** (349 Monroe, tel. 313/964–0007), while sports trivia is served up with beer and burgers at the **Lindell A.C.** (1310 Cass, tel. 313/964–1122), filled with fans—and an occasional pro athlete—replaying that night's hockey or baseball game.

*Comedy Clubs*
The area's oldest is still the best: **Mark Ridley's Comedy Castle** (2593 Woodward, Royal Oak, 313/542–9900) regularly imports top acts. **Chaplin's** (34244 Groesbeck, Fraser, tel. 313/792–1902) features a mix of national and local performers.

## Jazz Clubs

The world's oldest jazz club, **Baker's Keyboard Lounge** (20510 Livernois, tel. 313/864–1201), is a smoky gem worth visiting just for its legendary keyboard-design bar. The **Soup Kitchen Saloon** (1585 Franklin, tel. 313/259–1374) serves up Blues Burgers and name acts at its gritty Rivertown location. **The Rhinoceros Restaurant** (265 Riopelle, tel. 313/259–2208), an occasional haunt of Governor James Blanchard, is an old speakeasy filled with antiques and oddities. A good place to people-watch and listen to quality acts.

## For Singles

The nighttime meeting place for the younger set has long been **Galligan's** (519 E. Jefferson, tel. 313/963–2098). If you prefer impromptu singalongs to comparing portfolios, make it over to the freewheeling **Woodbridge Tavern** (289 St. Aubin, tel. 313/259–0578), a former speakeasy where downtown's thirtysomething crowd loosens its ties and stomps its feet. **Clubland** (2115 Woodward Ave., tel. 313/961–5450) is a 2,000-plus-capacity dance dome in the freshly refurbished State Theatre. The **Woodward Jukebox** (4616 N. Woodward Ave., Royal Oak, tel. 313/549–2233) is a '50s-style dance club where the waitresses wear letter sweaters and do the Mashed Potato.

# Houston

*by Mary Davis Suro*

Many first-time visitors to Houston expect to see down-town streets crowded with oil-men dressed in tooled-leather boots and cowboy hats when, in fact, the style now leans more toward dark suits and Gucci loafers. Oil is no longer the only show in this town, and while you may notice it first on the streets, its effects reach much further.

Since the worst days of the oil bust and the ensuing recession of the 1980s, "diversification" has become Houston's new gospel. Today, facilities like the Texas Medical Center, NASA's Johnson Space Center, and the Port of Houston, the nation's third largest (after New Orleans and New York), are considered the incubators of new businesses that will be more reliable in the long run than the forest of oil rigs in the Gulf of Mexico. With the exception of a few big companies like Compaq Computers, however, much of the nonoil growth has come in the formation of relatively small firms. Although the process has begun, the shape of Houston's economic future is still being defined.

The oil business is now leaner, and, its boosters would say, meaner, than before prices plunged in the 1980s and swept the marginal companies off the map. Most of the majors, though, still have a sizable presence in Houston, led by the U.S. headquarters of Exxon and Shell. A variety of pipeline, service, and oil technology companies are alive and well, too.

Some signs of the bust still linger, like the aftermath of a deluge brought by one of the frequent tropical storms. Although all the major banks have been bought out or bailed out, the process of settling bad loans still consumes a lot of attention. And the construction industry is thoroughly in the doldrums.

The years of unemployment, bankruptcies, and bailouts were so chastening that very little is now taken for granted. The optimism generated by the rise in oil prices caused by the gulf crisis is tempered by the awareness of the tenuousness of such booms. A competitive spirit pervades all aspects of business, and visitors will have trouble finding a discourteous store clerk, or a hotel employee not trying hard to please.

## Top Employers

| Employer | Type of Enterprise | Parent*/ Headquarters |
|---|---|---|
| **Brown & Root Inc.** | Engineering construction & maintenance | Halliburton Co./ Dallas |
| **Continental Airlines Inc.** | Airline | Houston |
| **Exxon Company, USA** | Oil | Exxon Corp./ Dallas |
| **Foley's Department Store** | Retail | The May Co./ St. Louis |
| **Houston Industries, Inc.** | Holding co. including utilities | Houston |
| **The Kroger Company** | Supermarkets | Kroger Co./ Cincinnati |
| **Randall's Food Markets** | Supermarkets | Houston |
| **Shell Oil Company** | Oil | Royal Dutch Shell Group/ Houston |
| **Southwestern Bell** | Telecommunications | Southwestern Bell Corp./St. Louis |
| **University of Texas Cancer Center** | Medical research | Houston |

*if applicable

## ESSENTIAL INFORMATION

### Climate

What follows are the average daily maximum and minimum temperatures for Houston.

| | | | | | | | | |
|---|---|---|---|---|---|---|---|---|
| **Jan.** | 63F | 13C | **Feb.** | 65F | 18C | **Mar.** | 72F | 22C |
| | 45 | 7 | | 47 | 8 | | 54 | 12 |
| **Apr.** | 79F | 26C | **May** | 85F | 29C | **June** | 90F | 32C |
| | 61 | 16 | | 67 | 19 | | 72 | 22 |
| **July** | 92F | 33C | **Aug.** | 94F | 34C | **Sept.** | 88F | 31C |
| | 74 | 23 | | 74 | 23 | | 70 | 21 |
| **Oct.** | 81F | 27C | **Nov.** | 72F | 22C | **Dec.** | 63F | 17C |
| | 61 | 16 | | 52 | 11 | | 45 | 7 |

### Airports

**Houston Intercontinental Airport** is 15 miles north of downtown via I–45 North or U.S. 59 via North Belt. Continuing road construction on I–45 North often doubles driving time from downtown. The **William P. Hobby Air-**

**port,** nine miles southeast of downtown via I-45 and Broadway Boulevard, handles only domestic flights.

## Airport Business Facilities

The **Marriott** (between terminals B and C, tel. 713/443–2310) has fax machines, photocopying, notary public, baggage storage, conference rooms with catering service, day rates for rooms, and a health club.

## Airlines

Houston Intercontinental is served most frequently by Continental, Hobby Airport by Southwest Airlines. Most domestic carriers serve both airports.

**American Airlines,** tel. 713/650–1116 or 800/433–7300.
**Continental,** tel. 713/821–2100 or 800/525–0280.
**Delta,** tel. 713/448–3000 or 800/221–1212.
**Northwest,** tel. 800/225–2525.
**Pan Am,** tel. 800/221–1111.
**Southwest,** tel. 713/237–1221 or 800/442–1616.
**USAir,** tel. 713/872–0096 or 800/428–4322.

## Between the Airport and Downtown

From both airports, passengers have a variety of transportation options, but taxi service is the most efficient way to get downtown.

*By Taxi*
The trip downtown takes about 30 minutes from either airport. However, rush hours (7–9 and 3–6) and construction delays can double the traveling time. Taxi fares from Intercontinental Airport are based on zone rates and cost $26–$45, depending on the destination. From Hobby Airport, the fare is based on meter rates, which run $2.25 for the first mile and $1.15 for each additional mile. Average fare is $25.

*By Bus*
**Airport Express** (tel. 713/523–5694) buses run every 30 minutes from 6:50AM to 12:20AM between Houston Intercontinental and three city terminals (Hyatt Regency, 1200 Louisiana St., downtown; Medical Center, S. Main St., 2301 Holcombe Blvd.; Galleria/Post Oak/Greenway Plaza, 5000 Richmond Ave.). Cost: $7.95. Most hotels near these three terminals provide courtesy transportation.

*By Limousine*
Rates vary; **TowneCar** (tel. 713/236–8877) charges $2.40 for the first mile and $1.15 for each additional mile from either airport. Passengers must reserve a day in advance.

## Car Rentals

The following companies have offices in both airports:

**Avis,** tel. 800/331–1212.
**Budget,** tel. 713/449–0145 (Intercontinental); tel. 713/643–2684 (Hobby); or 800/527–0700.
**Dollar,** tel. 713/641–2806 (Intercontinental); tel. 713/821–4532 (Hobby); or 800/421–6868.
**Hertz,** tel. 800/654–3131.

## Emergencies

*Doctors*

**The Diagnostic Clinic** (6448 Fannin St., tel. 713/797–9191). **The Doctors at the Galleria** (Galleria I, Level 3, tel. 713/960–9926).

*Dentists*

Dentists also operate out of the **Galleria** (*see* above).

*Hospitals*

**St. Lukes Episcopal Hospital** (6720 Bertner Ave., tel. 713/791–2011).

## Important Addresses and Numbers

**Audiovisual rentals.** A/V Texas (4715 Main St., tel. 713/526–3687), Houston Audio Video (1217 West Loop N., tel. 713/681–1100).

**Chamber of Commerce** (1100 Milam Bldg., 25th fl., tel. 713/651–1313).

**Computer rentals.** Computerland Rentals (2121 West South Loop S., tel. 713/964–4730 or 800/441–2707), Computer Leasing Exchange (1003 Wirt Rd., tel. 713/467–9384).

**Convention and exhibition centers.** George R. Brown Convention Center (1001 Convention Center Blvd., tel. 713/853–8000).

**Fax service.** Kinko's (1430 San Jacinto St., tel. 713/654–8161).

**Formal-wear rentals.** Al's Formal Wear (7807 S. Main St. at Kirby Dr., tel. 713/791–1888), Gingiss Formalwear International (U.S. Hwy. 290 & Loop 610, Northwest Mall, tel. 713/688–5986).

**Gift shops.** Confectioners: Sweet Taste of Texas (540 Memorial City Shopping Center, tel. 713/465–5848); Flowers: Breen's Florist (2403 Rice Blvd., tel. 713/528–5551 or 800/548–5551), Hannah Niday Florists & Gifts (817 Walker St., tel. 713/644–7571).

**Graphic design studios.** PPC Graphics (810 Hwy. 6 S., Suite 116, tel. 713/493–9659).

**Hairstylists.** Unisex: Tova Hair Salon (2694 Marilee La., tel. 713/784–4848), Visible Changes (1154 Galleria I, tel. 713/627–7234).

**Health and fitness clubs.** *See* Fitness, below.

**Information hot lines.** Downtown Events Hot Line (tel. 713/650–1470), Quicklink (tel. 713/777–LINK or 800/747–LINK).

**Limousine services.** Houston Luxury Limousine Service (tel. 713/781–5478), Niccos River Oaks Limousines (tel. 713/789–0809 or 713/880–5466), Towne Car (tel. 713/236–8877).

**Liquor stores.** Richard's Liquors & Fine Wines (2124 N. Shepherd Dr., tel. 713/529–4849), Spec's (2410 Smith St., tel. 713/526–8787).

**Mail delivery, overnight.** DHL Worldwide Express ( 713/442–4500), Federal Express (tel. 713/667–2500), TNT

Skypak (713/443–2020), UPS (tel. 713/820–1880), U.S. Postal Service Express Mail (tel. 713/226–3403).

**Messenger service.** A & W Carriers (tel. 713/868–6122).

**Office space rental.** The Poole Company (12 Greenway Plaza, Suite 1100, tel. 713/623–6655).

**Pharmacies, late-night.** Walgreen Drug Stores has a 24-hour prescription service (822 S. Main St., tel. 713/223–1513, 10826 Beechnut St., tel. 713/530–6210).

**Radio stations, all-news.** KACO 1090 AM; KPRC 950 AM; KTRH 740 AM.

**Secretarial services.** Kelly Services (1100 Milam St., tel. 713/654–9432), Norrell Temporary Services (Texas Commerce Bank Bldg. 712 Main St., tel. 713/227–6673).

**Stationery supplies.** Kwik Kopy (4101 San Jacinto St., tel. 713/526–6364), Office Depot, phone orders (tel. 713/947–7896).

**Taxis.** Fiesta Cab (tel. 713/225–2666), United Taxi (tel. 713/699–0000), Yellow Cab (tel. 713/236–1111).

**Theater tickets.** *See* The Arts, below.

**Train information.** Amtrak (902 Washington Ave., tel. 713/224–1577 or 800/872–7245).

**Travel agents.** American Express Travel Related Service (3435 Galleria, 5015 Westheimer Rd., tel. 713/626–5740), Windsor Travel (600 Travis St., Suite 2875, tel. 713/228–1111 or 713/627–0111).

**Weather** (tel. 713/228–8703).

## LODGING

Houston has a multitude of first-class hotels and good accommodations in every price range. Because public transportation is a far cry from what it should be in this traffic-congested city, and taxi service in town is sporadic at best, it's a good idea to stay at a hotel convenient to your business destination.

If your destination is the Galleria complex, where several major oil companies have headquarters, you might look for a hotel that offers complimentary transportation. If business keeps you downtown, which has its share of oil companies but is also the banking and financial services center, consider staying in a hotel connected to Houston's air-conditioned tunnel system. This underground network of shops and restaurants was designed to alleviate the vagaries of the city's tropical climate.

All of the hotels listed below have corporate rates; most also offer weekend discounts. Inquire when making reservations.

Highly recommended lodgings in each price category are indicated by a star ★.

| Category | Cost* |
|---|---|
| $$$$ (Very Expensive) | over $150 |
| $$$ (Expensive) | $120–$150 |
| $$ (Moderate) | under $120 |

*All prices are for a standard double room, single occupancy, excluding 14% tax.*

*Numbers in the margin correspond to numbered hotel locations on the Houston Dining and Lodging maps.*

## Downtown

**㉔**
$$$$
**La Colombe d'Or.** This elegant establishment was once the private estate of Walter Fondren, a founder of Humble Oil, a forerunner of today's Exxon. The European-style luxury of the hotel's six suites, adorned with an eclectic array of antiques and modern art, will make you feel as though you're staying in a château. Suites have sitting and writing areas, and each has a dining room with seating for 10—very suitable for meetings. Every room is unique, but all are elegantly decorated with arrangements of silk brocade couches, Oriental rugs, and lush, velvet wingbacks. Avoid the Van Gogh suite, where you can hear much of the noise from the lobby directly below. This is a favorite spot for international business travelers who appreciate European style more than American convenience. The hotel's restaurant is renowned for its fine French cuisine (*see* Dining, below); two bars/lounges (*see* After Hours, below) are good for meetings with associates. *A Relais & Châteaux hotel. 3410 Montrose Blvd., 77006, tel. 713/524–7999, fax 713/524–8923. Gen. manager, Stephen Zimmerman. 6 suites, 1 penthouse. AE, CB, DC, MC, V.*

**㉚**
$$$
**The Doubletree at Allen Center.** This hotel's cold, formal lobby has a minimalist decor, with beige-tone furniture and marble walls. The staff, however, is gracious and eager to please. Standard guest rooms are small but nicely appointed in tones of salmon; corner queen rooms are considerably larger. Fitness facilities are noteworthy: In addition to the 6.2-kilometer jogging trail located just across the street, the hotel also provides access to three nearby health clubs. *400 Dallas St., 77002, tel. 713/759–0202 or 800/528–0444, fax, 713/752–2734. Gen. manager, Mike Hughes. 341 rooms, 20 suites. AE, CB, D, DC, MC, V.*

**★ ㉝**
$$$$
**Four Seasons Hotel, Houston Center.** This elegant hotel is in the Houston Center redevelopment area on the eastern edge of downtown, within walking distance of the convention center. The lobby is serene and inviting, with plush carpeting, comfortable conversation areas, and a majestic staircase to the second floor. Rooms are bright and spacious, with custom-made work tables and large bay windows; suites provide a good place for small meetings. The DeVille restaurant (*see* Business Breakfasts, below) is a popular spot for business entertaining; the chef is highly esteemed. An upscale crowd gathers at the Terrace Café (*see* After Hours, below) for drinks. Guests may use the fitness facilities at the Houston Center Club for a nominal fee. *1300 Lamar St., 77010, tel. 713/650–1300, fax 713/650–1300, ext. 4240. Gen. manager, Francisco Gomez. 399 rooms, 12 suites. AE, CB, DC, MC, V.*

**㉛** **Hyatt Regency.** The dramatic 30-story atrium lobby, typi-
$$$ cal of this chain, has two lounges and two restaurants that
draw a lot of activity to this downtown hotel. In fact, the
lobby is often chaotic. For business travelers, the recently
renovated Regency Club floors offer upgraded rooms, con-
cierge service, and Continental breakfast. Rooms have ad
equate lighting with neutral furnishings and color
schemes. In general, though, accommodations are small
and provide little space to spread out and work. Ask for a
room on the south side, which has the best views. The
Hyatt is connected to Houston's tunnel system, so it's an
especially good choice during the summer. *1200 Louisi-
ana St., 77002, tel. 713/654–1234, fax 713/654–1549. Gen.
manager, Tom Netting. 907 rooms, 52 suites. AE, CB, D,
DC, MC, V.*

**★ ㉜** **The Lancaster.** This hotel, in the heart of the city's theater
$$$$ and business districts, is elegant without being stuffy,
and functional but charming. Reproductions of antiques,
brass fixtures in the bathrooms, and miles of chintz create
the unhurried, dignified atmosphere of an English manor
house. Rooms are luxurious, each with three or four tele-
phones, comfortable seating areas, fresh flowers daily,
umbrellas, and supplies of artesian water. Guests can
travel around town in the hotel's silver London taxi. The
Texas Club is one of the most luxurious health clubs in the
city. The Lancaster Grille (*see* Dining, below) is a popular
breakfast spot. *A Lancaster Group hotel. 701 Texas Ave.,
77002, tel., in Texas, 713/228–9500, outside Texas, 800/
231–0336, fax 713/223–4228. Gen. manager, Roberta
Sroka. 85 rooms, 8 suites. AE, D, DC, MC, V.*

**㉗** **The Wyndham Warwick.** Located in Houston's museum
$$$ district, across the street from the Fine Arts Gallery and
near Rice University, this newly restored, 12-story hotel
has sumptuous furnishings in its public rooms—18th-
century Aubusson tapestries on the walls, Baccarat chandeliers in the lobby, and antique French couches and love
seats that provide intimate groupings for conversation.
Rooms in this 60-year-old property are individually
decorated with tasteful antique furnishings and reproductions. Not all rooms have desks or suitable work areas, so
it's best to make your needs known when making reservations. Floors 8 and 9 provide the best views of either downtown or the medical center, both only minutes away, and
rooms in the new wing have balconies. *5701 Main St.,
77005, tel. 713/526–1991 or 800/822–4200, fax 713/639–
4545. Gen. manager, Larry Brown. 307 rooms, 45 suites.
AE, CB, DC, MC, V.*

## Galleria

**➒** **Guest Quarters.** Business travelers who miss the comforts
$$$ of home will like this 26-story, all-suites property, built 10
years ago next door to the Galleria. The one- or two-bed-
room suites boast full kitchens. Rooms are spacious and
have balconies—a real rarity in Houston—recently refur-
bished living rooms, and dining areas with soothing pastel
colors and comfortable furniture. Best views are in rooms
facing north to the downtown skyline, especially impres-
sive at night. *A Guest Quarters Suite hotel. 5353
Westheimer Rd., 77056, tel. 713/961–9000, fax 713/877–
8835. Gen. manager, Mike Hirsch. 335 suites. AE, D, DC,
MC, V.*

# DOWNTOWN HOUSTON

**Lodging**

Astro Village Hotel Complex, **21**
La Colombe D'Or, **24**
Doubletree at Allen Center, **30**
Four Seasons Hotel, Houston Center, **33**
Hobby Airport Hilton, **35**
Hotel Luxeford, **22**
Hyatt Regency, **31**
The Lancaster, **32**
The Wyndham Warwick, **27**

**Dining**

Brennan's, **28**
Carrabba's, **18**
La Colombe d'Or, **24**
Damian's, **29**
Goode Co. Barbeque, **19**
Hunan River, **23**
The Lancaster Grille, **32**
Mussel's Seafood and Bistro, **20**
Ninfa's on Navigation, **34**
River Café, **26**
Ruggles Grill, **25**

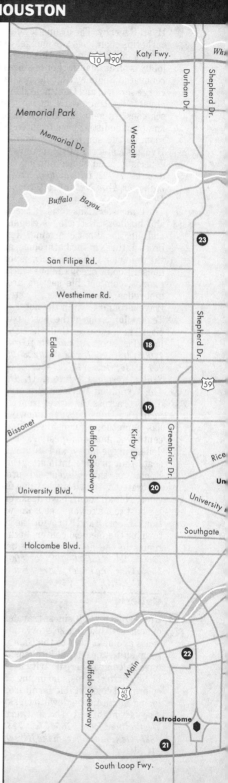

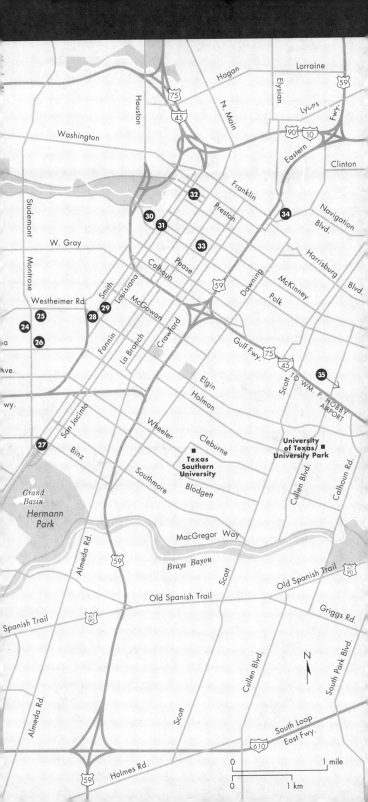

# GREATER HOUSTON

**Lodging**

Guest Quarters, **9**

Holiday Inn Crown Plaza, **15**

The Houstonian, **7**

Inn on the Park, **8**

J.W. Marriott, **10**

Quality Inn, Intercontinental Airport, **6**

Ritz-Carlton, **17**

The Westin Oaks, Galleria, **14**

Wyndham Hotel Greenspoint, **5**

**Dining**

Café Annie, **11**

Carrabba's, **2**

Churrasco's, **3**

Goode Co. Barbeque, **1**

Luling City Market BBQ, **16**

La Reserve, **8**

Ruth's Chris Steak House, **4**

Sam's Café, **12**

Tony's, **13**

**⑮** **Holiday Inn Crown Plaza.** One of the best values in the up-
**$$** scale Galleria area, this Holiday Inn was built in 1984 dur-
ing the lean years of Houston's oil bust. Although the hotel
lacks the elegant trappings of other nearby hotels, it of-
fers the business traveler a wide range of amenities at
a reasonable price. Guest rooms are large and bright;
executive-level rooms on the 23rd floor are clearly the
most desirable, with limited key access for security, a
minibusiness center, and free breakfast and cocktail re-
ceptions. Complimentary transportation within a five-mile
radius of the hotel is another plus. *2222 West Loop S, 77027,
tel. 713/961–7272 or 800/465–4329, fax 713/961–3327.
Gen. manager, Al Stento. 477 rooms, 7 suites. AE, D,
DC, MC, V.*

**★ ❼** **The Houstonian.** George Bush stays here when he comes
**$$$** to Houston, but even without the presidential seal of ap-
proval this lodgelike hotel set in a 22-acre wooded park
near the Galleria would have much to recommend it. The
lobby, with skylights and large picture windows, takes
full advantage of its forested surroundings. Rooms, which
are small but nicely appointed in pastels and floral prints,
face either the woods or the pool. Ambassador House
rooms, on the first three floors, are slightly larger than
regular rooms and have canopied beds. All bathrooms are
small. Conference facilities are notable: There are 34
meeting rooms and a 20-station personal computer center.
Fitness facilities are first class as well, and include two
Olympic-size swimming pools, courts for nearly every
sport, and an indoor and outdoor running track. *111 N.
Post Oak La., 77024, tel. 713/680–2626. Dial main number for fax access. Gen. manager, Jim Sugarman. 297
rooms, 19 suites. AE, CB, D, DC, MC, V.*

**★ ❽** **Inn on the Park.** While George Bush stays at the
**$$$$** Houstonian, his entourage can usually be found at this elegant nearby hotel. Located at the edge of Memorial Park,
and within minutes of the Galleria area, the hotel has an
inviting, parklike setting. An aura of unhurried grace
pervades the public rooms, where fresh flower arrangements brighten intimate conversation areas. Rooms are
spacious, with marble-top desks, and accents of Oriental
art. Floors 8–10 overlook the pool and a small pond.
Rooms farthest from the elevators are the largest and quietest. The hotel's four-star restaurant, La Reserve (*see*
Dining, below), is reason alone to stay here; the Black
Swan (*see* After Hours) is a popular after-work watering
hole. *A Four Seasons hotel. 4 Riverway, 77056, tel. 713/
871–8181, fax 713/871–0719. Gen. manager, Philip
Barnes. 368 rooms, 13 suites. AE, CB, DC, MC, V.*

**❿** **J.W. Marriott.** This Galleria hotel looks like an upended
**$$$** brick cracker box. The lobby is sunny, although much
of its space is taken up with marble columns and an
overabundance of furniture. The staff is efficient, and
the hotel does a good job of catering to businesspeople.
Rooms are small, but provide a functional work area and a
little space to move around in; all have three phones
and two TV sets. Some rooms have special amenities, in-
cluding irons and ironing boards, makeup mirrors, and ad-
ditional toiletries. Ask for a room with a view of the Gal-
leria. Facilities include a small but workable health
club with an indoor/outdoor pool, two racquetball
courts, and basketball and tennis courts. *5150 Westheim-*

# HOUSTON HOTEL CHART

| HOTELS | Price Category | Business Services Banquet capacity | No. of meeting rooms | Secretarial services | Audiovisual equipment | Teletype news service | Computer rentals | In-room modem phonejack | All-news cable channel | Desk | Desk lighting | Bed lighting |
|---|---|---|---|---|---|---|---|---|---|---|---|---|
| Astro Village Hotel Complex | $$ | 1800 | 18 | - | ✓ | - | - | - | ✓ | ◐ | ◐ | ● |
| La Colombe d'Or | $$$$ | 100 | 0 | ✓ | ✓ | - | ✓ | ✓ | ✓ | ◐ | ◐ | ● |
| The Doubletree at Allen Center | $$$ | 450 | 11 | - | ✓ | - | - | - | ✓ | ● | ● | ● |
| Four Seasons Hotel Houston Center | $$$$ | 400 | 13 | ✓ | ✓ | - | ✓ | ✓ | ✓ | ● | ● | ● |
| Guest Quarters | $$$ | 150 | 7 | ✓ | - | - | - | - | ✓ | ◐ | ◐ | ◐ |
| Hobby Airport Hilton | $$ | 800 | 15 | - | ✓ | - | - | - | | ● | ● | ● |
| Holiday Inn Crown Plaza | $$ | 450 | 16 | ✓ | ✓ | - | ✓ | ✓ | | ● | ● | ● |
| The Houstonian | $$$ | 500 | 33 | ✓ | ✓ | - | ✓ | ✓ | | ● | ● | ● |
| Hyatt Regency | $$$ | 1800 | 30 | ✓ | ✓ | ✓ | ✓ | ✓ | ✓ | ◐ | ● | ● |
| Inn On The Park | $$$$ | 490 | 13 | ✓ | ✓ | - | - | - | ✓ | ● | ● | ● |
| J.W. Marriott | $$$ | 1200 | 11 | ✓ | ✓ | - | - | - | ✓ | ● | ● | ● |
| The Lancaster | $$$$ | 56 | 3 | ✓ | ✓ | - | - | - | - | ● | ● | ● |
| Luxeford | $$ | 150 | 4 | - | - | - | - | - | ✓ | - | - | ● |
| Quality Inn, Inter-Continental Airport | $$ | 150 | 8 | ✓ | ✓ | - | - | - | - | ◐ | ◐ | ● |
| Ritz-Carlton | $$$$ | 300 | 6 | ✓ | ✓ | - | - | - | ✓ | ● | ● | ● |
| The Westin Oaks, Galleria | $$$$ | 1400 | 27 | ✓ | ✓ | - | ✓ | ✓ | ✓ | ◐ | ◐ | ◐ |
| Wyndham Hotel Greenspoint | $$ | 1500 | 25 | ✓ | ✓ | - | - | - | ✓ | ● | ● | ● |
| Wyndham Warwick | $$$ | 550 | 10 | - | ✓ | - | - | - | ✓ | ● | ● | ● |

**$$$$** = over $150, **$$$** = $120-$150, **$$** = under $120.
● good, ◐ fair, ○ poor.
All hotels listed here have photocopying and fax facilities.

| In-Room Amenities | | | | | | | | | | Hotel Amenities | | | | | | |
|---|---|---|---|---|---|---|---|---|---|---|---|---|---|---|---|---|
| Nonsmoking rooms | In-room checkout | Minibar | Pay movies | VCR/Movie rentals | Hairdryer | Toiletries | Room service | Laundry/Dry cleaning | Pressing | Concierge | Barber/Hairdresser | Garage | Courtesy airport transport | Sauna | Pool | Exercise room |
| ✓ | – | – | – | – | – | ◐ | ● | ● | ● | ✓ | ✓ | – | – | – | ● | – |
| ✓ | ✓ | ✓ | – | – | – | ◐ | ● | ● | ● | ✓ | – | ✓ | ✓ | – | – | – |
| ✓ | – | – | ✓ | – | – | ● | ● | ● | ● | ✓ | ✓ | ✓ | – | – | – | – |
| ✓ | – | ✓ | – | – | ✓ | ◐ | ● | ● | ● | ✓ | – | – | – | ✓ | ● | – |
| ✓ | – | – | ✓ | – | ✓ | ◐ | ● | ● | ● | ✓ | – | ✓ | – | – | ● | ● |
| ✓ | ✓ | – | ✓ | – | – | ◐ | ● | ● | ● | – | – | – | – | – | ● | ◐ |
| ✓ | – | ✓ | ✓ | – | ✓ | ◐ | ● | ● | ● | ✓ | – | ✓ | ✓ | – | ● | ◐ |
| ✓ | – | ✓ | ✓ | ✓ | – | ◐ | ● | ● | ● | ✓ | – | ✓ | ✓ | – | ● | ● |
| ✓ | ✓ | – | ✓ | – | – | ◐ | ● | ● | ● | ✓ | ✓ | – | – | – | – | – |
| ✓ | ✓ | ✓ | – | – | ✓ | ● | ● | ● | ● | ✓ | – | ✓ | – | – | ● | ● |
| ✓ | – | ✓ | – | – | ✓ | ● | ● | ● | ● | ✓ | ✓ | ✓ | ✓ | ✓ | ● | ● |
| ✓ | – | – | ✓ | – | – | – | ◐ | ● | ● | – | – | ✓ | – | – | ◐ | ◐ |
| ✓ | – | – | ✓ | ✓ | – | ◐ | ● | ● | ● | – | – | – | – | – | – | – |
| ✓ | ✓ | – | ✓ | – | – | ● | ● | ● | ● | ✓ | – | ✓ | – | – | ● | – |
| ✓ | ✓ | ✓ | ✓ | – | – | ◐ | ◐ | ● | ● | ✓ | – | ✓ | ✓ | ✓ | ● | ● |
| ✓ | ✓ | – | ✓ | – | – | ◐ | ● | ● | ● | ✓ | – | ✓ | – | – | ● | ◐ |
| ✓ | ✓ | – | – | – | ✓ | ◐ | ● | ● | ● | ✓ | – | ✓ | ✓ | ✓ | ● | ● |

**Room service:** ● 24-hour, ◐ 6AM-10PM, ○ other.
**Laundry/Dry cleaning:** ● same day, ◐ overnight, ○ other.
**Pressing:** ● immediate, ◐ same day, ○ other.

*er Rd., 77056, tel. 713/961–1500, fax 713/993–9907. Gen. manager, Robert Pittenger. 503 rooms, 46 suites. AE, CB, DC, MC, V.*

**⑰** **Ritz-Carlton.** Formerly the Remington Hotel, this Hous-
$$$$ ton landmark was fastidiously renovated by new owners in 1989, and it remains a favorite of local businesspeople and distinguished visitors. Fine antiques and art works adorn the public rooms of this well-located property, near the Galleria and a wooded park. Guest rooms, decorated with soothing pastel colors, are exceptionally spacious and have comfortable sitting areas and three telephones. Business facilities are noteworthy, including multilingual translation services, a research library, and audiovisual equipment with a technician available 24 hours a day. Particularly appealing are rooms on the second floor that open up to a lovely landscaped deck and heated swimming pool. The staff is first rate and service is personal and thoughtful. *1919 Briar Oaks La., 77027, tel. 713/840–7600 or 800/ 241–3333. Gen. manager, Philip von Hardenberg. 221 rooms, 27 suites. AE, D, MC, V.*

**⑭** **The Westin Oaks, Galleria.** This hotel and its sister
$$$$ property, the Westin Galleria, are favorites with convention-eers. Both have choice locations in the Galleria shopping complex. Unfortunately, much of the activity from the Galleria's shops, restaurants, and movies—activities that make the area so attractive—often spills over into the hotel. The lobby is usually noisy; shoppers use the hotel as a shortcut to the mall. All the accommodations were renovated in 1987, but some rooms are starting to show signs of wear. Some standard guest rooms are a tacky blend of loud, floral wallpaper and Oriental-style furniture. The Executive Level and Premiere rooms are more tastefully styled and feature VIP amenities. *5011 Westheimer Rd., 77056, tel. 713/623–4300 or 800/228–3000, fax 713/960– 6551. Gen. manager, Louis Martinelli. 406 rooms, 11 suites. AE, CB, D, DC, MC, V.*

## Medical Center

**㉑** **Astro Village Hotel Complex.** Judge Roy Hofheinz, who
$$ built the Houston Astrodome, also built this hotel across the highway. The 20-year-old complex, which is land-scaped with tropical plants and maintains a resortlike atmosphere, is beginning to show its age. An ongoing major renovation and expansion is expected to freshen the property and bring amenities up to date. For now, rooms are a hodgepodge of designs and decor, often with out-of-style wall coverings and mismatched furniture. Visiting sports teams and entertainers booked at the Dome often stay here. The hotel is convenient to the Texas Medical Center (complimentary transportation is provided), and NASA's Johnson Space Center is less than a half-hour drive away. *An Sheraton Astrodome hotel. 2350 South Loop W., 77054, tel. 713/748–3221, fax 713/ 796–9371. Gen. manager, Bill Havey. 725 rooms, 75 suites. AE, CB, D, DC, MC, V.*

**㉒** **Hotel Luxeford.** Don't expect fresh flowers in your room;
$$ the Luxeford is a centrally located, basic all-suites hotel with rather gloomy public areas—and extremely reasonable rates. Single or double suites have two rooms, two telephones, and complete kitchens. Accommodations are clean, and decor is practical, with dark carpeting and

wear-resistant upholstery. Laundry facilities are located on every floor. A complimentary full breakfast buffet is served in the lobby, and there's a cocktail hour Monday–Thursday evenings. Free transportation to the Medical Center and the Astrodome is also provided. *1400 Old Spanish Trail, 77054, tel. 713/796–1000, or 800/662–3232, fax 713/796–8055. Gen. manager, Judi Bikulege. 190 suites. AE, DC, MC, V.*

## Airport

**㉟** **Hobby Airport Hilton.** This hotel, just two blocks from the
**$$** airport, is a favorite of airline personnel. The sunny lobby, with its floor-to-ceiling windows, is a great spot from which to watch the planes take off. Considering its proximity to the airport, the hotel is surprisingly quiet. The nine-year-old property has an attractive, Southwestern look, with lots of plants and blue-and-mauve decor. Rooms in the Tower section have Jacuzzis and skylights. Upper Tower floors are recommended for somewhat more quiet and privacy. Small meeting rooms/parlors with fold-out beds are available 8AM–5PM for a daytime rate. *8181 Airport Blvd., 77061, tel. 713/645–3000 or 800/445–8667, fax 713/645–3000, ext. 902. Gen. manager, Baron Hobbs. 277 rooms, 33 suites. AE, D, DC, MC, V.*

**❻** **Quality Inn, InterContinental Airport.** Pure function is
**$$** what you get at this two-story brick hotel, about two miles east of the airport. Rooms are clean and bright, with basic furnishings that include small reading tables with lamps. Frills are few, but there are VCRs in every room and a complimentary movie rental service; a few rooms have whirlpools and steam baths. There is a travel agency and a car rental booth in the lobby, and complimentary transportation to the airport. *6115 Will Clayton Pkwy., 77205. tel. 713/446–9131 or 800/228–5151, fax 713/446–2251. Gen. manager, Ron Jordan. 174 rooms, 2 suites. AE, DC, D, MC, V.*

**★ ❺** **Wyndham Hotel Greenspoint.** Built in 1983 as part of the
**$$** Greenspoint Business Center, the Wyndham has an especially airy, spacious lobby, constructed around a 45-foot atrium. An indoor garden with tropical plants and skylights makes the lobby's café a pleasant spot for a light meal or a drink. Rooms are comfortable, if small, with standard modern furnishings. Ask for a room above the third floor, or you may find yourself looking out on a gravel roof. A nearby health club has a running track and racquetball, squash, and basketball courts. The newest hotel in the area, this is the top choice for accommodations near the airport. *12400 Greenspoint Dr., 77060, tel. 713/875–2222, fax 713/875–1652. Gen. manager, Pat Lupsha. 472 rooms, 50 suites. AE, D, DC, MC, V.*

## DINING

Houston's restaurants are not concentrated downtown; in fact, some of the best are in suburban strip malls. Local cuisine can be characterized as Southwestern cooking sparked with Cajun accents, and there are enough ethnic places to surprise out-of-towners, many of whom arrive thinking that a Texan's idea of foreign food is an Idaho potato. Also, visitors tend to forget that Houston is less than an hour away from the Gulf of Mexico, and that the seafood can be as fresh as the day's catch.

Highly recommended restaurants in each price category are indicated by a star ★.

| Category | Cost* |
|---|---|
| *$$$$* (Very Expensive) | over $35 |
| *$$$* (Expensive) | $21–$35 |
| *$$* (Moderate) | $6–$20 |
| *$* (Inexpensive) | under $6 |

*\*per person, including appetizer, entrée, and dessert, but excluding drinks, service, and 8% sales tax.*

*Numbers in the margin correspond to numbered restaurant locations on the Houston Lodging and Dining maps.*

## Business Breakfasts

Most top law firms, investment houses, and oil companies have membership privileges for their top executives at private downtown clubs; this is where early-morning wheeling and dealing generally takes place in town. The hotel dining rooms listed below are other likely spots for Houston's powerbrokers to begin the day.

The **Lancaster Grille** (Lancaster Hotel, tel. 713/228–9502; *see* review, below) is where top businesspeople start the day with a stack of hotcakes and strong coffee. It's in walking distance of all major downtown hotels. The **DeVille** (Four Seasons, Houston Center, tel. 713/650–1300) is just three blocks from the convention centers and features light breakfasts from 6:30AM; of the two this is the better for meetings, with larger, more widely spaced tables than the Lancaster Grille.

## Downtown

★ ㉘ **Brennan's.** This downtown restaurant has the same
*$$$$* Southern appeal and Cajun specialties as its French Quarter namesake, although it's no longer connected with the New Orleans establishment. A clubby decor with lots of wood molding, ornate mirrors, and discreet service make it a popular lunch spot for city lawyers and financial types. Regulars like the tables with a courtyard view. Turtle soup is a popular appetizer. Recommended entrées include angel hair pasta with gulf shrimp and mild andouille sausage; grilled mahi mahi with smoked cream-corn salsa; and a perfectly grilled veal chop with a port, brandy, and peppercorn sauce. For dessert, call ahead to order a chocolate soufflé—it will satisfy a lifetime of cravings. *3300 Smith St., tel. 713/522–9711. Jacket and tie advised. Reservations advised. AE, CB, D, MC, V.*

⑱ ❷ **Carrabba's.** Pasta is the name of the game at this no-non-
*$$* sense eatery with locations downtown and in the suburbs west of the Galleria. The room is sparsely decorated with white-tile walls, wooden shelves filled with pasta boxes, and a wood-burning pizza oven behind the bar. Reservations are not accepted, and there's always a wait in the bar, which is usually filled with customers sporting everything from blue jeans to tuxes. House classics are lasagne bolognese, spaghetti with meatballs, and ravioli in a

porcini mushroom sauce. For lunch, flavorful options include the *insalata carrabba*, a mix of greens, grilled chicken, cheese, and vegetables in a vinaigrette dressing; or the mussels steamed in white wine, spices, and olive oil. Service is quick and efficient, and there's a respectable selection of reasonably priced Italian wines. Come for a social, rather than serious, meal with colleagues or business associates. *2 locations: 3115 Kirby Dr., tel. 713/522–3131; 1399 South Voss Rd., tel. 713/468–0868. Casual dress. No reservations. AE, DC, MC, V.*

★ ❸ **Churrascos.** Nicaraguan specialties make this one of the
$$ more interesting, as well as one of the more exotic, places to eat, but the noise and crowds reduce opportunities for quiet conversation. The menu's unfamiliar but savory dishes include *cerdo a la plancha* (baby tenderloin of pork flavored with tamarind and guava sauce) and *pechuguitas asadas* (grilled chicken breast basted with a salsa criolla). *Churrascos*, the house specialty, is charcoal-grilled beef tenderloin basted and served with *chimichurri* sauce (olive oil, garlic, and parsley). If you like things hot, add a spoonful of one of the sauces on the tray that accompanies each meal. An excellent and unusual selection of Spanish and South American wines is available. *9788 Bissonnet St. (between U.S.59 & Beltway 8), tel. 713/541–2100. Casual dress. Reservations advised. AE, D, V.*

★ ㉔ **La Colombe d'Or.** The best French food in Houston is
$$$$ served in this tiny jewel of a restaurant in the small luxury inn that was once the mansion of the late Walter Fondren, a founder of a predecessor of Exxon Corporation. The dining room, adorned with antiques and modern art, has become a gathering spot for influential politicians. Well-prepared specialties usually include fillet of red snapper topped with crabmeat in a lemon-pepper sauce; and braised *ris de veau* (calf's sweetbread). For dessert, try *la palette de Concorde*, a selection of dessert offerings, including white- and dark-chocolate mousse and homemade pistachio ice cream; it's enough for four to share. *3410 Montrose Blvd., tel. 713/524–7999. Jacket and tie required. Reservations required. AE, CB, D, DC, MC, V.*

★ ㉙ **Damian's.** This fine downtown restaurant has a loyal
$$$ following of local business types who like the classic Northern Italian food and the warm and soothing atmosphere. Peach stucco walls, brown carpets, subtle lighting, and soundproof ceilings make it an attractive setting for business discussions, even at its most crowded. The kitchen has been known to have off days, but when it's good, it produces the closest thing to authentic Italian cuisine that Houston has to offer. The noodles in cream sauce with prosciutto, mushrooms, peas, and Parmesan is a good choice, as is the cannelloni. Entrées, including chicken, veal, and fish dishes, are well prepared, but often could use more seasoning. The wine list features an excellent selection of reasonably priced Italian wines. *3011 Smith St., tel. 713/ 522–0439. Jacket and tie advised. Reservations advised. AE, DC, MC. Closed Sun.*

❶ ⑲ **Goode Co. Barbeque.** If you want to see where locals go
$$ when they have nothing more serious in mind than some real, down-home barbecue, check out this old gray barn decorated with such wild West memorabilia as buffalo heads, rodeo posters, and silver belt buckles. You'll be greeted by the heady aromas of meats roasting over wood

fires and vats of simmering tomato sauce. It's difficult to call a best pick. Duck, chicken, pork sausage, and beef brisket are all done well and can be made extra zingy with a ladleful of spicy sauce. Jalapeno corn bread is served with every order and is the perfect solution for mopping up the plate. Locals rate the beans the best in Texas. The pecan pie is similarly esteemed. The downtown Kirby Drive restaurant is the original, more lively, locale. *Two locations: 5109 Kirby Dr., tel. 713/522–2530; 8911 Katy Frwy., tel. 713/464–1951. Casual dress. No reservations. AC, DC, MC, V.*

**㉓ Hunan River.** An ultramodern room with black-marble ta-
**$$** ble tops, stainless steel chairs, and dark, industrial ceilings makes an appropriately trendy setting for good Chinese food on the edge of the exclusive River Oaks neighborhood. Society matrons in tennis skirts and jogging togs dine next to professionals in corporate gray flannel. Service is efficient and discreet, making Hunan River a comfortable spot for a business meal. The steamed dumplings, either pork or shrimp, are nice starters. House specialties include a Hunan-style seafood platter with lobster, crabmeat, shrimp, and scallops, and filet Mignon with shrimp and vegetables cooked in a flower-pepper sauce. In general, dishes tend to be mild, even the ones noted on the menu as spicy. If you like things hot, advise your waiter. *2015 W. Gray St., tel. 713/527–0200. Casual but neat. Reservations advised. AE, DC, MC, V.*

**㉜ Lancaster Grille.** Its clubby setting—dark-green walls,
**$$$** wood and leather trim—combined with a convenient location in the downtown financial district and a menu of Continental and Southwestern American fare attract many businesspeople for lunch. However, this popular restaurant is small and usually so crowded that privacy is at a premium. The salads are just right for lunch on a hot summer day. For dinner, you might start with a warm duck salad with a Grand Marnier vinaigrette. Poached salmon steak or rack of lamb with Dijon mustard make fine entrées. *The Lancaster hotel 701 Texas Ave., tel. 713/ 228–9502. Jacket and tie suggested. Reservations advised. AE, D, DC, MC, V.*

**⑯ Luling City Market BBQ.** At lunch the lines of business-
**$** people waiting to order at this rustic ribs joint often spill out the front door and onto the sidewalk. Its location—in the shadows of the Galleria and a 15-minute drive from downtown—accounts for some of the popularity. But the main draw here is the beef brisket, pork ribs, and beef links that are sold by weight and served cafeteria style. Potato salad and cole slaw are extras, as are pickles and jalapeño peppers that sit in plastic tubs along the serving line. Shaker bottles filled with the house special red sauce sit on every table. While the concrete floors, small wooden tables, and neon beer signs might make the setting too rough-edged for some, the restaurant has achieved a cult following for those in town who would do almost anything for good barbecue. *4726 Richmond Ave., tel. 713/871– 1903. Casual dress. No reservations. AE, DC, MC, V.*

**⑳ Mussel's Seafood and Bistro.** If you're looking for a light
**$$** meal in the Village shopping area near Rice University, this neighborhood seafood restaurant is a reliable and well-priced option; you can have a nice, quiet business discussion at one of the corner tables. The small room is spot-

less, with black-and-white-tile floors and mauve table-cloths and chairs. Mussels are naturally the specialty, but the steamed mussels appetizer is bland; crab cakes served with a picante sauce as an appetizer or entrée are just right, and the sandwiches are hearty. *2512 Times Blvd., tel. 713/524–8684. Casual but neat. Reservations suggested. AE, DC, MC, V.*

**③④ Ninfa's on Navigation.** This is the original location of a
**$** Tex-Mex chain that has expanded across the state. It is conveniently located for downtown businesspeople who overlook the noisy, fiesta-style ambience. The widowed Mama Ninfa and her five children who opened the place in an abandoned tortilla factory are local legends. Try the *tacos a la Ninfa* (either grilled chicken or beef wrapped in soft flour tortillas); they're the local favorites. Also recommended are the *fajitas* (seasoned pieces of grilled meat or shrimp served with a variety of sauces). *2704 Navigation Blvd., tel. 713/228–1175. Casual dress. No reservations. AE, DC, MC, V.*

**㉖ River Café.** This popular bistro and bar is located in Mont-
**$$** rose, Houston's version of Greenwich Village, about 10 minutes from the downtown business area. It caters to a mixed crowd of young professionals and local artists: The decor is spare, with brick walls, exposed ductwork along the ceiling, and sparse cactus arrangements in the corners. The cuisine is an innovative take on Southwestern specialties. Consider starting with the poblano pepper, stuffed with fontina and cheddar cheeses and crabmeat, topped with a cheese sauce, and served with black beans. The red-chili pasta with smoked sausage in a tomato sauce is a robust novelty, as is the shrimp étouffée, sautéed shrimp with rice, covered with a spicy creole sauce. On clement days, there are tables outdoors—a rare find in Houston. *3615 Montrose Blvd., tel. 713/529–0088. Casual dress. Reservations advised. AE, DC, MC, V.*

**★ ㉕ Ruggles Grill.** This lively Montrose bistro attracts many of
**$$** the city's young professionals at lunch and dinner time; the bar area, with its stained glass, cozy booths, and ceiling fans, is always busy. Chef Bruce Molzan lends a creative Southwestern touch to everything from pizza to pasta. Both black-bean pasta and chicken sausage pizza are highly recommended. Daily seafood specials, ranging from shrimp to snapper cooked adventurously well, are also worth investigating. *903 Westheimer Rd. (east of Montrose), tel. 713/524–3839. Casual dress. Reservations advised. AE, DC, MC, V. Closed Mon., and Sat. lunch.*

## Galleria

**★ ⑪ Café Annie.** A popular Galleria restaurant, modern and
**$$$$** uncluttered, Café Annie has high ceilings, mirrored walls, and wide aisles. The cuisine blends nouvelle American specialties with downhome Southern flavor. Notable dishes include yellowfin tuna seared rare with spicy jalapeño-lime butter, and grilled T-bone steak with pecan-and-maple steak sauce. The à-la-carte dinner menu changes daily. Game specialties may include quail with potato tacos and smoked-chili sauce, or roast pheasant with green-olive pesto and tomato butter. The toasted pound cake with ice cream and chocolate sauce is worth saving room for. There are two dining levels, both suitable for serious conversations. *1728 Post Oak Blvd., tel. 713/840–*

*1111. Jacket and tie advised. Reservations required. AE, DC, MC, V.*

**8** **La Reserve.** An elegant setting, fine nouvelle cuisine, and
**$$$$** a convenient location in the Inn on the Park, near the Galleria, draw an upscale crowd of visiting businesspeople and Houstonians. The richly paneled dark-wood walls create a tranquil atmosphere. The fixed-price menu is recommended: It offers a choice of two appetizers, an entrée, a dessert, and a selection of wines. Fettucine with Gulf Shrimp and sea scallops in pesto; grilled swordfish with couscous; and paillard of veal with asparagus and red onions are among the excellent entrée possibilities. The menu also features a creative list of low-cholesterol, low-calorie dishes. *4 Riverway, tel. 713/871–8177. Jacket and tie advised. Reservations advised. AE, CB, DC, MC, V.*

**4** **Ruth's Chris Steak House.** The decor of this quintessential
**$$$$** business restaurant is no-frills oil-man's chic: Oil company logos and photos of oil rigs adorn the walls along with a New York Stock Exchange ticker. The steak-and-potatoes crowd will find lots of old favorites: New York strip steak, fillet, T-bone, and Porterhouse, all cooked to order in sizzling butter and served without garnish. Side dishes, ordered separately, include potatoes, creamed spinach, and asparagus with hollandaise. Ice cream freezes, the dessert specialty, are made with liqueurs. *6213 Richmond Ave., tel. 713/789–2333. Casual but neat. Reservations advised. AE, D, DC, MC, V.*

**12** **Sam's Café.** This Houston outpost of a successful New
**$$** York City bistro owned by Mariel Hemingway is dressed up with lots of cactus, rough-hewn timbers, and desert hues of mauve and blue. It has one of the city's most respected chefs and a fashionable location in the Saks Pavilion, so Sam's draws a chic crowd. Tables are well spaced; if you want even more privacy, ask to sit in the upstairs dining area. The cuisine is a mix of standard American favorites and Southwestern specialties. Locals rate the sautéed crab cakes the best in Houston; spicy grilled shrimp with a seafood boudin, and jicama salad are also popular. The menu includes many variations on a basic pasta-and-pizza theme. Service can be spotty. *1800 Post Oak Blvd., tel. 713/622–9292. Casual but neat. Reservations suggested. AE, DC, MC, V.*

**13** **Tony's.** This trendy Galleria restaurant is the place to see
**$$$$** and be seen for the denizens of Houston's society columns and top-echelon businesspeople. The dining room is spacious, but the decor features too much of everything—gilt and glass and the color red. Best tables are reserved for the regulars, but all afford enough space to keep conversations confidential. The cuisine is basic Italian, with some Continental specialties. The *fedelini Marinara* (thin pasta with a tomato and basil sauce) is a fine starter, as is crabmeat ravioli. In general, it's wise to steer clear of more complicated dishes and order simpler options such as veal chops. *1801 Post Oak Blvd., tel. 713/622–6778. Jacket and tie advised. Reservations necessary. AE, DC, MC, V.*

# FREE TIME

## Fitness

*Hotel Facilities*
Many Houston hotels have excellent health clubs, but they are open only to hotel guests (or to locals who've purchased long-term memberships).

*Health Clubs*
The facilities at the **Downtown YMCA** (1600 Louisiana St., tel. 713/659–8501) are open free of charge to YMCA-chain members (be sure to bring your membership card) and cost $15 for the day for nonmembers.

*Jogging*
Downtown, the **Buffalo Bayou Trail** has a 4.8-mile and a 6.8-mile route. In the Galleria area, **Memorial Park** offers five miles of jogging trails.

## Shopping

The **Galleria** (tel. 713/622–0663), at Post Oak Boulevard and Westheimer Road, has the biggest names in department stores: Neiman-Marcus, Marshall Field, Lord & Taylor, Macy's, and hundreds of smaller stores, including many top names in retailing like Gumps and Tiffany. The tony **Saks** Pavilion (tel. 713/627–0500) draws an upscale crowd with designer stores such as Krizia, Hermes, and Cartier's jewelers.

For a good selection of Southwest pottery, rugs, or jewelry, try **Edith Brown Southwest Collections** (Suite 2705, Galleria, tel. 713/961–4462 or 713/681–7799). For Western wear, **Stelzig's** (3123 Post Oak Blvd., tel. 713/629–7799) should have what you're looking for.

## Diversions

**Bayou Bend Collection** (1 Westcott St., tel. 713/529–8773) has early-American furniture from the colonial period through the Victorian era; it's housed in the historic 28-room mansion of philanthropist Ima Hogg.

The **Galleria** (Westheimer Rd. and Post Oak Blvd.) is not only Houston's premier shopping center, it's also a good place to watch the ice-skaters and to sip a cappuccino at one of the cafés around the rink.

**Hermann Park,** in the heart of Houston's museum district, offers many diversions for a spare morning or afternoon, including beautiful walks in the Rose Garden, horseback riding on oak-lined trails, and a visit to the city's small zoo.

**Houston Arboretum and Nature Center** (4501 Woodway, tel. 713/681–8433) provides more than 100 acres of wilderness, with hiking trails ideal for bird and animal watching.

**Menil Collection** (1500 Sul Ross St., tel. 713/524–9028) has a permanent holding of modern and ancient work, including impressive displays of Mediterranean antiquities and African art.

**Museum of Fine Arts** (1001 Bissonet St., tel. 713/526–1361), Houston's largest art museum, features the Straus Collection of Renaissance and 18th-century works. There is also a pleasant café for a light lunch.

**Museum of Natural Science** (1 Hermann Circle Dr., tel. 713/639–4600) features the Wortham IMAX Theatre where you can see such documentaries as "The Dream is Alive," filmed by 14 astronauts during shuttle missions.

**Rothko Chapel** (3900 Yupon St., tel. 713/524–9839) was designed and created by artist Mark Rothko 20 years ago for meditation and prayer. His paintings provide a serene setting for quiet reflection.

## Professional Sports

Houston's basketball team, the **Rockets,** plays at The Summit (tel. 713/627–0600). The city's football club, the **Oilers,** appear at the Astrodome (tel. 713/797–1000), as does Houston's baseball team, the **Astros** (tel. 713/799–9500).

## The Arts

All theaters are centrally located downtown. Top productions are usually performed at the nationally known **Alley Theater** (615 Texas Ave., tel. 713/228–8421). The **Wortham Theatre Center** (501 Texas Ave., tel. 713/237–1439) is home to the Houston Ballet and the Houston Grand Opera, one of the most highly esteemed opera companies in the country. Directly across the street is **Jones Hall for the Performing Arts** (615 Louisiana St., tel. 713/237–1439), home of the Houston Symphony Orchestra.

Ticket agencies include **Ticketron** (2990 Richmond Ave., No. 601, tel. 713/621–0637) and **Ticketmaster** (15 Houston locations, tel. 713/799–9555).

## After Hours

For entertaining clients after work, many Houston businesspeople head for the bars and lounges in the Galleria or downtown hotels. There are some boisterous places as well, such as the Cadillac Bar (*see* below), that offer a downhome Texas experience for a less-formal night out.

*Bars and Lounges*
The **Black Swan** at the Inn on the Park (tel. 713/871–8181) is modeled on an English pub and draws a young professional crowd. The **Terrace Café** in the Four Seasons Hotel (tel. 713/650–1300) provides a handsome backdrop for a distinctly well-heeled crowd to enjoy drinks and discussions. The leather couches at either of the two elegant bar/lounges at **La Colombe d'Or** (tel. 713/524–7999) offer opportunities for intimate conversation. The bar at **Brennan's** (3300 Smith St., tel. 713/522–9711), complete with gaslights, white trellises, and garden views, provides a New Orleans–style respite for after-work and before-dinner drinks.

*Comedy Clubs*
The **Laff Stop** (1952A W. Gray St., tel. 713/524–2333) is where professional stand-up comedians perform. **Radio Music Theatre** (2623 Colquitt St., tel. 713/522–7722) features original musical comedy revues.

*Jazz Clubs*
**Cody's** (3400 Montrose St., tel. 713/522–9747) is noted for its music and four-star view of the city from its rooftop terrace. **Rockefeller's** (3620 Washington Ave., tel. 713/861–

9365) features big-name entertainers whose repertoire runs the musical gamut from jazz to bluegrass; noisy crowds can detract from enjoyment of the music. The **Blue Moon** (1010 Banks St., tel. 713/523–3773) has an upscale clientele that stops in for late-night listening.

*For Singles*

**XIT** (1971 W. Gray St., tel. 713/523–1919; 777 Walker St., tel. 713/228–4400) is packed at both locations. **Birraporetti's** (1997 W. Gray St., tel. 713/529–9191) is also popular. **Sam's Place** (5710 Richmond Ave., tel. 713/781–1605) is lively at all hours; on summer Sundays the party moves outdoors. The **Cadillac Bar** (1802 Shepherd Dr., tel. 713/862–2020) has waitresses who wear holsters stuffed with tequila bottles, and is about as raucous as a local night spot gets.

# Indianapolis

*by Ann Hughes*

Ever since U.S. 40 was routed through Indianapolis, the city has been known as the Crossroads of America. It is crisscrossed by more interstates and federal highways than any other city in the nation. It also has had some other nicknames—Naptown, India-no-place—that projected a less positive image. That was back in the '50s, when Indianapolis made John Gunther's list of the dirtiest U.S. cities.

What followed was a generation of aggressive city leadership and a tremendous outpouring of public and private development money. Creative legal minds found a way to consolidate the city and county governments, thus preserving the city's tax base and doubling its population. Indianapolis built new museums and expanded old ones. Crews of workmen demolished crumbling and dilapidated eyesores in the central business district and erected chrome and granite office buildings that act as foils for landmark structures, such as the Indiana Soldiers & Sailors Monument and old Christ Church. The city constructed new sports complexes, such as Market Square Arena and the Hoosier Dome, and in 1987, it played host to the Pan Am Games. In 1988, Keep America Beautiful named Indianapolis the cleanest U.S. city of its size.

Old money in Indianapolis comes from hog-processing, milling, and downtown real estate. After the Civil War, the city became—and it still is—a key player in the manufacture and distribution of pharmaceuticals. The automobile was invented in Indiana, and Indianapolis was once home to the shops where Stutz Bearcats and Duesenbergs were handcrafted before the era of mass production rendered those shops obsolete.

Today, Indianapolis has a service-oriented economy. It is a headquarters city for national associations—many of them sports- and health-related—but not for national industrial and financial firms, though a respectable number of them have satellite or back-room operations here. Because of a strong work ethic based in part on the city's farming roots, the rate of unemployment is among the lowest of major U.S. cities. So is the cost of living.

Although the quality of life in Indianapolis is now good, it is rather homogeneous. Indianapolis has no Little Italy, no Greektown, no Chinatown. Every autumn, third- and fourth-generation German-Americans get together for a day-long feast of bratwurst, hot potato salad, and beer, but that halfhearted Octoberfest is about as close to an ethnic festival as you'll get around here. And, in general, geared toward residents rather than visitors, Indianapolis has little or no nightlife.

Indianapolis and Washington, D.C., are the only two U.S. cities that were planned to be capitals. The Hoosier capital and the nation's capital have something else in common: They were laid out by the same team of urban designers, who gave them both a traffic pattern of circles with avenues radiating from them and cross streets laid out on a grid. The logical order in which the streets are numbered makes it easy to find your way around.

## Top Employers

| Employer | Type of Business | Parent* / Headquarters |
|---|---|---|
| **Community Hospital** | Health care | Indianapolis |
| **Eli Lilly and Co.** | Pharmaceuticals | Indianapolis |
| **General Motors Corp.** | Automotive | Detroit |
| **Indiana Bell Telephone Co.** | Telecommunications | Indianapolis |
| **Marsh Supermarkets** | Food stores | Yorktown, IN |
| **Methodist Hospital of Indiana** | Health care | Indianapolis |
| **St. Vincent Hospital** | Health care | Indianapolis |

*if applicable

## ESSENTIAL INFORMATION

### Climate

What follows are the average daily maximum and minimum temperatures for Indianapolis.

| | | | | | | | | |
|---|---|---|---|---|---|---|---|---|
| **Jan.** | 36F | 2C | **Feb.** | 40F | 4C | **Mar.** | 49F | 9C |
| | 22 | −6 | | 23 | −5 | | 32 | 0 |
| **Apr.** | 61F | 16C | **May** | 72F | 22C | **June** | 83F | 28C |
| | 43 | 6 | | 54 | 12 | | 63 | 17 |
| **July** | 86F | 30C | **Aug.** | 85F | 29C | **Sept.** | 77F | 25C |
| | 67 | 19 | | 65 | 18 | | 58 | 14 |
| **Oct.** | 65F | 18C | **Nov.** | 50F | 10C | **Dec.** | 40F | 4C |
| | 47 | 8 | | 36 | 2 | | 27 | −3 |

### Airport

**Indianapolis International Airport** is 7 miles west of downtown, via I–70, and is accessible to all parts of the city due to its location just off I–465, the city's beltway. The airport underwent a $171-million renovation and expansion in 1987 that added a new runway and parking garage, expanded the baggage-handling system, and upgraded the main terminal.

## Airport Business Facilities

The **Airport Information Center** (on the upper level) has a fax machine and coin-operated photocopier. A conference room in the second floor of the Administrative Building can be rented from the **Airport Authority** (tel. 317/248–7243). **The Mutual of Omaha Insurance Counter** (on the upper level across from Delta, tel. 317/241–0440) has Western Union and travel insurance.

## Airlines

Indianapolis is a hub city for USAir.

**Air Canada,** tel. 800/776–3000.
**American,** tel. 317/262–1054 or 800/433–7300.
**Continental,** tel. 317/635–0291 or 800/525–0280.
**Delta,** tel. 317/634–3200 or 800/221–1212.
**Midway,** tel. 800/621–5700.
**Northwest,** tel. 800/225–2525.
**Pan Am,** tel. 800/221–1111.
**Southwest,** tel. 317/637–1717 or 800/531–5601.
**TWA,** tel. 317/635–4381 or 800/221–2000.
**United,** tel. 317/638–6363 or 800/241–6522.
**USAir,** tel. 317/248–1211 or 800/428–4322.

## Between the Airport and Downtown

Getting to and from the airport is easiest by taxi or limo, unless your hotel has an airport shuttle service.

*By Taxi or Limousine*
Catching a cab isn't much of a problem if you're coming in on a red-eye flight or going out on a milk run, but when you're traveling at peak hours and several flights are converging upon the airport, expect to queue up for a 5–10-minute wait. If it's smooth sailing, the 7-mile ride downtown takes 10–15 minutes during a normal rush hour (7–8:30 AM and 4:30–6 PM). On Friday evenings, with big rigs and heavy weekend traffic on the interstate, the ride takes a few minutes more. If you're going to the north side, allow an extra 25 minutes; to the northeast side, add 35 minutes. The most direct routes are by interstate. Cab fare to downtown is $6; to the north side, $20; to the far-northeast side, $30. Gratuities are extra.

*By Bus*
The **AAA Airport Shuttle Express** (tel. 317/247–7301) runs between the airport and downtown every half hour from 4 AM to midnight, stopping at the major hotels. The trip takes 15–20 minutes, depending on your stop. Cost: $4.

## Car Rentals

The following companies have terminals near the airport:

**Ace,** tel. 317/243–6336.
**Avis,** tel. 317/244–3307 or 800/331–1212.
**Budget,** tel. 317/248–1100 or 800/527–0700.
**Dollar,** tel. 317/241–8206 or 800/421–6868.
**Enterprise,** tel. 317/243–8988 or 800/325–8007.

**Hertz,** tel. 317/243–9321 or 800/634–3131.
**National,** tel. 317/243–1177 or 800/227–7368.

## Emergencies

*Doctors*
**Harcourt Road Internists** (St. Vincent Professional Bldg., No. 705, tel. 317/872–5431, on call 24 hours), **Meridian Medical Group** (1801 N. Senate Blvd., tel. 317/929–5800 or 317/926–3466 in emergencies), **Northside Cardiology** (8402 Harcourt Rd., tel. 317/872–5050, on call 24 hours), **Northside Internal Medicine** (2010 W. 86th St., No. 203, tel. 317/872–6551 or 317/926–3466 in emergencies).

*Dentists*
**Downtown Dental Specialists** (324 E. New York St., No. 300, tel. 317/262–4838) is available 24 hours.

*Hospitals*
Emergency service is available round the clock at the following: **Methodist Hospital of Indiana** (1701 N. Senate Blvd., tel. 317/929–2000), **St. Vincent Hospital** (2001 W. 86th St., tel. 317/871–2345), and **Wishard Memorial Hospital** (1001 W. 10th St., tel. 317/639–6671).

## Important Addresses and Numbers

**Audiovisual rentals.** Cosler Communications (6330 E. 75th St., tel. 317/842–9580), Markey's Audio-Visual (2909 S. Meridian St., tel. 317/783–1155), Shoemaker Motion Picture Company (3901 Meadows Dr., tel. 317/547–8000), Visual Aids Electronics (50 S. Capitol Ave., 317/638–8110).

**Chambers of Commerce.** Indiana Chamber of Commerce (1 N. Capitol Ave., tel. 317/634–6407), Indianapolis Chamber of Commerce (320 N. Meridian St., tel. 317/464–2200).

**Computer rentals.** Micro Rental Plus (5937 W. 71st St., tel. 317/299–6298), Micro-Rental USA (5129 E. 65th St., tel. 317/253–7788), Personal Computer Rentals (6201 Coffman Rd., tel. 317/297–7676 or 800/922–8646), Rex Business Machines (121 S. Pennsylvania St., tel. 317/639–6453).

**Convention and exhibition centers.** Indiana Convention Center & Hoosier Dome (1 S. Capitol Ave., tel. 317/632–4321), Indianapolis Convention and Visitors Association (1 Hoosier Dome, tel. 317/639–4292), Indiana State Fairgrounds (1202 E. 38th St., tel. 317/927–7500), University Place Conference Center (950 W. Michigan St., tel. 317/269–9000).

**Fax services.** Just the Fax (546 S. Meridian St., tel. 317/638–9462), Kinko's Copies (333 N. Pennsylvania St., tel. 317/631–6862), Pip Printing Centers (1 N. Capitol, tel. 317/236–8383; 445 N. Pennsylvania St., tel. 317/634–2963).

**Formal-wear rentals.** Black Tie Formal Wear (Glendale Center, 6101 N. Keystone Ave., tel. 317/254–8899), D C Designers Tux Shops (6258 Carrollton Ave., tel. 317/253–3422), Gingiss Formalwear (6020 E. 82nd St., tel. 317/849–9081), Indiana Tux Shops (5518 E. 82nd St., tel. 317/849–3427), Leon Tailoring (809 N. Delaware St., tel.

317/634–8559), Warren Tailors Formal Wear (30 E. Georgia St., Suite 100, tel. 317/636–3535).

**Gift shops.** Chocolates: Rocky Mountain Chocolate Factory (28 Monument Circle, tel. 317/636–6555), Sweet Things (11 W. Washington St., tel. 317/236–1911); Flowers: Andrews Florist (251 N. Illinois St., tel. 317/237–3030), Wells (2160 W. 86th St., tel. 317/872–4267).

**Graphic design studios.** Caldwell Van Riper Design (1314 N. Meridian St., tel. 317/632–6501), The Design Group (3444 Washington Blvd., tel. 317/924–2444), DesignMark (4640 W. 71st St., tel. 317/291–0300).

**Hairstylists.** Unisex: The Hair Closet (155 W. Washington St., No. 3–A, tel. 317/635–1331), L.S. Ayres & Co. (1 W. Washington St., tel. 317/262–2261), Meridian Design Group (210 S. Capital Ave., tel. 317/237–5353).

**Health and fitness clubs.** *See* Fitness, below.

**Information hot lines.** Fun Fone (tel. 317/237–5210), Indianapolis City Center (tel. 317/237–5206 or 800/323–INDY).

**Limousine services.** A Touch of Class Limoservice (tel. 317/846–4743), Dynasty Limousines (tel. 317/241–9900), Hoosier Alternative Limousine Service (tel. 317/243–0000), Indy Connection Limousine Service (tel. 317/271–2522), Solid Gold Limousine Service (tel. 317/259–4653).

**Liquor stores.** John's Spirits, Decanters & Fine Wines (25 N. Pennsylvania St., tel. 317/637–5759), Reliable Drug Stores (310 N. New Jersey St., tel. 317/639–4539). The Twenty-first Amendment (2209 N. Meridian St., tel. 317/925–4211).

**Mail delivery, overnight.** DHL Worldwide Express (tel. 317/241–4464), Federal Express (tel. 317/636–4845), UPS (tel. 317/875–0060), U.S. Postal Service Express Mail (tel. 317/464–6489).

**Messenger services.** Fast Package Delivery (tel. 317/635–3278), Pony Express Courier (tel. 317/241–0611), Purolator Courier (tel. 317/247–5566 or 800/645–3333).

**Office space rentals.** Group Systems (36 S. Pennsylvania St., tel. 317/633–4220; 10 W. Market St., tel. 317/464–8250), May & Steele The Executive Workplace (11711 N. Meridian St., tel. 317/843–5500), Officeplus of Keystone Crossing (8888 Keystone Crossing, tel. 317/575–4000).

**Pharmacies, late-night.** Hook's Drugs Stores (1315 W. 86th St., tel. 317/253–6427; 27 N. Lyndhurst Dr., tel. 317/241–8901; 1744 N. Illinois St., tel. 317/923–1491), Reliable Drug Stores (8405 Ditch Rd., tel. 317/253–4821; 1535 N. Meridian St., tel. 317/631–9229; 140 S. Girls School Rd., tel. 317/271–8329).

**Radio stations, all-news.** WIBC 1070 AM; WFYI 90 FM (public radio).

**Secretarial services.** Dunhill Temporary Systems (950 N. Meridian St., tel. 317/237–7878), Everyday Typesetting & Typing (5 E. Market St., No. 832, tel. 317/636–2767), Group Systems (10 W. Market St., No. 500, tel. 317/464–

8250; 36 S. Pennsylvania St., tel. 317/633–4220), Olsten Services (107 N. Pennsylvania St., tel. 317/634–6601).

**Stationery supplies.** Stationers (36 N. Pennsylvania St., tel. 317/635–2461).

**Taxis.** Hoosier Cab Company (tel. 317/243–8800), Metro Taxi (tel. 317/634–1112 or 317/545–1111), Yellow Cab (tel. 317/637–5421).

**Theater tickets.** *See* The Arts, below.

**Train information.** Amtrak (Union Station, 350 S. Illinois St., tel. 317/632–1905 or 800/872–7245), CSX Transportation (Union Station, *see* above, tel. 317/267–3000).

**Travel agents.** American Express-Allen Travel Services (201 N. Illinois St., tel. 317/237–2230), Hoosier Travel Service (130 E. Washington St., tel. 317/632–7553), Ross & Babcock Travel Bureau (210 S. Capitol Ave., 317/637–4300; 2601 Fortune Circle E., tel. 317/244–8444).

**Weather** (tel. 317/222–2362).

## LODGING

The major chains (many of them new properties) are strategically located downtown, but they offer few surprises. Airport hotels are convenient to the interstate roads and the industrial complexes on the west side. If you're going to be traveling around the area, an airport hotel may be your best bet. Commercial centers and office parks in the suburbs are well-served by first-class accommodations.

Most hotels listed here offer special corporate rates and weekend discounts; inquire when making reservations.

Highly recommended lodgings are indicated by a star ★.

| Category | Cost* |
| --- | --- |
| $$$$ (Very Expensive) | over $120 |
| $$$ (Expensive) | $90–$120 |
| $$ (Moderate) | under $90 |

*All prices are for a standard double room, single occupancy, excluding 5% state and 5% city sales taxes.*

*Numbers in the margin correspond to numbered hotel locations on the Indianapolis Lodging and Dining maps.*

### Downtown/Center City

★ ⑲  **The Canterbury Hotel.** This 60-year-old, 12-story hostelry
$$$$  near Indianapolis Union Station, once serving city transients, has been brought back to life as a plush European-style hotel where gentlemen play backgammon in the evening and ladies sip tea in the afternoon. The elegant Beaulieu restaurant (*see* Dining, below) draws a business crowd all day long. The public rooms are beautifully appointed—a parlor with a fireplace, a clublike wood-paneled bar with leather furniture and lamplight, an atrium with Chinese Chippendale, ginger jars, and cloisonné urns. Hallways are brightened with both original artwork and fine reproductions. Though rejuvenated guest rooms are lavish, armoires and queen poster beds take up a lot of

space. A compensating feature is the bathroom, with telephone, television set, and heated towel bar. *A member of Preferred Hotels Worldwide. 123 S. Illinois St., 46225, tel. 317/634–3000, fax 317/634–3000, ext. 7397. Gen. manager, Pamela Hacker. 99 rooms, 15 suites. AE, CB, DC, MC, V.*

**⑰ Embassy Suites Downtown.** This is the third hotel on this
$$$ site, a corner equidistant from Monument Circle and the statehouse. President Lincoln spoke from the balcony of the Bates House, the first hotel to be built here. Old-timers remember this as the site of the Claypool Hotel (hence the name Claypool Court [*see* Shopping, below] for the maze of 30-plus gift shops and specialty stores on the first two floors, today). But there's nothing old-fashioned about this contemporary property. The 15-story atrium boasts a simulated tropical rain forest. Rooms are done in shades of mauve, pink, and aqua and appointed with modernistic ivory-color wood furniture, etched-glass mirrors, and Art Deco prints. Suites have separate living rooms with convertible sofas and minikitchens. Dining areas with eating space for four have tables that can double as work space. *110 W. Washington St., 46204, tel. 317/236–1800 or 800/362–2779, fax 317/236–1816. Gen. manager, Bill Mabrey. 360 suites. AE, CB, DC, MC, V.*

**⑱ Hilton at the Circle.** This 21-story high rise, just a half-
$$$ block from Monument Circle, opened in 1970 and was renovated in 1985. Its biggest plus is its location in the heart of the financial district, close to the headquarters of two major banks and city-county and federal offices. Day or night, the lobby is a hive of activity. Decor in the standard rooms is chain-motel traditional, but that's offset by pastel walls, colorful prints, and lots of lamplight. Things take a more elegant turn in the Tower Club, where there is a private lounge, a billiard room, and concierge service. *31 W. Ohio St., 46204, tel. 317/635–2000 or 800/445–8667, fax 317/638–0782. Gen. manager, Vicki Jackson. 371 rooms, including 45 executive suites. AE, CB, DC, MC, V.*

**★ ㉓ Holiday Inn Union Station.** This hotel occupies a remod-
$$ eled train shed adjacent to the Indianapolis Union Station. Baggage carts on the sidewalk are piled high with steamer trunks, foot lockers, and valises to set a nostalgic mood. The lobby is in the old express pick-up and delivery area, and the Louisiana Street Bar (*see* After Hours, below) used to be the loading dock. Thirteen sleeper cars-cum-suites are named for such personalities as Greta Garbo and Rudolph Valentino, and furnished with appropriate antiques and memorabilia. There are two suites in each Pullman, and although they're fun and popular, they're not as spacious as standard rooms in the main part of the hotel. In case of an earthquake, though, this is probably the safest place in town— the Carnegie Steel superstructure was built at the turn of the century to withstand the weight of some 200 trains that used to rumble in overhead each day. *123 Louisiana St., 46206, tel. 317/631–2221 or 800/465–4329, fax 317/236–7474. Gen. manager, William Townsend. 243 rooms, 33 suites. AE, CB, DC, MC.*

**⑯ Hyatt Regency Indianapolis.** Built in 1977, the Hyatt is an
$$$ easy stroll from the statehouse, the Indiana Convention Center, and Hoosier Dome, as well as dozens of first-rate restaurants. Club chairs and sofas grouped amid the greenery give the lobby the ambience of a conservatory, a

# GREATER INDIANAPOLIS

**Lodging**
Adam's Mark, **11**
Hilton at the Airport, **9**
Holiday Inn Airport, **10**
Omni Indianapolis
North Hotel, **8**
Radisson Plaza and
Suite Hotel, **6**
Signature Inns,
**1, 2, 7, 12**

**Dining**
Dodd's Town House, **4**
Shapiro's Delicatessen
& Cafeteria, **3**
Something Different, **5**

# DOWNTOWN INDIANAPOLIS

**Lodging**
Canterbury Hotel, **19**
Embassy Suites Downtown, **17**
Hilton at the Circle, **18**
Holiday Inn Union Station, **25**
Hyatt Regency Indianapolis, **16**
Omni Severin Hotel, **24**
Ramada Downtown Indianapolis, **14**
University Place Hotel, **13**
Westin Hotel Indianapolis, **15**

**Dining**
Beaulieu, **18**
Benvenuti, **21**
Fletcher's American Grill & Café, **23**
King Cole, **20**
Milano Inn, **27**
Peter's, **28**
St. Elmo Steak House, **22**
Severin Bar & Grill, **24**
Shapiro's Delicatessen & Cafeteria, **26**

look that contrasts with the down-home appeal of the rockers outside the Front Porch restaurant on the mezzanine. Interior rooms open onto balconies overlooking the 20-story atrium. All rooms have work areas; some have computer hutches. A renovation added a 14-foot waterfall to the atrium, a health club, and a full service in-house business center. The Eagle's Nest (*see* After Hours, below) is a good spot for a quiet drink. *1 S. Capitol Ave., 46204, tel. 317/632–1234 or 800/228–9000, fax 317/231–7569. Gen. manager, Earl Nightingale. 484 rooms, 22 suites. AE, CB, DC, MC, V.*

**㉔** **Omni Severin Hotel.** Omni has brought new life to this his-
**$$$** toric grande dame of Indianapolis hotels, nearly doubling its size and blending contemporary styling with classic elegance. A two-story, skylighted atrium with a 20-foot waterfall is the focal point in the new tower; the old Italian Renaissance Revival section boasts meticulously restored crystal chandeliers, ceiling medallions, a curving marble staircase, and cast-iron mezzanine railings. Built in 1913 as the Hotel Severin at a cost of $400,000, the hotel underwent a more recent renovation costing $40 million. The location, across from Union Station, is still prime. Renovated guest rooms have nine-foot ceilings; rooms in both new and old sections have similar furnishings and decor, with writing tables. Deluxe suites have balconies with views of the Pan American Plaza and Hoosier Dome. *40 W. Jackson Pl., 46225, tel. 317/634–6664 or 800/843–6664, fax 317/687–3619. Gen. manager, John Berta. 385 rooms, 36 suites, 11 2-story penthouses. AE, CB, DC, MC, V.*

**⑭** **Ramada Downtown Indianapolis.** Guests appreciate the
**$$** combined advantages of roadside motel and downtown property that this hotel offers. It has plenty of street-level parking, yet it's right at the hub of activity, just a stone's throw from the convention center and across the street from the Capitol and the state-office complex. This used to be a Howard Johnson's, but the aqua-and-orange look has been replaced with wood veneers, marble tiles, and elevators with polished brass doors. Card-accessed guest rooms have easy chairs with ottomans, and writing desks with wall-mounted, swing-away lamps. The hotel is air-conditioned, but the windows can be opened to let in fresh air. Another plus is a coin-operated laundry. An amiable staff and a T.G.I.Friday's (*see* After Hours, below) bistro that's action-packed from noon to midnight make this a lively place. *510 W. Washington St., 46204, tel. 317/635–4443 or 800/666–5397, fax 317/687–0029. 233 rooms, 3 suites. AE, CB, DC, MC, V.*

**⑬** **University Place Hotel.** This new hotel near the Indianapo-
**$$$$** lis campus of Indiana and Purdue universities (IUPUI) is where academics and medical professionals congregate. Presidential suites have canopy beds, Queen Anne writing desks with leaded-crystal lamps, and double sinks in the master baths. Standard rooms are handsomely appointed with desks, easy chairs, and traditional furniture. Museum-quality original oils and watercolors add interest to the common areas. Services for business travelers include a fiber-optics telecommunications system, fully equipped computer lab, and meeting rooms with simultaneous language-translation capabilities. There's no in-house health club, but guests have access to the excellent athletic facilities on the nearby campus. *850 W. Michigan*

# INDIANAPOLIS HOTEL CHART

| HOTELS | Price Category | Banquet capacity | No. of meeting rooms | Secretarial services | Audiovisual equipment | Teletype news service | Computer rentals | In-room modem phone jack | All-news cable channel | Desk | Desk lighting | Bed lighting |
|---|---|---|---|---|---|---|---|---|---|---|---|---|
| Adam's Mark | $$$ | 800 | 17 | ✓ | ✓ | - | - | - | ✓ | ● | ● | ● |
| The Canterbury | $$$$ | 0 | 3 | ✓ | ✓ | - | - | - | ✓ | ◖ | ◖ | ● |
| Embassy Suites Downtown | $$$ | 350 | 5 | ✓ | ✓ | - | - | - | - | ● | ● | ● |
| Hilton at the Airport | $$$ | 700 | 12 | ✓ | ✓ | - | ✓ | - | ✓ | ● | ● | ● |
| Hilton at the Circle | $$$ | 650 | 6 | ✓ | ✓ | - | - | - | ✓ | ● | ● | ● |
| Holiday Inn Airport | $$ | 440 | 15 | ✓ | ✓ | - | - | - | ✓ | ● | ● | ● |
| Holiday Inn Union Station | $$ | 600 | 16 | - | ✓ | - | - | ✓ | ✓ | ● | ● | ● |
| Hyatt Regency | $$$ | 788 | 19 | ✓ | ✓ | - | ✓ | - | ✓ | ● | ● | ● |
| Omni Indianapolis North | $$$ | 250 | 9 | - | ✓ | - | ✓ | ✓ | ✓ | ● | ● | ● |
| Omni Severin | $$$ | 254 | 16 | - | ✓ | - | - | - | ✓ | ● | ● | ● |
| Radisson Plaza and Suite | $$$ | 750 | 15 | ✓ | ✓ | - | - | - | ✓ | ● | ● | ● |
| Ramada Downtown | $$ | 300 | 8 | - | ✓ | - | - | - | ✓ | ● | ● | ● |
| Signature Inns | $$ | 0 | 0 | ✓ | ✓ | - | ✓ | - | ✓ | ● | ● | ● |
| The Westin Hotel | $$$$ | 800 | 22 | ✓ | ✓ | - | - | ✓ | ✓ | ● | ● | ● |
| University Place | $$$$ | 250 | 30 | ✓ | ✓ | - | - | - | ✓ | ● | ● | ● |

$$$$ = over $120, $$$ = $90-$120, $$ = under $90.
● good, ◖ fair, ○ poor.
All hotels listed here have photocopying and fax facilities.

| In-Room Amenities | | | | | | | | | | Hotel Amenities | | | | | | |
|---|---|---|---|---|---|---|---|---|---|---|---|---|---|---|---|---|
| Nonsmoking rooms | In-room checkout | Minibar | Pay movies | VCR/Movie rentals | Hairdryer | Toiletries | Room service | Laundry/Dry cleaning | Pressing | Concierge | Barber/Hairdresser | Garage | Courtesy airport transport | Sauna | Pool | Exercise room |
| ✓ | – | – | ✓ | – | ✓ | ◐ | ◐ | ◐ | ◐ | – | – | – | ✓ | ✓ | ● | ◐ |
| ✓ | ✓ | – | – | – | – | ● | ● | ● | ● | ✓ | – | – | ✓ | – | – | – |
| ✓ | – | ✓ | – | ✓ | ✓ | ◐ | ◐ | ● | ● | – | – | ✓ | – | ✓ | ● | – |
| ✓ | – | – | ✓ | – | – | ◐ | ◐ | ◐ | ◐ | – | – | – | ✓ | – | ◐ | ◐ |
| ✓ | – | ✓ | – | – | – | ◐ | ● | ◐ | ◐ | ✓ | – | – | – | – | ● | – |
| ✓ | – | – | – | – | – | ◐ | ◐ | ◐ | ◐ | – | – | – | ✓ | ✓ | – | ◐ |
| ✓ | – | – | – | – | – | ◐ | ● | ◐ | ◐ | ✓ | – | ✓ | ✓ | ✓ | ● | ◐ |
| ✓ | ✓ | – | ✓ | – | – | ◐ | ● | ◐ | ◐ | – | – | ✓ | – | ✓ | ● | ◐ |
| ✓ | ✓ | ✓ | ✓ | – | ✓ | ◐ | ◐ | ◐ | ○ | – | – | – | – | ✓ | ● | ◐ |
| ✓ | – | ✓ | ✓ | – | – | ◐ | ● | ◐ | ◐ | ✓ | – | ✓ | ✓ | ✓ | ● | ● |
| ✓ | ✓ | – | – | ✓ | – | ◐ | ◐ | ◐ | ◐ | ✓ | – | ✓ | – | ✓ | ● | – |
| ✓ | – | – | – | – | – | ◐ | ◐ | ◐ | ◐ | ✓ | ✓ | – | – | ✓ | ◐ | – |
| ✓ | – | – | – | – | – | – | – | – | – | – | – | – | – | – | ● | – |
| ✓ | ✓ | – | ✓ | – | – | ◐ | ● | ◐ | ◐ | ✓ | – | ✓ | – | – | ● | – |
| ✓ | ✓ | – | ✓ | – | – | ◐ | ◐ | ◐ | ◐ | – | – | – | – | ✓ | ◐ | ◐ |

**Room service:** ● 24-hour, ◐ 6AM–10PM, ○ other.
**Laundry/Dry cleaning:** ● same day, ◐ overnight, ○ other.
**Pressing:** ● immediate, ◐ same day, ○ other.

*St.*, *46202, tel. 317/269–9000 or 800/627–2700, fax 317/231–5168. Gen. manager, Per Moller. 262 rooms, 16 suites. AE, CB, DC, MC, V.*

**⑮ The Westin Hotel Indianapolis.** This sleek, cosmopolitan
$$$$ hotel is adjacent to the Indiana Convention Center and has
a view of the Hoosier Dome on one side and the Indianapolis Zoo on the other. Rooms are done in soothing beiges
and lime colors, and original watercolors hang on the
walls. Executive-level rooms have sleeper sofas, minibars,
two telephones, valet stands, and added amenities such as
complimentary Continental breakfast, newspapers, and
terry robes. The 1,000-car parking garage, 38,000 square
feet of column-free exhibit space, and 22 meeting rooms
make this a convention center in and of itself. *50 S. Capitol
Ave., 46204, tel. 317/262–8100 or 800/228–3000, fax 317/
231–3928. Gen. manager, Thomas Hosea. 572 rooms (32
on executive level), 38 suites. AE, CB, DC, MC, V.*

## Airport

**⑪ Adam's Mark.** The industrial complexes and office parks on
$$$ the Indianapolis west side are accessible from this 11-
year-old low rise that was renovated in 1989. Tufted leather sofas, wood paneling, and leaded glass give it a clubby
English ambience that compensates for the sterile, concrete-block facade. Bright colors and striped fabrics lend
the refurbished guest rooms an individuality missing from
standard hotel rooms. Some accommodations have panoramic views of the Indianapolis skyline; all have ample
writing desks. There are sleeper sofas in the minisuites;
full suites add oak conference tables and wet bars.
Quincy's (*see* After Hours, below) attracts yuppies to its
live band music. *2544 Executive Dr., 46241, tel. 317/248–
2481 or 800/231–5858, fax 317/248–2481, ext. 7135. Gen.
manager, Bob Von Esmarch. AE, CB, DC, MC, V.*

**⑨ Hilton at the Airport.** This 1962 hotel is right on airport
$$$ turf, but don't worry—it's been soundproofed, and none
of the air lanes is directly overhead. If you're not burdened
with heavy baggage, you can easily walk here from the
terminal. The Sri Lankan rattan chairs in the lobby create
a visual alternative to the usual homegrown Hoosier look.
Standard rooms have standard hotel fixtures. This place
has evolved as a favorite for local meetings and social functions, but guests can escape from the hubbub on an outdoor putting green or with a drink at poolside in the
atrium. *2500 S. High School Rd., 46241, tel. 317/244–3361
or 800/445–8667, fax 317/241–9202. Gen. manager, Robert
Meyer. 256 rooms, 20 studios, 9 suites. AE, CB, DC,
MC, V.*

**⑩ Holiday Inn Airport.** This Holiday Inn franchisee's corpo-
$$ rate headquarters are on the premises, so the staff is attentive and everything is especially clean and orderly. The
building has a new facade and a new wing, but once you're
inside, you won't know whether you're in the original
building or the addition. All guest rooms are roadside
modern, with new bathrooms. Suites have wet bars and
tables big enough for small meetings. Inside rooms open
out onto a five-story atrium with natural lighting and tropical plants that screen an indoor pool. The lobby has areas
where discreet conversations can be held. *2501 S. High
School Rd., 46241, tel. 317/244–6861 or 800/465–4329, fax*

317/243–1059. Gen. manager, Douglas Allison. 270 rooms, 4 suites. AE, CB, DC, MC, V.

**❶ ❷ ❼ ⑫** **Signature Inns.** These business-traveler oriented inns were
**$$** developed by their owner to supply the needs he noted
were not being met by other highway lodgings. Signature
Inns, contemporary inside and out, offer a complete range
of business services, including interview centers, meeting
rooms for as many as 100 people, and least-cost long-dis-
tance call routing. Corridor-accessed guest rooms have
sturdy, commercial-grade furniture, recliner chairs, and
corner desks with track lighting. Newspapers delivered to
your door during the week are another perk. The inns
have outdoor pools, but no food or beverage service, ex-
cept for complimentary Continental breakfast in the lob-
by. Consequently, inns are always situated next to family
restaurants and close to interstate highways. This may or
may not mean there's a cocktail lounge nearby, so BYOB
may be in order. *Several Indianapolis locations: west, I–
465 and 38th St., tel. 317/299–6165; northwest, I–465 and
U.S. 421, tel. 317/875–5656; northeast, I–465 and
Allisonville Rd., tel. 317/849–8555; east, I–465 and U.S.
40, tel. 317/353–6966. All inns: tel. 800/822–5252. AE,
DC, MC, V.*

## Keystone Crossing/Castleton

**❽** **Omni Indianapolis North Hotel.** Located in the far north-
**$$$** east corner of Marion County, this two-year-old, full-ser-
vice hotel is adjacent to Community Hospital North and
the rapidly expanding business complexes in the Castleton area. The contemporary, two-story lobby is resplendent with marble columns and a three-tier fountain/plant-
er, anchored with patterned carpeting in the theme
colors of turquoise and burgundy. Rooms are ample in
size and attractively appointed with Queen Anne chairs,
spacious desks, and matching print bedspreads and
draperies. Conveniences include a coffee center, and refrigerators in some rooms. Some suites have separate living rooms with bars; none has a kitchenette. Nine meeting
rooms are available. The Café offers casual dining;
Abruzzi's restaurant has good Italian fare. The Lobby Bar
is a relaxing spot for cocktails, and the Blue Moon Bar (*see
After Hours, below*) is one of the city's hottest, high-energy nightclubs. *8181 N. Shadeland Ave., 46250, tel. 317/
849–6668, fax 317/849–4936. Gen. manager, Caren Zaft.
222 rooms, 11 suites. AE, CB, DC, MC, V.*

**★ ❻** **Radisson Plaza and Suite Hotel.** This suburban property
**$$$** just off the beltway combines two hotels in one. The Plaza
has a sparkling, glittery, glass-canopied public space that's
partitioned by railings and planter boxes into restaurants,
lounges (including the Lobby Lounge—*see After Hours,
below*—a good place to take a client for a drink), and con-
versation groupings. Its lobby bustles all day long. The
more sedate Suite Hotel has the ambience of a private club
with Oriental rugs, camel-back sofas, and chess tables.
Complimentary breakfast and an afternoon hors d'oeuvre
buffet are served in the lobby. Plaza rooms have lamp-
lighted desks and club chairs or love seats. Units in the
Suite Hotel have sleeper sofas and dinette-size work space
with overhead lighting. Don't lay in a supply of frozen en-
trées, however. Suites have no microwaves and the refrig-
erators are about big enough for a bottle of wine and a

banana. *8787 Keystone Crossing, 46240, tel. 317/846–2700 or 800/228–9822, fax 317/846–2700, ext. 402. Gen. manager, Frank Klare. 393 rooms, 159 suites. AE, CB, DC, MC, V.*

## DINING

*by Marge Hanley*

Indianapolis has moved from corncrib cooking, past classic cuisine, into eclectic Americana. You can still find Hoosier home-style fare, such as pan-fried chicken and sugar cream pie, but newly trendy tables offer sophisticated presentations and a surprising marriage of fresh, fine American ingredients. Some chefs reinterpret regional specialties from throughout the country; others draw inspiration from the ethnic diversity of the American cookpot. Indiana's primary home-grown contributions, all featured on upscale menus, include Black Angus beef, corn-fed pork, ducklings, and farm-raised pheasant. Beef remains big in Indiana; you can find a fine steak almost everywhere. The local winery is Château Thomas, which "imports" vinifera grapes from some of California's premier vineyards and turns them into notable varietals such as chardonnay and cabernet sauvignon.

Hoosiers offer comfortable hospitality; the dress code has been relaxed in some white-cloth dining rooms. Men, however, may feel more comfortable in jacket and tie for evening dining.

Most restaurants recommended here are in the central downtown area, but there are two other districts worth trying as well. The Northside, a wealthy residential area about 20 minutes from the center by taxi, boasts a number of upscale restaurants. The area about a mile south of downtown, known as near-Southside, drew large groups of Irish, German, and Jewish immigrants in the mid-19th century. This historic neighborhood, still somewhat run-down, is in the process of slow gentrification.

Highly recommended restaurants in each price category are indicated by a star ★.

| Category | Cost* |
|---|---|
| *$$$$* (Very Expensive) | over $45 |
| *$$$* (Expensive) | $36–$45 |
| *$$* (Moderate) | $20–$35 |
| *$* (Inexpensive) | under $20 |

*per person, including appetizer, entrée, and dessert, but excluding drinks, service, and 6% sales tax.*

*Numbers in the margin correspond to numbered restaurant locations on the Indianapolis Dining and Lodging maps.*

### Business Breakfasts

Two hotel dining rooms (*see* reviews, below), the **Beaulieu** (tel. 317/634–3000) and **Severin Bar & Grill** (tel. 317/634–

6664), are good choices for breakfast meetings. The following are also recommended:

**Le Peep.** As the name implies, this breakfast-and-lunch spot specializes in egg dishes, including a wide variety of omelets and house specialties. "Panhandled" dishes are showered with everything from cheese to chorizo; the "pampered" eggs are scrambled mixtures of meat, seafood, vegetables, and cheeses. For quiet talks, ask to be seated in the private dining area. *2 locations: 301 N. Illinois St., tel. 317/237–3447; 8255 Craig St., Castleton, tel. 317/576–0433.*

**Original Pancake House.** This chain was built on hot air—baked into puffed-up German Dutch Babies: The balloonlike signature dishes rise some seven inches above the plate, but the bubble bursts as you top them with powdered sugar, whipped butter, and lemon juice. Pancakes, waffles, crèpes, and omelets complete the menu. This downtown greenhouse-style, glass-enclosed restaurant is adjacent to the Holiday Inn at Union Station and Pan Am Plaza; another Pancake House recently opened on the Northside. Sections of the dining room can be closed off for business meetings. *121 W. Louisiana St., tel. 317/266–0304; 1518 W. 86th St., tel. 317/843–1122.*

## Downtown

**⑱ Beaulieu.** This intimate dining room of the Canterbury
$$$ Hotel serves an impressive business breakfast, lunch, or dinner in a graceful European setting. Dark, paneled walls are adorned with oil paintings, and shades of pink in the seating, carpet, and marbelized china soften the look. The menu has been influenced by the nouvelle wave, but avoids the pitfalls of superfluous presentation and exaggerated experimentation. For lunch, businesspeople often order English scallop chowder, salmon with cilantro cream sauce, angel hair pasta with fresh vegetables, or grilled sea scallops with goat cheese. The wine list is notable. The restaurant draws a young, sophisticated clientele. Attractive private dining rooms are available for business meals. *123 S. Illinois St., tel. 317/634–3000. Jacket and tie preferred. Reservations advised. AE, CB, DC, MC, V.*

**★ ㉑ Benvenuti.** Miguel Santana, the young chef at Benvenuti,
$$$ reinterprets and embellishes standard Northern Italian cuisine with his innovative saucing and elaborate presentations. The menu includes cream of roasted red bell pepper soup with sautéed onions and chardonnay; linguine tossed with smoked salmon, asparagus tips, and Montrachet cream sauce; and grilled veal chop with prosciutto, fontina cheese, and spinach. Wines are thoughtfully selected. The ambience is sophisticated and the service polished. Rich woods, tapestry-covered banquettes, and lavish floral arrangements add warmth and elegance to the cosmopolitan setting. Banquette seating is conducive to business discussions during lunch or dinner; a private dining room is available, too. *36 S. Pennsylvania St., tel. 317/633–4915. Jacket and tie advised. Reservations preferred. AE, CB, DC, MC, V.*

**㉓ Fletcher's American Grill & Café.** The two levels here offer
$$$ two styles of dining. The upstairs grill with bar has a casual, contemporary ambience and an eclectic New American

menu. Etched glass panels between booths afford privacy. The Thai chef blends seasonings from the Pacific Rim, American Southwest, Italy, and the Caribbean to enhance the marinades, relishes, and compound butters for the mesquite-grilled fresh fish, steaks, lamb, and chicken breasts. Popular choices include Canadian crab meat soup; grilled Indiana goat cheese with dried tomatoes and basil wrapped in romaine; grilled "egg roll" shrimp, marinated in plum sauce and hot mustard and wrapped in bacon; and Midwestern salmon prepared with a tarragon-apple vinaigrette. Cuisine in the formal downstairs Café has more classic overtones, but sauces are lightened for health-conscious customers. The dining room is quiet, rendered in soothing shades of aqua and mauve. There's a knowledgeable selection of wines. *107 S. Pennsylvania St., tel. 317/ 632–2500. Jacket and tie preferred. Reservations preferred. AE, MC, V.*

**㉟ King Cole.** Warm woods and authentic Gainsborough and
$$$ Reynolds paintings give this downtown restaurant some of the feeling of a London gentlemen's club. Spacious booths afford privacy for quiet talks. The traditional Continental menu adapted in the 1950s has been modified but has never completely forsaken its classic French roots. Businesspeople like the refined comfort of the white-cloth dining rooms for lunch, and most order the fresh fish of the day, chicken Kiev, or chicken Cordon Bleu. This enduring standard has been attracting an older, established business crowd for years. *7 N. Meridian St., tel. 317/638–5588. Casual dress; jacket and tie preferred. Reservations advised. AE, CB, DC, MC, V.*

**㉒ St. Elmo Steak House.** This no-frills, New York–style
$$$ steak house and bar has had a loyal clientele since it opened in 1902. Customers seem to enjoy the bustling atmosphere and the sight of raw meat aging in a showcase near the bar. The popular shrimp cocktail has a power-packed sauce fueled with freshly grated horseradish. One dining area can be closed off for private business dinners. *127 S. Illinois St., tel. 317/635–0636. Casual dress. Reservations advised. AE, CB, DC, MC, V.*

**㉔ Severin Bar & Grill.** This spacious dining room in the Omni
$$$ Severin Hotel features fresh seafood, meat, and poultry cooked on its open exhibition grill. With its muted ivory and mulberry decor, comfortable Louis XV chairs around pedestal tables, and quiet, sedate atmosphere, this is a good place for business meetings. Among popular entrées are Colorado lamb chops with goat cheese and fresh rosemary; red snapper with tomato-cucumber relish and capers; veal T-bone steak with wild mushroom-shallot compote; poussin with cornbread-apple dressing and summer savory; and duckling with apricot chutney and basmati rice. Samplings from American microbreweries and wineries are available. *40 W. Jackson Pl., tel. 317/ 634–6664. Casual dress; jacket and tie preferred. Reservations suggested. AE, CB, DC, MC, V.*

## Near-Southside

**㉗ Milano Inn.** This convivial restaurant was a neighborhood
$$ favorite when it began in 1934 in this blue-collar Italian area, but its appeal today is citywide. The rustic look, crowded tables, and raucous atmosphere remain. This is not a place to do business; relax and enjoy Indy's version

of a good, although not great, trattoria. Popular with the yuppie/business clientele are the *pasta e fagioli* soup (pasta and beans), an assortment of veal dishes, and pastas with homemade sauces: Bolognese, marinara, white or red clam, or pesto. *231 S. College Ave., tel. 317/ 264-3585. Casual dress. Reservations advised. AE, CB, DC, MC, V.*

**28** **Peter's.** Located southeast of the Circle in an area yet to
**$$$** experience its predicted renaissance, this sophisticated restaurant has gained nationwide recognition. Owner Peter George, Jr., and Chef Joseph Kalil emphasize the best from the Midwest, but pair regional ingredients with tastes from around the world. For instance, you could start dinner with cilantro fettuccine tossed with mussels, sun-dried tomatoes, mild chilies, and cumin-sour-cream sauce; then proceed to roasted tenderloin of Black Angus beef with spinach and pine nut stuffing, or pan-browned fillets of freshwater fish with avocado hollandaise. Decor is sleek but understated, with a crisp, clean look. Tables are positioned to make maximum use of the limited floor space in the narrow dining room, but there's sufficient room for the servers to work efficiently and for private conversation. Corporate customers prefer the two private dining rooms upstairs. The wine list is excellent. *936 Virginia Ave., tel. 317/637-9333. Jacket and tie advised. Reservations preferred. DC, MC, V.*

**3** **26** **Shapiro's Delicatessan & Cafeteria.** White- and blue-collar
**$** types, the frugal elderly, and harried executives all meet in this near-Southside landmark, the daddy of the delis since 1904. What draws them together is the kosher-style cooking: Cafeteria breakfasts include bagels and lox, corned beef hash, and matzoh and salami omelets. At lunch and dinner, guests line up for deli sandwiches, stuffed cabbage rolls, hot plate specials, pastries, towering slices of cheesecake, and much, much more. A Northside Shapiro's is more recent and a bit more polished. At both locations, part of the dining area can be closed off for large business groups. *2 locations: 808 S. Meridian St., tel. 317/631-4041; 2370 W. 86th St., Northside, tel. 317/ 872-7255. Casual dress. No reservations, no credit cards, no personal checks.*

## Northside

**4** **Dodd's Town House.** For a taste of informal family din-
**$$** ing, come to this well-preserved historic landmark frame house on the fashionable Northside, where Betty and Jim Dodd's family dishes up down-home Indiana fare. Best bets are the pan-fried chicken dinner, steaks seared on hot metal in the time-honored Hoosier way, and a slice of traditional buttermilk pie. *5694 N. Meridian St., tel. 317/ 257-1872. Casual dress. Reservations advised. AE, CB, DC, MC, V.*

**★ 5** **Something Different.** The adventurous young chef/own-
**$$$** ers, Drew and Susan Goss, consistently turn out an eclectic variety of interesting dishes in this stylish dining room incongruously sited on a Northside shopping strip. The Gosses, trained in New York, cross culture and food frontiers with ease. The menu, which changes weekly, might include smoked lobster and curried capellini with spinach-garlic vinaigrette; Southwest sushi; steamed salmon with

romaine-wrapped sea scallops and yogurt-scallion sauce; or grilled duck breast with dried cherry-duck chili on garlic-potato pancakes. There's a small, well-selected wine list. *2411 E. 65th St. at Keystone Ave., tel. 317/257–7973 or 317/257–6368 for menu recording. Casual dress. Reservations advised. AE, CB, DC, MC, V.*

## FREE TIME

## Fitness

*Hotel Facilities*
Most Indianapolis hotel fitness facilities are not open to nonguests for day use. However, visitors staying at hotels without a health center can use the athletic facilities, including an indoor pool, on the **IUPUI** campus (901 W. New York St., tel. 317/274–3517) for a per-visit rate of $1.50. You must present your hotel room key, and bring your own towel and padlock.

*Health Clubs*
**Peak Performance** (5030 E. 62nd St., tel. 317/257–6218), offering aerobics, weight room, cardio room, and sauna has a per-visit rate of $6.

*Jogging*
Trails around the **IUPUI campus** vary in length from ½ to 3 miles. A jog to the campus from Monument Circle and back takes you over a 2½-mile course on city streets. Three routes along the city's east side wind around the curving streets in the **historic Irvington neighborhood.** A map, available from the Indianapolis City Center, indicates these routes.

## Shopping

As a center for shopping, downtown Indianapolis has lost out to the malls. **L.S. Ayres & Co.** (1 W. Washington St., tel. 317/899–4411) is still the city's flagship department store, but new owners have yet to reverse its current decline. **Claypool Court,** on the first two levels of the Embassy Suites (110 W. Washington St., tel. 317/236–1839) has a few upscale retailers, such as Talbots, plus scores of specialty food and gift shops.

Castleton, 30 minutes from downtown, has the sprawling **Castleton Square Mall** (6020 E. 82nd St., tel. 317/849–9993) and several strip malls anchored by such retail giants as Sears Roebuck, JC Penney, and K mart. A mile west of Castleton on 82nd Street, the **Fashion Mall at Keystone at the Crossing** (8701 Keystone Crossing, tel. 317/574–4000) has upscale fashions at more than 90 shops, including Brooks Brothers, Jacobson's, and Gidding Jenny, plus art galleries and home-furnishing stores.

## Diversions

**Benjamin Harrison Memorial Home** (1230 N. Delaware St., tel. 317/631–1898) is the carefully preserved residence of the United States's 23rd president.

**Broad Ripple Village** is a Northside community 20 minutes from downtown where clapboard houses and old storefronts have been turned into art galleries, sidewalk cafés, and shops that sell used books, second-hand clothing, and antiques. At night, the area's saloons and nightclubs are lively.

**Eiteljorg Museum of American Indian and Western Art** (500 W. Washington St., tel. 317/636–WEST), an adobe building opened in June 1989, houses fine collections of American Indian and Western art. On display are works from the original art colony in Taos, New Mexico, as well as paintings by Frederic Remington, Charles Russell, and Georgia O'Keeffe.

**Indiana Medical History Museum** (3000 W. Washington St., tel. 317/635–7329) has more than 15,000 medical and health-care artifacts from the 19th and early 20th century housed in the landmark Pathology Building on the Central State Hospital grounds. The teaching amphitheater, where students gathered for lectures, shows what it was like to be a medical student at the turn of the century.

**Indianapolis Motor Speedway Hall of Fame Museum** (4790 W. 16th St., tel. 317/241–2500) displays 33 Indianapolis 500-mile-race winning cars and other racing, classic, and antique autos. This is one of the city's most frequented tourist attractions, in part because visitors may take a van-tour around the famous speedway.

**The Indianapolis Museum of Art** (1200 W. 38th St., tel. 317/923–1331) is noted for its extensive collection of works by J.M.W. Turner, as well as paintings and objets d'art acquired through donations from prominent Indianapolis art collectors. A museum shop sells regionally made gift items.

**The Indianapolis Zoo** (1200 W. Washington St., tel. 317/630–2030), ¾ mile from downtown, exhibits animals in simulated natural habitats. The zoo's centerpiece is an enclosed, environmentally controlled whale and dolphin pavilion.

**Lockerbie Square,** a revitalized 19th-century neighborhood that begins at the corner of New York and Alabama streets, is a good place for a quiet stroll; you'll come across the 1872 house where "The Hoosier Poet," James Whitcomb Riley, lived.

**Scottish Rite Cathedral** (650 N. Meridian St., tel. 317/635–2301), designed by Indianapolis architect George F. Schreiber, is a 1929 Gothic-Tudor structure that was listed by the International Association of Architects as one of the seven most beautiful buildings in the world.

## Professional Sports

Indianapolis's basketball team, the **Indiana Pacers** (tel. 317/639–2112), competes at Market Square Arena. The city's football players, the **Indianapolis Colts** (tel. 317/297–7000 or 317/262–3309), play at Hoosier Dome. The **Indianapolis Ice** (tel. 317/924–1234) hockey players appear at the Indiana State Fairgrounds Coliseum. For baseball, see the **Indianapolis Indians** (tel. 317/269–3540 or 317/632–5371) at Bush Stadium.

## The Arts

Clowes Hall on the Butler University campus is host to the Indianapolis Opera and the Indianapolis Ballet Theatre as well as to a series of Broadway road shows, student performances, and local art exhibits. Dance Kaleidoscope, a modern-dance troupe, shares a home with the Indiana Repertory Theatre in a restored downtown movie palace. Other offerings are dinner theater at Beef & Boards, experimental theater at the Phoenix, and a Shakespeare festival and community theater at the Indianapolis Civic. The Indianapolis Symphony Orchestra performs at the Circle Theatre, another restored movie palace downtown.

Tickets for plays and concerts may be obtained through **Court Side Tickets** (6100 N. Keystone Ave., tel. 317/254–9500), **Karma** (3540 W. 86th St., tel. 317/876–9603), **Tickets Up Front** (1099 N. Meridian St., tel. 317/633–6400), and **TicketMaster** (2 W. Washington St., tel. 317/239–1000 or 317/239–5151).

**Beef & Boards Dinner Theatre,** 9301 N. Michigan Rd., tel. 317/872–9664.
**Circle Theatre,** 42 Monument Circle, tel. 317/635–6541.
**Clowes Memorial Hall,** 4600 Sunset La., tel. 317/283–9696.
**Indiana Repertory Theatre,** 140 W. Washington St., tel. 317/635–5252.
**Indianapolis Civic Theatre,** 1200 W. 38th St., tel. 317/923–4597.
**Phoenix Theatre,** 749 N. Park Ave., tel. 317/635–7529.

## After Hours

Downtown Indianapolis has never been known for its nightlife. Most people who work downtown go home to the suburbs at the end of the day. Consequently, pub crawling is best in the out-of-the-way neighborhoods and on the outskirts of town.

*Bars and Lounges*
The city's only revolving rooftop restaurant, **The Eagle's Nest** at the Hyatt (tel. 317/632–1234) is where businesspeople go when they want to stay in town for a drink after work. The **Flag Room** at the Indianapolis Motor Speedway Motel (4400 W. 16th St., tel. 317/241–2500) appeals to the curious visitor; it's frequented by Indy car drivers. The **Lobby Lounge** at the Radisson (tel. 317/846–2700) has a soft piano background, and is a good place for a quiet talk if you're in the Keystone Crossing area. The **Louisiana Street Bar** at Holiday Inn Union Station (tel. 317/631–2221), a brick and brass New Orleans–style bistro in the downtown area, features a piano bar, and offers enough privacy for a quiet tête-à-tête. **Rick's Café Americain** at Union Station (39 Jackson Pl., tel. 317/634–6666) is a boisterous place downtown that appeals to the under-30 crowd. The **Slippery Noodle Inn** (372 S. Meridian St., tel. 317/631–6974), which was a stop on the Underground Railroad before the Civil War, offers blues, drinks, and good food. Take a client here to celebrate, but be sure to take a cab, because the neighborhood is iffy. Four TV monitors at **Sports, A Bar & Grill** (231 S. Meridian St., tel. 317/631–5838) draw Monday-morning quarterbacks. **T.G.I.Friday's** at the Ramada Downtown (tel. 317/685–

8443) attracts yuppies on Friday nights. It's a place for loosening your tie and relaxing.

### Cabaret
**The Indiana Repertory Theatre Cabaret Club** (140 W. Washington St., tel. 317/635–5252) stages musical revues with big-name talent in an intimate nightclub setting.

### Comedy Clubs
**Crackers Comedy Club** (8702 Keystone Crossing, tel. 317/846–2500) features nationally known comics. **Indianapolis Comedy Connection** (247 S. Meridian St., tel. 317/631–3536) brings in two Los Angeles–based stand-up comics each week.

### Jazz Club
**Chatterbox Tavern** (435 Massachusetts Ave., tel. 317/636–0584), in the city's art gallery district, attracts actors, artists, and young professionals to listen to the top-notch jazz musicians who play here.

### Clubs
**Bentley's** (711 E. Thompson Rd., tel. 317/782–1618) features top-40 dance and rock bands. The **Blue Moon Bar** (tel. 317/849–6668) at the Omni North Hotel attracts a young, single, working crowd, who go to dance and relax after work. Neon decor and disco lights set the tone at **Celebrity** (247 S. Meridian St., tel. 317/639–6369). **The Patio** (6308 N. Guilford Ave., tel. 317/253–0799) is a laid back rock club that features regional and local groups. At **Quincy's** in the Adam's Mark (tel. 317/248–2481) tomorrow's business leaders play backgammon to the accompaniment of live band music. The **Razz-Ma-Tazz** (6380 W. 34th St., tel. 317/298–8093) attracts diehards from the big-band era. The **Safari Bar and Restaurant** (5910 E. 82nd St., tel. 317/842–2968) has a DJ and dance floor in a tropical setting for the under-40 set.

# Kansas City

*by Jane Cigard and Shifra Stein*

Anyone who still believes Kansas City is a classic American cowtown should take another look. The city's recent growth and development, unprecedented since the 1880s, has turned this heartland metropolis into a booming market for corporate relocation. Large private-sector employers such as Allied-Signal Aerospace, U.S. Sprint, Hallmark Cards, Butler Manufacturing, and the country's largest farm cooperative, Farmland Industries, all have headquarters here.

The low rent and high quality of life are the biggest draws, along with the city's location at the confluence of the Missouri and Kansas rivers, which makes it an important inland port. The Foreign Trade Zones are among the largest in the nation. The city also lays claim to be first in the world in producing greeting cards, storing frozen food, marketing hard winter wheat, and distributing farm equipment.

Kansas City's 1.4 million residents straddle the state line that divides Missouri and Kansas. The urban core of the city, on the Missouri side, holds turn-of-the-century neighborhoods, stately boulevards, and fountains, while the Kansas side has kept pace with demand by sprouting suburbs, business offices, and shopping centers where prairie grasses and wheat fields once stood.

If you ask to be taken to "downtown" or "midtown," you'll be driven to the urban core on the Missouri side of town, where the biggest cluster of better restaurants, hotels, and night spots can be found. The downtown hub is centered on the convention center at 13th and Wyandotte streets, with shops, restaurants, and accommodations within easy walking distance of one another. Farther south, still on the Missouri side, is the Crown Center Complex of hotels and boutiques. Nightlife and entertainment are in midtown's Westport and Country Club Plaza district, where you'll find excellent dining and shopping. Buses run infrequently, except at rush hour, and they do not cross the state line into suburban Kansas.

The community of Overland Park, Kansas, on the southwest edge of Kansas City, is home to the College Boulevard corridor, a growing business district that runs from 105th Street to 127th Street between Stateline Road and I–35. Although the area is bustling with office complexes, restaurants, and shopping malls, it is an expensive 25- to

40-minute cab ride from downtown Kansas City, Mo. Bus service is spotty. The best way to get around is by car.

## Top Employers

| Employer | Type of Enterprise | Parent*/ Headquarters |
|---|---|---|
| Allied-Signal Aerospace Co. | Manufacturing | Kansas City |
| AT&T | Telecommunications | New York City |
| Ford Motor Co. | Automotive | Dearborn, MI |
| General Motors | Automotive | Detroit |
| Hallmark Cards | Greeting cards | Kansas City |
| J.C. Penney Co. Inc. | Retail | Dallas |
| Trans World Airlines | Airline | St. Louis |
| U.S. Sprint | Telecommunications | Kansas City |
| University of Kansas Medical Center | Health care | Kansas City |

*if applicable

## ESSENTIAL INFORMATION

### Climate

What follows are the average daily maximum and minimum temperatures for Kansas City.

| | | | | | | | | |
|---|---|---|---|---|---|---|---|---|
| Jan. | 38F 21 | 4C −6 | Feb. | 42F 24 | 6C −4 | Mar. | 53F 34 | 12C 1 |
| Apr. | 65F 46 | 19C 8 | May | 75F 56 | 24C 14 | June | 84F 66 | 29C 19 |
| July | 89F 70 | 32C 21 | Aug. | 88F 69 | 31C 21 | Sept. | 80F 61 | 27C 16 |
| Oct. | 69F 49 | 21C 10 | Nov. | 54F 36 | 12C 2 | Dec. | 42F 26 | 6C −3 |

### Airports

**Kansas City International Airport** is about 20 miles northwest of downtown. Three C-shaped terminals allow passenger parking in the center and aircraft loading around the perimeters. It's only a 75-foot walk from curbside to aircraft, but there are no walkways connecting the three terminals, and shuttle bus service may be slow, so allow extra time to make connections between airlines. The **Downtown Airport** is in Kansas City, MO, just north of downtown and across the Missouri River, and is used primarily for private and charter aircraft.

## Airlines

Major carriers with the most flights are USAir and Southwest.

**America West,** tel. 800/247–5692.
**American,** tel. 800/433–7300.
**Continental,** tel. 816/471–3700 or 800/525–0280.
**Delta,** tel. 816/471–1828 or 800/221–1212.
**Northwest,** tel. 800/225–2525.
**Southwest,** tel. 816/474–1221 or 800/531–5601.
**TWA,** tel. 816/842–4000 or 800/221–2000.
**USAir,** tel. 800/428–4322.
**United,** tel. 816/471–6060 or 800/631–1500.

## Between the Airport and Downtown

The best route to downtown is via I–29 south to the Broadway Bridge (25¢ toll). Hotels near the airport have courtesy transportation; downtown and midtown hotels rely on the KCI Airport Express bus (*See* By Bus, below).

*By Taxi*
Each company sets its own metered rates, so fares vary. A trip from the airport to downtown takes about 30 minutes in normal traffic and about 45 minutes during morning and evening rush hours. The cost from airport to downtown may range from $18 to $35, but most companies charge around $25. If you're not in a hurry, it pays to ask several drivers before agreeing on a fare.

*By Bus*
The **KCI Airport Express Bus** (tel. 816/243–5950) runs every 45 minutes from 5:45 AM to 11 PM. The cost is $9 to downtown, $10 to Crown Center, and $11 to the Plaza. The trip takes 30 minutes to downtown and 40–45 minutes to Crown Center. Allow 60 minutes to the Plaza. The bus departs from Gate 63, Terminal C.

## Car Rentals

The following companies rent cars at or near the airport, with pickup service at terminals:

**Alamo,** tel. 816/964–5151 or 800/327–9633.
**Avis,** tel. 816/243–5760 or 800/331–1212.
**Budget,** tel. 816/243–5757 or 800/527–0700.
**Dollar,** tel. 816/243–5600 or 800/800–4000.
**Hertz,** tel. 816/243–5765 or 800/654–3131.
**National,** tel. 800/227–7368.
**Sears,** tel. 816/243–5757 or 800/527–0770.

## Emergencies

*Doctors and Hospitals*
**St. Luke's Hospital** (4400 Wornall Rd., tel. 816/932–2000), **Trinity Lutheran Hospital** (3100 Wyandotte St., tel. 816/753–4600), **Ask-A-Nurse** (tel. 816/676–7777), **Kansas City Medical Society** (tel. 816/531–8432).

*Dentists*
**Dental Society** (tel. 816/333–5454).

## Important Addresses and Numbers

**Audiovisual rental.** Hoover's Audiovisual (2540 W. Pennway, midtown, tel. 816/221-7663).

**Chamber of Commerce** (920 Main St., downtown, tel. 816/221-2424), Convention and Visitor's Bureau (1100 Main St., Suite 2550, downtown, tel. 816/221-5242 or 800/767-7700).

**Computer rental.** Computer Express (10312 Metcalf Ave., tel. 913/341-4152) delivers to downtown and Plaza locations.

**Convention and exhibition centers.** Kansas City Convention Center (downtown, tel. 816/274-2900), Kansas City Market Center (15 minutes east of downtown, tel. 816/241-6200), Kemper Arena/American Royal Complex (downtown, tel. 816/274-1900).

**Fax service.** Buzz Print (1009 Main St., downtown, tel. 816/842-0889; 3959 Broadway, midtown, tel. 816/931-6494).

**Formal-wear rental.** American Formal and Bridal (1331 Main St., downtown, tel. 816/221-7971).

**Gift shops.** Chocolates: Annedore's Fine Chocolates (106 E. 43rd St., tel. 816/753-5012); Flowers: Babb Floral and Gift (1100 Main St., downtown, tel. 816/471-7673); Gift baskets and locally made gifts: Catch Kansas City (Allis Plaza Hotel, 200 W. 12th St., downtown, tel. 816/421-6800, ext. 4474), The Best of Kansas City (108 Crown Center Shops, tel. 816/842-0200).

**Graphic design studio.** Hedrick, Daniel, Richter and Rood (1828 Walnut St., Crown Center, tel. 816/221-7067).

**Hairstylists.** Unisex: Jones (1201 Main St., downtown, tel. 816/391-7173), Salon Klaus (444 Ward Pkwy., Plaza, tel. 816/531-1835), Naturally (Crown Center, tel. 816/471-8138), Supercuts (3915 Broadway, midtown, tel. 816/753-4511, no appointment necessary).

**Health and fitness clubs.** *See* Fitness, below.

**Information hot line.** Convention and Visitors Bureau recorded information (tel. 816/474-9600).

**Limousine services.** American Limousine Company (tel. 816/471-6050 or 800/221-9165), Metropolitan Transportation (tel. 816/471-6050).

**Liquor stores.** Berbiglia (4300 Main St., midtown, tel. 816/531-1725; 1816 Westport Rd., midtown, tel. 816/931-9463), Quality Hill Liquors (621 W. 12th St., downtown, tel. 816/471-6783).

**Mail delivery, overnight.** Federal Express (tel. 816/661-0255), UPS (tel. 913/281-1000), U.S. Postal Service/Express Mail (tel. 816/374-9760).

**Messenger services.** Apple Courier (tel. 816/356-5900), Quick Delivery (tel. 913/888-4600).

**Pharmacies, late-night.** Quality Hill Pharmacy (1020 Broadway, downtown, tel. 816/221-5449), Bruce Smith Drugs (4700 Broadway, midtown, tel. 816/753-1225).

**Radio Stations, all-news.** KCMO 81 AM.

**Stationery supplies.** Demaree Stationery (1111 Main St., downtown, tel. 816/842–5694 and 4706 Central, Plaza, tel. 816/931–1333), Buzz Print (1009 Main St., downtown, tel. 816/842–0889).

**Taxis.** Airport Transportation Service (tel. 816/421–7000), Bill's Taxi Express (tel. 816/765–6366), Yellow Cab (tel. 816/471–5000).

**Trains.** Amtrak (2200 Main St., tel. 816/421–3622).

**Travel agents.** Passport Travel (1101 Walnut St., downtown, tel. 816/221–6666), American Express (114 W. 47th St., Plaza, tel. 816/531–9114).

**Weather** (tel. 816/844–4444).

## LODGING

Visitors can choose between the familiarity of the large chains and a good variety of locally owned establishments. In Kansas City, MO, the three main business districts are downtown (from the Missouri River to 31st Street); midtown (31st to 47th streets, including Westport and the Country Club Plaza); and the airport (northwest of the Missouri River). If you're without a car, you'll find it easiest to get around by taxi and trolley from a central base in midtown or downtown. And you'll be close to some of the city's best dining and entertainment spots. If you have business in Kansas City, KS, or one of the Johnson county, Kansas, suburbs, pick the hotel chain with which you're most familiar and rent a car. Traveling back and forth across the state line and getting around the Kansas side of town is difficult without your own wheels.

All the hotels listed here offer special corporate rates and weekend discounts; inquire when making reservations.

Highly recommended lodgings in each price category are indicated by a star ★.

| Category | Cost* |
|---|---|
| *$$$$* (Very Expensive) | over $125 |
| *$$$* (Expensive) | $75–$125 |
| *$$* (Moderate) | under $75 |

*\*All prices are for a standard double room, single occupancy, excluding a 6.425% sales tax and 5.5% convention and facilities tax.*

*Numbers in the margin correspond to numbered hotel locations on the Kansas City Lodging and Dining maps.*

### Downtown

**❺**
*$$$$*
**Allis Plaza.** Downtown's premier meeting and convention hotel is connected by underground tunnel to the Bartle Hall Convention Center. Don't be fooled by the exterior of this 22-story high rise built in 1985. The massive block of unappealing gray concrete contains a warm, inviting interior. An atrium skylight highlights the waterfall and tropical plants in the two-story lobby, which has a jazz-era

# DOWNTOWN KANSAS CITY

**Lodging**

Airport Hilton Plaza Inn, **2**

Allis Plaza, **5**

Historic Suites of America, **3**

Hyatt Regency Crown Center, **10**

Kansas City Airport Marriott, **1**

Radisson Suite Hotel, **6**

Residence Inn by Marriott, **11**

The Westin Crown Center, **8**

**Dining**

American Restaurant, **9**

Arthur Bryant's, **7**

Benton's Steak & Chop House, **8**

Peppercorn Duck Club, **10**

Savoy Grill, **4**

# MIDTOWN KANSAS CITY

decor. Aside from its appeal to conventioneers, the hotel also draws bankers, lawyers, and others doing business with downtown firms. Shops and restaurants are within walking distance, and the trolley to Crown Center, Westport, and the Plaza stops in front. The hotel is undergoing a $1.5 million renovation, starting with floors 17–21. Rooms have a traditional English country decor and are being redecorated in shades of plum and mauve. South-facing rooms overlook the fountain-filled Barney Allis Plaza, where downtown office workers often brown-bag lunch in nice weather. For complimentary Continental breakfast and evening cocktails, ask for an Executive Club room on the 20th or 21st floor. *200 W. 12th St., 64105, tel. 816/421– 6800 or 800/548–4782, fax 816/421– 6800, ext. 4418. Gen. manager, Michael J. Brenan. 550 rooms, 23 suites, AE, CB, DC, MC, V.*

**❸ Historic Suites of America.** In the old garment district,
$$$ two historic buildings have been converted into downtown's newest all-suite hotel. Both have generous-size accommodations, but rooms in the Old Builders and Traders Exchange, built in 1898, are arranged around a five-story atrium with the original wrought-iron railings, oak woodwork, and rooftop skylight, all restored. The hotel is primarily suited for visitors who need to be near the convention center and travelers who want additional space for extended stays. Five types of suites—studios to two-bedrooms—have high vaulted ceilings, oversize-windows, and fully equipped kitchens. The hotel has Nautilus-equipped fitness areas, and offers complimentary breakfast. Several restaurants are within walking distance. A hotel courtesy van will take you anywhere-within a 5-mile radius. *612 Central, 64105, tel. 816/842–6544 or 800/733–0612, fax 816/842–6544. Gen. manager, Marilyn Townsend. 101 suites. AE, CB, D, DC, MC, V.*

**❿ Hyatt Regency Crown Center.** The Hyatt anchors the
$$$$ northeast end of the Crown Center complex, and is connected to stores, restaurants, theaters, and the Westin hotel by the Link, a three-block long, glass-enclosed walkway above street level. The lobby's five-story atrium court connects the 42-story high-rise tower with the hotel's recreational and meeting facilities. Built in 1980 and last remodeled in 1988, the Hyatt's rooms are decorated in soft pastel colors with a Southwest flavor, and are furnished with either a king-size bed or two double beds. For a better-than-average room, ask for the Regency Club accommodations on the 39th and 40th floors. Skies (*see* After Hours), the revolving restaurant on the top floor, is a good place to meet business associates for a quiet after-work drink while enjoying a great view of the city. You'll find some of the best dining in town at the Peppercorn Duck Club (*see* Dining, below), 40 floors below. *2345 McGee St., 64108, tel. 816/421–1234 or 800/233–1234, fax 816/435– 4190. Gen. manager, Stephen G. Trent. 689 rooms, 42 suites. AE, CB, D, DC, MC, V.*

**★ ❻ Radisson Suite Hotel.** This registered National Historic
$$$ Landmark, two blocks from the convention center, has undergone a $12.5 million facelift that has restored much of its Art Deco heritage. The original marble pillars, dark walnut woodwork, and bronze statuary highlight the lobby. Studio and one-bedroom suites have traditional, solid cherry furnishings, including an armoire, minibar, and

# KANSAS CITY HOTEL CHART

| HOTELS | Price Category | Business Services Banquet capacity | No. of meeting rooms | Secretarial services | Audiovisual equipment | Teletype news service | Computer rentals | In-room modem phonejack | All-news cable channel | Desk | Desk lighting | Bed lighting |
|---|---|---|---|---|---|---|---|---|---|---|---|---|
| Airport Hilton Plaza Inn | $$$ | 700 | 13 | ✓ | ✓ | - | ✓ | ✓ | ✓ | - | - | ◐ |
| Airport Marriott | $$$ | 500 | 22 | ✓ | ✓ | - | ✓ | ✓ | ✓ | ◐ | ◐ | ◐ |
| Allis Plaza | $$$$ | 1200 | 22 | ✓ | ✓ | - | - | ✓ | ✓ | ○ | ● | ● |
| Doubletree | $$$ | 640 | 18 | ✓ | ✓ | - | - | - | ✓ | - | - | ◐ |
| Embassy Suites | $$$ | 250 | 11 | - | ✓ | - | - | - | ✓ | ◐ | ◐ | ◐ |
| Hilton Plaza Inn | $$$ | 800 | 15 | - | ✓ | - | ✓ | ✓ | ✓ | - | - | ◐ |
| Historic Suites of America | $$$ | 50 | 3 | ✓ | ✓ | - | ✓ | - | ✓ | ◐ | ● | ● |
| Holiday Inn Crowne Plaza | $$$ | 450 | 15 | ✓ | ✓ | - | ✓ | ✓ | ✓ | ● | ● | ● |
| Hyatt Regency Crown Center | $$$$ | 1700 | 23 | ✓ | ✓ | - | - | - | ✓ | - | - | ◐ |
| Quarterage | $$ | 0 | 4 | - | ✓ | - | - | ✓ | ✓ | ● | ● | ◐ |
| Radisson Suite | $$$ | 130 | 8 | ✓ | ✓ | - | ✓ | ✓ | ✓ | ◐ | ◐ | ◐ |
| The Raphael | $$$$ | 0 | 0 | ✓ | ✓ | - | - | - | ✓ | ◐ | ◐ | ◐ |
| Residence Inn By Marriott | $$$ | 30 | 2 | - | ✓ | - | - | ✓ | ✓ | ● | ● | ● |
| Ritz-Carlton | $$$$ | 1000 | 19 | ✓ | ✓ | - | ✓ | ✓ | ✓ | ◐ | ◐ | ● |
| The Westin Crown Center | $$$$ | 1000 | 28 | ✓ | ✓ | - | ✓ | ✓ | ✓ | ◐ | ● | ● |

**$$$$** = over $125, **$$$** = $75-$125, **$$** = under $75.
● good, ◐ fair, ○ poor.
All hotels listed here have photocopying and fax facilities.

| In-Room Amenities | | | | | | | | | | Hotel Amenities | | | | | | |
|---|---|---|---|---|---|---|---|---|---|---|---|---|---|---|---|---|
| Nonsmoking rooms | In-room checkout | Minibar | Pay movies | VCR/Movie rentals | Hairdryer | Toiletries | Room service | Laundry/Dry cleaning | Pressing | Concierge | Barber/Hairdresser | Garage | Courtesy airport transport | Sauna | Pool | Exercise room |
| ✓ | ✓ | ✓ | ✓ | - | ✓ | ○ | ◐ | ◐ | ◐ | - | - | - | ✓ | ✓ | ● | ● |
| ✓ | ✓ | - | ✓ | - | ✓ | ● | ◐ | ● | ◐ | ✓ | - | - | ✓ | ✓ | ● | ● |
| ✓ | ✓ | ✓ | - | - | ✓ | ● | ◐ | ● | ● | ✓ | - | - | - | ✓ | ● | ● |
| ✓ | - | - | ✓ | ✓ | ✓ | ○ | ◐ | ● | ◐ | - | - | - | - | ✓ | ● | - |
| ✓ | ✓ | ✓ | ✓ | - | ✓ | - | ◐ | ● | ◐ | - | - | ✓ | - | - | ◐ | - |
| ✓ | ✓ | ✓ | ✓ | - | - | ○ | ◐ | ● | ◐ | - | ✓ | ✓ | - | - | ● | - |
| ✓ | - | - | - | ✓ | ✓ | ● | ● | ● | ◐ | - | - | ✓ | - | ✓ | ◐ | ● |
| ✓ | - | ✓ | ✓ | - | ✓ | ○ | ◐ | ◐ | ◐ | ✓ | - | ✓ | - | - | ● | ● |
| ✓ | ✓ | ✓ | ✓ | ✓ | ✓ | ● | ● | ◐ | ◐ | ✓ | - | ✓ | - | ✓ | ◐ | ◐ |
| ✓ | - | - | ✓ | - | - | - | - | ● | ◐ | - | - | ✓ | - | ✓ | - | ◐ |
| ✓ | ✓ | ✓ | ✓ | - | ✓ | ● | ◐ | ● | ◐ | - | - | ✓ | - | - | ○ | ◐ |
| ✓ | - | ✓ | ✓ | ✓ | ✓ | ● | ◐ | ● | ● | - | - | ✓ | - | - | ○ | ○ |
| ✓ | - | - | - | - | - | ○ | - | ● | ● | - | - | - | - | - | ● | ◐ |
| ✓ | ✓ | ✓ | - | ✓ | ✓ | ● | ● | ● | ● | ✓ | - | ✓ | - | ✓ | ◐ | ● |
| ✓ | - | ✓ | - | - | ✓ | ● | ● | ● | ● | ✓ | ✓ | ✓ | - | ✓ | ● | ● |

**Room service:** ● 24-hour, ◐ 6AM-10PM, ○ other.
**Laundry/Dry cleaning:** ● same day, ◐ overnight, ○ other.
**Pressing:** ● immediate, ◐ same day, ○ other.

desk. The 20th-floor business center is equipped with a fax machine, photocopier, computer, and ample work space. A free, full American breakfast is served in The Haberdashery (named for the haberdashery where Harry Truman once worked). Complimentary cocktails are served daily on the terrace overlooking the two-story lobby. *106 W. 12th St., 65105, tel. 816/221–7000 or 800/333–3333, fax 816/221–7000, ext. 387. Gen. manager, Janet Kinney. 33 rooms, 181 suites, AE, CB, D, DC, MC, V.*

**⑪** **Residence Inn by Marriott.** This suite hotel has the look
**$$$** and ambience of a suburban apartment complex. The three-story, Colonial-style buildings were built in 1988 and designed to complement the traditional architecture of the surrounding Union Hill neighborhood. There are one-level studios with queen- or king-size beds, or two queen-size beds; and bilevel penthouses with two bedrooms and two baths. With a more casual atmosphere than the downtown suite hotels, the Residence Inn is a good choice if you're relocating or attending lengthy meetings or training sessions. The blue, burgundy, and mauve interiors are cozy and comfortable, and include fully equipped kitchens. Many suites have working fireplaces. There's a trolley stop on the corner to downtown, Crown Center, and Westport or the Plaza. Exercise facilities are limited to free weights and an exercise bicycle; there is an indoor Jacuzzi, however, and a small outdoor pool. To make guests feel at home, the management sponsors poolside barbeques and evening social hours. *2975 Main St., 64108, tel. 816/561–3000 or 800/331–3131, fax 816/931–0967. Gen. manager, Carl Galbreath. 80 studios, 16 penthouses. AE, CB, D, DC, MC, V.*

**★ ⑧** **The Westin Crown Center.** Kansas City's primary conven-
**$$$$** tion hotel—in an excellent location about midway between downtown and the Plaza—has also housed its share of celebrities, from Gerald Ford to Michael Jackson. The five-story tropical garden and waterfall, which was built into the natural limestone hillside, is unique in Kansas City. Fresh, contemporary rooms, decorated in quiet tones of rose and beige, are the norm. An Executive Club on the 17th floor offers such extra amenities as a private lounge, Continental breakfast, and mini-TVs in bathrooms. A full-service health club provides workout equipment, saunas, steam rooms, tanning beds, a pool, jogging track, and tennis courts. The hotel also offers a 24-hour mail message service. Benton's Steak and Chop House (*see* Dining, below) sits atop the hotel. *1 Pershing Rd., 61408, tel. 816/474–4400 or 800/228–3000, fax 816/391–4438. Gen. manager, Parker J. Smith. 725 rooms, 49 suites. AE, CB, D, MC, V.*

## Midtown/Westport District

**⑮** **Embassy Suites.** With its hot pink stucco exterior and tur-
**$$$** quoise, wrought-iron railings, this 12-story, all-suite hotel is a can't-miss-it landmark located between the Plaza and Westport. Within walking distance of Westport's dining and entertainment spots, the Embassy Suites is also just across the street from St. Luke's Hospital and nearby medical offices and clinics. All rooms have direct access to the atrium, and each has a kitchenette, a bedroom, and a living room with queen-size sofa sleeper. Spanish-style furnishings complement the Spanish decor throughout

the hotel. Amenities include a complimentary breakfast and two-hour cocktail reception each evening. The indoor pool, whirlpool, and sauna are fine for relaxing, but don't expect complete workout facilities. Joggers can run the 1.2-mile paved trail across the street in Mill Creek Park. *220 W. 43rd St., 64111, tel. 816/756-1720 or 800/362-2779, fax 816/756-3260. Gen. manager, Dick Nogosek. 266 suites. AE, CB, D, DC, MC, V.*

**18** **Hilton Plaza Inn.** With 13 meeting rooms, a ballroom
**$$$** equipped with a permanent stage, and 17,500 square feet of exhibit space, the Hilton attracts plenty of convention business. Located a few blocks from the Country Club Plaza, it draws a fair number of corporate types as well. Though two decades older than its next-door neighbor, the Holiday Inn Crowne Plaza, the Hilton underwent a $7-million renovation in 1987 and now has fresh, traditional furnishings in all rooms. If you need a desk, ask for a room with a king-size bed; standard doubles have only small tables and chairs, inadequate for serious work. The outdoor pool is large enough to swim laps in, and the Mill Creek jogging trail is down the street, but health and fitness enthusiasts will be disappointed by the lack of exercise facilities. *1 45th St., 64111, tel. 816/753-7400 or 800/525-6321, fax 816/753-4777. Gen. manager, Richard Arey. 239 rooms, 11 suites. AE, CB, D, DC, MC, V.*

**17** **Holiday Inn Crowne Plaza.** Sandy colors, palm trees, and
**$$$** rattan furniture give the lobby and rooms in this high-rise hotel a casual Caribbean look and a kick-off-your-shoes ambience. South-facing rooms afford views of the Plaza's Spanish towers and red-tiled roofs. Rooms on the concierge level (19th floor) include upgraded amenities such as bathrobes, hair-dryers, and Continental breakfast. First-rate facilities include a four-tiered indoor amphitheater with a state-of-the-art audiovisual system. The Plaza Bar (*see* After Hours, below) features live music. *4445 Main St., 64111, tel. 816/531-3000 or 800/228-9290, fax 816/531-3007. Gen. manager, Clyde Guinn. 270 rooms, 15 suites. AE, CB, D, DC, MC, V.*

**14** **Quarterage Hotel.** This no-frills property, only footsteps
**$$** from Westport's top restaurants and nightspots, is a sensible place to stay if you don't need the extra amenities of a full-service luxury hotel. Rooms are small, and outfitted with basic, functional furnishings, including a swivel chair and desk. A complimentary light breakfast and cocktails are available to guests in the hospitality suite, but there is no restaurant or room service. With Westport so near, however, it hardly matters; and when you're too tired to venture out, several Westport restaurants will deliver hot meals to your room. If you're looking for a large convention hotel, stay elsewhere; meeting rooms here can accommodate only small groups of 10–35 people. *560 Westport Rd., 64111, tel. 816/931-0001 or 800/942-4233, fax 816/931-0001, ext. 157. Gen. manager, Mike Mitko. 123 rooms, 8 suites. AE, CB, D, DC, MC, V.*

**21** **The Raphael.** The many renovations of this 1920s-vintage
**$$$$** apartment building have carefully preserved its genteel, Old World charm since it became a hotel in the 1970s. Fashioned after small, elegant European hotels, The Raphael is for visitors who care more about an intimate atmosphere and gracious service than pools, exercise clubs, or banquet-size rooms. Most of the accommodations are

suites of varying sizes, with double, queen, or king-size beds. Rooms are outfitted with traditional furnishings and equipped with refrigerators and minibars; suites facing the Plaza offer the best views. The inviting café atmosphere of The Raphael restaurant makes it a good place for business lunches or dinners. *325 Ward Pkwy., 64112, tel. 816/756–3800 or 800/821–5343, fax 816/756–3800, ext. 123. Gen. manager, Maxine Hill. 27 rooms, 96 suites. AE, DC, MC, V.*

★ ⑳ **Ritz-Carlton.** Honduran mahogany wainscoting, original
$$$$ 18th- and 19th-century European paintings, and attentive service earn the Ritz its rightful reputation as Kansas City's prime luxury hotel. All rooms offer extra amenities such as bathrobes, phones, and mini-TVs in bathrooms. Room TVs are tucked inside Queen Anne-style cherrywood armoires. Club rooms on the 10th and 11th floors have private access, complimentary food and bar service, and a full-time concierge. Rooms facing the Plaza have better views. The Café (*see* Business Breakfasts, below) is an elegant spot for morning meetings. The lobby, with its high-back wing chairs, is the perfect place for an informal afternoon chat over tea and pastries. The Grill (*see* Dining, below), offers traditional American fare and the Top of the Ritz (*see* After Hours) is perfect for an after-dinner drink. *401 Ward Pkwy., 64112, tel. 816/756–1500 or 800/ 241–3333, fax 816/756–1500, ext. 114. Gen. manager, Mark Caney. 346 rooms, 28 suites. AE, CB, D, DC, MC, V.*

## Airport/Northwest of Missouri River

❷ **Airport Hilton Plaza Inn.** The boxy concrete exterior of
$$$ this 11-story high rise is typical of hotels built in the mid-1970s. The 10th floor has been redone with new carpeting and wallpaper, and a major renovation of all guest rooms, including new furnishings, is beginning in the spring of 1991. Guest rooms do not have desks, and the small parlor tables don't allow much work space. VIP service on the 10th and 11th floors includes evening turndown, free newspaper and coffee, and extra bath amenities. Located just 2.5 miles from the airport, the Hilton provides 24-hour courtesy shuttle service. A plus for business travelers is the in-house business center staffed by a full-time secretary. Facilities include tennis on lighted courts, basketball, indoor and outdoor pools, and a health club with Nautilus equipment, sauna, and whirlpool. *I–29 and N.W. 112th St., 64195, tel. 816/891–8900 or 800/525–6322, fax 816/891–8030. Gen. manager, Richard Arey, 348 rooms, 30 suites. AE, CB, D, DC, MC, V.*

❶ **Kansas City Airport Marriott.** This is the only hotel on air-
$$$ port grounds, and all rooms have a view of the airport runways or the Marriott lake. Rooms have been soundproofed to eliminate airplane noise. The hotel was built in 1969, guest rooms were last renovated in 1988, and a new, 125-room wing was completed in 1989. Rooms are spacious, with either king-size or double beds. Furnishings have little charm and are basic-hotel functional. The concierge rooms on the ninth floor are extra large, with vaulted ceilings, floor-to-ceiling windows, and extra amenities. Facilities include an indoor pool, sauna, whirlpool, and exercise equipment. *775 Brasilia, 64153, tel. 816/464–2200 or 800/*

*228–9290, fax 816/464–5915. Gen. manager, Costa Androulakis. 382 rooms, 35 suites. AE, D, DC, MC, V.*

## Overland Park, Kansas

**㉓** **Doubletree Hotel.** Its prime location on the College Boule-
$$$ vard corridor (Johnson County's executive, primarily
business, district) makes this hotel a favorite for travelers
with business in the Corporate Woods office park. The ho-
tel provides courtesy transportation to Corporate Woods
offices and to Oak Park Mall and other nearby shopping
and dining centers. Rooms are designed along clean, con-
temporary lines with a muted Scandinavian look, but
there are no desks. Deluxe rooms have better views.
There are two indoor racquetball courts, and the hotel is
adjacent to a bicycle and jogging trail that winds through
Corporate Woods for about 27 miles. *10100 College Blvd.,
66210, tel. 913/451–6100 or 800/528–0444, fax 913/451–
3873. Gen. manager, Gary D. Walton, 340 rooms, 17
suites. AE, CB, D, DC, MC, V.*

## DINING

In recent years, this meat-and-potatoes city has become a
center for corporate transplants who have created a
strong demand for culinary excellence. In the '90s, Kansas
City has caught up with the rest of the country, with ec-
lectic and cross-cultural cuisine that can match almost
anything California has to offer. Some of the best restau-
rants are conveniently clustered together in the down-
town and midtown area. Three offer superb city views,
and all have excellent wine lists. One restaurant, Jasper's,
on the south end of the city, is 10 minutes from down-
town—but it's worth the drive.

Highly recommended restaurants in each price category
are indicated by a star ★.

| Category | Cost* |
|---|---|
| $$$$ (Very Expensive) | over $25 |
| $$$ (Expensive) | $15–$25 |
| $$ (Moderate) | under $15 |

*per person, including appetizer, entrée and dessert, but
excluding drinks, service, and 6% sales tax.*

*Numbers in the margin correspond to numbered restau-
rant locations on the Kansas City Lodging and Dining
maps.*

### Business Breakfasts

One of the best places to hold a quiet power breakfast, the
**Café at the Ritz-Carlton** (tel. 816/756–1500) offers everything from lamb chops with eggs to hickory-smoked salmon with potato pancakes and eggs. The pleasant dining
area is complemented by elegant furnishings and tables
spaced far enough apart to hold intimate conversations. **La
Bonne Bouchée** (618 Ward Pkwy., tel. 816/931–5230)
opens at 7 AM and is a good place for a quick, light meal. The
French restaurant's bakery is renowned for its puffed pastries, crisp-crusted breads, and excellent coffee. This bus-

tling spot is a favorite of local businesspeople, but tables are too close for confidential conversations.

## Downtown/River to 18th Street

★ ❾ **American Restaurant.** An exponent of fine American cui-
$$$$ sine for more than 16 years, this is one of the most beautiful restaurants in the country. Located atop Hall's Crown
Center, the American boasts a splendid view, with windows rising from the floor to the three-story height of the
ceiling. Deep burgundy upholstery, white oak columns,
and a gorgeous brass serpentine railing add richness to
the dramatically lighted surroundings. Tables are spaced
conveniently apart for privacy and many a deal has been
made here. The expert staff is helpful, but not hovering.
The food is expensive, but worth every penny. Innovative
dishes here merge the exotic with heartland cooking; try
the cured salmon with corn griddle cakes and crème
fraiche; grilled veal medallions with chanterelle mushrooms and blackberries; or grilled lamb loin chops with
tamarind-curry sauce. If you have dietary restrictions,
phone ahead and the chef can tailor something to meet
your needs. *2450 Grand, tel. 816/426–1133. Reservations
recommended during the week; required on weekends.
Jacket required. AE, CB, DC, MC, V. Closed lunch.*

★ ❼ **Arthur Bryant's.** There are people who claim that Arthur
$$ Bryant's offers the best barbecue in the world. Certainly,
it has captured the limelight as a Kansas City tradition. In
the '30s, you could slide all the way up to the counter on
the grease-encrusted floor. Today, Bryant's has been
cleaned up, to the chagrin of some and the delight of
others. It's still a roadhouse, however, and guests yell or-
ders to the blockman who slices up brisket and layers it in
a mountain of white bread and cumin-colored sauce.
Served with a side of sizzling lard-cooked fries and an icy
mug of beer, this is barbecue, Kansas City-style. At
lunch, the Formica tables are filled with three-piece
suiters who dive in up to the pits, with only a handful of
napkins to protect them. The place is noisy and crowded at
noon. The only serious business conducted here is doctor-
ing ribs with sauce, and trying to wrap your mouth around
a four-inch-high sandwich without looking ridiculous.
About a 10-minute cab ride from downtown hotels. *1727
Brooklyn Ave., tel. 816/231–1123. Reservations not re-
quired. Casual dress. No credit cards.*

★ ❽ **Benton's Steak & Chop House.** Benton's, located atop the
$$$ Westin Crown Hotel, was named after Kansas City artist
Thomas Hart Benton. The rich woods and floral arrange-
ments are enhanced by Benton lithographs placed strategically around the room. Booths offer more seclusion, but
tables afford more dramatic views of the city skyline. The
specialties are grilled seafood and steaks, but lamb and
pork chops are also available. An all-you-can-eat bucket of
fresh shrimp is included in the price. Try to save room for
one of the rich desserts. *1 Pershing Rd., Westin Crown
Center Hotel, tel. 816/391–4460. Reservations recommended. Jacket preferred. AE, CB, D, DC, MC, V. Closed
lunch.*

★ ❿ **Peppercorn Duck Club.** This restaurant in the Hyatt Re-
$$$$ gency Crown Center has a quiet, elegant feel, but it's definitely not stuffy. The staff is amiable and accommodating, the lighting subdued. The decor, a warm mix of dark

woods, burnished copper, and rich burgundy, is accented with floral arrangements. Plush banquettes, and tables large enough to accommodate modest-size groups, are spaced well apart and are conducive to conversation. Local businesspeople come for lunch, out-of-towners and "special occasion" guests come for dinner. Although the restaurant, which specializes in American and Continental cuisine, has a good reputation for its beef, veal, and lamb dishes, the main attraction is crisp, tender duck, served with a peppercorn brandy or raspberry bourbon sauce. Appetizers are a meal in themselves; try the lemon and black pepper pasta, tossed with escargot in an artichoke garlic sauce. Guests who make reservations find their names engraved on matchbook covers when they arrive. The wine list is one of the best in town. *Hyatt Regency Crown Center, 2345 McGee St., tel. 816/435–4199. Reservations recommended. Jacket required. AE, DC, MC, V.*

**④** **Savoy Grill.** This vintage gem, tucked away in the heart of
*$$$* downtown, is a charming reminder of yesteryear. Cloth-covered tables and fine silver and crystal have been the norm since the Grill opened in 1903. Antique stained-glass windows, flecked with gold and red, let in a pleasant light at lunch. President Truman used to feast on the famed steak and seafood served here. (His favorite booth, number four, has a plaque in his honor.) The plush, eight-foot-high booths have to be reserved in advance, but they're great for holding private discussions. Lobster Thermidor and prime steak are what the Savoy does best. Make reservations for the main dining room, or you might be stuck in one of the newer annexes. Single business travelers, while not overlooked, are seated at side tables. *219 W. 9th St., tel. 816/842–3890. Reservations recommended. Jacket advised. AE, CB, D, DC, MC, V.*

## Midtown/Westport District

**★ ⑫** **Café Allegro.** Seasonal, new American cuisine has made
*$$$* this casual, New York-style bistro one of Kansas City's "in" places to dine. Part of the cluster of innovative offbeat restaurants nestled along 39th Street between State Line and Southwest Trafficway, Café Allegro has a character all its own. Small, intimate alcoves break the room into private conversation areas. Antique posters, carved glass, and works by local artists add to the restaurant's style. The cuisine is consistently creative, and the unusual is always usual. Seasonal dishes include crab cakes with roasted tomato salsa and cilantro, veal chops with Calvados cream and Granny Smith apples, and duck breast seared and served with caramelized garlic sauce. *1815 W. 39th St., tel. 816/561–3663. Reservations advised. Jacket recommended. AE, CB, DC, MC, V.*

**★ ⑬** **Metropolis American Grill.** Pinpoint lighting adds a soft
*$$* luminosity to Metropolis's contemporary high-tech setting. The Grill—off the beaten path in Westport—is tiny, so when it gets busy the noise level tends to rise. Businesspeople prefer window tables, which offer a degree of privacy. The owner has trained his staff never to ask, "Only one for lunch today?" The menu reflects his sensitivity to various tastes with its cross-cultural fare that features farm-fresh produce mixed with imported items from around the world. Specialties include smoked Norwegian salmon stuffed with a mild chorizo sausage and bathed in

caviar cheese; grilled tender flank steak, served with papaya and black bean and corn relish; and a vegetable plate featuring seasonal items. *303 Westport Rd., tel. 816/753–1550. Reservations recommended. Casual dress. AE, DC, MC, V.*

## Midtown/Country Club Plaza District

**⑯** **Fedora.** This European-style bistro has kept up with eclec-
$$$ tic tastes by offering a variety of unusual dishes in a polished, upscale environment. Ecru-color tablecloths, tile floors, and soft lighting provide the backdrop for people who want to see and be seen. Fedora is usually crowded with a business-and-briefcase crowd at lunch; dinner brings a mix of local socialites, politicians, couples, singles, and executives looking for a fun night on the town. Fedora has successfully covered all bases with Kansas City strips and grilled sturgeon for the traditionalists; and, for cross-cultured tastes, new American dishes such as squid-ink pasta with shirred medallions of salmon, and barbecqued shrimp quesadillas. For dessert, don't miss the pecan pie with butter pecan ice cream and caramel sauce, or tartufo—white chocolate ice cream coated with white chocolate and served in a pool of warm fudge. *210 W. 47th St., tel. 816/561–6565. Reservations suggested. Jacket required. AE, CB, D, DC, MC, V.*

**⑳** **The Grill in the Ritz-Carlton.** Hearty traditional American
$$$$ cuisine blended with a touch of Continental elegance and a terrific view of the famed Country Club Plaza make this place a good bet for businesspeople. Wood-paneled walls are adorned with brass and crystal sconces, and antique furnishings complete the setting. Everything here is discreet and understated, from the dinner music to the fine bone china and damask linen tablesettings. The atmosphere is refined, but portions are hefty. Specialties include 2½-pound Maine lobsters, thick, smoked pork chops, and 24-ounce Porterhouse steaks. For an appetizer, you might try Kansas City corn chowder, or spicy duck sausage braised with cabbage. Service is sometimes slow. The wine list is one of the best in town. *401 Ward Pkwy., tel. 816/756–1500. Reservations recommended. Jacket required. AE, CB, D, DC, MC, V.*

**⑲** **Plaza III: The Steakhouse.** This traditional steakhouse re-
$$$$ calls the turn-of-the-century era when rich, dark woods and thick, tufted banquettes were preferred by Kansas City's cigar-toting financiers and moneyed aristocracy. The restaurant's Western art and artifacts, including Remington prints, add to the beefy legend of this steak-and-potatoes town. Lettuce nibblers beware; this is the home of certified Black Angus steaks, including a thundering 20-ounce Porterhouse, and a 32-ounce Kansas City strip. Those with daintier appetites opt for fresh seafood, chicken, lobster, veal, or ribs. The restaurant can quickly string tables together to accommodate parties of 12. Singles are also welcome. *4749 Pennsylvania St., tel. 816/753–0000. Reservations recommended. Jacket required. AE, CB, D, DC, MC, V.*

## South/Waldo District

**★ ㉒** **Jaspers.** This famed Northern Italian restaurant is a
$$$$ throwback to the days when tableside cooking was the rule. Politicians, celebrities, and businesspeople are

drawn to the sumptuous, baroque surroundings, with velvet banquettes moderately spaced for privacy. House favorites are *scampi livornese*, served with a hint of sherry, garlic, and cayenne; and lobster *raviolo arogosta* (ravioli stuffed with lobster and ricotta and served with a creamy lobster sauce). Peppered steak and decadent desserts like cherries jubilee are flamed tableside. Consistently excellent food and attentive service make Jasper's worth the 10-mile drive from downtown. *405 W. 75th St., tel. 816/363-3003. Reservations required. Jacket required. AE, CB, DC, MC, V. Closed lunch.*

## FREE TIME

### Fitness

*Hotel Facilities*
None of the hotels listed above has health club facilities open to nonguests.

*Health Clubs*
**The Plaza Athletic Club** (4711 Central, tel. 813/756–0067) offers guests at The Raphael and Embassy Suites Hotel a $5 discount on its $10-per-day rate. **Westport Bodyworks** (4050 Pennsylvania Ave., tel. 816/531–1876) offers aerobics and weights for $7 a day.

*Jogging*
The 1.2-mile exercise trail in **Mill Creek Park** (47th St. and J.C. Nichols Pkwy.) is across the street from the Embassy Suites Hotel and down the street from the Hilton Plaza Inn and Kansas City Marriott Plaza. **Loose Park** (55th St. and Wornall Rd.) is an uphill climb from The Raphael or Ritz-Carlton, but once you get there you can jog 2 miles along a paved trail, past a lake and municipal rose garden.

### Shopping

Built in 1922 as the nation's first shopping center, Kansas City's **Country Club Plaza** district at 47th Street and J.C. Nichols Parkway is the city's version of Rodeo Drive. A 5- to 10-minute cab ride from downtown, this historic area boasts ornate Spanish architecture, fountains, and sculpture, as well as 150 stores offering everything from diamonds and art to high fashion and exotic kitchen items. Within the 14-block district are upscale stores such as Brooks Brothers, Gucci's, Saks, Crabtree and Evelyn, and Laura Ashley, along with locally owned establishments such as **Halls** (211 Nichols Rd. tel. 816/274–3222). Named for the founder of Hallmark Cards, this unusual store contains a complete line of Hallmark greeting cards, clothing, and fine housewares.

Adjoining the plaza district to the north is midtown's colorful, renovated **Westport** area, a thriving mix of night spots, trendy restaurants, and unusual stores that sell everything from jewelry to art. A few blocks west of Westport is the **State Line Antique and Arts Center** (45th St. and State Line Rd., tel. 913/362–2002). This district is one of the best and most convenient places to shop for everything from collectibles and primitives to old world furniture and fine art.

Between downtown and midtown is **Crown Center** (25th St. and Grand, tel. 816/274–8444), across the street from the world headquarters of Hallmark Cards. This multi-level shopping center is crammed with boutiques, high-fashion clothing and specialty stores, restaurants, and theaters.

## Diversions

**The Board of Trade** (4800 Main St., tel. 816/753–7500), headquarters of the world's second busiest grain exchange, has a two-story trading floor and a visitor's gallery where you can watch the frantic process of buying and selling grain.

River City U.S.A. (1 Kaw Point, tel. 816/281–5300), a riverboat company, provides daily lunch aboard ship, plus one-hour sightseeing **cruises on the Missouri River.** Relaxing dinner cruises are offered Tues.–Sun., with moonlight cruises on weekends.

**Harry S. Truman Library and Museum** (U.S. 24 at Delaware St., Independence, MO, tel. 816/833–1400), a 20-minute cab ride from downtown, contains historical documents and memorabilia from the Truman era.

**Liberty Memorial** (100 W. 26th St., tel. 816/221–1918) is the only U.S. museum specializing in World War I memorabilia.

**Nelson-Atkins Museum of Art** (4525 Oak St., tel. 816/561–4000), one of the country's largest art museums, is internationally known for its collection of Oriental art.

**Thomas Hart Benton Home and Studio Historic Site** (3516 Belleview, tel. 816/931–5722) offers guided tours of the famed artist's home and studio, built in 1903.

## Professional Sports

For football, catch the **Chiefs** at the Arrowhead Stadium, tel. 816/924–9300. The town's baseball team, the **Royals,** can be seen at **Royal Stadium,** tel. 816/921–8000. The soccer team, the **Comets,** competes at Kemper Arena, tel. 816/421–7770.

## The Arts

Kansas City's commitment to culture is evidenced by a virtual explosion of interest in the fine arts. Several theaters, located in a five-block downtown district bounded by Main Street and Broadway, offer everything from the offbeat to the commercial. The **Folly Theater** (300 W. 12th St., tel. 816/474–4444) is a restored turn-of-the-century burlesque house presenting theatrical shows and chamber-music concerts. National touring companies book dates at the **Midland Center for the Performing Arts** (1288 Main St., tel. 816/421–4700), which is housed in a sumptuously restored '20s movie palace. **The State Ballet of Missouri** (706 W. 42nd St., tel. 816/931–2232), the only fully professional ballet company in Missouri, presents classical and contemporary works in Kansas City's **Music Hall** at 13th Street and Wyandotte.

For tickets to concerts, plays, and sporting events, call **Ticket-Master** (tel. 816/931–3330).

## After Hours

*Bars and Lounges*

For a relaxing drink with business associates, **The Top of the Ritz-Carlton** (tel. 816/756–1500) is an elegant, upscale choice. **Skies** (tel. 816/421 1234), the revolving restaurant at the top of the Hyatt Regency, offers quiet conversation and a great view of the city. **The Bristol Bar & Grill** (4740 Jefferson, tel. 816/756–0606) attracts a younger, livelier, after-work crowd. **The Quaff Buffet** (1010 Broadway, tel. 816/471–1918) has an unsophisticated, poolhall atmosphere, but it's popular with a casual, 25–35 yuppie crowd. **The Plaza Bar** in the Marriott Plaza (tel. 815/531–3000) has live contemporary pop music and dancing on the weekends. A few blocks south of the Plaza is **The Peanut** (5000 Main St., tel. 816/753–9499), a casual neighborhood bar that is popular with all ages.

*Comedy Clubs*

Two teams of comedians match wits and compete for highest honors with the help of the audience at **ComedySportz** in the **8th Street Café Theater** (323 W. 8th St., tel. 816/842–2744). **Stanford's Comedy House** (543 Westport Rd., tel. 816/756–1450) is Kansas City's original comedy shop.

*Jazz Clubs*

The **Grand Emporium** (3832 Main St., tel. 816/531–1504) is the place for blues and reggae. Drop into **The Levee** (16 W. 43rd St., tel. 816/561–2821) for live jam sessions. Another good place for jazz, and a popular spot for singles, is **City Light Restaurant** (7425 Broadway, tel. 816/444–6969) a few miles south of the Plaza.

*For Singles*

In nice weather, the sidewalk café at **Parkway 600 Grill** (600 Ward Pkwy., tel. 816/931–6600) attracts the 25–35 professional crowd.

# Las Vegas

*by Shari Silk*

Las Vegas is the largest American city founded in the 20th century (1905), though many would argue that the significant year was 1946, when Bugsy Siegal's Fabulous Flamingo opened for business. In the 1950s and '60s, Vegas had a resortlike atmosphere: Couples relaxed in the sun and perhaps gambled a bit by day, then dined and went to shows at night, dressed in gowns and furs, jackets and ties. Those were the days of the high rollers, many of them oilmen, who found that their hotels provided women to stand by them as they dropped their money on the table.

The days of the oilmen are over, and what high rollers there are come chiefly from other countries, primarily Asia. Vegas today includes visitors in open collars looking for cheap fun, and dancers, singers, acrobats, and comedians dreaming of making it in the self-proclaimed Entertainment Capital of the World.

Gambling is not the only industry—Nellis Air Force Base employs 8,000 people, and 6,000 more work at the Nevada Test Site—yet 80% of the Vegas work force, many of them Mormon, labor in the so-called hospitality industry. Although the Strip is considered the principal commercial area of the city, 700,000 people live on the east and west sides of town. There you'll find rows of three-bedroom houses, often with a mom, a dad, two kids, and a car in the garage. What makes some of these homes different from those in other cities is that Mom is a show girl, Dad is a casino dealer, and both work nights rather than days.

## Top Employers

| Employer | Type of Enterprise | Parent*/ Headquarters |
|---|---|---|
| **Cashman Equipment** | Construction equipment manufacturers | Caterpillar Inc./ Peoria, IL |
| **Central Telephone** | Telecommunications | Centel Corp./ Chicago |
| **Citibank** | Banking | Citicorp/New York City |
| **EG&G Energy Measurements Group** | Engineering and research development | EG&G Inc./ Wellesley, MA |

| Ford Aerospace | Electronic training equipment manufacturers | San Jose, CA |
| --- | --- | --- |
| Levi Strauss | Clothing manufacturers | San Francisco |
| McDonnell Douglas | Aircraft manufacturers | St. Louis |
| Reynolds Electrical and Engineering | Nuclear testing management and energy research | EG&G, Inc./ Wellesley, MA |
| Titanium Metals | Titanium manufacturers | Baroid Corp./ Houston |

*if applicable

## ESSENTIAL INFORMATION

### Climate

What follows are the average daily maximum and minimum temperatures for Las Vegas.

| Jan. | 60F 16C 28 −2 | Feb. | 66F 19C 33 1 | Mar. | 71F 22C 39 4 |
| --- | --- | --- | --- | --- | --- |
| Apr. | 80F 27C 44 7 | May | 89F 32C 51 11 | June | 98F 37C 60 16 |
| July | 102F 39C 68 20 | Aug. | 102F 39C 66 19 | Sept. | 95F 35C 57 14 |
| Oct. | 84F 29C 46 8 | Nov. | 71F 22C 35 2 | Dec. | 60F 16C 30 −1 |

### Airports

Ultramodern **McCarran International Airport** is 1 mile east of the Strip, 3 miles south of the Las Vegas Convention Center, and 6 miles south of downtown. **Hughes Air Terminal,** part of McCarran, handles charter flights and private planes.

### Airport Business Facilities

**Mutual of Omaha Business Service Center** (at the main ticketing area between America West and Delta, tel. 702/739–5650) has fax machines, photocopying, notary public, secretarial service, baggage storage, Western Union, travel insurance, cash advance, and phone suites.

### Airlines

Las Vegas is a hub city for American West Airlines.

**American,** tel. 702/385–3871 or 800/433–7300.
**America West,** tel. 702/736–1737 or 800/247–5692.
**Continental,** tel. 702/383–8291 or 800/525–0280.
**Delta,** tel. 702/731–3111 or 800/221–1212.
**TWA,** tel. 702/385–1000 or 800/221–2000.
**United,** tel. 702/385–3222 or 800/241–6522.
**USAir,** tel. 702/382–1905 or 800/428–4322.

## Between the Airport and the Strip/Downtown

*By Taxi or Limousine*

Taxis are the fastest way to the Strip (5–7 minutes; $7–$10, depending on your destination) or downtown (15 minutes; $13–$15). Airport traffic is moderately heavy at rush hours (8–9:30 AM and 4–6 PM) and on busy weekends, so add 10–15 minutes travel time to both the Strip and downtown during these times. For the scenic route downtown, take a left on Tropicana Avenue and a right straight down the Strip. For the quick route, go down Paradise Road or take I–15, depending on the traffic. Airport limos, which wait for passengers outside the terminals along with cabs, generally make several stops but are a less expensive alternative ($3 to the Strip; $4.25 downtown).

*By Bus*

**Bell Trans** (tel. 702/736–4428) runs buses every half-hour from 6 AM to 6 PM or you can call for reservations until 2 AM. Cost: $4.25. **Grey Line** (tel. 702/384–1234) leaves every 20 minutes from 6 AM to 6:30 PM. Cost: $4.25. Both companies have booths at McCarran and Hughes.

## Car Rentals

The following companies have booths in or near the airport, with free shuttle service to and from their nearby locations.

**Alamo,** tel. 702/737–3111 or 800/327–9633.
**Allstate,** tel. 702/736–6147 or 800/634–6186.
**Avis,** tel. 702/739–5595 or 800/331–1212.
**Budget,** tel. 702/736–1212 or 800/527–0700.
**Dollar,** tel. 702/739–8408 or 800/421–6868.
**Hertz,** tel. 702/736–4900 or 800/654–3131.
**National,** tel. 702/739–5391 or 800/328–4657.
**Sav Mor,** tel. 702/736–1234.
**Thrifty,** tel. 702/736–4706 or 800/367–2277.

## Emergencies

All major hotels have physicians and dentists on call.

*Doctors*

**Las Vegas Medical Centers,** 3111 Joe Brown Dr., tel. 702/731–6060, plus three other locations, is open 24 hours.

*Dentists*

**Clark County Dental Society,** tel. 702/435–7767, is a 24-hour referral hot line.

## Important Addresses and Numbers

**Audiovisual rentals.** Bauer/Southam Audio Video (6000 S. Eastern Ave., Bldg. 10, Suite H, tel. 702/795–8960), Greyhound Audio Visual and Creative Services (1730 Mojave Rd., tel. 702/457–2376).

**Chamber of Commerce** (2301 E. Sahara Ave., tel. 702/457–4664).

**Computer rentals.** BRS Leasing (918 E. Sahara Ave., tel. 702/732–4422), PCR Personal Computer Rentals (3002A Rigel Ave., tel. 702/365–1103).

**Convention and exhibition centers.** Cashman Field Center (850 N. Las Vegas Blvd., tel. 702/386–7100), Las Vegas Convention Center (3150 Paradise Rd., tel. 702/733–2244).

**Fax service.** Mail Boxes Etc. has 15 outlets in town. Call tel. 702/732–0024 for nearest location.

**Formal-wear rentals.** Casino Clothiers (Commercial Center, 2560 Maryland Pkwy., tel. 702/732–9792), Tuxedo Junction (3540 W. Sahara Ave., tel. 702/873–8830).

**Gift shops.** Chocolates: Ethel M Chocolates (6 locations: Fashion Show Mall, California Club, Flamingo Hilton, Holiday Casino, Stardust Hotel, Tropicana Hotel, tel. 702/796–6662); Flowers: Bloom Saloon Florist (3547 S. Maryland Pkwy., tel. 702/731–1711 or 316 Bridger St., tel. 702/384–8863); Gift baskets: Dial-A-Gift (2800 W. Sahara Ave., tel. 702/368–0001).

**Graphic design studios.** Graphic Art Services (2141 Industrial Rd., tel. 702/382–7612), High Profile (3220 E. Flamingo Rd., Suite 246, tel. 702/564–4822).

**Hairstylists.** Men: Gentleman's Choice Hair Design (4417 W. Charleston Blvd., tel. 878–0366). Women: Cleopatra's Salon (Caesars Palace, tel. 702/731–7791).

**Health and fitness clubs.** *See* Fitness, below.

**Information hot lines.** Road conditions (tel. 702/486–3116), tourist information (tel. 702/739–1482 or 702/733–2323).

**Limousine services.** Bell Transportation (tel. 702/739–7990), Presidential (tel. 702/731–5577).

**Liquor stores.** Sherry's Fine Food & Liquor (44 Convention Center Dr., tel. 702/735–1276), Town Pump Liquors (953 E. Sahara Ave., tel. 702/735–8515).

**Mail delivery, overnight.** Federal Express (tel. 702/385–7628), UPS (tel. 702/385–3636), Express Mail (tel. 702/361–9397).

**Messenger services.** Fleet Courier Service (tel. 702/876–9666), Las Vegas Bonded Messenger Service (tel. 702/734–4800).

**Office space rentals.** Professional Center (1601 E. Flamingo Rd., tel. 702/794–2402), The Office (514 S. 3rd St., tel. 702/387–0404).

**Pharmacies, late-night.** The Health Pharm (3059 Las Vegas Blvd. S, tel. 702/369–3222), Landmark Pharmacy (252 Convention Center Dr., tel. 702/731–0041), White Cross Drugs, open 24 hours (1700 Las Vegas Blvd. S, tel. 702/382–1733).

**Radio station, all-news.** KNEWS 970 AM.

**Secretarial services.** A Gal Friday (3001 E. Charleston Blvd., tel. 702/386–1717), Manpower Temporary Services (4 locations, tel. 702/386–2626).

**Stationery supplies.** Rose Office Supplies (3909 W. Sahara Ave., tel. 702/362–1103), TAC Office Products (4800 S. Maryland Pkwy., tel. 702/736–2657).

**Taxis.** Whittlesea Blue (tel. 702/384–6111), Yellow-Checker Cab (tel. 702/873–2227).

**Theater tickets.** *See* The Arts, below.

**Train information.** Amtrak (Union Plaza, behind Union Plaza Hotel Downtown, 1 N. Main St., tel. 702/386–6898 or 800/872–7245).

**Travel agents.** Ask Mr. Foster/Prestige Travel (11 locations, tel. 702/362–1555), Abbey Travel (1801 E. Tropicana Ave., tel. 702/795–7055).

**Weather** (tel. 702/734–2010).

# LODGING

Sprawling megaresorts dominate the scene, but a variety of chain-owned and independent smaller properties and motels are interspersed throughout the city. Las Vegas has two major districts, the Strip and downtown, both heavily populated with hotels, casinos, and restaurants. The 6-mile long Strip is convenient to almost everything—the airport, convention center, and the University of Nevada at Las Vegas. Unfortunately, guest rooms in many casino hotels are cramped and amenities are few, because casinos prefer that customers spend their time gambling, not sleeping or relaxing in their rooms. But with the influx of conventioneers and other business travelers, several large Strip hotels have undergone major renovations, resulting in larger, more comfortable rooms. The governmental, financial, and legal communities, Cashman Field Center, and the casinos of Glitter Gulch are downtown. The hotels in this area focus exclusively on gaming, and none of the properties was designed with the needs of the business traveler in mind.

Because this city is so much defined by its lodgings—and because there is not generally a great deal of distinction among them—a number of alternative accommodations in both locations are given at the end of each geographical section.

Highly recommended lodgings in each price category are indicated by a star ★ .

| Category | Cost* |
|---|---|
| *$$$$* (Very Expensive) | over $100 |
| *$$$* (Expensive) | $70–$100 |
| *$$* (Moderate) | under $70 |

*\*All prices are for a standard double room, single occupancy, excluding 7% city tax. (All prices are based on average daily rates. Room rates in Las Vegas tend to vary widely based on the expected occupancy. Rates go up during citywide trade shows and holiday weekends; rates go down in summer and other off-times.)*

*Numbers in the margin correspond to numbered hotel locations on the Las Vegas Lodging and Dining map.*

## On and Around the Strip

★ ❷⑨ **Alexis Park Resort.** This self-contained oasis, just 2 miles
$$$ from the convention center, is designed for upscale travelers who want full services and all-suite comfort away from the neon, the gaming tables, and the slots. Cool tile floors, abundant foliage, and comfortable seating make the quiet, airy lobby a good spot for a quick meeting, while the lushly landscaped 20-acre property is perfect for a morning jog. Tennis courts and a putting green are added outdoor attractions. Spacious standard suites range in decor from pastel French Provincial to black-and-white Art Deco. Coffee makers help get the day started, and the well-lighted breakfast bar doubles as a desk. Most suites boast fireplaces and Jacuzzis, and there's full concierge service. The Pegasus restaurant is recommended for dinner (*see* Dining, below); Cafinao is fine for a morning meeting (*see* Business Breakfasts, below) and there's dancing at the Club Pisces. *A Princeton hotel. 375 E. Harmon Ave., 89109, tel. 702/796–3300 or 800/453–8000, fax 702/796–0766. Gen. manager, Stu Platt. 410 standard suites. No casino. AE, CB, DC, MC, V.*

❷③ **Caesars Palace.** If Las Vegas is a fantasy, Caesars does the
$$$$ best job of any resort of keeping the dream alive. Setting the tone for lavish accommodations in Las Vegas since 1966, this garish Strip hotel is awash with marble statuary, towering fountains, Cleopatra-costumed cocktail waitresses, world-famous entertainers, and two casinos. Guest rooms come in many shapes and sizes; some look like they belong in a honeymoon resort, with large baths and Roman Jacuzzi tubs, and an assortment of bed shapes and sizes, topped off with canopies or mirrored ceilings. Glitzy, yes, but rooms are also designed for comfort, with large seating areas, desks, and plenty of amenities. Lowest-priced rooms, however, are cramped and offer no frills. Higher floors have good views and afford the most peace and quiet. Service is prompt and reliable, if not always friendly. *3570 Las Vegas Blvd. S, 89109, tel. 702/731–7110 or 800/634–6661, fax 702/731–7331. Gen. manager, Brent Vockrodt. 942 kings and queens, 197 double queens; 100 suites. AE, CB, D, DC, MC, V.*

❷⑤ **Center Strip Inn.** On the south end of the Strip, and the low
$$ end of the price range, this motel is well located for the airport. Although it has no casino, it's within walking distance of Bally's, Aladdin, and Dunes casinos, and offers spacious, clean rooms with such amenities as VCRs and refrigerators. There is no room service, however. Bathrooms are small but functional. The furniture is motel style, but the upkeep is excellent. Free coffee is offered 24 hours a day in the small lobby, and a Continental breakfast is included in the price. *3688 Las Vegas Blvd. S, 89109, tel. 702/739–6066 or 800/877–7737, fax 702/736–2521. Gen. manager, Larry Williams. 29 singles, 58 doubles, 6 suites. AE, CB, D, DC, MC, V.*

❶⑧ **Courtyard.** This 1989 property from the Marriott cookie
$$$ cutter is adjacent to the Convention Center and a few blocks from the Strip. Well designed for the business traveler, the rooms are spacious and functional, with large desks, good lighting, and extra-long phone cords. Breakfast and dinner are available in a small airy café, but hours are limited and there is no room service. Perhaps to com-

# LAS VEGAS

Bonanza Rd.
95
Rancho Dr.
Alta Dr.
Alta D
Charleston Blvd.
11
Rancho Dr.
15
Sahara Ave.
Ci
Circ
15
Stardust Rd.
Spring Mountain Rd.
17
Tw
Sands
Ave.
21
Dauphine
19
20
23
24
Dunes Rd.
Flaming
26
25
Las Vegas Blvd.
THE STRIP
Tropicana Ave.
27
Reno Av

# LAS VEGAS HOTEL CHART

| HOTELS | Price Category | Business Services<br>Banquet capacity | No. of meeting rooms | Secretarial services | Audiovisual equipment | Teletype news service | Computer rentals | In-room modem phone jack | All-news cable channel | Desk | Desk lighting | Bed lighting |
|---|---|---|---|---|---|---|---|---|---|---|---|---|
| **Alexis Park Resort** | $$$ | 800 | 3 | ✓ | ✓ | - | ✓ | ✓ | ✓ | ◐ | ● | ● |
| **Best Western McCarran Inn** | $$ | 15 | 1 | - | ✓ | - | - | - | ✓ | ◐ | ◐ | ◐ |
| **Caesar's Palace** | $$$$ | 3000 | 17 | ✓ | ✓ | - | ✓ | ✓ | ✓ | ◐ | ● | ◐ |
| **Center Strip Inn** | $$ | 0 | 0 | - | - | - | - | - | ✓ | ◐ | ● | ◐ |
| **Desert Inn** | $$$$ | 800 | 6 | ✓ | ✓ | - | ✓ | - | - | ◐ | ◐ | ● |
| **Golden Nugget** | $$ | 400 | 13 | ✓ | ✓ | - | ✓ | - | ✓ | - | - | ● |
| **Las Vegas Hilton** | $$$ | 10000 | 41 | ✓ | ✓ | ✓ | ✓ | ✓ | - | ● | ● | ● |
| **Marriott Courtyard** | $$$ | 30 | 1 | ✓ | ✓ | - | ✓ | - | ✓ | ● | ● | ● |
| **Marriott Residence Inn** | $$$ | 0 | 0 | ✓ | ✓ | - | ✓ | ✓ | ✓ | ◐ | ● | ● |
| **Mirage** | $$$$ | 3200 | 15 | ✓ | ✓ | ✓ | ✓ | ✓ | ✓ | ● | ● | ● |
| **Ramada Hotel San Remo** | $$ | 250 | 9 | - | ✓ | - | - | - | ✓ | ● | ● | ● |
| **St. Tropez** | $$$ | 200 | 2 | ✓ | ✓ | - | ✓ | ✓ | ✓ | ◐ | ● | ● |
| **Sheffield Inn** | $$ | 100 | 2 | - | ✓ | - | - | - | ✓ | - | - | ◐ |

**$$$$** = over $100, **$$$** = $70-$100, **$$** = under $70.
● good, ◐ fair, ○ poor.
All hotels listed here have photocopying and fax facilities.

| In-Room Amenities | | | | | | | | | | | Hotel Amenities | | | | | | |
| Nonsmoking rooms | In-room checkout | Minibar | Pay movies | VCR/Movie rentals | Hairdryer | Toiletries | Room service | Laundry/Dry cleaning | Pressing | | Concierge | Barber/Hairdresser | Garage | Courtesy airport transport | Sauna | Pool | Exercise room |
|---|---|---|---|---|---|---|---|---|---|---|---|---|---|---|---|---|---|
| ✓ | ✓ | ✓ | ✓ | - | - | ◐ | ● | ● | ● | | ✓ | ✓ | - | ✓ | ✓ | ● | ◐ |
| ✓ | ✓ | - | ✓ | - | - | ◐ | - | ◐ | ◐ | | - | - | - | ✓ | - | ◐ | - |
| ✓ | - | - | ✓ | - | - | ◐ | ● | ● | ● | | ✓ | ✓ | ✓ | - | ✓ | ● | ● |
| - | - | - | ✓ | ✓ | - | ◐ | - | ◐ | - | | - | - | - | - | - | ◐ | - |
| ✓ | - | - | ✓ | - | - | ● | ● | ● | ● | | ✓ | ✓ | - | - | ✓ | ● | ● |
| ✓ | - | - | - | - | - | ○ | ● | ● | ● | | - | ✓ | ✓ | - | ✓ | ● | ● |
| ✓ | ✓ | ✓ | ✓ | - | ✓ | ◐ | ● | ● | ● | | ✓ | ✓ | ✓ | ✓ | ✓ | ● | ● |
| ✓ | ✓ | - | ✓ | - | - | ○ | - | ● | ◐ | | - | - | - | ✓ | - | ◐ | ○ |
| ✓ | - | - | ✓ | - | - | ◐ | - | ● | ◐ | | ✓ | - | - | ✓ | - | ● | - |
| ✓ | ✓ | ✓ | ✓ | - | - | ● | ● | ● | ● | | ✓ | ✓ | ✓ | - | ✓ | ● | ● |
| ✓ | - | ✓ | - | - | - | ● | ● | ◐ | ◐ | | - | - | ✓ | ✓ | - | ● | - |
| ✓ | - | ✓ | - | ✓ | - | ◐ | ● | ● | ● | | ✓ | - | - | ✓ | - | ● | ◐ |
| ✓ | - | - | - | ✓ | - | ○ | - | ● | ◐ | | - | - | ✓ | ✓ | - | ◐ | - |

**Room service:** ● 24-hour, ◐ 6AM–10PM, ○ other.
**Laundry/Dry cleaning:** ● same day, ◐ overnight, ○ other.
**Pressing:** ● immediate, ◐ same day, ○ other.

pensate, each room has a boiling water tap and coffee machines. There's no on-site casino. *3275 Paradise Rd., 89109, tel. 702/791-3600 or 800/321-2211, fax 702/796-7981. Gen. manager, Dan Thorn. 87 singles, 50 doubles, 12 suites. AE, CB, D, DC, MC, V.*

★ ❶ **Desert Inn.** This full-scale Strip resort with outstanding
$$$$ sports and spa facilities is a fine place to relax after work. Guest rooms are far above the Las Vegas norm, both in terms of size and amenities, with such extras as terry robes and bathroom telephones. Standard rooms have a Southwestern decor. St. Andrews tower rooms, done in soothing French country fashions, are the largest and feature deluxe Roman-style baths. Some rooms and suites are spread across 200 acres of landscaped grounds, with not a neon sign in sight. The resort's country-club atmosphere is reinforced by a PGA-tournament caliber championship golf course and tournament-class tennis courts. There's a strong emphasis on service at this relaxed property, which lacks the pretentiousness of Caesars, but not the comfort or quality. Concierge service is all that it should be—interested, attentive, and efficient. The hotel's La Vie En Rose restaurant is worth a visit (*see* Dining, below), as is the upscale Promenade Coffee Shop (*see* Business Breakfasts, below). *3145 Las Vegas Blvd. S, 89109, tel. 702/733-4444 or 800/634-6906, fax 702/733-4437. Gen. manager, Vince Matthews. 500 singles and doubles, 250 suites and minisuites. AE, CB, D, DC, MC, V.*

❶ **The Las Vegas Hilton.** There's a good chance that if you're
$$$ traveling on business to Las Vegas you'll end up in this hotel, a few blocks east of the Strip. The city's huge convention center is right next door, and most convention bookers place their delegates here. The hotel is huge, and getting from one part of it to another takes longer than one might anticipate. During a big convention, room service can get backed up, because many executives like to have meetings in their suites. But elevators come quickly, phone messages are delivered, and parking is plentiful. In-room check-out is another business-oriented amenity. Guest rooms tend to be large, with soft chairs and large beds, and expansive views of the golf course on the east side and views of the Strip on the west side. *3000 Paradise Rd., 89109, tel. 702/732-5111 or 800/732-7117, fax 702/732-5249. Gen. manager, Mike Maggiore. 1,389 kings, 1,546 double queens, 239 suites. AE, CB, D, DC, MC, V.*

❷ **The Mirage.** If the Hilton is the hotel you'll most likely end
$$$$ up at, the Mirage is the one you'll most likely want to see. The newest hotel and casino on the Strip, this $630 million, 3,049-room resort is the talk of the town: Among its attractions are an outdoor volcano that erupts every 15 minutes after dark and illusionists Siegfried and Roy's rare white tigers on display 24 hours a day. Yes, this is definitely a tourist attraction, a place you'd probably be more comfortable visiting than staying in, especially if you're in town on business. The crowds are generally huge, getting into the parking lot through the traffic is a hassle, it's a trek to get from one part of the hotel to another, and the hotel's food, shows, and room rates are very expensive. The rooms are on the small side, and nowhere near as spectacular as the hotel itself. The Mirage's Caribe Cafe (*see* Business Breakfasts, below) is a good early meeting spot.

*3400 Las Vegas Blvd., 89109, tel. 702/791–7111, 800/639–3403, fax 702/791–7414. Gen. manager, Steve Kyle. 1,299 king rooms, 1,299 double queen rooms, 159 suites. AE, CB, D, DC, MC, V.*

**28 Ramada Hotel San Remo.** An alternative to the hustle and
$$ bustle of the large Strip hotels, this charming, relatively small hotel combined the former Treasury and Polynesian hotels and gave them a $40-million facelift in 1990. Granted, it's missing many of the amenities of the larger hotels (such as in-room check-out, hairdresser, and health club), but it's also missing crowds, parking problems, and restaurant lines. Gambling rates are also rather low ($1 blackjack tables are plentiful), and rooms are spacious and colorful and overlook the hotel's swimming pool and/or Tropicana Boulevard, just off the Strip. *115 E. Tropicana Blvd., 89109, tel. 702/739–9000, 800/522–7366. Gen. manager, Michael Hessling. 322 rooms, 200 kings, 122 double queens. AE, CB, D, DC, MC, V.*

**16 Residence Inn.** Business travelers planning an extended
$$$ stay will like this townhouse-style Marriott with its well-furnished and roomy executive suites that aim to make you feel at home. It's convenient to the Strip (about ¼ mile away) and right across the road from the Convention Center. Studios have full kitchens with a well-lighted breakfast bar that doubles as a desk; the hotel will take care of your grocery shopping and the housekeeping staff will do the dishes. The comforts are enhanced by a fireplace, a VCR, and a patio or balcony. The cozy lounge with books, games, and magazines, is an appealing place to relax or to meet colleagues after work. A complimentary breakfast and cocktail hour are offered, as well as dinner three nights a week. Laundry facilities are a useful extra, and there is full concierge service. Curbside parking is a plus. Two-story penthouse suites are suitable for sharing. *3225 Paradise Rd., 89109, tel. 702/796–9300 or 800/331–3131, fax 702/796–9300 ext. 6120. Gen. manager, John Fiore. 144 standard suites, 48 2-bedroom suites. AE, CB, D, DC, MC, V.*

**30 Sheffield Inn.** Moderately priced and suitable for extended
$$ visits, this converted time-share resort is noted for its quiet, spacious, and well-equipped suites. The hotel is a short walk from both the Strip and the Convention Center, but it does show some signs of wear, and could benefit from a fresh coat of paint and new carpets. Bathrooms and closets are small, and rooms have no desks; suites have only one TV set. Amenities in the executive suites include a microwave and a VCR. Avoid the cramped double/double accommodations, unless you need two double beds. A complimentary Continental breakfast is offered, and virtually next door are seven restaurants. There is no casino. Substantial discounts are offered to business travelers who ask for "executive club" rates. *A Colony hotel. 3970 Paradise Rd., 89109, tel. 702/796–9000 or 800/632–4040, fax 702/796–9000, ext. 410. Gen. manager, James Riker. 120 singles, 57 doubles, 51 suites. AE, CB, DC, MC, V.*

**31 St. Tropez.** This small, all-suite hotel rates high for per-
$$$ sonal service, luxury amenities, and sedate surroundings. It's also only a five-minute drive (or free shuttle ride) to the Strip, the Convention Center, and the airport. One-room suites are well lighted, and have VCRs and two-line phones; other niceties include complimentary breakfast

and afternoon cocktails. The two-story resort surrounds a first-class pool and garden area. The Super Suites are suitable for meetings, but separate meeting facilities are also available. Concierge service is helpful, as is the staff. The hotel's Savoia Restaurant is a good choice for a casual lunch or dinner (*see* Dining, below). *A Ramada Suite hotel. 455 E. Harmon Ave., 89109, tel. 702/369–5400 or 800/ 666–5400, fax 702/369–5400, ext. 2999. Gen. manager, Floyd Benedict. 72 standard suites, 74 2-room suites, 4 super suites. AE, CB, DC, MC, V.*

*More on the Strip*

⑬ Other Strip resorts include the **Riviera** (2901 Las Vegas Blvd. S, 89109, tel. 702/734–5110 or 800/634–3420), the city's first (1955) high-rise hotel. Today this moderately priced megahotel for conventioneers and trade show attendees has 2,200 guest rooms and is growing to a planned 4,000 by 1992. The property is somewhat confusing to get around in, and accommodations are uneven (the best ones are in the Monte Carlo and Monaco towers), but the hotel's

㉗ business center is very good. The 2,000-room **Tropicana** (3801 Las Vegas Blvd. S, 89109, tel. 702/739–2222 or 800/ 826–9200) boasts a 5-acre water park that is a big attraction in summer. Older rooms are nothing more than small hotel units; try to stay in the newer Island Tower. Prices are moderate to expensive, depending on the time of year.

㉒ The **Mardi Gras Inn** (3500 Paradise Rd., 89109, tel. 702/ 731–2020 or 800/634–6501) is a moderately priced offering that houses a cramped and noisy casino. But the minisuites are spacious and the location convenient to the convention center.

Clean, inexpensive, well-located motels with upscale
㉖ amenities include the **Vagabond Inn** (4155 Koval Ln.,
⑮ 89109, tel. 702/731–2111 or 800/634–6541) and the **Monaco Motel** (3073 Las Vegas Blvd. S, 89109, tel. 702/735–9222).

## Downtown

★ ❺ **Golden Nugget.** This splashy resort casino in Glitter Gulch
*$$* is downtown's best bet, particularly if you stay in the quiet 22-story south tower. Here, guest rooms have a tropical look, with bright colors and wicker furniture. In the 18-story north tower, rooms have a Victorian look with four-posters and period mirrors and furniture. In both towers, in-room amenities are few. Suites are multilevel; some have a personal room-service waiter. The restaurants are recommended, especially the elegant Elaine's, The Buffet, which offers the city's best spread, and The Carson Street Café (*see* Business Breakfasts, below). Meeting facilities are well designed, and extensive business services are handled with a friendly, willing attitude. The Nugget's main drawback is its location. If you plan a lot of activities in Vegas, you'll have to endure the traffic when traveling between the Strip and downtown. *129 E. Fremont St., 89101, tel. 702/385–7111 or 800/634–3454, fax 702/386–8362. Gen. manager, Bob Hilton. 1,805 singles and doubles, 195 suites. AE, CB, D, DC, MC, V.*

*More in Downtown*

❹ The **Las Vegas Club** (18 E. Fremont St., 89101, tel. 702/ 385–1664 or 800/634–6532) is a cozy casino/hotel with 224 soundproof, relatively inexpensive rooms. Also reasona-

**7** bly priced, the **Lady Luck** hotel and casino (206 N. 3rd St., 89101, tel. 702/477–3000) has a brand-new 25-story tower with in-room refrigerators and Jacuzzis. Two nongaming
**3** motels, the **Best Western Downtown Convention Center Inn** (1000 N. Main St., 89101, tel. 702/382–3455 or 800/528–
**6** 1234) and the **Comfort Inn** (525 E. Bonanza Rd., 89101, tel. 702/366–0456 or 800/331–3504), are located near Cashman Field Center. Both are clean, have large guest rooms with standard motel-issue furniture and few ameni-
**9** ties, and are moderately priced. Similarly, the **Downtowner Motel** (129 N. 8th St., 89101, tel. 702/384–1441 or 800/
**8** 777–2566) and the **Crest Inn** (207 N. 6th St., 89101, tel. 702/382–5642 or 800/777–1817) are within walking distance of downtown's Glitter Gulch.

## Near Nellis Air Force Base

This Air Force installation dominates the northeast corner of the Las Vegas Valley, but those with business there might be better off staying downtown, as accommodation
**1** options are few in the area. Two motels, the small **Best Western Nellis Motor Inn** (5330 E. Craig Rd., 89115, tel.
**2** 702/643–6111 or 800/528–1234) and the larger **Barcelona Motel** (5100 E. Craig Rd., 89115, tel. 702/644–6300 or 800/223–6330), are nearby but offer small rooms and limited services.

## Airport

**32** **Best Western McCarran Inn.** Less than 1 mile from
**$$** McCarran Airport, this clean property has no casino, just functional rooms with standard motel furnishings. Continental breakfast, newspapers, and airport transportation from 6 AM to 8 PM are complimentary. For diversion, there are in-room movies and a pool that's open 24 hours. *4970 Paradise Rd., 89119, tel. 702/798–5530 or 800/626–7575, fax 702/798–7627. Gen. manager, Frederick Walter. 36 kings, 54 doubles, 6 suites. AE, CB, D, DC, MC, V.*

# DINING

Las Vegas offers visitors an enormous range of options: ride down the Strip or through downtown's Glitter Gulch and you'll see everything from 99¢ breakfasts to steak houses and elegant French restaurants, with Italian, Mexican, Japanese, and Chinese restaurants interspersed. Every large hotel offers a buffet—food is used as a lure for casino customers—and every major hotel has at least one so-called gourmet room. The ethnic restaurants are not as authentic as those in cities with large immigrant populations, and the hotel dining rooms rarely match their counterparts in more cosmopolitan locations, but a number of places offer reasonably good meals in pleasant surroundings. Generally speaking, single diners, including women, will feel comfortable wherever they choose to go.

Highly recommended restaurants in each price category are indicated by a star ★.

| Category | Cost* |
|----------|-------|
| $$$$ (Very Expensive) | over $40 |
| $$$ (Expensive) | $25–$40 |
| $$ (Moderate) | under $25 |

*per person, including appetizer, entrée, and dessert, but excluding drinks, service, and 6% sales tax.*

*Numbers in the margin correspond to numbered restaurant locations on the Las Vegas Lodging and Dining map.*

## Business Breakfasts

Upscale coffee shops in the better hotels are the standard for business breakfasts in Las Vegas. **La Promenade** (tel. 702/733–4444) at the Desert Inn is among the best, with linen tablecloths, a view of the pool, attentive service, and a telephone in every booth. The Alexis Park's **Cafinao** (tel. 702/796–3300), a bright, airy spot where a quiet table can be found, also has an excellent Sunday brunch. **The Caribe Café** (tel. 702/791–7111) in the Mirage offers all-American breakfasts in a festive atmosphere suggestive of a Caribbean village, but like all the hotel's restaurants, its acoustics were designed for private conversation.

Downtown, the Golden Nugget's **Carson Street Café** (tel. 702/385–7111) is appropriate for quiet business breakfasts. The best of the casual breakfast spots is the western-style coffee shop in **Binion's Horseshoe** (9128 Fremont St., tel. 702/382–1600); the ham steak is a meal in itself.

## The Strip

**㉔**
**$$**
**Battista's Hole in the Wall.** This is a reliable standby for an informal Italian meal in a boisterous setting. The opera-singing owner serves up large portions and, occasionally, an Italian melody during the dinner hour. Unlimited carafes of red and white wine are among the extras that accompany entrées of homemade pasta with sausage cacciatore, meatballs, pesto, or seafood sauces. Other choices include a robust *ciaoppino* (seafood stew) and a fresh fish of the day. Every inch of wall space is covered with celebrity photos, posters, business cards, fruit baskets, and chianti bottles. This large restaurant (seating for 300 plus) is designed with intimate dining alcoves, but don't expect a quiet meal—this place is all noisy fun. *4041 Audrie St., across from Bally's, tel. 702/732–1424. Dress: casual but neat. Reservations advised. AE, MC, V. Open daily. Dinner only.*

**㉙**
**$$$**
**Bhalla's Cuisine of India.** This exotic looking restaurant offers a change of pace from the city's usual Continental fare. Indian scenes, hanging bronze lanterns, and a mounted tiger skin are the backdrop for North Indian Mogul cuisine and tandoori (clay oven) specialties. This is not a place to try to impress a client, but it's good for a casual, relaxing dinner. *4433 W. Flamingo Rd., tel. 702/367–4900. Jacket suggested. Reservations suggested for dinner. AE, MC, V. Closed for lunch weekends.*

**㉑**
**$$$**
**Kokomo's.** In keeping with the general tone of the Mirage, this steak-and-seafood restaurant in the hotel's tropical rainforest atrium replicates a Hawaiian village, complete

with waterfalls, palm trees, and an interior lagoon. Kokomo's may be a bit kitschy for some, but the sounds of the waterfall are soothing, and it's possible to have a quiet business lunch or a casual dinner here in the middle of one of the world's largest casinos. Daily fresh fish specialties are usually excellent, as are the Caesar salads, prepared at tableside. The fried onion shavings are hard to resist. *The Mirage Hotel and Casino, 3400 Las Vegas Blvd., 89109, tel. 702/791-7111. Jacket suggested. Reservations required for dinner. AE, CB, D, DC, MC, V.*

★ **17** **La Vie En Rose.** Both the cuisine and elegant atmosphere
$$$$ in this classic French restaurant are highly esteemed, and the staff is knowledgeable, attentive, and unobtrusive. Tables are well spaced, and classical music plays softly in the background. Starters might include creamy seafood soup with flaming cognac in a scooped-out loaf of bread. A popular entrée is veal sautéed with demiglacé and fresh cream, served with caramelized apples flamed with brandy. The fixed-price menu, a seven-course feast of the chef's favorite dishes, is usually a good choice. The wine cellar holds a fine selection of vintages in every price range. All in all, an excellent choice for a business discussion or celebration. *Desert Inn, 3145 Las Vegas Blvd. S, 89109, tel. 702/733-4444. Jackets required. Reservations required. AE, CB, D, DC, MC, V. Dinner only.*

**12** **Pamplemousse.** This classic French restaurant, in a small
$$$ building just off the Strip, is patronized by locals who appreciate high-quality fare at a reasonable price. The friendly service and relaxed French country atmosphere are well suited for a low-key business dinner. Offerings may include succulent roast duck with three sauces or Norwegian salmon in orange cream sauce. *400 E. Sahara Ave., tel. 702/733-2066. Jacket advised. Reservations required. AE, CB, DC, MC, V. Dinner only. Closed Mon.*

**29** **Pegasus.** This pretty nouvelle French restaurant, with its
$$$$ etched-glass murals, hand-blown Italian glass chandeliers, deep banquettes, and soft harp music, provides a comfortable and intimate setting for serious negotiating or for celebrating the closing of a deal. Consider following the complimentary hors d'oeuvres with breast of pheasant with chopped truffles and Madeira sauce, or fresh abalone with pecan butter. The wine list has a number of award-winning vintages, many of them offered by the glass. *Alexis Park Hotel, 375 E. Harmon Ave., 89109, tel. 702/ 796-3300. Jacket and tie suggested. Reservations required. AE, CB, DC, MC, V. Dinner only.*

★ **31** **Savoia.** This eclectic Italian restaurant in the St. Tropez
$$ hotel, with its upscale pizzas and large fish menu, is a fine place for a relaxed business dinner or a more casual business lunch—either al fresco on one of the patios, or indoors in a comfortable booth. An oak-fired oven, located in view of most diners, creates a variety of imaginative pizzas, from Cajun (with andouille sausage) to baby eggplant and smoked gouda. Recommended specialties include *bouillabaisse antiboise*, a chowder of lobster, shrimp, crab claws, clams, mussels, fresh fish, and vegetables in a saffron-flavored broth, and braised quail on a bed of spaghetti squash with port wine. *St. Tropez Hotel, 455 E. Harmon Ave., 89109, tel. 702/731-5446. Casual but neat. Reservations suggested. AE, CB, DC, MC, V.*

## Downtown

★ ⑩ **Andre's.** This local favorite in an old white stone house sur-
$$$$ rounded by lush foliage resembles a French country man-
or, but is just a few blocks from downtown's Glitter Gulch.
Beamed ceilings, burgundy velvet chairs, lace-covered tables, and European objets d'art in four intimate dining
rooms provide a serene, Old World setting for business
talks and fine dining. Owner/chef Andre Rochet has
crafted an imaginative nouvelle French/Continental
menu, which changes nightly. Favorites include lobster
sausage with crayfish sauce, followed by magret of duck
with blueberry sauce, or a reliable, well-prepared cha-
teaubriand. Andre's carries both rare vintages and more
moderately priced labels in one of the largest wine cellars
in Las Vegas. *401 S. 6th St., tel. 702/385–5016. Jacket and
tie suggested. Reservations required. AE, DC, MC, V.
Dinner only.*

## West Side

⑲ **Santa Fe.** This large, airy Southwestern restaurant, off
$$ the beaten path, is worth finding for a stylish but casual
lunch or dinner. Mexican tile floors, high ceilings, stained
glass, and desert plants set the tone for the cuisine, an in-
teresting synthesis of Mexican, Spanish, American Indi-
an, and early American ingredients and cooking styles.
Specialties include sizzling beef, chicken, or pork fajitas,
served with tortillas freshly baked in the restaurant's own
tortilleria. The unusual Aztec soup is a rich chicken broth
with vegetables over tortilla strips topped with cheese.
*4930 W. Flamingo Rd., tel. 702/871–7119. Casual but
neat. Reservations suggested for dinner. AE, CB, D, DC,
MC, V.*

## Northwest

★ ⑪ **Aristocrat.** This elegant, quietly sophisticated spot is off
$$$ the beaten track (about 10 minutes off the Strip), but lo-
cals consider it one of the top restaurants in Las Vegas.
The setting is dark and intimate and each of the 13 tables is
surrounded by hanging plants on trellises, which creates
small private dining areas. The relaxed ambience and impeccable service are well suited for a quiet business dinner
or for celebrating a deal. The menu features such Continental classics as beef Wellington and osso bucco, as well
as occasionally flown-in fresh swordfish. The extensive
wine list is thoughtfully chosen. The mood is set by soft
violin music and after-dinner dancing. *850 S. Rancho Dr.,
Town and Country Center, tel. 702/870–1977. Jacket and
tie required. Reservations required. AE, CB, DC, MC, V.
Closed for lunch weekends.*

## Near the University of Las Vegas

㉝ **Marrakech.** For a taste of Morocco, Las Vegas style, this
$$ restaurant has it all: traditionally garbed servers, pillow
seating, inlaid tables, and a belly dancer. Sure it's corny,
but it's also good fun, and the food transcends the fuss.
The fixed-price menu includes Pastilla Royal, a mixture of
ground chicken, almonds, and eggs encased in phyllo
dough and rolled in sugar; flaming lamb brochette on
spears impaled in a whole pineapple; and couscous, the
Moroccan national dish, a bed of tasty semolina topped

with chicken or lamb and vegetables. Patrons are encouraged to eat with their fingers—come with colleagues or business contacts with whom you're willing to let loose. *4632 Maryland Pkwy., across from UNLV, tel. 702/736-7655. Casual but neat. Reservations suggested. AE, MC, V. Dinner only. Closed Mon.*

# FREE TIME

## Fitness

*Hotel Facilities*
Spas in most major casino hotels accept nonguests for a daily fee; best are in the **Desert Inn** (tel. 702/733-4444), which charges $17.50 plus tax for use of the whirlpool, sauna, pool, and weight room; **Caesar's** (tel. 702/731-7110), with a steam sauna, whirlpool, and gym, charges $15 a day.

*Health Clubs*
Guests at Strip resorts pay a $15 fee to use the **Sports Club Las Vegas** (3025 Industrial Rd., tel. 702/733-8999). The **Las Vegas Athletic Club** at four locations (1070 E. Sahara Ave., tel. 702/733-1919; 3315 Spring Mountain, tel. 702/362-3720; 5090 S. Maryland Pkwy., tel. 702/795-2582; 3830 Flamingo Rd., tel. 702/451-2526) offers everything from a pool and weight room, to Nautilus and racquetball for $10 a day or $25 for a week-long pass.

*Jogging*
Good places to jog are the University of Las Vegas campus, a five-minute drive from the Strip, or the grounds of most resort hotels, such as the Desert Inn and the Mirage.

## Shopping

For unique gaming gifts try **Bonanza—World's Largest Gift Shop** (across from the Sahara Hotel; 2440 Las Vegas Blvd. S, tel. 702/385-7359) or the **Gambler's General Store** (800 S. Main St., tel. 702/382-9903). The best boutiques for upscale clothing and jewelry are in the major hotels on the Strip; the **Esplanade**, in the Mirage (tel. 702/791-7111), has the trendiest stores in town; Caesars Palace's arcade features Gucci, Ted Lapidus and Cino. **Fashion Show Mall** (3200 Las Vegas Blvd. S, tel. 702/369-8382), located on the Strip across the street from the Desert Inn, has 140 stores, including Neiman Marcus, Saks, Dillards, and Goldwaters.

## Diversions

It's hard to ignore the wide variety of options for **gambling**. Players can choose from blackjack, baccarat, poker, craps, roulette, wheel of fortune, keno, pai gow, slots, red dog, bingo, sports, and race book. Many casinos offer free lessons.

Next door to the Riviera is the **Candlelight Wedding Chapel** (2855 Las Vegas Blvd. S, tel. 702/735-4179) where couples line up for 15-minute ceremonies. Just walk in and take a seat.

**Hoover Dam,** one of the wonders of the modern world, is just 25 miles from Las Vegas on lovely Lake Mead. Ask at your hotel about half-day bus tours or drive there yourself.

The **Imperial Palace Automobile Museum** (3535 Las Vegas Blvd. S, tel. 702/731–3311) displays more than 200 vintage cars on the first level of the hotel's parking garage.

The **Liberace Museum** (1775 E. Tropicana Ave., tel. 702/798–5595) has the flamboyant showman's costumes, pianos, candelabras, and customized cars on show.

At **Red Rock Canyon** (visitors center, tel. 702/363–1921), about 20 miles west of town, brilliant colors turn magnificent sandstone formations into works of art.

**Ripley's Believe It or Not** (202 E. Fremont St., tel. 702/385–4011), downtown in the Four Queens Hotel, features more than 1,000 artifacts, inventions, and wax figures.

**University of Nevada, Las Vegas Museum of Natural History** (4504 Maryland Pkwy., tel. 702/739–3381) features exhibits of live desert animals, and displays relating to the archaeology, anthropology, and natural history of Nevada and the Southwest.

The 56,000-acre **Valley of Fire State Park** is 55 miles northeast of Las Vegas. The unusual colors of the rock formations, as well as the petroglyphs and pictographs—believed to be the work of the Basket Maker and Anasazi Pueblo Indians—make this a worthwhile excursion. The visitor center (Hwy. 169, Overton, tel. 702/397–2088) has exhibits, films, lectures, and slide shows.

## Professional Sports

The city's baseball club, the **Las Vegas Stars** (tel. 702/386–7200), plays at Cashman Field. Catch the basketball team, the **Las Vegas Silver Streaks** (tel. 702/798–6464), at the Thomas Mack Center.

## The Arts

What Las Vegas excels in are big productions—a combination of multimillion dollar shows and top-name stars such as Frank Sinatra, the Pointer Sisters, Bill Cosby, and Wayne Newton. The most lavish productions take place at the Flamingo, the Hilton, Bally's, the Riviera, and the Tropicana. There is also less glitzy entertainment in town, however. The Las Vegas Civic Ballet performs at the **Charleston Heights Art Center** (300 S. Torrey Pines Dr., tel. 702/386–6383). Film classics are shown here as well. The **Reed Whipple Cultural Center** (821 Las Vegas Blvd. N, tel. 702/362–6211) hosts concerts and film festivals. The University of Las Vegas's **Ham Hall** and **Bayley Theater** (4505 S. Maryland Pkwy., tel. 702/739–3801) offer performances by the Las Vegas Symphony and the Nevada Dance Theater. For rock music, the **Aladdin Theatre for the Performing Arts** (3667 Las Vegas Blvd. S, tel. 702/736–0250) and **Thomas and Mack Center** (4505 S. Maryland Pkwy., tel. 702/739–3900) are the main venues.

For major concerts and sporting events, call **Ticketron** (2303 E. Flamingo Ave., tel. 702/791–3344 or 800/992–2128). **USA Hosts** (tel. 800/634–6133) will mail you a show guide or take reservations (tel. 702/733–3451) when you're in town; or you can stop at their booth in the Flamingo Hilton Hotel on the Strip.

## After Hours

Hotel lounges provide some of the best, least-expensive shows in the city and offer everything from sophisticated blues and country to hard rock.

*Bars and Lounges*
For a place subdued enough for private conversation, try the mid-Strip **Peppermill Inn** (2985 Las Vegas Blvd. S, tel. 702/735–7635) or **Capo's** (1487 E. Flamingo Rd., tel. 702/737–0727), an insider place where celebrities often congregate. An upscale crowd mingles and dances in the chic **Botany's** (1700 E. Flamingo Rd., tel. 702/737–6662). **TGI Friday's** (1800 E. Flamingo Rd., tel. 702/732–9905) is popular with young suit-and-tie locals after work. **Tarkanians** (4550 Maryland Pkwy., tel. 702/795–4667) and **Sneakers** (2250 E. Tropicana Ave., tel. 702/798–0272) draw a sports-minded set.

*Hotel Lounge Acts*
**Cleopatra's Barge** (tel. 702/731–7110) in Caesars Palace has continuous entertainment on a unique floating barge from 10 PM. The **Winner's Choice Lounge** (tel. 702/733–4444) in the Desert Inn features music for the more conservative, from 3:30 PM. Sixties rock 'n' roll is the mainstay from 8 PM at the **Landmark's Casino Lounge** (364 Convention Center Dr., tel. 702/733–1110). Downtown swings with the best jazz at the **French Quarter Lounge** (202 E. Fremont St., tel. 702/385–4011) in the Four Queens Hotel.

*Comedy Clubs*
The top choices are **The Comedy Store** at the Dunes (3650 Las Vegas Blvd. S, tel. 702/737–4110) and the **Improv Room** (tel. 702/734–5110) at the Riviera.

*Dance Clubs*
The **Shark Club** (75 E. Harmon Ave., tel. 702/795–7525) has a multilevel dance floor. Rock to sounds of the '60s at **The Hop** (1650 E. Tropicana Ave., tel. 702/736–2020), or kick up your heels to country and western 24 hours a day at the **Silver Dollar Saloon** (2501 E. Charleston Blvd., tel. 702/382–6921). For hard rock try **Moby Grape** (1131 E. Tropicana Ave. tel. 702/736–3311), where the jeans and T-shirt set listen to live bands after 11 PM nightly.

*For Singles*
Places listed above are all good choices for singles. Add **Tramps** (4405 W. Flamingo Rd., tel. 702/871–1424) to the list of cocktail-hour spots for the under-35 set, and **Carlos Murphy's** (4770 S. Maryland Pkwy., tel. 702/798–5541) for rowdy, shoulder-to-shoulder dancing. Those with more mature tastes might enjoy the **Atrium Lounge** in the Holiday Casino (3475 Las Vegas Blvd. S, tel. 702/369–5000), which features music from the '30s, '40s, and '50s.

# Los Angeles

*by Norman Sklarewitz and Deborah Sroloff*

While other parts of the country worried about sluggish business conditions in recent years, Angelenos remained typically upbeat. To a large extent, the area's wide range of industries helped insulate it from wide economic swings. However, the country's budget deficit crisis has triggered nervous talk of slashed orders for military aircraft and missiles, which are manufactured in Southern California, and aerospace industry layoffs were reaching an alarming level in 1990. In addition, a recession in real estate, another focus of the Southern California economy, has had a carryover effect on construction-related businesses.

There's hope, however, that Pentagon cutbacks will be offset by a surge of orders for commercial jetliners and commercial communications satellites. Moreover, a lowering in the cost of housing is likely to draw businesses for which relocation costs had previously been prohibitive. And foreign investors, particularly the Japanese, have continued to acquire everything from "trophy" skyscrapers to golf clubs and resorts, reflecting continuing investor confidence in the city's future.

Supermarket tabloids to the contrary, not all Angelenos are narcissistic diet fanatics who make three-picture deals via cellular car phones while they navigate the freeways in convertibles. While admittedly not Hometown U.S.A., Los Angeles is, in the main, a normal (albeit fun-loving) city—or more precisely, a collection of cities and communities. A stockbroker may live in quiet, bucolic Thousand Oaks and commute 90 minutes each way to Downtown L.A. Or a studio executive may live in sunny Manhattan Beach and drive up to Century City to work.

L.A.'s business pace is often more relaxed than most Easterners are accustomed to. But that doesn't mean people don't work hard. Because of the time difference with the East Coast, stockbrokers and others connected with the financial and commodity markets are at their screens by 6:30 AM. Those who deal with Asia, on the other hand, are waiting at 5 PM for fax and phone calls, when the business day starts in Tokyo and Hong Kong. In the aerospace and high-tech industries, engineers and technicians start work at 8 AM, and many first production shifts begin at 7. However, toilers in the less structured industries are convinced that a script draft, marketing proposal, or financial plan can be read just as effectively at poolside as in an office. And an astounding amount of business is done over lunch and dinner, often at much trendier restaurants than businesspeople frequent in other cities.

## Top Employers

| Employer | Type of Enterprise | Parent*/ Headquarters |
| --- | --- | --- |
| Douglas Aircraft Corp. | Aircraft manufacturer | McDonnell Douglas/ St. Louis |
| General Telephone Co. of Calif. | Telecommunications | Santa Monica, CA |
| Hughes Aircraft Co. | Satellites manufacturer | General Motors/ Detroit |
| Lockheed Corp. | Aircraft manufacturer | Calabasas, CA |
| May Department Stores | Retail | May Co./ St. Louis |
| Northrop Corp. | Aircraft manufacturer | Los Angeles |
| Pacific Bell | Telecommunications | Pacific Telesis/ San Francisco |
| Rockwell International | Aerospace, electronics manufacturer | El Segundo, CA |
| Southern California Gas Co. | Utility | Pacific Enterprises/Los Angeles |
| The Vons Companies, Inc. | Supermarkets | El Monte, CA |

*if applicable

## ESSENTIAL INFORMATION

### Climate

Los Angeles enjoys pleasant weather most of the year: warm, sometimes hot, days and cool evenings. Rain does fall from time to time in winter, but even in January it's common to have brilliant, sunny days with temperatures into the 60s and 70s. Spring and early summer are marked by gloomy, overcast mornings; the low clouds invariably burn off by early afternoon. Summers are hot and smoggy—L.A. is making progress in cleaning its air, but those suffering from asthma or other respiratory problems will want to take it easy on smoggy days.

By no means is the entire Los Angeles basin subject to uniform temperatures. In summer, temperatures in the inland valleys—San Fernando and San Gabriel—can climb into the 100s while the coastal communities are in the 70s or 80s.

What follows are the average daily maximum and minimum temperatures for Los Angeles.

| Jan. | 64F | 18C | Feb. | 64F | 18C | Mar. | 66F | 19C |
|------|-----|-----|------|-----|-----|------|-----|-----|
|      | 44  | 7   |      | 46  | 8   |      | 48  | 9   |
| Apr. | 66F | 19C | May  | 69F | 21C | June | 71F | 22C |
|      | 51  | 11  |      | 53  | 12  |      | 57  | 14  |
| July | 75F | 24C | Aug. | 75F | 24C | Sept.| 75F | 24C |
|      | 60  | 16  |      | 62  | 17  |      | 60  | 16  |
| Oct. | 73F | 23C | Nov. | 71F | 22C | Dec. | 66F | 19C |
|      | 65  | 13  |      | 48  | 9   |      | 46  | 8   |

## Airports

**Los Angeles International Airport,** or LAX, as it is called, fronts the ocean in the southwest corner of the city, 20 miles from Downtown and 12 miles from Beverly Hills. Thanks to a $700-million modernization and expansion program carried out for the 1984 Olympics, LAX has solved most of its congestion problems (except on major holidays, when you should allow up to an extra hour to reach your terminal). Some 80 airlines now serve Southern California through LAX. Most foreign airlines use the Bradley International Terminal; the U.S.-based carriers use the seven other main terminals. All are connected by well-marked shuttles. On the edge of LAX is the West Imperial Terminal, which is used for charter and corporate aircraft as well as MGM Grand Air and LA Air flights. LAX has both nearby short-term parking and less expensive long-term parking on lots served by frequent shuttle buses. For parking information, call tel. 213/646–5707. For general airport information, call tel. 213/646–5252.

The **Burbank-Glendale-Pasadena Airport,** known to locals as Burbank Airport, is a small, low-hassle airport that is ideal for travelers headed to the San Fernando Valley, Glendale/Pasadena area, and Downtown L.A., which is just 13 miles away. Eight major airlines, including Alaska, American, Delta, TWA, United, and USAir, fly in and out of Burbank. Call tel. 818/840–8847 for general information.

**Ontario International Airport,** in neighboring San Bernardino County, is served by 12 airlines, including United, American, Continental, Delta, Alaska, USAir, Northwest, and Southwest. Ontario, which is 35 miles east of downtown L.A., serves communities in eastern L.A. County as well as such cities as San Bernardino and Riverside. Call tel. 714/983–8282 for information.

## Airport Business Facilities

**Los Angeles International Airport. Mutual of Omaha Business Service Centers** (in Terminals 1, 4, and 7, tel. 213/646–7934) all have fax machines, photocopying, notary public, secretarial service, baggage storage, Western Union, travel insurance, cash advance, Federal Express dropoff, portable fax and cellular phone rentals, phone suites, and conference rooms with catering service. **Skytel** (International Terminal, tel. 213/417–0200) is a mini-hotel with rooms rented by the hour.

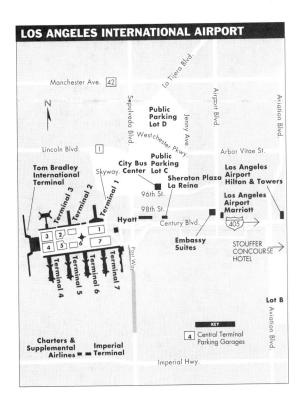

**LOS ANGELES INTERNATIONAL AIRPORT**

Manchester Ave. 42
La Tijera Blvd.
Airport Blvd.
Aviation Blvd.
Sepulveda Blvd.
Jenny Ave.
Public Parking Lot D
Westchester Pkwy.
Lincoln Blvd. 1
Arbor Vitae St.
Public Parking Lot C
City Bus Center
Skyway
Tom Bradley International Terminal
Sheraton Plaza La Reina
Los Angeles Airport Hilton & Towers
Terminal 3
Terminal 2
Terminal 1
96th St.
Los Angeles Airport Marriott
98th St.
405
Hyatt
3 2 1
4 5 6 7
Century Blvd.
Post Way
Terminal 4
Terminal 5
Terminal 6
Terminal 7
Embassy Suites
STOUFFER CONCOURSE HOTEL
Lot B
Aviation Blvd.
KEY
4 Central Terminal Parking Garages
Charters & Supplemental Airlines
Imperial Terminal
Imperial Hwy.

## Airlines

**Alaska Airlines,** tel. 800/426–0333.
**American,** tel. 213/935–6045 or 800/433–7300.
**America West,** tel. 800/247–5692.
**Continental,** tel. 213/271–8733, 213/772–6000, or 800/525–0280.
**Delta,** tel. 213/386–5510, 818/247–0700, or 800/221–1212.
**Hawaiian Air,** tel. 800/367–5320.
**Midway,** tel. 800/621–5700.
**Northwest,** tel. 213/380–1511 (domestic), 800/447–4747 (international).
**Pan Am,** tel. 800/221–1111.
**Southwest Airlines,** tel. 213/485–1221 or 800/531–5601.
**TWA,** tel. 213/858–8811, 213/484–2244, or 800/221–2000.
**United,** tel. 213/550–1400, 213/772–2121, or 800/241–6522.
**USAir,** tel. 213/935–5005 or 800/428–4322.

## Between LAX and L.A. Destinations

*By Taxi*
Cab stands are at the arrival level. Cabs take about 30 minutes in the best of conditions to get Downtown, but during rush hours (6–9 AM and 3–7 PM) and sometimes throughout the day, the trip can take an hour. Cost: about $24 to Downtown and about $22 to the Beverly Hills/Century City area. **LA Taxi** (tel. 213/412–8000) has a flat $24 rate

from Downtown to LAX, but the fare isn't offered the other way.

*By Shuttle Van*
The explosion in shuttle vans has given airport travelers a convenient, less expensive alternative to taxis. Vans charge a flat rate per person (about $11 to Downtown and $9–$15 to the Century City/Beverly Hills area; the second person in the same party pays less), and they make no more than three stops per vanload. Vans pick up passengers at clearly marked stops outside each baggage-claim area. For return runs to any of the airports, call the shuttle company 24 hours in advance for a pickup. Depending on your hotel's location, allow 1½–3 hours before flight departure. The major shuttle firms are **Super Shuttle** (tel. 213/338–1111), which has the largest fleet and courtesy phones in all terminal baggage-claim areas; **City Shuttle** (tel. 213/419–4000 or 800/262–7433); **Amtrans Shuttle** (tel. 213/532–5999 or 800/356–8671), which travels throughout Southern California; **Airway Shuttle** (tel. 213/769–5555 or 800/446–5766); and **Flightline Airport Shuttle** (tel. 213/971–8265).

*By Bus*
L.A.'s sprawl makes bus travel by far the slowest, least convenient way to get from LAX to town. If you must take the bus, head for the **Rapid Transit District (RTD)** (tel. 213/626–4455) bus center just outside parking lot C. From the arrival area, take the free airport shuttle bus marked "Lot C" to the parking lot, then walk over to the bus departure islands. Buses depart regularly for Downtown, West Hollywood, Long Beach, the South Bay communities, and Van Nuys. Cost: $1.10; seniors and the disabled, 55¢.

## Car Rentals

At LAX, rental cars are kept in surrounding areas, but the major rental companies have reservation desks at arrival levels, outside each baggage claim area. Pickup vans from rental car lots circle the airport regularly.

**Alamo,** tel. 800/327–9633.
**Avis,** tel. 800/331–1212.
**Budget,** tel. 800/527–0700.
**Dollar,** tel. 800/421–6878.
**Hertz,** tel. 800/654–3131.
**LAX Express,** tel. 800/523–9773.
**Luxury Line,** tel. 213/659–5555 or 800/826–7805 (reserved luxury and sports cars are delivered to customers at LAX; car phones available).
**National,** tel. 800/227–7368.
**Rent-A-Wreck,** tel. 213/478–0676 or 800/423–2158.

## Emergencies

*Doctors*
**Physicians Referral Service** of the L.A. County Medical Association (tel. 213/483–6122), **Psychiatric Referral Service** of the Southern California Psychiatric Society (tel. 213/450–4611).

*Dentists*
**Dentists Referral Service** of the L.A. Dental Society (tel. 213/380–7669).

*Hospitals*
The following hospitals and medical centers have 24-hour emergency rooms and outpatient facilities for nonemergency medical problems: **Cedars-Sinai Medical Center** (8700 Beverly Blvd., L.A., tel. 213/855–5000; emergency room, tel. 213/855–6517); **Hospital of the Good Samaritan** (616 S. Witmer St., Downtown, tel. 213/977–2121; physicians referral, tel. 213/977–2533; 24-hour Ambulatory Care Center, tel. 213/975–1239); **St. Vincent Medical Center** (2131 W. 3rd St., Downtown, tel. 213/484–7111; physicians referral, tel. 213/484–7444); **UCLA Medical Center,** 10822 Le Conte, Westwood, tel. 213/825–0881; emergency room, tel. 213/825–2111).

## Important Addresses and Numbers

**Audiovisual rentals.** AIMM/MFI-Rents (5057 W. Washington Blvd., tel. 213/931–2466 or 800/356–2466), Audio Visual Headquarters (Beverly Hilton Hotel, 9876 Wilshire Blvd., Beverly Hills, tel. 213/205–0054), Visionmaster (1470 W. Hold Ave., Pomona, tel. 714/622–3306 or 800/851–5415).

**Chambers of Commerce.** Beverly Hills Chamber of Commerce (239 S. Beverly Dr., Beverly Hills, tel. 213/271–8126), Los Angeles Chamber of Commerce (404 S. Bixel St., tel. 213/629–0602), West Hollywood Chamber of Commerce (147 N. Robertson Blvd., West Hollywood, tel. 213/859–8613).

**Computer rentals.** Computer Rental Center (975 Michillinda Ave., Pasadena, tel. 213/231–6784 or 800/727–3685), Ganton Temporary Computer (1201 S. Flower St., Downtown, tel. 213/785–9319), Micro Computer Rental (1244 Westwood Blvd., Westwood, tel. 213/470–1421), Rent-a-Mac (3944 Wilshire Blvd., tel. 213/651–2011).

**Convention & exhibition centers.** Los Angeles Convention & Exhibit Center (1201 S. Figueroa St., Downtown, tel. 213/741–1151), Long Beach Convention & Entertainment Center (300 E. Ocean Blvd., Long Beach, tel. 213/436–3636).

**Fax services.** A Super Facsimile (400 S. Beverly Dr., suite 214, Beverly Hills, tel. 213/553–6161), Copy Mat (24 hours; 6301 Sunset Blvd., Hollywood, tel. 213/461–1222; 5750 Wilshire Blvd., Mid-Wilshire, tel. 213/938–0653; 11988 Wilshire Blvd., West L.A., tel. 213/207–5952), Kinko (731 W. 7th St., Downtown, tel. 213/627–6441), Telex All Services (512 S. San Vincente, West Hollywood, tel. 213/658–6341).

**Formal-wear rentals.** Gary's Tux Shop (8621 Wilshire Blvd., Beverly Hills, tel. 213/659–7296), Tuxedo Center (7360 Sunset Blvd., Hollywood, tel. 213/874–4200, 4738 Woodman Ave., Sherman Oaks, tel. 818/784–8242, 930 Wilshire Blvd., Santa Monica, tel. 213/393–6707), Wilshire Tuxedo (3822 Wilshire Blvd., Mid-Wilshire, tel. 213/388–2297).

**Gift shops.** Candy: Ultimate Nut & Candy Co. (Farmer's Market, 3rd and Fairfax, Wilshire district, tel. 213/938–1555); Florists: Broadway Florists (218 W. 5th St., Downtown, tel. 213/626–5511), Crossley's Flowers (7819 Beverly Blvd., Beverly Hills, tel. 213/274–4990); Gift Baskets: Jurgensen's (2 locations: 316 N. Beverly Dr., Beverly Hills, tel. 213/858–7814; 601 S. Lake Ave., Pasadena, tel. 213/681–4861), Lawry's California Center (570 W. Ave. 26, East L.A., tel. 213/224–6800).

**Graphic design studios.** The Art Director (5512 Wilshire Blvd., Mid-Wilshire, tel. 213/933–9668), Gonz Graphics (3325 Wilshire Blvd., Suite 305, Mid-Wilshire, tel. 213/385–4815).

**Hairstylists.** Unisex: Alex Roldan Salon (Le Bel Age Hotel, 1020 N. San Vicente Blvd., West Hollywood, tel. 213/855–1113), Juan-Juan Salon (9667 Wilshire Blvd., Beverly Hills, tel. 213/278–5826), José Eber (2 Rodeo Dr., Beverly Hills, tel. 213/278–7646), Style Council (924 Wilshire Blvd., Santa Monica, tel. 213/395–7892), Vidal Sassoon (405 N. Rodeo Dr., Beverly Hills, tel. 213/451–8586).

**Information hot lines.** Highway conditions (tel. 213/626–7231), L.A. Convention and Visitors Bureau (tel. 213/689–8822), Traveler's Aid (tel. 213/686–0950).

**Limousine services.** Dav-El Livery, Beverly Hills, 24-hour service (tel. 213/550–0070 or 213/645–8865), Fleetwood Limousine, West L.A. (tel. 213/208–0209), Fox Limousine Service, LAX area, multilingual chauffeurs, 24-hour service (tel. 213/641–9626), V.I.P. Limousine Service, West L.A., also vans and wagons, tel. 213/273–1505).

**Liquor stores.** Beverly Hills Liquor Castle (212 S. Beverly Dr., Beverly Hills, tel. 213/273–6000), Liquor Locker (8161 Sunset Blvd., Hollywood, tel. 213/656–1140), Gil Turner's (9101 Sunset Blvd., West Hollywood, tel. 213/271–0030), Gourmet Wine & Spirits (505 S. Flower St., Downtown, tel. 213/489–2666), King's Liquors (3102 Santa Monica Blvd., Santa Monica, tel. 213/828–7100).

**Mail delivery, overnight.** Airborne Express (tel. 800/826–0144), DHL Worldwide Express (tel. 213/973–7300), Federal Express (tel. 213/687–9767), UPS (tel. 213/626–1551), U.S. Postal Service/Express Mail (24-hour; tel. 213/337–8846).

**Messenger services.** A & S Messenger & Courier (tel. 213/657–0808), Express Messenger Service (tel. 213/658–6793 in Beverly Hills, 213/629–9159, Downtown), Modern Messenger & Delivery Service (tel. 213/873–4262), Red Arrow Messenger (tel. 213/276–2388 in Beverly Hills/Century City, 213/626–6881, Downtown), Superrush (tel. 213/622–6541).

**Office space rentals.** Gateway Suites (1801 Ave. of the Stars, Century City, tel. 213/553–6341), Professional Suites at Wilshire (6500 Wilshire Blvd., Suite 500, Wilshire District, tel. 213/651–2333), Raleigh Executive Suites (11444 W. Olympic Blvd., 10th floor, West L.A., tel. 213/312–9500), Roxbury Executive Suites (445 S. Figueroa Blvd., Downtown, tel. 213/612–7700), United Business Center (624 S. Grand Ave., Downtown, tel. 213/689–1454).

**Pharmacies, late-night.** Horton & Converse Pharmacies (several locations: 7th Street Marketplace, 735 S. Figueroa St., Downtown, tel. 213/623–2838; 11600 Wilshire Blvd., West L.A., tel. 213/478–0801; 9201 Sunset Blvd., West Hollywood, tel. 213/272–0488; 6625 Van Nuys Blvd., Van Nuys, tel. 818/782–6251; 2001 Santa Monica Blvd., Santa Monica, tel. 213/829–3401), Rexall Square Drug (8490 Beverly Blvd., West Hollywood, tel. 213/653–4616).

**Radio stations, all-news.** KFWB 980 AM, KNX 1070 AM.

**Secretarial services.** California Transcribing Service (6010 Wilshire Blvd., Suite 400, West L.A., tel. 213/857–5566), Century Secretarial Service (2040 Ave. of the Stars, Century City, tel. 213/277–3329), Helen's Legal Support Services (601 W. 5th St., Suite 500, Downtown, tel. 213/614–1142), McCullough Transcribing Service (527 W. 7th St., Suite 301, Downtown, tel. 213/628–7173), Nancy Ray Secretarial Service (9401 Wilshire Blvd., Suite 650, Beverly Hills, tel. 213/273–7244).

**Stationery Supplies.** The Green Butterfly (136 Santa Monica Pl., Santa Monica, tel. 213/451–8485), McManus and Morgan (2506 W. 7th St., Downtown, tel. 213/387–4433).

**Taxis.** There are taxi stands outside major hotels, but otherwise you'll have to call for a cab—and you'll have to call a cab company in your area. Airport: LA Taxi (tel. 213/412–8000); Beverly Hills and West L.A.: Beverly Hills Cab (tel. 213/273–6611) and Rodeo Cab (tel. 213/659–9722); Downtown: LA Taxi (tel. 213/627–7000) and L.A. Checker Cab (tel. 213/393–8905 or 213/201–0775); Hollywood: United Independent Taxi (tel. 213/653–5050); West L.A.: Blue & Yellow Cab (tel. 213/205–0656) and Independent Cab (tel. 213/659–8294).

**Train information.** Amtrak (Union Station, 800 N. Alameda St., tel. 213/624–0171).

**Travel agencies.** American Express (several locations: 901 W. 7th St., Downtown, tel. 213/627–4800; 8493 W. 3rd St., West Hollywood, tel. 213/659–1682; 327 N. Beverly Blvd., Beverly Hills, tel. 213/272–9778), Carlson Travel (2040 Ave. of the Stars, Century City, tel. 213/556–2506; 6916 Hollywood Blvd., Hollywood, tel. 213/466–7771; 633 W. 5th St., 25th floor, Downtown, tel. 213/622–3418; 8271 Melrose Ave., West Hollywood, tel. 213/655–4103), Travel Unlimited (9107 Wilshire Blvd., Suite 711, Beverly Hills, tel. 213/274–8826).

**Weather** (tel. 213/554–1212, 213/209–7211).

# LODGING

Visitors to Los Angeles soon find out what the natives have long known: that one spends an inordinate amount of time in automobiles, traveling from one destination to another. Since, as one wag put it, Los Angeles is a series of suburbs in search of a city, everything seems incredibly far away from everything else. With that caveat in mind, choose your hotel carefully. If you have television industry business to conduct, roost yourself near your particular network—the CBS, NBC, and ABC studios are all miles apart. Lockheed Aircraft is over the horizon in Calabasas, while Douglas is down Long Beach way, and Northrup is in Century City. As for film studios, they tend to stay as far apart as snakes and mongooses.

A large number of aerospace and high-tech industries, including Hughes, Rockwell, Ford Aerospace, TRW, and McDonnell Douglas—as well as U.S. Air Force space-related operations and oil refineries—are located near LAX. Consequently, many major hotel chains are in this area, along with upscale motels. Because of their location (and convenience to the San Diego Freeway), these hotels accommodate major conferences and conventions as well as smaller business meetings.

The major airport hotels are located on or just off Century Boulevard, which leads directly into the LAX terminals. Century is not beneath flight paths, so aircraft noise isn't a problem. Unless otherwise indicated, hotel vans cruise the terminals every 10 minutes or so to pick up and drop off guests. Because the hotels at LAX are business-traveler oriented, standard rooms tend to be small.

Fortunately, nearly every urban area and suburban satellite commercial zone features a first-rate hostelry—sometimes, even a world-class one. Many of the older hotels, such as the Regent Beverly Wilshire and the Beverly Hills Hotel, have recently undergone extensive refurbishing. And, considering the rather eclectic local architecture, you're bound to find an inn to suit any aesthetic sensibility, from nouveau mission to postmodern to glitzy.

For organizational purposes, the hotels in this section are grouped into five main areas: Downtown, Hollywood/West Hollywood, Westside (including Beverly Hills, Century City, Bel Air, and Westwood), San Fernando Valley (including Universal City, Burbank, and Warner Center), and Airport/South Bay (LAX and the L.A. Harbor area).

Most hotels listed here offer special corporate rates and weekend packages; inquire when making reservations.

Highly recommended lodgings in each price category are indicated by a ★.

| Category | Cost* |
|---|---|
| $$$$ (Very Expensive) | over $175 |
| $$$ (Expensive) | $125–$175 |
| $$ (Moderate) | under $125 |

*All prices are for a standard double room, single occupancy, excluding tax (12% in L.A., 12.2% in Beverly Hills).*

*Numbers in the margin correspond to numbered hotel locations on the Los Angeles Lodging and Dining maps.*

## Downtown

**Biltmore.** With its Spanish rococo and Italian Renaissance decor, this gorgeous 1920s landmark underwent a painstaking $10-million renovation in 1987. This lush, opulent beauty has soaring, vaulted ceilings, richly colored frescoes, and chandeliers fairly dripping with crystal. The
$$$

# COASTAL LOS ANGELES

# BEVERLY HILLS AND HOLLYWOOD

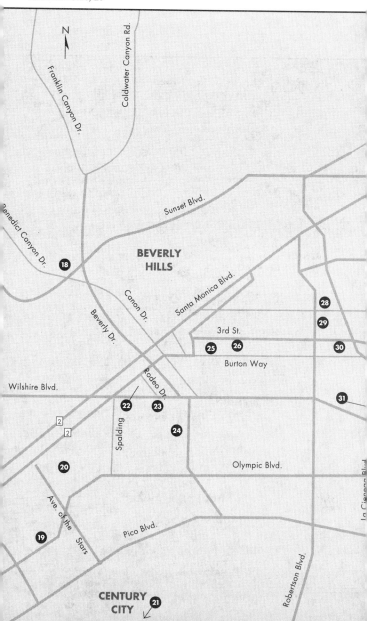

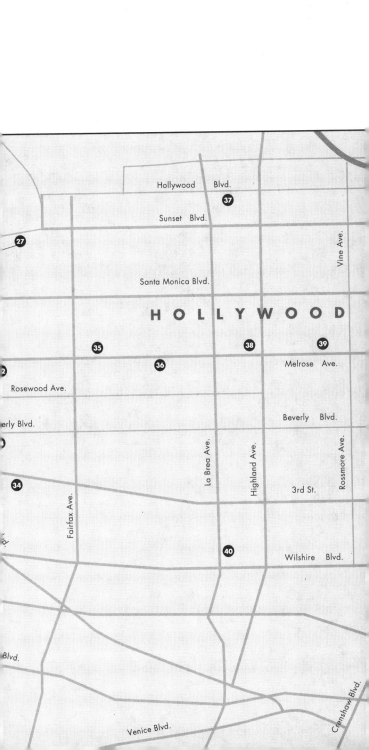

# DOWNTOWN LOS ANGELES

**Lodging**
Biltmore, **50**
Bonaventure, **47**
Checkers, **49**
Hyatt Regency, **44**
Los Angeles Hilton and Towers, **41**
New Otani Hotel and Gardens, **52**
Sheraton Grande, **46**

**Dining**
Bernard's, **50**
Checkers, **49**
Crocodile Cafe, **53**
Empress Pavilion, **51**
Engine Co. No. 28, **42**
Parkway Grill, **54**
Rex, Il Ristorante, **48**
Seventh Street Bistro, **45**
The Tower, **43**

reasonably large, high-ceilinged guest rooms feature most of the modern amenities, although bathrooms still need some upgrading, and the single-line bedside phones don't reach the fold-down work desk. Some rooms have had their original millwork, fine moldings, and other Beaux-Arts details lovingly restored; other rooms are decorated in a more sleek, contemporary fashion. Biltmore is home to the largest hotel health facility (*see* Fitness, below) in the city. Bernard's (*see* Dining, below), the hotel's restaurant, is highly regarded. The Biltmore is well located for Downtown businesspeople—the Grand Avenue and Gallery bars (*see* After Hours, below) are popular afterwork meeting places. However, this is a neighborhood in transition, and Pershing Square, adjacent to the hotel, is a haven for the homeless. *506 S. Grand Ave., 90013, tel. 213/624–1011; in CA, 800/252–0175; in U.S., 800/421–8000; fax 213/612–1628. Managing dir., Randall Villareal. 660 rooms, 40 suites. AE, CB, DC, MC, V.*

**47**
**$$** **Bonaventure.** A staple location for numerous futuristic Hollywood films, the Blade Runner-esque Bonaventure is a 35-story hotel comprising five slick, cylindrical glass-sheathed towers. Inside, conventioneers and tour groups swarm like drones, milling in confusion around the circular atrium lobby, with its byzantine network of concrete ramps, whooshing glass elevators, and often-long check-ins lines. Thirty meeting rooms, including one that holds 3,000, make this the largest convention hotel smack in the center of Downtown. Rooms, many with great views, and all with generic, contemporary corporate decor, are on the cramped side. The 24th floor was recently converted into an executive club floor as part of a major renovation. The Bonaventure is almost a city unto itself—albeit a rather chilly, incoherently planned one: There are 24 shops, a disco, 19 restaurants, and two lounges, including the revolving BonaVista on the 34th floor. *A Westin hotel. 404 S. Figueroa St., 90071, tel. 213/624–1000 or 800/228–3000, fax 213/612–4800. Managing dir., William P. Lucas. 1,408 rooms, 66 suites. AE, D, DC, MC, V.*

**★ 49**
**$$$$** **Checkers.** Owned by the Ayala Group, which also runs the exquisite Campton Place in San Francisco, Checkers is as intimate and luxurious as a private club, without being the least bit pretentious or stuffy. This elegant, service-oriented smaller hotel is extremely popular with top corporate executives, attorneys, and fast-trackers, and for good reason: Checkers makes you feel important and pampered. This phoenix rose out of the $49-million gutting and renovation of the 1926-vintage Mayflower Hotel in the heart of Downtown. Rooms are on the compact side, but are quietly opulent in muted, soothing shades with expanses of marble, and brass fixtures in the bathrooms. Each room has three two-line phones (with voice mail), and fax machines are available for in-room use at a nominal charge. Among Checkers' many distinctive touches is the cozy mezzanine library, a perfect spot for informal meetings or simply for relaxing. Sports-minded guests are loaned workout garb, and there's a heated lap pool on the rooftop. The eponymous restaurant (*see* Business Breakfasts and Dining, below) is top rate—a destination

# LOS ANGELES HOTEL CHART

| HOTELS | Price Category | Business Services / Banquet capacity | No. of meeting rooms | Secretarial services | Audiovisual equipment | Teletype news service | Computer rentals | In-room modem phone jack | All-news cable channel | Desk | Desk lighting | Bed lighting |
|---|---|---|---|---|---|---|---|---|---|---|---|---|
| Airport Hilton and Towers | $$$ | 2500 | 40 | ✓ | ✓ | - | ✓ | - | ✓ | ◐ | ● | ● |
| Airport Marriott | $$$ | 850 | 37 | ✓ | ✓ | - | - | - | ✓ | ● | ● | ● |
| Beverly Hills Hotel and Bungalows | $$$ | 550 | 6 | ✓ | ✓ | - | ✓ | ✓ | | ● | ● | ● |
| The Biltmore | $$$ | 1000 | 16 | - | ✓ | - | ✓ | - | ✓ | ● | ● | ● |
| Bonaventure | $$ | 2000 | 22 | ✓ | ✓ | - | - | - | ✓ | ◐ | ◐ | ◐ |
| Century City Inn | $$ | 0 | 0 | ✓ | - | - | ✓ | - | ✓ | ◐ | ● | ● |
| Century Plaza | $$$$ | 2500 | 23 | ✓ | ✓ | - | ✓ | ✓ | ✓ | ● | ● | ● |
| Checkers | $$$$ | 70 | 4 | ✓ | ✓ | - | ✓ | ✓ | ✓ | ● | ● | ● |
| Compri Hotel Los Angeles Harbor | $$ | 500 | 7 | - | ✓ | - | - | - | ✓ | ● | ● | ● |
| Embassy Suites | $$ | 180 | 5 | - | - | - | - | ✓ | ✓ | ● | ● | ◐ |
| L'Ermitage | $$$ | 80 | 2 | ✓ | ✓ | - | ✓ | ✓ | | ● | ● | ● |
| Four Seasons | $$$$ | 280 | 11 | ✓ | ✓ | - | ✓ | ✓ | | ● | ● | ● |
| Hilton and Towers | $$$ | 666 | 28 | ✓ | ✓ | - | ✓ | ✓ | | ● | ● | ● |
| Hollywood Roosevelt | $$ | 600 | 9 | - | - | - | - | - | | ● | ● | ● |
| Hotel Bel-Air | $$$$ | 180 | 2 | ✓ | ✓ | - | ✓ | ✓ | | ● | ● | ● |
| Hyatt Regency | $$ | 1500 | 15 | - | ✓ | - | ✓ | - | ✓ | - | - | ◐ |
| New Otani Hotel and Gardens | $$$ | 750 | 8 | - | - | - | - | - | | ● | ● | ● |
| Regent Beverly Wilshire | $$$$ | 800 | 8 | ✓ | ✓ | - | - | ✓ | ✓ | ● | ● | ● |
| St. James's Club | $$$$ | 75 | 3 | ✓ | ✓ | - | ✓ | - | ✓ | ● | ● | ● |

$$$$ = over $175, $$$ = $125 -$175, $$ = under $125.
● good, ◐ fair, ○ poor.
All hotels listed here have photocopying and fax facilities.

| In-Room Amenities | | | | | | | | | | Hotel Amenities | | | | | | |
| Nonsmoking rooms | In-room checkout | Minibar | Pay movies | VCR/Movie rentals | Hairdryer | Toiletries | Room service | Laundry/Dry cleaning | Pressing | Concierge | Barber/Hairdresser | Garage | Courtesy airport transport | Sauna | Pool | Exercise room |
|---|---|---|---|---|---|---|---|---|---|---|---|---|---|---|---|---|
| ✓ | ✓ | - | ✓ | ✓ | ✓ | ● | ◐ | ● | ● | ✓ | ✓ | ✓ | ✓ | ✓ | ● | ● |
| ✓ | ✓ | - | ✓ | - | ✓ | ● | ● | ◐ | ◐ | ✓ | ✓ | ✓ | ✓ | ✓ | ● | ● |
| - | - | - | - | ✓ | ✓ | ● | ● | ● | ● | ✓ | ✓ | ✓ | - | ✓ | ● | ● |
| ✓ | - | ✓ | ✓ | ✓ | ✓ | ● | ● | ● | ● | ✓ | ✓ | ✓ | - | ✓ | ● | ● |
| ✓ | ✓ | ✓ | ✓ | ✓ | ✓ | ◐ | ● | ● | ● | ✓ | ✓ | ✓ | - | - | ● | ○ |
| ✓ | - | - | - | ✓ | - | ◐ | - | ● | ● | - | - | ✓ | - | - | - | - |
| ✓ | ✓ | ✓ | ✓ | ✓ | ✓ | ● | ● | ● | ● | ✓ | ✓ | ✓ | - | ✓ | ● | ● |
| ✓ | - | ✓ | ✓ | - | ✓ | ◐ | ● | ● | ● | ✓ | - | - | - | - | ● | ◐ |
| ✓ | - | ✓ | ✓ | - | - | ◐ | - | ● | ● | ✓ | ✓ | - | ✓ | ✓ | ● | ● |
| ✓ | ✓ | - | - | ✓ | - | ◐ | ● | ● | ● | - | - | ✓ | ✓ | ✓ | ● | ● |
| ✓ | - | ✓ | ✓ | ✓ | ✓ | ● | ● | ● | ● | ✓ | - | ✓ | - | - | ● | - |
| ✓ | - | ✓ | ✓ | ✓ | ✓ | ● | ● | ● | ● | ✓ | - | ✓ | - | - | ● | ● |
| ✓ | ✓ | - | ✓ | ✓ | - | ◐ | ● | ● | ◐ | ✓ | ✓ | ✓ | - | - | ● | ● |
| ✓ | - | ✓ | ✓ | ✓ | - | ◐ | ◐ | ● | ◐ | ✓ | - | ✓ | - | - | ● | ● |
| - | - | ✓ | - | - | ✓ | ● | ● | ● | ● | ✓ | - | - | - | - | ● | - |
| ✓ | ✓ | - | ✓ | - | - | ◐ | ● | - | - | ✓ | - | ✓ | - | - | - | ◐ |
| ✓ | - | ✓ | ✓ | - | - | ◐ | ● | ● | ● | ✓ | ✓ | ✓ | - | ✓ | - | - |
| - | - | - | ✓ | - | ✓ | ● | ● | ● | ● | ✓ | - | ✓ | - | ✓ | ● | ● |
| - | - | ✓ | - | ✓ | ✓ | ● | ● | ● | ● | ✓ | - | ✓ | - | ✓ | ● | ● |

**Room service:** ● 24-hour, ◐ 6AM-10PM, ○ other.
**Laundry/Dry cleaning:** ● same day, ◐ overnight, ○ other.
**Pressing:** ● immediate, ◐ same day, ○ other.

# LOS ANGELES HOTEL CHART

| HOTELS | Price Category | Business Services | | | | | | | | | | | |
| --- | --- | --- | --- | --- | --- | --- | --- | --- | --- | --- | --- | --- |
| | | Banquet capacity | No. of meeting rooms | Secretarial services | Audiovisual equipment | Teletype news service | Computer rentals | In-room modem phone jack | All-news cable channel | Desk | Desk lighting | Bed lighting |
| **Sheraton Grande** | $$$ | 0 | 0 | ✓ | ✓ | - | ✓ | ✓ | ✓ | ● | ● | ◐ |
| **Sheraton Plaza La Reina** | $$ | 650 | 99 | ✓ | ✓ | - | ✓ | ✓ | - | ● | ● | ● |
| **Sheraton Universal** | $$$ | 1000 | 15 | ✓ | ✓ | - | ✓ | ✓ | ✓ | - | - | ● |
| **Stouffer Concourse** | $$ | 1500 | 42 | ✓ | ✓ | - | ✓ | ✓ | ✓ | ● | ● | ● |
| **Warner Center Hilton and Towers** | $$ | 0 | 0 | ✓ | ✓ | - | - | - | ✓ | ● | ● | ◐ |
| **Warner Center Marriott** | $$ | 800 | 16 | - | ✓ | - | - | - | ✓ | ● | ● | ● |
| **Westwood Marquis Hotel and Garden** | $$$$ | 120 | 6 | ✓ | ✓ | - | ✓ | - | ✓ | ● | ● | ● |

**$$$$** = over $175, **$$$** = $125 -$175, **$$** = under $125.
● good, ◐ fair, ○ poor.
All hotels listed here have photocopying and fax facilities.

| In-Room Amenities | | | | | | | | | | Hotel Amenities | | | | | | |
| Nonsmoking rooms | In-room checkout | Minibar | Pay movies | VCR/Movie rentals | Hairdryer | Toiletries | Room service | Laundry/Dry cleaning | Pressing | Concierge | Barber/Hairdresser | Garage | Courtesy airport transport | Sauna | Pool | Exercise room |
|---|---|---|---|---|---|---|---|---|---|---|---|---|---|---|---|---|
| ✓ | ✓ | ✓ | ✓ | - | - | ◐ | ● | ◐ | ● | ✓ | - | ✓ | - | - | ● | - |
| ✓ | ✓ | ✓ | ✓ | - | - | ◐ | ● | ● | ● | ✓ | ✓ | ✓ | ✓ | - | ● | ● |
| ✓ | ✓ | ✓ | ✓ | - | - | ◐ | ● | ● | ● | ✓ | - | ✓ | - | - | ● | - |
| ✓ | ✓ | ✓ | ✓ | - | ✓ | ● | ● | ◐ | ● | ✓ | - | ✓ | ✓ | ✓ | ● | ● |
| ✓ | - | ✓ | ✓ | - | ✓ | ● | ● | ● | ◐ | ✓ | ✓ | - | | ✓ | ● | - |
| ✓ | ✓ | - | ✓ | - | - | ◐ | ◐ | ● | ◐ | ✓ | ✓ | - | | ✓ | ● | ● |
| ✓ | - | ✓ | - | ✓ | ✓ | ● | ● | ● | ● | ✓ | ✓ | ✓ | - | ✓ | ● | ● |

**Room service:** ● 24-hour, ◐ 6AM-10PM, ○ other.
**Laundry/Dry cleaning:** ● same day, ◐ overnight, ○ other.
**Pressing:** ● immediate, ◐ same day, ○ other.

even if you're not staying here. *An Ayala International hotel. 535 S. Grand Ave., 90071, tel. 213/624–0000, 800/ 628–4900, fax 213/626–9906. Gen. manager, Mark McGuffie. 173 rooms, 15 suites. AE, CB, DC, MC, V.*

**44**
**$$**
**Hyatt Regency.** If location is indeed everything, then the Hyatt reigns supreme for doing business Downtown. It is situated in a mixed-use office and retail complex that is within walking distance of the Convention Center and most Downtown businesses. Without leaving the premises, guests have access to the 32-story Broadway Plaza office building, the Broadway department store, as well as two floors of shops, restaurants, and various services. A recent, massive renovation and remodeling have essentially made this a new hotel. Standard rooms are more comfortable and roomy than is the norm, each equipped with a desk, good lighting, and a telephone that allows for modem and portable fax transmissions. If you reserve well in advance, for the same rate you can get a larger corner room with city views, but alas, no desk. The top two floors are occupied by the executive-class Regency Club. The Lobby Bar (*see* After Hours, below) offers evening entertainment. *711 S. Hope St., 90017, tel. 213/683–1234, 800/ 233–1234, fax 213/629–3230. Gen. manager, Ralph Suda. 444 rooms, 41 suites. AE, D, DC, MC, V.*

**41**
**$$$**
**Los Angeles Hilton and Towers.** Although it recently underwent a $70-million renovation and expansion, the Hilton remains a rather cold, impersonal hostelry. Yes, it's been considerably glamorized, and the public areas are picture-perfect, but the ambience is one of rather icy perfection. However, the redo has reversed the Hilton's downward slide, and once again it's a hub for conferences, business meetings, and tour groups. Room decor varies, but generally speaking, the style is soulless corporate contemporary, with inoffensively neutral colors and furnishings. In the Towers—the executive class hotel-within-a-hotel on the top two floors—rooms are exceptionally large and perks include complimentary Continental breakfast and evening hors d'oeuvres. A full-service business center and a variety of shops, services, and restaurants (including Cardini, a swanky, sophisticated Italian eatery, and a 24-hour coffee shop) are among the amenities. Within walking distance are the semichic Seventh Street Marketplace mall, many of Downtown's newer office buildings, and good restaurants such as Engine Co. 28 and Seventh Street Bistro (*see* Dining, below). *930 Wilshire Blvd., 90017, tel. 213/629–4321, 800/445–8667, fax 213/488–9869. Gen. manager, Larry Kirk. 868 rooms, 32 suites. AE, DC, MC, V.*

★ **52**
**$$$**
**New Otani Hotel and Gardens.** It's no surprise that this recently refurbished, Japanese-owned hotel, located in the heart of Little Tokyo (on the northeast edge of Downtown), is a favorite of visiting Japanese executives and tour groups. But it's also a peaceful haven for travelers who appreciate a bit of serenity in the middle of the city. Ideally located near city, state, and federal courts and government agencies, it's also close to a gaggle of terrific Japanese restaurants, like Kokekokko (on 2nd St.) and Kappo Kyara (in Little Tokyo Square on Alameda St.). The Japanese Experience package includes a Japanese-style room and some meals (your choice of either Jap-

anese or Western fare). Most rooms, however, have regular beds and faceless, modern decor, with minibars inexplicably located in the bathrooms, and adequate working spaces (though the phones are goofily placed across the room from desks). On the fourth floor is a fine Japanese restaurant, A Thousand Cranes, and a serene half-acre garden complete with ponds and walkways. *120 S. Los Angeles St., 90012, tel. 213/629–1200; in CA, 800/252–0197; in U.S. and Canada, 800/421–8795; fax 213/622–0980. Gen. manager, Kenji Yoshimoto. 434 rooms, 6 suites. AE, DC, MC, V.*

★ **46** **Sheraton Grande.** Though it's Downtown—an easy walk
$$$ from the Stock Exchange and many major office centers—the Grande possesses a rare feeling of seclusion. In the afternoon, a pianist plays in the spacious marble lobby, floor butlers bring pots of coffee with wake-up calls, and a complimentary limo shuttles guests to Beverly Hills. There are no workout facilities on the premises, but guests may use the new YMCA down the street (except during peak late afternoon hours). There's even a blessedly uncrowded movie multiplex next door. The recently renovated rooms, pleasingly decorated, are among the largest Downtown; each has a fine marble bathroom, a desk, and a two-line phone with a modem port and a 10-foot cord. The quiet lobby has many comfortable nooks for informal meetings. *345 S. Figueroa St., 90071, tel. 213/617–1133, 800/325–3535, fax 213/613–0291. Gen. manager, H. Karl Schaefer, 339 rooms, 36 suites. AE, CB, DC, MC, V.*

## Hollywood/West Hollywood

**37** **Hollywood Roosevelt Hotel.** This once-famous 12-story ho-
$$ tel, closed in 1984, reopened a year later after new owners undertook a complete renovation and sensitive restoration of the original Spanish colonial style (intricate tile work, woodwork, arches, and such, updated with a subtle rose-and-taupe color scheme). Rooms have been modernized, and are very tasteful if not truly distinctive. A marvelous fillip was added by having artist David Hockney paint the bottom of the hotel's swimming pool—life imitating art imitating life. Guests include lots of starry-eyed tourists (who, unfortunately, won't see too many stars around here), but business travelers wanting to be near major recording studios or other entertainment industries appreciate the hotel's location, as well as its beautiful old meeting rooms, moderate prices, and the Cinegrill (*see* After Hours, below), a terrific, '40s-style jazz supper club. *7000 Hollywood Blvd., Hollywood, 90028, tel. 213/466–7000, fax 213/462–8056. Gen. manager, Bruno Fava. 360 rooms, 20 suites, 80 poolside cabanas. AE, CB, DC, MC, V.*

**27** **St. James's Club.** The former Sunset Towers, an imposing
$$$$ apartment building popular with Hollywood stars such as Jean Harlow and Clark Gable, was placed in the National Registry of Historic Places in 1979, and in 1985, a London-based firm spent a bundle turning it into a small hotel with opulent '30s decor and great city views from most of the rooms. Most rooms are suites; there are also some spacious doubles, but practical working space is limited in nonsuite rooms. Although many of the lavish furnishings are costly copies of Art Deco pieces in the Metropolitan Museum in New York, you get a little too much of a good

thing in the suites, which are done in a sort of *uber*-Deco, with overscaled furniture and garish colors. However, the public rooms are as sleek as the sets of *The Gay Divorcée*. The gimmick is that this is a private club—though, in fact, anyone may buy a membership for $8 a day, which will be tacked onto your room rate. In keeping with the club atmosphere, there's a dining room that mimics the great supper clubs of yesteryear in both look and service; a pool; health spa; business center; and secretarial service. *8358 Sunset Blvd., West Hollywood, 90069, tel. 213/654-7100, 800/225-2637, fax 213/654-9287. Gen. manager, Allan Blest. 18 rooms, 44 suites. AE, CB, MC, V.*

## Westside/West Los Angeles

★ ❻
$$$$

**Hotel Bel-Air.** A night at Hotel Bel-Air is akin to an escape to a parallel universe—a tranquil, luxury-laden Arcadia where swans drift lazily in ponds, towering trees provide a sylvan canopy, and fragrant blooms abound throughout a lush, 12-acre glade, in which the hotel is half hidden. It's a short drive down a canyon road to Sunset Boulevard and Westwood Village, but this isn't the place to stay if you wish to be centrally located; it's really convenient to nowhere. No matter. Guests, many of whom register under assumed names, don't dash in and out to make sales calls—their meetings come to them. The hotel was recently sold to a Japanese company (for a record-setting $110 million—that's $1.2 million per room), but the Bel-Air still bears the imprint of its previous owner, Caroline Hunt Schoellkopf, who had beautifully renovated and expanded it. The hotel's individuality—no two rooms are alike—was greatly due to Schoellkopf's decision to employ five big-name designers, including the late Kalef Aleton, Louis Cataffo, and Betty Garber. Though rooms reflect each designer's style, all share elements like wood-burning fireplaces, and architectural details like window seats, French doors, and hand-stenciled ceiling beams. Rooms and suites are located in six single story California mission-style buildings spread across the grounds; many also have private patios and Jacuzzis. The Hotel Bel-Air Restaurant is one of the classiest, most romantic eateries in town, and the food is imaginative and fabulous, as well. *701 Stone Canyon Road, Bel Air, 90077, tel. 213/472-1211, fax 213/476-5890. Managing dir., Paul Zuest. 59 rooms, 33 suites. AE, CB, DC, MC, V.*

❶⑧
$$$

**Beverly Hills Hotel and Bungalows.** A sprawling, three-story pink main building and 21 fabled bungalows (recently outfitted with central air and marble bathrooms) are set amid palm trees and wide lawns on a 12-acre site not far from central Beverly Hills, but not really within walking distance, either. This place is a haven for executives and celebrities who prefer their presence to be known (as opposed to the seclusion and privacy of the Hotel Bel-Air). Amenities include tennis courts, a pool embraced by private cabanas, an exercise room, shops, and restaurants. Rooms in the main building are done in pastels with relatively simple furnishings (although some rooms border on the shabby and reek of cigarette smoke); the standard ones aren't particularly large. A better bet are the "superior" rooms on the main floor, many of which, for the same price, have large private patios. Two-line phones with modem outlets are on all desks, and rooms have VCRs and access to a video library. Unless you're a "somebody," service can be awfully sniffy. The legendary Polo Lounge (*see* Business Breakfasts, below) remains a show-business power-meal institution in which the right seat (which is the booth that faces the entrance) is a sure sign of success—the food is decidedly mediocre. The coffee shop, however, is wonderful. *9641 Sunset Blvd., Beverly Hills, 90210, tel. 213/276–2251, fax 213/281–2919. Gen. manager, Kerman Beriker. 247 rooms and 21 bungalows. AE, CB, D, MC, V.*

★ ⑲ **Century City Inn.** It's as difficult to find a well-located,
$$ moderately priced Westside hotel as it is a cruising cab in L.A., which makes this modest businessperson's hotel worth knowing about. Opened in 1988, it's perfectly located for those doing business in Century City or West L.A., and though there are just 46 generic, California-contemporary style rooms, it has a big hotel-style business center complete with copiers, computers, and fax machines. Each room is conveniently equipped with a microwave, refrigerator, and VCR. Service is limited but friendly. *10330 W. Olympic Blvd., Century City, 90064, tel. 213/553–1000, fax 213/277–1633. Gen. manager, Trout Felker. 34 rooms, 12 suites. AE, CB, DC, MC, V.*

⑳ **Century Plaza Hotel.** The Century Plaza rises out of what
$$$$ was once the Twentieth Century-Fox studio backlot, and remains the practical place to stay if you need to be a short walk from Century City's high-rise business and entertainment offices. It's not the city's best or most beautiful hotel—indeed, many think this sweeping, '60s-style, arc-shaped hotel and its adjoining 30-story tower has too many rooms, too much hustle and bustle. All the characterless, blandly contemporary rooms in the massive main building and tower addition have private balconies and views. A thorough renovation marked the hotel's 25th anniversary in 1991. Guests paying corporate rates receive a 50% discount on Super Shuttle van service to LAX, and are entitled to complimentary limo rides to nearby Beverly Hills or Westwood. *A Westin hotel. 2025 Ave. of the Stars, Century City, 90067, tel. 213/277–2000; in U.S., 800/228–3000; in Canada, 800/268–8383; fax 213/551–3355. Managing dir., Bodo Lemke. 683 doubles, 67 suites in main building; 313 rooms, 9 suites in Tower. AE, CB, DC, V.*

★ ㉕ **L'Ermitage.** With baroque music wafting through the inti-
$$$ mate reception area (no grand lobby here), and an impressive collection of original Impressionist paintings on the walls, this all-suite, eight-story hotel, built in 1976, is the closest L.A. comes to a small, luxurious European inn. A recent renovation and added room lighting have brightened the heretofore somber color scheme. Also installed were huge Jacuzzi tubs and showers with steam jets in some of the suites, duvets on beds, and color TVs in the bathrooms. The suites, which resemble plush apartments more than they do hotel rooms, also feature kitchens, dining rooms, and multiple-line phones; and there is free limo service provided to the Beverly Hills-West Hollywood area. Corporate executives and celebrities such as Placido Domingo prefer the large Town House suites. Service throughout the hotel is superb. Le Petit Ermitage next door is a hidden, swanky hospice for stars recovering from plastic surgery. *9291 Burton Way, Beverly Hills, 90210,*

*tel. 213/278–3344; in U.S. and Canada, 800/424–4443; fax 213/278–8247. Gen manager, Alexis Eliopulos. AE, MC, V.*

★ ❷❻ **Four Seasons.** For executives and publishing and enter-
$$$$ tainment industry folk who find the Bel-Air a little too out of the way and the Beverly Hills Hotel a tad too glitzy/ tacky, the Four Seasons, opened in 1987, has become the hotel of choice. Its location on the border of Beverly Hills and Los Angeles is convenient to West Hollywood, the Wilshire District, and Beverly Hills. The staff is unfailingly friendly and helpful. Public rooms, which open onto beautifully landscaped terraces and gardens, are appointed with cozy, overstuffed sofas and sink-into chairs. Antiques, spectacular flower displays, and original art, combined with a sense of urban seclusion, make this one of L.A.'s premiere hotels, home to guests ranging from President Bush to the Rolling Stones. Though guest rooms aren't huge, they're flawlessly appointed. Each room offers bathroom TVs, marble vanities, and good desks. Guests who arrive before check-in or whose flights leave after check-out may use an executive suite at no charge. And there's also no tariff for use of in-room fax machines, exercise bikes, shoe shines, and limo rides to Beverly Hills. Windows (*see* After Hours, below) is perfect for tea or a late-evening drink. *300 S. Doheny Dr., L.A., 90048, tel. 213/273–2222; in U.S., 800/332–3442; in Canada, 800/268–6282; fax 213/859–3824. Gen. manager, Kurt Stielhack. 106 rooms, 179 suites. AE, CB, D, MC, V.*

★ ❷❸ **Regent Beverly Wilshire.** In 1987, the Hong Kong-based
$$$$ Regent group purchased this tired, landmark hotel, closed it for two years, and spent some $68 million to totally renovate the original (1926) building. Then, in 1990, a health spa was added and the "new" wing, built in 1971, underwent renovation (which is still in progress). This venerable institution, right in the thick of Beverly Hills, once again draws the crème de la crème of the business and entertainment fields. Public rooms are decorated in an elegant Regency/Directoire style; guest rooms follow suit. Accommodations have been enlarged, and are accessorized with antiques. Deluxe-class rooms have sitting areas with sofas and chairs, as well as three TVs and phones. Baths in all rooms have glass shower stalls, separate, spacious bathtubs, and full-length mirrors. Steward service on each floor is impeccable. The business center provides all the customary services, along with space for informal meetings. The Dining Room (*see* Dining, below) is a culinary destination for locals as well as hotel guests. The Cafe (*see* Business Breakfasts, below) is fine for an early meeting, and the Bar (*see* After Hours, below) is a good place to unwind. *9500 Wilshire Blvd., Beverly Hills, 90212, tel. 213/275–5200, 800/421–4354, fax 213/274–2851. Gen. manager, Alain M. Longatte. AE, DC, MC, V.*

❼ **Westwood Marquis Hotel & Garden.** The understated ele-
$$$$ gance of this 15-story, all-suite hotel appeals to the likes of Lee Iacocca and Dustin Hoffman; media and entertainment executives from New York also fill its suites—not bad for a place that used to be a UCLA dorm. Attractive features include efficient yet personable service, a location on a quiet residential street in Westwood Village, and a half-acre garden with two swimming pools. UCLA, Westwood's abundant shops, theaters, restaurants, and

many Wilshire Boulevard office buildings are within walking distance. The one-, two-, and three-bedroom suites are spacious and have comfortable parlors, complete with desks, but are of undistinguished design. The china cabinets housing faux-antique items in the rooms are locked—a rather tacky inference that some guests may be light-fingered. There are several two-line phones in each suite, with voice-mail and modem/fax capabilities. Complimentary limos transport guests to Century City and Beverly Hills. *930 Hilgard Ave., Westwood, 90024, tel. 213/208–8765, 800/421–2317, fax 213/824–0355. Gen. manager, Jacques Camus. 285 suites. AE, CB, DC, MC, V.*

## San Fernando Valley

❸
$$$
**Sheraton Universal.** On the same property as Universal Studios and MCA's monolithic headquarters, this 20-story hotel is also close to The Burbank Studios and the many businesses in Burbank and Studio City. A tram takes guests to the MCA building, specialty restaurants (although what most of them specialize in is lousy food), and the studio tour. Built in 1969, the Sheraton completed an extensive renovation in 1990; now marble floors (in the baths and entries), minibars, and safes are standard in all rooms. Unfortunately, the lobby still looks like the leftover set from a Gothic horror movie. Also added was a sports bar named for Telly Savalas, who has lived in the hotel for 20 years. The contemporary rooms, done in the ubiquitous corporate/Southwestern mode endemic to current hotel redos, are a bit larger than the norm, and most have terrific views of the Valley. Its size and amenities make this hotel popular for meetings and conferences of all sizes. *333 Universal Terrace Pkwy., Universal City, 91608, tel. 818/980–1212, 800/325–3535, fax 818/985–4980. Gen. manager, Creston Woods. 423 rooms, 23 suites. AE, CB, DC, MC, V.*

❶
$$
**Warner Center Hilton and Towers.** Opened in late 1989, this 15-story business-oriented hotel is located in the western end of the Valley, in the middle of the sprawling, prefab Warner Center business/retail/residential megalopolis. Rooms, decorated in an inoffensive, phony Art Deco fashion, are relatively large; those on the Towers floors have such extras as two-line phones with call-waiting. The Towers has the usual executive-class services, along with complimentary breakfast and hors d'oeuvres. Use of the large athletic club next door is available to guests for $10 a day (no charge for Towers patrons), but use of the pool is free. There's no business center, but the hotel will send and receive faxes, make copies, and provide guests with computers. *6360 Canoga Ave., Woodland Hills, 91367, tel. 818/595–1000, 800/445–8667, fax 818/595–1090. Gen. manager, Uwe Holtorf. 313 rooms, 23 suites. AE, CB, DC, V.*

❷
$$
**Warner Center Marriott.** Opened in 1986 at a cost of $55 million, this humongous hotel was the first property in the then newly developed Warner Center. The focus here is on business; 80% of the clientele consists of folks dealing with the major insurance companies, defense contractors, and high-tech industries that have relocated to the area in recent years. It's also a major center for meetings and conventions, boasting meeting rooms of every size, and two huge kitchens to service them all, including one kosher

kitchen. Rooms, done in the usual soft pastels, have sitting areas and good work space. The top two floors are devoted to an executive-class hotel-within-a-hotel. *21850 Oxnard Ave., Woodland Hills, 91367, tel. 818/887–4800, 818/228–9290, fax 818/340–5893. Gen. manager, Rene Boskoff. 453 rooms, 20 suites. AE, DC, MC, V.*

## Airport/South Bay

**⓱** **Compri Hotel Los Angeles Harbor.** Opened in 1989 in
**$$** L.A.'s port community of San Pedro, this is a business hotel with some resort amenities. The three-story property is located on a multi-acre parcel overlooking a marina, and is well positioned for travelers doing business in the South Bay and the industrial areas around the L.A. Harbor. Rooms are compact yet functional. The Compri Club, a large, informal meeting and working area—sort of a grown-up rumpus room—off the main lobby, is complete with big-screen TV, telephone-equipped desks, and a library. Here a complimentary, cooked-to-order breakfast is served, along with early evening cocktails and late-night snacks. There are also two lighted tennis courts. *2800 Via Cabrilla Marina, San Pedro, 90731, tel. 213/ 514–3344, fax 213/547–9612. Gen. manager, Jeffrey K. Protzman. 212 rooms, 12 suites. AE, CB, DC, MC, V.*

**⓬** **Embassy Suites Hotel.** It's difficult to take a hotel corpora-
**$$** tion that "hires" Garfield as its spokescat too seriously, but practicality and economy are the strong suits at the second of the Embassy chain's properties at LAX (the other, just off the Imperial Terminal on the south side of LAX, is named Embassy Suites Hotel-LAX/Imperial, so if you hop aboard a courtesy van upon arrival, make sure you're headed for the right one). The spacious rooms, amenities, and color schemes are standard for the chain, yet are a cut above most hotels in this range. A full breakfast is complimentary. Facilities include an indoor pool, 4,100 square feet of banquet or meeting space, seven conference suites, and guest laundry facilities. *9801 Airport Blvd., L.A., 90045 tel. 213/215–1000, 800/634–0066, fax 213/215–1952. Gen. manager, Anthony Lovoy. 215 suites (7 for disabled). AE, CB, DC, MC, V.*

**⓮** **Los Angeles Airport Hilton and Towers.** More than 85,000
**$$$** square feet of meeting and conference space make this 17-story hotel, with its dramatic smoked-glass and granite exterior, one of the world's largest airport hotels and conference centers. The top two floors are devoted to the executive-class Towers, which offer a complimentary Continental breakfast, evening hors d'oeuvres, and a boardroom for informal meetings. The lounge has the same view of the south runways as the LAX control tower. There are five restaurants and a fully equipped business center, yet the generic, corporate-looking rooms lack good workspace. However, despite its immense size and all the hustle and bustle, this is a good place to stay if you need to be in the area. *5711 W. Century Blvd., L.A., tel. 213/410– 4000, 800/445–8667, fax 213/410–6250. Gen. manager, John Elford. 1,200 rooms, 79 suites. AE, CB, DC, MC, V.*

**⓭** **Los Angeles Airport Marriott.** Formerly the flagship of the
**$$$** Marriott chain, this 1973-built hotel was one of LAX's first luxury properties. Though large and very busy, the Marriott manages to maintain a friendly, warm atmos-

phere that sets it apart from other airport inns. It recently underwent a major renovation; the top two of the 18 floors are concierge levels, offering a private lounge, complimentary Continental breakfast, evening hors d'oeuvres, and space for small meetings. Standard rooms are reasonably spacious and contemporary in style, with two phones and good desks. A business center provides secretarial services, including word processing. Three restaurants, retail shops, a laundry room (something few hotels have), and a pool complete with swim-up bar are on the grounds. *5855 W. Century Blvd., L.A., 90045, tel. 213/641–5700, fax 213/337–5358. Gen. manager, Charlton W. Hines. 993 rooms, 19 suites. AE, DC, MC, V.*

**⓫** **Sheraton Plaza La Reina.** With more than 100 meeting
*$$* rooms ranging from the intimate to the grand, the Sheraton lives and breathes business—the overall mood is one of cool functionality, not elegance. Though the ambience is somewhat cold, the staff more than makes up for that with its amiability and helpfulness. The modern rooms, in requisite pastels, get larger the higher up they are; you can request one with a sitting area or work desk. As with the other airport hotels, this place has a variety of services, including retail shops, self-service laundry, business center, three lounges, and two restaurants. A free shuttle runs every few hours to Manhattan Beach and a nearby mall. *6101 W. Century Blvd., L.A., 90045, tel. 213/642–1111, fax 213/410–1267. Gen. manager, Jerry Golenor, 641 rooms, 166 suites. AE, DC, MC, V.*

**⓯** **Stouffer Concourse Hotel.** In addition to providing plenty
*$$* of work-related facilities, this efficient, 12-story hotel has 18 corner suites with terraces equipped with private spas—a nice, sybaritic touch for the business traveler. The top two stories are the Club Floors, which have standard-size rooms with upgraded amenities and a lounge that serves complimentary Continental breakfast. Guests in the regular rooms (which are comfortable, contemporary, and characterless) are brought coffee and a morning paper with wake-up calls. Meeting facilities include a large, tiered theater and a range of conference rooms. TV monitors in the lobby display flight information from the major airlines. *5400 W. Century Blvd., L.A., 90045, tel. 213/216–5858, 800/468–3571, fax 213/645–8053. Gen. manager, John Reiss. 703 rooms, 47 suites. AE, DC, MC, V.*

## DINING

*by Merrill Shindler*

When it comes to eating in Los Angeles, the first thing you must understand is that this is a city without a center. Even if you're searching for what cynics consider to be L.A.'s best-known contribution to American regional cuisine—surf 'n' turf—you're probably going to have to drive some distance to find it. But the drive is often worth it, for hidden in the midst of this urban and suburban sprawl are culinary treasures that rival the finest in the world. After decades of slavishly following the cooking styles of other cities (as in "New York-style Italian" or "Hong Kong-style Chinese"), L.A.'s chefs, especially its young chefs, have headed for regions not formerly explored—or even imagined. At cocktail parties, the conversation may begin with housing prices, but it inevitably works its way to restaurants. In L.A., eating well keeps the wheels of commerce and entertainment well lubricated.

A note about dress: Ties are not expected in any but a very few formal restaurants (though they're common at the Downtown places, just because the locals have to wear them to work). L.A.'s large entertainment, design, and fashion industries are notoriously casual, and you'll look like an out-of-towner if you wear a businesslike pin-striped suit (unless it's an Armani) to such trendy spots as Trumps or Citrus; men are well advised to pack a hip sportcoat, and women a casual-chic ensemble, for fashionable L.A. dining.

The restaurants that follow are scattered all over the L.A. basin, though most are in the most central areas popular with travelers and residents alike. They are divided into these categories: Downtown, Hollywood/West Hollywood (including the central L.A. area), Westside (including Beverly Hills, West L.A., and Santa Monica), San Gabriel Valley, and South Bay (not far from LAX).

Highly recommended restaurants in each price category are indicated by a ★.

| Category | Cost* |
|---|---|
| $$$$ (Very Expensive) | over $50 |
| $$$ (Expensive) | $26–$50 |
| $$ (Moderate) | $10–$25 |
| $ (Inexpensive) | under $10 |

*per person, excluding drinks, service, and 6½% sales tax.*

*Numbers in the margin correspond to numbered restaurant locations on the Los Angeles Lodging and Dining maps.*

## Business Breakfasts

Unlike New York, home of the power breakfast, Los Angeles is not a city where many residents go out for breakfast, even to do business. The morning ritual for most Angelenos consists of a 3-mile jog and a hearty breakfast of Ultra Slim-Fast, followed by an hour stuck in traffic. But for those who must meet for breakfast, certain spots predominate. Downtown, there's a superb breakfast at the elegant **Checkers** (Checkers Hotel, tel. 213/624–0000). Breakfast at the **Polo Lounge** (Beverly Hills Hotel, tel. 213/276–2251) is not a wonderful meal, but the local power brokers (most in show business) feel a sentimental attachment to it. Nearby, in the **Cafe at the Regent Beverly Wilshire** (tel. 213/274–8179), the food is much better, the setting more convenient, and the service great. And both writers and actors love informal **Hugo's** (8401 Santa Monica Blvd., West Hollywood, tel. 213/654–3993), whose Italian dishes include an exceptionally filling spaghetti carbonara mixed with scrambled eggs.

## Downtown

**50** **Bernard's.** After a multimillion-dollar restoration, the
$$$$ Biltmore has returned from its dowdy decline to the ranks
of one of L.A.'s great hotels. And its tastefully ornate dining room has returned as well, revived after the departure
of its founding father, Bernard Jacoupy (who now runs
West L.A.'s Lunaria). The room is noted for its indirect
lighting, its quiet atmosphere, and the privacy of its few,
widely spaced tables, making it especially appropriate for
discreet business meetings. The menu is a paean to
nouvelle cuisine—modest portions of chartreuse of lobster and sweetbreads with a "butter" of fresh peas, and
steamed red snapper served on a bed of creamed parsley.
A harp player fills the room with soothing sounds.
*Biltmore Hotel, 515 S. Olive St., tel. 213/612–1580. Jacket
and tie required. Reservations essential. AE, CB, DC,
MC, V.*

★ **49** **Checkers.** Checkers sits ever so elegantly in the rear of the
$$$$ hotel of the same name, the Southern California branch of
San Francisco's fine Campton Place. Open for breakfast,
lunch, and dinner, it's one of downtown's best business
restaurants. Its quiet, soothing space, with peachy-pastel
colors, soft lighting, abundant flowers, and white linens, is
tucked in the midst of the high-rise frenzy that's busily
giving L.A. its long-awaited skyline. The menu is best described as new American: sweet-potato waffles and duck
hash for breakfast, smoked ham shanks with roasted crab
apples for lunch, hickory smoked duck with a chestnut flan
for dinner. It sounds eccentric, but it tastes wonderful.
You'll certainly impress your guests here—and please
yourself as well. *535 S. Grand Ave., tel. 213/624–0000.
Jacket and tie advised. Reservations essential. AE, CB,
DC, MC, V.*

**51** **Empress Pavilion.** This is the premier Hong Kong-style
$$ Chinese restaurant in Chinatown, capable of seating some
800 diners in an elegantly appointed room that swarms
with hosts, waiters, and busboys. Come lunchtime, much
of Chinatown shows up for the dim sum, a wide assort-
ment of dumplings served from rolling carts that criss-
cross the dining room, feeding groups of 10 or 12 at a time.
The noise level remains high at dinnertime, as banquet ta-
bles are piled high with steaming bowls of shark's fin soup
and heaping platters of Peking duck emerging at a frantic
rate from the kitchen. Despite the size of the place, and
the huge menu, the service is superb—but the noise
makes it more a place for fun, not work. *Bamboo Plaza,
988 N. Hill St., tel. 213/617–9898. Informal dress. Reser-
vations essential. AE, MC, V.*

★ **42** **Engine Co. No. 28.** An old firehouse, on the verge of being
$$ demolished, was saved as an historical landmark and
turned into one of downtown's best American restaurants
(and bars, *see* After Hours, below). The high-ceilinged
room is reminiscent of the grills of San Francisco—filled
with gleaming woodwork and booths, serviced by bar-
tenders who know how to make a proper martini and a
kitchen that can cook a steak black and blue. This is Guy
Food—steaks and chops, chili, meatloaf, superb onion
rings, and thin, crisp fries sprinkled with chili pepper.
The comfortable upholstered booths offer a good sense of
privacy for conversation, and the larger tables in back are

comfortable for meetings. *644 S. Figueroa St., tel. 213/624–6996. Business casual dress. Reservations essential. AE, MC, V.*

**㊽** **Rex, Il Ristorante.** What is arguably the most expensive
**$$$$** restaurant in town is inarguably the most elegant. A virtual museum of Art Deco, it occupies the ground floor of the Art Deco Oviatt Building, a beacon of taste in the midst of L.A.'s transitional Downtown area. Even the doors were made by Lalique. Inside is a superb bar on the upstairs balcony, with a black marble dance floor and a pianist who plays like Bobby Short. Below, in the dining room (a one-time haberdashery), tables sit far apart, offering a maximum of privacy. After years of serving miniature portions of Italian *nuova cucina*, Rex has a skilled new chef whose cooking is a bit heartier in style and larger in portion; dishes include a potato soup with tuna, pappardelle noodles with quail and artichoke hearts, and incomparable veal chops. The large wine list is predictably pricey. In all, expect to be wowed—and to pay a pretty penny. Though this is a fine spot for top-drawer business entertaining, the sheer dazzle of the room makes meetings seem distinctly out of place. *617 S. Olive St., tel. 213/627–2300. Jacket and tie advised. Reservations essential. AE, CB, DC, MC, V.*

**㊺** **Seventh Street Bistro.** Along with Rex, Checkers, and
**$$$$** Bernard's, this place completes the quadrumvirate of downtown's most elegant restaurants. The surprisingly modern space is situated within the exquisitely restored Fine Arts Building (don't miss the adjacent lobby, with its remarkable fountains and murals). Don't let the word "bistro" fool you—this is a formal nouvelle French restaurant, with elegant service, subdued lighting, and one of the best chefs in town. Try the cold cream of watercress soup served with Santa Monica bay shrimp fritters, duck breast with rhubarb purée, or crayfish salad wrapped in sautéed eggplant. In the staid world of Downtown dining, chef Laurent Quenioux's creations would be considered outlandish if they didn't work so well—you'd never believe a celery-root purée could taste so good. *815 W. 7th St., tel. 213/627–1242. Jacket and tie advised. Reservations required. AE, CB, MC, V.*

**㊸** **The Tower.** Though Los Angeles stretches from the moun-
**$$$** tains to the sea, there are few restaurants that afford vistas of the basin. The Tower, which sits atop the Transamerica Building, offers the best view of any restaurant in town (you can even helicopter to the roof of the building and walk down the stairs into the restaurant, a decidedly memorable experience). On a very clear evening, you can watch planes land and take off at distant LAX and admire the sunset over Santa Monica. After several years of serving dated Continental cuisine, the Tower has become one of L.A.'s few remaining classic French restaurants, featuring chicken au Grand Marnier, steak au poivre, and duckling with olives. The restaurant is on several levels, so every table offers a view. This is a fine setting for a business meeting. *1150 S. Olive St., 32nd floor, tel. 213/746–1554. Jacket and tie strongly advised. Reservations required. AE, CB, DC, MC, V.*

## Hollywood/West Hollywood

★ ❸❻ **Angeli Caffe.** There's hardly a restaurant more definitively
$$ casual—or more constantly crowded—than Angeli, which
sits in the very heart (and indeed may actually *be* the
heart) of the ultratrendy Melrose district. Angoli is noth-
ing more than a pair of busy, minimalist rooms, with floor-
to-ceiling windows facing the street and an open kitchen
balancing the back of each room. Tables are small and
crowded, not the sort of setting for a business deal—but a
great spot for very amusing people-watching. The anti-
pasto plates are like no others: an assortment of smoked
meats, baked ricotta tartlets, fried eggplant, grilled ol-
ives, and small rice and potato croquettes. The pizzas are
among the most authentic this side of Naples. *7274 Mel-
rose Ave., Hollywood, tel. 213/936–9086. (Also:* **Trattoria
Angeli,** *11651 Santa Monica Blvd., West L.A., tel. 213/
478–1191; and* **Angeli Mare,** *Marina Marketplace, 13455
Maxella Ave., Marina del Rey, tel. 213/822–1984.) Casu-
al dress. Reservations essential. AE, MC, V.*

❹❶ **Campanile.** Named for the tower that crowns this 1928,
$$$ Charlie Chaplin-built landmark, Campanile is run by the
married team of Mark Peel and Nancy Silverton, veterans
of Michael's, Spago, and Maxwell's Plum in New York.
Campanile is a wonderful-looking restaurant. You enter
through a fine café, with a bar off to one side, a rustic fountain in the middle of the room, and a skylight overhead
that allows you to look up at the looming campanile. Beyond the café is a long, cloisterlike room, with tables on
one side and the kitchen on the other. In back is a dining
room with an isolated balcony running around its perimeter (some think the balcony is too removed from the action,
but it's much preferred for doing business). The food is, at
once, Californian, French, Italian, Mediterranean, and
many permutations in between, and virtually everything
is cooked with olive oil. The poached mozzarella with pesto
and the grilled prime rib are memorable; every table re-
ceives incredible breads from the adjacent bakery and a
steaming plate of grilled vegetables. Silverton made her
name as a pastry chef for very good reason. Service can
sometimes drag. *624 S. La Brea Ave., Wilshire District,
tel. 213/938–1447. Studied casual dress. Reservations required. AE, MC, V.*

❸❺ **Chapo.** The owners are Philipe and Hilde Leiaghat, whose
$$ previous restaurant was the De Pottekyker (The Curi-
osity) in Antwerp. Their latest effort is a moderate-
ly priced California-French-Italian-Belgian restaurant
which serves, among other things, a spectacular tomato-
corn soup. The menu includes baked goat cheese with fat
croutons flavored with olive tapenade, and grilled chicken
with a light goat cheese sauce and a heap of french fries,
something the Belgians make better than anyone else. If
you pretend the rice tart is rice pudding, you'll be in com-
fort-food heaven. Located in the middle of too-hip Mel-
rose, the setting is serenely quiet and candlelighted, a
nice spot for an impromptu business meeting. *7661 Mel-
rose Ave., Hollywood, tel. 213/655–2924. Casual dress.
Reservations helpful. AE, MC, V.*

❷❾ **Chaya Brasserie.** This fashionable celebrity haunt is
$$$ owned by the Tsunodas, a family of restaurateurs in Japan
since the 17th century. Despite the family's venerable tra-

dition, Chaya Brasserie is radically modern. Situated next door to Cedars-Sinai Medical Center on the edge of West Hollywood, it serves food that's mostly Franco-Californian, with some Japanese touches. You dine under a high beamed ceiling, in a room awash with mirrors and potted palms, with a casual brasserie atmosphere. The menu lists grilled smoked eel on pumpernickel points, poached red snapper stuffed with artichoke, lamb chops with a rosemary pesto sauce, and pan-fried oysters in a puff pastry with a sorrel cream sauce. Portions can be substantial, and it's all delicious. Only meet here with those who are tolerant of more than a little ambient noise. *8741 Alden Dr., central L.A., tel. 213/859–8833. Casual dress. Reservations essential. AE, MC, V.*

★ **38** **Citrus.** Citrus is the brainchild of chubby, avuncular
$$$ Michel Richard, who spent many years being L.A.'s favorite French pastry chef before becoming the city's overall favorite chef. This is perhaps the best restaurant in town, a perfect combination of superb food and the casual Los Angeles style that's evident in every aspect of Citrus: the oversize white patiolike room with its curious indoor umbrellas; the spotless glass-walled kitchen, where you can see chefs and assistants bustling about; and chatty, well-informed waiters who help customers put together the best meal possible. The Hollywood Power People love Citrus, which has remained (along with Spago) the hottest ticket in town for several years. The undeniable bottom line is that the food is remarkable—Richard is always there, tasting in the kitchen, greeting customers at their tables, worrying that something's wrong. Business meetings work especially well in the privacy of the small room to the right of the hostess's desk. *6703 Melrose Ave., Hollywood, tel. 213/857–0034. Casual dress (many in jacket and tie). Reservations strongly advised. AE, MC, V.*

★ **34** **Indigo.** It's hard to be blue in Indigo, which is basically one
$$ big room, where you can see who's eating what with whom. Behind a window at the far end is a garden, complete with a faux waterfall and a little fisherman trolling in it, an offbeat memento from the Thai restaurant that once filled this space near West Hollywood. With its small, kitschy touches, Indigo doesn't seem quite real. There's more than just a creative menu writer at work here—the food tastes as great as it sounds. It's hard to choose between such starters as Chinese crisp-fried baby squid in a spicy chili sauce and chicken and spinach potstickers with a mint dipping sauce. Main dishes include a Thai shrimp and papaya salad, a super grilled chicken (with rosemary and garlic), and wonderful charred lamb loin brochettes and flank steaks—really charred, not faux charred as at too many places. They make their own bread, too, flavored with rosemary and garlic. It's a good space for casual meetings or just a good time. *8222-½ W. 3rd St., central L.A., tel. 213/653–0140. Casual dress. Reservations advised. AE, MC, V.*

★ **30** **Locanda Veneta.** This small, incredibly popular trattoria
$$ may be across the street from Cedars-Sinai Medical Center and down the block from the Beverly Center, but when you're at your table you'll swear you're in Venice on a warm summer's night, with the evening breeze flowing through the windows. The image of Venice is further reinforced by the green olive oil being poured over the carpac-

cio and the sizzle of the roast lamb (served in a mustard and walnut sauce). Close your eyes (or drink enough Pinot grigio) and you'll imagine you hear the songs of the gondoliers. It's hard to choose from the simple menu—perhaps the *frittura di bianchetti* (pan-fried whitebait served with a fine pile of vinegared onions cooked to a mush) or the *trittico di mozzarelle*, a trio of freshly made mozzarellas with tomatoes, basil, and olive oil. Unfortunately, the noise level of this fine but extremely cozy spot makes it inappropriate for meetings; come here for the pleasure of the cuisine, and the company. *8368 W. 3rd St., central L.A., tel. 213/274–1893. Casual dress. Reservations required. AE, MC, V.*

**㉝** **Mandarette.** Like sushi, dim sum is a recent discovery for
**$** most Americans. But unlike sushi, it was never intended to be eaten at any old time of the day. Dim sum is meant to be eaten during late morning, or in the early afternoon as a sort of pick-me-up. But at this offspring of the far grander Mandarin, dim sum and then some are served into the small hours of the morning. Located near the Beverly Center and West Hollywood, the room is as spare as can be—a big shoebox with a high ceiling and lots of industrial appointments. The dishes range from dim sum standbys (dumplings, pastries, and so forth) to miniature versions of full-fledged Chinese dishes. Under the *Binh* and *Bao* (Breads and Pancakes) heading are a hot dog Mandarette (actually a Chinese pork sausage), onion pancakes, and a spiced-beef sandwich. The menu continues through garlic catfish, clams in black-bean sauce, and Szechuan noodles—none bigger than a snack, at snack prices. A good restaurant for fun food, but not a great one for meetings. *8386 Beverly Blvd., central L.A., tel. 213/655–6115. Casual dress. Reservations advised. AE, MC, V.*

**★ ㊉** **Patina.** Its exterior is so understated that you can easily
**$$$$** drive by without noticing the place at all. Even after you've left your car with a parking valet, it's tricky to find the front door—it looks like the delivery entrance. But that's just a little witticism, for as soon as you walk in, you're in an elegant space filled with muted tones, soft light, and lots of little tables placed so close together that it looks as though they've tried to squeeze a large restaurant into a very small space. Superchef Joachim Splichal has pulled out all the stops in creating a menu that keeps fans coming back again and again. Consider the whimsy (stronger at lunch than dinner) of dishes like a corn blini "sandwich" filled with marinated salmon; a soufflé (how French) of grits (how American) with Herkimer cheddar and an apple-smoked bacon sauce; and a red bell pepper soup served with a tiny bacon, lettuce, and tomato sandwich. Quiet discussions are best held in the smaller room to the right of the entrance. This is an excellent place for entertaining clients who are serious about food. *5955 Melrose Ave., Hollywood, tel. 213/467–1108. Jacket and tie advised. Reservations essential. AE, MC, V.*

**★ ㉘** **Trumps.** In many ways, this is the quintessential Los An-
**$$$** geles restaurant. From its ultracool look (white walls hung with Major Art, white ceiling rafters, huge concrete tables) to its power tea (wedged in between the power lunch and power dinner), it is a gathering spot for the Angelenos of the future. Sitting among the designers, agents, and assorted beautiful people, you don't just feel

like you're on the cutting edge, you feel like you're the edge itself. There's food (and service) to match: potato pancakes with goat cheese and sautéed apples; tuna grilled rare with eggplant caviar; superb fried chicken with mashed potatoes and gravy. Chef Michael Roberts shares his recipes in a fine book, *Secret Ingredients*. But every day in this restaurant, he proves it takes more than recipes to make great food. Despite the noise, lots of business (usually in the creative fields) is done here; for meetings, there's an excellent private space right next to the bar, with a fine view of the celebrities coming and going across the street at Morton's. *8764 Melrose Ave., West Hollywood, tel. 213/855–1480. Casual-chic dress. Reservations required. AE, MC, V.*

**32** **Tulipe.** This large, glass-walled, fairly stark place with a
**$$$** sizable open kitchen is warmed by both the people who work here and the people who eat here. It's a pleasure far beyond the sum of its parts, though that sum is a significant one. In the kitchen are owners/chefs Roland Gilbert (ex of Bernard's and Califia) and Maurice Peguet (ex of the California Club). Their food has French roots, though there's plenty of California tossed in for good measure. Duck is grilled with acacia honey and Oriental spices; a most commendable braised veal shank comes with an assortment of vegetables and crunchy cabbage; and Louisiana shrimp are wrapped in savoy cabbage leaves and served in a ginger sauce. There's a Chinese/Japanese edge to the food, adding one more set of ingredients to this particular mélange. They may not recognize this food in Paris, but melting-pot Angelenos have no trouble making it their own. Both the food and the wine list are very fairly priced. This is a good space for quiet talks, though there's no private room. *8360 Melrose Ave., West Hollywood, tel. 213/655–7400. Jacket advised. Reservations strongly advised. AE, MC, V.*

## Westside

**24** **Chez Helene.** This light and airy Beverly Hills cottage is
**$$** reminiscent of the small French bistros popular in the late '50s and early '60s, the friendly little places where the service was casual, the food better than decent, and the ambience conducive to lingering. Despite its location in Beverly Hills, it looks like it's in the middle of Provence, with its sweet outdoor patio, polished wood, and farmhouse interior. The menu is quite small and reasonably priced. Try the rich, intensely flavored cream of tomato soup. The onion soup is a straightforward rendition of one of the most beloved clichés of French cuisine, as are the escargots de Bourgogne, the trio of quiches (eaten by the occasional real man), and the house pâté. You can talk comfortably here, but it isn't wholly appropriate for serious business meetings. *267 S. Beverly Dr., Beverly Hills, tel. 213/276–1558. Casual dress. Reservations advised. AE, MC, V.*

**★ 23** **The Dining Room at the Regent Beverly Wilshire.** The
**$$$** many dining rooms at the old Beverly Wilshire hotel have boiled down to just The Dining Room at the new Regent Beverly Wilshire. The room is at once highly classical and stringently modern; trompe l'oeil, gleaming woodwork, and bucolic murals blend with a massive kitchen-under-glass. It's a formal room but a comfortable one, and it's one

of L.A.'s best for an elegant working breakfast, lunch, or dinner, or for fine business entertaining. The daily-changing menu is less formal (and less expensive) than you'd expect, given the dazzling decor and excellent service. The food is basically American, lightly influenced by France, Italy, and Japan. You can have an excellent meal here that's as American as anything you'll find in the Midwest: clam chowder, Cobb salad (infinitely better than the one served at the Brown Derby), veal chops with garlicked mashed potatoes, and cheesecake. It's a winning combination. *9500 Wilshire Blvd., Beverly Hills, tel. 213/275–4282. Jacket advised. Reservations advised. AE, CB, DC, MC, V.*

**③①** **Ed Debevic's.** After a hard day crunching numbers on your
**$** laptop, there's nothing like the old-fashioned fun at Ed's. It doesn't take reservations, but it's not a bad place to wait—and wait you will. This is L.A.'s best re-creation of a '50-style diner, which is no small praise in a town that has been buried beneath a mudslide of born-again meatloaf and gum-cracking waitresses. Signs on the walls proclaim "The more you tip—the nicer we are" and "Eat it—then beat it." The staff hams it up, occasionally bursting into song. The food is pure nostalgia, only better—and for Beverly Hills, it's dirt cheap. The cheeseburger comes topped with a combination of American, Cheddar, Swiss, and Velveeta. The tasty Five-Way Chili is mixed with macaroni, cheese, and onions. The meatloaf is a hash-house classic, and it comes with—says the menu—frozen vegetables. Honesty this rare is worth waiting for. This is a place for after-work zaniness, not meetings. *134 N. La Cienega Blvd., Beverly Hills, tel. 213/659–1952. Very casual dress. No reservations. No credit cards.*

**⑤** **Four Oaks.** Nestled in the midst of Beverly Glen, this place
**$$$$** spent years being the prettiest restaurant in town with the most mediocre food. And then, after several failed attempts at being revived, it was finally reborn. The new chef, Peter Roelant, is a young graduate of Girardet and L'Orangerie. And though he's clearly learned his classical lessons well, the food has evolved into a tidy sort of California-French, with small touches from Italy and Japan—in other words, an eminently modern menu. Dishes include white-potato soup with smoked morels, a homemade terrine of duck foie gras with a kumquat chutney, and baby chicken in a rock-salt crust with country vegetables. The exceptional beauty and serenity of the setting make this an excellent place for small meetings and refined entertaining. *2181 N. Beverly Glen Blvd., Beverly Glen, tel. 213/470–2265. Jacket advised (many in tie). Reservations required. AE, MC, V.*

**⑩** **The Heritage.** One feels obliged to dress properly here
**$$$** (though not all do—this is Santa Monica, after all). Nearly a century ago, when this grand old Victorian was designed by one Summer P. Hunt, it was known as the Kyte House. Today, it is a traditionalist's haven, a handsome, old-money-style American setting that would do Ralph Lauren proud. The food is gentrified American—things get no wilder than the wild honey with which the California quail is glazed. There's a fine braised veal shank, terrific steak tartare, and an excellent culotte steak broiled over bay leaves. It's worth noting that the entrée prices,

which are mostly in the mid-teens, include big plates with lots of side dishes, so you probably won't need to order the à la carte vegetables. This is ideal for dignified working meals, and the many rooms upstairs are excellent private meeting spots. *2640 Main St., Santa Monica, tel. 213/392-4956. Jacket and tie advised. Reservations advised. AE, MC, V.*

★ ㉒ **The Mandarin.** When the Mandarin was gutted by fire sev-
$$$ eral years ago, everyone thought owner Cecilia Chiang would rebuild it and continue to produce some of the best, most elegant Chinese food in town. But instead she passed on ownership to her son Philip, who had shown his wit in a casual Chinese bistro called Mandarette. The result is a restaurant that's best described as an upscale version of Mandarette know-how. The portentousness of the old place is gone; this is a place for those who wear Armani, and wear him well. It serves what may be the best Chinese food in L.A.—it's certainly the best in Beverly Hills. It's also highly ideal for meetings, especially in the small alcove rooms; be sure to preorder the meal so your guests won't be distracted with menus. *430 N. Camden Dr., Beverly Hills, tel. 213/272-0267. Jacket advised. Reservations advised. AE, CB, DC, MC, V.*

★ ㉑ **Primi.** At the heart of casual dining in L.A. is that '80s
$$ phenomenon called grazing. And L.A.'s prime grazing spot is a casually elegant room, with angels hidden in the decor, called Primi, short for *primi piatti*, Italian for "first plates." Several dozen Italian appetizers are served in both the main room, with its open kitchen, and the garden room. The best way to go is to order the tasting menu of three cold appetizers, three hot appetizers, three pastas, and dessert. Expect such dishes as shreds of grilled pigeon served with soft white cannellini beans and black truffles; gnocchetti, little potato dumplings in the colors of the Italian flag (red, green, and white); and risotto with seafood with porcini or herbs. Each dish is just a nibble, proof that tasty things come in small packages. It's a good meeting space, though the multiplicity of the dishes may be a bit distracting. *10543 W. Pico Blvd., West L.A., tel. 213/475-9235. Casual dress. Reservations advised. AE, MC, V.*

④ **Shane.** Hidden in back of the Beverly Glen Circle shopping
$$ center, this Italian-Southwestern restaurant is unique while being quintessentially L.A. The wild, colorful Southwestern decor is pure love-it-or-hate-it stuff, with tile snakes crawling around the room—it's anything but neutral and beige. Even the dishware makes a statement. Oddly, the food that sits atop these plates is fairly recognizable, despite its eccentric Italian-Southwestern roots. The pizzas are all tasty (lamb sausage, sage, and red chili; or chicken and tomatillo salsa; or pancetta and shiitake mushrooms), and the duck tostada and the beef quesadilla are unusually good. Although this is an informal spot, you can have quiet talks in the upstairs dining area. *2932 Beverly Glen Circle, Beverly Glen, tel. 213/470-6223. Casual dress. Reservations advised. AE, MC, V.*

⑨ **Valentino.** That the food has always been superb at Valen-
$$$$ tino is something few would deny. That the ambience at Valentino was dreary was also something few would argue

against. So master restaurateur Piero Selvaggio shut down his place several years ago and redid everything. Though the exterior still looks like a stucco bunker, the inside has been opened up and stylized, a series of rooms painted in muted, powdery pastels, with a Milanese stylishness in the lighting and decorative touches. Ask Selvaggio to create a meal for you, and out of the kitchen will come such things as bread crusts with beautiful glass pitchers of obscure olive oils; buffalo ricotta with basil leaves; prosciutto with white beans and Parmesan; small pancakes filled with radicchio and cheese—in other words, Italian cooking as it's eaten in Italy. One caveat: Leaving yourself in Selvaggio's hands is not inexpensive. But it certainly is good. Valentino's is also excellent for business meals of all sizes and types. *3115 Pico Blvd., Santa Monica, tel. 213/829-4313. Jacket and tie advised. Reservations required. AE, CB, DC, MC, V.*

## San Gabriel Valley

🟑53  **Crocodile Café.** This is the creation of the nearby Parkway
$   Grill, which has been described as the "Spago of Pasadena." It's a successful attempt to create a place where people can go for fun and good, cheap California cuisine. The café setting—a pleasant outdoor patio and a bright, minimalist interior designed around the hectic open kitchen—is noisy, cheerful, and easygoing. The food can be strikingly good, in particular the black bean and sirloin chili. Then there are the chubby red Anaheim chilies stuffed with smoked jack cheese; the excellent oakwood-grilled burgers, which come with a small mountain of very crisp fries; and the barbecued-chicken and smoked-gouda pizza. For those in Pasadena or in not-far-away Downtown L.A., this is a great spot for a lively, casual night off. *140 S. Lake St., Pasadena, tel. 818/449-9900. Casual dress. No reservations. MC, V.*

★ 🟑54  **Parkway Grill.** This is a warm and wonderfully open place,
$$$   with brick walls, high ceilings, and a small forest of plants and trees. When you enter, you stand on a platform that overlooks an open kitchen in which a bevy of chefs is making pizzas and composing salads. It's a nearly perfect piece of design, blending the traditional with the modern. The design of the menu is equally successful. The dishes are utterly revisionist Americana; for the most part, they never existed in anyone's past. Consider such appetizers as delicate corn cakes with warm oysters, small sausages, and a slightly spicy tomatillo sauce; black-bean soup with smoked pork and a lime cream; and roasted chilies filled with smoked chicken, corn, cilantro, and cheese. Think of marvelous pizzas topped with lamb sausage, grilled eggplant, smoked chicken and cilantro, or even black beans and smoked pork. It sounds odd, but it tastes good. This is an excellent spot for business lunches and dinners, and there's a fine private room for larger meetings. *510 S. Arroyo Pkwy., Pasadena, tel. 818/795-1001. Jacket advised. Reservations advised. AE, MC, V.*

## Airport/South Bay

🟑16  **Fino.** This is a child of the South Bay's widely acclaimed
$$   Chez Melange, a three-ring culinary circus that makes you

wonder why more places aren't doing it this way—and this well. Tucked in a mini-mall south of Pacific Coast Highway, Fino is an assortment of smallish rooms on several levels, with rough white walls, a red-tile interior "roof," Mediterranean decorative touches, and a semiopen kitchen raging on the ground floor. Waiters who work the upper floor develop legs of steel; bounding up those steps laden with plates of lamb loin, duck with white beans and sausage, and braised escarole stuffed with prosciutto balanced on their forearms takes a lot of skill. Fino defines itself as, "a bistro featuring the rustic foods of Spain, France, and Italy," though you taste mostly Italy, and its requisite garlic and olive oil. The quieter upstairs dining area is good for informal business meetings; downstairs is the place for a good time. *24530 Hawthorne Blvd., Torrance, tel. 213/373–1952. Casual dress. Reservations strongly advised. AE, MC, V.*

## FREE TIME

### Fitness

*Hotel Facilities*
Downtown's **Biltmore Health Club** (tel. 213/612–1567) is the city's largest hotel club. Hotel guests are charged $8 during the week, nonguests pay $10 a day.

*Health Clubs*
There are many **Holiday Spa Health Clubs** around town (tel. 800/669–3200, for locations and information); most have a decent collection of gym equipment, pools, and fitness classes. Fees vary, and there's usually a one-week minimum membership. The new **Ketchum Downtown YMCA** (401 S. Hope St., tel. 213/624–2348) has outstanding facilities and charges $10 daily ($15 if you arrive prime-time, between 4:30 and 7:30 PM). The **Sports Connection** (8612 Santa Monica Blvd., West Hollywood, tel. 213/652–7440; 2929 31st St., Santa Monica, tel. 213/450–4464; and locations in outlying areas), a good health-club chain with extensive facilities, admits out-of-town guests for $15 a day.

*Jogging*
Runners and walkers staying Downtown will have to make their course on the wide sidewalks, or drive north to **Griffith Park,** which has many hillside trails. Visitors to the Westside can jog on the grassy median on **Burton Way** between La Cienega Boulevard and Beverly Hills. In Beverly Hills, there are gravel paths along **Sunset Boulevard** and **Santa Monica Boulevard.** Crisscrossing Beverly Hills are many wide, quiet, tree-lined side streets that are excellent for running or walking. The best (and most smogfree) Westside running area is the grassy median on **San Vicente Boulevard** between Brentwood and Santa Monica, ending at Ocean Avenue overlooking the beach. And of course, there are many options for those who like to run on sand; *see* Beaches, in the Diversion section, below.

### Shopping

Los Angeles is a great shopping town, but as with everything here, it often involves a trip by car. Most shoppers head for one of the many sprawling malls scattered throughout the city; they may have a rather depressing uniformity and preponderance of chain stores, but for a busy traveler they're perfect for one-stop shopping. There are also some excellent neighborhood shopping areas throughout town, most notably the expensive, tourist-thronged shops of Beverly Hills's **Rodeo** (pronounced "Ro-DAY-o"), **Cañon** (pronounced "Canyon"), and **Beverly** drives, and **Wilshire Boulevard.** Other good streets to walk and shop are yupscale **Montana Avenue** in Santa Monica, arty **Main Street** in Venice, hip **Melrose Avenue** in Hollywood, small-town **Larchmont Boulevard** in Hancock Park, **Sunset Plaza** in West Hollywood, and conservative **Lake Street** in Pasadena.

*Downtown*
**ARCO Plaza** (Fifth & Flower Sts., tel. 213/625–2132), with its 7 acres of shopping and dining on two levels, is one of the largest subterranean shopping centers in the country, and one of the most disappointing. Downtown's **Seventh Street Marketplace** (Figueroa St. at 7th St., tel. 213/955–7150) is home to a good Bullock's, a small but choice array of upscale shops, like Ann Taylor and Godiva, and a fast-food court. Bargain-hunters flock to the **Cooper Building** (860 S. Los Angeles St., tel. 213/622–1139), in which some 70 shops sell heavily discounted, major-label men's, women's, and children's clothing and accessories, along with cosmetics and linens.

*West Hollywood, Westside, Beverly Hills*
The famed **Beverly Center** (8500 Beverly Blvd., tel. 213/854–0070), on the edge of the Wilshire District and West Hollywood, is home to more than 200 shops and restaurants, including a 13-screen cinema complex. The mix of shops slants toward the young and aggressively chic. On the street level is the legendary (and *always* mobbed) Hard Rock Café. The **Century City Shopping Center & Marketplace** (10250 Santa Monica Blvd., Century City, tel. 213/553–5300) is a large, very pleasant outdoor mall with lots of upscale shops (Charles Jourdan, Ann Taylor, The Pottery Barn), a 14-theater complex, and dozens of places to eat. In West L.A., the **Westside Pavilion** (10800 W. Pico Blvd., tel. 213/474–6255) is a striking three-story atrium-style center with a good mix of shops (The Cashmere People, Victoria's Secret), restaurants, and movie theaters. The most famous shopping area, **Rodeo Drive,** is often compared to Fifth Avenue in New York or Via Condotti in Rome. Along several blocks of North Rodeo Drive, between Wilshire and Santa Monica boulevards, are such stores as Giorgio (327 Rodeo Dr., tel. 213/274–0200), Battaglia (306 Rodeo Dr., tel. 213/276–7184), Polo/Ralph Lauren (444 Rodeo Dr., tel. 213/281–7200), Theodore (453 Rodeo Dr., tel. 213/276–9691), Montana (463 Rodeo Dr., tel. 213/273–7925), Giorgio Armani (436 Rodeo Dr., tel. 213/271–5555), Krizia (410 Rodeo Dr., tel. 213/276–5411), Alaïa (313 Rodeo Dr., tel. 213/275–7313), and Chanel (301 Rodeo Dr., tel. 213/278–5500).

## Diversions

The new **Gene Autry Western Heritage Museum** (4700 Zoo Dr., Griffith Park, tel. 213/667–2000) displays a worthwhile collection of art and artifacts from the early West.

**Beaches** abound in Southern California; the widest, most popular, and most convenient beach is Santa Monica Beach (tel. 213/394–3266); check to be sure its waters are clean enough for safe swimming. Take the Santa Monica Freeway about 20 miles west from Downtown. Swimmers can also head north on Pacific Coast Highway to **Zuma** (tel. 213/457–9891) or the beaches near the Ventura County Line.

The **California Afro-American Museum** (600 State Dr., Exposition Park, tel. 213/744–7432) documents the Afro-American experience in the Americas.

The recently expanded **California Museum of Science & Industry** (700 State Dr., Exposition Park, tel. 213/744–7400) is filled with fascinating exhibits on science, technology, and health.

**Card clubs** in the communities of Gardena and Bell Gardens (5 miles from Downtown) offer legal table (mostly poker) gaming. **The Bicycle Club** (7301 Eastern Ave., Bell Gardens, tel. 213/806–4646) is the world's largest such casino. Another card room is the **Normandie Casino & Dinner Theater** (1045 W. Rosecrans Ave., Gardena, tel. 213/715–7400).

**Downtown walking tours** of L.A.'s marvelous old buildings (yes, L.A. has a history) are led on Saturday mornings by the Los Angeles Conservancy (tel. 213/623–CITY or 213/623–TOURS).

Early risers staying Downtown should visit the **Flower Market** (Wall St. between 7th and 8th Sts.) around 5–6 AM. In scenes reminiscent of Holland, local growers and importers deliver truckloads of fragrant blooms to some 100 wholesalers. In the same area is the bustling **Produce Market,** where, in similar scenes of bustling predawn activity, fresh fruits and vegetables are unloaded and transferred to trucks from supermarkets and grocers.

The spectacularly sited **J. Paul Getty Museum** (17985 Pacific Coast Hwy., Malibu, tel. 213/459–7611) is home to an extensive collection of Greek and Roman antiquities, plus pre-20th-century Western art, all housed in a re-creation of a first-century A.D. Roman country villa.

**Golf West** (tel. 818/340–9202) organizes corporate and organizational golf outings and tournaments for groups only.

**Grand Central Market** (317 S. Broadway, Downtown) may be in L.A., but it's a scene straight out of a Latin American market town. Local Latino shoppers come to shop for familiar groceries and household goods; terrific Latino fast food is available.

**Heli LA** (tel. 213/553–4354) offers various dramatic sightseeing dinner helicopter flights over Los Angeles. It's not cheap at $299 per person, but it's an unforgettable experience.

**Hollywood On Location** (8644 Wilshire Blvd., Beverly Hills, tel. 213/659–9165) sells (for $29) a daily list and precise map of some 35 locations where movies, TV series, and music videos are being shot. It's a great chance to see how Hollywood works—and perhaps even to see a few stars.

The **Los Angeles County Museum of Art** (5905 Wilshire Blvd., Wilshire District, tel. 213/857 6111) attempts with some success to be L.A.'s cultural heart and soul. The five museum buildings around a spacious central court include the new Pavilion for Japanese Art and the Atlantic Richfield Gallery of Modern Art. Classic films are also screened regularly.

The **Los Angeles Zoo** (5333 Zoo Dr., Griffith Park, tel. 213/666–4650) is the sprawling (and intriguing) home to more than 2,000 rare and exotic mammals, birds, and reptiles in naturalistic settings.

The **Museum of Contemporary Art** (250 S. Grand Ave., Downtown, tel. 213/626–6222) is both a spectacular building (designed by Arata Isozaki) and an excellent center for new art, including media and performing arts. The gift shop and café alone are worth a visit.

The **Museum of Flying** (2771 Donald Douglas Loop, Santa Monica, tel. 213/392–8822) at the Santa Monica Airport details L.A.'s rich aviation history, with its restored historical military and commercial aircraft.

The **George C. Page Museum of La Brea Discoveries** (5801 Wilshire Blvd., Wilshire District, tel. 213/857–6311 or 213/936–2230) houses the collection of Ice Age fossils recovered from the asphalt deposits (the famed La Brea Tar Pits) that surround the museum.

**Power and sail boats** of all sizes are rented by the hour from Rent-a-Sail in Marina del Rey (tel. 213/271–2677).

The **Southwest Museum** (234 Museum Dr., Highland Park, tel. 213/221–2164 or 213/221–2163) is an excellent museum that holds exhibits on Native American cultures from Alaska to South America, with a particular emphasis on local tribes.

The **Wells Fargo History Museum** (333 S. Grand Ave., Downtown, tel. 213/253–7166) uses stagecoaches, photos, and other relics to illustrate California's Gold Rush days.

## Professional Sports

**Baseball: Los Angeles Dodgers** (Dodger Stadium, 1000 Elysian Park Ave., L.A., tel. 213/224–1400), **California Angels** (Anaheim Stadium, Anaheim, tel. 714/634–2100). **Basketball: Los Angeles Lakers** (Great Western Forum, 3900 W. Manchester Blvd., Inglewood, tel. 213/419–3142), **Los Angeles Clippers** (Los Angeles Memorial Sports Arena, 3939 S. Figueroa St., tel. 213/748–0500). **Football: Los Angeles Rams** (Anaheim Stadium, Anaheim, tel. 714/937–6767 or 213/227–4748), **Los Angeles Raiders** (scheduled to play in the Los Angeles Coliseum but still negotiating for a new home; tel. 213/322–5901). **Hockey: Los Angeles Kings** (Great Western Forum, tel. 213/480–3232).

## The Arts

Although movies and television dominate the performing arts in Los Angeles, the stage is still quite active; in fact, it's not unusual for major Hollywood performers, nostalgic for the live theater, to appear in one of the area's small houses. For the most complete listing of weekly events, get the current issue of *Los Angeles* or *California* magazine. The Calendar section of the Los Angeles *Times* also offers a wide survey of Los Angeles arts events, as do the more irreverent free publications, the *L.A. Weekly* and the *L.A. Reader.* The largest venue for live theater is downtown's Music Center, which comprises the Ahmanson Theatre (seating 2,071); the Dorothy Chandler Pavilion, the 3,200 seat home to musical extravaganzas; and the Mark Taper Forum, a more intimate and experimental theater. The other major L.A. theaters are the Shubert Theater in Century City, and Hollywood's James A. Doolittle Theatre and Henry Fonda Theater. Smaller, more avant-garde venues include the Canon Theatre, Colony Studio Theatre, Park Plaza, and Taper, Too, a 99-seat space at the John Anson Ford Theater near the Hollywood Bowl.

The Los Angeles Philharmonic makes its summer home at the famous Hollywood Bowl; a concert under the stars here is a memorable experience. From October to May, the Philharmonic performs at the Dorothy Chandler Pavilion, which also showcases major dance troupes.

The following are good venues for tickets: **Al Brooks Tickets** (900 Wilshire Blvd., Downtown, tel. 213/626–5863); **Front Row Center** (404 S. Figueroa, Suite 105, Downtown, tel. 213/488–0020); **Murray's Tickets** (740 W. Martin Luther King Jr. Blvd., Downtown, tel. 213/234–0123); **Ticketmaster** (tel. 213/480–3232); **Ticketron** (6060 W. Manchester, Westchester, tel. 213/642–5708); **Ticket Times** (9925 Venice Blvd., Culver City, tel. 213/202–0053).

**Ahmanson Theatre,** 135 N. Grand Ave., Downtown, tel. 213/972–7403.
**Canon Theatre,** 205 N. Canon Dr., Beverly Hills, tel. 213/466–9966.
**Colony Studio Theatre,** 1944 Riverside Dr., Beverly Hills, tel. 213/665–3011.
**Dorothy Chandler Pavilion,** 135 N. Grand Ave., Downtown, tel. 213/972–7200.
**Henry Fonda Theater,** 6126 Hollywood Blvd., Hollywood, tel. 213/410–1062.
**Hollywood Bowl,** 2301 N. Highland Ave., Hollywood, tel. 213/850–2000.
**James A. Doolittle Theatre,** 1615 N. Vine St., Hollywood, tel. 213/410–1062.
**Mark Taper Forum,** 135 N. Grand Ave., Downtown, tel. 213/972–7337.
**Park Plaza,** 607 S. Park View, Downtown, tel. 213/466–1767.
**Shubert Theater,** 2020 Ave. of the Stars, Century City, tel. 800/233–3123.
**Taper, Too,** 2580 Cahuenga Blvd. E, Hollywood, tel. 213/972–7392.

## After Hours

Clubs are scattered across the city, but many of the best are in the Hollywood/West Hollywood area; not surprisingly, they tend to attract the young and the restless. Despite the high energy level, this is an early-to-bed city, and its safe to say that by 2 AM most clubs are closed. The accent is on trendy rock clubs, smooth country-western establishments, intimate jazz spots, and comedy clubs. City residents usually don't gravitate to hotels, except for a quiet evening of soft piano music, often accompanied by sentimental vocalists.

*Bars and Lounges*

**Downtown:** The small bar at **Engine Co. No. 28** (644 S. Figueroa St., tel. 213/624–6996) is a traditional spot popular with the Brooks Brothers set. The **Lobby Bar** (Hyatt Regency, tel. 213/683–1234) is an unpretentious, comfortable, and convenient gathering spot that offers live entertainment and a happy hour buffet. The **Grand Avenue Bar** (Biltmore Hotel, tel. 213/624–1011) is a cool, sophisticated marble hideaway with good music and hors d'oeuvres.

**Westside:** The serenely sophisticated **Windows** (Four Seasons Hotel, tel. 213/273–2222) is something of a mecca for Beverly Hills business types. Afternoon tea is poured, and there's a pianist in the evening. Perhaps the best Westside bar for doing business and unwinding is **The Bar, Regent Beverly Wilshire** (tel. 213/275–5200), a very elegant spot with the atmosphere of a gentleman's club in which women feel right at home. There's piano music from 4 PM and complimentary hors d'oeuvres from 5 to 7. **Jimmy's Bar** (201 Moreno Dr., Beverly Hills, tel. 213/879–2394), located just off the restaurant's main dining room, is a gathering spot for local society, celebrities, and show-business dealmakers. Those wanting to people-watch and check out the trendy side of L.A.'s bar scene might consider **DC3** (Santa Monica Airport, 31st St. entrance, Santa Monica, tel. 213/399–2323), the **West Beach Café** (60 N. Venice Blvd., Venice, 213/823–5396), **Eureka** (1845 S. Bundy Dr., West L.A., tel. 213/447–8000), and **Maple Drive** (345 N. Maple Dr., Beverly Hills, tel. 213/274–9800).

*Nightclubs/Dancing*

**Bar One** (9229 Sunset Blvd., West Hollywood, tel. 213/271–8355) is an intimate combination of restaurant and disco; a DJ plays rap, hip hop, and rock. Don't expect to get in unless you're with someone the door host recognizes. The trendy **China Club** (1600 Argyle St., Hollywood, tel. 213/469–1600) serves California cuisine for late dinners and showcases live music during the week and DJs on weekends. The clientele is casually well dressed and well heeled. **Club Lingerie** (6507 W. Sunset Blvd., Hollywood, tel. 213/466–8557) is a fashionable spot to hear live rock and check out hip Angelenos. For a classic disco (with live music and an adjoining restaurant), head for **Spice** (7070 Hollywood Blvd., Hollywood, tel. 213/856–9638). **The Troubadour** (9081 Santa Monica Blvd., Hollywood, tel. 213/276–6168), once L.A.'s folk/rock center, is now a haven for heavy metal. You have to like it loud if you come here. Young execs, entertainment industry folk, and offbeat trendsetters frequent **Vertigo** (333 S. Boylston St., Downtown, behind the Pacific Stock Exchange, tel. 213/

747–4849), a huge, stylish nightclub that features live music and dancing. Also check out **Roxbury** (8225 W. Sunset Blvd., W. Hollywood, tel. 213/656–1750) and **Highland Grounds** (742 N. Highland Ave., Hollywood, tel. 213/466–1507).

### Comedy Clubs

The most famous are the **Comedy Store** (8433 W. Sunset Blvd., West Hollywood, tel. 213/656–6225) and **The Improvisation** (8162 Melrose Ave., West Hollywood, tel. 213/651–2583). Also good are the **Laugh Factory** (8001 W. Sunset Blvd., West Hollywood, tel. 213/656–1336) and **Igby's** (11637 W. Pico Blvd., West L.A., tel. 213/477–3553). For a change of pace and lots of laughs, don't miss the show at the **Groundlings Theatre** (7303 Melrose Ave., Hollywood, tel. 213/934–9700), a very funny mix of improvisation and ensemble sketch comedy.

### Cabarets

**Café Largo** (432 N. Fairfax, Hollywood, tel. 213/852–1073) has taken the cabaret to new heights, with its cutting-edge live entertainment, jazz, performance art, readings, and good dinners. Traditionalists will adore **The Cinegrill** (Hollywood Roosevelt Hotel, 7000 Hollywood Blvd., Hollywood, tel. 213/466–7000), a beautiful, sophisticated '40s-style supper club featuring great torch singers and jazz music. **Oscar's** (8210 Sunset Blvd., West Hollywood, tel. 213/654–3457) serves up jazz and the blues in an English pub atmosphere. **Verdi** (1519 Wilshire Blvd., Santa Monica, tel. 213/393–0706) combines Northern Italian food and a chic decor with fairly serious performances of opera and light opera.

### Jazz Clubs

The gorgeous former lobby area of the Biltmore Hotel, the **Gallery** bar (tel. 213/624–1011), is a popular gathering spot for businesspeople after work and on into the evening. The live jazz is mellow and pleasant. **Café Mondrian** (Le Mondrian Hotel, 8440 Sunset Blvd., West Hollywood, tel. 213/650–8999) showcases jazz and pop artists in an intimate lounge setting. Big-name jazz acts perform in the large room at the **Catalina Bar & Grill** (1640 N. Cahuenga Blvd., Hollywood, tel. 213/466–2210). **Nucleus Nuance** (7267 Melrose Ave., Hollywood, tel. 213/939–8666) is a small, lovely spot in which to dine (Continental cuisine), dance, and listen to traditional jazz and jazz-tinged pop. The comfortable **Vine Street Bar & Grill** (1610 N. Vine St., Hollywood, tel. 213/463–4375) attracts such fine performers as Etta James and George Shearing.

# Memphis

*by Tom Martin*

Memphis, once a sleepy river town, woke up in the 1980s. After the turbulent period that followed the assassination of Dr. Martin Luther King, Jr., in 1968, and culminated in a divisive strike by firemen and policemen in the late '70s, Memphis began a slow but steady recovery. With the growth of Memphis-based Federal Express as a catalyst, the city emerged as a major distribution center and effective capital of the mid-South. It is rapidly expanding to the east, and along its western boundary, the Mississippi River.

International Paper moved its center of operations from Manhattan to Memphis in the late 1980s and boosted the city's business ego enormously. The city continues to serve as headquarters for Holiday Inns (now owned by the Bass, PLC of England) and its former parent, Promus, which owns Harrah's Casinos, Embassy Suites, and other hotel chains. The consumer operations of Schering-Plough are also here, though most of the decision-making authority has moved to New Jersey. Other major sources of jobs include health care (Memphis has two of the nation's largest private hospitals), government service (a naval air station and large defense depot are located in the area), and education (Memphis State University has more than 25,000 students).

Like many mid-American cities, Memphis isn't dominated by large manufacturing companies. Instead, small- to medium-size companies, mainly in the service sector, account for the majority of the work force. Tourism has become a fast-growing industry, helped by the popularity of Elvis Presley's Graceland, which by the end of the decade was drawing more than 600,000 visitors annually. Tourists also visit Beale Street, birthplace of blues music, which has been revitalized as a restaurant and nightclub area.

## Top Employers

| Employer | Type of Enterprise | Parent*/ Headquarters |
|---|---|---|
| **BellSouth Corp.** | Telecommunications | Atlanta |
| **Federal Express** | Air freight carrier | Memphis |

| First Tennessee National Corp. | Banking | Memphis |
|---|---|---|
| Fleming Cos. | Wholesalers of grocery products | Oklahoma City, OK |
| Holiday Inns, Inc. | Hotels and Casinos | Bass, PLC/ London |
| Kroger Co. | Food, convenience, & drug stores | Cincinnati |
| NWA, Inc. | Transportation & airlines | St. Paul |
| Schering-Plough Corp. | Drugs and personal care products | Madison, NJ |
| Sears Roebuck & Co. | Merchandising, financial services | Chicago |
| T.P.I. Restaurants Inc. | Operator of restaurants | Memphis |

*if applicable*

## ESSENTIAL INFORMATION

### Climate

The city's changeable weather is affected by both Gulf Coast warm fronts and Canadian cold fronts. Winters are usually mild, with occasional ice storms but little snow. Summers can be unbearably hot, with humidity high from late June to early September.

What follows are average daily maximum and minimum temperatures for Memphis.

| | | | | | | | | |
|---|---|---|---|---|---|---|---|---|
| Jan. | 48F | −5C | Feb. | 53F | −2C | Mar. | 61F | 2C |
| | 31 | −15 | | 34 | −13 | | 42 | −9 |
| Apr. | 73F | 9C | May | 81F | 13C | June | 88F | 17C |
| | 52 | −3 | | 61 | 2 | | 69 | 7 |
| July | 92F | 20C | Aug. | 90F | 18C | Sept. | 84F | 15C |
| | 73 | 9 | | 71 | 8 | | 64 | 4 |
| Oct. | 75F | 10C | Nov. | 61F | 2C | Dec. | 52F | −3C |
| | 51 | −3 | | 41 | −9 | | 34 | −13 |

### Airport

**Memphis International Airport** is 9½ miles south of downtown. Few international flights come here, but as the major hub for Federal Express, it's the world's busiest airport from midnight to 4 AM.

### Airport Business Facilities

**Mutual of Omaha Business Service Center** (Central Terminal Building, upper level, tel. 901/922–8090) has fax machines, photocopying, notary public, secretarial service, baggage storage, Western Union, travel insurance, cash advance, and check cashing. **The Skyport Inn** (in Terminal A, tel. 901/345–3220) has a two-hour rate for beds and showers, and five conference rooms with catering service.

## Airlines

Memphis is a hub city for **Northwest.**

**American,** tel. 800/433–7300.
**Delta,** tel. 901/761–5441 or 800/221–1212.
**Midway,** tel. 800/621–5700.
**Northwest,** tel. 901/525–7681 or 800/225–2525.
**TWA,** tel. 901/526–8414 or 800/221–2000.
**United,** tel. 800/241–6522.
**USAir,** tel. 901/526–7691 or 800/428–4322.

## Between the Airport and Downtown

*By Taxi*
A ride from the airport takes 15–20 minutes (there is no real traffic congestion at any time) and costs about $10 on the meter to downtown, $15 to suburban hotels (rates are $1.85 for the first mile and $1 for each additional mile). Taxis that are not metered offer fixed rates approximating those noted for the metered cabs.

*By Limousine*
An airport limousine that serves the major hotels downtown can be picked up outside the baggage claim area; the cost one way is $6.

## Car Rentals

All major car-rental companies are located just north of the airport on Democrat Road, a five-minute shuttle ride.

**Avis,** tel. 800/331–1212.
**Budget,** tel. 901/332–2222 or 800/527–0700.
**Hertz,** tel. 901/345–5680 or 800/654–3131.
**National,** tel. 901/345–0070 or 800/328–4567.

## Emergencies

*Doctors*
**Baptist Memorial Hospital Physician Referral Service** (tel. 901/362–8677), **Baptist Minor Medical Clinic** (five locations, tel. 901/274–3336), **Med-Emergency Clinic** (5270 Knight Arnold Rd., tel. 901/362–2811), **Methodist Med-Search** (tel. 901/762–8686).

*Dentists*
**Care-Dent** (tel. 901/345–1153), 24-hour telephone referral.

## Important Addresses and Numbers

**Audiovisual rental.** Nolans (675 Poplar Ave., tel. 901/527–4313).

**Chamber of Commerce** (22 Front St., tel. 901/575–3500).

**Computer rental.** Computerland (80 Monroe Ave., tel. 901/521–8088).

**Convention and exhibition centers.** Agricenter International (7777 Walnut Grove Rd., tel. 901/757–7777), Memphis and Shelby County Convention Center (255 N. Main, tel. 901/576–1200), Mid-South Coliseum (Mid-South

Fairgrounds, 996 Early Maxwell Blvd., tel. 901/274–3982).

**Fax services.** Executive Business Center (1355 Lynnfield Rd., tel. 901/761–2420), VIP Express (2600 Poplar Ave., tel. 901/454–6050) for pickup and delivery.

**Formal-wear rental.** Formal Shop (4722 Poplar Ave., tel. 901/683–5297).

**Gift shops.** Chocolates: Dinstuhl's (The Peabody Hotel, 149 Union Ave., tel. 901/529–9845); Flowers: John Hoover Flowers (2206 Union Ave., tel. 901/274–1853); Gift Baskets: Partytime (10 Timber Creek Dr., Germantown, tel. 901/756–4751).

**Graphic design studios.** Allan and Akin (1995 Nonconnah Blvd., tel. 901/345–3686), Graphic Creations (3566 Walker Ave., tel. 901/458–8187), Nixon and Associates (5575 Poplar Ave., tel. 901/767–8933).

**Hairstylist.** Unisex: Hudson-Barnett Hair Studio (1086 W. Rex Rd., tel. 901/682–9320).

**Health and fitness clubs.** *See* Fitness, below.

**Information hot lines.** Commercial Appeal Sports Information Line (tel. 901/529–5800), LINC (tel. 901/725–8895) community information and referral service.

**Limousine services.** Airport Limousine Service (tel. 901/577–7700), Tennessee Limousine Service (tel. 901/366–5616).

**Liquor stores.** Arthur's Wine and Liquors (964 June Rd., tel. 901/767–9463), Buster's Liquors (191 S. Highland St., tel. 901/458–0929).

**Mail delivery, overnight.** DHL Worldwide Express (tel. 901/795–9911), Federal Express (tel. 901/345–5044), TNT Skypak (tel. 901/527–0501), UPS (tel. 800/342–8357), U.S. Postal Service Express Mail (tel. 901/521–2180).

**Messenger service.** Financial Courier Services (6099 Mt. Moriah Extended, tel. 901/761–4555).

**Office space rentals.** HQ Headquarters Companies (6055 Primacy Pkwy., tel. 901/682–4090), Morgan Keegan Tower Executive Suites (50 N. Front St., tel. 901/576–8120).

**Pharmacies, late-night.** Walgreen's (1801 Union Ave., tel. 901/272–2006; 6680 Poplar Ave., tel. 901/754–1472; 3515 Park Ave., tel. 901/458–1611).

**Secretarial services.** EBC Office Centers (5865 Ridgeway Center Pkwy., tel. 901/682–4934), Morgan Keegan Executive Suites (50 N. Front St., tel. 901/576–8120).

**Stationery supplies.** Michael's Pen and Paper (1229 Park Place Center, tel. 901/685–2340).

**Taxis.** United Cab (tel. 901/525–0521), Yellow/Checker Cab (tel. 901/577–7777).

**Theater tickets.** *See* The Arts, below.

**Train information.** Amtrak (545 S. Main St., tel. 901/526–0052).

**Travel agents.** A & I Travel (8 S. 3rd St., tel. 901/525–0151), Omega Travel (5050 Poplar Ave., tel. 901/767–0761), Regency Travel (6410 Poplar Ave., tel. 901/683–3003).

**Weather.** WEZI FM Weather Line (tel. 901/363–9494).

## LODGING

Memphis may have grown into a major distribution center, but its hotels, especially those that court business travelers, have some catching up to do. Amenities that have become common in hotels elsewhere, such as stocked mini-bars and indoor pools, won't be found at many of the hotels reviewed here. Major hotels can be found in two areas: downtown and east Memphis, near the Poplar Avenue exit of I–240. Only a few hotels, and only one deserving of mention here, are located near the airport. The medical center and most government, legal, and banking activity are downtown. East Memphis is home to large real-estate development companies, the operations headquarters of International Paper, and the headquarters of the Promus Companies. Federal Express is located near the airport. Fortunately, getting around the Memphis area is much easier than travel in many cities of similar size; expect a downtown-to-east-Memphis trek (about 15 miles) to take only about 20–25 minutes. (Note, however, that taxi service is not terrific in Memphis; don't depend on a cab to arrive in less than 15 minutes from the time you call.)

Most of the hotels listed below offer corporate rates and weekend discounts. Inquire when making reservations.

Highly recommended lodgings in each price category are indicated by a star ★.

| Category | Cost* |
|---|---|
| $$$$ (Very Expensive) | over $95 |
| $$$ (Expensive) | $70–$95 |
| $$ (Moderate) | under $70 |

*All prices are for a standard double room, single occupancy, excluding 7 ¾% sales tax and 5% room tax.*

*Numbers in the margin correspond to numbered hotel locations on the Memphis Lodging and Dining maps.*

### Downtown/Center City

**18** $$$ **The Brownstone Hotel.** This 11-story high rise, built in 1970, was the convention-center hotel before it was displaced by the Holiday Inn Crowne Plaza across the street. Though the current, partial renovation may help, the hotel has definitely lost its luster. It's understaffed, especially to serve the needs of the business traveler; room service is offered only a few hours a day, and the on-premises restaurant is disappointing. The rooms are modern, functional, and spare; bathrooms are small and offer few amenities. Lighting, both on desks (which not all rooms have) and at bedside, is poor. The lobby is small and somber. Avoid the 11th floor, where sleeping rooms are interspersed with meeting rooms. The hotel's primary merit is its location, making it a second choice for convention-goers when the Crowne Plaza is full. *300 N. 2nd St., 38105, tel. 901/525–2511 or 800/468–3515, fax 901/525–2511, ext. 1220. Gen. manager, Robert Beck. 48 singles, 183 doubles, 12 suites. AE, CB, D, DC, MC, V.*

❷ **The French Quarter Inn.** This intimate all-suites hotel,
$$$$ with its plant- and fountain-filled atrium, achieves the New Orleans atmosphere its name evokes. Situated in the Overton Square entertainment district, it is convenient to midtown and medical center businesses. The four-story hotel, built in 1985, had a new wing added in 1988. The rooms are among the best in the city, and the hotel offers a complimentary breakfast buffet. Two-room suites have a sitting area and separate dressing tables; larger suites have a separate sitting room and living room. Both types are well furnished with cherry and mahogany and deco-rated with soft pastel colors and floral draperies. All baths have a large Jacuzzi. Avoid the first floor, which has meet-ing rooms as well as sleeping rooms; the newer east wing is quieter and better furnished than the original building. The staff is energetic and emphasizes personal service. *2144 Madison Ave., 38104, tel. 901/728–4000 or 800/843–0353, fax 901/278–1262. Gen. manager, Ronald Drowns. 65 2-room suites, 36 3-room suites. AE, CB, D, DC, MC, V.*

❿❾ **Holiday Inn Crowne Plaza.** This 18-floor high rise adjacent
$$$ to the Memphis Convention Center was built in 1985. The hotel no longer offers the crisp professionalism it did in its early years, despite a recent million-dollar renovation. Its restaurant, Chervil's, was closed in 1989, and the con-cierge floor is used only to fulfill special requests, but all the rooms are spacious and tastefully decorated with mod-ern furniture and subtle mauves and grays in the carpet-ing and draperies. Bathrooms are especially large and well lighted. The pool area is large, too, with a high ceil-ing, huge windows, and an outdoor terrace. The spar-kling, terraced lobby has polished faux-marble tile, brass railings, and several fountains. *250 N. Main St., 38103, tel. 901/527–7300 or 800/466–4329, fax 901/526–1561. Gen. manager, Bob Bekart. 163 kings, 208 doubles, 13 suites. AE, CB, D, DC, MC, V.*

★ ㉑ **The Peabody.** Located in the heart of downtown, The Pea-
$$$$ body has been something of a barometer of the fortunes of Memphis—grand and glorious from 1925 until after World War II, tired and declining in the 1950s and '60s, and closed altogether in the '70s. But 1981 marked its return as the city's best. In the lobby, live mallard ducks (the ho-tel's symbol) march to their marble fountain each day at 11 AM to the tune of the "King Cotton March," and return to their penthouse on the roof at 5. The hotel offers much more than ducks: Service is the most comprehensive in the city, with a hairdresser, health club, pool, and two of the city's best restaurants, Dux and Chez Philippe (*see* Dining, be-low); Cafe Espresso is a good place for breakfast (*see* Busi-ness Breakfasts, below). Compared with the splendor of the public areas, the basic-class rooms are small and sparsely furnished. But at each successive price level the appointments improve dramatically, and deluxe rooms have rich fabrics and French-provincial reproductions. Bathrooms throughout are small and old-fashioned. The clientele is a mix of well-heeled business travelers and

# GREATER MEMPHIS

**Lodging**
Embassy Suites, **13**
French Quarter Inn, **2**
Holiday Inn Memphis East, **12**
Memphis Airport Hilton, **17**
Memphis Hilton East, **7**
Memphis Marriott, **16**
Omni Memphis, **10**

Radisson Ridgeway Inn, **11**

**Dining**
Ben's, **1**
Folk's Folly, **6**
Frank Grisanti's, **13**
Genghis Khan's / Chef's Bistro, **9**
Hemming's, **14**

John Will's Barbeque Bar and Grill, **8**
Justine's, **4**
La Patisserie Bistro, **15**
Sekisui, **5**
La Tourelle, **3**

# DOWNTOWN MEMPHIS

**Lodging**
The Brownstone Hotel, **18**
Holiday Inn Crowne Plaza, **19**
The Peabody, **21**

**Dining**
Chez Philippe, **21**
The Rendezvous, **20**

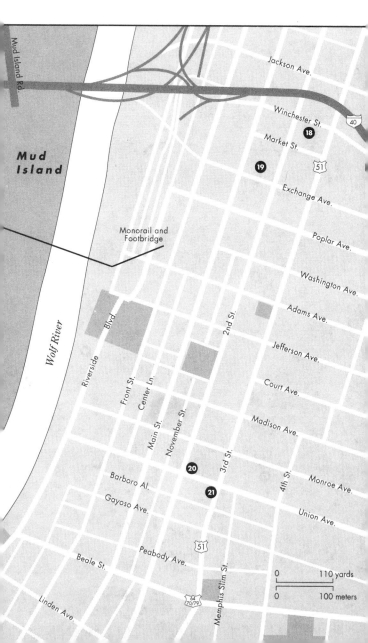

tourists, and the lobby can get congested. *A Belz hotel. 149 Union Ave., 38103, tel. 901/529–4000 or 800/732–2639, fax 901/529–9600. Gen. manager, John Voegler. 85 basic, 50 standard, 204 superior, 87 deluxe, 16 suites. AE, CB, D, DC, MC, V.*

## East Memphis

**⑬ Embassy Suites.** This four-story all-suites hotel was com-
$$$$ pleted in 1989. The appeal of its accommodations is under-
standable; for rates only slightly higher than those at
first-class hotels, you'll get a spacious suite, complimentary cooked-to-order breakfast, and nightly cocktail reception. The modern rooms are not plush, but do include a
sitting area with wet bar, refrigerator, microwave, and
coffee maker. The lobby leads into a large atrium, with
bold colors accenting the tropical theme. The staff is
friendly and enthusiastic. In the heart of the east Memphis business district, the hotel is adjacent to the Regalia
shopping center and near the headquarters of International Paper. An excellent Italian restaurant, Frank
Grisanti's (*see* Dining, below), is on the premises. *1022 S. Shady Grove Rd., 38119, tel. 901/684–1777 or 800/362–2779, fax 901/685–6185. Gen. manager, Dave Lagarce. 157 king suites, 60 standard suites, 3 conference suites. AE, CB, D, DC, MC, V.*

**⑫ Holiday Inn Memphis East.** Memphis is the birthplace of
$$$ Holiday Inns, and this property is a good representative
of that chain. Although it's not as upscale as the Crowne
Plaza downtown, this 10-story high rise off of I-240 is a cut
above the city's other Holiday Inns. Don't expect many
surprises in the rooms, which are plainly decorated with
modern furniture. Best value are the health suites, large
corner rooms priced only slightly higher than standard
rooms and equipped with stationary bicycles. The Iris
Room restaurant serves respectable food. Avoid the third
floor, which has a chlorine smell from the pool and is noisy
with the traffic of guests headed for a swim. *5795 Poplar Ave., 38119, tel. 901/682–7881 or 800/833–4463, fax 901/682–7881, ext. 7760. Gen. manager, Jim Meeker. 136 singles, 73 doubles, 18 suites. AE, CB, D, DC, MC, V.*

**❼ Memphis Hilton East.** This eight-story glass-and-brick ho-
$$ tel opened in 1987, practically next door to the Racquet
Club, home of the U.S. National Indoor tennis tourna-
ment. It is also convenient to two east Memphis office
buildings, Clark Tower and White Station Tower. The decor is plain and functional, with a small, skylit lobby, compact pool area, and guest rooms decorated in somber
colors (except for the garish geometric-print bedspreads).
Though some rooms have refrigerators, other amenities
are scarce; some doubles don't have desks. A concierge
level offers complimentary Continental breakfast. Avoid
the first floor, where cramped meeting rooms are barely
distinguishable from sleeping rooms in the same hallway.
*5069 Sanderlin Ave., 38117, tel. 901/767–6666 or 800/342–7336, fax 901/767–6666, ext. 167. Gen. manager, Jeff Manis. 185 singles, 79 doubles, 6 suites. AE, CB, D, DC, MC, V.*

**★ ⑯ Memphis Marriott.** This 14-story suburban high rise
$$$$ opened in 1987 and has established itself as a favorite of
business travelers. The spacious lobby sparkles with
chandeliers and polished marbled tile. Rooms are large

# MEMPHIS HOTEL CHART

| HOTELS | Price Category | Banquet capacity | No. of meeting rooms | Secretarial services | Audiovisual equipment | Teletype news service | Computer rentals | In-room modem phone jack | All-news cable channel | Desk | Desk lighting | Bed lighting |
|---|---|---|---|---|---|---|---|---|---|---|---|---|
| Airport Hilton | $$$ | 900 | 14 | - | ✓ | - | - | ✓ | ✓ | ◐ | ◐ | ◐ |
| Brownstone | $$$ | 250 | 4 | ✓ | - | - | - | ✓ | ✓ | ○ | ○ | ○ |
| Embassy Suites | $$$$ | 250 | 6 | ✓ | ✓ | - | - | ✓ | ✓ | ◐ | ◐ | ● |
| French Quarter Inn | $$$$ | 125 | 7 | - | ✓ | - | - | - | ✓ | ◐ | ◐ | ◐ |
| Holiday Inn Crowne Plaza | $$$ | 360 | 7 | - | - | - | - | ✓ | ✓ | ◐ | ○ | ◐ |
| Holiday Inn Memphis East | $$$ | 320 | 6 | ✓ | ✓ | - | - | - | ✓ | ◐ | ○ | ● |
| Marriott | $$$$ | 800 | 12 | ✓ | ✓ | - | - | ✓ | ✓ | ● | ◐ | ◐ |
| Memphis Hilton East | $$ | 300 | 8 | ✓ | ✓ | - | - | ✓ | ✓ | - | - | ◐ |
| Omni | $$$ | 1000 | 19 | ✓ | ✓ | - | - | ✓ | ✓ | ◐ | ◐ | ◐ |
| The Peabody | $$$$ | 1100 | 32 | ✓ | ✓ | - | - | ✓ | ✓ | ◐ | ○ | ○ |
| Radisson Ridgeway Inn | $$$ | 700 | 4 | - | - | - | - | ✓ | ✓ | ○ | ○ | ○ |

$$$$ = over $95, $$$ = $70-$95, $$ = under $70.
● good, ◐ fair, ○ poor.
All hotels listed here have photocopying and fax facilities.

| In-Room Amenities | | | | | | | | | | Hotel Amenities | | | | | | |
| --- | --- | --- | --- | --- | --- | --- | --- | --- | --- | --- | --- | --- | --- | --- | --- | --- |
| Nonsmoking rooms | In-room checkout | Minibar | Pay movies | VCR/Movie rentals | Hairdryer | Toiletries | Room service | Laundry/Dry cleaning | Pressing | Concierge | Barber/Hairdresser | Garage | Courtesy airport transport | Sauna | Pool | Exercise room |
| ✓ | ✓ | – | ✓ | – | – | ○ | ◐ | ● | ◐ | – | – | – | ✓ | ✓ | ◐ | ○ |
| ✓ | – | – | ✓ | ✓ | – | ○ | ○ | ● | ◐ | – | – | – | – | – | ○ | – |
| ✓ | ✓ | – | – | – | – | ○ | ◐ | ● | ◐ | – | – | – | ✓ | ✓ | ◐ | ◐ |
| ✓ | – | ✓ | – | – | – | ◐ | ● | ◐ | ◐ | – | – | – | ✓ | – | ○ | ◐ |
| ✓ | ✓ | – | ✓ | – | – | ○ | ◐ | ● | ◐ | ✓ | – | ✓ | – | ✓ | ● | ◐ |
| ✓ | – | – | ✓ | – | – | ○ | ◐ | ● | ◐ | – | – | – | ✓ | ✓ | ◐ | ◐ |
| ✓ | ✓ | – | ✓ | – | ✓ | ◐ | ● | ● | ● | ✓ | – | – | ✓ | ✓ | ◐ | ● |
| ✓ | – | ✓ | ✓ | – | ✓ | ○ | ◐ | ◐ | ◐ | ✓ | – | – | – | – | ○ | ◐ |
| ✓ | – | – | ✓ | – | – | ○ | ● | ● | ● | – | – | – | ✓ | – | ○ | ◐ |
| ✓ | ✓ | – | ✓ | – | – | ◐ | ● | ● | ● | ✓ | ✓ | – | ✓ | ✓ | ● | ● |
| ✓ | ✓ | – | ✓ | ✓ | – | ○ | ◐ | ● | ◐ | ✓ | – | – | ✓ | – | ◐ | – |

**Room service:** ● 24-hour, ◐ 6AM-10PM, ○ other.
**Laundry/Dry cleaning:** ● same day, ◐ overnight, ○ other.
**Pressing:** ● immediate, ◐ same day, ○ other.

and are decorated in sedate green tones with traditional furniture and oriental art. Bathrooms are especially roomy and have detached, lighted vanities. The best views are to the west from the fifth floor and above; avoid the second floor on the wing that sits over Kicks (*see* After Hours, below), the city's noisiest disco. The main restaurant, Stacy's Sea Grille, is not lavish but does offer fresh seafood. The hotel's main drawback is its somewhat out-of-the-way location, but it is near an I–240 interchange and no more than 15 minutes from downtown. *2625 Thousand Oaks Blvd., 38118, tel. 901/362–6200 or 800/228–9290, fax 901/360–8836. Gen. manager, Mike Barnett. 160 singles, 156 doubles, 4 suites. AE, CB, D, DC, MC, V.*

★ ⑩ **Omni Memphis.** Since it opened in 1975, this 27-story mirrored-glass tower has been the largest east-Memphis hotel, offering the greatest range of services. The hotel benefited greatly from a 1987 facelift, and since its takeover by the Omni group in 1988, service and staffing have improved. All rooms in the circular tower have panoramic views of the tree-lined suburbs; those with a western exposure (from about the eighth floor up) look toward the downtown skyline 15 miles away. Though rooms are oddly shaped because of the tower layout, they are well furnished in a modern style. The hotel entrance is through a spacious lounge that looks out onto a terraced lawn and reflecting pool complete with swans. The lobby is graced with oriental sculpture and caged multicolored finches. The hotel's one restaurant, Sawyer's, offers no surprises in decor or cuisine; the lounge, Breezes, features live music and has a local following. *939 Ridgelake Blvd., 38119, tel. 901/684–6664 or 800/843–6664, fax 901/762–7411. Gen. manager, John Kuhn. 169 singles, 190 doubles, 16 suites. AE, CB, D, DC, MC, V.*

⑪ **Radisson Ridgeway Inn.** A somewhat dated exterior conceals an otherwise excellent, smaller hotel. Built in 1959 as a Holiday Inn, the seven-story hotel was transformed in 1986 by the Belz Hotel group, which manages it as part of the Radisson chain. Rooms are of average size, but brightly decorated in Colonial style, giving the hotel the feel of an inn. A concierge floor offers guests complimentary Continental breakfast and an honor bar each evening. Café Expresso (*see* Business Breakfasts, below), the hotel's excellent restaurant, is a fine place to start your day. *A Belz hotel. 5679 Poplar Ave., 38119, tel. 901/766–4000 or 800/778–7000, fax 901/763–1857. Gen. manager, Hector Venegas. 91 singles, 63 doubles, 2 suites. AE, CB, D, DC, MC, V.*

## Airport

⑰ **Memphis Airport Hilton.** The most reliable of a sprinkling of hotels (most are budget chains) in the airport area, the Hilton is run by the same group that owns The Peabody and the Radisson Ridgeway Inn. The staff reflects the group's skill in training. Both the original main building (opened in 1975) and a 1984 addition are built around skylight atria; the wings connect at the third of five floors. Rooms in the newer wing are more tastefully furnished, with small sitting areas and dark-wood furniture. Older rooms have a more institutional look. Avoid rooms on the first floor, which also has meeting rooms and banquet facilities; they can be noisy and dark. Second-floor accommodations are better, though there are meeting rooms here, too. *A Belz hotel. 2240 Democrat Rd., 38132, tel. 901/332–1130 or 800/445–8667, fax 901/398–5206. Gen. manager, Bo Laterveer. 120 singles, 174 doubles, 8 suites. AE, CB, D, DC, MC, V.*

## DINING

Memphis dining offered visitors relatively few choices until the 1980s, but during the last decade both the quality and variety of restaurants improved. Although Memphis may not be the culinary equal of such southern cities as Dallas, New Orleans, or Atlanta, you can find good food here from Thailand, Vietnam, Germany, Japan, and Greece, in addition to the ever-popular French, Italian, and Chinese fare. The area specialty is, without question, pork barbecue, and you can find dozens of barbecue restaurants, from plain to fancy, serving barbecued pork shoulder and ribs, along with smoked sausages, freshly made onion rings, and lemon ice-box pie. It may be folksy, but it's good enough to keep a number of barbecue mail-order businesses going.

Highly recommended restaurants in each price category are indicated by a star ★.

| Category | Cost* |
| --- | --- |
| *$$$$* (Very Expensive) | over $40 |
| *$$$* (Expensive) | $25–$40 |
| *$$* (Moderate) | under $25 |

*per person, including appetizer, entrée, and dessert, but excluding drinks, service, and 7¾% sales tax.*

*Numbers in the margin correspond to numbered restaurant locations on the Memphis Lodging and Dining maps.*

### Business Breakfasts

The two locations of **Cafe Expresso** (The Peabody, tel. 901/529–4160; and Radisson Ridgeway Inn, 5679 Poplar Ave., tel. 901/763–3888) are at opposite ends of the city. Both restaurants, often frequented by business people, offer excellent, freshly baked breads and pastries in bright surroundings. The Peabody location doesn't offer egg dishes. **La Patisserie Bistro** (5689 Quince Rd., tel. 901/767–0069), convenient to the Ridgeway and Lynnfield office developments, is one of the city's foremost bakeries, and the breakfast menu reflects this; omelets are also available. **Zack's** (Memphis Airport Hilton, tel. 901/398–3828) offers a full range of breakfast dishes, including bagels and lox, and fresh-fruit plates, in a whitewashed, southwestern-style dining room. Private dining rooms are available for meetings.

### Downtown/Midtown

★ ❶
*$$*
**Ben's.** This downtown restaurant offers classic French specialties at attractive prix-fixe rates. It's the creation of chef Jean Claude Prevot and is named for his young son. The decor is Mediterranean, with pink stucco walls and a flowing fountain in one dining room; there's a view of the

Mississippi River from the bar. It's popular with business-people for both lunch and dinner. Prevot's menu changes frequently; typical of his creations are sautéed scallops with curry; lamb stew; and medallions of veal in red wine. The prix-fixe meal includes an appetizer or soup, an entrée, and dessert. *110 Wagner Pl., tel. 901/521–8215. Casual but neat dress. Reservations advised. AE, MC, V. Closed Sun. and Mon.*

★ ❷ **Chez Philippe.** Firmly established as the city's best res-
$$$$ taurant, Chez Philippe owes its success to the mastery of chef Jose Gutierrez. The restaurant, adjacent to The Peabody lobby, has three levels: The uppermost is the most quiet and roomy. The room is majestic, with high ceilings, faux-marble columns, and large murals. The nouvelle French cuisine is exceptional in quality, creativity, and presentation. Specialties include fresh pasta shaped into a pouch and filled with seafood; cold mousse of salmon and scallops with lobster aspic; and medallions of veal and tuna in paprika vinegar. This is the place to come to celebrate a deal, with live harp music and waiters in black-tie setting the tone. The wine list is extensive and, not surprisingly, high-priced. *The Peabody, 149 Union Ave., tel. 901/529–4188. Jacket and tie required. Reservations advised. AE, CB, D, DC, MC, V. Closed Sun. and lunch.*

❹ **Justine's.** Six dining areas are filled with piano music ema-
$$$$ nating from the foyer in this restored, 1843 mansion. In summer, fresh roses from the restaurant's gardens adorn each table. Justine's is a favorite of the Memphis establishment, both for business entertaining and marking special occasions. The New Orleans–influenced menu is not innovative, but the cooking is reliable. Fresh seafood dishes include crabmeat sautéed in butter, and broiled pompano with chives, parsley, and lemon. Beef tenderloin with artichoke hearts and bearnaise sauce is also recommended. *919 Coward Pl., tel. 901/527–3815. Jacket and tie advised. Reservations advised. AE, CB, D, DC, MC, V. Closed Sun. and lunch.*

❸ **La Tourelle.** The quiet setting is reminiscent of a French
$$$ country inn, with lace curtains, polished wood floors, and crisp green-and-white linens. It may be too sedate for a large group, but the food is excellent. Four-course prix-fixe meals are available, or you can order à la carte. Menus change regularly, but expect dishes like grilled scallops with sage butter; shrimp-and-crab mousse with ginger and mushrooms; poached salmon with lobster sauce; and beef filet with juniper-berry sauce. Excellent desserts include the Queen Mother cake, a triple-chocolate wonder. The restaurant is located in the Overton Square entertainment district, a 10-minute drive from downtown. *2146 Monroe Ave., tel. 901/726–5771. Jacket and tie advised. Reservations advised on weekends. AE, MC, V. Closed Mon. and lunch.*

❷⓿ **The Rendezvous.** Charlie Vergos has become something of
$$ an ambassador of Memphis barbecued ribs; not only does his downtown basement restaurant draw thousands of tourists and businesspeople each year, but he also ships his ribs all over the country. The walls are filled with memorabilia and bric-a-brac, from old newspaper clippings to Essolene gas signs. The mood runs from convivial to raucous, and the pork-loin plates and ribs are a down-home slice of Memphis cuisine. This is a good place to relax after

work. *52 S. 2nd St., tel. 901/523-2746. Casual dress. No reservations. AE, MC, V. Closed Sun., Mon.*

## East Memphis/Germantown

**❻** **Folk's Folly.** The city's busiest and most-popular steak
**$$$** house, this simple and straightforward restaurant is a favorite with local businesspeople. Though the food offers few surprises, the steaks are properly prepared and consistently well flavored. For those who seek other options, the restaurant serves a respectable veal chop, blackened or broiled fish, and king crab legs. The main dining rooms can be noisy, but several small private rooms are available. The east Memphis location is a 20-minute drive from downtown and less than a 10-minute drive from suburban hotels. A serviceable wine list, especially for reds, is available. *551 S. Mendenhall Rd., tel. 901/762-8200. Casual but neat dress. Reservations advised. AE, CB, D, DC, MC, V. Closed lunch.*

**❸** **Frank Grisanti's.** One of the city's better Italian restau-
**$$$** rants, Frank Grisanti's, in the Embassy Suites hotel, offers seating in a dark, clubby dining room and in a tropical atrium (though the tables in the latter are too small for more than two people to dine comfortably). The restaurant, like the hotel, appeals especially to business travelers, but the locals have found it, too, and tables are hard to come by on weekends. The food is a mix of traditional Italian dishes (manicotti, ravioli, and eggplant Parmesan) and more innovative fare, including steamed mussels over angel-hair pasta; and broiled swordfish with oregano marinade. A velvety chocolate-hazelnut ice cream is one of several freshly made ice creams and sorbets. *1022 S. Shady Grove Rd., tel. 901/761-9462. Casual but neat dress. Reservations advised. AE, CB, D, DC, MC, V.*

**❾** **Genghis Khan's/Chef's Bistro.** In a storefront on the
**$$** ground floor of Clark Tower in east Memphis, chef Bernard Chang serves flavorful and tastefully presented Chinese specialties at Genghis Khan's. Step a few feet into the restaurant's back room and you've entered the Chef's Bistro, an experimental restaurant launched by Chang and his Swiss collaborator, Roland Schnider. Genghis Khan's features Hunan, Szechuan, and Mandarin specialties in a formal, jade-green dining room. The menu at the bistro blends Oriental and Continental themes in specialties like veal curry, shrimp-filled dumplings, and moist broiled salmon with a dark, sweet Szechuan topping. *5100 Poplar Ave., tel. 901/763-0272. Casual but neat dress. Reservations advised. AE, DC, MC, V.*

**★ ❿** **Hemming's.** This restaurant opened in 1988 in the Saddle
**$$$** Creek shopping center in Germantown, an east Memphis suburb, and has since then been added to many best-restaurant lists of local and national publications. The menu, which features California and Southwest cuisine, changes frequently. Expect combinations like venison cutlets over grilled corn-cakes with tomato salsa; roasted breast of duck with bok choy and papaya-chili sauce; and roasted quail with andouille and corn relish. Tall windows illuminate pale-blue, paneled walls and mauve-and-ivory linens. Noise can be a problem, and a dining room is available for groups of 15 or more. *7615 W. Farmington Rd., tel. 901/757-8323. Jacket advised. Reservations advised. AE, CB, DC, MC, V. Closed lunch weekends.*

★ ❽ **John Will's Barbecue Bar and Grill.** John Wills parlayed
$$ two victories in the International Pork Barbecue Cooking
Contest into this successful restaurant. This eatery has a
huge wooden bar, high ceilings, and Art Deco furnishings.
Try the barbecue pizza, a Memphis favorite, as an appetiz-
er. The pork ribs are the "wet" variety, with a tomato-
based sauce. Pork shoulder, beef brisket, and smoked sau-
sage are also available. *5101 Sanderlin, tel. 901/761–5101.
Casual dress. No reservations. AE, MC, V.*

❶❺ **La Patisserie Bistro.** This surprising little country-French
$$ bistro is located in an east Memphis shopping center. The
restaurant's kitchen and bakery open into the dining
room, allowing diners to glimpse the behind-the-scenes
action. Owners Guy Pacaud and Yves Albaret are masterful bakers so the breads and desserts are particularly
good, but the rest of the menu is also commendable, with
selections including beef tournedos with mushroom sauce;
chicken blanquette (in a white-wine sauce, served in a hollow baguette), and creamy curry soup garnished with
chopped fresh apple. *5689 Quince Rd., tel. 901/767–0069.
Casual dress. Reservations advised on weekends. MC, V.
Closed Sun.*

❺ **Sekisui.** This storefront restaurant in the newly opened
$$$ Humphrey's Center in east Memphis has the city's most
elaborate sushi selection as well as a wide range of other
Japanese dishes. This is a gathering spot for the younger
business crowd in search of something more exotic than
steak or grilled fish. The menu offers sushi, tempura, gyo-
za and shu-mai dumplings, teriyaki, and kushiyaki
(broiled) meats and seafood. The decor is simple and clean,
with blond oak, rice-paper screens, and a choice of seating
at booths or on floor cushions. *50 Humphrey's Blvd., tel.
901/747–0001. Casual dress. Reservations advised on
weekends. AE, MC, V. Closed lunch.*

## FREE TIME

### Fitness

*Hotel Facilities*
**The Peabody**'s (tel. 901/529–4000) well-equipped athletic
club caters to local fitness enthusiasts at $10 daily, as well
as to hotel guests at $3 a day.

*Health Clubs*
**Wimbleton Sportsplex** (6161 Shelby Oaks Dr., tel. 901/388–
6580) offers Holiday Inn guests a $10 day rate; guests from
other hotels pay $20. **YMCA** branches downtown (245
Madison Ave., tel. 901/527–9622) and in east Memphis
(5885 Quince Rd., tel. 901/682–8025) offer visitors one
complimentary visit to their excellent facilities.

*Jogging*
The **Memphis Airport Hilton** (2240 Democrat Rd.) is on a
2-mile jogging path in the landscaped Nonconnah office
park.

### Shopping

Like most of America, Memphis shops at the malls: the
**Mall of Memphis,** a stone's throw from the Memphis
Marriott on American Way at Perkins Road; **Hickory
Ridge Mall** in the southeastern part of the city, a few miles

from the Omni Memphis, Radisson Ridgeway, and Holiday Inn Memphis East; and **Oak Court Mall,** the newest, which includes Lord and Taylor among its tenants.

Kitsch is now king where Elvis once reigned: Visitors to Graceland will find every imaginable Elvis souvenir at the stores across the street on (what else?) Elvis Presley Boulevard. Easily the most unusual store in town is **A. Schwab's** (163 Beale St., tel. 901/523–9782), an authentic dry-goods store in the Beale Street historic district. The only store on the street that's been there since the blues were born, 114-year-old Schwab's carries everything from Mad Hatter hats to size-74 overalls.

## Diversions

On the two-block restored section of **Beale Street** (between 2nd and 4th streets), you'll find a mix of night clubs, restaurants, and specialty shops. To get a sense of the street's past, spend a few moments at A. Schwab's dry-goods store (*see* Shopping, above), the Old Daisy Theatre (built in 1918), and the W.C. Handy Memphis Home and Museum.

**Dixon Gallery and Gardens** (4339 Park Ave., tel. 901/761–5250), a 17-acre estate donated to the city by the late local art patrons Margaret and Hugo Dixon, houses a permanent collection of French and American Impressionist art, the Stout collection of 18th-century German porcelain, and British landscapes.

**Graceland** (3717 Elvis Presley Blvd., tel. 901/332–3322) is the most popular of Memphis attractions. Elvis Presley's home is virtually unchanged since his death here in 1977. The guided tour includes his living quarters, gold-record museum, and gravesite. Separate tours of his four-engine personal jet, the *Lisa Marie*, are also available. Crowds peak during the days surrounding the anniversary of his birth, in January, and his death, in August. Reservations are advised in summer.

Recently expanded as part of a multimillion-dollar facelift, the **Memphis Brooks Museum of Art** (Overton Park, tel. 901/722–3500) houses a collection that spans eight centuries. Its focus is American Modernist paintings.

**Memphis Pink Palace Museum and Planetarium** (3050 Central Ave., tel. 901/454–5600) is the region's principal museum. The museum's collection is partially housed in a pink-granite mansion that once belonged to Clarence Saunders, creator of the Piggly Wiggly grocery stores that paved the way for modern supermarkets. Holdings include artifacts from the mid-South's past and displays on the region's geology, history, plant and animal life, and archaeology.

Though the name may be less than compelling, **Mud Island,** a 52-acre, $63 million park, is a fascinating tribute to the Mississippi River. Included in the sprawling complex is a five-block-long scale replica of the Mississippi River, as well as a river museum, 5,000-seat amphitheater, shops, and restaurants. A mid-1991 expansion adds the Great American Pyramid, a new sports arena and museum complex. Either drive across Auction Street Bridge and park on the island, or take the monorail from the terminal at Front Street and Poplar Avenue.

## The Arts

The Memphis Symphony Orchestra (tel. 901/324–3627) and Opera Memphis (tel. 901/454–2706) usually perform at the **Memphis Convention Center** (255 N. Main St., tel. 901/576–1200). Community theater productions can be seen at **Theatre Memphis** (630 Perkins Rd. Extended, tel. 901/682–8323). Concerts and touring Broadway shows are at the **Orpheum Theatre** (203 S. Main St., tel. 901/525–3000). **Playhouse on the Square** (51 S. Cooper Ave., tel. 901/726–4656) features repertory theater.

For a complete listing of weekly events, check the Playbook section in the Friday *Memphis Commercial Appeal*. *Memphis Magazine* also publishes a monthly calendar of events, as does the weekly *Memphis Flyer*, a free newspaper distributed throughout the city.

Ticket agencies include **Ticket Hub** (149 N. Angeles, tel. 901/725–4822) and **Ticketmaster** (tel. 901/274–7400), which has locations at the Park Place, Raleigh Springs, and Southland malls.

## After Hours

*Bars and Lounges*
**The Peabody Lobby** (149 Union Ave., tel. 901/529–4000) is the city's most famous, complete with marble fountain and live ducks. **Sleep Out Louie's** (88 Union Ave., tel. 901/527–5337) attracts the downtown after-five crowd. It's casual, and there's outdoor seating in the warmer months. **The Gazebo/Café Toulouse** (2144 Madison Ave., tel. 901/728–4000), in the atrium of the French Quarter Inn, features live New Orleans–style jazz. **Pepper's Sport Bar and Grill** (3569 S. Mendenhall Rd., tel. 901/276–3200) offers large-screen viewing of professional and collegiate games.

*Comedy Clubs*
**Comedy House Café** (4095 American Way, tel. 901/366–7711) is in a suburban shopping center and is the newer of the two comedy clubs in town. The more-established club, **Sir Lafs-A-Lot** (535 S. Highland St., 901/324–5653), is in the Highland Strip area near Memphis State University and caters to a younger crowd.

*Jazz/Blues Clubs*
Beale Street has a number of excellent jazz and blues clubs, including **Blues Hall/Rum Boogie** (182 Beale St., tel. 901/528–0150), a pair of blues clubs with a shared kitchen; **King's Palace** (162 Beale St., tel. 901/521–1851), with jazz and jazz-fusion artists; and **Club Royale** (349 Beale St., tel. 901/527–5404), with R & B groups. Away from Beale Street, you'll find excellent jazz, blues, and rockabilly at **Lou's Place** (94 S. Front St., tel. 901/528–1970), **Marmalade** (153 Calhoun Ave., tel. 901/522–8800), and in the Overton Square entertainment district at **Huey's** (1927 Madison Ave., tel. 901/726–4372).

*For Singles*
Set near the foot of Beale Street, overlooking the Mississippi, **Captain Bilbo's** (263 Wagner Pl., tel. 901/526–1966) is a perennial favorite of the dance crowd, with a mix of

rock-and-roll and oldies bands. **Kicks** (Memphis Marriott, 2625 Thousand Oaks Blvd., tel. 901/362–6200) offers its upscale crowd live contemporary and Top-40 dance music in a swirl of brass, mirrors, and flashing lights. Those in search of alternative music (and who don't mind a punk rock crowd) might try out the **Antenna Club** (1588 Madison Ave., tel. 901/276–4052).

# Miami

*by Roger Lowenstein*

Visitors to Miami have the sense of arriving at a foreign port of call—a blend of every culture that can be found in the Caribbean, thoroughly bilingual, and fraught with opportunity and danger as only the tropics are. What is strange about this palm-laden, visually seductive city is that many of its natives have come to feel like foreigners too. Although the "Miami Vice" image of high-profile crime is inaccurate (you are unlikely to see a drug arrest, except on the evening news), the TV show accurately conveys the city's pace of change. Where it once was sleepy, Miami is vibrant; where it once was a cultural backwater, Miami is trendy; where it formerly was the preserve of Southern gentlemen, it has been transformed by émigrés from Cuba, New York, Philadelphia, and Chicago. The mayor, for one, was born in Las Villas, Cuba.

The vibrancy has reawakened Miami's economy, among other things. The visible signs include the modernized airport and port; the metrorail and light rail people-mover; and the brazen architecture that has invented, out of almost nothing, a Miami skyline. International banking (there are 40 foreign banks here), import-export, and manufacturing each contributes as much to Miami's economy as tourism; and new industries, such as high-tech medical research and fashion photography, are gaining. Miami leads the nation as a port of disembarkation for cruise ship passengers—3 million a year. Those who get ahead seem to be those most adept at marketing to two languages and two cultures.

The rapid change has, however, produced some dislocations for the economy and for society at large. Miami's real estate industry continues to feel the chill from Latin America's long recession. Condos intended for Latin buyers remain unsold; 23% of the office space downtown is empty. Florida's banks, having financed development all over the state, have a growing number of bad loans. Miami's gaudiest skyscraper, the colorfully lit, 42-story Centrust Tower, has been seized by the U.S. Government—along with the defunct savings and loan which built it. And the city is still adjusting to the waves of Cubans, Nicaraguans, and Haitians that arrived in the 1980s. The visitor should find a buoyant, unfinished city, rife with opportunity, still defining itself.

## Top Employers

| Employer | Type of Enterprise | Parent*/ Headquarters |
| --- | --- | --- |
| **American Capital** | Savings and loan | Miami |
| **Burdines Department Stores** | Retail | Campeau/Toronto |
| **Burger King Corp.** | Fast food | Grand Metropolitan PLC/London |
| **Florida Power & Light Co.** | Utility | North Palm Beach, Fla. |
| **Jackson Memorial Hospital** | Hospital | Miami |
| **Mount Sinai Medical Center** | Hospital | Miami |
| **Sears Roebuck & Co.** | Retail | Chicago |
| **Southeast Banking Corp.** | Bank | Miami |
| **Southern Bell** | Telecommunications | BellSouth/Atlanta |
| **University of Miami** | Education | Miami |

*\*if applicable*

## ESSENTIAL INFORMATION

### Climate

What follows are the average daily maximum and minimum temperatures for Miami.

| | | | | | | | | |
| --- | --- | --- | --- | --- | --- | --- | --- | --- |
| **Jan.** | 74F | 23C | **Feb.** | 76F | 24C | **Mar.** | 77F | 25C |
| | 63 | 17 | | 63 | 17 | | 65 | 18 |
| **Apr.** | 79F | 26C | **May** | 83F | 28C | **June** | 85F | 29C |
| | 68 | 20 | | 72 | 22 | | 76 | 24 |
| **July** | 88F | 31C | **Aug.** | 88F | 31C | **Sept.** | 86F | 30C |
| | 76 | 24 | | 77 | 25 | | 76 | 24 |
| **Oct.** | 83F | 28C | **Nov.** | 79F | 26C | **Dec.** | 76F | 24C |
| | 72 | 22 | | 67 | 19 | | 63 | 17 |

### Airport

**Miami International Airport** is 7 miles west of downtown Miami. It's especially convenient to Coral Gables, which lies just to the south. The airport ranks second in the United States in international passenger traffic.

## Airport Business Facilities

**Hotel MIA** (Concourse E, on the departure level, tel. 305/871–4100) has fax machines, photocopying, notary public, Western Union, travel insurance, conference rooms with catering service, day rates for rooms, and a fitness center.

## Airlines

Miami is the principal U.S. destination from Latin America and it is served by 50 foreign airlines, which use it as a hub city. Major domestic carriers are listed below.

**American,** tel. 800/433–7300.
**Continental,** tel. 305/871–1400 or 800/525–0280.
**Delta,** tel. 305/448–7000 or 800/221–1212.
**Northwest,** tel. 800/225–2525 or 800/225–2525.
**Pan Am,** tel. 305/874–5000 or 800/221–1111.
**United,** tel. 800/241–6522.
**USAir,** tel. 305/358–3396 or 800/428–4322.

## Between the Airport and Downtown

*By Taxi*
The ride downtown costs about $12 and takes 20–30 minutes. Fares to other areas are roughly as follows: Coral Gables, $8; Coconut Grove, $14; Key Biscayne, $20.

*By Bus*
Dade County operates buses from the airport to downtown and to various other areas. See the information desk on the second level in Concourse E. If you're travelling alone the most economical way to go is by Super Shuttle which operates a van/limousine service to your hotel for $5–$10. The vans are located outside of the baggage claim area.

## Car Rentals

The following companies have booths at the airport.

**Avis,** tel. 305/637–4900 or 800/331–1212.
**Budget,** tel. 305/871–3053 or 800/527–0700.
**Hertz,** tel. 305/871–0300 or 800/654–3131.
**National,** tel. 305/328–4567 or 800/227–7368.
**Thrifty,** tel. 305/871–2277 or 800/367–2277.

## Emergencies

*Doctors*
**Baptist Hospital,** Physician Referral Service (tel. 305/596– 6557); **Cedars Physician Referral** (tel. 305/325–5000); **South Miami Hospital,** physician referral and appointment service (tel. 305/633–2255); **Doctors Hospital of Coral Gables,** doctors referral and appointment service (tel. 305/663–1380).

*Dentists*
**The Dental Office** (7900 S.W. 104th St., tel. 305/595–4548), open weekdays 10 AM–8 PM, weekends 10 AM–4 PM. **Dade Dental Center East Coast District Dental Society** (tel. 305/667–3647 or 305/944–5668), 24-hour emergency referral.

*Hospitals*
**South Miami Hospital** (U.S. 1 at S.W. 62nd Ave., tel. 305/661–4611); **Golden Glades** (17300 N.W. Seventh Ave., tel. 305/652–4200); **Mercy Hospital** (3663 S. Miami Ave., tel. 305/854–4400); **Jackson Memorial Hospital** (University of Miami, 1611 N.W. 12th Ave., tel. 305/325–7429).

## Important Addresses and Numbers

**Audiovisual rentals.** Miami Audio Visual (555 N.W. 95th St., tel. 305/757–5000).

**Chamber of Commerce.** Coral Gables (50 Aragon Ave., tel. 305/446–1657), Great Miami Chamber (1601 Biscayne Blvd., tel. 305/350–7700).

**Computer rentals.** Personal Computer Rentals (800 Douglas Rd., Coral Gables, tel. 305/444–6300), Southern Business Rentals (7827 N.W. 15th St., tel. 305/591–2233).

**Convention and exhibition centers.** Miami Convention Center (400 S.E. Second Ave., tel. 305/372–0277), Coconut Grove Exhibition Center (3360 Pan American Dr., tel. 305/579–3310), Miami Beach Convention Center (1901 Convention Center Dr., tel. 305/673–7311). For more information, call the Greater Miami Convention & Visitors Bureau, tel. 305/539–3000.

**Fax services.** Brickell Mail Receiving (444 Brickell Ave., tel. 305/371–4046), Fax & Telex Service by Telephone (4700 N.W. Seventh St., tel. 305/443–2243, near the airport), Sunset Quickprint (2205 Ponce De Leon Blvd., Coral Gables, tel. 305/444–1265).

**Formal-wear rentals.** Ace Formal Wear (1102 W. Flagler St., tel. 305/545–5621), University Formal Shop (2980 Ponce De Leon Blvd., Coral Gables, tel. 305/445–3679), Black Tie (2270 Coral Way, tel. 305/854–8535), Sacino's Formal Wear (6939 Red Rd., South Miami, tel. 305/662–5757).

**Gift shops.** Chocolates: Sweet Treat Emporium (1565 Sunset Dr., Coral Gables, tel. 305/665–0233); Flowers: Blossoms on Brickell (600 Brickell Ave., tel. 305/358–0560), Gift Baskets: City Basket of Florida (6101 Sunset Dr., tel. 305/669–1000); A Balloon Fantasy, takes phone orders for deliveries of champagne and other gifts (tel. 305/595–9536).

**Graphic design studios.** Adcom International (4111 N. Miami Ave., tel. 305/856–2393), Graphic Dimensions (4200 Aurora St., Coral Gables, tel. 305/448–9696), Original Impressions (12900 S.W. 89th Ct., tel. 305/233–1322).

**Hairstylists.** Unisex: Hair Designers of Alhambra (300 Alhambra Circle, Coral Gables, tel. 305/443–4247), Peter of London Designer Hair Salon (550 Biltmore Way, Coral Gables, tel. 305/445–2621, and other locations in greater Miami).

**Health & fitness clubs.** *See* Fitness, below.

**Limousine services.** International Limousine (tel. 305/324–1088), Limousines of South Florida (tel. 305/940–5252), Royal Limousine Service (tel. 305/442–1414).

**Liquor stores.** Chevalier Wine Cellar (4040 Red Rd., South Miami, tel. 305/661–6782), 27 & 27 Liquor Store (2700 S.W. 27th Ave., tel. 305/443–0635).

**Mail delivery, overnight.** DHL Worldwide Express (tel. 305/471–0490), Federal Express (tel. 305/371–8500), TNT Skypak (tel. 305/594–2221), UPS (tel. 305/238–0134), U.S. Post Office Express Mail (tel. 305/470–0202).

**Messenger services.** All-Pro Courier (tel. 305/758–1558), Baron Messenger Service (tel. 305/688–0074).

**Office space rental.** Abacus Secretarial Center Office & Desk Space Rental Service (1444 Biscayne Blvd., tel. 305/576–8310).

**Pharmacies, late-night.** Omega Pharmacy (9537 S.W. 72nd St., tel. 305/279–9999), South Dixie Discount Center (8865 S. Dixie Hwy., tel. 305/667–2586), Sunset Drug Store (5640 Sunset Dr., South Miami, tel. 305/667–7577).

**Secretarial services.** Business & Secretarial Services Inc. (2320 S. Dixie Hwy., Coconut Grove, tel. 305/856–8877), Coral Gables Secretarial Services (334 Minorca Ave., Coral Gables, tel. 305/443–8973).

**Stationery supplies.** Dussault Stationery Co. (5822 Sunset Dr., South Miami, tel. 305/666–2575), Jaffe's Stationery & Office Supplies (3100 Ponce De Leon Blvd., Coral Gables, tel. 305/444–7937), Office Depot (8665 S.W. 40th St., tel. 305/223–1912), T-Square Office Supplies (998 W. Flagler St., tel. 305/324–1234).

**Taxis.** Central Cab (tel. 305/532–5555), Metro Taxi (tel. 305/888–8888), Yellow Cab (tel. 305/444–4444).

**Theater tickets.** *See* The Arts, below.

**Train information.** Amtrak (8303 N.W. 37th Ave., tel. 800/872–7245).

**Travel agents.** American Express Travel Service (32 Miracle Mile, Coral Gables, tel. 305/446–3381), Brickell Executive Travel (600 Brickell Ave., tel. 305/358–7030), Coconut Grove Travel Agency (3139 S.W. 27th Ave., Coconut Grove, tel. 305/ 445–8538).

**Weather** (tel. 305/661–5065).

## LODGING

Miami is spread out in typical sunbelt fashion, so most business travelers will want to stay near their place of work. Coral Gables is the business area of choice; its compact downtown area, only minutes from the airport, is a headquarters for numerous international companies and a home to many businesses, banks, and law firms. Some travelers enjoy staying here even when their appointments are in downtown Miami. Most of the area's hotels are within walking distance of restaurants and shopping, and the Mediterranean-style residential area, built by the utopian George Merrick in the 1920s and preserved by strict zoning, is the classiest in Miami. Airport hotels are a reasonable second choice for people working in the Gables; they are conveniently located and—unlike airport hotels in some other cities—not at all drab.

Downtown hotels are recommended only for travelers spending most of their time working in the central business district—roughly defined as the old area cordoned off by U.S. 395, U.S. 95, the Miami River, Biscayne Bay, and the modern high-rise extension to downtown along Brickell Avenue. By day the area is alive with the activity at Miami's biggest banks, law firms, and businesses, but after hours—with the exception of Bayside Marketplace and scattered restaurants, the area is generally quiet. Coconut Grove has many hotels that are a short drive from downtown as well as from Coral Gables. This eclectic area will entice—or irritate—travelers depending on whether they appreciate the swell of shoppers, tourists, and traffic. The area is jam-packed with restaurants, stores, arts and crafts shops, and night clubs that run the gamut from rich and tasteful to tacky.

Miami's hotels are crisp and corporate, but—with a few exceptions—they suffer from a feeling of sameness and are short on character or charm. One way to break the mold is to stay on Key Biscayne. It's further from the city's business districts, but after hours you have the sun, sand, and water.

Most of the hotels listed below offer corporate rates, and some give weekend discounts. Inquire when making reservations.

Highly recommended lodgings in each price category are indicated by a star ★.

| Category | Cost* |
| --- | --- |
| $$$$ (Very Expensive) | over $160 |
| $$$ (Expensive) | $125–$160 |
| $$ (Moderate) | under $125 |

*All prices are for a standard double room, single occupancy, during the winter high season, excluding 11% a day tax. Off-season rates are available at some hotels.*

*Numbers in the margin correspond to numbered hotel locations on the Miami Lodging and Dining map.*

## Coconut Grove

★ ㉒ **Grand Bay.** This brassy, modern high-rise, overlooking
$$$$ Biscayne Bay, is one of Miami's ritziest hotels. Pavarotti stays here (in a suite with a baby grand) and so do Michael Jackson and Pete Rozelle, but you're more likely to run into corporate CEOs. The hotel is close to Coconut Grove restaurants and shops (but not on a noisy street) and within 10 minutes of the downtown office and banking district. Guests get amenities such as mineral water with the nightly turndown service; the staff is notably attentive. Plants and flowered spreads in the rooms make for a light, contemporary (though somewhat bland) decor; every room has a terrace overlooking the bay. Make sure your room isn't one of the few that don't have desks. Guests have access to Regine's, a chic, members-only restaurant and disco in the penthouse; Grand Café (*see* Dining, below) is also on the premises. *Ciga hotels. 2669 South Bayshore Dr., Coconut Grove, 33133, tel. 305/858–9600 or 800/327–*

# MIAMI

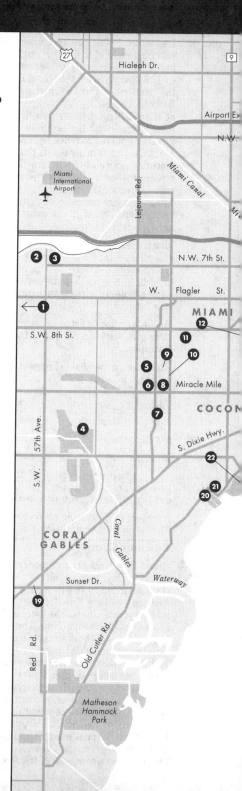

# MIAMI HOTEL CHART

| HOTELS | Price Category | Business Services Banquet capacity | No. of meeting rooms | Secretarial services | Audiovisual equipment | Teletype news service | Computer rentals | In-room modem phone jack | All-news cable channel | Desk | Desk lighting | Bed lighting |
|---|---|---|---|---|---|---|---|---|---|---|---|---|
| **Airport Hilton** | $$$ | 900 | 22 | ✓ | ✓ | - | ✓ | ✓ | ✓ | ○ | ◐ | ○ |
| **Biltmore** | $$$ | 250 | 14 | ✓ | ✓ | - | ✓ | - | ✓ | ◐ | ◐ | ● |
| **Colonnade** | $$$ | 400 | 7 | ✓ | ✓ | - | - | ✓ | ✓ | ● | ● | ● |
| **Grand Bay** | $$$$ | 250 | 7 | - | ✓ | - | ✓ | ✓ | ✓ | ◐ | ◐ | ● |
| **Hotel Sofitel** | $$$ | 700 | 10 | ✓ | ✓ | - | - | ✓ | ✓ | ● | ● | ● |
| **Hyatt Regency Coral Gables** | $$$$ | 250 | 13 | ✓ | ✓ | - | - | ✓ | ✓ | ◐ | ◐ | ● |
| **Hyatt Regency Miami** | $$ | 800 | 21 | ✓ | ✓ | - | - | ✓ | ✓ | ● | ● | ● |
| **InterContinental** | $$ | 1300 | 25 | ✓ | ✓ | - | ✓ | ✓ | ✓ | ● | ● | ● |
| **Mayfair House** | $$$$ | 200 | 3 | ✓ | ✓ | - | ✓ | - | ✓ | ● | ● | ● |
| **Park Central** | $$ | 150 | 1 | - | - | - | - | - | - | - | - | ◐ |
| **Place St. Michel** | $$ | 200 | 0 | - | - | - | - | ✓ | ✓ | ● | ○ | ● |
| **Sheraton Brickell Point** | $$$ | 500 | 12 | ✓ | ✓ | - | ✓ | - | ✓ | ● | ● | ● |
| **Sonesta Beach** | $$$$ | 700 | 16 | - | ✓ | - | - | ✓ | ✓ | ◐ | ● | ● |

**$$$$** = over $160, **$$$** = $125-$160, **$$** = under $125.
● good, ◐ fair, ○ poor.
All hotels listed here have photocopying and fax facilities.

| In-Room Amenities | | | | | | | | | | Hotel Amenities | | | | | | |
|---|---|---|---|---|---|---|---|---|---|---|---|---|---|---|---|---|
| Nonsmoking rooms | In-room checkout | Minibar | Pay movies | VCR/Movie rentals | Hairdryer | Toiletries | Room service | Laundry/Dry cleaning | Pressing | Concierge | Barber/Hairdresser | Garage | Courtesy airport transport | Sauna | Pool | Exercise room |
| ✓ | ✓ | ✓ | ✓ | - | - | ◐ | ● | ● | ● | ✓ | - | ✓ | ✓ | ✓ | ● | ● |
| ✓ | ✓ | ✓ | ✓ | - | - | ◐ | ● | ● | ● | ✓ | - | ✓ | ✓ | ✓ | ● | ● |
| ✓ | - | ✓ | ✓ | - | ✓ | ● | ● | ● | ◐ | ✓ | ✓ | ✓ | - | ✓ | ● | ◐ |
| ✓ | ✓ | ✓ | - | ✓ | ✓ | ● | ● | ● | ● | ✓ | ✓ | ✓ | - | ✓ | ◐ | ◐ |
| ✓ | ✓ | - | ✓ | - | - | ● | ◐ | ● | ● | ✓ | - | - | ✓ | ✓ | ● | ● |
| ✓ | ✓ | ✓ | ✓ | ✓ | ✓ | ◐ | ◐ | ● | ◐ | ✓ | - | ✓ | - | ✓ | ● | ◐ |
| ✓ | ✓ | ✓ | ✓ | ✓ | - | ● | ● | ● | ◐ | ✓ | - | ✓ | - | - | ○ | - |
| ✓ | ✓ | ✓ | ✓ | - | ✓ | ◐ | ● | ● | ◐ | ✓ | - | ✓ | ✓ | - | ◐ | ◐ |
| ✓ | - | ✓ | ✓ | - | ✓ | ● | ● | ● | ● | ✓ | ✓ | ✓ | ✓ | ✓ | ○ | - |
| - | - | - | - | - | ✓ | ◐ | ◐ | ● | ◐ | ✓ | - | - | - | - | - | - |
| - | ✓ | - | ✓ | - | - | ○ | ◐ | ● | ● | - | - | ✓ | - | - | - | - |
| ✓ | ✓ | - | ✓ | - | - | ◐ | ◐ | ● | ◐ | ✓ | - | ✓ | - | - | ○ | ◐ |
| ✓ | - | ✓ | ✓ | - | ✓ | ◐ | ◐ | ● | ◐ | ✓ | ✓ | ✓ | - | ✓ | ● | ● |

**Room service:** ● 24-hour, ◐ 6AM-10PM, ○ other.
**Laundry/Dry cleaning:** ● same day, ◐ overnight, ○ other.
**Pressing:** ● immediate, ◐ same day, ○ other.

*2788, fax 305/858–1532. Gen. manager, Thomas Ax-macher. 132 rooms, 49 suites. AE, CB, DC, MC, V.*

**㉑** **Mayfair House.** The Mayfair adjoins a shopping mall, but
$$$$ don't let that fool you. It's one of Miami's most exclusive
(and private) all-suite hotels. There is little in the way of
public or lobby space; guests (including Frank Sinatra and
Liza Minelli) come for the plush Deco and contemporary
decor in the rooms. Thanks to a few apt touches—some
well-chosen art, mahogany valets, and beds that border on
romantic—the quarters look more like private bedrooms
than hotel suites. The one-room suites have fridges and
raised balconies with Jacuzzis. Bathrooms have big tubs,
plenty of marble, and television sets. The elegant hotel
restaurant, Ensign Bitters, is open only to club members
and hotel guests. Mayfair caters to corporate guests (and
Coconut Grove shoppers) and gets plenty of repeat customers, but it's longer on snob appeal than charm. *3000
Florida Ave., Coconut Grove, 33133, tel. 305/441–0000 or
800/433–4555, fax 305/447–9173. Gen. manager, Alvaro
Soto. 181 suites. AE, CB, DC, MC, V.*

## Coral Gables

**❹** **Biltmore Hotel.** The Biltmore, a grand hotel built by Ga-
$$$ bles founder George Merrick in 1926, housed, in various
decades, Al Capone's gambling suite and a military hospi-
tal run by Uncle Sam. With a $50 million, 1987 restoration,
the reopened hotel has become a mecca for corporate exec-
utives. The arched and hand-painted cathedral ceiling,
supported by 26 keystone-finished columns, makes for a
stunning entry; the Spanish-tiled balcony, overlooks a
courtyard and fountain. Guests have the run of the 155-
acre grounds, which include tennis courts, an 18-hole golf
course, and a spectacular pool; those in the Premier Club
get the use of a business center, a lounge, complimentary
breakfasts, and entry to members-only dining in the
private Biltmore Club. Rooms, furnished in French
Provincial style, lack the grandeur of the restored public
spaces. *Premier Resorts & Hotels. 1200 Anastasia Ave.,
Coral Gables, 33134, tel. 305/445–1926 or 800/223–6620,
fax 305/448–9976. Gen. manager, Heinz Schutz. 237
rooms, 36 suites. AE, CB, D, DC, MC, V.*

**★❻** **Colonnade Hotel.** The Colonnade, opened in 1988, is a
$$$ vastly refurbished version of a building constructed in
1926 by George Merrick. The hotel owes its stately look to
a restored, 75-foot-high domed rotunda, and to the unusual assemblage of materials used in the reconstruction:
imported Mexican marble, Argentine hand-blown chandeliers, French and English antiques, and mahogany furnishings and woodwork from a factory in Guatemala. The
relaxed outdoor café caters to hotel guests and office workers alike. Rooms are spacious and the baths are plush. The
big draw is the Coral Gables locale—near to restaurants
and offices and minutes from the airport. The Colonnade
attracts some models and film crews, but the hotel's bread
and butter are international executives and staffs of companies with offices in the Gables. Rooms with the best
views face the Miami skyline. The staff, which is unusually
helpful, greets each new guest with a bottle of bubbly. *180
Aragon Ave., Coral Gables, 33134, tel. 305/441–2600 or
800/533–1337, fax 305/445–3929. Gen. manager, Jad
Shor. 140 rooms, 17 suites. AE, D, DC, MC, V.*

★ **❾** **Hotel Place St. Michel.** One of the few hotels in greater Mi-
$$ ami that isn't all brass and glass, the St. Michel, in a re-
stored 1926 stone building is small, warm, and charming
(which explains its popularity with women travelers).
Regular guests include some well-known names (Jimmy
Buffet is one), but most of the clientele are people doing
business at Coral Gables companies. Rooms have modern
baths, plenty of work and living space, and Scottish and
French antique furnishings. The lobby has hand-tiled
floors, vaulted ceilings, and a manually operated elevator.
There is a lively piano bar and an upscale French restau-
rant (*see* Dining, below) on the main floor; Continental
breakfast (with homemade croissants) is on the house. *162
Alcazar Ave., Coral Gables, 33134, tel. 305/444–1666 or
800/247–8526, fax 305/495–1356. Gen. manager, Stuart
Bornstein. 27 rooms, 3 suites. AE, CB, DC, MC, V.*

**❿** **Hyatt Regency Coral Gables.** The pink stone exterior and
$$$$ elegant lobby give this 14-floor high rise a faintly Spanish
flavor, but, given the price, the blond wood furnishings
and otherwise unremarkable room decor are a bit disap-
pointing. However, the location, just off the main street
but within walking distance of Gables restaurants and of-
fices, is ideal. North American executives convene here
with those from Latin America; executives from Europe
are numerous, too. The Hyatt's Two Sisters is a fine Medi-
terranean restaurant. But if the weather's good, don't
overlook the Court of Lions, a courtyard restaurant with
light meals and a bright fountain setting. Guests on the
Regency Club floors get morning newspapers, free Conti-
nental breakfasts, evening coffee, hors d'oeuvres, and the
run of a private lounge. *50 Alhambra Plaza, Coral Ga-
bles, 33134, tel. 305/441–1234 or 800/233–1234, fax 304/
441–0520. Gen. manager, Monica Newman. 182 rooms,
60 suites. AE, CB, D, DC, MC, V.*

## Downtown

**⓮** **Hyatt Regency Miami.** This 24-floor high rise, adjacent to
$$ the Miami Convention Center in the heart of downtown, is
a beehive of activity. In the big, glitzy atrium in the lobby,
a steady traffic of conventioneers adds to the hubbub. Bob
Hope and Ronald Reagan (as President) stayed here, but
the clientele is basically business. The location—on the
Miami River, close to the city's banks and insurance and
law firms, and overlooking Biscayne Bay—is the big
draw. Rooms have plenty of space and walk-in closets, and
the plain vanilla decor follows the patented Hyatt formula. Bay rooms have the best views; rooms on the drawbridge side are noisy. A helpful staff is a plus. Guests on
Regency Club floors have a private lounge for complimentary breakfast, hors d'oeuvres, and wine. *400 SE Second
Ave., 33131, tel. 305/358–1234 or 800/232–1234, fax 305/
358–1234 ext. 3138. Gen. manager, Stuart Meyerson. 554
rooms, 61 suites. AE, CB, D, DC, MC, V.*

★ **⓲** **InterContinental Miami.** The location—overlooking Bis-
$$ cayne Bay and Bayfront Park at the foot of downtown Mi-
ami—is superb. Bankers, insurance people, and other
financial types dominate the guest list, but the InterCon-
tinental also draws foreign royalty and plenty of tourists,
conventioneers, and cruise-goers. The Bayside shopping
and entertainment market is a short walk away. Rooms
are spacious and modern. Best views from the 34-story

marble and granite high rise are of the Bay and the nearby port, but newcomers to the city may also enjoy the dramatic Miami skyline, visible from rooms on the opposite side. There are a ¼-mile jogging track and a squash court on the fifth floor. The hotel also has a business center with PCs and other services. The hotel's Pavillon Grill (*see* Dining, below) is very good. Rates are surprisingly reasonable. *100 Chopin Plaza, 33131, tel. 305/577-1000 or 800/332-4246, fax 305/577-0384. Gen. manager, Marcello Pigozzo. 612 rooms, 34 suites. AE, CB, DC, MC, V.*

**⑮** **Sheraton Brickell Point.** The ambience is relaxed, thanks
$$$ to lavish gardens that help to insulate the hotel from downtown. Nonetheless, this 18-story high rise is in the thick of Miami's financial district, overlooking the Bay. Spacious rooms are furnished with mahogany furniture, and many have stupendous views (take your choice of the Bay, the Port of Miami, or the futuristic city skyline). The lobby is light and airy; if only the piped-in music were piped-out!. Pro basketball teams stay here, as does the cruise crowd, but bankers, financiers, and government business people dominate the guest list. *455 Brickell Ave., 33131, tel. 305/373-6000 or 800/325-3535, fax 305/ 374-2279. Gen. manager, Bill Ripple. 584 rooms, 14 suites. AE, CB, D, DC, MC, V.*

## Key Biscayne and Miami Beach

**㉔** **Park Central.** This six-story, lavender and blue landmark
$$ is the premier hotel in Miami Beach's Art Deco district, the 10-block stretch of faithfully restored hotels fronting the beach. The Park Central, about 10 minutes by car from downtown Miami, is not for guests who want the amenities of a conventional business hotel, but for those who appreciate the rich detail of an earlier era. The sharp lines and soft pastel colors, the ersatz porthole windows, and the mix of high-tech metal and period piece Deco furniture are spellbinding, especially in the public spaces. Rooms are simple and neat, with period photographs and ceiling fans. Continental breakfast is on the house. The clientele includes film crews and models from European fashion magazines. *640 Ocean Dr., 33139, Miami Beach, tel. 305/ 538-1611, fax 305/534-7520. Gen. manager, Diana Stirling. 80 rooms. AE, DC, MC, V.*

**★ ㉗** **Sonesta Beach.** This oceanfront resort, designed like a
$$$$ Mayan temple, doesn't seem overburdened by having to cater to both vacationers and business people. There is a full complement of tennis, sailing, and fitness activities as well as a heated outdoor, Olympic-size pool. It's a 15-minute drive from the downtown office district, but the hotel gives up nothing in the way of business services, and the rooms are spacious. Club Floor rooms provide free newspapers, Continental breakfasts, evening cocktails, and hors d'oeuvres. Best rooms overlook the ocean. The hotel does a big convention business; it's also a refuge, depending on political winds south of the border, for elite Central American families. Pastel Florida colors set the mood, decidedly informal. Andy Warhol drawings of Mick Jagger decorate the hotel disco, Desires (*see* After Hours, below). *Sonesta Hotels. 350 Ocean Dr., Key Biscayne, 33149, tel. 305/361-2021 or 800/343-7170, fax 305/361-3096. Gen. manager, Felix Madera. 278 rooms. 14 suites. AE, CB, DC, MC, V.*

## Airport

**❸** **Airport Hilton.** This mostly business hotel is close to the
**$$$** airport and within five to 10 minutes of the Coral Gables
office district. The guest list leans toward international
business travelers—many in import-export and from Lat-
in America. The hotel is on a lagoon bordered by a jogging
track. A tropical motif makes the Hilton a bit more exotic
than the usual airport high rise. Rooms, though, have all
the charm of a suburban shopping mall. Airport noise is
kept to a minimum, thanks to double-insulated windows.
However, the hotel could have better insulated its own
disco, the Club Mystique. The Cove, a seafood restaurant,
is worth checking out. *5101 Blue Lagoon Dr., 33126, tel.
305/262–1000 or 800/445–8667, fax 305/267–0038. Gen.
manager, Peter Kretschmann. 350 rooms, 150 suites. AE,
CB, D, DC, MC, V.*

**★ ❷** **Hotel Sofitel.** Don't let the airport locale fool you—the
**$$$** Sofitel re-creates a South-of-France ambience from the
truffles and red roses left at bedside to the French bakery
that opens six days a week at 6 AM. You'll want to spend
some time—possibly with a client—in the oak-paneled
bar, where in the evenings a pianist plays popular jazz
tunes. The hotel has an informal café with American/
French bistro cooking, and a formal nouvelle restaurant,
Café Royal, that is perfect for business meals. Room decor
is French, with antique desks, marbletop dressers, and
plenty of work space. The clientele is North American,
European, and Latin American. Many guests do business
near the airport—in computer software, medical supplies, and insurance—and in nearby Coral Gables. *Hotel
Sofitel. 5800 Blue Lagoon Drive, 33126, tel. 305/264–4888
or 800/221–4542, fax 305/264–4888. Gen. manager, Cyn-
thia Johnson. 260 rooms, 25 suites. AE, CB, DC, MC, V.*

## DINING

Major Miami hotels have the proper ambience for business
meals, and so do a number of restaurants in Coral Gables
and downtown, but the more interesting eating is off the
beaten track, in Miami Beach, Coconut Grove, Little
Haiti, and in Latin restaurants all over town. No longer a
backwater, Miami offers a variety of ethnic cuisines, with
more and more Thai, Indian, and Haitian restaurants
cropping up among the standard Continental French and
Italian restaurants. The predominant ethnic food, of
course, is Cuban, and the easiest way to test it is to sample
the informal restaurants that line **Calle Ocho**, or Southwest Eighth Street, the heart of Little Havana. Be sure to
have a bowl of black bean soup and to sample the sweet
Cuban platanos and the strong Cuban café. Miami's ethnic
mix makes it difficult to identify any one cuisine as the local specialty, but seafood is a unifying favorite. It pays to
order one of the local fish, such as grouper, pompano, or
dolphin, which in other areas are uncommon and in Miami
are fresh, inexpensive, and tasty.

Highly recommended restaurants in each price category
are indicated by a star ★.

| Category | Cost* |
|---|---|
| $$$$ (Very Expensive) | over $25 |
| $$$ (Expensive) | $16–$25 |
| $$ (Moderate) | under $15 |

*per person, including appetizer, entrée, and dessert, but excluding drinks, service, and 6% sales tax.

*Numbers in the margin correspond to numbered restaurant locations on the Miami Lodging and Dining map.*

## Business Breakfasts

The power breakfast has yet to take hold as an institution in Miami, but a few places stand out for their convenience and ambience. **Grand Café** (tel. 305/858–9600), the brassy restaurant at the Grand Bay Hotel in Coconut Grove, is the biggest morning draw for Miami politicians and businesspeople. Buckwheat crêpes filled with fruit and lowfat cottage cheese is a Grand specialty. A relaxed way to start the day in Coral Gables is over croissants and café au lait in the intimate, European-style dining room of The **Hotel Place St. Michel** (tel. 305/444–1666). For a more informal restaurant and robust servings of waffles, pancakes, and other American fare, try **J.J.'s American Diner** (*see* Dining, below) in South Miami and in Coral Gables. **Ashley's** (tel. 305/373–6000) in the Sheraton Brickell Point Hotel serves breakfast (buffet style, if you like) accompanied in good weather by a stunning view of the morning sun rising over Biscayne Bay.

## Calle Ocho

**⑫** **Casa Juancho.** This is the place for movers and shakers of
**$$$** Miami's Cuban community. With its dark wood interior and colorful plates adorning the walls, Casa Juancho is unmistakably Spanish. The cuisine hails from various regions: roast pig (Seville), paella (Valencia), sautéed trout (the Pyrenees), shellfish (Catalonia), and Dover sole in rum and butter sauce (Costa del Sol). Caldo Gallego, the thick white bean soup with potatoes, collard greens, and Spanish ham, is a house favorite. The wine list includes many labels from Spain's Rioja region. The ambience is a bit too lively for working dinners (balladeers are apt to stroll by your table), but for entertaining a business (or other) associate and soaking up some local character, Casa Juancho can't be beat. *2436 S.W. Eighth St., tel. 305/642–2452. Semiformal dress: jackets suggested at dinner. Reservations advised. AE, CB, DC, MC, V.*

**⑪** **Versailles.** This is one the best of the informal Cuban res-
**$$** taurants that line Calle Ocho, just north of Coral Gables. The multimirrored and gold-trimmed Versailles is right out of the Louis XIV period, but the cuisine is pure Little Havana. Specialties include *pollo Versailles*, a grilled half chicken with onions and garlic served with plantains, rice, and black beans; roast pork; grilled steak; and *arroz con pollo* (chicken with yellow rice). The restaurant is open until 2 AM; the *media noche*, or "midnight sandwich" of ham and cheese on sweet Cuban bread, is a late-hours favorite. Tables are close together, and the sense of intrigue is palpable. Most customers, however, are engaged in Miami's favorite pastime—sipping sweet, strong Cuban

coffee and heatedly discussing Caribbean politics. *3555 S.W. Eighth St., tel. 305/444–0240. Casual dress. No reservations. AE, CB, DC, MC.*

## Coconut Grove

22 *$$$$* **Grand Café.** The sun-bathed, open, and plant-filled restaurant in the Grand Bay Hotel is known for its power-lunch buffets. City Hall is across the street, and many a politician wines and dines over the Grand's pink tablecloths and floral bouquets. In the evening, the atmosphere is quieter and more intimate (especially appropriate for solitary diners). The cuisine is an eclectic mix of standard Continental (rack of lamb, Dover sole) and international foods with a Caribbean accent. Swordfish is grilled and served in a light cream of curry sauce. Conch is on the menu; so is lobster in a coconut curry sauce. The diverse wine selection has labels from France, Italy, and California. *2669 South Bayshore Dr., tel. 305/858–9600. Jackets required. Reservations advised. AE, CB, DC, MC, V.*

20 *$$$* **Kaleidoscope.** This breezy restaurant is perched one flight above a busy shopping street in Coconut Grove. The eclectic clientele reflects the neighborhood—local businesspeople, politicians, artists, and pretheater diners. The cuisine favors seafood and pasta, such as grilled swordfish on a bed of spinach with lemon caper sauce; snapper with glazed bananas broiled in white wine and lemon; and julienned strips of duck fettucini with andouille sausage, wild mushrooms, tomatoes, herbs, and garlic. A guitar livens up the mood at night. Solitary diners should ask for a balcony table overlooking the street (Coconut Grove offers the most interesting people-watching in Miami). The Kaleidoscope manages to combine elegance with a casual air. *3112 Commodore Plaza, tel. 305/446–5010. Formal to casual dress; almost anything goes. Reservations advised. AE, CB, MC, V.*

## Coral Gables

7 *$$$* **Christy's.** This one-story, pink brick steakhouse has deep red walls, comfortably spaced tables, and a subdued, elegant ambience. Fresh fish and lobster are on the menu, but the raison d'être for Christy's is beef. Prime ribs, New York sirloin, filet Mignon, and lamb chops are house favorites. All entrées come with a tasty Caesar salad. Christy's also has an uncommonly good pureed black bean soup spiced with sherry. The wine list has mostly American labels. Coral Gables business people are the main clientele at lunch, but Christy's draws steak lovers from all over Miami. *3101 Ponce de Leon Blvd., tel. 305/446–1400. Jacket and tie suggested. Reservations advised. AE, CB, DC, MC, V. Dinner only weekends.*

★ 8 19 *$$* **J.J.'s American Diner.** This informal diner—fine for men or women eating alone—is heavy on atmospherics and is especially good for casual brunches and lunches. The open grill (chefs are right behind the counter), black and white tiles, and Wurlitzer jukebox have a high-gloss, 1990s look ("Miami Vice" has filmed here), but the American Graffiti-era ambience, big portions, and simple American foods recall the 1950s. Breakfast favorites include waffles, pancakes, yogurt, fruit, and granola. Best bets at lunch: the oversized burger 'n fries, cobb salad, grilled dolphin, and blackened swordfish. *Two locations: 2320 Galiano St., Coral Gables, tel. 305/448–6886 and 5850 Sunset Dr., South Miami, tel. 305/665–5499. Casual dress. No reservations. AE, MC, V.*

★ ❺ **Le Festival.** This elegant French restaurant, a favorite of
$$$ Richard Nixon's, serves classic (but not too heavily sauced) dishes to the Coral Gables elite. Specialties include chicken niçoise—a boneless breast of chicken on a bed of angel hair pasta with tomatoes, mushrooms, onions, and garlic—and red snapper in a light white wine and cream sauce with shrimp and scallops. Le Festival also wows you with its desserts of fresh strawberries, apple pie topped with caramel, chocolate mousse, and cheese cake. The wines are French and American. The decor is distinctly French, down to the Arc de Triomphe painting, and the ambience is perfect for business lunches and dinners. *2120 Salzedo St., tel. 305/442–8545. Jackets suggested. Reservations advised. AE, MC, V. Dinner only Sat.; closed Sun.*

❾ **Place St. Michel.** Chef Curtis Whitticar has expanded the
$$$ Continental menu to include game specialties such as buffalo steak grilled in a cabernet wine sauce, pan-roast quail, and, on occasion, elk sausage. His flair for regional American cooking extends to sweetbreads and to local fruits such as mango and papaya, which grace some of his seafood dishes. Less ambitious specialties include rack of lamb and various pastas. The selection of French and California wines isn't unusually large, but it has been carefully and tastefully chosen. The restaurant is located in what is easily Miami's quaintest hotel, in the Coral Gables business district, and the French inn ambience is appropriate for business meals and for solitary diners as well. *162 Alcazar Ave., Coral Gables, tel. 305/444–1666. Neat, casual dress. Reservations advised. AE, CB, DC, MC, V.*

★ ❶ **Vinton's.** This charming, white stucco haunt fitted with
$$$$ Impressionist art is a favorite of Coral Gables locals and of wine connoisseurs from around the world (*Wine Spectator* rates the wine among the top 100 in the United States). The French/Continental cuisine features dishes prepared with local ingredients, such as black grouper served on a bed of endives in a ginger and vinegar sauce, and yellowtail with spinach in a red cabernet sauce. The roast duck, served in an orange or raspberry sauce, is especially crisp. Vinton's, which attracts its share of local celebrities, has a number of small rooms that are perfect for throwing business dinners. When the weather is right, you can also eat in an outdoor courtyard. *116 Alhambra Circle, tel. 305/445–2511. Jacket suggested. Reservations advised. AE, CB, DC, MC, V. Closed Sun.*

## Downtown

⓰ **Brasserie de Paris.** This French/Continental restaurant is
$$$ a lunchtime favorite of bankers, cruise line executives, and other pinstripes. It's located in the Everglades Hotel, in the heart of downtown. The dark wood paneling sets a serious tone, but it's brightened by Toulouse-Lautrec posters. Tables are spaced with enough room for discreet conversation. Cold salmon, split pea soup, and salads are light, midday favorites. The Dover sole and grilled snapper are popular entrées. Heartier eaters may opt for grilled lamb chops or veal in a light cream sauce. There is a

diverse and tempting array of desserts. *244 Biscayne Blvd., tel. 305/374–0122. Jackets suggested. Reservations generally aren't necessary. AE, CB, DC, MC, V. Lunch only weekdays; closed weekends.*

**⑬** **Firehouse Four.** This recent addition to downtown Miami,
*$$$* housed in a restored, 1923 fire station, is a hot attraction for young professionals, bankers, politicians, and journalists. The 35-foot mahogany bar, the brightly polished fire poles, and every other aspect of the decor, recall the building's past. The cuisine is American, with an emphasis on fish, pasta, and steaks—all simply prepared. Popular entrées include fettuccine with fresh vegetables and prosciutto; and Firehouse's grilled chicken in Key-lime sauce, served in a salad, sandwich, or platter. The upstairs dining area is elegant and roomy. There is music downstairs by the bar, and a live band on Fridays. Happy hour is jammed with yuppies. *1000 South Miami Ave., tel. 305/379–1923. Jacket suggested; neat and casual is fine. Reservations advised for large parties. AE, MC, V. Closed Sun.*

**★ ⑰** **Los Ranchos.** Julio Somoza, the owner and a nephew of the
*$$$* late Nicaraguan dictator Anastasio, has carried on a tradition that began with the original Los Ranchos in prerevolutionary Managua. The crowd tends to be Latin, well-dressed, and upscale. Nicaraguans love beef, and the ranch-house decor and cowhide menus are of a piece with the cuisine. The house specialty is *churrasco* (tenderloin) with a choice of *chimichurri* (a green sauce of chopped parsley, garlic, oil, and vinegar), sweet and sour sauce, and a hot pepper sauce. Other favorites include *chorizo* (sausage) and sautéed shrimp in a creamy jalapeño sauce. Most meals are served with generous portions of rice, beans, and platanos. Los Ranchos is a festive restaurant with live music that is most fun when you're traveling in a group. Start with a plate of mixed appetizers—ranging from yuca to cheese to sausages—and a pitcher of sangria. *Two locations: 401 Biscayne Blvd. (in Bayside Marketplace, downtown) tel. 305/375–8188 and 135 S.W. 107th Ave., Sweetwater, tel. 305/221–9367. Casual to dressy. Reservations advised. AE, DC, MC, V.*

**⑱** **Pavillon Grill.** This private lunch club, on the ground floor
*$$$$* of the Hotel InterContinental, throws open its doors in the evening to bankers, lawyers, and executive types. The leather chairs, mahogany paneling, and green marble set a boardroom ambience that is appropriate for entertaining clients and for conducting business dinners. The menu is described as gourmet American. A house specialty is Two-Act Duck, roasted breast of duck in balsamic vinegar sauce, followed by a leg of duck shredded and sautéed with fresh greens and a light herb vinaigrette. The four-course Surprise Menu changes daily, according to what's freshest. The Pavillon uses domestic ingredients and local seafood and features California labels on its wine list. *100 Chopin Plaza, tel. 305/577–1000. Jackets suggested. Reservations advised. AE, CB, DC, MC, V. Open to the public for dinner only, closed Sun.*

## The Beaches

**㉓** **Café des Arts.** This small, nouvelle French restaurant
*$$$* faces the ocean on Miami Beach, and it has an almost sensual appeal. The walls are covered with Deco paintings,

and diners eat in one of three intimate rooms or outside on a patio. Pasta des arts (with smoked salmon and artichokes), baked salmon with grape sauce, and duck à l'orange are popular entrées. The extensive wine list includes labels from France, Italy, and Chile. Some nights a guitarist or pianist plays, adding to the relaxing atmosphere. This is a good spot to soothe a recalcitrant client. *918 Ocean Dr., Miami Beach, tel. 305/534-6267. Casual but neat. Reservations suggested. AE, MC, V. Dinner only. Closed Mon.*

**②⑤** **Joe's Stone Crab Restaurant.** Joe's, an informal family res-
$$$ taurant now in its fourth generation, is the one place, Miamians say, that tourists *must* visit. After 75 years, Joe's is still serving the same basic entrée—local stone crabs with drawn butter, lemon, and Joe's own tangy mustard sauce. Joe's is also famous for its coleslaw, creamed garlic spinach, and Key-lime pie with graham cracker crust and whipped cream. Be prepared for a long wait. Building an appetite in Joe's crowded bar is part of the tradition. This boisterous restaurant is definitely not a place to dine alone, or to bring your work. *227 Biscayne St., Miami Beach, tel. 305/673-0367. Informal dress. No reservations. AE, D, DC, MC, V. Dinner only Sun., Mon.; closed June–Sept.*

**★ ②⑥** **Stefano's.** The homemade pasta at this Key Biscayne hot
$$$ spot is Miami's best. Specialties on the Northern Italian menu include veal scaloppine stuffed with spinach and imported mushrooms on a bed of creamy radicchio; risotto with seafood; linguine with basil and garlic; and fresh clams or mussels in marinara sauce. The hot and cold antipasti are the genuine articles. Stefano's has 700 wines from Italy, France, Spain, Chile, and elsewhere. This is a place for entertaining clients, not for serious negotiations. A soft, saxophone-led dance band plays from 7:30 PM. At 11 PM a DJ picks up the tempo—and the decibel level—with Latin and American disco. The dining-by-dance floor setting is elegant. *24 Crandon Blvd., Key Biscayne, tel. 305/361-7007. Casual but elegant. Reservations advised. AE, DC, MC, V. Dinner only.*

## FREE TIME

### Fitness

*Hotel Facilities*
Hotel health clubs are generally open only to hotel guests and regular members. But several independent clubs accept day-at-a-time walk-ins. Outsiders can sign up for aerobics classes or use the free weights, cycles, sauna, and cardiovascular equipment at the **Sonesta Beach** (tel. 305/361-2021) for a daily rate of $10. Or you can indulge in a massage at the **Biltmore Hotel** (tel. 305/445-1926) for $36 for a half hour, and have the run of its health club facilities included in the fee.

*Health Clubs*
The **Downtown Athletic Club** (200 S. Biscayne Blvd., tel. 305/358-9988) has a full complement of cardiovascular equipment, including treadmills facing TVs. It also has a whirlpool, steam room, sauna, toning and aerobics classes, raquetball, squash, volleyball, basketball, track, free weights, and Nautilus—all available at a daily rate of

$15.90. **Grove Fitness** (Coconut Grove Mall, 2901 Florida Ave., tel. 305/442–2107) has aerobics classes, Nautilus, stationary cycles, sauna and free weights; a one-day membership costs $15. **Jazzercise,** with 20 locations in Miami (tel. 305/661–0106), has aerobics classes on a per-class rate of $5. **Utmost Fitness Center** (5741 S.W. 40th St., Coral Gables, tel. 305/665–6604) has aerobics classes, free weights, steam room, sauna, stationary cycles, and Nautilus; the daily rate is $10.

*Jogging*

There are plenty of parks and running courses in Miami, but you'll see locals jogging just about anywhere all year round. Some favorite courses include the path around the Granada Golf Course, on either side of Granada Avenue in Coral Gables; Cape Florida State Park in Key Biscayne; along South Bayshore Drive in Coconut Grove; along Brickell Avenue, near downtown; and in Tropical Park, west of the Palmetto Expressway and adjacent to S.W. 40th Street.

## Shopping

Miamians shop in malls. The best is **Dadeland Mall** (7535 N. Kendall Dr., tel. 305/665–6226). It's a world of its own with five department stores and 180 specialty stores. At **Mayfair Shops** in the Grove (2911 Grand Ave., Coconut Grove), stores are spread around waterfalls and tropical greenery and are decidedly more upscale. The downtown **Bayside Marketplace** (401 Biscayne Blvd., tel. 305/577–3344) has an international flavor and features tourist items, artifacts, and fashions—try it when you're shopping with no fixed item in mind (*see* Diversions, below). Miami's most popular department store is **Burdines** (22 E. Flagler St., downtown, tel. 305/835–5151 and in Dadeland Mall).

Miami has three prime areas for out-of-doors street shopping: the hyperkinetic **downtown in Coconut Grove; Sunset Drive in South Miami,** and **Miracle Mile,** a small-town-America strip in Coral Gables. In addition, an artists' colony is spawning a strip of galleries and studios on **Lincoln Road** in South Miami Beach. Though Miami is well stocked with gift shops, an unusual one is **Zanjabil** (3442 Main Hwy., Coconut Grove), which has an eclectic selection of imports, tropical fashions, leather handbags, exotic incense, and other items.

## Diversions

Tour the **Art Deco** district in South Miami Beach as far east as you can, especially the hotels on Ocean Drive. The rows of buildings with geometric lines and pastel colors evoke tropical images and fantasies of 1920s and '30s romance. The mile-square district was the first area in the United States dating from the 20th century to be designated as a national historic district.

**Bass Museum of Art** (2121 Park Ave., Miami Beach, tel. 305/673–7533) has a diverse permanent collection of European paintings, sculpture, and tapestries, including works by Rubens and Toulouse-Lautrec.

**Bayside Marketplace** (401 Biscayne Blvd.), a waterside mall built by the Rouse Company, combines outdoor entertainment with shops, pushcarts, and restaurants. If you have time to kill downtown, it's the perfect place to shop, eat, drink, or people-watch.

The **beach** is at your doorstep. Crandon Park, on Crandon Park Boulevard, an Atlantic Ocean beach on Key Biscayne, is minutes from downtown Miami.

**Center for the Fine Arts** (101 W. Flagler St., tel. 305/375–1700) has exhibits from museum and art collections around the world. The downtown building is part of the Metro-Dade Cultural Center, a postmodern complex designed by Philip Johnson.

**Cuban Museum of Arts & Culture** (1300 S.W. 12th Ave., tel. 305/858–8006) features paintings and drawings by Cuban artists and temporary cultural exhibits.

**Everglades National Park** (tel. 305/247–6211) is an hour away and well worth the drive. Take the Florida Turnpike south to the Florida City exit and follow signs to the park visitors center. The ¼-mile raised boardwalk called Anhinga trail, just inside the park entrance, is ideal for starters. You'll see alligators, fish, and unforgettable varieties of tropical birds darting amid the mangroves.

Take a tram ride and guided tour through a wondrous display of tropical plants and flowers at the 83-acre **Fairchild Tropical Gardens** (10901 Old Culter Rd., Coral Gables, tel. 305/667–1651).

**Parrot Jungle** (11000 S.W. 57th Ave., tel. 305/666–7834) has 1,100 parrots, toucans, palm cockatoos, and other exotic birds in vivid technicolor. Peacocks and flamingos run free in the landscaped gardens, and alligators lurk in protected canals.

## Professional Sports

Miami's football team, the **Miami Dolphins,** plays at Joe Robbie Stadium (tel. 305/620–5000). The city's basketball team, **Miami Heat,** competes at the Miami Arena (tel. 305/577–4328).

## The Arts

Miami has more fine sand than fine arts, but as the city has grown it has begun to devote more resources to culture. Although Miami lacks a resident symphony orchestra, the New World Symphony, a unique training symphony for young musicians who have finished their academic studies, helps fill the void. The Miami City Ballet, though only a few years old, has rapidly become prominent, and Miami's opera ranks with the nation's best. Miami also boasts an annual series of chamber concerts with internationally known guest ensembles. The city has several live theaters—most notably the Coconut Grove Playhouse, which stages current and vintage Broadway plays, musical reviews, and original productions. Others include the Minorca Playhouse, home to the Florida Shakespeare Festival and productions of other dance and theater companies; the Hirschfeld Theater, which features musicals from Broadway on national tour; and the University of Miami's Ring Theater.

Ticket agencies include **RR Ticket Service** (tel. 800/888–1840) and **TicketMaster** (tel. 305/358–5885). For more information, consult **Miami's Guide to the Arts** (tel. 305/854–1790), a monthly guide to music of all kinds, art gallery openings, theater, and cultural events, sold at newsstands throughout Miami.

**Coconut Grove Playhouse,** 3500 Main Hwy., Coconut Grove, tel. 305/442–2662.
**Friends of Chamber Music,** Univ. of Miami, tel. 305/372–2975.
**Greater Miami Opera Association,** Dade County Auditorium, 305/854–7890.
**Hirschfeld Theater,** Clarion Castle Hotel & Resort, 5445 Collins Ave., Miami Beach, tel. 305/865–7529.
**Miami City Ballet,** Gusman Center, tel. 305/532–4880.
**Minorca Playhouse,** 232 Minorca Ave., Coral Gables, tel. 305/441–1330.
**New World Symphony,** Gusman Center or Lincoln Theater, tel. 305/673–3330.

## After Hours

There are night spots in Coconut Grove, Little Havana, the Kendall area, and on the fringes of downtown. In recent years, Miami Beach has become the hottest area for singles and yuppies as the revitalization of the Deco district has spawned a burst of trendy new nightspots.

*Bars and Lounges*
If you're meeting a business associate or want to unwind with a quiet drink, hotels are usually best. In Coconut Grove, the **Tiffany Lounge** in the Mayfair House Hotel (tel. 305/441–0000) is an intimate spot for a drink. Downtown, the lobby lounge in the **Hotel InterContinental** (tel. 305/577–1000) overlooks the Henry Moore sculpture, The Spindle; **Cye's Rivergate Restaurant** (444 Brickell Ave., tel. 305/358–9100) is an old-time Miami favorite; and **Bayview Lounge** (lobby of the Dupont Plaza Hotel, 300 Biscayne Blvd. tel. 305/358–2541) offers a view of Biscayne Bay and classical jazz guitar on weeknights. **Stuart's Bar & Lounge** in the Hotel Place St. Michel (tel. 305/444–1666) is an appealing spot in Coral Gables and frequently has live music. Also in the Gables, the **Lobby Bar** in the Hyatt Regency Coral Gables (tel. 305/441–1234) is a relaxed place for a drink. **Doc Dammers Saloon,** in the Colonnade Hotel (tel. 305/441–2600), draws yuppies after hours during the week and a college crowd on weekends. The **Rendevous Lounge,** in the Hotel Sofitel (tel. 305/264–4888), is an upscale, oak-paneled bar with a French ambience. The lobby in the **Miami Airport Hilton** (tel. 305/262–1000) has a piano bar with a lakeside view. For a hip, tropical ambience on Miami Beach, try the **Clevelander Poolside Bar** (1020 Ocean Dr., tel. 305/531–3485), or the lively **Island Club** (701 Washington Ave., tel. 305/538–1213).

*Cabarets*
**Les Violins Supper Club** (1751 Biscayne Blvd., tel. 305/371–8668) has musical revues, dinner, and dancing. In **Club Tropigala** (Fontainebleau Hilton Resort & Spa, 4441 Collins Ave., Miami Beach, tel. 305/672–7469), made up to look like a jungle, an orchestra plays Latin salsa and Top 40, and costumed shows are given nightly. The Latin mu-

sic and dance show at **Copacabana Supper Club** (3600 S.W. 8th St., tel. 305/443–3801) re-creates the tropical night-club scene from Havana's pre-Castro heyday.

### Comedy Clubs

New performers each week do adult and somewhat risqué acts at **Uncle Funny's Comedy Clubs** at the Dadeland Marriott Hotel (9090 S. Dadeland Blvd., tel. 305/670–2022), and also at Holiday Inn (21485 N.W. 27th Ave., North Miami, tel. 305/948–6887).

### Jazz Clubs

The most renowned Miami nightspot is **Tobacco Road** (626 S. Miami Ave., tel. 305/374–1198), an offbeat, two-story nightclub on the site of a Prohibition-era speakeasy that is home to local and national blues bands, as well as occasion-al jazz artists. A jazz trio plays Thurs.–Sat. in the **Ciga Lounge** in the Grand Bay Hotel (tel. 305/858–9600). **Andiamo** (1717 N. Bayshore Dr., tel. 305/579–2001) has live jazz and occasional Latin rhythms Tues.–Sun.—along with plenty of pasta. **Greenstreets** (Coral Gables Holiday Inn, 2051 LeJeune Rd., tel. 305/443–2301) books jazz pi-anists or small groups most evenings. A jazz pianist plays at **Lucky's** restaurant in the Park Central Hotel (tel. 305/538–1611) on Friday and Saturday. However, schedules and styles are subject to change. For current listings, it's a good idea to consult the *Miami Herald* or Miami's *Guide to the Arts*.

### For Singles

**Currents** in the Hyatt Regency Miami (tel. 305/358–1234) draws a 20s-to-30s crowd with bands in the Miami Sound Machine mode. **Coco Loco's** has Top 40 and high-intensity Latin sounds and dancing, Thurs.–Sat. in the Sheraton Brickell Point Hotel (tel. 305/373–6000). Latin disco thrives at **Desires** in the Sonesta Beach Hotel (tel. 305/361–2021). Take a moment out from the music to admire the Andy Warhol drawings of Mick Jagger. **Club Mystique** in the Miami Airport Hilton (tel. 305/262–1000) draws a young crowd for high-energy Latin and rock. The happy hour Wed.–Fri. at the **Alcazaba** in the Hyatt Regency Coral Gables (tel. 305/441–1234) is stocked with Coral Gables professionals. Downtown's young professionals con-verge on **Firehouse Four** (1000 South Miami Ave., tel. 305/379–1923) for happy hour, especially for the live band that plays there Fridays. **Stringfellow's** (Mayfair in the Grove, 3390 Mary St., tel. 305/446–7555) is a popular disco in Co-conut Grove with high-tech video, sound, and lighting. If you want to sample the hip bars and restaurants on Miami Beach you might start with the bistro-like **Strand** (671 Washington Ave., tel. 305/532–2340); the juke-box-infor-mal **Island Club** (701 Washington Ave., tel. 305/538–1213); **Lucky's** (Park Central Hotel, tel. 305/538–1611); and **Club Nu** (245 22nd St., tel. 305/672–0068), which reinvents its own decor every few months and features offbeat (and at times off-color) revues, acts, and fashion shows.

# Minneapolis/ St. Paul

*by Carla Waldemar*

The Mississippi River that separates the twin cities of Minneapolis and St. Paul is also responsible for their progress from mere trading posts to major centers of commerce over a century ago, when the waterway's power was leashed to build fortunes in lumber and flower milling. Today, the early grain mills have evolved into giant food industries, including General Mills, Pillsbury, Cargill, and International Multifoods. The river also bisects the campus of the University of Minnesota, whose graduates are recruited by Minnesota Mining and Manufacturing (3M), Honeywell, and Control Data, all based here. The Twin Cities are the home base of Northwest Airlines and maintain close business and cultural ties with neighboring Canada. Bell Canada Enterprises Developers (BCED) has become a major landlord of large local commercial properties.

For a metropolitan area of its size—around 2,250,000 in the seven county region—there are proportionately few blue-collar industries, and few of the social and economic problems that often accompany the vicissitudes of these industries. The cities remain clean and safe, and boast an unusually high level of education, support for the arts, and government involvement in civic and social affairs.

While the business climate is healthy, aided by a new, state-of-the-art convention center in Minneapolis and an ambitious World Trade Center in St. Paul (the locus of the area's business contacts with such countries as Canada, Japan, and the Soviet Union), the geographical climate can be daunting. To combat long and bitter winters, downtown buildings are connected by an elaborate network of skyways. And to combat potential brain drain to more temperate zones, the Twin Cities have actively promoted leisuretime amenities, including one of the country's oldest and most extensive park systems. Minneapolis, which means City of Lakes, boasts six interconnected, inner-city lakes, as well as miles of public trails along the Mississippi.

Likewise, a savvy business community has generously supported the arts; in fact, it's here that the idea of the nation's Five Percent Clubs, in which participating companies donate a part of their gross income to the arts, originated. As a result, this cultural oasis on the arid plain between the coasts is emerging as a mecca for cutting-edge performers, film makers, publishers, and advertising and public relations firms such as Fallon, McElligott, & Rice. World-class theaters, orchestras, and museums contribute to what national pollsters tout as an enviable quality of life.

Differences between the two cities began with their earliest settlers. Minneapolis translates a strong Scandinavian heritage to an almost single-minded work ethic and disdain for conspicuous consumption. To outsiders, the city seems to have greater energy and to be more open. St. Paul is smaller, and probably somewhat more insular; it's home to the cities' oldest names and money, born of conservative Irish Catholic roots. Despite the inevitable rivalry between the two cities, a spirit of economic and political cooperation has begun to emerge.

## Top Employers

| Employer | Type of Enterprise | Parent*/ Headquarters |
|---|---|---|
| **Cargill Inc.** | Agricultural | Minnetonka, MN |
| **Carlson Cos.** | Service | Minneapolis |
| **Control Data** | Computer management systems | Bloomington, MN |
| **Dayton-Hudson** | Retail stores | Minneapolis |
| **General Mills** | Food manufacturing | Golden Valley, MN |
| **Honeywell** | Defense, energy systems, home heating products | Minneapolis |
| **NWA** | Transportation | Eagan, MN |
| **St. Paul Cos.** | Insurance | St. Paul |
| **Super Valu** | Wholesaler/ retailer | Eden Prairie, MN |
| **3M Co.** | Consumer electronics, automotive, surgical and other manufacturing | Maplewood, MN |

*if applicable

## ESSENTIAL INFORMATION

### Climate

Expect the kind of bitterly cold and snowy winters that legends are made of from November to March. The good news, however, is that roads are cleared quickly and the airport rarely closes down. During July and August temperatures may soar to the high, humid 80s, but nights generally bring relief.

What follows are the average daily maximum and minimum temperatures for Minneapolis-St. Paul.

| Jan. | 22F | −6C | Feb. | 25F | −4C | Mar. | 38F | 3C |
|------|-----|-----|------|-----|-----|------|-----|-----|
|      | 7   | −14 |      | 9   | −13 |      | 22  | −6 |

| Apr. | 56F | 13C | May | 68F | 20C | June | 77F | 25C |
|------|-----|-----|-----|-----|-----|------|-----|-----|
|      | 36  | 2   |     | 49  | 9   |      | 58  | 14  |

| July | 83F | 28C | Aug. | 81F | 27C | Sept. | 72F | 22C |
|------|-----|-----|------|-----|-----|-------|-----|-----|
|      | 63  | 17  |      | 61  | 16  |       | 52  | 11  |

| Oct. | 59F | 15C | Nov. | 40F | 4C | Dec. | 27F | −3C |
|------|-----|-----|------|-----|-----|------|-----|-----|
|      | 41  | 5   |      | 27  | −3  |      | 13  | −11 |

## Airport

**Minneapolis-St. Paul International Airport** serves all domestic and international flights. It is 12 miles south of Minneapolis and 8 miles southwest of St. Paul. Domestic flights leave from the main terminal, the Charles Lindbergh building. International flights depart from the Hubert H. Humphrey terminal, a 10-minute shuttle bus ride from the main terminal.

## Airport Business Facilities

The **Airport Director's Office** (tel. 612/726–5555) rents conference rooms in the center of the mezzanine level. **Host International** (tel. 612/726–5341) rents a conference room on the main floor with catering service. **Teleticket** (main floor across from United Airlines, tel. 612/726–9338) has fax machines, photocopying, notary public, secretarial services, baggage storage, phone suites, IBM PCs, and a conference room. **Mutual of Omaha Insurance Counter** (main floor, tel. 612/726–5848) offers Western Union and travel insurance.

## Airlines

Northwest Airlines is headquartered here.

**Air Canada,** tel. 800/422–6232.
**American,** tel. 800/433–7300.
**Continental,** tel. 612/332–1471 or 800/525–0280.
**Midway,** tel. 800/621–5700.
**Northwest,** tel. 612/726–1234 or 800/225–2525.
**Pan Am,** tel. 800/221–1111.
**TWA,** tel. 612/333–6543 or 800/221–2000.
**United,** tel. 612/339–3671 or 800/241–6522.
**USAir,** tel. 612/338–5841 or 800/428–4322.

## Between the Airport and Downtown

*By Taxi*
Travel time between the airport and either downtown area takes 25–30 minutes, about 45 minutes during rush hours (4–6 PM). The fare is about $16 to Minneapolis, $13 to St. Paul. A cab stand is outside the airport's lower level, near the baggage claim area.

*By Van*
**Airport Express** (tel. 612/726–6400) operates to and from the airport and most of the larger downtown Minneapolis hotels every half hour 5 AM–11 PM; the 30-minute trip (or longer, depending on distance to your hotel) costs $7.50 one way, $11.50 round-trip. The **St. Paul-Airport Limousine Service** (tel. 612/726–5479) operates every half hour

5 AM–1 AM; it takes about 20 minutes to most hotels and costs $5.50 one way, $9.50 round-trip. All vans leave from the airport's lower level outside baggage claim area No. 7.

*By Bus*

**Metropolitan Transit Commission** (tel. 612/827–7733) buses offer inexpensive ($1 or less) but somewhat unreliable passage to both downtowns. Both trips take about an hour. Service runs from 4 AM to 1 AM; buses depart every 20 minutes to an hour. Passengers for both St. Paul and Minneapolis board a No. 7 bus at a bus shelter at the west end of the airport's lower level; St. Paul-bound passengers must transfer to a No. 9 bus.

## Car Rentals

The following companies have airport locations, except for Dollar and Rent-A-Wreck, which operate shuttle services to nearby offices.

**Budget,** tel. 612/727–2000 or 800/527–0700.
**Dollar,** tel. 612/726–9494 or 800/421–6868.
**Hertz,** tel. 612/726–1600 or 800/654–3131.
**National,** tel. 612/726–5600 or 800/227–7368.
**Rent-a-Wreck,** tel. 612/854–0123 or 800/535–1391.

## Emergencies

*Doctors*

**Park Nicollet Medical Center** (2001 Blaisdell Ave. S, Minneapolis, tel. 612/871–8144) and **Ramsey Clinic** (640 Jackson St., St. Paul, tel. 612/221–3000).

*Dentists*

**Park Nicollet Medical Center** (*see* Doctors, above), **The Medical Center,** at the airport (7775 26th Ave. S., Suite 190, tel. 612/726–1490) and **Ramsey Clinic** (*see* Doctors, above) offer emergency dental treatment.

*Hospitals*

**Hennepin County Medical Center** (701 Park Ave. Minneapolis, tel. 612/347–3131) and **St. Paul-Ramsey Medical Center** (640 Jackson St., St. Paul, tel. 612/221–3456).

## Important Addresses and Numbers

**Audiovisual rentals.** *See* Computer rentals, below.

**Chamber of Commerce** (81 S. 9th St., Suite 200, Minneapolis, tel. 612/370–9132 and 445 Minnesota St., 600 NCL Tower, St. Paul, tel. 612/223–5000).

**Computer rentals.** Blumberg Communications (525 Washington Ave. N., Minneapolis, tel. 612/333–1271), Rent-A-Center (509 University Ave. W, St. Paul, tel. 612/227–9985).

**Convention and exhibition centers.** The Minneapolis Convention Center (1301 2nd Ave. S, tel. 612/335–6000); Civic Center (143 W. 4th St., St. Paul, tel. 612/224–7403).

**Fax and copying services.** Kinko's Copies (9 outlets, including: IDS Center, 80 S. 8th St., Suite 180, Minneapolis, tel. 612/338–1541; 1669 Grand Ave., St. Paul, tel. 612/699–9671; 708 W. 66th St., Richfield, tel. 612/866–1900).

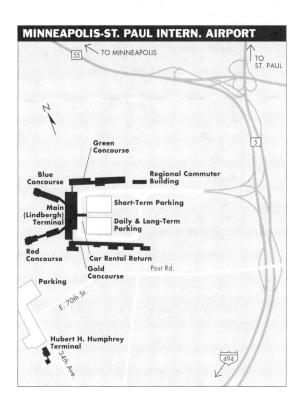

**Formal-wear rentals.** Men: Skeffingtons Men's Formal Wear (1032 Nicollet Mall, Minneapolis, tel. 612/333–6249 and 1636 University Ave., Midway District, St. Paul, tel. 612/645–6102); Women: Formal Princess (2508 Hennepin Ave., Uptown, tel. 612/377–6427).

**Gift shops.** Candy: Godiva Chocolatier (IDS Center, 7th St. and Nicollet Mall, Minneapolis, tel. 612/338–6800), Maud Borup Chocolates (Carriage Hill Plaza, 5th St. near St. Peter St., St. Paul, tel. 612/293–0530); Flowers: Bachman's City Center (40 S. 7th St., Minneapolis, tel. 612/333–3450 or 612/851–7311), Holm & Olson (14 W. 5th St., St. Paul, tel. 612/224–9641.

**Graphic design studios.** Type House (3030 2nd St. N, Minneapolis, tel. 612/588–7511), Typeshooters (4524 Excelsior Blvd., St. Louis Park, tel. 612/927–9260), Forum Graphics (485 Selby Ave., St. Paul, tel. 612/224–4081).

**Hairstylists.** Unisex: Horst and Friends (Lumber Exchange Building, 10 S. 5th St., Minneapolis, tel. 612/332–3644), Rocco's Altobelli Hair Stylists (665 S. Snelling Ave., St. Paul, tel. 612/690–5491).

**Health and fitness clubs.** *See* Fitness, below.

**Information hot lines.** The Connection, for music, sports, theater, and restaurant and bar information (tel. 612/929–9000).

**Limousine services.** Twin Star Limousine (Minneapolis, tel. 612/641–1385), Kjell Bergh's Borton Limousine (Bloomington, tel. 612/884–4668).

**Liquor stores.** For fine wines: Haskell's (81 S. 9th St., Minneapolis, tel. 612/333–2434 and 2251 Ford Pkwy., St. Paul, tel. 612/698–8844). Other liquor stores include Surdyk's (E. Hennepin at University Ave. NE, Minneapolis, tel. 612/379–3232), Kappy's Liquor (347 N. Wabasha St., St. Paul, tel. 612/222–8407).

**Mail delivery, overnight.** DHL (tel. 612/681–0100), Express Mail-U.S. Postal Service (tel. 612/349–4720), Federal Express (tel. 612/340–0887), UPS (tel. 612/378–0700).

**Messenger services.** Bicycle Express (Minneapolis, tel. 612/340–0059), Midwest Delivery Service (St. Paul, tel. 612/644–8724).

**Office space rentals.** Lumber Exchange Building (10 S. 5th St., Minneapolis, tel. 612/375–9555), The 701 Building (701 4th Ave. S, Minneapolis, tel. 612/337–9500), World Trade Center (30 E. 7th St., St. Paul, tel. 612/220–2025).

**Pharmacies, late-night.** Walgreen Drug Stores, open 24 hours (12 W. 66th St., Richfield, tel. 612/861–7276 and in the Midway Shopping Center, 1530 University Ave., St. Paul, tel. 612/646–6165).

**Radio stations, all-news.** KNOW 1330 AM, public radio station KSJN 91.3 FM.

**Secretarial services.** Dolphin Temporary Help Services (258 Hennepin Ave. S, Minneapolis, tel. 612/338–7581), Kelly Services (330 2nd Ave. S, No. 765, Minneapolis, tel. 612/339–7311), Manpower Temporary Services (445 Minnesota St., No. 514, St. Paul, tel. 612/227–9111).

**Stationery supplies.** St. Paul Book and Stationery (11 stores, including: Town Square, 6th and Cedar Sts., St. Paul, tel. 612/227–9156 and First Star Metro Bank Building, skyway level, 6th St. and Marquette Ave., Minneapolis, tel. 612/338–1883).

**Taxis.** Yellow Taxi (tel. 612/222–4433, covers St. Paul and the suburbs), Minneapolis Yellow Cab (tel. 612/824–4000, covers Minneapolis and its suburbs), Premier Taxi (tel. 612/522–2222, covers Minneapolis and the airport), Town Taxi (tel. 612/331–8294, covers the Twin Cities' suburbs).

**Theater tickets.** *See* The Arts, below.

**Train information.** Amtrak (St. Paul/Minneapolis Minnesota Midway Station, 730 Transfer Rd., near Prior Ave. and University Ave., St. Paul, tel. 612/644–1127 or 800/872–7245).

**Travel agents.** American Express (Pillsbury Center, 200 S. 6th St., Minneapolis, tel. 612/343–5500 and the National Bank Building, 30 E. 7th St., St. Paul, tel. 612/291–7081), Carlson Travel Network (several locations, including 514 Nicollet Mall, Minneapolis, tel. 612/332–4323).

**Weather** (tel. 612/725–6090).

# LODGING

Twin Cities hotels tend toward the monumental, could-be-anywhere towers that are stronger on serving business needs than on creating enclaves with personality. However, several newer properties along the Minneapolis stretch of the Mississippi have begun a move toward creating gracious environments; furthermore, in response to the fitness craze, new conference center hotels in the suburbs are touting recreational facilities as their lure. In readiness for the opening of the remodeled Convention Center, the new sports stadium, and the arrival of Saks Fifth Avenue and Neiman Marcus in the city center, many Minneapolis hotels are undergoing renovations in order to satisfy the expected surge of business guests. St. Paul offers fewer options, not only in range of style and services, but in location. A corridor of hotels near the Minneapolis-St. Paul International Airport lies within a 20-minute drive of both downtowns.

Most of the hotels listed here offer special corporate rates and weekend discounts; inquire when making reservations.

Highly recommended lodgings in each price category are indicated by a star ★.

| Category | Cost* |
| --- | --- |
| *$$$$* (Very Expensive) | over $120 |
| *$$$* (Expensive) | $90–$120 |
| *$$* (Moderate) | under $90 |

*All prices are for a standard double room, single occupancy, excluding 12% tax.*

*Numbers in the margin correspond to numbered hotel locations on the Minneapolis-St. Paul Lodging and Dining maps.*

## Downtown Minneapolis

**㉒**
*$$$$*

**Hyatt Regency Minneapolis.** The Hyatt's greatest asset is its location at the prestigious south end of the Nicollet Mall, close to Orchestra Hall and to the city's finest shops, the financial district, and the new Convention Center. However, the hotel is charmless. The 24-story early 1980s building features a modernistic fountain and a piano, both trilling away in the otherwise anonymous lobby, which is frequently filled with name-tagged conventioneers. A renovation promises to brighten the spacious but blandly decorated guest rooms, which offer spectacular skyline views from the upper floors. For VIP treatment, request the Regency Club floor: It has upgraded accommodations and amenities, concierge service, and complimentary breakfasts and cocktails in the private lounge. The Hyatt is attached to the well-equipped Greenway Athletic Club, open to guests on a per-diem basis (*see* Fitness, below). Hotel pluses include such good on-premises restaurants as Manny's Steakhouse (*see* Dining, below), and 24-hour hot-food room service. *1300 Nicollet Mall, 55403, tel. 612/370–1234 or 800/228–9000, fax 612/370–1463. Gen. manager,*

*Richard Mogensen. 511 rooms, 23 suites. AE, CB, DC, MC, V.*

★ ⑲  **Hotel Luxeford Suites.** The public spaces in this hotel are
$$$  small but charming, with antique reproduction furniture
in a homey arrangement. Guests in this all-suites proper-
ty get a modest living room area with comfortable furnish-
ings in which to hold small meetings; the bedroom can be
closed off. Although the hotel is a few blocks off the beaten
downtown path, it's proved popular with business travel-
ers on extended trips because of such homelike features as
a minikitchen in each room and washer and dryer on each
floor. A hotel van shuttles guests throughout the loop
area, and complimentary Continental breakfast is served
in the intimate lobby. The exercise-sauna-whirlpool facili-
ties are standard, but a YWCA (for men and women) with
extensive facilities is just around the corner. *1101 La Salle
Ave., 55403, tel. 612/332–6800, fax 612/332–8246. Gen.
manager, Edward Nee. 230 suites. AE, DC, MC, V.*

★ ⑰  **Marquette Hotel.** It's as fancy as they come in Minneapo-
$$$$  lis—particularly after a 1989 refurbishing of the public
areas that created a street-level lobby-cum-bar done in
creamy marble, with Louis XV-style furniture with pie-
bald ponyskin coverings, and original contemporary art
on the walls. The Marquette's location is just as pedigree,
for it's a part of the landmark IDS tower of Philip Johnson
design, connected by skyways to major banks, retail es-
tablishments, and legal offices. Guest rooms, arguably the
largest in town, are decorated in pastel hues, and have
windows with double exposures. Guests may use facilities
at the Greenway Athletic Club (*see* Fitness, below) for a
per diem rate. The tony bar (*see* After Hours, below)
draws the local power crowd. The Marquette justly prides
itself on its service (even accommodating Mrs. Frank
Lloyd Wright's dogs during her stay). Mary Tyler Moore
filmed her show's mealtime sequences in the hotel's
Juliette Restaurant on the atrium balcony (*see* Business
Breakfasts, below); however, discerning diners prefer the
50th floor Windows on Minnesota (*see* Dining, below). *A
Hilton International hotel, 7th & Marquette, 55402, tel.
612/332–2351 and 800/ 328–4782, fax 612/332–7007. Gen.
manager, Martin Lawrence. 281 rooms, 12 suites with
steam baths. AE, CB, DC, MC, V.*

⑬  **Minneapolis Marriott City Center.** Built as Amfac's flag-
$$$  ship in 1984, this is not a typical Marriott property. Its
fourth floor lobby overlooks the throngs shopping at City
Center below, as does its new Wall Street Club, a lounge
outfitted with table telephones, business journals, and 24-
hour stock market listings. However, it's not only the followers of Dow Jones from nearby banks and brokerage
firms who frequent this 31-story hotel, but conventioneers
of every ilk, crowding the small, street-level lobby and elevators. Rooms are decorated in soft colors and inoffensive contemporary furnishings. The hotel's health club
(*see* Fitness, below) offers saunas and massages. The
Marriott's posh Fifth Season restaurant, with a greenhouse ambience and regional American menu, offers well-
spaced tables, adequate food, and adept service. The
Northern Italian restaurant, Gustino's, is suitable for the
celebratory dinner only—its opera-singing waiters preclude serious conversation. Women are advised to take a
cab rather than stroll to and from this foyer at night, when

# MINNEAPOLIS

# ST. PAUL

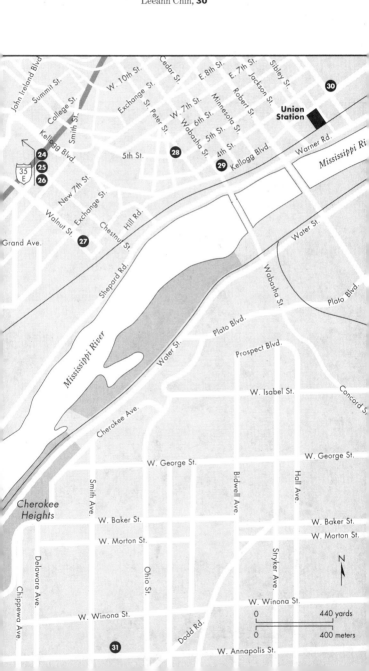

transients replace the men in Brooks Brothers suits. *30 S. 7th St., 55402, tel. 612/349–4000 or 800/228–9290, fax 612/ 332–7165. Gen. manager, Tom Chase. 584 rooms, 62 suites, and 23 bilevel suites. AE, CB, DC, MC, V.*

**⓮ Radisson Plaza Hotel.** Curt Carlson is the wealthiest man
$$$$ in Minnesota, and this is his flagship property: pink-and-pewter postmodern pyramids, constructed in 1987 on the site of his original venture into the hotel industry. It's competing successfully with the Marriott (*see* above) for the convention trade, and capturing a bit more of the upscale market as well. Three floors have been upgraded for business travelers. The lobby and public rooms on the third level are dressed in a monied mix of timeless modern and Art Deco, with Oriental fillips from Carlson's travels. The hotel's excellent service includes a well-informed concierge staff and such extras as an iron and ironing board in every closet. Request a room with a city view rather than one looking out on the vapid atrium. *35 S. 7th St., 55402, tel. 612/339–4900 or 800/333–3333, fax 612/337–9766. Gen. manager, John Kelly. 339 rooms and 31 suites. AE, CB, DC, MC, V.*

**❽ Regency Plaza Best Western Hotel.** For years this circa
$$ 1962 three-story, no-frills hotel has been a favorite of traveling salespeople and price-conscious business guests whose budgetary needs have been largely ignored by other downtown properties. These days there's a new appeal as well. Its location, on the arid "far side" of downtown, where strolling hasn't been advised at night, has become hot property, thanks to the newly constructed basketball arena just a block away and urban development projects reclaiming the rather seedy vistas out its front door. The hotel itself has caught the spirit, and it has undertaken major renovations of the wood-panel lobby, restaurant, and lounge. Shuttle service throughout downtown is available. Guest rooms conform to Best Western "hotel basic" style. *41 N. 10th St., 55403, tel. 612/339–9311 or 800/523–4200, fax 612/339–4765. Gen. manager, Douglas Anderson. 197 rooms, 7 suites. AE, CB, DC, MC, V.*

**★ ⓫ The Whitney Hotel.** Right on the bank of the Mississippi,
$$$$ with a newly created pocket park and jogging lanes along the water's edge, the Whitney is also a good ½ mile from the downtown loop and surrounded by unused railroad tracks and parking lots (a complimentary stretch limo compensates). Built in the mid-80s, this six-floor hotel has a small lobby that is warmed with sparkling brass, ornate antique reproduction furniture in comfortable seating arrangements, a grand piano, and a classic spiral staircase. Guest rooms are quiet and elegant, too, with mahogany furniture, high ceilings, and full-length mirrors, as well as practical two-line phones. The chic first-floor bar (*see* After Hours, below) is a good spot for a discreet chat. The clubby dining room has a fireplace, alcoves, sequestered booths for privacy, and a straightforward American menu. The top floor river-view suite hosts touring politicians and international entertainers. *A Preferred Hotel. 150 Portland Ave., 55401, tel. 612/339–9300 or 800/248–1879, fax 612/339–1333. Gen. manager, Brian R. Snell. 53 rooms, 40 bilevel suites, 3 penthouses. AE, CB, DC, MC, V.*

# MINNEAPOLIS/ST. PAUL HOTEL CHART

| HOTELS | Price Category | Business Services | | | | | | | | | | | |
|---|---|---|---|---|---|---|---|---|---|---|---|---|---|
| | | Banquet capacity | No. of meeting rooms | Secretarial services | Audiovisual equipment | Teletype news service | Computer rentals | In-room modem phone jack | All-news cable channel | Desk | Desk lighting | Bed lighting |
| Comfort Inn | $$ | 275 | 9 | ✓ | - | - | - | ✓ | ✓ | ● | ● | ● |
| Hotel Luxeford Suites | $$$ | 85 | 3 | - | ✓ | - | ✓ | - | - | ● | ● | ● |
| Hyatt Regency | $$$$ | 2000 | 13 | ✓ | ✓ | - | ✓ | ✓ | ✓ | ● | ● | ● |
| Marquette | $$$$ | 450 | 13 | ✓ | ✓ | - | ✓ | ✓ | ✓ | ◑ | ● | ● |
| Marriott City Center | $$$ | 1300 | 20 | ✓ | ✓ | ✓ | ✓ | ✓ | ✓ | ● | ● | ● |
| Nicollet Island Inn | $$$ | 80 | 5 | ✓ | ✓ | - | ✓ | - | - | ◑ | ● | ● |
| Northland Inn | $$$ | 600 | 25 | ✓ | ✓ | - | ✓ | ✓ | ✓ | ● | ● | ● |
| Radisson Hotel Saint Paul | $$$ | 1800 | 12 | ✓ | ✓ | - | ✓ | ✓ | ✓ | ◑ | ● | ● |
| Radisson Plaza | $$$$ | 400 | 9 | ✓ | ✓ | - | ✓ | ✓ | ✓ | ◑ | ● | ● |
| Regency Plaza Best Western | $$ | 300 | 8 | ✓ | ✓ | - | ✓ | - | ✓ | ◑ | ● | ● |
| Registry | $$$ | 600 | 16 | ✓ | ✓ | - | ✓ | ✓ | ✓ | ● | ● | ● |
| Saint Paul | $$$ | 400 | 7 | ✓ | ✓ | - | ✓ | ✓ | ✓ | ● | ● | ● |
| Scanticon - Minneapolis | $$$ | 500 | 32 | ✓ | ✓ | - | ✓ | ✓ | ✓ | ● | ● | ● |
| Sheraton Inn Midway | $$ | 300 | 5 | ✓ | - | - | - | ✓ | ✓ | ◑ | ● | ● |
| The Whitney | $$$$ | 150 | 5 | ✓ | ✓ | - | ✓ | ✓ | ✓ | ◑ | ● | ● |

$$$$ = over $120, $$$ = $90 -$120, $$ = under $90.
● good, ◑ fair, ○ poor.
All hotels listed here have photocopying and fax facilities.

| In-Room Amenities | | | | | | | | | | Hotel Amenities | | | | | | |
| Nonsmoking rooms | In-room checkout | Minibar | Pay movies | VCR/Movie rentals | Hairdryer | Toiletries | Room service | Laundry/Dry cleaning | Pressing | Concierge | Barber/Hairdresser | Garage | Courtesy airport transport | Sauna | Pool | Exercise room |
|---|---|---|---|---|---|---|---|---|---|---|---|---|---|---|---|---|
| ✓ | ✓ | - | ✓ | - | - | ◐ | ○ | ● | - | - | - | ✓ | ✓ | - | ◐ | - |
| ✓ | ✓ | ✓ | ✓ | - | ✓ | ◐ | ◐ | ● | ◐ | - | - | - | - | ✓ | - | ◐ |
| ✓ | ✓ | - | ✓ | ✓ | - | ◐ | ● | ● | - | ✓ | ✓ | ✓ | - | ✓ | ● | - |
| ✓ | ✓ | - | ✓ | - | - | ◐ | ◐ | ● | ◐ | ✓ | - | - | - | - | - | - |
| ✓ | ✓ | ✓ | ✓ | - | ✓ | ● | ◐ | ● | ◐ | ✓ | - | - | - | ✓ | - | ● |
| - | - | - | - | ✓ | ✓ | ◐ | ◐ | ● | ◐ | ✓ | - | ✓ | - | - | - | - |
| ✓ | ✓ | ✓ | ✓ | - | - | ● | ◐ | ● | - | ✓ | - | ✓ | - | ✓ | ● | ● |
| ✓ | - | - | ✓ | - | ✓ | ◐ | ◐ | ● | ● | - | ✓ | ✓ | - | - | ◐ | - |
| ✓ | - | - | ✓ | - | ✓ | ◐ | ◐ | ● | ◐ | ✓ | - | ✓ | - | ✓ | - | ◐ |
| ✓ | - | - | - | - | - | ◐ | ◐ | ● | ○ | ✓ | - | - | ✓ | - | ◐ | - |
| ✓ | - | - | ✓ | ✓ | - | ● | ◐ | ● | ● | ✓ | - | ✓ | ✓ | ✓ | ● | ● |
| ✓ | ✓ | - | - | - | ✓ | ◐ | ◐ | ● | ● | ✓ | - | ✓ | - | - | ● | ● |
| ✓ | - | ✓ | ✓ | - | - | ◐ | ◐ | ● | - | ✓ | - | ✓ | - | ✓ | ● | ● |
| ✓ | - | - | ✓ | - | - | ◐ | ◐ | ● | ◐ | - | - | ✓ | - | ✓ | ◐ | ◐ |
| ✓ | - | - | - | - | ✓ | ● | ● | ● | ● | ✓ | ✓ | ✓ | ✓ | - | - | - |

**Room service:** ● 24-hour, ◐ 6AM–10PM, ○ other.
**Laundry/Dry cleaning:** ● same day, ◐ overnight, ○ other.
**Pressing:** ● immediate, ◐ same day, ○ other.

## Nicollet Island

★ ❿ **Nicollet Island Inn.** This historic, three-story fieldstone
$$$ building is as close as Minneapolis comes to the little hide-
away with charm and personality. It began life as the Is-
land Sash & Door Company in 1893 and reemerged as a
country inn in the city in 1982. Don't expect exercise sa-
lons and typing pools; instead, the Inn, which occupies a
leafy island in the middle of the Mississippi, seduces the
world-weary with rooms individually decorated in quaint
Victoriana and possessed of terrific pastoral views (except
for those with the dreary north exposure). It's a 10-min-
ute stroll from the heart of town and connected by historic
bridges to the Riverplace shopping-entertainment com-
plex; the University of Minnesota campus is nearby, too.
The restaurant, which offers lovely vistas, is an acceptable
venue for breakfast meetings (*see* Business Breakfasts,
below), though the food and service are mediocre. *95
Merriam St., 55401, tel. 612/331–1800, fax 612/331–6528.
Gen. manager, Gordon Schutte. 24 rooms. AE, CB, DC,
MC, V.*

## Northern Minneapolis Suburbs

❶ **Northland Inn.** The Northland is one of two new hotels
$$$ (the other is the Scanticon, *see* below) that combines the
best features of a destination resort with the amenities of
a good midtown convention hotel. Facilities include electronic audiovisual gadgetry such as satellite dishes for
in-house meetings. After business hours, guests can
unwind with extensive recreational options, including
an indoor running track. Traditionally furnished suites
are wrapped around an eight-story atrium; some provide
conference tables for small group meetings. America's
Harvest, an excellent, informal restaurant, features
Minnesota cuisine at its prime. The hotel is located on
I-94, 15 minutes north of downtown. *7101 Northland
Circle, Brooklyn Park, 55428, tel. 612/536–8300, fax
612/536–8790. Gen. manager, Wim Pastoor. 210 2-room
suites and 21 suites with adjoining conference rooms.
AE, CB, DC, MC, V.*

❹ **Scanticon-Minneapolis.** Like the Northland Inn (*see*
$$$ above), the Scanticon was built to combine an exceptional
range of meeting services and facilities with an array of
recreational perks. This wooded suburban enclave over-
looks a wildlife marsh and lake, 9 miles west of Minneapo-
lis. Its Scandinavian owners have reproduced the blond
wood, clean lines, bright fabrics, and 21st-century design
elements business travelers abroad will recognize. Meet-
ing facilities are state-of-the-art, including in-house au-
diovisual technicians and graphic artists. Guest rooms are
grouped in a separate wing that re-creates a street in Co-
penhagen with overhanging staircases and potted trees
lining the hallway promenade; a skylight enhances the
out-of-doors feel. Recreational facilities include racquet-
ball and tennis courts, aerobics classes, and jogging
paths. *3131 Campus Dr., Plymouth, 55441, tel. 612/559–
6600 or 800/327–7397, fax 612/559–7516. Gen. manager,
Richard Harrison. 203 rooms and 20 suites. AE, DC,
MC, V.*

## Downtown St. Paul

**㉙** **Radisson Hotel Saint Paul.** From a bluff above the Missis-
$$$  sippi, the Radisson commands a dynamic view of the river
traffic. Request a room with this vista, or at least take the
exterior glass elevator 22 stories up to the revolving res-
taurant, Le Carousel, a quiet, semisophisticated dining
option for meat-and-potatoes-plus. The hotel's lobby, res-
taurants, and guest rooms benefitted from a 1988 renova-
tion that introduced soft colors and plush furniture and
carpeting. Commercial travelers, drawn by the broad rep-
ertoire of business equipment and services, including up-
graded suites with two phone lines, are frequent guests.
However, the hotel's size and location, next to the World
Trade Center and the Civic Center, make it equally popu-
lar with athletic teams and conventioneers, who arrive in
buses and cluster around clots of luggage in the lobby. *11
E. Kellogg Blvd., 55101, tel. 612/292–1900 or 800/333–
3333, fax 612/292–1900, ext. 6200. Gen. manager, Richard
Mason. 423 rooms, 52 suites. AE, CB, MC, V.*

**★ ㉘** **Saint Paul Hotel.** Distinguished architecture and discreet
$$$  service are the hallmarks of this grande dame, which has
welcomed visiting VIPs at its carriage drive since 1910.
Scott and Zelda Fitzgerald stayed here in the 1920s; more
recent celebrities, like Pincus Zuckerman and Julie Harris, have stayed here when they were performing at the
Ordway Theatre, just across Rice Park. The hotel is near
the Civic Center, World Trade Center, and the upscale
shops of Carriage Hill, so its guests even include foreign
trade commissioners. The drawing room–like lobby, with
glittering chandeliers, ornate antiques, and jewel-tone
carpets, glories in the good old days. Guest rooms (for the
best view, seek a corner suite), renovated in soft blues and
yellows, suggest the decor of an English country house.
Other draws are l'Etoile, the hotel's fine restaurant (*see*
Dining, below); The Café (*see* Business Breakfasts, below), a good spot for a morning meeting; and the hotel bar
(*see* After Hours, below), where the power brokers recon-
vene at night. *350 Market St., 55102, tel. 612/292–9292,
fax 612/228–9506. Gen. manager, William Morrissey. 235
rooms, 29 suites. AE, CB, DC, MC, V.*

## Midway

**㉖** **Sheraton Inn Midway.** This unassuming, four-story hotel
$$  has had its faltering days, but is moving ahead with rea-
sonable rates and a good location, right on I-94, between
the two downtowns. A dim, characterless foyer leads to a
similarly austere skylighted atrium with a swimming pool
that often echoes with children's squeals. Above the pool,
guest rooms form utilitarian, charmless circles around the
atrium. They were renovated in 1989 with Formica furni-
ture and tones of pale green and peach. Nonetheless, re-
quest an atrium exposure; the alternative is a view onto
the busy highway. The Inn serves as a convenient base for
business travelers who need to cover the widespread
metro area by car and for trainees at Twin Cities-based
companies. The Blue Horse (*see* Dining, below), just a few
blocks away, is a bright alternative to the Inn's cookie-cut-
ter coffee shop. *400 Hamline Ave. N, 55104, tel. 612/642–
1234 or 800/535–2339, fax 612/642–1126. Gen. manager,
Robert Gramowski. 197 rooms. AE, DC, MC, V.*

**Airport**

㉒ **Comfort Inn.** Although the Comfort Inn is a standard mo-
$$ tel with basic amenities and nondescript contemporary
furnishings, it attracts its share of business travelers be-
cause of its location near the Mall of America and the large
corporations headquartered nearby in Bloomington. Also
attractive are the free airport shuttle and the flight-de-
parture monitoring system. When present management
acquired the former Rodeway Inn in 1989, the public
rooms were redone in a softer look with peach, blue, and
pewter. Rooms are reliably clean and serviceable; request
one facing the courtyard to avoid dreary highway and
parking-lot vistas. *1321 E. 78th St., Bloomington, 55425,
tel. 612/854-3400 or 800/228-5150, fax 612/854-2234.
Gen. manager, Don Peterson. 276 rooms, 2 suites. AE,
CB, DC, MC, V.*

㉓ **Registry Hotel.** Although it's located in the grim airport/
$$$ interstate area, the Registry is way above a standard air-
port hotel in style, comfort, and ambience. A spacious,
airy lobby, with low, comfortable furniture, a fireplace,
crystal chandeliers—and even a hospitable bowl of apples—sets the scene. President Bush stayed in the 15th
floor executive suite. The hotel boasts excellent tele- and
video-conferencing capabilities. Upgraded executive
rooms are on the top floor, and there's a complimentary
airport shuttle. Service is outstanding, both in the hotel
and in its fine dining room, La Tour, where nouvelle American specialties outdistance the dated, formal decor. *7901
24th Ave. S, Bloomington, 55425, tel. 612/854-2244 or 800/
328-1927, fax 612/854-4421. Gen. manager, Harvey
Moore. 315 rooms, 7 suites. AE, CB, DC, MC, V.*

## DINING

This used to be a two-martini, meat-and-potatoes town.
And, although a Midwestern show-me attitude still colors
the food scene, California trends have infiltrated the corn
belt; Italian trattorias have graduated from red sauce to
lobster ravioli, and French cuisine, for long the only acceptable alternative to prime rib, has found its rival in
modern American (even distinctly regional) cooking,
thanks to young, homegrown chefs and a new breed of sophisticated travelers, responsive to their talents. Business meals have moved from musty private clubs to
popular new restaurants, and hotel dining room menus,
recently treated to a much needed facelift, promise to give
them a run for their money, too. Although downtown is
fast becoming revitalized with the addition of a new convention center, sports arena, and upscale shopping venues, most movers and shakers and their underlings still
choose to live outside the urban core, so several good restaurants have opened on the Western Corridor (Hwy. 394/
12). Known as the Uptown area (even though it's two miles
south of downtown), this is where CEOs, heading to their
Lake Minnetonka estates, often stop for a status bite.

The other good news is that this is not New York, and one
does not need to tip the mâitre d' for a prime table. In the
egalitarian Midwest, status does not deliver—or depend
on—seating. Business is assiduously conducted over

lunch, which is likely to be light, lean, and nonalcoholic. Dinner meetings certainly are feasible, although less customary, and they are conducted at a relatively early hour (6:30 or 7). Women holding business dining parties are accorded top-notch treatment. St. Paulites tend to be more conservative than Minneapolitans—more clubby and traditional in their dining preferences and less inclined to devote evening hours to business.

Highly recommended restaurants in each price category are recommended with a ★.

| Category | Cost* |
| --- | --- |
| $$$$ (Very Expensive) | over $35 |
| $$$ (Expensive) | $26–$35 |
| $$ (Moderate) | $15–$25 |
| $ (Inexpensive) | under $15 |

*per person, including appetizer, entrée, and dessert, but excluding drinks, service, and 6.5% sales tax.*

*Numbers in the margin correspond to numbered restaurant locations on the Minneapolis-St. Paul Lodging and Dining maps.*

## Business Breakfasts

Minneapolitans are an early-to-work crowd whose business breakfasts are short and to the point—and mostly held in corporate boardrooms or private clubs. Business breakfasts in the dining rooms of quiet, upscale hotels are also eminently suitable, whether they're in the centrally located **Northstar** (618 2nd Ave. S, tel. 612/338–2288) and **Marquette** (tel. 612/332–2351) hotels, or the **Nicollet Island Inn** (tel. 612/331–1800), ½ mile from the city center on a leafy island in the Mississippi. Restaurants have been slow to open their doors to this opportunity. **Rupert's American Café** (5410 Wayzata Blvd., Golden Valley, tel. 612/544–4993), 3 miles west of downtown, attracts the decision makers of commerce on their way to work from western exurban estates, offering eggs-plus and private conversation in a tastefully masculine polished wood-and-brass setting. Within the downtown Warehouse District, the city's answer to New York's Soho, the **New French Café** (128 N. 4th St., tel. 612/338–3790) serves the best croissants and café au lait this side of Chicago in a quiet and spartanly chic room that attracts arts funders, publishers, high-power architects, and advertising executives.

St. Paul businesspeople, even more than their Minneapolis compatriates, power-breakfast (if at all) in their clubs, which offer reciprocity to affiliates in other cities. Those who prefer to entertain in their hotels will find both the privacy and tasteful presentation they require at the **Saint Paul Hotel's Café** (tel. 612/292–9292), a bright room with country-French flavor and food, such as eggs and bacon and omelets of smoked salmon and brie. Politicians and lobbyists at the State Capitol regularly start their day at nearby **Serlin's** (1124 Payne Ave., tel. 612/776–9003, closed Sundays), a long-established hole-in-the-wall

where Al Serlin himself will scold if you reject a second
stack of flapjacks on the house.

## Downtown Minneapolis

★ ⑮   **Azur.** The newest star in the crown of wunderkinder
$$$$   brothers Richard and Larry D'Amico achieves a Moderne-
meets-Milano look: Deep purple columns, inky green
high-gloss floors, chairs of Italian leather, and marble-top
tables lend credibility to a business meal, as do a well-
drilled staff and spacious layout, including super-private
banquettes. Azur dominates the top floor of the posh new
Gaviidae Commons, home of Saks Fifth Avenue and Anne
Klein, whose status couturiers dine here when they blitz
through town. A glass turret overlooking downtown's busiest crossroads showcases the café's most coveted tables.
Specialties, based on the lusty flavors of the Côte d'Azur,
include snapper sautéed with artichokes and garlic, and
an update of the classic cassoulet with duck and garlic sausage. The wine list offers a premier selection of Provençal
and Spanish wines. *651 Nicollet Mall, tel. 612/342–2500.
Casual chic to formal dress. Reservations recommended.
AE, DC, MC, V. Closed Sun.*

★ ⑨   **D'Amico Cucina.** Two Italian princelings have pitched
$$$   camp in a grand brick dowager of a building in the newly
chic Warehouse District, within walking distance of down-
town hotels. Richard D'Amico has dressed the room's his-
toric blond bricks and heavy timbers in a modish Milano
combo of peach and pewter marble, contemporary frosted
glass, and leather Matteo Grasso chairs, occupied by
equally stylish members of the legal and financial worlds.
Chef Larry D'Amico oversees a kitchen devoted to cut-
ting-edge cuisine that is often just short of being precious:
Italian and Cal-Ital compositions such as ricotta ravioli
with herbs, greens, and pistachio sauce; duck and arti-
choke stew with pancetta and rosemary biscuits; and tuna
sautéed with fennel and apricot-tomato oil. Window and
banquette tables are private enough for business discus-
sions in these sometimes noisy rooms. The staff is pol-
ished. A well-assembled list of Italian wines adds to the
dolce vita. *Butler Square, 100 N. 6th St., tel. 612/338–
2401. Jacket advised. Reservations advised. AE, MC, V.*

② **510 Restaurant.** The 510 is a stroll away (through innercity
$$$$   Loring Park) from downtown hotels and across the street
from the Guthrie Theater/Walker Art Center/Sculpture
Garden arts complex. The grande dame of local fine dining
was renovated recently, and a hint of the '90s has crept
into the patrician, pearl gray, chandelier-hung parlor.
This is the favorite haunt of author Judith Guest and
maestro de Waart's guest artists, as well as blueblood
bankers, university professors, and top physicians, who
know they can converse in privacy as tuxedoed waiters
pace service in deference to their guests. A nightly chang-
ing fixed price menu shows off chef Scott Bergstrom's way
with modern French-meets-Minnesota cooking, as do en-
trées such as grilled pork with cabbage spring rolls and
caramelized citrus sauce; and grilled duck breast with
poached turnips, apples, and duck confit in sherry vinegar
sauce. The list of French and California wines is excep-
tional. *510 Groveland Ave., tel. 612/874–6440. Jacket sug-
gested. Reservations advised. AE, CB, DC, MC, V.
Closed Sun.*

★ ⑱  **Goodfellow's.** Financier John Dayton and chef Stephan
$$$$  Pyles, the whiz kid behind two hot Dallas restaurants, de-
cided Minneapolis was ripe for their brand of vanguard
cooking and upscale digs. Located at the top of The Conservatory, a deluxe collection of designer shops in the
heart of downtown, their restaurant woos the city's CEOs
and their social-register spouses. A serene, uncluttered
air, well-spaced tables, and savvy, almost telepathic servers make this an ideal business rendezvous (there's a new
private dining room that seats up to 25, too). Museum-
quality modern art on the walls vies with artforms from
the kitchen that marry Texas and Midwest flavors such as
smoked pheasant with wild rice-game sausage compote
and pear sauce, or loin of lamb with griddled pasta and
roasted pepper sauce. The wine list, touting more than
400 labels, is one of the town's top, both in quality and
depth. *800 Nicollet Mall, tel. 612/332–4800. Jacket required. Reservations required. AE, DC, MC, V. Closed
Sun.*

⑳  **Manny's Steakhouse.** Manny's is Minneapolis's answer to
$$$  New York's The Palm—except here the waiters are more
polite. With dish towels tied across their middles, they
trundle a cart of viands for your inspection: Goliath-size
cuts of prime Midwest beef, huge lobsters, and only slight-
ly less grand portions of chops and chicken, with à la carte
options that include thickets of broccoli and huge pota-
toes. "Our most complicated sauce is butter," grins host
Fred Onello, stolen from Tavern on the Green in New York
City. The wine list is impressive, especially the magnums
of California reds. Bare floors, well-spaced tables in semi-
private alcoves, and hunting prints on the walls all make it
a very clubby place to sit down and do business. *Hyatt Re-
gency, 1300 Nicollet Mall, tel. 612/339–9900. Jackets sug-
gested. Reservations advised. AE, DC, MC, V. Dinner
only.*

★ ㉑  **Market Bar-B-Que.** You name 'em, they've been here—
$  Lena Horne, Perry Como, Mickey Mantle, Bob Hope are
all honored by brass plaques that hang on vintage wooden
booths where each itinerant luminary licked fingers after
chowing down on the stringy, chewy, pitsmoked pork
ribs. The Market, on the south fringe of downtown near
the Convention Center, boasts the tin ceiling, checkered
tablecloths, vintage juke, and career waitresses that have
greeted locals of all walks of life for three generations.
Funky, yes; fancy, no, but this temple of down-home cook-
ing has proved a favorite late-night place to unwind. *1414
Nicollet Ave. S, tel. 612/872–1111. Casual dress. Reserva-
tions not necessary. AE, CB, DC, MC, V.*

⑫  **Murray's.** These are the folks who invented steak, at least
$$$$  in Minneapolis. The Murray family has been serving the
town's VIPs and visiting celebrities from the political, en-
tertainment, and sports arenas since the '40s; and noth-
ing's changed in those years except the price. The long,
windowless dining room in the heart of downtown is a
throwback to the supper club era of swags, grillework,
and mirrors, underscored by déjà vu dinner music from a
ruffle-shirted trio on a pocket stage. Career waitresses,
known by name to Murray's legion of regulars, hoist trays
of anything from salmon with hollandaise to chicken
breast in herbs and garlic, but they'll look at you as if
you're touched if you settle for anything less than the leg-

endary Murray's trademark—Silver Butterknife steak. The astonishingly deep wine list comes as a pleasant surprise. Forging important business deals here is no surprise—it's a given with the good old boys. *26 S. 6th St., tel. 612/339–0909. Jacket advised. Reservations advised. AE, DC, MC, V.*

**⑤** **Patti's.** Texas-based Trammel Crow developers put up
**$$** postmodern office towers in all prosperous corners of the metropolitan area, then invited young, effervescent Patti Soskin to realize her fantasy in the foremost of them, located 3 miles west of downtown on the important Hwy. 12 corridor to the monied suburbs. In Patti's, tables for smokers flow into the building's greenhouse atrium, while the clean-air crowd of middle management types (with spouses, come evening) sit on pastel banquettes, pinwheeled around floral pedestals for privacy, under a talk-of-the-town Sistine Chapel creation, painted on the ceiling by a local Michelangelo. Patti's upbeat yet relaxed aura extends to its accommodating, though at times slow-paced, staff and its menu—an update of American classics such as potato pancakes with sour cream-apple jalapeño sauce, dry-aged Kansas strip steak with roasted garlic hollandaise, lamb chops on roasted onions, and a banana split on crème anglaise. Across the street you'll find Rupert's Nightclub, should you be motivated to dance off the calories to a big band sound. *5500 Wayzata Blvd., tel. 612/546–4000. Jackets advised. Reservations advised. AE, DC, MC, V. Closed Sun.*

**⑯** **Windows on Minnesota.** Like many a sky-high restaurant,
**$$$** the Orion Room packaged a stellar view with food that was far from celestial. Early in 1990, this landmark dining room was acquired by Hilton International, operators of Manhattan's Windows on the World, and its food and beverage manager, Adel Boutros, was dispatched to resuscitate the menu and revive the staff. Mission accomplished: The dining experience today is as impressive as the vista and lures big-name bankers, lawyers, and top university staffers. The surroundings are clean-cut and contemporary, and, nowadays, so's the food, with such specialties as roast duck with green peppercorns and glazed cantaloupe, rack of lamb in a Minnesota wild rice crust and herb-garlic sauce, and straight-arrow cuts of Certified Angus beef, with a suitable list of heavy hitting California and French wines. Choose the tableside Caesar salad, chateaubriand, and bananas Foster and your waiter may join the party; otherwise, privacy's a given. *Hilton International, 5000 IDS Center, 701 Nicollet Mall, tel. 612/ 349–6255. Jacket suggested. Reservations advised. AE, MC, V.*

## Western Corridor

**★ ⑥** **CocoLezzone.** A glitzy, see-and-be-seen trattoria, 3 miles
**$$** west of the city's skyscrapers, Coco's has high ceilings, marble columns, trendy art, and trendy diners—everyone from culture czars to owners of major airlines air-kissing from closely packed tables. There's a semiprivate back room and front greenhouse area for those who require more privacy, which the savvy staff members respect. The Northern Italian menu offers designer pizzas from the display kitchen, which make good starters. Pasta options include *spaghetti ai gamberi* (shrimp, garlic, light

tomato sauce, and hot peppers). Entrées worth trying are *vitello alla boscaiola* (veal chop sautéed with asparagus and mushrooms) and *spiedini di carne*, a brochette of beef tenderloin, chicken, Italian sausage, onions, and peppers. All are easily paired with selections from a consummate Italian wine list. Lunch, dinner, and late-night seating allow the business traveler to clinch the deal, then celebrate it. *5410 Wayzata Blvd., tel. 612/544–4014. Casual chic dress. Reservations advised. AE, MC, V.*

★ ❸ **Shelly's Woodroast.** This costly and painstakingly ren-
$$ dered facsimile of a north woods lodge has handhewn logs, fieldstone fireplaces (complete with lap robes to fend off the Minnesota windchill), soft leather booths, and table appointments picked up on the owner's global travels. Local small-business people come to this unique, informal spot 3 miles west of the city center at every opportunity. Privacy and pacing pose no problem for business lunches, as manufacturers' reps and medical professionals have noticed, and the jackets-off dinner works well either for negotiating contracts or casual entertaining. Shelly's woodroast cooking method gives a campfire flavor to game birds, local trout and walleye, and beef, from ribs to brisket, abetted by corn cob chowder soup and herb-roasted potatoes (nothing wrong with the green apple pie for dessert, either). Although there's a full bar stocked with rare Scotch and Irish whiskies, Shelly's exclusive microbrewery beers are the drinks of choice. *Hwy. 12 at Turner's Crossroads, St. Louis Park, tel. 612/593–5050. Casual dress. No reservations. AE, CB, DC, MC, V.*

## Uptown

❼ **Figlio.** Uptown is as close as this city gets to a vibrant
$$ street scene, and Figlio is its darling. Anchoring a corner 2 miles south of downtown, Figlio's boasts the greatest people-watching outside of a rock concert at its body-to-body bar and casual bistro (*see* After Hours, below); those beyond thirtysomething line up in the more sedate, white tablecloth side of the restaurant, close to the display kitchen where cooks flip pizzas with Italian fervor. The menu borrows a page from L.A.'s chef Wolfgang Puck with trendy pastas like angelhair tossed with spinach, garlic, Parmesan, olive oil, and pine nuts; wood-grilled tenderloins rubbed with sage and garlic in red wine butter; and seafood such as swordfish sautéed with artichokes, mushrooms, and sweet peppers. All are accompanied by a respectable range of Italian and California wines. Expect a wait during peak hours; once you're seated, however, service is exceptionally deft. If a business discussion is on the agenda, tables on the south wall afford the most privacy. For Vikings football heroes, Guthrie performers, and card-carrying yuppies, it's where the action is. *Calhoun Square, 3001 Hennepin Ave. S, tel. 612/822–1688. Casual dress. No reservations. AE, MC, V.*

## Downtown St. Paul

❸❶ **Cherokee Sirloin Room.** Ask a cabbie where locals go for a
$ great steak, and he'll take you across the river from the bright lights to this sprawling neighborhood roadhouse, 10 minutes south of the city center. Three generations of Caspers have served as proprietor/hosts in this warm, in-

formal steakhouse that seems not to have changed a whit since its 1930s opening. It has a standard dark bar, wall mural, and vintage appointments. Small-business owners and middle-management types rub elbows with civic leaders playing host to foreign delegations over some of the largest bargain cuts of beef this side of the stockyards, along with au gratins and a token iceberg salad whose only redeeming feature is a dynamite French-blue cheese dressing. There's nothing to preclude a business discussion at the Cherokee—particularly if you favor cocktails to fine wines, which are minimally represented—but relaxing or celebratory dinners are more appropriate. *886 Smith Ave. S, tel. 612/457–2729. Casual dress. Reservations suggested. AE, DC, MC, V.*

**㉗** **Forepaugh's.** In the 1870s, drygoods magnate Joseph
**$$$** Forepaugh entertained Governor Ramsay (whose house, across the street, still stands and is open to visitors) and lumber barons in his opulent Victorian gingerbread manse. Today its rooms, furnished in period antiques, are just as popular with business leaders. Tables that overlook leafy Irvine Park and its old-fashioned bandstand are in high demand, as is the sprawling porch for summer dining. French chef Bernard La Grande re-creates both classic and modern dishes from his homeland, such as veal in cream and Calvados, duck sauced with lime and honey, and shrimp basted with a white wine-garlic butter sauce. A complimentary van shuttles guests to Ordway Theatre events. *276 S. Exchange St., tel. 612/224–5606. Jacket advised. Reservations advised. AE, MC, V.*

**㉘** **l'Etoile.** Ornate l'Etoile, reached by descending a grand
**$$$$** curving staircase from the lobby of the St. Paul Hotel, has no rival in downtown St. Paul when the agenda calls for discretion and formality. The intimate, Empire-style salon attracts national and international entrepreneurs from the nearby World Trade Center as well as top-name artists performing at the Ordway Theatre, just across Rice Park. A bright young chef earns his keep with French-American dishes like spinach-wrapped lamb loin encased in puff pastry with green peppercorn sauce, and Dover sole in fennel butter, as well as housemade ice creams and dessert soufflés. Service is friendly rather than correct and stuffy. *Saint Paul Hotel, 350 Market St., tel. 612/292–9292. Jacket and tie required. Reservations advised. AE, CB, DC, MC, V. Closed Sun.*

**㉚** **Leeann Chin.** It's been more than two decades since a train
**$$** has pulled into St. Paul's grand old Union Station, but the stately Greek Revival building still draws commuter crowds. Cantonese-born Leeann Chin has resurrected its vast, high-ceiling waiting room as a restaurant of contemporary flavor, where quiet, well-spaced tables share space with precious Chinese art. The art that flows from the kitchen is more Everyman than exotic, however. A stylishly designed buffet line (with tableside beverage service) includes three appetizers highlighted by Leeann's legendary cream cheese wontons, fried rice, salad, and a quartet of entrées such as kung pao shrimp, sesame beef, moo shu pork, and her signature lemon chicken. *Union Depot Place, 214 E. 4th St., tel. 612/224–8814. Business or casual dress. Reservations advised 1 day in advance. AE, MC, V. Closed Sun. for dinner.*

## Midway

★ ㉕ **The Blue Horse.** Stabled among auto dealerships on a com-
$$$$ mercial corridor just off the expressway connecting the
Twin Cities' downtowns, The Blue Horse is St. Paul's pioneer and still-leading fine dining restaurant. Host John
Warling, son of its founder, has led the clubby restaurant
into the '90s with new contemporary art and paneling on
the walls, and a subtly fresher Continental menu with
dishes such as walleye in dill beurre blanc, and duckling
with rosemary and Chartreuse. Classics not to be sup-
planted include The Blue Horse's legendary Stroganoff,
tableside steak tartare, and cherries jubilee, with a well-
chosen list of California wines to set them off. Don't be de-
ceived by the lack of glitz: This is unquestionably the power center of St. Paul, where business moguls vie with
political movers and shakers from the nearby state capitol. Important power-lunching tables are the ones close to
John's host stand and the sequestered booths in the corner. *1355 University Ave., tel. 612/645–8101. Jackets advised. Reservations advised. AE, DC, MC, V. Closed Sat.
for lunch, and Sun.*

㉔ **Dakota Bar & Grill.** A 10-minute cab ride from downtown
$$ St. Paul brings diners in-the-know to this turn-of-the-cen-
tury railroad roundhouse-turned-shopping-mecca, whose
culinary anchor is the Dakota. Its weathered brick walls
hold a most contemporary restaurant swathed in subtly
lighted pewter-gray, mauve, and teal, and the menu's an
equally daring mix of old and vanguard. Chef Ken Goff has
been winning national kudos for his classy updates of
strictly regional cuisine, displayed in dishes like sautéed
walleye with yellow tomatoes and tarragon, and grilled
quail on a compote of apple and dried cranberries with
corn cakes and wild rice. The wine list, which explores
rare vintages and little-known American wineries, is own-
er Lowell Pickett's pride. Lunches are mere teasers; din-
ner's when the crowd and the kitchen come alive, and
intense conversations give way to pure enjoyment as
Dakota's top-rated jazz performers begin to percolate af-
ter 9 PM (*see* After Hours, below). *Bandana Square, 1021
E. Bandana Blvd., tel. 612/642–1442. Casual chic or busi-
ness dress. AE, CB, DC, MC, V.*

## FREE TIME

### Fitness

*Hotel Facilities*
The **Marriott City Center** (tel. 612/349–4000) offers a day
pass for $5 for nonguests; some Twin City hotels have re-
ciprocal arrangements with the Marriott and can offer
guests a daily pass—inquire at your hotel.

*Health Clubs*
**Greenway Athletic Club** (1300 Nicollet Mall, tel. 612/343–
3131), with its lavish facilities—including rooftop, domed
tennis courts—is the best. Out-of-towners staying at any
downtown hotel pay $10.95 ($8 for Hyatt guests) per day.
**Northwest Racquet Swim and Health Clubs** (tel. 612/454–
8790) has several suburban locations, and accepts guests
at a day rate of $15. The **U.S. Swim and Fitness** centers
(tel. 612/893–1319), with facilities in St. Paul's Midway

area and suburbs, welcome day users for $10. The well-equipped downtown **Minneapolis YWCA** (1130 Nicollet Mall, tel. 612/332–0501) charges $6 per visit.

*Jogging*

Minneapolis-St. Paul joggers can run around most of the 22 lakes within city limits, including **Lake Calhoun** and **Lake of the Isles,** both within 2½ miles of downtown. They can also run through **Loring Park** or the **West River Parkway** along the Mississippi, both in the downtown loop. In St. Paul, joggers run along **Summit Avenue,** a calm, 5-mile-long stretch of Victorian mansions.

## Shopping

For regional gifts (Indian carvings, wild rice, maple syrup) try **Hello, Minnesota** (7 S. 7th St., Minneapolis, tel. 612/332–1755) and **Accent Minnesota** (444 Cedar St., St. Paul, tel. 612/224–2888).

*Minneapolis*

The best shopping avenue in Minneapolis is the Nicollet Mall, which houses the city's chief department stores, scores of specialty shops, boutiques, and bookstores. **Gaviidae** (the Latin name for loon) **Common** (tel. 612/372–1222) at 7th Street and Nicollet Mall boasts 60 upscale shops (Anne Klein, Burberry's, Cole-Haan, Lenox China, etc.), and **The Conservatory** (tel. 612/332–4649) at 8th Street and Nicollet Mall offers Mark Shale, Coach Leather, Ann Taylor, and an F.A.O. Schwartz toy store. **Dayton's** (tel. 612/375–2200), the locally owned grande dame of department stores, and Chicago-based **Carson Pirie Scott** (tel. 612/347–7611) are the Macy's and Gimbel's of the Twin Cities. They are located across from each other on Seventh Street. A **Saks Fifth Avenue** (tel. 602/333–7200) is at the same intersection.

*St. Paul*

Shopping is scattered throughout the downtown malls and avenues, but the **Saint Paul Center** (7th and Cedar Sts., tel. 612/291–1715) includes both **Dayton's** and **Carson's** (*see* Minneapolis, above), as well as smaller specialty stores. **Grand Avenue** is a neighborhood shopping street. From Dale Street to Lexington Avenue are boutiques, bookstores, antiques shops, and restaurants.

## Diversions

*Minneapolis*

Even if you're not blonde and blue-eyed, as is much of Scando Minnesota, you're invited to the programs of folk music, recitals, and arts and crafts at the **American Swedish Institute** (2600 Park Ave., tel. 612/8781–4907), housed in a whimsical palace with towers and carved griffins, 2 miles south of downtown and built by a successful Swedish immigrant.

**The Minneapolis Institute of Arts** (2400 3rd Ave. S, 612/870–3046) is noted for its collection of Rembrandts, French Impressionists, German Expressionists, and Chinese jade.

**The Walker Art Center and Sculpture Garden** (725 Vineland Pl., tel. 612/375–7600), founded in 1879 by Minneapolis lumber baron T.B. Walker, has evolved into one of the premier collections of cutting-edge modern art in the country. Across the street, in the sculpture garden, elaborate plantings are interspersed with large-scale works by modern masters, including a huge Pop Art spoon by Claes Oldenburg and Coosje van Bruggen.

**West River Parkway's** walkway, along the Mississippi, is perfect for a solitary moment.

*St. Paul*
**James J. Hill House** (240 Summit Ave., tel. 612/297–2555) is a massive feudal castle constructed in 1891 for the man who held a virtual railroad monopoly between Washington state and Chicago in the late 19th century. Tour guides lead visitors through many of the house's 32 convention-size rooms. The mansion makes a good starting point for a stroll down Summit Avenue to view the grand Victorian mansions where St. Paul's monied set came to roost.

**The Minnesota Museum of Art** (305 St. Peter St., tel. 612/ 292–4355), housed in an Art Deco caprice beside the Mississippi River in downtown St. Paul, specializes in regional American art. Its Deco restaurant (lunch only) offers both a panoramic river view and outstanding Scandinavian food.

**The Alexander Ramsey House** (265 S. Exchange St., tel. 612/296–8760), within walking distance of downtown St. Paul, was built in 1872 as the home of Minnesota's first governor. The gracious French Second Empire mansion has been carefully restored to provide a glimpse of cultivated Minnesota family life of the time.

**Summit Avenue** takes you along several miles of historic mansions to the river.

## Professional Sports

The Twin Cities baseball club, the **Minnesota Twins** (tel. 612/375–7444) and the football team, the **Vikings** (tel. 612/ 333–8828), play at the Hubert H. Humphrey Metrodome. Timberwolves Stadium hosts the **Timberwolves** (tel. 612/ 337–3865), the cities' basketball team. For a hockey match, see the **Minnesota North Stars** (tel. 612/853–9310) at the Met Center.

## The Arts

A vibrant scene of 100-plus professional troupes include the world-famous **Tyrone Guthrie Theater** (700 Vineland Pl., Minneapolis, tel. 612/377–2224), adjacent to the Walker Art Center, the **Children's Theatre Company** (2400 3rd Ave., Minneapolis, tel. 612/887–4040), and a spectrum of avant-garde companies that perform at the **Hennepin Center for the Arts** (6th St. and Hennepin Ave., Minneapolis, tel. 612/332–4478). Both cities are equally rich in music, with the Minnesota Orchestra occupying **Orchestra Hall** in downtown Minneapolis (1111 Nicollet Mall, tel. 612/371– 5656) and the St. Paul Chamber Orchestra tuning up in the jewelbox **Ordway Music Theatre** (345 Washington Ave., St. Paul, tel. 612/224–4222) fronting Rice Park—also home to the Minnesota Opera and traveling shows.

For complete listings, check the Friday arts section of the *Minneapolis Star Tribune*, the Thursday listings in the

St. *Paul Dispatch,* and the Wednesday listings of the *Twin Cities Reader.*

**Ticketmaster** sells tickets to all events; outlets are located in all Dayton's department stores (tel. 612/375–2200).

## After Hours

*Bars and Lounges*

**Minneapolis.** Hotel bars at **The Marquette** (tel. 612/332–2351) and **The Whitney** (tel. 612/339–9300) provide chic, quiet settings for business conversations. The **Fine Line Music Café** (318 1st Ave. N, tel. 612/338–8100) is where stylish young professionals pause nightly in their climb up the corporate ladder to catch equally stylish local and touring jazz, rock, and folk groups. The **Pacific Club** (downtown at 6th St. and Hennepin Ave., tel. 612/339–6100) is dolled up in a palms-and-surf motif, made all but invisible by the nightly body count at the bar stools and dance floors. Ad agency and other three-piece-suit under-30 types are lured as much by each other as by the lavish happy hour buffet. **First Avenue** (701 1st Ave. N, tel. 612/332–2771) attracts a funky, younger crowd hoping for a glimpse of rock superstar Prince on a visit home. **Rupert's Night Club,** adjoining CocoLezzone (5410 Wayzata Blvd., Golden Valley, tel. 612/544–5035), dispenses Motown and Big Band sounds to a slightly older, dressier set. At **Figlio** (tel. 612/822–1688), the only music is the cling of the cash register, almost inaudible in the festive jostle of jocks, preps, and their somewhat more sedate elders.

**St. Paul.** The bar at the **Saint Paul Hotel** (tel. 612/292–9292) is where you can head for a quiet business talk. The **Heartthrob Café and Philadelphia Bandstand** (St. Paul Center, 30 E. 8th St., tel. 612/224–2783) draws junior execs on both sides of thirty to the dance floor with hits from the '50s and drinks delivered by barmaids on roller skates. **Dixie's Bar and Smokehouse Grill** (695 Grand Ave., tel. 612/222–7345) packs in the locals with a Southern theme (great ribs, too). The **Dakota Bar & Grill** (tel. 612/642–1442) is the city's most sophisticated venue for local and touring cool jazz and blues talent.

*Comedy Clubs*

**Dudley Riggs' Brave New Workshop** (2605 Hennepin Ave. S, Uptown, tel. 612/332–6620) and **Didley Riggs' ETC** (1430 Washington Ave., Minneapolis, tel. 612/332–6620) brought topical satire to the Twin Cities in the 1960s. Scott Hansen, whose home base is Minneapolis, has **Comedy Galleries** in several locations: near the Nicollet Island Inn, 25 SE Main St.; Uptown, at 2911 Hennepin Ave. S; and in suburban St. Paul at 1780 County Rd. E, Maplewood. **David Wood's Rib Tickler and Magic Club** (716 N. 1st St., Minneapolis, tel. 612/339–9031) is a plush club that lures comics straight from the David Letterman and Johnny Carson shows.

# Montréal

*by Patricia Lowe*

Montréal has made good business sense since 1611, when entrepreneur and explorer Samuel de Champlain first set up a fur-trading post on a strategic 32-mile-long island in the St. Lawrence River. Settlement by the French followed in 1642, a milestone that will be marked by 350th-anniversary celebrations in Montréal in 1992.

The city's history as first a French then a British possession has led to endless language and power feuds between its French- and English-speaking populations. Officially, Montréal is French-speaking, but unofficially, it's English as well, as evidenced in the names of its early tycoons— Allan, Drummond, McGill, McTavish, Shaughnessy, and Van Horne—which live on in museums (the Shaughnessy House of the Canadian Centre for Architecture, for example), the leading university (McGill), and many street signs.

Today, with the approach of celebrations that will mark Montréal's founding, major multinationals, like Lavalin, the homegrown engineering firm, and Teleglobe Canada, are erecting the city's tallest (51-story) office tower, at 1000 rue la Gauchetière. IBM is building an enormous complex at 1250 blvd. René-Lévesque. Other consortiums and private foundations are renovating museums (including the McCord Museum) and restoring monuments.

The municipality is also rebuilding sidewalks and major arteries. The downside of all this activity is that city streets are a tangle of muddied walkways, workmen, cement trucks, and cranes. What should be a five-minute cab ride may stretch to almost half an hour. It's fortunate for the business traveler that most office towers and shopping complexes are clustered in a downtown core. Cabs are abundant, and the subway system is linked with "the city below," Montréal's unique response to its harsh climate. In winter, Montréalers can travel below ground on more than eight miles of walkways leading to métro, train, and bus stations, major hotels, businesses, boutiques, restaurants, banks, movie theaters, and the two main convention centers, the Palais des Congrès and Place Bonaventure.

Translation and simultaneous interpretation services abound, international firms and banks from Shanghai, Paris, Italy, and the United States do business here; and the Federal Business Development Bank operates from Place Victoria. Montréal is the headquarters of the International Air Transport Association and the United Nations International Civil Aviation Organization. Long a center for high-level international meetings, the city is well equipped with support services, which make this a good place to do business, whatever your language.

## Top Employers

| Employer | Type of Enterprise | Parent*/ Headquarters |
|---|---|---|
| **Alcan Aluminum** | Aluminum manufacturing | Montréal |
| **BCE** | Investment and holding company | Montréal |
| **Canadian National** | Freight services | CPI Rail/ Montréal |
| **Canadian Pacific** | Transportation | Montréal |
| **Canada Post Corp.** | Postal service | Montréal |
| **Hydro-Quebec** | Electric company | Montréal |
| **Power Corporation** | Investment and holding company | Montréal |
| **Provigo** | Food and convenience distribution | Montréal |
| **Steinberg** | Supermarket chain | Montréal |

*if applicable

## ESSENTIAL INFORMATION

### Climate

What follows are the average daily maximum and minimum temperatures for Montréal.

| | | | | | | | | |
|---|---|---|---|---|---|---|---|---|
| **Jan.** | 23F<br>9 | −5C<br>−13 | **Feb.** | 25F<br>12 | −4C<br>−11 | **Mar.** | 36F<br>23 | 2C<br>−5 |
| **Apr.** | 52F<br>36 | 11C<br>2 | **May** | 65F<br>48 | 18C<br>9 | **June** | 74F<br>58 | 23C<br>14 |
| **July** | 79F<br>63 | 26C<br>17 | **Aug.** | 76F<br>61 | 24C<br>16 | **Sept.** | 68F<br>53 | 20C<br>12 |
| **Oct.** | 57F<br>43 | 14C<br>6 | **Nov.** | 42F<br>32 | 6C<br>0 | **Dec.** | 27F<br>16 | −3C<br>−9 |

### Airports

**Montréal International Airport** is divided into two terminals. The first is in Dorval, a suburb 14 miles west of the city; the second is called Mirabel, and is about 30 miles north. The Dorval terminal is used for all domestic and U.S. flights and Mirabel serves all other destinations.

## Airport Business Facilities

**Mirabel Terminal. Le Château de l'Aeroport Mirabel** (connected by walkway to the Main Terminal, tel. 514/476–1611) has fax machines, photocopying, conference rooms with catering service, a fitness center, and day rates for rooms. **Dorval Terminal** has no business facilities.

## Airlines

Montréal is a hub city for Air Canada.

**Air Canada,** tel. 514/393–3333 (U.S. and Canadian destinations), 514/393–1111 (other destinations), or 800/776–3000.
**Air France,** tel. 514/284–2825 or 800/237–2747.
**Air Ontario,** tel. 514/393–3333 or 514/393–3888.
**American,** tel. 800/433–7300.
**British Airways,** tel. 514/287–9133 or 800/247–9297.
**Canadian Airlines International,** tel. 514/286–1212 or 800/387–2737.
**City Express,** tel. 514/485–2489 or 800/387–3060.
**Delta,** tel. 514/337–5520 or 800/221–1212.
**United,** tel. 514/875–4333 or 800/241–6522.

## Between the Airports and Downtown

*By Taxi*
From Dorval, taxis take 30–60 minutes during rush hour (8:30–10 AM and 4:30–5:30 PM) and 20–30 minutes at nonpeak times. From Mirabel, a cab ride generally takes 45 minutes to one hour. Dispatchers (who do not accept tips) at both airports hail the taxis, and fares are legally set: Unmetered rates are Can$19 from Dorval and Can$45 from Mirabel.

*By Limousine*
Limousines, also reserved through airport dispatchers at the arrivals exit, are on a set-fare system as well. The cost is Can$27.50 from Dorval and Can$55 from Mirabel.

*By Bus*
**Aerocar** (tel. 514/397–9999) is the cheapest way to get downtown, and, if a bus is standing ready to depart, it's often quicker than taking a cab. The buses stop at various hotels in the downtown area. Buses begin running at about 5 AM to both terminals; the Dorval bus runs until 11:10 PM, the Mirabel bus runs until 2 AM. They leave every 20 minutes from Dorval and every ½ hour from Mirabel (every 30 minutes and every hour, respectively, on weekends). The cost is Can$7 from Dorval and Can$9 from Mirabel.

## Car Rentals

**Avis,** tel. 514/636–1902 (Dorval), 514/476–3481 (Mirabel) or 800/331–1212.
**Budget,** tel. 514/636–0052 (Dorval), 514/476–2687 (Mirabel) or 800/527–0700.
**Hertz,** tel. 514/636–9530 (Dorval), 514/476–3385 (Mirabel) or 800/654–3131.
**Thrifty/Viabec,** tel. 514/631–5567 (Dorval), 514/476–0496 (Mirabel) or 800/367–2277.

**Tilden,** tel. 514/636–9030 (Dorval), 514/476–3460 (Mirabel) or 800/227–7368.

## Emergencies

*Doctors*
**Jewish General Hospital** (3755 rue Côte-Ste-Catherine, tel. 514/340–8222), **Montréal General Hospital** (1650 av. Cedar, tel. 514/937–6011), **Royal Victoria Hospital** (687 av. Pine ouest, tel. 514/842–1231).

*Dentists*
**Côte-des-Neiges Dental Centre** (5845 rue Côte-des-Neiges, Suite 100, tel. 514/731–7721), **Dental Centre** (1414 rue Drummond, Suite 412, tel. 514/281–1023), **Emergency Dental Services** (800 blvd. René-Lévesque ouest, tel. 514/875–7971).

## Important Addresses and Numbers

**Audiovisual rentals.** Audio-Visual and Video (pl. Bonaventure and 475 av. President Kennedy, tel. 514/844–9865), NDG Photo (1197 Sq. Phillips, tel. 514/866–2965), Photo Service (222 rue Notre-Dame ouest, tel. 514/849–2291), Visual Planning (6805 blvd. Décarie, tel. 514/739–3116).

**Chamber of Commerce.** Montréal Board of Trade (1080 Côte Beaver Hall, tel. 514/878–4651).

**Computer rentals.** Centre Micro-Informatique CIAP (1690 rue Gilford, tel. 514/522–2427), Co-Rent (500 rue Sherbrooke ouest, tel. 514/843–8888), Ordiloc (4425 rue Ste-Catherine ouest, tel. 514/934–1348).

**Convention and exhibition centers.** Palais des Congrès (201 rue Viger ouest, tel. 514/871–8226), Place Bonaventure (pl. Bonaventure, tel. 514/397–2355).

**Fax services.** Canadac (7520 rue Côte-de-Liesse, tel. 514/735–1411), Officium (475 av. du Président Kennedy, tel. 514/284–2246), Ricoh Facsimile (1150 rue Golf, Verdun, tel. 514/769–2552).

**Formal-wear rentals.** Classy Formal Wear (486 rue Ste-Catherine ouest, tel. 514/861–5416 and 1227 carré Phillips, tel. 514/875–9938).

**Gift shops.** Flowers: Cupidon (2288 rue Fleury est, tel. 514/382–6111), McKenna (4509 rue Côtes-des-Neiges, tel. 514/731–4992), Pinkerton Flower (5127 rue Sherbrooke ouest, tel. 514/487–7330); Gift Baskets and Candy: Eaton Department Store Gourmet Shop (677 rue Ste-Catherine ouest, tel. 514/284–8361), Laura Secord (1 pl. Ville-Marie, tel. 514/861–7867 and 1007 rue Ste-Catherine ouest, tel. 514/843–5708).

**Graphic design studios.** Graf 18 (1130 rue Sherbrooke ouest, tel. 514/849–1784), Graphème Communication Design (1558 av. Dr. Penfield, tel. 514/932–2615), Montréal Creative Centre (407 rue Dowd, Vieux-Montréal, tel. 514/861–6323).

**Hairstylists.** Unisex: La Coupe (1115 rue Sherbrooke ouest, tel. 514/288–6131), Gibson's (Le Reine Elizabeth, 900 blvd. René-Lévesque, tel. 514/866–6639), Vag (pl. Bonaventure, Centrale Station tunnel, tel. 514/866–9279 and 2015 rue Crescent, tel. 514/844–9656).

**Health and fitness clubs.** *See* Fitness, below.

**Information hot lines.** Bus and métro (tel. 514/288–6287), Canadian Automobile Association (tel. 514/861–1313 for emergencies, or 514/861–7111 for information), Entertainment (CHOM-FM, tel. 514/790–0718 and Montréal Today, tel. 514/352–2500), Road conditions (tel. 514/861–1313 or 514/873–4121).

**Limousine services.** Contact (tel. 514/875–8746), G. T. V. (tel. 514/871–8888), Murray Hill (tel. 514/937–5466).

**Liquor stores.** Maison des Vins (505 av. President Kennedy, tel. 514/873–2274), Société des Alcools du Québec (1 pl. Ville-Marie, tel. 514/861–6616; 1067 pl. Bonaventure, tel. 514/861–7037; 800 pl. Victoria, tel. 514/875–6180; and 426 Complexe Desjardins, tel. 514/844–8721).

**Mail delivery, overnight.** DHL International Express (tel. 514/636–8703), Federal Express (tel. 514/345–0130), TNT Skypak (tel. 514/636–6983).

**Messenger services.** Blitz 24 (tel. 514/321–0646), Express Service Courier (tel. 514/526–4434), Purolator Courier (tel. 514/731–1000).

**Office space rental.** Travelex Business Centre (1253 av. McGill College, tel. 514/871–8616).

**Pharmacies, late-night.** Cumberland Drug (1004 rue Ste-Catherine ouest, tel. 514/866–7791), Jean Coutu (1836 rue Ste-Catherine ouest, tel. 514/933–4221).

**Secretarial services.** A&A (1117 rue Ste-Catherine ouest, tel. 514/288–3795), ExecuCentre (1200 av. McGill College, tel. 514/393–1100), Travelex Business Centre (1253 av. McGill College, tel. 514/871–8616).

**Stationery supplies.** Pilon (1 pl. Ville-Marie, tel. 514/861–9497; 280 rue St-Jacques, tel. 514/842–4171; and Windsor building, 1170 rue Peel, tel. 514/861–4640), Wilson Stationers (Place Montréal Trust, tel. 514/499–9851 and Alexis Nihon Plaza, tel. 514/937–3579).

**Taxis.** Diamond (tel. 514/273–6331), LaSalle (tel. 514/277–2552), Veteran's (tel. 514/273–6351).

**Theater tickets.** *See* The Arts, below.

**Train information.** Amtrak (Central Station, 935 rue la Gauchetière ouest, tel. 800/426–8725), Via Rail (Central Station, 935 rue la Gauchetière ouest, tel. 514/871–1331).

**Travel agents.** American Express Travel Services (in all La Baie department stores and at 1141 blvd. de Maisonneuve ouest, tel. 514/284–3300), Thomas Cook (2020 rue University, tel. 514/398–0555 or 514/842–2541).

**Weather** (tel. 514/636–3026 or 514/636–3282).

## LODGING

Travelers do well in most Montréal hotels, even in those that are moderately priced. Most of the major hotels are downtown, between rue Guy and rue Berri, a generally safe area even after dark. Some motels on the outskirts of town and tiny "bargain hotels" in the city can be a disappointment.

Most of the hotels listed below offer corporate rates and weekend discounts; inquire when making reservations.

Highly recommended lodgings in each price category are indicated by a star ★.

| Category | Cost* |
|---|---|
| *$$$$* (Very Expensive) | over Can$150 |
| *$$$* (Expensive) | Can$121–Can$150 |
| *$$* (Moderate) | under Can$120 |

*All prices are for a standard double room, single occupancy, excluding the 10% provincial accommodation tax, 7% federal goods and service tax, and 15% service charge.*

*Numbers in the margin correspond to numbered hotel locations on the Montréal Lodging and Dining map.*

### Downtown

**⑥**
**$$**
**Auberge Ramada Centre-Ville.** The exterior of this seven-story building in a dreary section of rue Guy is unexceptional, but inside you'll find a friendly staff and a welcoming lobby. Corridors on unrenovated floors are a bit dingy and the worse for wear. However, the renovated plum-and-mauve rooms are neat, clean, and well furnished, each with bedside tables, a coffee table, and two armchairs. Rooms with queen-size beds are reserved for single guests and are spacious and fully equipped, but their white-tile bathrooms are small and toiletries are skimpy. The sixth and seventh floors are reserved for business clientele who place a premium on peace and quiet. The neighborhood, just below bustling boulevard René-Lévesque, can be a bit threatening at night. La Buisonnière restaurant is a good choice if you're dining alone. *1005 rue Guy, H3H 2K4, tel. 514/866–4611 or 800/268–8930, fax 514/866–8718. Gen. manager, Michel Garnier. 199 doubles, 6 suites. AE, CB, D, MC, V.*

**★ ⑰**
**$$$$**
**Bonaventure Hilton International.** This hotel is perched atop the Place Bonaventure Center, with its busy mall and exhibition space, and overlooks 2½ acres of gardens and streams. It is also connected to Central Station and Place Ville-Marie's underground shopping complex. Contemporary comfort characterizes the spacious doubles and suites, which were redecorated in 1989. All have brightly lighted desks, work/dining tables, love seats, and easy chairs framed by large windows. Inside garden units are recommended; those facing west may have their view cut off by the rapidly rising building next door. Lobby restaurants include the imposing Castillon (*see* Dining, below) and Le Portage (*see* After Hours, below); the Belvedere Bar (*see* After Hours, below) is a classy piano lounge. *A*

*Hilton International hotel. 1 pl. Bonaventure, H5A 1E4, tel. 514/878–2332 or 800/445–8667; in Canada, 800/268–9275; fax 514/878–3881. Gen. manager, Robert Frigère. 374 doubles, 13 suites, 7 executive suites. AE, CB, D, MC, V.*

**⑫** **Le Centre Sheraton.** This utilitarian, 37-story concrete
**$$$$** tower is near the financial high rises on boulevard René-Lévesque and has been a prime location for business travelers since 1982. The staff is welcoming, and the concierge is particularly helpful. Smallish double rooms are outfitted with creamy pastel tones and pale-wood furnishings. Guests staying in executive-class rooms, on levels 30 and 31, can take tea at the lounge on 32. The lounge also serves the more luxurious Towers floors (32–36) that, for higher rates, offer better accommodations, private check-in/check-out, and a boardroom. A health club, the relaxing L'Impromptu bar (*see* After Hours, below), and the rooftop restaurant, Le Point de Vue, are three more pluses. *1201 blvd. René-Lévesque ouest, H3B 2L7, tel. 514/878–2000 or 800/325–3535, fax 514/878–3958. Gen. manager, Alfred Heim. 800 doubles, 18 suites, 60 business-class. AE, CB, D, MC, V.*

**⑮** **Le Château Champlain.** Facing Windsor Station and Do-
**$$$$** minion Square, the 36-story skyscraper with distinctive half-moon-shape windows is favored by British guests, such as Prince Phillip, who stayed in the 35th-floor Royal Suite. A cage of tiny tropical birds is a grace note in the gold-ceilinged, marble-floored lobby, which gives way to wide, quiet halls. The rooms are clustered in groups of three in small alcoves off the corridors, adding a feeling of privacy. Brocade-pattern wallpaper and upholstery appear worn in some rooms, but reproductions of Louis XVI, Second Empire, and Queen Anne furnishings lend touches of luxury. Every unit has a dressing room. Guests staying on the three business floors get express check-in/check-out and a lounge. The Château is home to Le Caf' Conc' (*see* After Hours, below) and the Escapade, on the 36th floor, which offers a good buffet dinner nightly. *A Canadian Pacific hotel. 1 pl. du Canada, H3B 2L7, tel. 514/878–9000 or 800/268–9411; in Canada, 800/828–7447; in Ontario or Quebec, 800/268–9420; fax 514/878–6761. Gen. manager, Paolo de Pol. 516 doubles, 40 suites, 60 business-class. AE, CB, D, MC, V.*

**④** **Château Versailles.** Four Edwardian, semidetached, lime-
**$$** stone townhouses in a quiet downtown residential section are a find if you like Old World charm at bargain prices. Guests must put up with a few inconveniences such as the lack of cable TV. In 1989 the Villeneuve family, which owns the complex, added a 12-story, 1960s-style wing across rue Sherbrooke. Called La Tour Versailles, it provides modern though spartan accommodations. Visiting journalists usually opt for the old-fashioned rooms, with decorative fireplaces and chaise longues; however, some rooms lack desks, and back rooms may face a brick wall. In comparison to the townhouse complex, the annex feels brand-new and empty, although some rooms on the upper floors have fine views southward to the St. Lawrence. The Scandinavian-style furnishings are appropriate in the airy rooms, many of which are equipped with kitchenettes. *1659 rue Sherbrooke ouest, H3H 1I3, tel. 514/933–*

# MONTRÉAL

# MONTRÉAL HOTEL CHART

| HOTELS | Price Category | Business Services — Banquet capacity | No. of meeting rooms | Secretarial services | Audiovisual equipment | Translation Service | Computer rentals | In-room modem phone jack | All-news cable channel | Desk | Desk lighting | Bed lighting |
|---|---|---|---|---|---|---|---|---|---|---|---|---|
| Auberge Ramada Centre-Ville | $$ | 175 | 11 | ✓ | - | - | - | - | ✓ | ● | ◐ | ● |
| Bonaventure Hilton International | $$$$ | 1600 | 19 | ✓ | ✓ | ✓ | - | ✓ | ✓ | ● | ● | ● |
| Le Centre Sheraton | $$$$ | 1000 | 11 | ✓ | ✓ | ✓ | - | ✓ | ✓ | ● | ● | ◐ |
| Le Château Champlain | $$$$ | 620 | 11 | ✓ | ✓ | - | - | ✓ | ✓ | ◐ | ◐ | ● |
| Château de L'aéroport | $$$ | 360 | 28 | - | ✓ | - | - | - | ✓ | ● | ◐ | ◐ |
| Château Versailles | $$ | 0 | 4 | - | ✓ | - | - | ✓ | - | ○ | ○ | ◐ |
| Delta | $$$ | 400 | 15 | - | ✓ | - | - | ✓ | ✓ | ◐ | ● | ◐ |
| Le Grand | $$$ | 1100 | 13 | - | ✓ | - | - | - | ✓ | ○ | ○ | ◐ |
| Holiday Inn Crowne Plaza | $$$ | 600 | 9 | - | ✓ | - | - | ✓ | ✓ | ● | ● | ● |
| Hôtel de la Montagne | $$$ | 100 | 2 | - | - | - | - | ✓ | ✓ | ● | ● | ● |
| Le Méridien | $$$$ | 800 | 18 | - | ✓ | ✓ | - | ✓ | ✓ | ○ | ○ | ◐ |
| Montreal Airport Hilton International | $$$ | 500 | 18 | ✓ | ✓ | ✓ | - | ✓ | ✓ | ● | ● | ◐ |
| Le Nouvel | $$ | 150 | 6 | - | ✓ | - | - | ✓ | ✓ | - | - | ◐ |
| Le Quatre Saisons | $$$$ | 650 | 12 | ✓ | ✓ | ✓ | - | ✓ | ✓ | ● | ● | ◐ |
| Ramada Renaissance du Parc | $$$ | 550 | 21 | ✓ | ✓ | - | - | ✓ | ✓ | ● | ● | ◐ |
| Le Reine Elizabeth | $$$$ | 2800 | 23 | ✓ | ✓ | - | ✓ | ✓ | ✓ | ● | ◐ | ◐ |
| Ritz-Carlton | $$$$ | 350 | 12 | - | ✓ | - | - | ✓ | ✓ | ● | ● | ◐ |
| Shangrila | $$$ | 450 | 10 | - | ✓ | - | - | ✓ | ✓ | ◐ | ◐ | ● |

**$$$$** = over Can $150, **$$$** = Can $120-Can $150, **$$** = under Can $120.
● good, ◐ fair, ○ poor.
All hotels listed here have photocopying and fax facilities.

| In-Room Amenities | | | | | | | | | | Hotel Amenities | | | | | | |
| Nonsmoking rooms | In-room checkout | Minibar | Pay movies | VCR/Movie rentals | Hairdryer | Toiletries | Room service | Laundry/Dry cleaning | Pressing | Concierge | Barber/Hairdresser | Garage | Courtesy airport transport | Sauna | Pool | Exercise room |
|---|---|---|---|---|---|---|---|---|---|---|---|---|---|---|---|---|
| ✓ | ✓ | - | ✓ | - | - | ○ | ○ | ● | ○ | ✓ | - | ✓ | - | ✓ | ● | ● |
| ✓ | ✓ | ✓ | ✓ | - | - | ● | ● | ● | ◐ | ✓ | - | ✓ | - | ✓ | ● | ○ |
| ✓ | ✓ | ✓ | ✓ | ✓ | - | ◐ | ● | ◐ | ● | ✓ | ✓ | ✓ | - | ✓ | ● | ● |
| ✓ | - | ✓ | ✓ | ✓ | ✓ | ● | ● | ◐ | ○ | ✓ | ✓ | ✓ | - | ✓ | ◐ | ● |
| - | - | - | ✓ | ✓ | - | ◐ | ○ | ◐ | ◐ | ✓ | ✓ | - | - | ✓ | ◐ | - |
| ✓ | - | ✓ | - | - | ✓ | ○ | - | ◐ | - | - | - | - | - | - | - | - |
| ✓ | - | ✓ | ✓ | - | - | ◐ | ◐ | ◐ | ○ | - | ✓ | ✓ | - | ✓ | ● | ● |
| ✓ | - | ✓ | ✓ | - | ✓ | ◐ | ◐ | ● | ○ | ✓ | - | ✓ | - | ✓ | ◐ | ◐ |
| ✓ | - | ✓ | ✓ | - | - | ○ | ◐ | ◐ | ○ | ✓ | ✓ | ✓ | - | ✓ | ◐ | ◐ |
| - | - | ✓ | - | ✓ | ✓ | ● | ◐ | ● | ◐ | ✓ | - | ✓ | - | - | ◐ | - |
| ✓ | - | ✓ | ✓ | - | ✓ | ◐ | ● | ◐ | ◐ | ✓ | ✓ | ✓ | - | ✓ | ● | - |
| ✓ | ✓ | ✓ | ✓ | ✓ | - | ◐ | ● | ◐ | ● | ✓ | - | ✓ | ✓ | ✓ | ● | ◐ |
| - | - | ✓ | - | - | - | - | - | ◐ | - | ✓ | - | ✓ | - | - | ◐ | - |
| ✓ | ✓ | ✓ | ✓ | - | ✓ | ● | ● | ● | ● | ✓ | - | ✓ | - | ✓ | ◐ | ● |
| ✓ | - | - | ✓ | - | ✓ | ◐ | ◐ | ● | ◐ | ✓ | ✓ | ✓ | ✓ | ✓ | ● | ● |
| ✓ | - | ✓ | ✓ | - | ✓ | ◐ | ◐ | ◐ | ◐ | ✓ | ✓ | ✓ | - | - | - | - |
| ✓ | - | ✓ | - | - | ✓ | ● | ● | ● | ◐ | ✓ | ✓ | ✓ | - | - | - | - |
| ✓ | - | ✓ | ✓ | - | ✓ | ● | ◐ | ● | ◐ | ✓ | ✓ | - | - | - | - | - |

**Room service:** ● 24-hour, ◐ 6AM-10PM, ○ other.
**Laundry/Dry cleaning:** ● same day, ◐ overnight, ○ other.
**Pressing:** ● immediate, ◐ same day, ○ other.

*3611 or 800/361-3664; in Canada, 800/361-7199; fax 514/933-7102. Gen. manager, Germain Villeneuve. 70 deluxe doubles in Château, 105 doubles and 2 penthouse suites in La Tour. AE, MC, V.*

★ ⑲ **Delta Hotel.** Built as a 24-story condominium, this is one of
$$$ the better choices visitors can make for convenience, comfort, and cost. It's in the commercial core, near the McGill métro station, and caters to a business, convention, and group clientele. Staff is polite and friendly. Accommodations are comfortably traditional, and the rose or pale blue color scheme blends well with the Velveteen armchairs with ottomans, and the stained-wood cabinets concealing minibars and televisions. Bathrooms, however, are on the small size and towels are skimpy. Most units, with the exception of those on the corners, have concrete balconies. Signature Service, designed for business travelers, offers better rooms with more amenities; however, all units are roughly the same size. The hotel is at its best in summer, when the garden courtyard off rue Sherbrooke is in bloom and the outdoor pool is open. Cellular phone rentals are a handy plus. *A Delta hotel. 475 av. President Kennedy, H3A 2T4, tel. 514/286-1986 or 800/877-1133; in Canada, 800/268-1133; fax 514/284-4342. Gen. manager, Carel Forlkesma. 400 doubles, 8 suites, 50 business-class. AE, CB, D, MC, V.*

⑱ **Le Grand Hôtel.** Opened in 1977, this 30-story property at-
$$$ tracts business people with its proximity to the convention center and underground access to Place Victoria's stock exchange and métro station. However, the hotel does have drawbacks. Public areas are sparsely furnished with worn modular-style chairs and chipped marble tables and some rooms reflect this general neglect. Panoramic-view glass elevators and the vine-bedecked atrium lobby are holdovers from the hotel's early days as a Hyatt. Standard rooms are '60s contemporary; all, including twin-bedded accommodations for single travelers, are the same size. Ongoing refurbishment will add desks to every room; now only 100 rooms have them. From the sixth story up, sweeping views from floor-to-ceiling windows give rooms a feeling of spaciousness. A concierge oversees the 24-floor Le Privé, which offers extra amenities. The hotel hosts Montréal's only revolving restaurant, Le Tour de Ville. *A Hôtel des Gouverneurs hotel. 777 rue University, H3C 3Z7, tel. 514/879-1370 or 800/361-8155, fax 514/879-1761. Gen. manager, Anthony Tuor. 673 doubles, 47 singles, 10 suites, and 1 business-class suite. AE, CB, DC, MC, V.*

⑳ **Holiday Inn Crowne Plaza.** Near McGill métro station and
$$$ the university, this 20-story hotel is invaded by college students every fall weekend and by business travelers year-round on weekdays. Despite the hotel's heavy traffic, the overworked staff is efficient and relatively friendly. Entirely renovated between 1987 and 1988, the '60s-era building was given a glittering marquee above the entrance. In contrast, rooms are decorated in peaceful gray-blues and pastels. Although the bathrooms are tiny, alcoves provide separate sinks and vanities. Some suites have lovely views of Mont Royal, and all resemble model-home rooms, down to the parquet floors. Two executive floors offer express check-in/check-out, priority reservations, and a lounge. Cellular phones can be rented at the front desk. Of the two restaurants, Les Verrières is the

better. *420 rue Sherbrooke ouest, H3A 1B4, tel. 514/842–6111 or 800/465–4329, fax 514/842–9381. Gen. manager, Guy Lemieux. 425 doubles, 6 suites, 58 business-class. AE, CB, D, MC, V.*

**❾** **Hôtel de la Montagne.** A rather ordinary apartment build-
**$$$** ing when it was built in 1982, this property has been ele-
gantly transformed and now contains the city's most
inviting lobby, graced by an eclectic collection of Edward-
ian, Neo-Classic, and Biedermeier furnishings. A gilded
nymph adorns the central fountain, and around her cavort
elephants and sphinxes. The upstairs corridors are nar-
row, dim, and occasionally stuffy, but the plush rooms are
spacious and feature golden-oak or dark wood French-Co-
lonial furnishings. In the suites, handsome four-poster
beds are hung with fabric that matches the spreads and
drapes. There's no health club, but suites are equipped
with their own rowing machines; guests in any type of
room will be provided with a machine at no charge upon
request. Luxurious bathrooms in the suites include
Jacuzzis. The hotel's owner is also the proprietor of
Thursday's/Les Beaux Jeudis, a restaurant and night spot
on rue Crescent that is connected by a tunnel with the lob-
by. The two lobby bars are popular with locals and thirty-
forty-something visitors; the restaurant, Le Lutetia (*see*
Dining, below) is highly esteemed. *1430 rue de la
Montagne, H3G 1Z5, tel. 514/288–5656 or 800/361–6262;
in Canada, 800/361–6262; fax 514/288–9658. Gen. manag-
er, Alain J. M. Pauquet. 122 doubles, 14 suites. AE, CB,
D, MC, V.*

**★ ㉑** **Hôtel Ramada Renaissance du Parc.** This 14-story brick
**$$$** tower targets a business clientele by means of incentives
and packages. The hotel is often, and undeservedly, over-
looked, partially due to its location in a quieter part of
downtown, 2½ blocks north of rue Sherbrooke. Much of
the darkish lobby is occupied by the Puzzles bar (*see* After
Hours, below); otherwise, there's not much public space.
The building resembles a modern apartment complex and
is part of the La Cité housing-and-commercial project; elevators from the lobby give direct access to a newly rede-
veloped underground mall. All rooms are pleasantly
decorated; those with northwest exposures offer unique
views of the Mont Royal cross. The top-floor Club Renaissance is for executives who want private check-in/check-
out, buffet, and bar service, and a boardroom for private
meetings. Cellular phones can be rented. This is the only
hotel in the city with an outdoor tennis court. *3624 av. du
Parc, H2X 3P8, tel. 514/288–6666 or 800/228–9898; for the
hearing impaired, 800/228–3232; in Canada, 800/268–
8930; fax 514/588–2469. Gen. manager, Marc Hamel. 416
doubles, 10 suites, 28 kings, 2 business-class suites. AE,
CB, D, MC, V.*

**㉔** **Le Méridien.** Built for the 1976 Summer Olympics (Mick
**$$$$** and Bianca Jagger were the first guests to stay in the
Presidential Suite that August), this 12-story appendage
to the Complexe Desjardins is the only hotel directly
linked to the convention center. The Place des Arts cultural complex is just across the street. Although the chain is
known for its elegance, the Montréal Méridien may be a
disappointment to guests expecting more-posh surroundings; the lobby, for instance, opens onto the bustling mall.
The rooms, decorated in soft tones, are on the small side

for a luxury hotel. Tiny vanities, beneath make-up mirrors, must double as desks; perhaps the hotel's business center is meant to compensate. Business travelers have a separate floor called Le Club President with additional perks: a lounge, express check-in/check-out, and a private boardroom. Le Club Restaurant is recommended for quiet, candlelit business dinners. *4 Complexe Desjardins, H5B 1E5, tel. 514/285–1450 or 800/543–4300; in Canada, 800/361–8234; fax 514/285–1243. Gen. manager, Jean-Claude Andrieux. 574 doubles, 22 suites, 5 executive suites. AE, CB, D, MC, V.*

★ ❸ **Le Nouvel Hotel.** A complex of three high-rises built be-
$$ tween 1985 and 1987, this convenient, moderately priced hotel in western downtown is known for its young, eager staff. The hotel itself may not have much personality, but its expansive studio and apartment suites are cheerful and spotless and boast wide balconies. All apartment-style units have kitchenettes and dining areas. Furnishings are contemporary boxy, in salmon, pink, and aqua tones; and every living room and studio has an added sofa bed. Although dining tables are wide enough to substitute for desks, their overhead lighting is more suited to romantic dinners. The quietest units are on the 10th–12th floors, where rooms with a northwest exposure have the best views. Bathrooms are basic. There are minibars in suites, but no room service; breakfast, lunch, and dinner are available in the Entr'acte restaurant. *A Nouvel Hôtel. 1740 blvd. René-Lévesque, H3H 1R3, tel. 514/931–8841 or 800/363–6063. Gen. manager, Jean Baervoets. 124 studios, 124 2½-room units. AE, MC, V.*

★ ⓮ **Le Quatre Saisons.** The most luxurious of Montréal's ho-
$$$$ tels, this 31-story tower has commanded the prime Peel-Sherbrooke intersection since 1976. Travelers who want every amenity will prefer this hotel to the Ritz-Carlton, its rival down the street; however, the Quatre Saisons does not have the reputation for old-European charm or fine dining that its neighbor has cultivated. Contemporary elegance prevails, from the stunning flower arrangements in the Oriental lobby to the dark wood cabinets that enclose the guest room television sets. Cheerful, satiny chintz brightens many standard doubles, and mahogany desks with brass lamps look ready for business. Suites are expansive and offer exhilirating views. French doors divide living rooms and bedrooms. Le Restaurant (*see* Business Breakfasts, below) is the home of the power breakfast or lunch, and the L'Apero Bar (*see* After Hours, below) is the place to go after work or after hours. *A Four Seasons hotel. 1050 rue Sherbrooke ouest, H3A 2R6, tel. 514/284–1110 or 800/332–3442; in Canada, 800/268–6282; fax 514/845–3025. Gen. manager, Kuno Fasel. 272 doubles, 28 suites. AE, CB, D, MC, V.*

⓰ **Le Reine Elizabeth.** Built in 1957 and still the biggest hotel
$$$$ in town, this downtown establishment near the train station caters to business travelers and tour groups. It has also hosted Queen Elizabeth, Neil Armstrong, and Charles de Gaulle and is still celebrated as the site of John and Yoko's bed-in for peace. The hotel's ground floor, frequently likened to a train station, could put off first-time visitors, who will find the lobby cavernous and loud; ongoing renovations should change its glitzy '50s decor. Standard rooms are cozy and restful and are furnished

with love seats and pine desks and cabinets. The dark-green-marble bathrooms are cramped. Business-class guests stay on floors 16 and 17 and enjoy extra amenities, including Continental breakfast, fresh plants, minibars, and a separate check-in/check-out. A glass elevator leads from these floors to Montréal's most intimate business lounge, with a woodburning fireplace in winter and a buffet. The Beaver Club (*see* Dining, below) is well known and one of the best restaurants in the city. Les Voyageurs (*see* After Hours, below) is good for quiet business talks over drinks. *A Canadian Pacific hotel. 900 rue René-Lévesque ouest, H3B 4A5, tel. 514/861–3511 or 800/828–7447; in Canada, 800/268–9420; fax 514/861–3536. Gen. manager, George Villedary. 276 singles, 495 doubles, 158 regular suites, 35 studios, 60 mini-suites, 19 executive suites. AE, CB, D, MC, V.*

★ ⓫ **Hôtel Ritz-Carlton.** Within two blocks of McGill University and the Montréal Museum, the Ritz has drawn execu-
$$$$ tive travelers since 1912, when Canadian-born publishing tycoon Lord Beaverbrook made the nine-story, neoclassical limestone building his preferred hotel. The Ritz is still a favorite with those who like to travel in style and don't care about in-house fitness facilities. The spacious black-and-gold lobby is set off by a curving staircase. Elegant doubles and suites feature crystal chandeliers and some antique furnishings as well as desks with inlaid leather and brass lamps. Each smart white-and-slate marble bathroom has built-in shelves for mounds of fluffy towels and robes. Better suites are fitted with working fireplaces. French doors separate the bedrooms from sitting rooms, which segue into compact dining areas with buffet and bar. Uninspiring views of surrounding offices don't seem to faze repeat visitors. The hotel's Café du Paris (*see* Dining, below) is excellent for business breakfasts and dinners; the Ritz Garden (*see* Diversions, below) offers lovely afternoon teas; and Le Grand Prix (*see* After Hours, below) provides a refined setting for a drink with associates. *Member of the Leading Hotels of the World. 1228 rue Sherbrooke ouest, H3G 1H6, tel. 514/842–4212 or 800/223–6800; in Canada, 800/363–0366; fax 514/842–3383. Gen. manager, René Gounel. 205 doubles, 35 suites. AE, CB, D, MC, V.*

⓭ **Shangrila Hotel.** Although it shares the Peel-Sherbrooke
$$$ locale with Le Quatre Saisons, this 20-story concrete tower is on a more modest scale. The lobby is small and serene, with an Oriental motif. The Eastern theme continues in the rooms, which are spacious and bright, except for the queen-bedded units (for single guests), which are small and overwhelmed with furniture. Suites feel airy, thanks to their cityscape panoramas, some from glass doors leading to private terraces. Bathrooms are unremarkable. Fitness addicts can stay in rooms that have private mini gyms. Corporate Class offers upgraded rooms, express check-in/check-out, and a lounge. The hotel's restaurants, the Dynastic de Ming (try the peanut-butter-flavor Chinese ravioli; it tastes better than it sounds) and Cafe Park Expresse (offering counter service) are both good. *A Best Western Hotel. 3407 rue Peel, H3A 1W7, tel. 514/288–4141 or 800/648–7200; in Canada, 800/361–7791; fax 514/288–3021. Gen. manager, Pierre Quintal. 153 doubles, 15 suites. AE, CB, D, MC, V.*

## Airport

*Dorval*

★ ❷ **Montréal Airport Hilton International.** Considering its lo-
$$$  cation in a dreary expanse alongside the Dorval terminal,
the Hilton is an unexpectedly pleasant stopover. A 1989
renovation spruced up the hotel, adding a marble lobby
and a solarium between the restaurant and garden-pool
area. A proficient staff has perfected the airport/hotel
transfer routine, carefully settling half-dazed early-morn-
ing travelers into shuttles for the two-minute trip to
Dorval, next door. Guest rooms are small but capture the
ambience of a private club, with dark wood and sturdy
wingback chairs. All rooms are soundproof, but units in
the Tower annex are the quietest. There are studio suites,
meeting facilities, and an executive floor with added
amenities. *A Hilton International hotel. 12505 chemin
Côte-de-Liesse, Dorval, H9P 1B7, tel. 514/631-2411 or
800/445-8667, fax 514/631-0192. Gen. manager, Gaston
Viallet. 483 doubles, 20 suites. AE, CB, D, MC, V.*

*Mirabel*

❶ **Château de l'Aéroport.** Conveniently connected to the air-
$$$  port at Mirabel, this location is ideal for passengers arriv-
ing or leaving on late-night flights. The hotel is built
around an atrium and spacious indoor pool, a setting that
attracts Montréalers on weekend escape packages.
*Aéroport International de Montréal, C.P. 60, Mirabel,
J7N 1A2, tel. 514/476-1611; in Quebec, 800/361-0924.
Gen. manager, Regis Nadeau. 362 rooms. AE, CB,
MC, V.*

## DINING

There are more than 3,500 restaurants in Montréal, over
10,000 if the surrounding suburbs are included. Nouvelle
cuisine, once a staple in French restaurants, is no longer
new; and menus seem to be returning to heartier fare. Recently, a few Mexican restaurants have opened along with
places that look to other parts of North America, especially California, for inspiration. However, traditional French
restaurants are still most popular with both residents and
visitors, and restaurants serving regional favorites like
meat pies, Gaspé salmon, *moules* (mussels), maple-syrup
dishes, and sugar pie continue to hold their own.

Highly recommended restaurants in each category are indicated by a star ★.

| Category | Cost* |
|---|---|
| $$$$ (Very Expensive) | over $30 |
| $$$ (Expensive) | $20–$30 |
| $$ (Moderate) | under $20 |

*All prices are per person, including appetizer, entrée,
and dessert, but excluding drinks, service, and 10% meal
tax.*

*Numbers in the margin correspond to numbered restau-
rant locations on the Montréal Lodging and Dining map.*

## Business Breakfasts

**A. L. Van Houtte.** Fresh-ground coffee, café au lait, and muffins are a successful formula for the more than 50 outlets of this café, most of them downtown and in major complexes like place Bonaventure and place Ville-Marie. *1083 Beaver Hall Hill, tel. 514/861–4604, and 1001 blvd. de Maisonneuve ouest, tel. 514/845–5922.*

**Café de Paris.** The Ritz-Carlton's highly esteemed restaurant (*see* Downtown, below) serves a wide choice of breakfasts in formal surroundings characterized by crisp white napery and careful, hushed service. Newspapers are available at the entrance, and there is a generous buffet for business people on the run. *Hôtel Ritz-Carlton, tel. 514/842–4212.*

**Lux.** This trendy restaurant-bar-cum-newsstand serves breakfast 24 hours a day in an off-the-beaten-track neighborhood that locals like to compare to New York's Soho. Vestiges of the building's former life—as a factory—are retained in the metal stairways around the bar. *5220 blvd. St-Laurent (Laurier métro, bus no. 55), tel. 514/271–9272.*

**Picnic.** Downstairs from the William Tell Restaurant, this cheerful Swiss chalet offers sit-down and takeout breakfasts beginning at 8 AM. Waitresses in dirndles preside while the regulars from surrounding office towers pick up fresh-baked blueberry muffins. Those with more time can relax over one of the most reasonable breakfasts in town. In summer a tiny outdoor terrace serves the same morning menu. *2055 rue Stanley, tel. 514/288–0139.*

**Le Restaurant.** The dining room of Le Quatre Saisons is best known as the originator of the Montréal power breakfast. You can get a welcoming cup of coffee and complimentary paper in the downstairs room, and the Captain's Table at the back can seat up to 12, for power get-togethers. Chrome-and-black leatherette chairs look like office furnishings, but fresh tulips and baby orchids brighten each table. A low-calorie, -sodium, and -fat menu is available. *Le Quatre Saison, tel. 514/284–1110.*

**La Tulipe Noire.** For most of the day, this café is jammed. However, breakfast is a quiet time, and employees of Alcan Aluminium upstairs make this an early morning rendezvous, as do guests from the nearby Ritz-Carlton and Quatre Saisons. It's a pretty spot, with frosted-glass sconces, and an open courtyard in summer. The youthful staff is friendly, even on gray November mornings. Some people prefer to sit at the coffee bar in back for a quick chocolate-chip muffin and cappuccino. *2100 rue Stanley, tel. 514/285–1255.*

## Chinatown

**㉕** **Tai Kim Lung.** This small restaurant in the heart of China-
**$$** town draws a loyal lunchtime crowd from neighboring federal offices at Complex Guy-Favreau, as well as delegates escaping the convention center down the street. Wedged between two larger establishments, the restaurant, with its beige, nondescript facade, is easy to miss. The decor is also simple; the leatherette-quilted bar dates back some 30 years. Reasonably priced business lunches include four or five selections of Szechuan or Cantonese dishes, such as beef with Chinese vegetables, or fillet of doré (walleye

pike) in garlic sauce. At dinner, when business is slower, more extensive menus are featured, along with tropical drinks. *74 rue Lagauchetière ouest, tel. 514/861–7556. Casual dress. AE, MC, V. Closed Sun. lunch.*

## Downtown

★ **⑯** **Beaver Club.** Maitre d' Charles Ploem oversees Montréal's
$$$$ most famous dining room, a favorite of former mayor Jean Dapeau and just about every Québec politician, including Canadian prime minister Brian Mulroney. Named for a private club started by fur-trading voyageurs in the 18th century, it's been a part of Le Reine Elizabeth hotel since 1958. Executives like to be seen here, and there are still some members whose copper plates engraved with their names share the back brick wall with an aging buffalo hide. Best for quiet business meetings in the evening, the restaurant can be cheerfully noisy at noon. Regulars like the special, a thick slice of roast beef au jus accompanied by a baked potato. Lighter meals might start with consommé of feathered game and morels beneath a crust, and include an entrée of roasted, lightly smoked salmon with a champagne-vinegar sauce. The dessert cart displays tiers of pastries, Black Forest cakes, and cheesecakes. The wine list ranges from a rare Sauternes to an enjoyable Entre-Deux Mers. *Le Reine Elizabeth, 900 blvd. René-Lévesque ouest, tel. 514/861–3511. Jacket and tie required. Reservations required. AE, CB, D, MC, V.*

**㉓** **La Cabane Grecque.** A good selection of reasonably priced
$$ Greek dishes; sunny, plant-filled dining rooms; and friendly service make this an inviting place to relax after work. Glassed-in on two sides, it's a fine vantage point for watching rue Prince Arthur, the city's first and most-popular pedestrian mall and a mecca for McGill University students as well as an older, trendy crowd. The generous shish kebab platter is a good bet, as is the moussaka, made with eggplant, squash, potatoes, and ground beef. *102 rue Prince Arthur est, tel. 514/849–0122. Casual dress. AE, MC, V.*

★ **⑪** **Café de Paris.** Don't be misled by the informal name—this
$$$$ café in the Ritz-Carlton is an elegant establishment with ornate gilt mirrors and lovely floral arrangements framing clusters of fawn-colored banquettes. Its walls are covered in golden watered silk, and a row of French doors at the back opens onto a private garden. Present and former prime ministers Mulroney and Trudeau drop by, and retired Canadian governor general Jeanne Sauvé enjoys summertime dining on the terrace around the duck pond. Most diners opt for one of the room's classic dishes, which includes light Dover sole with wild rice. The chef also prepares a six-course menu de degustation, with venison or veal as the entrée. There are low-calorie, salt-free dishes. Strawberries with whipped cream go well with the little cookies and bonbons served at the end of every meal. *Hôtel Ritz-Carlton, 1228 rue Sherbrooke ouest, tel. 514/842–4212. Jacket and tie required. Reservations required. AE, CB, D, MC, V.*

★ **⑰** **Le Castillon.** The Bonaventure Hilton's dining room is a
$$$$ modern-day replica of a baronial castle. In winter a roaring fire greets guests as they enter the lobby and in summer glass sliding doors open onto a terrace shaded by firs and birches. Wherever diners sit they have a view of trees

and sky. The stone walls are hung with tapestries, and the beamed ceiling supports huge, carved-wood chandeliers. Maroon banquettes offer the most comfortable and private areas. Waiters in knee breeches serve food that is surprisingly light and nouvelle. A favorite dish is scallops braised with butter and dill, surrounded by baby carrots and new potatoes. Roast pheasant is the house specialty; other recommended selections are the medallions of lamb with braised peppers, and the roast of the day, always good and reasonably priced. At lunchtime the front dining area by the fireplace features a 55-minute business menu. *Bonaventure Hilton International. 1 pl. Bonaventure, tel. 514/878–2332. Jacket and tie required. Reservations advised. AE, CB, D, MC, V.*

**⑱** **Chez Antoine.** Stockbrokers gravitate to this popular bis-
**$$$** tro and grill in the tunnel that links Le Grand Hôtel with the Place Victoria exchange. Even during the busy lunch hour you can find privacy in a tranquil corner. Tiffany-style lamps, frosted glass, and Art Deco tilework depicting romantic Edwardian figures create a cheery ambience. Chez Antoine excels at grilled selections, prepared over mesquite, Canadian maple, or hickory woods. Grilled quail is a specialty, as is grilled scampi with curry. Luncheon fare also includes salads and sandwiches. Abstainers will appreciate the nonalcoholic "wine list." *Le Grand Hôtel, 777 rue University, tel. 514/879–1370. Casual dress. Reservations advised for dinner. AE, CB, D, MC, V.*

**❺** **Chez Pauzé.** Established in 1862, this is one of the few re-
**$$$** maining fine restaurants that once clustered on rue Ste-Catherine. The somewhat outdated maritime decor sets the stage for seafood specialties. Sconces and chandeliers are replicas of ships's wheels, and a swordfish trophy guards the bar entrance. Lone diners are fussed over by attentive waitresses. Reasonably priced business lunches are featured Tuesday through Friday 11:30–2:30. The à la carte menu may feature creamy lobster stew or a thick lobster sandwich on brown bread. Clam chowder makes an economical, filling meal. Dinner is more extensive and expensive and is especially good when lobster is in season. *1657 rue Ste-Catherine ouest, tel. 514/932–6118. Casual dress. Reservations advised for dinner. AE, CB, D, MC, V. Closed Mon.*

**★ ❽** **Les Halles.** An evening here will take you back to the era of
**$$$$** Paris's old market district. It's the most talked-about restaurant in Montréal, and all four dining rooms are usually full. On the first floor a charcuterie serves a high-spirited crowd. For a quiet meeting sit upstairs, where the atmosphere is more restrained. The menu offers a selection of classic French and nouvelle cuisine, and appetizers include a hare pâté with apples and juniper berries. Among the main dishes are *magret de canard de Barbarie* (breast of duck with Cumberland sauce), and filet of beef with mushrooms and foie gras. For dessert try the homemade sorbet or the pastries. A reasonably priced business lunch is offered Tuesday through Friday 11:45–2:30. *1450 rue Crescent, tel. 514/844–2328. Jacket advised in the evening. Reservations required. AE, CB, D, MC, V. Closed Mon. and some holidays.*

**❿ Katsura.** Located near the Hôtel Ritz-Carlton, this Japa-
**$$$** nese restaurant, the most elegant in the city, is always
jammed with local and international clientele. Business
groups meet in private tatami rooms or in the relatively
quiet alcove off the sushi bar. Service in the alcove is not
always efficient, and the area can become hot and stuffy.
Tastefully decorated with Japanese screens and prints,
the restaurant manages to be both contemporary and
cozy, and knowledgeable waitresses are exceptionally
helpful. Although there is a good wine list, most diners
start off with hot saki. The generous sushi-and-sashimi
combination platter is a comprehensive selection. Shabu-
shabu is prepared here for two with slices of beef and veg-
etables thinly cut and boiled in broth at the table. Fixed-
price, eight- to 12-course dinners provide a good sampling
of the house specialties. *2170 rue de la Montagne, tel. 514/
849–1172. Casual dress. Reservations required, except at
the sushi bar. AE, CB, D, MC, V.*

**❾ Le Lutetia.** This valentine of a dining room in the Hôtel de
**$$$** la Montagne is a frothy confection of needlepoint chairs,
cabbage-rose rugs, lacey tablecloths, and candy-box mu-
rals of clouds and cherubs. Popular for power breakfasts
and lunches, as well as for Sunday brunch, Lutetia's kitch-
en is highly regarded for its nouvelle cuisine. All-inclusive
lunches range from mushroom quiche to roast beef. The
fresh fettuccine with shredded vegetables and shrimp is
light, yet as satisfying as the steak tartare, and the lamb
medallions "perfumed" with fresh mint. Oenophiles
praise the wine cellar, which, in 1987, won a gold medal as
the best in Québec. *Hôtel de la Montagne, 1430 rue de la
Montagne, tel. 514/288–5656. Jacket advised. Reservations advised. AE, D, MC, V.*

**★ ❼ Le Mas des Oliviers.** This restaurant's name ("The Olive
**$$$** Grove") and its white stucco walls and black wrought-iron
grillwork conjure images of Provence. Although the food
is not quite so lyrical as the images suggest, the restau-
rant has come into its own since it was taken over by
Jacques Muller a decade ago. You'll like the look of the
place: the fresh green napery, the imposing refectory ta-
ble displaying wine and cheese, and the dark wood bar.
The soup of the day, simmering in an old black cauldron, is
a good way to start. Some entrées are exceptional. A wise
choice is the grilled, lightly seasoned lamb chops, or the
steak *sauvage*, marinated in white wine, thyme, sage,
rosemary, laurel, and garlic. Frogs' legs, and the tender
double entrecôte in a red-wine sauce flavored with shal-
lots, are also excellent. Crêpes suzette and rich chocolate
profiteroles are popular desserts. *1216 rue Bishop, tel.
514/861–6733. Casual dress. Reservations advised. AE,
D, MC, V. Closed weekend lunch.*

**★ ㉒ Moishe's Steak House.** Those who have business with the
**$$$** clothing concerns around boulevard St-Laurent, Mon-
tréal's "Main," which divides the city into east and west,
and visitors in the area will enjoy this institution, famous
among beef-lovers since 1938. The down-at-the-heels
storefront—and the restaurant's dirty white siding and
green plastic awnings—shouldn't put off first-time visitors. The pace is hectic, and the expert waiters busy and
often brusque, but the atmosphere is clubby and comfortable and the steaks are prime quality, particularly the
tender Red Brand filet mignon broiled over charcoal.

Other offerings include marinated shish kebab, mixed grill, lamb chops, and boiled beef. Deli mainstays uch as pickled herring, chopped liver, and fresh pickled salmon are also available as appetizers. *3961 blvd. St-Laurent, tel. 514/845–3509. Casual dress. AE, D, MC, V.*

## Vieux-Montréal

★ **26** **Chez Delmo.** This Vieux-Montréal restaurant, near the
**$$$$** Notre-Dame Basilica, has been an institution for fresh seafood since 1910. Delmo's offers communal lunch in the front room at two long, polished, wood bars for a crowd of individual diners and couples, and more private tables in the back dining room. A lunchtime favorite with the regular clientele of judges, lawyers, journalists, and actors is the seafood plate, offering crab, lobster, shrimp, and scallops on a bed of Boston lettuce. Curried-shrimp casserole with rice; and Dover sole belle meunière are also house specialties. Thanks to two experienced chefs, Luigi Bordi and Enja Bertoli, almost any selection is a good choice. The white house wine, a Muscadet, is available by the glass at the bar and is reasonably priced. However, the wine list includes a good selection of labels and can be expensive. For dessert, the crème caramel is exceptional. *211 rue Notre-Dame, tel. 514/849–4061. Casual dress. Reservations advised for dinner. AE, CB, D, MC, V. Closed Sun., two weeks in mid-summer, Christmas week.*

★ **29** **Les Filles du Roy.** Although it's been called corny, this res-
**$$$** taurant seems to please everyone from summertime tourists to busy executives. Named in honor of the women sent by Louis XIV to marry colonists in New France, the restaurant has cream-color wainscoting, casement windows, and fluffy curtains that frame a view of the Historic Quarter's cobblestoned rue Bonsecours. Today's "filles" wear 18th-century garb and are happy to describe typical Québécois fare featured at the luncheon buffet and dinner. The hearty platters are not for everyone, but the menu is balanced with such lighter dishes as salmon, fillet of sole, and chicken and veal dishes. The enormous Québec platter holds *tourtière* (meat pie), meatballs, sausage, and mashed potatoes in gravy. Other regional dishes include *cipaille St-Jean* (three-meat pie), and ham in maple syrup. Sweet sugar pie is another local favorite. There is an extensive wine list and a good house wine, Cuvée des Filles du Roy. *415 rue Bonsecours, tel. 514/849–3535. Jacket advised in evening. Reservations advised; required for opera evening. AE, CB, D, MC, V.*

**27** **La Sorosa.** Always busy with diners from nearby office
**$$** towers and the courthouse, this Italian restaurant in Vieux-Montréal is a barn of a place with exposed beams and brick walls adorned with collectibles that include an old-fashioned baby's sleigh and faded wedding photos. Sterno candles light the room and keep the pizzas hot, too. The quietest area is the mezzanine balcony overlooking rue Notre-Dame; by noon there is usually a line and most of these tables are taken. Salads, pastas, and *croques-monsieurs* are popular. The wine list favors Italian labels; red house wine, in half liters and smaller carafes, can be harsh but goes down well with the pizza. Service is often brusque. *56 rue Notre-Dame ouest, tel. 514/844–8595. Casual dress. AE, MC, V. Closed Sun.*

**㉘** **Le St-Amable.** Cozily ensconced in an 18th-century field-
$$$$ stone building off place Jacques Cartier, this is a splurge
even for visitors on an expense account. But everything
about the restaurant bolsters Montréal's reputation for
fine dining in artful surroundings. Thick exposed brick
walls give a sense of history to the upstairs dining room.
The intimate bar is lit by candles. Usually quiet, except
during the holiday season, the setting is an excellent background for a business lunch or dinner. Waiters are solici-
tous but never intrusive. Evening meals feature classics
for which the restaurant is known—breast of duckling in
cream sauce with red peppercorns and apples; and medallions of veal in sherry. The thick and flavorful chateaubri-
and—filet mignon with truffles for two—is just the dish
with which to seal a business agreement. The fare is
hearty and filling, but try to leave room for the desserts,
which range from millefeuilles to cherries jubilee. *188 rue
St-Amable, tel. 514/866–3471. Jacket advised. Reservations advised. AE, CB, D, MC, V. Closed weekend lunch.*

## FREE TIME

### Fitness

*Hotel Facilities*
The **Centre Sheraton** (tel. 514/878–2000) is the only hotel
health club open to nonguests; a Can$8 daily fee or special
weekly rates are available.

*Health Clubs*
The **YMCA** (1450 rue Stanley, across from Peel mètro, tel.
514/849–8393), downtown, is open to visitors for a Can$8
fee. The **YWCA** (1355 blvd. René-Lévesque ouest, tel. 514/
866–9941), downtown, is open to visitors for Can$6 week-
days, Can$4 weekends and holidays.

*Jogging*
**Mont Royal** is a favorite jogging route and offers challenging trails. Stairs at the top of rue Peel, rue Drummond,
and avenue du Musée lead to avenue Pine, across which
you jog to reach the main mountain path. Le Quatre
Saisons provides guests with maps of various park routes.
Another joggers' rendezvous is the **Vieux-Port** bicycle
path along the harbor.

### Shopping

**Le Rouet Métiers d'Art** craft stores (136 rue St-Paul,
Vieux-Montréal, tel. 514/875–2333, and 700 rue Ste-Catherine ouest, tel. 514/861–8401) are good bets for tasteful and reasonably priced Québec-made items such as
ceramics, hand-embroidered clothing, copper and enamel
jewelry, and wooden toys. Fine carvings, prints, and tapestries are available at the **Eskimo Art Gallery** (1434 rue
Sherbrooke ouest). **Henry Birks and Sons** (1240 Carré
Phillips, tel. 514/397–2510), a longtime Montréal firm at
square Phillips, is the place for jewelry, china, and silver.

The central shopping area extends from **Baie** department
store (585 rue Ste-Catherine ouest, tel. 514/281–4422), at
square Phillips, westward to **Ogilvy** department store
(1307 rue Ste-Catherine ouest, tel. 514/842–7711). Rue
Ste-Catherine cuts through this roughly 20-square-block
zone and is lined with boutiques and major stores. With

the exception of **Holt Renfrew** (1300 rue Sherbrooke ouest, tel. 514/842–5111), all department stores have Ste-Catherine addresses, as do a number of major complexes, like the **Eaton Centre** (677 rue Ste-Catherine ouest). If you don't have much time, the **Eaton** department store at the Centre is your best bet. Here you can find anything from Canadian souvenirs to Canadian furs. Other leading shopping complexes include the underground mall at **Place Ville-Marie, Place Bonaventure, Place Victoria, Complexe Guy-Favreau** (connected to the convention center), and **Complexe Desjardins.** Rue St-Denis eastward, and rue Crescent westward of blvd. St-Laurent are the two streets for trendy fashions. Rue Sherbrooke ouest, with which they both intersect, is lined with expensive designer salons, antiques shops, and art galleries. High-fashion shops for men include **Brisson & Brisson** (1472 rue Sherbrooke ouest, tel. 514/937–7456), **Giorgio de Montréal** (1176 rue Sherbrooke ouest, tel. 514/287–1928), and **Uomo Moda** (1452 rue Peel, tel. 514/844–1008). Among dozens of women's haute couture salons are **Bruestle** (1490 rue Sherbrook ouest), **Raffinati,** and **Valentino,** at Ogilvy; **Ralph Lauren** (1300 rue Sherbrooke ouest, tel. 514/284–3988, for men and children, too) next door to Holt Renfrew on rue Sherbrooke ouest, and **Ungaro** (1430 rue Sherbrooke ouest, tel. 514/844–8970).

## Diversions

**Montréal Harbour Cruises** (Victoria Pier at the Vieux-Port, tel. 514/842–3871) let you drift down the St-Lawrence on any one of six daily trips, including an evening cocktail-and-dinner cruise. Tickets are available at Info-Touriste on square Dorchester. Cruises run from May to October.

**The Montréal Museum of Fine Arts** (1379 rue Sherbrooke ouest, tel. 514/285–1600), the oldest in Canada (1861), holds a large collection of European and North American fine and decorative art. A massive expansion is underway across rue Sherbrooke.

**Mont Royal** offers a quick escape, particularly in fall, when Montréal maples burst into scarlet and orange. Jogging, biking, a restful lake, acres of rolling lawns, and wooded trails are all easily accessible via steps at the top of rues Drummond, Peel, and du Musée downtown.

**Murray Hill Tours** (1380 rue Barré, tel. 514/937–5311) gives a general overview of the city on a four-hour bus tour leaving from square Dorchester's InfoTouriste center and major hotels. Tickets are on sale at the hotels and the main departure point (1001 sq. Dorchester).

In summer drop by the **Ritz Garden** (Hôtel Ritz-Carlton, tel. 514/842–4212) for tea near the fluffy Brome ducklings, and relax amid the flowers and sculptures in Canada's most famous backyard.

A walk along **rue Sherbrooke** eastward to rue University, and west as far as rue Guy, introduces visitors to Montréal's "Square Mile," where wealthy families lived a century ago. The turreted limestone mansions look much as they did before the street became a center for museums, sculpture cafés, outdoor terraces, and intriguing art and antiques galleries.

Take a **sleigh ride** over Mont Royal and view the cityscape from the wooded mountaintop lookout. Bring your skates, or rent them at the chalet (tel. 514/653–0751) for a quick spin around Beaver Lake, to the accompaniment of the "Skater's Waltz."

**Vieux-Montréal** (Champ-de-Mars métro) is for browsers who want to stroll among historic greystone houses and stop off at a bistro or sidewalk café for a pick-me-up.

## Professional Sports

Hockey fans can see the **Canadiens** at the Forum (2313 rue Ste-Catherine ouest, tel. 514/932–2582). The baseball team, the **Expos,** plays in the Olympic Stadium (4545 av. Pierre-de-Coubertin, tel. 514/253–3434 for information); 514/253–0700 or 800/361–0658, in Québec and Ottawa, for tickets). **Supra de Montréal** play soccer in Centre Claude-Robillard (1000 rue Emile-Journault, tel. 514/739–6266).

## The Arts

The **Place des Arts** (PdA) complex (1501 rue Jeanne-Mance, tel. 514/842–2112) is the main center for the performing arts and home to the Montréal Symphony Orchestra, Les Grands Ballets Canadiens, and the Opéra de Montréal. The renovated **Théâtre Saint-Denis** (1594 rue St-Denis, tel. 514/849–4211) and the **Spectrum** (318 rue Ste-Catherine ouest, tel. 514/861–5851) are venues for musicals and jazz. Most drama is aimed at French-speaking audiences, but the **Centaur Théâtre** (453 rue St-Francoís-Xavier, tel. 514/288–3161) concentrates on English productions. The **Saidye Bronfman Centre** (5170 rue Côte-Ste-Catherine, tel. 514/739–2301) has had uneven success with English-language plays but highlights first-rate Yiddish (simultaneous-translation) drama twice a year.

Ticket agencies include **Ticketron** (sq. Phillips, tel. 514/277–2552, and Sears Store branches) and **Teletron** (tel. 514/288–2525).

## After Hours

*Bars and Lounges*
**Le Grand Prix,** in the Hôtel Ritz-Carlton (tel. 514/842–4212), is a sophisticated rendezvous for a drink with clients. **Moby Dick** (1188 rue Sherbrooke ouest, tel. 514/285–1637) is flush with young professionals at happy hour. In the lobby of the Hôtel Ramada Renaissance du Parc, **Puzzles** (tel. 514/288–6666) features jazz during the week and dancing cheek-to-cheek on Saturday. Hotel piano bars are usually good for a quiet business tête à tête. Try, among others, the Bonaventure Hilton's **Belvedere Bar** (tel. 514/878–2332); **L'Impromptu,** the lobby bar at Le Centre Sheraton (tel. 514/878–2000); Le Quatre Saisons' **L'Apero** (tel. 514/284–1110); the Manoir LeMoyne's **Bar Frédéric** (2100 De-Maisonneuve, tel. 514/931–8861); and Le Reine Elizabeth's **Les Voyageurs** (tel. 514/861–3511).

*Cabarets*
**Le Portage** (Bonaventure Hilton International, 1 pl. Bonaventure, tel. 514/878–2332) spotlights singers, jazz musicians, small combos, and occasionally a comedy act. **Le Caf' Conc'** (Le Château Champlain, pl. du Canada, tel. 514/878–9000) offers a can-can show and variety acts.

*Comedy Clubs*
Try the **Comedy Nest** (1459 rue Crescent, tel. 514/849–6378), one of the sites for the "Just for Laughs" festival. This annual summer festival (tel. 514/845–3155) is an international, multilingual celebration of comedy at various theaters around Montréal.

*Jazz Clubs*
Owner and bassist Charlie Biddle and a host of guest musicians play at **Biddle's** (2060 rue Aylmer, tel. 514/842–8656). Other possibilities include: **L'Air du Temps** (191 rue St-Paul ouest, tel. 514/842–2003) and **Le Grill Café** (183 rue St-Paul ouest, tel. 514/397–1044).

*For Singles*
**Thursday's/Les Beaux Jeudis** (Hôtel de la Montagne, 1430 de la Montagne, tel. 514/288–5656) stands out as the most popular singles meeting place in town. A couple of disco choices: **Metropolis** (59 rue Ste-Catherine est, tel. 514/288–5559), the biggest disco in town, is awash in high-tech lasers, throbbing music, and multiple dance floors. **L'Esprit** (1234 rue de la Montagne, tel. 514/397–1711) is another favorite of young singles.

# New Orleans

*by Honey Naylor*

New Orleans is among the top convention cities in the nation, and with good reason. In addition to turning out terrific food and red-hot music, the city has considerable experience in entertaining visitors—some 6 million annually.

During Mardi Gras, probably the nation's best-known festival, a million or so people throng to the Central Business District (called the CBD by the locals) and the nearby French Quarter, pumping millions of dollars into the economy. And the city has played host to professional football's Super Bowl more often than any other city: seven times, including 1990.

The Crescent City (so called because it was built within a great bend of the Mississippi River) was long dominated by the Creole culture, and the French influence is still apparent in the city's architecture and its place names.

New Orleans's role as the birthplace of jazz and its fabulous past as a trading center during the Western expansion contribute to the city's continuing reputation for glamour, elegance—and wickedness. But then again New Orleans is also a port city, vying with New York over the years for the position of top U.S. port.

Thirty-one percent of the region's manufacturing work force is employed in either shipbuilding or aerospace. Avondale Industries, one of the nation's leading Marine fabricators, is headquartered here, as is the Michoud NASA complex of Martin Marietta Manned Space Systems.

Like most Gulf cities, New Orleans suffered setbacks in the 1980s because of the drop in the price of oil. However, the Economic Development Council here reports a pattern of recovery that began in 1989. Moreover, oil and gas account for only about 25% of the city's economy; the other 75% is diversified, and includes industries such as financial services, wholesale trade, retail trade, and distribution and handling.

## Top Employers

| Employer | Type of Enterprise | Parent*/ Headquarters |
|---|---|---|
| **Avondale Ship-yards Inc.** | Ship builders | New Orleans |
| **Dillard's** | Department store | Little Rock, AR |
| **Martin Marietta Corporation** | Defense contractor | Baltimore |
| **National Super-markets Inc.** | Grocery chain | National Tea Co./ Rosemont, IL |
| **Ochsner Founda-tion Hospital and Clinic** | Medical treatment and research | Ochsner Founda-tion/New Orleans |
| **Schwegmann Bros. Giant Super Markets** | Grocery chain | New Orleans |
| **Shell Oil Company** | Petroleum | Houston |
| **South Central Bell Telephone Co.** | Communications | Birmingham, AL |
| **Tulane University** | Education | New Orleans |
| **Winn Dixie Stores, Inc.** | Grocery chain | Jacksonville, FL |

*if applicable

## ESSENTIAL INFORMATION

### Climate

In July and August the heat in New Orleans, aggravated by the humidity, can be unbearable, but the hotels are all air-conditioned. Mild winters rarely see temperatures drop below 40F. The temperate days of spring and fall average a pleasing 68–70F.

What follows are the average daily maximum and minimum temperatures for New Orleans.

| Jan. | 62F 17C<br>47   8 | Feb. | 65F 18C<br>50   10 | Mar. | 71F 22C<br>55   13 |
|---|---|---|---|---|---|
| **Apr.** | 77F 25C<br>61   16 | **May** | 83F 28C<br>68   20 | **June** | 88F 31C<br>74   23 |
| **July** | 90F 32C<br>76   24 | **Aug.** | 90F 32C<br>76   24 | **Sept.** | 86F 30C<br>73   23 |
| **Oct.** | 79F 26C<br>64   18 | **Nov.** | 70F 21C<br>55   13 | **Dec.** | 64F 18C<br>48   9 |

## Airports

**New Orleans International Airport** (a.k.a. Moisant Field, tel. 504/464–0831) is located in Kenner, 15 miles west of New Orleans. Private and corporate craft fly into **Lakefront Airport** (tel. 504/243–4010) in eastern New Orleans.

## Airport Business Facilities

**Mutual of Omaha Business Service Center** (second floor, next to Delta, tel. 504/465–9647) has fax machines, photocopying, secretarial services, Western Union, travel insurance, and cash advance.

## Airlines

Delta is the leading carrier here.

**American,** tel. 800/433–7300.
**Continental,** tel. 504/581–2965 or 800/525–0280.
**ComAir,** tel. 800/354–9822.
**Delta,** tel. 504/529–2431 or 800/221–1212.
**L'Express,** tel. 504/466–1295 or 800/344–1970.
**Midway,** tel. 800/621–5700.
**Northwest,** tel. 800/225–2525.
**Pan Am,** tel. 800/221–1111.
**Southwest,** tel. 504/523–5683 or 800/531–5601.
**TWA,** tel. 504/464–9393 or 800/221–2000.
**United,** tel. 800/241–6522.
**USAir,** tel. 504/469–6214 or 800/428–4322.

## Between the Airport and Downtown

*By Taxi*
The fastest way to get downtown is by taxi. The trip takes 20–30 minutes during nonpeak hours and 45 minutes during rush hours (7 AM–8:30 AM from the airport and 3:30 PM–6:30 PM from the city). Cost: $18 for up to three passengers; $6 for each additional passenger.

*By Van*
Airport Rhodes runs small vans to and from the airport round the clock. The vans leave the airport when they're loaded, and drop passengers off at hotels downtown. Your arrival time will depend entirely upon whether your hotel is the first or the last drop-off. Plan on at least 40 minutes. For your return trip to the airport, call 504/469–4555 to make a reservation. Cost: $7.

*By Bus*
The least expensive, but most time-consuming way to get to and from the airport is by bus. The **Louisiana Transit** system (tel. 504/737–9611) runs a bus every 10–12 minutes between the airport and Elks Place (corner of Tulane and Loyola in the Central Business District [CBD]). Buses run from 5:30 AM–5:40 PM; allow 45 minutes to an hour. Cost: $1.10.

## Car Rentals

The following companies have outlets at the airport as well as in the CBD. There are no drop-off charges if you pick up the car in the CBD and drop it off at the airport.

**Avis,** tel. 504/464–9511 or 800/331–1212.
**Budget,** tel. 504/467–2277 or 800/527–0700.

**Dollar,** tel. 504/468–3643 or 800/421–6868.
**Hertz,** tel. 504/468–3695 or 800/654–3131.
**Thrifty,** tel. 504/467–8796 or 800/367–2277.

## Emergencies

*Doctors*
Close to the CBD and the French Quarter, there are 24-hour emergency rooms at **Charity Hospital** (1532 Tulane Ave., tel. 504/468–2311) and the **Tulane University Medical Center** (220 Lasalle St., tel. 504/588–5711). Uptown, there is a 24-hour emergency room at **Touro Infirmary** (1401 Foucher St., tel. 504/897–8250).

*Dentists*
Contact the **New Orleans Dental Association** (3101 W. Napoleon St., Suite 119, Metairie, tel. 504/834–6449) or **Elk Place Dental Center** (144 Elk Pl., tel. 504/561–5771). For 24-hour dental emergency treatment: **Touro Emergency Dental Service** (1401 Foucher St., tel. 504/897–8250).

## Important Addresses and Numbers

**Audiovisual rentals.** Audio Visual Communications (210 Decatur St., French Quarter, tel. 504/522–9769), AVW Audio Visual (805 Convention Center Blvd., tel. 504/522–7937).

**Chamber of Commerce** (201 Camp St., tel. 504/527–6962).

**Computer rentals.** NYNEX (1515 Poydras St., tel. 504/524–6024).

**Convention and exhibition centers.** Louisiana Superdome (Sugar Bowl Drive, tel. 504/587–3663), New Orleans Convention Center (900 Convention Center Blvd., tel. 504/582–3000 or 800/521–NOCC), The Rivergate (No. 4 Canal St., tel. 504/592–2000).

**Fax services.** Convention Copy Center (807 Convention Center Blvd., tel. 504/524–2679), Kinko's Copies (762 St. Charles Ave., tel. 504/581–2541), Mule Durel (241 Dauphine St., French Quarter, tel. 504/529–7484).

**Formal-wear rentals.** Gentlemen's Quarter (232 Royal St., French Quarter, tel. 504/522–7139), Mitchell's Formal Wear (3442 St. Charles Ave., tel. 504/525–7636).

**Gift shops.** Chocolates: Godiva's Chocolatier (Canal Place, 333 Canal St., tel. 504/524–1175), Laura's Fudge & Praline Shop (600 Conti St., French Quarter, tel. 504/525–3880); Flowers: Eastside Westside Flowers (901 Convention Center Blvd., tel. 504/522–9747), French Quarter Florist (223 Dauphine St., French Quarter, tel. 504/523–5476); Gourmet foods: Creole Delicacies (533 St. Ann St., Jackson Sq., French Quarter, tel. 504/525–9508).

**Graphic design studios.** Design Partners (6901 Pritchard Place, tel. 504/866–8264), Tom Varisco Graphic Design (1925 Esplanade Ave., French Quarter, tel. 504/949–2888).

**Hairstylist.** Unisex: Lulu Buras (Canal Place, 333 Canal St., tel. 504/523–5858).

**Health and fitness clubs.** *See* Fitness, below.

**Information hot lines.** The 24-hour television Tourist Channel (channel 55), available in most hotels, provides information on weather, news, and local events and attractions.

**Limousine services.** A Touch of Class Transportation Service (tel. 504/522–7565 or 800/821–6352), London Livery (tel. 504/944–1984).

**Liquor stores.** Package liquor can be purchased 24 hours in drugstores or grocery stores: K&B (3401 St. Charles Ave., tel. 504/895–0344), Royal St. A&P (701 Royal St., tel. 504/523–1353), Vieux Carre Wine & Spirits (422 Chartres St., French Quarter, tel. 504/568–9463), Walgreen's (900 Canal St., tel. 504/523–7201).

**Mail delivery, overnight.** DHL Worldwide Express (tel. 504/733–9717), Federal Express (One Shell Sq., drop-off box in Canal Place, tel. 800/238–5355), TNT Skypak (tel. 504/767–1631), UPS (tel. 504/733–9717), U.S. Postal Service Express Mail (tel. 504/589–1012).

**Messenger services.** New Orleans Messenger Service (tel. 504/586–0036), United Cabs (tel. 504/522–9771).

**Office space rentals.** HQ Services & Offices (One Canal Pl., Suite 2300, tel. 504/525–1175), International Office Centers (Energy Centre, 1100 Poydras St., tel. 504/585–7333).

**Pharmacies, late-night.** Eckerd (3400 Canal St., tel. 504/488–6661), K&B (3100 Gentilly Blvd., tel. 504/947–6611), Walgreen's (900 Canal St., tel. 504/523–7201).

**Radio station, all-news.** WWL 87 AM.

**Secretarial services.** Executemps (1001 Howard Ave., tel. 504/581–3886), Kelly Services (1515 Poydras St., tel. 504/529–1451).

**Stationery supplies.** Dameron-Pierson Co. (400 Camp St., tel. 504/525–1203), Mule-Durel (241 Dauphine St., French Quarter, tel. 504/529–7464).

**Taxis.** United Cabs (tel. 504/522–9771), White Fleet (tel. 504/948–6605), Yellow-Checker (tel. 504/525–3311).

**Theater Tickets.** *See* the Arts, below.

**Train information.** Amtrak and Union Passenger Terminal (1001 Loyola Ave., tel. 800/872–7245).

**Travel agents.** American Express Travel Service (158 Baronne, tel. 504/586–8201), Thomas Cook Travel (201 St. Charles Ave., tel. 504/568–1964).

**Weather** (tel. 504/465–9212), Marine Recreational Forecast (tel. 504/465–9215).

## LODGING

The lion's share of the city's 27,000 hotel rooms are in the historic French Quarter and in the CBD. In the French Quarter, which is adjacent to the CBD, you can find accommodations in luxury hotels and quaint Creole guest houses. As this is a major convention city, most CBD hotels are typically high-rise, high-tech. The residential

Garden District, about a 10-minute drive from downtown, is home to one of the city's landmark hotels, the Pontchartrain.

As a result of inflated hotel rates during Super Bowl weekend and Mardi Gras, the New Orleans City Council has passed legislation requiring that rates be posted in rooms and filed with the city. Many hotels have a five-night minimum during special events, and some want payment in advance. It is wise to book well ahead of busy seasons, as much as a year in advance for Mardi Gras.

Most of the hotels listed below offer corporate rates and weekend discounts; inquire when making reservations.

Highly recommended lodgings in each price category are indicated by a star ★.

| Category | Cost* |
|---|---|
| $$$$ (Very Expensive) | over $120 |
| $$$ (Expensive) | $90–$120 |
| $$ (Moderate) | under $90 |

*All prices are for a standard double room, single occupancy, excluding 11% tax.*

*Numbers in the margin correspond to numbered hotel locations on the New Orleans Lodging and Dining maps.*

## Central Business District

**㉑**
$$$
**Doubletree.** Across the street from the chic Canal Place shops, and near the Riverwalk festival marketplace, the 17-story modern Doubletree occupies a prime site. The Convention Center is within walking distance. Built in 1971, this upscale chain hotel has a small, comfortable lobby graced with flower arrangements, Italian-marble floors, and Oriental rugs. Decor is country French and rooms have an open, airy feeling with matching pastel draperies and spreads and light-color furniture. Rooms with numbers ending in 05 are larger, and the eighth floor is nonsmoking. There are a restaurant, lounge, mezzanine bar, an outdoor pool, and—a nice touch—a self-service laundry for guests. *300 Canal St., 70140, tel. 504/581–1300 or 800/528–0444, fax 504/582–1300. Gen. manager, Pico Bevier. 363 rooms, 15 suites. AE, CB, DC, MC, V.*

**㉖**
$$$$
**Fairmont.** Awash with gold leaf, glittering chandeliers, and scarlet carpeting, this New Orleans landmark fits everybody's idea of a grand hotel. (Arthur Hailey took copious notes here for his novel *Hotel*.) Its three buildings occupy almost a full block, and the huge lobby runs the full length of the hotel. The rooms vary in size, but all are tastefully furnished with marble appointments. Spacious individually decorated suites are equipped for lavish entertaining. All baths are roomy. The Sazerac Bar (*see* After Hours, below) attracts local movers and shakers. Legend has it that Huey Long built Airline Highway to connect Baton Rouge with the Roosevelt Hotel, now the Fairmont. Eight U.S. presidents, from Coolidge to Ford, have stayed here. *University Pl., 70140, tel. 504/529–7111 or 800/527–4727, fax 504/522–2303. Gen. manager, Bernard Wohlschlaeger. 685 rooms, 50 suites. AE, CB, DC, MC, V.*

**⑰** **Hotel InterContinental.** This sleek, 14-story glass- and
$$$$ rose-granite hotel opened in 1984. High-tech features include teleconferencing via satellite, which can be received
through TV sets in individual guest rooms. The marble
lobby has indirect lighting and is adorned with modern
art. Large, sunny rooms decorated in pastel tones have
lighted cedar double closets. Baths are not very large, but
include vanity areas, mini-TVs, and phones. Spacious luxury suites come with marble foyers, Jacuzzis, full kitchens, and a maid's room. Guests include the NFL team
managers and owners. Nearby Lafayette Square, safe
during the day, should be avoided at night. *444 St. Charles
Ave., 70130, tel. 504/525–5566 or 800/332–4246, fax 504/
523–7310. Gen. manager, Michael Tourniaire. 467 rooms,
30 suites. AE, CB, DC, MC, V.*

**⑮** **Hyatt Regency Hotel.** A glass atrium connects the hotel,
$$$$ built in 1976, with the Superdome and the New Orleans
Centre shopping mall. Unfortunately, the multilevel public areas are complex and gloomy, despite fountains,
greenery, and the atrium. Corner rooms have two walls of
windows that give a sense of space; some offer a good view.
Lanai rooms face the pool and have a private patio or balcony. Special rooms for women travelers are larger and
close to the elevators. Of the 100 suites, 44 are conference
suites, with separate areas for meetings. The Superdome
area is safe during the day, but should be avoided at night
when there's no activity. *500 Poydras Plaza, 70140, tel.
504/561–1234 or 800/228–9000, fax 504/523–0488. Gen.
manager, Norm Howard. 1,196 rooms, 100 suites. AE,
CB, DC, MC, V.*

**★ ㉔** **Le Meridien Hotel.** Built in 1984, Air France's marble pal-
$$$$ ace is deluxe all the way from the lobby waterfall to the
Tower Suite's 30th-floor duplexes. Gleaming brass, bev-
eled glass, and vases of fresh flowers create contemporary
elegance. The large, well-lighted rooms are done in shades
of beige and have marble baths; deluxe, split-level corner
rooms offer the best views, as well as space for small meetings. Dixieland is played nightly in the lobby (*see* After
Hours, below). Oprah Winfrey is among the celebs who've
stayed here. The French restaurant, Henri (*see* Dining,
below) is excellent. *614 Canal St., 70130, tel. 504/525–
6500 or 800/543–4300, fax 504/525–8068. Gen. manager,
Louis Daniel. 497 rooms, 5 bilevel suites. AE, CB, DC,
MC, V.*

**㉕** **Marriott New Orleans.** The vast lobby of the Marriott is al-
$$$$ ways busy. This big convention hotel, which consists of
two towers, was built in 1973 and renovated in 1987. The
41-story River Tower boasts some spacious suites with wet
bars and entertainment/meeting facilities. Some suites
have bath phones. Decor is traditional, in shades of rose
and pink. The 21-story Quarter Tower's rooms have concierge service. Between the two towers is an outdoor pool
and a well-equipped health club. The Riverview restaurant has exceptional views, good food, and a Sunday jazz
brunch. *555 Canal St., 70140, tel. 504/581–1000 or 800/
228–9290, fax 504/581–5749. Gen. manager, Ray Warren.
1,275 rooms, 54 suites. AE, CB, DC, MC, V.*

**★ ⑲** **New Orleans Hilton Riverside & Towers.** Headquarters for
$$$ the 1988 Republican Convention and for President Bush
when he's in town, the Hilton is a splashy, vast complex

# NEW ORLEANS

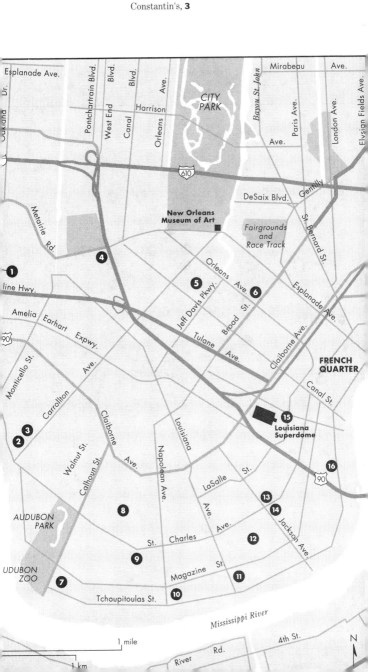

# NEW ORLEANS FRENCH QUARTER

**Lodging**
De La Poste Motor Hotel, **36**
Doubletree, **21**
Fairmont, **26**
Hotel Inter-Continental, **17**
Hotel Maison de Ville, **41**
Marriott New Orleans, **25**
Le Meridien Hotel, **24**
Monteleone, **30**
New Orleans Hilton Riverside & Towers, **19**

Omni Royal Orleans, **39**
Le Richelieu, **43**
Royal Sonesta, **35**
Sheraton New Orleans, **23**
Soniat House, **42**
Westin Canal Place, **22**
Windsor Court, **20**

**Dining**
Acme Oyster and Seafood House, **27**
Arnaud's, **33**
Bayona, **34**
Bon Ton Café, **18**

Brennan's, **37**
Galatoire's, **32**
Grill Room, **20**
Henri, **24**
Le Jardin, **22**
La Louisiane, **28**
Louis XVI, **31**
Mr. B's Bistro, **29**
Rib Room, **38**
Seb's, **40**

with several wings extending from a soaring atrium lobby that's always busy. Concierge services and in-room check-in/out are available in the high-rise Towers section, but the Riverside wing has the high-tech business center. Riverside rooms are large, decorated in French Provincial style with attractive wicker, and the view of the Mississippi is unmatched. The Rivercenter Racquet and Health Club is top-notch; facilities include an outdoor jogging path (*see* Fitness, below). Clarinetist Pete Fountain has had his nightclub in the hotel since it opened in 1977. *No. 2 Poydras St., 70140, tel. 504/561–0500 or 800/445–8667, fax 504/525–8636. Gen. manager, Paul Buckley. 1,602 rooms, 86 suites. AE, CB, DC, D, MC, V.*

**㉓** **Sheraton New Orleans.** This big, white high-rise chain ho-
**$$$** tel opened in 1982 on Canal Street, across from the French Quarter. Its large lobby boasts a broad expanse of glass, a sweeping spiral staircase, and jazz nightly. An extensive renovation program added a five-story conference center, two restaurants, and a health club. Rooms are done in contemporary style, with carpets and wall coverings of blue and mauve. Preferred rooms are on the Executive Level, which has a private lounge, concierge service, express check-in/out, turndown service, cushy robes, and TVs and phones in the bathrooms. *500 Canal St., 70130, tel. 504/ 525–2500 or 800/325–3535. Gen. manager, Robert Foster. 1,200 rooms, 84 suites. AE, CB, DC, MC, V.*

**㉒** **Westin Canal Place.** This 30-story luxury hotel was built in
**$$$$** 1984 over the Canal Place mall. Glass-and-brass elevators soar to the 11th-floor lobby, a cavernous space with pink Carrara marble, Oriental rugs, giant jardinieres, 19th-century furnishings, and a somewhat impersonal air; windows 26-feet high frame the great bend in the Mississippi and the neighboring French Quarter. Rooms are done in restful shades of peach, green, or rose, and have marble foyers, armoires, stocked minibars, and spacious marble baths. Artwork and antiques are used extensively throughout. Plush suites provide ample meeting space. All rooms benefit from a sophisticated phone system that includes call waiting. The 11th-floor Le Jardin restaurant (*see* Dining, below) offers excellent—and scenic—dining. *100 Iberville St., 70130, tel. 504/566–7006 or 800/228– 3000, fax 504/523–2549. Gen. manager, Ray Sylvester. 400 rooms, 35 suites. AE, MC, V.*

**★ ㉒** **Windsor Court.** This opulent, British-style hotel is a 23-
**$$$$** story structure of rose granite, opened in 1984. Scenes of Great Britain and portraits of the royal family adorn the lobby and guest quarters, all of which feel typically upper-class English, with Oriental rugs, fresh flowers, and period furnishings. Most accommodations are one- and two-bedroom suites with foyer, sitting room, and kitchen or wet bar, and afford ample room for small meetings and cocktail parties. Each has three telephones with two incoming lines and dataports for facsimiles or computers. Baths have marble vanities and oversize mirrors. You can have fine fare in the Grill Room (*see* Dining, below), take tea with scones and chamber music in Le Salon (*see* After Hours, below), the lobby lounge, and work off your excesses in a pool with an underwater sound system. The hotel has been host to such diverse personages as Dan Rather, Lee Iacocca, and the Lord Mayor of London. *300 Gravier St., 70140–1035, tel. 504/523–6000 or 800/262–*

# NEW ORLEANS HOTEL CHART

| HOTELS | Price Category | Business Services / Banquet capacity | No. of meeting rooms | Secretarial services | Audiovisual equipment | Teletype news service | Computer rentals | In-room modem phone jack | All-news cable channel | Desk | Desk lighting | Bed lighting |
|---|---|---|---|---|---|---|---|---|---|---|---|---|
| Airport Hilton | $$$ | 500 | 18 | ✓ | ✓ | - | ✓ | ✓ | ✓ | ● | ● | ● |
| De la Poste Motor Hotel | $$$ | 0 | 1 | - | ✓ | - | - | ✓ | ✓ | ● | ● | ◐ |
| Doubletree | $$$ | 600 | 15 | ✓ | ✓ | - | - | ✓ | ✓ | ● | ● | ● |
| Fairmont | $$$$ | 2800 | 20 | ✓ | ✓ | - | ✓ | - | ✓ | ● | ● | ◐ |
| Hilton Riverside and Towers | $$$ | 2500 | 38 | ✓ | ✓ | - | ✓ | ✓ | ✓ | ● | ● | ● |
| Hotel Maison de Ville | $$$$ | 25 | N/A | - | - | - | ✓ | - | ✓ | ● | ● | ● |
| Hyatt Regency | $$$$ | 2400 | 15 | ✓ | - | - | - | ✓ | ✓ | ● | ● | ● |
| InterContinental | $$$$ | 900 | 30 | ✓ | ✓ | - | ✓ | ✓ | ✓ | ● | ● | ◐ |
| Marriott | $$$$ | 0 | 36 | ✓ | ✓ | - | - | ✓ | ✓ | ● | ● | ● |
| Le Meridien | $$$$ | 1000 | 16 | ✓ | ✓ | - | ✓ | ✓ | ✓ | ● | ● | ● |
| Monteleone | $$$ | 500 | 16 | ✓ | ✓ | - | ✓ | ✓ | ✓ | ◐ | ◐ | ◐ |
| Omni Royal Orleans | $$$$ | 400 | 16 | ✓ | ✓ | - | - | ✓ | - | ● | ● | ● |
| Pontchartrain | $$$ | 300 | 5 | - | ✓ | - | ✓ | ✓ | ✓ | ● | ● | ● |
| Le Richelieu | $$ | 0 | 0 | ✓ | ✓ | - | - | - | - | ● | ● | ● |
| Royal Sonesta | $$$$ | 450 | 19 | ✓ | ✓ | - | - | ✓ | ✓ | ● | ● | ● |
| Sheraton | $$$ | 1980 | 34 | ✓ | ✓ | - | ✓ | - | ✓ | ● | ◐ | ◐ |
| Soniat House | $$$$ | 0 | 1 | ✓ | ✓ | - | - | ✓ | - | ● | ● | ● |
| Westin Canal Place | $$$$ | 0 | 0 | ✓ | ✓ | - | ✓ | ✓ | ✓ | ● | ● | ● |
| Windsor Court | $$$$ | 160 | 10 | ✓ | ✓ | - | ✓ | ✓ | ✓ | ● | ◐ | ● |

$$$$ = over $120, $$$ = $90-$120, $$ = under $90.
● good, ◐ fair, ○ poor.
All hotels listed here have photocopying and fax facilities.

| In-Room Amenities | | | | | | | | | | Hotel Amenities | | | | | | |
| Nonsmoking rooms | In-room checkout | Minibar | Pay movies | VCR/Movie rentals | Hairdryer | Toiletries | Room service | Laundry/Dry cleaning | Pressing | Concierge | Barber/Hairdresser | Garage | Courtesy airport transport | Sauna | Pool | Exercise room |
|---|---|---|---|---|---|---|---|---|---|---|---|---|---|---|---|---|
| ✓ | ✓ | ✓ | ✓ | - | - | ● | ◐ | ● | ● | ✓ | - | - | ✓ | - | ● | ● |
| ✓ | ✓ | ✓ | - | - | - | - | ◐ | ● | - | - | - | ✓ | - | - | ◐ | - |
| ✓ | ✓ | - | ✓ | - | - | ○ | ◐ | ● | ◐ | ✓ | - | - | - | - | ◐ | ● |
| ✓ | ✓ | - | ✓ | - | ✓ | ● | ● | ● | ● | ✓ | ✓ | ✓ | - | - | ● | - |
| ✓ | ✓ | ✓ | - | - | - | ● | ● | ● | ● | ✓ | - | ✓ | - | ✓ | ● | ● |
| - | ✓ | ✓ | - | ✓ | ✓ | ● | ◐ | ● | ● | ✓ | - | ✓ | - | - | ● | - |
| ✓ | ✓ | ✓ | ✓ | - | ✓ | ● | ● | ● | ● | ✓ | ✓ | ✓ | - | - | ● | - |
| ✓ | ✓ | ✓ | ✓ | - | ✓ | ● | ● | ● | ● | ✓ | ✓ | ✓ | ✓ | - | ◐ | - |
| ✓ | ✓ | - | ✓ | - | - | ◐ | ● | ● | ● | ✓ | - | ✓ | - | ✓ | ● | ● |
| ✓ | ✓ | ✓ | ✓ | - | - | ● | ● | ● | ● | ✓ | ✓ | ✓ | - | ✓ | ● | ● |
| ✓ | - | ✓ | ✓ | - | - | ◐ | ◐ | ● | ◐ | ✓ | ✓ | ✓ | - | ✓ | ● | ● |
| ✓ | ✓ | - | ✓ | - | - | ● | ● | ● | ● | ✓ | - | ✓ | - | - | ● | ● |
| - | - | ✓ | ✓ | - | - | ● | ● | ● | ● | - | - | ✓ | ✓ | - | - | - |
| ✓ | ✓ | ✓ | - | - | - | ◐ | ◐ | ● | ◐ | - | - | ✓ | ✓ | - | ● | - |
| ✓ | ✓ | ✓ | - | - | ✓ | ● | ◐ | ● | ● | ✓ | - | ✓ | - | - | - | ● |
| ✓ | ✓ | ✓ | ✓ | - | ✓ | ● | ● | ● | ● | ✓ | - | ✓ | - | ✓ | ● | ✓ |
| - | - | - | - | - | - | ● | ● | ● | ● | ✓ | - | ✓ | ✓ | - | - | - |
| ✓ | - | ✓ | ✓ | - | - | ● | ● | ● | ● | ✓ | ✓ | ✓ | - | - | ● | ● |
| ✓ | - | ✓ | - | ✓ | ✓ | ● | ● | ● | ● | ✓ | - | ✓ | - | ✓ | ● | ● |

**Room service:** ● 24-hour, ◐ 6AM-10PM, ○ other.
**Laundry/Dry cleaning:** ● same day, ◐ overnight, ○ other.
**Pressing:** ● immediate, ◐ same day, ○ other.

2662, fax 504/596-4513. Gen. manager, Jean Mestriner.
60 rooms, 250 suites. AE, CB, DC, MC, V.

## French Quarter

**㊱** **De la Poste Motor Hotel.** From the front, this upscale mo-
$$$ tel appears to be a plain, gray three-story building with
columns, dormer windows, and a driveway leading to a
small, ordinary lobby. But the building extends around a
spacious courtyard with trees, shrubs, a pool, and a re-
stored carriage house, which also has guest quarters.
Rooms and suites have mahogany furniture, with quilted
spreads and matching drapes. Desks are in a cramped foy-
er where there is little room to spread out. The suites are
large bed/sitting rooms with a sofa, coffee table, armoire,
and more desk space. Balcony rooms on the street are
noisy; the quieter carriage house suites have private pati-
os. Built in 1971, the motel is convenient to the CBD. *316
Chartres St., 70130, tel. 504/581-1200 or 800/448-4927.
Gen. manager, Lucian Cusimano. 92 rooms, 8 suites.
AE, CB, DC, MC, V.*

★ **㊶** **Hotel Maison de Ville.** An etched-glass door leads into the
$$$$ cozy lobby of this three-story European-style hotel. The
tiny rooms, done in 18th- and 19th-century antiques and
French country prints, are in a main house and attached
old slave quarters. Some rooms have four-posters; all have
small marble baths with brass fittings. Some units open
onto a charming courtyard where privacy can only be
achieved by keeping the curtains drawn. The main build-
ing can be noisy. However, the hotel's nearby, luxurious
Audubon Cottages are quiet and secluded; they have pri-
vate patios, kitchens, concierge service, and ample space
for meetings and entertaining. The complimentary Conti-
nental breakfast arrives in style on a silver tray with a
rose. *717 Toulouse St., 70130, tel. 504/561-5858 or 800/
634-1600, fax, same as switchboard. Gen. manager, John
Gioscia. 14 rooms, 2 suites, 7 cottages. AE, CB, DC,
MC, V.*

★ **㊸** **Le Richelieu.** Five 19th-century Greek Revival row houses
$$ make up this intimate hotel in a residential section of the
French Quarter. The small lobby has a black-and-white
tile floor and crystal chandelier. There's a pretty, plant-
filled courtyard and on-site parking. Individually decorated rooms have custom-made draperies, brass ceiling
fans, and oil paintings. Some have mirrored walls, huge
walk-in closets, minifridges or wet bars, and areas suitable for small meetings. The lavish, three-bedroom VIP
suite has cypress floors, Oriental rugs, marble bath, a
well-equipped kitchen, and a steam room. Chartres is one
of the safest streets in town; however, Decatur Street is
one block away, and this is not a good area in which to wan-
der alone at night. *1234 Chartres St., 70116, tel. 504/529-
2492 or 800/535-9653, fax 504/524-8179. Gen. manager,
Joanne Kirkpatrick. 69 rooms, 17 suites. AE, CB, DC,
MC, V.*

**㉚** **Monteleone.** The grande dame of French Quarter hotels
$$$ has been on the scene since 1886 and is operated by the
fourth generation of Monteleones. Paul Newman is one of
the many celebrities who've stayed in this prime location,
just two blocks from Canal Street and one block off Bour-
bon. Rooms here are extra large and luxurious—but not
all of the baths are equally large. Junior suites are spa-

cious combination bedrooms and sitting rooms; some have four-posters with mirrored canopies and tooled leather tables. Extra pampering is provided in the sumptuous VIP suites. There's a rooftop pool and lounge. The slowly revolving Carousel Bar in the lobby is a local landmark. *214 Royal St., 70140, tel. 504/523–3341 or 800/535–9595, fax 504/528–1019. Gen. manager, Howard Goodman. 600 rooms, 35 suites. AE, CB, DC, MC, V.*

**③⑨** **Omni Royal Orleans.** A five-story light-gray building with
$$$$ black wrought-iron balconies, this elegant hotel was built in 1960, and is said to be an exact replica of the grand St. Louis Hotel of the 1800s. Its lobby is adorned with white marble, gilt mirrors, Oriental rugs, statuary, and huge chandeliers. Rooms, though not exceptionally large, are well appointed with marble baths (phone in each), dressers, and tabletops. One-, two-, and three-bedroom suites are individually decorated; some have draped canopy beds, velvet chairs, floral wallpaper, French Provincial dining-room furnishings, and huge baths done in bold colors, with Jacuzzi and sauna. Local politicos do a lot of power-lunching in the Rib Room (*see* Dining, below); many meet for drinks in the Esplanade Lounge (*see* After Hours, below). *621 St. Louis St., tel. 504/529–5333 or 800/ 843–6664, fax 504/529–7089. Gen. manager, Ronald Pincus. 335 rooms, 16 suites. AE, CB, DC, MC, V.*

**③⑤** **Royal Sonesta.** Awnings and iron balconies adorn this sev-
$$$$ en-story luxury hotel, built in 1969, which occupies a city block. A fountain is the centerpiece of the spacious marble lobby, which has a country French feel. Small dormer rooms decorated in light colors have sloped ceilings, window seats, desks, and reading areas. Balcony rooms/suites facing Bourbon Street can be very noisy. Suites come in a variety of sizes and shapes, including split-level. Some suites have oriental rugs, Jacuzzi, and French doors that open onto a large balcony. Larger suites have canopy beds; all have baths with phone extensions. The Tower concierge level offers extra perks. *300 Bourbon St., 70140, tel. 504/586–0300 or 800/343–7170, fax 504/586–0126. Gen. manager, Hans Wandfluh. 468 rooms, 32 suites. AE, CB, DC, MC, V.*

**★ ④②** **Soniat House.** Two restored 1830s town houses with
$$$$ wrought-iron balconies make up this small, charming hotel. Staying here is like visiting an antiques-filled private home. Empire chairs grace the small drawing room; an honor bar is in the brick courtyard. No two rooms are alike; most have four-poster or canopied beds. Second-floor rooms require a steep climb. A private, key-access elevator leads to the two rooms in the renovated attic: No. 30 has a skylight, a high-vaulted ceiling, and the ambience of a hunting lodge, with heavy tan leather chairs, zebra-striped pillows, and a table that seats 12. Many rooms and suites have Jacuzzis; all have huge marble baths with phones. *1133 Chartres St., 70115, tel. 504/522–0570 or 800/ 544–8808, fax 504/522–7208. Gen. manager, Rodney Smith. 17 rooms, 6 suites. AE, MC, V.*

## Garden District

**★ ⑬** **Pontchartrain Hotel.** This New Orleans landmark, built in
$$$ 1927, is subdued elegance all the way. Although it offers no pool, gift shop, or separate VIP section, this elegant hotel does provide personal attention to each guest. Each

unit is decorated individually with a mix of antique and contemporary furnishings. There are large, sumptuous suites with full kitchens and four-poster beds; one suite has a solarium, another a grand piano. But there are also small, dark "pensions," and not all units have full baths—some only offer shower stalls. The guest register at times lists William Bennett and Tom Brokaw. The Bayou Bar (*see* After Hours, below) is a good place for drinks with associates. A courtesy limousine takes guests to the CBD and the French Quarter. While St. Charles Avenue is safe, the surrounding areas are not. This is not a neighborhood to explore after dark. *2031 St. Charles Ave., 70140, tel. 504/524–0581 or 800/777–1700, fax 504/529–1165. Gen. manager, Tom Gaskill. 65 rooms, 35 suites. AE, CB, DC, MC, V.*

## Airport

❶ **New Orleans Airport Hilton & Conference Center.** This
$$$ soundproof property opened in 1989 across from the airport. A six-story high-tech building of pink stone that surrounds a courtyard, it has a broad marble lobby with huge windows, ultramodern chairs, and muted pastel colors. Rooms are almost identical, with wicker chairs, two phones, double closets with mirrored panels, and contemporary furnishings in light or dark woods. Not all rooms have desks, and none has a separate dressing area; baths are average size. Complimentary Continental breakfast and other perks are available on the Executive Level. Former President Reagan was a guest in 1990. *901 Airline Hwy., 70062, tel. 504/469–5000 or 800/445–8667, fax 504/466–5473. Gen. manager, David Villarrubia. 313 rooms, 2 suites. AE, CB, DC, MC, V.*

# DINING

*by Gene Bourg*

Newcomers to south Louisiana food are often struck by its innovative variations. With a few well-chosen meals in equally well-chosen restaurants, they learn that the Creole and Cajun are slightly differing aspects of a singular cuisine, as original and multifaceted as the French, Italian, or Chinese. The definitive New Orleans meal is a true hybrid, the end product of 200 years of improvisation and fine tuning. The foundation was laid by the French, Spanish, and African settlers, with help from the local Indians. Later influences came from almost every culture that found its way up the Mississippi River to the swampy town. Over the decades, West Indians, Germans, Sicilians, and even Yugoslavs added to the melting pot. The creativity is now accelerating with a new generation of resident chefs adding lightness and delicacy to the heavier, spicier traditions. Today's distinctive New Orleans gastronomy offers something for every species of eater, from the die-hard fan of buttery sauces to the seeker of surprises in a sophisticated, contemporary mode. The list that follows describes a representative sampling—including both the culinary landmarks of New Orleans and some less renowned, but equally worthy, in the Central Business District, the French Quarter, and a bit farther afield. Though this is not a hard-and-fast rule, you'll find most of the old-line Creole restaurants in the French Quarter, hotel dining rooms in the CBD, and the trendier eateries uptown. Most are fine for small-scale business entertaining, some for large groups as well. Several restaurants are earmarked for after-hours exploring, when time is not a factor, but tasting the pleasures of New Orleans' distinctive cuisine is.

Highly recommended restaurants in each price category are indicated by a star ★.

| Category | Cost* |
|----------|-------|
| *$$$$* (Very Expensive) | over $35 |
| *$$$* (Expensive) | $26–$35 |
| *$$* (Moderate) | $15–$25 |
| *$* (Inexpensive) | under $15 |

*All prices are per person, including appetizer, entrée, and dessert, but excluding drinks, service, and a 9% meal tax.*

*Numbers in the margin correspond to numbered restaurant locations on the New Orleans Lodging and Dining maps.*

## Business Breakfasts

No restaurant matches the range of the superb **Grill Room's** (300 Gravier St., tel. 504/522–1992) breakfast dishes—from broiled Aberdeen kippers to eggs *en cocotte* with goose liver. The city's best Continental breakfasts are served in the charming and casual **Croissant d'Or** (617 Ursulines St., tel. 504/524–4663), either inside or alfresco in the pretty courtyard. The day's first meal can be memorable when the view from the dining room is equally memorable: At **Brennan's** (417 Royal St., tel. 504/525–9711), the traditional poached-egg dishes, stacked with spinach, artichoke bottoms, or fried fish, are paired with a beautifully planted patio. Tables at **Louis XVI** (730 Bienville St., tel. 504/581–7000), which serves traditional Creole and American breakfasts, overlook a courtyard. The Westin Canal Place's **Le Jardin** (tel. 504/566–7006), perched above the Mississippi River in the French Quarter, offers a sweeping variety of breakfast foods and a fixed-price Sunday jazz brunch. The **Rib Room** in the Omni Royale Orleans (tel. 504/529–7045) affords a sidewalk-level look at the Quarter's busiest corner.

## Central Business District

**❶❽** **Bon Ton Café.** Long before all the blackening and jalapeño *$$$* hoopla, this unaffected and comfortable bistro was serving creditably done food with strong connections to Louisiana's Cajun country. If the crawfish etouffée and bisque are a bit old-fashioned, they're also hearty and sanely seasoned. The oyster omelet is one favorite of the legion of businesspeople who pack the dining room at midday. The turtle soup, seafood gumbo, and crawfish jambalaya carry gilt-edged Louisiana birth certificates. The warm, very sweet bread pudding fits right in with the waitresses' amiability. An open-but-cozy bar sits at the rear of the single large dining room, lined in brick and done up in attractive, nostalgic fashion—duck prints, potted azaleas, wrought-iron chandeliers. *401 Magazine St., tel. 504/524–3386. Jacket required for dinner. Reservations advised. AE, MC, V. Closed Sat. and Sun.*

★ **⓰ Emeril's.** The hard-edged, high-tech look of this young
$$$ restaurant fits right in with the atmosphere of New Orleans' trendy Warehouse District. And Emeril's is where you'll find some of the city's most innovative local cooking. Boldness and energy are the trademarks of chef Emeril Lagasse's food, Creole in spirit but charged with a contemporary American vigor. Oyster cakes are lavished with a satiny, heartily seasoned ragout of more oysters. Sautéed crawfish tails embellish a peppery jambalaya of seafood and sausage. Black Louisiana caviar is served with a crisp-edged corn crêpe and sour cream. And roasted quail arrives stuffed with wild mushrooms and andouille sausage in a port sauce. Prominent among the many elaborate desserts are the knockout banana cream pie and the chocolate-pecan terrine. The carefully chosen wines include a good number from very small but high-quality California producers. A huge abstract-expressionist oil sets the mood, along with bare wood floors, exposed brick, and lots of glass and metal. This restaurant has become so popular that it's often too noisy for any serious business discussions. *800 Tchoupitoulas St., tel. 504/ 528–9393. Informal dress. AE, CB, DC, MC, V.*

★ **⓴ The Grill Room.** An island of upper-class English-style
$$$$ luxury, this restaurant sets the standard with lavish appointments, not the least of which are the large canvases depicting the British aristocracy during the Edwardian era. Body-hugging banquettes alternate with cushy oak armchairs. Heavy damask, bronze, and crystal appear in every niche. No request is taken lightly by the polished service staff, and the voluminous wine list is excellent. The food usually is, too. Menus change daily, and cover a wide range of styles. The bill of fare at lunch and dinner can range from oysters baked under a béchamel sauce spiced with horseradish and Parmesan, to cold smoked partridge with lobster and herbed goat cheese. There's also a fine chocolate-hazelnut mousse. The day's fish might be sardines from Brittany or Dover sole. *Windsor Court Hotel, 300 Gravier St., tel. 504/522–1992. Jacket required for dinner; tie optional. Reservations advised. AE, CB, DC, MC, V.*

★ **㉔ Henri.** Refinement pervades this luxurious French res-
$$$$ taurant, by far the city's leading source of French haute cuisine in the contemporary mode. Chef Marc Haeberlin of Alsace's star-studded Auberge de l'Ill composes the regular menus and comes to town twice a year to introduce new dishes. Among the permanent menu fixtures are his soufflé of poached salmon under a creamy, yet feather-light seafood mousse; braised venison fillets in wild mushrooms with Alsatian cheese noodles; and a cream of cauliflower soup with nuggets of puff pastry filled with caviar. A typical dessert is dark cherries submerged in cinnamon ice cream. Deep green is the dominant color in the multilevel complex of rooms, lined in brass accents. Small mural panels whimsically depict formal garden scenes. Service is dependably correct, and the sommelier is on hand to elaborate on the very serviceable list of wines. *Hotel le*

*Meridien, 614 Canal St., tel. 504/527-6708. Jacket required. Reservations advised. AE, CB, DC, MC, V. Closed Sun., lunch Sat.*

㉒ **Le Jardin.** At sunrise or dusk, the sweeping, 11th-floor
$$$ view of the Mississippi is breathtaking in this lavish hotel dining room. Any sound bouncing off the immense glass wall is muffled by the thickest carpeting and upholstery in town. Pale-wood veneers and beiges make up the soothing color scheme. Seafood takes center stage, and cream is what usually holds it all together. The gratinée of crabmeat and avocado scores high, along with pan-seared shrimp and scallops in a peppery and lemony butter sauce. Soups lean toward the hearty, and meats are of excellent quality. Chocolate addicts have several good choices on the dessert list. Wines and service are adequate, if not exceptional. *Atop the Westin Canal Place Hotel, 100 Bienville St., tel. 504/566-7006. Jacket advised at dinner. Reservations accepted. AE, CB, DC, MC, V.*

## French Quarter

㉗ **Acme Oyster and Seafood House.** Laid-back and unpreten-
$ tious, the Acme is fine for a quick refueling at midday or early evening. Dew-fresh, plump raw oysters are shucked at an always-crowded counter as they're ordered. Po-boy sandwiches are competently composed with fresh and crusty French bread and good fried shrimp, oysters, or lean roast beef in a thick and dark gravy. Other food is of the blue-plate-special species, New Orleans–style. Red beans and rice are creamy and well seasoned with sausage. Beer signs and the like are the major decorative elements in the dim and cavernous dining room. Table service is optional and anything but formal. *724 Iberville St., tel. 504/522-5973. Casual dress. No reservations. AE, MC, V. Closes 8 PM.*

㉝ **Arnaud's.** Both the cuisine and the atmosphere in this glit-
$$$$ tery old French Quarter establishment are classic Creole. In the lofty, early-19th-century main dining room, tuxedoed waiters scurry along the patterned ceramic floor tiles while the flames from café brûlot reflect against a huge expanse of etched, leaded glass. Inside the two-story labyrinth are other dining and banqueting rooms and bars, all soft-edged and elegant. Some of the old standbys are the shrimp rémoulade Arnaud, creamy oyster stew, sautéed fish with crab or crawfish toppings, and crème brûlée. The more elaborate desserts include flambéed crêpes prepared tableside. On busy weekends, the service deteriorates. If conversation is important, ask for a table in the quieter mezzanine. Private rooms for business dinners are a specialty here. *813 Bienville St., tel. 504/523-5433. Jacket required at dinner. Reservations required. AE, MC, V.*

★ ㉞ **Bayona.** A refreshing sense of adventure marks the food
$$$ in this sophisticated, contemporary restaurant in the French Quarter. Chef Susan Spicer's admirable culinary style blends Mediterranean, country French, Latin, and Asian sensibilities. On the plate, this usually means such clever concoctions as grilled quail with sage polenta and red wine sauce, sautéed rabbit tenderloin with artichokes and orange, and grilled shrimp with black-bean cake and coriander sauce. Fish dishes are offbeat, too, as in pan-

roasted salmon with sauerkraut and *gewurtztraminer* (spicey white wine) sauce. Wine choices are limited, but every bottle has been chosen with the menu in mind, and the price range is good. Traditional and modern decorative elements are combined inside the cozy, early 19th-century cottage. Mistily surreal photographs line the walls of the main room, brightened with bursts of flowers. In pleasant weather, cocktails are served in the pretty courtyard at the rear. *430 Dauphine St., tel. 504/525–4455. Jacket preferred at dinner. AE, DC, MC, V.*

**㊲ Brennan's.** A stem-to-stern redecoration has put lots of
**$$$$** new sparkle into this legendary Royal Street fixture. The menus have been reworked, too, although the original lavish Creole breakfasts and classic dinners remain. The second-floor rooms, done in the softly elegant style of 19th-century New Orleans, are the prettiest and cushiest of any old-line Creole restaurant. Tables on the rear balcony offer views of the quintessential New Orleans courtyard, shaded by trees and tropical flora. Hollandaise, meunière, marchand de vin and béarnaise sauces, ladled onto exceptionally fresh fish and top-quality meats, are menu staples. The headliners are the seafood gumbo and oysters Rockefeller, which are unbeatable. Flambéed bananas Foster was born here, and the inch-thick wine list is awesome. Note that the typical, all-inclusive cost of breakfast is on a par with what you'd expect to pay for a complete, very expensive dinner at most restaurants. *417 Royal St., tel. 504/525–9711. Jacket advised for dinner; no jeans. Reservations strongly advised. AE, DC, MC, V.*

**★ ㉜ Galatoire's.** Galatoire's remains the paragon of the turn-
**$$** of-the-century Creole-French bistro. In bentwood chairs around starched linen cloths, seersuckered locals down the definitive Creole shrimp rémoulade, bouillabaisse, two-fisted veal chops in béarnaise sauce, and golden lyonnaise potatoes. Light from the polished brass fixtures overhead bounces against the wide ribbon of wall mirrors, topped with a phalanx of brass coat hooks. The closeness of the tables adds to the festive air, but does not make this a good place to come for confidential conversation. The no-reservations policy means that at peak hours there may be a half-hour wait in the humidity outside. Still, for lovers of solid, traditional Creole cooking, Galatoire's is indispensable. Seafood dishes are the kitchen's strengths, but beefsteak in bordelaise has its charms, too. The tuxedoed, veteran waiters wield considerable power. The best strategy is to be assertive and demand to know the day's freshest fish or shellfish. *209 Bourbon St., tel. 504/525–2021. Jacket required for dinner; no jeans or shorts at lunch. No reservations. No credit cards. Closed Mon.*

**㉘ La Louisiane.** Embossed wall coverings, inch-thick car-
**$$$** pets, huge vases of silk flowers, and crystal prisms inhabit this dependable standby—a series of plush dining rooms in a town house that's functioned as a restaurant since 1881. A taste of the traditional Italian often pops up on a menu that otherwise toes the classic Creole line. Pasta dishes—carbonara, primavera, Alfredo, and pesto—blaze no new trails. Baked oysters are deservedly a hit. So is the sautéed shrimp Mavis, in a subtly seasoned cream sauce. The ambitious kitchen also produces a good selection of elaborately sauced trout dishes and a sterling white veal chop blanketed in cream. The brandy sauce on the hot

bread pudding is definitively super-sweet. The respectable wine list contains a few offbeat but good Italian labels. Experienced waiters perform efficiently. *725 Iberville St., tel. 504/523–4664. Jacket advised for dinner. Reservations advised, especially on weekends. AE, CB, DC, MC, V. Closed Sun., lunch Sat.*

**③① Louis XVI.** Two handsomely decorated dining rooms and
$$$$ an elegant bar border one of the French Quarter's prettiest courtyards. The plush decor includes lavender walls, mirrors bordered in black lacquer and brass, and old prints. The menu is mostly classical French with several nods to upscale Creole cuisine. Creole dishes (shrimp or crab rémoulade, baked oysters Rockefeller, turtle soup) are competently done, but the richly sauced Gallic ones are better. Bits of oyster appear in a fine velouté, a smooth heavy-cream sauce, with aromatic vegetables. A classic Madeira sauce overflows from puff pastry filled with silky-textured sweetbreads. Provençal influences show up in a fine rack of lamb. The dessert list offers a profusion of mousses, sorbets, Chantilly cream, chocolate, and fresh fruit. The mostly French wine list is appealing. Executive dinner meetings are expertly handled. *St. Louis Hotel, 730 Bienville St., tel. 504/581–7000. Jacket required in main dining rooms. Reservations strongly advised on weekends. AE, CB, DC, MC, V. Breakfast and dinner only.*

**★ ②⑨ Mr. B's Bistro.** The bustle rarely lets up in this sophisti-
$$$ cated contemporary bistro, usually filled and always festive. The dining room's large size is scaled down excellently with partitions of dark wood and etched glass. Lacy café curtains are the backdrop for green vinyl banquettes lining the walls. The real center of activity is a large grill fueled with aromatic woods. From it come expertly prepared fish, shellfish, and meats. Spicy, New Orleans–style barbecued shrimp is a good bet, as are the fish beignets and pasta jambalaya, a clever mix of shrimp, andouille sausage, duck, and chicken in a deep-flavored sauce on spinach fettuccine. Bread pudding, in a warm Irish-whiskey sauce, is a stand-out. Daily specials can be as satisfying as they are creative, and the wine cellar boasts one of the city's best collections from California. Service is knowledgeable and well organized. *201 Royal St., tel. 504/523–2078. Casual dress. Reservations required. AE, CB, DC, MC, V.*

**③⑧ Rib Room.** Its comfortable elegance and consistently good
$$$$ food have made this hotel dining room a lunchtime favorite of local business types for years. The lofty room's size is reduced by warm brick-and-maroon tones and such decorative touches as antique lanterns and other nostalgic memorabilia. Large windows along Royal Street provide fine views of the Quarter. Top-quality beef, game birds, and lamb from the central rotisserie and grill are a big draw. So are the seafood dishes, led by such winners as pompano in herbed lemon butter, and giant spit-roasted shrimp. Roast prime rib of beef au jus with potatoes and Yorkshire pudding is the house specialty, and it's consistently satisfying. The dessert cart is filled with the usual hotel-style abundance of pastries. Daily lunch specials usually feature local favorites such as red beans and rice with sausage, and pasta salads with seafood. *Omni Royal Orleans Hotel, 621 St. Louis St., tel. 504/529–7045. Jacket*

*required. Reservations advised for dinner. AE, CB, DC, MC, V.*

**40** **Seb's.** The French Quarter's best river views are at Seb's,
$$$ in the window-lined dining room or on one of the terraces. The kitchen's clever improvisations on the Creole theme can be almost as impressive. The split-level interior's angular, neomodern look is softened considerably by thick carpets and cushy chairs, as well as stylized wall sculptures of catfish, a creature that rarely shows up on the menu. What often does is competently grilled amberjack, mahi-mahi, or other gulf fish, fresh lumps of backfin crab in a spicy mayonnaise, and pasta salads with seafood. Meat dishes are reliably good as well. Creole favorites take over at lunchtime, in the form of seafood gumbo, red beans and rice, and nicely done po-boy sandwiches. The Sunday jazz brunch centers on the familiar roster of New Orleans–style poached eggs in rich butter sauces with ham, fried oysters, and other supplements. Service is conscientious, and the wine list shows some thought. *Jackson Brewery Millhouse, 5th level, 600 Decatur St., tel. 504/ 522–1696. Casual dress for lunch; jacket advised for dinner. Reservations advised. AE, MC, V.*

## Mid-City

**4** **Bayou Ridge Café.** Its out-of-the-way location makes Bay-
$$$ ou Ridge rather undesirable for business meals. But, if time is not a factor, it's a solid recommendation for seekers of food that match deep New Orleans flavors with contemporary lightness. From a stone, wood-burning oven come terrific baked fish in innovative sauces and some interesting pizzas. Pasta dishes, especially the fried oysters saltimbocca (served on penne in meunière sauce), are consistent winners. Desserts, especially the unsurpassed crème brûlée, are exceptional, too. The sleek and neat environment is brightened with boldly colored art work and large windows. Service is brisk and intelligent. Good, reasonably priced wines, domestic and foreign, populate the moderate list. *Pontchartrain Blvd. (enter from Metairie Rd.), tel. 504/486–0788. Casual dress. Reservations accepted. AE, CB, DC, MC, V.*

**5** **Christian's.** Few of those who regularly fill this cavernous
$$$ dining room, carved out of a medium-size, wooden church, come for the dishes tagged low-cholesterol. The more likely motivation is the crunchy soft-shell crab or the nicely textured fish drenched in a cream sauce dotted with green peppercorns. The filet Mignon stuffed with oysters and brushed with a rich demi-glaze sauce is another favorite on the extensive French-Creole menu. The loftiness of the vaulted ceiling is partly obscured by suspended plants and lights. Banquettes line the walls under the stained glass that's framed in dark wood. On busy nights, even reserved tables often require a 10- or 15-minute wait in a ridiculously small bar. Wines are well chosen and sensibly marked up. Waiters tend to rush the meal unless they're forewarned that you're not on your way to the airport. *3835 Iberville St., tel. 504/482–4924. Jacket advised. Reservations required. AE, MC, V. Closed Sun. and for lunch.*

**6** **Ruth's Chris Steak House.** The standard-setter among
$$$$ New Orleans steak houses operates on the principle that a market still exists for aged, U.S. prime beefsteak, charbroiled in slabs and served sizzling in seasoned butter. At

the Broad Street location, local politicians huddle over 18-ounce New York strips and ribeyes in the large, carpeted dining room, adorned with serene landscapes and still lifes in gilded frames. If the group can handle it, there's a huge porterhouse for four, soft-textured and full of flavor. The filet Mignon is as tall as it is wide. The potato options are wide, ranging from fries in several thicknesses to lyonnaise and au gratin. Shunners of beef are courted with thick, top-quality chops of pork and white veal or fresh steamed lobsters and a few other seafoods. Dessert headliners are cheesecakes and bread pudding. The veteran staff of fleet-footed waitresses keeps things moving. *Two locations: 711 N. Broad St., Mid-City, tel. 504/486–0810; 3633 Veterans Blvd., Metairie, tel. 504/888–3600. Casual dress. Reservations advised, especially on weekends. AE, CB, DC, MC, V.*

## Uptown

★ **②** **Brigtsen's.** Grace and earthiness meet in chef Frank
$$$ Brigtsen's cooking, a fusion of the Creole, Cajun, and contemporary American styles. His cream of oysters Rockefeller soup is a masterpiece worthy of his mentor, Paul Prudhomme. The daily changing menu might include admirably sautéed rabbit livers, dusted with sesame flour and moistened with a port sauce and caramelized onions; or a fillet of broiled amberjack, encased in a crawfish croustade and sauced with a lemon mousseline. Among the night's simpler desserts might be the fresh banana ice cream, worth every calorie. The setting is a small Victorian frame cottage, with three off-white rooms, minimally decorated but reasonably comfortable (although table spacing is too close for private talks). Service is informal, and the wine list is modest but imaginative. *723 Dante St., tel. 504/861–7610. Casual dress; no jeans or cutoffs. Reservations required (call a week or more in advance). AE, MC, V. Closed Sun., Mon., and for lunch.*

**⑩** **Casamento's.** What looks like the world's cleanest public
$ shower is actually uptown New Orleans's premier purveyor of down-to-earth seafoods. The spotless oyster bar with tables up front and the small dining room behind it are encased in glistening white wall and floor tiles almost dating back to the restaurant's 1919 founding. Only a few manicured house plants and odd, nostalgic artifacts interrupt the pristine expanse. Blue-ribbon oysters are served freshly shucked on the half shell or fried and placed on special loaves of white bread. The oyster stew features gently poached ones in milk with a sprinkle of green seasonings. The fried shrimp and trout match the oysters' quality. Shunners of seafood have to make do with an egg, ham, or cheese sandwich, or the old-fashioned spaghetti. Don't expect coddling at the clothless tables. *4330 Magazine St., tel. 504/895–9761. Casual dress. No reservations. No credit cards. Closed Mon. and early June–late Aug.*

**❼** **Clancy's.** No one is distracted by the decor in this popular
$$$ gathering place for upscale, uptown couples. White walls, ceiling fans, and a band of mirrors above the gray wainscoting are about all there is. The draw instead is a menu of updated Creole dishes marked by a good balance between richness and restraint. If the smoked shrimp with honey-mustard is a disappointment, there are bracingly

good chunks of mildly spicy rabbit sausage in a compatible puff-pastry, or a coquille of crawfish tails in a peppery cream sauce under mozzarella. The clinker ratio in entrées is usually very low. Sautéed trout with pecans is light and crisp, and filet Mignon in Madeira sauce is close to flawless. The fine dessert pies include a towering wedge of peppermint ice cream under a frothy meringue. The moderate-size wine list shows more thought than the rough-edged table service. *6100 Annunciation St., tel. 504/895–1111. Casual dress. Reservations advised. AE, MC, V. closed Sun., lunch Sat.–Tues.*

★ ⑫ **Commander's Palace.** To many locals, Commander's is the
$$$$ quintessential New Orleans restaurant—colorful, elegant, and many-faceted. The moods inside this large, 19th-century Garden District mansion vary from understated refinement in the main room to the spectacle of the upstairs Garden Room, with sweeping views of graceful oaks through two glass walls. In good weather, the leafy courtyard is the place for the celebrated jazz brunch. The ambitious menu covers all the bases. Any roster of the Commander's classics would include oysters Trufant, poached in lightly seasoned cream and crowned with Oregon caviar; crabmeat cakes with oyster sauce; and a soul-warming bread pudding soufflé. The brisk service operates on a team system, and usually comes off well. The impressive wine list focuses on California. *1403 Washington Ave., tel. 504/899–8221. Jacket required. Reservations required. AE, DC, MC, V.*

❸ **Constantin's.** Chef Patti Constantin keeps coming up with
$$$ all kinds of eclectic surprises in this bright and crisply decorated old cottage. Examples of her contemporary style are pork chops stuffed with zucchini and earthy andouille sausage in a rich brown sauce, and a luscious cream of garlic soup studded with batter-fried escargots. Among the made-from-scratch desserts is the delicious Snappy's Polar Chip, with alternating strata of vanilla ice cream, thin chocolate-chip cookies, and chocolate sauce. Greenery and boldly colored prints interrupt the whiteness of the walls in the roomy bar and two dining rooms, as waitresses in sneakers dash between the white-linened tables. The wine cellar is small, but carefully put together. *8402 Oak St., tel. 504/861–2111. Casual dress. Reservations advised for dinner. AE, MC, V. Closed Sun., lunch Sat.*

⓫ **Flagons.** What began in the early 1980s as a smartly
$$$ turned out wine bar in trendy uptown has grown into a restaurant, fashionably minimal in decor and very modern in its culinary outlook—contemporary American with occasional Creole touches. From the fine-tuned wine cellar comes a great array of old favorites and the latest releases. Typical and good dishes are charbroiled shrimp atop fettuccine, seasoned with Louisiana ham, and a sauté of rabbit tenderloin with cabbage steeped in champagne. The gumbo of smoked chicken and andouille sausage is a fine tribute to Louisiana traditions. Caviar addicts can sample Petrossian's beluga, ossetra, and sevruga, as well as Boyajian's American Palaid sturgeon. Past the always bustling wine bar are two pale-gray and burgundy-trimmed dining rooms decorated with paintings by local artists. The wine bar serves light dishes and cheese boards inside or on a pleasant patio. *3222 Magazine St.,*

*tel. 504/891–4444. Casual dress; jacket advised at dinner. Reservations advised for weekends. AE, MC, V.*

★ ❽ **Gautreau's.** Nostalgia and chic meet in this intimate bistro
$$$ almost hidden among the oaks of the Uptown residential area. Fewer than 50 seats fill the simply decorated room, fashioned from an old neighborhood drugstore. Chef Larkin Selman's up-to-date cooking is charged with creativity, a possible reflection of his New York training, but it's often boldly flavored in the style of his native New Orleans. Although the seasonal menu changes almost daily, risks are few. The crab cakes at Gautreau's, served with basil tartar sauce, are as good as you'll find in the city. Luscious Louisiana shrimp might appear tossed with pasta and bits of tomato and zucchini in a parsley pesto. A hearty risotto with prunes escorts sliced breast of guinea hen in sage sauce. And the crème brûlée, laced with orange, is a revelation. The wine list is brief but selective. Space is at a premium in the oxblood-enamel dining room, dominated by the pharmacy's handsome old original cases of glass and polished wood. Hard surfaces also raise the noise level, making Gautreau's chancy for serious discussions. *1728 Soniat St., tel. 504/899–7397. Jacket preferred at dinner. MC, V.*

★ ❾ **Upperline.** Behind an unassuming facade, this fashionably
$$$ streamlined spot has become popular with upscale foragers. Colorful paintings and prints by local artists enliven the dead-white walls. The third dining room, in the rear, looks out on illuminated sago palms outside the bare, floor-to-ceiling windows. The menu dips into several cultures, including Creole and Indian. A creamy trout mousse served with crouton disks is a marvelous overture. Five baked oysters, each under a different sauce, are deliciously hearty. The entrée list stars veal escallops in Madeira, a crisply sautéed soft-shell crab stuffed with more crabmeat, and a refreshing boiled beef brisket with horseradish sauce. Aside from the very good lemon and chocolate mousses, desserts lean toward the tropical—rum trifle, coconut-banana layer cake, and the like. Service is intelligent and well paced, and the wine list's brevity compensates with careful choices, especially in the white California category. *1413 Upperline St., tel. 504/891–9822. Casual dress, but jacket advised. Reservations required on weekends. AE, MC, V. Closed for lunch.*

❿ **Versailles.** This cluster of imaginatively furnished rooms
$$$$ takes on an Old World aspect with lace tablecloths, soft lighting, and warm colors. Little gets past the service staff, whose performance is consistently correct. The best tables flank the large glass wall along St. Charles Avenue. Regulars come for the menu's fusion of rich sauces with local ingredients, especially seafoods. Creamed crab is spooned onto oysters on the half shell and gratinéed to marvelous effect. Snails and a bourguignon sauce fill little French rolls. Main entrée attractions include an excellent fillet of salmon with artichoke bottoms and asparagus in a basil beurre blanc, and tournedos in a dense and winey truffle sauce with mushrooms. The cold lemon soufflé and warm Grand Marnier mousse are but two winners among a wide array of elaborate desserts. Wines are carefully selected and rather pricey. *2100 St. Charles Ave., tel. 504/524–2535. Jacket required. Reservations strongly advised. AE, CB, DC, MC, V. Closed Sun. Dinner only.*

## FREE TIME

### Fitness

*Hotel Facilities*
Guests at most midtown hotels pay a $10 fee for a one-day membership in the **Rivercenter Racquetball and Tennis Center** at the Hilton (tel. 504/587–7242). For Hilton and Le Meridien guests, the fee is $6. A one-day membership in the **Euro/Vita Spa** atop the Avenue Plaza Hotel (2111 St. Charles Ave., Garden District, tel. 504/566–1212) is $15.

*Health Clubs*
**Heritage Sports Central** (Heritage Plaza, 111 Veterans Blvd., tel. 504/832–5982) has Nautilus, aerobic classes, racquetball and handball courts, and a pool. Cost: $7 a day. **Racquetball One Fitness** (1 Canal Pl., Suite 380, tel. 504/525–2956) has racquetball courts, Nautilus, free weights, and aerobics. Facilities are $12 a day, though the gym has arrangements with some downtown hotels. **The New Orleans International YMCA** (936 St. Charles Ave., tel. 504/568–9622) has Universal and Nautilus machines, a jogging track, and a lap pool. Guests at the Hyatt Regency pay $5 a day; others pay $10.

*Jogging*
The 1.5-mile jogging path in lush **Audubon Park** has a leafy canopy of Live Oaks. There are 18 exercise stations along the route. Joggers also favor the levee at **Riverbend,** where St. Charles Avenue turns onto Carrollton Avenue.

### Shopping

Leathery, feathery Mardi Gras masks, Mardi Gras and Jazz Fest posters, chicory coffee and pralines, and jazz records are all popular souvenirs of the Crescent City. New Orleans is also noted for its chic antiques shops. In the latter category, the greatest concentrations of shops are on **Royal Street** in the French Quarter and along **Magazine Street** uptown. In the **French Quarter,** a 96-square-block area bounded by Canal, Decatur, and Rampart streets, and Esplanade Avenue, shops abound in the picturesque Creole cottages and renovated 19th-century buildings. **Canal** and **Poydras streets** are the two major shopping thoroughfares downtown. **Riverwalk,** at the foot of Poydras Street, is jam-packed with boutiques and eateries. Saks Fifth Ave. (tel. 504/524–2200), Gucci (tel. 504/524–5544), Brooks Brothers (tel. 504/522–4200), and Laura Ashley (tel. 504/522–9403) are among the many shops of **Canal Place** (333 Canal St.). Lord & Taylor (tel. 504/581–5673) and Macy's (tel. 504/592–5985) are in the **New Orleans Centre** (1400 Poydras St.). Innovative custom-design fashions, French lingerie, and a full array of shoes and accessories (including frilly millinery) are at **Yvonne La Fleur** (8131 Hampson St., uptown, tel. 504/866–9666).

### Diversions

In addition to fine antique stores, Royal Street from Canal on past Jackson Square is lined with **art galleries.**

**Audubon Park and the Zoo** (6500 Magazine St., tel. 504/861–2537) is a luxuriant 400-acre park for a jog, a stroll, golf, tennis, or a visit with more than 1,100 animals. You should do none of the above after dark.

If you take the Canal Street Ferry across to Algiers and stroll along the levee to your right, you'll come to **Blaine Kern's Mardi Gras World** (223 Newton St., tel. 504/362–8211), the den of the world's largest float-builder, where you can watch Mardi Gras in the making all year round.

For a fascinating look at the city's famous graveyards, contact **Cemetery Tours** (916–918 N. Peters St., tel. 504/589–2636). In addition, park rangers of the Jean Lafitte National Park Service conduct daily walking tours of St. Louis Cemetery No. 1, the oldest of New Orleans's unique Cities of the Dead.

Noted for its majestic oaks draped in Spanish moss, **City Park** (City Park Ave. at Marconi Dr., tel. 504/482–4888) is a 1,500-acre expanse with four golf courses, a driving range, 54 tennis courts, lagoons and boat rentals, and the New Orleans Museum of Art.

The "Astronomical Gastronomical Tour of New Orleans" (tel. 504/649–3137) is designed for visitors who want to sample several restaurants, but are short on time. Created and hosted by local writer John DeMers, the **culinary tours** are custom-designed progressive meals that might start at Arnaud's and finish at Brennan's.

The Vieux Carré ("Old Square"), the original colony founded by French Creoles in 1718, laid out in a perfect grid, is an easily navigable 96-square-block area now known as the **French Quarter**. Jackson Square has been its hub and heartbeat since Colonial days. St. Louis Cathedral, the country's oldest cathedral, is located on the square along with several 18th- and 19th-century structures. The quarter is home to Bourbon Street, to many but not all of the jazz clubs, and to all manner of shops and boutiques housed in tiny pastel Creole houses. Most of the famous French Creole restaurants are located in the quarter. Bourbon Street runs right down its center.

Designed in 1857 by famed architect James Gallier, Jr., as a home for his family, **Gallier House** (1118–32 Royal St., tel. 504/523–6722) is one of the best-researched of the many house museums, and gives you an idea of how well-heeled Creoles lived.

The city's most palatial mansions are in the residential area bounded by St. Charles, Jackson, and Louisiana avenues, and Magazine Street, called the **Garden District**. Take the St. Charles Streetcar from Canal and Carondelet streets, get off at Sixth Street, and look at the exquisite digs on St. Charles Avenue, and Prytania, Third, and Fourth streets.

A noted authority on the subject conducts two-hour **literary walking tours** that take in the former haunts and homes of Tennessee Williams, William Faulkner, Truman Capote, and some 70 other authors. Contact Heritage Tours (tel. 504/949–9805).

On the Great River Road west of town, several restored **plantation homes** are open for visitors. For escorted tours, contact Tours by Isabelle (tel. 504/367–3963); you can also drive out yourself and follow signs to the plantations.

If you want to **ride a riverboat,** the *Steamboat Natchez* (Toulouse St. Wharf behind the Jackson Brewery, tel. 504/586–8777) and the *Creole Queen* (Riverwalk, tel. 504/529–4567) both offer two-hour harbor cruises daily and festive dinner-plus-jazz cruises at night.

If you're curious about Voodoo Queen Marie Laveau and her cult, take a look in the one-of-a-kind **Voodoo Museum** (724 Dumaine St., tel. 504/523–7685). It's a small, dimly lighted place with displays of *gris-gris* (pronounced gree gree) charms and voodoo potions; in the back room there is a voodoo altar. The museum also offers tours of voodoo sites in the city, including a church and the grave of Marie Laveau. A longer and more exotic tour takes in a haunted plantation in the swamps.

## Professional Sports

**Football.** The **New Orleans Saints** play at the Superdome, (tel. 504/733–0255).

## The Arts

The New Orleans Ballet and New Orleans Opera companies perform at the **Theatre for the Performing Arts** (801 N. Rampart St., tel. 504/522–0592). The New Orleans Symphony performs at the **Orpheum Theatre** (129 University Pl., tel. 504/525–0340). Top performers and touring companies can be seen at the **Saenger Performing Arts Center** (143 N. Rampart St., tel. 504/524–2490). The **UNO Lakefront Arena** (University of New Orleans, Lakeshore Dr., tel. 504/586–6805) is also a venue for headliners. **Le Petit Theatre du Vieux Carré** (616 St. Peter St., tel. 504/522–2081), one of the nation's oldest community theaters, does comedies, dramas, and musicals in an historic French Quarter building.

Tickets for events at the Saenger and the UNO Lakefront Arena are available through **Ticketmaster** (tel. 504/888–8181). The **Hospitality Hotline** (tel. 504/522–9200) arranges ticket purchases for a wide range of events, including the arts.

## After Hours

New Orleans is a 24-hour town, which means there are no legal closing times. Jazz, of course, was born here, and the Dixieland beat keeps up right along with rhythm and blues, rock 'n' roll, Cajun zydeco music, gutbucket (lowdown, mean blues), Irish music, and even an occasional bagpiper. The music begins on Bourbon around noonish. Some bars are open round the clock, some don't rev up till midnight, some close around 1 AM. Hours tend to be changeable, so call before tooling out at 2 AM. Music is not confined to Bourbon Street and the French Quarter. There are some good, popular uptown spots such as Tipitina and the Maple Leaf (*see* below). There are also some considerably quieter piano bars, as well as just plain bars and lounges.

*Bars and Lounges*
A *lot* of business is done each afternoon over tea, scones, and champagne in **Le Salon** (Windsor Court Hotel, tel.

504/523–6000), which is the most luxurious lounge in town. The **Esplanade Lounge** (Omni Royal Orleans, tel. 504/529–5333) is also a chic place to meet associates. The **Napoleon House** (500 Chartres St., tel. 504/524–9752), the best place to soak up Old New Orleans atmosphere, is a favorite with local writers and artists. The **Bayou Bar** (Pontchartrain Hotel, tel. 504/524–0581) is popular with businesspeople and uptowners. Many a business deal is done in the **Sazerac Bar** (Fairmont Hotel, tel. 504/529–7111). Business people from the CBD like to stop off after work at the **Victorian Lounge** (The Columns Hotel, 3811 St. Charles Ave., tel. 504/899–9308). It's far too dark (day and night) in **Lafitte's Blacksmith Shop** (941 Bourbon St., tel. 504/ 523–0066) to get any work done, and the laid-back atmosphere makes you not care much. Writers have been lured to Lafitte's long before Tennessee Williams used to hang out here. A New Orleans institution, **Pat O'Brien's** (718 St. Peter St., tel. 504/525–4823) is loud and loaded with college folks and tourists.

*Jazz Clubs*

At the **Absinthe Bar** (400 Bourbon St., tel. 504/525–8108) things get started about midnight with hard-driving R&B that rocks into the wee hours. The Dukes of Dixieland hold forth (when they're not on tour) at **Lulu White's Mahogany Hall** (309 Bourbon St., tel. 504/525–5595). **Pete Fountain's Club** (Hilton Hotel, tel. 504/523–4374) is a posh spot to listen to some great clarinet music (Pete is on tour a lot, so check the schedule). The **Palm Court Jazz Café** (1204 Decatur St., tel. 504/525–0200) features some of the city's best musicians; the proprietors know everything there is to know about jazz and can tell you who's playing where. Neither pub nor club, **Preservation Hall** (726 St. Peter St., tel. 504/523–8939) is in a class by itself. This is the place to hear jazz legends like Kid Sheik and the Humphrey Brothers. **Storyville Jazz Club** (1104 Decatur St., tel. 504/525–8199) is a cavernous place where locals gather to listen to jazz and rock. **Tipitina's** (501 Napoleon Ave., tel. 504/895–8477) is among the best music clubs in town. If it looks familiar to you, it's because this is where Dennis Quaid romanced Ellen Barkin in *The Big Easy*. The Neville Brothers play here when they're in town. Loaded with very laid-back locals and great R&B, **The Maple Leaf** (8316 Oak St., tel. 504/866–5323) is funky, friendly, and the best place in town for Cajun music and dancing. Cozy, colorful **Tyler's** (5324 Magazine St., tel. 504/891–4989) turns out jazz and R&B, and on weekends showcases the great saxophonist James Rivers with his band, the Movement. All ages gather at **Snug Harbor** (626 Frenchmen St., tel. 504/949–0696) to hear Charmaine Neville, Johnny Adams, Steve Masakowski, and a host of other greats. Music really pops at **Benny's Bar** (938 Valence St., tel. 504/895–9405), a honky-tonk where the music is mostly blues. Dixieland holds its own in the handsome marble halls of **Le Meridien Hotel** (tel. 504/525–6500).

*For Singles*

Many of the above clubs are great places to mix and meet, notably the Maple Leaf, Snug Harbor, Tipitina's and Storyville. All of them draw a mixed crowd of locals and tourists. **City Lights** (310 Howard Ave., tel. 504/568–1700), a discolike club in the gentrified Warehouse District, features oldies-but-goodies for an upwardly mobile crowd. **4141** (4141 St. Charles Ave., tel. 504/891–9873) is a classy avenue bar with a disco area where young professionals flock in droves after work and linger into the night.

# New York

*by Roger Lowenstein*

The 1980s were, in general, a prosperous time for New York—a welcome rebound from its 1970s brush with bankruptcy. With the notable exception of the 1987 crash, Wall Street and other white-collar industries boomed; employment soared; new hotels and skyscrapers changed the skyline; and whole neighborhoods on the West Side, Lower East Side, and Brooklyn were reclaimed from blight. New York's retail establishments—from groceries to boutiques—never looked brighter.

Tourists and natives benefited from a new convention center, a renovated zoo, a new waterfront district at Battery Park City, and, more important, an overhauling of the subway system. New graffiti-free cars were installed and stations began to get long-overdue facelifts. As real estate prices soared, some of New York's most famous buildings, including parts of Rockefeller Center and Citicorp Center, were sold to cash-rich foreigners.

But the real estate boom that fed the city's coffers and seemed at times to be the inescapable conversation topic at any gathering of New Yorkers also brought problems. The city's residents were joined by some of its corporations in being unable to afford the rents. Exxon, Mobil, and J.C. Penney left town. NBC and Chase Manhattan threatened to leave, but were given generous inducements by City Hall to stay. And as the 1990s got under way, the prosperous times were clearly coming to an end. Wall Street, still under the shadow of the 1987 stock market crash, continued to cut back on its employees and its bonuses. Advertising, another major New York industry, slumped, and development stalled. And the City Government was again badly strapped for funds.

Violent and drug-related crime, as in other cities, has been on the rise, but tourists, with a few notable exceptions, have usually been unaffected by it. What average citizens have been unable to avoid is the striking juxtaposition between rich and poor. A seemingly endless stream of homeless people often disconcert and disturb visitors and New York residents alike.

That said, New York still has twice the verve of almost any other town. To get the most out of it, remember to allow for a little delay, even confusion, in getting from one place to another, and try to indulge in, rather than just tolerate,

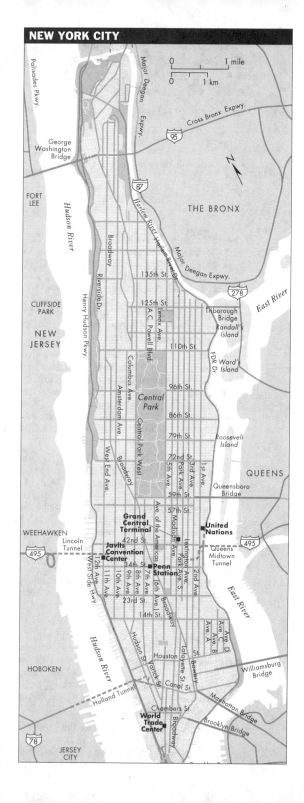

# NEW YORK CITY

Palisades Pkwy.

Major Deegan Expwy.

Cross Bronx Expwy.

95

87

George Washington Bridge

FORT LEE

Hudson River

THE BRONX

278

Harlem River, Harlem River D.

Major Deegan Expwy.

East River

CLIFFSIDE PARK

NEW JERSEY

135th St.

125th St.

Broadway

Riverside Dr.

Henry Hudson Pkwy.

A.C. Powell Blvd.

Lenox Ave.

110th St.

Triborough Bridge

Randall's Island

FDR Dr.

Ward's Island

Columbus Ave.

Amsterdam Ave.

West End Ave.

96th St.

Central Park

86th St.

79th St.

Roosevelt Island

Central Park West

Broadway

72nd St.

1st Ave.

3rd Ave.

5th Ave.

Park Ave.

59th St.

QUEENS

Queensboro Bridge

57th St.

Grand Central Terminal

Ave. of the Americas

Madison Ave.

Lexington Ave.

Park Ave. S.

United Nations

WEEHAWKEN

Lincoln Tunnel

495

42nd St.

Javits Convention Center

34th St.

Penn Station

12th Ave.

11th Ave.

10th Ave.

9th Ave.

8th Ave.

7th Ave.

6th Ave.

Broadway

2nd Ave.

495

Queens Midtown Tunnel

East River

23rd St.

14th St.

West Side Hwy.

Ave. A

Ave. B

Ave. C

Ave. D

HOBOKEN

Hudson River

Houston St.

Lafayette St.

Bowery

Williamsburg Bridge

Hudson St.

Varick St.

Canal St.

Holland Tunnel

Manhattan Bridge

Chambers St.

World Trade Center

Broadway

Brooklyn Bridge

78

JERSEY CITY

0 — 1 mile
0 — 1 km

the city's diversity. As always, the best way to mine the city's riches is to walk its streets (with reasonable care).

## Top Employers

| Employer | Type of Enterprise | Parent*/ Headquarters |
|---|---|---|
| **American Express/ Shearson Lehman Hutton** | Travel, credit card, broker- age firm | New York |
| **Chase Manhattan Bank** | Bank | New York |
| **Citicorp** | Bank | New York |
| **Consolidated Edison** | Utilities | New York |
| **R.H. Macy** | Department store | New York |
| **Manufacturers Hanover Trust Co.** | Bank | New York |
| **Merrill Lynch & Co.** | Financial services | New York |
| **New York Telephone** | Telephone company | NYNEX/ New York |
| **New York University** | University | New York |
| **Pan American** | Airline | New York |

*if applicable

## ESSENTIAL INFORMATION

### Climate

What follows are the average daily maximum and mini- mum temperatures for New York.

| | | | | | | | | |
|---|---|---|---|---|---|---|---|---|
| **Jan.** | 41F 29 | 5C −2 | **Feb.** | 43F 29 | 6C −2 | **Mar.** | 47F 34 | 8C 1 |
| **Apr.** | 61F 45 | 16C 7 | **May** | 70F 54 | 21C 12 | **June** | 81F 63 | 27C 17 |
| **July** | 85F 70 | 29C 21 | **Aug.** | 83F 68 | 28C 20 | **Sept.** | 76F 61 | 24C 16 |
| **Oct.** | 69F 52 | 19C 11 | **Nov.** | 56F 43 | 13C 6 | **Dec.** | 43F 31 | 6C −1 |

### Airports

**John F. Kennedy International Airport** is 15 miles east of midtown Manhattan. Though few will be unimpressed by its vital statistics (31 million passengers a year, 16,000 parking spaces, and a total surface area equal to one third of Manhattan Island), the airport is unwieldy and is the least convenient of the three that serve New York. Half the traffic is from overseas.

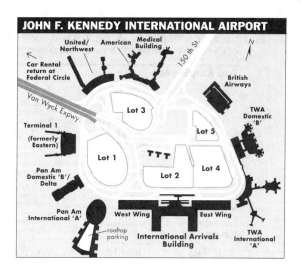

**JOHN F. KENNEDY INTERNATIONAL AIRPORT**

**LaGuardia Airport,** eight miles east of Manhattan, primarily handles short-haul domestic flights. Though much smaller than JFK, it accommodates 24 million people a year and is growing—perhaps too quickly. In recent years, its on-time record has been among the worst in the U.S.

**Newark International Airport,** 16 miles southwest of midtown, handles 22 million passengers a year, making it one of the country's biggest. Unlike the other metropolitan-area airports, however, Newark is not operating beyond its designed capacity. That, plus a user-friendly and accessible roadway system, make this a good choice, especially for those staying in downtown Manhattan. About 10% of the traffic is international.

## Airport Business Facilities

**John F. Kennedy International Airport.** There are no business service centers or hotels in the terminals.

**LaGuardia Airport.** Mutual of Omaha Business Service Center (Second fl., Main Terminal, near USAir and United, tel. 718/478–1414) has fax machines, photocopying, baggage storage, Western Union, travel insurance, cash advance, and phone suites. Another branch at the Delta terminal (tel. 718/651–6725) has baggage storage and travel insurance.

**Newark International Airport.** There are no business services here except the airline clubs and insurance machines.

## Airlines

In general, the major domestic carriers serve all three airports. The Trump and Pan American shuttles connecting New York with Washington and Boston operate out of LaGuardia. Continental is the primary carrier out of Newark.

**Air Canada,** tel. 212/869–1900 or 800/776–3000.
**American,** tel. 800/433–7300.
**Continental,** tel. 212/319–9494 or 800/525–0280.
**Delta,** tel. 212/239–0700 or 800/221–1212.
**Midway,** tel. 800/621–5700 or 800/621–5700.
**Northwest,** tel. 212/736–1220 or 800/225–2525.
**Pan Am,** tel. 212/687–2600 or 800/221–1111.
**TWA,** tel. 212/290–2121 or 800/221–2000.
**Trump Shuttle,** tel. 800/247–8786.
**United,** tel. 800/241–6522.
**USAir,** tel. 800/428–4322.

## Between the Airports and Downtown

*By Helicopter*

This is the fastest way to get into town. **New York Helicopter** (tel. 800/645–3494) flies from JFK (TWA Terminal A) to midtown, at 34th Street on the East River, in 10 minutes; flights leave every half hour from 1:45 PM until 7:15 PM. Cost: $65.88, though the ride is free for first-class passengers on some airlines. **Trump Air Helicopter Service** (tel. 800/448–4000 or 800/247–8786) flies between LaGuardia (Trump Shuttle terminal) and its Pier 6 Wall Street terminal (at South St. and Water St.) in six minutes, from 8 AM until 6:15 PM. Cost: $60.

*By Taxi*

The trip to midtown is about 30 minutes from LaGuardia, 30–45 minutes from Newark, and an hour from JFK, but travelers should allow for considerable traffic delays, especially (but not exclusively) during rush hours. From LaGuardia the most direct route into midtown is via the Queens-Midtown Tunnel, but during rush hours the Triboro Bridge route is often quicker. From JFK, take the Belt Parkway and Brooklyn Battery Tunnel into lower Manhattan and the 34th Street Tunnel into midtown. The Holland Tunnel is the best route from Newark. Cost: about $17 from LaGuardia, $30–$35 from JFK, and $30–$35 from Newark, plus tolls and tip. At Newark, "Share-and-Save" group rates are available for up to four passengers between 8 AM and midnight; make arrangements with the airport's taxi dispatcher.

*By Ferry*

Pan Am operates a water shuttle (tel. 800/543–3779) from LaGuardia's Marine Air Terminal, which serves the Pan Am Shuttle. It runs from 7:45 AM–6:45 PM, and stops at Pier 11, at Wall Street and South Street, and at 35th Street on the East River. The trip takes 45 minutes to downtown and 30 minutes to midtown. Cost: $20.

*By Minibus or Van*

**Gray Line Air Shuttle** (tel. 212/757–6840) will take you from the three area airports directly to your midtown hotel for $11 per person from LaGuardia, $14 from Kennedy, and $16 from Newark; prices are slightly higher for locations from 30th to 14th streets and from 64th to 95th streets. Buses leave every 15 minutes from JFK and LaGuardia, every 20 minutes from Newark; they run from 7 AM to midnight at JFK, 8 AM to midnight at LaGuardia and Newark. Make arrangements at the ground transportation counter.

*By Bus*

**Carey Airport Express** (tel. 718/632–0500, 718/632–0506, and 800/284–0909) runs buses from both New York airports to six hotels and terminals in midtown Manhattan. Buses from LaGuardia run every 20 minutes from 7 AM to midnight; travel time is 25–45 minutes, depending on traffic. Cost: $7.50. Buses from JFK run every half hour from 6 AM to midnight. Travel time is 45–75 minutes. Cost: $9.50. **Olympia Trails** (tel. 212/964–6233) runs buses every 15 minutes from 6 AM to midnight between Newark and Manhattan. The trip is 25 minutes to the World Trade Center and 35–45 minutes to Grand Central Station. Cost: $7.

For information on bus service between the three metropolitan airports call 800/AIR–RIDE.

## Car Rentals

The following companies have booths at all three metropolitan airports:

**Avis,** tel. 800/331–1212.
**Budget,** tel. 800/527–0700.
**Hertz,** tel. 800/654–3131.
**National,** tel. 800/328–4567.
**Thrifty,** tel. 800/367–2277.

## Emergencies

*Doctors*

**Affiliated Physicians of St. Vincent's** (5 World Trade Center, tel. 212/775–1218), **Central Park West Medical** (2 W. 86th St., tel. 212/769–1700, doctors always on call), **Lincoln Medical Practice** (1995 Broadway, tel. 212/787–8770, doctors always on call).

*Dentists*

**Concerned Dental Care** (30 E. 40th St., tel. 212/696–4979), **Preventative Dental Associates** (200 Madison Ave., tel. 212/213–2004 and 210 E. 86th St., tel. 212/685–7169).

*Hospitals*

**Beth Israel Medical Center** (First Ave. & 16th St., tel. 212/420–2000), **Mount Sinai Hospital** (100th St. & Fifth Ave., tel. 212/241–6500), **New York Eye & Ear Infirmary** (310 E. 14th St. & Second Ave., tel. 212/598–1313), **New York Hospital-Cornell Medical Center** (525 E. 68th St., tel. 212/472–5454), **New York University Medical Center** (560 First Ave., between 32nd & 33rd Sts., tel. 212/340–7300), **St. Vincent's Hospital & Medical Center** (153 W. 11th St. at Seventh Ave., tel. 212/790–7000).

## Important Addresses and Numbers

**Audiovisual rentals.** Olden Camera & Lens (1265 Broadway bet. 33rd St. and 32nd St., tel. 212/725–1234), VRI Scharff (599 11th Ave., tel. 212/582–4400).

**Chamber of Commerce** (200 Madison Ave., tel. 212/561–2020).

**Computer rentals.** The Computer Factory (219 E. 44th St., tel. 212/953–2233; 11 W. 52nd St., tel. 212/664–0170), Microrent (14 Leonard St., tel. 212/925–6455).

**Convention and exhibition centers.** Jacob J. Javits Convention Center (36th St. and 11th Ave., tel. 212/216–2000).

There is also convention space at Pier 88 (tel. 212/466–7985), and at Pier 90 (tel. 212/466–7974). For more information, call the New York Convention & Visitors Bureau (tel. 212/397–8222).

**Fax services.** AAA Service Resource Industries (07 Wall St., tel. 212/943–1111), Abco Typing & Mail Service (60 E. 42nd St., tel. 212/697–1360), Electronic Systems Plus (120 W. 44th St., tel. 212/302–5477), Mailboxes Etc. USA (217 E. 86th St., tel. 212/996–7900).

**Formal-wear rentals.** A.T. Harris (47 E. 44th St., tel. 212/682–6325), Jack & Co. Formal Wear (128 E. 86th St., tel. 212/722–4455).

**Gift shops.** Chocolates: Godiva Chocolatier (560 Lexington Ave., tel. 212/980–9810; 33 Maiden Lane, tel. 212/809–8990; and 701 Fifth Ave., tel. 212/593–2845), Jo-Ann's Nut House (25 W. 33rd St. [lobby of the Empire State Building], tel. 212/279–1809); Flowers: Christatos & Koster (201 E. 64th St., tel. 212/838–0022, New York's most famous florist), Christie's Flowers (71 Broadway, tel. 212/425–2644).

**Graphic design studios.** Bloch, Graulich, Whelan (333 Park Ave., tel. 212/473–7033), Commercial Arts (122 W. 27th St., tel. 212/243–1905).

**Hairstylists.** Unisex: Jean-Louis David (Roosevelt Hotel, 45 E. 45th St., tel. 212/661–9600, where no appointment is necessary), Vidal Sassoon (767 Fifth Ave., tel. 212/535–9200); Women: Elizabeth Arden (691 Fifth Ave., tel. 212/832–3225).

**Health and fitness clubs.** *See* Fitness, below.

**Information hot lines.** Movies (tel. 212/777–3456), Sports (tel. 212/976–1313).

**Limousine services.** Battery City Car & Limousine Service (tel. 212/947–9696), Concord Luxury Limousine (tel. 212/230–1600), Limousine and Chauffeur Service (tel. 212/222–8247), Limousine by Ari (tel. 212/472–2226), London Town Cars (tel. 212/988–9700).

**Liquor stores.** Famous Wines & Liquors (27 William St., tel. 212/422–4743), Morrell & Co. (535 Madison Ave., tel. 212/688–9370), Sherry Lehmann (679 Madison Ave., tel. 212/838–7500).

**Mail delivery, overnight.** DHL Worldwide Courier Express (tel. 718/917–8000), Federal Express (tel. 212/777–6500), TNT Skypak (tel. 800/558–5555), UPS (tel. 212/695–7500), U.S. Postal Service Express Mail (212/330–5250).

**Messenger services.** Able Motorized Delivery Service (tel. 212/687–5515), Allboro Messenger Service (tel. 212/532–5959), Bullit Courier (tel. 212/952–4343, downtown; and tel. 212/983–7400, midtown).

**Office space rental.** World-Wide Business Centres (575 Madison Ave., tel. 212/605–0200).

**Pharmacies, late-night.** Jaros Drug (25 Central Park West, tel. 212/247–8080), Kaufman Pharmacy (557 Lexington Ave., tel. 212/755–2266), Star Pharmacy (1540 First Ave., tel. 212/737–4324).

**Radio stations, all-news.** WCBS, 880 AM; WINS, 1010 AM.

**Secretarial services.** Dial-A-Secretary (521 Fifth Ave. and 149 E. 81st St., tel. 212/348–9575), HQ Services & Offices (730 Fifth Ave., tel. 212/333–8700; 237 Park Ave., tel. 212/949–0722; 666 Fifth Ave., tel. 212/541–3800), Wordflow (162 Madison Ave., tel. 212/725–5111).

**Stationery supplies.** Airline Stationers (284 Madison Ave., tel. 212/532–6525), Grolan Stationers (1800 Broadway, tel. 212/247–2676), Ropal Stationery (1283 Third Ave., tel. 212/988–3548), Times Circle East (61 E. 45th St., tel. 212/682–0820).

**Taxis.** Minute Men Taxi (tel. 718/899–5600), Taxi Town (tel. 212/315–1490), Uptown Taxi (tel. 212/304–3989).

**Theater tickets.** *See* The Arts, below.

**Train information.** Amtrak (tel. 212/582–6875 or 800/872–7245) and the Long Island Railroad (tel. 718/454–5477) depart from Pennsylvania Station at Seventh Ave. and 33rd St; Metro North (tel. 212/532–4900) departs from Grand Central Station, at Lexington Ave. and 42nd St.

**Travel agents.** American Express (150 E. 42nd St., tel. 212/687–3700; American Express Tower C, World Financial Center, 200 Vesey St., tel. 212/640–5130; and 374 Park Ave., tel. 212/421–8240), Liberty Travel (1430 Third Ave., tel. 212/772–3808; 298 Madison Avenue, tel. 212/689–5600; 50 Broad St., tel. 212/363–2320), Thomas Cook Travel (2 Penn Plaza, tel. 212/967–4390; 160 E. 53rd St., tel. 212/755–9780).

**Weather** (tel. 212/976–1212).

## LODGING

New York's hotels are concentrated in midtown (usually defined as the area between 42nd and 59th streets and between the East River and Avenue of the Americas). This is home base for the lion's share of New York's major law firms and large corporations. However, the boundary lines of midtown have blurred as development has pushed west into the theater district. Hotels there are a bit farther from the heart of the business zone, but not much. The big difference is one of style. Midtown is consistently fast-paced, corporate, and somewhat sterile; the theater area, a blend of small businesses—including those that make the garment and diamond trade, as well as show business—is serious by day and colorful (some would say raffish) by night. Female travelers especially should note: this neighborhood has been coming back for a long time but still has a way to go.

Travelers who want a break from the monotony of skyscrapers when the work day is over should consider hotels on the Upper East Side, just a short taxi ride or a longish walk from midtown. Enticing restaurants cater to the area's well-to-do locals, and the streetscape is dotted with museums, galleries, and boutiques. Hotels in the residential streets south of midtown (grouped here with midtown hotels) offer convenience and quiet, though the area is somewhat short on pizzazz.

The downtown financial district has only one hotel, and it's easily the most convenient for those doing business on Wall Street. The airport hotels may suffice for people on one-night stopovers, but are not advisable for those planning repeated trips to midtown.

Most hotels listed here offer special corporate rates and weekend discounts; inquire when making reservations.

Highly recommended lodgings in each price category are indicated by a star ★.

| Category | Cost* |
| --- | --- |
| $$$$ (Very Expensive) | over $210 |
| $$$ (Expensive) | $150–$210 |
| $$ (Moderate) | under $150 |

*All prices are for a standard double room, single occupancy, excluding 13.25% and $2 a day taxes.*

*Numbers in the margin correspond to numbered hotel locations on the New York Lodging and Dining maps.*

## Wall Street

★ **52**
$$$ **Vista International.** The style is plain-vanilla functional, but rooms are comfortable, and the location makes the hotel a must for those who need to be near Wall Street. Among its other standard amenities, the Vista offers computers for hire and a 22nd-floor fitness center with a 50-foot pool, jogging track, and weight room overlooking the Hudson River. Guests on two executive floors have the run of a lounge and open bar. The best rooms are those overlooking the World Trade Center plaza, stunning when lit up at night. Book in advance; though other developments are in the works, at press time this remained the Wall Street area's only hotel. *A Hilton International hotel, 3 World Trade Center, 10048, tel. 212/938–9100 or 800/445–8667, fax 212/372–2231. Gen. manager, Roman Rickenbacher. 769 rooms, 25 suites. AE, CB, D, DC, V.*

## Midtown/Theater District/Gramercy

★ **36**
$$ **Algonquin.** Famous writers put the hotel on the map by holding court in the Blue Bar, today a hangout of the theater set as well as literary types. The Oak Room is still a good bet to view cabaret acts and to enjoy pretheater dinner, and the oak-paneled lobby, a cozy place for reading and subdued conversation, doesn't seem to have changed since 1902. It's a good place to have a drink with a highbrow client, but you'll go upstairs to a cramped bedroom and smallish bath. Rooms on all 12 floors have recently been refurbished, so they no longer have a boarding house feel; most of them now have desks. Still, it's best to come for the scene and the location, convenient to midtown—but not if you need to spend a lot of time working in your room. *An Aoki hotel. 59 W. 44th St., 10036, tel. 212/840–6800 or 800/548–0345, fax 212/944–1419. Gen. manager, Edward Pitt. 139 rooms, 24 suites. AE, CB, DC, MC, V.*

# MIDTOWN NEW YORK CITY

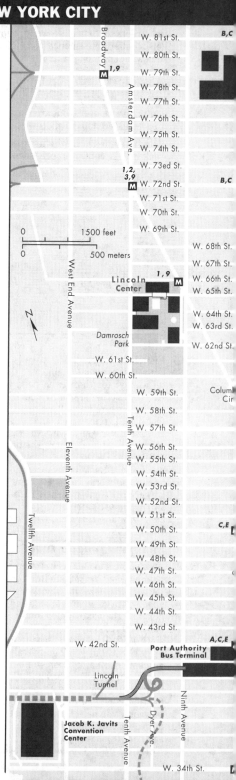

# DOWNTOWN NEW YORK CITY

# NEW YORK CITY HOTEL CHART

| HOTELS | Price Category | Business Services Banquet capacity | No. of meeting rooms | Secretarial services | Audiovisual equipment | Teletype news service | Computer rentals | In-room modem phone jack | All-news cable channel | Desk | Desk lighting | Bed lighting |
|---|---|---|---|---|---|---|---|---|---|---|---|---|
| Algonquin | $$ | 100 | 3 | - | - | - | - | - | ✓ | - | - | ◐ |
| Beekman Towers | $$$ | 125 | 1 | - | - | - | - | - | - | ◐ | ◐ | ● |
| The Carlyle | $$$$ | 120 | 2 | - | ✓ | - | - | ✓ | ✓ | ● | ◐ | ● |
| Gramercy Park | $$$$ | 200 | 5 | - | - | - | - | - | - | ◐ | ◐ | ○ |
| Grand Hyatt | $$$$ | 150 | 20 | ✓ | ✓ | - | - | ✓ | ✓ | - | - | ◐ |
| Hilton and Towers | $$$ | 2800 | 47 | ✓ | ✓ | ✓ | ✓ | - | ✓ | ● | ● | ◐ |
| Hotel Elysée | $$$ | 50 | 0 | - | - | - | - | - | ✓ | ◐ | ● | ● |
| JFK Plaza | $$ | 250 | 12 | - | ✓ | - | - | ✓ | ✓ | ◐ | ● | ◐ |
| Kitano | $$ | 0 | 0 | - | - | - | - | - | - | ◐ | ◐ | ○ |
| LaGuardia Marriott Airport Hotel | $$$ | 400 | 13 | - | - | - | - | - | - | ◐ | ◐ | ◐ |
| Lowell | $$$$ | 50 | 1 | - | ✓ | - | - | ✓ | ✓ | ● | ● | ● |
| Marriott Marquis | $$$$ | 200 | 47 | - | ✓ | - | - | ✓ | ✓ | ● | ● | ● |
| Mayfair Regent | $$$$ | 40 | 2 | ✓ | ✓ | - | - | ✓ | ✓ | ● | ● | ● |
| Mayflower | $$ | 100 | 3 | - | - | - | - | - | ✓ | ◐ | ◐ | ◐ |
| Parc 51 | $$$$ | 70 | 2 | ✓ | ✓ | - | - | ✓ | ✓ | ● | ● | ◐ |
| Le Parker Meridien | $$$$ | 300 | 7 | ✓ | ✓ | ✓ | - | ✓ | ✓ | ◐ | ● | ● |
| Park Lane | $$$ | 20 | 1 | - | ✓ | - | - | ✓ | ✓ | ◐ | ◐ | ◐ |
| Peninsula | $$$$ | 180 | 6 | - | ✓ | - | - | ✓ | ✓ | ● | ● | ○ |
| Penta | $$ | 1500 | 34 | - | ✓ | - | - | ✓ | ✓ | ◐ | ◐ | ◐ |

$$$$ = over $210, $$$ = $150 -$210, $$ = under $150.
● good, ◐ fair, ○ poor.
All hotels listed here have photocopying and fax facilities.

| In-Room Amenities | | | | | | | | | | Hotel Amenities | | | | | | |
|---|---|---|---|---|---|---|---|---|---|---|---|---|---|---|---|---|
| Nonsmoking rooms | In-room checkout | Minibar | Pay movies | VCR/Movie rentals | Hairdryer | Toiletries | Room service | Laundry/Dry cleaning | Pressing | Concierge | Barber/Hairdresser | Garage | Courtesy airport transport | Sauna | Pool | Exercise room |
| – | – | – | – | – | – | ○ | ◐ | ● | ● | ✓ | – | – | – | – | – | – |
| – | – | – | ✓ | – | – | ● | ◐ | ● | ● | – | – | – | – | – | – | – |
| – | – | ✓ | – | ✓ | ✓ | ● | ● | ● | ● | ✓ | ✓ | ✓ | – | ✓ | – | ● |
| – | – | – | – | – | – | – | ◐ | ◐ | ● | ✓ | ✓ | – | – | – | – | – |
| ✓ | ✓ | – | ✓ | ✓ | – | ● | ● | ● | ● | ✓ | – | ✓ | – | – | – | – |
| ✓ | ✓ | – | ✓ | – | – | ● | ● | ◐ | ◐ | ✓ | ✓ | – | – | – | – | ● |
| – | – | – | – | – | ✓ | ● | ○ | ● | ◐ | – | – | ✓ | – | – | – | – |
| ✓ | – | – | – | – | ✓ | ● | ● | ◐ | ● | ✓ | – | ✓ | ✓ | ✓ | ◐ | ◐ |
| – | – | – | ✓ | – | – | ○ | – | ○ | ◐ | ✓ | – | – | – | – | – | – |
| ✓ | – | – | ✓ | – | – | ○ | ◐ | ● | ◐ | – | – | ✓ | ✓ | ✓ | ● | ◐ |
| – | – | ✓ | – | ✓ | – | ● | ◐ | ● | ● | ✓ | – | ✓ | – | ✓ | – | – |
| ✓ | ✓ | – | ✓ | – | ✓ | ○ | ● | ● | ○ | ✓ | – | ✓ | – | ✓ | – | ● |
| – | – | – | – | – | ✓ | ● | ● | ● | ● | ✓ | – | – | – | – | – | – |
| – | ✓ | – | – | – | – | ○ | ◐ | ● | ◐ | – | – | – | – | – | – | – |
| ✓ | – | – | – | ✓ | – | ● | ● | ● | ● | ✓ | – | ✓ | – | ✓ | – | – |
| ✓ | ✓ | ✓ | ✓ | ✓ | ✓ | ● | ● | ● | ● | ✓ | – | ✓ | – | ✓ | ● | ● |
| ✓ | – | – | ✓ | ✓ | ✓ | ● | ● | ● | ● | ✓ | ✓ | ✓ | – | – | – | – |
| ✓ | – | ✓ | – | – | ✓ | ● | ● | ● | ● | ✓ | – | ✓ | – | ✓ | ● | ● |
| ✓ | – | – | ✓ | – | – | – | ◐ | ● | ◐ | – | ✓ | ✓ | ✓ | ✓ | – | – |

**Room service:** ● 24-hour, ◐ 6AM-10PM, ○ other.
**Laundry/Dry cleaning:** ● same day, ◐ overnight, ○ other.
**Pressing:** ● immediate, ◐ same day, ○ other.

# NEW YORK CITY HOTEL CHART

| HOTELS | Price Category | Business Services Banquet capacity | No. of meeting rooms | Secretarial services | Audiovisual equipment | Teletype news service | Computer rentals | In-room modem phone jack | All-news cable channel | Desk | Desk lighting | Bed lighting |
|---|---|---|---|---|---|---|---|---|---|---|---|---|
| The Plaza | $$$$ | 700 | 18 | - | ✓ | - | - | ✓ | ✓ | ● | ● | ● |
| Regency | $$$$ | 150 | 3 | - | - | - | - | - | ✓ | ● | ● | ● |
| The Royalton | $$$ | 0 | 0 | - | - | - | - | ✓ | ✓ | ● | ● | ● |
| San Carlos | $$ | 0 | 0 | - | - | - | - | - | ✓ | ● | ● | ● |
| Sheraton Park Avenue | $$$ | 100 | 3 | - | ✓ | - | - | ✓ | ✓ | ● | ● | ● |
| Sheraton Squire | $$$ | 400 | 7 | - | ✓ | - | - | - | ✓ | ◐ | ● | ◐ |
| Sherry Netherland | $$$ | 400 | 0 | - | - | - | - | ✓ | ✓ | ◐ | ◐ | ◐ |
| Waldorf-Astoria | $$$$ | 1600 | 25 | ✓ | ✓ | - | - | - | ✓ | ● | ● | ◐ |
| Vista International Newark Airport | $$ | 600 | 6 | ✓ | ✓ | - | ✓ | - | ✓ | ◐ | ◐ | ◐ |
| Vista International Wall Street | $$$ | 1000 | 16 | ✓ | ✓ | - | ✓ | ✓ | ✓ | ◐ | ◐ | ◐ |
| Westbury | $$$$ | 250 | 5 | - | ✓ | - | - | ✓ | ✓ | ● | ● | ◐ |

$$$$ = over $210, $$$ = $150 -$210, $$ = under $150.
● good, ◐ fair, ○ poor.
All hotels listed here have photocopying and fax facilities.

| **In-Room Amenities** Nonsmoking rooms | In-room checkout | Minibar | Pay movies | VCR/Movie rentals | Hairdryer | Toiletries | Room service | Laundry/Dry cleaning | Pressing | **Hotel Amenities** Concierge | Barber/Hairdresser | Garage | Courtesy airport transport | Sauna | Pool | Exercise room |
|---|---|---|---|---|---|---|---|---|---|---|---|---|---|---|---|---|
| ✓ | - | ✓ | ✓ | - | - | ● | ● | ● | ● | ✓ | ✓ | ✓ | - | ✓ | - | - |
| - | - | - | ✓ | ✓ | ✓ | ● | ● | ● | ● | ✓ | ✓ | ✓ | - | ✓ | - | ● |
| ✓ | ✓ | - | - | ✓ | - | ● | ● | ● | ● | ✓ | - | ✓ | - | ✓ | ● | ● |
| - | ✓ | - | - | - | - | ○ | ◐ | ● | ○ | - | - | - | - | - | - | - |
| ✓ | ✓ | - | ✓ | - | ✓ | ● | ● | ● | ◐ | ✓ | - | ✓ | - | ✓ | - | - |
| ✓ | - | - | ✓ | - | - | ● | ● | ● | ● | ✓ | ✓ | - | - | - | ● | - |
| - | - | - | - | ✓ | - | ● | ◐ | ● | ● | ✓ | ✓ | - | - | - | - | - |
| ✓ | ✓ | ✓ | ✓ | - | - | ● | ● | ◐ | ● | ✓ | ✓ | ✓ | - | - | - | - |
| ✓ | ✓ | - | ✓ | - | - | ● | ● | ◐ | ◐ | ✓ | - | ✓ | ✓ | ✓ | ◐ | ● |
| ✓ | ✓ | ✓ | ✓ | - | ✓ | ○ | ● | ● | ◐ | ✓ | ✓ | ✓ | - | ✓ | ● | ● |
| ✓ | - | ✓ | ✓ | - | ✓ | ● | ● | ● | ● | ✓ | - | ✓ | - | - | - | - |

**Room service:** ● 24-hour, ◐ 6AM-10PM, ○ other.
**Laundry/Dry cleaning:** ● same day, ◐ overnight, ○ other.
**Pressing:** ● immediate, ◐ same day, ○ other.

**㉜** **Beekman Tower.** This good-value, all-suite hotel is recom-
**$$$** mended for travelers seeking an extended stay in a quiet,
homelike environment. Favored by business people and
by diplomats serving the nearby United Nations, the 1929
Art Deco establishment sports Top of the Tower, a cock-
tail lounge and famed nightspot. The homey rooms have
traditional mahogany furnishings as well as kitchens with
enough counter space to be the envy of many New
Yorkers; the upper floors afford East River views. Avoid
the studio suites, however, if you need a desk. As part of
an ongoing room-by-room restoration, the Beekman re-
cently added a health club and restaurant. *Manhattan
East Suite Hotels. 3 Mitchell Pl., 10017, tel. 212/355–7300
or 800/637–8483, fax 212/753–9366. Gen. manager, Bob
Hansen. 172 suites. AE, CB, DC, MC, V.*

**㊸** **Gramercy Park.** A nice change from the many soulless
**$$$$** brass-and-chrome midtown hotels, this 18-story estab-
lishment offers its guests the key to one of Manhattan's
only private parks. Set in a quiet residential neighbor-
hood, a couple of subway stops closer to Wall Street, the
Gramercy Park offers a personal touch, catering to even
unusual requests with efficiency and grace. But the warm,
wood-paneled lobby and alluring bar have a disappointing
follow-through. Rooms are poorly lighted, bathroom tiles
are chipped, and the cheerless mood pervades even those
rooms that have been recently renovated. The lower
floors, on occasion, are noisy—attributable in part to the
rock bands that stay here (along with clothing manufac-
turers and gift and toy industry people). *2 Lexington
Ave., 10010, tel. 212/475–4320 or 800/221–4083, fax 212/
505–0535. Gen. manager, Thomas O'Brien. 220 rooms,
140 suites. AE, DC, MC, V.*

**㊳** **Grand Hyatt.** People move about the brassy, floodlit lobby
**$$$$** of this 34-story hotel, revamped in 1981, at an almost fre-
netic pace. You may not admire such flourishes as the
lobby's marble waterfall (subtlety was never the strong
suit of Donald Trump, the developer and part-owner), but
the hotel has an energy that captures the spirit of the city.
One apt touch: Diners in the glass-walled Crystal Foun-
tain can watch the 42nd Street traffic reflected in mirrored
ceilings. The mostly business clientele enjoy the proximi-
ty to the transportation hub of Grand Central Station, as
well as the spacious, quiet rooms, but the absence of desks
is a shortcoming. Sports fans, note: You could run into
Magic Johnson in the elevator—the hotel is a favorite with
out-of-town athletic teams. *Park Ave. at Grand Central,
10017, tel. 212/883–1234 or 800/233–1234, fax 212/697–
3772. Gen. manager, Gale Garvin. 1,293 rooms, 54 suites.
AE, CB, D, DC, MC, V.*

**㉒** **Hotel Elysée.** Via word of mouth, this small hotel has
**$$$** developed a loyal clientele who prize its intimate, French
country-inn ambience. Close to a wealth of fine restau-
rants, the Elysée is valued by business travelers—especially Europeans and Japanese—who want character and
charm along with the convenience of midtown. The rooms
are spacious, comfortable, and warmly furnished, if not
plush; all have terraces, some overlooking 54th Street.
Other pluses are the seafood restaurant and the Monkey
Bar, which has comedy and cabaret acts. *60 E. 54th St.,
10022, tel. 212/753–1066, fax 212/980–9278. Gen. manager, Sy Pinto. 95 rooms, 15 suites. AE, CB, DC, MC, V.*

**㊲ Kitano.** Tokyo newspapers are delivered daily to this Japanese-owned and -staffed hotel, whose clientele is about 70% Japanese. The Kitano is also popular with fashion buyers doing business in the nearby garment district. It offers good value and a helpful staff; the location, in a quiet area, just south of midtown, is also a plus. But the ambience—from the piped-in lobby music to the flourescent lighting—owes more to a suburban shopping mall than it does to the Orient, and room desks are the sort seen at garage sales. *66 Park Ave., 10016, tel. 212/685–0022, fax 212/532–5615. Gen. manager, Yoshiomi F. Nakajima. 86 rooms, 12 suites. AE, CB, DC, MC, V.*
**$$**

**㉟ Marriott Marquis.** This huge, 48-floor hotel, part of the upgrade of the still sleazy theater district, opened in 1985 and largely caters to groups attending the city's Jacob Javits Convention Center. Every detail of the design—rooms wrapping around an atrium, glass elevators, revolving rooftop restaurant—is familiar, but the patented look, cloned from sunbelt establishments, seems out of place on Times Square. Though the lower seven floors of stores, restaurants, and meeting places are reminiscent of a shopping mall, the rooms and baths are unusually spacious and comfortable; those on the front side, though a trifle noisy, offer spectacular views of Broadway. *1535 Broadway, 10036, tel. 212/398–1900 or 800/228–9290. Gen. manager, Thomas Reese. 1,733 rooms, 141 suites. AE, CB, D, DC, MC, V.*
**$$$$**

**★ ㉓ New York Hilton & Towers.** This no-nonsense hotel is probably the best in midtown for purely business needs, as is evidenced by a largely business clientele. Guests can give dictation 24 hours a day and get prompt, printed transcripts. A business center has private work stations with personal computers as well as a Dow Jones news ticker and information services. Those staying in the hotel's executive tower get complimentary breakfasts and drinks with free hors d'oeuvres on a 39th-floor lounge. The rooms have slick, black-top furniture and a clean, corporate look. A new, Manhattan-style steakhouse has a lot of old-fashioned character, but unless you favor pulsating music and flashing lights, you can skip the nightclub, which is oddly out of place. *1335 Ave. of the Americas, 10019, tel. 212/586–7000 or 800/445–8667, fax 212/315–1374. Gen. manager, John Power. 1,922 rooms, 112 suites. AE, CB, D, DC, MC, V.*
**$$$**

**㉖ Parc 51.** Opened in 1986 as the Grand Bay, this is perhaps the most luxurious of the new hotels springing up in the theater district. Catering to law firms, accounting firms, and other businesses pioneering on the west side, the hotel has only seven floors; guests who want to avoid the noise of Seventh Avenue should ask for an interior room. Compensations are a pampering staff and 24-hour-a-day concierge service, along with plush, French provincial rooms with ample sitting areas, and luxurious baths with 60-gallon tubs as well as bidets, TVs, and telephones. The lobby, with its classical paintings and quiet fern bar, has an understated elegance, and the mezzanine breakfasts are perfect for morning business meetings. *Park Lane Hotels International. 152 W. 51st St., 10019, tel. 212/765–1900, fax 212/541–6604. Gen. manager, Guenter Richter. 126 rooms, 52 suites. AE, CB, DC, MC, V.*
**$$$$**

⑫ **Parker Meridien.** This distinctly French hotel boasts a
$$$$ warm and lively lobby animated by a jazz piano bar. Visitors from nearby Carnegie Hall and the theater district come for the ground-floor buffets. In addition to a full health club, Le Parker Meridien has a skylit penthouse swimming pool. The only disappointment is the rooms, furnished in spare, contemporary style; they seem a bit too modest for a hotel in this price category. The higher floors are quietest. The mostly business clientele draws heavily from West Coast entertainment industry people visiting the nearby networks. *A Meridien hotel. 118 W. 57th St., 10019, tel. 212/245–5000 or 800/543–4300, fax 212/307–1776. Gen. manager, Serge Denis. 494 rooms, 207 suites. AE, CB, DC, MC, V.*

⑩ **Park Lane Hotel.** If you're not from Miami Beach you may
$$$ find this 1972, 46-floor hotel a bit overstated. The lobby is done up in light marble, wood paneling, mirrors, and the inevitable crystal chandeliers, but the effect is of glitz rather than grandeur. Still, the Central Park views are second to none, and the location is within walking distance of most of midtown. The rooms are spacious and come with fridges, scales, shoe-shine facilities, and phones by beds and desks; their old-fashioned furnishings are surprisingly plain, however. Guests are lavished with attention by the staff, and the hotel seems undisturbed by the myriad legal problems of its most famous long-time resident— who also happens to be its owner—Leona Helmsley. *Helmsley Hotels. 36 Central Park S., 10019, tel. 212/371–4000 or 800/221–4982, fax 212/319–9065. Gen. manager, Anton Gotsche. 601 rooms, 25 suites. AE, CB, DC, MC, V.*

⑱ **Peninsula New York.** The hotel was known as Maxim's un-
$$$$ til 1988, when it reopened under its present name. The new management has made mostly superficial changes; the accent is still French, and still luxurious, the tone somewhat formal. The Fifth Avenue location appeals mainly to Fortune 500 executives, but celebs stay here, too. Practically every room has a photograph of Sara Bernhardt, one of the many Art Nouveau touches in the establishment. Everything about the rooms is plush— note the large bathtubs and gold fixtures. The three-floor health spa is one of the city's best. *A Peninsula Group hotel. 700 Fifth Ave., 10019, tel. 212/247–2200 or 800/262–9467, fax 212/903–3949. Gen. manager, Manfred Timmel. 220 rooms, 30 suites. AE, DC, MC, V.*

㊶ **Penta.** A hangout of Glenn Miller in the Big Band era, this
$$ 1919 Beaux Arts classic (designed by McKim Mead & White) has lost some of its shine with the decline of the neighborhood, which suffers from an overabundance of panhandlers and a general social malaise. Still, the hotel is popular with convention-goers and business groups. The rooms are adequate, although the decor leans to tacky still-life prints. The upper floors are a bit worn; the lower floors, refurbished in 1985, are the best bet. Guests staying on the sixth floor can go from the conference center to their quarters without stepping in an elevator. Another plus: young, energetic staff members. Many have been hired recently and most are bubbling over with an eagerness to help. The Penta is convenient to the subway and to shopping (Macy's is a block away). *401 Seventh Ave., 10001, tel. 212/736–5000 or 800/447–3682, fax 212/502–*

*8712. Gen. manager, Kenneth Walles. 1,680 rooms, 25 suites. AE, CB, DC, MC, V.*

★ ⑪ **The Plaza.** Owner Donald Trump has too many copies of
$$$$ his autobiography on display in the hotel store, but the
Plaza is arguably still the grandest of New York's hotels,
attracting show biz guests as well as business and sports
VIPs. The original 1907 moldings and crystal chandeliers
lend an elegance to the guest quarters, but save for the
suites, they are otherwise surprisingly ordinary and the
rates quite steep. The Plaza's appeal is in its location, on
the high-rent border of Central Park, and in its Baroque
public spaces. The dark panelled Oak Room, with painted
murals and leather armchairs, is ideal for business meals.
Most notable is the gold-trimmed Palm Court, serving
light fare and desserts—perfect for listening to piano and
violin duets and for just passing time. *Fifth Avenue at
Central Park S., 10019, tel. 212/759–3000 or 800/228–
3000, fax 212/759–3167. Gen. manager, Richard Wilhelm.
705 rooms, 109 suites. AE, CB, D, DC, MC, V.*

㊲ **The Royalton.** This super-chic hotel, whipped up in 1988
$$$ by the duo that created Studio 54, has the same flair as
that disco for capturing a sense of scene. The museum gal-
lery-like interior, the creation of avant garde designer
Philippe Starck, includes a hypermodern lobby with horn-
shaped lights, harpoon-legged stools, and employees in se-
vere black Mao jackets. The comfortable rooms have a se-
ductive charm—the beds are tucked between pairs of
portholes, and the bathrooms are done in green slate;
many of them have five-foot round tubs. An in-house tape
library holds 500 films. Not surprisingly, movie, record,
design, and entertainment types figure prominently on
this midtown hotel's guest list. Indeed, everything and
everyone here is beautiful, but some will find the self-con-
scious and unrelenting attention to design tiresome. *44 W.
44th St., 10036, tel. 212/869–4400 or 800/635–9013, fax
212/869–8965. Gen. manager, Alex de Toth. 154 rooms, 16
suites. AE, CB, DC, MC, V.*

★ ㉚ **San Carlos.** This small, owner-operated hotel offers priva-
$$ cy, reasonable rates, and a residential feeling in the heart
of midtown. U.N. diplomats and Japanese and Brazilian
businessmen who stay here lend an international accent,
and all are well attended by the efficient staff. The rooms
are equipped with sleek, modern furnishings and small
kitchens, and the decor is bright, spare, and uncluttered.
Rooms in the back, off the street, are recommended. *150
E. 50th St., 10022, tel. 212/755–1800 or 800/722–2012, fax
212/688–9778. Gen. manager, Robert Kaminsky. 140
rooms, 60 suites. AE, CB, DC, MC, V.*

㊵ **Sheraton Park Avenue.** This hotel has about as much per-
$$$ sonality and charm as one might expect from a chain, but
its location, just south of midtown, is perfect for no-non-
sense business travelers. The rooms, recently renovated,
are comfortable, and have telephones in the bath. The low-
er floors on the 37th Street side can be noisy; the rooms
overlooking Park Avenue have the best views. Garment
industry people, executives with business on Wall Street,
and Europeans of various interests are among the guests.
Try out the jazz (four nights a week) in the Judge's Cham-
ber. *45 Park Ave., 10016, tel. 212/685–7676 or 800/325–
3535, fax 212/889–3193. Gen. manager, James Bennett.
133 rooms, 18 suites. AE, CB, D, DC, MC, V.*

㉕ **Sheraton Squire.** This hotel is generally packed with busi-
$$$ ness travelers, but it's hard to tell why. The ground-floor
coffee shop is neon depressing, the lobby has all the ambi-
ence of an airport lounge, and the room decor is tacky. The
last room renovation was in 1983 and the next is overdue:
paint is peeling on some walls, and some bedboards are
spotted. Rooms overlooking Seventh Avenue are noisy,
and the smallish lobby is jammed with patrons and a bit
confused. One plus is the staff, many of whom have been
here for years and do their best to overlook the chaos and
keep the guests content. The west side location is close to
midtown, Broadway, and the Jacob Javitz Convention
Center. *790 Seventh Ave., 10019, tel. 212/581–3300 or 800/
325–3535, fax 212/541–9219. Gen. manager, Andrew
Katz. 713 rooms, 7 suites. AE, CB, D, DC, MC, V.*

★ ㉛ **Waldorf-Astoria.** The Waldorf, built in 1931 and restored
$$$$ in 1986, evokes an era when great public places were re-
vered as monuments and meeting grounds. The Art Deco
lobby is a sort of idealized, bustling city, where no one
seems to be at cross purposes, and elegance transcends all
the hubbub—see especially the Cocktail Terrace, where a
harpist sets the tone. Rooms are plush and luxurious,
from the gold bath fixtures to the separate dressing areas
and solid mahogany furnishings. The hotel has a well-
equipped business center, and a staff capable of translat-
ing 60 languages. Although the salad to which the hotel
gave its name is still served here, a Japanese restaurant,
Inagiku, is becoming the most admired of the Waldorf's
various dining spots. *A Hilton hotel. 301 Park Ave.,
10022, tel. 212/355–3000 or 800/445–8667, fax 212/872–
4799. Gen. manager, Per Hellman. 1,410 rooms, 300
suites. AE, CB, DC, MC, V.*

## Upper East Side and Lincoln Center

★ ❶ **The Carlyle.** A favorite of celebrities—Jack Nicholson is a
$$$$ regular—who are wont to wave at each other in the hotel
tea room, the Carlyle is also a haven for corporate big-
wigs, who sail in and out in limousines to offices down-
town. The decor may be English country, but modern
amenities abound: most of the large, ultra-plush rooms in-
clude Jacuzzi, bidet, pantry with fridge, compact disk
player, stereo, bathroom phone, and fax machine. The up-
per floors facing south offer stunning views of the midtown
skyline. The Carlyle has twice as many staff members as
rooms, yet its muraled bar, restaurant, and nightclub are
what make this hotel a New York institution. Jazz pianist
Bobby Short—also an institution—is in his third decade
at the Café Carlyle (*see* Bars and Lounges, below). *35 E.
76th St., 10021, tel. 212/744–1600 or 800/227–5737, fax
212/717–4682. Gen. manager, Dan Camp. 100 rooms, 90
suites. AE, CB, DC, MC, V.*

★ ❺ **The Lowell.** This small, mostly suite hotel is the ultimate
$$$$ for those looking for a European flavor and elegant, spa-
cious quarters. The rooms, with their eclectic mix of En-
glish and French furnishings, wood-burning fireplaces,
and 18th- and 19th-century prints, are very homey, and in-
clude desks both practical *and* stylish; all also feature full
kitchens, and bathroom telephones. The Pembroke Room,
serving Continental cuisine and afternoon tea, is a good
hideaway for business meals. Few hotels are pricier than
the Lowell, but few have better service (the staff outnum-

bers the guests). On a quiet, east-side street, close to galleries and bookstores as well as to midtown, the hotel is a favorite of executives traveling with spouses. *28 E. 63rd St., 10021, tel. 212/838-1400, fax 212/319-4230. Gen. manager, Lynne Hunter Gray. 13 rooms, 48 suites. AE, CB, DC, MC, V.*

**❹ Mayfair Regent.** A fine location—in an upscale residential
$$$$ district, but close to midtown—and Continental-style attention to detail help this gracious hotel draw a large number of European business travelers and dignitaries. The rich terra cotta color of the walls in the elegant lobby is accented by the upholstery of the dark-wood furniture; the arches, palm fronds, and Oriental vases of an adjoining lounge make it a lovely setting for a light lunch or afternoon tea. The complete refurbishing in 1988–89 of the original 1925 structure left the spacious, light rooms and suites with charm intact while adding such modern business amenities as 4-line telephones (at least two in each accommodation). There are no on-premises exercise facilities, but stationary bikes are available on request. Umbrellas, unlimited free local calls, and humidifiers in each room are among the other special touches. The superlative Le Cirque restaurant (*see* Dining, below) has an entrance off the hotel lobby. *A Regent International hotel; member of Leading Hotels of the World. 610 Park Ave., 10021, tel. 212/288-0800 or 800/223-0542, fax 212/737-0538. Gen. manager, Dario Mariotti. 27 singles, 69 doubles, 105 suites. AE, CB, DC, MC, V.*

**❻ Mayflower.** If you're seeking a crisp, corporate look, you
$$ won't find it here. The lobby is dreary and a bit run-down. The spacious rooms and suites, recently redone, have pantries, fridges, and oversized closets (one reason the hotel is a favorite of actors and Bolshoi Ballet members), but the nondescript modern decor is nothing to write home about. What the Mayflower does offer is a friendly and informal ambience and a Central Park West location, appreciated by conventioneers, Lincoln Center- and theater-goers, and all who prefer Manhattan's more relaxed and heterogeneous West Side. Park-front rooms have views as good as any, but be prepared for street noise. Music in the hotel's Conservatory Bar and Restaurant is a neighborhood favorite. *15 Central Park W., 10023, tel. 212/265-0060 or 800/223-4164, fax 212/265-5098. Gen. manager, Michael Fenn. 190 rooms, 410 suites. AE, CB, D, DC, MC, V.*

**❼ Regency.** The exclusive and residential Park Avenue ad-
$$$$ dress may explain why Dustin Hoffman and Frank Sinatra—as well as many wealthy South Americans—are frequent guests. All the amenities, and most of the luxuries, are here (an executive favorite: telephones are placed on desks as well as on nightstands). The restaurant, "540 Park," is famed for power breakfasts, and the rooms, recently restored, combine modern baths with reproductions of 18th-century furniture. But the Regency doesn't have the grandeur to justify its price, and it's a bit too stuffy to qualify as intimate. Though it bills itself as "residential," music from weddings in the hotel ballroom is audible in the lobby. *Loews Hotels. 540 Park Ave., 10021, tel. 212/759-4100 or 800/243-1166, fax 212/826-5674. Gen. manager, John Beier. 320 rooms, 70 suites. AE, DC, MC, V.*

★ **8** **Sherry Netherland.** Considering its Old New York reputa-
$$$ tion, its Fifth Avenue location, and its air of elegance, this
vintage 1927 hotel offers surprising value. Its chief attri-
butes are the spacious, traditional rooms—try for one
with a Central Park view—the quiet, subdued tone, and a
staff that prides itself on knowing its guests. (The bell
captain has been on the job for more than 30 years.) CEOs,
Hollywood celebrities, and fashion moguls are among the
clientele, and many come for long stays. A room renova-
tion is on-going, but some guests say it isn't necessary.
The wooden, hand-painted elevator is a gem. *781 Fifth
Ave., 10022, tel. 212/355–2800 or 800/223–0522, fax 212/
319–4306. Gen. manager, Louis Ventresca. 98 rooms, 25
suites. AE.*

**2** **Westbury.** With a restaurant called The Polo, this hotel in
$$$$ the heart of New York's gallery district is perfect for the
prep school set. And with socialites, diplomats, foreign
dignitaries, and camera-shy celebrities heading the guest
list, is it any wonder the lobby is a tad stiff? Thanks to the
staff's policy of catering to guests' whims, the hotel has a
high ratio of regular customers. The understated elegance
of the rooms, recently renovated in English manor house
style, should appeal to business travelers, as should their
noiselessness. The Westbury's rates are as exclusive as its
ambience. *Trusthouse Forte Hotels. 15 E. 69th St., 10021,
tel. 212/535–2000 or 800/225–5843, fax 212/535–5058.
Gen. manager, Stefan Simkovics. 180 rooms, 55 suites.
AE, CB, DC, MC, V.*

## Airport

$$ **JFK Plaza Hotel.** This contemporary-style, 12-story hotel, a 5- to 10-minute drive from the terminals at John F.
Kennedy International airport, is out of the flight path of
most of the airport's traffic. Guests on the concierge level
get free Continental breakfasts and hors d'oeuvres; general amenities include a weight room. *Heller-White Hotels. 135–30 140th St., 11436, tel. 718/659–6000 or 800/
445–7177, fax 718/659–4755. Gen. manager, Bill McGlad-
dery. 349 rooms, 21 suites. AE, CB, D, DC, MC, V.*

$$$ **LaGuardia Marriott Airport Hotel.** A quarter-mile from
the airport and—barring traffic—within 20 minutes of
Manhattan, this 1981 hotel is out of the direct line of most
of the flights. A concierge floor with a bar and free Conti-
nental breakfasts recently opened. *102–05 Ditmars
Blvd., East Elmhurst, 11369, tel. 718/565–8900 or 800/
228–9290, fax 718/899–0764. Gen. manager, William
Archard. 432 rooms, 5 suites. AE, CB, D, DC, MC, V.*

$$ **Vista International.** Opened in 1988, the Vista is five minutes from Newark airport and 20 minutes, in light traffic,
from Manhattan. Triple-glazed glass doors keep airport
noise to a minimum. The hotel caters to businesspeople,
but guests who need to go into Manhattan should bear in
mind that traffic in the Jersey–New York tunnels can be
especially slow (in both directions) at rush hours and at
various other unpredictable times. *A Hilton International hotel. 1170 Spring St., Elizabeth, NJ, 07201, tel. 201/
351–3900 or 800/678–4782, fax 201/355–8059. Gen. manager, Cindy Estis. 370 rooms, 6 suites. AE, CB, D, DC,
MC, V.*

# DINING

*by Elaine Hamilton*

The restaurant scene in New York, like the city itself, is constantly changing as new places open and close, new cuisines come and go, and chefs hop around from one kitchen to another. Along with "spa" cuisine and Northern Italian food, bistro cooking has become the current craze. Even if no one knows what next year will bring, one thing is certain: there are few places in the world where one can eat as well as in New York City. In the past decade, many top French and Italian chefs have moved here, and their influence has spread throughout the city's better restaurants. Many of the top hotels have upgraded their eateries—some of the best food in town is now to be found in hotel dining rooms. At the same time, the quality of the produce available has improved dramatically. There has never been such a variety of fresh ingredients for the chef to choose from.

The following guide lists restaurants that are congenial either to business discussion or entertaining. It includes well-known and less-discovered places. In addition, after the reviews is a listing of some of the best or most unusual ethnic restaurants the city has to offer. Although most are not appropriate for business meals, they help represent what makes dining in New York a unique experience.

Highly recommended restaurants in each of these categories are indicated by a star ★.

| Category | Cost* |
|---|---|
| *$$$$* (Very Expensive) | over $55 |
| *$$$* (Expensive) | $38–$55 |
| *$$* (Moderate) | under $38 |

*\*per person, including appetizer, entrée, and dessert, but excluding drinks, service, and 8¼% sales tax.*

*Numbers in the margin correspond to numbered restaurant locations on the New York Lodging and Dining maps.*

## Business Breakfasts

Many of the city's top hotels also serve the now legendary "power breakfast." **Café Pierre** in the Hotel Pierre (2 E. 61st St., tel. 212/940–8185) has a dining room in the grand style of the '30s and '40s and serves a business breakfast that includes chipped beef and (for the health conscious) Egg Beaters. **The Carlyle Restaurant** (Carlyle Hotel, tel. 212/744–1600) presents a top-notch breakfast buffet in an elegant, classic Georgian-style setting. **The Regency** (Regency Hotel, tel. 212/749–4200) is the place where the power breakfast originated. On any weekday morning you can find the city's business leaders wheeling and dealing here over kippers and eggs.

## Midtown

**Adrienne.** International business travelers, many from the Far East, congregate in this second-floor dining room of the Hotel Peninsula. Comfortable chairs, thick carpets, and a low noise level make this a good place for serious business talk, although the Art Nouveau decor is uninspired and the atmosphere just slightly stuffy. The food, however, is first-rate. The chef, Gray Kunz, a young Swiss protégé of master chef Fredy Girardet, is unquestionably a rising star; his cooking is a fascinating blend of East and West (he worked for a while in Hong Kong). Some of his dishes are dazzling, especially those featuring fish, such as snapper with curry and cardamom, or steamed sole. The cheese tray is exceptional and the wine list excellent. *Peninsula Hotel, 700 Fifth Ave. at 55th St., tel. 212/903–3918. Jacket and tie required. Reservations advised. AE, CB, DC, MC, V. Closed Sun. dinner.*

**20** **Aquavit.** Aquavit offers the best and most sophisticated
**$$$** Scandinavian food New York City has seen for years. Christer Larsson, a Swedish-born chef who trained in restaurants and hotels in Europe, does wonders with such exotic specialties as juniper-smoked salmon, moose, Arctic venison, snow grouse, and cloudberries. You walk into a sleek café that serves inexpensive light meals and Danish open-face sandwiches; in the handsome formal dining room beneath it, a seven-story atrium between two townhouses, the leaves of silver birch trees rustle as endless sheets of water pour down a gray tiled wall. In addition to the extensive wine list, there is a choice of seven kinds of beer and eight kinds of aquavit. *13 W. 54th St., tel. 212/307–7311. Jackets required downstairs, no dress code upstairs. Reservations suggested downstairs, not accepted upstairs. AE, MC, V. Closed Sun.*

**34** **Aurora.** At lunchtime Joseph Baum's restaurant resem-
**$$$$** bles a corporate dining room, so packed is it with business-people. Sometimes it can be hard to get reservations, as this has become one of the city's major business lunch places. Comfortable leather chairs, tables placed far apart, wood paneling, and a soothing pink glow make this a relaxed spot for a serious discussion. A special grill menu is served at the long horseshoe-shaped bar. Chef Andrew Wilkinson produces classic but innovative French food. Try ravioli with sea scallops, oysters on the half shell with spicy veal sausage, roast pigeon with garlic sauce, salmon in a horseradish crust, and, for dessert, saffron ice cream and warm chocolate mousse cake. Service is professional and unobtrusive. *60 E. 49th St., tel. 212/692–9292. Jacket and tie required. Reservations advised. AE, CB, DC, MC, V. Closed Sun.*

**24** **The Four Seasons.** No other restaurant in New York serves
**$$$$** up quite such a big-league lunch as the Four Seasons in the Seagram's Building. Every working day in the Grill Room, a no-nonsense masculine setting of leather and wood, with enormous hanging brass rod sculptures by Richard Lippold, the big guns in publishing, finance, and politics make deals over small bottles of Seagram's soda water and spa cuisine. At night, the Pool Room with its gurgling waters and tubs of ficus trees caters to out-of-town businesspeople. Chef Christian Albin is skilled and inventive (especially with game, polenta, and terrines) but not all the dishes are a success. Try frog's legs in flaky pastry, fettucine primavera, roast pigeon, and any of the desserts. Service can be offhand and if you are unknown you may be seated in "Siberia"—upstairs in the back. Private rooms accommodate 10–22 people. *99 E.*

52nd St., tel. 212/754–9494. Jacket and tie required. Reservations advised. AE, DC, MC, V. Closed Sun. and major holidays.

**⑭ La Caravelle.** With its lipstick-red banquettes and post-
$$$$   war murals of Paris, this restaurant is a throwback to the
1950s; you could picture the Duke and Duchess of Windsor walking in at any minute. Bright and elegant, this is a good setting for business or post-business pleasure at lunch as well as dinner. Chef Frank Chanpli produces exciting variations on classic French themes. Try the fresh foie gras, roast duck with cranberries, crab ravioli, and such exceptional desserts as chocolate Charlotte or apple tart from the trolley. The impeccable service is of the old school, with dishes prepared at tableside. *33 W. 55th St., tel. 212/586–4252. Jacket and tie required. Reservations advised. AE, CB, DC, MC, V. Closed Sun. and major holidays.*

**⑮ La Côte Basque.** The noise and table hopping can be dis-
$$$$   tracting for serious business, but this restaurant also
turns out superb classic French cooking. Pretty murals of the French coast, red banquettes, and a chic clientele lend a touch of glamour. You can feel a bit out of things, though, if you are seated in the newer dining room to the left—and indeed, customers not known to the management are often placed here. Tables in front of the bar, as you walk in, are quieter than those in the main dining room. Jean-Jacques Rachoux now looks after the customers and staff, while Michel Fitoussi oversees the kitchen. The food is elaborate, intensely flavored, and highly decorated with two-tone sauces painted with fanciful designs. Particularly recommended are the charcuterie, pâtés and terrines, roast duck, rack of lamb, and cassoulet Toulousain. Fresh berries and hot soufflés are the best desserts. *5 E. 55th St., tel. 212/688–6525. Jacket and tie required. Reservations advised. AE, CB, D, MC, V. Closed Sun. and major holidays.*

**⑬ Lafayette.** The Swiss-owned Drake Hotel's plush, quiet
$$$$   dining room is a little bland and dowdy, but the food—
French with Mediterranean and Southeast Asian influences—is not. The menu is overseen by Louis Outhier, who had a three-star restaurant in the French Riviera, and his protégé, Jean-Georges Vongerichten, who trained at L'Auberge de L'Ill in Alsace. Among the stellar choices are sweetbreads with foie gras, whole sea bass in pastry crust, baby goat with chick peas, and chocolate soufflé gratin. Lafayette now serves a special three-course lunch for hurried businesspeople and guarantees to get you out within half an hour. *Drake Hotel, 65 E. 56th St., tel. 212/ 832–1565. Jacket and tie required. Reservations advised. AE, CB, D, MC, V. Closed Aug.*

**★ ㉝ La Reserve.** Without fanfare, La Reserve has taken its
$$$$   place among the city's best French restaurants. The cook-
ing is classically based but with a light touch. The restaurant's two dining rooms are large, quiet, and comfortable, with enormous chandeliers, beige-and-peach banquettes, and chairs generously proportioned to accommodate those accustomed to a steady diet of rich French food. Owner Jean-Louis Missud is a conservationist, and named his restaurant after the wetlands reserve on the New Jersey shore overlooking Manhattan, pictured in huge murals in the first room. Some good choices are a jellied crayfish

consommé, bavarois of smoked salmon topped with red caviar, grilled quail in hazelnut vinaigrette, and lamb noisettes with green peppercorns. Save room for dessert. *4 W. 49th St., tel. 212/247–2993. Jacket and tie required. Reservations advised. AE, CB, DC, MC, V. Closed Sun.*

**㉗** **Le Bernardin.** This French fish restaurant on the ground
$$$$ floor of the Equitable building is both luxurious and clubby, with high teak ceilings and dark blue walls decorated with large oil paintings of fishermen. Tables are well spaced, making this an ideal spot for private conversations—and indeed, virtually all the clientele look to be here on business. The fish is as fresh as you'll get anywhere, and chef Gilbert LeCoze's food can be dazzling, even if inconsistent. Among the more arresting preparations are a carpaccio of tuna, oysters cooked with truffles and served on seaweed, and salmon dishes such as gravlax potato salad or roulade of salmon, stuffed with spinach. Finish off with a caramel sampler, which includes caramel ice cream, crème caramel, oeuf à la neige, and caramel mousse. *155 W. 51st St., tel. 212/489–1515. Jacket and tie required. Reservations advised well in advance. AE, CB, V. Closed Sun.*

**★ ❹** **Le Cirque.** This is less a restaurant in which to do business
$$$$ than a place to celebrate after a deal has been made. It's boisterous, noisy, amusing, and filled with celebrities and society types blowing kisses across the crowded dining room. Owner Sirio Maccioni is a New York legend and a master at making it all work. The classic French food prepared by the young Burgundian chef, Daniel Boulud, is nothing short of great—and the menu is vast. Try the scallops with black truffles (listed as "sea scallops fantasy in black tie"), sautéed fresh foie gras, pot au feu, or roast chicken with lemon garlic and herbs. The crème brûlée is justifiably renowned. The wine list is one of the city's best, with many good choices at reasonable prices. *58 E. 65th St., in the Mayfair-Regent Hotel, tel. 212/794–9292. Jacket and tie required. Reservations advised well in advance. AE, CB, DC. Closed Sun., major holidays, and first 3 weeks of July.*

**㉑** **Le Cygne.** Despite handsome new quarters, this restau
$$$$ rant went into decline for a few years until the arrival of chef Jean Michel Bergougnoux, who formerly worked at Lutèce. Now the pretty pastel dining rooms (on two floors of a townhouse) are a fitting backdrop to the fine French cuisine being produced here. A dual winding staircase leads to the upper level, which has arched ceilings and opaque glass panels; the downstairs is decorated with bright murals of wildflowers. Parties of more than four should request upstairs seating—tables are larger and more widely spaced. On both floors the noise level is low and the service first-rate. Among the many excellent entrées are bouillabaisse, breast of chicken with leeks and truffles, and fettuccine with wild mushrooms; top the evening off with a cassis delight. *55 E. 54th St., tel. 212/759–5941. Jacket and tie required. Reservations advised. AE, DC, MC, V. Closed Sun., major holidays, and 3 weeks in Aug.*

**★ ㉘** **Lutèce.** Also on two floors of a townhouse, with a garden
$$$$ room in back, Lutèce is one of New York's best French restaurants, but you may have to wait a month for a reservation. André Soltner is a dedicated chef whose classic

French and Alsatian dishes make the wait worthwhile. (He also consistently tours the dining room to make suggestions and check on the meal; if he makes a recommendation, follow it.) People are often surprised at the informality of Lutèce—it doesn't have the stiffness of many haute cuisine establishments. In some ways it sees itself as a high-class bistro—and the customers who come here tend to be passionate about food. Try the Alsatian onion tart, choucroute garni, roast pheasant or venison, chicken sauté au Riesling, or tarte tatin. The prix fixe lunch is a very good value. *249 E. 50th St., tel. 212/752–2225. Jacket and tie required. Reservations advised well in advance. AE, DC, CB. Closed Sun., Mon. lunch, Sat. in June and July, all major holidays, and Aug.–Labor Day weekend.*

**⑰** **Michael's.** Chef Michael McCarty recently brought his
**$$$** brand of California cuisine from Santa Monica to New York. The large dining rooms are hung with lithographs by Jasper Johns, Frank Stella, and David Hockney, and bas-reliefs by Robert Graham. During the day, the restaurant is bright and cheerful, with a view onto the street, and, in the back, a skylight and courtyard gardens. Despite a menu that spells out the life-history of each ingredient, much of the food at Michael's is superior. Try the Malpèque oysters, gravlax with mustard dill sauce and brioche toast, lobster salad, grilled rabbit in mustard cream sauce, or grilled saddle of lamb with red wine, blackcurrants, and thyme. Michael's has a particularly impressive wine list with many unusual choices from small California vineyards at reasonable prices. *24 W. 55th St., tel. 212/753–7295. Casual dress. Reservations advised. AE, DC, CB, MC, V.*

**㊷** **Park Bistro.** If you are doing business near or around low-
**$$** er Park Avenue, this is a good place for a casual lunch. Publishers and magazine editors congregate here for superior Provençal cooking at reasonable prices. The restaurant feels like an authentic old-style bistro, complete with French film posters, lace curtains, leather banquettes, and a bustling, glassed-in kitchen at the back. Jean-Michel Diot's dishes are redolent of the Mediterranean, infused with garlic, olive oil, and fresh herbs, plus out-of-the-ordinary seasonings, such as whole baby onions, fennel, and salsify. Try cold shellfish soup, codfish (cabillaud) with fried leeks and mashed potatoes, leg of lamb with flageolets, and roasted rabbit. The short wine list (on the back of the menu) is reasonably priced and interesting, with some good selections from Provence. *414 Park Ave., tel. 212/689–1360. Casual dress. Reservations advised. AE, DC. Closed Sun. and Sat. lunch.*

**★ ⑯** **The Quilted Giraffe.** The most expensive restaurant in
**$$$$** New York—usually filled with rich foreign businessmen—The Quilted Giraffe is also one of the most impressive both in decor and cuisine. The dramatic new quarters in the AT&T building on Madison Avenue at 55th Street feature stainless steel walls, gray leather banquettes, and speckled granite floors; lavish flower arrangements add color and warmth. Chef Barry Wine turns out food that is out of the ordinary and unforgettable. Among the delights are beggar's purses (tiny crêpes filled with caviar and crème fraiche), home-smoked salmon, confit of duck, and rack of lamb with Chinese mustard. Some desserts worth

the calories are pecan squares and chocolate soufflé with espresso ice cream. *550 Madison Ave., tel. 212/593–1221. Jacket and tie required. Reservations advised well in advance. AE, MC, V. Closed Sun., lunch.*

**㉙ The Rainbow Room.** The famous 1930s supper club has undergone extensive renovations under the supervision of restaurateur Joseph Baum and designer Milton Glaser. Now, complete with revolving dance floor, seating on three levels, silk walls, and giant bandstand, it brings back a more glamorous era. It's an experience not to be missed—a great place to celebrate a business deal. The room itself, with one of the most magnificent views in Manhattan, is a stunning example of Art Moderne. In addition to contemporary French fare, much of the menu is deliberately retro—some of the dishes, such as lobster thermidor, tournedos Rossini, and oysters Rockefeller, date back to the 1930s and '40s. For a finishing touch you can order a baked Alaska flambé. *30 Rockefeller Plaza, tel. 212/632–5100. Jacket and tie required. Reservations advised several weeks in advance. AE. Dinner only; closed Mon.*

$$$$

**⑲ Restaurant Raphael.** A quiet spot in bustling midtown, this intimate, demure townhouse is understandably popular with French business visitors. With its fireplace and outdoor garden (where you can dine in the summer), it fits everyone's image of the quintessential Parisian dining room. A new chef, Kurt Beverly, has taken over the kitchen, but to date, this restaurant, supervised by owners Mira and Raphael Edery, has consistently produced classic French cooking at its best. Among the commendable choices on the current menu are wild mushroom flan, grilled jumbo shrimp, roast loin of lamb with ratatouille purée, Gascogny-style duck breast with celery root and apple, and, to finish, chocolate soufflé with crème anglaise or apple tart in a thin pastry shell. Service is impeccable but the wine list, while offering many French vintages to go with the food, is predictable. *33 W. 54th St., tel. 212/ 582–8993. Jacket and tie required. Reservations advised. AE, CB, DC, MC, V. Closed Sun., Sat. from Memorial to Labor Day.*

$$$$

**⑨ San Domenico.** New York's most expensive Italian restaurant caters to lawyers, businesspeople, wealthy Europeans, and followers of fashion. The large, comfortable dining rooms have terra cotta floors, ocher-tinted walls, and lots of marble and leather. Chefs Paul Bartolotta and Valentino Marcatulii produce refined Northern Italian cuisine—plus "spa" dishes at lunchtime for those watching their waistlines. Pasta dishes are superior (especially seafood ravioli); also recommended are the sautéed goose liver with fried onions, rabbit in a casserole with grilled polenta, and roast squab with borlotti beans. The wine list is extensive and offers many unusual and interesting Italian vintages—but also complements the food in price. *240 Central Park S., tel. 212/265–5959. Jacket and tie required. Reservations advised. AE, CB, DC, MC, V. Closed Sun., Sat. lunch.*

$$$$

**③ Sign of the Dove.** After years of serving appalling food at outrageous prices to an audience largely from out of town, this restaurant, with the help of consultant Clark Wolf and chef Andrew D'Amico, has finally become one of the city's most exciting spots. The rooms are elegant and romantic,

$$$

separated by brick arches and decorated with beautiful flower arrangements; the lighting is soft and flattering, and an attractive piano bar near the entrance is a nice spot for cocktails. Tables are well spaced for conversation but service can be slow; be prepared to linger over your meal. The food is French/American with oriental influences. Try, according to season, ravioli stuffed with duck confit and mushrooms, homemade pastas, or venison with polenta. Desserts, especially crème brûlée, are also excellent, and the wine list superior, with reasonable prices. *1110 Third Ave., tel. 212/861–8080. Jacket required. Reservations advised. AE, CB, DC, MC, V. Closed Mon. lunch.*

## Lower Manhattan

**45** **Alison on Dominick Street.** Alison Price took a chance
**$$** when she opened this discreet, attractive restaurant in a landmark townhouse tucked away on a downtown side street, but it quickly became a hit, especially among downtown artists and Wall Street executives. Now it is hard to get a table here at peak hours without a week's notice. Dark-blue velvet curtains, cream colored walls, and framed photographs create a pleasant, understated ambience. Customers whose local hangout is Lutèce find no cause to complain about the food here: Chef Thomas Valenti's cooking, with its Provençal overtones, is creative, boldly seasoned, and flavorful. Try roast guinea hen with wild mushroom risotto, pan-seared breast of Muscovy duck, lamb shank with fava and white beans, bread pudding, or pear and walnut tart. *38 Dominick St., between Hudson and Varick, tel. 212/727–1188. Casual dress. Reservations advised. AE, CB, DC, MC, V. Closed Sun. and major holidays.*

**47** **Arqua.** Light Italian cooking is served here in a soaring
**$$** dining room with mottled amber-ocher walls that could be in a palazzo in Venice. The contrast between the huge space and the stark decor of this restaurant has been much imitated all over the city. Some of the customers come straight from their Wall Street offices, briefcases in hand, after work. Come for lunch if a quiet discussion is what's on the agenda. The small menu (in Italian only) focuses on Venetian dishes: fresh pasta, risotto, polenta, seafood. The food can be superb, but it's uneven; first courses and pastas are the best. The carpaccio, radicchio with melted cheese, homemade pastas (especially papardelle with sausage and radicchio), and the cheesecake with lemon and raspberry sauces are all highly recommended. *281 Church St. at White St., tel. 212/334–1888. Casual dress. Reservations advised. AE. Closed Sun.*

**49** **Bouley.** The beautiful formal dining room here is reminis-
**$$$$** cent of that in a top French country hotel, with high arched ceilings, flattering lighting, and Impressionist landscapes. Even though the tables are well spaced, the room can get noisy at night, and service can be distracted—all of which does not deter the Wall Street crowd that frequents the place. David Bouley, a young American chef, serves New American cuisine that is often brilliant but at times erratic. His best dishes are game and fish. Among the top choices are guinea hen in port wine sauce, pigeon with savoy cabbage and grilled foie gras, roasted halibut with rosemary oil, monkfish with garlic, bacon, and cabbage, and for dessert, bitter chocolate sorbet. The

wine list is excellent, with many unusual choices. *165 Duane St. between Hudson and Greenwich Sts., tel. 212/ 608–3852. Jacket and tie required. Reservations advised. AE, CB, DC, MC, V. Closed Sun.*

**48** **Chanterelle.** This austere French restaurant in a soaring
**$$$$** post-modern dining room is a perfect spot for business— and given the location, it predictably attracts a Wall Street clientele (as well as many Japanese business travelers). The effect here is grandeur mixed with functionalism. The starkness of the decor is alleviated by magnificent, immense flower arrangements. Chef David Waltuck turns out some inspired creations of New American cuisine, although there are some misfires. Among the recommended choices are the grilled seafood sausage, seared foie gras, or rack of lamb with thyme and mustard; for finishers, there's a superior cheeseboard, lemon tart with blackberry coulis, or chocolate mille feuille with coffee sauce. The wine is interesting but exorbitant, and the sommelier is extremely helpful. *2 Harrison St. at Hudson St., tel. 212/966–6960. Jacket and tie required. Reservations advised. AE, CB, D, DC, MC, V. Dinner only; closed Sun., Mon., major holidays, first week of Jan., and July.*

**50** **Duane Park Café.** Two Japanese chefs with backgrounds
**$$** in Cajun, Italian, and American food have opened a restaurant that serves another new style of cooking: Northern Italian and American regional with a dash of Japanese and French. Dishes are grounded in the classics but are at the same time esoteric and subtle; the oriental touch comes in the seasonings. The modern brown-and-black dining room is comfortable, quiet, and attractive in an understated way. A well-heeled art crowd, plus business people from Wall Street, are the usual customers. The wine list is short but reasonably priced (wine tastings are held here in the early evening during the week). For entrées, the crisp-skinned roast mackerel, risotto with shrimp, mussels and scallops, skate wings with ponzu sauce (a Japanese vinegar), and duck with balsamic vinegar are all commendable; pear hazelnut tart with raspberry coulis is a good dessert choice. *157 Duane St., tel. 212/ 732–5555. Casual dress. Reservations advised. AE, CB, DC, MC, V. Closed Sat. lunch, Sun.*

**★ 46** **Montrachet.** Among the New Wave of downtown restau-
**$$$** rants with spare interiors and a reverential focus on the food, Montrachet is the least stiff, and attracts a following both from midtown and downtown business communities. Prices are lower than at comparable restaurants, and the prix-fixe menus are a real bargain. The setting is vaguely post-modern—a softly-lit converted industrial space with light-green walls, rust-colored banquettes, and a small, attractive bar. Chef Debra Ponzek's style has evolved from a modern French tradition. Her cooking is exceptional: bold and innovative, with clever combinations that work, such as salmon with lentils and red wine, or baby pheasant with orzo and olives. The distinguished wine list has interesting selections at all prices. *239 W. Brdwy. at White St., tel. 212/219–2777. Casual dress. Reservations advised. AE. Dinner only except Fri. when lunch is served. Closed Sun.*

**51** **The Odeon.** After nearly a decade, the Odeon has evolved
**$$** into a genuine bistro, and it is extremely popular both

with Wall Street executives and local artists. The occasional limousine purrs outside the door, but prices are reasonable and the restaurant has become the sort of place people can drop in casually without a reservation on slow nights and expect to get a table before they've finished their second drink at the bar. The decor is simple, comfortable and attractive, a former 1930s working man's cafeteria updated to serve the new breed of workers in the area. Chef Stephen Lyle turns out good, straightforward but updated bistro specialties, among them squid in cornmeal with red-pepper garlic mayonnaise, grilled salmon, and steak frites; some light finishers are a pucker-inducing lemon tart or fruit sorbets. *145 West Broadway at Thomas St., tel. 212/233-0507. Casual dress. Reservations advised. AE, CB, DC, MC, V.*

★ ❹ **Union Square Café.** Book publishers have made this their
$$ downtown club at lunchtime, perhaps because the eclectic menu, with a Northern Italian flair, is good and reasonably priced. Of the three informal dining rooms, decorated with splashy paintings or murals, the most comfortable is the main one a few steps down in front of the bar. The signature of the cooking here is freshness. Try risotto made with fried sage leaves, spinach, and prosciutto; green gnocchi in a yèllow tomato sauce topped with melted cheese; palliard of lamb; or fried calamari with anchovy mayonnaise. Also recommended are the oysters—different kinds are on the menu, fresh daily—and the generous hamburgers. The wine list is distinguished. *21 E. 16th St., tel. 212/243-4020. Casual dress. Reservations advised. AE, MC, V. Closed Sun.*

❺ **Windows on the World.** Don't come here for the food; the
$$$$ view makes better eating. Stick to plain dishes such as oysters on the half shell, marinated salmon with cucumber and yogurt sauce, rack of lamb, and lemon tart. The view and the wine list, however, are unbeatable, and if the former doesn't distract too much from the conversation, this is an impressive spot for a business dinner (for lunch during the workday week the restaurant is a private club; there is a surcharge for nonmembers). The large rose, cream, and beige dining room is reminiscent of that in an ocean liner—it's built on tiers with brass railings so all the tables get a view. In keeping with the nautical motif, members of the staff wear white uniforms with gold epaulettes; in addition, they're extremely helpful, especially when you are trying to make your way through the remarkable wine list. (For oenophiles, there is another restaurant here, Cellar in the Sky, which lacks a view but specializes in matching wines with a special four- or five-course menu.) *One World Trade Center, 107th floor, tel. 212/938-1111. Jacket and tie required. Reservations required. AE, CB, DC, MC, V.*

## Ethnic

*Chinese*
There are Chinese restaurants on almost every block of the city, some better than others, but almost all offer a great variety of dishes. Chinatown is, of course, a prime source for an authentic meal. Three recommended Chinatown restaurants are **The Oriental Pearl Restaurant** (103 Mott St., tel. 212/219-8388); the **Nice Restaurant** (35 E. Broadway, tel. 212/406-9510) for dim sum; and the **Silver**

**Palace** (50 Bowery, tel. 212/964–1204). Uptown, near Lincoln Center, **Shun Lee West** (43 W. 65th St., tel. 212/595–8895) provides an elegant preconcert meal, with the **Shun Lee Café** right next door for a more casual, dim sum experience.

*Japanese*
Some good Japanese restaurants are **The Tatany Restaurant** (388 Third Ave., tel. 212/686–1871) and **Tatany Village** (62 Greenwich Ave., tel. 212/675–6195); **Japonica** (90 University Pl., tel. 212/243–7752) has some of the freshest sushi in the city.

*Delicatessans*
**Carnegie Restaurant & Delicatessan** (854 Seventh Ave., between 54th and 55th Sts., tel. 212/757–2245) is a classic place to indulge in New York deli "cuisine"; for the scene and the hot dogs, try **Katz's** (205 E. Houston St., tel. 212/254–2246); also for the experience, **Sammy's Famous Roumanian** (157 Chrystie St., tel. 212/673–5526); and for kosher rather than kosher-style there's the **Second Avenue Delicatessan** (156 Second Ave., tel. 212/677–0606).

*Indian*
Good, inexpensive Indian restaurants abound on Sixth Street between First and Second avenues. If you don't mind roughing it (in most places you bring your own alcohol), it's well worth the trip. On that block **Passage to India** (308 E. Sixth St., tel. 212/529–5770), one of the few places with a liquor license, is good; uptown, the chef at **Dawat** (210 E. 58th St., tel. 212/355–7555) was advised by the cookbook author and chef Madhur Jaffrey; and **Akbar** (475 Park Ave., tel. 212/838–1717) has a staff that is particularly friendly.

*Others*
**Periyali** (35 W. 20th St., tel. 212/463–7890) serves good Greek food and attracts a publishing crowd. **Teresa Coffee Shop and Restaurant** (103 First Ave., tel. 212/228–0604), casual and inexpensive, offers hearty authentic Polish fare. **Sun Lee Oak** (77 W. 46th St., tel. 212/869–9958) lets you barbecue Korean-style at the table. For spicy Thai cuisine, **Tommy Tang's** (323 Greenwich Ave., tel. 212/334–9190) is a good pick. **Zarela's** (953 Second Ave., tel. 212/644–6740) serves out-of-the-ordinary Mexican food in a relaxed atmosphere. For a Brazilian meal in a lively, fun setting, try **Cabana Carioca** (123 W. 45th St., tel. 212/581–8008; and 133 W. 45th St., tel. 212/730–8375).

## FREE TIME

### Fitness

*Hotel Facilities*
Hotel health clubs in New York generally are open only to hotel guests and regular members, but several independent health clubs accept guests on a walk-in, one-day basis.

*Health Clubs*
**Battery Park Fitness** (375 South End Ave., tel. 212/321–1117) has a 50-foot pool, aerobics, free weights, Nautilus, Jacuzzi, rowing machines, treadmills, and stationary cycles. A one-day pass is $26. **ABC Health Spa** (500 E. 83rd

St., tel. 212/772–8760) has a 44-foot pool, sauna, steam, Jacuzzi, weights, and stationary cycles. Daily cost: $12.50. The **Vanderbilt YMCA** (224 E. 47th St., tel. 212/755–2410) and the **West Side YMCA** (5 W. 63rd St., tel. 212/787–4400) have 75-foot pools. The Vanderbilt branch has aerobics, Nautilus, free weights, and an indoor track and gym. Daily cost: $10. The West Side branch has weights, Nautilus, rowing machines, an indoor track, stationary cycles, racquetball, and squash. Daily cost: $12.

*Jogging*
The best, by far, is the 1½-mile reservoir track and 6-mile roadway in **Central Park,** a pastoral setting enlivened by views of the skyline. During the day the park fairly swarms with runners and cyclists; still, side roads or paths should be avoided. If you must run after dark, don't go alone, and stay south of 96th Street (women especially should never run alone at night). On the west side, **Riverside Park,** from 72nd to 96th streets is also popular and offers Hudson River views. On the east side, joggers can run through **Carl Schurz Park** from 90th to 84th streets and then follow the East River walkway to the United Nations, but the ambience is marred by the East River Drive expressway.

## Shopping

In New York, unlike in most American cities, shopping has yet to become dependent on the automobile. New Yorkers shop wherever they walk, and they walk just about anywhere. One of the most quintessentially New York stores is **Zabar's** (2245 Broadway, tel. 212/787–2000), a temple of hanging sausages and coffee beans from around the world where the act of buying gourmet foods and housewares is transformed into an almost religious experience. A toy store that is similarly connected to the Manhattan zeitgeist—and where the looking is almost as much fun as the buying—is **F.A.O. Schwarz** (767 Fifth Ave., tel. 212/644–9400). **Mythology Unlimited** (370 Columbus Ave.) has a funky array of antique toys, alligator rafts, Mexican art, cookie jars, etc. The **Metropolitan Museum gift shop** (82nd St. and Fifth Ave., tel. 212/570–3726) has prints, date books, jewelry, neckties, scarves, and other gifts based on reproductions from the museum collection. **47th St. Photo** (67 W. 47th St.; 115 W. 45th St., both at tel. 212/398–1410; or downtown on 116 Nassau St., tel. 212/732–3370) has the last word in watches, electronics, computers, radios and yes, even camera equipment and supplies, at low prices.

**Macy's,** the world's biggest store (Sixth Ave. and 34th St., tel. 212/695–4400), is one of New York's best for clothing, housewares, and linens. **Bloomingdale's** is its uptown rival (59th St. and Lexington Ave., tel. 212/725–2000). **Barney's New York** (106 Seventh Ave. at 17th St., tel. 212/929–9000) is one of the city's most popular stores for its wide and well-chosen selection of men's suits and women's wear. **Paul Stuart** (45th St. and Madison Ave., tel. 212/682–0320) is very exclusive and has a superb array of men's wear and a smaller, though equally smart, selection of women's clothes. **Henri Bendel** (10 W. 57th St., tel. 212/247–1100) is an upscale favorite of women executives.

The toniest **jewelry stores** are on **Fifth Avenue** between 42nd and 59th streets. Cheaper prices can be found in the diamond district, on **West 47th Street** between Fifth and Sixth avenues, but be prepared to haggle with the local merchants.

## Diversions

For a wonderful walk, just slightly off the beaten path, cross the **Brooklyn Bridge.** Supported by a spider web of cables, the bridge, completed in 1883, has a drama and beauty matched by few; the same may be said for its views of the lower Manhattan skyline.

**Central Park,** designed by Frederick Law Olmstead and Calvert Vaux, keeps 843 acres of New York out of the mitts of real estate developers. Its woodlands and open knolls look much as they might have before the arrival of Dutch settlers. Contemporary natives use it as a giant backyard for cycling, jogging, walking, softball, concerts, and people-watching. The renovated zoo is beautifully landscaped.

Circle Line (42nd St. & 12th Ave., tel. 212/563–3200) **cruises around Manhattan Island** in three hours. Those pressed for time might prefer the lesser known Seaport Line (Pier 16, at Fulton and South Sts., tel. 212/669–9400), which tours the southern end of the island and returns in only 90 minutes. Both are open March–Nov.

**Fifth Avenue** is the main drag for elegant and pricey window shopping. Good destinations are **Rockefeller Center** (48th to 52nd Sts.), with its statue of Atlas, shopping, and wintertime skating, and **St. Patrick's Cathedral** (50th to 51st Sts.), an arched, granite, French Gothic structure dating to 1879.

If you don't mind heights, **New York's best views** are from the Observation Deck of Two World Trade Center (tel. 212/466–7377), and from the Observatory of the Empire State building (350 Fifth Ave., between 33rd and 34th Sts., tel. 212/736–3100).

**Madison Avenue** from 50th to 86th streets is lined with galleries, shops, boutiques, and coffee shops.

**Metropolitan Museum of Art** (82nd St. and Fifth Ave., tel. 212/535–7710) runs the gamut from the ancient Near East, Egypt, and the Orient to contemporary European and American styles. But it's the daunting collection of European Old Masters, à la Rembrandt and Raphael, that makes this one of the world's great museums.

**Museum of Modern Art** (11 W. 53rd St., tel. 212/708–9480) is notable for Picasso's *Desmoiselles d'Avignon*, perhaps the landmark work of cubism, and Monet's soothing *Water Lilies*. Picasso's *Pregnant Goat*, a hauntingly realistic sculpture, is itself worth the price of admission.

**Neighborhoods** in New York are too numerous to name. One good one is SoHo, a collection of small streets between Houston and Canal where browsers will find a wealth of art galleries, as well as fashions, merchandise, and cafés with an artsy tone. Another one worth visiting, just a bit to the east and teeming with restaurants, is Chinatown. For an endless choice of cafés and small artsy shops, visit Greenwich Village between 10th and Houston streets and from Broadway to the Hudson River.

**Short stops**—perfect for chance run-ins and stolen hours—abound. The **International Center of Photography** has a branch at 1133 Avenue of the Americas and 43rd St. (tel. 212/768-4680). The **Frick Collection,** housed in the splendid old home of a steel baron (1 E. 70th St. and Fifth Ave., tel. 212/288-0700), houses such gems as Rembrandt's Polish Rider and Holbein's portrait of Sir Thomas More. AT&T's **InfoQuest** (550 Madison Ave. between 55th and 56th Sts., tel. 212/605-5140) features interactive science exhibits on robotics, electronic voice recognition, and other high-tech topics. The **IBM Gallery of Science of Art** (590 Madison Ave., between 56th and 57th Sts., tel. 212/745-6100) has a permanent computer exhibit, visiting art collections, and an atrium café. In addition to its main, 75th Street and Madison locus, The **Whitney Museum of American Art** (tel. 212/570-3676) has bite-sized, rotating samples of American artists—including, at times, such figures as Warhol and Hopper—at three downtown and midtown branches (33 Maiden Lane; Equitable Center, Seventh Ave. between 51st and 52nd Sts.; Philip Morris, 120 Park Ave., between 41st and 42nd Sts.). A good place to kill time in midtown is the lobby of **Citicorp Center** (Lexington Ave. between 53rd and 54th Sts.), with its restaurants, shops, and concerts. Downtown, try the magnificent, palm-shaded, glass-enclosed atrium at the **Winter Garden** in the World Financial Center, also offering shops, restaurants, and concerts (West St. between Liberty and Vesey Sts., tel. 212/945-0505).

**South Street Seaport** (Fulton St., tel. 212/732-7678) is New York's answer to the national craze for waterfront marketplaces. Open-air entertainment, a maritime museum, and tall sailing ships round out the usual collection of restaurants and trendy stores facing the East River. The wholesale Fulton Fish Market, still in business during the early morning hours and still pungent, is a New York original.

**Wall Street,** the country's financial center, was the first part of Manhattan settled by the Dutch. Any walking tour of its narrow, crooked streets should include the New York Stock Exchange (Wall & Broad Sts., tel. 212/656-5167), and Fraunces Tavern (Broad & Pearl Sts., tel. 212/269-0144), the site of General Washington's emotional farewell dinner for his officers, and one of the few remaining restored Colonial buildings (1719) in New York.

For more: the New York Convention & Visitors Bureau, tel. 212/397-8222, has a complete and yet wonderfully concise calendar of events.

## Professional Sports

**Baseball. Mets,** Shea Stadium, Flushing, Queens, tel. 718/507-8499; **Yankees,** Yankee Stadium, the Bronx, tel. 212/293-6000. **Football. Giants,** Giant Stadium, East Rutherford, NJ, tel. 201/935-8222; **Jets,** Giant Stadium, tel. 212/421-6600. **Basketball. Knicks,** Madison Square Garden, Manhattan, tel. 212/563-8000; **Nets,** Brendan Byrne Arena, East Rutherford, NJ, tel. 201/935-3900. **Hockey. Rangers,** Madison Square Garden, tel. 212/563-8000; **Dev-**

**ils,** Brendan Byrne Arena, East Rutherford, NJ, tel. 201/935–3900; **Islanders,** Nassau Veteran's Memorial Coliseum, Uniondale, Long Island, tel. 516/794–4100.

## The Arts

Anyone who doubts that New York is the country's arts capital should talk to a waiter or waitress. Nearly everyone, it seems, is an aspiring (or moonlighting) actor, actress, dancer, or musician. Besides its 30 or so Broadway theaters, New York has dozens of Off Broadway houses and scores of neighborhood Off Off Broadway theaters. The city's diverse selection of music and dance argues against singling out any one stage, but Carnegie Hall must be mentioned as the best place to hear concerts. Lincoln Center is home to the Metropolitan Opera, the American Ballet Theatre, the New York Philharmonic, the New York City Ballet, the New York City Opera, and a first-rate (and moderately priced) Broadway stage, the Vivian Beaumont. Two modern dance groups appear at City Center Theater: Alvin Ailey American Dance Theater and Martha Graham Dance Company. At Christmastime and other times, the Rockettes kick up their legs at Radio City Music Hall.

New York is also replete with smaller stages and music halls where the setting is more intimate and the talent is first-rate. One that is close to East Side hotels and features classical and other concerts is the 92nd Street YMHA. Travelers should consult the listings in local newspapers or magazines. (The New York Convention & Visitors Bureau calendar of events is also a good guide; *see* Diversions, above.)

Ticket agencies include **Miller Ticket Service** (2 E. 61st St., lobby of the Pierre Hotel, tel. 212/757–5210), **Nite on New York Town Inc.** (430 W. 34th St., tel. 212/947–0819), and **Downtown Theater Ticket Agency** (71 Broadway., tel. 212/425–6410). **TKTS (Times Square Theater Center)** has half-price tickets to same-day performances (if you're willing to wait in line and to take your chances on what's available) of Broadway and Off Broadway shows. Two locations: Broadway & 47th St. at Times Square and in the mezzanine of Two World Trade Center (which is less crowded). For information on hours call tel. 212/354–5800. The **Theater Development Fund NYC/ON STAGE** hot line for information on theater, dance, and music is 212/587–1111 or, outside of New York State, 800/782–4369.

**Alice Tully Hall,** Lincoln Center, 65th St. and Broadway, tel. 212/362–1911.
**Avery Fisher Hall,** Lincoln Center, tel. 212/874–2424.
**Brooklyn Academy of Music,** 30 Lafayette Ave., Brooklyn, tel. 718/636–4100.
**Carnegie Hall,** 57th St. and Seventh Ave., tel. 212/247–7800.
**City Center Theater,** 131 West 55th St., tel. 212/581–7907.
**Joyce Theater,** 175 Eighth Ave., tel. 212/242–0800.
**Metropolitan Opera,** Lincoln Center, tel. 212/362–6000.
**New York State Theater,** Lincoln Center, tel. 212/870–5570.
**92nd St. YMHA,** 92nd St. & Lexington Ave., tel. 212/996–1100.

Radio City Music Hall, 1260 Ave. of the Americas, tel. 212/247-4777.

Town Hall, 123 W. 43rd St., tel. 212/840-2824.

## After Hours

There is life after dark all over town, but night crawling can be classified into four geographic turfs: Greenwich Village and SoHo, midtown, the upper east side, and the upper west side. The Village and SoHo, in lower Manhattan, are trendiest; midtown is favored by establishment types. Uptown night spots, both east and west, draw hordes of young professionals, many of them singles, but the west-side crowd is ethnically diverse and informal. On the east side, the accent is glitzier and the bills are larger.

*Bars and Lounges*

For a quiet drink with clients, hotel bars are usually best. Try, among others, the **Plaza**, the **Carlyle**, the **Algonquin**, and the **Westbury** (*see* Lodging, above). The **Palio** (151 W. 51st St. at Seventh Ave., tel. 212/245-4850) is flush with executives. The open bar overlooking the main terminal area at **Grand Central Station** (enter at Vanderbilt and 42nd Sts., tel. 212/883-0009) is jammed with people-watchers. If you want to wow clients—or yourself—with views and elegance, try the **Rainbow Room** (RCA Building, 30 Rockefeller Plaza, tel. 212/632-5100); **Windows on the World** (1 World Trade Center, tel. 212/938-1100); and **River Café** (1 Water St., Brooklyn, tel. 718/522-5200). Sports nuts will enjoy the big screens and, if they're lucky, catch a glimpse of the restaurant's namesake, at **Mickey Mantle's Restaurant Sports Bar** (42 Central Park S., tel. 212/688-7777).

*Cabarets*

For the likes of the Gershwins, Rodgers and Hart, Cole Porter, et al sung in lively, intimate settings, the **Algonquin** and the **Carlyle** hotels are the best bets (*see* Lodging, above). **Rainbow & Stars** (RCA Building, 30 Rockefeller Plaza, tel. 212/632-5000) sports spectacular views in a glitzier, 65th-floor setting. Dinner and music are offered at **Jan Wallman's** (49 W. 44th St., tel. 212/764-8930). Hotels with pianists and/or singers include the **Drake** (440 Park Ave. at 56th St., 212/421-0900), **Parc 51**, the **Marriott Marquis**, the **Parker Meridien**, the **InterContinental** (111 E. 48th St., tel. 212/755-5900), and the **Westbury** (*see* Lodging, above, for addresses and telephone numbers).

*Clubs*

The club scene in New York is constantly changing, practically from week to week. What's in today can, literally, be gone tomorrow. There are no guarantees that the following will still be open by the time you visit, but they've proved to have some staying power.

**Heartbreak** (179 Varick St., tel. 212/691-2388) pays homage to the '50s with a bust of the King on the bar, a linoleum dance floor, a luncheonette, and kitschy touches everywhere. **Mars** (10th Ave. at 13th St., tel. 212/691-6262) is still hot after over a year as *the* place to go. Take your pick among five levels. The door staff is *very* particular. **M.K.** (204 5th Ave., tel. 212/779-1340) has a SoHo-chic design that attracts a celebrity crowd to this supper club noted for its number of film premiere parties. **Nell's** (246

W. 14th St., tel. 212/675–1567) reintroduced sophistication to nightlife. The tone in the upstairs jazz salon is Victorian; downstairs is for tête-à-têtes and dancing. **Regine's** (502 Park Ave., tel. 212/806–0990) attracts the international set for dancing and listening to a variety of contemporary sounds. **Stringfellows** (35 E. 21st St., tel. 212/254–2444), a British import, is for the jet-and-blank-check set. At 11, mirrored panels unveil a dance floor, where commodities traders, TV commentators, and famous fashion designers invade each other's personal space.

*Comedy Clubs*

The talent varies but is often quite good. The best-known clubs are on the upper east side, including **Catch A Rising Star** (1487 First Ave., tel. 212/794–1906), **Comic Strip** (1568 Second Ave., tel. 212/861–9386), and **Dangerfield's**—owned by Rodney, who on rare occasions performs here (1118 First Ave., tel. 212/593–1650). In midtown try **Monkey Bar,** in the Elysée Hotel (*see* Lodging, above). **Stand-Up New York** (236 W. 78th St., tel. 212/595–0850), a bit off the beaten track, draws a local Upper West Side crowd.

*Jazz Clubs*

The Village is the place for jazz. The list (by no means complete) includes **Village Gate** (160 Bleecker St., tel. 212/475–5120), **Village Vanguard** (178 Seventh Ave. S., tel. 212/255–4037), **Sweet Basil** (88 Seventh Ave. S., tel. 212/242–1785), and **Blue Note** (131 W. 3rd St., tel. 212/475–8592). **Sounds of Brazil (S-O-B's)** (204 Varick St. at W. Houston St., tel. 212/243–4940) has music from exactly where you'd expect, and also from the Caribbean and elsewhere. In midtown, in addition to the many hotels with jazz bars, there is **Michael's Pub** (211 E. 55th St., tel. 212/758–2272) and **Red Blazer Too** (349 W. 46th St., tel. 212/262–3112). For egg rolls with rhythm, **Fortune Garden Pavilion** (209 E. 49th St., tel. 212/753–0101) combines a greenhouse ambience with jazz and Chinese food.

*For Singles*

With the exception of grand, formal settings, singles feel comfortable just about anywhere in New York. The hotel lounges and low-key bars on the east side are generally more relaxed than the pick-up joints. You can meet people or enjoy the scene, no questions asked. A few choices: **Ravelled Sleave** (1387 Third Ave., tel. 212/628–8814), **Brighton Grill** (1313 Third Ave., tel. 212/988–6663), **Island** (1305 Madison Ave., tel. 212/996–1200), **Elio's** (1621 Second Ave., tel. 212/772–2242), **Sam's Cafe** (1406 Third Ave., tel. 212/988–5300), which is owned by Mariel Hemingway, and the celebrity/literary salon, **Elaine's** (1703 Second Ave., tel. 212/534–8103).

# Philadelphia

*by Julie Amparano Lopez and Beatrice E. Garcia*

The city of Brotherly Love, founded in 1681 as a Quaker settlement by William Penn, was the seat of the Continental Congress, and then was chosen as the first capital of the new nation. Philadelphia's early history is enshrined in the midtown Independence National Historical Park, which includes Independence Hall, where the Declaration of Independence was signed and the Liberty Bell is kept; Congress Hall, where Congress met after its inception; and Carpenters Hall, where the First Continental Congress met.

Sleek glass skyscrapers now overshadow the 37-foot statue of William Penn that tops the City Hall tower, Philadelphia's tallest structure for almost a century. The tradition that no city building could go higher than Alexander Milne Calder's Penn statue was broken when Willard G. Rouse III completed One Liberty Place, a steel and blue-glass tower whose neon-lighted crown is reminiscent of New York City's Chrysler Building. A companion tower, which houses Cigna's insurance operations, was completed in late 1990. The Liberty Place complex, which occupies an entire city block between Market and Chestnut streets along South 17th Street, includes a new Ritz-Carlton Hotel.

Along with the city's skyline, Philadelphia's airport, train station, and highways have undergone major transformation. A new terminal was added to the airport. Penn Station, more commonly known as 30th Street Station, was modernized to house trendy new shops and restaurants. And almost every major artery into the city is being expanded. The Vine Street Expressway, connecting Routes I–95 and I–76, was completed in early 1991.

Philadelphia's heavy manufacturing days have long vanished, although an occasional smokestack remains. Today, the city is known for its growing service economy industries, especially health care and finance. New industry has been aggressively pursued—and successfully in the case of Eastman Kodak, which recently moved some operations to the area. Philadelphia still is home to some of the nation's largest and most prestigious law firms.

William Penn's city plan, based on a grid system, makes Philadelphia's compact downtown, nestled between the Delaware River on the east and the Schuylkill River on the west, easy to navigate. City Hall stands at Broad and Market streets, Penn's original center square. From here, the city fans out to the north, south, and west, covering some 130 square miles.

## Top Employers

| Employer | Type of Enterprise | Parent*/ Headquarters |
|---|---|---|
| Alco Standard Corp. | Paper and office products | Valley Forge, PA |
| Bell Atlantic Corp. | Telecommunications | Philadelphia |
| Campbell Soup Co. | Food products | Camden, NJ |
| Cigna Corp. | Insurance | Philadelphia |
| Consolidated Rail | Railroad | Philadelphia |
| Philadelphia Electric Co. | Utility | Philadelphia |
| Scott Paper Co. | Paper products | Philadelphia |
| SmithKline Beecham Corp. | Pharmaceuticals | London |
| Sun Co. | Oil refinery | Radnor, PA |
| Unisys | Computers | Blue Bell, PA |

*if applicable

## ESSENTIAL INFORMATION

### Climate

What follows are the average daily maximum and minimum temperatures for Philadelphia.

| | | | | | | | | |
|---|---|---|---|---|---|---|---|---|
| Jan. | 40F | 4C | Feb. | 41F | 5C | Mar. | 49F | 9C |
| | 26 | −3 | | 27 | −3 | | 33 | 1 |
| Apr. | 61F | 16C | May | 72F | 22C | June | 80F | 27C |
| | 43 | 6 | | 54 | 12 | | 62 | 17 |
| July | 85F | 29C | Aug. | 83F | 28C | Sept. | 76F | 24C |
| | 68 | 17 | | 67 | 19 | | 60 | 16 |
| Oct. | 66F | 19C | Nov. | 53F | 12C | Dec. | 43F | 6C |
| | 50 | 10 | | 39 | 4 | | 30 | −1 |

### Airport

**Philadelphia International Airport** is 8 miles southwest of downtown, but road construction makes the trip seem longer.

### Airport Business Facilities

**Mutual of Omaha Insurance Counters** (in Terminals B, D, E, and Overseas, tel. 215/492–8880) have fax, photocopying, Western Union, and travel insurance. **American Express Business Service Center** (Terminal B, tel. 215/492–4200) is only for American Express cardholders, and has fax machines, photocopying, traveler's checks, cash advance, moneygrams, phone suites with computer hookups, typewriters, and a small conference room.

## Airlines

Philadelphia is a hub city for USAir.

**Allegheny Commuter,** tel. 215/563–8055 or 800/428–4322.
**American,** tel. 215/365–4000 or 800/433–7300.
**American Eagle,** tel. 800/433–7300.
**Continental,** tel. 215/592–8005 or 800/525–0280.
**Delta,** tel. 215/928–1700 or 800/221–1212.
**Pan Am Express,** tel. 215/492–2740 or 800/223–1115.
**TWA,** tel. 215/923–2000 or 800/221–2000.
**United,** tel. 215/568–2800 or 800/241–6522.
**USAir,** tel. 215/563–8055 or 800/428–4322.

## Between the Airport and Downtown

During nonrush hours, a taxi is the fastest way to get downtown. During peak times (6–9 AM; 4–6 PM), Southeastern Pennsylvania Transportation Authority (SEPTA's) Airport Express train is your best bet. Generally, allow 30 minutes to get to the airport during nonrush hours, about 45–60 minutes during rush hours.

*By Taxi*
Cab stands are located at all the terminals. The ride to Center City costs $15–$25, with tip, depending on how long the cab stands in traffic or is delayed by road construction.

*By Train*
The Airport Express trains run every ½ hour 6:10 AM–12:10 PM. Directions to the train from inside all the terminals are well marked. The train stops at 30th Street Station, where cabs can be taken to the Center City hotels; at Suburban Station, which is within walking distance of most hotels; and at Market East and North Broad stations. Cost: $4. For more information and schedules, call the Airport Information desk (tel. 215/492–3333) or SEPTA (tel. 215/580–7800).

*By Shuttle Bus*
Vans charge about $8 per person and drop you off at most Center City hotels; they run from 7 AM to about midnight, but nighttime service is less frequent. Late-night arrivals would do better to take the Airport Express train or a taxi.

## Car Rentals

Business travelers staying in Center City don't really need to rent a car. Most major businesses and city attractions in the downtown area are only a short stroll away or easily accessible by public transportation. But for those who need to travel to outlying areas, rental cars can be picked up at the airport, downtown, or at the 30th Street train station.

The following companies have booths in or near the airport:

**Alamo,** tel. 215/492–3960 or 800/732–3232.
**American International,** tel. 215/492–1750 or 800/527–0202.

**Avis,** tel. 800/331–1212.
**Budget,** tel. 215/492–9447 or 800/527–0700.
**Dollar,** tel. 215/365–2700 or 800/421–6868.
**Hertz,** tel. 800/654–3131.
**National,** tel. 215/492–2750 or 800/328–4567.
**Thrifty,** tel. 215/365–3900 or 800/367–2277.

## Emergencies

*Doctors*
**Jefferson Medical Care** (2305 Fairmount Ave., tel. 215/978–7800), **Pine Medical Center** (1335–37 Pine St., tel. 215/735–3833), **Presbyterian University of Pennsylvania Medical Center** (39th and Market Sts., tel. 215/662–8150), **Thomas Jefferson University Clinic** (11th and Walnut Sts., tel. 215/928–6000).

*Dentists*
**Center City Dental** (1616 Walnut St., Suite 1000, tel. 215/732–9376), **Pennsylvania Hospital Dental Clinic** (8th and Spruce Sts., tel. 215/829–3359), **Temple University Dental Clinic** (3401 N. Broad St., tel. 215/221–2000).

## Important Addresses and Numbers

**Audiovisual rentals.** American Video (65 E. Lancaster Ave., tel. 215/644–2001), Kosmin's Camera Exchange (927 Arch St., tel. 215/627–8231), Visual Sound (485 Pkwy., tel. 215/544–8700), Webb Taylor (241 N. 12th St., tel. 215/923–8380), Williams Brown & Earl (904 Chestnut St., tel. 215/923–1800).

**Chamber of Commerce** (1346 Chestnut St., Suite 800, tel. 215/545–1234).

**Computer rentals.** Campus Computer Rentals (812 Lombard St., tel. 215/440–9979), PC Computer Rental (1810 Rittenhouse Sq., tel. 215/735–2901), The Computer Factory (1624 Chestnut St., tel. 215/977–9302).

**Convention and exhibition centers.** Philadelphia Civic Center (34th St. and Civic Center Blvd., tel. 215/823–7031).

**Fax services.** Copy Systems (5211 Oxford Ave., tel. 215/537–8289), HQ Headquarters Companies (10 Penn Center, tel. 215/569–9969), Sir Speedy (1920 Chestnut St., tel. 215/567–4959), Society Hill Mail & Parcel Service (614 S. 8th St., tel. 215/627–1750).

**Formal-wear rentals.** Smalls Formal Wear & Rentals (1109 Walnut St., tel. 215/923–1230), Tuxedo Outlet, has same-day service (3642 N. 2nd St., tel. 215/427–1388), One Night Stand, for women (132 S. 17th St., tel. 215/568–9200).

**Gift shops.** Chocolates: Godiva Chocolatiers (1625 Chestnut St., tel. 215/963–0810); Flowers: Thoughts in Blooms (18th and Locust Sts., tel. 215/732–1100); Jewelry, bags, and gifts: Touches (225 S. 15th St., tel. 215/546–1221).

**Graphic design studios.** AJ Graphic Service (2061 E. Clearfield St., tel. 215/425–4114), Philadelphia Graphics Center (1311 Sansom St., tel. 215/546–3454), Royal Graphics (3117 N. Front St., tel. 215/739–8282), Stephenson Brothers (1422 Chestnut St., tel. 215/557–7437).

**Hairstylists.** Unisex: Estetica (242 S. 17th St., tel. 215/ 569–9618), Pileggi on the Square (717 Walnut St., tel. 215/ 627–0565), Thunder (110 S. 19th St., tel. 215/563–2665).

**Health and fitness clubs.** *See* Fitness, below.

**Information hot lines.** Cultural Connection (tel. 215/564– 4444), Music Book (tel. 215/787–1529), Philly Fun Phone (tel. 215/568–7255), Visitors' Information (tel. 215/636– 1666).

**Limousine services.** Ali Baba Limousine (tel. 215/842– 0328), American Express Travel Agency (tel. 215/587– 2350), Classic Limousine Service (tel. 215/925–9335), Deluxe Transportation (tel. 215/463–8787), Sterling Limousine Services (tel. 215/328–1999).

**Liquor stores.** All liquor stores are run by the state. Society Hill Wine & Spirit Shop (326 S. 5th St., tel. 215/ 922–4224), Wine Reserve (205 S. 18th St., tel. 215/560– 4529), Wine & Spirit Shop at the Bourse (5th and Market Sts., tel. 215/560–5504), State Liquor Store (1913 Chestnut St., tel. 215/567–0257; 2109 Walnut St., tel. 215/563– 8994).

**Mail delivery, overnight.** DHL Worldwide Express (tel. 215/461–8111), Federal Express (tel. 215/923–3085), TNT Skypak (tel. 215/521–5260), UPS (tel. 215/463–7300), U.S. Postal Service Express Mail (tel. 215/895–8630).

**Messenger services.** Intercept Delivery Service (tel. 215/ 567–1730), Kangaroo Couriers (tel. 215/561–5132), Philadelphia Express Courier (tel. 215/627–6700), Silver Top Delivery Service (tel. 215/751–1166).

**Office space rentals.** American Executive Centers (1411 Walnut St., tel. 215/569–2649), Center City Executive Offices (230 S. Broad St., tel. 215/546–3336), Executive Office Network (5 Great Valley Pkwy., tel. 215/251–0144).

**Pharmacies, late-night.** Brog Pharmacy (701 N. 7th St., tel. 215/627–5571), Corson's Pharmacy (15th and Spruce Sts., tel. 215/735–1386), CVS Pharmacy (6501 Harbison Ave., tel. 215/333–4300), Medical Tower Pharmacy (255 S. 17th St., tel. 215/545–3525).

**Radio stations, all-news.** KYW, 1060 AM; WHYY, 91 FM (National Public Radio).

**Secretarial services.** A Careful Stenographer (801 Arch St., tel. 215/592–9280), Ames Personnel Services (3 Penn Center, tel. 215/569–3737), B & B Associates Secretarial Services (3900 Chestnut St., tel. 215/662–0695), Standby Secretarial Support Services (305 S. 15th St., tel. 215/ 546–7277).

**Stationery supplies.** A. Pomerantz & Co. (1525 Chestnut St., tel. 215/864–3000), Details (131 S. 18th St., tel. 215/ 977–9559), Goodrich & Co. (7th and Chestnut Sts., tel. 215/925–9100), Market Street Stationers (231 Chestnut St., tel. 215/627–2226), Stationery Stop (1824 Chestnut St., tel. 215/568–8214).

**Taxis.** Crescent Cab (tel. 215/365–3500), Quaker City Cab (tel. 215/728–8000), United Cab Association (tel. 215/625– 9170), Yellow Cab (tel. 215/922–7186).

**Theater tickets.** *See* The Arts, below.

**Train information.** Amtrak (30th and Market Sts., tel. 215/824–1600), Southeastern Pennsylvania Transportation Authority (SEPTA, tel. 215/574–7800).

**Travel agents.** AAA Keystone Travel Agency (2040 Market St., tel. 215/864–5050), American Express Travel Services (16th St. and John F. Kennedy Blvd., tel. 215/864–5050), Liberty Travel (1737 Chestnut St., tel. 215/972–0200), Rosenbluth Vacation Centers (1515 Walnut St., tel. 215/563–1070), Travel Now (One Franklin Plaza, tel. 215/988–0848).

**Weather** (tel. 215/936–1212).

## LODGING

Philadelphia's compact downtown now has a glut of luxury hotels vying for the business trade. If you want to be near the banking and legal centers, City Center hotels such as the Warwick, Latham, Rittenhouse, Four Seasons, Ritz-Carlton and Barclay are convenient. The Bellevue and Hershey Philadelphia are also good places to stay if your business is with the law firms clustered on Broad Street. If you want to be near the teaching hospitals, and textbook and legal publishers, stay at the Society Hill Sheraton, in the Historic District (8th St. to the Delaware River, north and south of Market St.), the Holiday Inn Independence Mall, or the Holiday Inn Midtown.

Most hotels listed here offer special corporate rates and weekend discounts; inquire when making reservations.

Highly recommended lodgings in each price category are indicated by a star ★.

| Category | Cost* |
| --- | --- |
| *$$$$* (Very Expensive) | over $140 |
| *$$$* (Expensive) | $90–$140 |
| *$$* (Moderate) | under $90 |

*All prices are for a standard double room, single occupancy, excluding 6% state tax and 5% city occupancy tax.*

*Numbers in the margin correspond to numbered hotel locations on the Philadelphia Lodging and Dining map.*

### Center City

**❿**
*$$$*

**Barclay.** Despite a lobby decked with marble-tile floors, dark-wood panel walls, and crystal chandeliers, this hotel is past its prime. Management says renovations are ongoing, but some rooms and halls are showing signs of wear. This 1929 hotel nevertheless attracts the carriage trade. The furniture is antique, with some reproductions, and nearly half the rooms have four-poster beds, some with canopies. The Barclay's central location on tony Rittenhouse Square is a plus, but don't expect all the amenities and business conveniences offered at the city's newer luxury hotels such as the Four Seasons or the Rittenhouse. The restaurant, tucked into a corner of the lobby, is a good, quiet choice for a business breakfast. *Rittenhouse*

*Sq. E, 19103, tel. 215/545–0300 or 800/421–6662, fax 215/ 545–2896. Gen. manager, Barry Pollard. 240 rooms. AE, DC, MC, V.*

**❻ Four Seasons.** This eight-story hotel, built in 1983, over-
$$$$ looks one of the prettiest green spots in the city, Logan Square. The hotel has all the details that have become synonymous with luxury—polished marble, crystal chandeliers, extravagant displays of fresh flowers, and high tea every afternoon. Guests are provided with terry robes and complimentary shoe shines. All standard rooms have desks; suites have an extra table and chairs that can be used for small meetings. The Presidential Suite is a favorite with visiting glitterati, such as singer Billy Joel. A 45-foot pool and well-equipped spa, though not as decked out as the Bellevue's Sporting Club (*see* Fitness, below), make this a good stop for travelers who want to maintain exercise programs. The Fountain Restaurant, in the lobby, is where many of Philadelphia's power brokers meet for breakfast (*see* Business Breakfasts, below). The Swann Lounge, also in the lobby, is appropriate for informal meetings or drinks with business colleagues. *One Logan Sq., 19103, tel. 215/963–1500 or 800/332–3442, fax 215/ 963–9562. Gen. manager, John Indrieri. 371 rooms. AE, DC, MC, V.*

**㉒ The Hershey Philadelphia Hotel.** This busy high-rise hotel
$$$ was built in 1983 in the heart of the theater district. Though sheathed in smoked glass, the four-story atrium lobby catches the morning and afternoon sun. In the summer months, baseball fans might see some of their favorite players milling around the lobby because visiting ball clubs often stay here. Rooms are comfortable but a bit worn, and decorated with modern furnishings in somewhat outdated earth tones. The hotel's angled design gives each room a bay window—and a 180-degree view. The eastside rooms get a panoramic view of the city and the Delaware River. The hotel is home to The Bar, one of the hottest jazz clubs in town (*see* After Hours, below). *Broad and Locust Sts., 19107, tel. 215/893–1600 or 800/ 553–3131, fax 215/893–1664. Gen. manager, Felix Rappaport. 428 rooms. AE, DC, MC, V.*

$$$ **Holiday Inns.** Downtown Philadelphia has three well-located Holiday Inns. All have rooms that are clean, relatively comfortable, and functional, although the decor is institutional; a soft mauve-and-beige color scheme is nearly identical throughout all the hotels. Some rooms have desks, all have an extra chair or two for reading. Staffs are helpful and friendly. Holiday Inn Center City is near the office towers on Market Street, Holiday Inn Independence Mall is close to the Liberty Bell and other historic sites, and Holiday Inn Midtown is close to several major hospitals and the shopping and theater districts. Women traveling alone should be warned that the Midtown hotel sits across the street from a liquor store, which draws pan
★ ❺ handlers both day and night. *Holiday Inn Center City, 1800 Market St., 19103, tel. 215/561–7500 or 800/465– 4329, fax 215/561–4484. Gen. manager, Arthur Yue. 450*
㉖ *rooms. Holiday Inn Independence Mall, 4th and Arch Sts., 19106, tel. 215/923–8660 or 800/465–4329, fax 215/ 923–8660, ext. 3369. Gen. manager, Ken Kodish. 367*
㉓ *rooms, 7 suites. Holiday Inn Midtown, 1305 Walnut St., 19107, tel. 215/735–9300 or 800/465–4329, fax 215/*

# PHILADELPHIA

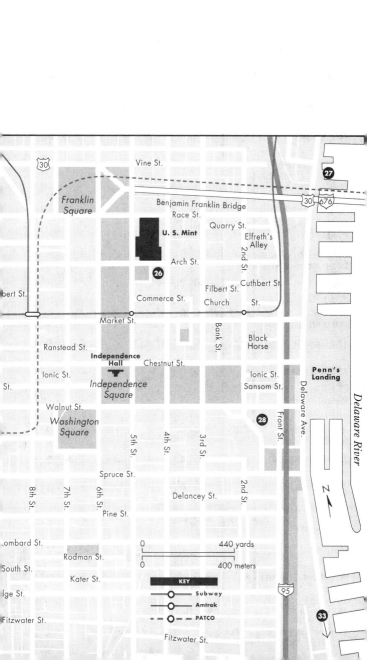

# PHILADELPHIA HOTEL CHART

| HOTELS | Price Category | Business Services Banquet capacity | No. of meeting rooms | Secretarial services | Audiovisual equipment | Teletype news service | Computer rentals | In-room modem phone jack | All-news cable channel | Desk | Desk lighting | Bed lighting |
|---|---|---|---|---|---|---|---|---|---|---|---|---|
| Airport Hilton Inn | $$$ | 540 | 16 | - | ✓ | - | - | ✓ | ✓ | ● | ◐ | ◐ |
| Barclay | $$$ | 180 | 10 | - | - | - | - | - | ✓ | ● | ● | ● |
| Days Inn | $$ | 100 | 7 | - | ✓ | - | - | ✓ | ✓ | - | - | ◐ |
| Four Seasons | $$$$ | 0 | 16 | ✓ | ✓ | - | - | ✓ | ✓ | ● | ● | ● |
| Guest Quarters | $$$$ | 125 | 9 | - | ✓ | ✓ | ✓ | ✓ | ✓ | ● | ● | ● |
| The Hershey Philadelphia | $$$ | 600 | 21 | - | ✓ | - | ✓ | ✓ | ✓ | ● | ● | ● |
| Holiday Inn, Center City | $$$ | 550 | 12 | - | ✓ | - | - | ✓ | ✓ | - | - | ◐ |
| Holiday Inn, Independence Mall | $$$ | 300 | 6 | - | ✓ | - | ✓ | - | ✓ | - | - | ◐ |
| Holiday Inn, Midtown | $$$ | 300 | 2 | - | ✓ | - | - | - | ✓ | - | - | ● |
| Hotel Atop the Bellevue | $$$$ | 800 | 9 | ✓ | ✓ | - | ✓ | ✓ | ✓ | ● | ◐ | ◐ |
| The Latham | $$$ | 50 | 2 | ✓ | ✓ | - | ✓ | ✓ | ✓ | ● | ● | ● |
| Marriott Hotel Airport | $$$$ | 0 | 0 | - | - | - | - | - | ✓ | ◐ | ◐ | ● |
| Penn Tower | $$$ | 500 | 7 | - | - | - | - | ✓ | - | - | - | ◐ |
| Radisson Suite Hotel | $$$ | 20 | 4 | - | ✓ | - | - | - | - | ● | ● | ◐ |
| The Rittenhouse | $$$$ | 300 | 4 | ✓ | ✓ | - | ✓ | ✓ | ✓ | ● | ● | ● |
| Ritz-Carlton | $$$$ | 500 | 8 | ✓ | ✓ | - | ✓ | ✓ | ✓ | ● | ● | ● |
| Sheraton Society Hill | $$$$ | 900 | 18 | ✓ | ✓ | - | ✓ | ✓ | ✓ | ● | ● | ◐ |
| Warwick | $$$ | 1200 | 7 | - | - | - | - | - | ✓ | ● | ● | ● |
| Wyndham - Franklin Plaza | $$$ | 2500 | 25 | ✓ | ✓ | - | - | ✓ | - | ● | ● | ◐ |

**$$$$** = over $140, **$$$** = $90-$140, **$$** = under $90.
● good, ◐ fair, ○ poor.
All hotels listed here have photocopying and fax facilities.

| In-Room Amenities | | | | | | | | | | Hotel Amenities | | | | | | |
| Nonsmoking rooms | In-room checkout | Minibar | Pay movies | VCR/Movie rentals | Hairdryer | Toiletries | Room service | Laundry/Dry cleaning | Pressing | Concierge | Barber/Hairdresser | Garage | Courtesy airport transport | Sauna | Pool | Exercise room |
|---|---|---|---|---|---|---|---|---|---|---|---|---|---|---|---|---|
| ✓ | - | - | ✓ | - | - | ◐ | ◐ | ◐ | ◐ | - | - | - | ✓ | - | ◐ | - |
| ✓ | - | - | - | - | - | ● | ◐ | ● | ◐ | ✓ | - | ✓ | - | - | - | - |
| ✓ | ✓ | - | ✓ | - | - | ◐ | ○ | ◐ | ◐ | - | - | - | ✓ | - | ◐ | - |
| ✓ | ✓ | ✓ | - | - | ✓ | ● | ● | ● | ◐ | ✓ | - | ✓ | - | ✓ | ● | ● |
| ✓ | ✓ | ✓ | - | - | - | ◐ | ◐ | ● | ◐ | ✓ | - | ✓ | ✓ | ✓ | ◐ | ◐ |
| ✓ | - | ✓ | ✓ | - | - | ● | ◐ | ● | ◐ | ✓ | - | ✓ | - | ✓ | ◐ | ● |
| ✓ | - | ✓ | ✓ | - | - | ◐ | ◐ | ○ | ○ | ✓ | - | - | - | - | ○ | ◐ |
| ✓ | - | ✓ | ✓ | - | - | ◐ | ◐ | ○ | ○ | ✓ | - | ✓ | - | - | ○ | - |
| ✓ | - | - | - | - | - | ● | ◐ | ● | ◐ | ✓ | - | ✓ | - | - | ○ | - |
| ✓ | ✓ | ✓ | ✓ | - | ✓ | ● | ● | ● | ● | ✓ | ✓ | ✓ | ✓ | ✓ | ◐ | ◐ |
| - | ✓ | ✓ | - | - | ✓ | ● | ◐ | ● | ◐ | ✓ | - | ✓ | ✓ | - | - | - |
| ✓ | - | - | ✓ | ✓ | - | ◐ | ◐ | ● | ◐ | ✓ | - | ✓ | ✓ | ✓ | ● | ◐ |
| ✓ | ✓ | ✓ | ✓ | - | - | ◐ | ● | ● | ◐ | ✓ | - | ✓ | - | - | - | - |
| ✓ | - | - | - | ✓ | ✓ | ◐ | ● | ● | ● | ✓ | - | ✓ | - | - | - | - |
| ✓ | ✓ | ✓ | ✓ | ✓ | ✓ | ● | ◐ | ● | ● | ✓ | ✓ | ✓ | ✓ | ● | ● | ● |
| ✓ | - | ✓ | ✓ | ✓ | ✓ | ● | ● | ● | ● | ✓ | ✓ | ✓ | ✓ | ✓ | ● | ● |
| ✓ | ✓ | ✓ | - | - | - | ◐ | ● | ● | ◐ | ✓ | - | ✓ | - | - | - | - |
| ✓ | - | - | - | - | - | ● | ○ | ● | ● | ✓ | - | ✓ | - | - | - | - |
| ✓ | ✓ | ✓ | ✓ | - | - | ◐ | ● | ◐ | ◐ | ✓ | ✓ | ✓ | ✓ | ✓ | ● | ● |

**Room service:** ● 24-hour, ◐ 6AM–10PM, ○ other.
**Laundry/Dry cleaning:** ● same day, ◐ overnight, ○ other.
**Pressing:** ● immediate, ◐ same day, ○ other.

*732–2682. Gen. manager, Richard Sheibley. 161 rooms. All take AE, DC, MC, V.*

**⑲** **Hotel Atop the Bellevue.** This grande dame of Philadelphia
**$$$$** hotels, listed on the National Register of Historic Places,
closed for several years after the outbreak of legionnaire's
disease in the mid-1970s and a renovation in the mid-1980s
that failed to restore the hotel's reputation. In 1988, following a two-year, $100-million renovation that included
new plumbing and air-conditioning systems, the 1904
French Renaissance–style building reopened. Most of the
hotel's public rooms, including its grand, two-tier ballroom, were restored and their original details retained.
The luxury guest rooms now occupy the top seven floors,
above several floors of offices, and three floors of smart
shops such as Ralph Lauren, Pierre Deux, Gucci, and Tiffany (*see* Shopping, below). The hotel has several fine restaurants, including the Barrymore Room, where high tea
and lunchtime fondues are served; and Founders, an appropriate spot for an early Morning meeting. The Philadelphia Library Lounge (*see* After Hours) is a good place
for a quiet drink. Hallways and many rooms are decorated—some might say overwhelmed—in mint-green wallpaper and carpeting; some rooms have a quieter pink or
blue color scheme. The rich oak furnishings are in keeping
with the building's architectural style. Executive rooms
are equipped with desks. *A Cunard hotel. 1415 Chancel-
lor Ct., 19102, tel. 215/893–1776 or 800/221–0833, fax 215/
893–9868. Gen. manager, Alex DeToth. 170 rooms, 11
suites. AE, DC, MC, V.*

**⑫** **The Latham.** Originally an apartment house, this 14-story
**$$$** building in the heart of the city's office and shopping dis-
trict was converted into a hotel in 1973. The lobby is small,
cozy, and elegant. Marble floors and lavish floral arrange-
ments adorn the entranceway. Guest rooms are large and
comfortable, each with a desk and a second phone in the
bathroom. Flowery chintz drapes and marble-top dressers
and nightstands are reminiscent of European hostelries.
Bogart's (*see* Business Breakfasts, below), one of two res-
taurants on the lobby floor, is a good choice for breakfast,
and Crickett's Bar is a good place to unwind after hours.
The staff is friendly, and doormen dressed in vests and
riding boots do their best to make guests feel welcome.
*135 South 17th St., 19103, tel. 215/563–7474 or 800/528–
4261, fax 215/563–4034. Gen. manager, Ron Gilbert. 139
rooms. AE, DC, MC, V.*

**⑧** **Radisson Suite Hotel.** Formerly known as The Palace, this
**$$$** 28-story residential hotel is where the late Grace Kelly
stayed when she visited her native city. The old name has
been discarded, along with the period furniture and Oriental rugs in the lobby. The hotel was bought in 1989 by a
young developer who redesigned the lobby in an Art Deco
style, upgrading the building's infrastructure, and giving
the hotel a more contemporary feel. The hotel's freshness
and its location on Ben Franklin Parkway make it an attractive alternative, but be sure to inquire if construction has been completed. *18th St. at Benjamin Franklin
Pkwy, 19103, tel. 215/963–2222 or 800/225–5843, fax 215/
963–2299. Gen. manager, Ted Knighton. 260 suites, 28
singles. AE, DC, MC, V.*

**❹ The Rittenhouse.** For nearly two decades, until it was com-
$$$$ pleted in mid-1989, this hotel and condominium tower was
a steel-and-concrete skeleton spoiling Philadelphia's most
fashionable neighborhood. The building's saw-tooth facade gives the hotel's 98 rooms an unusual layout. A wall of
large windows on one side of the building offers wide panoramic views of the skyline to the north, south, and east, as
well as of Rittenhouse Square. Suites, decorated in navy
and beige, have spacious sitting rooms and separate bedrooms. Some of the single rooms, with their oversize mahogany furniture, including armoires that hide the TV and
VCR, feel a bit cramped. The hotel is well stocked with
amenities for business travelers: marble baths with separate walk-in shower and tub, two-line phones in each
room, large desks, comfy armchairs for reading, secretarial and messenger services, offices for rent, an ATM machine in the back lobby, and a foreign-exchange desk. The
lobby, decorated in soothing beige tones, with marble
floors and overstuffed sofas and chairs, is a quiet place for
an informal meeting. The staff, eager to establish a steady
clientele among business travelers, is young, energetic,
and eager to please. *210 W. Rittenhouse Sq., 19103, tel.
215/546–9000 or 800/635–1042, fax 215/732–3364. Gen.
manager, Paul Seligson. 87 rooms, 10 suites. AE, DC,
MC, V.*

**❾ The Ritz-Carlton.** This new (opened November 1990) mem-
$$$$ ber of the luxury chain is an elegant addition to the heart
of Philadelphia's business center. Crystal chandeliers
shed a soft light on the 18th- and 19th-century oils and furnishings, richly paneled walls, and marble floors of the
lobby. Rooms feature antique reproductions, with large
mahogany desks, Waterford crystal lamps, three phones
with modem jacks, and imported Italian marble in spacious baths. Club floor accommodations entitle guests to
extras such as access to a lounge offering complimentary
Continental breakfast and cocktails, and private concierge service. The fitness center is state of the art. The
hotel also has several good restaurants, including the clubby Grill for steaks and seafood. *1650 Market St., 19103,
tel. 215/563–8215 or 800/241–3333, fax 215/851–9457.
Gen. manager, Darrell Shaeffer. 290 rooms, 16 suites.
AE, DC, MC, V.*

**⓫ Warwick.** First opened in 1924 and renovated in 1976 (indi-
$$$ vidual rooms have been redone in subsequent years), this
23-story hotel today attracts a theatrical clientele. Peter
Nero, the London Pops, and the casts of touring Broad-
way shows stay here. The lobby, adorned with gilded mir-
rors and 18-foot Palladian windows, is always busy. About
half of the building's rooms are for hotel guests; the rest
are apartments for permanent residents. Rooms and
suites have armchairs and desks with lamps. Decor is gen-
erally comfortable and appealing; some rooms are done in
Schumacher wallpapers and fabrics. The hotel's business
center offers temporary office space and secretarial ser-
vices, but is closed during the slower winter months.
Capricco, a European-style café with marble-top tables
and wrought-iron chairs, serves desserts and espresso un-
til 11 PM from Sunday to Wednesday and until 2 AM other
nights; it's the place in Center City to indulge a sweet tooth
when other spots have shut down. Polo Bay is the hotel's
disco (*see* After Hours, below). *17th and Locust Sts.,*

*19103, tel. 215/735–6000 or 800/523–4210, fax 215/790–7766. Gen. manager, Irving Anderson. 200 rooms. AE, DC, MC, V.*

**❼ Wyndham-Franklin Plaza Hotel.** This 760-room high rise
$$$ is the city's main convention hotel, thanks to its size and excellent meeting facilities. The imposing pile of buff-color brick occupies an entire city block. The vast 70-foot atrium lobby has sleek, beige marble walls that tower over numerous restaurants, lounges, and sitting areas. The busy hotel shows signs of wear in its hallways, but accommodations are kept surprisingly well. Rooms are large, and most have desks and an extra chair for reading. Decor is modern, with chrome tubular chairs and a gray-and-purple color scheme. Rooms facing south have good views of the skyline. The hotel is just one block from Benjamin Franklin Parkway, a shady boulevard modeled after the Champs Élysées in Paris and lined with most of the city's museums—an ideal place for an afternoon stroll. Fitness facilities—pool, aerobic center, and racquetball, squash, and tennis courts—are among the best of any hotel in town (*see* Fitness, below). Another plus is a resident masseuse. *17th and Vine Sts., 19103, tel. 215/448–2000 or 800/822–4200, fax 215/448–2864. Gen. manager, Chuck McCaffree. 760 rooms. AE, DC, MC, V.*

## Society Hill

**㉘ Sheraton Society Hill.** Located in the center of the city's
$$$$ historic district and a few blocks from Penn's Landing, this sprawling four-story hotel, built in 1986, has a splendid atrium lobby. Mexican tile pathways meander through archways and verandas that are filled with trees and plants and lighted by hanging wrought-iron lanterns. Rooms in this red-brick, neo-Colonial building have a traditional motif, with armoires and Chippendale pieces, but are enhanced with modern conveniences such as wet bars. All rooms have large desks and good reading lamps. The best views are from the fourth-floor rooms that face east and toward the Delaware River. The hotel staff is young and helpful. *1 Dock St., 19106, tel. 215/238–6000 or 800/325–3535, fax 215/922–2709. Gen. manager, Fred Corso. 365 rooms, 17 suites. AE, DC, MC, V.*

## West Philadelphia

**❸ Penn Tower.** This 21-floor hotel, a former Hilton, sits
$$$ across the street from the University of Pennsylvania's hospital, a short walk from the university's campus and next door to the civic center. The university purchased and renovated the hotel in 1987. The spacious and comfortable rooms are furnished in pastel colors with Colonial-style furniture; those facing east have spectacular views of the city's skyline. The lobby's deep burgundy decor gives it a somber air, but fresh flowers brighten it up a bit. The hotel has restaurants and lounges, as well as a large sitting area in the lobby. *34th St. and Civic Center Blvd., 19104, tel. 215/387–8333 or 800/356–7366, fax 215/386–8306. Gen. manager, Marcia Rafig. 227 rooms, 10 suites. AE, DC, MC, V.*

## South Philadelphia

**㉙** **Airport Hilton Inn.** The name is misleading, since the hotel
$$$ is 5 miles from the airport and is better known for its prox-
imity to the city's two arenas, the Spectrum and Veterans
Stadium. The hotel's lounge, Cahoots, is a favorite for ath-
letes and fans; often, after a game, the crowd in the lounge
spills out into the lobby, which is rather small. The 11-
story hotel was renovated in 1986 and has sizable rooms,
bathrooms, and closets. An Oriental floral print is used for
bedspreads and wallpaper, kelly-green solids are used for
the furniture upholstery. The hotel also features an out-
door swimming pool. Views of downtown, about 3 miles
away, are best from rooms that face north. *10th St. and
Packer Ave., 19148, tel. 215/755–9500 or 800/445–8667,
fax 215/462–6947. Gen. manager, Ken Kapikian. 238
rooms, 22 suites. AE, DC, MC, V.*

## Airport

**㉜** **Days Inn.** Price and location are the draws of this four-sto-
$$ ry, L-shape hotel across the street from the airport, near
the highway. Despite its location, the noise level is accept-
able thanks to special sound-proofing materials used in the
building's construction. Though it's a no-frills establishment, corridors are sunny pastel green and rooms are spacious, most with a desk. Amenities are minimal, but
include a coin-operated launderette, a restaurant, and
free airport shuttle service. *2 Gateway Center, 4101 Island Ave., 19153, tel. 215/492–0400 or 800/325–2525, fax
215/365–6035. Gen. manager, Barbara Griffin. 177
rooms. AE, DC, MC, V.*

**㉚** **Guest Quarters.** Rooms in this all-suites hotel open out on
$$$$ plant-filled balconies overlooking an eight-story circular
atrium. Guest Quarters, renovated on the upper floors in
early 1990, offers many perks for business travelers, including complimentary cocktail hour and Continental
breakfast. All accommodations have a king-size bed in the
bedroom and a queen-size foldout in the living room. Each
suite has three telephones, two remote-control television
sets, a bar, and a full kitchen; some have an extra-large
living room that can be used as a conference room, and
come equipped with a VCR, overhead projector, and
screen. Basketball teams stay here when they come to
play the Philadelphia 76ers. Exercise facilities include an
indoor pool, rowing machine, weights, and whirlpool.
*Gateway Center, 4101 Island Ave., 19153, tel. 215/365–
6600 or 800/424–2900, fax 215/492–9858. Gen. manager,
Chris Pfohl. 250 suites. AE, DC, MC, V.*

**㉛** **Marriott Hotel Airport.** Located just across from the air-
$$$$ port's Overseas Terminal, this hotel has set aside a floor
for business travelers. It offers such amenities as a lounge
with several telephones, a fax machine, and a conference
table, as well as complimentary beverages and fresh fruit.
Guest rooms are decorated with wood and wicker furnishings, and nearly all have desks and electric shoe buffers.
Lighting is insufficient. The main attraction in the lobby is
a pool, which is enclosed in glass and partly hidden by
plants. There's also a small but adequate workout room.
*4509 Island Ave., 19153, tel. 215/365–4150 or 800/228–
9290, fax 215/365–3875. Gen. manager, Greg Doyle. 331
rooms. AE, DC, MC, V.*

## DINING

Philadelphia underwent a culinary renaissance about 10 years ago, with the arrival of Continental-style bistros and elegant cafés that have taken the city well beyond the indigenous cheesesteak, soft pretzels, and TastyKakes. Although Frog, the restaurant that epitomized the dining renaissance, closed in 1988, other old favorites and some newcomers offer a wide selection of regional American, classic French, and ethnic specialties. Atmosphere is informal in many restaurants, and a good meal here tends to be more affordable than in other major East Coast cities. The business crowd stays in Center City for lunch, but some interesting dining options are available if you have time to visit the waterfront area (a five-minute ride) or West Philadelphia (a 15-minute trip).

Highly recommended restaurants in each price category are indicated by a star ★.

| Category | Cost* |
| --- | --- |
| $$$$ (Very Expensive) | over $35 |
| $$$ (Expensive) | $26–$35 |
| $$ (Moderate) | $20–$25 |
| $ (Inexpensive) | under $20 |

*per person, including appetizer, entrée, and dessert, but excluding drinks, service, and 6% sales tax.*

*Numbers in the margin correspond to numbered restaurant locations on the Philadelphia Lodging and Dining map.*

### Business Breakfasts

Overlooking Swann Fountain and Logan Square, **The Fountain** (Four Seasons, tel. 215/963–1500) is where many of the city's power brokers come for croissants and fresh fruit platters starting at 6 AM. Reservations are suggested. **Bogarts** (Latham Hotel, tel. 215/563–9444) has a similar ambience, but neither a location nor menu quite as interesting. **Founders** (The Hotel Atop the Bellevue, 19th floor, tel. 215/790–2814) offers breakfast (and lunch and dinner) overlooking the city and is convenient to office towers.

Outside of the hotels, an option is **Apropros** (211 Broad St., tel. 215/546–4424), a sleek and modern restaurant whose European-style bakery turns out delicious pastries, muffins, and breads. The central location is ideal for a business meeting, and the place is neither noisy nor rushed. If you and your associates need a lox and bagels fix and don't mind paper plates and plastic utensils, try **Famous 4th Street Delicatessen** (4th and Bainbridge Sts., tel. 215/922–3274); it's less than a 10-minute cab ride from most hotels.

### Center City

**⑭** **Le Bec-Fin.** Peach-color silk damask wall coverings, crystal chandeliers, and polished silver gleaming in the candlelight provide an elegance befitting one of the best French restaurants on the East Coast. The menu is classic

$$$

French, emphasizing the season's best ingredients. It's also one of the most expensive restaurants in town, a good place to dazzle clients, though the service can be stiff and off-putting. The five-course fixed-price dinner starts with a choice of appetizers, perhaps soup or homemade pâté, a salad of quail or scallops, fish in season, then a veal, chicken, or duck entrée. If it's on the menu, try the sweetbreads on cabbage with a black truffle sauce. Recommended from the bounteous dessert cart are profiteroles—cream puffs stuffed with ice cream and drizzled with dark chocolate sauce. Guest menus without prices are usually presented to female diners, so women hosts should notify the headwaiter in advance. *1523 Walnut St., tel. 215/567–1000. Jacket and tie required. Reservations for weekday lunches and dinners require one week advance notice; 10 weeks needed for dinner on weekends. AE, DC, MC, V. Closed Sun.*

**㉕** **Deux Cheminées.** After a fire destroyed chef Fritz Blank's
**$$$** first restaurant on Camac Street in 1988, he reopened a year later in this elegantly restored 19th-century mansion. Several of the private dining rooms—available at no extra charge—have fireplaces and are decorated with gilded mirrors, silver candelabras, and antiques. The menu is nouvelle French. A popular opener is crab soup Marguerite, which is cream based and enlivened by a shot of Scotch. Rack of lamb is the local favorite, but you usually can't go wrong with the fresh fish of the day. Lemon hazelnut cake is the dessert of choice. The extensive wine list includes selections from France and California. This is the spot to close an important business deal or impress clients. The staff paces meals slowly and pampers diners, but never patronizes them. *1221 Locust St., tel. 215/790–0200. Jacket and tie required. Reservations suggested. AE, DC, MC, V.*

**⑳** **Dilullo Centro.** Etched glass, brass partitions, rich dark
**$$$** wood, and murals set a romantic, elegant mood for this dimly lighted restaurant. The menu is Northern Italian; among the chef's most noted dishes are aragosta (lobster), prepared in a white-wine sauce with ginger; rack of lamb sautéed in rosemary and served with grilled eggplant; and medallions of salmon in white-wine and saffron sauce. The restaurant, once home of the former Locust Theater and located across from the Academy of Music, also has lighter fare for the after-theater crowd. For the most part the food is excellent, although some entrées are overpriced. It's a quiet and centrally located spot, good for a business lunch. An extraordinary wine list carries some rare Italian selections. *1407 Locust St., tel. 215/546–2000. Jacket and tie required. Reservations suggested. AE, DC, MC, V. Closed Sun.*

**⑱** **15th Street Bookbinder's Seafood House.** Although the
**$$$** Bookbinder's on Walnut Street in Society Hill calls itself Old Original Bookbinder's, this one on 15th Street is the restaurant founded by the Bookbinder family in the 1880s. Today, the fourth generation, Sam and Richard Bookbinder, are hosts to the lawyers and investment bankers who favor this spot for lunch. Nautical decor, featuring wall-mounted swordfish and fishermen's nets draped from the ceiling, provides a backdrop for such local favorites as lobster Coleman (chunks of lobster in a Newburg sauce), fresh stone crabs, and snapper soup; steak and chicken are

also available. Although the place is usually full at lunch-time, tables are adequately spaced and the atmosphere is still conducive to business talks. This Bookbinder's is less pricey than the one on Walnut Street, which tends to attract a tourist rather than a business crowd. *215 S. 15th St., tel. 215/545–1137. Business or casual dress. Reservations suggested. AE, DC, MC, V.*

**13** **The Garden.** Set in a town house near Rittenhouse Square,
$$$ The Garden offers indoor dining in the mahogany-paneled first-floor dining room, or outdoor seating in the garden at umbrella-covered tables. The house specialty is Dover sole, dusted with seasoned breadcrumbs, grilled, and served with hollandaise sauce. All desserts are home-made, including ice creams and sorbets, which are particularly refreshing. Investment bankers are among the business types who often lunch here. The staff is less accommodating of special requests than one would expect. *1617 Spruce St., tel. 215/546–4455. Jacket and tie required for dining room; casual for garden. Reservations required. AE, DC, MC, V.*

**17** **Il Gallo Nero.** Behind a nondescript facade is an elegant
$$$ dining room with candlelighted tables, lacy curtains, and an ebony and brass-rail bar. Philadelphia Orchestra conductor Ricardo Muti has a permanent table assigned to him. The chef, Carla Fusaro, who is also the owner's wife, creates such variations on Northern Italian cuisine as a pepper-and-garlic pasta with shrimp and scallops. The menu changes seasonally. Husband Enzo concocts desserts worth saving room for. It's an appropriate spot for a business dinner. *254 S. 15th St., tel. 215/546–8065. Business to casual dress. Reservations advised. AE, DC, MC, V. Closed Sun., Mon., July, and 1st week in Aug.*

**24** **Odeon.** This former flower shop, converted into a chic bis-
$$$ tro, attracts both businesspeople and upscale couples for lunch, dinner, and drinks. The wine bar has a 16-spout Cruvinet as well as an extensive wine list. The restaurant has two levels connected by a sweeping staircase; mirrored walls, Art Deco wall sconces, and green marble columns make an appealing and sophisticated setting. The menu ranges from simple to complicated regional French specialties. Try the fresh goose liver, served with a chestnut garnish, as an appetizer. The chef has adapted a dish typical of southwestern France, breast of duck, by adding Szechuan peppercorn sauce. Also good for entrées are the fillet of beef with shallot sauce and the salmon with gazpacho sauce. Hearty eaters may find the portions small. Because the restaurant can be noisy and crowded in the evening, it's best to conduct serious business here at lunch. *114 S. 12th St., tel. 215/922–5875. Casual dress. Reservations advised. AE, DC, MC, V. Closed Sun.*

**21** **Ruth's Chris Steakhouse.** Next door to the Academy of
$$$ Music, this newcomer to Philadelphia is giving Morton's of Chicago some stiff competition among businesspeople who like a good steak for lunch or dinner. Located on the first floor of an office building, the dining room is sufficiently large so that seating isn't cramped. Although there's wood paneling and a clubby feel, large windows let in lots of light. Beef is the star here—still sizzling as it's rushed to the table and served with a large green salad and potatoes. *260 S. Broad St., tel. 215/790–1515. Business to casual dress. Reservations suggested. AE, MC, V.*

**16** **Susanna Foo.** Chinese food takes on an elegant dimension
**$$$** in Susanna and Hsin Foo's spacious dining room, where ta-
bles are set with starched white linens, crystal, and blue-
and-white china. The menu, which features dishes typical
of China's Mongolian region but often prepared French-
style with stock-based sauces, changes seasonally. House
specialties include sautéed quail with shiitake mushrooms
and filet Mignon with pepper sauce. Tables and ban-
quettes along one side of the restaurant are a bit cramped
and offer little privacy; ask for a table in the center of the
room. A five-minute walk from Market Street's high-rise
office towers, this spot is popular for both lunch and din-
ner. *1512 Walnut St., tel. 215/545–2666. Business to casu-
al dress. Reservations advised, especially at lunchtime.
AE, MC.*

**15** **Tequila's.** This Mexican restaurant doesn't offer chimi-
**$$** changas or nachos smothered in cheese, but rather a more
refined Mexican cuisine that includes chicken breast with
mole, a chocolate and chili-based sauce. The nachos on this
menu are light and crispy and come with ground beef,
beans, and a chunky guacamole. Many of the ingredients
are imported directly from Mexico, as are the blue ceramic
china, barware, and artifacts that decorate the whitewashed walls. This is a fun place to share a business meal
with associates or clients, although it's usually busy until
8 PM with theater- and concert-goers (it's near the city's music hall and main theaters). The room can be a bit noisy and
cramped when full, but the staff is always friendly and efficient. Avoid the two tables near the bar, which are the noisiest when the bar gets crowded. *1511 Locust St., tel. 215/
546–0181. Casual dress. AE, DC, MC, V.*

## Waterfront

**33** **Chef Theodore.** Once just a tiny storefront, this Greek
**$** restaurant moved to larger quarters near the waterfront
(a 10-minute cab ride from Center City hotels) in 1989. Although the decor is now more upscale, with soft lighting
and huge potted plants, the menu is still surprisingly reasonable. The spinach pie is excellent, but the chef's real
specialty is lamb, prepared in a variety of ways each
night. Desserts are a little too sugary, but they can be
tempered with strong Greek coffee. This isn't the spot to
close a deal, but a place to unwind or celebrate afterward
with colleagues. The staff is eager to please. The chef often greets diners and regales them with a song or two
when the kitchen slows down. *1100 S. Delaware Ave., tel.
215/271–6800. Casual dress. BYOB (liquor store located
in same mall). Reservations taken only for parties of 6 or
more. AE, CB, DC, MC, V. Closed Mon.*

**27** **Meiji-En.** This large Japanese restaurant, with indoor
**$$$** rock gardens and waterfalls, is housed on the second floor
of an old pier. A seat at the bar offers fine waterfront
views. An extensive menu features fresh sushi and excel-
lent tempura. Diners in the Teppanyaki Room sit around a
grill and watch a chef prepare their meal tableside—a
procedure that inhibits conversation. About a 10-minute
cab ride from most hotels and office towers, Meiji-En is a
quiet spot, good if you and your client have time for a long-
er weekday lunch or dinner. *Pier 19, N. Delaware Ave.,
tel. 215/592–7100. Casual dress. Reservations advised.
AE, CB, DC, MC, V.*

## West Philadelphia

**❶ Thai Garden.** Tucked away in a residential neighborhood
$ in West Philadelphia, this little restaurant has won a big
following since it opened in 1988. Its pastel-color interior,
with soft lighting and delicate floral-print curtains framing bay windows, is inviting. A popular choice among
some 40 entrées is crispy duck with raspberry sauce (large
enough to share, but so good you'll want to keep it all to
yourself). Fried bananas with sweet coconut-milk sauce is
a good bet for dessert. Thai Garden is a 15-minute cab ride
from Center City hotels, but it's worth the trek for a more
relaxing, informal business meal. On weeknights, the dining room is quiet and guests are easily accommodated. Expect a wait for tables on weekends. *Garden Court
Apartments, 349 S. 47th St., tel. 215/471–3663. Casual
dress. Reservations suggested on weekends to avoid a
wait. MC, V.*

**★ ❷ White Dog Café.** Nestled in a rowhouse just off the Univer-
$$ sity of Pennsylvania campus in West Philadelphia, this
well-regarded spot is where faculty often dines out and
visiting parents treat their offspring on homecoming
weekends. The cuisine is a mix of regional specialties and
new American dishes. The dining rooms are reminiscent
of those in a cozy country inn, with rustic oak tables, lace
curtains, blue-and-white gingham table linens, and fresh
wild flowers. The swordfish is seasoned with a delicate
peppercorn sauce. The basic apple crumbcake à la mode
tastes like something Grandma should have made. The bar
in the front attracts a young professional crowd; prices are
beyond most student budgets. Come for a business lunch
or a relaxing dinner, except on fall weekends during the
university's football season and in early March when the
Philadelphia Flower Show attracts hordes of tourists to
the area. *3420 Samson St., tel. 215/386–9224. Reserva-
tions required for dinner. AE, DC, MC, V.*

# FREE TIME

## Fitness

*Hotel Facilities*
The **Wyndham Franklin Plaza** (tel. 215/448–2000) has an
aerobics center and racquetball, squash, and tennis
courts, which costs $10 a day for Wyndham guests and $20
for guests at other hotels in the city.

*Health Clubs*
The **12th Street Gym** (204 S. 12th St., tel. 215/985–4092)
offers one-day memberships for $10 a day. **Fourth Street
Gym** (325 Bainbridge St., tel. 215/627–5874) offers a $5
day pass. **Rittenhouse Fitness Club** (2002 Rittenhouse Sq.,
tel. 215/985–4095) allows nonmembers to use its facilities
for $10 a day.

*Jogging*
The **Philadelphia Museum of Art** is the starting block for
an 8-mile loop along the Schuykill River, on Kelly Drive,
across Falls Bridge, and West River Drive to the museum.
**Wissahickon Park** offers 5 miles of scenic jogging on For-
bidden Drive, a dirt path along a meandering creek.

## Shopping

Philadelphia's most fashionable shops are **along Walnut Street between Broad and 21st streets:** Ann Taylor, Honeybee (women's clothes), Burberry's, Allure (women's shoes), Wayne Edwards (men's clothing), Eddie Bauer (sports equipment and sports clothes), Laura Ashley, and Deschamps (French bath and bed linens). **Palladio** (132 S. 18th St., tel. 215/972–7272) and **Knit-Wit** (208 S. 17th St., tel. 215/735–3642), both a ½ block from Walnut Street, offer stylish clothing for women for business and play. For reliable department-store selections, visit **John Wannamaker's** (13th and Market Sts., tel. 215/432–2000) or **Strawbridge & Clothiers** (8th and Market Sts., tel. 215/629–6000). In 1989, **Nan Duskin** (tel. 215/735–6400), a haven for the city's well-heeled and well-dressed women, moved from its Walnut Street address to the ground floor of the new Rittenhouse Hotel. But this venerable Philadelphia establishment is facing stiff competition from such trendy new arrivals as Ralph Lauren, Gucci, Alfred Dunhill, Pierre Deux, and Tiffany, all located in the nearby refurbished Bellevue Hotel (tel. 215/893–1776) at Broad and Walnut streets.

Neighborhood shops **along Spruce and Locust streets, from 13th to 23rd streets** are fun for browsing and offer a unique assortment of gifts, collectibles, and antiques. Antiques shops line **Pine Street, from 6th to 18th streets,** offering everything from quilts and Shaker furniture to jewelry and prints. No real bargains, but it's fun to browse. For the true antique buyer, **Freeman/Fine Arts of Philadelphia** (1808 Chestnut St., tel. 215/563–9275) holds estate auctions on Wednesdays; the viewing of each week's auction lots is on Monday and Tuesday.

## Diversions

**Fairmont Park** (tel. 215/235–1776), the largest landscaped park in the United States, offers peaceful walks through woodlands and rolling hills. The park also has some 200 pieces of outdoor art, exercise courses, and several early American country house-museums.

**Franklin Institute** (20th St. and Benjamin Franklin Pkwy., tel. 215/448–1200) offers computers, gadgets, buttons, and devices to hold, touch, and play with. The Futures Center, opened in May 1990, showcases emerging technologies. The center's Omniverse Theater projects 70-mm films on a 79-foot-wide domed ceiling with sound emerging from 56 speakers.

**Independence National Historical Park,** which you enter at the Visitor's Center at 3rd and Chestnut streets (tel. 215/597–8974), must be America's most historic square mile. Red-brick paths bordered by groomed lawns and shaded by ancient oaks and maples lead to **Independence Hall,** the **Liberty Bell, Congress Hall,** the **Betsy Ross House,** and **Elfreth's Alley** (the oldest continuously occupied residential street in the United States). Most attractions are free, and several guided tours are available.

**Penn's Landing,** on the Delaware River waterfront, features outdoor concerts, jamborees, festivals, and other events, including Friday-night jazz concerts during the summer (check local papers, such as the *Philadelphia Inquirer*'s Friday Weekend section and the *Welcomat* for upcoming week's concerts).

**Philadelphia Museum of Art** (26th St. and Ben Franklin Pkwy., tel. 215/763–8100) is one of the country's finest art museums, boasting a collection of more than 300,000 works in some 200 galleries. The newly renovated American Wing houses fine collections of furniture, silver, and paintings, including the large canvases of Thomas Eakins, who was charmed by the rowers on the Schuylkill River.

**Reading Terminal Market,** at 12th and Market streets, offers everything from produce carted in by Amish farmers to fresh meats, used books, and fresh-cut flowers. More than a dozen counter-top restaurants offer a wide selection of tastes, including Chinese, Greek, and Mexican. The **Down Home Diner** (tel. 215/627–1955) is the place to go for home-style cooking and generous helpings. Many city workers stop here at midday to get fresh groceries or pick up lunch.

**The Rodin Museum** (22nd St. and Benjamin Franklin Pkwy., tel. 215/787–5431), guarded outside by a statue of "The Thinker" (an original—Auguste Rodin made three; the others are in Detroit and Paris), has the largest collection of Auguste Rodin's works outside of France. The museum doors are his Gates of Hell.

**South Street** from Front to 9th streets is lined with funky boutiques, outdoor cafés, thrift shops, galleries, and arts-and-crafts shops. This Philadelphia version of New York's Greenwich Village is pleasant for browsing and people-watching.

## Professional Sports

At Veteran's Stadium, catch Philadelphia's football team, the **Eagles** (tel. 215/463–5500) and the city's baseball club, the **Phillies** (tel. 215/463–1000). Philadelphia's basketball team, the **76ers** (tel. 215/339–7676), and its hockey team, the **Flyers** (tel. 215/755–9700), play at the Spectrum.

## The Arts

The city's proximity to New York brings many top-notch touring Broadway shows to town, usually to the **Forrest Theater** and the **Walnut Street Theatre.** The **Academy of Music** is home to one of the world's finest symphony orchestras, the Philadelphia Orchestra, and to various traveling ballet companies and the local favorite, the Pennsylvania & Milwaukee Ballet. For avant-garde performances, try the **Wilma Theater, Philadelphia Theater Company of Plays and Players,** and the **Society Hill Playhouse.** The **Annenberg Center** and the **Shubert Theater** at the University of the Arts provide a potpourri of entertainment that includes musicals, ballets, and popular entertainers. **Freedom Theater,** the oldest and most active black theater, is housed in Heritage House, the former home of American actor Edwin Forrest.

Ticket agencies include **Culture Connection** (16th St. and John F. Kennedy Blvd., tel. 215/564–4444) and **Central City Ticket Office** (1312 Sansom St., tel. 215/735–1350).

**Academy of Music,** Broad and Locust Sts., tel. 215/893–1935.

**The Annenberg Center,** 3680 Walnut St., tel. 215/898–6791.

**Forrest Theater,** 1114 Walnut St., tel. 215/923–1515.

**Freedom Theater,** 1346 N. Broad St., tel. 215/765–2793.

**Philadelphia Theater Company of Plays and Players,** 1714 Delancey St., tel. 215/592–8333.

**Shubert Theater** at the University of the Arts, 250 S. Broad St., tel. 215/732–5446.

**Society Hill Playhouse,** 507 S. 8th St., tel. 215/923–0210.

**Walnut Street Theatre,** 9th and Walnut Sts., tel. 215/574–3550.

**Wilma Theatre,** 2030 Sansom St., tel. 215/963–0249.

## After Hours

*Bars and Lounges*

The **Swann Lounge** (Four Seasons Hotel, tel. 215/963–1500) and the **Philadelphia Library Lounge** (The Bellvue, tel. 215/893–1776) offer elegant and tranquil settings for drinks with clients. After work, young, single professionals cruise the **Top of Centre Square** (15th and Market Sts., tel. 215/563–9494), a loud, crowded bar with a panoramic view of the city. For those who really want to let loose, try **Downey's** (Front and South Sts., tel. 215/629–0525), a smokey Irish bar frequented by local athletes, especially baseball and hockey players.

*Cabaret*

The **Chestnut Cabaret** (3801 Chestnut St., tel. 215/382–1201) offers everything from New Age music to reggae, rhythm-and-blues, heavy metal, and rock 'n' roll. The club is near the University of Pennyslvania and caters mostly to those in their 20s.

*Comedy Clubs*

The **Comedy Factory Outlet** (31 Bank St., tel. 215/922–5997) features big-name comics as well as local amateurs. The larger and less intimate **Comedy Works** (126 Chestnut St., tel. 215/386–6911) seats 300 and brings in young comedians from Los Angeles and New York.

*Jazz Clubs*

The intimate **Café Borgia** (406 S. 2nd St., tel. 215/574–0414) serves up local singers à la Billie Holiday. The century-old **Orlieb Jazz Haus** (847 N. 3rd St., tel. 215/922–1035) has jam sessions on Tuesdays. A newcomer to the jazz scene is **The Bar Lounge** (Hershey Hotel, tel. 214/893–1600), which recruits headliners from across the country for weekend performances.

*For Singles*

**Polo Bay** (Warwick Hotel, tel. 215/546–8800) is a tropical oasis renowned for its happy hours. The dance floor is small, but the music is energetic. About a 30-minute drive from downtown, **Pulsations** (Rte. 1, Glen Mills, tel. 215/459–4140) has a 25,000-watt sound system that keeps people on their feet into the wee hours. **Metropolis** (1515 Locust St., tel. 215/546–1515) is a favorite with Center City's yuppie crowd. The brass-and-glass watering hole has a small dance floor, a separate lounge, and a restaurant.

# Phoenix

*by Mark Hein*

In the late '80s, the much publicized collapse of overpriced real-estate developments and underregulated S & Ls put a brake on two decades of steadily accelerating Sunbelt growth. Arizona, which had known land booms and busts before, was among the hardest hit states. But this time, something different happened: Led by metropolitan Phoenix, the state continued to grow—less rapidly, but steadily.

Phoenix's resilience can be attributed partly to the diversified economic base it has built over the last 30 years. High- and mid-tech manufacturing—Phoenix is the nation's third largest electronics center and manufactured-goods exporter—transportation, and communications continued their steady expansion, the former receiving an unexpected boost from the Persian Gulf war. Meanwhile, the area's infrastructure, as well as its retail and service industries, have yet to meet the needs of the current, still growing population. If apartments and office space are two to three years overbuilt, the metro area's freeways, parkways, and mass-transit systems are 10 to 15 years behind, keeping construction industries busy. And many Valley service industries already are extending their reach into the wider markets for which Phoenix is a metro center—the state, the Southwest, the West Coast, and Mexico.

Phoenix is now getting serious about the ecological costs of growth. By the mid-80s, it had one of the worst smog problems in the United States, aggravated by desert dust; in 1990, alternative-fuel legislation and carpool incentives cut emission levels by 20% from 1989. The city plans to plant a million desert trees by 1995—a major step in alleviating air pollution and controlling urban heat absorption and energy use.

Unless you plan to stay in or near your hotel for your entire visit to the Valley, you will need a car. The Valley's mass transit system is a sketchy linkup of city bus and minibus systems and Dial-a-Ride services; it is not recommended for business travelers. Allow generous travel time when driving: The freeway system, all but nonexistent until the mid-'80s, is still being built. And virtually all the Valley's cities—Phoenix, Scottsdale, Mesa, Tempe, Glendale, the Sun Cities, and smaller suburbs—are plotted on a single grid-system street layout, stretching 40 miles east to west, and more than 20 miles north to south, with almost no diagonals (not even the freeways). The grid makes it easy to find places, but it can double the driving time from point A to point B, because you must trace two legs of a right triangle to get there.

## Top Employers

| Employer | Type of Enterprise | Parent*/ Headquarters |
|---|---|---|
| **Allied Signal Corp.** | Aerospace manufacturing | Morristown, NJ |
| **American Express** | Travel and financial services | New York, NY |
| **America West Airlines** | Airline | Phoenix |
| **Arizona Public Service** | Electric utility | Phoenix |
| **Honeywell** | Aircraft electronics | Minneapolis |
| **McDonnell Douglas** | Helicopter manufacturing, research & development | St. Louis |
| **Motorola** | Electronics manufacturing, research & development | Schaumberg, IL |
| **Samaritan Health Services** | Health care | Phoenix |
| **Smitty's/ SuperValu** | Groceries, retail drugs | Phoenix |
| **U.S. West** | Telecommunications | Denver |
| **Valley National Bank** | Financial services | Phoenix |

*if applicable

## ESSENTIAL INFORMATION

### Climate

What follows are the average daily maximum and minimum temperatures for Phoenix.

| Jan. | 64F 18C<br>39 4 | Feb. | 69F 21C<br>42 6 | Mar. | 75F 24C<br>46 8 |
|---|---|---|---|---|---|
| Apr. | 82F 28C<br>53 12 | May | 91F 33C<br>60 16 | June | 100F 38C<br>69 21 |
| July | 104F 40C<br>77 25 | Aug. | 100F 38C<br>75 24 | Sept. | 96F 36C<br>69 21 |
| Oct. | 86F 30C<br>55 13 | Nov. | 75F 24C<br>44 7 | Dec. | 66F 19C<br>39 4 |

## Airport

**Sky Harbor International Airport** is 3 miles east of downtown. Freeway links connect it to every part of the metro area except Scottsdale (to the northeast, a 45-minute drive by surface streets) and the Sun Cities area (to the far northwest, also about 45 minutes, by way of I–17 and surface streets).

## Airport Business Facilities

**Host International** (tel. 602/273–3820) leases out five conference rooms in Terminal 3, and has fax machines, photocopying, and catering service. Coin-operated showers are in the rest rooms of Terminal 3.

## Airlines

Sky Harbor is the home airport for America West Airlines, and a hub for Southwest Airlines.

**American,** tel. 800/433–7300.
**America West,** tel. 602/693–0737 or 800/247–5692.
**Aviacion del Noroeste,** tel. 602/275–7950 (Mexico).
**Continental,** tel. 602/258–8911 or 800/525–0280.
**Delta,** tel. 602/258–5930 or 800/221–1212.
**Mesa,** tel. 800/637–2247 (commuter).
**Northwest,** tel. 800/225–2525.
**Southwest,** tel. 602/273–1221 or 800/531–5601.
**StatesWest,** tel. 602/220–0700 (commuter).
**United,** tel. 602/273–3131 or 800/241–6522.
**USAir,** tel. 602/258–7355 or 800/428–4322.

## Between the Airport and Downtown

Sky Harbor is served by several taxi and shuttle services, including a few hotel courtesy shuttles.

*By Taxi*
It takes 10–15 minutes to reach downtown and Tempe, even during rush hours (6–9 AM, 4–7 PM), since both are less than 5 miles away. It takes 20–30 minutes to reach Metrocenter in the West Valley. Taxi fares to downtown and Tempe run about $7, to Metrocenter $15 or more.

*By Van*
**Super Shuttle's** blue and gold vans (tel. 602/244–9000) offer door-to-door service for about 25% less than taxis. The van stop, outside the baggage claim area, is marked by a red diamond-shape sign.

*By Bus*
Phoenix Transit buses (tel. 602/253–5000) will get you directly to downtown Phoenix from the airport in 15–25 minutes for less than $1. Getting to other Valley cities (Tempe, Mesa, Scottsdale) takes a transfer, usually to the smaller city's minibus system. Buses run every 30 minutes from about 5:45 AM to 6 PM.

## Car Rentals

The following companies have booths at the airport or free pickup and delivery service from nearby lots.

**Alamo,** tel. 602/244–0897 or 800/327–9633.
**Avis,** tel. 602/273–3222 or 800/331–1212.
**Avon,** tel. 602/258–1918 or 800/822–2866.

**Budget,** tel. 602/267–4000 or 800/527–0700.
**Hertz,** tel. 602/267–8822 or 800/654–3131.
**Thrifty,** tel. 602/244–0311 or 800/367–2277.

## Emergencies

*Doctors*
*See* Hospitals, below.

*Dentists*
The Valley chapter of the **American Dental Association** has a 24-hour referral hot line (tel. 602/957–4864).

*Hospitals*
The four Samaritan hospitals in the Valley—**Good Samaritan,** downtown, **Desert Samaritan,** Mesa, **Maryvale Samaritan,** south West Valley, and **Thunderbird Samaritan,** north West Valley, near Metrocenter—share a 24-hour referral line (tel. 602/230–2273) with the network's satellite emergency clinics. **Scottsdale Memorial Hospital** has three campuses in the northeast Valley (tel. 602/481–4411). County-run **Maricopa Medical Center,** downtown (tel. 602/267–5011) has been rated one of the nation's best public hospitals.

## Important Addresses and Numbers

**Audiovisual rentals.** Arizona Audio-Visual Center (9332 N. 95th Way, Suite 105, Scottsdale, tel. 602/345–9155), Audio-Video Recorders of Arizona (3830 N. 7th St., Phoenix, tel. 602/277–4723), Audio Video Specialists (333 E. Camelback Rd., Phoenix, tel. 602/264–9911), Audio Visual Services (1425 W. 12th Place, Suite 102, Tempe, tel. 602/968–0202), Video West (3733 E. Atlanta Ave., Phoenix, tel. 602/470–0880).

**Chamber of Commerce** (34 W. Monroe St., tel. 602/254–5521), Phoenix & Valley of the Sun Convention & Visitors Bureau (502 N. 2nd St., tel. 602/254–6500).

**Computer rentals.** Abcor Computer Rental (8940 N. 19th Ave., Suite 103, Phoenix, tel. 602/870–3717), AccuRent (521 S. 48th St., Suite 101, Tempe, tel. 602/829–6500), Photo & Sound Co. (4246 E. Wood St., Suite 560, Phoenix, tel. 602/437–1560), Scott Tellier (3302 E. Indian School Rd., Phoenix, tel. 602/954–8933).

**Convention and exhibition centers.** Phoenix Civic Plaza (225 E. Adams St., tel. 602/262–6225), Mesa Community & Conference Center (263 N. Center St., Mesa, tel. 602/644–2178).

**Fax services.** AlphaGraphics (23 Valley locations, including Phoenix, tel. 602/271–9525; Tempe, tel. 602/968–7821; Scottsdale, tel. 602/994–1514), Courier Fax (tel. 800/877–2329) provides pickup & delivery service.

**Formal-wear rentals.** Azteca (1010 E. Washington St., Phoenix, tel. 602/258–2568), Fairy Godmothers (3 locations: 702 W. Camelback Rd., Phoenix, tel. 602/222–8838; 725 S. Rural Rd., Tempe, tel. 602/968–0238; 9070 E. Indian Bend Rd., Scottsdale, tel. 602/443–3060), Hanny's (2 locations: 3100 N. Central Ave., Phoenix, tel. 602/264–5857; 2426 E. Camelback Rd., Phoenix, tel. 602/997–5831).

**Gift shops.** Gift Baskets: C. Steele & Co. (7303 E. Indian School Rd., Scottsdale, tel. 602/994–4180), The Better Basket and Bouquet (1219 E. Glendale Ave., Phoenix, tel. 602/235–9500; nationwide delivery); Flowers: Green Forest (Valley Bank Center, 201 N. Central Ave., tel. 602/271–9506); Jewelry: Goldcraft Jewelers (Valley Bank Center, 201 N. Central Ave., tel. 602/256–7323).

**Graphic design studios.** AlphaGraphics (23 Valley locations; *see* Fax services, above), Contemporary Graphics (122 E. University Dr., Tempe, tel. 602/967–5625), Wayzgoose (7515 E. 1st St., Scottsdale, tel. 602/645–0289), Wizzard Supergraphics (812 W. Earll Dr., Phoenix, tel. 602/258–3126), Zuniga Designs (1616 N. 16th St., Phoenix, tel. 602/258–3126).

**Hairstylists.** Unisex: B'Anne (2 locations: 14 E. Camelback Rd., Phoenix, tel. 602/252–3908; 5402 E. Lincoln Dr., Scottsdale, tel. 602/951–0423), Executive Towers Barber Salon (207 W. Clarendon Ave., Phoenix, tel. 602/265–6975), Golden Razor (10413 N. 35th Ave., Phoenix, tel. 602/866–9868), Hair Design (24 W. Monroe St., Phoenix, tel. 602/253–1879), Sebring Hair International (824 E. Indian School Rd., Phoenix, tel. 602/266–9019).

**Health and fitness clubs.** *See* Fitness, below.

**Information hot lines.** Pressline (tel. 602/271–5656) offers updates and information on more than 75 topics including stock and bond prices, sports scores, soap-opera plots, local restaurants, movie sets, and television, and local and national weather.

**Limousine services.** Arizona's Puttin' on the Ritz (tel. 602/483–6151), Continental Limousines (tel. 602/941–9340), Jackson Limousines (tel. 602/242–5567), Limousine Referral Hotline (tel. 602/957–1117).

**Liquor stores.** Dave's Fine Wines & Liquors (5031 N. 16th St., Phoenix, tel. 602/277–7887), Drinkwater's Liquor & Cheese (10802 N. Scottsdale Rd., Scottsdale, tel. 602/948–0520), Norman's Liquor Barn (8 locations, including: 3601 E. Indian School Rd., Phoenix, tel. 602/954–0137).

**Mail delivery, overnight.** DHL Worldwide Express (tel. 800/225–5345), Federal Express (tel. 602/244–4662), TNT Skypak (tel. 602/431–1211), UPS (tel. 602/272–5555), U.S. Postal Service Express Mail (602/244–8811).

**Messenger services.** A Minute Messenger (tel. 602/224–9886), Arizona Messenger (tel. 800/231–6768), Direct Delivery (tel. 602/946–0690).

**Office space rentals.** Forum Executive Suites (6 locations: tel. 602/631–3555 for the closest one), Home Office Executive Suites (6900 E. Camelback Rd., Scottsdale, tel. 602/994–0944), Legal Suite (3225 N. Central Ave., Phoenix, tel. 602/274–4827), Los Olivos Executive Suites (202 E. McDowell Rd., Phoenix, tel. 602/252–1832).

**Pharmacies, late-night.** Kristal-Lahr (9220 N. Central Ave., Phoenix, tel. 602/944–3326), Walgreen's (3 locations: 5121 W. Indian School Rd., tel. 602/247–1014; 3722 E. Thomas Rd., Phoenix, tel. 602/275–7507; 1717 E. Southern Ave., Tempe, tel. 602/838–3642).

**Radio stations, all-news.** The Valley has no all-news radio station, but KFNN 1510 AM broadcasts business news during daylight hours.

**Secretarial services.** Absolute Perfection (10410 N. 31st Ave., Phoenix, tel. 002/978–9211), Home Office Executive Suites (*see* Office rentals, above), Kelly Temporary Services (6 locations: tel. 602/264–0717 for the closest one), Manpower Temporary Services (6 locations: tel. 602/264–0237 for the closest one).

**Stationery supplies.** Bronwals (8220 N. Hayden Rd., Scottsdale, tel. 602/991–0888), Scottsdale Stationery & Office (7221 E. 1st Ave., Scottsdale, tel. 602/945–8148), State Office Supply (4015 N. 16th St., Phoenix, tel. 602/232–1956), Wilke's (229 N. 1st Ave., Phoenix, tel. 602/258–1581).

**Taxis.** American Handicapped Transport (tel. 602/272–7211), Checker Cab (tel. 602/257–1818), Courier Cab (tel. 602/232–2222), Super Shuttle (tel. 602/244–9000), Yellow Cab (tel. 602/252–5252).

**Train information.** Amtrak (tel. 800/872–7245), Conrail (tel. 800/932–9292), Mexican National Railway (Nogales, tel. 800/344–1865), Southern Pacific (tel. 602/256–0556). Each railway has its own depot. Call for schedules and locations.

**Travel agents.** CEFRA (12 locations: tel. 602/258–0200 for the closest one), Laird Travel (4166 N. Scottsdale Rd., Scottsdale, tel. 602/947–4375), Travel Concepts (2525 E. Indian School Rd., Phoenix, tel. 602/263–7779), Wild Adventures (7521 E. McKnight St., Scottsdale, tel. 602/946–0775).

**Weather.** Pressline (tel. 602/271–5656, ext. 3333).

# LODGING

Central Phoenix is the seat of Arizona's government and the heart of its corporate, financial, and communication networks. In the '70s and '80s, it burst into life as a modern urban center, including hotels, the Civic Plaza convention complex, historic Heritage Square, futuristic Patriots Park, and a bright neo-Mexican Mercado. Although it still has scant nightlife and few 24-hour services, it is a compact, quietly active city center. The only time noise and street life really build is in August, when heat empties its office towers, and during Grand Prix week (time alternates from year to year, check ahead), when Formula One race cars roar through its streets.

Business travelers also may find it convenient to stay in one of several other areas, depending on what business brings them to Phoenix.

The airport is only 3 miles from both downtown and Tempe, making it a logical home base for business travelers.

The fast-growing East Valley communities—Tempe, Mesa, Chandler and Gilbert—are home to Arizona State University and to most of metro Phoenix's electronics and aerospace firms. This is also the area closest to central Arizona's major agricultural and mining operations.

Biltmore and Scottsdale, both upscale areas, are northeast of downtown, in the shadow of Camelback Mountain. The Biltmore area of Phoenix, along Camelback Road adjacent to the luxurious Biltmore Estates, has become the epicenter of Valley financial and investment industries and a key area for fine dining and shopping. Just east is downtown Scottsdale, home to many of Arizona's best-known luxury resorts, and one of the Southwest's art capitals (the other is Santa Fe, New Mexico).

West Valley, long a vast expanse of farm fields broken only by Luke Air Force Base, took off in the '60s with electronic manufacturing and the Sun Cities—the nation's pioneer active-retirement subdivisions—and has kept growing since. Light manufacturing and insurance industries are here, too, as well as the American Graduate School for International Management and an ASU campus.

Most of the hotels listed below have corporate rates and weekend discounts. Inquire when making reservations.

Highly recommended lodgings in each category are indicated by a star ★.

| Category | Cost* |
| --- | --- |
| $$$$ (Very Expensive) | over $160 |
| $$$ (Expensive) | $110–$160 |
| $$ (Moderate) | under $110 |

*All prices are for a standard double room, single occupancy, excluding 6½% city and state sales tax.*

*Numbers in the margin correspond to numbered hotels on the Phoenix Lodging and Dining map.*

## Downtown

★ ⑯ **Executive Park.** This is downtown's hidden jewel, a small,
$$ eight-story hotel on Central Avenue at the new Deck Park (built and landscaped atop I–10 as it passes under the heart of the city). Finished in 1983 and managed by Doubletree Inns, it's simply but elegantly decorated with Southwestern master prints and unpainted antique reproductions. Moderate-size rooms have comfortable beds and large, well-lighted desks, compact baths with coffeemakers, and commanding city views above the first two floors. The eighth-floor suites are dramatic, with ample balconies and sitting rooms; off the bedroom is a double dressing room and large Roman-style tub, in addition to a standard bathroom with shower. Business services are good, with facilities for small conferences and a helpful staff. The Phoenix Art Museum and the Heard Museum are walking distance; corporate and governmental centers are within a mile or two. Besides charm and location, the other good news is price. *1100 N. Central Ave., 85004, tel. 602/252–2100 or 800/872–3932, fax 602/340–1989. Gen. manager, David Dunavin. 105 rooms, including 9 suites. AE, CB, D, DC, MC, V.*

★ ⑩ **Hilton Suites.** This beautiful hotel is a model of excellent
$$ design within tight limits. Opened in August 1990, it is

Hilton's fourth entry nationwide into the frequent-traveler niche occupied by the Marriott Courtyard Hotels; but luxury extras bring it back into the $100-plus category. On Central Avenue, just 2 miles from downtown, the 11-story atrium structure is dwarfed by the stunning office towers surrounding it in the Phoenix Plaza cluster; but it holds its own. The marble-floored, pillared lobby, with its giant urns, opens into an atrium with fountains, palms, and a multilevel, neo-New Orleans restaurant and lounge. Fauvist art hangs on the walls. The thematic colors—sand and bright teal blue—and the Navajo-inspired motifs are carried throughout the suites, which also feature bleached wood furniture and custom rough-cut metal chandeliers. Space is used thoughtfully; each large bathroom opens to both living room and bedroom, windows open for fresh airflow, and every couch is a sofabed. A breakfast can be ordered from 6 AM. The gift shop sells food for the microwave that is in each room. VCR movies are free. Travel agencies, spas, beauty salons, and dining options are only steps away in the plaza. This hotel is likely to become a classic, and at bargain rates. *10 E. Thomas Rd., 85012, tel. 602/222–1111 or 800/445–8667, fax 602/265–4841. Gen. manager, Bob Yeoman. AE, CB, D, DC, MC, V.*

**19** **Hyatt Regency Phoenix.** This hotel facing Civic Center is a
$$$ landmark, with its disk-shape rotating restaurant sitting atop 24 floors of dark sandstone. Completed in 1975 and renovated in early 1990, it has Hyatt's trademark atrium design and skyview elevators. Desert and Indian decor dominate; shops, meeting rooms, and an on-site visitors bureau attest to its focus on tourism and conventions, which crowd it in the spring. Airline crews stay here, but business services are less extensive than at other metro-area hotels. Rooms, closets, and baths are comfortably utilitarian and of moderate size; only singles have desks. There are balcony rooms on floors 3–7 and poolside rooms on 3. The atrium's roof mars east views on floors 8–10. The Southwestern cuisine at the Theater Terrace Café is a cut above hotel fare; the rooftop Compass Room (*see* Dining, below) and The Plaza Bar (*see* After Hours, below) both have splendid views. *122 N. 2nd St., 85004, tel. 602/252–1234 or 800/233–1234, fax 602/254–9472. Gen. manager, Roger Naumann. 711 rooms, including 42 suites. AE, D, DC, MC, V.*

**9** **La Mancha.** Adjacent to several corporate headquarters,
$$ only 3–5 miles from the downtown hub, La Mancha is Phoenix's best best for sports-loving business visitors. Carved out of the ballroom, conference rooms, and poolside wing of the 25-year-old Del Webb TowneHouse in 1987, La Mancha houses a sports bar (noisy and crowded), 12 racquetball courts (a national tournament site), an aerobics room, 40-station machine workout center, a full basketball court, and large waterfall pool. The ambience is bright and modern, but more athletic than aesthetic; and the staff is decidedly informal. Rooms range in size from moderate (in the cabana wing, where baths have bidets) to small (tower wing). Some first-floor rooms have poolside patios. Room decor is sparse, but in the locker rooms, no amenity is spared. Visiting pro teams stay here. And rates are exceptionally reasonable. *100 W. Clarendon, 85013, tel. 602/279–9811 or 800/422–6444, fax 602/*

# PHOENIX

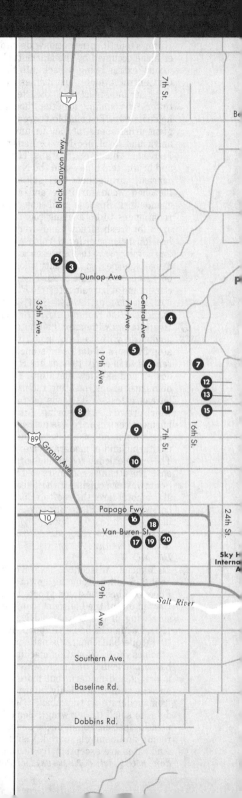

# PHOENIX HOTEL CHART

| HOTELS | Price Category | Business Services Banquet capacity | No. of meeting rooms | Secretarial services | Audiovisual equipment | Teletype news service | Computer rentals | In-room modem phone jack | All-news cable channel | Desk | Desk lighting | Bed lighting |
|---|---|---|---|---|---|---|---|---|---|---|---|---|
| Arizona Biltmore | $$$$ | 1250 | 16 | ✓ | ✓ | - | - | ✓ | ✓ | ● | ● | ● |
| Crescent | $$$ | 550 | 18 | ✓ | ✓ | - | ✓ | ✓ | ✓ | ● | ● | ◖ |
| Doubletree Suites | $$$ | 250 | 8 | ✓ | ✓ | - | ✓ | ✓ | | ● | ● | ● |
| Executive Park | $$ | 100 | 3 | - | ✓ | - | - | ✓ | ✓ | ● | ● | ● |
| Hilton Pavilion | $$ | 600 | 12 | ✓ | ✓ | - | - | ✓ | ✓ | - | - | ● |
| Hilton Suites | $$ | 80 | 5 | ✓ | ✓ | - | ✓ | ✓ | ✓ | ● | ● | ● |
| Hotel Westcourt | $$$ | 400 | 22 | ✓ | ✓ | - | - | ✓ | ✓ | - | - | ● |
| Hyatt Regency Phoenix | $$$ | 1100 | 26 | - | ✓ | - | - | ✓ | ✓ | ◖ | ◖ | ● |
| Hyatt Regency Scottsdale/Gainey | $$$$ | 1800 | 14 | ✓ | ✓ | - | ✓ | ✓ | ✓ | - | - | ● |
| La Mancha | $$ | 75 | 4 | ✓ | ✓ | - | - | - | ✓ | - | - | ◖ |
| Marriott Courtyard | $$ | 50 | 3 | ✓ | ✓ | - | - | ✓ | ✓ | ● | ● | ● |
| The Pointe on South Mountain | $$$$ | 600 | 27 | - | ✓ | - | - | ✓ | ✓ | ● | ● | ● |
| Ritz-Carlton | $$$$ | 540 | 10 | ✓ | ✓ | - | ✓ | - | ✓ | ● | ◖ | ● |
| Sheraton | $$$ | 1000 | 15 | ✓ | ✓ | - | - | ✓ | ✓ | ○ | ◖ | ◖ |
| Tempe Mission Palms | $$ | 1000 | 16 | ✓ | ✓ | - | - | ✓ | ✓ | ● | ◖ | ● |
| Westcourt In The Buttes | $$$ | 1000 | 9 | ✓ | ✓ | - | - | ✓ | ✓ | - | - | ● |

$$$$ = over $160, $$$ = $110-$160, $$ = under $110.
● good, ◖ fair, ○ poor.
All hotels listed here have photocopying and fax facilities.

| In-Room Amenities | | | | | | | | | | Hotel Amenities | | | | | | |
| Nonsmoking rooms | In-room checkout | Minibar | Pay movies | VCR/Movie rentals | Hairdryer | Toiletries | Room service | Laundry/Dry cleaning | Pressing | Concierge | Barber/Hairdresser | Garage | Courtesy airport transport | Sauna | Pool | Exercise room |
|---|---|---|---|---|---|---|---|---|---|---|---|---|---|---|---|---|
| ✓ | ✓ | ✓ | ✓ | ✓ | ✓ | ● | ● | ● | ● | ✓ | ✓ | - | - | ✓ | ● | ◐ |
| ✓ | ✓ | ✓ | ✓ | - | ✓ | ● | ◐ | ● | ● | ✓ | - | ✓ | - | ✓ | ● | ● |
| ✓ | ✓ | ✓ | - | - | - | ◐ | ◐ | ● | ◐ | ✓ | - | ✓ | ✓ | ● | ● | ● |
| ✓ | ✓ | - | ✓ | - | ✓ | ● | ◐ | ● | ● | - | - | ✓ | - | - | ● | ◐ |
| ✓ | - | ✓ | ✓ | - | - | ○ | ● | ● | ◐ | - | ✓ | - | - | - | ◐ | - |
| ✓ | ✓ | - | ✓ | ✓ | - | ◐ | - | ● | ● | - | - | ✓ | - | - | ◐ | ◐ |
| ✓ | ✓ | ✓ | ✓ | ✓ | - | ● | ◐ | ◐ | ● | ✓ | - | - | - | ✓ | ● | ◐ |
| ✓ | ✓ | - | ✓ | - | - | ◐ | ◐ | ● | ● | ✓ | - | ✓ | - | ✓ | ◐ | ○ |
| ✓ | ✓ | ✓ | ✓ | ✓ | ✓ | ● | ● | ● | ● | ✓ | ✓ | - | - | ✓ | ● | ● |
| ✓ | - | - | ✓ | - | - | ○ | ◐ | ● | ◐ | ✓ | ✓ | - | - | ✓ | ● | ● |
| ✓ | ✓ | - | ✓ | - | - | ○ | - | ◐ | ◐ | - | - | ✓ | - | - | ● | ○ |
| ✓ | ✓ | ✓ | ✓ | - | ✓ | ◐ | ◐ | ● | ● | ✓ | - | ✓ | - | ✓ | ◐ | ◐ |
| ✓ | ✓ | ✓ | ✓ | ✓ | ✓ | ● | ◐ | ● | ● | ✓ | - | ✓ | - | ✓ | ◐ | ● |
| ✓ | ✓ | ✓ | - | - | - | ○ | ◐ | ● | ● | ✓ | ✓ | ✓ | - | ✓ | ● | ● |
| ✓ | - | - | ✓ | - | ✓ | ● | ◐ | ● | ◐ | - | - | - | ✓ | ✓ | ◐ | ◐ |
| ✓ | ✓ | ✓ | ✓ | - | ✓ | ● | ● | ● | ● | ✓ | - | - | ✓ | ✓ | ● | ● |

**Room service:** ● 24-hour, ◐ 6AM-10PM, ○ other.
**Laundry/Dry cleaning:** ● same day, ◐ overnight, ○ other.
**Pressing:** ● immediate, ◐ same day, ○ other.

279–9811 ext. 2846. Gen. manager, Chuck Griffin. 171 rooms, including 8 suites. AE, DC, MC, V.

**⑰** **Sheraton Phoenix.** The city's oldest hotel is also its biggest
$$$ disappointment. After a major fire, total rebuilding, and a series of owners, the historic Adams is only a memory; in its place is a 19-story modern shell cleverly crafted for the desert, with sand-color walls and arcaded sidewalks, and arches shading each entry and window. But inside is a worn looking hostelry that seems to scrape by on overflow from the next-door Hyatt. It has a willing staff and the scale and services of a major hotel, but vacant shop spaces and deservedly empty restaurants give it away. Rooms are small and cheaply decorated—small desks, minibars that don't match the furniture, thin towels. Not worth the price. *111 N. Central Ave., 85004, tel. 602/257–1525 or 800/325–3535, fax 602/253–9755. Gen. manager, Coyne Edmison. 534 rooms, including 32 suites. AE, CB, D, DC, MC, V.*

## Airport

**㉑** **Doubletree Suites.** In the Gateway Center, just a mile
$$$ north of the airport, this five-year-old all-suite hotel is the best of a dozen choices for the traveler who wants to get off the plane and into the room. Past the lobby full of modernist regional art lies a honeycomb of six-story towers, linked by mazes of walkways and richly landscaped gardens. The compact sitting rooms have sofabeds and stocked minibars, the kitchenettes have microwaves and coffeemakers. Bedrooms and bathrooms also are modest in size but not cramped; the decor is plain, with comfy furniture. Poolside breakfast and cocktail hour, and evening hors d'oeuvres in the lobby lounge, are complimentary. Business services and sports facilities are extensive, with meeting space for groups of up to 360. Topper's bar (*see* After Hours, below) is an excellent venue for a drink with an associate. The casual elegance and easy access attract visiting celebrities and the Oakland A's during spring training. Rates drop mid-May–Dec. *320 N. 44th St., 85008, tel. 602/225–0500 or 800/528–0444, fax 602/225–0957. Gen. manager, Bob Dimberg. 242 suites. AE, CB, D, DC, MC, V.*

**★ ㉛** **The Pointe on South Mountain.** The Southwest's largest
$$$$ resort (at 1,000 acres), this Mexican-Mediterranean extravaganza opened in 1987 next to the nation's largest city park (South Mountain, a 16,000-acre desert preserve). Of all the Valley's luxury resorts, this is the most conveniently situated for the business traveler—less than 3 miles from the airport, and less than 10 miles from downtown Phoenix and the East Valley. Three lavishly designed and decorated suite hotels (one set on winding hillside streets like a coastal village), a four-story sports center, and four restaurants are linked by walkways and roadways; carts and drivers are on 24-hour call. Spacious, high-ceiling suites combine the undyed fabrics, whitewashed timbers, and fireplaces of a mountain lodge with dark wood-accent furniture, cinnamon-colored carpets, and Mexican handicrafts. Golf course, tennis courts, riding trails, and several pools are among the amenities; business services are extensive. If you have extra time, this is a wonderful place to play—and with corporate discounts, the exorbitant resort-level prices come all the way down to moderate dur-

ing the off-season (May–mid-September). *7777 S. Pointe Pkwy., 85044, tel. 602/438–9000 or 800/528–0428, fax 602/438–0577. Gen. manager, Bruce Berres. 648 suites. AE, CB, D, DC, MC, V.*

★ ③⓪ **Westcourt in the Buttes.** Two miles east of Sky Harbor,
$$$ nestled in desert buttes at I–10 and U.S. 360, is the metro area's best hotel buy. Built in 1986, it combines dramatic architecture (the lobby's back wall is the volcanic rock itself), classic Southwest design (pine and ocotillo furniture, works by major regional artists), and stunning views of the valley. Rooms are moderate in size and comfortable, each with live cactus, stocked minibar, compact bath and half-closet (but no desk); concierge-floor amenities are well worth the slightly higher cost. "Radial" rooms are largest with widest views; inside rooms face the huge free-form pool in its natural rock amphitheater, with waterfall, Jacuzzis, and cantina. Business services are complete, conference facilities impressive, service attentive. The elegant Top of the Rock restaurant, the adjacent lively lounge (*see* After Hours, below), and the quiet Market Cafe, open dawn–11 PM, are also assets. Rates drop June–Dec. *2000 Westcourt Way, Tempe, 85282, tel. 602/225–9000 or 800/843–1986, fax 602/438–8622. Gen. manager, C.V. Healy. 298 rooms, including 7 suites. AE, CB, D, DC, MC, V.*

## East Valley

③⑤ **Hilton Pavilion.** This eight-floor atrium hotel, built in 1985
$$ and redone in mid-1989, is in the heart of the East Valley, just off its main artery, the Superstition Freeway (U.S. 360). The East Valley's largest shopping mall is almost next door, and downtown Phoenix is 18 miles away. Public spaces are fitted out with etched glass and brass, tropical greenery, and Art Deco furniture. The staff is young and eager to help. Business services are not extensive but are being upgraded. Rooms are moderately spacious and decorated in dark earth-tones, with small baths and closets and a large lighted table (no desk) in each; corner suites and rooms on the top two floors have the best views. *1011 W. Holmes Ave., Mesa, 85210, tel. 602/833–5555 or 800/445–8667, fax 602/649–1886. Gen. manager, Robert Patterson. 228 rooms and 38 suites. AE, CB, D, DC, MC, V.*

③② **Tempe Mission Palms.** Set snugly between the ASU cam-
$$ pus and Old Town Tempe, this informal six-year-old courtyard hotel is convenient to the East Valley and downtown Phoenix. The tone is set by the spacious adobe and copper-green lobby and the young staff in green polo shirts. Many visitors come for ASU sports and pro football (the stadium is next door). Business services are good; Tempe's Chamber of Commerce and visitors bureau both have headquarters here. Rooms are done in bright, simple Southwestern style and are comfortable. The hotel has a pleasant, quiet sports bar, a café, and a creditable restaurant (The Cloister); guests also can enjoy Old Town's wide array of restaurants, shops, and clubs. *A Sheraton hotel. 60 E. 5th St., Tempe, 85281, tel. 602/894–1400 or 800/325–3535, fax 602/894–1400, ext. 566. Gen. manager, Michael Keeler. 303 rooms, including 12 suites. AE, CB, D, DC, MC, V.*

## Scottsdale and Biltmore

**⑫** **Arizona Biltmore.** The 62-year-old grande dame of Arizo-
**$$$$** na's resorts was designed by Frank Lloyd Wright's colleague, Albert Chase McArthur, who used his ideas to
create a masterpiece in the hills north of downtown. Since
restoring it after a 1973 fire, Wright's protégés at Taliesin
West do all design and refurbishing at the historic landmark. Last expanded in 1983 and renovated in mid-1990,
the Biltmore remains a sedate classic: Its custom-woven
carpets, stained-glass skylights, glass-brick lamps, and
wrought-iron pilasters make a walk to the lobby a fascinating tour. Rooms in the main building feature bold 1930s
color schemes (orange drapes and bedspreads, royal blue
carpet, and gold-foil ceilings), inventive teak furnishings,
and brown-and-pink marble bathrooms. Suites in the newer wings, separated from the main buildings by geometric
lawns and lush flowerbeds, are larger but in the same
style. Business services are extensive (you can rent cellular phones) and recreation befits a world-class resort—17
lighted tennis courts, three pools, two PGA-rated championship golf courses, canalside jogging, bike and raft rentals, and more. *A Westin hotel. 24th St. & Missouri Ave.,
Biltmore, 85016, tel. 602/955–6600 or 800/528–3696, fax
602/954–0469. Gen. manager, Hud Hinton. AE, CB, D,
DC, MC, V.*

**㉕** **Hyatt Regency Scottsdale at Gainey Ranch.** Thoroughly
**$$$$** modern and dramatically styled, this is Scottsdale's finest
resort. Built in 1987, it's the anchor of a planned residential community with a shopping mall next door, yet from
its palm- and saguaro-lined entry drive to its manmade lagoon, it creates a sense of place and peace. Inventive architecture (copper pyramids on the roof; a massive,
naturally cooled lobby that opens to the desert) and a sure
sense of aesthetic detail (local stone and woods, an impeccable collection of Southwestern art and decor) keep the
lavish from becoming garish. Even the Hyatt atrium is
humanized into a series of cozy miniatriums defining the
four main guest areas. The staff is young and skillful; business services are extensive. Rooms, in stone and sand
with rose and blue accents, range from compact to spacious; each has a safe, stocked minibar, and wide balcony,
but no desk. Recreation includes gondola and hot-air balloon rides. Resort prices drop sharply in summer, and
creep halfway back from Sept. to Jan. *7500 E. Doubletree
Ranch Rd., Scottsdale, 85258, tel. 602/991–3388 or 800/
233–1234, fax 602/483–5550. Gen. manager, Jim Petrus.
490 rooms. AE, CB, D, DC, MC, V.*

**⑧** **Marriott Courtyard.** This trim four-story hostelry, opened
**$$** in 1990, is tucked into the Town and Country village-style
mall, less than a ½ mile from the Ritz-Carlton. A smart,
viable alternative for frequent travelers who watch the
bottom line, it delivers compact elegance in its public
areas and "no frills" comfort in its 155 rooms. The white-
tiled lobby's inviting restaurant (breakfast buffet from
6 AM, dinner until 10 PM) and lounge area are furnished in
smartly upholstered neo-Queen Anne mahogany. A medium-
size lap pool and whirlpool fill the courtyard, landscaped
with granite boulders and palms. Beneath the red tile roofs,
standard doubles are carpeted and draped in rose colors;
suites are done in gray with rose accents; both have

mahogany trim and sand-color walls. A full 70% of the beds are kings, the desks are large and well lighted, and the bedside phone's cord reaches throughout the room. Bathrooms are small but clean, with mirrored closets, coffee set-ups, and "superhot" taps; suites add a wet bar (unstocked) and minifridge in the living room. Business services are good, with small, well-equipped meeting rooms. The hotel keeps expenses down by dropping room service and relying on the attached mall for gift and grooming shops, travel services, and the like. *2101 E. Camelback Rd., 85016, tel. 602/955–5200 or 800/321–2211, fax 602/955–1101. Gen. manager, Mike Frazin. AE, CB, D, DC, MC, V.*

★ ⓯   **Ritz-Carlton.** This thin, flat, sand-color neo-Federal
$$$$   midrise (11-stories) facing Biltmore Fashion Square mall is undistinguished, but an unpromising shell hides a graceful, well-appointed luxury hotel that pampers the business traveler. Built in 1988, it has large public rooms decorated with antique reproductions, fine carpeting and Oriental rugs, early 19th-century European paintings, and handsomely displayed china collections. Rooms are moderately spacious with two desks, an armoire holding a TV and a built-in refrigerator (stocked), a safe, and a well-supplied marble bathroom. The pricey concierge club floor has a conference suite with meeting room for up to 16. The compact, elegant health club and the daily high tea (2:30–4:40 PM) are highlights, and The Restaurant, modestly named, is among the Valley's best for Southwest-style Continental fare. For the cost-conscious, rooms on floors 2–4 go for about 70% of the price of those on floors 8–10. *2401 E. Camelback Rd., Biltmore, 85016, tel. 602/468–0700 or 800/241–3333, fax 602/468–0793. Gen. manager, James Veil. 287 rooms, including 16 suites. AE, CB, D, DC, MC, V.*

## West Valley

❸   **Crescent Hotel.** This eight-story, terraced white concrete
$$$   hostelry on I–17 across from the state's largest shopping mall was built in 1987 by financier Charles Keating. In 1989, it was taken over (along with Lincoln Savings & Loan and the rest of Keating's empire) by the federal government, and professional managers were hired. They appear to have made the Crescent a viable upper-end hotel. Mrs. Keating's "Southwestern Imperial" decor remains— vast public rooms with massive stone arches and concrete columns, terra-cotta tile floors and bleached wood wall paneling, and rose carpets in the hallways. The sizable rooms continue the look with deep rose carpets, mauve bedspreads and drapes, and pale-tone furnishings; each has a well-stocked red marble bathroom. Business services are good, and the staff is young and helpful. The full-size pool and tennis courts are well kept; the health club is small but well appointed. *2620 W. Dunlap Ave., 85021, tel. 602/943–8200 or 800/423–4126, fax 602/371–2856. Gen. manager, Graham Asher. 344 rooms, including 12 suites. AE, CB, D, DC, MC, V.*

❷   **Hotel Westcourt.** This undistinguished looking brown
$$$   block sits on the outer circle of the huge Metrocenter shopping mall, but in a small space, it packs 300 rooms around a large central pool, even managing a miniatrium that rises the full five floors above the lobby. Rooms (identical to those in the stunning sister hotel, Westcourt in the

Buttes) offer modest space with live palms and overstuffed decorator pillows, bentwood chairs, compact bath and half-closet; there's no desk, however. Corner suites are popular for receptions and small meetings; business services are fair, and facilities for large meetings or small conventions are good. A tiny lobby bar offers respite from the popular night club; Trumps restaurant is expensive and often worth it, and more modest meals abound within a short walk. *10220 N. Metro Pkwy. E, 85051, tel. 602/997–5900 or 800/858–1033, fax 602/997–1034. Gen. manager, Michael Byrd. 300 rooms, including 15 suites. AE, DC, MC, V.*

## DINING

Phoenix's longstanding stock-in-trade included Sonoran Mexican food (robust, simple ranch-style food that features lots of beef and few complicated sauces), an ample supply of steakhouses and Western-style eateries, numerous Cantonese restaurants, and a few of those American-Continental sauce houses that pass for fancy in every small American city. In the last half-dozen years, however, the city has suddenly come into its own as a place to enjoy sophisticated dining. The reason? Maybe it was an influx of Thais that began about 15 years ago, bringing their finely chopped, peppery food. Perhaps it was the arrival of other Asian refugees, and immigrants fleeing Central and South America, each bringing spicy, delicate variations on their themes. Iranian and Afghani exiles settled here, too, adding their own influences and styles. Whatever the cause, the "Southwestern international cuisine" that took hold in the late '80s was born here, and continues to thrive—developing new, eclectic offshoots—in the hands of dozens of inventive master chefs and clever restaurateurs.

Highly recommended restaurants in each category are indicated by a star ★.

| Category | Cost* |
| --- | --- |
| $$$$ (Very Expensive) | over $30 |
| $$$ (Expensive) | $21–$30 |
| $$ (Moderate) | $10–$20 |
| $ (Inexpensive) | under $10 |

*per person, including appetizer, entrée, and dessert, but excluding drinks, service, and 6½% sales tax.*

*Numbers in the margin correspond to numbered restaurant locations on the Phoenix Lodging and Dining map.*

### Business Breakfasts

**Caf' Casino.** This innovative, cafeteria-style restaurant offers a good selection of fresh breads, egg dishes, waffles, fruit juices and coffees. In a pleasant, gardenlike setting, this is a good spot for an informal business breakfast; across from the Ritz-Carlton and Biltmore Fashion Park, it opens at 7 AM daily. (Avoid its rundown namesake in Scottsdale.) *4824 N. 24th St., tel. 602/264-3127.*

**Fina Cocina.** This bright, order-at-the-counter eatery in the heart of downtown, hung with Hispanic-American modern art, opens at 6 AM weekdays for Mexican breakfasts, including egg-and-chorizo burros and steaming bowls of *menudo* (tripe soup). Popular as a business lunch spot, it offers a quiet, uncrowded breakfast in a decidedly informal café setting. *130 N. Central Ave., tel. 602/258–5315.*

**Matador.** Another option for a Mexican breakfast downtown, this Phoenix institution serves up authentic, reliable south-of-the-border fare, as well as American breakfast favorites. In the morning, the red vinyl banquettes and long tables fill up with local politicians and meetings of civic groups. *125 E. Adams St., tel. 602/254–7563.*

**Tom's Tavern.** This lively, nostalgic re-creation—of a legendary Phoenix bar and poolroom—with wood and green leather booths, wainscoted walls hung with pictures and memorabilia—offers an unbeatably convenient spot to meet a downtown client before the workday gets rolling. Servers are snappy and personable and the 7–10:30 AM menu runs from a Continental breakfast to banana-pecan pancakes, name-your-ingredients omelets and grilled ham, with no item reaching $5. *2 N. Central Ave., tel. 602/257–1688.*

There are two good local scrambled-egg chains, both offering creative takes on standard morning dishes in pleasant surroundings: **The Eggery** (off Camelback Rd., 5109 N. 44th St., tel. 602/840–5734; at the Paradise Valley Mall, 4326 E. Cactus Rd., tel. 602/953–2342; and 70 W. Warner Rd., Chandler, tel. 602/786–0195) and **The Good Egg** (906 E. Camelback Rd., tel. 602/274–5393; 2957 W. Bell Rd., tel. 602/993–2797; 6149 N. Scottsdale Rd., Scottsdale, tel. 602/991–5416; and 1457 W. Southern Ave., Mesa, tel. 602/834–1957). Phoenix also has two good New York-style delis to satisfy that craving for lox and bagels, blintzes or chopped liver: the homey **Munch-a-Bagel** (central, just above Camelback Rd., at 5111 N. 7th St., tel. 602/264–1975) and the flawless **Tradition** (near Paradise Valley Mall, 13637 N. Tatum Blvd., tel. 602/996–2202).

## Downtown

**④ ㉝** **Char's.** Phoenix's brood of Thai eateries began here, in
$$ this spartan pair of restaurants that still are run under the watchful eye of granddaddy Char. Careful preparation and courteous service are Char's hallmarks. A meal here might include snappy *satay* (skewered chicken appetizer) or *tom yum gai* (hot and sour soup), *yum yai* (pickled salad), and a noodle-rich *pad Thai* or soul-warming curry. If you want the pepper meter set on medium or low, tell your server; Thais like it hot. This is for business associates who care more about food than decor. *2 locations: 7810 N. 12th St., Phoenix, tel. 602/246–1077; 927 E. University Dr., Tempe, tel. 602/967–6013. Casual dress. Reservations advised for groups. AE, MC, V.*

**⑥** **Christo's.** The sign says "ristorante," and the Northern
$$$ Italian food is fine. But Christo and Connie Panagiotakopoulos's cuisine reaches throughout the Mediterranean, from the light, tempuralike fried calamari to adroitly handled duck, à l'orange or in raspberry sauce. From a strip shopping center, you step into dimly lighted elegance, the mirrors and glass-block dividers adding sparkle and a sense of space. The service is skillful, and

business lunches and dinners are where Christo's really shines, offering an understated ambience and food worth twice the price. *6327 N. 7th St., tel. 602/264–1784. Casual dress. Reservations advised. AE, MC, V.*

★ ⑲ **Compass Room.** Spectacular views have always made the
$$$ Hyatt Regency's elegant rotating dining room an attraction. Since 1989, chef Mark Ching has prepared food to match. The menu may include smoky eggplant soup, a salad of peppered lamb slivers and greens, and a choice of fiery Southwestern cioppino or beef tenderloin in a jalapeno reduction and cilantro-lime Hollandaise. Don't miss Cajun croutons—crusty fried oysters in red-pepper mayonnaise. And after the room turns 90 more degrees, try one of Ching's cobblers or his chocolate pâté. *122 N. 2nd St., tel. 602/252–1234. Jacket and tie. Reservations required. AE, CB, D, DC, MC, V.*

★ ⑪ **Eddie's Grill.** Part of a new office complex 4 miles north of
$$ downtown, the location and look of this restaurant are upscale—black-trimmed Art Deco furniture, neon wall art, and fine handmade ceramics on the tables. The cuisine, as eclectic as the decor, makes this one among a half dozen of Phoenix's hottest eateries. Chef-owner Eddie Matney's "Ameriterranean" dishes reflect a playful, shifting love affair between Southwestern and North African fare. Try succulent Mo' Rockin' Shrimp in *chermoula* sauce (lime juice, olive oil, four kinds of pepper, coriander, cilantro, and mustard) or baked goat cheese with black beans and pita chips for starters. Move to a classic Moroccan lamb-pork-beef stew with tabouli, or grilled chicken breasts on lemon-mint pasta. The tastes are subtle, the presentations artistic, and the portions large. This is a quiet, classy setting for lunch or dinner meetings; there is intimate seating in the wine cellar, and a glass-enclosed gazebo can be reserved for parties. *4747 N. 7th St., tel. 602/ 241–1188. Jacket advised. Reservations advised. AE, MC, V.*

⑱ **1895 House.** In this charmingly restored downtown Victor-
$$ ian, there's always soft music—taped New Age, live jazz, or classical guitar—and always a small new menu. It's intimate and understated, with semiformal service and delightful nouvelle-cuisine surprises—turkey divan on sourdough under light dill sauce, seabass with pineapple salsa, and roast duck in pomegranate sauce. And it's very convenient to downtown for a small business lunch or dinner. But plan ahead: The hours are as compact as the rooms (lunch, 11:30–2:30; dinner, 5:30–8:30). *362 N. 2nd Ave., tel. 602/254–0338. Casual dress. Reservations advised. AE, MC, V.*

❺ **Greekfest.** Decorated like a tasteful Athenian taberna in
$$$ bold blue and white with painted vines and racked wines, this small but immaculate restaurant handles classic Greek dishes—feather-light *spanakopitas* (spinach pies), sweet succulent lamb, nutty *dolmades* (vine leaves) stuffed to bursting, and sour-light *avgolimon* (lemon soup) as both soup and sauce—with haute cuisine skill. This is a quietly festive location for discussing or celebrating a deal. *1219 E. Glendale Ave., tel. 602/265–2990. Casual dress. Reservations advised. AE, DC, MC, V.*

⑳ **La Tasca.** From this comfortable indoor-outdoor café that
$$ blends Mexican and Art Deco styles, you look onto the cobbled lanes and pastel shopfronts of Phoenix's new

Mercado center. A Spanish sherry or Mexican beer may help you enjoy the unhurried service (meals will take 90 minutes or more). Fare ranges from light, warm *sopes* (fat minitortillas piled with chicken, black beans, shaved cheese, lettuce, and a smart but gentle salsa) to a hefty *barbacoa torta* (tender chunks of meat in light green barbecue sauce, stuffed in fresh-baked split rolls) or a dramatic *cochinita pibil* (spiced, marinated pork baked in banana leaves). Hispanic business and community leaders, and political and media people lunch here; dinner is early (until 9 PM) and popular with theater- and concert-goers headed for the nearby Herberger Center or Symphony Hall. *541 E. Van Buren St., tel. 602/340–8797. Casual but neat. Reservations accepted. AE, MC, V.*

## Airport

**㉗ Delhi Palace.** Midway between downtown and Tempe,
*$$* right across from Motorola's semiconductor plant, is a storefront restaurant that offers attentive service and authentic northeast Indian dishes. Nibble on naan and kulcha breads while perusing the lengthy menu; best bets are tandoori chicken and yogurt lamb. The inclusive dinner provides a sampling tour of the cuisine, as does the lunch buffet. This is a good spot for informal business meals. *5050 E. McDowell Rd., tel. 602/244–8181. Casual but neat. No reservations. MC, V.*

★ **㉘ The Stockyards.** When Arizona had cattle barons, they cut
*$$* their deals and their steaks here, amid one of the nation's largest feedlot complexes. The neighborhood has been cleaned up (cattle and barons are gone), but the restaurant has remained, a Phoenix landmark. Its refurbished Victorian interior still features the ornate old brass-trimmed bar and three dining rooms—the Cattle Room, with black leather booths and wood shutters; the red-carpeted, gold-wallpapered Gold Room; and the Rose Room, with chandeliers, mauve carpeting, and handpainted murals. The menu still features beef handled with respect. Beside steaks and prime ribs, the cooks prepare calf liver and calf fries (Rocky Mountain oysters) just right. There's also fish, if you must. *5001 E. Washington St., tel. 602/ 273–7378. Casual but neat. Reservations suggested. AE, MC, V.*

## Northeast Phoenix and Scottsdale

**㉖ Coyote Café.** There's indoor eating (black-top tables, black
*$$* and white tiles, a tiny bar), but strollers and after-theater diners prefer the redwood terrace of this casual café, tucked into a niche of shops on Scottsdale's civic plaza. The innovative Southwestern menu changes weekly, depending on local ingredients. Creamy pumpkin soup or nutty black bean cakes may be your appetizers; sun-dried tomato sandwiches or chicken in blackberry Cabernet sauce might turn up among the main courses. Desserts are light and delightful. Spa cuisine options cater to the diet-conscious. Best for a two- to four-person lunch or dinner. No smoking. *7373 Scottsdale Mall, tel. 602/947–7081. Casual dress. Reservations suggested for dinner. AE, MC, V.*

**㉔ La Bruschetta.** In a tiny space squeezed between a comedy
*$$$* club and a gas station, Gianni and Linda Scorza have recreated a bit of Tuscany. The atmosphere is cozy, with 14 linen-draped tables, a mural of Florence on one wall, and

huge antique olive jars with palms. The tasty *bruschetta* (toasted bread topped with tomato and olive oil) comes first. For an appetizer, try the delicate-flavored marinated and cooked vegetables; for an entrée, pasta in a light Gorgonzola sauce, a roast Cornish hen dusted in herbs, or succulent squid. *4515 N. Scottsdale Rd., tel. 602/946-7236. Jacket advised. Reservations advised. AE, MC, V.*

★ ❶ **La Hacienda.** About 20 miles northeast of Phoenix, in the
$$$$ Scottsdale Princess resort, is a tile-roofed hacienda with huge beehive fireplaces and rug-covered Saltillo tile floors. Its heavy, handcarved tables are the Valley's premier showplace for Sonoran Mexican food done as haute cuisine. The *quesadilla* (cheese melted on a flour tortilla) is laced with crab; the *chili relleno* (a stuffed, batter-fried green chili) has pork loin and nuts with a cheese glaze. Entrées include *cochinillo asado* (roast stuffed suckling pig), the sea-sweet *cabrilla rellena de salpicon* (bass stuffed with crab in lime mayonnaise), and a masterful *codorniz rellena* (quail stuffed with spicy chorizo sausage in chipotle chili sauce). *7575 E. Princess Dr., Scottsdale (1 mile north of Bell Rd., a.k.a. Frank Lloyd Wright Blvd.), tel. 602/585-4848. Jacket and tie advised. Reservations needed. AE, DC, MC, V.*

★ ❶ **Marquesa.** Also at the Scottsdale Princess (along with La
$$$$ Hacienda, *see* above) is this soft-hued, intimate pair of rooms where Catalan Spanish cuisine gets a Southwestern interpretation. The stunning presentations match the flavors—authentic ingredients (dried chorizo sausage, Serrano ham), fresh greens, vegetables, and seafood. Wines are well selected, desserts inspired. Service is thoughtfully paced and attentive. Eating here is an experience to savor, for executives who appreciate quality and style. *7575 E. Princess Dr., Scottsdale (1 mile north of Bell Rd., a.k.a. Frank Lloyd Wright Blvd.), tel. 602/585-4848. Jacket and tie. Reservations required. AE, DC, MC, V.*

㉓ **Moroccan.** Seated on cushions at a low table, you rinse
$$ your hands in warm rosewater from a brass ewer, then begin your meal by pulling apart hot, nutty pita bread and dipping it in garbanzo-eggplant paste. With fork or fingers, you feast on such specialties as *fassi* (chicken in cilantro curry), *m'rouzia* (honeyed lamb with raisins and almonds), or classic couscous. Moroccan red wine is simple but complements the fare well, as do the music and the belly dancer. A meal for celebrating or socializing rather than serious talk: Take associates who can let their hair down a bit together. *4228 N. Scottsdale Rd., tel. 602/947-9590. Casual but neat. Reservations advised. AE, MC, V.*

★ ⑬ **Roxsand.** Chef-owner Roxsand Scocos has woven together
$$$ Greek, Asian, Continental, and Caribbean influences to create her "transcontinental" cuisine. In this trendy but very friendly restaurant and café, a solo snacker is as welcome as a hungry dinner foursome. Be on the lookout for such surprises as sizzling sea scallop salad, Mongolian fajitas, Jamaican jerked rabbit, and an ever-changing array of desserts. The lively decor, with its liberal use of concrete and granite tiles and the multicolored plates atop small linen-covered tables, injects an eclectic, modernist note into the casual elegance of Biltmore Fashion Square. A business meal here is for entrepreneurs, not bean coun-

ters. *2594 E. Camelback Rd., tel. 602/381–0444. Casual but neat. Reservations advised. AE, CB, DC, MC, V.*

**7** **Timothy's.** In a cozy, converted cottage north of Camel-
**$$$** back Road, Tim Johnson's contemporary art collection hangs on maroon- and pink-accented white walls. Tim offers Continental and Cajun cuisine and live jazz. The jambalaya, steak au poivre, and veal Genovese are well-prepared standards; like the music, the food gets hotter as the voices blend, as in Cajun prime rib, or salmon in filo dough with chili Hollandaise. The separate rooms afford privacy; the regulars give it a clubby atmosphere. Service is brisk and dinner is available until midnight. *6335 N. 16th St., tel. 602/277–7634. Casual dress. Reservations advised. AE, CB, DC, MC, V.*

**★ 14** **Vincent Guerithault's on Camelback.** Guerithault is ac-
**$$$$** knowledged as one of the West's master chefs. One of the handful who originated Southwestern cuisine, he used his classical country French training and Mexican ingredients to create such entrées as duck tacos, crab cakes in avocado salsa, and lobster with chipotle chili pasta. Racks of lamb and symphonic pâtés are here, too; so are a full "Heart Smart" menu, an intelligent wine list, and a risky but romantic list of dessert creations. The candlelighted decor is all French country—blue carpeting, blue-flower cushions on walnut chairs, Villeroy & Boch china, and taped classical music. *3930 E. Camelback Rd., tel. 602/224– 0225. Jacket and tie advised. Reservations advised. AE, DC, MC, V.*

**27** **Voltaire.** This restaurant offers the Valley's most consist-
**$$$** ently excellent classical French cuisine. Hidden in a cinderblock building on a street corner in a residential area of Scottsdale, Voltaire's interior is simple and elegant—silver tableware, white china, fine linen, indirect lighting. Nothing's nouvelle; there may not be a recipe less than 100 years old. But when Valley dwellers want to savor escargots, onion soup, and perfectly handled lamb, this is where they come. Then there's the hard work: Will it be crêpes suzette, cherries jubilee, or an exquisite crème caramel? *8340 E. McDonald Dr., Scottsdale, tel. 602/948– 1005. Jacket and tie advised. Reservations required. AE, MC, V. Closed June–Oct.*

## East Valley

**29** **Chopandaz.** Afghanistan's gift to the Valley is "The Horse-
**$$** man," which features crisp, succulent kebabs, nutty rice, and a wonderful mash of sweet-spicy lentils. The rug collection almost transforms the former pizzeria into an exotic locale; the owner-manager and his staff educate newcomers to the Afghan plateau's hearty cuisine and its subtly spiced surprises. This is a relaxing place to take associates for a very informal dinner, with time to talk and linger over dark coffee. *1849 N. Scottsdale Rd., Tempe, tel. 602/947–4396. Casual dress. Reservations accepted. MC, V.*

**34 36** **Jasmine Cafe.** If you want to sample a range of Asian reg-
**$** ional foods in one stop, visit one of these East Valley restaurants. The "trans-Asian" menu embraces Chinese, Thai, Japanese, and Korean dishes, with a little poetic license. The result is a fun, varied array of tastes; portions are small and inexpensive, so feel free to experiment. The neon-art-and-palms decor is a bit California cutesy, the

service is a bit uneven, but the dining is an adventure. This is a good setting for an informal meal, perhaps with younger clients. *1805 E. Elliot Rd., Tempe, tel. 602/491–0797; and 5761 E. Brown Rd., Mesa, tel. 602/981–0399. Casual dress. DC, MC, V.*

## FREE TIME

### Fitness

*Hotel Facilities*
The best general exercise and sports facilities are at **La Mancha.** The **Pointe on South Mountain** has an elaborate sports-health complex, including an 18-hole golf course. Both are open to nonguests.

*Health Clubs*
**The Arizona Athletic Club** (1425 W. 14th St., Tempe, at the Scottsdale border, tel. 602/894–2281), near the airport, is the Valley's largest facility and has a day rate of less than $15. In downtown Phoenix, **Life Centers of Arizona** (4041 N. Central Ave., tel. 602/265–5472) also serves the day visitor, with a similarly low rate. For women, **Naturally Women** (3320 S. Price Rd., Tempe, tel. 602/838–8800) offers one free drop-in day, with a day rate of under $10 afterward. The Valley also has 36 franchised sites offering regular Jazzercise programs (tel. 602/420–1006).

*Jogging*
Phoenix's dozens of miles of canal banks, all naturally cooled and many landscaped, are popular for sunrise and sunset jogging. The Arizona Canal runs from near Sun City in the northwest, past Metrocenter and over to the Biltmore Estates, then into downtown Scottsdale, where it loops through the resort area. The **Grand Canal,** further south, begins in western Glendale and runs just north of downtown Phoenix, then southeast past the zoo and into Tempe. **Encanto Park,** just 3 miles from the heart of downtown, is the city's one large, green park, with lagoons and a golf course that are fine for jogging, too. A similar green belt, with lagoons, runs for more than 5 miles along Scottsdale's Indian Bend Wash.

### Shopping

*Southwestern*
The finest selection of authentic Southwestern Indian arts and crafts is sold at the gift shop in the **Heard Museum** (22 E. Monte Vista Rd., tel. 602/252–8848). Shops at **The Mercado** (7th and Van Buren Sts.) offer fine selections of gifts, art, and clothing, mostly from Mexico but also from the Caribbean and Africa. In the Old West-style shops along Fifth Avenue in downtown Scottsdale, you'll see everything from cowboy boots to the bright trinkets you'd find in the stalls at Nogales or Tijuana. A great souvenir shop is **Mexican Imports** (3933 N. Brown Ave., tel. 602/945–6746); across the street, **Herman Atkinson's Indian Trading Post** (3957 N. Brown Ave., tel. 602/949–9750) has both a wide variety of tourist mementos and Indian, Mexican, and even African handiwork for the serious collector. On the west side of Scottsdale Road are the art galleries and shops.

The best place to learn about and buy Southwestern jewelry is at **Godber's** (7542 E. Main St., tel. 602/949–1133), started 60 years ago by a reservation trading-post family. For handmade Southwestern decor and furniture, check **Santa Fe West** (7121 E. 5th Ave., tel. 602/994–9611); for Southwestern folk art, don't miss **Folklorico** (7126 E. Main St., tel. 602/947–0758). And a walk down **Craftsman Court** will run the gamut from cowboy art to European masters to the best in modern Southwestern painting and sculpture.

*Malls and Boutiques*
The nearest mall to downtown is the open-air **Park Central** (Central Ave. and Earll Drive). The state's largest is the covered **Metrocenter,** on the west side (I–17 and Peoria Ave., tel. 602/997–2641); its sister, **Fiesta Mall,** serves the East Valley (U.S. 360 and Alma School Rd., Mesa, tel. 602/833–5450). Most of the Valley's chic boutiques and high-fashion outlets are represented at or near **Biltmore Fashion Square,** an open-air mall in northeast Phoenix (24th St. and Camelback Rd., tel. 602/955–8400); and **The Borgata** (6166 N. Scottsdale Rd., tel. 602/998–1822) recreates an Italian walled village and fills it with stylish shops.

## Diversions

The **Arizona State Capitol** at 16th Avenue and Washington Street is a copper-domed monument to recent history and current politics. From January through May, you can watch both houses of the legislature at work, and the 48th state's 80-year history is showcased in the **Capitol Museum** (1700 W. Washington St., tel. 602/542–4675).

**Artist's studios** flourish in the older buildings downtown, and many—especially group studio/galleries, such as MARS Artspace, Alwun House, Ariztlan, Faux Café, and the city's Visual Arts Center—welcome drop-in visitors. Call **Artlink** (City Hall, 251 W. Washington St., tel. 602/256–7539) to help arrange visits.

**Four-wheel vehicle tours** are an exciting way to see the amazing variety of **Sonoran desert** landscapes, especially during the wildflower season (roughly February through May). Tours range from 4 hours to 5 days, in the Valley's several mountain ranges; all include at least one meal, and most offer hotel pickup for 1–250 people. Some recommended operators are: **Arizona Awareness Jeep Tours** (tel. 602/947–7852), **Arizona Scenic Tours** (tel. 602/971–3601), and **Trail Blazer Tours** (tel. 602/481–0233).

**Guadalupe,** a Yaqui Indian reservation, is a rural Mexican village in the urban area. Amid its handmade homes and lean-tos, a lovely mission-style church stands on the zocalo, or square. Nearby are a turquoise adobe *tianguis* or mall, with restaurants and craft shops; the fine **Flores Bakery** (8402 S. Avenida del Yaqui, tel. 602/831–9709), and a tiny diner next door, **Filito's** (tel. 602/839–5814), that almost gives away its tasty tamales.

**The Heard Museum** (22 E. Monte Vista Rd., tel. 602/252–8848), the nation's leading museum of Native American art, focuses on Southwestern tribal artists, ancient and modern. Its slide shows, dioramas, and frequent live demonstrations animate the collections; the annual spring Indian Fair (dates vary) is a treat. Don't miss the kachina room.

The Valley is rich in **hiking** opportunities. A two-hour classic is up **Squaw Peak,** about 7 miles north of downtown, with spectacular 2,000-square-mile views; slightly harder trails ascend **Camelback Mountain,** 3 miles east; similar trails visit the Indian caves on the peaks in **Papago Park,** between Phoenix and Tempe; and hikers at all skill levels can spend from an hour to a day on the network of trails crisscrossing the ridges and canyons of magnificent, 16,000-acre **South Mountain Park.** (Note: From May 1 to Oct. 1, when midday temperatures often hit 100 and more, jogging and hiking can be unsafe between 9 AM and 6 PM. Even in winter, be sure to use strong sunscreen—rated 15 or above—and carry at least one pint of water per person for each hour hiked. And wear strong UV-rated sunglasses.)

If you want to do your nature viewing on **horseback,** the following are among the operators who offer trail rides lasting from 1½ hours to a half-day (with meal): **Trailmasters Adventure Tours** (3805 N. Scottsdale Rd., Scottsdale, tel. 602/947–4565), **Trailhead Ranch** (35013 N. 49th St., Cave Creek, tel. 602/254–6376), and **Rio Verde Ranch** (Rio Verde, tel. 602/471–7281).

The **Mercado** and **Heritage Square,** adjacent sites at Seventh and Van Buren streets, celebrate the Mexican and U.S. influences on Phoenix and the Southwest. The Mercado's bright shops, cafés and alleys are a modern variation on a Mexican village theme; the restored Victorian and turn-of-the-century homes in Heritage Square recapture Phoenix as a fledgling city in Arizona Territory.

A **paddleboat ride** on **Encanto Park lagoon** (15th Ave. and Encanto Blvd., tel. 602/262–4539) is a unique way to unwind after a busy day, listening to ducks and birds as you lean back and watch sunset paint the palms and skyscrapers. Or try **gondola rides** at the Hyatt Regency at **Gainey Ranch** (7500 E. Doubletree Ranch Rd., tel. 602/991–3388); 15-minute sunset rides include a glass of wine.

The **Phoenix Zoo** and **Desert Botanical Garden** are in Papago Park, about 7 miles east of downtown. The 125-acre zoo provides natural habitats for 1,200 animals, including Sonoran desert species, and has an extensive children's zoo as well (5810 E. Van Buren St., tel. 602/273–7771). The garden has more than half of the world's 1,800 cactus species (1202 N. Galvin Pkwy., tel. 602/941–1217).

**Pueblo Grande Museum** (4619 E. Washington St., tel. 602/275–3452) is an active archeological dig at a large pueblo-style dwelling complex just a mile from the airport. Well-designed displays and a self-guided site walk reveal the life and crafts of the Hohokam, a farming people who first irrigated the Sonoran desert.

**Taliesin West** (13201 N. 108th St. Scottsdale, tel. 602/860–2700) was Frank Lloyd Wright's second architectural school-cum-colony (the first was in rural Wisconsin). Wright's desert masterpiece, built in 1938 using natural lighting and local materials, is open for tours daily. The school still thrives, with students living in habitats of their own design; the tour, led by students, includes models of many of Wright's later, more visionary works.

## Professional Sports

Phoenix's football team, the **Cardinals** (tel. 602/967 1402), plays at the Sun Devil Stadium at ASU, Tempe. The basketball team, the **Suns** (tel. 602/263–7867), competes at America West Arena. The **Roadrunners** (tel. 602/340–0001), the city's hockey team, play at Veterans Memorial Coliseum.

## The Arts

Phoenix performing arts groups have grown rapidly as the Valley has expanded, and the completion of the downtown Symphony Hall and Herberger Theater Center (facing each other across the Civic Plaza mall) has given many of them a well-equipped permanent home in elegant surroundings.

The **Phoenix Symphony Hall** (225 E. Adams St., tel. 602/262–7272) is home to Arizona Opera and the Phoenix Symphony Orchestra. **Herberger Theater Center** (222 E. Monroe St., tel. 602/252–8497) houses Actors Theater of Phoenix and the Phoenix season of the Tucson-based Arizona Theatre Company. The Herberger also is host to touring plays and musicals, and pre-Broadway runs. Arizona State University operates **Gammage Auditorium** in Tempe (tel. 602/965–3434) and the **Sundome Center** in Sun City West (tel. 602/975–1900), two of the Valley's largest venues for touring musicals and popular music performers. ASU's **Kerr Cultural Center** in Scottsdale (tel. 602/965–5377) is an intimate setting for chamber music and one-person shows.

The best ticket agencies are **Dillard's** (13 Valley locations, including: Phoenix Civic Plaza, tel. 602/267–1246) and the **Arizona State University ticket office** (Gammage Auditorium, Tempe, tel. 602/965–3434). For popular and rock music, try **Trails** (5 Valley locations, tel. 602/265–6653) and **Hot Tickets** (2 locations, tel. 602/234–0664).

## After Hours

*Bars and Lounges*
For a quiet drink with a sparkling city view, the **Plaza Bar** at the Hyatt Regency Phoenix (tel. 602/252–1234) is an ideal place to discuss an idea or close a deal; uptown, the **Top of Central** (8525 N. Central Ave., tel. 602/861–2438) offers intimacy and soft music and can accommodate groups comfortably. Near the airport, the elegant **Topper's** (Doubletree Suites, tel. 602/225–0500) even has a wine bar, a sophisticated setting for serious decision-making or celebrating with senior-level clients; the **Top of the Rock Lounge** at Westcourt in the Buttes (tel. 602/225–9000) offers the city's best view and a noisy, upscale crowd.

*Cabaret and Comedy Clubs*
The Valley's one cabaret club is **Yesterday's** (9035 N. 8th St., tel. 602/861–9080). Standup comics perform at **Finney Bones** (502 W. Camelback Rd., tel. 602/234–1717) and **Fun Seekers** (4519 N. Scottsdale Rd., Scottsdale, tel. 602/949–1100). **The Improv** (University Dr. and Rural Rd., Tempe,

tel. 602/921–9877) and **The Last Laugh** (8041 N. Black Canyon Hwy., tel. 602/995–5653) have both improv groups as well as solo standups.

*Jazz Clubs*

Soft solos in a San Francisco–style lounge (plus a very credible Southwestern/Cajun grill) are at both **American Grills** (6113 N. Scottsdale Rd., Scottsdale, tel. 602/948–9907; and 1233 S. Alma School Rd., Mesa, tel. 602/844–1918). Many top local artists work at **The French Corner** (50 E. Camelback Rd., tel. 602/234–0245).

*For Singles*

The **Acapulco Bay Beach Club** (3837 E. Thomas Rd., tel. 602/273–6077) and **Depot Cantina** (300 Ash Ave., Tempe, tel. 602/966–6677) are always crowded, the former with young business types and the latter with ASU folks. Both have above-average Mexican restaurants. **Char's** (4631 N. 7th Ave., tel. 602/230–0205) and **Chuy's** (410 S. Mill Ave., Tempe, tel. 602/968–6362) are top blues clubs, the former more traditional and the latter younger, more rock-based. Among sports bars, **McKenna's Club** (La Mancha Hotel, tel. 602/264–0792) is lively and loud. Or don jeans and boots and larn the two-step at Phoenix's classic cowboy dancin' bar, **Mr. Lucky's** (3660 Grand Ave., tel. 602/246–0687).

# Pittsburgh

*by Clare Ansberry*

Pittsburgh remains loyal to its industrial roots as the home of the nation's largest steelmaker, USX, as well as of other manufacturing and industrial giants—including Westinghouse Electric and PPG Industries. And in spite of losing such corporate powers as Gulf Oil, Pittsburgh still rates as the fifth largest headquarters city in the U.S., and recently was ranked eighth by *Fortune* magazine for its favorable business climate.

Once described as hell with a lid off, Pittsburgh has shaken its image as a grimy steel center by capitalizing on its respected educational and medical base, which includes Carnegie Mellon University and Presbyterian University Hospital. The massive, shutdown steel plants remain, but the city's downtown, on a point of land bordered by the Allegheny and Monongahela rivers (which join here to form the Ohio), is squeaky clean. Dominated by the Gothic-style all-glass headquarters of PPG Industries, the skyline is almost breathtaking as you emerge from the tunnels that lead into the city.

When you get downtown, it's easy to find your way around; the central area is only about 10 blocks long. In rain or snow, use the transit system (also called the trolley), which offers free rides between three downtown stops; it's a lot easier than trying to find cabs, which rarely seem to budge from their stands outside hotels.

People like living in Pittsburgh. There's a relatively low crime rate, living costs are reasonable, and the school system is respected. About the only drawback is the city income tax, which local officials may lower to entice more people to live, as well as work, in the city.

## Top Employers

| Employer | Type of Enterprise | Parent*/ Headquarters |
|---|---|---|
| **Giant Eagle** | Supermarket | Pittsburgh |
| **Kaufmann's** | Department store | May Co./ St. Louis |
| **Mellon Bank Corp.** | Financial services | Pittsburgh |

| University of Pittsburgh | University | Pittsburgh |
|---|---|---|
| USAir | Airline | USAir Group Inc./Arlington, VA |
| USX Corp. | Steel, energy | Pittsburgh |
| Westinghouse Electric Corp. | Financial services, broadcasting, electronics | Pittsburgh |

*\*if applicable*

## ESSENTIAL INFORMATION

### Climate

What follows are the average daily maximum and minimum temperatures for Pittsburgh.

| | | | | | | | | |
|---|---|---|---|---|---|---|---|---|
| Jan. | 36F | 2C | Feb. | 38F | 3C | Mar. | 47F | 8C |
| | 20 | −7 | | 22 | −6 | | 29 | −2 |
| Apr. | 61F | 16C | May | 72F | 22C | June | 79F | 26C |
| | 40 | 4 | | 49 | 9 | | 58 | 14 |
| July | 83F | 28C | Aug. | 81F | 27C | Sept. | 76F | 24C |
| | 61 | 16 | | 61 | 16 | | 54 | 12 |
| Oct. | 65F | 18C | Nov. | 52F | 11C | Dec. | 38F | 3C |
| | 54 | 12 | | 34 | 1 | | 23 | −5 |

### Airports

**Greater Pittsburgh International Airport** is 16 miles west of downtown. USAir dominates the overcrowded airport and dominates traffic here. A major expansion is under way, but until it's further along, expect delays. **Allegheny County Airport,** 8 miles south of downtown, caters to private and corporate jets.

### Airport Business Facilities

**Mutual of Omaha Business Service Center** (on the main floor of the International Airport near the USAir ticket counter, tel. 412/472–0241) has fax machines, photocopying, notary public, ticket pickup, baggage storage, Western Union, travel insurance, traveler's checks, and cash advance.

### Airlines

Pittsburgh is a hub city for USAir.

**American,** tel. 412/771–4437 or 800/433–7300.
**British Airways,** tel. 412/281–6920 or 800/247–9297.
**Canada Airlines International,** tel. 800/426–7000.
**Continental,** tel. 412/391–6910 or 800/525–0280.
**Corporate Jets,** tel. 412/466–2500 or 800/245–0230, located at the county airport.
**Delta,** tel. 412/566–2100.
**Midway,** tel. 800/621–5700.
**Northwest,** tel. 800/225–2525.
**Pan Am,** tel. 800/221–1111.

**TWA,** tel. 412/391–3600 or 800/221–2000.
**United,** tel. 800/241–6522.
**USAir,** tel. 800/428–4322.

## Between the Airport and Downtown

There's virtually one route from Pittsburgh International Airport to downtown: SR 60, a four-lane highway that is frequently under construction and easily becomes congested.

*By Taxi*
Taxis take 30–40 minutes at nonpeak hours and up to 70 minutes at rush hour (7–9 AM from the airport and 4–6 PM from the city). The cost is about $25 plus tip.

*By Bus*
Because none of the major downtown hotels has courtesy vans, your best bet is to use the buses run by **Airlines Transportation** (tel. 412/471–8900 or 412/471–2250), which stop at all major downtown hotels and take a little longer than a taxi. Buses leave about every ½ hour from outside the main terminal. The cost is $10 one way.

## Car Rentals

Pittsburgh's car rental rates are among the lowest in the nation, but downtown parking is limited and hotel garages charge as much as $10 a day. A car will be useful if you plan to do most of your business on the outskirts of the city—either along the parkway (Rte. 279) into downtown or at the universities and hospitals on the east side of the city.

The following companies have booths in or near the airport. No rental cars are returned directly to the airport; companies have stations either along Route 279 or less than a mile away.

**Avis,** tel. 412/262–5160 or 800/331–1212.
**Budget,** tel. 412/262–1500 or 800/527–0700.
**Dollar,** tel. 412/262–1300 or 800/800–4000.
**Hertz,** tel. 412/262–1705 or 800/654–3131.
**National,** tel. 412/262–2312 or 800/227–7368.

## Emergencies

*Doctors*
**Falk Clinic** (3601 5th Ave., tel. 412/648–3000), **Pittsburgh Diagnostic Clinic** (4815 Liberty Ave., tel. 412/683–0034).

*Dentists*
**Downtown Dentistry Associates** (204 5th Ave., tel. 412/281–7330 or 412/362–3144), **West Penn Dental Group** (100 5th Ave., tel. 412/281–8166).

*Hospitals*
**Allegheny General Hospital** (320 E. North Ave., tel. 412/359–3131), **Central Medical Center and Hospital** (1200 Centre Ave., tel. 412/562–3000), **Mercy Hospital** (1400 Locust St., tel. 412/232–8111).

## Important Addresses and Numbers

**Audiovisual rentals.** KVL Audio Visual (Vista International Hotel, 1000 Penn Ave., tel. 412/281–3700), Visual Aids Center of Pittsburgh (Westin William Penn Hotel, 530 William Penn Pl., tel. 412/566–1898).

**Chamber of Commerce** (3 Gateway Center, tel. 412/392–4500).

**Computer rental.** Personal Computer Rentals (550 William Pitt Way, tel. 412/826–3060).

**Convention and exhibition centers.** A. J. Palumbo Center (Duquesne University, 1304 Forbes Ave., tel. 412/434–6058), David L. Lawrence Convention Center (1001 Penn Ave., tel. 412/565–6000), Greater Pittsburgh Convention & Visitors Bureau (4 Gateway Center, tel. 412/281–7711).

**Fax services.** Copy Boy (328 Forbes Ave., tel. 412/391–4997), Mail Boxes Etc., USA (8 Market Sq., tel. 412/391–1911), QuikPrint (4 Gateway Center, tel. 412/456–1084).

**Formal-wear rentals.** Grande Affaires (710 Smithfield St., tel. 412/281–9339), Master Tuxedo (Westin William Penn Hotel, 530 William Penn Pl., tel. 412/261–9189).

**Gift shops.** Gift Baskets: A Basket of Pittsburgh (1401 McLaughlin Run Rd., tel. 412/221–4406); Flowers: Ed & Jim Ludwig Flowers (7th Ave. and William Penn Way, tel. 412/281–3322).

**Graphic design studios.** Alphagraphics Printshops of the Future (1 Oliver Plaza, 6th and Liberty Aves., tel. 412/-391–3664), Skyline Displays of Pittsburgh (105 26th St., tel. 412/562–0300).

**Hairstylists.** Unisex: Domeniques Hair Studio (305 Forbes Ave., tel. 412/281–3155), Philip Pelusi (One Oxford Center, Grant St. and 4th Ave., tel. 412/261–6550).

**Health and fitness clubs.** *See* Fitness, below.

**Information hot lines.** Convention and Visitors Bureau Events Line (tel. 412/391–6840), Pittsburgh Council for International Visitors (tel. 412/624–7800), Traveler's Aid (tel. 412/281–5474), 24-hour Visitor Information Hot Line (tel. 412/281–9222).

**Limousine services.** Landmark Limousine Service (tel. 412/321–0802), The Limo Center (tel. 412/787–3421).

**Liquor stores.** Fifth Avenue Wine & Spirits (223 5th Ave., tel. 412/565–3664), Liberty Avenue Wines & Spirits (959 Liberty Ave., tel. 412/281–6448).

**Mail delivery, overnight.** Airborne Express (tel. 412/788–2500), DHL Worldwide Express (tel. 412/262–2764), Federal Express (tel. 800/238–5355), TNT Skypak (tel. 412/695–8500), UPS (tel. 412/323–1500), U.S. Postal Service Express Mail (tel. 412/359–7890).

**Messenger service.** First Courier (1301 Beaver Ave., tel. 412/771–1000).

**Pharmacy, late-night.** Giant Eagle Pharmacy (Penn and Shady Aves., tel. 412/361–5248).

**Radio station, all-news.** KQV 1410 AM (tel. 412/281–1505).

**Secretarial services.** Allegheny Personnel Services (2 Oliver Plaza, tel. 412/391–2044), Choice Personnel (701 Smithfield St., tel. 412/261–4130), Executaries Four (4 Gateway Ctr., tel. 412/456–1070).

**Stationery supplies.** Curry McCloy Office Products (550 Wood St., tel. 412/281–2224), J. R. Weldin (415 Wood St., tel. 412/281–0123).

**Taxis.** Peoples Cab (tel. 412/681–3131), Yellow Cab (tel. 412/665–8100).

**Theater tickets.** Tix Booth (tel. 412/642–2787). Also *see* The Arts, below.

**Train information.** Amtrak (Liberty Ave. and Grant St., tel. 800/872–7245).

**Travel agents.** A-1 Adventure Travel (710 Smithfield St., tel. 412/263–2929), Carlson Travel Network (1 Mellon Bank Center, tel. 412/391–1650), Mon Valley Travel (4 Smithfield Bldg., tel. 412/255–6056).

**Weather** (tel. 412/936–1212).

## LODGING

Pittsburgh is a city of chains, which is great if you like familiarity and consistency, but disappointing if you want class or variety. Indeed, most of the hotels seem to have hired the same interior design consultant who was enamored of seafoam green, turquoise, and a dozen shades of pink. If you have business downtown, it's best to stay in one of the seven downtown-area hotels listed below. Hotels along Route 279 (the two airport category properties and the one in Greentree) are convenient if you're in Pittsburgh to meet with a company located near the airport, or if you need to travel and want a central base. Anyone doing business at the universities or hospitals on the east side of the city has slim pickings (one exception is cited in the East Side section); it's often easiest to stay downtown and use taxis to get to meetings.

Most hotels listed here offer special corporate rates and weekend discounts; inquire when making reservations.

Highly recommended lodgings in each price category are indicated by a star ★.

| Category | Cost* |
|---|---|
| $$$$ (Very Expensive) | over $125 |
| $$$ (Expensive) | $95–$125 |
| $$ (Moderate) | under $95 |

*All prices are for a standard double room, single occupancy, excluding 6% sales tax and 3% city tax.*

*Numbers in the margin correspond to numbered hotel locations on the Pittsburgh Lodging and Dining map.*

### Downtown

**⑲**
*$$$*  **Hyatt Pittsburgh at Chatham Center.** A much-needed interior renovation is transforming this former Howard Johnson's. It's too bad that little can be done with the hotel's drab, boxy exterior. The cramped, wood-paneled lobby has been enlarged and redone in bold green, black, and burgundy, and the old, dark restaurant has been replaced by an upbeat Italian bistro; the respected chef stays. Most guest rooms—the largest in the city—have been re-

# PITTSBURGH

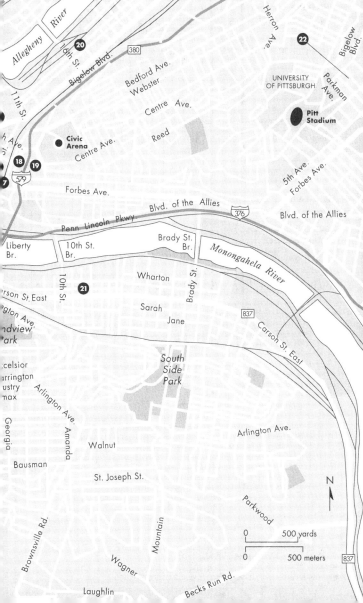

# PITTSBURGH HOTEL CHART

| HOTELS | Price Category | Business Services | | | | | | | | | Desk | Desk lighting | Bed lighting |
| | | Banquet capacity | No. of meeting rooms | Secretarial services | Audiovisual equipment | Teletype news service | Computer rentals | In-room modem phone jack | All-news cable channel | | | |
|---|---|---|---|---|---|---|---|---|---|---|---|---|
| **Airport Hilton Inn** | $$ | 375 | 8 | - | ✓ | - | - | ✓ | ✓ | ◐ | ◐ | ◐ |
| **Airport Marriott** | $$$$ | 1900 | 20 | ✓ | ✓ | - | ✓ | ✓ | ✓ | ◐ | ◐ | ◐ |
| **Greentree Marriott** | $$$ | 400 | 19 | - | ✓ | - | - | ✓ | ✓ | ◐ | ◐ | ◐ |
| **Hilton and Towers** | $$$ | 600 | 27 | ✓ | ✓ | - | ✓ | ✓ | ✓ | ◐ | ◐ | ○ |
| **Holiday Inn at University Center** | $$ | 900 | 13 | ✓ | ✓ | - | - | ✓ | ✓ | ◐ | ◐ | ◐ |
| **Hyatt Pittsburgh at Chatham Center** | $$$ | 350 | 12 | - | ✓ | - | - | ✓ | ✓ | ◐ | ◐ | ◐ |
| **The Priory** | $$ | 40 | 1 | - | - | - | - | - | ✓ | ◐ | ◐ | ◐ |
| **The Ramada** | $$ | 60 | 5 | - | ✓ | - | - | ✓ | ✓ | ◐ | ◐ | ◐ |
| **Sheraton Hotel at Station Square** | $$$ | 900 | 21 | ✓ | ✓ | - | - | - | ✓ | - | ◐ | ◐ |
| **Vista International** | $$$$ | 950 | 18 | ✓ | ✓ | - | - | ✓ | ✓ | ◐ | ● | ◐ |
| **Westin William Penn** | $$$ | 1200 | 39 | ✓ | ✓ | - | - | ✓ | ✓ | ◐ | ● | ◐ |

$$$$ = over $125, $$$ = $95-$125, $$ = under $95.
● good, ◐ fair, ○ poor.
All hotels listed here have photocopying and fax facilities.

| In-Room Amenities | | | | | | | | | | Hotel Amenities | | | | | | |
| Nonsmoking rooms | In-room check-out | Minibar | Pay movies | VCR/Movie rentals | Hairdryer | Toiletries | Room service | Laundry/Dry cleaning | Pressing | Concierge | Barber/Hairdresser | Garage | Courtesy airport transport | Sauna | Pool | Exercise room |
|---|---|---|---|---|---|---|---|---|---|---|---|---|---|---|---|---|
| ✓ | - | - | - | - | - | ○ | ○ | ● | ● | - | - | - | ✓ | - | ◐ | ○ |
| ✓ | ✓ | ✓ | ✓ | ✓ | - | ○ | ◐ | ● | ● | ✓ | ✓ | - | - | ✓ | - | ○ |
| ✓ | - | - | ✓ | ✓ | - | ○ | ◐ | ● | ● | ✓ | - | ✓ | - | ✓ | ◐ | ◐ |
| ✓ | - | ✓ | ✓ | ✓ | - | ○ | ◐ | ◐ | ● | - | ✓ | - | ✓ | ✓ | ◐ | ○ |
| ✓ | - | - | ✓ | - | - | ○ | ◐ | ● | ● | ✓ | - | ✓ | - | ✓ | ◐ | ◐ |
| ✓ | ✓ | - | ✓ | - | - | ○ | ◐ | ● | ● | - | - | - | ✓ | ✓ | ◐ | ◐ |
| - | - | - | - | - | - | ○ | - | ● | ● | - | - | - | - | - | - | - |
| ✓ | ✓ | - | - | - | - | ○ | ◐ | ● | ● | ✓ | ✓ | ✓ | - | ✓ | - | - |
| ✓ | - | - | ✓ | ✓ | - | ○ | ◐ | ● | ● | ✓ | ✓ | - | - | ✓ | ◐ | ○ |
| ✓ | ✓ | ✓ | ✓ | - | - | ◐ | ● | ● | ● | ✓ | - | - | - | - | - | ○ |
| ✓ | ✓ | ✓ | ✓ | - | ✓ | ○ | ● | ● | ● | - | ✓ | - | - | - | - | ○ |

**Room service:** ● 24-hour, ◐ 6AM-10PM, ○ other.
**Laundry/Dry cleaning:** ● same day, ◐ overnight, ○ other.
**Pressing:** ● immediate, ◐ same day, ○ other.

modeled. On the topmost, executive-level floor, the renovation is expanding the private lounge and updating the rooms, which are the only ones in the hotel with desks. The Hyatt is on the outskirts of downtown, although in this compact city that doesn't mean much. It's the hotel closest to the city's civic arena, in case you plan to go to a hockey game. *112 Washington Pl., 15219, tel. 412/471–1234 or 800/233–1234, fax 412/355–0315. Gen. manager, Don Schmid. 400 rooms, 19 suites. AE, CB, D, DC, MC, V.*

★ ❽ **Pittsburgh Hilton and Towers.** A longtime local favorite, $$$ the Hilton is respected for its trusty service. One of the few hotels that isn't dominated by green and pink, its light browns and creams give the lobby a warm, low-key atmosphere. With the largest ballroom between New York and Chicago—and the largest brass revolving door in the country—the Hilton caters to large groups. But it also offers a panoramic view of the city and the three rivers and is across the street from the only downtown park. Rooms with the best views face the front. For deluxe service, request the Tower Level, where rooms are equipped with VCRs (there is a video bookshelf in the Tower lounge) and serviced with an express elevator and a concierge for speedy check-in and check-out. If you're traveling with a companion, ask for a mini-suite, which has two full baths. *600 Commonwealth Ave., 15222, tel. 412/391–4600 or 800/445–8667, fax 412/594–5161. Gen. manager, Patrick Duffy. 714 rooms, 31 suites. AE, CB, D, DC, MC, V.*

❿ **The Priory.** This renovated Benedictine monastery $$ doesn't pretend to cater to travelers looking for fax service, computers, or ballrooms. Instead, it prides itself on homey, personal service in immaculate, Victorian-style rooms furnished with antiques. A complimentary Continental breakfast with homemade breads is a cut above the cardboard-Danish fare at chain hotels. In comfortable, do-it-yourself style, guests serve themselves in a central dining room overlooking a small courtyard and mix their own drinks from a modestly stocked honor bar in the tiny library. Complimentary drinks are offered from 5 PM to 11 PM. The inn is located across the river from downtown, but morning shuttles are offered from 7 to 10 in a black vintage Chrysler Imperial. *614 Pressley St., 15212, tel. 412/231–3338. Gen. manager, Tracy Callison. 24 rooms. AE, D, DC, MC, V.*

⓭ **The Ramada Hotel.** Downtown's only suite hotel, the 20-$$ story, orange-brick building—a typical 1950s structure—draws longer-term residents as well as the corporate transient. It's remarkably low priced, so don't expect fresh-cut flowers in the rooms. About 100 rooms remain unrenovated, which means dull-orange bedspreads and brown carpets and no control over the central heating and air conditioning. Ask for a room on the recently renovated fourth or fifth floor, decorated in more-subdued blue and dark wood and equipped with a full kitchen and work area with computer hookup. But forget about trying to organize large meetings in this hotel: The largest room holds about 65 people, and the next largest can squeeze in about 20. *1 Bigelow Sq., 15219, tel. 412/281–5800, fax 412/281–8467. Gen. manager, George Remmers. 400 rooms, 150 business suites. AE, CB, D, DC, MC, V.*

**❾ Sheraton Hotel at Station Square.** Near this riverfront
$$$ hotel are a couple of diverting attractions: a historic-
landmark warehouse with about 70 trendy shops and
restaurants, and the Gateway Clipper Fleet, which has
sightseeing and dinner-dance cruises. Some guests object
to staying across the Monongahela River from downtown;
others are content to use the subway or the hotel's shuttle
to the city center. Riverfront rooms are slightly more ex-
pensive but worth it: Among these are the parlor rooms,
which are less cramped and have a desk and real-wood fur-
niture instead of the plastic pieces found in standard ac-
commodations. If you can't get a riverfront room, you can
still watch the river traffic from the lounge in the huge lob-
by, which has a ceiling of exposed pipes and grillwork, like
a high school gymnasium. *7 Station Square Dr., 15219, tel.
412/261–2000 or 800/325–3535, fax 412/261–2932. Gen.
manager, Anthony DeCarolis. 293 rooms, 11 suites. AE,
CB, D, DC, MC, V.*

**★ ⓭ Vista International.** Pittsburgh's newest hotel, the Vista
$$$$ draws an assortment of stylish guests—including Prince
Charles—with its casual elegance and smart service.
Built around an airy, four-story atrium, the granite-and-
glass structure boasts a covered walkway to the conven-
tion center and proximity to federal buildings and the civic
arena. It offers first-rate amenities; gym shorts and T-
shirts are provided for your workout in the well-equipped
exercise club. (Bring your own shoes, and be prepared for
a mandatory physical, administered by a staff physiolo-
gist.) More extras pamper guests on the three upper, ex-
ecutive floors, especially the 26th, where the concierge
provides hassle-free check-in and check-out. *1000 Penn
Ave., 15222, tel. 412/281–3700 or 800/367–8478, fax 412/
281–2652. Gen. manager, Paul J. Kelly. 616 rooms, 68
suites. AE, CB, D, DC, MC, V.*

**★ ⓮ Westin William Penn.** One of the last (1916) building ven-
$$$ tures of industrialist Henry Clay Frick, this downtown
hotel has hosted movie stars, world-renowned fashion de-
signers, and princes. It's also a favorite among business
travelers who admire the elegance of crystal chandeliers
and marble staircases and don't mind the somewhat stiff,
formal atmosphere that goes along with this decor. Rooms
are spacious; all were tastefully redecorated in 1983.
Newer furnishings and additional amenities, including
a minibar and Continental breakfast, distinguish the
eighth-floor "crown-service" rooms, revamped in 1986.
The newly introduced voice-mail service is an up-to-the-
minute plus, but for fitness buffs the lack of a pool and sauna is a disappointment. *530 William Penn Pl., 15219, tel.
412/281–7100 or 800/245–4728, fax 412/553–5239. Gen.
manager, Wayne Bodington. 595 rooms, 47 suites. AE,
CB, D, DC, MC, V.*

## East Side

**★ ㉒ The Holiday Inn at University Center.** Built in 1988, this is
$$ the best bet for anyone with business at Pittsburgh's uni-
versities or hospitals on the east side. And the hotel pro-
vides a complimentary shuttle service downtown. It's a
typical, squeaky-clean Holiday Inn with an energetic staff
hired largely from the nearby universities. The look is a
mix of Art Deco and Greco-Roman, with marble columns
in the restaurant and pencil drawings of ruins in the

rooms. If you want a desk, be sure to ask for business class or you'll be stuck with a small, useless table with poor lighting. Don't be put off by the appearance of Foster's Bar and Grille, which looks like a New Age college cafeteria. The menu features New Orleans–style dishes. *100 Lytton Ave., 15213, tel. 412/682–6200, fax 412/681–4749. Gen. manager, Dennis Burrell. 253 rooms, 3 suites. AE, CB, D, DC, MC, V.*

## Greentree

★ ❹ **Greentree Marriott.** Situated between downtown and the
$$$ airport, the Marriott in Greentree draws business travelers who need an accessible base of operations, and groups who want to avoid downtown traffic for their meetings or training seminars. A no-nonsense hotel with efficient and friendly service, this Marriott also caters to women and single diners. Rooms on the third floor have been set aside for women executives, offering such added amenities as hair dryers, makeup mirrors, irons, and ironing boards. One section of the Prime House restaurant has rows of small tables equipped with reading lights for single diners who want to relax over dinner with complimentary magazines and newspapers. A racquetball club with tennis and squash courts is just out the back door and available to guests at a discount rate. *101 Marriott Dr., 15205, tel. 412/922–8400, fax 412/922–8981. Gen. manager, Barbara McMahon. 467 rooms, 5 suites, 12 parlors. AE, CB, D, DC, MC, V.*

## Airport

❷ **Pittsburgh Airport Hilton Inn.** This hotel is pure function.
$$ Rooms are tidy and clean, and service is attentive—all that's necessary for those who simply want a place to sleep between trips around the area on business. Most rooms don't even have a desk. However the third-floor, executive-level rooms offer a desk, hair dryer, makeup mirror, and complimentary Continental breakfast and sparkling water. The hotel is easily accessible from the airport, but coming from downtown you must dart across congested Route 279. Also, in the snow, the long, uphill driveway might prove daunting. *Parkway West, Box 12411, 15231, tel. 412/262–3800 or 800/445–8667, fax 412/695–1068. Gen. manager, Timothy Winter. 140 rooms. AE, CB, D, DC, MC, V.*

❸ **Pittsburgh Airport Marriott.** If you're doing business any
$$$$ where near the airport and don't need to venture downtown, this is your place. The Marriott aims for elegance, with piped-in classical music and lots of dark wood, brass, and glass chandeliers. But it doesn't want to turn away the lobby lizard either, which explains why a grand piano and big-screen television share the crowded lobby bar. If you want anything other than a typical room, stay on the 14th (concierge) floor, and you'll also get a complimentary Continental breakfast and hors d'oeuvres. As the glitziest of the dozens of airport hotels, the Marriott doesn't have to try as hard as others to attract guests. Maybe that explains the sometimes reluctant staff. *100 Aten Rd., Coraopolis 15108, tel. 412/788–8800 or 800/328–9297, fax 412/788–0743. Gen. manager, Robert Hermany. 314 rooms, 5 suites, 13 minisuites. AE, D, DC, MC, V.*

# DINING

Pittsburgh isn't an outpost of culinary innovation, but its chefs do a creditable job of copying from the current stars and adding their own special twists. Business travelers will find their local counterparts enjoying traditional American cuisine at downtown restaurants. A five-minute cab ride from the center will take you to Mt. Washington (see the three listings below), which affords a spectacular view of downtown from across the Monongahela River. And if you have the time or the inclination to go farther afield, check out Café Allegro on the south side; Primanti's in the Strip District; or Hyeholde, near the airport.

Highly recommended restaurants in each price category are indicated by a star ★.

| Category | Cost* |
| --- | --- |
| *$$$$* (Very Expensive) | over $25 |
| *$$$* (Expensive) | $15–$25 |
| *$$* (Moderate) | under $15 |

*per person, including appetizer, entrée, and dessert, but excluding drinks, service, and 6% sales tax.*

*Numbers in the margin correspond to numbered restaurant locations on the Pittsburgh Lodging and Dining map.*

## Business Breakfasts

The combination hot-and-cold buffet at the **Orchard Café** (1000 Penn Ave., tel. 412/281–3700) is ideal for those who are as serious about eating as about business. If you have a lighter appetite, stick to the cold buffet, with yogurts, cereals, and fruits. The **Terrace Room** (tel. 412/553–5235), the formal dining room of the Westin William Penn, has become a favorite for breakfast meetings. Round tables are well spaced, and the service is attentive but not overbearing. **Warburton's Bakery** (USX Tower, tel. 412/471–0198) opens at 6 AM, so early risers can sit at a small booth and hold an informal meeting over some of the biggest and best muffins in the city.

## Downtown/Center City

★ ⑬
$$$
**American Harvest Restaurant.** Six chefs, each from a different country, make this one of downtown's most interesting places to dine. Elegant mahogany-paneled walls complement the rich burgundy decor. The lighting is subdued, with candles on the tables and sconces on the wall, but the room is not so dark that you can't read your menu. Well-spaced tables are ideal for serious conversation, but for even more privacy ask for a booth on the second level. The menu stresses American basics of beef and seafood, but the fare is hardly standard. Consider pan-fried veal tenderloin, coupled with crab cakes; or an appetizer of shrimp and scallops steamed in a corn husk and topped with chive-butter sauce and American-sturgeon caviar. The pastry chef is first class, as is the black-tie staff. *1000*

Penn Ave., tel. 412/281–3700. Jacket required. Reservations advised. AE, CB, D, DC, MC, V.

**⓱ The Carlton.** Dark paneling, a warm, peach-tone interior,
**$$$** and well-spaced tables cosset diners at this lunchtime favorite. If you want complete privacy, request a booth by the window. The staff does its best to get time-pressed guests in and out without rushing them; single diners are also accorded good tables and attentive service. The mostly American dishes of grilled prime meats and seafood are consistently good, with tuna and salmon highly recommended. Wooing the health conscious, the restaurant offers a handful of low-cholesterol and cholesterol-free dishes, including fire-roasted lobster, and swordfish steak with tomato and basil. There is complimentary limousine service to events at Heinz Hall and Benedum Center. *One Mellon Bank Center, tel. 412/391–4099. Casual dress. Reservations advised. AE, CB, D, DC, MC, V. Closed Sun.*

**⓰ Common Plea.** Not surprisingly, this restaurant courts
**$$$** many of the city's lawyers and judges. You have your choice of two dining rooms: The downstairs is subdued with dark wood, and the newer Wine Room upstairs is a little flashier, with emphasis on glass and mirrors. Although some items are available à la carte, most diners opt for the seven-course dinner, which consists of soup, three appetizers (usually including clams and marinated mushrooms), salad, entrée, and a selection from a fruit-and-cheese tray. Recommended are the fresh seafood and the veal dishes, including veal Romano (tender veal sautéed in egg-and-Romano-cheese batter). *310 Ross St., tel. 412/281–5140. Jacket and tie advised. Reservations advised. AE, CB, DC, MC, V.*

**★ ⓫ Jake's Above the Square.** Jake's has the best wine list in the
**$$$$** city, with 220 selections and more on the way. Diners can request two or three 2-ounce tastings to help narrow down their options. The owner personally oversees the food preparation and service at this classy spot, and both are top notch. The cuisine relies on regional American and northern Italian fare; house specialties are mesquite-grilled seafood and homemade pasta, including porcini pasta, and a spinach lasagna with a rich béchamel sauce. Save room for the spumoni or soufflés. Most tables are a little too close together for privacy, but those at the window overlooking Market Square are more secluded, and also great for people- and pigeon-watching. *430 Market St., tel. 412/338–0900. Jacket and tie advised. Reservations advised. AE, CB, D, DC, MC, V.*

**★ ⓯ Juno Trattoria.** The regional Italian cooking here was
**$$** good enough to lure Luciano Pavarotti when he was in town performing *Tosca* with the Pittsburgh Opera. This clean, bright restaurant attracts a casual crowd that can't get enough of the homemade pastas and desserts. Favorites include chicken with angel-hair pasta and homemade plum sauce; various ravioli, filled perhaps with lobster; and chicken and broccoli. Don't pass up the focaccia, an Italian flat bread layered with two cheeses, sundried tomatoes, and prosciutto, and grilled with olive oil. Portions come in three sizes, with prices adjusted accordingly, for those who do and don't have a Pavarotti-size appetite. *One Oxford Center, Grant St. and 4th Ave., tel. 412/392–0225*

*Casual dress. Reservations advised for dinner. AE, MC,
V. Closed Sun.*

## South Side

㉑ **Café Allegro.** This European-style restaurant and espres-
$$ so bar, about a 10-minute cab ride from downtown, is
tucked into one of the city's oldest neighborhoods, where a
refreshing mix of tony restaurants and used-furniture
stores share high-Victorian architecture. Simply deco-
rated in black and white and graced with fresh-cut flow-
ers, the restaurant is classy but cozy—almost too cozy for
important business meetings. (A second-floor dining area
is more conducive to a business talk.) The menu's Mediter-
ranean dishes vary seasonally, but you can't go wrong
with the grilled veal or the moist salmon baked in parch-
ment; or with any of the starters, including grilled
calamari. Chocolate fanatics can indulge in Death by
Chocolate—layers of chocolate meringue, cake, and fudge
icing. After dinner, walk across the street to Cardillo's
Club Café, where a father-and-son jazz team entertain on
dueling pianos. *51 S. 12th St., tel. 412/481–7788. Casual
dress. Reservations advised. MC, V.*

⑩ **Grand Concourse.** This former waiting room of the Pitts-
$$$ burgh & Lake Erie Railroad Station has the most impres-
sive interior of any Pittsburgh restaurant. When con-
versation lags you can marvel at the stained-glass windows and marble columns, and if you're lucky enough to
get a riverfront table you can admire the downtown skyline or watch barge traffic on the river. This is a seafood
place, so you can't go wrong with the chowders and the
fresh daily specials, which are simply prepared and not
overwhelmed by sauces. A nice touch is the complimentary bluefish pâté served before dinner. If you want a more
casual meal, belly up to the bar at the adjoining Gandy
Dancer for chowder, pasta, or a dozen oysters—but note:
On Friday night, diners are packed in here like sardines. *1
Station Sq., tel. 412/261–1717. Casual dress. Reservations advised. AE, CB, D, DC, MC, V.*

## Strip District

⑳ **Primanti's.** This no-nonsense sandwich joint was once a
$$ filling station for hungry truck drivers delivering produce
to the city's street market. Now it's a Pittsburgh institu-
tion, albeit still an unpretentious one. It's noisy and
crowded, and service can be surly at times. But those han-
kering for a Dagwood-style sandwich don't seem to mind:
Everything from eggs to pastrami is buried in coleslaw
and french fries and then sandwiched between two thick
slabs of bread. Open 24 hours a day, the place is a favorite
haunt for college students and young executives who need
a quick, satisfying bite. *46 18th St., tel. 412/263–2142. Ca-
sual dress. No reservations. No credit cards.*

## Mt. Washington

⑤ **Christopher's.** Diners here can catch the view as they ride
$$$$ up 10 stories in a glass-enclosed elevator to a huge—al-
most too big—dining room. Three sides of the restaurant
offer a panoramic view, and the fourth is occupied by a
huge wall embedded with chunks of coal, a tribute to the
city's industrial roots. A roving violinist entertains, as
does the chef, who prepares at tableside such specialties

as steak Diane (medallions of filet sautéed with mushrooms, onions, sweet peppers, red wine, and brandy) and lobster ravioli. *1411 Grandview Ave., tel. 412/381–4500. Jacket required. Reservations advised. AE, D, DC, MC, V. Closed lunch.*

**❻ Cliffside.** Between LeMont and Christopher's, Cliffside
**$$$** has the same view but is slightly less showy and expensive. The menu is limited and not too ambitious. House specialties include veal Lafayette (sautéed with artichokes and black olives) and chicken Dragina (stuffed with cheddar and apples and served in a honey-raisin sauce). *1208 Grandview Ave., tel. 412/431–6996. Jacket and tie advised. Reservations advised. AE, CB, DC, MC, V.*

**❼ LeMont.** Down the street from Christopher's is this
**$$$** glitzy-bordering-on-gaudy restaurant. It, too, has a spectacular view, but be sure to reserve a window booth if possible. The menu, which is a little hard to read because it's so dark in here, offers smoked duck and escargots for starters. The specialty of the house is rack of lamb. *1114 Grandview Ave., tel. 412/431–3100. Jacket required. Reservations advised. AE, D, DC, MC, V. Closed lunch.*

## Airport

**❶ Hyeholde Restaurant and Cabaret.** You'll feel as if you've
**$$$$** been invited to dine in an elegant home at this mansion hidden in a grove of trees. Slate floors, an oak interior, and candlelight are just the right accompaniment for a relaxing meal. Service is attentive and professional; and the menu, while limited, offers a good variety with such bestsellers as rack of lamb, and Virginia Spots (tiny, delicate fish fillets). The chef's nightly specials, which include venison when in season, are highly esteemed. On Friday and Saturday night, you can have your white-chocolate cheesecake and coffee in the stark, white-and-gray cabaret downstairs while you listen to a local jazz group. The restaurant, only a few minutes from the airport, is a 20- to 30-minute cab ride from downtown, depending on traffic. *190 Hyeholde Dr., Coraopolis, tel. 412/264–3116. Jacket advised. Reservations advised. AE, CB, D, DC, MC, V.*

## FREE TIME

### Fitness

*Hotel Facilities*
There is a $10 fee for nonguests to use the impressive fitness club at the **Vista International** (tel. 412/281–3700); among the facilities are treadmills and exercise bikes, pool, and sauna.

*Health Clubs*
You can't get a better deal than at the **YMCA;** your first visit to the center at 330 Boulevard of the Allies (tel. 412/227–6420) is free (the next costs $7, or, if you want sauna, steam, and whirlpool, $10); a large body-sculpting area, double gymnasium, aerobic equipment, racquetball and squash courts, and a 25-meter pool are all available here. **City Club** (119 Sixth St., tel. 412/391–3300) offers visitors an indoor track, basketball court, swimming pool, weight room, fitness machines, sauna, and Jacuzzi for $10 a day.

*Jogging*

Downtown's only real patch of green, **Point State Park,** has a number of nice paths. Or you can create your own route by tracing downtown's triangular perimeter along the two rivers.

## Shopping

For a true taste of Pittsburgh, walk along colorful East Carson Street on the city's south side, where antiques stores, used-book shops, and art galleries are housed in Victorian-style storefronts. Stop at the Chamber of Commerce (1413 E. Carson St., tel. 412/481–0650) for a map of the area. Visit Penn Avenue, adjacent to downtown and known as the Strip District, for marinated olives from a barrel at **Pennsylvania Macaroni** (2012 Penn Ave., tel. 412/471–8330) or biscotti and cappuccino at **La Prima Espresso** (205 21st St., tel. 412/281–1922). Also on the Strip is the **Society for Art in Crafts** (2100 Smallman St., tel. 412/261–7003), where local artists show and sell their work.

The best downtown department stores are **Saks Fifth Avenue** (513 Smithfield St., tel. 412/263–4800), **Kaufmanns** (400 5th Ave., tel. 412/232–2000), and **Hornes** (Penn Ave. and Stanwix St., tel. 412/553–8000). Two major office/retail complexes house high-end shops: **One Oxford Center** (Grant St. and 4th Ave., tel. 412/391–5300) has **Ann Taylor, Polo–Ralph Lauren,** and **Benetton.** The relatively new **Arcade at Fifth Avenue Place** (at the intersection with Liberty, Stanwix, and Penn), offers **Eddie Bauer, Caswell Massey,** and **The Narragansett.**

You can walk or take the subway or a taxi across the Monongahela River to **Station Square,** a renovated rolling mill and historic landmark now filled with 70 restaurants and specialty shops that sell everything from coffee to baseball shirts.

## Diversions

**The Aviary** (Western Ave. and Arch St., tel. 412/323–7234) is the nation's largest zoo for birds, with more than 800 specimens.

**Carnegie Institute** (4400 Forbes Ave., tel. 412/622–3131), Pittsburgh's cultural center, houses the Museum of Art, Museum of Natural History (with one of the world's most complete dinosaur collections), Carnegie Music Hall, and the Library of Pittsburgh.

**Cathedral of Learning** (4200 5th Ave., tel. 412/624–4141) is a 42-story Gothic skyscraper that houses the library of the University of Pittsburgh. It's also noted for the "nationality rooms" representing typical classrooms of 22 different nations.

For the best view of the city, take the cable car up the side of Mt. Washington to the observation deck of the **Duquesne Incline** (1220 Grandview Ave., tel. 412/381–1665).

**Falling Water** (Rte. 381, Mill Run, tel. 412/329–8501) is a Frank Lloyd Wright masterpiece that boasts indirect lighting, windows without curtains or blinds, and "floating" furniture. The house is about a 1½- to two-hour drive from Pittsburgh.

**Gateway Clipper Fleet** (9 Station Square Dock, tel. 412/355-7980) offers daily sightseeing cruises as well as a dinner-dance cruise, weather permitting.

**Phipps Conservatory** (Schenley Park, tel. 412/622-6915) is one of the nation's largest, with 13 display rooms and 2.5 acres of gardens enclosed in glass.

**Point State Park,** at the tip of downtown, where the Monongahela and Allegheny rivers join to form the Ohio, is downtown's only patch of green. Sit at the fountain's edge and watch the river traffic, or, if you're a history buff, check out the park's Fort Pitt Museum, which commemorates the fort's capture by George Washington.

## Professional Sports

Pittsburgh's hockey team, the **Penguins** (tel. 412/642-1985), play at the Civic Arena. The city's baseball team, the **Pirates** (tel. 412/321-2827; or 800/289-2827), and football team, the **Steelers** (tel. 412/323-1200), play at Three Rivers Stadium.

## The Arts

Although the arts scene in Pittsburgh is not as well developed as it is in other, larger cities, there are a number of venues here worth visiting. A renovated 1928 movie palace, **Benedum Center for the Performing Arts** (719 Liberty Ave., tel. 412/456-6666) is home to the Pittsburgh Opera, Pittsburgh Ballet, Civic Light Opera, and Pittsburgh Dance Council. The Pittsburgh Symphony Orchestra plays at **Heinz Hall** (600 Penn Ave., tel. 412/ 392-4800). The **Pittsburgh Playhouse** (222 Craft Ave., tel. 412/621-4445) offers a range of entertainment, from revivals of Broadway musicals, to children's theater, to film series. The Shriners' **Syria Mosque** (4423 Bigelow Blvd., tel. 412/682-2200) hosts such performers as Don Henley and other musical and theatrical acts.

The main ticket agency is **Network Ticket Agency** (5th Ave. and Smithfield St., tel. 412/391-7427). There is also a **TIX Booth** (USX Tower Plaza at Grant St., tel. 412/642-2787).

## After Hours

*Bars and Lounges*
The suit-and-tie group meet at **The Bar** (Vista International Hotel, tel. 412/281-3700) over cocktails or vintage wines by the glass, and no-nonsense beer lovers head to the **Allegheny Brewery & Pub** (Troy Hill Rd. and Vinial St., tel. 412/237-9402). The crowd is loud and happy; a cheer goes up when the bell signals that the hot pretzels are done and on their way with mustard and white radishes. Sports nuts wanting to check on their home team might head to the 20,000-square-foot **Sports Garden** (1 Station Square Dr., tel. 412/281-1511). Tune in one of the 40 television sets or three big screens. Unless you like standing, don't go on the weekend.

*Cabaret*
**Hyeholde Cabaret** (190 Hyeholde Dr., tel. 412/264-3116) is the place for fine cognac, port, and live jazz on weekends.

### Comedy Clubs

**Funny Bone** (Station Sq., tel. 412/281–3130) is your best and only bet for a comedy club close to downtown.

### Jazz Clubs

Two places, only a few blocks from each other and both a 15-minute cab ride from downtown, are worth checking. There's the **Balcony** (5520 Walnut St., tel. 412/687–0110), which has a jazz brunch on Sunday; and **Clearwater** (5401 Walnut St., tel. 412/621–8881). Another worthwhile stop is **Cardillo's Club Café** (56–58 S. 12th St., tel. 412/381–3777), home to Bobby and Harry Cardillo, a father-son team who play jazz on two pianos.

### For Singles

**Metropol** (1600 Smallman St., tel. 412/261–2221), a former appliance warehouse that has been converted into a nightclub, is where the young and hip meet to dance, people-watch, and mingle. The dress code seems to be anything black. Beware of strobe lights. **Chauncy's** (The Shops at Station Square, tel. 412/232–0601) offers dancing nightly to classic hits of the 1960s through '80s.

# St. Louis

*by Nancy Milton*

Earlier in this century, St. Louis was described as being "First in shoes, first in booze, and last in the American League." Many things have changed since that ill-fated baseball team (the Browns) left in 1954, but St. Louis remains home to Anheuser-Busch, the world's largest brewer, and the headquarters of footwear giants Brown Group and Edison Brothers. The St. Louis area now boasts the corporate headquarters of 10 of the Fortune 500; McDonnell Douglas is a major force in aerospace here; and two other important defense contractors, General Dynamics and Emerson Electric, also make the city their headquarters.

Transportation, on land and water, has been important to St. Louis since its beginnings as a French fur-trading center in 1764. Today, the city has the second largest inland port in the U.S., the third largest rail center, and the country's seventh busiest airport. St. Louis's automobile production for Chrysler, Ford, and General Motors is second only to Detroit's.

To encourage the convention and meeting industry, a major growth area of the local economy, the convention center is being expanded to include a connecting exhibition/stadium facility. New hotels are planned, too, to keep pace with an expected increase in demand.

## Top Employers

| Employer | Type of Enterprise | Parent*/ Headquarters |
|---|---|---|
| **Anheuser-Busch Inc.** | Brewer | St. Louis |
| **Emerson Electric Co.** | Electronic products | St. Louis |
| **General Dynamics Corp.** | Defense contractor | St. Louis |
| **Interco Inc.** | Apparel and furniture manufacturer and retailer | St. Louis |
| **May Department Stores** | Retail chain | St. Louis |

| McDonnell Douglas Corp. | Aerospace | St. Louis |
|---|---|---|
| Monsanto Co. | Chemicals | St. Louis |
| Ralston Purina Co. | Consumer products | St. Louis |
| Southwestern Bell Corp. | Communications | St. Louis |
| Wetterau Inc. | Food distributor and retailer | St. Louis |

*\*if applicable*

## ESSENTIAL INFORMATION

### Climate

What follows are the average daily maximum and minimum temperatures for St. Louis.

| Jan. | 40F | 4C | Feb. | 43F | 6C | Mar. | 54F | 12C |
|---|---|---|---|---|---|---|---|---|
| | 25 | −4 | | 27 | −3 | | 36 | 2 |
| Apr. | 65F | 18C | May | 76F | 24C | June | 85F | 29C |
| | 47 | 8 | | 58 | 14 | | 67 | 19 |
| July | 88F | 31C | Aug. | 88F | 31C | Sept. | 81F | 27C |
| | 72 | 22 | | 70 | 21 | | 63 | 17 |
| Oct. | 68F | 20C | Nov. | 54F | 12C | Dec. | 43F | 6C |
| | 50 | 10 | | 38 | 3 | | 29 | −2 |

### Airports

All international and domestic flights use **Lambert-St. Louis International Airport,** 13 miles northwest of downtown. Spirit of St. Louis Airport, 17 miles to the west, and St. Louis Downtown Parks Airport, within sight of the city, handle only small, private flights.

### Airport Business Facilities

**Lambert-St. Louis International Airport.** The Main Terminal has fax machines and photocopiers on the lower level, and a Western Union desk next to the baggage claim.

### Airlines

St. Louis is the domestic hub for TWA, which controls more than 80 percent of the traffic at Lambert. TWA has St. Louis's only direct international flights—to Paris, London, and Frankfurt.

**American,** tel. 314/231–9505 or 800/433–7300.
**Continental,** tel. 314/241–7205 or 800/525–0280.
**Delta,** tel. 314/421–2600 or 800/221–1212.
**Northwest,** tel. 800/225–2525.
**Southwest,** tel. 314/421–1221 or 800/527–0770.
**TWA,** tel. 314/291–7500 or 800/221–2000.
**United,** tel. 314/454–0088 or 800/241–6522.
**USAir,** tel. 314/421–1018 or 800/428–4322.

## Between the Airport and Downtown

*By Taxi*
I–70 east is the fastest, most direct route. The 13-mile trip should take no more than 20 minutes, even during rush hour. Cost: $18, plus tip.

*By Airport Limousine*
Call the limo (tel. 314/429–4940) from a booth on the lower level of the main terminal, between luggage carousels 5 and 6. The limousines are actually passenger vans, so there may be a number of stops before your hotel, but they are in good condition and the drivers are helpful. Cost: $6.

*By Bus*
The **Natural Bridge** bus (tel. 314/231–2345) leaves from the arriving flights (lower) level of the terminal at about 15 minutes past every hour from 8 AM until 9 PM. This is a local route making many stops and will take you about an hour to arrive downtown. Cost: 85¢.

## Car Rentals

Of the following agencies, all but four—Ajax, American International, Enterprise, and Thrifty—have booths at the airport. The other four are nearby, and all have shuttle service to the terminal.

**Ajax,** tel. 314/428–1111 or 800/252–9756.
**American International,** tel. 314/423–1200.
**Avis,** tel. 314/426–7766 or 800/331–1212.
**Budget,** tel. 314/731–6000 or 800/527–0700.
**Dollar,** tel. 314/423–4004 or 800/421–6868.
**Enterprise,** tel. 314/427–7757 or 800/325–8007.
**Hertz,** tel. 314/426–7555 or 800/654–3131.
**National,** tel. 314/426–6272 or 800/328–4567.
**Sears,** tel. 314/731–3400.
**Thrifty,** tel. 314/423–3737 or 800/367–2277.

## Emergencies

*Doctors*
**St. Louis Health Center** (401 Pine St., tel. 314/241–8181) is located in the heart of downtown. Closed weekends. **St. Mary's of Clayton** (112 S. Hanley Rd., tel. 314/721–8859) is in the Clayton business district. **Primedical** (seven area offices, tel. 314/878–2337) offers walk-in service daily.

*Dentists*
**Downtown Dental Associates, Inc.** (223 N. Seventh St., tel. 314/241–4232), **St. Louis Health Center** (*see* Doctors, above) also offers emergency treatment.

*Hospitals*
**Barnes Hospital** (4949 Barnes Hospital Plaza, tel. 314/362–5000) is affiliated with Washington University, **St. Louis University Medical Center** (1325 S. Grand Blvd., tel. 314/577–8000).

## Important Addresses and Numbers

**Audiovisual rentals.** Hoover (200 N. Leffingwell Ave., tel. 314/652–1114), Swank (211 S. Jefferson Ave., tel. 314/534–1940).

**Chamber of Commerce** (100 N. Fourth St., tel. 314/231–5555).

**Computer rentals.** Computer Access International (11B Worthington Dr., tel. 314/878–1670), Houlihan Office Systems (745 Craig Rd., tel. 314/567–7794), West Port Desktop Publishing (631 West Port Plaza, tel. 314/878–6885).

**Convention & Visitors Commission** (10 S. Broadway, Suite 300, tel., 314/421–1023 or 800/325–7962).

**Convention and exhibition centers.** Cervantes Convention Center (801 Convention Plaza, tel. 314/342–5000), The Arena (5700 Oakland Ave., tel. 314/644–0900), The Kiel (1400 Market St., tel. 314/621–4089).

**Fax services.** Business Centers (13035 Olive Street Rd., tel. 314/469–0500), Mail Boxes Etc. (7536 Forsyth Blvd., tel. 314/862–3700), Office Plus in West Port (111 West Port Plaza, tel. 314/434–9500).

**Formal-wear rentals.** Castelli, 10 locations (tel. 314/645–1776), Stallone's, 3 locations (tel. 314/721–5750).

**Gift shops.** Chocolates: Bissinger's Chocolates (4742 McPherson Ave., tel. 314/534–2400); Gift Baskets: Capricorn Gift Baskets (15444 Clayton Rd., Suite 207, tel. 314/256–8066); Flowers: Walter Knoll Florist (5501 Chippewa St., tel. 314/352–7575).

**Graphic design studios.** Obata Kuehner (5585 Pershing Ave., tel. 314/361–3110), Robert Falk Group (4425 West Pine, tel. 314/531–1410).

**Hairstylists.** Unisex: Executive Salon (707 Olive Street Rd., tel. 314/421–2222), Facade (8211 Clayton Rd., tel. 314/725–2911), Jon Tomas (6510 Clayton Rd., tel. 314/644–3667).

**Health and fitness clubs.** *See* Fitness, below.

**Information hot lines.** Sports Information (tel. 314/321–1111), St. Louis Fun Phone, for what's on in town (tel. 314/421–2100).

**Limousine services.** Admiral (tel. 314/991–5466), Show Me (tel. 314/382–6003).

**Liquor stores.** Bussone's (1011 Olive Street Rd., tel. 314/241–1083), West End Wines (309 Belt Ave., tel. 314/367–3049), Westport Liquor & Deli (1913 Schuetz Rd., tel. 314/432–4795).

**Mail delivery, overnight.** DHL Worldwide Express (tel. 314/423–8663), Federal Express (tel. 314/367–8278), TNT Skypak (tel. 314/429–4646), UPS (tel. 800/392–3730), U.S. Postal Service Express Mail (tel. 314/436–3880).

**Messenger services.** Laclede Cab (tel. 314/652–3456), National Courier (tel. 314/423–8484).

**Office space rentals.** Home Office (47 Village Square Center, tel. 314/731–8261), LaSalle Office Suites (509 Olive Street Rd., tel. 314/231–5255), Professional Business Services (734 West Port Plaza, tel. 314/434–1174).

**Pharmacies, late-night.** Walgreen's (4 Hampton Village Plaza, tel. 314/351–2100).

**Radio station, all-news.** KMOX 1120 AM.

**Secretarial services.** Clayprice Business Service (1760 S. Brentwood Blvd., tel. 314/961–1450), Kelly Services (200 N. Broadway, tel. 314/421–4111).

**Stationery supplies.** Service Bureau (9208 Clayton Rd., tel. 314/991–1104).

**Taxis.** Airport Cab (tel. 314/843–3571), Allen Cab (tel. 314/531–4545), Laclede Cab (tel. 314/652–3456).

**Theater tickets.** *See* The Arts, below.

**Train information.** Amtrak (550 S. 16th St., tel. 314/241–8806 or 800/872–7245).

**Travel agents.** American Express Travel (One Mercantile Center, tel. 314/241–6400), Ask Mr. Foster (1850 Craigshire Rd., Suite 100 N., tel. 314/434–1220).

**Weather** (tel. 314/321–2222).

## LODGING

Large chains, residential suites, and small luxury facilities are available in St. Louis. Downtown hotels are convenient if your business is in that compact section; parking fees are not expensive by large-city standards, but high for St. Louis, about $8–$10 overnight. Six miles west of downtown St. Louis is Clayton, which is becoming known as "the other downtown," and offers some good options as well. Hotel parking is free in Clayton; shopping is nearby. The airport hotels are close to St. Louis's many large manufacturers, and most have good conference facilities.

Most hotels listed here offer special corporate rates and weekend discounts; inquire when making reservations. Hotels may also offer substantial discounts from December through March.

Highly recommended lodgings in each category are indicated by a star ★.

| Category | Cost* |
|---|---|
| $$$$ (Very Expensive) | over $125 |
| $$$ (Expensive) | $90–$125 |
| $$ (Moderate) | under $90 |

*All prices are for a standard room, excluding 13.175% hotel tax and a $2 occupancy fee.*

*Numbers in the margin correspond to numbered hotel locations on the St. Louis Lodging and Dining maps.*

### Downtown

**⓱** **Adam's Mark.** An unassuming facade belies the elegance
$$$$ of this first-class hotel built in 1986 in the heart of downtown's business and financial district. The bustling lobby's centerpiece—Italian bronze horses—has become a favorite meeting place, and the hotel's bars, restaurants, and lounges, tastefully decorated with Oriental and walnut touches, are seldom without their share of advertising, banking, and media powerbrokers. Pierre's Lounge is a popular place for quiet talks with clients in the evening, and several well-appointed board rooms are well set up for

# GREATER ST. LOUIS

**Lodging**
Daniele Hilton, **5**
Oakland Park Inn, **2**
Residence Inn-Galleria, **8**
Seven Gables Inn, **6**
Sheratons in West Port, **1**
Stouffer Concourse Hotel, **3**

**Dining**
Al Baker's, **7**
Blueberry Hill, **9**
Cardwell's, **4**
Chez Louis, **6**
Cunetto House of Pasta, **11**
Riddle's Penultimate Cafe & Wine Bar, **10**

# DOWNTOWN ST. LOUIS

**Lodging**
Adam's Mark, **17**
Drury Inn-Union Station, **12**
Hotel Majestic, **16**
Hyatt Regency-St. Louis Union Station, **13**

**Dining**
Faust's, **17**
Miss Hulling's, **14**
Tony's, **15**

large meetings. Rooms have contemporary furniture and Oriental accents. The best rooms are the 17 on each floor with full views of the Gateway Arch. All bathrooms have exterior dressing rooms. Two Concorde level executive floors offer extra amenities and a lounge with bar service, Continental breakfast, and space for private dinner parties. *Fourth and Chestnut Sts., 63102, tel. 314/241-7400 or 800/231-5858, fax 314/241-6618. Gen. manager, Maurice Briquet. 910 rooms, 94 suites, 97 rooms on Concorde level. Racquetball courts. AE, D, DC, MC, V.*

★ ⑫ **Drury Inn-Union Station.** A chain specializing in family
$$ hotels renovated a turn-of-the-century hostel for YMCA workers and brought into being this down-to-earth establishment, which is simply decorated but interesting for its architectural detail. Rooms are small but spotless, with cherry furniture several steps up from standard chain hotel issue. A complimentary American-style breakfast is served each morning in the lobby. Proximity to the St. Louis Union Station's entertainment, shopping, and restaurant complex is a plus. The hotel is popular with clubs and groups, so its public areas are usually bustling. The parking garage is free to hotel guests, a rarity downtown. *20th and Market Sts., 63103, tel. 314/231-3900 or 800/325-8300, fax 314/231-3900. Gen. manager, Gail Turnbull. 176 rooms, 98 doubles, 57 business class kings, 6 business class king doubles, 11 mini-suites. AE, D, MC, V.*

★ ⑯ **Hotel Majestic.** Classical music and a simple concierge's
$$$$ desk in the lobby set the tone for this quietly elegant hotel built in 1915. On the National Register of Historic Places, it reopened in 1987 after an extensive renovation. Personalities as diverse as the Rolling Stones and Henry Kissinger have enjoyed the hotel's attentive service. Rooms are done in early 18th-century style with cherry and mahogany furnishings and flowered curtains and bedspreads. Rooms are spacious; bathrooms are small but have separate dressing areas. The Hotel Majestic Dining Room (*see* Business Breakfasts, below) is a favorite power breakfast site and is fine for dinner, too. *Small Luxury Hotels & Resorts. 1019 Pine St., 63101, tel. 314/436-2355 or 800/451-2355, fax 314/436-2355. Gen. manager, John Hurley. 91 rooms, 3 suites, 18 double doubles, 70 kings. AE, CB, D, DC, MC, V.*

⑬ **Hyatt Regency-St. Louis Union Station.** In 1985, the Rouse
$$$$ Company which created the South Street Seaport in New York and Faneuil Hall in Boston, turned the Romanesque Union Station (*see* Diversions, below) into a hotel and shopping complex. The cavernous former waiting room became the lobby, and the old terminal hotel became the concierge section of this elegant Hyatt. The 13-acre former train shed now houses the standard hotel rooms—decorated in tasteful, if not out-of-the-ordinary, contemporary style—as well as the festival hall, with upscale shops and a large food court. The Gothic Corridor, a quiet lounge off the lobby, is conducive to business discussions. The best rooms are the 61 located in what was once the station headhouse: they are served by a private elevator, and decorated in traditional dark wood furnishings, with elegant, rich-toned carpeting. This is not a low-key establishment, but it has the advantages of a central location and of the myriad eating and shopping options close at hand. *One St. Louis Union Station, 63103, tel. 314/231-1234 or*

# ST. LOUIS HOTEL CHART

| HOTELS | Price Category | Business Services Banquet capacity | No. of meeting rooms | Secretarial services | Audiovisual equipment | Teletype news service | Computer rentals | In-room modem phonejack | All-news cable channel | Desk | Desk lighting | Bed lighting |
|---|---|---|---|---|---|---|---|---|---|---|---|---|
| Adam's Mark | $$$$ | 2400 | 32 | - | ✓ | - | - | ✓ | ✓ | ● | ● | ◕ |
| Daniele Hilton | $$$ | 150 | 4 | ✓ | ✓ | - | - | ✓ | ✓ | ● | ● | ● |
| Drury Inn-Union Station | $$ | 45 | 3 | - | ✓ | - | - | ✓ | ✓ | ● | ● | ● |
| Hyatt Regency-St. Louis Union Station | $$$$ | 1350 | 21 | ✓ | ✓ | ✓ | - | ✓ | ✓ | - | - | ● |
| Majestic | $$$$ | 64 | 3 | ✓ | ✓ | - | - | ✓ | ✓ | ● | ● | ◕ |
| Oakland Park Inn | $$ | 150 | 9 | ✓ | ✓ | - | - | ✓ | ✓ | ◕ | ◕ | ● |
| Residence Inn-Galleria | $$$ | 30 | 1 | ✓ | ✓ | - | - | ✓ | ✓ | ○ | ○ | ◕ |
| Seven Gables Inn | $$$ | 45 | 3 | ✓ | ✓ | - | - | - | ✓ | ● | ● | ● |
| Sheraton Plaza West Port | $$$ | 320 | 10 | ✓ | ✓ | - | - | - | ✓ | ◕ | ◕ | ● |
| Sheraton West Port Inn | $$$ | 350 | 12 | ✓ | ✓ | - | - | - | ✓ | ◕ | ◕ | ● |
| Stouffer Concourse | $$$ | 1000 | 34 | ✓ | ✓ | - | - | ✓ | ✓ | ● | ● | ● |

**$$$$** = over $125, **$$$** = $125-$90, **$$** = under $90.
● good, ◕ fair, ○ poor.
All hotels listed here have photocopying and fax facilities.

| In-Room Amenities | | | | | | | | | | Hotel Amenities | | | | | | |
| Nonsmoking rooms | In-room checkout | Minibar | Pay movies | VCR/Movie rentals | Hairdryer | Toiletries | Room service | Laundry/Dry cleaning | Pressing | Concierge | Barber/Hairdresser | Garage | Courtesy airport transport | Sauna | Pool | Exercise room |
|---|---|---|---|---|---|---|---|---|---|---|---|---|---|---|---|---|
| ✓ | ✓ | – | ✓ | – | – | ● | ● | ● | ◐ | ✓ | ✓ | ✓ | ✓ | – | ● | ● |
| ✓ | – | – | – | – | – | ○ | ◐ | ● | ● | – | – | – | – | – | ◐ | – |
| ✓ | – | – | ✓ | – | – | – | – | ● | ● | – | – | ✓ | ✓ | – | ◐ | – |
| ✓ | ✓ | – | – | ✓ | ✓ | ○ | ◐ | ● | ● | ✓ | – | – | ✓ | – | ◐ | ◐ |
| ✓ | – | ✓ | – | – | ✓ | ◐ | ● | ● | ● | ✓ | – | – | – | – | – | – |
| – | – | – | – | – | – | ○ | ◐ | ● | ● | – | – | – | ✓ | ✓ | ◐ | ○ |
| ✓ | – | – | ✓ | ✓ | – | ● | – | ● | ● | – | – | – | ✓ | – | ◐ | – |
| – | – | – | – | ✓ | – | ● | ◐ | ● | ● | ✓ | – | – | – | – | ◐ | – |
| ✓ | – | – | ✓ | ✓ | ✓ | ◐ | ● | ● | ● | ✓ | – | – | ✓ | – | ◐ | – |
| ✓ | – | – | ✓ | ✓ | ✓ | ◐ | ● | ● | ● | ✓ | – | – | ✓ | – | ◐ | – |
| ✓ | ✓ | ✓ | – | – | – | ● | ● | ● | ● | ✓ | – | – | ✓ | ✓ | ◐ | ● |

**Room service:** ● 24-hour, ◐ 6AM-10PM, ○ other.
**Laundry/Dry cleaning:** ● same day, ◐ overnight, ○ other.
**Pressing:** ● immediate, ◐ same day, ○ other.

800/233–1234, fax 314/436–6827. Gen. manager, Gary Dollens. 550 rooms, 61 Regency Club. AE, CB, MC, V.

## Clayton

**⑤** **The Daniele Hilton.** Furnishings vary from Chippendale
$$$ reproductions to Art Deco in this recently remodeled hotel. The spacious, airy rooms are newly decorated in neutral colors and the hotel's location on a quiet street, but just a short walk from Clayton's office buildings, shops, and restaurants, make this Hilton a good bet. The hotel's meeting rooms are suitable for small corporate functions including private dinner parties. The staff is efficient and eager to please. The London Grill draws an executive lunch crowd during the week. *216 N. Meramec, 63105, tel. 314/721–0101 or 800/325–8302, fax 314/721–0609. Gen. manager, David Morgan. 91 rooms, 6 suites. AE, CB, DC, MC, V.*

**⑧** **The Residence Inn-Galleria.** For frequent travelers tired
$$$ of hotel living, this small, apartment-like complex five minutes from downtown Clayton is an attractive option. Rates are competitive in this Marriott, built in 1986, and decrease with the length of stay. Each unit is decorated in a pleasingly neutral, contemporary style, and includes a fully equipped galley kitchen with ice maker, microwave, and refrigerator. Both studios and loft bedrooms are available, many with woodburning fireplaces. A breakfast bar separating the kitchen from the living space does double duty as a desk. Uncommon extras like free breakfasts, evening cocktails, and complimentary dinner on Wednesday nights bring guests together in the clubhouse-style lobby. Video rentals, babysitting services, and grocery shopping are available. The staff is service-oriented and friendly. A courtesy van operates within a five-mile radius, but the complex is within walking distance of the St. Louis Galleria mall. *A Marriott Hotel. 1100 McMorrow, 63117, tel. 314/862–1900 or 800/331–3131, fax 314/862–5621. Gen. manager, Linda Schuette. 128 units. AE, D, DC, MC, V.*

**★ ⑥** **The Seven Gables Inn.** Housed in a 3-story Tudor building
$$$ that's listed on the National Register of Historic Places, the Seven Gables is the Midwest's only member of the Relais & Châteaux association. Each room is decorated differently, and all are large, with pleasing country-French details. The best ones overlook a small courtyard, shaded with a towering old mulberry tree, where restaurant patrons dine in the summer. The staff's European insouciance is tempered by its efficiency. The Inn is popular with visiting physicians and top executives at Clayton's nearby corporations, some of which are within walking distance. Bernard's Bistro, off the lobby, is a popular meeting place for breakfast and for weekend brunch. Request a lower-level room if you don't want to climb stairs; there is no elevator. Continental breakfast is complimentary on Saturday, Sunday, and Monday. *A Relais & Châteaux property. 26 N. Meramec, 63105, tel. 314/863–8400 or 800/433–6590, fax 314/863–8846. Gen. manager, David Morgan. 32 rooms. AE, MC, V.*

## Airport

**②** **Oakland Park Inn.** A sleek, white facade leads, surpris-
$$ ingly, to a dark wood-paneled lobby with Georgian period

reproduction furnishings and the quiet, clubby atmosphere usually associated with a British country house. Conversation areas furnished with leather sofas are placed invitingly throughout the public spaces. The longtime staff is friendly and remembers frequent guests. Guest rooms are good-sized and continue the English manor house theme. The best rooms are in the newest addition. Not all of the rooms have desks; ask for one when making reservations. This is a good choice if you're tired of cookie-cutter chain hotels and are looking for personal service. *4505 Woodson Rd., 63134, tel. 314/427–4700 or 800/426–4700, fax 314/427–4700, ext. 624. Gen. manager, Brian McMahon. 155 rooms, 15 suites. AE, D, DC, MC, V.*

**❶** **Sheratons in West Port.** The Sheraton Plaza is a contempo-
**$$$** rary high rise, the Sheraton Inn is a faux Swiss chalet. They're located on opposite ends of West Port Plaza, a commercial and residential development, about 5 miles west of the airport near Hwy. 70. Each hotel has a concerned staff and there are a variety of entertainment and business services on hand in the West Port development. The Plaza's public spaces and rooms have contemporary Oriental decor, plush and comfortable in deep mauves and greens; the Inn favors dark woods in an Old World setting. The Inn's tower section is newer, and rooms there are slightly larger; lake views are available in both parts of the hotel. The Plaza has no restaurant, the Lucerne Room at the Inn serves meals in a pleasing Swiss atmosphere. *900 West Port Plaza, 63146, tel. 314/434–5010, fax 314/434–0140. Gen. manager, Mitch Bolen. 209 rooms/Plaza, 300 rooms, 9 suites/Inn. AE, CB, D, DC, MC, V.*

**★ ❸** **The Stouffer Concourse Hotel.** This 12-story black mono-
**$$$** lith at the southern tip of Lambert-St. Louis International Airport goes further than any other airport hotel in catering to the business traveler. The staff is young and eager to be helpful. Guest rooms, all recently renovated, have an airy, contemporary look in light pastels. Club level rooms are a good value—guests have access to a lounge with a pool table. Complimentary coffee and newspaper come with the morning wake-up call in all rooms. Rooms facing the runways can get noisy when the Missouri Air National Guard roars off in fighter formation. Ample ballroom and conference space makes this a good choice for meetings. *9801 Natural Bridge Rd., 63134, tel. 314/429–1100 or 800/468–3571, fax 314/429–3625. Gen. manager, Doug Browne. 400 rooms, 20 suites. AE, CB, D, DC, MC, V.*

## DINING

A new appreciation for American food, specifically midwestern, has swept through St. Louis in recent years. In its wake, restaurants are using seasonal, regional produce and meats in creative combinations. St. Louis is also known for fine Italian food, thanks mostly to immigration from Lombardy in the early part of this century. Cooking that started in family kitchens quickly spread to mom-and-pop trattorias and has blossomed into elegant restaurants. Most restaurants listed below are in the downtown and Clayton business areas, but for those willing to go a little farther afield, there are other dining options. University City, about 15 minutes west of downtown by car, is the kind of neighborhood you might expect to find near Washington University; it's an arty area with a diverse mix of residents and lots of ethnic restaurants—including Ethiopian, Jamaican, and Chinese—on the strip of Delmar Boulevard called the Loop. South St. Louis, about 12 minutes southwest of downtown, is a stable working class district, which includes the Hill, St. Louis's Italian enclave.

Highly recommended restaurants in each price category are indicated by a star ★.

| Category | Cost* |
| --- | --- |
| *$$$$* (Very Expensive) | over $28 |
| *$$$* (Expensive) | $20–$28 |
| *$$* (Moderate) | under $20 |

*per person, including appetizer, entrée, and dessert, but excluding drinks, service, and 5.925% sales tax in the county and 7.425% sales tax in the city.*

*Numbers in the margin correspond to numbered restaurant locations on the St. Louis Lodging and Dining maps.*

## Business Breakfasts

Paintings of trees decorate **The Oak Room** (tel. 314/427–4700), a small, plush room in the Oakland Park Inn near the airport. Quiet, rather formal, and a bit dark, the atmosphere is right for business breakfast discussions and hearty American fare. Reservations are suggested during the week. **Hotel Majestic Dining Room** (tel. 314/436–2355) is known for its well-prepared meals—not its speedy service. The menu includes locally smoked ham and banana pancakes with honey-pecan butter. The plush green velvet booths, formal table service, and cherry-paneled walls create a comfortable, clubby, but rather somber atmosphere.

St. Louis's political power brokers often eat at the **Cheshire Inn** (6303 Clayton Rd., tel. 314/647–7300) because of its hearty fare and its location on the city-county border. **Uncle Bill's Pancake House** (3427 S. Kingshighway, tel. 314/832–1973) is open 24 hours, serving breakfast all day. The **Hyatt Regency-St. Louis Union Station** (tel. 314/231–1234) serves the Pullman Country Classic breakfast, an eggs and bacon feast.

A Belgian waffle station and a restful view of the sculpture garden make the **Museum Café** (Art Museum in Forest Park, tel. 314/721–5325) a crowded Sunday favorite and a good spot for a business meeting if you have time to spare. For less leisurely meals, there's **Earhardt's** at the Stouffer Concourse Hotel (tel. 314/429–1100), which serves a brunch buffet within view of the runways at Lambert-St. Louis International Airport.

## Downtown

★ **⑰** **Faust's.** The Adam's Mark Hotel has re-created the atmos-
*$$$$* phere of a famous Victorian restaurant. Featuring an excellent Continental menu, this eatery lends itself to quiet

social or business discussions. The private Library Room is appropriate for dinner parties of up to 12 people. Try the pounded, lightly sautéed abalone, served in an herb-butter sauce with jumbo shrimp; or the homemade saffron pasta with red and yellow peppers. Desserts are rich; save room for the white-chocolate cheesecake. The excellent wine list leans toward California Cabernets and Chardonnays. *Fourth and Chestnut Sts., 314/342–4664. Jacket required. Reservations advised. AE, D, DC, MC, V.*

**⑭** **Miss Hulling's.** This self-service restaurant is the place to
**$$** come if you're in need of comfort food: real mashed potatoes, sliced roast beef, steaming chicken pot pies with flaky pastry crusts, and three-bean salad. Prices are moderate, quality and cholesterol-content high. Specialty pastries include split lemon cake filled with lemon custard and covered with a tart-sweet frosting. The standard cafeteria-style atmosphere is mitigated by the pink decor and awnings hanging from the ceiling. Catfish and Crystal, the attached table-service restaurant, serves many of the same dishes. *1103 Locust St., tel. 314/436–0840. Dress: informal. No reservations. AE, D, DC, MC, V.*

**★ ⑮** **Tony's.** The winner of many national and international
**$$$$** awards, Tony's has been long acknowledged as the area's finest Italian restaurant. Red velvet banquettes suit the plush decor, and formal, impeccably trained waiters serve the classic Italian cuisine. Choose an entrée, and let your waiter design a dinner to complement it. Lobster Albanello, chunks of the sweet shellfish in a creamy sauce, is excellent, as are the veal chops. Most dishes are finished tableside with a flourish. Local and national celebrities come here; the wall along the stairway to the second floor is lined with photos of famous patrons. *826 N. Broadway, tel. 314/231–7007. Jacket and tie required. Reservations advised. AE, CB, D, DC, MC, V. Closed Sun.*

## Clayton

**❼** **Al Baker's.** Among the city's many Italian restaurants, Al
**$$$$** Baker's comes out ahead in many categories, but consistently so in the preparation of fish. Flown in fresh, the fish can range from Alaskan miniature Coho salmon to Florida red snapper. A "heart smart" menu offers diners the chance to feel good about shrimp marinara or linguini with tomato basil. Though the decor is a peculiar mix—half Italian, half Oriental, with red flocked wallpaper—the regulars don't seem to mind. The wine cellar is the best in town. Personal attention from the staff makes this a good choice for business dinners. *8101 Clayton Rd., tel. 314/ 863–8878. Jacket and tie advised. Reservations advised. AE, CB, D, DC, MC, V.*

**❹** **Cardwell's.** This is the "in" lunch spot for young business
**$$$** people who appreciate well-spaced tables and who care more about food than decor. The main dining area opens onto a large patio facing busy downtown Clayton. The patio is open from late spring to early fall, and can get noisy with an after-work crowd in the early evening; there are fewer distractions in the back of the restaurant near the open kitchen. A private dining room is available for entertaining. The menu focuses on regional dishes and game. The cream-of-five-onions soup is a good start for lunch, followed by a sandwich or salad. Medallions of buffalo served with wild mushrooms in a zinfandel sauce is a house spe-

cialty. White chocolate macadamia nut layer cake from the dessert tray is worth the calories. *8100 Maryland Ave., tel. 314/726–5055. Jacket suggested. Reservations advised. AE, MC, V.*

**❻** **Chez Louis.** Located in Clayton's historic Seven Gables
**$$$$** Inn, this simple but elegant restaurant serves classic French food. Mauve linens and flowery-patterned china set the scene. The best tables are in the hotel's courtyard, where it's pleasant to dine in early summer. Convenient to Clayton's many corporate headquarters, the restaurant lends itself to business lunches (try the shrimp salad) and special occasion dinners. Best entrées are usually the chef's daily suggestions, which can include sautéed frogs legs with garlic and lemon or medallions of veal with lemon butter. *26 N. Meramec Ave., tel. 314/863–8400. Jacket and tie advised. Reservations required. AE, D, MC, V.*

## South St. Louis

**⓫** **Cunetto House of Pasta.** No reservations are accepted, so
**$$** expect a considerable wait at this popular restaurant on the Hill, St. Louis's Italian neighborhood. Exceptional value, well-placed tables, and fast, friendly service from a long-time staff keep customers satisfied. Linguini tutto mare, with crab, shrimp, and clams in a rich butter-based sauce, is a house favorite. This is also the place to try a local favorite: toasted ravioli, filled with meat, lightly breaded, deep fried, then served with a hearty meat sauce. *5453 Magnolia Ave., tel. 314/781–1135. Dress: casual but neat. No reservations. AE, DC, MC. Closed Sun.*

## University Circle

**❾** **Blueberry Hill.** If you want to see where St. Louisans un-
**$$** wind, check out this restaurant and bar, a nostalgic flashback for baby boomers. A neighborhood place with scrubbed wooden booths, Blueberry Hill is a shrine to rock'n'roll, with what must be one of the best jukeboxes in the U.S. Walls are adorned with souvenirs from rock's early days, and display cases are filled with '50s and '60s memorabilia, including cartoon-character lunchboxes and everything Howdy Doody. The fare is appropriate: an impressive list of imported beers, and oversize hamburgers topped with cheese or sautéed vegetables. St. Louis's Walk of Fame (patterned after Hollywood's) is outside. *6504 Delmar, tel. 314/727–0880. Dress: informal. No reservations. AE, D, MC, V.*

**★ ❿** **Riddle's Penultimate Cafe & Wine Bar.** Locals flock to the
**$$** University City area known as the "Loop" (after an old streetcar turnaround) for the special wine dinners, beer dinners (seven courses, seven beers), and mystery dinners scheduled here throughout the year. The interior is dark and small, and the background music favors Dave Brubeck. Riddle's huge wine list offers a wider selection of Missouri bottles (mid-Missouri topography is similar to that of Germany's Rhine River valley) than you'll find in any other St. Louis restaurant. Service is extremely informal but knowledgeable, and the suit and tie lunch crowd seems out of place in this unassuming barroom. Cool orange apricot soup is a summer favorite. Spaghetti Conroy is made with a garlic-butter sauce of white wine, sautéed onions, mushrooms, and green peppers. Ice creams are homemade: Try the chocolate-raspberry and coconut-

macadamia. *6307 Delmar Blvd., tel. 314/725–6985. Casual dress. Reservations advised. AE, DC, MC, V. Closed Mon.*

## FREE TIME

### Fitness

*Hotel Facilities*
A number of St. Louis hotels have excellent health clubs, but they are open only to guests.

*Health Clubs*
**Modern Fitness** (9977 Manchester Rd., tel. 314/962–0800) has good facilities, free for a one-time visit. The plush, private atmosphere at the **Marquette YMCA** (314 N. Broadway, tel. 314/436–7070) draws lunchtime crowds from downtown businesses. Guests at downtown St. Louis hotels pay $4, other visitors pay a $8 day rate. The 25-yard pool at the **Downtown YMCA** (1528 Locust St., tel. 314/436–4100) opens at 5:45 AM for early risers. Also on the premises are an indoor track and handball court. Cost: $10 per visit. Facilities at **Body Builders** (8111 Clayton Rd., tel. 314/727–2639) include Universal circuits and free weights. Day rates are $10.

*Jogging*
Paths on the grounds of the Gateway Arch are convenient for both runners and walkers staying at downtown hotels. Forest Park's tree-lined bicycle paths double as a 10k-run past golf courses, softball diamonds, 1904 World's Fair relics, and stately mansions.

### Shopping

**Plaza Frontenac mall** (South Lindbergh at Hwy. 40, tel. 314/432–0604) is an upscale complex anchored by Saks and Neiman-Marcus. Antiques are sold in the restored homes on lower Cherokee Street on the near south side. Try **Neon Lady** (1959 Cherokee St., tel. 314/771–7506) for 20th-century collectibles. At St. Louis's Union Station, **Accessory Lady** (tel. 314/621–4422) has a good selection of up-to-date purses, belts, and jewelry; and **John Pils** (190 St. Louis Union Station, tel. 314/421–1838) specializes in interesting framed views of St. Louis. **Famous-Barr** and **Dillard's**, St. Louis's top local department stores, are in most malls. Their flagship stores anchor St. Louis Centre at 515 N. Sixth Street. Fashions, antiques, fine gift items, and unusual jewelry can be found in boutiques in the Central West End.

### Diversions

**Anheuser-Busch Brewery** (One Busch Place, tel. 314/577–2626), five minutes south of downtown, has free tours and tastings on Mon.–Sat.

**Cathedral of St. Louis** (Lindell Blvd. and Newstead Ave., tel. 314/533–2824), in the Central West End, is notable for its interior, covered with mosaics depicting religious scenes and figures who played a vital role in St. Louis's history.

**Gateway Arch** (Riverfront, tel. 314/425–4465) is the nation's tallest memorial; visitors can ride to the top for a 30-

mile panoramic view. An underground museum honors the westward expansion of the United States.

**Gateway Riverboat Cruises** (Riverfront, tel. 314/621–4040) offers one-hour narrated cruises on the Mississippi.

**Missouri Botanical Garden** (4344 Shaw Blvd., tel. 314/577–5100) is a peaceful spot, 10 minutes southwest of downtown, where visitors can stroll through the largest Japanese garden in the United States.

**St. Louis Art Museum** (in Forest Park, tel. 314/721–0067) has an important collection of German Expressionist works as well as special exhibits throughout the year.

**St. Louis Sightseers** (tel. 314/355–6374) has tour buses that pick up at most hotels and run regularly scheduled half- and full-day tours.

**St. Louis Union Station** (18th and Market Sts., tel. 314/421–6655), the largest and busiest train station in the world when it was built in 1894, is now a festival marketplace of shops, entertainment venues, restaurants, and rail history exhibits.

**St. Louis Zoo** (in Forest Park, tel. 314/781–0900), known for its innovative displays, is an ideal place for a pleasant walk.

## Professional Sports

**Baseball.** St. Louis Cardinals, Busch Stadium, tel. 314/421–4040; **Hockey.** St. Louis Blues, The Arena, tel. 314/781–5300; **Soccer.** St. Louis Storm, The Arena, tel. 314/781–6475.

## The Arts

St. Louis boasts a lively and progressive arts community, heavily supported by local corporations and philanthropists. National touring companies play the **Fox Theatre** and the **Muny** in Forest Park. The St. Louis Symphony offers a full season at **Powell Hall,** and **Dance St. Louis** hosts visiting companies. The two repertory theater companies are popular. The **Opera Theatre** stages classics and new works each year. A full season of plays is produced by the avant-garde **Theatre Project Company.** Many St. Louis performing groups are in the newly developed **Grand Arts Center** along Grand Boulevard west of downtown.

Ticket agencies include **Dialtix** (tel. 314/434–6600), **Metrotix** (tel. 314/534–1111), **Ticketmaster** (2229 Pine St., tel. 314/652–5000), and **Tickets Now** (5700 Oakland Ave., tel. 314/644–2466).

**Black Repertory Company,** 634 N. Grand., tel. 314/534–3807.
**Dance St. Louis,** 149 Edgar Rd., tel. 314/968–4341.
**Fox Theatre,** 527 N. Grand Blvd., tel. 314/652–5000.
**Grand Arts Center,** N. Grand Blvd., between Lindell and Delmar Sts., tel. 314/533–1884.
**Muny,** Forest Park, tel. 314/361–1900.
**Opera Theatre,** Loretto-Hilton Center, tel. 314/961–0171.
**Repertory Theatre of St. Louis,** 130 Edgar Rd., tel. 314/968–4925.

**St. Louis Symphony,** 718 N. Grand Blvd., tel. 314/534–1700.
**Theatre Project Company,** 4219 Laclede Ave., tel. 314/531–1301.

## After Hours

Laclede's Landing, a restored 1800s warehouse district along the Mississippi, is home to many clubs and restaurants; the streets are original cobblestone, attractive but difficult to negotiate in heels. The West Port area and St. Louis Union Station both offer a variety of entertainment, from billiards to biergartens. The weekly *Riverfront Times*, published on Wednesdays, contains a complete entertainment guide. The Thursday Calendar section of the *St. Louis Post-Dispatch* also prints entertainment listings.

*Bars and Lounges*
**Pierre's** in Adam's Mark Hotel (tel. 314/241–7400) is a good place to take a client for a drink; it's fairly quiet, except for some light jazz and the subdued conversation of an elegant crowd. **Rupert's** (5130 Oakland Ave., tel. 314/993–6669) has a 16-piece pop orchestra for dancing. **John D. McGurk's Irish Pub** (12th and Russell, tel. 314/776–8309) features traditional Irish music and friendly regulars of all ages each night. In the summer, the **Biergarten** (Union Station, tel. 314/231–1234), under the Station's train shed, serves appetizers and beer to an after-work clientele. **Ozzie's** (645 West Port Plaza, tel. 314/434–1000), owned by shortstop Ozzie Smith, is filled with Cardinal baseball memorabilia. **Mike Shannon's** (100 N. Seventh St., tel. 314/421–1540) is a clubby bar/steak and seafood restaurant named for the Cardinal announcer. **Powerhouse Billiards** (Union Station, tel. 314/621–5900) has 10 tables and a '50s menu.

*Comedy Club*
The two **Funny Bone** clubs (940 West Port Plaza and 19 Ronnie's Plaza, tel. 314/469–6692) bring up-and-coming comics together.

*Jazz and Blues Clubs*
The historic Soulard neighborhood is the place to find good jazz from home-grown talent. **Hilary's** (1017 Russell Blvd., tel. 314/421–3126) and the nearby **Broadway Oyster Bar** (736 S. Broadway, tel. 314/621–9606) are two favorites. **Mike and Min's** (925 Geyer Ave., tel. 314/421–1655) is the best choice for blues.

*For Singles*
**AJ's** (Adam's Mark Hotel, tel. 314/241–7400) draws an under-45, after-work group for a happy-hour buffet, videos, and live bands. For casual chic, **Café Balaban** (405 N. Euclid, tel. 314/361–8085), in the Central West End neighborhood, is where a young upscale crowd comes together. A more mature gathering can be found in the piano bar at **Al Baker's** (8101 Clayton Rd., tel. 314/863–8878), where a jacket and tie are de rigueur. **The Big Kahuna** (2136 Schuetz Rd., tel. 314/993–9669) surf-style bar has no dress code, no cover, and a young, casual crowd.

# San Diego

*by Dan Janeck*

The first of a chain of 21 missions was established here by Junipero Serra in 1769, giving rise both to the town and to the Mission style of architecture. Since then, San Diego has grown steadily under Spanish, Mexican, and U.S. rule.

First-time visitors invariably marvel at the city's natural beauty, excellent location, and nearly perfect weather.

Despite these advantages, however, tourism ranks as only the third greatest revenue producer, after manufacturing (including the high-profile shipbuilding companies along the harbor) and the military (including activities such as aerospace engineering). The Navy continues to have a major presence here.

Housing development and construction were very strong in the late 1980s, but escalating costs may slow growth in the '90s. San Diego looks to higher education (the country's newest university is being built in North San Diego County), health care, communications, and tourism for expansion. Biotechnology is also burgeoning, with almost 100 companies engaged in extensive research and development throughout the county. And the opening of San Diego's $165-million convention center in late 1989 gave the city the opportunity to compete for sorely needed West Coast convention business. The waterfront complex, topped by an eye-catching sail-like roof, accommodates groups of more than 70,000 people.

The primary business communities in this very spread out city are downtown, Mission Valley, Kearny Mesa, La Jolla, North University City (more frequently called the Golden Triangle), Sorrento Mesa, and Otay Mesa in the South Bay. (Otay Mesa is also one of the main locations for San Diego county's *maquiladoras*, or twin-plant industries—a phenomenon of border cities in which management is headquartered in the United States while manufacturing operations are located in Mexico.) Long-time San Diego residents decry the city's "Los Angelization"—smog, freeway congestion, hordes of new residents, and disappearing wildlands. But development has brought a revitalized downtown, a cosmopolitan arts and theater community, and plenty of new office space—a familiar tradeoff, with the final accounting of gains and losses yet to be reckoned.

## Top Employers

| Employer | Type of Enterprise | Parent*/ Headquarters |
|---|---|---|
| Cubic Corp. | Electronics | San Diego |
| General Dynamics | Defense | St. Louis |
| Kaiser Permanente | Health maintenance | Kaiser Permanente Medical Care Program/ Oakland, CA |
| Pacific Bell | Telephone company | Pacific Telesis Group/ San Francisco |
| Rohr Industries | Aerospace | Chula Vista, CA |
| San Diego Gas & Electric | Utility | San Diego |
| Scripps Clinic | Health care & biomedical research | La Jolla, CA |
| Scripps Memorial Hospitals | Health Care | San Diego |
| Sharp HealthCare | Hospital & medical services | San Diego |
| University of California, San Diego | Education & research | University of California, Oakland, CA |

*if applicable

## ESSENTIAL INFORMATION

### Climate

What follows are the average daily maximum and minimum temperatures for San Diego.

| Jan. | 62F 17C<br>46 8 | Feb. | 62F 17C<br>48 9 | Mar. | 64F 18C<br>50 10 |
|---|---|---|---|---|---|
| Apr. | 66F 19C<br>53 12 | May | 66F 19C<br>55 13 | June | 69F 21C<br>59 15 |
| July | 73F 23C<br>62 17 | Aug. | 73F 23C<br>64 18 | Sept. | 73F 23C<br>62 17 |
| Oct. | 71F 22C<br>57 14 | Nov. | 69F 21C<br>51 11 | Dec. | 64F 18C<br>48 9 |

### Airport

San Diego's airport, **Lindbergh Field,** is just three miles northwest of downtown.

## Airport Business Facilities

The airport has fax machines open to the public in the East Terminal by the United gate. **Mutual of Omaha's Insurance Counter** (East Terminal, tel. 619/295–1501) has Western Union, travel insurance, and traveler's checks. **Union Bank** (East Terminal, tel. 619/230–4340) offers cash advances.

## Airlines

**Alaska,** tel. 800/426–0333.
**American,** tel. 619/232–4051 or 800/433–7300.
**American Eagle,** tel. 800/433–7300.
**American West,** tel. 619/560–0727 or 800/247–5692.
**British Airways,** tel. 619/298–0550 or 800/247–9297.
**Continental,** tel. 619/232–9155 or 800/231–0856.
**Delta,** tel. 619/235–4344 or 800/221–1212.
**Northwest,** tel. 619/239–0488 or 800/447–4747.
**Pan Am,** tel. 800/221–1111.
**Skywest/Delta,** tel. 800/453–9417.
**Southwest,** tel. 619/232–1221 or 800/531–5601.
**TWA,** tel. 619/295–7009 (domestic), 619/295–0094 (international) or 800/221–2000.
**United,** tel. 619/234–7171 or 800/241–6522.
**USAir,** tel. 619/574–1234 or 800/428–4322.

## Between the Airport and Downtown

*By Taxi*
Taxis can generally do the trip downtown in 7–10 minutes. Cost: $6–$8. Trips to other business areas—La Jolla, Kearny Mesa, Mission Valley, Sorrento Mesa, Mira Mesa, and South Bay—range from 15–45 minutes, depending on highway traffic. Cost: $15

*By Public Bus*
San Diego Transit bus line No. 2 is the direct public transportation link between Lindbergh and downtown. Buses leave every 30 minutes from 5:10 AM to midnight from East Terminal. Buses also stop at the West Terminal and take about 20 minutes to reach downtown, where they make two stops: 3rd St. & Broadway and 15th St. & Broadway. Cost: $1; 50¢ for seniors or disabled.

*By Private Bus*
**SuperShuttle** provides 24-hour, door-to-door service in bright blue vans. Dial 69 on the airport's courtesy phone or call 619/278–5700. To request service to the airport, call 619/278–8877. Cost: about $5. **Peerless Shuttle** (tel. 619/695–1766) also provides service to downtown. Cost: $5–$8.

## Car Rentals

The following car rental companies have booths at Lindbergh Field or very near the airport:

**Alamo,** tel. 619/297–0311 or 800/327–9633.
**Avis,** tel. 619/231–7171 or 800/331–1212.
**Budget,** tel. 619/279–2900 or 800/527–0700.
**Dollar,** tel. 619/234–3388 or 800/421–6868.
**Hertz,** tel. 619/231–7000 or 800/654–3131.
**National,** tel. 619/231–7000 or 800/227–7368.
**Thrifty,** tel. 619/239–2281 or 800/367–2277.

## Emergencies

*Doctors*

**Info Line** (tel. 619/549–0997), and **San Diego County Medical Society** (tel. 619/565–8161) offer referral services. **Ask-A-Nurse** is an information line (tel. 619/696–8100). **Assured Health Care** (1075 Camino del Rio S., Mission Valley, tel. 619/295–3355) and **Sharp Rees-Stealy Medical Group** (2001 4th Ave., downtown, tel. 619/234–6261, and other locations in San Diego) are emergency clinics.

*Dentists*

**San Diego County Dental Society** (tel. 619/223–5391) is a referral service.

*Hospitals*

**KaiserPermanente** (4647 Zion Ave., Mission Valley area, tel. 619/528–5000), **Scripps Memorial Hospitals** (9888 Genesee Ave., La Jolla, tel. 619/457–4123 and 435 H St., Chula Vista, tel. 619/691–7000), **Sharp Memorial Hospital** (7901 Frost St., Kearny Mesa, tel. 619/541–3400), **UCSD Medical Center** (225 Dickinson St., Hillcrest, tel. 619/543–6222).

## Important Addresses and Numbers

**Audiovisual rentals.** Audio Visual Headquarters (10950 N. Torrey Pines Rd., La Jolla, tel. 619/558–7662), AV West (5097 Santa Fe St., near Pacific Beach, tel. 619/270–7800), Photo and Sound (3553 California St., near Old Town, tel. 619/291–3380).

**Chamber of Commerce** (Downtown: Emerald-Shapery Center, 402 W. Broadway, 10th floor, tel. 619/232–0124; North San Diego County: 4275 Executive Sq., La Jolla-Golden Triangle, tel. 619/450–1518).

**Computer rentals.** Computer Rents (4934 Voltaire St., Ocean Beach, tel. 619/223–2202), Micro-Rent (8950 Villa La Jolla Dr., Suite 1200, La Jolla-Golden Triangle, tel. 619/232–8707), Personal Computer Rentals county-wide phone service (tel. 619/576–8500).

**Convention and exhibition centers.** Convention and Performing Arts Center (202 C St., downtown, tel. 619/236–6500), San Diego Convention Center (111 W. Harbor Dr., downtown, tel. 619/525–5000).

**Fax services.** American Mail & Fax Center (3808 Rosecrans St., near Pt. Loma, tel. 619/291–3421), Mail Boxes Etc. USA (35 locations, including 341 W. Broadway, downtown, tel. 619/232–0332), Postal Annex (30 locations, including 1043 University Ave., Hillcrest, tel. 619/298–7155), Words Etc. (3111 Camino del Rio N., Mission Valley, tel. 619/283–8060).

**Formal-wear rentals.** Gary's Tux Shop (9 locations, including 24 Horton Plaza, downtown, tel. 619/233–4277), Night & Day Formalwear (7 locations, including 114 Fashion Valley, Mission Valley, tel. 619/291–7810), Perfect Penguin (3 locations, including 3740 Sports Arena Blvd., near Pt. Loma, tel. 619/223–2677).

**Gift shops.** Gift Baskets: Dial-a-Gift of La Jolla (tel. 619/456–2888), Flowers: The Floral Emporium (441 Washington St., Hillcrest, tel. 619/293–7200), Chocolates: Godiva Chocolatier (Mission Valley Center, tel. 619/291–6775).

**Graphic design studios.** Covi Corp. (5333 Mission Center Rd., Mission Valley, tel. 619/295–1711), Design Group West (853 Camino del Mar, Del Mar, tel. 619/450–9200).

**Hairstylists.** Unisex: Haircut Store (18 locations, including 10450 Friars Rd., Mission Valley, tel. 619/279–5171), Razors Edge (122 Fashion Valley, Mission Valley, tel. 619/291–5330); Men: Westgate Hotel Barber Shop (1055 2nd Ave., downtown, tel. 619/234–1951).

**Health and fitness clubs.** *See* Fitness, below.

**Information hot lines.** San Diego Convention & Visitors Bureau's recorded announcements of events (tel. 619/239–9696), What's Happening (tel. 619/560–4094).

**Limousine services.** A Touch of Class (tel. 619/265–1995), La Jolla Limousine Service (tel. 619/459–5891), The Livery (tel. 619/234–3600), Paul the Greek's (tel. 619/287–6888), Presidential Limousine (tel. 619/291–2820).

**Liquor stores.** Chip's Liquor Store (1926 Garnet Ave., Pacific Beach, tel. 619/273–1536), Liquor Barn (6 locations, including 4175 Park Blvd., near Hillcrest, tel. 619/291–1890), Liquor Land Discount (5 locations, including 4001 W. Point Loma Blvd., tel. 619/223–4397).

**Mail delivery, overnight.** Airborne Express (tel. 619/293–7570), DHL Worldwide Express (tel. 619/571–0271), Emery & Purolator Worldwide (tel. 800/645–3333), Federal Express (tel. 619/295–5545), Flying Tigers (tel. 619/295–5304), TNT Skypak (619/270–0681), UPS (tel. 619/565–1551), U.S. Post Office Express Mail (tel. 619/574–5230).

**Messenger services.** Executive Express (tel. 619/280–0600), Marathon Messenger San Diego (tel. 619/270–6300), Road Runners (tel. 619/544–1200), United Couriers (tel. 619/278–1000).

**Office space rentals.** Coronado Plaza Executive Offices (1330 Orange Ave., Coronado, tel. 619/437–1871), La Jolla Management Group (7825 Fay Ave., Suite 200, La Jolla, tel. 619/456–3500), Prestige Executive Offices (555 W. Beech, downtown, tel. 619/231–4425).

**Pharmacies, 24-hour.** Sharp Cabrillo Hospital (3475 Kenyon St., near Point Loma, tel. 619/221–3711), Sharp Memorial Hospital (7901 Frost St., Kearny Mesa, tel. 619/541–3711).

**Radio stations, all-news.** XTRA 690 AM, KSDO 1130 AM.

**Secretarial services.** HQ–Headquarters (4350 La Jolla Village Dr., Golden Triangle, tel. 619/546–5000), The Total Office (964 5th Ave., downtown, tel. 619/544–1433), Words Etc. (3111 Camino del Rio N., Mission Valley, tel. 619/283–8060).

**Stationery supplies.** International Office Supply (4186 Sorrento Valley Blvd., Mira Mesa, tel. 619/457–0335), The Office Supply Store (9340 Clairemont Mesa Blvd., Kearny Mesa, tel. 619/571–3423), San Diego Office Supply (8 locations, including 1035 7th Ave., downtown, tel. 619/232–7661).

**Taxis.** Checker Cab (tel. 619/234–4477), Coast Cab (tel. 619/226–8294), La Jolla Cab (tel. 619/453–4222), Orange Cab (tel. 619/291–3333), Yellow Cab (tel. 619/234–6161).

**Theater tickets.** *See* The Arts, below.

**Train information.** Amtrak (1050 Kettner Blvd., downtown, tel. 619/239–9021 or 800/872–7245); San Diego Trolley, light rail service from downtown to South Bay and East County (tel. 619/231–8549).

**Travel agents.** American Express Travel Service (1020 Prospect St., La Jolla, tel. 619/459–4161), Draper World Travel (1551 4th Ave., downtown, tel. 619/531–0070), Travel Headquarters (9665 Chesapeake Dr., Kearny Mesa, tel. 619/541–1710).

**Weather** (tel. 619/289–1212).

## LODGING

Many business areas, shopping centers, and cultural attractions are very close to downtown and the airport, which means that business travelers don't have to spend much time in a taxi or rental car. Hotels listed below are in centrally sited areas of town; each location has its particular advantages. Downtown hotels are close to the financial district, the Convention Center, and many of the city's law offices. Hostelries in Coronado offer a quiet refuge from the hubbub of downtown, just across the bay. Mission Valley lodgings, 10 minutes from downtown and the airport, are convenient to two major shopping centers, numerous insurance companies, and development and real estate companies. The area is also close to Kearny Mesa and points east. Beach and bay hotels have good recreational benefits—and are minutes away from the airport and La Jolla, which has its own financial and legal district. Close to La Jolla is the Golden Triangle, one of San Diego's newest business districts, where development companies and banks continue to establish offices. Even with the proximity of San Diego's hotels to offices and attractions, it's important to factor in the increased freeway congestion at rush hour.

A number of the hotels listed below offer corporate rates; inquire when making reservations.

Highly recommended lodgings in each price category are indicated by a star ★.

| Category | Cost* |
| --- | --- |
| *$$$$* (Very Expensive) | over $165 |
| *$$$* (Expensive) | $126–$165 |
| *$$* (Moderate) | under $125 |

*All prices are for a standard double room, single occupancy, excluding 9% tax.*

*Numbers in the margin correspond to numbered hotel locations on the San Diego Lodging and Dining map.*

# SAN DIEGO

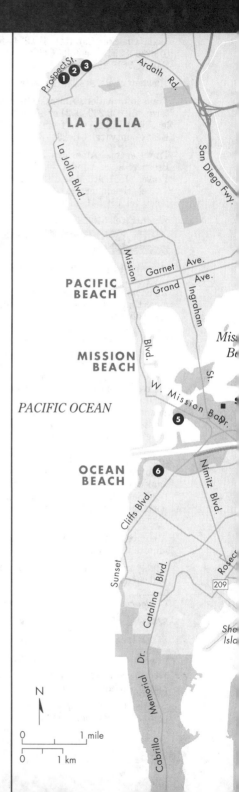

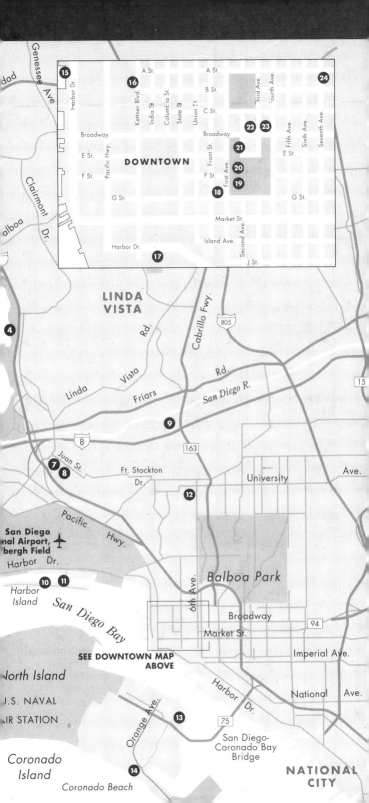

# SAN DIEGO HOTEL CHART

| HOTELS | Price Category | Business Services | | | | | | | | | | | |
|---|---|---|---|---|---|---|---|---|---|---|---|---|---|
| | | Banquet capacity | No. of meeting rooms | Secretarial services | Audiovisual equipment | Teletype news service | Computer rentals | In-room modem phone jack | All-news cable channel | Desk | Desk lighting | Bed lighting |
| Hilton Beach and Tennis Resort | $$$ | 900 | 10 | ✓ | ✓ | ✓ | ✓ | ✓ | ✓ | ● | ● | ● |
| Hotel del Coronado | $$$$ | 1500 | 45 | ✓ | ✓ | - | ✓ | ✓ | ✓ | ● | ● | ● |
| Hyatt Islandia | $$$ | 500 | 15 | ✓ | ✓ | - | ✓ | ✓ | ✓ | ◑ | ◑ | ● |
| Marriott Hotel and Marina | $$$ | 1000 | 40 | ✓ | ✓ | - | ✓ | ✓ | ✓ | ● | ● | ● |
| Marriott Suites at Symphony Towers | $$$ | 100 | 6 | - | ✓ | - | - | ✓ | ✓ | ● | ● | ● |
| Le Meridien San Diego at Coronado | $$$$ | 630 | 16 | ✓ | ✓ | - | ✓ | ✓ | ✓ | ● | ● | ● |
| Omni San Diego | $$$ | 864 | 18 | ✓ | ✓ | - | ✓ | ✓ | ✓ | ● | ● | ● |
| Sheraton Grande on Harbor Island | $$$$ | 400 | 10 | - | ✓ | - | ✓ | ✓ | ✓ | - | - | ◑ |
| Sheraton Harbor Island | $$$ | 4000 | 29 | ✓ | ✓ | - | ✓ | ✓ | ✓ | ● | ● | ● |
| Town and Country | $$ | 3000 | 21 | ✓ | ✓ | - | - | ✓ | ✓ | - | - | ● |
| U.S. Grant | $$$$ | 680 | 17 | ✓ | ✓ | - | ✓ | - | ✓ | ● | ● | ● |
| La Valencia | $$$$ | 175 | 4 | ✓ | ✓ | - | ✓ | ✓ | ✓ | ● | ● | ● |
| Westgate | $$$$ | 240 | 14 | ✓ | ✓ | - | ✓ | ✓ | ✓ | ● | ● | ● |

$$$$ = over $165, $$$ = $126-$165, $$ = under $125.
● good, ◑ fair, ○ poor.
All hotels listed here have photocopying and fax facilities.

| In-Room Amenities | | | | | | | | | | Hotel Amenities | | | | | | |
| Nonsmoking rooms | In-room checkout | Minibar | Pay movies | VCR/Movie rentals | Hairdryer | Toiletries | Room service | Laundry/Dry cleaning | Pressing | Concierge | Barber/Hairdresser | Garage | Courtesy airport transport | Sauna | Pool | Exercise room |
|---|---|---|---|---|---|---|---|---|---|---|---|---|---|---|---|---|
| ✓ | ✓ | ✓ | ✓ | – | – | ● | ◗ | ● | ◗ | ✓ | ✓ | – | ✓ | ✓ | ● | ● |
| – | ✓ | ✓ | – | – | – | ● | ● | ● | ● | ✓ | ✓ | – | – | ✓ | ● | ● |
| ✓ | ✓ | – | – | – | – | ● | ◗ | ● | ◗ | ✓ | – | ✓ | ✓ | – | ● | – |
| ✓ | ✓ | ✓ | ✓ | – | – | ● | ● | ● | ● | ✓ | ✓ | – | ✓ | – | ◗ | – |
| ✓ | ✓ | – | ✓ | – | – | ● | ◗ | ● | ◗ | ✓ | – | ✓ | ✓ | ✓ | ◗ | ◗ |
| ✓ | ✓ | ✓ | ✓ | – | – | ● | ● | ● | ● | ✓ | ✓ | ✓ | – | ✓ | ● | ● |
| ✓ | ✓ | ✓ | ✓ | – | – | ● | ● | ● | ● | ✓ | – | ✓ | ✓ | – | ● | ● |
| ✓ | ✓ | ✓ | ✓ | – | – | ◗ | ● | ● | ◗ | ✓ | – | – | ✓ | – | ● | – |
| ✓ | ✓ | ✓ | ✓ | ✓ | – | ● | ● | ● | ◗ | ✓ | – | – | ✓ | ✓ | ● | ● |
| ✓ | ✓ | – | ✓ | – | – | ● | ● | ● | ● | ✓ | ✓ | ✓ | – | ✓ | ● | – |
| ✓ | – | – | ✓ | – | – | ● | ● | ● | ● | ✓ | – | ✓ | ✓ | – | – | ◗ |
| – | – | – | ✓ | – | – | ● | ◗ | ● | ◗ | ✓ | – | – | ✓ | – | ● | ◗ |
| ✓ | – | ✓ | – | – | ✓ | ◗ | ● | ● | ● | ✓ | ✓ | ✓ | ✓ | – | – | – |

**Room service:** ● 24-hour, ◗ 6AM-10PM, ○ other.
**Laundry/Dry cleaning:** ● same day, ◗ overnight, ○ other.
**Pressing:** ● immediate, ◗ same day, ○ other.

## Downtown

**㉔** **Marriott Suites at Symphony Towers.** This all-suites high-
$$$ rise hotel in San Diego's financial district opened in Janu-
ary 1990. With their marble bathrooms and French doors
that shut off the bedrooms from the parlors, the three-
room suites feel like cozy pied-à-terres. Amenities such as
two phones with modems and call waiting make these ex-
cellent homes-away-from-home for business travelers
(though the conference rooms, as well as the pool and exer-
cise rooms, are small). If a view is essential, request a
room that faces north toward Balboa Park; southern
rooms face offices in the adjoining tower that hosts the San
Diego Symphony. The hotel entrance is at ground level,
but the lobby is on the 12th floor, reachable by express ele-
vators. *701 A St., 92101, tel. 619/696–9800 or 800/228–
9290, fax 619/696–1555. Gen. manager, Ron Berger. 264
suites. AE, CB, D, DC, MC, V.*

**㉕** **Omni San Diego Hotel.** The 16-floor Omni is located in
$$$ Horton Plaza, an urban playground with a myriad of de-
partment and specialty stores, restaurants, cinemas, and
theaters, which is why such celebrities as Alec Baldwin
and Dudley Moore can be counted among its guests. It's
also close to the Convention Center and the many financial
and legal offices scattered along Broadway. Rooms have a
Southwestern ambience, with their soft peach and beige
tones, and bleached wood furnishings. Fitness facilities,
which include tennis courts, are excellent. The Omni Club
Level, on the top floor, has its own concierge, check-in
area, and private lounge. The Café San Diego (*see* Business Breakfasts, below) attracts the downtown business
crowd in the mornings. The hotel staff is enthusiastic and
courteous. *910 Broadway Circle, 92101, tel. 619/239–2200
or 800/843–6664, fax 619/239–0509. Gen. manager, Luis
Barrios. 429 rooms, 21 suites. AE, CB, DC, MC, V.*

**★ ㉗** **San Diego Marriott Hotel & Marina.** This hotel complex,
$$$ comprising two 25-story glass towers, employs nearly
2,000 people, ensuring attentive service in the restau-
rants, fitness club, and banquet facilities. All rooms in the
north tower, refurbished in October 1989, have balconies.
The views in both towers are generally superlative, but
the best are from rooms on the higher floors overlooking
San Diego Bay. Pluses for business travelers (among
them, Ted Turner) include the largest ballroom in San
Diego, some 40 meeting rooms, fully staffed office facili-
ties for rent, and concierge levels with private lounges,
complimentary breakfasts, and afternoon hors d'oeuvres.
Personal touches include fruit baskets in every room.
Among the recreational facilities are tennis courts and a
246-slip marina with boats for rent. *333 W. Harbor Dr.,
92101, tel. 619/234–1500 or 800/228–9290, fax 619/234–
8678. Gen. manager, Joel Rothman. 1,195 rooms, 97
suites. AE, CB, D, DC, MC, V.*

**★ ㉓** **U.S. Grant Hotel.** The premier downtown historic hotel,
$$$$ the Grant, was reopened in 1985 after a four-year, multi-
million-dollar revamp that restored much of its original
splendor. Built in 1910, the hotel has provided lodging to
U.S. presidents and continues to appeal to an upper-eche-
lon clientele, from heads of state to CEOs. The ornate lob-
by, with its grandiose Palladian columns and crystal
chandeliers, is the site of afternoon teas where executives

mingle with frazzled shoppers from Horton Plaza, just across the street. The Queen Anne-style rooms are sumptuously furnished in rich mahogany and feature four-poster beds, armoires, wing-back chairs, and travertine-marble baths; suites come with whirlpool bathtubs. Nearly all rooms face the street; the south-facing rooms, looking out toward Horton Plaza and Coronado, are the plums. All meeting rooms are elegantly appointed to reflect the luxury of the hotel, and the grand ballroom is the scene of some of this city's most spectacular functions. The Grant Grill (*see* Dining, below) is a gathering spot for the power brokers in town. Note: Contrasting with all this opulence is a rather seedy zone of transients between the hotel and Horton Plaza; the Grant staff will escort those wishing to cross to the shopping center at night. *A member of Preferred Hotels Worldwide. 326 Broadway, 92101, tel. 619/232–3121 or 800/237–5029, fax 619/232–3626. Gen. manager, John Roberts. 219 rooms, 64 suites. AE, CB, DC, MC, V.*

**㉒** **Westgate Hotel.** In the heart of downtown, this extrava-
$$$$ gantly opulent 20-floor hotel might seem more at home in Imperial-era Paris: Its public areas are filled with glittering Baccarat crystal chandeliers, 14-karat gold fixtures, tapestries, and antiques. Its rooms and suites, though definitely first-class, are not quite as extravagant. Marble bathrooms, high ceilings, armoires, two-line speaker phones, and city views are common to the rooms and suites, which show English Regency and Georgian influences. Private entry hallways for every two rooms afford extra security. Additional amenities include: Mercedes shuttle service to and from the airport; a Trolley stop right outside the hotel; and many airline ticket offices on site. The elegant restaurant, Le Fontainebleau Room (*see* Dining, below), features white-gloved service in keeping with the hotel's European style; afterwards, you can retire to the tony Plaza Bar (*see* After Hours, below). *A member of The Leading Hotels of the World. 1055 2nd Ave., 92101, tel. 619/238–1818 or 800/221–3802, fax 619/232–4526. Gen. manager, Billie Neff. 212 rooms, 11 suites. AE, CB, D, DC, MC, V.*

## Coronado

★ **⑭** **Hotel del Coronado.** It's a matter of dispute whether the
$$$$ Prince of Wales first met Wallis Simpson here, but there's no question that this is one of the most heralded historic hotels in the country. Considered extravagant when it was built in 1888 in Victorian style—its red-roofed turrets are instantly recognizable as you come over the San Diego-Coronado Bay Bridge from downtown—the Del has played host to 12 U.S. presidents, many foreign dignitaries, and countless screen stars. A recently completed renovation brings new polish to common areas, and Italian marble baths with Roman pedestal sinks, cherry-wood armoires, and quilted bedspreads were added in many of the rooms. Floors do creak—but that's part of the charm in this National Historic Landmark. Ocean-view rooms are the best bets, though those that face the serene garden patio are quite acceptable. Even though it's known to generations of well-heeled travelers as a resort hotel, the Del currently does much convention business; its Grande Hall Convention Center can accommodate up to 1,500. A piano

lounge, The Palm Court (*see* After Hours, below), and three top-notch restaurants also service the hotel: the Prince of Wales, the Ocean Terrace Lounge, and the Crown/Coronet Room. *1500 Orange Ave., Coronado, 92118, tel. 619/522–8000 or 619/435–6611, fax 619/435–6611. Gen. manager, Scott W. Anderson. 654 rooms, 37 suites. AE, CB, D, DC, MC, V.*

⑬ **Le Meridien San Diego at Coronado.** This resort hotel of-
$$$$  fers high-end accommodations with a Gallic ambience, attracting business travelers who like both its proximity to downtown (five minutes away) and the feeling of being worlds away from the city's hustle and bustle. The Meridien's rustic-looking three-story buildings are set amid bougainvillea and man-made lagoons, and its rooms are country-French-style, bathed in light colors. Luxurious villa suites, in outlying units, feature Berber carpets, wet bars, and light-wood armoires. An on-premises spa and the Clarins Institut de Beauté offer such sybaritic indulgences as hydrotherapy baths, herbal wraps, and massages (costs for these services are extra). Other pluses include a superb Continental restaurant and a hospitable staff. *2000 2nd St., Coronado, 92118, tel. 619/435–3000 or 800/543–4300, fax 619/435–3032. Gen. manager, Fabio Piccirillo. 265 rooms, 35 suites. AE, CB, DC, MC, V.*

## Mission Valley

⑨ **Town & Country Hotel.** This 32-acre property located in
$$  Mission Valley's Hotel Circle, just a few hundred yards from the Fashion Valley Shopping Center, was established in 1953. The original one- and two-story bungalows with wood-shingle roofs are set amid palm trees and close to four pools; rooms in these rustic accommodations are moderately priced—good for business people who are on a budget or are traveling with family. Rooms in the two high-rise towers, built in the 1970s and recently renovated, are Colonial style, with cherry-wood headboards, desks, armoires, floral bedspreads, and canopies. Hospitality suites, on the first level of the west tower, are decorated with light colors, large wall mirrors, and wicker furniture; these open out toward the pool area for typical Southern California entertaining. Although the hotel is close to major attractions such as Balboa Park and the San Diego Zoo, its primary draw for business travelers is its convention center, which offers 21 meeting rooms and a grand ballroom that accommodates groups of 3,000. *An Atlas Hotel. 500 Hotel Circle N., 92108, tel. 619/291–7131 or 800/854–2608, fax 619/291–3584. Gen. manager, Tom Schoch. 1,000 rooms, 62 suites. AE, CB, D, DC, MC, V.*

## Beach/Bay

❺ **Hyatt Islandia.** This could be considered *the* beach hotel—
$$$  the 18-floor tower, located in San Diego's aquatic playground, Mission Bay, is a frisbee's throw from beaches, marinas, and Sea World. Rooms face inland or overlook the shoreline to the west, and have just been through a multi-million-dollar spruce-up. Floors 8–10 are for members of Gold Passport, Hyatt Regency's frequent visitor program; benefits include express check-in and check-out, with the bill slipped under the door; morning newspaper delivery; and an express breakfast delivered in 10 minutes. Floors 16 and 17, the Regency Club levels, are acces-

sible only by elevator keys; rooms on these floors have upgraded amenities, and guests receive complimentary Continental breakfast and evening hors d'oeuvres in the concierge lounge. Marina suites, added in 1988 adjacent to the tower, have spacious rooms, appointed in desert colors, and equipped with a VCR, two TVs, and two phones. *1441 Quivira Rd., 92109, tel. 619/224–1234 or 800/233–1234, fax 619/224–0348. Gen. managers, Herb Rafetto and Edward G. Sullivan. 339 rooms, 84 suites. AE, CB, D, DC, MC, V.*

**①** **La Valencia Hotel.** This picturesque, pink, Mediterra-
**$$$$** nean-style hostelry in the heart of exclusive La Jolla evokes an era when locals could spot Hollywood luminaries strolling near the bougainvillea in the gardens or in the Spanish mosaic-tiled main arcade. The charming eight-story "La V" is still a favorite getaway for actors such as William Hurt and Barbra Streisand, who cherish its prime location near La Jolla Cove, and its overall romantic atmosphere. The hotel offers many amenities for business travelers as well, including bathroom phones. Most rooms were recently renovated in contemporary California-style, with oak-wood furnishings and mirrored ceilings at the entranceway. Accommodations facing the Pacific are the most requested and most expensive, but garden, courtyard, and street views are desirable, too. The devoted staff—many members of it have been with the hotel more than 30 years—is cordial and efficient. La Jolla movers and shakers can be found in The Mediterranean Room in the morning, and in the Whaling Bar & Grill (*see* Dining, below) later in the day. *A member of Preferred Hotels Worldwide. 1132 Prospect St., La Jolla, 92037, tel. 619/454–0771 or 800/451–0772, fax 619/456–3921. Man. director, Patrick Halcewicz. 90 rooms, 10 suites. AE, DC, MC, V.*

**④** **San Diego Hilton Beach and Tennis Resort.** Like the
**$$$** Hyatt Islandia, this hotel offers the lure of a prime bayside location, which makes it a good choice for recreation-minded business travelers, or those bringing along the family. Guests can rent bikes, jog along Mission Bay, sail, swim in the 25-meter pool, or play tennis. Located on I–5, the Hilton is convenient to business areas as well: it's only 10–15 minutes away from Mission Valley, Kearny Mesa, La Jolla, the Golden Triangle, and downtown. Rooms in the eight-floor tower were last renovated in late 1989; new carpets, drapes, floral bedspreads, and wall coverings were among the improvements. The Garden Court lanai rooms, built in 1985 primarily for corporate travelers, are close to the water and feature more spacious accommodations. In the evening contemporary jazz is offered at The Cargo Bar (*see* After Hours, below). *1775 E. Mission Bay Dr., 92109, tel. 619/276–4010 or 800/445–8667, fax 619/276–4010, ext. 7991. Gen. manager, H. L. Bert James. 335 rooms, 19 suites. AE, CB, D, DC, MC, V.*

## Airport

**⑩** **Sheraton Grand on Harbor Island.** Although the two
**$$$$** Sheratons on Harbor Island are separate properties (*see* below), they are only 300 yards apart and share facilities. The 12-story Grand is the grander of the two: its lobby boasts marble floors, recessed lighting, fountains, and original artwork. Rooms are expansive and considerably

more plush than those in the Sheraton Harbor Island (known as Sheraton East); the 11th floor is staffed by butlers. Rooms on one side of the hotel face the airport; rooms on the other side look toward the bay and are highly recommended, though they are pricier. The Grand does not offer as many business-related amenities as its sister property—secretarial services are referred to the Sheraton East's business center—nor does it have its sister hotel's extensive recreational facilities, but it has a lot more elegance and charm. *1506 Harbor Island Dr., 92101, tel. 619/291–6400 or 800/325–3535, fax 619/291–4847. Gen. manager, Ken Gifford. 328 rooms, 22 suites. AE, CB, D, DC, MC, V.*

**⑪ Sheraton Harbor Island Hotel.** This is the hotel closest to
**$$$** the airport and one of the most popular conference sites in the city, featuring two large ballrooms and a banquet capacity of nearly 4,000 people. Built in 1972, and completely renovated in 1990, the 12-floor hotel has spectacular skyline and harbor views (request floors eight and up). The upgrade gave the rather small rooms brighter colors and marble bathroom counters. The 200-unit lanai village features the hotel's most casual lodging, especially good for families. This recreational hub of the two Sheratons has a fully equipped health club and three swimming pools. It's no noisier here than at the Sheraton Grand; you can expect some jet sounds at both hotels, no matter which floor you book or which direction you face. *1380 Harbor Island Dr., 92101, tel. 619/291–2900 or 800/325–3535, fax 619/296–5297. Gen. manager, Larry Saward. 675 rooms, 35 suites. AE, CB, D, DC, MC, V.*

# DINING

Although the number of trendy restaurants in San Diego has skyrocketed in recent years, some longtime institutions—many cited here—are still *the* places to go for superb meals. Nor should one miss the opportunities this border town affords for good Mexican food; two options in San Diego's Old Town are listed below. And, as might be expected, the city also abounds in ocean- or bay-view restaurants that feature fresh seafood. However, don't think San Diego's restaurants have a beach town ambience; coat and tie, not resort wear, are expected in the better restaurants.

Highly recommended restaurants in each price category are indicated by a star ★.

| Category | Cost* |
|---|---|
| $$$$ (Very Expensive) | over $35 |
| $$$ (Expensive) | $26–$35 |
| $$ (Moderate) | $15–$25 |
| $ (Inexpensive) | under $15 |

*per person, including appetizer, entrée, and dessert, but excluding drinks, service, and 7.25% sales tax.*

*Numbers in the margin correspond to numbered restaurant locations on the San Diego Lodging and Dining map.*

## Business Breakfasts

Many San Diego business leaders aren't keen on eating big breakfasts, preferring to exercise or to catch up with their morning newspaper over a danish and coffee in the office—which means that the concept of the business breakfast has not completely caught on in this town. However, when they do go out for breakfast meetings, they're likely to head for **Hob Nob Hill** (2271 1st Ave., Bankers Hill, tel. 619/239–8176). San Diego's premier spot for breakfast, near downtown, opens at 7 AM, and its front booths quickly fill up with lawyers and politicians. Breakfast fare, served throughout the day, is above average, and includes the usual pancakes, waffles, egg dishes, and unusually good pecan rolls.

Other downtown breakfast spots include the U.S. Grant Hotel's **Grant Grill** (tel. 619/239–6806, also, *see* Downtown Restaurants, below) and the Omni San Diego Hotel's **Café San Diego** (tel. 619/239–2200). Open at 6:30 AM, the casual Café offers a breakfast buffet with eggs, omelets, and pancakes; waffles and salmon Benedict are among the items on the regular menu.

## Downtown

**⑮** **Anthony's Star of the Sea Room.** Anthony's chain of sea-
**$$$$** food restaurants has capitalized on San Diego's proximity to the ocean by offering consistently fresh seafood dishes. The Star of the Sea Room on the Embarcadero, the showcase restaurant of the chain, is where San Diegans go for special occasions. It is also well regarded by local business people, though the noise level does not generally allow for serious discussions. The elegant though somewhat stuffy dining room, with upholstered chairs and chandeliers, looks out on the bay—especially pretty at sunset. Anthony's is known for its abalone (be prepared to pay a hefty penny, though) and the vast selection of hot and cold appetizers. The cart service is a trademark here; most dishes are prepared tableside by the unobsequious staff. *1360 N. Harbor Dr., Embarcadero, tel. 619/232–7408. Jacket and tie required. Make reservations several days in advance. AE, MC, V. Dinner only.*

**⑫** **Celadon.** San Diego's toniest—and, many contend, best—
**$$** Thai restaurant, with dramatic glass-block partitions at the front and ceramics throughout the room, is a good place to come for an informal business lunch. In the evening, the restaurant's dimmed lights soften the pink and celadon green room to create a romantic, subdued atmosphere. The food is handsomely presented and innovatively prepared. Specialties, from mildly spiced to maximum burn, include such Thai standards as *mee krob*, an appetizer of rice vermicelli, chicken, and shrimp; chicken curry; and the picturesque pineapple boat, made with chicken, sausage, and rice. Prevail upon the pleasant serving staff for suggestions and for a gauge of the "heat" levels of the food. *3628 Fifth Ave., Hillcrest, near downtown, tel. 619/295–8800. Reservations accepted. Dress: casual but neat. MC, V. Closed Sun.*

**㉑** **Dobson's.** For years, Dobson's has been a mecca for local
**$$$** politicians, bankers, and lawyers, but it is also a perennial favorite for après-theater dining. The long, narrow, mahogany bar attracts a congenial crowd waiting to go up-

stairs to the dining area. Tables are close together, and those nearest to the railing are coveted for their high visibility; this is definitely a place to see and be seen (and, in some cases, overheard)—not one for delicate negotiations. The menu reflects a predilection for seafood—the savory mussel bisque is the restaurant's best-known dish. Dobson's has a superb selection of wines as well. *956 Broadway Circle, tel. 619/231–6771. Jacket and tie suggested. Reservations accepted. AE, MC, V.*

㉓ **Grant Grill.** A clubby haven for business dining, especially
$$$ at lunch, this highly regarded restaurant in the U.S. Grant Hotel consistently bustles with government officials, bankers, and PR and advertising reps. Those with a fondness for tradition will appreciate its richly stained mahogany paneling, antique wall lamps, and private leather booths. The luncheon menu in the main dining room offers such Grant signature dishes as mock turtle soup, Cobb salad, and its well-known hamburgers; an adjacent lounge features a copious buffet for quick-and-simple lunch meetings. Dinner selections emphasize grill items cooked on the large French rotisserie. Afternoon tea, with finger sandwiches and pastries, is served in the Grant's lobby daily. *326 Broadway, tel. 619/239–6806. Jacket and tie advised. Reservations advised at lunch, suggested at dinner. AE, MC, V.*

⑲ **Panda Inn.** Business travelers who are tired of steak and
$$ seafood often head to the Panda Inn, San Diego's most highly acclaimed Oriental restaurant. Mandarin/Szechuan cuisine is served in a room decorated in muted colors, with Chinese vases in niches. Standouts on the enormous menu include fried dumplings, sweet-and-pungent shrimp, orange-flavored beef, and lemon scallops. Service is gracious and quick, even during peak periods. Spacious booths can seat up to six people comfortably. *506 Horton Plaza, tel. 619/233–7800. Casual dress. Reservations accepted. AE, MC, V.*

⑯ **Rainwater's.** A few blocks from the county administration
$$$ building, this prime power-lunch and -dinner venue draws government officials, judges, attorneys, and sometimes even the mayor. Table No. 1 is the choice of judges (and the mayor); table 5 is the generic power table; table 51 is the best for visibility; and table 45, in the corner facing the train station, is known for its privacy. Perhaps deal-making is encouraged by the boardroom-style cherry-wood decor here. The chophouse fare follows the prenouvelle dining dictum, more is more: Massive cuts of Chicago corn-fed T-bone steak, prime rib, and Kansas City strip dominate. Also available are competently prepared lamb chops, catfish, lake perch, and free-range chicken. The sterling wine list puts a strong emphasis on California cabernets and chardonnays; an intimate wine room can be reserved for private meetings. A special snack menu makes Rainwater's a good place for late-night dining. *1202 Kettner Blvd., 2nd floor, tel. 619/233–5757. Jacket and tie advised. Reservations advised. AE, CB, DC, MC, V.*

★ ⑱ **Salvatore's.** On the bottom floor of an exclusive downtown
$$$ residential high rise, Salvatore's Northern Italian restaurant is elegantly turned out in soft colors, with columns and intricate moldings. You're likely to be greeted with *molto brio* by the Roman-born owner, a reception characteristic of the warm, personalized attention you'll find

here; those dining alone are treated exceptionally well. Pasta dishes are superb, especially the tagliatelle with cheese and ham in a cream sauce, and the rigatoni with peas, mushrooms, and prosciutto. Also outstanding is the saltimbocca topped with prosciutto and mozzarella and sprinkled with sage. The lunch crowd is heavily business-oriented; this is a place to get to know one another or celebrate a contract. At dinner, there's a good mix of theater-goers and foodies. *750 Front St., tel. 619/544–1865. Jacket and tie advised. Reservations advised. AE, MC, V. Closed Sun.*

## Along the Coast

**❻** **Belgian Lion.** Ocean Beach, about a 10-minute cab-ride
**$$** from downtown, is not an area known for sophisticated eateries, but this Belgian-French restaurant, with its lace curtains and tablecloths, tapestry-upholstered chairs, and Breughel prints, is a notable exception. The atmosphere is relaxed, but conducive to quiet conversations. Notable entrées in the owner/chef's repertoire include rabbit cooked in red wine; roast duckling with sauerkraut; and a sublime *cassoulet Castelnaudaray* (a hearty country-style casserole) of pork, lamb, sausage, beans, and confit of duck. Service is hospitable, and the wine list of some 400 selections has an even mix of California and French vineyards. *2265 Bacon St., Ocean Beach, tel. 619/223–2700. Casual but neat. Reservations advised. AE, DC, MC, V. Dinner only. Closed Sun. and Mon.*

**❸** **George's at the Cove.** A yuppie crowd now holds sway at
**$$$** this pastel-colored eatery, but George's has never lost the graciousness that endeared it to its first patrons, the La Jolla old-money establishment. The waiters are knowledgeable about entrée preparation and ingredients, and will help match the right wine to each dish. George's specializes in fresh seafood like ahi and shark prepared with light sauces in typical California-nouvelle fashion; pasta, beef, and poultry entrées are also above average. The tables are well spaced, and thus suitable for business discussions—if you can resist being distracted by the magnificent view of La Jolla Cove. Many locals just stop by for a drink at the upstairs bar (*see* After Hours, below). *1250 Prospect St., La Jolla, tel. 619/454–4244. Jacket and tie advised. Reservations advised. AE, CB, DC, MC, V.*

**★ ❷** **Top o' the Cove.** This exclusive dining room, with its
**$$$$** stained-oak furnishings and intimate banquettes, offers an excellent view of La Jolla Cove, as its name suggests. Huge Morton fig trees in the front make it easy to locate this converted late-19th-century beach cottage, on one of La Jolla's two main streets. At lunchtime the restaurant is filled with the attorneys, bankers, and stockbrokers who work in this posh community. Traditional Continental cuisine is favored here; the well-prepared entrées feature venison, beef, veal, and duckling in richly flavorful sauces. Pay particular attention to one of San Diego's best wine lists—it features 800 selections. A piano lounge near the entrance is a fine place to finish the business discussions begun at dinner (*see* After Hours, below). *1216 Prospect St., La Jolla, tel. 619/454–7779. Jacket and tie required. Reservations advised. AE, MC, V.*

**❶** **Whaling Bar & Grill.** The publike bar in La Valencia Hotel
**$$** is La Jolla's prime venue for business, attracting invest-
ment bankers, attorneys, and La Jolla's Old Guard as well
as UCSD professors, and scientists from nearby Scripps
Institute. The top table for visibility in the nautically dec-
orated bar/small dining area is No. 4; there's also a larger,
more formal dining room beyond. The cuisine is Continen-
tal, featuring lots of seafood entrées; the paella and *carne
asada* (roasted meat) are especially recommended. The
top-notch staff is extraordinarily helpful and polite. *1132
Prospect St., La Jolla, tel. 619/454-0771. Jacket and tie
advised. Reservations advised. AE, DC, MC, V.*

## Old Town

**❽** **Café Pacifica.** This seafood restaurant numbers local pub-
**$$** lic relations and media people among its regular lunch clientele. Although tables in the main dining room are too
close together for very private discussions, shop talk still
prevails at midday; if a really quiet conversation is de-
sired, reserve banquette No. 2 or 26. Rows of tiny lights
throughout the restaurant create a festive mood in the
evening, when people come here to relax. The fresh fish
may be ordered sautéed, baked, or broiled, or prepared in
more exotic fashion: Two recommended mainstays are
Cajun-style mustard catfish and Hawaiian ahi tuna with
shiitake mushrooms and ginger butter. The crème brûlée
**⑯** makes a fine finish. A sister restaurant downtown, **Pacifi-**
**$$** **ca Grill** (1202 Kettner Blvd., tel. 619/696-9226), specia-
lizes in imaginatively prepared Southwestern cuisine and
features firstrate *canarditas* (smoky-flavored duck
carnitas). This eatery is downstairs from Rainwater's (*see*
above), and attracts the same courthouse clientele. *Café
Pacifica: 2414 San Diego Ave., Old Town, tel. 619/291-
6666. Casual but neat. Reservations advised. AE, MC, V.*

**❼** **Old Town Mexican Café.** Sure it's a touristy place in a tour-
**$** isty area; but this long-time San Diego favorite, with its
boisterous Mexican market atmosphere and excellent
margaritas, is still one of the best places in town to ditch
the tie and the day's stress. Virtually all combinations on
the menu are good, but especially noteworthy are the beef
tacos and the carnitas—shredded, marinated meat
packed with cilantro, guacamole, and other Mexican con-
diments into freshly made tortillas. Expect to wait for a
table, even after 10 PM. *2489 San Diego Ave., Old Town,
tel. 619/297-4330. Casual dress. No reservations. AE,
MC, V.*

## FREE TIME

### Fitness

*Hotel Facilities*
The health club at the **Omni San Diego Hotel** offers tennis
and could easily compete with San Diego's larger member-
ship clubs; the day rate for nonguests is $5.

*Health Clubs*
**Bodyworks** (1130 7th Ave., tel. 619/232-5500; 2 other loca-
tions) has an extensive variety of machines available for
$10 daily or $25 weekly rates. **Family Fitness Centers** (12
locations in San Diego, tel. 619/281-5543 for Mission Val-
ley club) offer one-day memberships for $10. All have exer-

cise machines and weight rooms, and some Family Fitness facilities also offer racquetball. **Jack LaLanne's American Fitness and Athletic Club** has four locations in San Diego (3666 Midway Dr., tel. 619/223–5581, call for others) and charges a $10 day fee. **San Diego Athletic Club** (701 B St., tel. 619/239–3622), a choice spot for local corporate workouts if you're downtown, is open only to International Racquet Sports Association members for a daily rate of $10.

*Jogging*

San Diego offers a variety of scenic routes for joggers. **The Mission Bay Course,** from De Anza Cove to Fiesta Island and somewhat parallel to East Mission Bay Drive, covers about six miles and passes by the San Diego Hilton. The **Sheraton Harbor Island Hotel's** 9.8-mile jogging course that goes along Harbor Island, the harbor, Shelter Island, and out to the tip of Cabrillo National Monument is also open to the public. The **Mission Beach Boardwalk,** along Ocean Front Walk, is a great course, running 2.75 miles from Crystal Pier to the jetty, but it is somewhat crowded with bicyclists and skaters.

## Shopping

If you just want souvenirs of San Diego to take back for the kids, the best bet is **Seaport Village,** downtown, below the San Diego Marriott. If you prefer collectibles that reflect San Diego's multicultural heritage, take a swing by the historic Old Town district for a look in the various pottery places and curio shops, including, on the fringes of Old Town, **Bazaar del Mundo,** a colorful Mexican shopping village. For authentic Mexican handicrafts such as serapes, piñatas, and silver jewelry, it's best to head for **Tijuana,** across the Mexican border.

Downtown's shopping mecca, **Horton Plaza,** is a colorful, multilevel conglomeration of trendy boutiques, department stores, and reasonably priced specialty stores. **Prospect Street** is La Jolla's main artery for pricey specialty shops. European and high-end boutiques are on nearby **Girard Avenue.** For antiques, the western stretch of **Adams Avenue** is superb, as is downtown's **Gaslamp District.** Memorabilia shops can be found around **Park Boulevard** at University Avenue in Hillcrest. The heart of **Hillcrest,** around Fifth and University avenues, features trendy card stores and restaurants.

Some of the major department stores in San Diego include: **Nordstrom** (University Towne Centre, tel. 619/457–4575; Fashion Valley, tel. 619/295–4441; Horton Plaza, tel. 619/239–1700), **Saks Fifth Avenue** (Mission Valley Center, tel. 619/260–0030; 7600 Girard Ave., La Jolla, tel. 619/459–4123), **Neiman Marcus** (Fashion Valley, tel. 619/692–9100), **I. Magnin** (La Jolla Village Square, tel. 619/455–7111), **Bullock's** (Grossmont Center, La Mesa, tel. 619/698–6422; Mission Valley Center, tel. 619/299–9811), and **The Broadway** (Horton Plaza, tel. 619/231–4747; Fashion Valley, tel. 619/291–6011; Grossmont Center, tel. 619/465–1121; La Jolla Village Square, tel. 619/453–2060).

For gowns and festive apparel, head to La Jolla, especially **Capriccio** (6919 La Jolla Blvd., tel. 619/459–4189). Other standout boutiques include **Jaeger** (La Jolla Village Square, tel. 619/455–7449) and **Wagener** (7802 Girard

Ave., tel. 619/454–3301). Good clothing stores for businessmen, also in La Jolla, include **Gentlemen's Quarter** (1224 Prospect St., tel. 619/459–3351), **Igelman & Co.** (7643 Girard Ave., tel. 619/454–9699), and **Polo Ralph Lauren** (7830 Girard Ave., tel. 619/459–0554).

For leisure apparel, some of sun-crazy San Diego's top beachwear and activewear shops include **Pilar's Beachwear** (3745 Mission Blvd., Mission Beach, tel. 619/488–3056), **Hamel's Action Sports Center** (704 Ventura Pl., Mission Beach, tel. 619/488–5050), and **La Jolla Surf Systems** (2132 Avenida de la Playa, La Jolla, tel. 619/456–2777).

## Diversions

**Balboa Park,** in the heart of San Diego, reached by driving along Route 163 or taking Sixth Avenue north from downtown, has nearly 1,100 acres of greenery, flower gardens, and trails; it is also home to many of this city's museums and cultural attractions. If you have a day, it's worth coming here to explore the museums or to visit the zoo (*see* below). If you walk the main thoroughfare, El Prado, from the fountain at the east end to Sixth Avenue at the west end, you'll pass artisans, some of the Moorish-style buildings constructed for the 1915 Panama-California International Expo, and the California Tower, arguably the symbol of San Diego.

**Old Town** is considered the birthplace of San Diego, and Old Town State Historic Park (10 minutes north of downtown, off I–5) is a unique district comprised of museums, Mexican restaurants, Victorian houses, specialty shops, and the Whaley House Museum (2482 San Diego Ave., tel. 619/298–2482,) a Victorian house reputed to be haunted.

**Reuben H. Fleet Space Theater and Science Center** (east end of El Prado, Balboa Park, tel. 619/238–1168) shows documentaries filmed in lifelike Omnimax on a huge, dome-shaped screen, fun for both adults and children.

The world famous, 100-acre **San Diego Zoo** (Balboa Park, tel. 619/234–3153) features an impressive collection of animals, tropical greenery, and exhibits like Tiger River, where Sumatran tigers live in a tropical rain-forest setting. Because of its size, you may find the guided bus tour (takes about an hour) convenient.

Home of Shamu the Killer Whale, **Sea World** (1720 S. Shores Rd., Mission Bay, tel. 619/226–3901) is an ever-expanding aquatic park, featuring marine animals in simulations of their natural environments.

## Professional Sports

The **San Diego Padres,** the city's baseball club, play at the San Diego Jack Murphy Stadium (tel. 619/283–4494). The football club, the **San Diego Chargers,** also appear at the San Diego Jack Murphy Stadium (tel. 619/280–2121). **San Diego Sockers** play soccer at the Sports Arena (tel. 619/224–8497).

## The Arts

San Diego theaters, especially the **Old Globe** and the **La Jolla Playhouse,** are being used increasingly as testing grounds for plays aimed at Broadway. Companies that offer innovative theater in more intimate surroundings include **San Diego Repertory Theatre** and **Gaslamp Quarter Theatre Company (GQT)**. Light-opera productions are **Starlight's** mainstay. The **San Diego Symphony Orchestra** is based in elegant Symphony Hall, and musical organizations like **San Diego Opera** and **San Diego Master Chorale** perform throughout the city.

Ticket agencies include **Times Arts Tix** (Horton Plaza, tel. 619/238–3810), which offers day-of-performance seating at half price, cash only, **Buck's Ticket Service** (4450 Ingraham St., Pacific Beach, tel. 619/273–4567), **Advance Tickets** (4225 Balboa Ave., Kearny Mesa, tel. 619/581–1000), **Omni Tickets International** (3555 Rosecrans St., Sports Arena area, 619/224–3747), **Teleseat** (tel. 619/283–SEAT), **Ticketmaster** (tel. 619/278–8497), and **Ticketron** (tel. 619/268–9686).

**Hahn Cosmopolitan Theatre (GQT)**, 444 4th Ave., tel. 619/234–9583.
**La Jolla Playhouse**, Mandell Weiss Center, UCSD campus, tel. 619/534–3960.
**Lyceum Stage** and **Lyceum Space** (S.D. Repertory Theatre), Horton Plaza, tel. 619/235–8025.
**Elizabeth North Theatre (GQT)**, 547 4th Ave., tel. 619/234–9583.
**San Diego Repertory Theatre**, 1620 6th Ave., tel. 619/235–8025.
**Simon Edison Centre for the Performing Arts**, Balboa Park (includes the **Old Globe Theatre, Cassius Carter Centre Stage,** and **Lowell Davies Festival Theatre**), tel. 619/234–5623.
**Starlight Bowl**, Balboa Park, tel. 619/544–7827.
**Symphony Hall**, 1245 7th Ave., tel. 619/699–4200.

## After Hours

*Bars and Lounges*
The best spots for winding down to smooth piano stylings after a stress-filled day include the lounge at the old-line **Imperial House** (505 Kalmia St., Balboa Park area, tel. 619/234–3525), **The Palm Court** (Hotel del Coronado, tel. 619/435–6611), and **Top o' the Cove** (tel. 619/454–7779). Opera singers stop by the elegant **Plaza Bar** (Westgate Hotel, tel. 619/238–1818) and offer civilized entertainment for the price of a drink. The always-crowded bar above **George's at the Cove** (tel. 619/454–4244) attracts chicly dressed younger professionals.

*Cabarets/Nightclubs*
Clubs where the music is loud and danceable and the patrons spirited and youthful include **Club Diego's** (860 Garnet Ave., Pacific Beach, tel. 619/272–1241) and **Confetti** (5373 Mission Center Rd., Mission Valley, tel. 619/291–8635). Intimate clubs that offer first-rate concerts by local and nationally known performers and groups include **Bacchanal** (8022 Clairemont Mesa Blvd., Kearny Mesa, tel. 619/560–8022), **Belly Up Tavern** (143 S. Cedros Ave., Solana Beach, tel. 619/481–9022), and **Rio's** (4258 W. Point Loma Blvd., near Point Loma, tel. 619/225–9559). Clubs that showcase everything from rock to jazz to oldies include the **Old Pacific Beach Café** (4287 Mission Blvd., Pacific Beach, tel. 619/270–7522) and **Cannibal Bar** (Cata-

maran Hotel, 3999 Mission Blvd., Pacific Beach, tel. 619/488–1081).

## Comedy Clubs

Nationally known comics stop by **The Improv** (832 Garnet Ave., Pacific Beach, tel. 619/483–4521) and the **Comedy Store** (916 Pearl St., La Jolla, tel. 619/454–9176). **Comedy Isle** at the Bahia Resort Hotel (998 W. Mission Bay Dr., Mission Bay, tel. 619/488–6872) focuses on local talent.

## Jazz Clubs

Downtown professionals, 25–45, gather for after-work cocktails and banter and stay to listen to contemporary jazz at **Anthony's Harborside** (1355A N. Harbor Dr., tel. 619/232–6358), **B Street Café** (425 W. B St., tel. 619/236–1707), and **Croce's** (802 5th Ave., tel. 619/233–4355). The Hilton's **Cargo Bar** (tel. 619/276–4010) attracts a similar crowd in a nautical setting; **Diego's Loft** (860 Garnet Ave., Pacific Beach, tel. 619/272–1241) features selected local jazz artists, and **Humphrey's** on Shelter Island (2241 Shelter Island Dr., tel. 619/224–3577) hosts an extensive concert lineup of high-profile performers during the summer. Jazz purists usually prefer **Elario's** (7955 La Jolla Shores Dr., La Jolla, tel. 619/459–0541) or **Jazz Mine Records** (5726 La Jolla Blvd., La Jolla, tel. 619/454–9832) because of the traditional jazz artists booked.

## For Singles

Some of the most popular under-30 singles haunts, all energetic and boisterous, are in the Mission Valley and beach areas and include **El Torito** (445 Camino del Rio S., Mission Valley, tel. 619/296–6154), **T.G.I. Friday's** (403 Camino del Rio S., Mission Valley, tel. 619/297–8443), **José Murphy's** (4302 Mission Blvd., Pacific Beach, tel. 619/270–3220), **Confetti,** and **Club Diego's** (*see* Cabarets/Nightclubs, above). Older singles tend to congregate at **Club Mick's** (4190 Mission Blvd., Pacific Beach, tel. 619/581–3938), **Cannibal Bar** (*see* Cabarets/Nightclubs, above), and **Old Ox** (4474 Mission Blvd., Pacific Beach, tel. 619/275–3790).

# San Francisco

*by Barbara Koeth*

In 1848, gold was discovered in the sleepy settlement of San Francisco, which had been founded by the Spaniards in 1776. Periods of frantic building have marked the city's progress ever since. Developers now fight bitterly against residents who seek to preserve the city's architectural past and unusual natural beauty.

The city is one of the most scenic in the world: In clear weather its precipitously steep hillsides bring to mind a Mediterranean seaport with a compact city center and outlying residential areas glittering in the sun. On foggy days (and there are many) San Francisco takes on a surreal aspect as skyscrapers and apartment towers disappear into mist-shrouded hills.

Tourism is the number one industry, but San Francisco also attracts a wide range of businesses. The headquarters of many of the nation's leading corporations, including BankAmerica, Chevron, Pacific Telesis, Shaklee, Transamerica, and Wells Fargo, are located here. The financial district—dominated by the dark, looming Bank of America and the pyramid-shaped, glass-and-concrete Transamerica Building—centers on Montgomery Street, between Market Street and the Embarcadero. More than 200,000 people are employed in the area, which is home to the Pacific Stock Exchange. The city's vital foreign trade sector is served by more than 80 foreign banks, which maintain representative offices or agencies in the city.

The population of San Francisco is about 732,000, but the city draws heavily on the Bay Area for its work force. The Chamber of Commerce estimates that there are 285,000 intracity commuters, and as many as 225,000 commuters from outside the city limits. Salaries in the Bay Area run 15%–20% higher than the national average, with San Francisco in the lead.

## Top Employers

| Employer | Type of Enterprise | Parent*/ Headquarters |
|---|---|---|
| **American Building Maintenance** | Building services | San Francisco |

| AMFAC Inc. | Distribution and retail | San Francisco |
| --- | --- | --- |
| BankAmerica Corp. | Banking | San Francisco |
| Chevron Corp. | Oil and gas | San Francisco |
| McKesson Corp. | Wholesale services | San Francisco |
| Pacific Gas & Electric | Utility | San Francisco |
| Pacific Telesis Group | Telecommunications | San Francisco |
| Potlatch Corp. | Paper and forest products | San Francisco |
| TransAmerica Corp. | Financial services | San Francisco |
| Wells Fargo & Co. | Banking | San Francisco |

*if applicable

## ESSENTIAL INFORMATION

### Climate

What follows are the average daily maximum and minimum temperatures for San Francisco.

| Jan. | 55F | 13C | Feb. | 59F | 15C | Mar. | 60F | 16C |
| --- | --- | --- | --- | --- | --- | --- | --- | --- |
|  | 41 | 5 |  | 42 | 6 |  | 44 | 7 |
| Apr. | 62F | 17C | May | 66F | 19C | June | 69F | 21C |
|  | 46 | 8 |  | 48 | 9 |  | 51 | 11 |
| July | 69F | 21C | Aug. | 69F | 21C | Sept. | 73F | 23C |
|  | 51 | 11 |  | 53 | 12 |  | 51 | 11 |
| Oct. | 69F | 21C | Nov. | 64F | 18C | Dec. | 57F | 14C |
|  | 50 | 10 |  | 44 | 7 |  | 42 | 6 |

### Airports

**San Francisco International Airport** (tel. 415/761–0800) is about 16 miles south of the city, off U.S. 101. **Oakland International Airport** (tel. 415/577–4000) is about the same distance east of the city, across San Francisco Bay via I–80 east and I–580 south. There is still a lot of construction going on in the freeway area due to the earthquake in 1989. Roads from the airport to the city should be clearly marked for detours. If you're doing business in the city, use SFIA. If you have business in the East Bay area, consider booking a flight into OIA.

### Airport Business Facilities

**Mutual of Omaha Business Service Center** (upper level of SFIA the South Terminal, between Eastern and Southwest airlines ticket counters, tel. 415/877–0369) has fax machines, photocopying, a notary public, ticket pickup, Western Union, travel insurance, cash advance, Federal Express, phone suites, and a conference room. **AT&T** (SFIA International Terminal, by Phillipine Airlines, tel. 415/877–0269) has fax machines, a small meeting room, and phone suites. **Great Haircuts Barber Shop** (North Terminal, tel. 415/877–8440) has showers.

## Airlines

**Alaska Air,** tel. 800/426–0333.
**American,** tel. 415/398–4434 or 800/433–7300.
**Continental,** tel. 415/397–8818 or 800/525–0280.
**Delta,** tel. 415/552–5700 or 800/221–1212.
**Piedmont,** tel. 415/956–8636 or 800/251–5720.
**Southwest,** tel. 415/885–1221 or 800/531–5601.
**TWA,** tel. 415/864–5731 or 800/221–2000.
**United,** tel. 415/397–2100 or 800/241–6522.
**USAir,** tel. 415/956–8636 or 800/428–4322.

## Between the Airports and Downtown

*By Taxi*
Taxis from San Francisco International Airport (SFIA) to downtown take 20–30 minutes and cost about $30. The trip from Oakland International Airport (OIA) takes 30–45 minutes, 60 minutes during rush hour, when traffic snarls on the San Francisco-Oakland Bay Bridge. Morning rush hour is 6:30–8:30 AM; afternoon rush hour, 4–6 PM. Cost: about $35.

*By Bus*
The **Airporter** (tel. 415/673–2433) provides bus service between SFIA and several convenient locations downtown, including major hotels. Call for the stop nearest your destination. Buses run every 15–30 minutes, 5:30–12:45 AM. Cost: $4.

*By Van*
**Supershuttle** will take you from SFIA to anywhere within the city limits of San Francisco, 24 hours a day. At the airport, after picking up your luggage, call 415/871–7800 and a van will usually pick you up within five minutes. Cost: $10. **Yellow Airport Shuttle** (tel. 415/282–7433) also offers service 24 hours a day, leaving every 15 minutes from the upper level of SFIA. Cost: $9. The trip takes 20–30 minutes.

*By Rail*
Rail service is available from OIA during daytime and early evening hours via shuttle bus to the Oakland Coliseum Arena **BART** (Bay Area Rapid Transit, tel. 415/788–BART) station. However, this is the least convenient way to get downtown. The shuttle to the BART station costs $1. The BART fare to Montgomery Street in downtown San Francisco is $1.90.

## Car Rentals

Avis, Budget, Dollar, and Hertz have booths at both airports. National has one at Oakland International.

**Avis,** tel. 415/562–9000 or 800/331–1212.
**Budget,** tel. 415/568–4770 or 800/527–0700.
**Dollar,** tel. 415/638–2750 or 800/421–6868.
**Hertz,** tel. 415/568–6777 or 800/654–3131.
**National,** tel. 415/632–2225 or 800/328–4567.

## Emergencies

*Doctors*

**Access Health Care** provides drop-in medical care at three San Francisco locations daily, 8–8: 1604 Union St. at Franklin St., tel. 415/775–7766; 26 California St. at Drumm St., tel. 415/397–2881; 5748 Geary Blvd. at 22nd Ave., tel. 415/221–9233.

*Dentists*

The **San Francisco Dental Office,** 132 Embarcadero, between Mission and Howard Sts., tel. 415/777–5115, provides 24-hour emergency service. It also offers dental care by appointment.

*Hospitals*

Two hospitals have 24-hour emergency rooms: **San Francisco General Hospital,** 1001 Potrero Hill, tel. 415/821–8200, and the **Medical Center** at the University of California, San Francisco, 500 Parnassus Ave. at 3rd Ave., near Golden Gate Park, tel. 415/476–1000.

## Important Addresses and Numbers

**Audiovisual rentals.** McCune Audio/Visual/Video (tel. 415/777–2700), Photo & Sound (tel. 415/882–7600). Both have many locations; call for the one nearest you.

**Chamber of Commerce** (465 California St., tel. 415/392–4511).

**Computer rentals.** *See* Audiovisual rentals, above.

**Convention and exhibition centers.** Moscone Center (747 Howard St., tel. 415/947–4000), Brooks Hall/Civic Auditorium Complex (99 Grove St., Civic Center, tel. 415/974–4000), The San Francisco Fashion Center at Showplace Square (650 Seventh St., tel. 415/864–1561).

**Fax services.** Copymat (several locations: 705 Market St., downtown, tel. 415/882–7377; 1 Maritime Plaza, Embarcadero, tel. 415/392–1757; 505 Sansome St., financial district, tel. 415/421–2327; 1898 Union St., Marina district, tel. 415/567–8933; 120 Howard St., SoMa district, tel. 415/957–1700), Red Carpet Service (821 Market St., tel. 415/495–1910).

**Formal-wear rentals.** Black and White Formal Wear, for men and women (1211 Sutter St., tel. 415/673–0625).

**Gift shops.** Flowers and Gift Baskets: Podesta Baldocchi (2525 California St., tel. 415/346–1300), San Francisco Florists and Gifts (220 Montgomery St., tel. 415/781–5900); Gourmet foods: Williams-Sonoma (576 Sutter St., tel. 415/982–0295); Chocolates: Godiva (The Galleria, 50 Post St., tel. 415/982–6798).

**Graphic design studios.** One Stop Graphics (27 Sutter St., tel. 415/781–8600).

**Hairstylists.** Unisex: Mayer's for Hair, no appointment necessary (245 Powell St., tel. 415/981–1310), Transitions (166 Grant Ave., tel. 415/433–7174).

**Health and fitness clubs.** *See* Fitness, below.

**Information hot line** (tel. 415/391–2001 for a recorded message listing daily events and activities).

**Limousine services.** A Classic Ride, Vintage Limousines (tel. 415/626–0433), Carey of San Francisco/Nob Hill Limousine (tel. 415/468–7550), Opera Plaza Limousines (tel. 415/826–9636).

**Liquor stores.** Fred O. Foster (51 2nd St., tel. 415/362–4775), John Walker & Co. (175 Sutter St., tel. 415/986–2707), The Wine Shop (2175 Chestnut St., tel. 415/567–4725).

**Mail delivery, overnight.** DHL Worldwide Express (tel. 415/345–9400), Federal Express (tel. 415/877–9000), TNT Skypak (tel. 415/692–9600), UPS (tel. 415/952–5200), U.S. Postal Service Express Mail (tel. 415/621–6792).

**Messenger service.** Quicksilver Messenger Service (tel. 415/495–4360), Silver Bullet Courier (tel. 415/777–5100), Western Messenger Service (tel. 415/864–4100).

**Office space rental.** Roxbury Executive Offices (1 Sansome St., tel. 415/951–4600 and 388 Market St., tel. 415/296–2500).

**Pharmacies, late-night.** Walgreen Drugstore (135 Powell St., near Union Sq., tel. 415/391–4433) open to midnight. Also, Mandarin (895 Washington St., tel. 415/989–9292), though not open late, offers free delivery.

**Radio stations, all-news.** KGO 810 AM, KCBS 740 AM, KQED 88.5 FM.

**Secretarial service.** Support Office Services (tel. 415/391–4578).

**Stationery supplies.** Minden's Stationers (1 Market Plaza, tel. 415/777–2550), Russ Building Stationers (235 Montgomery St., tel. 415/392–7169).

**Taxis.** Luxor Cab (tel. 415/282–4141), Veteran's Taxicab Company (tel. 415/552–1300), Yellow Cab (tel. 415/626–2345).

**Theater tickets.** *See* The Arts, below.

**Train information.** Bay Area Rapid Transit (BART, tel. 415/788–BART), CalTrain Peninsula Commute Service (CALTRAIN, tel. 415/557–8661), San Francisco Municipal Railway System (MUNI, tel. 415/673–MUNI), Amtrak (First and Mission Sts., tel. 415/982–8512).

**Travel agents.** American Express (several locations: 237 Post St., downtown, tel. 415/981–5533; 295 California St., financial district, tel. 415/788–4367; 2500 Mason St., Sheraton Hotel, Fisherman's Wharf, tel. 415/788–3025), Tyree & Associates, Personalized Tours & Travel (tel. 415/333–3250).

**Weather** (tel. 415/936–0100).

## LODGING

Despite an unusually large number of hotel rooms for a city its size, San Francisco's hotel prices are high. The competitive situation provides good value, though, and just might spoil the hotel experience for you in other cities. Upgraded services and amenities are becoming standard: this is a city of complimentary papers, overnight shoe-shines, and terry-cloth robes. It's not unusual to be greeted by name by the hotel concierge and the doorman. Many of the ultra-deluxe modern hotels provide attentive, Asian-style hospitality. They offer personal service and European-style ambience at only slightly lower prices.

"The City," as it's called by northern Californians, is very compact. All of the Downtown/City Center hotels are within easy walking distance of the business and financial district.

Most of the hotels listed here offer special corporate rates and weekend discounts; inquire when making reservations.

Highly recommended lodgings in each price category are indicated by a star. ★

| Category | Cost* |
|----------|-------|
| $$$$ (Very Expensive) | over $225 |
| $$$ (Expensive) | $150–$225 |
| $$ (Moderate) | under $150 |

*All prices are for a standard double room, single occupancy, excluding 11% San Francisco hotel tax.*

*Numbers in the margin correspond to numbered hotels on the San Francisco Lodging and Dining map.*

## Downtown/City Center

❻ **Fairmont Hotel and Tower.** Built atop fashionable Nob Hill
$$$$ in 1907, this landmark hotel has a magnificent carriage entrance leading to an opulent lobby with more red velvet than one could imagine. Guest rooms in the Tower, which was added in 1961, have the best views, but have a modern, almost anonymous look. Those in the original building provide a more elegant ambience, with period architectural details restored. Although it caters to large convention groups, the hotel is quite luxurious; standard amenities include hair dryers, terry robes, and shoe-shine machines. Extensive renovations in 1989 included state-of-the-art phone services in each room, complete with voice-mail features and jacks for modems and computers; the concierge handles arrangements for other business support services. The exclusive Nob Hill Club, a spa and fitness center on the hotel's Terrace level, is available to guests. The Crown Room (*see* After Hours, below) is a good spot for a scenic drink. *950 Mason St., 94106, tel. 415/772–5000 or 800/527–4727, fax 415/772–5086. Gen. manager, Herman Wiener. 600 rooms, 62 suites. AE, CB, DC, MC, V.*

★ ㉕ **Four Seasons Clift Hotel.** This was the exclusive spot for
$$$ the exclusive set in the 1920s and '30s. Today, it's the only 5-star and 5-diamond hotel in San Francisco (the ultimate ratings by the Mobil Travel Guide and AAA, respectively), and it sets local standards for luxury accommodations, concierge services, and congenial atmosphere. Since 1981, more than $1 million dollars has been spent each year so that the 75-year-old landmark could give its more modern high-rise competition a run for the money. And it does—with aplomb. Almost all doubles are spacious enough for a comfortable seating area; deluxe rooms, created from two

smaller rooms have a larger seating area. Rooms have fine fabrics, original artwork, period reproduction furnishings, and tasteful appointments that create an elegant, residential atmosphere. Each room has two phone lines. Baths are small but have every amenity. The 16th and 17th floors house the Business Center, 11 deluxe penthouse rooms, and two large boardrooms for private meetings. The French Room is the place for power breakfasts and dinners; the Sunday brunch is outstanding (*see* Dining, below). High tea in the lobby is a San Francisco institution (*see* Diversions, below), and the Redwood Room (*see* After Hours, below) draws an upscale crowd at the end of the working day. *495 Geary St., 94102, tel. 415/775–4700 or 800/332–3442, fax 415/776–9238. Gen. manager, Paul V. Pusateri. 329 rooms, 18 suites. AE, CB, DC, MC, V.*

**㉒** **Galleria Park Hotel.** This European-style "boutique" ho-
**$$** tel in the heart of the financial district opened in 1984, and was refurbished and redecorated in 1988. It features Art Nouveau decor in the lobby, including a marble entry with striking etched glass, a sculpted wood-burning fireplace, and a glazed crystal skylight. Guest rooms are decorated in light-hued floral patterns and pale wood furniture. Rooms on the lower floors are quite small, as are all the bathrooms, but the soundproofing throughout is excellent, an important factor given the hotel's busy location. Business amenities are minimal, but each room has a well-lighted desk with direct-dial telephone. Three small meeting rooms accommodate groups of 12–60. Room service is limited; Bentley's, a commendable seafood restaurant, offers gourmet room service in the early morning and evening hours only. There is a rooftop park and jogging track. *A Kimco hotel. 191 Sutter St., 94104, tel. 415/781–3060 or 800/792–9855, fax 415/433–4409. Gen. manager, John Brocklehurst. 177 rooms, 8 suites. AE, CB, DC, MC, V.*

**★ ㉑** **Grand Hyatt San Francisco.** After a top-to-bottom $20 mil-
**$$$** lion renovation, completed in 1990, this 36-story hotel is indeed grand. Its large, open-air plaza area is a wonderfully extravagant use of space. The hotel is just steps from Union Square. Guest rooms are elegantly decorated in dark walnut and rich burgundy, and include two phones and television sets as standard amenities. The Executive Business Center is the most complete in San Francisco, providing a long list of business and on-line information services including stock market quotes and averages and the Dow Jones QuickSearch, which accesses corporate reports, as well as facilities for issuing airline tickets and boarding passes. *345 Stockton St., 94108, tel. 415/398–1234 or 800/233–1234, fax 415/392–2536. Gen. manager, Gunter Stannius. 693 rooms, including 92 concierge level, 25 suites, and 6 penthouse suites. AE, CB, DC, MC, V.*

**⑮** **Hyatt Regency San Francisco.** This luxury convention ho-
**$$$** tel is part of the eight-block Embarcadero Center business and shopping complex, just minutes from Moscone Convention Center, Union Square shopping, Fisherman's Wharf, and other visitor attractions. The 20-story building has a 300-foot-long sky-lighted lobby with full-size trees, a running stream, and enough greenery to landscape a small park. When it opened in 1973, the Hyatt's high-tech futuristic design was on the cutting edge. Times have changed, though, and in 1990 all rooms and most of the public spaces were redecorated to provide a warmer

# SAN FRANCISCO

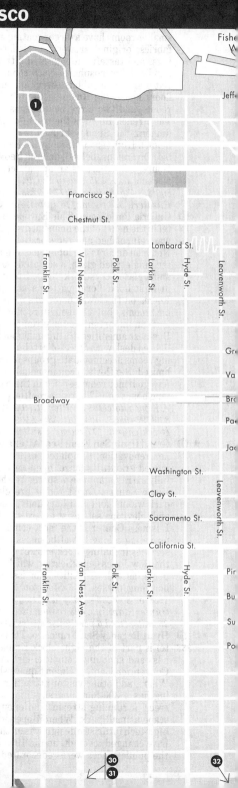

# SAN FRANCISCO HOTEL CHART

| HOTELS | Price Category | Business Services / Banquet capacity | No. of meeting rooms | Secretarial services | Audiovisual equipment | Teletype news service | Computer rentals | In-room modem phone jack | All-news cable channel | Desk | Desk lighting | Bed lighting |
|---|---|---|---|---|---|---|---|---|---|---|---|---|
| Airport Hilton | $$ | 700 | 27 | ✓ | ✓ | ✓ | ✓ | ✓ | ✓ | ● | ● | ● |
| Airport Marriott | $$ | 1200 | 7 | ✓ | ✓ | - | ✓ | ✓ | ✓ | ◐ | ◐ | ◐ |
| The Claremont Resort | $$$$ | 400 | 15 | ✓ | ✓ | - | ✓ | - | ✓ | ● | ● | ● |
| Fairmont Hotel and Tower | $$$$ | 1900 | 19 | ✓ | ✓ | - | ✓ | ✓ | ✓ | ● | ● | ● |
| Four Seasons Clift | $$$ | 180 | 9 | ✓ | ✓ | - | ✓ | ✓ | ✓ | ● | ● | ● |
| Galleria Park | $$ | 50 | 3 | ✓ | ✓ | - | ✓ | ✓ | ✓ | ● | ● | ● |
| Grand Hyatt | $$$ | 700 | 18 | ✓ | ✓ | ✓ | ✓ | ✓ | ✓ | ● | ● | ● |
| Hilton and Towers | $$$ | 3000 | 61 | ✓ | ✓ | - | ✓ | ✓ | ✓ | ● | ● | ● |
| Hyatt Regency | $$$ | 1500 | 35 | ✓ | ✓ | ✓ | ✓ | ✓ | ✓ | ◐ | ◐ | ◐ |
| The Inn at Union Square | $$ | 0 | 0 | ✓ | - | - | - | - | ✓ | ◐ | ◐ | ◐ |
| Mandarin Oriental | $$$$ | 100 | 3 | ✓ | ✓ | - | ✓ | ✓ | ✓ | ● | ● | ● |
| Marriott | $$$ | 3350 | 21 | ✓ | ✓ | - | ✓ | - | ✓ | ◐ | ◐ | ◐ |
| Meridian | $$$$ | 100 | 4 | ✓ | ✓ | - | ✓ | ✓ | ✓ | ● | ● | ● |
| Nikko | $$$ | 500 | 9 | ✓ | ✓ | - | ✓ | ✓ | ✓ | ● | ● | ● |
| Nob Hill Lambourne | $$$$ | 0 | 0 | ✓ | ✓ | - | ✓ | ✓ | ✓ | ● | ● | ● |
| The Pan Pacific | $$$ | 500 | 13 | ✓ | ✓ | - | ✓ | ✓ | ✓ | ◐ | ◐ | ◐ |
| Prescott | $$ | 0 | 0 | ✓ | - | - | ✓ | ✓ | ✓ | ● | ● | ● |
| The Stanford Court | $$$ | 400 | 2 | ✓ | ✓ | - | ✓ | ✓ | ✓ | ◐ | ● | ● |
| The Westin St. Francis | $$$ | 1100 | 27 | ✓ | ✓ | - | - | ✓ | ✓ | ◐ | ◐ | ◐ |

**$$$$** = over $225, **$$$** = $150-$225, **$$**= under $150.
● good, ◐ fair, ○ poor.
All hotels listed here have photocopying and fax facilities.

| In-Room Amenities | | | | | | | | | | Hotel Amenities | | | | | | |
|---|---|---|---|---|---|---|---|---|---|---|---|---|---|---|---|---|
| Nonsmoking rooms | In-room checkout | Minibar | Pay movies | VCR/Movie rentals | Hairdryer | Toiletries | Room service | Laundry/Dry cleaning | Pressing | Concierge | Barber/Hairdresser | Garage | Courtesy airport transport | Sauna | Pool | Exercise room |
| ✓ | ✓ | ✓ | ✓ | ✓ | ✓ | ● | ◐ | ● | ● | – | – | ✓ | ✓ | – | ● | ● |
| ✓ | ✓ | – | ✓ | – | ✓ | ◐ | ● | ● | ● | ✓ | – | ✓ | ✓ | ✓ | ● | ● |
| ✓ | ✓ | ✓ | ✓ | ✓ | – | ◐ | ◐ | ● | ● | ✓ | ✓ | ✓ | – | ✓ | ● | ● |
| ✓ | ✓ | ✓ | – | ✓ | ✓ | ● | ● | ● | ● | ✓ | ✓ | ✓ | – | ✓ | – | ● |
| ✓ | ✓ | ✓ | ✓ | ✓ | – | ● | ● | ● | ● | ✓ | – | ✓ | – | – | – | – |
| ✓ | – | ✓ | ✓ | ✓ | – | ◐ | ○ | ● | ● | ✓ | – | ✓ | – | – | – | – |
| ✓ | ✓ | ✓ | ✓ | – | – | ● | ● | ● | ● | ✓ | – | ✓ | – | – | – | ● |
| ✓ | ✓ | ✓ | – | – | – | ● | ● | ● | ● | ✓ | ✓ | ✓ | – | ✓ | ● | ● |
| ✓ | ✓ | ✓ | ✓ | – | – | ◐ | ● | ● | ● | ✓ | ✓ | ✓ | – | – | – | – |
| ✓ | – | ✓ | – | – | – | ◐ | ○ | ● | ● | ✓ | – | ✓ | – | – | – | – |
| ✓ | ✓ | ✓ | – | – | ✓ | ● | ● | ● | ● | ✓ | ✓ | ✓ | – | – | – | – |
| ✓ | ✓ | ✓ | ✓ | – | ✓ | ◐ | ● | ● | ● | ✓ | – | ✓ | – | ✓ | ● | ● |
| ✓ | ✓ | ✓ | ✓ | – | – | ● | ● | ● | ● | ✓ | – | ✓ | – | – | – | – |
| ✓ | ✓ | ✓ | ✓ | – | ✓ | ● | ● | ● | ● | ✓ | ✓ | ✓ | – | ✓ | ● | ● |
| ✓ | ✓ | ✓ | ✓ | ✓ | ✓ | ● | – | ● | ● | ✓ | – | ✓ | – | – | – | – |
| ✓ | – | ✓ | ✓ | ✓ | ✓ | ● | ● | ● | ● | ✓ | – | ✓ | – | – | – | – |
| ✓ | ✓ | ✓ | ✓ | – | – | ● | ○ | ● | ● | ✓ | – | ✓ | – | – | – | – |
| ✓ | ✓ | ✓ | ✓ | – | ✓ | ● | ● | ● | ● | ✓ | – | ✓ | – | – | – | – |
| ✓ | ✓ | ✓ | ✓ | ✓ | – | ◐ | ● | ● | ● | ✓ | ✓ | ✓ | – | – | – | – |

**Room service:** ● 24-hour, ◐ 6AM-10PM, ○ other.
**Laundry/Dry cleaning:** ● same day, ◐ overnight, ○ other.
**Pressing:** ● immediate, ◐ same day, ○ other.

atmosphere, though rooms are still standard Hyatt issue. The phone system was also upgraded to provide two lines in each room and voice mail features. Each room contains a work area with a well-lighted desk; a full range of business services including teleconference calling is available at the business center. Equinox, San Francisco's only revolving rooftop restaurant and cocktail lounge, is a good place for a drink with a view (*see* After Hours, below). *5 Embarcadero Center, 94111, tel. 415/788–1234 or 800/ 233–1234, fax 415/989–7448. Gen. manager, Charles McElroy 803 rooms, 110 concierge level, including 44 suites. AE, CB, DC, MC, V.*

**㉒** **The Inn at Union Square.** This small, elegant hotel in the
**$$** heart of downtown San Francisco offers service and comfort in the European tradition. Security-conscious travelers will appreciate the locked front door (with doorbell) and keyed access elevator. Built in 1924, the Inn was completely renovated in 1981. Each room is decorated differently, with Georgian-style furniture and designer fabrics; many have king-size canopied beds with goosedown pillows. Each of the four guest-room floors has its own intimate lobby where guests are served a complimentary Continental breakfast, afternoon tea, and wine and hors d'oeuvres in the evening. The sixth-floor penthouse boasts a wood-burning fireplace and private whirlpool bath and sauna. All business services are provided by the front desk staff; the penthouse will accommodate up to eight people for meetings. *440 Post St., 94102, tel. 415/397– 3510 or 800/288–4346, fax 415/989–0529. Gen. manager, Brooks Bayly. 31 rooms, 7 suites, 1 penthouse suite. AE, CB, MC, DC, V.*

**★ ⓭** **Mandarin Oriental, San Francisco.** In the middle of the
**$$$$** historic "Dollar Block," in the heart of the city's financial district, this hotel occupies the top 11 floors of the 48-story First Interstate Center. The unique positioning of the double towers ensures each of the guest rooms an unobstructed view of the city and the Bay. Because there are only 14 rooms on each floor, guests are ensured a high degree of quiet, privacy, and security. The luxuriously appointed rooms have a distinctly residential feeling, complete with a pleasantly chiming doorbell. The 22 Mandarin rooms have screened living areas and huge polished-marble bathrooms with floor-to-ceiling windows next to the extra-deep soaking tubs. All rooms have three phones with two phone lines, extra large desk, and remote control television and radio with speakers in the bathroom. Personal amenities are outstanding, including lightweight and terry-cloth robes, and Thai silk slippers to take home with you. The lobby level Business Center provides all professional services and includes a private conference room. The restaurant here, Silks (*see* Dining, below), is first-rate. *222 Sansome St., 94104–2792, tel. 415/885– 0999 or 800/622–0404, fax 415/433–0289. Gen. manager, Wolfgang K. Hultner. 154 rooms, 6 suites. AE, CB, DC, MC, V.*

**★ ㉙** **Hotel Meridien San Francisco.** When it opened in 1983,
**$$$$** this 36-story sky-rise hotel was at the cutting edge of the newly respectable SoMa (South of Market) area. Today, the opulent hotel, with expansive rooms, elegant furnishings, and fabulous floor-to-ceiling windows, is at the heart of the new downtown area, just a block from Moscone Cen-

ter. A $20 million redecoration, which began early in 1990, gilded the lily. Personal and business amenities are top notch; all rooms have desks and well-lighted work areas. The distinctively French atmosphere that pervades the hotel is best showcased in the Pierre restaurant (*see* Dining, below), which serves contemporary California-French cuisine. There's a fully staffed Business Center and a currency exchange in the lobby. *50 3rd St., 94103, tel. 415/974-6400 or 800/543-4300, fax 415/543-8268. Gen. manager, Cyril Isnard. 675 rooms, 26 suites. AE, CB, DC, MC, V.*

★ ㉗ **Hotel Nikko San Francisco.** Oriental-style tranquility
$$$ marks this sleekly modern hotel, just minutes from the downtown financial district. From the soothing sound of falling water in the white marble lobby, to the mauve and pearl-gray room decor, the mood throughout the 25-story hotel is serene. Guest rooms feature expansive windows, furniture with simple lines, and recessed lighting. Well-designed, contemporary desks and swivel reading lamps are standard, as are radio and television speakers in the bathrooms. The fifth-floor fitness center features two dry saunas, two traditional *ofuros* (Japanese soaking tubs), a *kamaburo* (Japanese sauna), and the city's only glass-enclosed swimming pool and whirlpool. Exercise clothing, towels, lockers, and full amenities are provided for guests at no extra charge. The Executive Assistance Center is staffed 12 hours every weekday, and offers complete business service support, including personal computers in small partitioned offices, a television monitor, VCR and video-editing equipment, and a paper shredder. *222 Mason St., 94102, tel. 415/394-1111 or 800/645-5687, fax 415/421-0455. Gen. manager, Andrews Kirmse. 522 rooms, 27 suites, 2 Japanese tatami suites. AE, CB, DC, MC, V.*

❽ **Nob Hill Lambourne.** At this high-tech hotel, a full range
$$$$ of business services is provided in the privacy of your own room; there's a fax machine with dedicated phone line, and a personal computer with preloaded software, including Lotus 1-2-3 and Wordperfect 5.0. On-line computer services include both Lexis and Nexis data bases. Opened late in 1989, the three-story hotel attracts many travelers in the legal and financial-services industry. And no wonder. Full secretarial support, personalized voice mail and answering services, desktop publishing, and boardroom facilities make the Nob Hill Lambourne seem like a San Francisco branch office. The accommodations are decorated with custom-designed furnishings that mix contemporary and period styles. Each room is oversized, with a queen-size bed, a separate work area, and a fully outfitted kitchen area. Although complimentary Continental breakfast is served, there is no other food service. Room rates include airport pickup in a London-style taxi. *725 Pine St., 94108, tel. 415/433-2287 or 800/274-8466, fax 415/433-0975. Gen. manager, Cyndi Weber. 20 rooms, 6 suites. AE, CB, DC, MC, V.*

❶❽ **The Pan Pacific Hotel San Francisco.** Known as the
$$$ Portman until it was acquired by the Pan Pacific Hotel and Resort chain in 1990, this 21-story hotel in the heart of downtown is noteworthy for its high degree of personal service and impeccable standards of privacy. There is round-the-clock concierge and valet service, a private club for off-hours meetings or relaxing, and no set check-

out time. The third-floor lobby is a riot of marble, glass, and chrome, complete with architect John Portman's signature glass capsule elevators. A sculpture of four dancing nudes, inspired by Matisse's *The Dance*, and a fountain are positioned directly under the 17-story atrium skylight. The rooms are spacious, and the rose-color marble baths are immense, with separate soaking tubs and shower stalls. The dressing areas have miniscreen TV sets. There are two-line phones at the desk, bedside, and in the bathroom, with call waiting and voice mail features. The Executive Conference Center has its own dining facility and a separate concierge staff. *500 Post St., 94102, tel. 415/771–8600 or 800/533–6465, fax 415/398–0267. Gen. manager, Patrick J. Mene. 330 rooms, 19 suites. AE, CB, DC, MC, V.*

★ ⑰ **Prescott Hotel.** This is one of San Francisco's newest "bou-
$$ tique" hotels, opened in 1989. Small and elegant, with a gracious lobby with blazing hearth-style fireplace and richly upholstered custom furniture, it offers a good location a block from Union Square. The accommodations conjure up a Ralph Lauren bedroom with deep green, rich burgundy, and dark wood decor. Terry robes, hair dryers, makeup mirrors, and limousine transportation to the financial district are standard amenities, and all rooms have desks and phone jacks for data transmission. The Mendocino penthouse takes up the entire seventh floor, and includes a secluded rooftop deck with hot tub and garden. Guests are guaranteed preferred seating at Postrio, Wolfgang Puck's restaurant sensation (*see* Dining, below), which also supplies room service during limited hours. *A Kimco hotel. 545 Post St., 94102, tel. 415/563–0303 or 800/283–7322, fax 415/563–6831. Gen. manager, Patrick Sampson. 109 rooms, 7 suites, 1 penthouse suite. AE, CB, DC, MC, V.*

㉖ **San Francisco Hilton and Towers.** A $210 million renova-
$$$ tion and expansion in 1988 made this the biggest hotel in San Francisco. Originally built in 1964, with a 1972 addition, it takes up an entire city block in the center of downtown with three towers of 19, 23, and 46 floors. The sleekly modern lobby bustles with activity, and each building serves a different market: business, convention, and leisure. The concierge-level rooms in the newest tower are the best bet for business travelers, with upscale furnishings, lots of greenery, and upgraded amenities; desks and two-line phones are standard. It's worth having a drink at Cityscape, the restaurant at the top of the highest tower; it commands a 360-degree view of the city and the Bay, and has a unique retractable skylight (*see* After Hours, below). There's a complete business center, and a health club with a heated outdoor pool on a sheltered deck—quite unexpected in the middle of the city. *1 Hilton Sq., 94102, tel. 415/771–1400 or 800/445–8667, fax 415/771–6807. Gen. manager, Holger Gantz. 1,891 rooms (107 concierge level, 190 suites). AE, CB, DC, MC, V.*

㉘ **San Francisco Marriott.** Part of the San Francisco redevel-
$$$ opment project known as "Yerba Buena Gardens," this huge 40-story hotel has changed the San Francisco skyline with its distinctive design—modern Art Deco with large fanlike windows across the top. This major meeting and convention facility, which opened in 1989, is one block from Moscone Center. It is a factory of sorts: Rooms are

small but functional, with standard California-pastel decor. The concierge level rooms on the 18th and 19th floors afford less anonymity. They feature upgraded amenities and a private lounge. Recreational facilities include a full-service health club, with the city's largest indoor swimming pool; weight, exercise, and massage rooms; whirlpool; and sauna. In addition to the largest ballroom west of Las Vegas, the hotel has 21 self-contained conference suites suitable for groups from 5 to 150. The Business Communications Center provides all business services, including paging devices and beepers. *777 Market St., 94103, tel. 415/896–1600 or 800/228–9290, fax 415/777–2799. Gen. manager, Alain Piallat. 1,500 rooms (98 concierge level, 134 suites). AE, CB, DC, MC, V.*

★ **❼** **The Stanford Court.** Acquisition by Stouffer Hotels and
$$$ Resorts in 1989 brought a number of immediate changes to this prestigious Nob Hill luxury hotel, including 24-hour room service. More important was the elimination of the 75¢ surcharge previously billed to guests to place phone calls, and the elimination of charges for incoming fax messages. The lobby area, which was refurbished in 1989, showcases Baccarat chandeliers, Carrara marble, and French Provincial furniture; it's a lovely setting for afternoon tea (*see* Diversions, below). All guest rooms were completely refurbished in 1990, and decorated with deep-tone floral print fabrics and dark wood furnishings; minibars and safes were added. But all this was icing on the cake: standard amenities at this nine-story hotel already included television sets in each bathroom, two telephones with call-waiting features in each bedroom, and all-day, complimentary car service anywhere in the city. Built in 1919 as a luxury apartment building, the hotel has spacious rooms, with high ceilings and detailed moldings. A fully staffed business center opened in 1990. *905 California St., 94108, tel. 415/989–3500 or 800/468–3571, fax 415/986–8195. Gen. manager, Creighton Casper. 402 rooms, 34 suites. AE, CB, DC, MC, V.*

**㉔** **The Westin St. Francis.** In 1972, the addition of a 32-story
$$$ tower doubled the number of rooms in this historic (1904) hotel, which dominates one side of famed Union Square and overlooks the financial district. A $53 million renovation, completed in 1987, preserved and enhanced historical details in the original lobby and guest rooms, but provided contemporary furnishings throughout. The Tower rooms are the best bet, featuring upgraded amenities and well-lighted work areas. Five bronze-tinted glass external elevators provide access to the Tower guest rooms, the much touted nightclub, Oz (*see* After Hours, below), the highly rated Victor's restaurant, and a breathtaking panorama of San Francisco and environs. The lobby's Compass Rose restaurant (*see* Diversions, below) offers high tea in style. *335 Powell St., 94102, tel. 415/397–7000 or 800/228–3000, fax 415/774–0124. Gen. manager, Hans Bruland. 1,202 rooms, 84 suites. AE, CB, DC, MC, V.*

## Airport

**㉟** **San Francisco Airport Hilton.** Unlike most airport hotels,
$$ this property has a resort look and feel to it. The hotel opened in 1960, but was renovated in 1989. Most rooms are oversized, with small bathrooms, and all have complete business amenities including two-line phones and well-

lighted desks and work areas. Many overlook the heated Olympic-size pool or the garden courtyard, and some have patios opening onto the pool area. The fully staffed business center has a PC work station and the latest office equipment. There's also a well-equipped fitness center. Though ideal for large meetings, the hotel also caters to smaller groups with well-designed and comfortable executive conference facilities. *San Francisco International Airport, 94128, tel. 415/589–0770 or 800/445–8667, fax 415/589–0770. Gen. manager, Richard Groves. 540 rooms, 9 suites. AE, CB, DC, MC, V.*

**36** **San Francisco Airport Marriott.** This 11-story hotel has a
**$$** bright and attractive public lobby, with picture windows that have panoramic views of the bay and the airport runways. The hallways, though, are narrow and dark. Standard rooms are small but functional, with adequate desks and lighting; concierge level rooms and suites are the best bets. There's a fully equipped health club complete with saunas, whirlpool, and indoor pool. *1800 Old Bayshore Hwy., Burlingame, 94010, tel. 415/692–9100 or 800/228–9290, fax 415/692–9861. Gen. manager, Steve Sharple. 684 rooms (55 concierge level, 21 suites). AE, CB, DC, MC, V.*

## Oakland

**★ 33** **The Claremont Resort.** This legendary Victorian-style ho-
**$$$$** tel, surrounded by 22 acres of landscaped gardens in the Oakland/Berkeley hills, celebrated its 75th anniversary in 1990. Less than 30 minutes from downtown San Francisco, it offers all the advantages of a self-contained resort in an urban setting, as well as a $6 million, 25,000-square-foot, European-style spa facility, opened in 1989. The high-ceilinged lobby showcases contemporary artwork— the largest collection by Pacific Northwest artists assembled outside of a museum. Guest rooms are unusually spacious, and many feature seating areas; all have upgraded bathrooms. The cuisine served in the Pavilion Restaurant is top notch, and the views across the bay to San Francisco and the peninsula and north to Mt. Tamalpais are exceptional. The Gallery is noted for premium wines by the glass; the Terrace Bar provides music and dancing. More than $28 million has been invested in the property over the past 10 years, much of it in the conference center, which draws major corporate clients. A staffed business center provides professional services. *41 Tunnel Rd., Box 23363, Oakland, 94623, tel. 415/843–3000, fax 415/843–6239. Gen. manager, Lenny Fisher. 239 rooms, 30 suites. AE, CB, DC, MC, V.*

## DINING

*by Colleen Dunn Bates*

For more than a century, San Francisco has reigned as the undisputed restaurant capital of the West. In the last two decades, excellent restaurants have opened in Los Angeles and San Diego and in towns from Seattle to Santa Fe. But San Francisco remains an eating town nonpareil. Its hotel restaurants are unsurpassed. Its Asian food—Cambodian, Vietnamese, Korean, Japanese, Chinese—is wonderful. Its classic "old San Francisco" eateries remain infused with charm and civility. And its California cuisine is inventive and flavorful.

Because of its compactness, San Francisco is ideal for the hungry business traveler. Within downtown's financial district/Union Square/Civic Center hub are some of the West's very best restaurants (Masa's, Fleur de Lys, Stars, and Postrio, to name just a few). Chinatown and North Beach (San Francisco's Little Italy) are just a short walk or cab ride north; trendy South of Market (SoMa) is an equally short hop south. The city's restaurants usually reflect the immediate neighborhood—more tourists in Union Square, more government employees and arts lovers in the Civic Center/Opera area, more bankers and business people in the financial district, more high-style yuppies in SoMa. But you'll usually find a refreshing mix of patrons almost everywhere.

San Francisco may be in California, but when it comes to wardrobe, don't expect the anything-goes attitude of Los Angeles. Thanks to a colder climate and more conservative populace, people dress up a bit at the city's best restaurants. Jackets and ties are the norm at practically all higher-end downtown establishments, even if they're not required. Things are a bit more casual in SoMa and, of course, at most of the ethnic restaurants.

Highly recommended restaurants in each price range are indicated by a star ★.

| Category | Cost* |
|---|---|
| $$$$ (Very Expensive) | over $50 |
| $$$ (Expensive) | $31–$50 |
| $$ (Moderate) | $20–$30 |
| $ (Inexpensive) | under $20 |

*per person, including an appetizer, entrée, and dessert, but excluding drinks, service, and 6.75% sales tax.*

*Numbers in the margin correspond to numbered restaurants on the San Francisco Lodging and Dining map.*

### Business Breakfasts

Hands down, the best business breakfast spot in the city is **Campton Place** (340 Stockton St., tel. 415/781–5155). It offers a dignified setting, exceptional contemporary American food (old-fashioned waffles topped with all sorts of tasty things, superb corned-beef hash, first-rate breads), and a convenient Union Square location. For another take on the all-American breakfast, this time in a chic farmhouse-kitchen setting, make the trek to the Marina district to **Doidge's** (2217 Union St., tel. 415/921–2149). Make a reservation, too, since the dreamy pancakes, nitrite-free bacon, and perfectly poached eggs keep the tables full. Despite the name, Union Square's **French Room,** at the Four Seasons Clift Hotel (tel. 415/775–4700), serves such tasty American standards as oatmeal and scrambled eggs; the setting is quiet and conservatively opulent—perfect for an important business breakfast. For something a bit different—and for a lively atmosphere and stunning decor of gleaming marble, polished wood, high ceilings, and an open kitchen—try **Il Fornaio** in the Embarcadero area (1265 Battery St., tel. 415/986–0100): Even bacon 'n' eggs are exceptional, particularly when ordered with Italian smoked bacon and toasted, triple-thick slices of Il Fornaio's famous breads. To make the trendiest breakfast scene in town, reserve a table at **Postrio,** at the Prescott Hotel in Union Square (tel. 415/776–7825). This glamorous multilevel restaurant is the latest project of California-cuisine King Wolfgang Puck, and serves such innovative dishes as soft scrambled eggs with lobster, mascarpone, and chives.

## Downtown

★ ❹ **Amelio's.** Like Ernie's (*see* below), Amelio's has been one
$$$$ of San Francisco's best known restaurants for decades. And like Ernie's, this once-tired North Beach warhorse was given a new lease on life by gifted chef Jacky Robert, who made Ernie's kitchen hum again before coming here. In an elegant, warmly decorated (rich woods, floral fabrics), quiet dining room, a smooth staff serves Robert's creative yet not too fussy contemporary French dishes, either à la carte or via one of two fine fixed-price menus. Dishes change regularly; you can expect such creations as woven bicolor pasta with Hawaiian prawns and scallops, a green salad with a brie "pancake," rack of lamb with an Oriental-style soy marinade, and exquisite chocolate desserts. The wine list is expensive but full of good choices. Amelio's is a short cab ride from downtown and an excellent spot for business entertaining. *1630 Powell St., tel. 415/397–4339. Jacket and tie advised. Reservations advised. AE, DC, MC, V. Dinner only. Closed Mon. and Tues. (closings vary).*

⓫ **The Blue Fox.** Redone from head to foot by a new owner,
$$$ the new Blue Fox combines an opulent decor (mirrored and draped walls, light colors, chandeliers) with equally opulent Northern Italian food, flawless service, and a well-dressed financial district clientele—making it an ideal spot for serious business entertaining. The food is almost too pretty to eat—almost. Try the venison carpaccio with essence of white truffle, any of the rich, perfect risotti, the first-rate veal dishes, and the fresh seafood, such as the simple, grilled red mullet with bitter greens. And take advantage of the excellent Italian wine list. The small, terribly refined bar serves as a predinner rendezvous. A short walk from downtown's office towers, The Blue Fox is probably the most elegant Italian restaurant in the city. *659 Merchant St., tel. 415/981–1177. Jacket and tie advised. Reservations advised. AE, CB, DC, MC, V. Dinner only. Closed Sun.*

㉓ **Campton Place.** Despite the departure of famed chef
$$$ Bradley Ogden, this hotel restaurant remains very good, turning out delicious contemporary American food. And it's as handsome as ever, in that luxury-hotel style that's currently popular: white linens on large tables, peach-color fabric walls, tall windows, upholstered chairs, and dramatic floral displays. It's a great place for both business meals and business entertaining; the well-spaced freestanding tables in the center of the room afford more privacy than the banquettes against the wall. The food combines American ingredients and inspirations with the creativity and technique normally associated with French

cooking. Breakfast is inspired (*see* Business Breakfasts, above), the lunchtime salads are marvels, and dinner is always intriguing, with such offerings as grilled asparagus with morels and a pancetta vinaigrette, spring lamb chops with a Gorgonzola crust, and guinea-hen with crisp potatoes and spinach. For sweets, try chocolate mousse torte with apricot brandy sauce, or butterscotch pie. *340 Stockton St., tel. 415/781–5155. Jacket and tie advised. Reservations advised. AE, CB, DC, MC, V.*

**⑤** **Cypress Club.** Located in the historic Jackson Square area
**$$$** of downtown, this wild new restaurant looks like a speakeasy designed for Ali Baba and Dick Tracy. You enter through a curtain into a room aswirl with curving, oversized shapes and exotic materials: fat, rounded dividers made of pounded copper, overstuffed mohair seats, a cartoonlike mural, and more. Even those who don't like the look admit that it's loads of fun. The contemporary American food isn't quite as weird as the decor, but it's definitely inventive. Seared scallops with fennel seed and a saffron vinaigrette, and charred pork loin with honey dates and ginger are among the tasty choices. The pastry chef is already legendary; people come here just for her caramel crème brûlée, and nut brioche pudding on warm poached fruit. The setting is a bit outlandish for serious business talks (though there's an excellent private room in back for meetings), but its a perfect spot for entertaining adventurous clients. *500 Jackson St., Financial District, tel. 415/296–8555. Jacket advised. Reservations strongly advised. AE, CB, DC, MC, V.*

**★ ⑲** **Donatello.** Haute Italian cuisine is the order of the day in
**$$$$** these adjoining dining rooms in the Donatello hotel. Both are ultraswank, almost stuffy visions of Old World splendor; mirrors and Italian marble dominate one, richly patterned Fortuny fabrics set a cozier tone in the other. Don't expect hearty fare—presentations are refined, almost a bit precious, and not exactly served with a generous hand. But there's no doubting that the kitchen is skilled and the flavors are outstanding. Popular dishes include sautéed fresh shiitake mushrooms with garlic, spinach, and pancetta; tasty eggplant and zucchini with tomato sauce, Fontina cheese, and oregano; and tender rack of lamb with rosemary, pancetta, and garlic. The service and wine list live up to the setting and the very high prices. The well-spaced tables and discreet atmosphere facilitate business conversation. *501 Post St., Union Square, tel. 415/441–7100. Jacket and tie advised. Reservations advised. Dinner only. AE, CB, D, DC, MC, V.*

**⑩** **Ernie's.** You may not believe it upon entering, but this
**$$$$** legendary spot began in 1934 as a humble Italian joint. Today, it is perhaps San Francisco's most elegant restaurant—popular with a moneyed, middle-aged crowd of locals and tourists, who appreciate the well-spaced tables, gleaming woodwork, silk-covered walls, fine silver, and unequaled service. And the wine list has done nothing but improve over the last half century. Many famous old restaurants stick with the tried and true, which then becomes tired and dull, but not Ernie's. The food has had its downs over the decades, but for the last several years it has been worthy of the decor and reputation. The dishes are updated French, neither too stodgy nor too strange; try the game pâté en croûte with seasonal mushrooms,

grilled tuna with a tropical-fruit coulis, rack of lamb in puff pastry with garlic sauce, and special-occasion desserts. If you need to impress someone, holding a dinner here will do the trick. On the border of the financial district and North Beach, Ernie's is a five-minute cab ride from most downtown hotels. *847 Montgomery St., tel. 415/ 397-5969. Jacket and tie required. Reservations advised. AE, CB, DC, MC, V. Dinner only.*

★ ⑯ **Fleur de Lys.** Rivaling Masa's (*see* below) as one of the best
$$$$ French restaurants in Northern California, Fleur de Lys deserves every bit of its national reputation. Chef/co-owner Hubert Keller turns out contemporary French masterpieces that taste as wonderful as they look. A hollowed baked potato hiding an herbed breast of squab, sautéed foie gras served on lettuce leaves with slices of duck breast, roasted lamb chops wrapped in an airy vegetable mousseline, a chocolate-mousse-and-meringue swan swimming on a raspberry pond—few restaurants outside of France serve such marvels. Hearty meat-and-potatoes types may find Fleur de Lys's food a bit precious, but gourmets will be in heaven—as will wine lovers. The dining room's dramatic use of hand-painted, rich red fabric draping the ceiling and walls, gives a feeling rather like that of a Sultan's banquet tent. The clientele is made up of soberly dressed executives and food lovers of all sorts; it's a good place for serious business entertaining and discussions, though it's more a place to pay attention to your meal, not your paperwork. Dinners are fixed-price only. *777 Sutter St., tel. 415/673-7779. Jacket and tie required. Reservations strongly advised. AE, DC, MC, V. Dinner only. Closed Sun.*

★ ❷ **Fog City Diner.** A rip-roaring hit from the day it opened,
$$ the Fog City Diner is a winning blend of old San Francisco charm and contemporary California-cuisine zing. San Francisco's mythical hard-boiled private eye Sam Spade would have felt at home in this waterfront hangout on the border of the financial district and North Beach, hunching over a steak and a scotch in one of the booths; also at home is a pride of wine-drinking Yuppies and well-dressed stockbroker types looking more for fun than shop talk. Fog City really does look like a diner, albeit a snazzy one, with polished wood, tile floors, upholstered booths, and '40s-style lighting. The food of chef/owner Cindy Pawlcyn is down-home American with a twist: crab cakes with a sherry-cayenne mayonnaise, skirt steak with a tomato aioli, sesame chicken with shiitake mushrooms, even a chili dog. Desserts—fruit pies, crème brûlée, chocolate cake—are richly satisfying. Service is helpful and efficient. Wines are rather pricey, and at peak times the noise level is considerable. *1300 Battery St., tel. 415/982-2000. Jacket advised, but anything goes. Reservations strongly advised. MC, V.*

❸ **Il Fornaio.** A chain of bakeries in Italy spawned an equally
$$ successful minichain of bakeries and cafés in America, which in turn spawned the crown jewels of the Il Fornaio empire: three full-fledged restaurants, this one on the edge of the financial district and North Beach, one north in Marin County, and one south in Del Mar. The stunning decor (gleaming white marble, polished dark wood, high ceilings, open kitchen, outdoor terrace) and appealing, well-prepared contemporary Northern Italian fare have

made this one of San Francisco's hot spots, particularly popular at lunch with a well-dressed business crowd. The noise level at lunch and dinner makes it a better place for entertaining than conducting serious business, but it's a superb spot for a breakfast meeting (*see* Business Breakfasts, above). The lengthy lunch and dinner menu includes a crisp, puffy *bomba* (pizzalike bread) topped with smoked prosciutto; intensely flavorful foccacia with Gorgonzola and Parmesan; lots of pastas and pizzas; and simple grilled fish and veal chops. And this is one place where you don't want to pass up the bread basket. *1265 Battery St., tel. 415/986–0100. Casual dress, but during the week most are in business attire. Reservations advised. AE, DC, MC, V.*

**㉕**
**$$$**
**French Room.** A grand old dining room in a grand old hotel, the French Room is a fine place for a business breakfast, lunch, or dinner. The Four Seasons management has skillfully kept the best of the old without neglecting contemporary comforts, amenities, and cuisine, which is why this place is so popular with executives from the worlds of fashion, retail, and real estate. Under a dazzling panoply of crystal chandeliers, a polished staff tends to the quietly wealthy clientele seated on richly upholstered chairs amid huge potted palms. If you're in the mood for familiar Continental fare, go for the excellent Caesar salad and the flawless prime rib with English popovers. If you're feeling a bit more adventurous, try some of chef Kelly Mills's fine Asian-influenced dishes, such as scallops and Chinese broccoli in a black-bean-and-ginger sauce, and crab cakes with a papaya and coriander relish. Even the firmest resolves weaken at the sight of the gleaming silver dessert cart. California's best are well represented on the wine list. The central Union Square location makes this a short walk from most downtown sites. *Four Seasons Clift Hotel, 495 Geary St., tel. 415/775–4700. Jacket and tie required. Reservations advised. AE, CB, DC, MC, V.*

**★ ❶**
**$$**
**Greens.** This vegetarian restaurant deserves all the acclaim it gets. Greens takes meatless eating to unprecedented levels—and it throws in such perks as a sweeping bay/Golden Gate Bridge view and a remarkable California wine list. Salads are exemplary, made with tasty organic greens and all sorts of good things—oranges, *frisée* (curly endive), and olives; assorted lettuces, mangoes, pecans. The menu also features rich, earthy breads, savory pizzas and pastas, herbed-cheese sandwiches on thick grilled bread, creative entrées, juicy cobblers, and a decidedly unhealthful chocolate hazelnut cake. Service can be a bit distracted. Located in one of Fort Mason's warehouse buildings (near Fisherman's Wharf), Greens has an homey, '70s-style decor, with polished wood floors, lots of plants, and huge windows. It's a great place to entertain vegetarian clients, and its meditative atmosphere allows for private talk. Friday and Saturday dinners are fixed-price only. *Building A, Fort Mason, tel. 415/771–6222. Casual dress. Reservations required. MC, V. Closed Sun. for dinner, and Mon.*

**★ ❾**
**$$$$**
**Masa's.** Quite likely the best restaurant in San Francisco — perhaps in all of California—Masa's remains the hottest culinary ticket in town; you'll probably need to make reservations three weeks in advance. It attained widespread notoriety in 1984 when chef Masa Kobayashi was mysteriously murdered (the case is still unsolved), but its real

claim to fame is its inspired contemporary French cuisine, now prepared by Julian Serrano. Although it's not exceptionally attractive, the small room is quiet and richly comfortable, with gray fabric walls, framed mirrors, vaguely contemporary black chairs, white linens, and elegantly simple appointments (oversize white china, clean-line crystal stemware). For maximum privacy, request a table along the wall. The wine list is full of treasures, the service is correct, if a tad haughty at times, and the food is unforgettable. Try the lobster-and-endive salad, incomparable foie gras, simple but perfect duck breast served with a poached winter pear, cheeses almost as good as those in France's best restaurants, and dreamy desserts, from the crème brûlée to the richly flavorful sorbets. The Union Square location is easily accessible, and the atmosphere and food make Masa's ideal for business entertaining of the first order. *648 Bush St., tel. 415/989–7154. Jacket and tie required. Reservations required. AE, DC, MC, V. Dinner only. Closed Mon.*

★ ㉙ **Pierre.** California cuisine is all well and good, but some-
$$$ times the occasion demands nothing but the finest classic French: decadent foie gras, sublime sauces, rich Bordeaux wines, petit fours with your coffee, and service by impeccably trained waiters who don't chat you up. That's exactly what you'll get at Pierre, the excellent dining room in the sleek Hotel Meridien, just south of Market Street and a quarter's throw from the financial district. You'll find all the components of a fine French meal here, plus a soothing, elegant dining room done in gray and cream, with candles on the tables and a baby grand in the corner. Game dishes such as roast pheasant with an orange and green-peppercorn sauce are specialties; also popular are roast lotte (monkfish) with sweet garlic, and an eggplant flan. The wine list, once exclusively French, is home to an increasing number of good Californian bottles. The frequent Master Chef's special dinners, prepared by some of the world's best chefs, are always worthwhile. Popular with well-dressed professionals, Pierre is good for both a working dinner and entertaining. *Hotel Meridien, 50 3rd St., tel. 415/974–6400. Jacket and tie required. Reservations advised. AE, CB, D, DC, MC, V. Dinner only. Closed Mon.*

★ ⓱ **Postrio.** L.A.-bashing is a favorite sport of San Francis-
$$$ cans, particularly when it comes to restaurants. So it came as quite a surprise to see how quickly and fervently the City by the Bay embraced this Union Square venture of L.A. wunderchef Wolfgang Puck. You'll need to make reservations at least a week in advance to get a table here, but the effort is well worth it. The most fashionable crowd in town, ranging from financial district whiz kids to society matrons, decorate a whimsical yet lovely three-level space that allows for great people-watching. Try to get a table on the lower level. It's the heart of the place, dominated by a sweeping staircase, large open kitchen, tall windows, and wacky space-age light fixtures. The second level is the next best thing. You'll eat excellent contemporary American food, even better than that served at Puck's legendary Spago in L.A. Try the crab cakes, the Chinese sausage on a bed of warm cabbage, the roast chicken with mashed potatoes, and the homey American desserts—actually, try anything, for it's all delicious. De-

spite the scene, the noise level isn't too daunting, though this is more a place for entertaining than working. Postrio is also a superb place for a breakfast meeting (*see* Business Breakfasts above). *Prescott Hotel, 545 Post St., tel. 415/776–7825. Jacket and tie advised. Reservations strongly advised. AE, CB, DC, MC, V.*

**⑬** **Silks.** Although hotel dining rooms are too often dreary
**$$$** places serving mediocre food, San Francisco has more than its share of first-rate hotel restaurants. One of the best is also one of the newest: Silks, in the dramatic Mandarin Oriental Hotel atop an office tower. (Unfortunately, the restaurant is on the second floor of the tower, so it doesn't have the same incredible views as the guest rooms.) Restaurants don't get much more attractive and serenely comfortable than this: extremely well-spaced tables set with white china and fine crystal; cream-color paneled walls inset with mirrors; thick gray carpeting; plush, fully upholstered armchairs; and a centerpiece laden with flowers, foodstuffs, and liqueurs. Despite the hotel's Asian roots, the intriguing, skillfully prepared cuisine is French-Californian: shrimp and corn chowder, grilled chicken wings in a red-sesame mole sauce, roast squab with chèvre tucked under its skin, gorgeous desserts. Service lives up to the food and decor. The financial district location means a big turnout by the business set. *Mandarin Oriental Hotel, 222 Sansome St., tel. 415/885–0999. Jacket and tie required. Reservations advised. AE, DC, MC, V.*

**⑭** **Tadich Grill.** You haven't been to San Francisco if you
**$$** haven't been to Tadich's, which has been around since the Gold Rush. The high-back wooden booths, starched white linens, crowded mahogany bar-counter, wonderfully brusque (some say surly) white-jacketed waiters, and heaps of tangy sourdough bread are all as San Franciscan as it gets. You'll have a long wait if you want a lunchtime booth, but the people-watching—middle-aged men in Brooks Brothers suits, younger financial district hotshots, tourists, old-timers, you name it—will keep you amused. No baby greens or Santa Barbara shrimp here; this is real food for unpretentious eaters, with an emphasis on fresh seafood: cioppino as good as it gets, grilled swordfish and salmon, wonderful sand dabs, textbook rice pudding, and simple wines served in small tumblers. A short walk from most downtown offices, Tadich's is a fun spot for business entertaining or a not-too-serious working meal, and its counter is perfect for the solo diner. *240 California St., tel. 415/391–2373. Jacket suggested (most diners are in business attire). No reservations. No credit cards. Closed weekends.*

**⑫** **Yank Sing.** For a delicious change of pace at lunch, head for
**$** this sophisticated dim sum restaurant. Most dim sum places are frenzied and noisy, with huge tables of Chinese families and swarms of women wheeling around carts laden with Chinese dumplings, pastries, and various small dishes. But Yank Sing, in the financial district, has successfully sought out a primarily non-Asian business-lunch crowd, which returns for the outstanding food, good service, relative quiet, and handsome, contemporary setting (flowers, white linens, parquet floors, etched-glass room dividers). The dim sum still comes by on carts, but the servers are more gracious than is the norm in such

eateries. Every offering is beautifully fresh and tasty; try the potstickers, spring rolls, sui mai, rice noodles, silver-wrapped chicken, and all sorts of dumplings filled with shrimp, chicken, pork, and vegetables. And by business-lunch standards, the prices are a bargain. *427 Battery St., tel. 415/362–1640. Informal dress. Reservations suggested. AE, DC, MC, V. Lunch only.*

## Civic Center

★ ③⓪ **Hayes Street Grill.** Curiously, the port town of San Fran-
$$ cisco isn't exactly thick with really good seafood restau-
rants. But it does have the Hayes Street Grill. The place doesn't look like much—an attractive but very simple two-room café, with bentwood chairs, hardwood floors, blackboard menus, and a good bit of noise—but the seafood is impeccably fresh and the service really hustles. Try any of the salads (especially smoked chicken and mango), then move on to one of the mesquite-grilled or sautéed fish dishes such as swordfish, snapper, salmon, or soft-shell crabs. Pasta fans will usually find a delicious shellfish pasta or two. A word of caution: The desserts, from the acclaimed crème brûlée to the retro fruit cobblers, will take away any virtuous feeling you had from eating fish. This is a good spot for a sociable Civic Center-area lunch or a casual business dinner before attending the nearby symphony or opera. *320 Hayes St., tel. 415/863–5545. Informal dress (jacket suggested). Reservations advised. MC, V. Closed Sun.*

★ ③① **Stars.** Stars owner/chef Jeremiah Tower is perhaps best
$$$ known for being profiled in a Dewar's Scotch ad. Fortunately, his celebrity status is matched with tremendous talent—despite the hype, Stars really does serve celestial food. Tower's kitchen crew turns out contemporary American dishes that almost always work, whether they be humble (the perfect hot dog served at the bar), homey (black-bean soup with sour cream and salsa), or inventive (Hawaiian tuna tartare with cilantro-chili vinaigrette, sesame cucumbers, and ginger cream). And the desserts—French silk pie, fresh berry pies, and cobblers—are incomparable. Several years after opening, Stars is still as vibrant as ever, always packed with the town's movers and shakers, along with curious tourists, devout foodies, and those attending the nearby opera or symphony. If you can't get a reservation, or are watching your pennies, drop in for a light meal and/or dessert at the bar or counter, which has a great view of the bustle in the open kitchen. At night, the noise level in this huge, handsome, bistro-style place (all gleaming wood and brass, with French posters, white linens, and old-fashioned glass light fixtures) is considerable. Stars is great for a working lunch—as long as you request a table in the quieter room to the right of the entrance—and for festive business entertaining at night. *150 Redwood Alley, tel. 415/861–7827. Jacket suggested. Reservations strongly advised. AE, CB, DC, MC, V.*

## South of Market

③② **Eddie Jacks.** If you want to eat well *and* make the trendy
$$ SoMa scene (just south of downtown), head for Eddie Jacks, an industrial looking modern place that offers terrific California fare and a wine list full of good values, in-

cluding excellent wines by the glass. And, unlike most SoMa eateries, the noise level isn't mind-numbing (though it isn't hushed, either). Dishes of note include addictive fried polenta sticks with a Gorgonzola dipping sauce, a delicious lamb sandwich with goat cheese and red onions, unusual pastas, and good seafood (savory seafood stew, rare tuna in a soy marinade). The atmosphere is vibrant yet not too chaotic, the decor is reminiscent of New York's SoHo (with a warehouse feel, high-tech black chairs, ceiling fans, and stage props decorating the walls), and the prices are quite fair. Though not appropriate for a serious business meal, this is a perfect place for hip business entertaining. *1151 Folsom St., tel. 415/626-2388. Casual dress. Reservations strongly advised. AE, MC, V. Closed Sun.*

## Berkeley

★ ㉞ **Chez Panisse and Café at Chez Panisse.** The years go by,
$$$$/$$ and Alice Water's Chez Panisse remains a shrine to California cuisine—you still need to call a month in advance for reservations. In a homey, almost plain setting of dark, clean-line woodwork, wooden banquettes, low-slung armchairs, and white linens, an eclectic mix of diners is served a single five-course fixed-price dinner, which changes nightly. Chef Paul Bertolli is an Italophile, so you may be treated to an excellent pasta or risotto, but in general his dishes are resolutely American/Californian. Preparations are usually extremely simple, and the quality of ingredients and cooking is exceptional. One recent dinner included delicious white-corn soup, a classic Chez Panisse baby-greens salad, and flavorful beef simply roasted with a rock-salt crust. Upstairs at the Café at Chez Panisse, where reservations aren't taken and the mood and food are more casual, you can lunch or dine on the famous pizzas and calzones topped with roasted garlic and goat cheese; hearty grilled radicchio with aioli; and satisfying roast chicken. Service can be snooty both upstairs and down. The wine selection in both places is superb. The Berkeley location doesn't make the two Chez Panisses convenient for most business-meal occasions, but they're worth the trek if you're a devout food-lover—or if you're entertaining one. *1517 Shattuck Ave. Chez Panisse: tel. 415/548-5525. Jacket advised. Reservations required. AE, DC, MC, V. Dinner only. Closed Sun. and Mon. Café: tel. 415/548-5049. Casual dress. AE, DC, MC, V. Closed Sun.*

## Ethnic

San Francisco is blessed with outstanding ethnic restaurants, particularly those representing the countries of the Pacific Rim. Following are some of the best ethnic places in the more accessible parts of the city.

**Angkor Palace** (1769 Lombard St., Marina District, tel. 415/931-2830) offers sophisticated Cambodian cuisine, lovely Cambodian-palace decor, and a good wine list. **Celadon** (881 Clay St., Chinatown, tel. 415/982-1168) is an elegant Hong Kong-style Chinese restaurant with first-rate food. **China Moon Café** (639 Post St., Union Square, tel. 415/775-4789), run by acclaimed chef Barbara Tropp, serves intriguing, creative Chinese/Californian dishes in a simple café setting. **Fuku-Sushi** (Japan Center West, 1581

Webster St., Japantown, tel. 415/346–3030) has excellent sushi, comfortable decor, and doting service. **Golden Turtle** (2211 Van Ness Ave., Van Ness, tel. 415/441–4419) serves up fabulous Vietnamese food in an opulent setting. **Kinokawa** (347 Grant Ave., Union Square, tel. 415/398–8226) is a good bet for fine sushi and good grilled dishes in a prime downtown location. **Peacock** (2800 Van Ness Ave., Van Ness, tel. 415/928–7001), set in a serene Victorian mansion, offers admirable Indian food. **Phnom Penh** (631 Larkin St., Polk Gulch, tel. 415/775–5979) is one of the city's finest Cambodian restaurants, with a friendly atmosphere, delicious food, and good French wines. **Royal Thai** (951 Clement St., Richmond district, tel. 415/386–1795) may be a bit out of the way, but it's worth the trek for wonderful Thai food, lovely decor, and an intimate, romantic atmosphere. **Wu Kong** (1 Rincon Center, 101 Spear St., financial district, tel. 415/957–9300) is the hottest Chinese restaurant in town, featuring Shanghai-style cuisine, a stylish decor, and a very good wine list.

## FREE TIME

### Fitness

*Hotel Facilities*
The following are the top fitness centers in San Francisco hotels; all are open to nonguests for a day rate. **Nikko Fitness Center,** Hotel Nikko San Francisco (tel. 415/394–1111), $20; **Nob Hill Club,** Fairmont Hotel, (tel. 415/772–5393), $15; **San Francisco Hilton Health Club,** (tel. 415/771–1400, ext. 6333), $10.

*Health Clubs*
The following health clubs have excellent facilities and day rates for guests: **24 Hour Nautilus Fitness Center** (1355 Sutter St., tel. 415/776–2200), **Northpoint Health Club** (2310 Powell St., tel. 415/989–1449), and **Physis** (1 Post St., tel. 415/989–7310).

### Shopping

**Union Square** recalls old San Francisco. It's a landmark park in the heart of downtown bounded by Powell, Stockton, Geary, and Post streets and is lined with traditional department stores, including Gump's, Macy's, I. Magnin, Neiman-Marcus, and Saks Fifth Avenue. The three-level **Crocker Galleria** (tel. 415/392–0100) at 50 Post Street has more than 50 shops and restaurants under a great glass vault. The newest and most elegant shopping mall is **San Francisco Centre** (tel. 415/495–5656), at Fifth and Market streets. Its spiral escalator leads to more than 100 stores, topped by Nordstrom's, which occupies five floors of the nine-story vertical mall. Its central location makes it perfect for one-stop quick shopping. There are more than 175 retail shops, boutiques, restaurants, cafés, and galleries in the **Embarcadero Center** (tel. 415/772–0500), a five-block complex at the foot of Market Street that looks out over San Francisco Bay.

**Ghirardelli Square** is a renovated 19th century chocolate-spice-coffee-woolen works complex overlooking Aquatic Park that attracts tourists to its more than 70 shops, galleries, outdoor cafés, and restaurants. Nearby, the **Can-**

**nery** (tel. 415/771–3112)—a refurbished produce cannery at Fisherman's Wharf—has 50 additional shops, galleries, restaurants, and cafés.

Not to be confused with Union Square is **Union Street,** a trendy upscale stretch of shops and restaurants five blocks south of the Golden Gate National Recreation Area, where you'll find expensive boutiques and gift shops. Even **Haight Street** shops have become sophisticated; you'll still find tie-dyed and vintage '40s and '50s clothing, as well as Art Deco jewelry, but prices are inflated.

## Diversions

Riding San Francisco's **cable cars** is a memorable experience: the views are spectacular, and clanging up the city's steepest hills is exhilarating. The Powell-Mason line (No. 59) and the Powell-Hyde line (No. 60) terminate at Fisherman's Wharf.

**Chinatown** is a 24-block city within a city, with the largest Chinese community outside of Asia. The area stretches from Bay Street south to California Street, and from downtown Sansome Street to Van Ness Avenue. Nighttime, the area is as busy as it is during the day.

**Cruise San Francisco Bay** day and night with Red & White Fleet (Pier 41 & 43½, Fisherman's Wharf, tel. 415/546–2896) or Blue & Gold Fleet (Pier 39, West Marina, tel. 415/781–7877).

**Embarcadero Center** (*see* Shopping, above) is a three-tiered pedestrian mall extending five blocks west from the landmark Ferry Building at the foot of Market Street. The complex has major outlet stores, like Ann Taylor and the Gap, as well as restaurants, but what's interesting here is the contemporary art, especially the immense Louise Nevelson sculpture.

**Ghirardelli Square,** the **Cannery, Fisherman's Wharf,** and **Pier 39** hug the promenade along the waterfront, with lots of shops and restaurants, and crowds of tourists—many of whom come to see the group of sea lions who have settled in at the end of Pier 39 (left-hand side).

Wear warm clothing and be prepared for wind and mist if you walk across the almost 2-mile-long **Golden Gate Bridge.** Mini Bus No. 28 takes you to the toll plaza on the city side; the view from the vista point on the Marin side is outstanding.

The eastern section of the 1,000-acre **Golden Gate Park** has three museums: the **M.H. de Young Memorial Museum** (tel. 415/221–4811), which has 44 galleries showing the development of Western cultures from the time of ancient Egypt to the 20th century; the **Asian Art Museum of San Francisco** (tel. 415/668–8921), which houses the world-famous Avery Brundage collection of more than 10,000 sculptures, paintings, and ceramics illustrating major periods of Asian art; and the **California Academy of Sciences** (tel. 415/750–7145), one of the top five natural-history museums in the country, featuring an aquarium and a planetarium.

**High tea** is served 3–4 in the Four Season Clift Hotel Lobby (tel. 415/775–4700), where you'll be treated as graciously as any guest. Tea is also served at the Stanford Court Hotel Lobby (tel. 415/989–3500); the Compass Rose in the Westin St. Francis Hotel (tel. 415/397–7000); and at the Rotunda, in the Neiman-Marcus store (150 Stockton St., tel. 415/362–3900).

**The Museum of Modern Art** (McAllister St. and Van Ness Ave., in the Civic Center, tel. 415/863–8800) includes works by contemporary masters Paul Klee, Jackson Pollock, Robert Motherwell, Alexander Calder, Henri Matisse, and Clyfford Still.

**The National Maritime Museum** (Aquatic Park, at the foot of Polk St., tel. 415/556–8177) showcases ship models, photographs, maps and other artifacts, and includes the **Hyde Street Pier** (two blocks east, tel. 415/556–6435), where the *Eureka*, a sidewheel ferry, and the *C.A. Thayer*, a three-masted schooner, can be boarded.

## Professional Sports

San Francisco's baseball club, the **San Francisco Giants,** plays at Candlestick Park (tel. 415/467–8000). The Oakland team, the **Oakland Athletics,** plays at Oakland Coliseum Stadium (tel. 415/638–0500). The city's **basketball** team, the **Golden State Warriors,** appears at Oakland Coliseum Arena (tel. 415/638–6000). And the **San Francisco 49ers,** the city's football team, keeps Candlestick Park (tel. 415/468–2249) packed in the autumn.

## The Arts

A single block of Geary Street makes up San Francisco's "theater row," but there are commercial theaters throughout the downtown area.

The city's major theater group, the **American Conservatory Theater,** sets the standard by which other Northern California resident theater companies are judged; performances are held at the **Herbst Theatre** (Van Ness Ave. at McAllister St., tel. 415/552–3656). Across the Bay, the **Berkeley Repertory Theatre** (2025 Addison St., Berkeley, tel. 415/845–4700) offers a more contemporary mix that includes classics and new plays, and is the major rival for leadership in the region.

Commercial, Broadway-style shows are the mainstay at the **Curran Theater** (445 Geary St., tel. 415/673–4400), the **Golden Gate Theatre** (Golden Gate Ave. at Taylor St., tel. 415/474–3800), and the **Orpheum Theater** (1192 Market St., tel. 415/474–3800).

The **San Francisco Symphony, San Francisco Opera,** and the **San Francisco Ballet**—the city's three major performing-arts organizations—perform in the downtown Civic Center complex, the first at **Louise M. Davies Symphony Hall** (Van Ness Ave. at Grove St., tel. 415/431–5400), the latter two at the **War Memorial Opera House** (Van Ness at Grove St., tel. 415/864–3300).

Ticket agencies include **City Box Office** (141 Kearny St., tel. 415/392–4400), **St. Francis Theatre and Sports Tickets,** Westin St. Francis Hotel (tel. 415/362–3500), **BASS** (tel. 415/762–2277), and **Ticketron** (tel. 415/392–SHOW). Try **STBS** (Stockton St. side of Union Square, Thurs.–Sat., noon–7:30; tel. 415/433–STBS for recorded information) for day-of-performance tickets for selected music, dance, and theater events at half-price, as well as advance, full-price tickets. Cash sales only; no reservations or telephone orders.

## After Hours

The greatest concentration of nightlife outside of the hotels is found in the North Beach/Broadway and South of Market (SoMa) areas, but there are bars and discos scattered throughout the waterfront and outer neighborhoods, too.

*Skyline Bars*
Not to be missed in scenic San Francisco, the city's skyline bars—many of them in the major hotels—are a good option for a drink with colleagues or business contacts. The best is **The Carnelian Room** (555 California St., tel. 415/433–7500) at the top of the 52-story Bank of America Building. It has a clubby feeling and a forever view. At the top of the 46-story San Francisco Hilton, **Cityscape** (tel. 415/771–1400) offers a spectacular 360-degree view under a unique retractable skylight. The view begins in the glass-enclosed elevator that takes you 24 stories to the **Crown Room** in the Fairmont Hotel (tel. 415/772–5131). At the top of the Hyatt Regency, the **Equinox** (tel. 415/788–1234) completes a 360-degree revolution every 45 minutes. The fabulous vistas are just part of the ambience at the elegant, landmark setting at the **Top of the Mark** in the Mark Hopkins Hotel (1 Nob Hill, tel. 415/392–3434).

*Bars*
**The Redwood Room** in the Four Seasons Clift Hotel (tel. 415/775–4700) is an Art Deco landmark where an upscale group in their 30s and 40s come to relax. The **House of Shields** (39 New Montgomery St., tel. 415/392–7732), just across from the Sheraton Palace Hotel, has the feel of an old-time San Francisco saloon. In the heart of downtown, **John's Grill** (63 Ellis St., tel. 415/986–0069) was featured in *The Maltese Falcon*, and mystery fans will revel in its Hammett memorabilia. Scores of office workers in the financial district enjoy friendly libations at **The Holding Company** (2 Embarcadero Center, tel. 415/986–0797), one of the area's most popular weeknight watering holes.

*Cabarets*
The wacky musical revue at **Club Fugazi** (678 Green St., tel. 415/421–4222) has been running for more than a decade; reservations are a must. Female impersonators have been the draw at **Finocchio's** (506 Broadway, tel. 415/982–9388) for 50 years. The **Plush Room** in the Hotel York (940 Sutter St., tel. 415/885–6800) provides big-name entertainment in an elegant atmosphere.

*Comedy Clubs*
Super stand-up comics perform at the crowded **Cobb's Comedy Club** (2801 Leavenworth St., in the Cannery, tel. 415/928–4329). There's a more local crowd at **Lipp's Bar and Grill** (201 9th St., tel. 415/552–3466), an all-improv club that showcases outstanding troupes; Robin Williams has been known to drop in. Jay Leno and Whoopie Goldberg launched their careers at the **Punch Line** (444 Battery St., tel. 415/397–7573), which continues to feature top talent.

## Jazz Clubs

Jazz greats, including Stan Getz, have performed at **Kimball's** (300 Grove St., tel. 415/861–5555). Johnny Coals and Clifford Jordan appear fairly regularly at **Milestones** (376 5th St., tel. 415/777–9997). **Roland's** (2313 Van Ness Ave. at Union St., tel. 415/567–1063) is a comfortable place that draws a local crowd.

## Rock Clubs

**City Nights** (715 Harrison St., tel. 415/546–7774) offers dancing to disks in sumptuous surroundings. In the SoMa area, the **DNA Lounge** (375 11th St., near Harrison St., tel. 415/626–2532) has live bands on Fridays and Saturdays. The **Great American Music Hall** (859 O'Farrell St., between Polk and Larkin Sts., tel. 415/885–0750) offers an eclectic schedule of live bands; call ahead to see who's appearing. Panoramic views are part of the decor at **Oz** (tel. 415/397–7000), an upscale disco at the top of the Westin St. Francis, reached via a glass elevator. You'll find crowds of young professionals, sometimes 2,000 strong, rocking at **Southside** (1190 Folsom St., tel. 415/431–3332).

## For Singles

**Channel's** (No. 1 Embarcadero Center, tel. 415/956–8768) is a financial district watering hole that's popular on weeknights. **Harry's Bar and American Grill** (500 Van Ness Ave., tel. 415/864–2779) attracts an upscale crowd. **Perry's** (1944 Union St. at Buchanan St., tel. 415/922–9022) is one of the city's best singles bars; it's usually jampacked. All of these clubs serve a 20s–40s crowd.

# Seattle

*by Mary Riordan Schactler*

Seattle is defined by water. There's no use denying the city's damp weather, or the fact that its skies are cloudy for much of the year. People in Seattle don't tan—goes the joke—they rust.

But Seattle is also defined by its rivers, lakes, and canals that bisect steep hills, creating a series of distinctive areas along the water's edge. Funky fishing boats and floating homes, swank yacht clubs and waterfront restaurants exist here side by side. Nearly everyone in Seattle shares a love of the outdoors. On the other hand, overcast days and long winter nights help make Seattle a haven for movie-goers and readers.

Shedding its sleepy-time image, Seattle is now ranked as one of the fastest growing cities in the country. Lumber accounts for a good portion of the local wealth, but the city is also the leading fishing port in the U.S. and the capital of the aerospace industry. Almost one of every two planes now serving the Western world was manufactured in Seattle—headquarters of Boeing Corp. As a major seaport, Seattle is also a vital link in Pacific Rim trade, and the evidence of internationalism is everywhere—from the discreet Japanese script identifying downtown department stores to the multilingual recorded messages at Seattle-Tacoma International Airport.

As the city grows, it is beginning to display big-city problems. With an increase in population has come sky-rocketing housing costs, clogged roads and bridges, and an increase in crime and racial tension. The homeless now haunt historic Pioneer Square and Pike Place Market, and nearby Bellevue has swollen in just a few years from a quiet farming community to the second largest city in the state.

On the positive side, the town that Sir Thomas Beecham once described as a cultural wasteland now has a world-renowned theater and music scene, as well as a new innovative convention center, and a covered dome for professional sports. And the city continues to enjoy a reputation as the most liveable city in the nation, and one of the ten most desirable urban destinations in the world.

## Top Employers

| Employer | Type of Enterprise | Parent*/ Headquarters |
|---|---|---|
| **Alaska Air Group** | Airline | Seattle |
| **Boeing** | Aerospace | Seattle |
| **Burlington Resources** | Energy and resources | Seattle |
| **Cosco** | Membership discount warehouses | Seattle |
| **Microsoft** | Computer software | Seattle |
| **Nordstrom** | Retailing | Seattle |
| **PACCAR** | Trucks | Seattle |
| **Safeco** | Insurance and financial services | Seattle |
| **Univar** | Industrial chemicals | Seattle |
| **Weyerhaeuser** | Forest products | Seattle |

*if applicable*

## ESSENTIAL INFORMATION

### Climate

The common perception of people who live outside the Pacific Northwest is that it rains all the time in Seattle. It's not true, though it sometimes seems that way. Seattle averages about 36 inches of rain annually (less than New York City and Chicago), but the skies are often gray from mid-October to June, and there's often a drizzle in the air. Snow is a rarity.

What follows are average daily maximum and minimum temperatures for Seattle.

| Jan. | 44F | 7C | Feb. | 48F | 9C | Mar. | 51F | 11C |
|---|---|---|---|---|---|---|---|---|
| | 35 | 2 | | 37 | 3 | | 39 | 4 |
| **Apr.** | 57F | 14C | **May** | 64F | 18C | **June** | 69F | 21C |
| | 42 | 6 | | 46 | 8 | | 51 | 11 |
| **July** | 71F | 22C | **Aug.** | 73F | 23C | **Sept.** | 66F | 19C |
| | 53 | 12 | | 55 | 13 | | 51 | 11 |
| **Oct.** | 59F | 15C | **Nov.** | 51F | 11C | **Dec.** | 46F | 8C |
| | 46 | 8 | | 41 | 5 | | 37 | 3 |

### Airport

Seattle-Tacoma International Airport is about 13 miles south of downtown.

### Airlines

United provides the most frequent service to Seattle from other major American cities.

**Alaska,** tel. 206/433–3100.
**American,** tel. 206/241–0920 or 800/433–7300.
**America West,** tel. 206/763–0737 or 800/247–5692.
**Continental,** tel. 206/624–1740 or 800/525–0280.
**Hawaiian,** tel. 800/367–5320.
**Northwest,** tel. 206/433–3500 or 800/225–2525.
**Pan Am,** tel. 800/221–1111.
**TWA,** tel. 206/447–9400 or 800/221–2000.
**United,** tel. 206/441–3700 or 800/241–6522.
**USAir,** tel. 206/587–6229 or 800/428–4322.

## Between the Airport and Downtown

*By Taxi*
Taxis can be found outside the airport baggage area or can be called from special curbside telephones. Travel time is about 20 minutes during nonpeak hours and up to 60 minutes in rush hour. The most frequently used route—and your best bet during peak periods—is Highway 518 east to I–5 north to downtown. A slightly shorter route is 518 west to 509 north to 99 north. The cost is $19–$23.

*By Van*
**Shuttle Express** (tel. 206/622–1424 or 800/942–0711) provides 24-hour door-to-door service. Travel time is 35 minutes during nonpeak hours and one hour at rush hour. To reserve space, pick up courtesy phone #48 as you leave the baggage area. The cost is $12 each way. Most airport-area hotels provide free shuttle service.

*By Bus*
**Gray Line's Airport Express** (tel. 206/626–6088) travels between the airport and major downtown hotels. It leaves the airport every 15–30 minutes between 6 AM and midnight. Return schedules vary by hotel. Scheduled travel time ranges from 25 to 50 minutes, but rush hour traffic can add 15–35 minutes. The cost is $10 round-trip and $5.50 one-way.

## Car Rentals

The following companies have locations at the airport:

**Avis,** tel. 206/433–5231 or 800/331–1212.
**Budget/Sears,** tel. 800/435–1880.
**Dollar,** tel. 206/433–6777 or 800/421–6868.
**Hertz,** tel. 206/433–5262 or 800/654–3131.
**Mini-Rate,** tel. 206/244–1701.
**National,** tel. 206/433–5501 or 800/328–4567.

## Emergencies

*Doctors*
The **Downtown Clinic** (509 Olive Way, No. 1664, tel. 206/682–3808) is open weekdays 9–5, Sat. 9–2. Just east of downtown, **FirstMed Prompt Medical Care** (St. Cabrini Hospital, Terry Ave. and Madison St., tel. 206/621–3702) offers immediate care 24 hours a day. **Virginia Mason Fourth Avenue** (1221 4th Ave., tel. 206/223–6490), open weekdays 7 AM–6 PM, is a walk-in health clinic for minor illness and injury.

*Dentists*

The **Medical Dental Building** (509 Olive Way, tel. 206/623–4096) welcomes walk-in patients.

*Hospitals*

**Highline Community** (16251 Sylvester Rd. SW, tel. 206/244–9970), 4 miles west of the airport; and in the downtown area, **Virginia Mason** (925 Seneca St., tel. 206/624–1144), **Swedish** (747 Summit Ave., tel. 206/386–2573), and **Harborview Medical Center** (325 9th Ave., tel. 206/223–3000).

## Important Addresses and Numbers

**Audiovisual rentals.** Entertainment Plus (334 NE Northgate Way, No. 123, tel. 206/524–7553), Lackey Sound & Light Rentals (3425 Stone Way N, tel. 206/632–7773).

**Chamber of Commerce** (600 University St., tel. 206/461–7200).

**Computer rental.** Coren Computer Rental (1100 Olive Way, No. 1140, tel. 206/624–1400).

**Convention and exhibition centers.** Kingdome (201 S. King St., tel. 206/340–2100), Seattle Center (305 Harrison St., tel. 206/684–7200), Seattle Trade Center (2601 Elliott Ave., 206/441–3000), Washington State Convention & Trade Center (800 Convention Pl., tel. 206/447–5000).

**Fax services.** Customer Satisfaction Services (15031–B Military Rd. S, tel. 206/431–8029), Mail Box (219 1st Ave. N, tel. 206/285–0919), Pony Express Seattle (2508 5th Ave., tel. 206/441–4949), Professional Business Services (1200 Westlake Ave. N, No. 414, tel. 206/285–3375).

**Formal-wear rental.** Tux Shop (1521 6th Ave., tel. 206/622–3900).

**Gift shops.** Chocolates: See's Candies (1206 4th Ave., tel. 206/621–0581, and 1527 4th Ave., tel. 206/682–7122); Flowers: Basket Case (15403 1st Ave., tel. 206/246–4902), Flower Shop (1304 Stewart St., tel. 206/622–1467), Long Stem Floral (1401 1st Ave., tel. 206/464–1030); Gift Baskets: Fruit for Thought (206 S.W. 153rd St., tel. 206/243–4501).

**Graphic design studios.** Aloha Graphics (817 5th Ave. N, tel. 206/283–2783), Globe Stat (105 S. Main St., tel. 206/583–0508).

**Hairstylists.** Unisex: Adam & Eve Hair Styling (19039 Pacific Highway S, tel. 206/244–5088), Designer Curls (701 Madison St., tel. 206/622–8310), Hair Masters (1631 6th Ave., tel. 206/624–9935), Innovations (309 Marion St., tel. 206/343–9211).

**Health and fitness clubs.** *See* Fitness, below.

**Information hot lines.** Arts events (tel. 206/447–ARTS), financial reports (tel. 206/641–7777, ext. 3), national news (tel. 206/641–7777, ext. 6), sports (tel. 206/464–2000, ext. 9600), travel weather (tel. 206/464–2000, ext. 9015).

**Limousine services.** American Limousine Service (tel. 206/467–1775), Elite Limousine Service (tel. 206/762–

3339), Encore Limousine Service (tel. 206/622–1640), Signature Limousine (tel. 206/364–2300).

**Liquor stores.** Washington State (600 2nd Ave., tel. 206/464–7850; 2105 6th Ave., tel. 206/464–7841; 710 Pike St., tel. 206/464–7910; and 317 Stewart St., tel. 206/404–6744).

**Mail delivery, overnight.** DHL Worldwide Express (tel. 800/225–5345), Federal Express (tel. 206/682–1557), TNT Skypak (tel. 206/251–3700), UPS (tel. 206/767–9700), U.S. Postal Service Express Mail (tel. 206/246–6788).

**Messenger service.** Bucky's (1916½ 4th Ave., tel. 206/448–9280).

**Office space rentals.** Business Service Center (1001 4th Ave., No. 3200, tel. 206/624–9188), Executive Suites (411 University St., No. 1200, tel. 206/467–9378), Premier Suites (1601 5th Ave., tel. 206/340–6411), Professional Business Services (1200 Westlake Ave. N, No. 414, tel. 206/285–3375).

**Pharmacy, late-night.** Jordan Drug (2518 E. Cherry St., tel. 206/322–3050).

**Radio station, all-news.** KIRO 710 AM.

**Secretarial services.** Business Service Center (1001 4th Ave., No. 3200, tel. 206/624–9188), Executive Suites (401 2nd Ave. S, No. 630, tel. 206/467–9260), Globe Secretariat (2001 6th Ave., No. 306, tel. 206/448–9441), Professional Business Services (1200 Westlake Ave. N, No. 414, tel. 206/285–3375).

**Stationery supplies.** Queen Anne Office Supply (524 1st Ave. N, tel. 206/284–0760).

**Taxis.** Checker Cab (tel. 206/622–8383 or 800/228–TAXI), Farwest (tel. 206/292–0569), North End (tel. 206/624–6666), Rainier (tel. 206/623–8294), Yellow Cab (tel. 206/622–6500).

**Theater tickets.** *See* The Arts, below.

**Train information.** Amtrak (303 S. Jackson St., tel. 206/464–1930 or 800/872–7245).

**Travel agents.** J.D. Cook Travel (801 2nd Ave., No. 1117, tel. 206/447–2667 or 800/547–1555), University Travel (515 Union St., tel. 206/296–3030).

**Weather** (tel. 206/641–7777, ext. 9).

# LODGING

Seattle offers both the familiar comfort of chain hotels and an array of first-class accommodations that range from country inns to hotels with turn-of-the-century elegance. The best hotels take advantage of the area's magnificent scenery by offering soul-expanding views of Puget Sound and the Olympic Mountains to the west, Lake Union to the north, and Lake Washington or the Cascade Mountains to the east.

Most hotels listed here offer special corporate rates and weekend discounts; inquire when making reservations.

Highly recommended lodgings in each price category are
indicated by a star ★.

| Category | Cost* |
| --- | --- |
| $$$$ (Very Expensive) | over $140 |
| $$$ (Expensive) | $110–$140 |
| $$ (Moderate) | under $110 |

*All prices are for a standard double room, single occu-
pancy, excluding 8.1% sales tax and 6% service charge.*

*Numbers in the margin correspond to numbered hotel lo-
cations on the Seattle Lodging and Dining map.*

## Downtown

★ ⓫
$$$
**Alexis.** Built in 1901 and listed on the National Register of
Historic Places, this four-story European-style hotel was
last remodeled in 1982. It's a serene and elegant spot, but
also close to the waterfront's shops and restaurants. The
lobby is quiet, well-lighted, and furnished with comfort-
able floral-print chairs. Guest rooms are decorated in pas-
tel colors, with antique furniture and overstuffed chairs;
the large, black-tile-and-marble bathrooms have robes,
telephones, and good mirror lighting. Some suites have
whirlpool bathtubs and wood-burning fireplaces. The
quietest rooms face the courtyard garden and Post
Alley; rooms facing the avenue can be noisy. Amenities
include a complimentary Continental breakfast and news-
paper. A private steam room is available. The young
hotel staff is polite, personable, and well informed. The
tiny Café Alexis offers fine seasonal American cuisine
in a friendly setting. *1007 1st Ave., 98104, tel. 206/
624–4844 or 800/426–7033, fax 206/623–1182. Gen.
manager, Noel Burk. 39 rooms, 15 suites. AE, CB, DC,
MC, V.*

★ ❹
$$
**Edgewater Inn.** You'll be able to enjoy the natural beauty
of Seattle's waterfront at this informal hotel on Pier 67, at
the fringe of the business district. Sweeping views of Elliott Bay and of the Olympic Mountains seem to bring the
outdoors into the quiet A-frame lobby, which is simply
furnished with colorful, overstuffed furniture grouped
near stone fireplaces. First opened in 1962 and completely
renovated in 1989, the hotel has attractive guest rooms
furnished with light wood. Spacious rooms on the water
provide mountain views. City-side accommodations face
the dingy warehouse buildings found on most water-
fronts. The casually dressed young staff is friendly
and helpful. A courtesy shuttle takes guests to and
from downtown, and the city's waterfront streetcar
stops in front of the hotel. Parking is free. *A Westgroup
hotel. 2411 Alaskan Way, 98121, tel. 206/728–7000 or 800/
642–0670, fax 206/441–4119. Gen. manager, Richard
A. Young. 63 singles, 171 doubles, 4 suites. AE, DC,
MC, V.*

★ ⓬
$$$$
**Four Seasons Olympic.** This Italian Renaissance-style hotel, Seattle's most elegant, opened in 1924 in the heart of
downtown and was restored to its original grandeur in
1982. Dignitaries and high power executives lounge in the
massive but subdued lobby, with its light-toned wood and
marble accents, large chandeliers, and comfortable seat-

ing areas. Off the lobby, the Garden Court (*see* After Hours, below), with large trees and floor-to-ceiling windows, offers a pleasant respite at the cocktail hour. Although the formality of the public areas may seem imposing, guest rooms are comfortable and intimate. Almost half the accommodations are mini suites, ideal for business use, with French doors separating sleeping from sitting areas. The even-numbered rooms in the west wing have the best views. The staff is knowledgeable and efficient but sometimes stuffy. *411 University Ave., 98101, tel. 206/621–1700 or 800/332–3442, fax 206/623–2271. Gen. manager, Peter Martin. 240 singles, 186 mini suites, 12 suites. AE, MC, V.*

**❽ Inn at the Market.** This modern but characterful seven-
$$ story hotel, built in 1984 of brick and glass in Pike Place Market on the waterfront, attracts tourists in summer and a young business crowd year-round. Service is friendly but sophisticated. The lobby won't win any design awards, but is furnished with comfortable, well-worn chairs and couches grouped near the fireplace. The spacious rooms wrap around a brick courtyard, and some have floor-to-ceiling bay windows that open. Duplex suites have a bedroom upstairs and living room/kitchen downstairs. Guest rooms are comfy rather than fancy, and most have views of Puget Sound; the city-side rooms are slightly smaller than the others. Bathrooms are large and well lit. Fresh-ground coffee is delivered each morning for in-room coffee makers. The respected Campagne restaurant (*see* Dining, below) shares the courtyard with the inn. Complimentary limousine service is provided within the downtown area. *An Alexis Distinctive hotel. 86 Pine St., 98101, tel. 206/443–3600 or 800/446–4484, fax 206/448–0631. Gen. manager, Connie Schneider. 58 rooms, 7 suites. AE, CB, D, DC, MC, V.*

**❾ Sheraton Hotel & Towers.** This large, modern high rise is
$$$$ across from the convention center and caters largely to conventioneers. Once you get past the bustle in the lobby, you'll find the decor tasteful and the service accommodating. The hotel boasts an exceptional, $1-million collection of Northwest art. An art tour, guided by the hotel's curator, is available. All guest rooms were recently renovated; for the best and quietest rooms, try the Towers section on floors 32–34, or the mini suites. A business center on the second floor offers a full complement of services. There are two recommended restaurants in the hotel, Fullers (*see* Dining, below) and the more-casual Banners, as well as a piano lounge. *1400 6th Ave., 98101, tel. 206/621–9000 or 800/325–3535, fax 206/621–8441. Gen. manager, Joseph Terzi. 483 singles, 367 doubles, 30 suites. AE, D, DC, MC, V.*

**⓮ Sorrento.** Seattle's society and distinguished visitors fre-
$$$ quent this turn-of-the-century property, on First Hill, about ten blocks from the central business district. At the palatial entrance, an Italian fountain plays inside a circular drive edged by palm trees. The elegant but noisy lobby looks like a private club, with rich mahogany walls and beams, floral carpeting, and a large fireplace. The largest accommodations are the corner suites; there are a few small rooms to avoid. The deluxe suite rooms have antique furnishings and lavishly appointed baths (scales included)

# SEATTLE

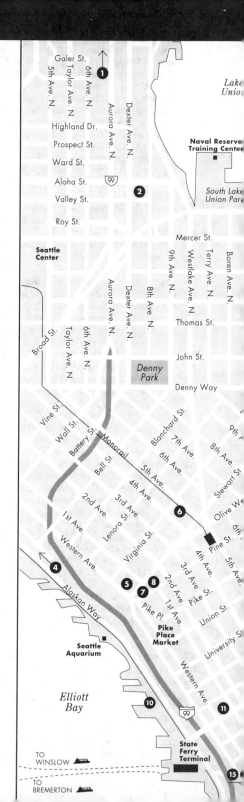

# SEATTLE HOTEL CHART

| HOTELS | Price Category | Business Services | | | | | | | | | | |
| --- | --- | --- | --- | --- | --- | --- | --- | --- | --- | --- | --- | --- |
| | | Banquet capacity | No. of meeting rooms | Secretarial services | Audiovisual equipment | Teletype news service | Computer rentals | In-room modem phone jack | All-news cable channel | Desk | Desk lighting | Bed lighting |
| Alexis | $$$ | 100 | 3 | ✓ | ✓ | - | - | - | ✓ | ◐ | ○ | ● |
| Edgewater Inn | $$ | 200 | 9 | ✓ | - | - | - | ✓ | ✓ | ◐ | ◐ | ◐ |
| Four Seasons Olympic | $$$$ | 500 | 13 | ✓ | ✓ | - | ✓ | ✓ | ✓ | ◐ | ● | ● |
| Inn at the Market | $$ | 40 | 1 | - | ✓ | - | - | - | ✓ | ● | ● | ◐ |
| Marriott Seattle-Tacoma | $$$ | 500 | 21 | ✓ | ✓ | - | - | - | - | ● | ● | ● |
| Ramada Seattle-Tacoma | $$ | 150 | 8 | - | ✓ | - | - | ✓ | ✓ | ● | ● | ● |
| Sheraton Hotel & Towers | $$$$ | 1300 | 25 | ✓ | ✓ | - | - | ✓ | ✓ | - | - | ◐ |
| Sorrento | $$$ | 80 | 3 | ✓ | ✓ | - | - | ✓ | ✓ | ◐ | ◐ | ● |
| Stouffer Madison | $$$$ | 448 | 16 | ✓ | ✓ | - | - | - | ✓ | ◐ | ● | ● |
| Westin | $$$ | 2200 | 24 | - | ✓ | - | - | - | ✓ | ◐ | ● | ◐ |

$$$$ = over $140, $$$ = $111 -$140, $$ = under $111.
● good, ◐ fair, ○ poor.
All hotels listed here have photocopying and fax facilities.

| In-Room Amenities | | | | | | | | | | Hotel Amenities | | | | | | |
| Nonsmoking rooms | In-room checkout | Minibar | Pay movies | VCR/Movie rentals | Hairdryer | Toiletries | Room service | Laundry/Dry cleaning | Pressing | Concierge | Barber/Hairdresser | Garage | Courtesy airport transport | Sauna | Pool | Exercise room |
|---|---|---|---|---|---|---|---|---|---|---|---|---|---|---|---|---|
| - | - | - | ✓ | - | ✓ | ◐ | ● | ● | ◐ | ✓ | - | ✓ | - | ✓ | - | - |
| ✓ | ✓ | ✓ | ✓ | ✓ | - | ◐ | ◐ | ● | ◐ | ✓ | - | - | - | - | - | - |
| ✓ | - | ✓ | - | ✓ | ✓ | ● | ● | ● | ● | ✓ | ✓ | ✓ | ✓ | ✓ | ● | ◐ |
| ✓ | - | ✓ | - | - | ✓ | ◐ | ◐ | ● | ◐ | ✓ | ✓ | ✓ | - | - | - | - |
| ✓ | ✓ | - | ✓ | ✓ | ✓ | ○ | ◐ | ◐ | ○ | ✓ | - | - | ✓ | ✓ | ● | ● |
| ✓ | - | - | ✓ | ✓ | ✓ | ◐ | ◐ | ● | ● | - | - | - | ✓ | - | ● | ● |
| ✓ | ✓ | ✓ | - | ✓ | ✓ | ◐ | ● | ● | ● | ✓ | ✓ | ✓ | - | ✓ | ● | ● |
| - | - | ✓ | ✓ | ✓ | ✓ | ◐ | ◐ | ● | ● | ✓ | - | ✓ | - | - | - | - |
| ✓ | ✓ | ✓ | ✓ | ✓ | ✓ | ◐ | ● | ● | ● | ✓ | ✓ | ✓ | - | ✓ | ◐ | ◐ |
| ✓ | ✓ | ✓ | ✓ | - | ✓ | ◐ | ● | ◐ | ● | ✓ | ✓ | ✓ | ✓ | ✓ | ● | ● |

**Room service:** ● 24-hour, ◐ 6AM–10PM, ○ other.
**Laundry/Dry cleaning:** ● same day, ◐ overnight, ○ other.
**Pressing:** ● immediate, ◐ same day, ○ other.

with separate dressing rooms. The employees are a mixed bag: some friendly and efficient, some inattentive. Visit the dimly lit Hunt Club for innovative Northwest cuisine and good traditional American fare. The hotel offers complimentary limousine service to downtown locations. A jogging route goes to Volunteer Park and back. *Preferred Hotels Worldwide, 900 Madison St., 98104, tel. 206/622–6400 or 800/426–1265, fax 206/625–1059. Gen. manager, Geoffrey A. Gelardi. 24 singles, 10 doubles, 42 suites. AE, DC, MC, V.*

**⑬** **Stouffer Madison.** This large, luxury chain hotel was built
**$$$$** in 1983. Business travelers usually stay on the club floors, which offer extra privacy and personal service. Overall, the staff is young, polite, and eager to serve. The rooms, like the lobby, are done in earth tones and have large, comfortable sitting areas. There are views from the 10th floor and up; views from rooms above the 20th floor are superb. Complimentary coffee and newspapers are delivered with a wake-up call. The multilevel Prego restaurant (*see* After Hours, below) doesn't rank with the best, but is worth a visit for a drink and the views. *515 Madison St., 98104, tel. 206/583–0300 or 800/468–3571, fax 206/622–8635. Gen. manager, Richard Whaley. 555 rooms. AE, CB, D, DC, MC, V.*

**⑥** **Westin.** Built in 1969 and fully renovated in 1982, this
**$$$** somewhat impersonal hotel is just a block from the city's major shopping area and an easy walk to the business district. A spacious lounge connects the hotel's two circular towers, which rise 40 and 47 stories. Don't be fooled by the rate schedule, which offers "view" rooms at premium prices; views can be found even in "medium" rooms above the 14th floor. The Westin takes justifiable pride in its dining rooms: Try the Palm Court for good Northwest cuisine. Also noteworthy is the spacious Market Café, modeled after Pike Place Market and decorated with color photos. The hotel's fitness facilities include an extensively equipped weight room and large pool; the locker room doesn't meet the same high standards. *1900 5th Ave., 98101, tel. 206/728–1000 or 800/228–3000, fax 206/728–2259. Gen. manager, Douglas Hales. AE, CB, D, DC, MC, V.*

## Airport

**⑯** **Marriott.** A well-trained, accommodating staff presides
**$$$** over this nine-story hotel perched on a hill above the airport. There is an attractive five-story tropical atrium with a large pool. However, the pool can attract a noisy crowd on weekends, and its chlorine smell permeates the rooms nearby. The largest rooms are the corner kings on the top floor of the tower, called the executive level; their vaulted ceilings are uncharacteristic of a chain hotel. The seventh and eighth floor concierge levels feature extra amenities and a comfortable lounge. The lobby and most guest rooms were recently renovated. Gambits lounge (*see* After Hours, below) offers jazz Wednesday through Sunday; it's an appealing room with a library area and some comfortable counter/stool setups. The Yukon Landing restaurant is noted for its fresh fish dishes. *3201 S. 176th St., 98188, tel. 206/241–2000 or 800/228–9290, fax 206/248–0789. Gen. manager, John Welt. 460 rooms, 3 suites. AE, CB, D, DC, MC, V.*

**⓯** **Ramada Inn Seattle-Tacoma International Airport.** Built
**$$** in 1988, this quiet, residential-style hotel is a pleasant sur-
prise. The Hearthside Lounge in the lobby is designed
like a modern living room—comfortable and friendly—
with music piped in or played on a baby grand. Just off the
lobby is the spare but elegant Café Fennel, with a lovely
garden setting accented by etched glass and polished
brass. The best rooms are on the east side of the upper
floors, facing away from the airport and toward Mount
Rainier. Unfortunately, the suites are all on the west side.
The single rooms are spacious, with comfortable seating
and excellent work areas. In all rooms there's a significant
buzzing sound when the bathroom lights are on. The staff
is polite and efficient. *18118 Pacific Highway S, 98188, tel.
206/244–6666 or 800/228–2828, fax 206/244–6666 ext. 510.
Gen. manager, Son H. Pham. 144 singles, 36 doubles, 24
suites. AE, D, DC, MC, V.*

## DINING

Seafood is a specialty here, and you'll rarely find a menu
that doesn't feature salmon, often broiled over an open
fire. Some of the hotel restaurants (Campagne, in the Inn
at the Market; Fuller's, in the Sheraton) are top choices
for business entertaining. Less-formal dining (Elliott's,
on Pier 56; Cutter's Bayhouse, near Pike Place Market)
will give you a taste of Seattle after-hours.

Highly recommended restaurants in each price category
are indicated by a star ★.

| Category | Cost* |
| --- | --- |
| *$$$$* (Very Expensive) | over $30 |
| *$$$* (Expensive) | $25–$30 |
| *$$* (Moderate) | under $25 |

*per person, including appetizer, entrée, and dessert, but
excluding drinks, service, and 8.1% sales tax.*

*Numbers in the margin correspond to numbered restau-
rant locations on the Seattle Lodging and Dining map.*

### Business Breakfasts

**The Georgian** (tel. 206/621–7889), the Four Seasons Olympic hotel's elegant dining room, offers privacy in a formal
but festive setting. The **Parkside Café** (6th Ave. and Seneca St., tel. 206/464–1980) at the Holiday Inn Crowne Plaza
is bright and cheerful. An artsy crowd gathers at the chic
but informal **Raison d'Etre Café**, (113 Virginia St., tel.
206/728–1113). **13 Coins** has two locations. The one next to
the Ramada Inn at the airport (1800 Pacific Hwy. S, tel.
206/243–9500) is where you'll find local politicians and entertainers. The booths are ultra-private at this small but
popular spot. The second, downtown location (125 Boren
Ave. N, tel. 206/682–2513) gets a business crowd at breakfast and is also a popular late-night spot. Both restaurants
are open 24 hours. **Von's Grand City Café & Martini-Man-
hattan Memorial** (619 Pine St., tel. 206/621–8667), in the
heart of downtown, is known for its breakfast egg bar

and country buffet. Sit in one of the back rooms for peace and quiet.

## Downtown

**❼ Campagne.** This intimate, urbane restaurant overlooking
$$$ Pike Place Market and Elliot Bay favors the lusty flavors of Provence. The young business crowd that flocks here tends to prefer the lounge area for its relative privacy. There is patio dining in warm weather. For starters try the salade Niçoise or the lamb salad served on a bed of greens with goat cheese. The menu incorporates fresh local ingredients in such dishes as chicken stuffed with goat cheese and fresh herbs, salmon in a cognac and Champagne sauce, or garlic sausage and duck leg served on red cabbage. Service can be grumpy. *86 Pine St., tel. 206/728-2800. Casual dress. Reservations advised. AE, MC, V.*

**❺ Cutter's Bayhouse.** Ask for a window seat so you can enjoy
$$ the waterfront views from this spacious, bustling—some would say raucous—bistro north of Pike Place Market. The kitchen and bakery are open to view. The atmosphere is at once noisy, exciting, and comfortable, with pop music playing in the background. The harried staff is not always accommodating. An eclectic menu emphasizes Northwest cuisine: The fresh king salmon is broiled over mesquite and basted with seasoned vermouth-lemon butter; and the Dungeness crab is broiled and basted with olive oil, garlic, and parsley. There is a regional emphasis to the wine list, and the beer selection is admirable. *2001 Western Ave., tel. 206/448-4884. Casual dress. Reservations advised. AE, MC, V.*

**★ ❿ Elliott's.** Many businesspeople lunch at this cheerful sea-
$$$$ food restaurant on Pier 56, and lots of tourists come on weekends, but the noise level never gets totally out of hand, and privacy is almost possible at the well-spaced tables. (The best ones overlook the pier.) There are also private booths in the back and plush seats at the counter for single diners. The staff is friendly and accommodating. You can't go wrong with fresh oysters, served at the oyster bar or at your table. Daily specials usually include king salmon, prepared in a number of ways. Mesquite figures prominently in the menu: Mesquite-grilled salmon with black beans and chilies is a local favorite, as is mesquite-blackened halibut with roasted red-pepper butter. Seafood pasta is highly recommended. *Pier 56, tel. 206/623-4340. Casual dress. Reservations accepted. AE, DC, MC, V.*

**★ ❾ Fullers.** Forget that Fullers is in a chain hotel (the Shera-
$$$$ ton); this is the top restaurant in town, despite the service. A loyal clientele of politicans, media types, and businesspeople enjoys the privacy afforded by comfortable booths, the "gallery" of paintings by Northwest artists, and the fresh, artfully presented Northwest cuisine, with Asian accents. Among the house specialties are cod with marinated vegetables; lamb loin with roasted garlic and forest mushrooms; and salmon broiled with orange roasted-shallot butter. *1400 6th Ave., tel. 206/447-5544. Jacket advised. Reservations advised. AE, DC, MC, V. Closed Sun.*

## Lake Union Area

**②** **Adriatica.** Expense account diners looking for a good, safe
**$$$** (not trendy) meal in elegant surroundings will be pleased
with this southern Mediterranean restaurant in a three-
story house on a hill overlooking Lake Union. The best ta-
bles are in the front room, which has a lovely nighttime
view; all are well spaced for privacy. For an entrée, try any
of the fresh grilled fish dishes or *raznjici* (leg of lamb mar-
inated in wine and rosemary, skewered, and charcoal-
grilled). The chef's favorite is boneless tenderloin of pork
marinated in olive oil and thyme, charcoal grilled, and
served with a port-and-sun-dried-cranberry sauce. Serv-
ice is attentive. *1107 Dexter Ave. N, tel. 206/285–5000. Ca-
sual dress. Reservations advised. DC, MC, V. Dinner
only.*

**①** **Canlis.** The flagship of a popular West Coast chain, five
**$$$$** minutes northwest of downtown, is more an institution
than a place for fine dining, but it rates well among
Seattle's business travelers, bankers, and executives.
Benefiting from its hilltop setting, Canlis has a spectacu-
lar view of Lake Union and boasts well-spaced tables set
with cream-colored linens, fine crystal, and silver. Huge
windows, a lofty beamed ceiling, and a large, stone fire-
place complete the quietly elegant picture. There's music
at the small piano bar from 7 PM until midnight. The menu
features fine Northwest cuisine in generous portions: The
specialties are Quilcene Bay oysters and prime steaks
grilled over charcoal. Recommended appetizers include
chilled lobster, scallops, and bay shrimp in Thousand Island
dressing, and shrimp Canlis Capri (gulf prawns sautéed in
oil, butter, garlic, and dry vermouth). The staff is friendly.
*2576 Aurora Ave. N, tel. 206/283–3313. Jacket required.
Reservations advised. AE, CB, DC, MC, V. Closed Sun.*

**③** **Kamon on Lake Union.** For Japanese food at a moderate
**$$** price, Kamon's is a reliable option. Located on the southeast side of Lake Union, it's often chosen for lunch by
young professionals, including real estate agents and
bankers. At night an older crowd comes to dine at the well-
spaced tables and capacious booths. Large windows have
panoramic views of the lake and marina. In warm weather
there's alfresco dining. The service and atmosphere are
cheerful, whether you're eating at the sushi bar, the
teppan yaki room (where a chef presides at your hibachi
table), or the main, international dining area that serves a
variety of ethnic cuisines. A combination of lobster tail
with sweet-ginger sauce and steak prepared with red
wine, soy sauce, and butter is a specialty here. Or choose
traditional Japanese sukiyaki—thin slices of sirloin
cooked in a broth with tofu, mushrooms, and vegetables.
*1177 Fairview Ave. N, tel. 206/622–4665. Casual but neat.
Reservations advised. AE, CB, DC, MC, V.*

## FREE TIME

### Fitness

*Health Clubs*
Guests at many downtown hotels pay $10 to visit the **Seat-
tle Club** (2020 Western Ave., tel. 206/443–1111). Also open
to the public are **Fitness Limited** (2001 6th Ave., tel. 206/
728–1500), and **Nautilus Northwest** (2306 6th Ave., tel.

206/443–9944) for $10 a day, and **Virginia Mason Sports Medicine Center** (904 7th Ave., tel. 206/223–6487) for $5 a day.

*Jogging*
You'll find good jogging routes at the **Washington Park Arboretum,** beginning from the main entrance at Lake Washington Boulevard and Madison Street; **Discovery Park;** and along the waterfront in **Myrtle Edwards Park,** from Pier 70 to Pier 92.

## Shopping

The new three-story, steel-and-glass **Westlake Center Mall** (1601 5th Ave., tel. 206/467–1600) is smack in the middle of downtown congestion, but contains some 80 upscale shops, as well as covered walkways to two of Seattle's top department stores, **Nordstrom's** (1501 5th Ave., tel. 206/628–2111) and **Frederick & Nelson** (506 Pine St., tel. 206/682–5500).

The colorful **Pike Place Market,** Seattle's waterfront market complex, has some 150 stands selling everything from spices to crafts. The Pioneer Square historic district is the place to go for Northwest Indian art and designer clothes.

For outdoor gear, try **North Face** (1023 1st Ave., tel. 206/ 622–4111), **Great Pacific Patagonia** (2100 1st Ave., tel. 206/622–9700), **Eddie Bauer** (5th and Union Sts., tel. 206/ 622–2766), and **REI** (1525 11th Ave., tel. 206/323–8333).

## Diversions

**Chittenden Locks** (tel. 206/783–7059), at the west end of the Lake Washington Ship Canal, draw visitors to see commercial and pleasure vessels being raised and lowered more than 20 feet between saltwater Puget Sound and freshwater Lake Union. Frequently, visiting California sea lions play outside the locks, and the fish ladder (with underwater viewing windows) is active July through January. The locks are bordered by seven acres of ornamental gardens.

**Discovery Park** (tel. 206/386–4236), located along the Puget Sound, covers 534 acres of forests, meadows, and sand dunes crisscrossed with hiking trails, including the easy half-mile **Wolf Tree Nature Trail.** The park's two miles of beaches—some sandy, some rocky—are good for swimming when the weather is warm enough. Also on park grounds is the **Daybreak Star Indian Cultural Center** (tel. 206/285–4425), which features a small collection of Native American art and a panoramic view of Puget Sound.

**Pike Place Market** (tel. 206/682–7453), Seattle's waterfront market complex, is built partly on stilts overlooking Elliott Bay. Be prepared to climb many steps and hills as you explore this seven-acre national historic district. Started in 1907, it calls itself the country's oldest farmer's market. A festival of local art and music takes place among the stands of some 250 local purveyors of spices baked goods, fresh fish, flowers, and crafts.

**Seattle Art Museum** (14th Ave. E. and E. Prospect St., tel. 206/625–8901), opened in 1933, is situated northeast of downtown, in Volunteer Park atop Capitol Hill. The museum is noted for its collections of Asian and African art and Renaissance paintings. The nearby **conservatory** and its five galleries include a cool rain forest and an arid cactus house.

**Seattle Center** (tel. 206/684–8582) is a 74-acre legacy of the 1962 World's Fair. A great place to take a stroll, it's especially appealing April through October, when the gardens are blooming. There's a magnificent view of the city, Puget Sound, and the snow-capped Cascade Range to the east and of the Olympic Mountains to the west. The five-building **Pacific Science Center** offers laser-light concerts, a planetarium, an IMAX theater, an interactive math-and-physics area, and a Northwest Native American longhouse. Visit **Center House** and its **Food Circus Court** for a wide range of international snacks. The **Alweg Monorail** runs 1.2 miles in 90 seconds, to Westlake Center in the commercial district.

Take a **Washington State Ferry** (tel. 206/464–6400 or 800/542–7052) to Bainbridge Island (one hour round-trip) or Bremerton (two hours round-trip). Ferries leave from Pier 52.

## Professional Sports

Seattle's baseball team, the **Mariners** (tel. 206/628–3555), and football team, the **Seahawks** (tel. 206/827–9777), play in the Kingdome. The city's basketball team, the **Super-Sonics** (tel. 206/281–5800), plays at the Seattle Center Coliseum.

## The Arts

The **Seattle Center** (tel. 206/684–8582; *see* Diversions, above) is the cultural heart of the city. Its Opera House is home to the Seattle Opera Association, the Seattle Symphony Orchestra, the Seattle Youth Symphony, and the Pacific Northwest Ballet. The **Bagley Wright Theater,** the **Intiman Theater,** and the **Bathhouse Theater** all present classical and contemporary drama. **A Contemporary Theater** focuses on works by living playwrights.

Ticket agencies include **Ticket/Ticket** (401 Broadway E, tel. 206/324–2744) and **Ticketmaster Northwest** (500 Mercer St. at Tower Records, tel. 206/628–0888).

**Bagley Wright/Seattle Repertory Theater,** 155 Mercer St., tel. 206/443–2222.
**Bathhouse Theater,** 7312 W. Green Lake Dr. N, tel. 206/524–9109.
**A Contemporary Theater,** 100 W. Roy St., tel. 206/285–5110.
**Intiman Theater,** Seattle Center, tel. 206/626–0782.

## After Hours

Pioneer Square has a number of nightspots, many of which offer a joint cover charge.

*Bars and Lounges*
For a power cocktail hour, the top choice is the elegant **Garden Court** (tel. 206/621–1700) at the Four Seasons Olympic Hotel. Only slightly less upscale is **Prego's** (tel. 206/583–0300), on the top of the Stouffer Madison.

**Ernie's,** at the Edgewater Inn (2411 Alaskan Way, tel. 206/244–3620), has piano entertainment and views of Elliott Bay. **The Top of the Hilton** (6th Ave. and University St., tel. 206/624–0500) has nightly music in its lounge.

### Cabaret

**Pink Door** (1919 Post Alley, tel. 206/443–3241) features cabaret-style singers on Tuesday and occasionally on other nights. Most guests are in their twenties.

### Comedy Clubs

**Comedy Underground** (222 S. Main St., tel. 206/628–0303), in Pioneer Square, has stand-up comedy nightly. Professional comedians are featured Wednesday through Sunday; open-mike amateurs on Monday and Tuesday. **Last Laugh Comedy Nightclub** (75 Marion St., tel. 206/622–5653) features national entertainers at a location near the waterfront.

### Jazz Clubs

**Dimitriou's Jazz Alley** (2033 6th Ave., tel. 206/441–9729) features name performers Monday through Saturday. **Patti Summers** (94 Pike St., tel. 206/621–8555), in Pike Place Market, is a small and casual club that attracts a local, professional crowd age 35–50. **Gambits** (tel. 206/241–2000), at the airport Marriott, has jazz Wednesday through Sunday.

# Toronto

*by Allan Gould and Suzanne McGee*

Local Indians gave the name "Toronto," believed to mean "a place of meetings," to the spot where the Humber and Don rivers come together and join with Lake Ontario. The site first hosted a busy Indian village, then a French trading post, and, in the late 1700s, a British town named York, before it was incorporated in 1834 as a Canadian city.

Toronto is still a place of meetings, the prime place to do business in English-speaking Canada. In response to growing separatist sentiment during the 1970s in Montréal, many national companies relocated here, and those companies have been joined by others. Hong Kong money is starting to flow into the city, along with that country's new entrepreneurs, who are fleeing the prospect of living the strictures of the People's Republic of China. At the same time, cost of living in Toronto has increased dramatically in recent years, and high rental fees have lead several major corporations to shift headquarters to the suburbs or away from the area altogether.

But although subject to typical big-city annoyances such as congested rush hours, Toronto is still a good place to live—if one can afford it. It is clean and relatively crime free. It is also the country's cultural capital. Once homogenous to the point of tedium, Toronto is now ethnically diverse; recent immigrant groups include Greeks, Portuguese, Italians, Vietnamese, Chinese, and Hungarians. With the conclusion of the free trade agreement between Canada and the United States, business travel has stepped up considerably, and services offered to business travelers have kept pace. Toronto is one of the few cities in North America where it is still possible to attend business meetings, dine in style, and attend an excellent concert or play before retiring for the night without having walked more than six blocks from your hotel.

## Top Employers

| Employer | Type of Enterprise | Parent*/ Headquarters |
|---|---|---|
| **A&P Food Stores** | Groceries | Toronto |
| **Canada Life Assurance** | Insurance | Toronto |

| | | |
|---|---|---|
| **Ellis Don Construction Limited** | Construction | London, Ontario |
| **F. W. Woolworth Co. Limited** | Retail | Toronto |
| **Honeywell Limited** | Computers | Toronto |
| **Indal Limited** | Manufacturing | Toronto |
| **Kodak Canada Inc.** | Photographic equipment | Toronto |
| **Maclean-Huntre Ltd.** | Communications | Toronto |
| **Royal Trust Company** | Real estate | Toronto |
| **Sun Life Assurance** | Insurance | Toronto |
| **Toronto Star Newspapers Ltd.** | Newspapers | Toronto |

*\*if applicable*

## ESSENTIAL INFORMATION

### Climate

What follows are the average daily maximum and minimum temperatures for Toronto.

| | | | | | | | | |
|---|---|---|---|---|---|---|---|---|
| **Jan.** | 30F | −1C | **Feb.** | 30F | −1C | **Mar.** | 37F | 3C |
| | 16 | −9 | | 15 | −9 | | 23 | −5 |
| **Apr.** | 50F | 10C | **May** | 63F | 17C | **June** | 73F | 23C |
| | 34 | 1 | | 44 | 7 | | 54 | 12 |
| **July** | 79F | 26C | **Aug.** | 77F | 25C | **Sept.** | 69F | 21C |
| | 59 | 15 | | 58 | 14 | | 51 | 11 |
| **Oct.** | 56F | 13C | **Nov.** | 43F | 6C | **Dec.** | 33F | 1C |
| | 40 | 4 | | 31 | −1 | | 21 | −6 |

### Airports

**Pearson International** (simply called "the Toronto airport"), 18 miles from the city center, serves Toronto and most of southwestern Ontario. Try to avoid arrivals at Terminal 1, which is overcrowded and has inadequate baggage handling facilities. (Although most flights use Pearson, **Toronto Island Airport,** about 25 minutes from downtown, also offers commuter service to nearby cities, notably Ottawa, Montreal, and Newark, NJ. Shuttle service from the Royal York Hotel to the Toronto Island Airport—by bus and then by ferry—is provided free by the airport's major carrier, City Express, but this airline's planes are small and propeller-driven, flights are less frequent, delays are not uncommon, and there are few alternative flights if delays are extensive.

## Airport Business Facilities

A **Swiss Hotel** with business facilities is planned to open in the summer of 1991 at Pearson International, within the new Terminal 3 currently under construction.

## Airlines

Toronto is a hub city for both Air Canada and Canadian Airlines International. Air Canada, USAir, and American Airlines fly between here and the northeastern U.S. most often; Northwest has frequent flights to and from Chicago.

**Air Canada,** tel. 416/925–2311 or 800/422–6232.
**American,** tel. 800/433–7300.
**Canadian Airlines International,** tel. 416/675–2211 or 800/387–2737.
**City Express,** tel. 416/360–4444 or 800/387–3060 (Island).
**Delta,** tel. 416/868–1717 or 800/843–9378.
**Midway,** tel. 800/621–5760.
**Northwest,** tel. 800/225–2525.
**United,** tel. 416/362–5000 or 800/241–6522.
**USAir,** tel. 416/361–1560 or 800/428–4322.

## Between Toronto Airport and Downtown

*By Taxi*
A cab downtown can take more than an hour during rush hour, 25–30 minutes if traffic is light. To avoid delays, travelers are advised to arrive or depart between 9 AM and 3 PM or after 7 PM. Fares from the airport are flat rates that depend on the destination. Taxis and limos to a hotel or business by the lake usually run more than Can$35. It is slightly more expensive to head uptown or to Yorkville, and about Can$40–Can$45 to go to the city's northeast corner (the area of Don Mills or Scarborough). Most limousine services have a minimum charge of Can$15, which gets you to an airport hotel. To Mississauga, charges run about Can$25.

*By Bus*
**Grey Coach** (tel. 416/393–7911) runs buses to most major downtown hotels at 20-minute intervals, from 6 AM to midnight daily. The fare is about Can$11. This is often a good bet when the airport is busy, as even at the best of times there is a dearth of taxis and limos. Grey Coach also transports travelers to three subway stops: two in the north (Yorkdale and York Mills) and one in the west (Islington).

*By Subway*
Subway travel is less expensive (Can$5–$8) but not recommended unless you're on a stringent budget and don't mind carrying your own luggage. Allow 1½–2 hours to reach center city. Buses run every 20 minutes from both terminals to Islington and Kipling stations (in the west end, on the Bloor line) and to Yorkdale (in the north of the city, on the Yonge line). The subway runs between 6 AM–12:30 AM.

## Car Rentals

The following companies have booths in the terminals.

**Avis,** tel. 416/964–2051 or 800/331–1212.
**Budget Rent-a-Car,** tel. 416/673–3322 or 800/527–0700.

**Hertz,** tel. 416/961–3320 or 800/223–6472; in NY, 800/522–5568.

**National,** tel. 416/488–2400 or 800/227–7368.

## Emergencies

*Doctors*
**Dial-a-Doctor** (tel. 416/492–4713).

*Dentists*
**Yonge Finch Dental Centre** (5650 Yonge St., tel. 416/222–6122), **Toronto Eaton Centre** (Dundas and Yonge Sts., tel. 416/585–9133), **Metro Central** (24-hour service, tel. 416/787–1275), **Metro West** (including airport, tel. 416/622–5235).

*Hospitals*
**Mount Sinai** (600 University Ave. near Dundas, tel. 416/596–4200), **Toronto General** (University Ave. and Dundas St., tel. 416/595–3111), **Toronto Western** (399 Bathurst St., at Dundas St., tel. 416/368–2581), **North York General** (4001 Leslie St., near the 401, tel. 416/756–6000), **Etobicoke General** (101 Humber College, near airport, tel. 416/747–3528).

## Important Addresses and Numbers

**Audiovisual rentals.** Metrocom (21 Goodridge St., tel. 416/259–1772).

**Chamber of Commerce.** The Board of Trade of Metropolitan Toronto (1 First Canadian Place, tel. 416/366–6811).

**Computer Rentals.** CO/RENT Computer Stores (2 Berkeley St., Suite 305, tel. 416/366–7368), Drexis Computer Rentals (100 Richmond St. E, Suite 320, tel. 416/366–9199), Vernon Computer Rentals (81st St. Clair Ave. E, tel. 416/963–9340).

**Convention and Exhibition Centers.** Canadian Exposition and Conference Centre (272 Attwell Drive, Etobicoke, tel. 416/675–6500), Exhibition Place (tel. 416/393–6076), International Centre (6900 Airport Rd., Mississauga, tel. 416/677–6131), Metro Toronto Convention Centre (255 Front St. W, tel. 416/585–8000).

**Fax services.** Businex Business Centres (801 York Mills; 3800 Steeles Ave. W; 833 The Queensway; 3100 Steeles Ave. W, 24-hour services; tel. 416/739–5000 for all stores).

**Formal-wear rentals.** Freeman Formalwear (556 Yonge St., tel. 416/920–2727), Syd Silver Formals (500 Yonge St., tel. 416/923–4611).

**Gift shops.** Chocolates: Chocolate Messenger (1574 Bayview, South of Eglinton, tel. 416/488–1414). Flowers: King Edward Florist (37 King St. E, tel. 416/366–6501), Queen's Quay Florist (at Harbourfront, tel. 416/865–1388, open daily). Fruit baskets: Gift O'Fruit (964 Eglinton St. W, tel. 416/787–4505).

**Graphic design studios.** GJW Graphics Services (1120 Tapscott Rd., Unit #3, Scarborough, tel. 416/298–7050), The Printing House (Citibank Pl., 123 Front St. W, tel. 416/865–1660), Syrograph International (517 Wellington St. W, Suite 301, tel. 416/599–8094).

**Hairstylists.** Unisex: De Berardini Salon (Eaton Centre, tel. 416/979–9292). Men: Roula's Exclusive Men's (Inn on the Park, Leslie and Englinton Ave. E, tel. 416/447–9780).

**Health and fitness clubs.** *See* Fitness, below.

**Information hot lines.** Metropolitan Toronto Convention and Visitors Association (tel. 416/368–9821), Canadian Auto Association Road Report (tel. 416/966–3000).

**Limousine services.** Airline Limousine (tel. 416/675–7181), Carey Limousine (tel. 416/466–8776 or 800/336–4747), Rosedale Livery (tel. 416/677–9444 or 800/268–4967).

**Liquor stores.** Pearson International Airport (Terminal 1, tel. 416/676–3945, Terminal 2, tel. 416/676–3695), Toronto Eaton Centre (Dundas and Yonge Sts., tel. 416/979–9978), Union Station (Front and Bay Sts., tel. 416/368–9644).

**Mail delivery, overnight.** DHL International (tel. 416/244–3278), Federal Express (tel. 416/897–9322), TNT Skypak (tel. 416/678–2770), UPS (tel. 416/736–3800).

**Messenger services.** Canada Post (tel. 416/973–5757), Win-Jam (tel. 416/431–5232).

**Office space rental.** Global Office (Drake International, 55 Bloor St. W, tel. 416/928–1300).

**Pharmacies, late-night.** Lucliff Place (700 Bay and Gerrard Sts., tel. 416/979–2424), Pharma Plus Drugmart (Wellesley and Church Sts., tel. 416/924–7760).

**Radio stations, all-news.** Canada's only all-news station closed in 1989 but CBC 740 AM and CBC 94.1 FM both have world news at the top of every hour.

**Secretarial service.** Support Office Systems (80 Richmond St. W, tel. 416/362–0859, open daily).

**Stationery supplies.** Grand & Toy (several locations, including: 120 Adelaide St. W, tel. 416/363–0022; 347 Bay St., tel. 416/366–0753; 777 Bay St., tel. 416/977–5100; 144 Bloor St. W, tel. 416/928–0213; Toronto Eaton Centre, Yonge and Dundas Sts., tel. 416/598–0144; 60 Yonge St., tel. 416/364–6481).

**Taxis.** Beck (tel. 416/449–6911), Co-op (tel. 416/364–8161), Diamond (tel. 416/366–6868), Metro (tel. 416/363–5611).

**Theater tickets.** *See* The Arts, below.

**Train information.** Union Station, Front St. W between Yonge and York Sts.: Amtrak (tel. 800/872–7245), Via Rail (tel. 416/366–8411).

**Travel agents.** Goliger's Travel (214 King St. W and other locations, tel. 416/593–6168), Marlin Travel (Commerce Ct., tel. 416/363–4911), P. Lawson Travel (131 Bloor St. W, tel. 416/926–6380; 33 Yonge St., tel. 416/365–7360; First Canadian Pl., tel. 416/862–0607).

**Weather** (tel. 416/676–3066).

# LODGING

As Canada's largest city and financial center, Toronto offers a wide variety of business-oriented hotels, many of which were built in the past 20 years. Business travelers who want to be within a few minutes' walk of their morning meetings often opt for hotels that belong to the Sheraton, Hilton, or Canadian Pacific chains. All are located in the downtown core, have similar rates, and cater primarily to business travelers or conventioneers. The downtown tends to be deserted early, except for theater- and concert-goers, but is within easy access of good restaurants and evening shopping. Many of the best Toronto hotels are located in the Yorkville area, a 5- to 10-minute cab ride from downtown, which has many excellent restaurants and upscale stores that stay open late on Thursday nights. It's not advisable to stay at airport hotels or in the northeast section of the city unless you're doing business in those areas. You'll have to fight rush-hour traffic if you want to get downtown—a fate many commuters feel no amount of luxury justifies. All but the airport and northeastern hotels are within easy access of Toronto's main attractions.

Most of the hotels listed offer corporate rates and weekend discounts; inquire when making reservations.

Highly recommended properties in each category are indicated with a star ★ .

| Category | Cost* |
| --- | --- |
| $$$$ (Very Expensive) | over Can$175 |
| $$$ (Expensive) | Can$125–Can$175 |
| $$ (Moderate) | under Can$125 |

*All prices are for a standard double room, single occupancy, excluding 8% city tax, 7% value-added tax, and 5% service charge.*

*Numbers in the margin correspond to numbers on the Toronto Dining and Lodging map.*

## Downtown/Center City

**❷❸** **Chestnut Park Hotel.** This 26-story hotel, which opened in
$$$ 1989, stands just behind the futuristic New City Hall and only steps from the financial district—an exceedingly convenient location for business travelers. The glass-enclosed lobby is handsomely turned out with Asian art, Chinese screens and vases, and handcarved rosewood chairs. The hotel's owner is a serious collector of exotic art, especially textiles, and the hotel is connected at the mezzanine level with a Museum of Textiles. Cozy guest rooms are furnished with bleached-pine furniture; bathrooms are standard. Executive suites have whirlpool tubs. *108 Chestnut St., M5G 1R3, tel. 416/977–5000 or 800/668–6600, fax 416/977–9513. Gen. manager, John Pye. 520 rooms, 8 suites. AE, CB, DC, MC, V.*

**❷⓪** **Delta Chelsea Inn.** One of the largest hotels in the British
$$ Commonwealth, the Chelsea recently finished several renovations and an $80-million expansion, including the addi-

tion of a business center, a glass-enclosed spa, an exercise room, and a pool. Rooms are bright and modern, with dark wood furniture; some are more spacious than others. Ask for the east- and west-facing rooms in the south wing, overlooking downtown and the lake. Signature Service Rooms include such extras as Continental breakfast. Because this is still one of the lowest-priced major hotels in the city and just a short walk from downtown, it draws many families and tour groups; tours alone represent 50% of the business. *33 Gerrard St. at Yonge St., M5G 1Z5, tel. 416/595–1975 or 800/877–1133, fax 416/585–4393. Gen. manager, Rekha Khote. 1,600 rooms. AE, CB, DC, MC, V.*

★ ⑫ **Four Seasons Toronto.** Built in 1972, this is the No. 1 choice
$$$$ for Toronto executives who need to lodge an important visitor. On the edge of Toronto's fashionable Yorkville district, it is a 5- to 10-minute cab ride from the financial center, and only a 5-minute walk to some of Toronto's best restaurants and shops. The elegant rooms are decorated in earth tones and feature tasteful artwork. Suites are filled with antiques and fresh flowers; those on the 31st floor come equipped with stereos and VCRs. The hotel's staff is renowned for its service. A business center on the fourth floor is staffed 9–5 weekdays, but never closes. A masseuse and a car rental office are on the premises. The Café (*see* Business Breakfasts, below) is a good place for a morning meeting, and the highly rated French restaurant has an intimate air and a substantial degree of privacy for lunch or dinner entertaining. *21 Avenue Rd., M5R 2G1, tel. 416/964–0411 or 800/332–3442, fax 416/964–2301. Gen. manager, Raymond Jacobi. 379 rooms, 47 twins, 70 queens, 95 kings, 30 suites, 7 penthouse suites. AE, CB, DC, MC, V.*

㊱ **Harbour Castle Westin.** A favorite with conventioneers,
$$$$ the hotel's two 30-story towers on the lakefront are just steps from the Harbourfront complex and the ferry to the Toronto Islands. The uptown business core is some distance away, but the hotel offers guests a shuttle service. All rooms have lake views; corner rooms also look north to the glittering towers of the city. This former Hilton was built in 1975; the North Tower was renovated in 1990. The swimming pool, squash courts, and health club are among the best in town. Guest rooms are all in pastel colors, with marble-top desks and night stands, and bathroom phones. The Executive Club floors (21–23) offer concierge service, a lounge with an honor bar, Continental breakfast, and access to the health club. *1 Harbour Sq., M5J 1A6, tel. 416/ 869–1600 or 800/228–3000, fax 416/869–0573. Gen. manager, Rick Layton. 950 rooms. AE, CB, DC, MC, V.*

㉜ **Hilton International Toronto.** The advantages here can be
$$$ summed up in one word: convenience. It's only a few minutes' walk to most major downtown office towers, restaurants, and shops. Built in 1979, this 32-story tower used to be a Westin hotel, and travel agents frequently confuse it with the Harbour Castle Westin; it's wise to double check (the Hilton is the better bet). The spacious rooms are standard fare with comfortable furnishings and requisite pastel decor. Business-class rooms are somewhat larger but have furniture disappointingly similar to that of standard rooms. Furnishings in the suites are Sears modern; guests may prefer to relax in the business-class lounge, with its

# TORONTO

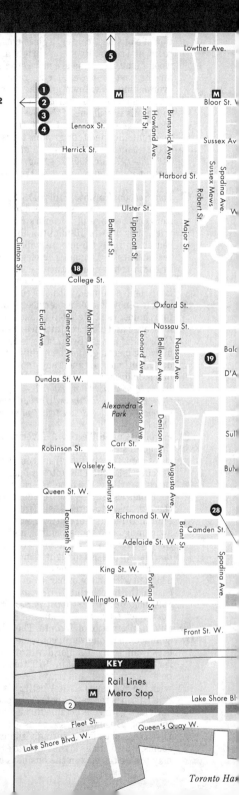

# TORONTO HOTEL CHART

| HOTELS | Price Category | Banquet capacity | No. of meeting rooms | Secretarial services | Audiovisual equipment | Teletype news service | Computer rentals | In-room modem phone jack | All-news cable channel | Desk | Desk lighting | Bed lighting |
|---|---|---|---|---|---|---|---|---|---|---|---|---|
| Bristol Place | $$$$ | 400 | 16 | ✓ | ✓ | ✓ | ✓ | – | | ◐ | ◐ | ● |
| Chestnut Park | $$$ | 400 | 19 | ✓ | ✓ | – | – | ✓ | ✓ | ◐ | ◐ | ● |
| Delta Chelea Inn | $$ | 1870 | 26 | ✓ | ✓ | – | – | ✓ | ✓ | ● | ● | ● |
| Four Seasons | $$$$ | 675 | 20 | ✓ | ✓ | – | ✓ | – | ✓ | ◐ | ● | ● |
| Harbour Castle Westin | $$$$ | 2500 | 25 | ✓ | ✓ | – | – | – | ✓ | ◐ | ◐ | ◐ |
| Hilton International | $$$ | 1000 | 18 | ✓ | ✓ | ✓ | ✓ | ✓ | – | ● | ● | ● |
| L'Hôtel | $$$ | 500 | 15 | ✓ | ✓ | – | – | – | – | ● | ◐ | ● |
| Ibis | $$ | 120 | 6 | – | ✓ | – | – | – | – | ● | ◐ | ● |
| Inn on the Park | $$$$ | 1400 | 26 | ✓ | ✓ | – | ✓ | – | ✓ | ✓ | ✓ | ✓ |
| Journey's End Hotel | $$ | 0 | 0 | – | – | – | – | ✓ | ✓ | ◐ | ◐ | ◐ |
| Journey's End Suites | $$ | 0 | 0 | ✓ | – | – | – | ✓ | ✓ | ◐ | ● | ◐ |
| King Edward | $$$$ | 350 | 12 | ✓ | ✓ | – | – | ✓ | ✓ | ● | ◐ | ● |
| Novotel Toronto Centre | $$ | 150 | 6 | ✓ | ✓ | – | ✓ | – | ✓ | ◐ | ◐ | ◐ |
| Park Plaza | $$$ | 400 | 12 | ✓ | ✓ | – | ✓ | ✓ | ✓ | – | – | ● |
| Regal Constellation | $$ | 2800 | 72 | ✓ | ✓ | – | – | – | ✓ | ◐ | ◐ | ◐ |
| Royal York | $$$ | 1380 | 34 | ✓ | ✓ | ✓ | ✓ | ✓ | ✓ | ◐ | ◐ | ● |
| Sheraton Centre | $$$ | 1800 | 36 | ✓ | ✓ | ✓ | ✓ | ✓ | | ● | ● | ● |
| Skydome | $$$ | 250 | 4 | ✓ | ✓ | – | ✓ | ✓ | ✓ | ● | ● | ● |
| Sutton Place | $$$$ | 350 | 17 | ✓ | ✓ | – | ✓ | ✓ | ✓ | ◐ | ◐ | ◐ |

**$$$$** = over Can$175, **$$$** = Can$125-Can$175, **$$** = under Can$125.
● good, ◐ fair, ○ poor.
All hotels listed here have photocopying and fax facilities.

| In-Room Amenities | | | | | | | | | | Hotel Amenities | | | | | | |
| Nonsmoking rooms | In-room checkout | Minibar | Pay movies | VCR/Movie rentals | Hairdryer | Toiletries | Room service | Laundry/Dry cleaning | Pressing | Concierge | Barber/Hairdresser | Garage | Courtesy airport transport | Sauna | Pool | Exercise room |
|---|---|---|---|---|---|---|---|---|---|---|---|---|---|---|---|---|
| ✓ | ✓ | ✓ | ✓ | ✓ | ✓ | ◐ | ● | ● | ● | ✓ | ✓ | – | – | ✓ | ◐ | ◐ |
| ✓ | – | ✓ | ✓ | – | ✓ | ● | ● | ● | ● | ✓ | – | ✓ | – | ✓ | ◐ | ◐ |
| ✓ | ✓ | ✓ | ✓ | – | – | ● | ● | ● | ● | ✓ | ✓ | ✓ | – | ✓ | ● | ● |
| ✓ | – | ✓ | – | ✓ | ✓ | ● | ● | ● | ● | ✓ | ✓ | ✓ | – | ✓ | ● | ● |
| ✓ | – | ✓ | – | ✓ | ✓ | ◐ | ● | ● | ● | ✓ | ✓ | ✓ | – | ✓ | ◐ | ◐ |
| ✓ | – | ✓ | ✓ | – | – | ◐ | ● | ● | ◐ | ✓ | ✓ | – | – | ✓ | ◐ | ◐ |
| ✓ | – | ✓ | ✓ | – | – | ◐ | ● | ● | ● | ✓ | – | – | ✓ | ✓ | ◐ | ● |
| ✓ | – | – | ✓ | – | – | ◐ | – | ● | ○ | – | – | – | – | – | – | – |
| ✓ | – | ✓ | ✓ | ✓ | ✓ | ● | ● | ● | ● | ✓ | ✓ | – | – | ✓ | ● | ● |
| – | – | – | ✓ | – | – | – | – | ● | ◐ | – | – | ✓ | – | ✓ | – | – |
| – | – | ✓ | ✓ | – | – | ◐ | ○ | ● | ● | – | – | ✓ | – | – | – | – |
| ✓ | – | ✓ | ✓ | – | – | ● | ● | ● | ● | ✓ | ✓ | ✓ | – | ✓ | – | ◐ |
| ✓ | – | ✓ | ✓ | ✓ | ✓ | ◐ | ◐ | ● | ● | – | – | ✓ | – | ✓ | ● | ◐ |
| ✓ | ✓ | ✓ | ✓ | – | ✓ | ◐ | ● | ● | ● | ✓ | – | – | – | ✓ | – | ◐ |
| ✓ | – | – | ✓ | – | ✓ | ◐ | ● | ● | ● | ✓ | ✓ | ✓ | – | ✓ | ● | ◐ |
| ✓ | ✓ | ✓ | ✓ | – | ✓ | ● | ◐ | ● | ● | ✓ | ✓ | ✓ | – | ✓ | ◐ | ● |
| ✓ | ✓ | ✓ | ✓ | – | ✓ | ● | ● | ● | ● | ✓ | ✓ | ✓ | – | ✓ | ● | ● |
| ✓ | – | ✓ | ✓ | – | – | ● | ● | ● | ◐ | – | ✓ | ✓ | – | ✓ | ◐ | ◐ |
| ✓ | – | ✓ | ✓ | ✓ | ✓ | ◐ | ● | ● | ● | ✓ | ✓ | ✓ | – | ✓ | ◐ | ◐ |

**Room service:** ● 24-hour, ◐ 6AM-10PM, ○ other.
**Laundry/Dry cleaning:** ● same day, ◐ overnight, ○ other.
**Pressing:** ● immediate, ◐ same day, ○ other.

large television set and billiards table. Other business-class perks include free local calls and in-house cable movies. *145 Richmond St. W, M5H 2L2, tel. 416/869-3456, fax 416/869-1478. Gen. manager, Horst Angelkotter. 601 rooms, 46 suites, 179 kings, 376 queens or doubles. AE, CB, DC, MC, V.*

★ **③** **L'Hôtel.** Open since 1984 and connected directly to
$$$ Toronto's convention center, this hotel is not only a favorite for conventioneers but also houses Canada's prime minister on his Toronto visits. The hotel is a few minutes' walk west from Union Station. Views are dismal—railway tracks, construction sites, office buildings, and only glimpses of the lake—but rooms are comfortable and in excellent repair (those on upper floors get less train noise). Nice touches include telephones with two lines and a hold button. Business-class rooms are larger and offer such features as stereos and full dining suites. Gold Class guests have private check-in service, free use of a boardroom, and a Victorian-style lounge where private breakfasts are served. The decor takes a turn toward the garish in some hospitality suites. Throughout, comfortable modern sofas and beds mix with the occasional reproduction antique sidetable or wingchair. The competent though not outstanding staff will provide most business services. *225 Front St. W, M5V 2X3, tel. 416/597-1400 or 800/828-7447, fax 416/597-8128. Gen. manager, Claude Sauve. 463 rooms, 36 suites, 427 doubles. AE, CB, D, DC, MC, V.*

**㉒** **Hotel Ibis.** This reasonably priced 11-story hotel is a mem-
$$ ber of the same French chain as the Novotel (*see* below). Opened in 1988, it is only a few blocks from the Eaton Centre and not much further from the business district. Although rates are attractive, the somewhat seedy neighborhood does not make women on their own feel at ease taking an evening stroll. The comfortable, standard-size rooms have the necessities, but few frills. Passes to a nearby health club are available. Staff members are cordial but not particularly knowledgeable. *Accor chain. 240 Jarvis St., M5B 2B8, tel. 416/593-9400 or 800/221-4542, fax 416/593-8426. Gen. manager, Patrice Basile. 294 rooms, 164 singles, 122 doubles, 10 for the disabled. AE, CB, DC, MC, V.*

**㊵** **Journey's End Hotel.** Rooms in this brick 14-story hotel,
$$ which opened in 1989, are spartan but spacious and well-lighted, with large work tables. Furniture and bathrooms are about what you would expect for the moderate price. On bright days, the modest lobby is flooded with sunlight. Amenities are few (free local phone calls are a plus), but the hotel is just a 10-minute walk from downtown. *111 Lombard St., near Jarvis, M5B 2B8, tel. 416/367-5555 or 800/668-4200; 416/624-8200, in Toronto, fax 416/367-3470. Gen. manager, Deidre Sloan. 196 rooms. AE, CB, DC, MC, V.*

★ **㊳** **King Edward Hotel.** After many years of neglect, this Ed-
$$$$ wardian classic has been thoroughly renovated. Some of the restoration was less than sensitive; the kitschy arbor in the dining room desecrates one of the city's great interiors. Still, the building is a splendid structure. Now restored to its pink marble grandeur, it attracts a well-heeled clientele (including royalty); one of the Shamrock Summits between Canada's prime minister, Brian Mulroney, and President Reagan took place here. Guest

rooms—all renovated by mid-1991—have an English country motif, and the floral wallpaper pattern is echoed in the curtains and bedspreads. The location, two blocks from King and Bay streets (the latter is Canada's Wall Street) is a plus, as is the hotel's Café Victoria, with its excellent business breakfasts (*see* Business Breakfasts, below). The Lobby Lounge (*see* After Hours, below) is a good spot for a quiet drink. *A Trusthouse Forte Exclusive Hotel. 37 King St. E, M5C 1E9, tel. 416/863–9700 or 800/225–5843, fax 416/863–5232; guest fax, 416/367–5515. Gen. manager, James Batt. 315 rooms. AE, CB, DC, MC, V.*

★ **③** **Novotel Toronto Centre.** This moderately priced hotel
$$ opened in late 1987. South of the main business district, it is within walking distance of downtown and caters to budget-conscious travelers who insist on service and quality. The stunning neoclassical gray building, fronted with columns and arches, promises—and delivers—a little more than the typical budget hotel. Rooms are basic but pleasant, with modern decor. The neighborhood is good, too; the O'Keefe Centre is just steps away, as is shopping along Front Street East. Among the cookie-cutter steak-and-seafood restaurants that dominate the area are a handful of attractive bistros. Unless you request a room facing north with a view of the city, you risk overlooking the city's railroad system. *Accor chain. 45 The Esplanade (one block below Front Street E, near Yonge St.), M5E 1W2, tel. 416/367–8900 or 800/221–3185, fax 416/360–8285. Gen. manager, Ricardo Perran. 226 rooms, 7 suites, 219 doubles. AE, CB, DC, MC, V.*

**⑪** **Park Plaza.** If there were desks in the 64 small rooms and
$$$ suites in the recently renovated South Tower, this half-century-old hostelry would give the nearby Four Seasons serious competition. Desks are planned for the larger rooms in the North Tower, being renovated, along with the lobby. Scheduled for completion in late 1992, these 200 rooms will do well to match the decor of those in the South Tower, where the atmosphere of a private home is created by individually decorated accommodations in pale earth tones, and the occasional antique vanity mixed among the Bauhaus-style furniture. Some suites feature added luxuries such as quilted comforters and TV sets in the marble bathrooms, which have separate vanity areas. A business center and fitness facilities are in the works. The elegant rooftop restaurant-and-bar (*see* Business Breakfasts, below) is a power breakfast spot in the morning and a favorite haunt for literati in the evening. The staff is generally gracious, but waiters can be supercilious. *Preferred Hotels Worldwide. 4 Avenue Rd., corner of Bloor St. W, M5R 2E8, tel. 416/924–5471 or 800/268–4928, fax 416/924–4933. Gen. manager, David L. Dennis. 64 rooms (264 by mid-1992), 20 suites. AE, CB, DC, MC, V.*

**㉟** **Royal York.** Until recently, the Royal York, built in 1929,
$$$ was the standard against which other Toronto hotels were measured. Most rooms, however, are on the small side, and although refurbished, they retain the somewhat dark, heavy air of Victoriana. Business-class rooms are a few square feet larger than standard rooms. Ask for accommodations on the upper floors with a southwest view, as far as possible from the noisy elevators. Some guests report problems with the aging heating system, which can over-

heat rooms. Bathrooms are dark marble and have new fixtures. The hotel's underground link to Toronto's railway station as well as to many of its major office towers helps explain why some 70% of the guests are business travelers. *A Canadian Pacific Hotel. 100 Front St. W, M5J 1E3, tel. 416/368–2511; 800/828–7447; in Canada, 800/368–9411, fax 416/368–2884. Gen. manager, Pietter Bougain. 1,438 rooms. AE, CB, DC, MC, V.*

**㉝ Sheraton Centre.** Those who prize convenience over all
**$$$** else will appreciate this central location and its labyrinthine underground connection to most major office buildings. The majority of guests are conventioneers, and the lobby resembles an airport lounge in size, decor, and volume of people rushing through it. The newly renovated rooms (floors 5–25) are standard Sheraton fare, with a pleasant decor in floral patterns. Desks are small, but rooms also have tables. Unrenovated rooms are rather dilapidated. Business-class travelers get a well-furnished lounge with free breakfast and hors d'oeuvres; however, their rooms are disappointingly small and some are in bad repair. The best bet for avoiding lobby noise are the "Cabana rooms," which open onto either the pool or a terrace garden. For a fee, male business-class travelers have access to a private health club within the hotel complex. The staff is cheerful but sometimes seems overburdened. *123 Queen St. W, M5H 2M9, tel. 416/361–1000; 800/325–3535; hearing impaired, 800/325–1717, fax 416/947–4874. Gen. manager, Marcel P. van Aelst. 1,430 rooms, 78 suites. AE, CB, DC, MC, V.*

**㉚ Skydome Hotel.** Not only is this one of the best values
**$$$** downtown, but guests in many of the rooms can watch baseball or football games at Toronto's new stadium from their bedroom windows. Other rooms have views of the downtown skyline. The decor throughout the hotel is slick and futuristic, but comfort hasn't been sacrificed to style. Some rooms are small, but rates for them are proportionately lower. Business-class accommodations are spacious, and occupants have access to a private lounge for breakfast or drinks. The friendly staff tends to get flustered when hordes try to check in as a ball game is starting. The surrounding area is safe, if a trifle bleak. The financial district is a 10-minute walk; cabs can take longer if there's a game on. *A Canadian Pacific Hotel. 45 Peter St. S, M5V 3B4, tel. 416/361–1400 or 800/828–7447. Gen. manager, Ray P. Thompson. 348 rooms, 71 suites. AE, CB, DC, MC, V.*

**★ ⑰ Sutton Place Hotel.** This European-owned luxury hotel,
**$$$$** one of the city's most impressive, occupies 16 stories of a 33-floor tower close to provincial government offices and thus is a favorite with lobbyists and lawyers. Afternoon tea is served off the lobby in an antique-filled lounge. Built in 1967, the hotel underwent renovations in 1988, including construction of a business center. Standard rooms are spacious and stylish, done in light, airy pastels; some adjoin parlors. Each suite has a different decor, though most include Oriental rugs and antiques. Butler service is available on the 18th floor, and also by special arrangement for all other guests. The neighborhood is a bit cut off from most business, shopping, and entertainment. To compensate, the hotel offers complimentary limousine service to the financial district. The staff is polite and efficient, but

warmth is reserved for favorite return guests. *A Kempinski Hotel. 955 Bay St., M5S 2A2, tel. 416/924–9221 or 800/268–3790, fax 416/924–1778. Gen. manager, Hans Gerhardt. 108 rooms, 72 suites. AE, CB, DC, MC, V.*

## Northeast of Toronto

**9** **Inn on the Park.** This resort hotel, part of the Four Sea-
$$$$ sons chain, is a 20-minute drive north of downtown. The advantages of the tranquil setting are offset by the distance from both the airport and downtown offices. The 600 acres have miles of trails for cross-country skiing, hiking, and jogging, as well as facilities for tennis, racquetball, squash, and horseback riding. The newly renovated lobby has marble floors, a rock garden, and a large fireplace. All rooms have dark wood armoires with matching headboards, side tables, and desks. The main building has 14 floors, the tower, 22. All deluxe accommodations are in the tower; these rooms are large, with spacious bathrooms, walk-in closets, and park or city views. Inner-courtyard rooms and the main building have balconies. Meeting facilities are superb, as is the service. *1100 Eglinton Ave. E, M3C 1H8. tel. 416/444–2561 or 800/332–3442. fax 416/446–3308. Gen. manager, Klaus Tenter. 568 rooms, 22 suites.*

## Airport

★ **1** **Bristol Place.** This 15-floor airport hotel has always been
$$$$ elegant, and after a major renovation in 1987, it is more attractive than ever. The three-story atrium/lobby has a traditional, European air, with soft colors, classical columns, Oriental carpets, and tasteful flower arrangements. Guest rooms have mahogany armoires, tables, desks, and minibars. Indoor and outdoor pools, a sauna, and a small exercise room add to the appeal. The hotel runs an airport bus from the arrival level; it's a two-minute ride. Airport noise should not be a problem for most, but rooms facing east are quietest. *950 Dixon Rd., M9W 5N4; tel. 416/675–9444, fax 416/675–4426. Gen. manager, Nick Vesely. 287 rooms, including 160 singles. AE, DC, MC, V.*

★ **3** **Journey's End Suites.** Like its downtown cousin (*see*
$$ *above*), this all-suite property is a reasonably priced option. Each suite is spacious, with a good-size table and four chairs in the living room, and French doors closing off the bedroom. The business center has all the basic facilities, and a courtesy bus runs to and from the airport every half-hour. Free local calls and a special day rate make this an excellent deal for budget travelers. *262 Carlingview Dr., Etobicoke, M9W 5G1, tel. 416/674–8442 or 800/668–4200. Gen. manager, Dykran Zabunyan. 258 suites. AE, D, MC, V.*

**2** **Regal Constellation.** This airport hotel has the facilities
$$ and sophistication of many downtown properties. It was built in 1960, and a new wing was added in 1984; all rooms were renovated between 1989 and 1991. The ballroom holds 3,000, and there are 75 individual meeting rooms. The executive floors offer minisuites with handsome desks, sitting areas, and attractive oak furniture—all in bright, contemporary colors that vary from room to room. An airport bus runs every 30 minutes between 4:30 AM and 1 AM. Airplanes do not fly over the hotel, so noise is not a

major problem. *A Regal Hotel. 900 Dixon Rd., M9W 1J7, tel. 416/675-1500 or 800/268-4838, fax 416/675-1738. Gen. manager, Michael Kalmar. 900 rooms. AE, D, MC, V.*

## DINING

Toronto's dining scene has gone far beyond the city's bland British meat-and-potatoes beginnings and now includes an encouraging selection of ethnic restaurants. Recent years have seen what the *Toronto Globe and Mail* restaurant critic has dubbed "the bistroization of Toronto," thanks to a new exciting generation of chefs. There are no real regional specialties as in, say, New Orleans, but the choices are wide and varied—the same as in any cosmopolitan U.S. city. Businesspeople frequent all the fine restaurants below, both for lunch and dinner. After-hours dining is available at most of them.

Highly recommended restaurants in each price category are indicated by a star ★.

| Category | Cost* |
| --- | --- |
| *$$$$* (Very Expensive) | over Can$35 |
| *$$$* (Expensive) | Can$27–Can$35 |
| *$$* (Moderate) | Can$15–Can$26 |
| *$* (Inexpensive) | under Can$15 |

*\*per person, including appetizer, entrée, and dessert, but excluding drinks, service, and 8% sales tax.*

*Numbers in the margin correspond to numbered restaurants on the Toronto Lodging and Dining map.*

### Business Breakfasts

**Café Victoria** (tel. 416/863-9700), on the main level of the King Edward Hotel, is popular for power breakfasts near the financial area; it's noted for poached eggs in phyllo dough with sautéed mushrooms and Canadian bacon, and broiled kippers with scrambled eggs on toast. **Le Café**, in the Four Seasons Hotel (tel. 416/964-0411), serves the old favorites—corned beef hash, bacon and eggs—as well as lighter fare. Service is attentive, and accommodates time restraints. Booths or secluded alcoves (seating 6–8) afford privacy. The **Prince Arthur Room** of the Park Plaza (tel. 416/924-5471) is Canada's primary business breakfast spot. Hearty repasts and a lighter Jogger's Breakfast come with a spectacular view.

### Downtown

★ ㉕  **The Avocado Club.** Until mid-1990, the Avocado Club was
$$  known as Beaujolais and was considered one of the city's best and most expensive restaurants. Then the same inspired owners and chef gave the place an entirely new, less expensive menu and look. In this converted warehouse, a few blocks east of the financial district, along the chic Queen Street West strip, Impressionist prints have given way to a riot of hot mustard, pink, and turquoise colors to match the menu's new spicy flavors. Appetizers include curried mussel salad with apples and new potatoes, and

soba noodle salad with sushi ginger. Main dishes include tandoori spiced pork loins with curried onions, and lamb chili. Publishers and ad execs continue to dine here at lunch, and a noisier sports and entertainment crowd pours in for dinner. The upstairs dining area is the best option for a quiet meeting. *165 John St., tel. 416/598–4656. Casual dress. Reservations required. AE, MC, V. Closed Sat. lunch, Sun. Moderate.*

★ ㉔  **Bamboo** An offbeat setting—a converted industrial laun-
$$  dry—and unusual Caribbean/Thai specialties have proved to be a draw for a young and chic TV, movie, and rock-music crowd. Because the dining area is always noisy, this is not a place for business meetings, but for relaxing after work. The decor is eclectic, with yellow walls, light green ceilings, and African and Indonesian art. Gado gado nut salad, Thai noodles, pan-fried sea bass, and red snapper are among the flavorful offerings. After 10 PM, there's live reggae and Caribbean music. *312 Queen St. W, tel. 416/593–5771. Casual dress, no reservations. AE, MC, V. Closed Sun.*

㉑  **Bangkok Garden.** The scent of teak and a faint odor of in-
$$$$  cense set the stage for some of Toronto's best Thai cuisine. Watch out for the fake crab, but don't miss the noodle dishes, which are the house specialties. The restaurant is elegant and quiet with teak paneling, Thai artifacts, and a small stream that runs through the dining area. Downstairs is The Brass Flamingo, a bar whose menu is more limited, though it still includes noodle dishes and the unique Boxing Stadium chicken. It's a good place to grab lunch, or even an early dinner. Menu items in both sections are thoughtfully coded according to spice level. *18 Elm St., near Eaton Centre, tel. 416/977–6748. Jacket and tie suggested, reservations recommended. AE, DC, MC, V. Closed Sat. lunch, Sun.*

★ ㉗  **Le Bistingo.** Claude Bouillet, one of Toronto's finest
$$$$  French chefs—part classic, part nouvelle—has his domain here among the Queen Street West shops, just a few blocks west of City Hall. This charming, low-key bistro has French windows with lace curtains, and large, round tables, well spaced for privacy. The prime minister is a regular, and lawyers, media stars, and business executives often lunch here, requesting the less noisy tables in the back when business is on the agenda. Reliable choices include the medallions of duck and any of the fresh fish dishes. The wine list is strong on French and California selections. *349 Queen St. W, tel. 416/598–3490. Casual dress. Reservations required. AE, MC, V. Closed Sat. lunch, Sun.*

★ ⑯  **Bistro 990.** This French Provençal-style bistro, complete
$$$  with open kitchen and mock-Chagall murals, is just across from the Sutton Place Hotel. Service tends to be quick at lunch and more leisurely at night. The place is packed for both meals, and low ceilings add to the noise level, but tables in the corners or at the back can be reserved for quiet talk. Roasted breast of duck, sea scallops, and salmon with peppercorns and olive oil all draw rave reviews. The wine list includes French, Australian, Californian, German, and Spanish labels. *990 Bay St., tel. 416/921–9990. Casual dress. Reservations advised. AE, MC, V. Closed Sat. afternoon and holidays.*

**④** **Bombay Palace.** Part of a chain that stretches from New
**$$** Delhi to New York, this offers the best tandoori chicken in
town, along with the usual North Indian fare. Another
tasty specialty is the vegetarian Navrattan curry. Al-
though the exterior and neighborhood are unprepossess-
ing, the red plush interior is upscale and the service is
nearly impeccable. The clientele is diverse and includes
the pretheater crowd. This is one of a handful of good
downtown restaurants open on Sunday. *71 Jarvi St., tel.
416/368–8048. Casual dress. Reservations suggested. AE,
DC, MC, V.*

**⑦ ⑲ ㉘** **Eating Counter.** This excellent Cantonese minichain has
**$** three locations: one near the Art Gallery of Ontario; a sec-
ond one near SkyDome; and a third uptown, on Yonge St.
near St. Clair Avenue West. Businesspeople and lawyers
flock to all three; meetings at the tables near the front
window and in the corners are quietest. The decor at these
eateries is nonexistent, but the food is top rate, particu-
larly the Szechuan shrimp, lobster, and chicken dishes, all
in garlic sauce. There are a few French wines available. *23
Baldwin St., near Dundas St., tel. 416/977–7028; 56 Peter
St. near SkyDome, tel. 416/977–2828; 1560 Yonge St., just
above St. Clair Ave. W, tel. 416/323–0171. Casual dress.
Reservations advised. AE, DC, MC, V.*

**★ ㉙** **La Fenice.** Convenient to both the Royal Alexandra thea-
**$$$$** ter and Roy Thomson Hall, this is a popular spot for
preperformance Northern Italian meals as well as for
business lunches. Though usually full and often noisy, it's
worth the hassle. The antipasto is a feast for the senses,
with treats such as mint-flavored grilled eggplant. Grilled
fish is the real specialty, but veal dishes also come highly
recommended. The extra virgin olive oil is pressed espe-
cially for the restaurant, and the chef's own watercolors
decorate the terra-cotta walls. *319 King St. W, tel. 416/
585–2377. Reservations recommended. Jacket and tie
suggested. Closed lunch, Sat.; Sun. AE, DC, MC, V.*

**㊴** **Nami.** This is where Japanese businesspeople like to wine
**$$$$** and dine their business contacts. Especially recom-
mended is the robata-yaki, or barbecue grill. Otherwise,
sample the seafood, the light and crispy tempura, or the
fresh sushi and sashimi. Some half-Western dishes have
crept on to the menu. The service ranges from mediocre to
attentive, depending on the day and the individual waiter.
The location is convenient to the business district. *55 Ade-
laide St. E, tel. 416/362–7373. Jacket and tie, reservations
recommended. AE, DC, MC, V. Closed lunch, Sat.; Sun.*

**㉖** **The Parrot.** For many years, this bistro near the financial
**$$$** district was Toronto's only high quality vegetarian res-
taurant; today carnivores have the most choices, but there
are still some good meatless dishes on offer. Track lighting, marble-top tables, black metal chairs, and changing
exhibits of oil paintings and photos offer a pleasant setting
for a blend of Continental and international specialties,
prepared by a French-Canadian chef. The menu changes
frequently, but the *gnocchi di spinaci* appetizer (dumplings of riccota and spinach in a rich gorgonzola cheese
sauce), sweetbreads, chicken breasts in amaretto cream
sauce garnished with cashews and almonds, and pastas
are all highly recommended. Quiet conversation is best at
tables 9 and 11 along the brick wall; elsewhere, it can be
noisy. The wine list is strong on American reds and

whites. *325 Queen St. W, near University Ave., tel. 416/ 593–0899. Casual dress. Reservations accepted. AE, MC, V. Closed Sun. and Mon. lunch, 2 weeks around Christmas, first 2 weeks of summer.*

**⑬** **Le Trou Normand.** As the name suggests, this restaurant
$$$ specializes in French dishes from Normandy. Calvados, an apple brandy, appears frequently in sauces; the omelets are renowned and make a good light lunch or dinner. Other Norman dishes include treats like duck livers sautéed with apple jelly, and grilled pork tenderloin with goat cheese sauce. Desserts, notably *clafouti*, a fruit tart with a custard base, are worth forgetting a diet for. The atmosphere is quiet and relaxed, and the restaurant, which contains three homelike rooms, resembles an unpretentious country inn. Generous portions and attentive service make this a pleasant alternative to fighting for tables and service at better known French restaurants. *90 Yorkville Ave., tel. 416/967–5956. Casual dress. Reservations recommended. AE, DC, MC, V. Closed Sun. lunch.*

**㉟** **Winston's.** Some of the city's top lawyers, politicians, and
$$$$ lawyers-turned-politicians lunch here daily at their personal tables, giving this resolutely nontrendy restaurant the feel of a private club rather than a public dining room. The vichyssoise is a highlight of the menu, much of which consists of good but predictable prenouvelle cuisine. Dependable entrées include beef Wellington and a range of soufflés. People come here because of the restaurant's reputation as a power meeting place; they don't expect an adventure in dining. *104 Adelaide St. W, tel. 416/363–1627. Tie and jacket required, reservations required. AE, DC, MC, V. Closed lunch Sat.; Sun.*

**⑭** **Zero.** True aficionados of Japanese cuisine are not de-
$$ terred by Zero's basement location or its unprepossessing appearance; in fact, the 30-seat room is consistently jammed with homesick Japanese businesspeople and students. The best bets are the set dinners, particularly tempura or *unagi* (broiled, marinated sea eel). Also offered are many dishes rarely found outside Japanese homes, such as *kimpira-gobo*, a mountain root chopped up and marinated with a tangy sesame-based sauce. The cuisine is simpler than that of Nami, but portions are bigger. *69 Yorkville Ave. (enter off street, down a flight of stairs), tel. 416/961–8349. Casual dress. Reservations suggested. AE, MC, V.*

## North Toronto

**❽** **Centro.** One of the best of the trendy Italian restaurants in
$$$$ the city, Centro sets a proper mood with soaring columns, photos of street scenes of the chef's hometown (Asolo, Italy), and warm, Mediterranean pinks and yellows. Large business groups request the quiet upstairs mezzanine; a private room in the wine cellar is often booked for parties. The menu is Northern Italian, with strong California overtones. Specialties include tuna carpaccio, grilled veal chop and roast American lamb, and polenta with gorgonzola mascarpone sauce. Desserts are made on the premises. Italian wines are very well represented, but there are California, French, and Australian labels as well. *2472 Yonge St., tel. 416/483–2211. Casual dress. Reservations required. AE, CB, DC, MC, V. Closed lunch; Sun., Christmastime.*

**⑱** **Palmerston.** Despite an out-of-the-way location, 1½ miles
**$$$$** from the financial district, lawyers, business executives,
and entertainers come here regularly to sample the
nouvelle American creations of chef Jamie Kennedy.
Among the light, tasty, and unfussy dishes are fresh lamb
and fish, cooked to near perfection, and trout fillets in
champagne sauce. Wonderful ice creams and fresh breads
and pastries are all made in-house. Menus change according to the availability of ingredients. The former storefront has pale pink walls hung with rotating exhibits of
paintings and photographs. The wood bar at the entrance
and the long, narrow dining area create a cozy and unpretentious atmosphere. The wine list includes Australian,
Californian, and Canadian varieties. *488 College St., at
Palmerston Ave., tel. 416/922–9277. Casual dress. Reservations advised. AE, CB, DC, MC, V. Closed lunch.*

★ **⑩** **Pronto.** This striking, bistro-style restaurant has an open
**$$$$** kitchen and a chic contemporary look to match its cuisine,
which can be described as Northern Italian with North
American twists. Mirrors and large abstract paintings
add to the flamboyant, stylish ambience; recessed lighting
adds an air of intimacy to an otherwise crowded, busy setting. Among dependable dishes on the seasonable menu
are barbequed shrimp with sweet potato fettuccine, and
peppered tuna steak—all with sauces that enhance rather
than disguise natural flavors. One sees world-class entertainers and the CEOs of Canada's Top 500 here, although
the usual noise level is not conducive to serious business
discussion; if you want to try to talk, request a table away
from the loud kitchen and front door. The private stock of
Italian, French, and California wines is impressive. *692
Mount Pleasant Rd., south of Eglinton Ave.; tel. 416/486–
1111. Jacket optional. Reservations required. Call weeks
ahead for weekends. AE, CB, D, MC, V.*

**⑥** **Scaramouche.** This elegant French restaurant, with fine
**$$$$** views of downtown Toronto, is located in a small apartment building on the peak of the Avenue Road hill, just
south of St. Clair and about 3 miles north of the financial
center. Tables are well spaced, but some are quieter than
others, and only six are directly in front of windows; call
early to request a table for serious conversation or good
views. The Continental cuisine is usually satisfying, if
rarely daring. Seasonal specialties include Atlantic salmon house-smoked and grilled with horse radish cream
sauce, organic filet Mignon with caramelized shallot
sauce, and a salmon tartare starter with caviar and cu-
cumber. The affiliated Pasta Bar next door is much less expensive; both have well-rounded wine lists. There is
complimentary valet parking. *1 Benevenuto Pl. (entrance
off Edmund Ave., on west side of Avenue Rd.; tel. 416/
961–8011. Jacket optional. Reservations recommended
starting Sept. Closed lunch Sat.; Sun. AE, CB, DC,
MC, V.*

★ **⑤** **United Bakers.** This superior dairy restaurant, about 15–
**$** 20 minutes by cab from downtown, is now overseen by a
third generation of the original owners, the Ladovsky
family. The soups are superlative, from the daily green
pea to twice-weekly barley, bean, vegetable, and potato,
to the Friday-only cabbage. Dishes such as gefilte fish,
carp, whitefish, cheese blintzes, vegetarian lasagna, and
Greek and Caesar salads match those found at downtown

establishments for three times the price. This place is worth the journey. *In Lawrence Plaza, corner of Bathurst and Lawrence Sts., tel. 416/789–0519. Casual dress. No reservations. MC, V.*

## Airport

❹ **Café Creole.** For many years this restaurant off the main
$$$ lobby of the Skyline Hotel was known for its Cajun specialties. The accent has shifted to such standard Continental fare as steamed salmon fillets and sautéed scallops in broth, but some old standards remain, such as the delicious potato pecan pie and bread pudding for dessert. Everything is prepared to order, so don't come here if you're in a hurry. Table 99, the "chef's table," is the quietest place in this large, 165-seat room. *655 Dixon Rd. at Martingrove, near the airport, tel. 416/244–5200. Jacket advised. Reservations advised. Closed Sat. lunch. AE, CB, DC, MC, V.*

# FREE TIME

## Fitness

*Hotel Facilities*
Some of the best fitness clubs can be found at the hotels, but the only one with daily fees (Can$5) for nonguests is the **Harbour Castle Westin** (tel. 416/869–1600).

*Health Clubs*
**Bloor Park Club,** inside Hudson's Bay Centre (at Bloor and Yonge Sts., tel. 416/922–1262), has a Can$10 guest pass. Facilities include a pool, squash courts, weights, an outdoor track, a sauna, and whirlpool. For facilities that include racquetball, squash, tennis, Nautilus, pool, and weights, **Parkview Club** (behind the Inn on the Park, tel. 416/441–6163) charges Can$15 a day.

*Jogging*
The **Martin Goodman Trail,** a 12-mile path along the waterfront from the Balmy Beach Club in the east end to the western beaches southwest of High Park, offers a scenic run; phone the *Toronto Star* (tel. 416/367–2000) for a map. **The Toronto Islands,** a 10-minute ferry ride from the foot of Bay Street, just beneath the Harbour Castle Westin, offer good paths and a spectacular view of downtown.

## Shopping

**Eaton's** and **Simpson's,** both large, moderately priced department stores, anchor the **Eaton Centre** (290 Yonge St., tel. 416/598–2322), downtown Toronto's major shopping area. With more than 300 stores convenient to the business district and enclosed from bad weather, this is the place to find virtually anything you need. It's also one of the city's major tourist attractions. Less expensive stores tend to be on the first floor, more expensive ones above.

The **Yorkville Avenue/Bloor Street area** is where you'll find the big fashion names. Yorkville Avenue, once Canada's equivalent of San Francisco's Haight Street, has become a mecca for those who would rather spend money than make love or war. Streets to explore include Cumberland and Scollard—both running parallel to Bloor Street—and Hazelton Avenue, running north from Yorkville Avenue near Avenue Road. The area is filled with famous designer boutiques, expensive jewelry shops, chichi cafés, and art galleries. Look for **Creed's** (45 Bloor St. W, tel. 416/923–1000) and **Holt Renfrew**, across the street (50 Bloor St. W, tel. 416/922–2333), for women's clothing (Holt's also has men's and children's departments); **Georg Jensen** (95 Bloor St. W, tel. 416/924–7707) for crystal; and **Boutique Quinto** (110 Bloor St. W, tel. 416/928–0954) or **David's** (89 Bloor St. W, tel. 416/928–9199) for shoes. On Yorkville Avenue, you'll find many antiques dealers. Bargain-hunters should check out **William Ashley** (50 Bloor St. W, tel. 416/964–2900) for discounted china and silverware.

If Bloor Street is Toronto's Rodeo Drive, the area around **Queen Street West** is its SoHo. Boutiques for young designers, new and used bookstores, vintage clothing shops, two shops devoted exclusively to comic books, and some of the city's most avant-garde galleries are to be found beginning at University Avenue and going westward past Bathurst Street, and along side streets. **Art Metropole** (788 King St. W, tel. 416/367–2304) specializes in limited edition art books. **Prime Canadian Crafts** (299 Queen St. W, tel. 416/593–5750) sells Canadian-made artifacts. **Atomic Age** (350 Queen St. W, tel. 416/977–1296) sells clothes by the trendiest young designers (no pinstripes allowed).

**Mirvish Village** (Markham St., a block south of Bloor St. W) is a one-block assortment of bookstores, antique shops, and boutiques. On Sunday, the Harbourfront features Canada's biggest antiques market (professional dealers are here Tues.–Fri.). Also at Harbourfront is the **Queen's Quay Terminal** (tel. 416/363–4411), a renovated warehouse that houses boutiques, crafts stalls, patisseries, and gift shops. There's a free shuttle bus from Union Station (parking is expensive).

## Diversions

**The Art Gallery of Ontario** (317 Dundas St. W, tel. 416/977–0414) offers an eclectic collection that ranges from medieval European to contemporary Canadian, as well as the world's largest collection of Henry Moore sculptures.

**The Beaches** area, in Toronto's east end from Coxwell Avenue eastward along Queen Street, has evolved from a village on the city's outskirts into a trendy Sunday and summer haunt for young professionals. It boasts a 4-mile boardwalk along the lakefront as well as a beach, but swimming isn't advised because of Lake Ontario's pollution.

**Casa Loma** (1 Austin Terr., tel. 416/923–1171), a European-style castle built in 1913 by an entrepreneur for $3 million, has 98 rooms, two towers, secret panels, and fine views of downtown Toronto. It's about a 10-minute cab ride from downtown.

Toronto's **Chinatown,** where more than 100,000 Chinese live, is a colorful setting for an afternoon stroll, particularly on Sunday. The area runs along Spadina Avenue, from Queen Street up to College Street, and along Dundas Street from Bay Street west almost to Bathurst Street. Visitors can eye cryptic medical labels at an herbalist, sniff the tantalizing aroma of roast duck hanging in shop windows, or buy pork buns to eat while strolling around.

**CN Tower** (301 Front St. W, tel. 416/360–8500) is Toronto's second most popular attraction (the Eaton Centre is the first, *see* Shopping, above). The tallest freestanding structure in the world (1,815 feet, or 147 stories tall), it offers spectacular views of the city—even extending to the spray of Niagara Falls, 80 miles to the south. Go on clear days only.

Toronto's nod to the waterfront "theme park" development trend is **Harbourfront** (at the foot of Bay Street by Lake Ontario, tel. 416/364–5665), which features galleries, boutiques, poetry readings, concerts, and boat tours of the harbor.

**Metropolitan Toronto Public Library** (789 Yonge St., tel. 416/393–7000), with its magnificent atrium, is one of the most inviting libraries in the world—open stacks, glass-enclosed elevators, audio carrels with headphones, and more than 10,000 albums to listen to. There's even an Arthur Canon Doyle Room for Sherlock Holmes fans.

It's a 30-minute ride from downtown to the **Metropolitan Toronto Zoo** (Meadowvale Rd., just north of Hwy. 401; tel. 416/392–5900), which was built to exhibit animals in natural habitats.

**Ontario Place** (South of Lakeshore Blvd., across from the Canadian National Exhibition grounds, tel. 416/965–7711) is a family-oriented waterfront complex, including a six-story movie theater, outdoor arena for concerts, a Children's Village, and a World War II destroyer. Open May–Sept.

**The Ontario Science Centre** (7700 Don Mills Rd., about 7 miles northeast of downtown, tel. 416/429–4100) has live demonstrations of lasers, glassblowing, papermaking, electricity, and a gift shop filled with science books and experiments.

**Royal Ontario Museum** (southwest corner of Bloor St. W and University Ave., tel. 416/586–5549) has a good dinosaur collection, an Evolution Gallery, a Roman Gallery, and a noted collection of Chinese art. Tickets include admission to **The Gardiner Museum** across the street, whose exhibits include a collection of Meissen porcelain.

Behind the Harbour Castle Westin Hotel, ferries debark regularly for the small group of **Toronto Islands** (tel. 416/363–1112), less than 10 minutes offshore. Here you can jog, ride a rented bike, fish, or just relax and enjoy the views.

## Professional Sports

The **Toronto Blue Jays** (tel. 416/595–0011, baseball) and the **Toronto Argonauts** (tel. 416/595–1131, football) appear at the Skydome. The city's hockey team, the **Toronto Maple Leafs** (tel. 416/977–1641), plays at Maple Leaf Gardens.

## The Arts

**Roy Thomson Hall** (60 Simcoe St., tel. 416/593–4828), home of the Toronto Symphony Orchestra, also hosts visiting orchestras as well as pop performers. **St. Lawrence Centre for the Arts** (Front St. at Scott St., tel. 416/366–7723) presents everything from live theater by the Canadian Stage Company to debates on political issues to chamber music. **The O'Keefe Centre** (1 Front St. E, tel. 416/872–2262), the largest of the city's halls, is home to the Canadian Opera Company and the National Ballet of Canada, as well as to those rock groups and other performers with the drawing power to fill it. **Royal Alexandra Theater** (260 King St. W, tel. 416/593–4211), a restored 1907 theater, offers everything from classic drama to Broadway musicals and new Canadian plays. The lavishly restored 1920-vintage vaudeville theater, **Pantages** (63 Yonge Street, tel. 416/362–3216), puts on Broadway road shows.

The best sources for information are the weekly "What's On" section of the *Toronto Star*, which appears on Fridays, the Saturday *Globe and Mail*, or the free weekly publications *Now* and *Metropolitan*.

Half-price tickets are available on the day of performance from **Five Star Tickets,** in the lobby of the Royal Ontario Museum (in winter), or at Yonge and Dundas streets outside the Eaton Centre the rest of the year. All sales are final and cash only, and a small service charge is added to the ticket price. Tickets are also sold through **Ticketmaster** (tel. 416/872–2233).

## After Hours

*Bars and Lounges*
**Club Twenty-Two** (22 St. Thomas St., tel. 416/979–2341), in the Windsor Arms Hotel, is a glamorous spot for an after-work drink. Local stockbrokers visit **The Amsterdam** (133 John St., tel. 416/595–8201) after work for excellent home-brewed beer (the food, unfortunately, isn't so good). Don't come if you want peace and quiet, however—especially on Fridays, when it turns into a singles bar. Reservations are a must. **The Bellari Café** (100 Cumberland St., near Bay and Bloor Sts., tel. 416/964–2222), in the upscale Yorkville area, has dancing to Top 40 music played by a DJ, and tables outside in summer for those who want to escape the noise. **The Madison Restaurant** (14 Madison Ave., tel. 416/927–1722) is a British-style pub on three floors with two outdoor terraces and wall-to-wall people, all playing darts and singing along with the pianist. For drinks or snacks, **Remy's** (115 Yorkville Ave., near Avenue Rd., tel. 416/968–9429) has brass, class, two outdoor patios, and a European atmosphere. **Movenpick** (165 York St., tel. 416/366–5234) has a wine bar that draws a business clientele from about 6 PM. **Quotes** (220 King St., tel. 416/979–7697) serves drinks and light snacks in a relaxing atmosphere. This is a favorite after-performance haunt for actors at the Royal Alexandra Theater next door. **Denison's** (75 Victoria St., tel. 416/360–5877) is another brew-pub, like the Amsterdam, but with a more relaxed atmosphere.

**The Barrister's Bar** at the Hilton (tel. 416/869–3456) offers a subdued, quiet setting for after-hours business discussions. **The Rooftop Bar** at the Park Plaza (tel. 416/924–5471), a favorite among Toronto's literary set, has a fireplace, which makes it a cozy spot for a drink on a winter evening. **The Lobby Bar** at The Four Seasons (tel. 416/964–0411) has window tables, which offer a fair amount of privacy for business discussions when the bar is full. Businesspeople from nearby offices gather at the quiet **Lobby Lounge** of the King Edward Hotel (tel. 416/863–9700).

*Cabaret and Comedy Clubs*
**Second City** (110 Lombard St., tel. 416/863–1111) usually offers great comedy fare, though much of the humor may be lost on those unfamiliar with Canadian politics and culture. **Yuk-Yuk's Komedy Kabaret** (1280 Bay St., just above Bloor St., and 2355 Yonge St., just above Eglinton, tel. 416/967–6425) has a dopey name, but Howie Mandel and many other top comics got their start here.

*Jazz Clubs*
**Café des Copains** (48 Wellington St. E, near Yonge St., tel. 416/869–0148) has a romantic yet casual atmosphere and a clientele of serious jazz lovers who come to hear a different solo jazz pianist every two weeks. **George's Spaghetti House** (290 Dundas St. E, tel. 416/923–9887) is in a fairly scruffy neighborhood but is the oldest continuously running jazz club in the city. **Meyer's Deli**, at two locations (185 King St. W, near University Ave., and 69 Yorkville Ave., near Bay and Bloor Sts., both tel. 416/593–4189), has solid deli food and good jazz, including late-night sets on Friday and Saturday.

*Rhythm and Blues*
**Club Bluenote** (128 Pears Ave., tel. 416/921–1109) is the champion of R&B in Toronto and attracts visiting musicians and singers; when Whitney Houston is in town, this is where she goes.

*For Singles*
An upscale 25-to-35-year-old crowd puts on its smartest outfits for a night at **Berlin** (2335 Yonge St., tel. 416/489–7777), a multilevel club with a Continental dinner menu and a seven-piece band for jazz, pop, and R&B. **P.W.D. Dinkel's** (88 Yorkville Ave., tel. 416/923–9689) is frequented by a thirtysomething crowd that comes to hear live bands play Top 40-style music. **StiLife** (217 Richmond St. W, tel. 416/593–6116) is a restaurant/bar/dancing club with metallic and modular decor, and a DJ. **Studebaker's** (150 Pearl St., tel. 416/591–7960) is the 1950s revisited, with colorful memorabilia, a jukebox, and a DJ. During the week, the business crowd comes here, more male than female. Celebrities frequently drop in, too.

# Vancouver

*by Terri Wershler*

Vancouver became a major port city when the Canadian Pacific Railroad reached here in 1887. With snow-capped mountains framing it to the north and 1,000-acre Stanley Park jutting between the city's inner and outer harbors, it also enjoyed an enviable natural setting.

The capital of British Columbia, Vancouver is strategically located to take advantage of the recent increase in trade with Japan and other Pacific Rim countries. In 1989, Japan overtook the United States as Canada's most important trading partner.

British Columbia has a resource-based economy, and forest products are the number one industry and number one export from the port of Vancouver. The port, a leader in cargo tonnage in the Americas, also ships large quantities of coal, potash, and sulfur.

During Expo '86, Vancouver's world's fair, the city caught the attention of international investors who were attracted by government initiatives, reasonably priced real estate, and a top provincial bond rating. Hong Kong businessman Li Ka-Shing has purchased the 180-acre Expo site in downtown Vancouver for a future massive residential and commercial development.

Not surprisingly, international investment, along with several other factors—low mortgage rates, a solid economy, and high immigration into the province—have caused property prices to soar. But Canadian businesspeople still compete for transfers to Vancouver. It's safe (drugs and crime are not serious problems), the surroundings are beautiful, and the climate is relatively temperate (this is one of the few spots in Canada where winters can pass without snow). And although there is concern about the effects of Vancouver's sudden new growth—especially its rising property values and massive immigration—the city is happy to be part of a boom economy again.

## Top Employers

| Employer | Type of Enterprise | Parent*/ Headquarters |
|---|---|---|
| **BC Hydro** | Utility | Vancouver |
| **BC Telephone** | Utility | GTE/Stamford, CT |

| Canfor | Forest products | Prentice-Bentley/Vancouver |
|---|---|---|
| C. Itoh & Co. | Wholesaler | Japan |
| Core-Mark Int'l. | Grocery wholesaler | Vancouver |
| Fletcher Challenge | Forest products | FC of New Zealand/New Zealand |
| Jim Pattison Group | Holding company (auto dealerships, supermarkets, etc.) | Vancouver |
| Kelly Douglas | Grocery wholesaler | Loblaw Companies, Ltd./Toronto |
| MacMillan Bloedel | Forest products | Noranda Mines Ltd./Toronto |
| Sumitomo Canada Ltd. | Wholesaler | C. Itoh/Japan |

*\*if applicable*

## ESSENTIAL INFORMATION

### Climate

Vancouver is never hot, never humid, and rarely cold. It *is* frequently wet, however, especially from November to February. July, August, and September are the warmest and driest months, but the temperature doesn't often go over 75 degrees Farenheit.

What follows are the average daily maximum and minimum temperatures for Vancouver.

| Jan. | 42F | 6C | Feb. | 45F | 7C | Mar. | 48F | 9C |
|---|---|---|---|---|---|---|---|---|
| | 33 | 1 | | 36 | 2 | | 37 | 3 |
| Apr. | 54F | 12C | May | 60F | 16C | June | 65F | 18C |
| | 41 | 5 | | 47 | 8 | | 52 | 11 |
| July | 70F | 21C | Aug. | 70F | 21C | Sept. | 65F | 18C |
| | 55 | 13 | | 55 | 13 | | 52 | 11 |
| Oct. | 56F | 13C | Nov. | 48F | 9C | Dec. | 43F | 6C |
| | 45 | 7 | | 39 | 4 | | 35 | 2 |

### Airport

**Vancouver International Airport** is on an island about 9 miles south of downtown. There is one main terminal building with three levels: departures, international arrivals, and domestic arrivals. The South Terminal, located in a small building, services flights to secondary destinations in the province.

Vancouver Airport has preclearance for customs and immigration for passengers traveling to the United States.

## Airport Business Facilities

The Main Terminal of the Vancouver International Airport has fax machines and a baggage check facility on Level 3 at the top of the escalator.

## Airlines

The two major domestic airlines are Air Canada and Canadian Airlines. Harbor-to-harbor service from Seattle is run by Lake Union Air.

**Air Canada,** tel. 604/688–5515 or 800/776–3000.
**American,** tel. 604/222–2532 or 800/433–7300.
**Canadian Airlines,** tel. 604/682–1411 or 800/387–2737.
**Continental,** tel. 604/222–2442 or 800/525–0280.
**Delta,** tel. 604/682–5933 or 800/221–1212.
**Horizon Air,** tel. 800/547–9308.
**Lake Union Air,** tel. 800/826–1890.
**United,** tel. 604/683–7111 or 800/631–1500.

## Between the Airport and Downtown

There's no direct service to downtown by public transit.

*By Taxi*
Taxi stands are in front of the main terminal building on the domestic and international arrivals levels. It's a 20-minute drive to downtown, but during rush hour (8–9 AM and 4–5:30 PM) allow about 45 minutes. Cost: about Can$20.

*By Limousine*
**Airlimo** (tel. 604/273–1331) has stands on both the domestic and international arrivals levels. Cost: Can$21 per person.

*By Bus*
The **Airport Express** bus (tel. 604/266–0376) leaves the domestic arrivals level every 15 minutes, stopping at major downtown hotels. It operates from 5:30 AM to 12:30 AM. Cost: Can$6.75 one way or Can$11.50 round-trip.

## Car Rentals

The following companies have booths in the airport terminal:

**Avis,** tel. 604/273–4577 or 800/268–2310.
**Budget,** tel. 604/278–3994 or 800/268–8900.
**Dominion,** tel. 604/278–7196.
**Hertz,** tel. 604/278–4001 or 800/263–0600.
**Thrifty,** tel. 604/276–0800 or 800/367–2277.
**Tilden,** tel. 604/273–3121 or 800/387–4747.

## Emergencies

*Doctors*
**Medicenter** (1055 Dunsmuir St., mall level, tel. 604/683–8138) is a drop-in clinic.

*Dentists*
**Dentacenter** (tel. 604/669–6700) is next door to Medicenter (*see* above).

*Hospitals*
**St. Paul's Hospital** (1081 Burrard St., tel. 604/682–2344) is a major downtown hospital with an emergency ward.

## Important Addresses and Numbers

**Audiovisual rentals.** Commercial Electronics (1305 Burrard St., tel. 604/669–5525), Freeman Smyth (1259 Frances St., tel. 604/251–2446).

**Chamber of Commerce** (400–999 Canada Place at Granville St., tel. 604/681–2111).

**Computer rentals.** Hamilton Computer Rentals (101–910 W. 6th Ave., tel. 604/734–7710), Microserve Business Computer Rentals (219–1675 W. 8th Ave., tel. 604/732–7368).

**Convention and exhibition centers.** Vancouver Trade and Convention Center (200–999 Canada Place at Granville St., tel. 604/641–1987), B.C. Place (777 Pacific Blvd., tel. 604/669–2300) is an enclosed downtown stadium used for large trade shows and conventions.

**Fax services.** Copy Time (714 W. Hastings St., tel. 604/682–8307 and credit-card operated machine in Bentall Center, lower level, Burrard St. at Melville St.), Zippy Print (849 Hornby St., tel. 604/681–5551; 1147 Melville St., tel. 604/683–8688).

**Formal-wear rentals.** Classy (1026 Robson St., tel. 604/684–4137).

**Gift shops.** Chocolates: Le Chocolate Belge Daniel (1105 Robson St., tel. 604/688–9642); Flowers: Bufton's Flowers (851 Hornby St., tel. 604/683–7781), The Flower Show (375 Water St., tel. 604/681–7285); Gift Baskets: Classic Greetings Baskets (B–3432 Sophia St., tel. 604/873–3932).

**Graphic design studios.** Koo & Company (200–1152 Mainland St., tel. 604/684–4466).

**Hairstylists.** Men: Jim's Barber Shop (Georgia Hotel, 801 W. Georgia St., tel. 604/683–5000); Women: Glemby's (Holt Renfrew, 633 Granville St., tel. 604/681–3121, ext. 421), Suki's (1025 Robson St., tel. 604/689–2859 and at the Pan Pacific Hotel, 300–999 Canada Pl., tel. 604/641–1342).

**Health and fitness clubs.** *See* Fitness, below.

**Information hot lines.** Arts Hotline (tel. 604/684–ARTS). Yellow Pages lists hot line numbers for weather, news, stock market, sports, ski conditions, entertainment, and community information.

**Limousine services.** Classic (tel. 604/669–5466), Star (tel. 604/875–9466).

**Liquor stores.** All liquor stores are government run in British Columbia. One of the better ones is downtown and has a specialty wine section (1120 Alberni St., tel. 604/660–4572).

**Mail delivery, overnight.** DHL International Express (tel. 604/278–3984), Federal Express (tel. 604/273–1544), TNT Skypak (tel. 604/270–2333), UPS (tel. 604/273–0014).

**Messenger services.** Loomis (tel. 604/665–4881), Purolator (tel. 604/273–7876).

**Office space rentals.** Summix Office Center (666 Burrard St., tel. 604/688–5884), Total Office Services (1500–701 W. Georgia St., tel. 604/688–1311).

**Pharmacy, late-night.** Shopper's Drug Mart (1125 Davie St., tel. 604/685–6445).

**Radio station, all-news.** CBU–CBC 690 AM.

**Secretarial services.** Laser's Edge (830–789 W. Pender St., tel. 604/662–3774), Total Office Services (1500–701 W. Georgia St., tel. 604/688–1311).

**Stationery supplies.** Murphy Stationery (644 Hornby St., tel. 604/877–6999), Wilson Stationery (419 Granville St., tel. 604/685–8407).

**Taxis.** Black Top (tel. 604/681–2181), MacLures (tel. 604/731–9211), Yellow (tel. 604/681–3311).

**Theater tickets.** *See* The Arts, below.

**Train information.** B.C. Railway (1311 W. 1st St., North Vancouver, tel. 604/984–5246), VIA Rail (1150 Station St., tel. 800/665–8630 in Canada).

**Travel agents.** American Express Travel Service (1040 W. Georgia St., tel. 604/669–2813), Hagen's Travel (210–850 W. Hastings St., tel. 604/684–2448), P. Lawson Travel (409 Granville St., tel. 604/682–4272).

**Weather** (tel. 604/666–1087).

## LODGING

Business and shopping centers are very close to one another, and most downtown hotels are within five minutes of both. The most popular hotels for business travelers are the three upscale chains: The Four Seasons, Pan Pacific, and Le Meridien. To be near nightlife, but away from the financial area—which is deserted at night—choose one of the hotels near Robson Street, Vancouver's promenade: Le Meridien, Wedgewood, Vancouver, O'Doul's, or The Four Seasons. The West End, where the Bayshore and the Sylvia Hotel are located, is also a good alternative; it's a high-rise residential neighborhood at the edge of downtown that is attractive, safe, and laced with beaches. Although there are no deluxe hotels at the airport, two members of the Delta chain in that area are viable options. No flights are permitted between midnight and 6 AM, so the noise factor is not much of an issue in Vancouver.

Most hotels listed here offer special corporate rates and weekend discounts; inquire when making reservations.

Highly recommended lodgings in each price category are indicated by a star ★.

| Category | Cost* |
|---|---|
| *$$$$* (Very Expensive) | over Can$180 |
| *$$$* (Expensive) | Can$120–Can$180 |
| *$$* (Moderate) | under Can$120 |

*All prices are for a standard double room, single occupancy, excluding 10% provincial accommodation tax, 7% federal goods and services tax, and 15% service charge.*

*Numbers in the margin correspond to numbered hotel locations on the Vancouver Lodging and Dining maps.*

# GREATER VANCOUVER

**Lodging**
Delta Airport Inn, **3**
Delta River Inn, **4**

**Dining**
Bishop's, **1**
Malinee's Thai, **2**
Phnom Pehn Restaurant, **7**
Pink Pearl, **8**
Rubina Tandoori, **10**
Seasons in the Park, **6**
Szechuan Chonkqing, **9**
Tojo's, **5**

# DOWNTOWN VANCOUVER

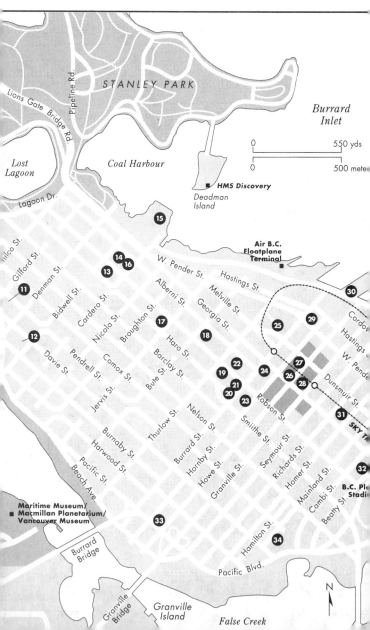

## Downtown

**㉙** **Day's Inn.** Even closer to the heart of the business district
**$$** than The Four Seasons and the Hyatt, the six-story, 70-
year-old Day's Inn is the only moderately priced hotel in
the financial core. The lobby is very small and rather plain,
but renovations, finished in 1990, enlivened the rooms
with bright colors and modern furniture. Standard rooms
are very large but don't include any extras. Suites 310,
410, 510, and 610 have views of the harbor. No room serv-
ice is available. The bar, the Bombay Bicycle Club, is a fa-
vorite with stockbrokers, bankers, and lawyers. *921 W.
Pender St., V6C 1M2, tel. 604/681–4335 or 800/663–1700,
fax 604/681–7808. Gen. manager, Zach Bhatia. 74 dou-
bles, 11 suites. Free parking. AE, CB, D, MC, V.*

**㉗** **Delta Place.** This 18-story hotel, built in 1985 for the luxu-
**$$$$** rious Hong Kong Mandarin chain, is now operated and
managed by Delta Hotels. The rates have gone down a bit,
but the hotel has retained its high standards. The lobby is
restrained and tasteful—one has to look for the registra-
tion desk; the Oriental theme of rugs and vases and rich,
dark mahogany furnishings runs throughout the hotel.
Most rooms have small balconies. Studio suites are recom-
mended for their spaciousness and views. A business cen-
ter is available with secretarial services, work stations,
cellular phones, and small meeting rooms. The location, at
most a five-minute walk from business and shopping, is an-
other asset. *645 Howe St., V6C 2Y9, tel. 604/687–1122 or
800/877–1133, fax 604/689–7044. Gen. manager, Alan
Sacks. 181 doubles, 16 suites. AE, D, MC, V.*

**㉘** **The Four Seasons.** Shoppers tend to use the lobby of this
**$$$$** hotel in the heart of the shopping district as a thorough-
fare, but the floors above are tranquil. Standard rooms are
somewhat small; the more spacious corner deluxe and de-
luxe Four Seasons rooms are recommended. All rooms are
comfortably furnished, some in burgundy tones, others in
more sophisticated black and white. The formal restau-
rant, Chartwell, is one of the best in the city (*see* Dining,
below). The hotel is adjacent to the Vancouver Stock Ex-
change, and complimentary limo service to other down-
town locations is available from noon to 8:30 PM. Service is
excellent, as are the amenities. *791 W. Georgia St., V6C
2T4, tel. 604/689–9333; or in Canada, 800/268–6282; in
U.S., 800/332–3442; fax 604/684–4555. Gen. manager,
Ruy Paes-Braga. 317 doubles, 68 suites. AE, CB, DC,
MC, V.*

**㉖** **Georgia Hotel.** Across from The Four Seasons and a five-
**$$** minute walk from the business district, this handsome 12-
story hotel was built in 1927. It has a warm, comfortable
ambience, with an oak-panel lobby and a friendly English-
style pub in the basement. If you don't need the extras
(bath robes, health club, concierge, etc.), the Georgia is
worth considering. Rooms are small but well furnished in
modern style, with gray-and-rose decor, and nothing
worn around the edges; those facing the art gallery have
the best views. Executive rooms have a separate sitting
area. *801 W. Georgia St., V6C 1P7, tel. 604/682–5566 or
800/663–1111, fax 604/682–8192. Gen. manager, Earl
Simmons. 310 doubles, 4 suites. AE, CB, DC, MC, V.*

**⑳** **La Grande Residence.** For stays of at least a month, this
**$$$** apartment high rise in the heart of Vancouver is a good op-

# VANCOUVER HOTEL CHART

| HOTELS | Price Category | Business Services — Banquet capacity | No. of meeting rooms | Secretarial services | Audiovisual equipment | Teletype news service | Computer rentals | In-room modem phone jack | All-news cable channel | Desk | Desk lighting | Bed lighting |
|---|---|---|---|---|---|---|---|---|---|---|---|---|
| Bayshore | $$$$ | 780 | 16 | ✓ | ✓ | - | ✓ | - | ✓ | ◐ | ◐ | ◐ |
| Day's Inn | $$ | 0 | 0 | - | ✓ | - | - | - | - | ◐ | ◐ | ◐ |
| Delta Airport Inn | $$$ | 600 | 18 | ✓ | ✓ | - | - | - | - | ○ | ● | ◐ |
| Delta Place | $$$$ | 90 | 7 | ✓ | ✓ | - | ✓ | ✓ | ✓ | ● | ● | ● |
| Delta River Inn | $$$ | 400 | 16 | ✓ | ✓ | - | - | - | ✓ | ● | ● | ● |
| The Four Seasons | $$$$ | 450 | 11 | ✓ | ✓ | - | ✓ | ✓ | ● | ● | ● | ● |
| Georgia | $$ | 300 | 7 | - | ✓ | - | - | - | ✓ | ● | ● | ● |
| La Grande Residence | $$$ | 350 | 11 | ✓ | ✓ | - | ✓ | - | - | ● | ● | ● |
| Hotel Vancouver | $$$ | 1000 | 21 | ✓ | ✓ | - | ✓ | - | ✓ | ● | ● | ● |
| Hyatt Regency | $$$$ | 1650 | 24 | ✓ | ✓ | - | - | - | ✓ | ● | ● | ● |
| Le Meridien | $$$$ | 350 | 11 | ✓ | ✓ | ✓ | ✓ | ✓ | - | ● | ● | ● |
| O'Doul's | $$$ | 230 | 3 | ✓ | ✓ | - | - | - | ✓ | ● | ● | ● |
| Pan Pacific | $$$$ | 400 | 15 | ✓ | ✓ | ✓ | ✓ | - | ✓ | ◐ | ◐ | ● |
| Sylvia | $$ | 0 | 0 | - | - | - | - | - | ✓ | ◐ | ◐ | ◐ |
| Wedgewood | $$$ | 20 | 3 | ✓ | ✓ | - | ✓ | ✓ | - | ● | ● | ● |

$$$$ = over $180, $$$ = $120-$180, $$ = under $120.
● good, ◐ fair, ○ poor.
All hotels listed here have photocopying and fax facilities.

| In-Room Amenities | | | | | | | | | | Hotel Amenities | | | | | | |
| Nonsmoking rooms | In-room checkout | Minibar | Pay movies | VCR/Movie rentals | Hairdryer | Toiletries | Room service | Laundry/Dry cleaning | Pressing | Concierge | Barber/Hairdresser | Garage | Courtesy airport transport | Sauna | Pool | Exercise room |
|---|---|---|---|---|---|---|---|---|---|---|---|---|---|---|---|---|
| ✓ | ✓ | ✓ | - | - | ✓ | ● | ● | ● | ● | ✓ | ✓ | - | - | ✓ | ● | ● |
| ✓ | - | - | - | - | - | - | - | ● | ● | - | - | ✓ | - | - | - | - |
| ✓ | ✓ | ✓ | ✓ | - | - | ● | ● | ◐ | ◐ | - | ✓ | ✓ | ✓ | ✓ | ● | ◐ |
| ✓ | ✓ | ✓ | - | - | - | ◐ | ● | ● | ● | ✓ | - | - | - | ✓ | ◐ | ○ |
| ✓ | - | ✓ | ✓ | - | - | ● | ● | ◐ | ◐ | - | - | ✓ | ✓ | ✓ | ◐ | - |
| ✓ | ✓ | ✓ | - | - | ✓ | ● | ● | ● | ● | ✓ | - | ✓ | - | ✓ | ● | ● |
| ✓ | - | - | - | ✓ | ✓ | ○ | ◐ | ● | ◐ | ✓ | ✓ | ✓ | - | - | - | - |
| - | - | - | - | - | ✓ | ○ | ● | ● | ● | ✓ | - | ✓ | - | ✓ | ◐ | ● |
| ✓ | ✓ | ✓ | ✓ | - | - | ◐ | ● | ● | ● | ✓ | ✓ | ✓ | - | ✓ | ● | ● |
| ✓ | ✓ | ✓ | ✓ | - | - | ● | ● | ◐ | ● | ✓ | - | ✓ | - | ✓ | - | ◐ |
| ✓ | ✓ | ✓ | ✓ | - | ✓ | ● | ● | ● | ● | ✓ | ✓ | ✓ | - | ✓ | ◐ | ● |
| ✓ | - | ✓ | ✓ | ✓ | ✓ | ● | ● | ● | ● | ✓ | - | ✓ | - | ✓ | ◐ | ○ |
| ✓ | ✓ | ✓ | ✓ | - | ✓ | ● | ● | ● | ● | ✓ | ✓ | ✓ | - | ✓ | ● | ● |
| - | - | - | - | - | - | - | ◐ | ● | ● | - | - | ✓ | - | - | - | - |
| ✓ | ✓ | ✓ | ✓ | - | ✓ | ● | ● | ● | ● | ✓ | - | ✓ | - | - | - | - |

**Room service:** ● 24-hour, ◐ 6AM-10PM, ○ other.
**Laundry/Dry cleaning:** ● same day, ◐ overnight, ○ other.
**Pressing:** ● immediate, ◐ same day, ○ other.

tion. The modern La Grande Residence shares facilities with the adjacent Le Meridien hotel (*see* below); the two are now under the same ownership. The elegant one- and two-bedroom apartments each have a balcony and are comfortably furnished; kitchens are well equipped, some with microwaves, and grocery shopping service is available. All rooms have good views, but the brightest are on the south side. The outstanding Meridien restaurant, café, and bar are just an indoor walkway away. *855 Burrard St., V6Z 2K7, tel. 604/682–5511 or 800/543–4300, fax 604/682–5513. Gen. manager, Jacques Ferriere. 131 1-bedrooms, 31 2-bedrooms. Minimum stay: 30 days. AE, CB, D, MC, V.*

★ ㉔ **Hotel Vancouver.** One of Canada's old-time railway hotels,
$$$ this château-style landmark has a weathered copper roof and a stone façade adorned with gargoyles and other fanciful details. Built in 1939, it commands a regal position in the center of town, across from the lawns and fountains of the Vancouver Art Gallery, the only green space downtown. Standard rooms are nothing special, but the hotel has set aside two floors as the Entree Gold accommodations, with extra services and amenities: Guests have on-the-floor check-in, a separate concierge, complimentary breakfast and canapés in a private lounge, fresh flowers, free use of a boardroom, morning limo service, and secretarial services. Entree Gold suites have a luxurious amount of space, with graceful wingback chairs and fine mahogany furniture. *900 W. Georgia St., tel. 604/684–3131; or in Ontario and Quebec, 800/268–9420; in rest of Canada, 800/268–9411; in U.S., 800/828–7447; fax 604/662–1937. Gen. manager, Michael Lambert. 466 doubles, 42 suites. AE, CB, DC, MC, V.*

㉕ **Hyatt Regency.** An electronically equipped boardroom,
$$$$ the largest hotel ballroom in Vancouver, and a prime location in the business district make the Hyatt Regency a good bet for the business traveler—as does a recent renovation of guest rooms and lobby. The two floors of Regency Club accommodations are entered by private elevators and offer concierge service, a private lounge, complimentary breakfast, and hors d'oeuvres. The Hyatt's standard rooms are the largest in the city; ask for a corner room with a balcony on the north or west side for harbor views. Regency Club rooms have robes and special toiletries. The atmosphere is lively and the food is good in the hotel's Fish & Co., a casual restaurant; the Gallery lounge (*see* After Hours, below) is one of the most pleasant in town. The hotel's health club is not as well equipped as most, however. *655 Burrard St., V6C 2R7, tel. 604/687–6543 or 800/233–1234, fax 604/689–3707. Gen. manager, Doug Forseth. 612 doubles, 34 suites. AE, CB, DC, MC, V.*

★ ㉑ **Le Meridien.** Making an appeal to business travelers world-
$$$$ wide with its excellent service and high quality restaurants, the Meridien chain is up to standard in its Vancouver branch. The lobby is sumptuous, with thick carpets and enormous bouquets of flowers, and rooms are elegantly appointed with rich wood furnishings, some with reproduction French Provincial details. The hotel's Café Fleuri serves the best Sunday brunch in town (*see* Dining, below), and the highly regarded, formal French dining room, Gerard, is a good place for special occasions. The bar (*see* After Hours, below) is a good place for an

after-work drink. The hotel's health club facilities are in the basement of the adjoining La Grande Residence suite-hotel (*see above*). *845 Burrard St., V6Z 2K6, tel. 604/682–5511, or 800/543–4300, fax 604/682–5513. Gen. manager, Jacques Ferriere. 350 doubles, 47 suites. AE, CB, DC, MC, V.*

⓱  **O'Doul's.** A five-minute walk from the heart of downtown
$$$  on a lively street of shops and restaurants, O'Doul's, built in 1986 in a long, low style, looks more like a deluxe motel. Its bright, contemporary California style is reinforced by the terra-cotta and blue-green color scheme throughout. Standard rooms face an alley; it's worth the small extra price for a deluxe room facing the front (double-glazing cuts out the street noise). There are three telephones in every room. The casual restaurant and bar are good places to relax and people-watch. *1300 Robson St., V6E 1C5, tel. 604/684–8461, or 800/663–5491, fax 604/684–8326. Gen. manager, Hart Molthagen. 119 doubles, 11 suites. AE, CB, DC, MC, V.*

★ ㉚  **Pan Pacific.** This first-class hotel, along with the Vancou-
$$$$  ver Trade and Convention Centre and a cruise ship termi-nal, is part of Canada Place, which sits on a pier adjacent to the financial district. Built for Expo '86 by the Japanese Pan Pacific chain, it was selected for Prince Charles and Princess Diana during their visit to the fair. The lobby area has a dramatic three-story atrium with a waterfall, and the lounge, restaurant, and café have huge expanses of glass that frame a view of the harbor and the mountains. Earth tones and bamboo patterns impart a Japanese feel and understated elegance to the guest rooms; try for one with a harbor view. The health club, with its indoor track and racquet and squash courts, is one of the best in Cana-da; in addition, the hotel offers outdoor paddle tennis courts. *300–999 Canada Place, V6C 3B5, tel. 604/662–3223; or in Canada, 800/663–1515; in U.S., 800/937–1515; fax 604/685–8690. Gen. manager, John Williams. 468 doubles, 40 suites. AE, CB, DC, MC, V.*

★ ㉓  **Wedgewood Hotel.** This small, elegant hotel, managed by
$$$  its owner, offers many personal touches: turn-down serv-ice, daily ice delivery to rooms, black-out drapes, balco-nies with flowers, complimentary shoe shine, and morning newspaper, as well as such business amenities as tele-conferencing. The rooms are spacious and suggest a European style with such touches as French Provincial re-production furniture and soft colors. During the week, the Wedgewood's clients are almost exclusively corporate and professional (the city's law courts are across the street); on weekends the hotel is favored by honeymoon couples. The view to the south is the best, but if you want late af-ternoon sun on your balcony, choose the north side. The first-class Bacchus Lounge serves good Northern Italian fare (*see* Business Breakfasts and After Hours, below). *845 Hornby St., V6Z 1V1, tel. 604/689–7777 or 800/663–0666, fax 604/688–3074. Gen. manager Eleni Skalbania. 60 doubles, 29 suites, 4 penthouses. AE, CB, DC, MC, V.*

## West End

⓯  **Bayshore.** Situated on 22 harborside acres, adjacent to
$$$$  Stanley Park, the Bayshore boasts a huge outdoor pool and great views. Because of its proximity to the water, it's

especially recommended during the summer. For business-people who travel with their families or have spare time for recreation themselves, other extras here include bicycle rentals, marina with fishing, and sailing charters. The location could be more convenient (it's a 15-minute walk from the heart of downtown), but the hotel provides free shuttle service. Most rooms are rather worn looking; those in the tower, built in 1978, are larger and better furnished than those in the 1960s low rise at the back of the complex (they're also the ones with the good views). Lake Union Air floatplanes from downtown Seattle land here. *1601 W. Georgia St., V6G 2V4, tel. 604/682–3377 or 800/228–3000, fax 604/687–3102. Gen. manager, Denis Forristal. 481 doubles, 38 suites. AE, DC, MC, V.*

★ ⑪ **Sylvia Hotel.** Recommended for budget watchers, the Syl-
$$ via boasts an exceptional location on the beachfront, just a five-minute cab ride from downtown. You won't find any business amenities in this charming establishment, but the plain rooms have fine views and all suites have kitchens. If you have some time to explore Vancouver, this is a good base from which to do so. Vancouverites are particularly fond of this ivy-covered brick building built in 1912. Until the 1950s, the eight-story hotel was the tallest building in the area (a neighborhood now dominated by high rises), and in 1954 it opened the first cocktail bar in the city; the building has been designated as a city landmark. *1154 Gilford St., V6G 2P6, tel. 604/681–9321. Gen. manager, Jill Davies. 97 doubles, 18 suites. AE, DC, MC, V.*

## Airport

❸ **Delta Airport Inn.** This 1960s-vintage airport hotel has the
$$$ atmosphere and facilities of a resort: It offers a 12-acre site with three swimming pools (one indoor), four all-year tennis courts with a pro, an outdoor fitness circuit, squash courts, aqua-exercise classes, outdoor volleyball courts, and a golf practice area. Though the hotel is large, the ambience is casual and friendly. There are two guest-room towers and a few low-rise buildings for conventions; meeting rooms open out onto patios. Unfortunately, guest rooms could use some updating and don't rate as highly as the other facilities. *10251 St. Edwards Dr., V6X 2M9, tel. 604/278–9611; or in Canada, 800/268–1133; in U.S., 800/877–1133; fax 604/276–1122. Gen. manager, William Sayce. 460 doubles, 4 suites. AE, CB, DC, MC, V.*

❹ **Delta River Inn.** The 11-story River Inn, two minutes from
$$$ the airport, has an appealing view from the edge of the Fraser River (best seen from rooms on the south side). Although the hotel, built in 1973, was renovated in 1990, rooms seem rather dark and old-fashioned. The hotel doesn't have its own health club, but offers shuttle service to all the athletic facilities at its sister hotel, the Delta Airport Inn *(see above)*. Fishing charters, leaving from the hotel's marina, are available. *3500 Cessena Dr., V7B 1C7, tel. 604/278–1241; or in Canada, 800/268–1133; in U.S., 800/877–1133; fax 604/276–1975. Gen. manager, John Orm. 410 doubles, 6 suites. AE, CB, D, MC, V.*

# DINING

*by Eve Johnson*

As a port city, Vancouver has always had a wide range of dining options. The city's growth in the past 10 years, particularly with immigration from Asia, has given restaurant patrons more choices than ever. There are intimate restaurants serving Northern Italian food, dim sum palaces that seat 600 for Cantonese brunch, sushi bars where Japanese tourists exclaim over the high quality and low price of the fish, and at least one restaurant for every ethnic group that has put down roots here: Thai, Cambodian, Vietnamese, Ethiopian, German, Portugese, and Spanish, to name a few.

Vancouver's businesspeople tend to like to eat near their offices, which are concentrated in the downtown peninsula. Dining is more casual in Kitsilano, the trendy west-side beach suburb, just across the Burrard Street Bridge from downtown; in the summer, "Kits" blossoms with sidewalk cafés along Fourth Avenue and down Yew Street to the beach. Broadway (Ninth Avenue) cuts a wide swathe through the city with Greek restaurants at the extreme west end and a more varied ethnic mix as you travel east.

Highly recommended restaurants in each price category are indicated by a star ★.

| Category | Cost* |
|---|---|
| *$$$$* (Very Expensive) | over Can$40 |
| *$$$* (Expensive) | Can$30–Can$40 |
| *$$* (Moderate) | under Can$30 |

*per person, including appetizer, entrée, and dessert, but excluding drinks, service, 10% sales tax on alcoholic beverages, and 7% goods and services tax.*

*Numbers in the margin correspond to numbered restaurant locations on the Vancouver Lodging and Dining maps.*

## Business Breakfasts

In the upscale category, **Bacchus,** the clubby dining room of the Wedgewood Hotel (tel. 604/689–7777), attracts lawyers from the courts across the street with its excellent coffee, hazelnut waffles, and French-toasted brioche; there's also a full complement of standard breakfasts. The impeccable Continental service makes breakfast at Le Meridien's **Le Fleuri** (tel. 604/682–5511) particularly pleasant. Coffee and orange juice arrive with the menu, which has the usual run of pancakes and bacon and eggs, but adds a French twist: crêpes as a breakfast special. Just a block from the Hyatt and Hotel Vancouver, the big pink and ivory room at **Jean-Pierre** (1055 Dunsmuir St., plaza level, tel. 604/669–0360) is a civilized if somewhat fussy-looking place to start the day. The breakfast menu features a papaya and strawberry fruit plate, eggs Benedict, and specialty omelets. Service is attentive, and there's plenty of privacy for breakfast meetings.

For more casual breakfasts, the Seattle coffee specialist, **Starbucks Coffee Co.,** has multiple outlets downtown that offer stand-up or takeout breakfasts, muffins, pastries, and cappuccino. The following Starbucks locations open by 6:30: 601 West Cordova St., in the Seabus Terminal; 700 W. Pender St.; 811 Hornby St.; and 1100 Robson St. The **Scanwich** (551 Howe St., tel. 604/687–2415) opens at 7 and serves good American breakfasts at modest prices until 10:30. **Bridges Bakery & Bagels** (1595 W. 6th Ave., tel. 604/736–3651, a 10-minute cab ride from downtown) open 7 AM–2 AM daily, features lox and cream cheese, and good cappuccino.

## Downtown

**❸❹ Il Barino.** This airy, modern, Italian-style dining room,
**$$$** with flowering plants, and tile floor, is on the ground floor of a warehouse in the Yaletown district, at the heart of the city's design and wholesale fashion center. A good place for a business lunch or an informal evening's entertaining, Il Barino has a big, open kitchen area displaying trays of potted herbs. Chef Julio Gonzalez turns out superb Northern Italian food: grilled oyster and shiitake mushrooms with a balsamic vinegar dressing, pear and goat cheese salad with hazelnuts, and buttery veal scallopini. Desserts, including a feather-light lemon meringue tart and a very rich macademia nut flan, are unusual and good. Service can be casual. Tables toward the rear of the restaurant are the most private. *1116 Mainland St., tel. 604/687–1116. Casual but neat. Reservations suggested. AE, MC, V.*

**❸❶ Bianco Nero.** Located on the street level of a modern, undistinguished downtown high rise just a block from the
**$$** Queen Elizabeth theater, Bianco Nero is a good choice for pretheater dining or for business dinner after 8 when curtain call empties the room. The restaurant is modern and appealing, with a sophisticated black and white decor. The best Italian wine list in the city complements a menu so large (and innovative) that it can take half an hour to read. Most dishes are hearty but imaginative; for example, homemade tortellini in a creamy mustard sauce, or veal chops with balsamic vinegar sauce and grilled fennel. Desserts are not memorable. Service varies, usually friendly and attentive, sometimes careless. *475 W. Georgia St., tel. 604/682–6376. Casual but neat. Reservations advised. AE, MC, V. Closed Sun.*

**★ ❷❽ Chartwell.** Named after Sir Winston Churchill's country home, a painting of which hangs over the green marble
**$$$$** fireplace, the flagship dining room at the Four Seasons Hotel is the city's closest equivalent to a British men's club. Floor-to-ceiling dark-wood paneling, deep leather chairs in which to sip claret, and quiet and privacy make this the city's top spot for power lunch. Chef Wolfgang von Weiser cooks robust Continental food. His loyal following includes brokers, lawyers, and forestry executives from nearby office buildings. Menu staples include an imaginative salad of smoked loin of wild boar with a sprinkling of hazelnuts and a walnut oil vinaigrette, and seafood pot au feu served with fennel bread and *aioli* (garlic mayonnaise). Port and stilton are served after dessert. *791 W. Georgia St., tel. 604/689–9333. Jacket required. Reservations advised.*

★ ⑬ **Chez Thierry.** Although this cozy bistro on the Stanley
$$ Park end of Robson Street isn't suitable for serious busi-
ness entertaining—it's too small and informal—it is a
good place to relax after work. Owner Thierry Damilano is
a friendly host whose country-style French cooking relies
heavily on local seafood. The watercress and smoked salm-
on salad is a worthy starter, and fresh tuna grilled with
artichokes, garlic, and tomatoes is hearty and well sea-
soned. The apple tarte tatin is superb. Expect noise and
jammed tables on the weekends. *1674 Robson St., tel. 604/
688-0919. Casual dress. Reservations required week-
ends. AE, DC, MC, V. Closed Dec. 24, 25, 26. Dinner
only.*

⑯ **Le Gavroche.** Time seems to stand still in this charming
$$$$ turn-of-the-century house, suitable for serious business
entertaining. On the main floor is a private dining room;
upstairs is a long, narrow room with a fireplace. Service is
knowledgeable and discreet. The kitchen turns out classic
French cooking, but tempers its richness. Mainstays
include smoked salmon with blinis and sour cream, and
smoked pheasant breast on a puree of celeriac, shallots,
and wine, with a light truffle sauce. The wine list is excel-
lent, especially the Bordeaux. Ask for a table by the front
window for a view of mountains and water. *1616 Alberni
St., tel. 604/685-3924. Jacket and tie suggested. Reserva-
tions advised weekends. AE, DC, MC, V. Closed Dec. 24,
25, Jan. 1.*

㉝ **Il Giardino di Umberto, Umberto's, Umberto's Fishhouse.**
$$$ First came Umberto's, a Florentine restaurant serving
classic Northern Italian food, installed in a century-
old, bright yellow house at the foot of Hornby Street, a
five-minute cab ride from the major hotels. Then Umberto Menghi built Il Giardino next door, a sunny, light-
splashed room styled after a Tuscan house, where a more
eclectic menu features such dishes as braised breast of
pheasant with polenta, and reindeer filet with crushed
peppercorn sauce. Finally he added Umberto's Fish
House, sandwiching the original yellow house between
the two new restaurants. Il Giardino attracts a Los Angeles crowd: actors, producers, and screenwriters who vie
for tables 20 and 21, and usually turn the tedious business
of ordering over to chef Gianni Picchi. Umberto's is quieter; favored tables are in the back room by the open kitch-
en. Umberto's Fish House, where less business and more
serious eating is done, is flower-filled and more casual in
style. Fish is prepared either Italian style (rainbow trout
grilled and served with sun-dried tomatoes, black olives,
and pinenuts) or with a taste of the Far East (yellowfin
tuna grilled with wasabi butter). *Il Giardino, 1382 Hornby
St., tel. 604/687-2422. Umberto's, 1380 Hornby St., 604/
687-6316. Umberto's Fish House, 1376 Hornby St., tel.
604/687-6621. Casual but neat. Reservations advised.
AE, DC, MC, V. Closed Sun. Dinner only, except Il
Giardino.*

⑱ **Kirin Mandarin Restaurant.** A short walk from most major
$$ hotels, the Kirin was one of the first Vancouver restau-
rants to serve Chinese food in elegant surroundings, and
at prices not much higher than those charged in China-
town kitsch palaces. Others have followed suit, but the
Kirin, with fish tanks set into slate-green walls, black lac-
quer chairs, and rose-color tablecloths, remains one of the

prettiest. Waiters are attentive, and tables in the large room are well separated. The menu is printed in Chinese, English, and Japanese in deference to Kirin's international clientele of tourists and businesspeople. Locals, both Asian and otherwise, eat here too. The menu, drawn from northern Chinese cuisines, features Shanghai-style smoked eel, Peking duck, and hot and spicy Szechuan scallops. A dessert worth trying is red-bean cooked pie, a crêpe filled with sweet red beanpaste, deep-fried, and served hot. *1166 Alberni St., tel. 604/682–8833. Casual but neat. AE, MC, V. Closed for 2 days, 15 days after Chinese New Year.*

**⑭** **The Raintree.** Vancouver's leading exponent of contempo-
$$$ rary West Coast cuisine draws businesspeople to its bright and spacious environment, highlighted by handsome bouquets of fresh flowers. The menu, which changes daily with market availability, sometimes seems willfully eccentric, other times, simple and inventive; for example, an entrée of abalone from the Queen Charlotte Islands and side-stripe shrimps stir-fried with scallions and spinach in chamomile essence shares the menu with grilled lamb chops with a mint-and-pear puree. Leon's Bar & Grill, on the ground floor, stocks local beers and a respectable number of single malt scotches. *1630 Alberni St., tel. 604/688–5570. Casual dress. Reservations suggested weekends. AE, DC, MC, V. Closed Dec. 24, 25, 26.*

**㉜** **The William Tell.** Swiss luxury and fine Continental cui-
$$$$ sine have maintained the well-established reputation of this restaurant in the Georgian Court Hotel, a 10-minute walk from the central business district. Silver dishliners, embossed linen napkins, and a silver vase on each table add a quiet gleam to this pale, elegant eatery. Among the dishes prepared by Chef Lars Trolle Jorgenson, a member of the gold-medallist Canadian team at the 1988 Culinary Olympics, are locally raised pheasant with glazed grapes and red-wine sauce, sautéed veal sweetbreads with red-onion marmalade and marsala sauce, and *Buendnerfleisch* (a Swiss specialty made from paper-thin slices of air-dried beef). Service is professional and discreet. A good choice for serious business or formal entertaining. *765 Beatty St., tel. 604/688–3504. Jacket required at dinner. Reservations advised. AE, DC, MC, V.*

## Kitsilano

**★ ❶** **Bishop's.** John Bishop opened his trend-setting restau-
$$$ rant five years ago on Fourth Avenue in newly gentrified Kitsilano, a 10-minute cab ride from downtown. The small white rooms (their only ornament some splashy, expressionist paintings) are favored by Robert de Niro when he's on location in Vancouver, and by a wide range of local businesspeople. The food is a blend of Northern Italian and nouvelle, with some Far Eastern touches. Appetizers to look for are squash and apple soup with sage, and Dungeness crab cakes. House favorites include some outstanding pastas, such as penne with grilled eggplant, roasted peppers, and basil. The marinated loin of lamb with ginger and sesame is a hearty, well-seasoned entrée. Bishop's signature dessert is Death by Chocolate, a dark chocolate terrine with raspberry sauce; daily dessert specials include a papaya flan. The wine list is an idiosyncratic mix of unusual, and often expensive, French wines and the

products of little-known West Coast estate wineries. The round table by the front window offers the best opportunity for private talk. Service is professional and friendly, but on weekend evenings, when people linger over dinner, reservations can back up. *2183 W. 4th Ave., tel. 604/738–2025. Casual dress. Reservations required. AE, DC, MC, V. Closed 1st wk. in Jan.*

## Queen Elizabeth Park

**⑥** **Seasons in the Park.** It's a 15-minute cab ride (due south of
**$$** downtown) to Queen Elizabeth Park, a comfortable postwar residential neighborhood. A commanding view of the park, city lights, and the mountains beyond distinguishes this warm, clean-lined room with lots of light wood and plush rugs. The menu, like the decor, is conservative. This is a good place for serious business discussions. The menu is a reliable mix of well-prepared staples such as grilled salmon with fresh mint, and roast duck with cherry sauce. The tables are well spaced; the service is unobtrusive. It's well worth taking a pre- or post-prandial walk in the park's lovely gardens. *Queen Elizabeth Park (33rd Ave. and Canby St.), tel. 604/874–8008. Casual but neat. AE, MC, V. Closed Christmas Day.*

## West Broadway

**★ ⑤** **Tojo's.** The handsome blond-wood tatami rooms are on the
**$$$** second floor of a new green-glass tower in the hospital district on West Broadway. Rooms are suitable for private business dinners, but the heart of Tojo is the 10-seat sushi bar. With Hidekazu Tojo presiding, this is a convivial place for those dining alone. Tempura and teriyaki dinners are available, of course, but the seasonal menu is more exciting. In October, ask for *dobbin mushi* (a soup made from pine mushrooms) served in a teapot. In spring, try sushi made from scallops and pink cherry blossoms. *202–777 West Broadway, tel. 604/872–8050. Casual but neat. Weekend reservations suggested. AE, MC, V. Closed Mon., and Dec. 24, 25, 26.*

## Ethnic

Most of Vancouver's ethnic restaurants are located outside the downtown peninsula, where rents are lower. If you have time to explore beyond downtown, you'll find these worthwhile stops.

*Asian*

**⑨** **Szechuan Chonkqing** (2495 Victoria Dr., tel. 604/254–7434) specializes in fiery Szechuan food that is well worth
**⑧** the 20-minute cab ride from downtown. The **Pink Pearl** (1132 E. Hastings St., tel. 604/253–4316) is a huge, noisy Cantonese restaurant with tanks full of live seafood. Crab dishes are excellent, particularly crab sautéed with five
**㉒** spices. **Chiyoda** (1050 Alberni St., tel. 604/688–5050) is a Japanese robata bar—a wide, curved sweep of wooden bar, where chefs wait to grill the fish or vegetables you se-
**⑩** lect. **Rubina Tandoori** (1962 Kingsway, tel. 604/874–3621) is a 25-minute cab ride from downtown, but some regulars drive from Seattle for this mix of tandoori specialties, south Indian seafood, and meat-rich Mogul dishes.
**②** **Malinee's Thai** (2153 W. 4th Ave., tel. 604/737–0097) is the city's most elegant and consistently interesting Thai res-

taurant. Part of the Fourth Avenue restaurant row, it's a ❼ 10-minute cab ride from downtown. **Phnom Pehn Restaurant** (244 E. Georgia St., tel. 604/682–5777) serves excellent Cambodian food with gentle, dignified hospitality. It's close to Chinatown, a 10-minute cab ride from downtown.

*Native American*

⓬ **Quilicum West Coast Native Indian Restaurant** (1724 Davie St., 604/681–7044) serves the original Northwest Coast cuisine: bannock bread, baked sweet potato with hazelnuts, and, of course, salmon, in a downstairs "longhouse" decorated with masks and totem poles.

## FREE TIME

### Fitness

*Hotel Facilities*
The health club at **Pan Pacific** (tel. 604/662–3223) has the best equipment, including an indoor track, a large heated outdoor pool, paddle tennis courts, and an aerobics room; rates for those not staying at the hotel are Can$10 per day, or Can$20 for four days.

*Health Clubs*
For women, the **YWCA** (580 Burrard St., tel. 604/683–2531) is a good, well-located, modern club; the charge is Can$6.50 per day, which includes classes as well as use of all facilities. The **Chancery Squash Club** (202–865 Hornby St., tel. 604/682–3752) charges nonmembers Can$5–Can$7 for use of their courts, depending on the time of day, and Can$3 for use of the weight room; the **Tower Courts Racquet and Fitness Club** (lower level, Bentall Four, 1055 Dunsmuir, tel. 604/689–4424) doesn't allow nonmembers to use the courts, but has drop-in aerobics classes for Can$5.

*Jogging*
The **Stanley Park Seawall** is a 6-mile route, which starts about a mile from downtown. If you don't want to do the 8-mile round-trip, you can take a cab to Lost Lagoon and start running the seawall from there.

### Shopping

One of the best places downtown to buy local crafts such as jewelry and ceramics is the gift shop at the **Vancouver Art Gallery** (750 Hornby St., tel. 604/682–5621). North Coast Indian art is available at **Images for a Canadian Heritage** (779 Burrard St., tel. 604/685–7046). If you call the **Salmon Shop** (tel. 604/669–3474), a fish shop in the Granville Island Public Market, a courier will land smoked salmon at your door packed for travel.

The huge **Pacific Center** mall is in downtown Vancouver, in the heart of the shopping area. It connects the two major department stores, **Eaton's** (tel. 604/685–7112) and **The Bay** (tel. 604/681–6211), which stand at opposite corners of Georgia and Granville streets. Pacific Center is on two levels and mostly underground.

**Sinclair Center** (Granville and W. Hastings Sts.) is an imaginatively renovated shopping complex in the financial district that caters to sophisticated and expensive tastes.

It continues along Pender Street, from Granville to Howe streets. If you're shopping for women's fashions, try **E.A. Lee** (466 Howe St., tel. 604/683–2457), **Wear Else?** (789 W. Pender St., tel. 604/662–7890), and **Leone** (757 W. Hastings St., tel. 604/683–1133). For men's clothes, there's **Edward Chapman** (833 W. Pender St., tel. 604/685–6207) or, in Pacific Center, **Harry Rosen** (tel. 604/683–6861) and **Holt Renfrew** (tel. 604/681–3121).

On the opposite side of Pacific Center, **Robson Street,** from Burrard to Bute streets, is the place for fashions. For shoes, try **Aldo** (1016 Robson St., tel. 604/683–2443), **Pegabo** (1137 Robson St., tel. 604/688–7877), and **Stephane de Raucourt** (1024 Robson St., tel. 604/681–8814). Clothing stores include **Ralph Lauren** (1123 Robson St., tel. 604/688–7656) and **Alfred Sung** (1143 Robson St., tel. 604/687–2153), the latter with high-end women's clothes perfect for the office. **Club Monaco** (1153 Robson St., tel. 604/687–8618) offers quality casual wear. (Robson Street is also the spot for people-watching in Vancouver; **Starbuck's** espresso bar, tel. 604/688–5125, at Robson and Thurlow streets has the best vantage point.)

## Diversions

After San Francisco, Vancouver has the largest **Chinatown** in North America. Pender Street from Carrall to Main, the heart of Chinatown, is a heritage area, and even new buildings must conform to traditional styles. Stroll through the markets, buy Chinese teas in fancy boxes, and visit the **Dr. Sun Yat-sen Classical Chinese Garden** (5778 Carrall St., tel. 604/689–7133).

**Granville Island,** connected by a causeway to the rest of Vancouver, has a lively food market, galleries, and boat charters. Come to check out the local crafts or to simply watch the boats go by. The island is at the south end of the Granville Street Bridge, a five-minute drive from downtown.

**The Maritime Museum** (north end of Cypress St., tel. 604/737–2211) traces the history of marine activities on the West Coast. Permanent exhibits depict the Port of Vancouver, the fishing industry, and early explorers. The museum sits on the top of Kitsilano Point—a five-minute walk from Kitsilano Beach, where there is swimming and tennis.

The **Museum of Anthropology** (6393 N.W. Marine Dr., tel. 604/228–3825), at the University of British Columbia, a 15-minute drive from Vancouver, focuses on the arts of the Pacific Northwest Indians, brilliant craftspeople who are finally getting worldwide recognition. The Great Hall, near the entrance, houses totems, ceremonial archways, and dugout canoes.

An asphalt path, called the **Stanley Park Seawall,** follows the shore past the Vancouver Rowing Club, the Yacht Club, totem poles, a cricket pitch, beaches, towering fir trees, and a fabulous view of downtown and the mountains. It's a two-hour walk or an easy one-hour bike ride. (Bicycles can be rented at the foot of Georgia Street near the park entrance.)

## Professional Sports

**Vancouver Canucks** (tel. 604/254–5141), the city's hockey team, play at the Coliseum. Vancouver's baseball team, the **Canadians** (tel. 604/872–5232), appears at the Nat Bailey Stadium. For football, the **BC Lions** (tel. 604/681–5466) can be seen at the BC Place Stadium.

## The Arts

Vancouver has a strong music scene. The **Orpheum Theater** (601 Smithe St., tel. 604/665–3050) presents choral groups and symphony performances; opera may be heard at the **Queen Elizabeth Theatre**, and chamber music at the smaller **Queen Elizabeth Playhouse** (both at 600 Hamilton St., tel. 604/873–3311). The two major theater companies, the **Arts Club** (1585 Johnston St., tel. 604/687–1644) and the **Vancouver Playhouse Company** (543 W. 7th Ave., tel. 604/873–3311), perform at the Queen Elizabeth Playhouse.

Call **Ballet BC** (tel. 604/669–5954) for information about dance performances in town, and the **Arts Hot Line** (tel. 604/684–ARTS) for information about the wide range of Vancouver cultural events.

Tickets to major events are available from **Ticketmaster** (Royal Center, mall level, tel. 604/280–4444; handiest access is Skytrain Station stairs at Burrard and Melville Sts.).

## After Hours

The after-work social scene takes place in bars after 5 PM and in restaurants at night. Clubs and cabarets attract a fairly young crowd of rock fans.

*Bars and Lounges*
The clubby bar at **Le Meridien** (tel. 604/682–5511), with fireplaces, wingback chairs, and dark wood and leather, is perfect for business talks. The **Bacchus Lounge** in the Wedgewood Hotel (tel. 604/689–7777) is stylish and sophisticated. The **Gallery Lounge** in the Hyatt (tel. 604/687–6543) is quiet and features a wall of windows overlooking a bustling street. In the Four Seasons, the **Garden Lounge** (tel. 604/689–9333) is bright and airy with lots of greenery, a waterfall, and big, comfortable chairs.

If you're just looking for a place to unwind, **Joe Fortes** (777 Thurlow St., tel. 604/669–1940) is where you'll meet like-minded young businesspeople. As you might suspect from the name, **Night Court** in the Georgia Hotel (801 W. Georgia St., tel. 604/682–5566) is where lawyers hang out. Go to **English Bay Café** (1795 Beach Ave., tel. 604/669–2225) to see the sun set over English Bay. The **Jolly Taxman** (828 W. Hastings St., tel. 604/681–3574) is an English-style pub usually crowded with stockbrokers. Two bars on Granville Island are popular nightspots: The nautically themed **Bridges Pub** (1696 Duranleau St., tel. 604/687–4400) is very casual, but you'll want to be well turned out for the **Pelican Bay** at the Granville Island Hotel (1253 Johnston St., tel. 604/683–7373), which attracts singles.

*Comedy Clubs*

**Yuk Yuks** (750 Pacific Blvd., tel. 604/687–5233) is your best bet.

*Jazz Clubs*

A jazz and blues hot line (tel. 604/682 0706) gives current information on concerts and clubs. **Carnegie's** (1619 W. Broadway, tel. 604/733–4141) and the **Alma Street Café** (2502 Alma St., tel. 604/222–2244), both restaurants, have good mainstream jazz; the food at the Alma Street Café is as good as the music.

# Washington, DC

*by Sharon Geltner*
*Introduction with Deborah Papier*

To a surprising degree, Washington is a city much like any other. True, it doesn't have a baseball team, but, in most other respects, life in the nation's capital is not that different from life elsewhere in the nation. People are born here, grow up, get jobs, and have children. Very often, they live out their lives without ever testifying before Congress, being indicted for influence peddling, or attending a state dinner at the White House.

Which is not to say that the government does not cast a long shadow over the city. "Washington means Business" is the city's slogan, but the biggest business of all is the Federal government, which employs about half a million local workers (out of a population of 630,000). Second is tourism, which brings in annual revenue of some $2 billion. Washington's downtown rents are the second highest in the nation, partly because developers can't build higher than the Capitol. This flat terrain has caused the business district to be called "K Street Canyon."

There's concern now over whether government spending cuts will level the city's economy. Local forecasters say not, because the economy is diversifying into high tech, financial, and information services. By the year 2000, professional workers should number 750,000—about 27% of all workers—clerical 26%, service 15%. Statistics aside, politics is still *the* business of this workaholic town, where people pride themselves on how early they get up.

It is often said that Washington does not have any real neighborhoods the way nearby Baltimore does. Although it's true that Washingtonians are not given to huddling together on their front stoops, each area of the city does have a clearly defined personality. Georgetown, one of the city's most inbred, exclusive communities—its residents successfully fought to keep out the subway—is a magnet for the young and the restless for miles around. Dupont Circle is Washington's bohemian neighborhood, where the artists and activists used to live before the rents got too high; now it's home to the most visible segment of the city's gay community. And adjacent Adams Morgan, the city's most intensely ethnic neighborhood, has begun to lose some of its Hispanic flavor, but you're still likely to hear more Spanish than English on the streets here.

Wealth and poverty have always coexisted here, but until recently poverty kept its distance. It's now omnipresent, wearing a very human face. Still, there's no denying that Washington, the world's first planned capital city, is also one of its most beautiful. And though the Federal government dominates the city psychologically, there are parts of the capital where you can leave politics behind. World-class museums and art galleries (nearly all of them free), tree-shaded and flower-filled parks and gardens, bars and restaurants that benefit from a large and creative immigrant community, and nightlife that seems to get better with every passing year are as much a part of Washington as floor debates or filibusters.

## Top Employers

| Employer | Type of Enterprise | Parent*/ Headquarters |
|---|---|---|
| **Federal Government** | | Washington, DC |
| **Gannett Company, Inc.** | Newspaper chain | Arlington, VA |
| **Giant** | Groceries | Landover, MD |
| **GEICO** | Insurance | Bethesda, MD |
| **Martin Marietta Corp.** | Defense, weapons manufacture | Bethesda, MD |
| **Marriott Corp.** | Hotels | Bethesda, MD |
| **MCI Communications** | Telecommunications | Washington, DC |
| **NVR L. P.** | Housing, construction | McLean, VA |
| **Potomac Electric Power Co. (PEPCO)** | Utility | Washington, DC |
| **USAir** | Airline | Arlington, VA |
| **Washington Post** | Newspaper | Washington, DC |

*if applicable

## ESSENTIAL INFORMATION

### Climate

What follows are the average daily maximum and minimum temperatures for Washington, DC.

| | | | | | | | | |
|---|---|---|---|---|---|---|---|---|
| **Jan.** | 47F | 8C | **Feb.** | 47F | 8C | **Mar.** | 56F | 13C |
| | 34 | −1 | | 31 | −1 | | 38 | 3 |
| **Apr.** | 67F | 19C | **May** | 76F | 24C | **June** | 85F | 29C |
| | 47 | 8 | | 58 | 14 | | 65 | 18 |
| **July** | 88F | 31C | **Aug.** | 86F | 30C | **Sept.** | 79F | 26C |
| | 70 | 21 | | 68 | 20 | | 61 | 16 |
| **Oct.** | 70F | 21C | **Nov.** | 56F | 13C | **Dec.** | 47F | 8C |
| | 52 | 11 | | 41 | 5 | | 32 | 0 |

## Airports

**National Airport** is just 3 miles south of downtown. **Dulles Airport** is 26 miles northwest, and principally handles international flights. **Baltimore Washington International** (BWI), in Maryland, is 28 miles from Washington and less convenient than the other two.

## Airport Business Facilities

**National Airport. Mutual of Omaha Business Service Center** (Main Terminal, close to the Trump Shuttle, tel. 703/685–2453) has fax machines, photocopying, secretarial service, ticket pickup, baggage storage, Western Union, travel insurance, cash advance, and conference rooms.

## Airlines

Dulles is the hub airport for United Airlines.

**America West,** tel. 800/247–5692.
**American,** tel. 202/393–2345 or 800/433–7300.
**Continental,** tel. 202/478–9700 or 800/525–0280.
**Delta,** tel. 202/468–2282 or 800/221–1212.
**Midway,** tel. 800/621–5700.
**Northwest,** tel. 202/737–7333 or 800/225–2525.
**Pan Am,** tel. 202/845–8000 or 800/221–1111.
**Trump Shuttle,** tel. 800/247–8786.
**TWA,** tel. 202/737–7400 or 800/221–2000.
**United,** tel. 202/742–4600 or 800/428–4322.
**USAir,** tel. 202/783–4500 or 800/428–4322.

## Between the Airports and Downtown

*By Taxi*
This is the fastest way to get downtown from National (less than 30 minutes, even during rush hours). Ask the dispatcher for a DC cab, which is on the zone system: it costs about $11 to get downtown. Virginia and Maryland cabs are not zoned by district but metered and therefore more expensive. The trip from Dulles costs about $36; from BWI, about $42.

*By Subway*
From National, walk about 15 minutes to the National Airport Metro station (you'll see it when you leave the terminal) or take a free shuttle bus that departs across from the North terminal. The ride downtown takes about 20 minutes and costs $1.25–$2.25. There is no metro connection to Dulles or BWI.

*By Train*
At BWI, free shuttle buses take passengers to and from the train station. Amtrak (tel. 800/872–7245) and MARC (Maryland Rail Commuter Service, tel. 800/325–7245) trains run between the station and Washington's Union Station from about 6 AM to 11 PM. The cost for the 40-minute ride is $11 on Amtrak ($21 on the Metroliner) and $4.25 on a MARC Train.

*By Bus*
Dulles and BWI are served by the buses of **Washington Flyer** (tel. 703/685–1400). The ride downtown costs $12 and takes 45–60 minutes. Buses go to the downtown terminal at 1517 K St. NW, and connect with vans that go to

major hotels. The **Metro Bus Service** runs from National, but it's much less complicated to take the subway.

*By Limousine*
Reserve ahead or call from all three airports for a **Diplomat** limousine or sedan (tel. 202/589–7620). The cost from National is $33 ($23 for a sedan); from Dulles, $60 (sedan, $42); from BWI, $90 (sedan, $75).

## Car Rentals

The following car rental companies have booths in or near National Airport:

**Alamo,** tel. 703/478–9597 or 800/327–9633.
**Avis,** tel. 202/467–6588 or 800/331–1212.
**Budget,** tel. 202/628–2752 or 800/527–0700.
**Enterprise,** tel. 202/393–0900 or 800/325–0700.
**Hertz,** tel. 703/979–6300 or 800/654–3131.
**National,** tel. 202/842–7454 or 800/328–4567.
**Thrifty,** tel. 202/783–0400 or 800/367–2277.

## Emergencies

*Doctors*
**Prologue Medical Referral** (tel. 202/362–8677), **Physicians Home Service** (2440 M St. NW, Suite 620, tel. 202/331–3888).

*Dentists*
**D.C. Dental Society** (tel. 202/547–7613), **Dental Referral Bureau** (tel. 202/723–5323).

*Hospitals*
**Capitol Hill Hospital** (700 Constitution Ave., NE, tel. 202/269–8750), **George Washington University Hospital** (2150 Pennsylvania Ave. NW, tel. 202/994–3211), **Georgetown University Hospital** (3800 Reservoir Rd. NW, tel. 202/784–2118).

## Important Addresses and Numbers

**Audiovisual rentals.** AVCOM (1006 6th St. NW, tel. 202/408–0444), Crews Control (1025 Thomas Jefferson St. NW, Suite 312, tel. 202/625–1900 or 800/545–2739).

**Chamber of Commerce** (1411 K St. NW, No. 500, tel. 202/347–7201).

**Computer rentals.** The Standard (1528 K St. NW, tel. 202/628–4940), ComputeRental (666 11th St. NW, Suite 1050, tel. 202/347–1582).

**Convention center** (9th & H Sts. NW, tel. 202/789–7000).

**Fax services.** AVCOM (1006 6th St. NW, tel. 202/408–0444), Lancaster Business Centers (16th & K Sts. NW, tel. 202/628–3614), Mail Boxes, Etc. (3220 N St. NW, tel. 202/342–0707; 2000 Pennsylvania Ave. NW, tel. 202/457–8166; 1718 M St. NW, tel. 202/785–3604), Presentation Group (2121 Wisconsin Ave. NW, Suite 55, tel. 202/337–5500).

**Formal-wear rental.** Royal Formal & Bridal (1328 G St. NW, tel. 202/737–7144).

**Gift shops.** Chocolates: Schoffs Belgian Chocolatier (2000 Pennsylvania Ave. NW, tel. 202/452–0924); Flowers: Blackistone's (1427 H St. NW, tel. 202/726–2700).

**Graphic design studios.** AlphaGraphics Printshops of the Future (1436 New York Ave. NW, tel. 202/638–1767), Balmar Printing, Graphics and 24-hour Copy Centers (1225 Eye St. NW, tel. 202/659–3610).

**Hairstylists.** Milton Pitts (Sheraton Carlton, 16th & K Sts. NW, tel. 202/638–2626, ext. 6733) has been barber to the presidents since 1969; at Rendezvouz in the Park (Park Hyatt, 24th & M Sts. NW, tel. 202/789–1234), Yves Graux cuts Barbara Bush's hair. When Nancy Reagan was in town she had hers done by Robin Weir (2134 P St. NW, tel. 202/861–0444).

**Health and fitness clubs.** *See* Fitness, below.

**Information hot lines.** Emergency (other than police/fire/ambulance, tel. 202/8DC–HELP), International Visitors Information Service (tel. 202/783–6540).

**Limousine services.** Bush-Martin Limousine Service (tel. 202/829–9719), Capital City Limousine (tel. 202/387–6217 or 800/441–6676), Carey Limousine (4345 42nd St. NW, Suite 300, tel. 202/537–5370).

**Liquor stores.** Capitol Hill Liquor (323 Pennsylvania Ave. SE, tel. 202/543–2900), Central Liquor Store (726 9th St. NW, tel. 202/737–2800), Connecticut Avenue Liquors (1529 Connecticut Ave. NW, tel. 202/332–0240), Dixie Liquor (3429 M St. NW, tel. 202/337–4412).

**Mail delivery, overnight.** DHL Worldwide Express (tel. 800/225–5345), Federal Express (tel. 800/238–5355), TNT Skypak (tel. 703/550–1000), UPS (tel. 301/595–9090), U.S. Postal Service Express Mail (tel. 202/636–1404).

**Messenger services.** Apple Courier (tel. 202/293–0930), Metro Delivery (tel. 202/387–8200), Quick Messenger Service, daily, 24 hours (tel. 202/783–3600), Washington Express Services (tel. 202/265–9200).

**Office-space rentals.** U.S. Office (1825 Eye St. NW, Suite 400, tel. 202/429–2000).

**Pharmacies, late-night.** Peoples at Dupont Circle (18th & Connecticut Ave. NW, tel. 202/785–1466), Peoples at Thomas Circle (14th St. & Massachusetts Ave. NW, tel. 202/628–0720).

**Radio stations, all-news.** WNTR 1050 AM, WTOP 1500 AM, WRC 980 AM.

**Secretarial services.** Advantage (1750 K St. NW, Suite 490, tel. 202/293–0232), Talent Tree Personnel (1101 17th St. NW, tel. 202/833–4880).

**Stationery supplies.** Ginns Office Products (7 locations, including: 1208 18th St. NW, tel. 202/833–6112), Jacobs Gardner Supply (10 locations, including: 1101 17th St. NW, tel. 202/293–3880 and 1353 Connecticut Ave. NW, tel. 202/872–9000).

**Taxis.** Capitol Cab (tel. 202/546–2400), Diamond Cab (tel. 202/387–6200), Yellow Cab (tel. 202/544–1212).

**Theater Tickets.** *See* The Arts, below.

**Train information.** Amtrak at Union Station (1st St. & Massachusetts Ave. NE, 800/872–7245 or 202/484–7540).

**Travel agents.** American Express Travel Service (3 locations: 1150 Connecticut Ave. NW, tel. 202/457–1300; 1776 Pennsylvania Ave. NW, tel. 202/289–8800; 1001 G St. NW, tel. 202/393–0095), Ask Mr. Foster Travel Service (4 locations: 1230 Connecticut Ave. NW, tel. 202/783–4255; 1120 Connecticut Ave. NW, tel. 202/466–8510; 1700 K St. NW, tel. 202/861–7700; 1800 G St. NW, tel. 202/682–9114).

**Weather** (tel. 202/936–1212).

## LODGING

Washington's new hotels are lavish and, to keep up, most of the older ones have been extensively—and expensively—refurbished. This competition makes amenities that might be noteworthy in other cities almost standard here—desks, minibars, two-line phones, modem hookups, cable TV sets hidden in armoires, robes, double beds, express checkout, hair dryers, and so on.

But this doesn't mean you always have to pay top dollar. Summertime rates at many top hotels are reasonable, even when Congress is in session. Note, however, that some of the less expensive downtown hotels, particularly those east of the business district, are no bargain because they're in borderline neighborhoods. Although all the hotels listed below are in safe areas, visitors going out alone at night would be wise, as a rule, to travel by cab.

Your business appointments needn't determine where you'll stay. The Convention Center area is a bit dreary. For a livelier stay near shopping and entertainment, Georgetown is probably a better bet. Capitol Hill is quiet after working hours, but more entertaining than the Convention Center area.

Almost all the hotels listed below offer corporate rates and weekend discounts; inquire when making reservations.

Highly recommended lodgings in each price category are indicated by a star ★.

| Category | Cost* |
| --- | --- |
| *$$$$* (Very Expensive) | over $195 |
| *$$$* (Expensive) | $150–$195 |
| *$$* (Moderate) | under $150 |

*All prices are for a standard double room, single occupancy, excluding 11% room tax and $1.50 occupancy charge.*

*Numbers in the margin correspond to numbered hotel locations on the Washington, DC, Lodging and Dining map.*

### Downtown

**㉓** **Hay-Adams.** With the White House as its near neighbor, *$$$$* this hotel on Lafayette Park has serious snob appeal—mostly for corporate executives and lawyers during the week, and couples on weekends. Built in 1927, it boasts a medieval-style lobby with a 17th-century Medici tapestry, arches, and shelves of leather-bound books. Women

# WASHINGTON DC

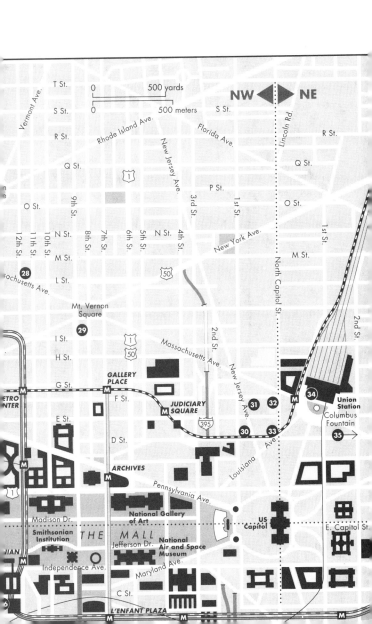

# WASHINGTON, DC HOTEL CHART

| HOTELS | Price Category | Banquet capacity | No. of meeting rooms | Secretarial services | Audiovisual equipment | Teletype news service | Computer rentals | In-room modem phone jack | All-news cable channel | Desk | Desk lighting | Bed lighting |
|---|---|---|---|---|---|---|---|---|---|---|---|---|
| Four Seasons | $$$$ | 500 | 4 | ✓ | ✓ | - | ✓ | ✓ | ✓ | ● | ● | ◐ |
| The Grand | $$$ | 220 | 5 | ✓ | ✓ | - | - | ✓ | ✓ | ● | ◐ | ◐ |
| Hay Adams | $$$$ | 200 | 3 | ✓ | ✓ | - | ✓ | ✓ | ✓ | ● | ● | ● |
| Hotel Washington | $$ | 600 | 8 | ✓ | ✓ | - | - | - | ✓ | ● | ● | ● |
| Hyatt Dulles | $$$ | 350 | 7 | ✓ | ✓ | - | - | ✓ | ✓ | ● | ● | ● |
| Hyatt Regency Capitol Hill | $$$ | 1500 | 12 | ✓ | ✓ | - | ✓ | - | ✓ | ● | ● | ● |
| Jefferson | $$$ | 65 | 5 | ✓ | ✓ | - | ✓ | ✓ | ✓ | ● | ● | ● |
| J.W. Marriott | $$$$ | 1300 | 10 | ✓ | ✓ | - | ✓ | ✓ | ✓ | ● | ◐ | ◐ |
| Mayflower | $$ | 700 | 20 | ✓ | ✓ | - | ✓ | ✓ | ✓ | ◐ | ○ | ○ |
| Morrison Clark Inn | $$$ | 125 | 2 | ✓ | ✓ | - | ✓ | ✓ | - | ● | ◐ | ◐ |
| Park Hyatt | $$$$ | 500 | 2 | ✓ | ✓ | - | ✓ | ✓ | ✓ | ● | ◐ | ● |
| Phoenix Park | $$ | 100 | 1 | ✓ | ✓ | - | ✓ | ✓ | ✓ | ◐ | ● | ◐ |
| Ramada Renaissance | $$ | 2000 | 20 | ✓ | ✓ | - | ✓ | ✓ | ✓ | ◐ | ◐ | ◐ |
| Ritz-Carlton Pentagon City | $$$ | 600 | 9 | ✓ | ✓ | - | ✓ | ✓ | ✓ | ● | ● | ● |
| Sheraton-Carlton | $$$$ | 650 | 7 | ✓ | ✓ | - | ✓ | ✓ | ✓ | ○ | ○ | ◐ |
| Washington Court | $$$ | 350 | 10 | ✓ | ✓ | - | ✓ | ✓ | ✓ | ◐ | ◐ | ◐ |
| Watergate | $$$$ | 500 | 9 | ✓ | ✓ | - | ✓ | ✓ | ✓ | ● | ● | ● |
| Westin | $$$ | 500 | 8 | ✓ | ✓ | - | ✓ | ✓ | ✓ | ◐ | ◐ | ◐ |
| Willard InterContinental | $$$$ | 400 | 13 | ✓ | ✓ | ✓ | - | - | ✓ | ● | ◐ | ● |

**$$$$** = over $195, **$$$** = $150-$195, **$$** = under $150.
● good, ◐ fair, ○ poor.
All hotels listed here have photocopying and fax facilities.

| In-Room Amenities | | | | | | | | | | Hotel Amenities | | | | | | |
|---|---|---|---|---|---|---|---|---|---|---|---|---|---|---|---|---|
| Nonsmoking rooms | In-room checkout | Minibar | Pay movies | VCR/Movie rentals | Hairdryer | Toiletries | Room service | Laundry/Dry cleaning | Pressing | Concierge | Barber/Hairdresser | Garage | Courtesy airport transport | Sauna | Pool | Exercise room |
| ✓ | ✓ | ✓ | ✓ | – | ✓ | ● | ● | ● | ● | ✓ | ✓ | ✓ | – | ✓ | ● | ● |
| ✓ | – | ✓ | ✓ | – | ✓ | ● | ● | ● | ● | ✓ | – | ✓ | – | – | ◐ | ◐ |
| ✓ | – | ✓ | ✓ | ✓ | ✓ | ● | ● | ● | ● | ✓ | – | – | – | – | – | – |
| ✓ | – | – | ✓ | – | ✓ | ● | ◐ | ● | ● | – | – | ✓ | – | – | – | ◐ |
| ✓ | – | – | ✓ | – | ✓ | ◐ | ● | ● | ● | – | – | – | ✓ | ✓ | ◐ | ◐ |
| ✓ | ✓ | ✓ | ✓ | ✓ | ✓ | ◐ | ● | ● | ● | ✓ | ✓ | ✓ | – | ✓ | ◐ | ● |
| ✓ | – | ✓ | ✓ | ✓ | ✓ | ● | ● | ● | ● | ✓ | – | – | – | – | – | – |
| ✓ | ✓ | ✓ | ✓ | – | ✓ | ○ | ● | ● | ● | ✓ | ✓ | ✓ | – | ✓ | ● | ● |
| ✓ | ✓ | ✓ | ✓ | ✓ | ✓ | ◐ | ● | ● | ● | ✓ | ✓ | – | – | – | – | – |
| ✓ | – | – | ✓ | ✓ | ✓ | ● | ◐ | ● | ● | ✓ | – | ✓ | – | – | – | – |
| ✓ | – | ✓ | ✓ | – | ✓ | ● | ● | ● | ● | ✓ | ✓ | ✓ | – | ✓ | ◐ | ● |
| ✓ | – | ✓ | ✓ | – | ✓ | ◐ | ◐ | ● | ● | ✓ | – | ✓ | – | – | – | – |
| ✓ | – | ✓ | ✓ | ✓ | – | ◐ | ● | ● | ● | ✓ | ✓ | ✓ | – | ✓ | ● | ● |
| ✓ | ✓ | ✓ | ✓ | – | ✓ | ● | ● | ● | ● | ✓ | – | ✓ | ✓ | ✓ | ● | ◐ |
| ✓ | ✓ | ✓ | ✓ | ✓ | ✓ | ● | ● | ● | ● | ✓ | ✓ | – | – | – | – | ◐ |
| ✓ | – | ✓ | ✓ | ✓ | ✓ | ● | ● | ● | ● | ✓ | – | ✓ | – | ✓ | – | ◐ |
| ✓ | – | ✓ | ✓ | – | ✓ | ● | ● | ● | ● | ✓ | ✓ | ✓ | – | ✓ | ● | ● |
| ✓ | – | ✓ | ✓ | ✓ | ✓ | ● | ● | ● | ● | ✓ | – | ✓ | – | ✓ | ● | ● |
| ✓ | ✓ | ✓ | ✓ | ✓ | ✓ | ● | ● | ● | ● | ✓ | – | ✓ | – | – | – | – |

**Room service:** ● 24-hour, ◐ 6AM-10PM, ○ other.
**Laundry/Dry cleaning:** ● same day, ◐ overnight, ○ other.
**Pressing:** ● immediate, ◐ same day, ○ other.

guests are usually booked in rooms decorated in pink and cream; men, in rooms with a blue-and-cream color scheme. All accommodations are decorated in English country house styles and are equally tasteful, even the smaller ones. Bathrooms tend to be small and worn; doors have original knobs and have to be slammed shut. Rooms on the south side have views of the White House. The best junior suite is 744. The Adams Room is a popular spot for power breakfasts (*see* Business Breakfasts, below). *Murdock Hotels. 1 Lafayette Sq. NW, 20006, tel. 202/638–6600 or 800/424–5054, fax 202/638–2716. Gen. manager, William Trimble. 144 rooms, 20 suites. AE, CB, DC, MC, V.*

★ ㉓   **Hotel Washington.** This oldest continuously operating ho-
$$   tel in town, and now a national monument, is neither big, flashy, well known—nor overly expensive. It boasts the best views and suites at prices one-third less than those of other luxury hotels. This elegant period piece was restored in 1988 for its 70th anniversary at a cost of $12 million. The hotel has retained its Edwardian character, and a Gibson girl would not feel out of place in the opulent lobby. The hotel's central location rear the Treasury is a plus. All rooms, some of which overlook White House grounds, are furnished with mahogany reproductions of 18th-century antiques; in keeping with the American Colonial tone, the dominant color is Williamsburg blue. Bathrooms are heavy with Italian marble. There are reasonably priced suites with Pennsylvania Avenue views. Washingtonians bring visitors to the rooftop bar for views of the White House grounds and the Washington Monument. The Two Continents restaurant (*see* Business Breakfasts, below) is a good venue for a morning meeting. *Gal-Tex. 15th & Pennsylvania Ave. NW, 20004, tel. 202/ 638–5900 or 800/424–9540, fax 202/638–5900, ext. 3999. Gen. manager, Muneer Deen. 350 rooms, 17 suites. AE, CB, DC, MC, V.*

★ ⓴   **Jefferson.** Built in 1923 and restored in 1989, the Jefferson
$$$   is just four blocks from the White House. The hotel has long been a favorite of Washington's elite; Cabinet members have stayed here, and George Bush's family settled in during the '89 inauguration. The staff remembers guests' names; laundry is hand-ironed and delivered in wicker baskets. The design touches are unusual and creative: Red-tipped white roses and oranges poked with cloves scent the lobby; black wallpaper with white sprigs gives character to one guest room, while a bright green Federal secretary desk brightens another. Striped divans, Japanese screens, grandfather clocks, antique lingerie chests, and Venetian glass reproductions are among the furnishings in the individually decorated rooms. Suites have phones with conference-call capability and speed dialing, as well as stereos and CD players; all rooms have VCRs and large desks. The Jefferson (*see* Business Breakfasts, below) dining room is a sunny spot for an early morning meeting. *Prudential-Bache. 16th & M Sts. NW, 20006, tel. 202/347–2200 or 800/223–6800, fax 202/331–7982. Gen. manager, Elmer Coppoolse. 100 rooms, 32 suites. AE, CB, DC, MC, V.*

㉗   **J. W. Marriott.** There's an even mix of tourists and
$$$$   businesspeople in this 15-story hotel, built in 1980, and attached to the National Press Building, National Theatre, and National Place shopping mall. Metro Center subway

is two blocks east, and Smithsonian museums and monuments are a few blocks south. Industrial-strength chandeliers hang above pink metal columns and white marble floors in the well-trafficked lobby of this massive hotel. (A nearby video arcade adds to the general hubbub.) Perks for Marriott guests include hair dryers on request and video check-out and breakfast order. VIPs stay on the 14th floor, with attractive parquet floors but some glass/brass bloopers; spectacular balcony views compensate for any decor deficiencies. Best views are on the Pennsylvania Avenue side. The executive lounge offers a free, light breakfast, snacks, an honor bar, and views of the Treasury park. There's also a health club with a lap pool, spacious sundeck, large Jacuzzi, and sauna. *1331 Pennsylvania Ave. NW, 20004, tel. 202/393–2000 or 800/228–9290, fax 202/626–6965. Gen. manager, John Dixon. 773 rooms, 51 suites. AE, CB, DC, MC, V.*

**⑲ Mayflower.** It seems that anyone who's anyone ends up at
$$ the Mayflower. Harry Truman and JFK lived here, and J. Edgar Hoover came for lunch daily for 25 years. Built in 1925, in what is now the heart of downtown, the 10-story hotel, now part of the Stouffer chain, was restored in 1984, although the west wing rooms are still to be done. The smallest rooms in the west wing have no desks, no bathroom amenities, and unsightly exposed pipes. Renovated rooms have Federal-period reproduction furnishings; bathrooms have been redone in marble. None of the rooms in either section of the hotel is huge, not even the suites. Lighting is a bit dim, but guests can borrow lamps from the front desk. Rooms facing bustling Connecticut Avenue have the best views, but those looking out on DeSales Street are quieter. The lobby, with its historical photos and large model of the *Mayflower*, is an ornate promenade stretching under a skylight for an entire block from Connecticut Avenue to 17th Street; it's *the* place to people-watch. Head to the mezzanine for quiet talks. Nicholas restaurant is well regarded for business meetings. The hotel offers Stouffer's systemwide "Meetings Express" service: with eight hours' notice, a guest can arrange a conference down to every detail—including catering, secretarial services, and audiovisual equipment (tel. 800/872–6338). *A Stouffer hotel. 1127 Connecticut Ave. NW, 20036, tel. 202/347–3000 or 800/468–3571, fax 202/466–9082. Gen. manager, Barry Swenson. 721 rooms, 85 suites. AE, CB, DC, MC, V.*

**㉒ Sheraton-Carlton.** This eight-story property was built in
$$$$ 1926 and underwent a major renovation in 1988 that enlarged many rooms and restored the hotel's grandeur. The hotel is in a bustling business sector, but the lobby is an opulent blend of Baroque and Rococo styles, with stucco arches, chandeliers, and a Florentine carpet of gold, green, and lavender. Even the elevators are decorated—with carved wooden griffins. Though rooms are furnished with antique reproductions, they don't quite live up to the promise of the lobby. The hotel provides 24-hour butler service, and exercise equipment will be delivered to rooms on request. Other in-room perks are three phones with call waiting, and a bathroom TV speaker. Desks, however, are the smallest of any major hotel in town. *A Sheraton hotel. 16th & K Sts. NW, 20006, tel. 202/638–2626 or 800/*

*325–3535, fax 202/638–4231. Gen. manager, Michel Ducamp. 200 rooms, 36 suites. AE, CB, DC, MC, V.*

★ ㉖ **Willard InterContinental.** The Willard, two blocks from
$$$$ the White House, was meticulously restored to its 1901 appearance in a renovation completed in 1986. Since then, 20 heads of state have stayed on the Secret Service-approved sixth floor. The hotel's rich history includes visits by Mark Twain and Nathaniel Hawthorne (who was covering the Civil War). The term "lobbyist" was inspired by those attempting to curry favor with prominent guests in the hotel's richly decorated lobby during the Grant administration. Martin Luther King, Jr., wrote his "I have a dream" speech here. The new Willard presents an opulent, Beaux-Arts feast for the eye. Book well in advance for the 45 rooms facing Pennsylvania Avenue and the Washington Monument; if they're not available, choose G Street over noisy 14th Street. Rooms are furnished with mahogany Queen Anne reproductions. Two restaurants, the Occidental and the Willard, have won national acclaim. Upon request, rooms can be outfitted with fax machines. *1401 Pennsylvania Ave. NW, 20004, tel. 202/628–9100 or 800/327–0200, fax 202/637–7326. Gen. manager, K.L. Jeffrey. 365 rooms, 37 suites. AE, CB, DC, MC, V.*

## West End

❾ **Grand.** The eight-story Grand, completed in 1984, has a
$$$ simple, understated lobby without gilt, chrome, or ornate flourishes. Good-size rooms are unfussy, too, with muted tones and clean lines. Windows open, phones have hold buttons, and tables are stocked with plenty of local magazines. Some rooms have French doors (no balconies) overlooking a European-style courtyard. Bathrooms are exceptionally opulent, with dark green marble sinks and tubs with whirlpool jets. Fax machines are installed in rooms upon request. The Grand Promenade, with its brass columns, murals, plush chairs, and courtyard views, is a good place for private talks. The Rose 'n' Crown pub is clubby, with plenty of privacy in an alcove hidden behind dark paneled walls. The hotel is a short walk from Georgetown and the Foggy Bottom Metro. *Kaempfer Company. 2350 M St. NW, 20037, tel. 202/429–0100 or 800/848–0016, fax 202/429–9759. Gen. manager, Samir Darwich. 236 rooms, 16 suites. AE, CB, D, MC, V.*

❽ **Park Hyatt.** Like its neighbors, the Grand and the Westin,
$$$$ this 10-story 1986 building on "hotel corner" is within walking distance of Georgetown, the State Department, "the K Street Corridor" of office buildings, and the shops and restaurants of Dupont Circle. Though it's a chain hotel, it's less bustling and more intimate than the representative of the Westin chain across the street. The lobby is decorated with flowers, ornate furniture, and a patterned marble floor. Rooms are less opulent, but spacious, with muted colors, good bed lamps, two-line telephones, and TVs in the bathrooms. The business center is open 24 hours. The health club is more for relaxing than working out; the pool is not big enough for lap swimming. *24th & M Sts. NW, 20037, tel. 202/789–1234 or 800/922–7275, fax 202/457–8823. Gen. manager, Paul Limbert. 224 rooms, including 130 suites. AE, CB, DC, MC, V.*

❻ **Watergate.** Though considered the top address in town,
$$$$ this famous 14-story hotel has some drawbacks. It has to

contend with a homeless shelter in the neighborhood, and it's part of the Watergate Complex, a serpentine configuration of curved black-and-white high rises faced with sawtooth balconies (ubiquitous maps guide guests through the labyrinth). Although the hotel, renovated by the designer who did the Westin and Willard, is fresh, with lots of pink and green and a sleek black-and-white marble lobby, there remains an odd underground feeling in many of the public areas, which are windowless. However, no other hotel offers views of the Potomac, Kennedy Center, and Key Bridge (less expensive rooms have a pleasant view of the pool and greenery). And though rooms are a bit prim, in a Ralph-Lauren-British-country-manor kind of way, they have such modern amenities as double-line phones. The health club is a chic outpost (*see* Fitness, below). There are many stores on site, including a bike rental shop. A complimentary limousine is available for rides to and from business appointments. *Pan American Properties. 2650 Virginia Ave. NW, 20037, tel. 202/965–2300 or 800/424–2736, fax 202/337–7915. Gen. manager, Alan Fitzgerald. 238 rooms, 119 suites. AE, CB, DC, MC, V.*

**7** **Westin.** Scenes in the movie *Broadcast News* were filmed
**$$$** in the high-tech auditorium, and Jesse Jackson exercises here in Washington's best hotel health club (*see* Fitness, below). Guests can walk to offices on K Street and environs, or to the shops and restaurants of Georgetown. The sand-color 10-story building is perfectly nondescript, but indoors the white marble lobby is elegantly spare and sunny, with a two-story glass enclosure overlooking a brick courtyard. Rooms are average size, if a bit narrow, in a restful blue. The Executive Club floor has upgraded rooms, a staff of 19, and complimentary breakfast and snacks. The velvet banquettes in the elegant Colonnade restaurant are ideal for private talks. *All Nippon Airways. 24th & M Sts. NW, 20037, tel. 202/429–2400 or 800/228–3000, fax 202/457–5010. Gen. manager, Michael Sansbury. 417 rooms, 4 suites. AE, CB, DC, MC, V.*

## Capitol Hill

**30** **Hyatt Regency.** When the Hyatt opened in 1976, it was an
**$$$** urban pioneer in shabby north Capitol Hill. Now, with the renovation of Union Station and the opening of other hotels, this 11-story convention hotel is trying to keep up. The lobby is an awkward triangle with a brown-tile floor that the skylight and chrome accents don't brighten much. Elsewhere in the hotel, browns are being replaced by more cheerful pastels. Still, the most light in the hotel is over the swimming pool and lounge area in the new health club. Rooms are a good size; upgraded rooms have bathroom phones, robes, and access to the 11th floor executive lounge. Ask for accommodations on the top floors, which still have views of, but are farther from, the rusty atrium roof. At night, from Hugo's Steakhouse, you can see the Capitol's lighted dome. The luncheon buffet in the lobby is a good value; the seafood stew in Jonah's Oyster Kitchen is excellent (Jonah's also has an upscale lunch counter for single travelers). Sunday brunch at the Park Promenade (*see* Business Breakfasts, below) is among the best in town. Video rentals are available in the lounge. *400 New Jersey Ave. NW, 20001, tel. 202/737–1234 or 800/223–*

*1234, fax 202/393–7927. Gen. manager, Charly Assaly. 834 rooms, 31 suites. AE, CB, DC, MC, V.*

**32** **Phoenix Park.** This eight-story hotel, built in 1921 and re-
**$$** furbished in 1986, is named after a park in Dublin, and the Irish theme is carried throughout. "Yards of beer" in glasses three feet tall are served in the bars around the hotel. The Dubliner bar is one of the most popular in town, and by day it serves as a casual meeting spot for businesspeople who hold informal talks at the small tables. The hotel lobby is fairly serene, with Oriental rugs on a marble floor and a handsome curving staircase. Rooms are furnished in tones of aqua or mauve. Desks are small. Draperies and spreads are in heavy floral patterns; furniture is boxy, except for the carved headboards. Corner rooms are preferable, but not on the floor over the bar. The Phoenix's greatest advantage for business travelers is its location—one block from the trains, shops, and restaurants at Union Station, and three blocks from the Capitol. *Irish Hospitality. 520 North Capitol St. NW, 20001, tel. 202/638–6900 or 800/824–5419, fax 202/393–3236. Gen. manager, Joseph Zarza. 87 rooms, 9 suites. AE, CB, MC, V.*

**31** **Washington Court.** Three blocks north of the Capitol,
**$$$** Washington's tallest hotel (15 stories) has a showpiece of a lobby, outfitted with salmon-color marble, glass elevators, and a one-story-high waterfall. Guest rooms are done in soothing pastels and include ornate armoires. Closets have such thoughtful touches as tie racks and padded hangers. All bathrooms have television sets. Some rooms have great views of the Capitol, others overlook the Washington Monument. All have comfortable couches. Exercise equipment is delivered to rooms on request. *Harbaugh Hotels. 525 New Jersey Ave. NW, 20001, tel. 202/628–2100 or 800/321–3010, fax 202/737–2641. Gen. manager, Marty Kaufman. 266 rooms, 14 suites. AE, CB, DC, MC, V.*

## Convention Center

**28** **Morrison Clark Inn.** Mamie Eisenhower held teas in these
**$$$** two Victorian townhouses that were built in 1865 and restored in 1987. Twelve guest rooms are decorated in turn-of-the-century style, with rich, dark colors and heavy fabrics. Some rooms have marble desks at bay windows, but you may need to request extra light for working. Rooms in the modern wing have a lighter, country feel, with pastel colors and wicker furniture. All baths are modern, with phones. Guest perks include complimentary limousine service, Continental breakfast, and newspapers. Try the restaurant, where, it's rumored, Barbara Bush favors the boneless chicken breast. *DEC Development. Massachussetts Ave. & 11th St. NW, 20001, tel. 202/898–1200 or 800/332–7898, fax 202/289–8576. Gen. manager, Michael Such. 54 rooms, 24 suites. AE, CB, DC, MC, V.*

**29** **Ramada Renaissance-Techworld.** Behind a bleak, black 15-
**$$** story facade is a skylighted lobby festooned with Christmas lights and a bar, hidden under a pagoda—a garish entrance to a good-value hotel built in 1989. This is a lobby that screams "Look at me," but you won't want to. In the guest rooms, cherrywood dressers and tables sit on teal-blue carpets. Bedspreads and curtains share a cinnamon-

and-teal floral pattern reflected in the requisite landscape paintings on the cream-color walls. There's a well-outfitted health club (*see* Fitness, below), executive lounge, decently priced restaurants with private alcoves, pay-fax machine, and shops—all just across from the convention center. The Techworld business complex is an easy walk through an Oriental-style garden. *999 9th St. NW, 20001, tel. 202/898-9000 or 800/228-2828, fax 202/789-4213. Gen. manager, Josef Ebner, 800 rooms, 61 suites.*

## Georgetown

❺ **Four Seasons.** A polished staff is at your service the mo-
$$$$ ment you approach the doors of this contemporary hotel between Georgetown and Foggy Bottom. The attractive lobby is lined with more than 2,000 plants set along brick paths, hanging from balconies, and encircling fountains. In the upstairs corridors, linens are stored in armoires, so chambermaids' carts never block the halls (instead, you'll find jars of Peruvian lilies in the hallways). Rooms were redecorated in 1990 with overstuffed goosedown armchairs, leather-top desks, and silk moiré wall coverings. Baths, heavy with beige Carrara marble, have fresh orchids or roses. Best accommodations face the C&O canal (and freeway), the quietest face the courtyard. Suites with locking desks and folding doors between bedrooms and parlors are suitable for meetings. The Aux Beaux Champs restaurant is well regarded locally. Free limo service is provided. *2800 Pennsylvania Ave. NW, 20007, tel. 202/342-0444 or 800/332-3442, fax 202/944-2076. Gen. manager, Stan Bromley. 197 rooms, 30 suites. AE, CB, D, MC, V.*

## Airport

❶ **Hyatt Dulles.** This 14-story hotel, built in 1989, is 3 miles
$$$ from Dulles International, and is linked to the airport by a free, half-hourly shuttle. Downtown is about 40 minutes away by taxi. Soundproof guest rooms are suite-sized. A parlor area, with seating for four, is set off from the bed by a credenza. All rooms have two-line telephones, and the women's rooms—closer to the elevators—have hair dryers in the bathrooms. A pianist performs near the fountain in the two-story atrium. This is a warmer and more elegant place to stay than the standard airport hotel. *2300 Dulles Corner Blvd., Herndon, VA, 22070, tel. 703/834-1234 or 800/223-1234, fax 703/742-3410. 300 rooms. AE, CB, DC, MC, V.*

❸❻ **Ritz-Carlton, Pentagon City.** This luxurious establish-
$$$ ment, in a vast and pricy shopping mall five minutes from National Airport, opened in the spring of 1990. It is a 15-minute taxi ride, and less than a half-hour subway ride, from downtown. Rooms have Federal reproduction furnishings, silk drapes, and framed botanical prints. Beds are covered with heavy quilted spreads. Two-line phones are standard. The building is insulated against jet noise. The lavish appointments and meticulous upkeep make this a splendid oddity among airport hotels. *1250 S. Hayes St., Arlington, VA 22202 tel. 703/415-5000 or 800/241-3333, fax 703/415-5061. 345 rooms, 41 suites. AE, CB, DC, MC, V.*

## DINING

In the last few years, Italian restaurants have come to rival French restaurants, which for a long time set the standards in fine dining in the city. There has also been an explosion of the kind of cooking usually called New American. You can find almost any kind of food in Washington, from Nepalese to Salvadoran to Ethiopian; in only one category is the city falling short these days, and that's Chinese. Many of the deluxe restaurants are in a 12-block area radiating northwest from 16th and K streets NW—also the location of many of the city's blue-chip law firms. These are the restaurants that feed expense-account diners and provide the most elegant atmosphere. The other area of town for dining, though more for pleasure than business, is Georgetown, whose central intersection is Wisconsin Avenue and M Street. Georgetown contains some of the city's trendiest dining spots, with elegant eateries right next door to hole-in-the-wall carryouts.

For an inexpensive meal when you're on your own, try one of the subsidized government cafeterias—at the Library of Congress, Federal Reserve Board, Supreme Court, or Congressional office buildings.

Highly recommended restaurants in each price category are indicated by a star ★.

| Category | Cost* |
| --- | --- |
| $$$$ (Very Expensive) | over $40 |
| $$$ (Expensive) | $20–$40 |
| $$ (Moderate) | under $20 |

*per person, including appetizer, entrée, and dessert, but excluding drinks, service, and 9% sales tax.*

*Numbers in the margin correspond to numbered restaurant locations on the Washington, DC, Lodging and Dining map.*

### Business Breakfasts

If the purpose of your meeting is to impress people, eat at **The Adams Room** in the Hay-Adams (tel. 202/638–6600), with its colorful, colonial-style decor and its views of Lafayette Park and the White House. Breakfasts are served up traditionally with meats; lighter fare is also available. **The Jefferson** (tel. 202/347–2200) is a bright, quiet spot with old-fashion wooden chairs and large tables—perfect for opening manila folders and getting down to business. **Two Continents,** at the Hotel Washington (tel. 202/638–5900), offers the best breakfast value with a large, varied buffet and a formal atmosphere suitable for quiet talks. The recently restored restaurant is still (unfairly) burdened with a ho-hum reputation, so privacy won't be a problem.

Best brunches (in order): **Key Bridge Marriott** (1401 Lee Hwy., Arlington, VA, tel. 703/524–6400), **Hyatt Regency** (tel. 202/737–1234), **Sheraton Washington** (2660 Woodley Rd. NW, tel. 202/328–2000), **Clyde's Georgetown** (3236

M St. NW, tel. 202/333–0294), **Vista International** (1400 M
St. NW, tel. 202/429–1700).

## Downtown

**㉑** **Bombay Club.** Many embassy and business types confer in
$$$$ this Indian restaurant. A block-and-a-half from both the
White House and the K Street business district, the restaurant smacks of Empire, with lots of rattan, spacious
banquettes, well-spaced side tables with lamps, and copper and brass antiques. Try lamb rogan josh, cooked with
saffron and yogurt, chicken tikka morsels with mint
sauce, tandoori chicken or shrimp, or Chesapeake
crabmeat masala with tomatoes, onions, and curry. The
combination (silver) platter gives you a choice of six
dishes. The service is more professional than warm. *815
Connecticut Ave. NW, tel. 202/659–3727. Jacket and tie.
Reservations advised. AE, CB, DC, MC, V. Closed lunch
Sat.*

**⑬** **C. F. Folks.** Located amid pricy power-lunch eateries is
$$ this popular white-collar lunch counter with a small out-
door patio for additional seating in warmer months. A tiny
spot for solo dining, it numbers among its specialties
thick, delicious soups, such as black bean. The clientele is
largely young office workers. Every day brings its own
cuisine, from Cajun on Mondays to Middle Eastern on Fri-
days. *1225 19th St. NW, tel. 202/293–0162. Casual dress.
No credit cards. Lunch only; closed weekends.*

**⑰** **Duke Zeibert's.** Washington's power elite—and more than
$$$ 400 others—lunch on designer deli dishes by the soaring
glass walls overlooking the bustle of Connecticut Avenue.
The staff is less than alert, except when serving celebrities, who get the prestigious center tables and slaps on the
back from Duke himself. Matzo ball soup is the signature
item; rich chopped chicken liver and beef hash are also dependable. The heavy cheesecake has a glutinous strawberry topping, omitted on request. The interior is more
subtle than the atmosphere. *1050 Connecticut Ave. NW,
tel. 202/466–3730. Jacket and tie. Reservations advised.
AE, DC, MC, V. Closed lunch Sun.*

**㉔** **Old Ebbitt Grill.** This Washington institution has settled
$$ into elegant, Victorian saloon digs. Lots of locals dine
here, notably "Schedule-C types" (political appointees)
from the Treasury Department and the White House next
door. Businesspeople come for friendly chats, not to con-
clude deals. Stick to simple dishes, such as grilled fish and
some of the best burgers in town. Service by young,
aproned staff members is briskly courteous. Open to 3 AM.
*675 15th St. NW, tel. 202/347–4801. Casual dress. Reser-
vations suggested. AE, CB, DC, MC, V.*

**⑫** **I Ricci.** Three weeks after his inauguration, George Bush
$$$$ ate at this restaurant, which features the earthy cuisine of
Tuscany. Immediately the most sought-after people be-
gan arriving in droves. Located on a major tributary of K
Street, this is a convenient and discreet-yet-glamorous
site for private-sector summits. The burnt orange walls
are painted with vines and flowers, with matching terra-
cotta and Ginori china from Italy. The open kitchen has a
huge wood-burning oven. Unusual meats, such as baby
goat, leg of rabbit, and quail, are featured. Appetizers in-
clude *la fettunta*, grilled garlic bread with white beans

and tomato; *topini*, potato dumplings with tomato sauce; and ricotta and spinach tortelloni. *1220 19th St. NW, tel. 202/835–0459. Jacket and tie. AE, CB, MC, V. Closed for lunch Sat.; Sun.*

⑱ **Tabard Inn.** With its artfully artless decor, absentminded
$$$ waiters, and quasihealth food menu, the Tabard is an idiosyncratic restaurant with a devoted clientele of baby boomers. The dark-panel club room is slightly shabby, but the courtyard is delightful. The Inn is suitable for relaxed lunch discussions, with just enough noise to foil eavesdroppers. At night, the atmosphere turns romantic with low lights and candles. The health-conscious chef is always inventing new treatments for the staple ingredients on her California/French nouvelle-style menu. Softshell crabs, for instance, have appeared sautéed with a cornmeal coating, and the chicken salad features walnut-bread croutons and a blue-cheese-and-buttermilk dressing. The wine list is laden with California labels, but also includes some organically grown Italian wines. The staff is friendly and knowledgeable. *1739 N. St. NW, tel. 202/785–1277. Casual dress. Reservations advised for dinner; accepted for lunch before 12:15; required anytime for parties of 5 or more. MC, V.*

⑮ **La Taberna del Alabardero.** The owner, who opened his
$$$$ first restaurant in Madrid, has achieved a formal Old World ambience in this upscale Spanish restaurant. Bilevel dining offers a chance to spot plenty of guests, but lawyers come here for a quiet place to talk. The restaurant is one block from 18th and K Streets, one of the busiest business-district intersections. The kitchen turns out creditable Basque shrimp with mushrooms, fried squid, filet Mignon with Rioja wine sauce, and paella and peppers stuffed with crab in a saffron sauce. The kitchen is visible in the main dining room. The staff comports itself with classic Spanish *cortesia*. *18th & Eye Sts. NW, tel. 202/429–2200. Jacket and tie. Closed for lunch Sat.; Sun. AE, DC, MC, V.*

⑯ **21 Federal.** Washington investors discovered the original
$$$$ in Nantucket and brought a branch to DC in 1988. A private dining room is separated from the main room by glass walls so that, as one critic said, "everyone can be aware of the exclusive gathering they weren't invited to." This trendy eatery is also staging ground for the Hollywood practice of taking phone calls at the table. The food is new American; among the specialties are mushroom streudel, lobster and corn chowder, scallops and shrimp fettuccine, roast goose, herb-crusted sole with chive butter, and lobster/crab cakes with corn okra relish. The place is noisy, so serious negotiations are out of the question. The bar and surrounding tables are of black granite—striking, against the black-and-white marble floor. The staff is helpful and only a trifle too familiar. Generally, the clientele is lower-middle-age, upper-middle-class, and highly fashion conscious. The wine list is French and Californian, with more than half a dozen available by the glass. *1736 L St. NW, 202/331–9771. Jacket and tie. Reservations advised. AE, CB, MC, V. Closed lunch Sat; Sun.*

⑪ **Vincenzo.** This Italian seafood restaurant is a popular
$$$ business spot, in part because of the pleasant Mediterranean-style decor, with red tile floors and white stucco

walls. Located in the trendy Dupont Circle neighborhood, near sidewalk cafés and art galleries, Vincenzo is within 10 blocks of most major law firms and corporate offices. Tables are decently spaced, making them suitable for negotiations. The main dining room downstairs is quieter and better lighted, but smoking is not permitted there. Try a whole grilled fish, such as grouper, red snapper, or pompano. Fish stews in spicy tomato broth, and grilled scallops are also delicious. Pasta is prepared with spicy sauces, but tends to be a bit chewy. Wines are exclusively Italian, and only two are available by the glass. *1606 20th St. NW, tel. 202/667–0047. Jacket and tie. AE, CB, MC, V. Closed for lunch weekends.*

## West End

★ **⓮** **Dominique's.** The front room is rustic, complete with
$$$ stuffed animal heads mounted on the wall; the back rooms have ornate tapestries, white columns, and stained glass—more fitting for a restaurant serving some of the best classic French food in town (few people actually order the rattlesnake and kangaroo appetizers Dominique's is so famous for). Local restaurant-goers voted Dominique's decor the city's prettiest. Specialties include shrimp in garlic sauce, fillet of beef, and duck pie. Near the World Bank complex, two blocks from the K Street lawyer-lobbyist promenade, and three blocks from the White House, this restaurant serves both private and public sectors. Tables are close together, inhibiting highly confidential talks; the noise level is acceptable. *1900 Pennsylvania Ave. NW, tel. 202/452–1126. Jacket and tie. Reservations advised. AE, MC, V. Closed for lunch weekends.*

★ **⓾** **Jockey Club.** Nancy Reagan ate here regularly, if you can
$$$$ call "just a salad" eating. People come in smug and curious, proud to be here and wondering who else is around. Order a Coke and the stiff and punctilious waiters insist upon adding "lay-mone." Still, the place isn't as intimidating as it may sound—and the food is excellent. The decor in three adjoining rooms is countrified, with heavy wooden beams, white stucco walls, red-and-white plaid tablecloths, and lots of paintings of dogs, horses, and ships. Commerce Secretary Robert Mosbacher and Lee Iacocca are regulars. Most diners want to sit in the first, most visible room, lining up against the back wall so they don't miss anyone. Tables in the back two rooms are farther apart and offer more privacy. On the whole, the menu is classic Continental. Crab cakes are distinguished by their meatiness rather than by unusual spicing; breast of duck is prepared with morels and port sauce; the double-grilled lamb chop is accompanied by rosemary and tomato sauce. The Grand Marnier chocolate tart is excellent. The wine list is evenly divided between France and California; a small selection is available by the glass. *Ritz-Carlton, 2100 Massachusetts Ave. NW, tel. 202/659–8000. Jacket and tie. Reservations advised. AE, MC, DC, V.*

## Capitol Hill

**㉞** **Adirondacks.** Inside Union Station is this restored 1907
$$$ Beaux Arts masterpiece, complete with soaring barrel-vault ceilings, gilded moldings, chandeliers, artwork by De Kooning, Hockney, and Motherwell on the walls, and Michael Graves china on the tables. The staff is friendly,

and the food is prepared in an unusual and appealing California style. Pork tenderloin is prepared with garlic and sun-dried tomatoes, and the roasted duck breast has a distinctive green peppercorn sauce. California labels dominate the pricy wine list, but France comes close; there are Australian and Spanish selections, too. Tables near the entrance are quietest. This is a perfect place to fête your Congressional representative, as the Capitol is practically next door. It's convenient, too, for those fresh off the Metroliner, or just about to board. *Union Station, 50 Massachusetts Ave. NE, tel. 202/682–1840. Jacket and tie. Reservations advised. AE, CB, DC, MC, V.*

**㉟** **La Brasserie.** Conveniently near the Capitol, La Brasserie
$$$ is noted as the place for Congressional working dinners over breast of duck or seafood prepared with a French flair. The salmon, smoked on the premises, is served as an appetizer with capers, chopped onions, and toast, or in a salad of mixed greens. The seafood is fresh and distinctively prepared; for instance, the unbreaded crab cakes are made with red peppers and shallots, and baked—not deep-fried. Lobster is baked in layers of pastry. The restaurant, which occupies two townhouses, has several small rooms (one holds only five tables) and a main dining room. Collectors' plates and scenes of France decorate the walls. Dim lighting, artwork in heavy gilt frames, and plenty of fresh flowers on the tables create a cozy ambience. In summer, diners prefer to sit outside on the patio. Private rooms seating 4–40 can be reserved. Service is efficient and polite, not fawning. Wines are mostly French, with a few Virginian labels among the Americans, which are otherwise from California; a dozen are available by the glass. *239 Massachusetts Ave. NE, tel. 202/546–9154. Jacket and tie. Reservations advised. AE, MC, V.*

**㉝** **La Colline.** Lunchtime meetings are the rule here among a
$$$ rogue's gallery of political photos (Ted Kennedy's is signed, "Let the Good Times Roll"). A bistro with lots of light and hanging plants, La Colline's best buy is the three-course fixed-price dinner. The menu, which changes daily, is reliable; most popular dishes are the bouillabaisse and cassoulet. The fricassée of shellfish includes scallops, shrimp, and lobster, and shiitake mushrooms in a dry vermouth-and-cream sauce. The breast of duck is served in an Oriental marinade. The wine list is two-thirds French, with the remainder Californian. Eight wines, plus one Champagne, are available by the glass. The service, efficient at midday, is very slow at night. Either time, you may spy a famous senator, but too many gladhanders will be stopping by his table for you to see him for long. The back-slapping and elbow-rubbing can be distracting, but otherwise your discussions will not be disturbed. Best tables for talks are near the captain's post. *400 North Capitol St. NW, tel. 202/737–0400. Jacket and tie. Reservations advised. AE, CB, MC, V.*

**㉚** **Mel Krupin's.** Krupin, Duke Ziebert's former head waiter
$$$ (*see above*), is usually on hand to greet diners at this bilevel Capitol Hill restaurant. Upstairs is Mel's Deli, fine for sandwiches or a solo breakfast or lunch. Downstairs, you're part of the macho Washington scene that includes athletes, reporters, and old-fashion politicos. The setting is subdued, with plenty of the expected dark wood, and surprisingly delicate upholstery on the Queen Anne

chairs in the section facing the lobby. Many booths are in the center of the room. Waiters are frank, even sassy, and—like the prime rib and crab cakes they serve—dependable. The sirloin is the outstanding item but, like the rest of the conventional menu, distinguished only by its consistency. *Washington Court, 525 New Jersey Ave. NW, tel. 202/628–2100. Jacket and tie. Reservations advised. AE, CB, MC, V.*

## Georgetown

**❷ Bamiyan.** Afghani food is largely unknown in the West.
**$$** That's a pity, because the country's cuisine is quite appealing, unusual enough to be interesting but not so strange as to be intimidating. Bamiyan is the oldest and arguably the best Afghani restaurant in the area, even though it does look like a motel that has seen better days. Kebabs—of chicken, beef, or lamb—are succulent. More adventurous souls should try the *quabili palow* (lamb with saffron rice, carrots, and raisins) or the *aushak* (dumplings with scallions, meat sauce, and yogurt). For a side vegetable, order the sautéed pumpkin; it will make you forget every other winter squash dish you've ever had. *3320 M St. NW, tel. 202/338–1896. Reservations accepted. Casual dress. AE, MC, V. Closed lunch.*

**❸ Germaine's.** This elegant Pan-Asian restaurant, over a
**$$$** video store in northern Georgetown, has a romantic story behind it. The eponymous Vietnamese owner met her husband, an American news photographer (whose work now hangs on the walls), in Saigon during the war. He returned to Vietnam to rescue his wife's family as Saigon fell, and many of Germaine's relatives now work in the restaurant. David Brinkley, Sam Donaldson, and the ambassadors from Japan, Singapore, and Germany eat here often. The tasty Korean-style beef is hot and spicy and has the chewy texture of beef jerky. The Southeast Asian menu includes a commendable "pine cone fish" that is both a specialty and a spectacle: Filleted and scored before it is deep-fried in a light tempura batter, it comes out looking like a pine cone split open. The lower-ceilinged front room, facing Wisconsin Avenue, is quieter than the atrium. In addition to an ample selection of international wines, the restaurant offers nearly 20 imported beers, including the rare Maui Lager. *2400 Wisconsin Ave. NW, tel. 202/965–1185. Jacket and tie. Reservations advised. AE, DC, MC, V.*

**❹ 1789.** Named not for the year of the French Revolution but
**$$$$** for the adoption of the U.S. Constitution and the founding of Georgetown University next door, this is an appropriately serene place to eat. Most diners are couples; for business purposes, the tone is right for toasting the conclusion of an agreement rather than for hammering out its details. Currier & Ives prints, wooden Venetian blinds, and an intricately carved antique mahogany sideboard lend to the main dining room the air of a sumptuous country inn. The livelier Pub Room has a five-stool bar. Waiters, in black tie, are reserved and attentive. The seasonal Continental menu is usually strong on fish dishes such as sautéed striped bass. Also popular are medallions of duck. Wines are from France and California and are reasonably priced. *1226 36th St. NW, tel. 202/965–1789. Jacket required. Reservations advised. AE, CB, DC, MC, V.*

## FREE TIME

### Fitness

*Hotel Facilities*

**Westin Fitness Center** at the Westin Hotel (tel. 202/457–5000) has the best facilities, including a two-lane pool, pounds of exercise equipment, and aerobics classes. **Hyatt Regency**, near Capitol Hill (tel. 202/737–1234), has similar facilities. **Ramada Renaissance Techworld** (tel. 202/898–9000) and the **Watergate** (tel. 202/965–2300) also have good clubs with lap pools. Nonguests pay $10–$15 a day.

*Health Clubs*

Most downtown facilities do not allow one-day members. Some hotels give passes to the modern, seven-story **YMCA** (1711 Rhode Island Ave. NW, tel. 202/862–9688), the largest downtown fitness center.

*Jogging*

The **Mall,** between the Capitol and Washington Monument, has a 3-mile gravel path. Some people continue west on the grass from the Monument to the Lincoln Memorial. The **Hains Point Loop** takes joggers along a scenic 3-mile waterfront path. Take a cab there, and don't go after dark.

### Shopping

Though **Georgetown** is not on a subway line and parking is next to impossible (take a cab), people still flock here for the antiques and craft shops and high-style clothing boutiques. From the intersection of Wisconsin Avenue and M Street, walk west on M Street and north on Wisconsin.

The city's department stores can be found in the "new" downtown, which is still being built. Its fulcrum is **Metro Center** (tel. 202/637–7000), which spans 11th and 12th streets NW along G Street. Here you'll find two of the best department stores, **Hechts** (12th & G Sts., tel. 202/628–6661) and **Woodward & Lothrop** (11th & F Sts., tel. 202/347–5300).

An even newer project is the renovation of **Union Station** (tel. 202/371–9441) at Massachusetts Avenue NE. Resplendent with marble floors and gilded, vaulted ceilings, this is now both a working train station and a mall with three levels of stores selling everything from designer jellybeans to trendy clothes.

For high quality country crafts, try **Appalachian Spring** (Union Station and 1415 Wisconsin Ave. NW, tel. 202/682–0505 or 202/337–5780). You can buy quality Americana at **Celebrate America!** (National Press Building, 14th & F Sts., tel. 202/638–4681) and the **Decatur House Museum Shop** (Lafayette Sq., tel. 202/842–1856). For American art, pottery, and antiques, try **Chenonceau** (2314 18th St. NW, tel. 202/667–1651). For unique, upscale gifts, visit the gift shops at the **Smithsonian** (tel. 202/357–2700).

### Diversions

First-time visitors to Washington will want to see the icons of American government: **Jefferson Memorial** (15th St. SW on the south shore of the Tidal Basin, tel. 202/426–6841); **Lincoln Memorial** (west end of the Mall at 23rd St.

NW, between Constitution & Independence Aves. NW, tel. 202/426–6841), with the **Vietnam Veterans Memorial** close by; **Washington Monument** (center of Mall, Constitution Ave. and 15th St. NW, tel. 202/426–6839); **White House** (1600 Pennsylvania Ave. NW, tel. 202/456–7041, tape, or 202/456–2000; the line forms at the Ellipse before noon, often around 9 AM); and the **U.S. Capitol** (east end of the Mall, tel. 202/225–6827).

The following are a selection of other options for those with extra time on their hands.

Walk up to 13 miles along the scenic **C&O Canal towpath,** starting in Georgetown.

**Georgetown,** with its trendy shops, restaurants, and galleries, is fun to explore (*see* Shopping, above).

The **National Museum of Women in the Arts** (1250 New York Ave. NW, tel. 202/783–5000) is the first museum in the world dedicated to women artists. The permanent collection of more than 500 works ranges from the Renaissance to the present and includes paintings, drawings, sculpture, prints, and photographs.

Cruise to **Mt. Vernon** (tel. 703/780–2000), George Washington's beautiful estate in Virginia, on the *Spirit of Washington* (Pier 4, 6th & Water Sts., tel. 202/554–1542). Before the cruise, stroll among seafood restaurants and fish stands along the waterfront.

The **National Archives** (Constitution Ave. between 7th & 9th Sts. NW, tel. 202/323–3000) house the Declaration of Independence and the U.S. Constitution.

The **National Gallery of Art** (Constitution Ave. at 4th St. NW, tel. 202/737–4215) has one of the world's foremost collections of paintings, sculptures, and graphics, including the only DaVinci outside of Europe. The domed west building has works from the 13th to the 20th century; I.M. Pei's angular east building displays modern art exclusively.

Not far from the Convention Center is the **National Portrait Gallery** (8th & F Sts. NW, tel. 202/357–1300). Its collection includes photographs from the Civil War era, and life casts of Abraham Lincoln's face and hands.

Stroll around the **Tidal Basin,** the small walled lake in front of the Jefferson Memorial, particularly in spring when the cherry blossoms are in bloom. Or rent a pedal boat at the Tidal Basin Boat House (15th St. & Maine Ave. NW, tel. 202/484–0206).

The **U.S. Botanic Garden** (Maryland Ave. & 1st St. SW, tel. 202/226–4082 or 202/225–7099) is especially delightful in the winter, with its conservatory offering sanctuary to cactii, ferns, and orchids.

Tour the **U. S. Supreme Court** (1st & East Capitol Sts. NE, tel. 202/479–3499) and the **Capitol** (tel. 202/225–6827) across the street.

## Professional Sports

DC's basketball team, the **Bullets** (tel. 301/350–3400), and the hockey team, the **Capitals** (tel. 301/350–3400), appear at Capital Centre. The town's football team, the **Redskins** (tel. 202/546–2222), plays at RFK Stadium.

## The Arts

In the past 20 years, this cultural backwater has been transformed into a cultural capital. **The Kennedy Center** is home to the National Symphony Orchestra and host to Broadway shows, ballet, modern dance, and opera. The Center is actually four stages under one roof: the Concert Hall, the Opera House, the Eisenhower Theater (usually for drama), and the Terrace Theater (for experimental works and chamber groups).

**The Arena Stage** is the city's most respected resident company—the first theater outside New York to win a Tony Award. There are three theaters: the theater-in-the-round Arena, the proscenium Kreeger, and the cabaret-style old Vat Room.

**Ford's Theatre,** looking much the way it did when President Lincoln was shot, is host mainly to musicals, many with family appeal. **National Theatre** presents pre- and post-Broadway shows. **Shakespeare Theatre** at the Folger presents works by the bard and his contemporaries in an Elizabethan-type setting. Several art galleries present highly regarded chamber concert series, including the **National Gallery** (which also offers free concerts Sun., 7 PM, in the Garden Court), **Corcoran Gallery of Art,** the **Folger Shakespeare Library,** and the **Phillips Collection** (free concerts Sun., 5 PM, Labor Day–Memorial Day).

The "Weekend" section in Friday's *Washington Post* is the best guide to coming events. The Post's daily "Guide to the Lively Arts" also lists cultural events. The *Washington Times's* "Weekend" section comes out on Thursday. Also consult the "City Lights" section in the monthly *Washingtonian* magazine.

**Instant-Charge** (tel. 202/857–0900) sells tickets to Kennedy Center only; **Metro Center TICKETplace** (F Street Plaza between 12th & 13th Sts. NW, tel. 202/842–5387) has day-of-performance tickets at half price; **TicketCenter** (tel. 202/432–0200 or 800/448–9009) sells tickets to Capital Centre, Wolf Trap, and Ford's Theatre. Tickets to most events are available through **Ticketron** (1101 17th St. NW, tel. 202/659–2601). **Premier Theatre Seats** (tel. 202/963–6161), **Top Centre Tickets** (tel. 202/452–9040), and **Ticket Connections** (tel. 202/587–6850) sell tickets on short notice, sometimes to otherwise sold-out productions, for a $15–$25 surcharge.

**Arena Stage** (6th St. & Maine Ave. SW, tel. 202/488–3300).
**Corcoran Gallery Concert Series** (17th St. & New York Ave. NW, tel. 202/638–3211).
**Folger Shakespeare Library Concerts** (201 E. Capitol St. SE, tel. 202/544–4600).
**Ford's Theatre** (511 10th St. NW, tel. 202/347–4833).
**John F. Kennedy Center for the Performing Arts** (one block

south of Virginia and New Hampshire Ave. NW, tel. 202/
254–3600 or 800/424–8504).
**National Gallery Concerts** (6th St. & Constitution Ave.
NW, West Building, tel. 202/737–4215).
**National Theatre** (1321 Pennsylvania Ave. NW, tel. 202/
783–3372 or 800/233–3123).
**Phillips Collection Concerts** (1600 21st St. NW, tel. 202/
387–2151).
**Shakespeare Theatre at the Folger** (201 E. Capitol St. SE,
tel. 202/546–4000).

## After Hours

*Bars and Lounges*
For a quiet talk with clients, **Madeo** (1113 23rd St. NW,
tel. 202/457–0057), with its indoor garden, is the most elegant. It is sophisticated but not stuffy, and offbeat types
come from the artsy cinema next door. **The Guards** (2915 M
St. NW, tel. 202/965–2350) has a hushed atmosphere, and
is favored by "cave dwellers" (old-money native Washingtonians). **The Dupont Plaza Hotel** (Dupont Circle NW, tel.
202/483–6000) has a piano lounge and a separate, quieter
room with views of Dupont Circle and its picturesque
fountain. **The Front Page** (19th & New Hampshire Sts.
NW, tel. 202/296–6500) is loud and jam-packed, especially
at Thursday Happy Hours, when under-30 office workers
come to let off steam.

*Cabarets*
Capitol Steps, a satirical group made up of Congressional
staffers, performs at **Chelsea's Georgetown** (1055 Thomas
Jefferson St. NW, tel. 202/683–8330). **Mrs. Foggybottom
& Friends/Marquee Cabaret** (Omni Shoreham Hotel, 2500
Calvert St. NW, tel. 202/745–1023) performs musical po-
litical satire.

*Comedy Clubs*
**Comedy Café** (1520 K St. NW, tel. 202/638–5653) brings in
comics from all over the east coast. Don't expect sophisticated political humor—not unless there's a crude and/or
silly angle. But the audience loves it. **Garvin's Comedy
Club** (1335 Greens Ct.; L St. between 13th & 14th Sts.
NW, tel. 202/726–1334) features top acts.

*Jazz Clubs*
**Blues Alley** (rear of 1073 Wisconsin Ave. NW, tel. 202/
337–4141) serves up jazz in an intimate, casual setting.
**Anton's 1201 Club** (1201 Pennsylvania Ave. NW, tel. 202/
783–1201), an Art Deco supper club, is one of the most sophisticated spots in town and a good place to take clients;
former Speaker of the House Jim Wright used to take refuge here when his fortunes were at their worst.

*For Singles*
**The Bayou** (3135 K St. NW, under Whitehurst Fwy., tel.
202/333–2897) features rowdy rock bands, rough wooden
tables, and an easy-going, beer-swigging crowd. **Bull-
feathers** (410 1st St. SE, tel. 202/543–5005) is for yuppies
and preppies, many of whom are from the nearby Congressional offices. **The Fifth Column** (915 F St. NW, tel.
202/393–3632) is a converted downtown bank where a
youngish crowd poses in black ensembles and punk hair-
dos amid neon sculpture and foreign videos.

## ADDRESSES

**Name**

*Address*

*Telephone*

*Fax*

**Name**

*Address*

*Telephone*

*Fax*

**Name**

*Address*

*Telephone*

*Fax*

**Name**

*Address*

*Telephone*

*Fax*

**Name**

*Address*

*Telephone*

*Fax*

## ADDRESSES

**Name**

*Address*

*Telephone*

*Fax*

**Name**

*Address*

*Telephone*

*Fax*

**Name**

*Address*

*Telephone*

*Fax*

**Name**

*Address*

*Telephone*

*Fax*

**Name**

*Address*

*Telephone*

*Fax*

## ADDRESSES

**Name**

*Address*

*Telephone*

*Fax.*

---

**Name**

*Address*

*Telephone*

*Fax*

---

**Name**

*Address*

*Telephone*

*Fax*

---

**Name**

*Address*

*Telephone*

*Fax*

---

**Name**

*Address*

*Telephone*

*Fax*

# FODOR'S TRAVEL GUIDES

## U.S. Guides

Alaska
Arizona
Boston
California
Cape Cod
The Carolinas & the
  Georgia Coast
The Chesapeake
  Region
Chicago
Colorado
Disney World & the
  Orlando Area
Florida
Hawaii
Las Vegas
Los Angeles

Maui
Miami & the
  Keys
New England
New Mexico
New Orleans
New York City
New York City
  (Pocket Guide)
Pacific North Coast
Philadelphia & the
  Pennsylvania
  Dutch Country
Puerto Rico
  (Pocket Guide)
The Rockies
San Diego

San Francisco
San Francisco
  (Pocket Guide)
The South
Texas
USA
The Upper Great
  Lakes Region
Vacations in
  New York State
Vacations on the
  Jersey Shore
Virgin Islands
Virginia & Maryland
Waikiki
Washington, D.C.

## Foreign Guides

Acapulco
Amsterdam
Australia
Austria
The Bahamas
The Bahamas
  (Pocket Guide)
Baja & the Pacific
  Coast Resorts
Barbados
Belgium &
  Luxembourg
Bermuda
Brazil
Budget Europe
Canada
Canada's Atlantic
  Provinces
Cancun, Cozumel,
  Yucatan Peninsula
Caribbean
Central America
China
Eastern Europe
Egypt
Europe
Europe's Great
  Cities
France

Germany
Great Britain
Greece
The Himalayan
  Countries
Holland
Hong Kong
India
Ireland
Israel
Italy
Italy 's Great Cities
Jamaica
Japan
Kenya, Tanzania,
  Seychelles
Korea
Lisbon
London
London Companion
London
  (Pocket Guide)
Madrid & Barcelona
Mexico
Mexico City
Montreal &
  Quebec City
Morocco
Munich

New Zealand
Paris
Paris
  (Pocket Guide)
Portugal
Rio de Janeiro
Rome
Saint Martin/
  Sint Maarten
Scandinavia
Scandinavian
  Cities
Scotland
Singapore
South America
South Pacific
Southeast Asia
Soviet Union
Spain
Sweden
Switzerland
Sydney
Thailand
Tokyo
Toronto
Turkey
Vienna & the
  Danube Valley
Yugoslavia

## Wall Street Journal Guides to Business Travel

Europe
International Cities

The Pacific Rim
USA & Canada

## Special-Interest Guides

Cruises and Ports
  of Call
Healthy Escapes
Fodor's Flashmaps
  New York

Fodor's Flashmaps
  Washington, D.C.
Shopping in Europe
Skiing in North
  America

Smart Shopper's
  Guide to London
Sunday in
  New York
Touring Europe